AF713908

A CONCISE ATLAS OF

ES DEVLIN

edited by
ANDREA LIPPS

T&H

BET AWARDS KANYE WEST **VOLCANO**
TOUR LENNY KRAVITZ **BLACK & WHITE AMERICA**
ROUNDABOUT THEATRE TREADWELL **MACHINAL**
ENO DONIZETTI **LUCREZIA BORGIA**
SADLER'S WELLS MALIPHANT **AFTERLIGHT I**
BELFAST MTV EMAS **STEEL SINEWS**
SADLER'S WELLS MALIPHANT **RODIN PROJECT**
GRAMMYS RIHANNA **PIXELS**
BRITS RIHANNA **PAINT**
MIF MASSIVE ATTACK V ADAM CURTIS **DOGS**
VIENNA BERLIOZ **BÉATRICE ET BÉNÉDICT**
GLYNDEBOURNE GOUGH **IMAGO**
PALLADIUM HILL / BROWN **I CAN'T SING**
WORLD TOUR LILY ALLEN **SHEEZUS**
PHILADELPHIA BEYONCÉ **MADE IN AMERICA**
PARIS LAPRISE **ROBIN DES BOIS**
TV MILEY CYRUS **DESERT BOX**
TIMES SQUARE U2 / SPRINGSTEEN / COLDPLAY **RED**
LV SS2015 GHESQUIÈRE **A BEGINNING**
MTV GLASGOW U2 **EVERY BREAKING WAVE**
MET OPERA NYC VERDI **OTELLO**
LV CRUISE 2015 GHESQUIÈRE **PALM SPRINGS**
TV SAM SMITH **AUDIENCE**
BRITS ED SHEERAN **PHOTOGRAPH**
MTV ED SHEERAN / RUDIMENTAL **CONFETTI**

DON GIOVANNI MOZART *ROYAL OPERA HOUSE* 276 656 740
BANGERZ MILEY CYRUS *WORLD ARENA TOUR* 284 842
CONNECTOME MARRIOTT / PÄRT *ROYAL BALLET* 287 628 735
OBSERVATORY GHESQUIÈRE *LOUIS VUITTON SS2015* 288
THE NETHER HALEY *ROYAL COURT THEATRE* 294
BLUE ORCHESTRA SAM SMITH *BRITS* 684

2015

RISE AND FALL OF MAHAGONNY BRECHT / WEILL *ROH* 293 854
LIGHT SHINING CHURCHILL *RNT* 297 633 690
HAMLET SHAKESPEARE *BARBICAN* 298 637
INNOCENCE + EXPERIENCE U2 *WORLD ARENA TOUR* 300 677 802
LV SERIES 3 GHESQUIÈRE *180 STRAND* 717
DER FREISCHÜTZ WEBER *ROYAL DANISH OPERA* 305
LIVE IN NEW YORK ADELE *RADIO CITY MUSIC HALL* 792

2016

HELLO ADELE *WORLD ARENA TOUR* 306 699 700 702
FAITH HEALER FRIEL *DONMAR THEATRE* 313 698
FORMATION BEYONCÉ *WORLD STADIUM TOUR* 314 662 664
PABLO STUDIES KANYE WEST 321
WITH NIEMEYER GHESQUIÈRE *LOUIS VUITTON CRUISE 2017* 44
RIO OLYMPICS *OPENING CEREMONY 2016* 322 818
MIRACLE BOX DEVLIN *SERPENTINE GALLERIES* 325 618
MIRROR MAZE DEVLIN *COPELAND PARK* 14 326 850
ORIGAMI POST-IT NOTE DEVLIN 333
TRIANGLE THE WEEKND *VOODOO MUSIC FESTIVAL* 681 776
LEGEND OF THE FALL THE WEEKND *WORLD ARENA TOUR* 334 682 768

2017

UGLY LIES THE BONE FERRENTINO *NATIONAL THEATRE* 337
ROOM 2022 DEVLIN *ART BASEL / EDITION HOTEL* 338 852
MELODRAMA COACHELLA LORDE *COACHELLA FESTIVAL* 343 667 814

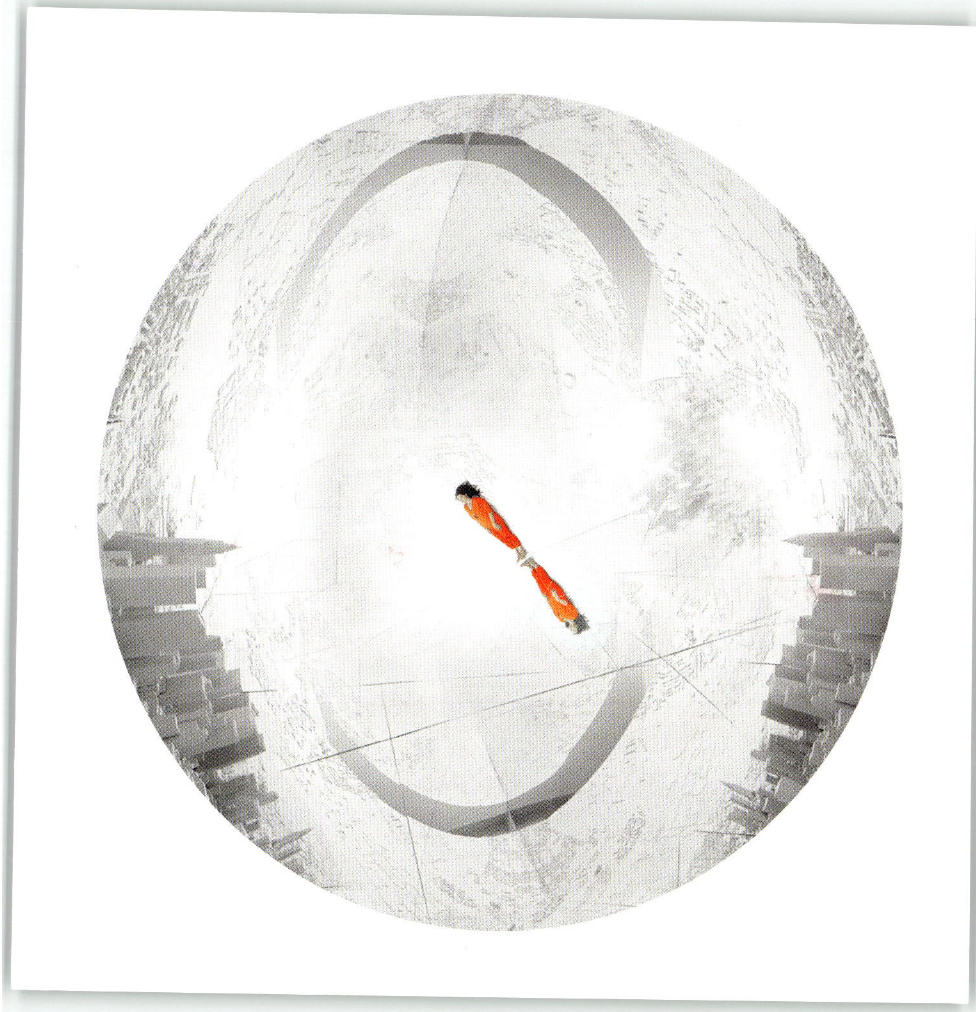

the
DESIGN
MUSEUM

First published in the United Kingdom in 2023
as *An Atlas of Es Devlin* by Thames & Hudson Ltd,
6–24 Britannia Street, London WC1X 9JD

First published in the United States of America in 2023
as *An Atlas of Es Devlin* by Thames & Hudson Inc.,
500 Fifth Avenue, New York, New York 10110

This new edition 2026

Published in conjunction with the exhibition *Es Devlin: Other Worlds* at the Design Museum, London

A Concise Atlas of Es Devlin © 2023 and 2026 Es Devlin

Book design by Daniel Devlin

Text © 2023 and 2026 Es Devlin, unless otherwise stated
'An Infinite Archive' © 2023 Andrea Lipps
'A New Renaissance Woman' © 2023 Donatien Grau
'Art As Ritual' by Johanna Agerman Ross
© 2026 Design Museum Enterprises Limited

Edited by Andrea Lipps
Copyedited by Jenny Wilson
Editorial assistance by Boo Devlin

All Rights Reserved. No part of this publication may be reproduced or transmitted in any form or by any means, electronic or mechanical, including photocopy, recording or any other information storage and retrieval system, without prior permission in writing from the publisher.

EU Authorized Representative: Interart S.A.R.L.
19 rue Charles Auray, 93500 Pantin, Paris, France
productsafety@thameshudson.co.uk
interart.fr

A CIP catalogue record for this book is available from the British Library

Library of Congress Control Number 2026940032

ISBN 978-0-500-29920-3
01

Printed and bound in China by Toppan Leefung Printing Limited

esdevlin.com

Be the first to know about our new releases, exclusive content and author events by visiting
thamesandhudson.com
thamesandhudsonusa.com
thamesandhudson.com.au

FSC MIX Paper | Supporting responsible forestry FSC® C104723

C O N T

COMEDY THEATRE GRAY THE HOLY TERROR
ROYAL COURT PENHALL DUMB SHOW
LINBURY ROH COCTEAU / GLASS ORPHÉE
ROYAL EXCHANGE LEATHER ALL THE ORDINARY ANGELS
SOHO THEATRE BROKS / GORDON ON EGO
ENO ASIAN DUB FOUNDATION GADDAFI
ROYAL COURT FEEHILY O GO MY MAN
HAMBURG BRITTEN BILLY BUDD
SHORT FILM KATE MOSS / FIGGIS DREAMS OF MISS X
SADLER'S WELLS MALIPHANT SMALL BOATS
FILM SALLY POTTER RAGE
VIDEO RAZORLIGHT / FIGGIS HOSTAGE OF LOVE
WORLD TOUR IMOGEN HEAP ELLIPSE
EUROPEAN STADIUM TOUR TAKE THAT CIRCUS
NETHERLANDS OPERA BELLINI I PURITANI
SADLER'S WELLS MALIPHANT AFTERLIGHT II
VH1 STORYTELLERS KANYE WEST TWO PLANES
BRITS PET SHOP BOYS TWIN HEADS
WORLD TOUR GOLDFRAPP HEAD FIRST
WORLD TOUR SHAKIRA THE SUN COMES OUT
WORLD TOUR MIKA IMAGINARIUM
GLYNDEBOURNE PHILIPS KNIGHT CREW
ARCOLA THEATRE WATSON PIECES OF VINCENT
PEACOCK THEATRE VAN LAAST BLAZE

a blank sheet of paper and a pencil.

SILVER & ZUBOFF MOLLY VS THE MACHINES
BRISBANE FESTIVAL DOYLE SALAMANDER
EXPO CITY UAE UNION DAY TAPESTRY
VINYL FACTORY AN ATLAS OF ES DEVLIN
SADLER'S WELLS ROSE & BLOOM PRIZES
TENNESSEE GORE CLIMATE UNDERGROUND
2024
LOS ANGELES SNAPCHAT THE COUNCIL
LV AW2025 GHESQUIÈRE ÉTOILE DU NORD
LV CRUISE 2026 GHESQUIÈRE PALAIS DES PAPES
COACHELLA GAGA THE ART OF PERSONAL CHAOS
MIT EUGENE MCDERMOTT AWARD
A CORUÑA ZARA 50 SONGS OF THE SEA
2025
ZARA 50 IRIS LAMP
OXFORD UNIVERSITY VISITING PROFESSORSHIP
FAENA MIAMI BEACH DEVLIN READING ROOM
MELBOURNE AUSTRALIAN OPEN SEA & SKY
ZORLU ISTANBUL MILLER DEATH OF A SALESMAN
OXFORD UNIVERSITY DEVLIN / MUHLY 360 VESSELS
2026
ROYAL COURT THEATRE JOSEPH ARCHDUKE
CASTLE HOWARD DEVLIN LIBRARY OF 4 WINDS
HOMO FABER AN ISLAND OF LIGHT
POWERHOUSE PARRAMATTA DEVLIN SOLO SHOW
FUTURA SEOUL DEVLIN POROSITY
DESIGN MUSEUM DEVLIN OTHER WORLDS

NEVADA ARK DEVLIN *U2:UV SPHERE LAS VEGAS* 54 56 534 862
FREE YOUR MIND BOYLE *MANCHESTER FACTORY INTERNATIONAL* 42 541
AN ATLAS OF ES DEVLIN DEVLIN *THAMES & HUDSON* 542
AN ATLAS OF ES DEVLIN DEVLIN *COOPER HEWITT SMITHSONIAN* 549
LUNAR CHRONICLES WARNER BROS 612
MOST WANTED BAD BUNNY *WORLD TOUR* 575 826
SCREENSHARE DEVLIN *REVERB 180 THE STRAND* 550 782
SURFACING DEVLIN *ART BASEL* 555 696 834
THERE IS NO OTHER DEVLIN *CANNES LIONS FESTIVAL* 556
IN A LANDSCAPE MAX RICHTER *WORLD TOUR* 577 626
CORIOLANUS SHAKESPEARE *NATIONAL THEATRE* 578 704
CONGREGATION DEVLIN & CO AUTHORS *ST MARY LE STRAND* 52 559
FACE TO FACE DEVLIN *SOMERSET HOUSE* 569
HAMLET SHAKESPEARE *ROYAL SHAKESPEARE COMPANY* 580 692
LIBRARY OF LIGHT DEVLIN *PINACOTECA DI BRERA MILAN* 28 587
MAYHEM BALL LADY GAGA *WORLD TOUR* 583
WOMEN'S PAVILION CARTIER *EXPO 2025 OSAKA* 584
LULLABY T4P *WEMBLEY ARENA* 603
LIBRARY OF US DEVLIN *FAENA ART MIAMI BEACH* 22 24 26 588
TRACING TIME DEVLIN *FAENA ART PROJECT ROOM MIAMI* 593
TAKE ME HOME DEVLIN *SHENZHEN BAY CULTURE PARK* 601
AMERICAN PSYCHO SHEIK & SACASA *ALMEIDA THEATRE* 604 778
TRISTAN UND ISOLDE WAGNER *MET OPERA* 606 622 624 794 828
SOU O OUTRO DO OUTRO DEVLIN *CASA BRADESCO SÃO PAULO* 16 58
THE EVERYTHINGISTS DEVLIN *V&A EAST STOREHOUSE* 611
A NATIONAL PORTRAIT DEVLIN *NATIONAL PORTRAIT GALLERY* 614

Every project starts like this:

OLD VIC MACGREGOR SNAKE IN THE GRASS	1995	**RAIDING PARADISE** *ROSE BRUFORD COLLEGE* 140
THEATRE PROJECT TOKYO GRIFFITH PIANO	1996	**EDWARD II** MARLOWE *OCTAGON THEATRE BOLTON* 143
BUSH THEATRE LUCIE LOVE YOU, TOO		**LOVE AND UNDERSTANDING** PENHALL *BUSH THEATRE* 144 638
ROYAL COURT THEATRE PRITCHARD YARD GAL	1997	**FIDELIO** BEETHOVEN *ENGLISH TOURING OPERA* 151 635
HAMPSTEAD THEATRE POLLOCK THE DEATH OF COOL	1998	**BETRAYAL** PINTER *ROYAL NATIONAL THEATRE (RNT)* 152
BUSH THEATRE BØLSTAD ONE LIFE AND COUNTING		**FOUR SCENES** RAMBERT *SADLER'S WELLS* 156 670
SCOTTISH OPERA HUMPERDINCK HANSEL AND GRETEL	1999	**HOWIE THE ROOKIE** O'ROWE *BUSH THEATRE* 155 631
GATE THEATRE UNEL PERA PALAS		**HAMLET** SHAKESPEARE *YOUNG VIC* 162
SOHO THEATRE OUT OF JOINT A STATE AFFAIR		**POWDER HER FACE** ADÈS *YSTAD FESTIVAL* 165 790
BBC 2 JACKSON BRILLIANT!	2000	**GOD'S PLENTY** RAMBERT *SADLER'S WELLS* 173 630 632 634
RSC SHAKESPEARE HENRY IV PARTS I & II	2001	**MEAT** O'DAVIES *THEATRE ROYAL PLYMOUTH* 639
RSC *EDGAR* THE PRISONER'S DILEMMA		**ANTONY AND CLEOPATRA** SHAKESPEARE *RSC* 161
COMEDY THEATRE NICHOLS JOE EGG	2002	**I REMEMBER RED** VELDMAN *CULLBERG BALLET* 167 669
ROYAL COURT WERTENBAKER CREDIBLE WITNESS		**FLAG : BURNING** WIRE *BARBICAN THEATRE* 174 644 646
ARTS THEATRE PSB / HARVEY CLOSER TO HEAVEN	2003	**MACBETH** BLOCH *THEATER AN DER WIEN* 182 642
SHORT FILM STUBBS SNOW ON SATURDAY	2004	**ESSENCE** WALKER / PARK *LINBURY ROYAL OPERA HOUSE* 168 836
SOHO THEATRE SCHIMMELPFENNIG ARABIAN NIGHT	2005	**TOUCH THE SKY** KANYE WEST *US TOUR* 179 648
NATIONAL THEATRE BARRY HINTERLAND		**HECUBA** EURIPIDES *ROYAL SHAKESPEARE COMPANY (RSC)* 187 736
NORTHERN BALLET THEATRE VELDMAN STREETCAR		**A MIDSUMMER NIGHT'S DREAM** BRITTEN *HAMBURG* 180 734
SHORT FILM PINTER / HODGE VICTORIA STATION	2006	**FUNDAMENTAL** PET SHOP BOYS *WORLD TOUR* 188
BUSH THEATRE FROST AIRSICK		**LA CLEMENZA DI TITO** MOZART *BARCELONA* 192 666 742 744
ALMEIDA THEATRE LAURENS FIVE GOLD RINGS		**DON GIOVANNI** MOZART *THEATER AN DER WIEN* 197 659
RSC DE VEGA THE DOG IN THE MANGER		**FLAMMEN** SCHULHOFF *THEATER AN DER WIEN* 198 739
OUT OF JOINT SHAKESPEARE MACBETH	2007	**CARMEN** BIZET *ENGLISH NATIONAL OPERA* 203 640 672 762
		SALOME WILDE / STRAUSS *ROYAL OPERA HOUSE (ROH)* 204 808
		GLOW IN THE DARK KANYE WEST *WORLD ARENA TOUR* 207

A PREFACE

When people ask me which is my favourite collaboration, I always answer: this book, although it's probably the smallest.

This edition, *A Concise Atlas of Es Devlin*, contracts the original 2023 volume to a quarter of the physical size, while expanding its content to include texts, sketches and images of 28 new projects and an essay by Johanna Agerman Ross, curator of the London Design Museum's monographic exhibition *Es Devlin: Other Worlds*.

Es Devlin, 2026

LV SS2016 GHESQUIÈRE **3 FORMS**

NRJ CANNES ADELE **WAVES**

LONDON O2 BRITS **FLYING ZOETROPE**

GRAMMYS ADELE **ALL I ASK**

BRITS ADELE **MIRRORED ZOETROPE**

LV AW2016 LOUVRE GHESQUIÈRE **ELECTRONIC OWL**

GLASTONBURY ADELE **SOMEONE LIKE YOU**

MTV ROTTERDAM THE WEEKND **PLANETARIUM**

MTV AMA THE WEEKND **MIRROR TUNNEL**

SNL THE WEEKND **CROSS / LIGHT**

ST JOHN AT HACKNEY DEVLIN **SHARED SKY**

TOUR ROBBIE WILLIAMS **HEAVY ENTERTAINMENT**

VIENNA HENZE **ELEGY FOR YOUNG LOVERS**

LV SS2017 GHESQUIÈRE **SPACESHIP LOUVRE**

LV AW2017 LOUVRE GHESQUIÈRE **NIGHT LOUVRE**

LV CRUISE 2017 GHESQUIÈRE **KYOTO TUNNEL**

SNL KATY PERRY **BACKPACK PARADE**

TV TOKIO MYERS **GAUZED PIANO**

GRAMMYS KATY PERRY **WHITE PICKET FENCE**

BRITS KATY PERRY **DONALD & THERESA**

DONMAR FRIEL **ARISTOCRATS**

LV SS2018 GHESQUIÈRE **LOUVRE FLOOD**

LV CRUISE 2018 GHESQUIÈRE **MAEGHT MAZE**

LV AW2019 GHESQUIÈRE **UNDER LOUVRE**

NRJ CANNES THE WEEKND **ZOETROPE**

ENTS

A CORRIDOR

Our own pulse beats in every stranger's throat

Barbara Deming, 'Spirit of Love'

I think we should not be in the persuasion business anymore … about ecological reality, we should be in the amazing people business. We should do some kind of magic … where people are so compelled by this miracle that before they realize they've changed their belief, they've already changed.

Timothy Morton

I remember standing in a long corridor of a music school when I was around 11 years old, hearing fragments of music from each glass-windowed door: a pianist playing a Bach fugue, a trumpeter playing Miles Davis, Led Zeppelin on a guitar, a soprano singing Mozart.

I remember admiring the virtuosity of each of these musicians and composers, and then observing that the place where I stood was equally miraculous – in that particular shaft of sunlight, where these fragments of music, light and atmosphere coalesced into something new and unnamable.

I see my practice in light, sculpture, theatre, music and text as a 31-year extension of that corridor: sometimes walking or reading alone, often running at speed, usually holding hands with collaborators – musicians, poets, engineers, activists, directors and dancers. This book is an attempt to collect the traces that have been left; to seek the connections, recurring interests and forms that have resurfaced throughout my practice. It aims to express the evolving intentions which have found their focus particularly over the past decade since I read Naomi Klein's *This Changes Everything*, which exposes the systemic roots of the climate crisis.

Many of us are seeking ways in which our crafts can resonate amidst the climate and broader civilizational crises we face. An artist's daily practice involves imagining worlds that don't yet exist. A theatre-making artist's work is inherently collaborative, made by an assembly of practitioners for a communal audience. We invite audiences into experimental perspectives that neither they nor we have previously inhabited. We see an audience as a temporary society, a community that arrives in one state, sits closely together, in thought, in the dark for a few hours, and departs in an altered state, the architecture of their minds redrawn by new thoughts and feelings. Whether in an art gallery, museum, theatre or public space, we use magic and illusion to destabilize entrenched beliefs and to encourage collective acts of imagination. Perhaps the techniques we have developed together to amaze our audiences may prove useful in the pursuit of broader cognitive shifts.

The book's opening images present the large-scale sculptural installations which have become my focus over the past decade. Their titles can be found in the visual index on page 872. Donatien Grau's essay introduces my practice and a conversation with Hans Ulrich Obrist discusses the past decade. Andrea Lipps's essay outlines the broad 31-year trajectory of my work, while Johanna Agerman Ross's essay explores the most recent work in the museum and gallery context. I have composed a series of texts to accompany the works that follow: '12 Things' offers a brief account of 1971–1985, 'A Student Sketchbook' assembles teenage and student drawings and paintings from 1985–1995, and 'A 31-Year Sketchbook' charts the process of 150 projects from 1995–2026, through a broadly chronological sequence of archive sketches and scale models. The sketchbook is interrupted by 'An Interval: Lockdown Conversations' – fragments of Zoom calls with colleagues during the 2020–2021 pandemic – and a conversation about ritual with Dorothea von Hantelmann.

Photographic illustrations of over 160 works are presented at the end of the book in 'A Series of Illuminated Forms' and 'A Sequence in Coloured Light'. We have included page numbers at the base of each of the commentaries to help you navigate between early sketches and final photographs which are arranged by form and colour rather than chronology.

The names of works often evolve during the process and I have sometimes retained the early working titles which are lodged most strongly in my memory. When I say

‘We’ throughout the texts, I’m referring to myself and my collaborators: the curators, composers, choreographers, directors, studio associates, lighting designers, production managers, musicians, writers and fabricators, whose names encircle the opening apertures of this book: their collaboration has made my practice possible.

A SELECTION OF WORKS: 2012–2026

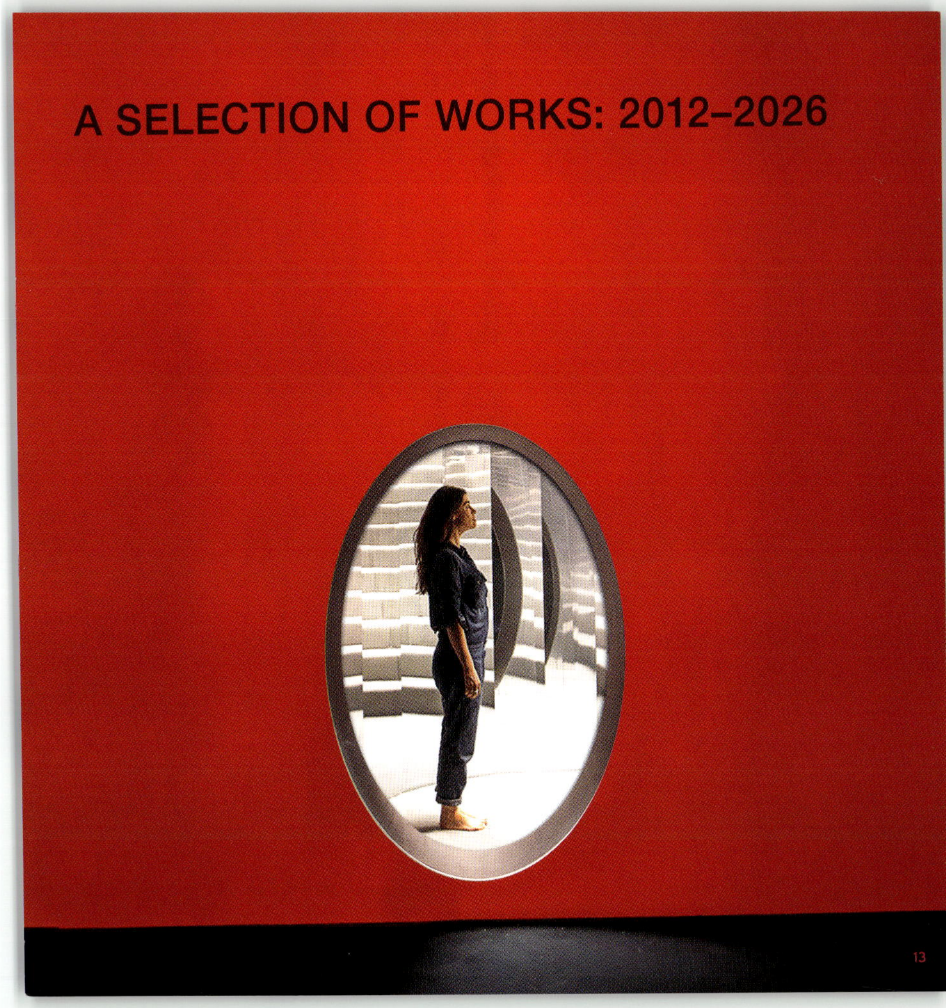

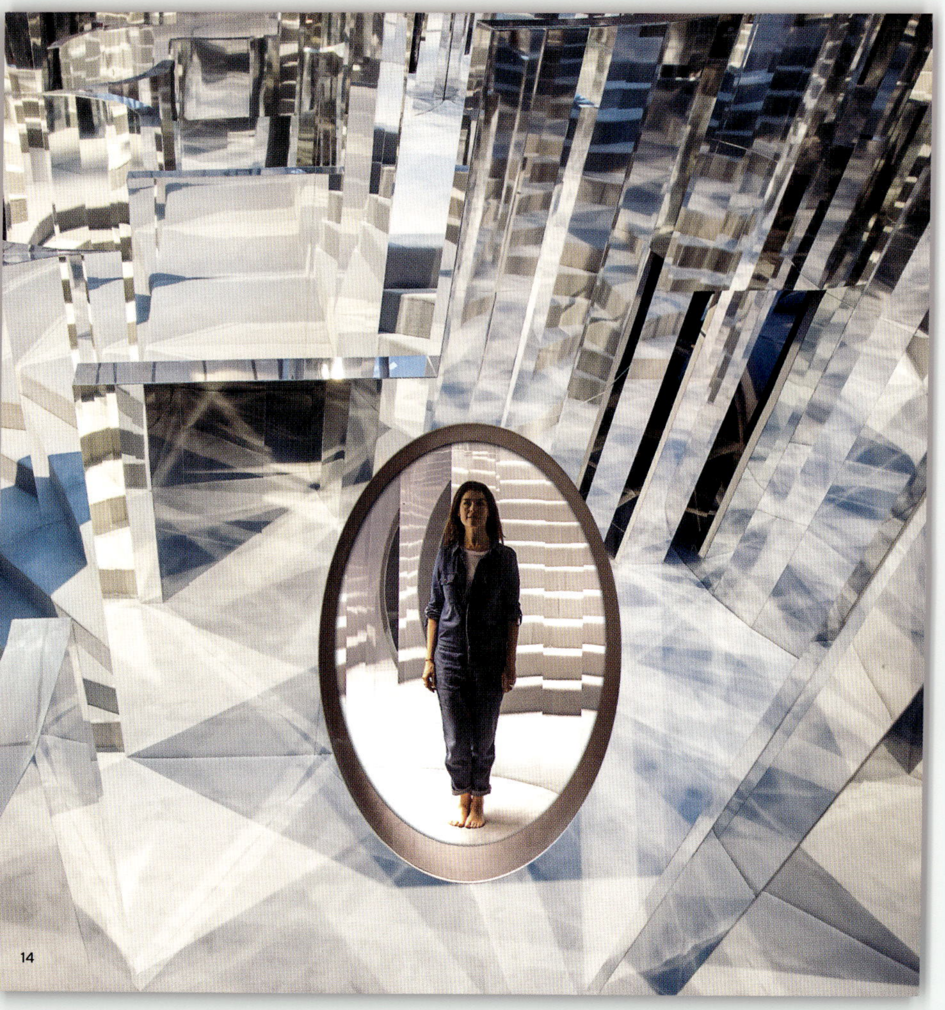

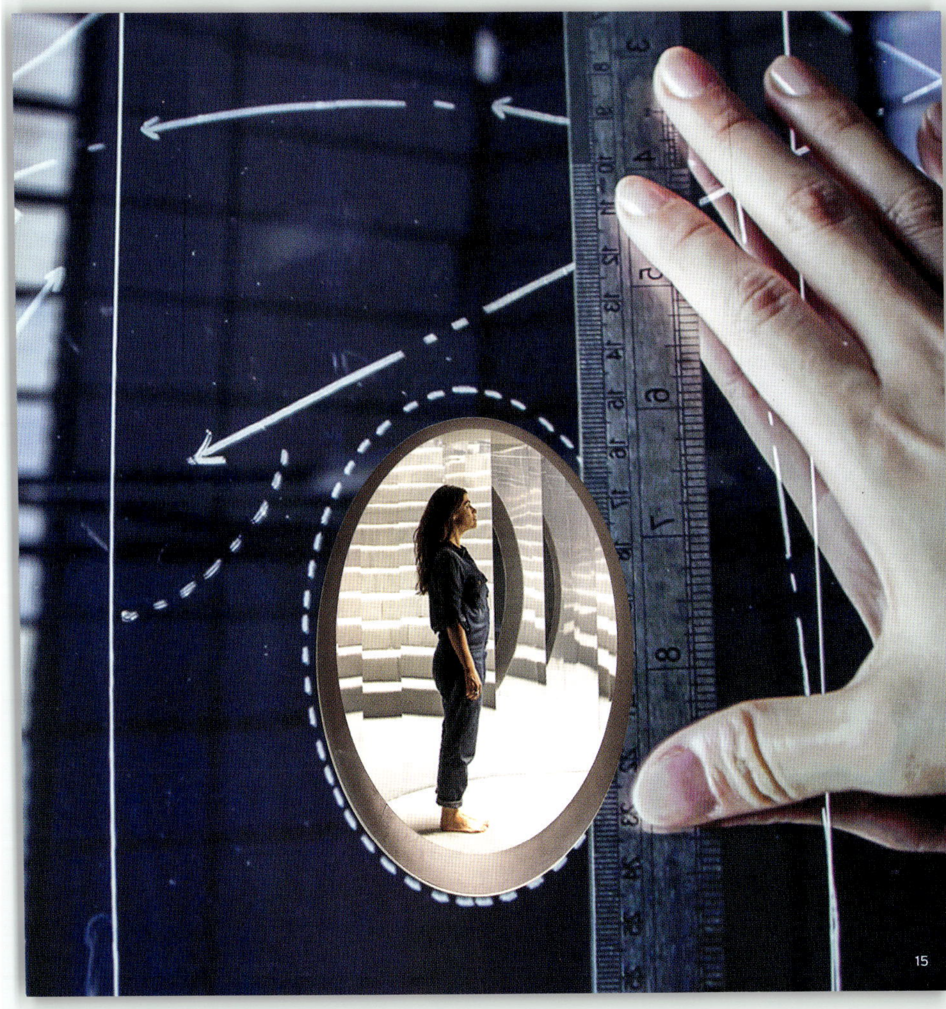

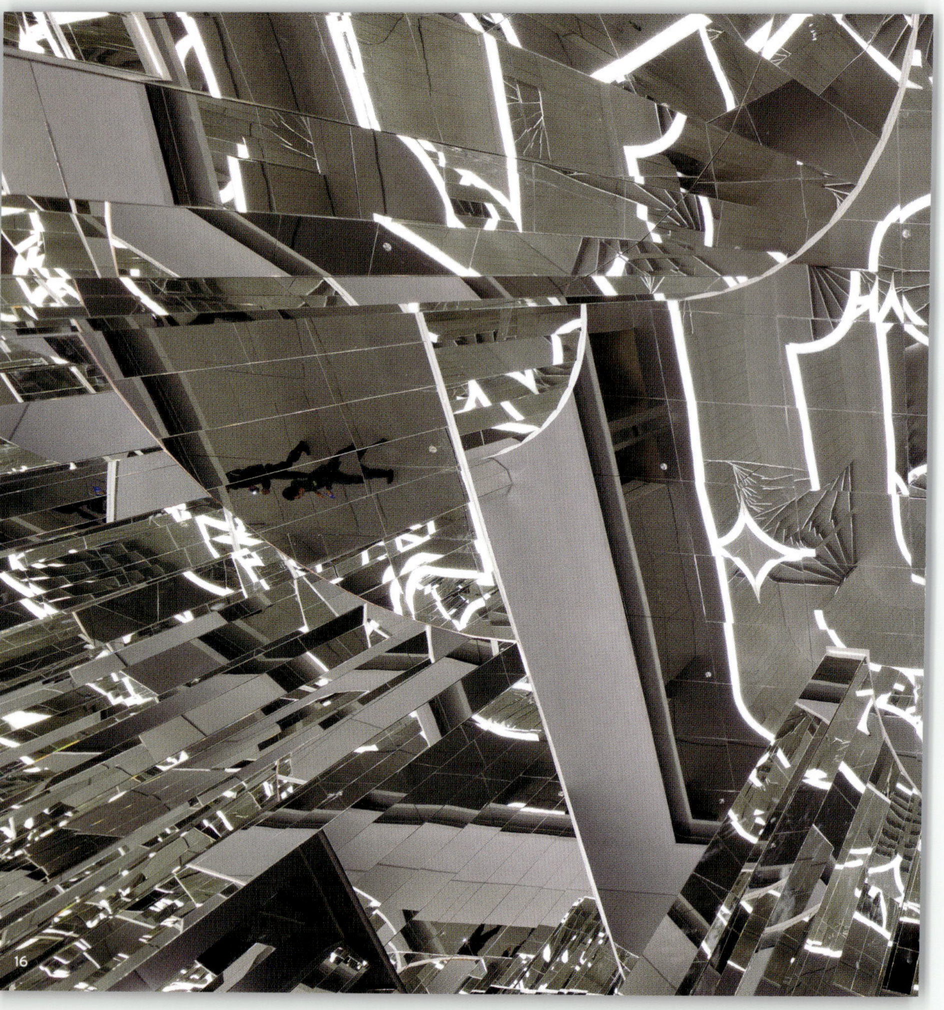

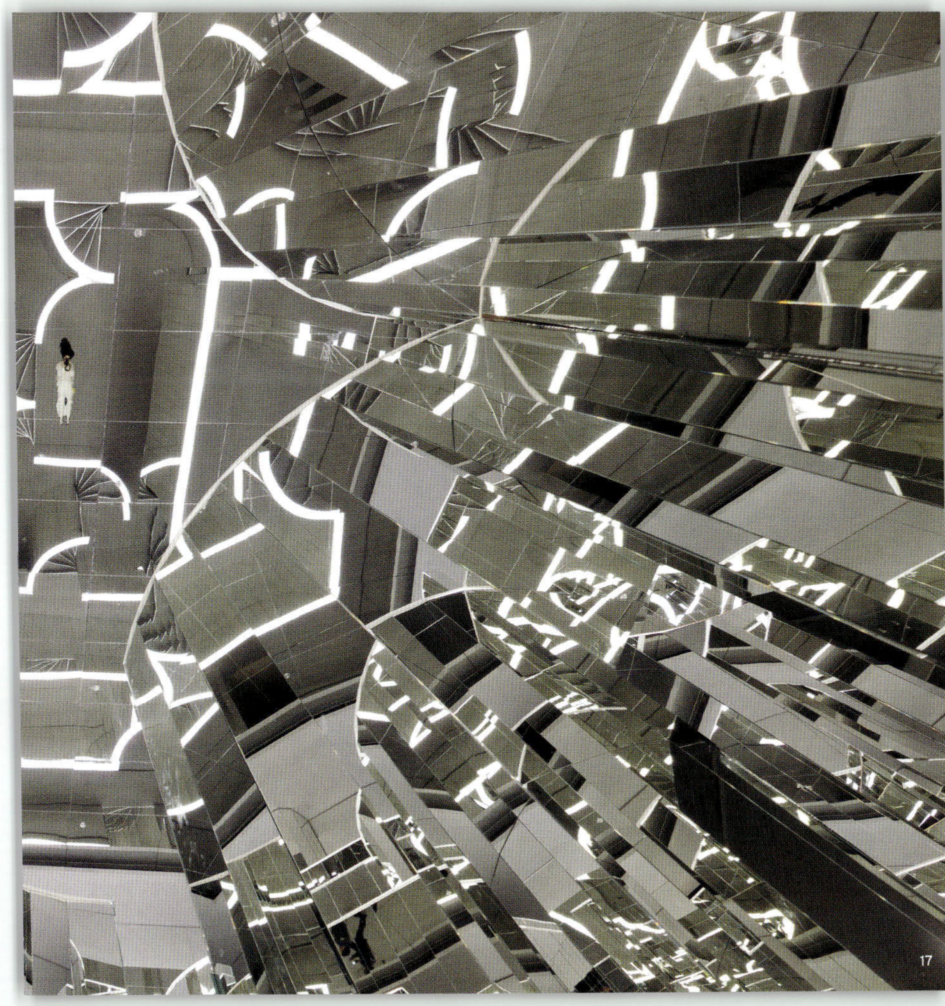

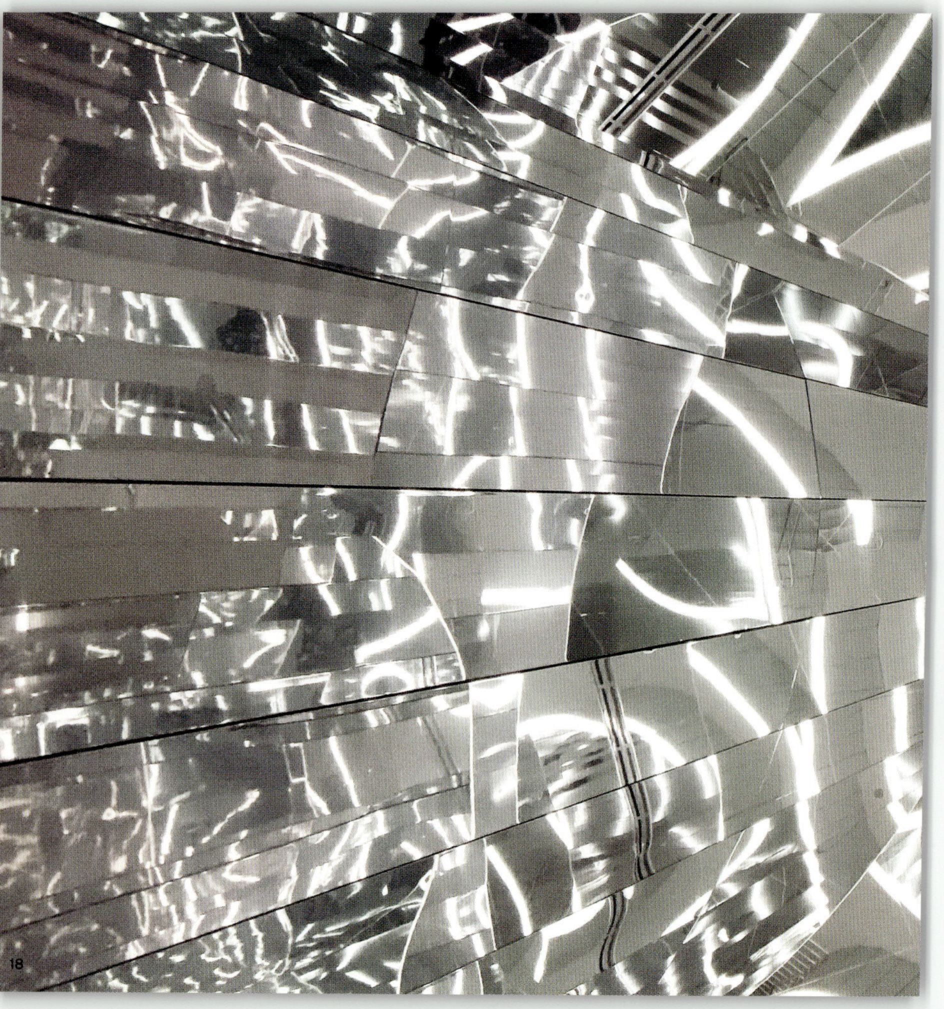

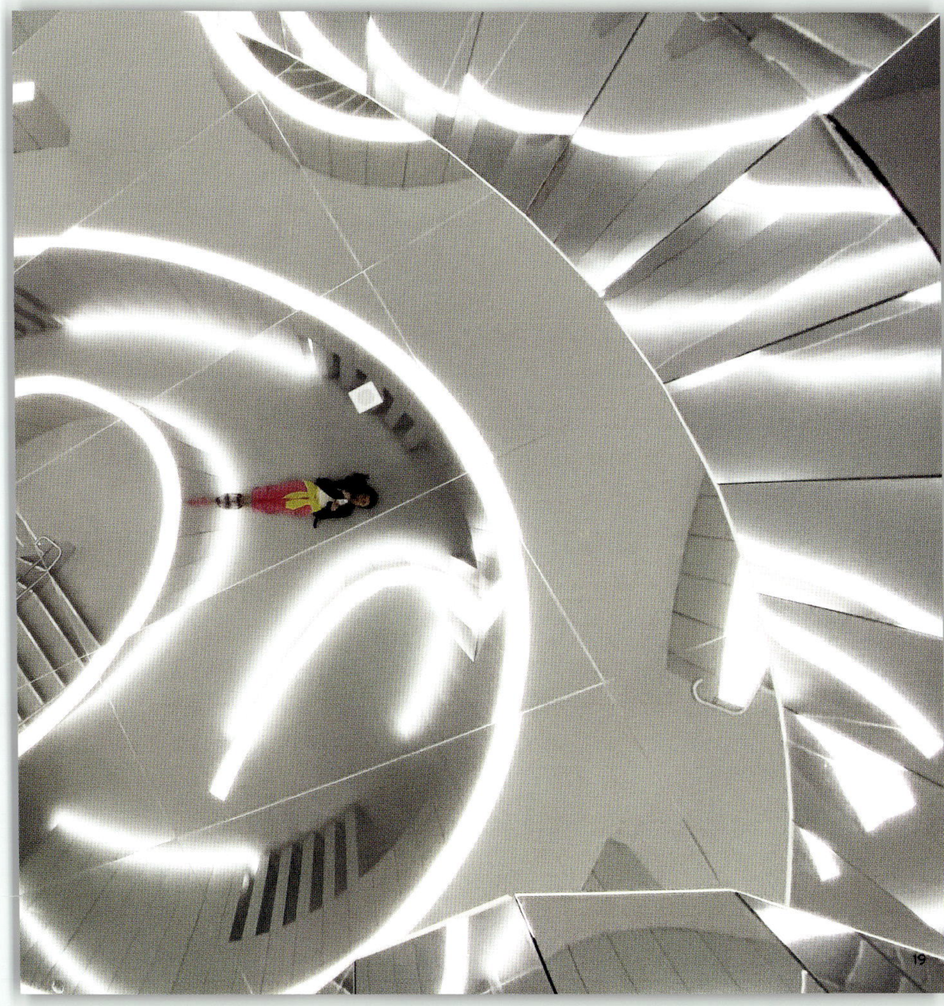

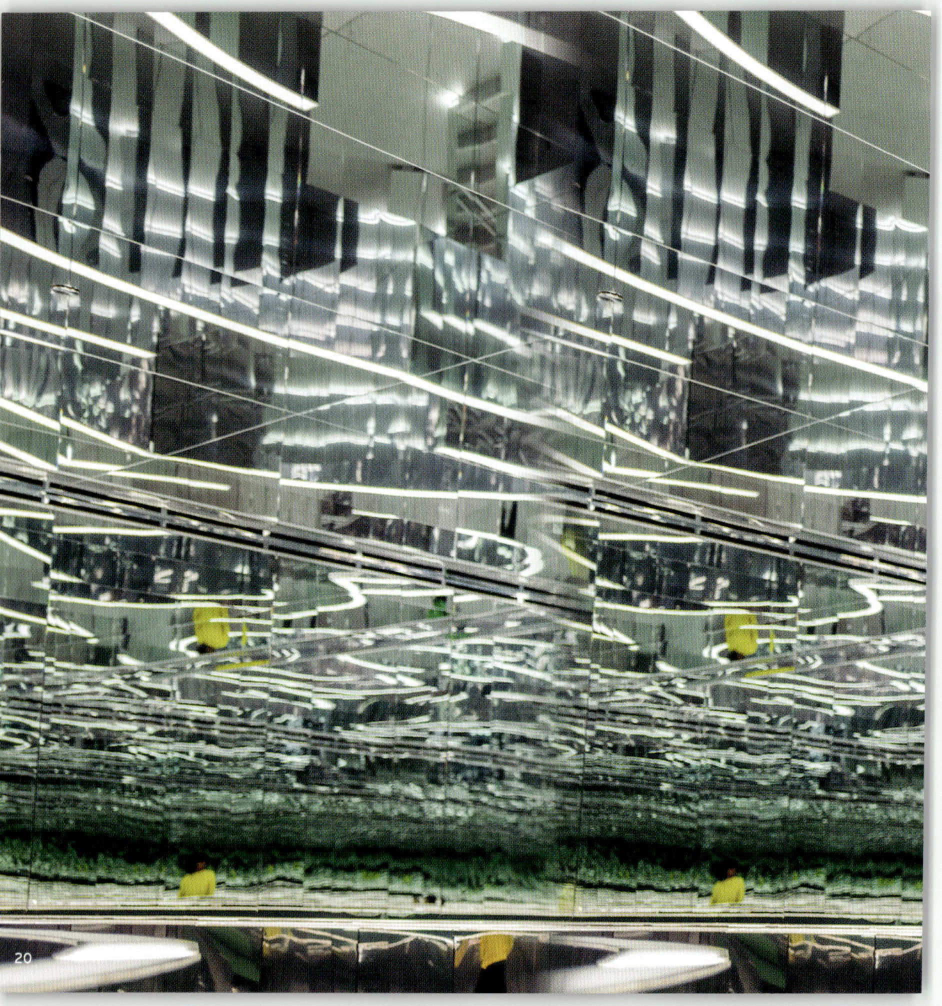

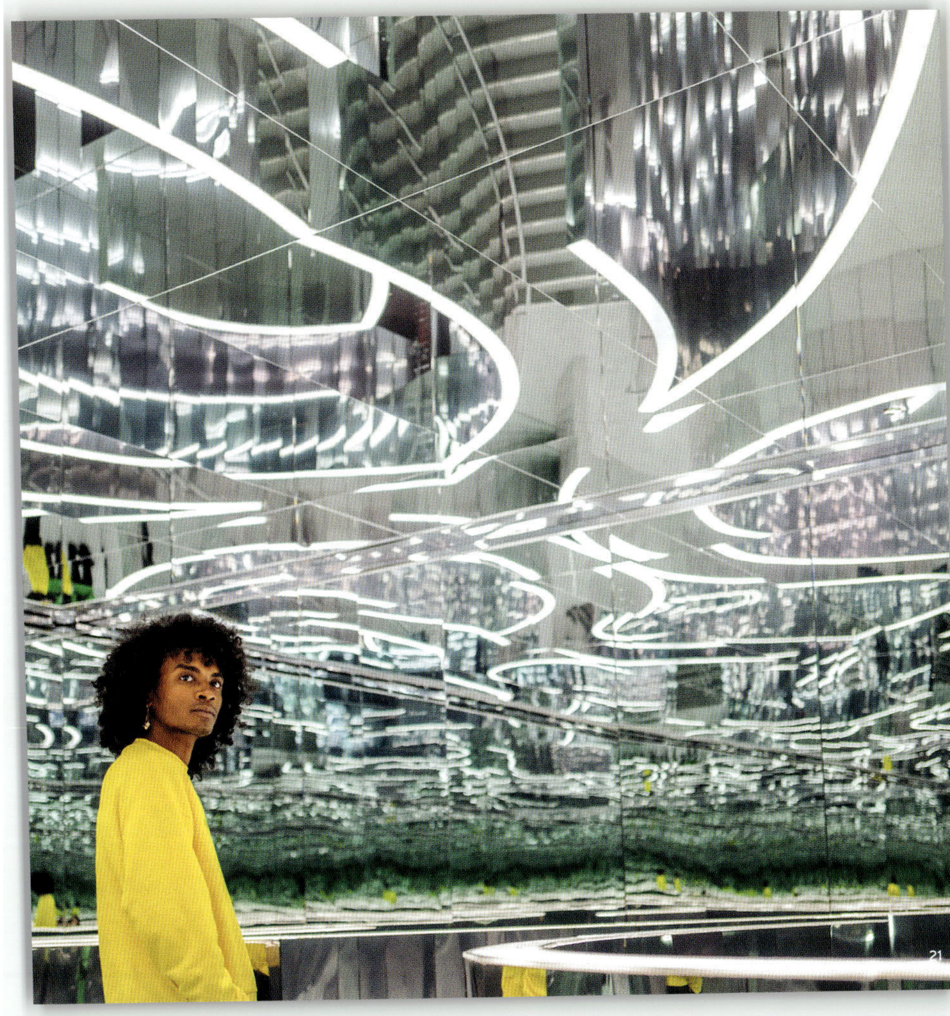

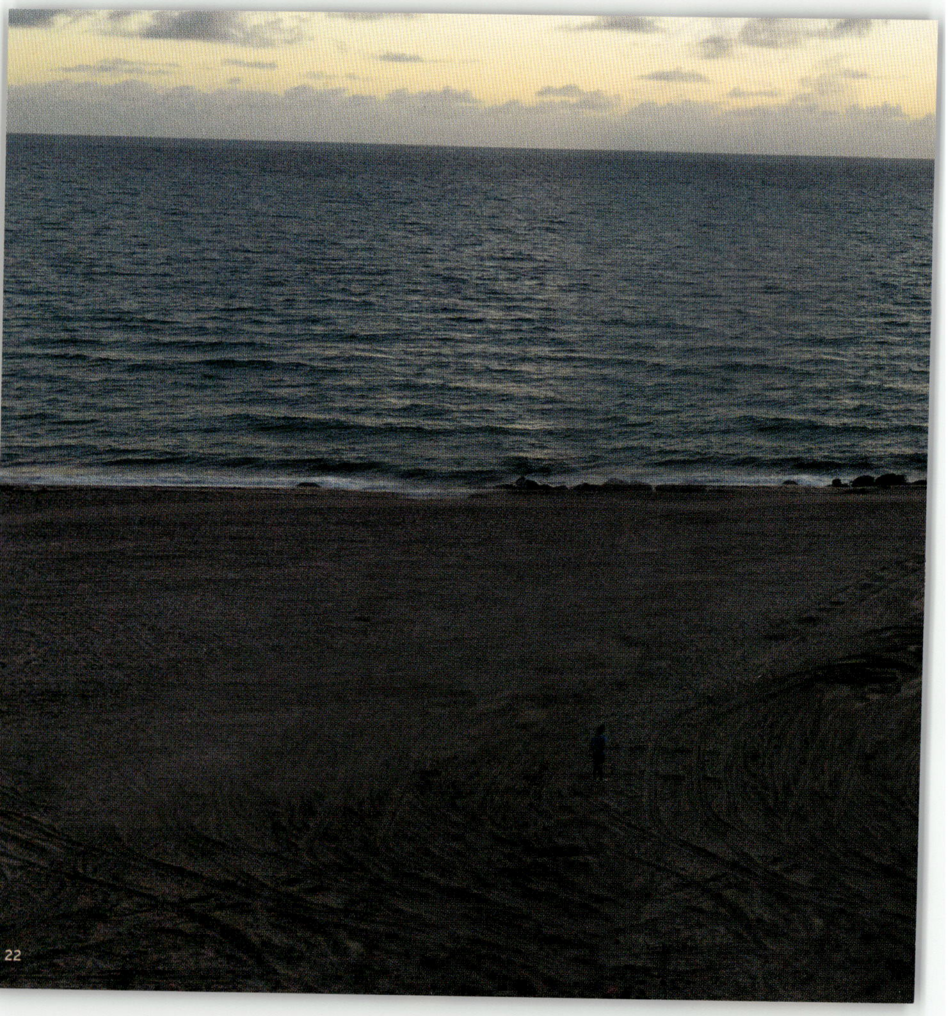

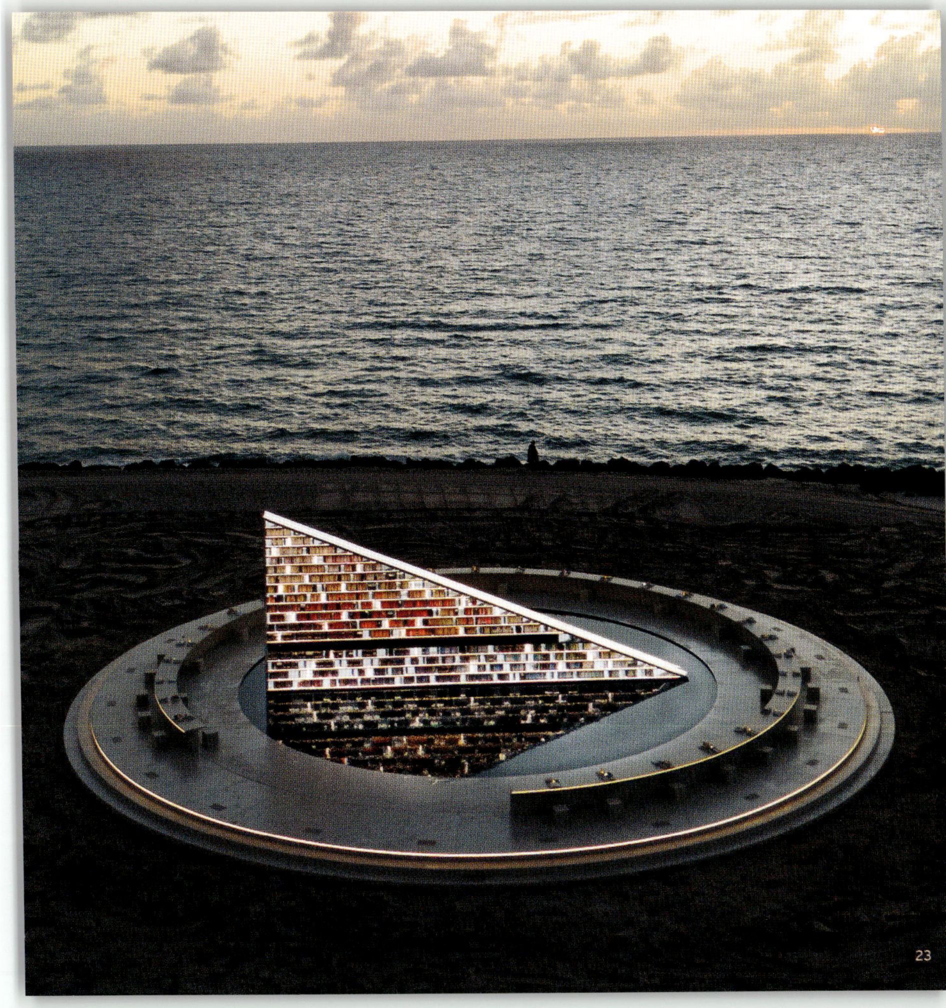

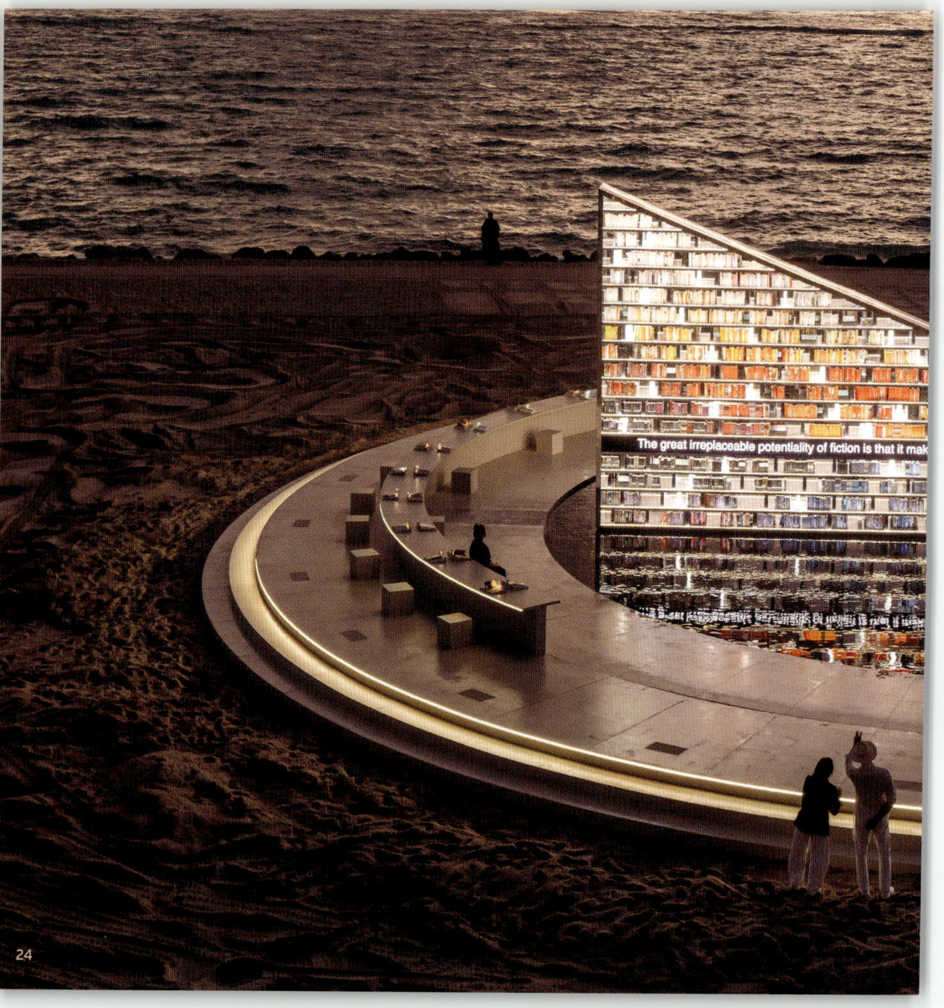
The great irreplaceable potentiality of fiction is that it mak

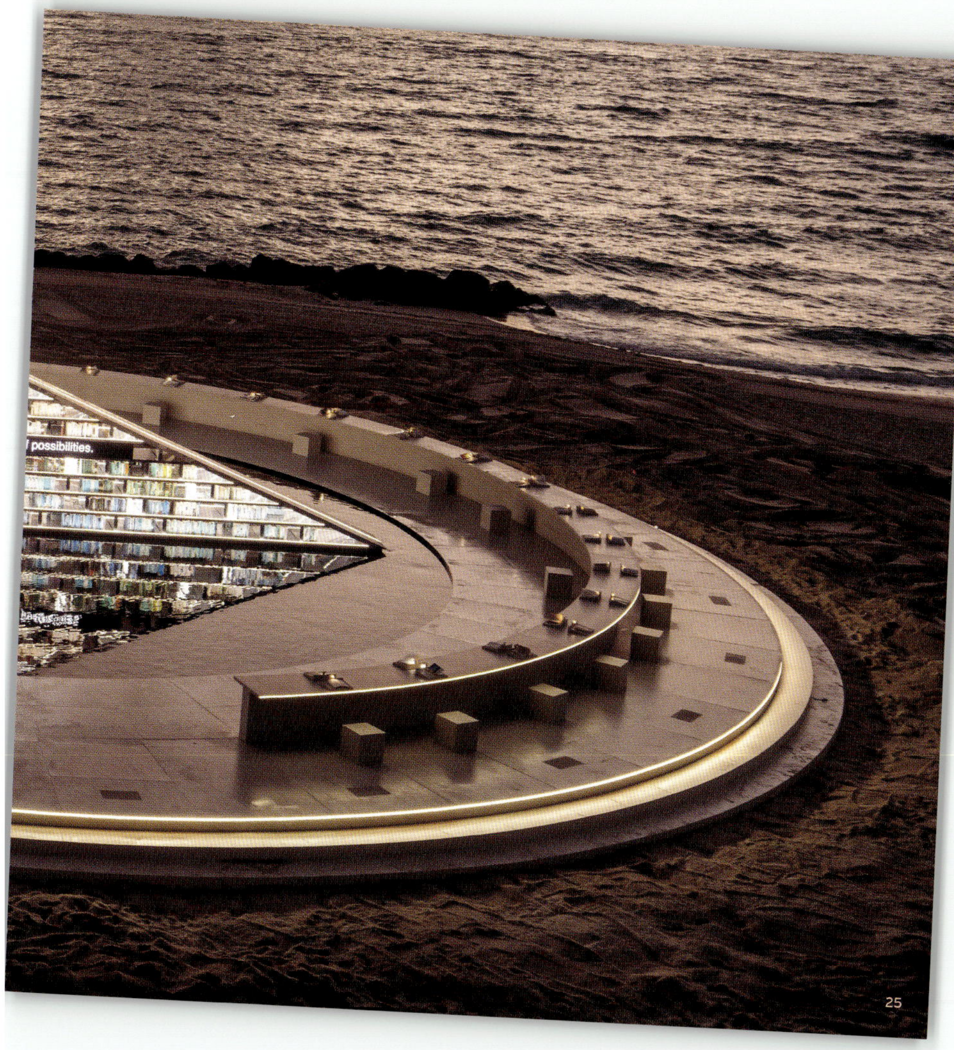
possibilities.

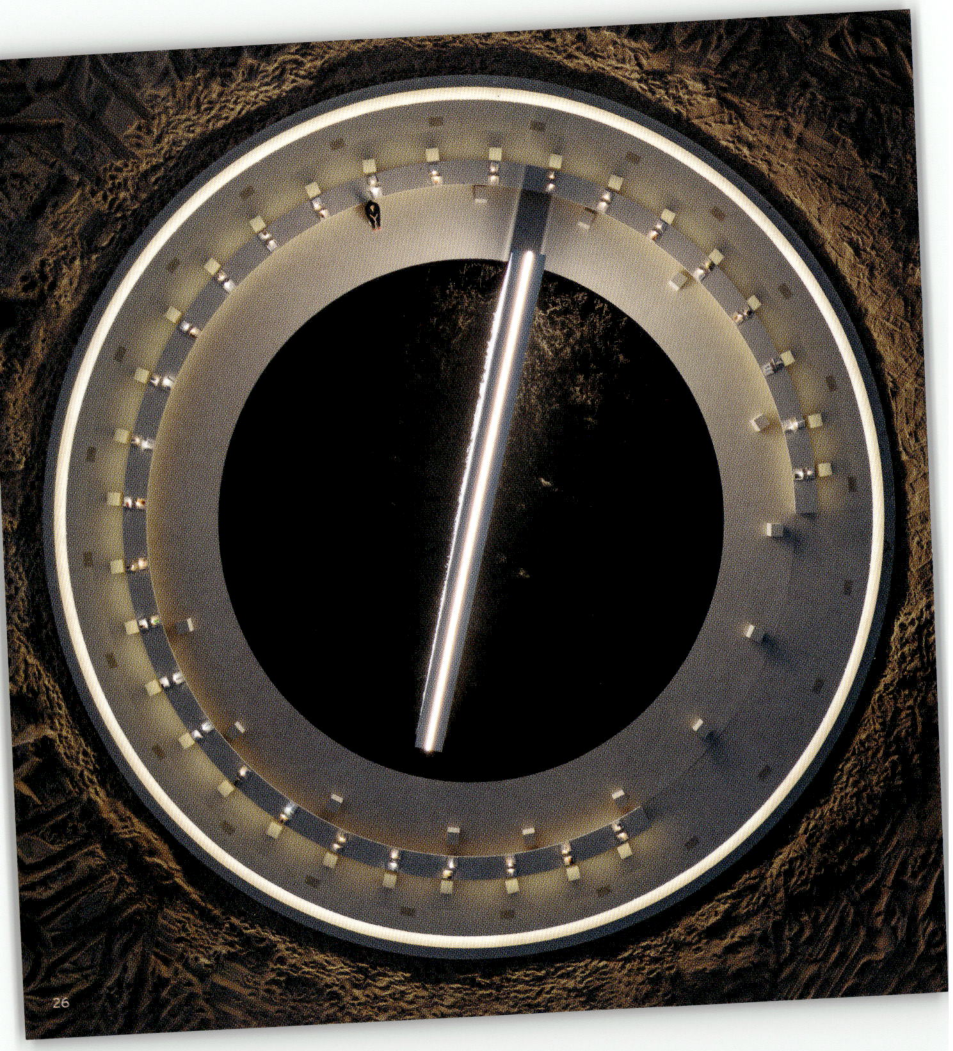

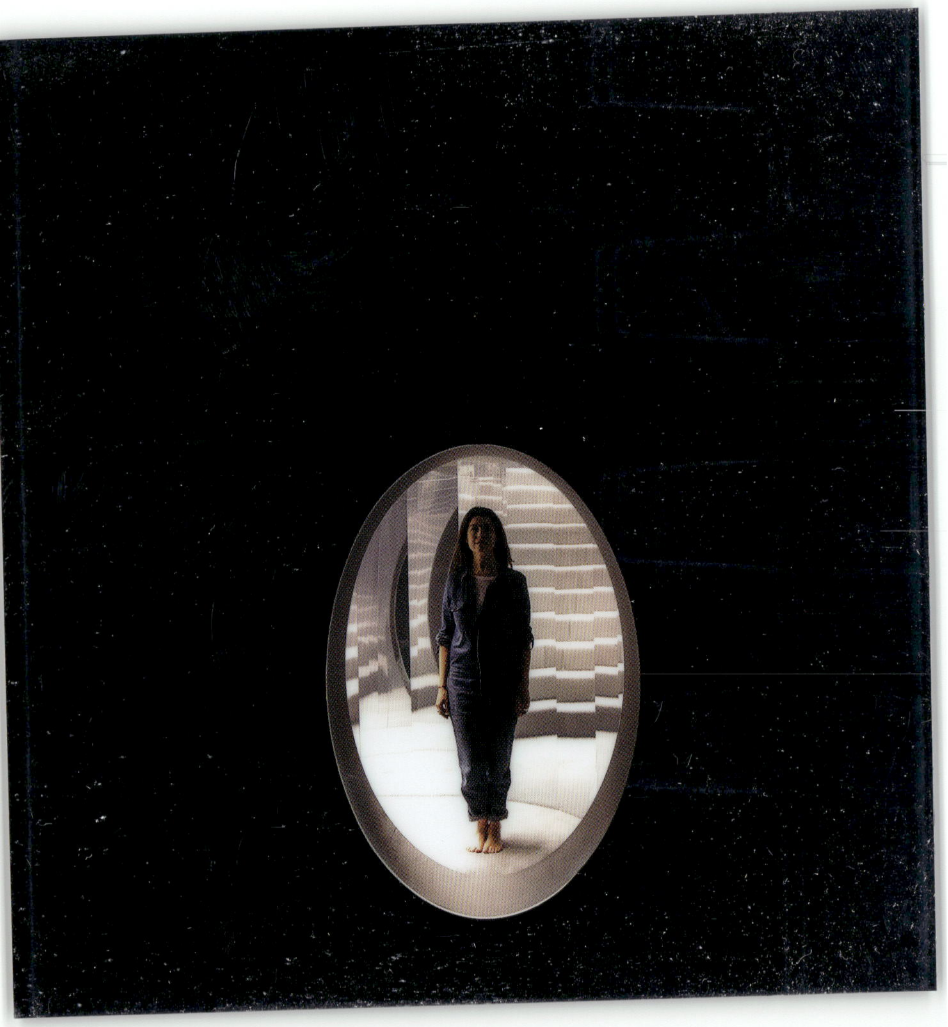

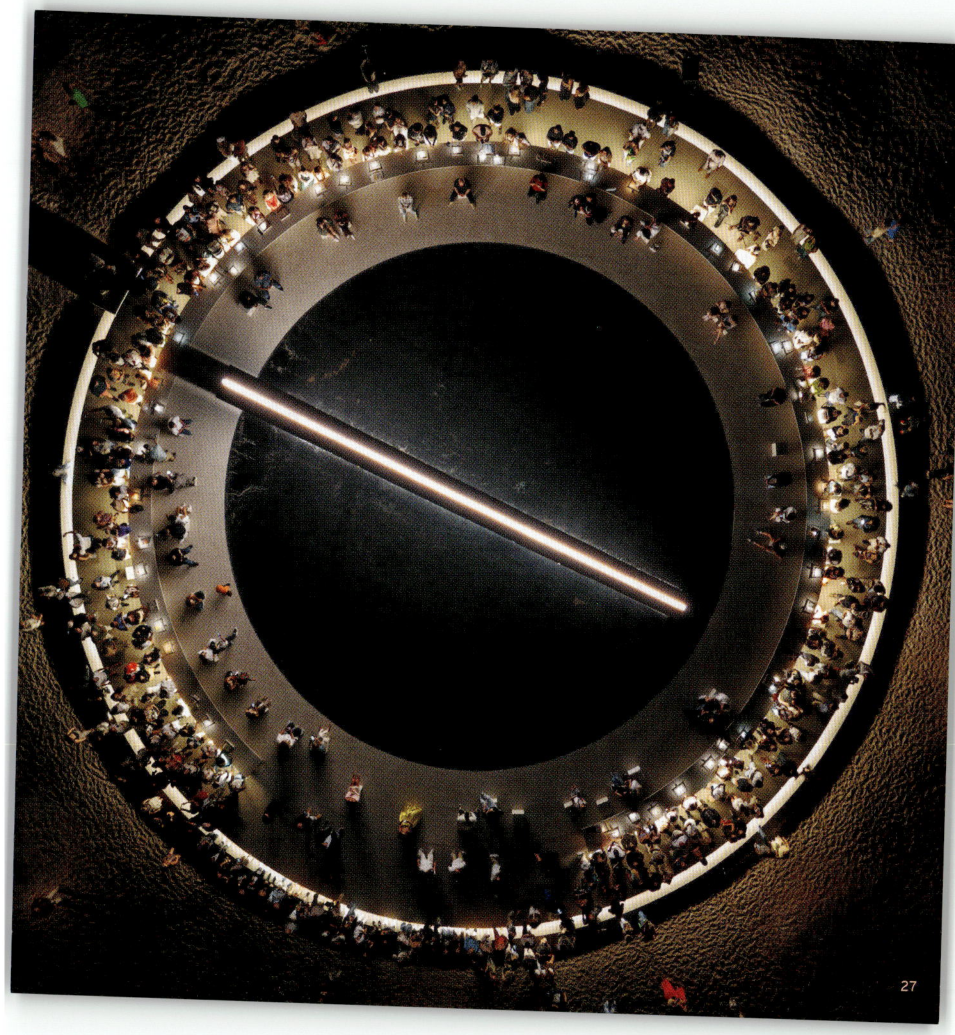

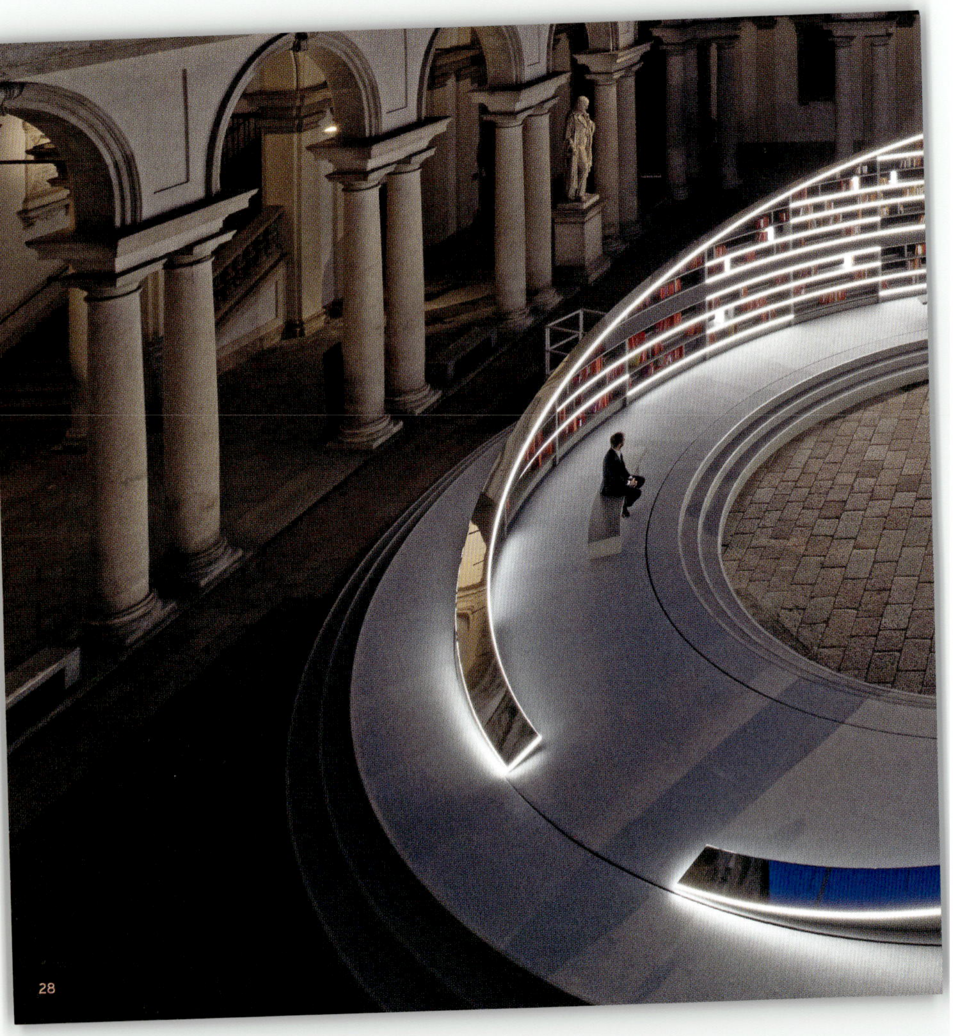

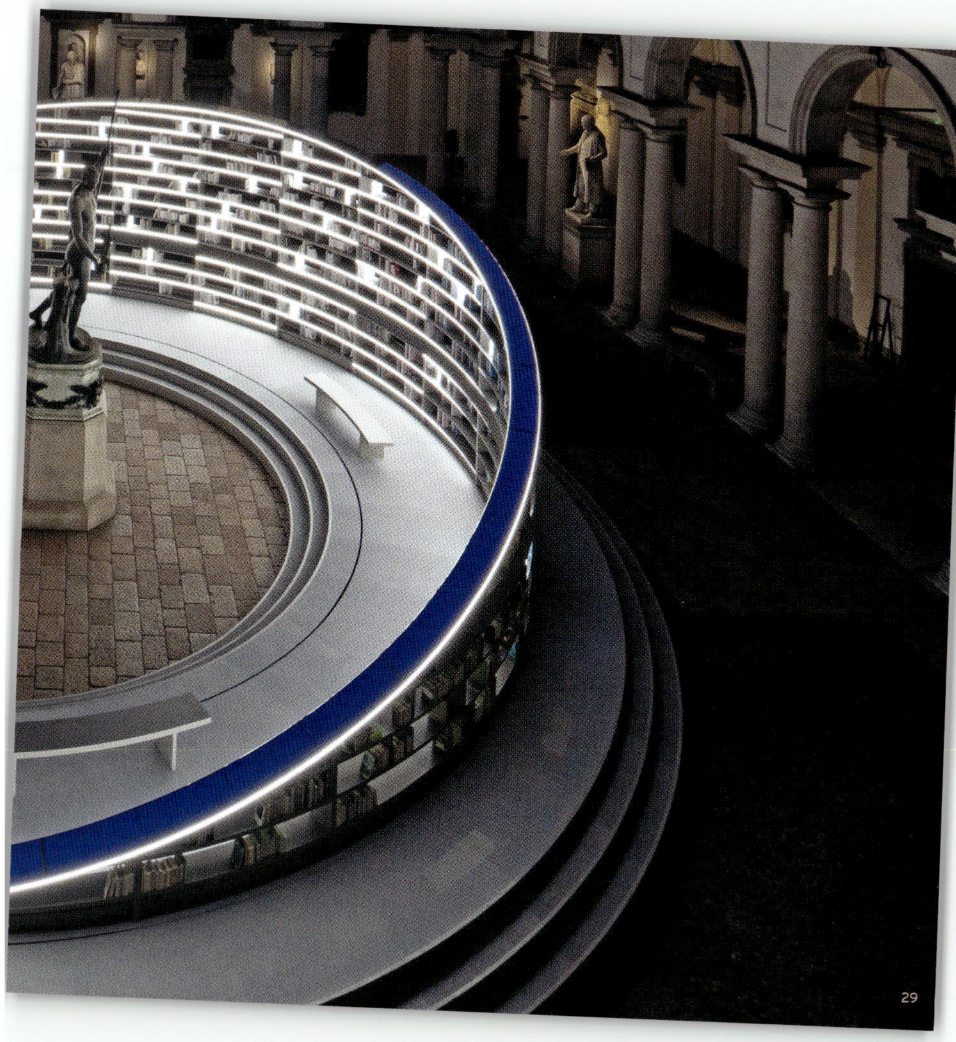

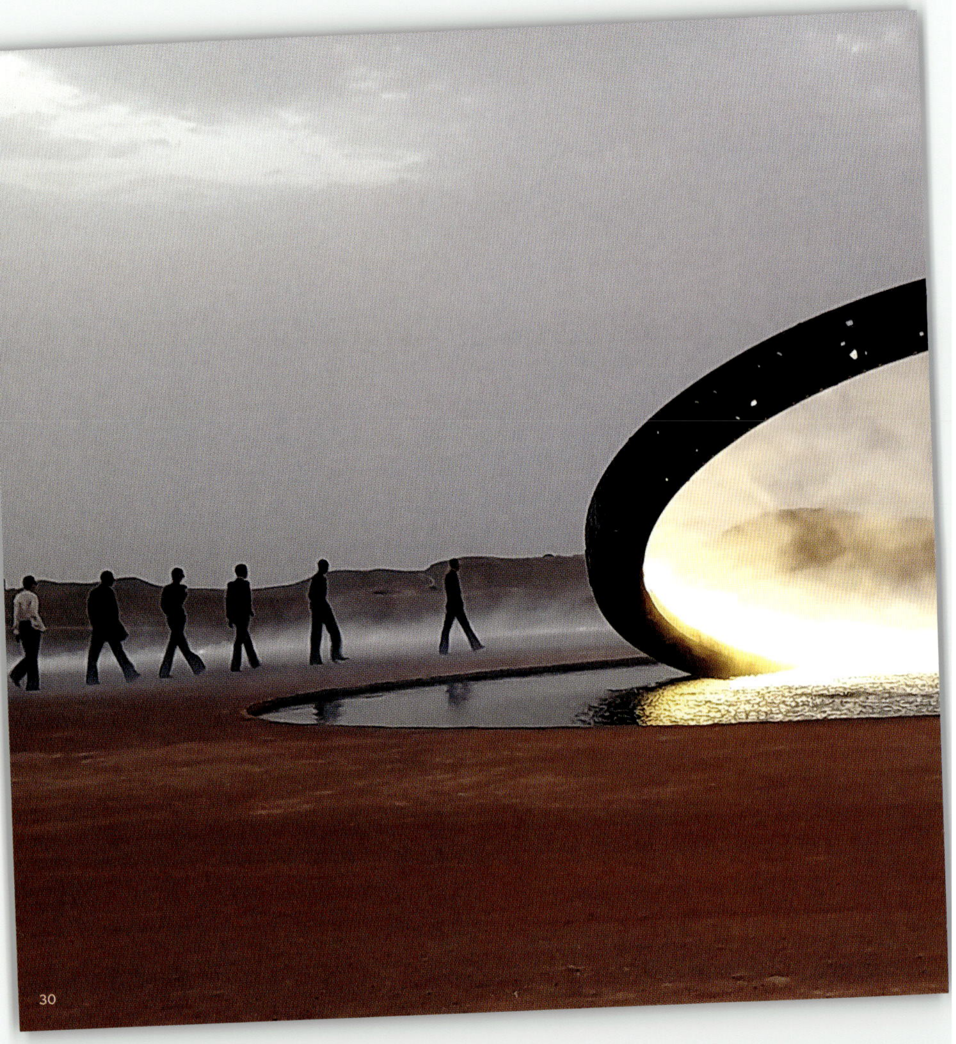

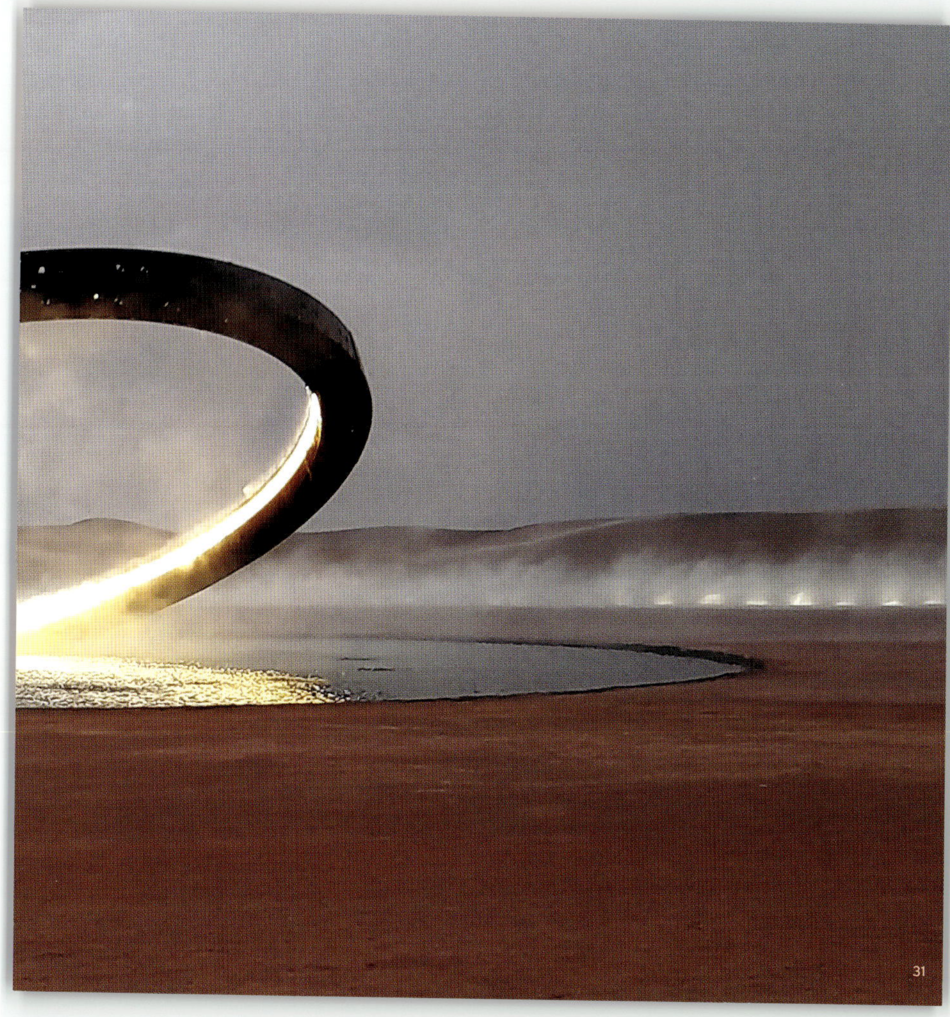

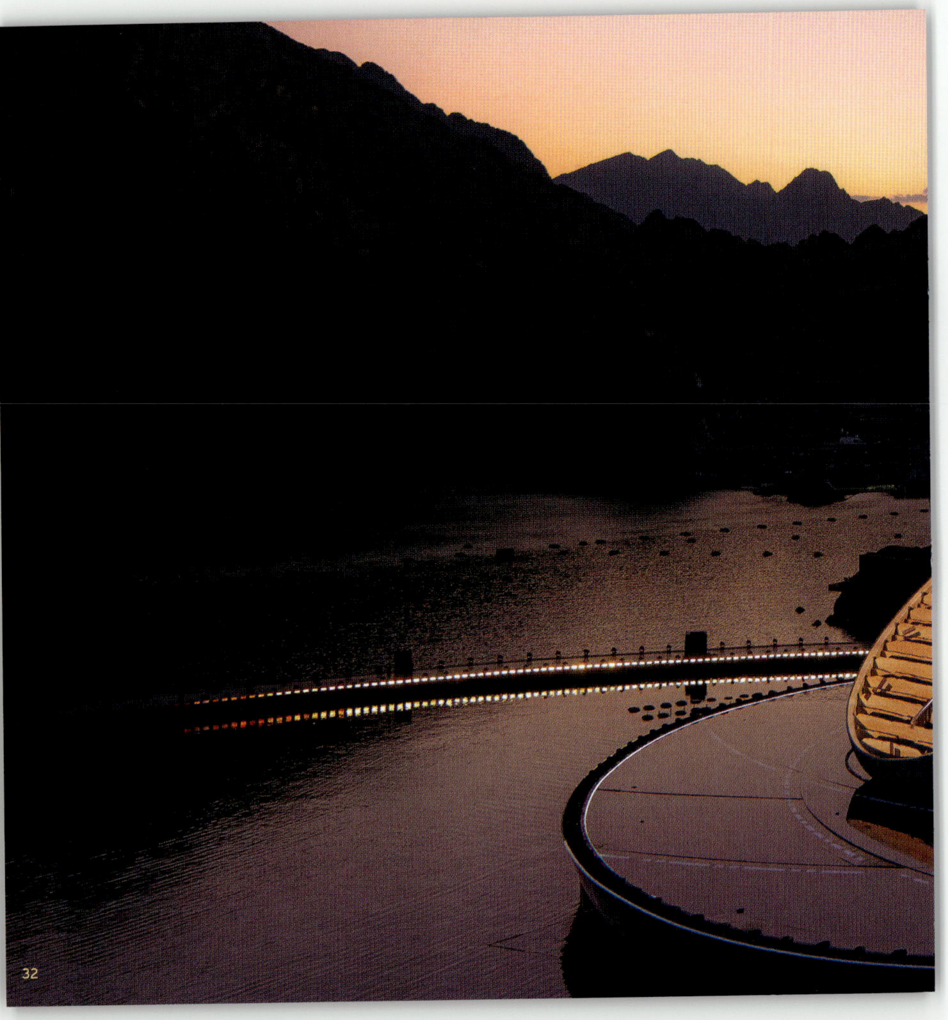

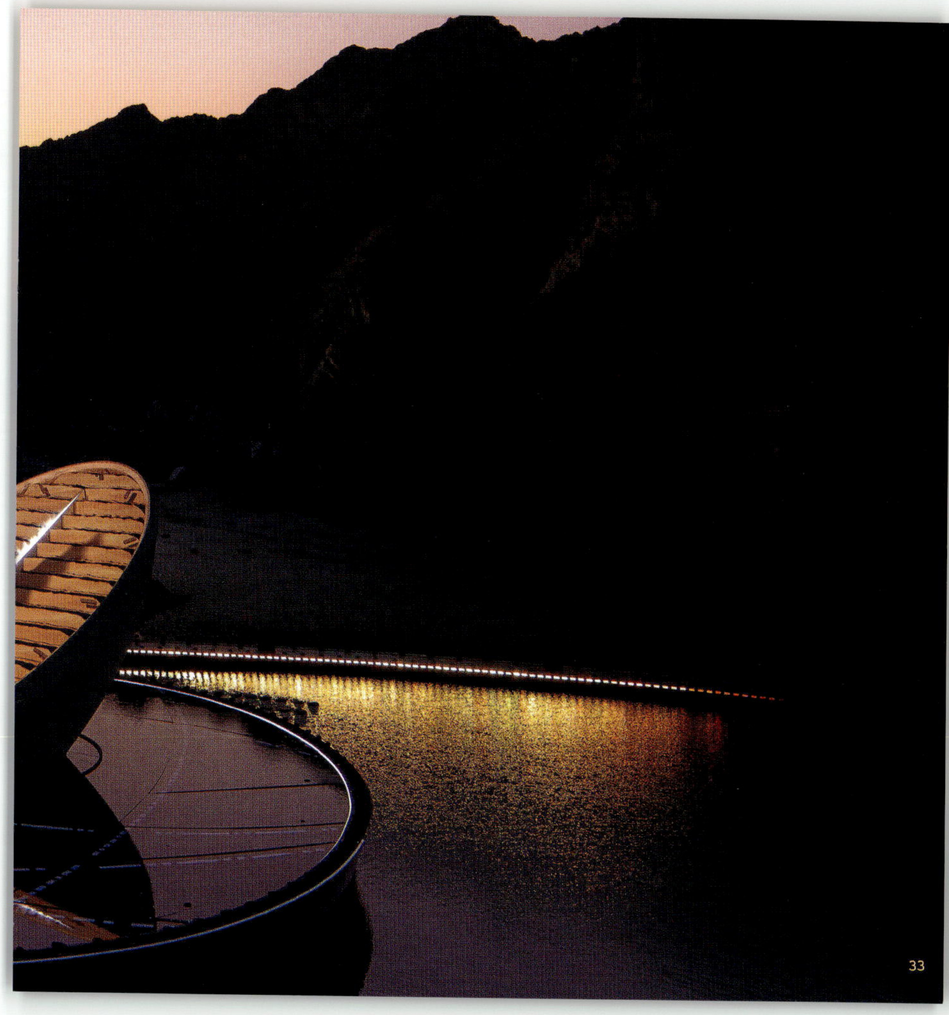

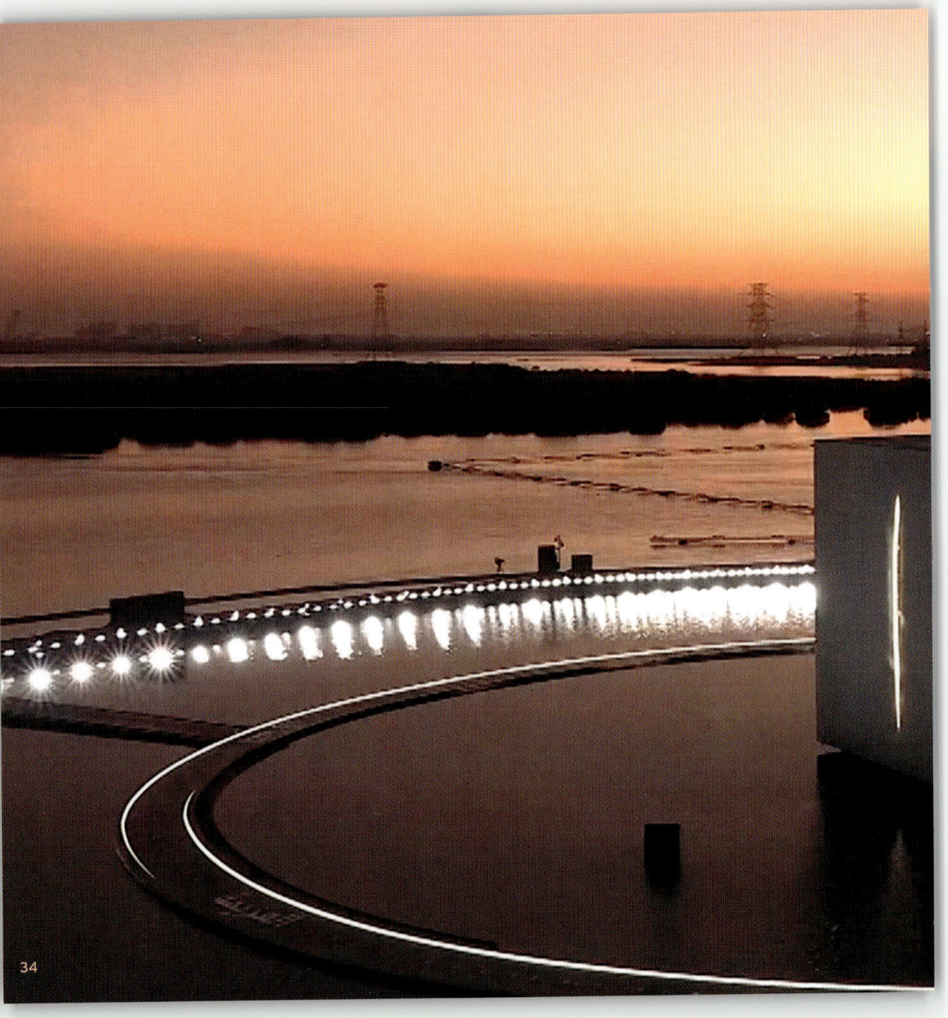

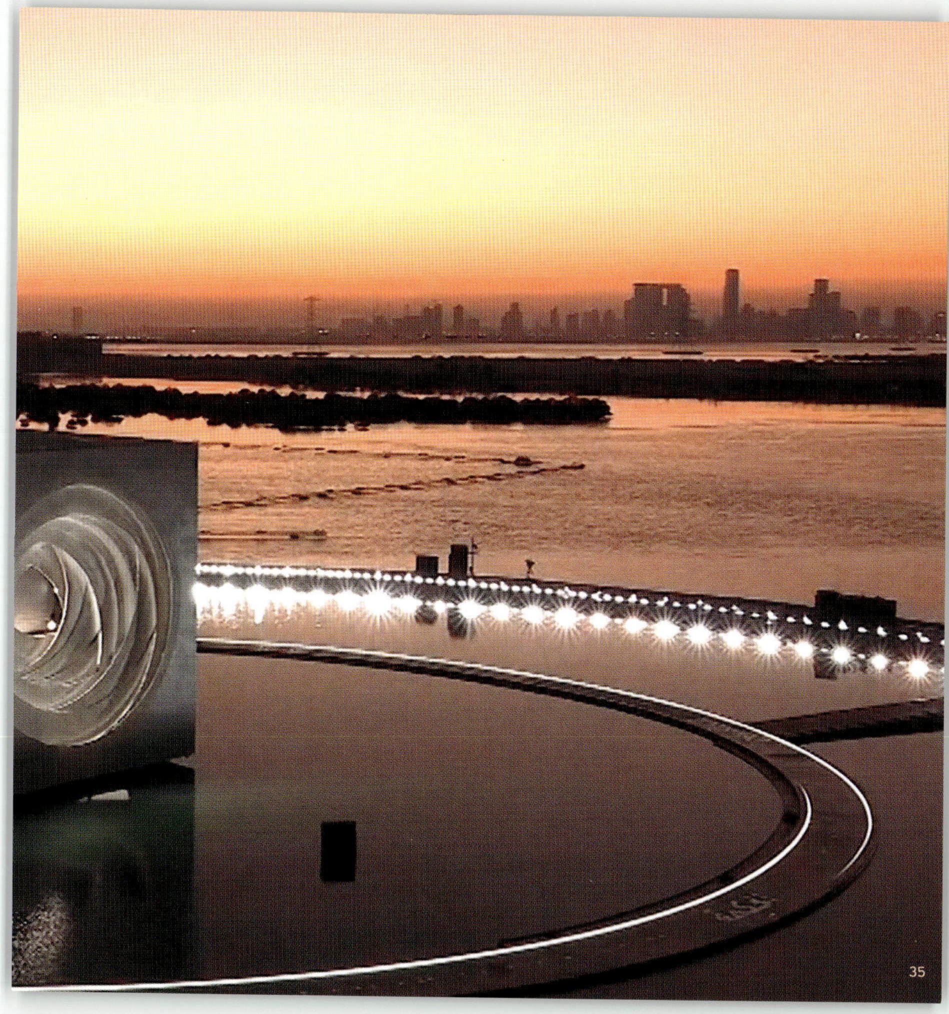

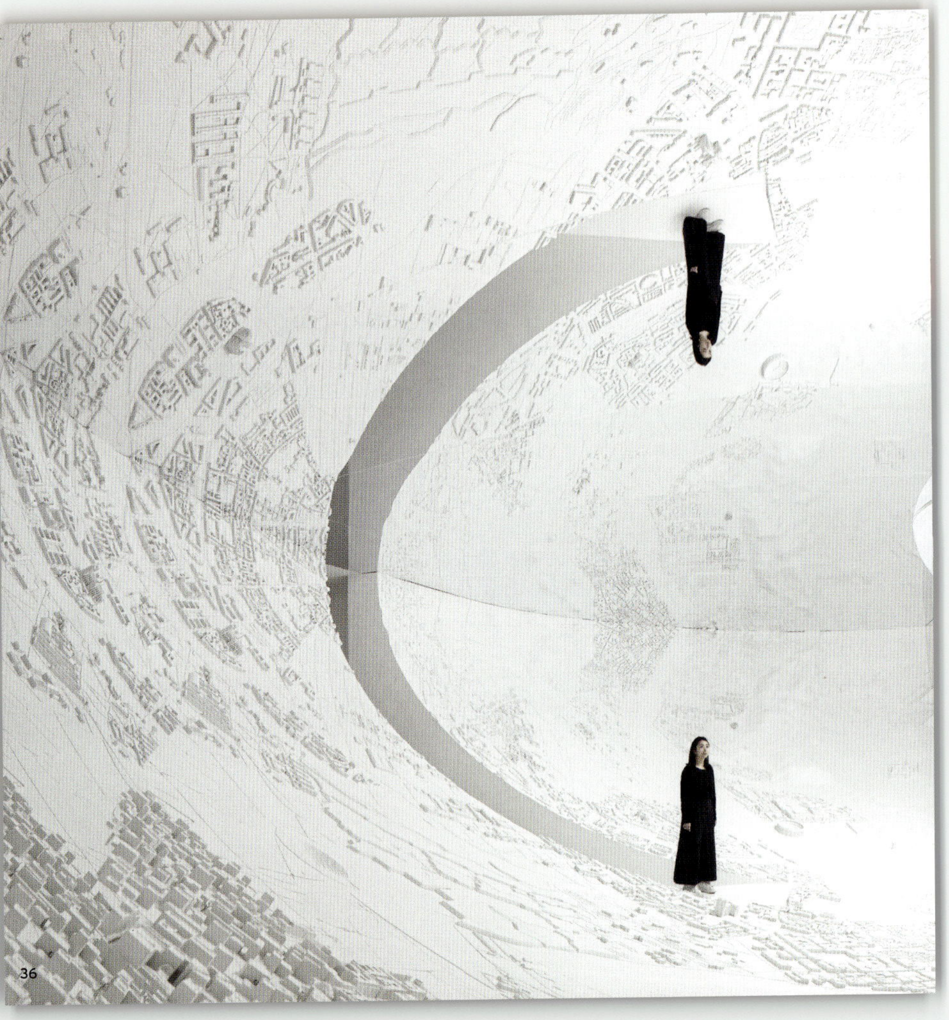

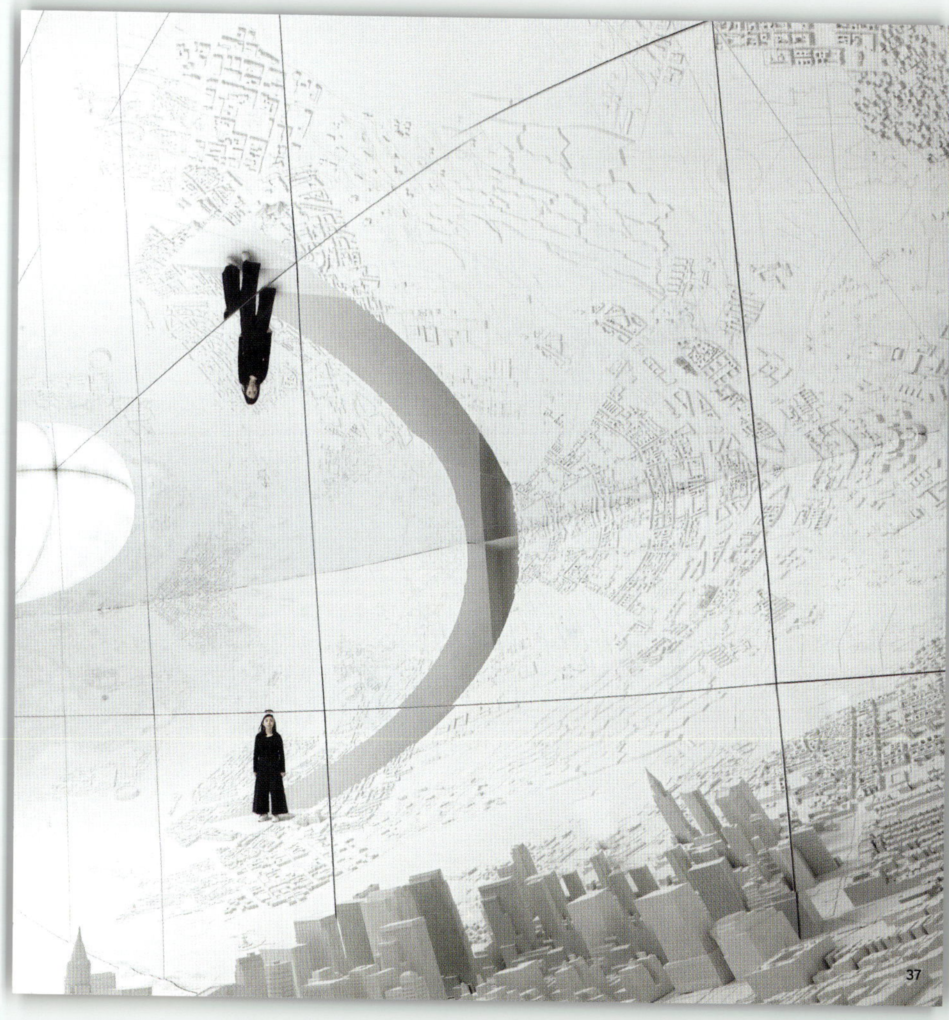

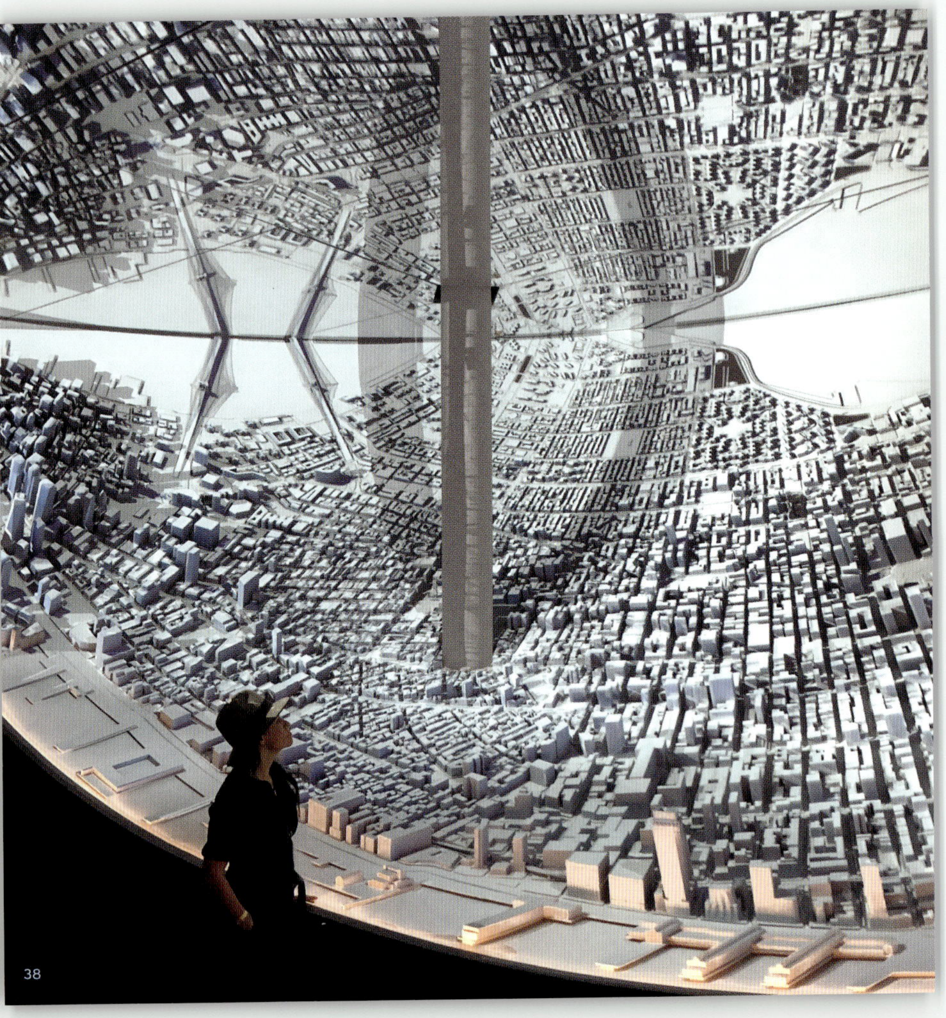

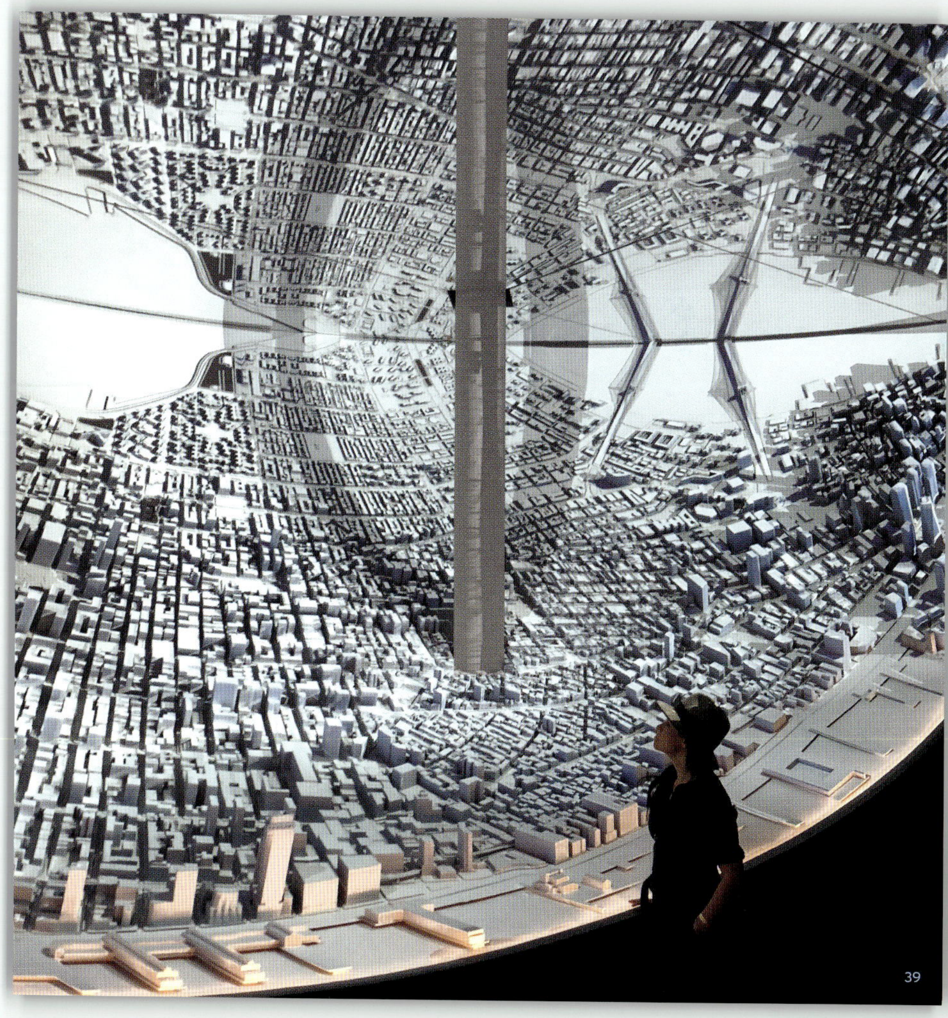

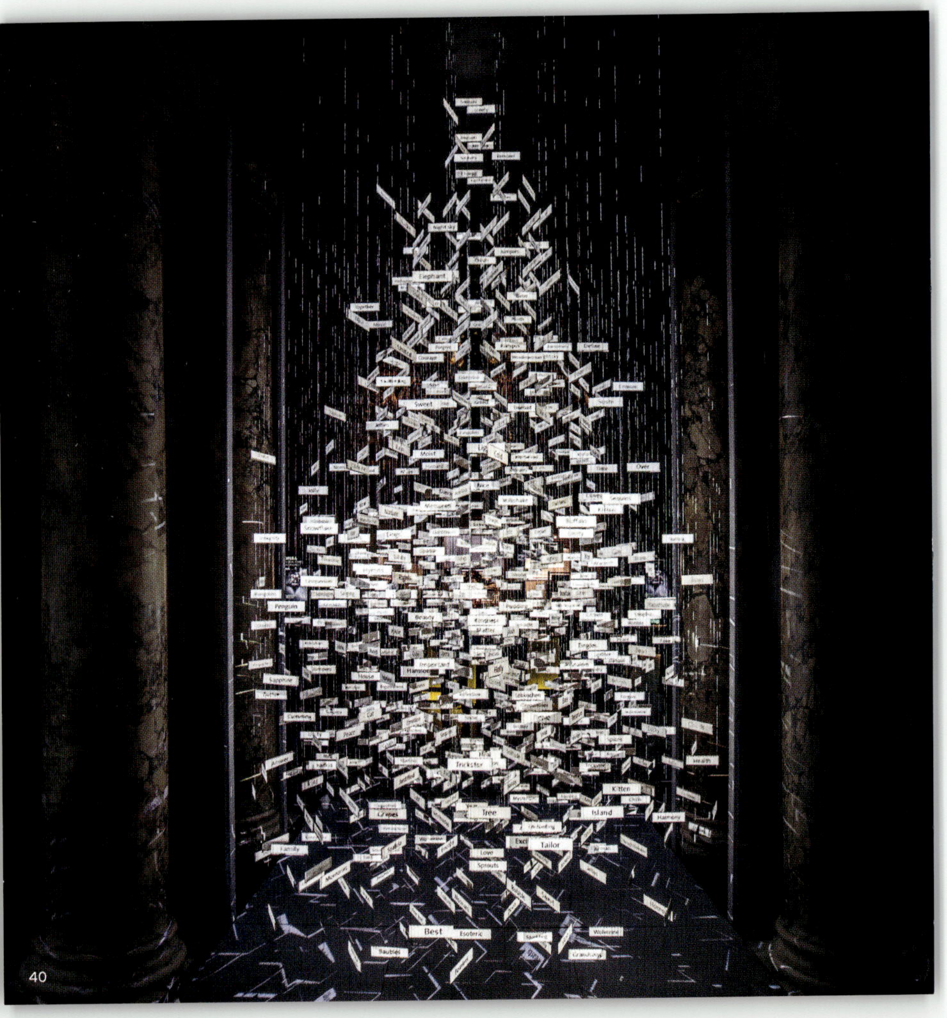

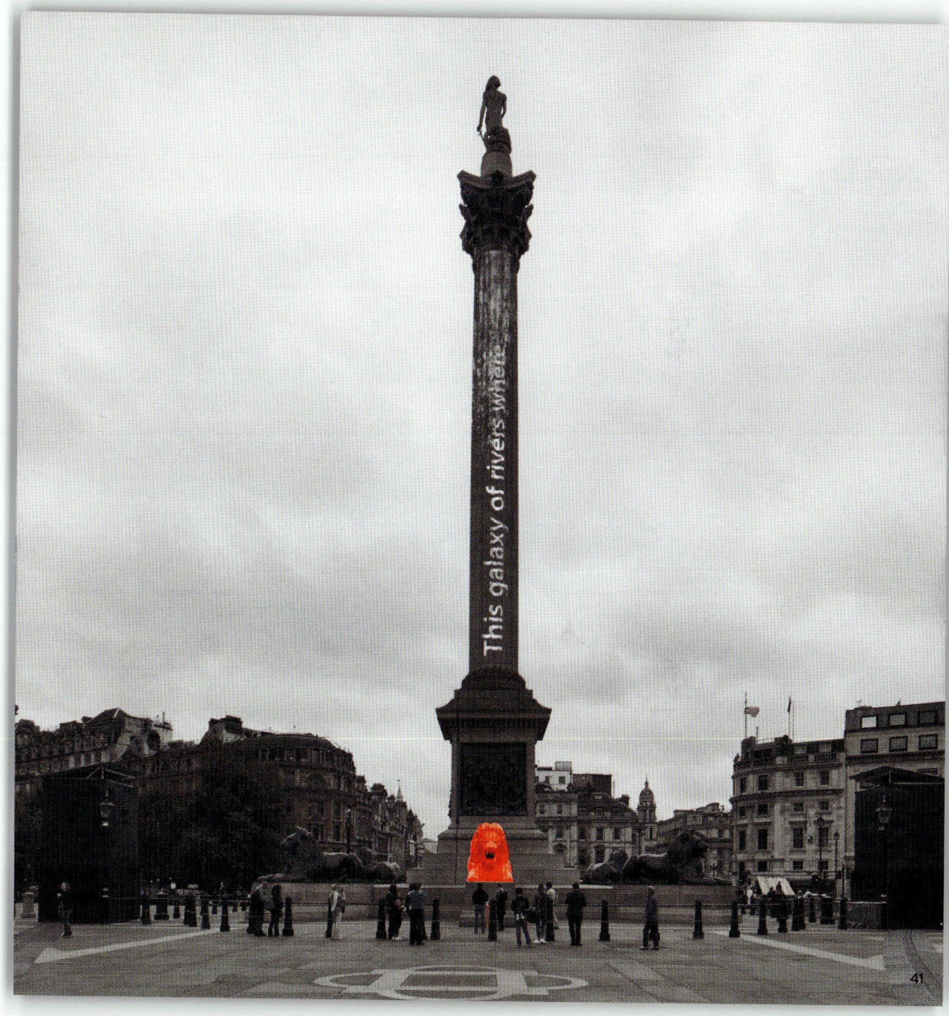
This galaxy of rivers where

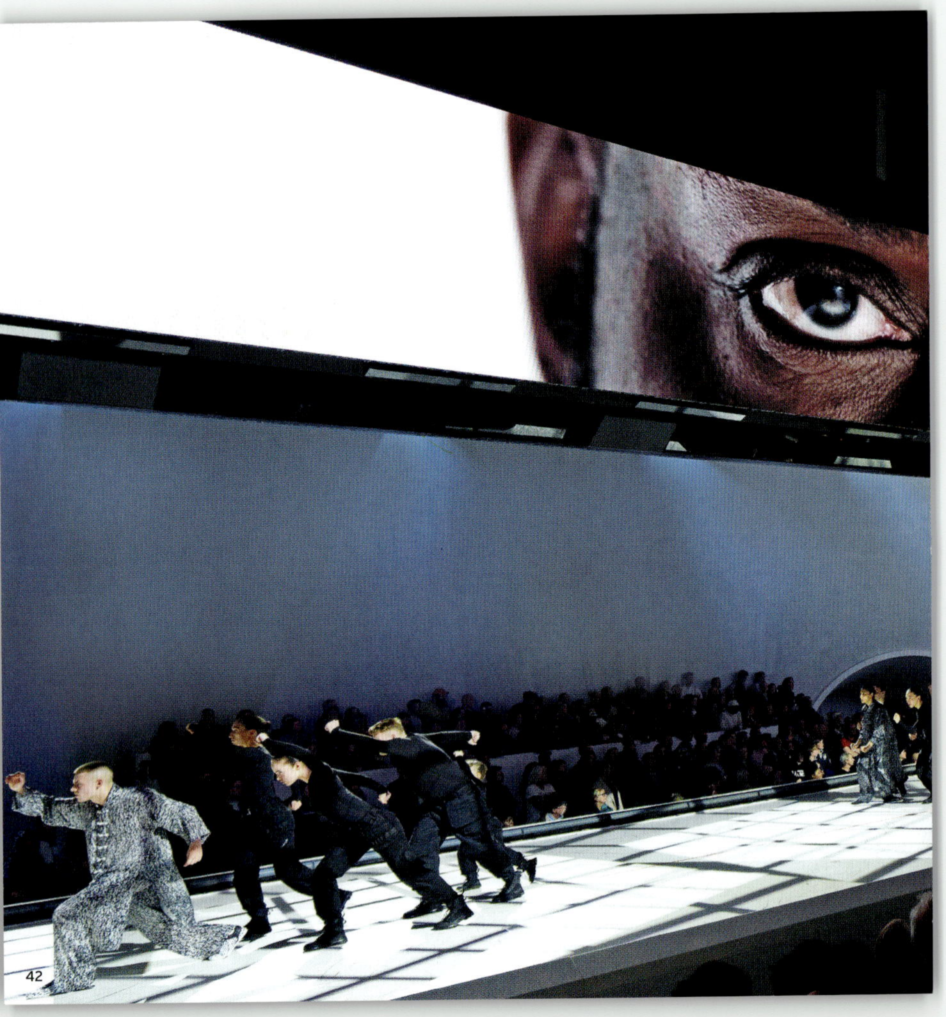

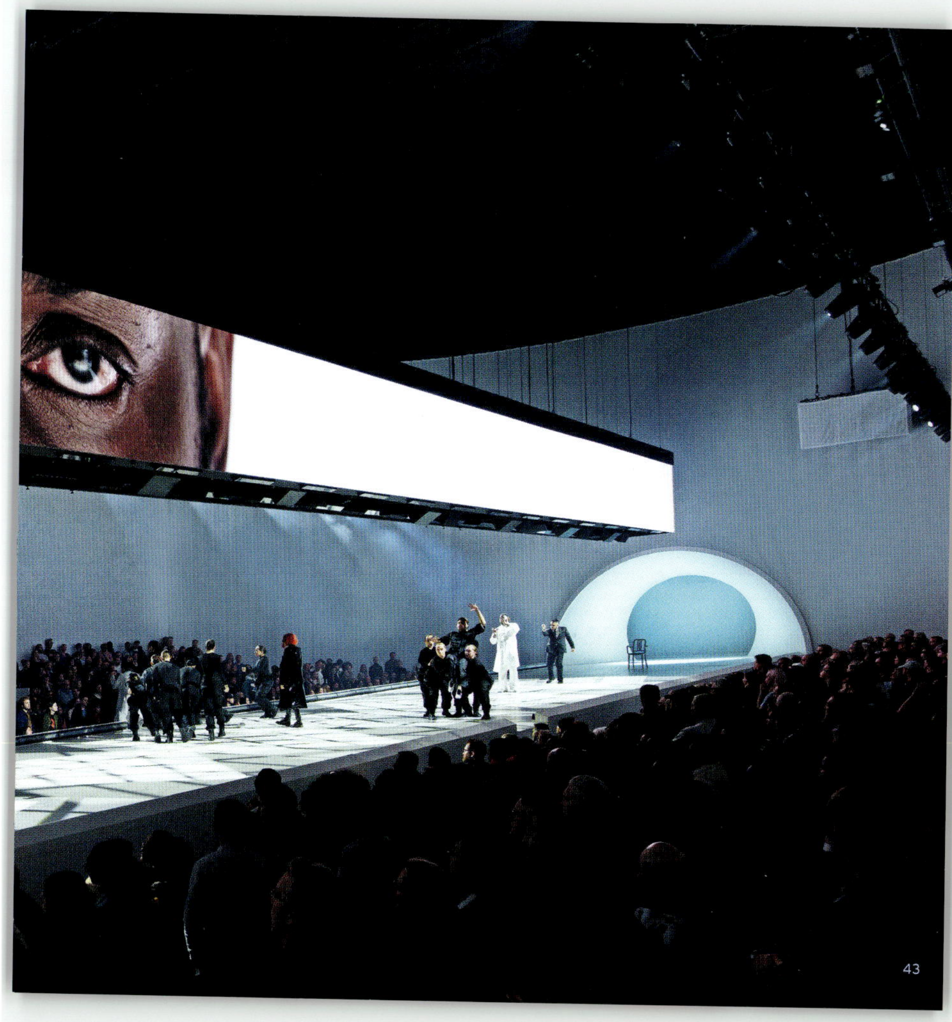

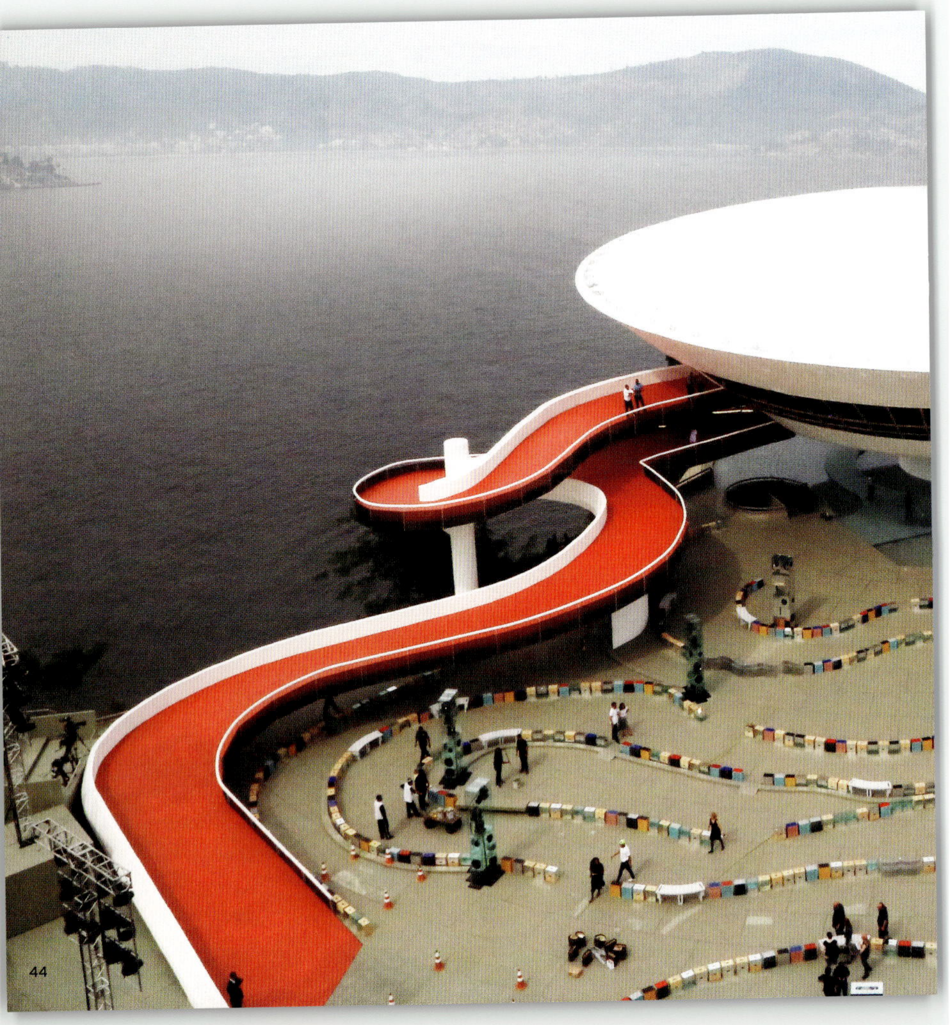

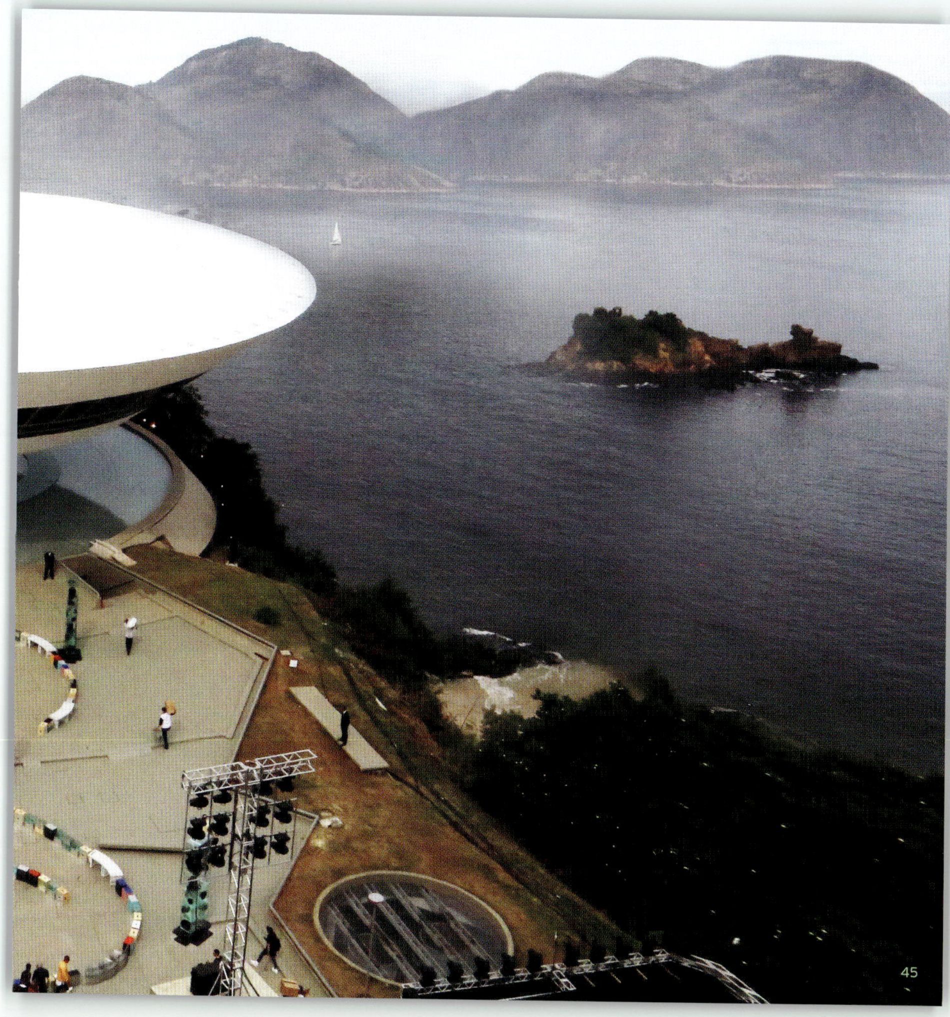

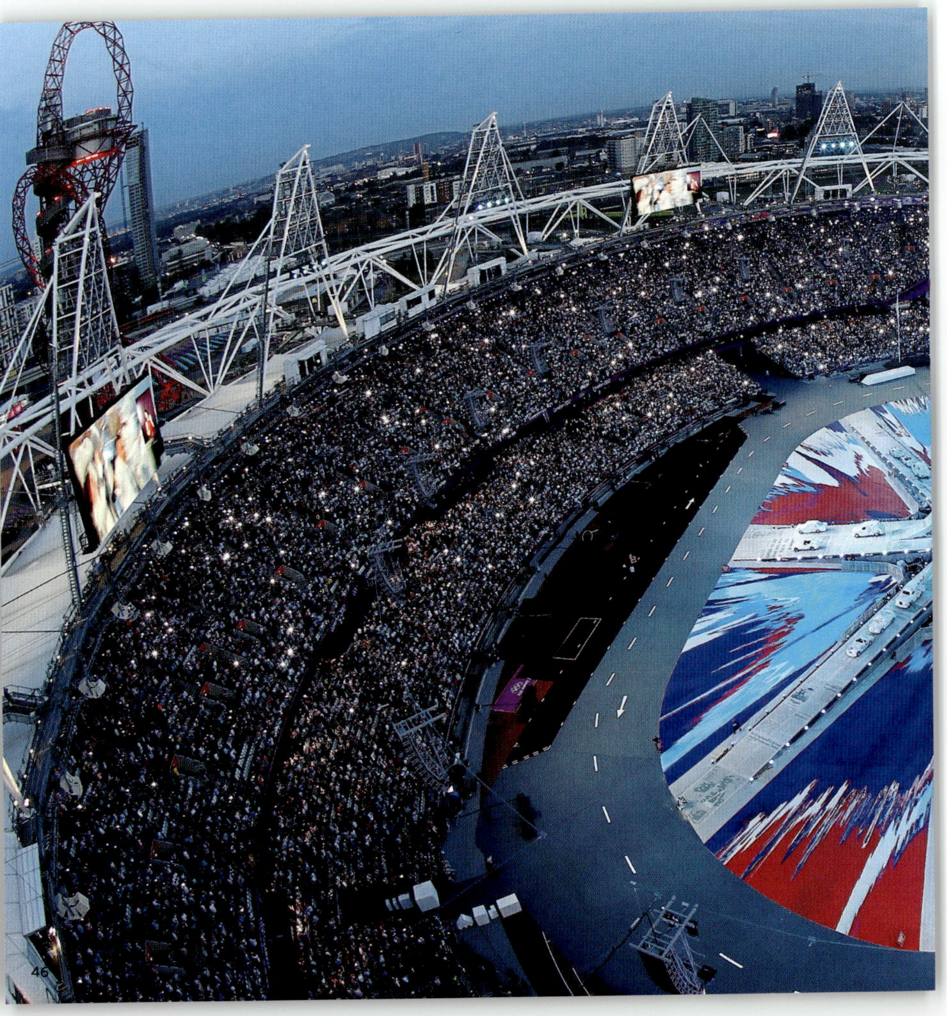

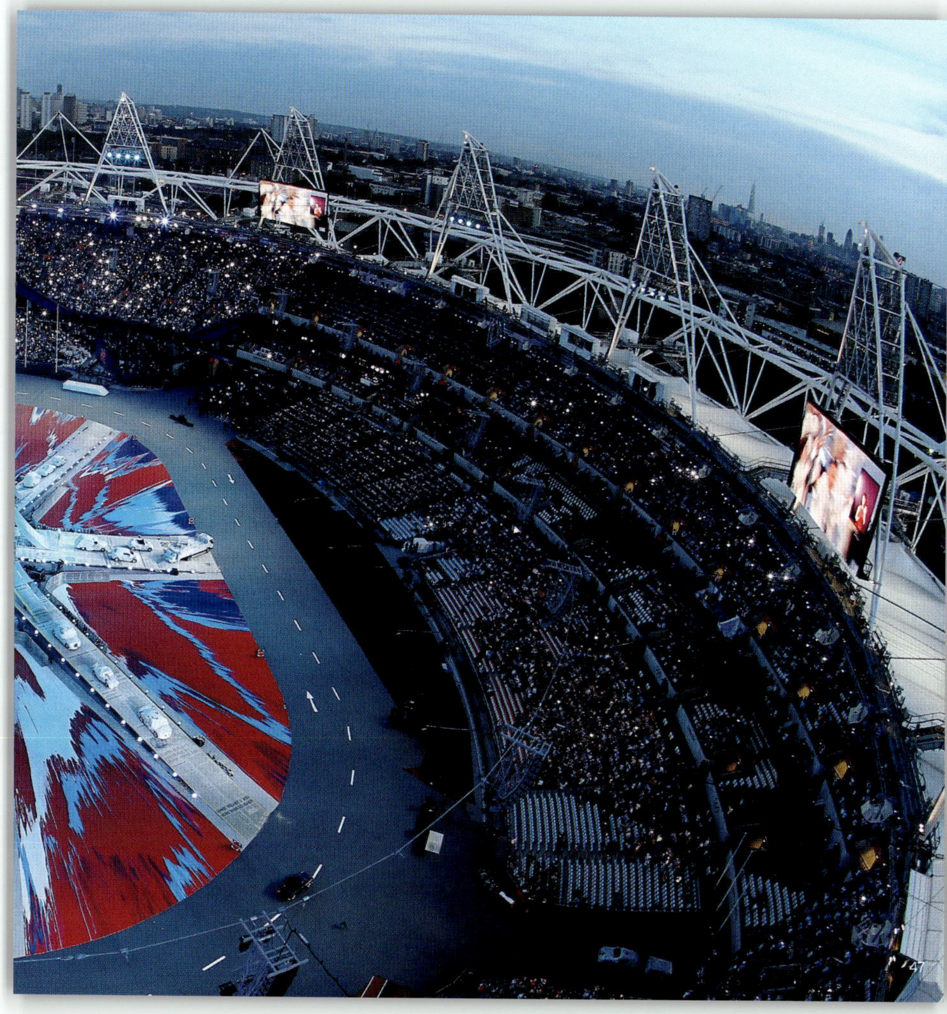

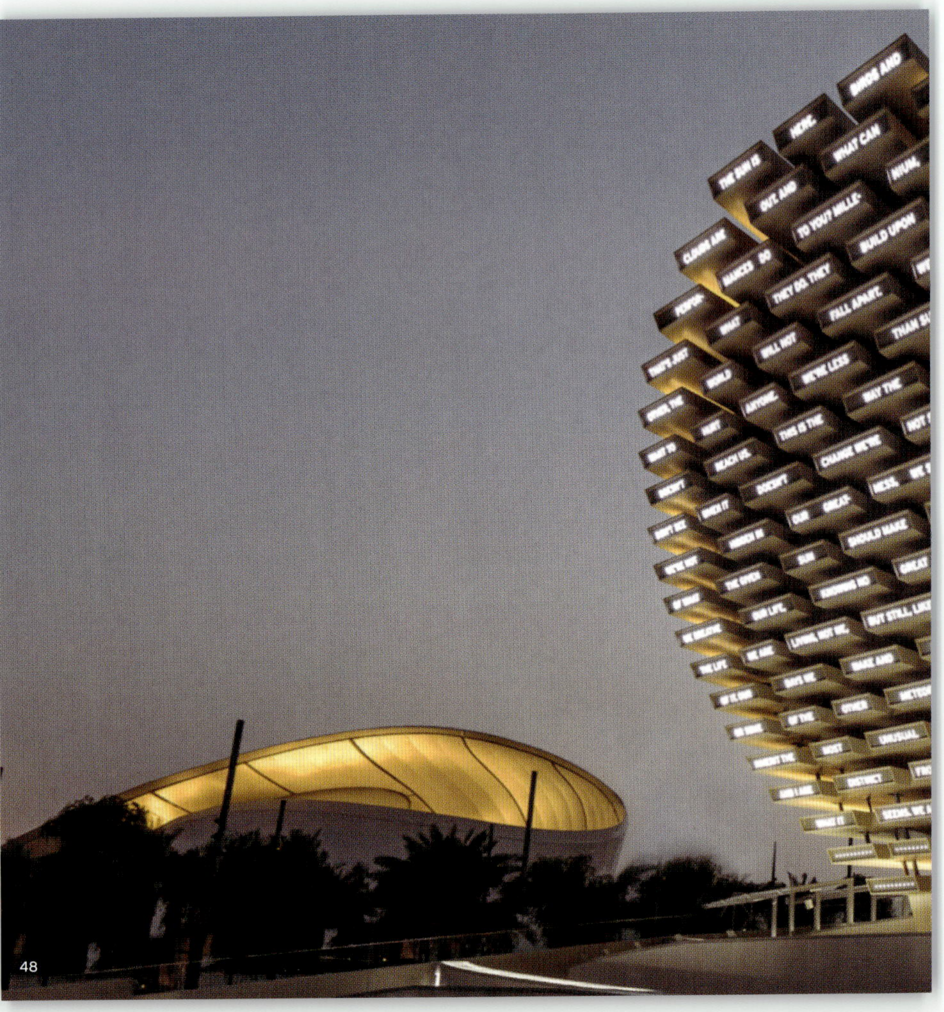
HERE.
THE SUN IS
WHAT CAN
OUT, AND
TO YOU? HILLS,
BUILD UPON
THEY DO. THEY
FALL APART.
WILL NOT
WE'RE LESS
THIS IS THE
REACH US.
SHOULD MAKE

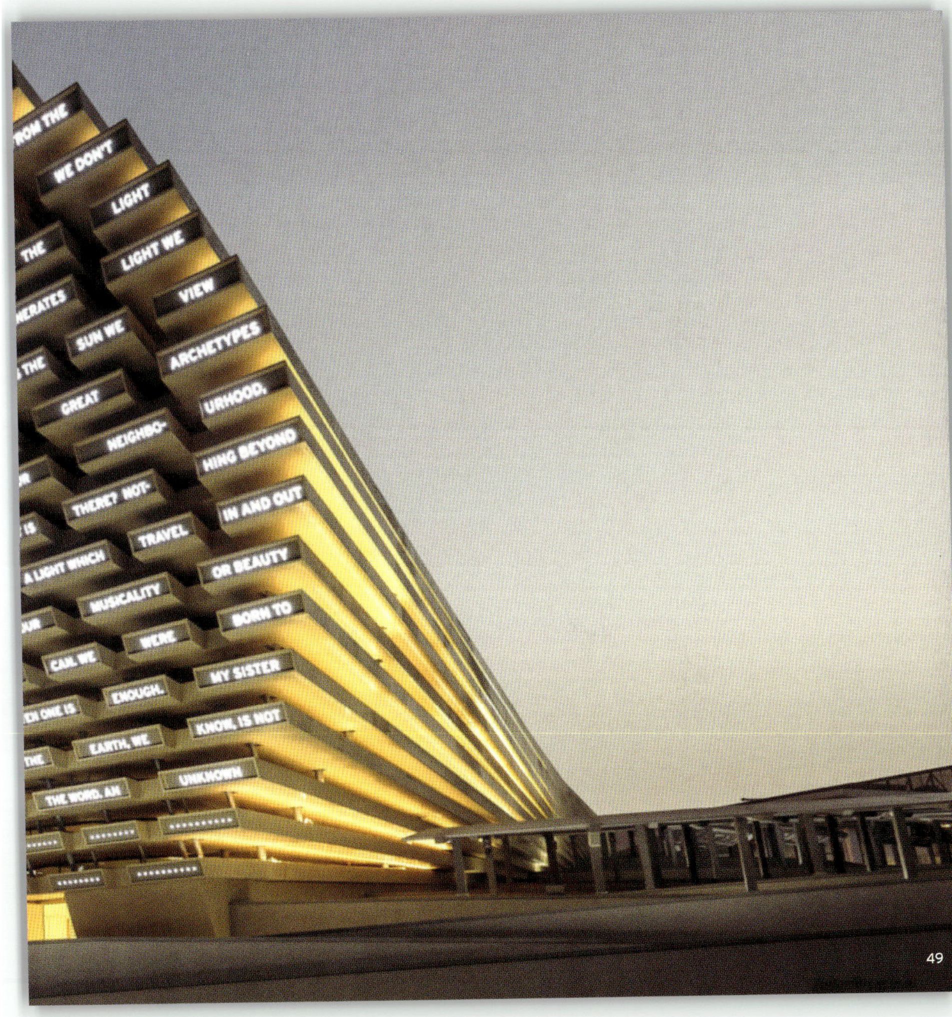
WE DON'T
LIGHT
LIGHT WE
VIEW
SUN WE
ARCHETYPES
GREAT
URHOOD,
NEIGHBO-
HING BEYOND
THERE? NOT-
IN AND OUT
TRAVEL
A LIGHT WHICH
OR BEAUTY
MUSICALITY
BORN TO
WERE
CAN. WE
MY SISTER
ENOUGH.
KNOW, IS NOT
EARTH, WE
UNKNOWN
THE WORD, AN

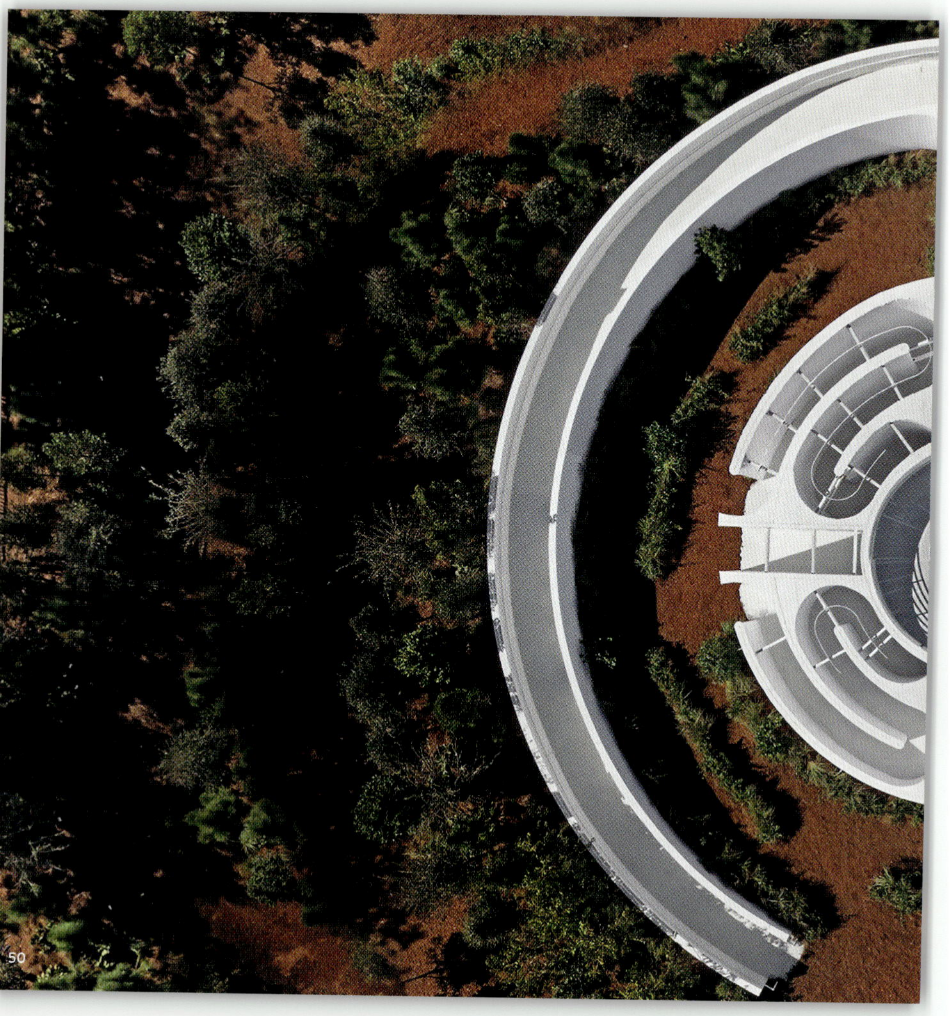

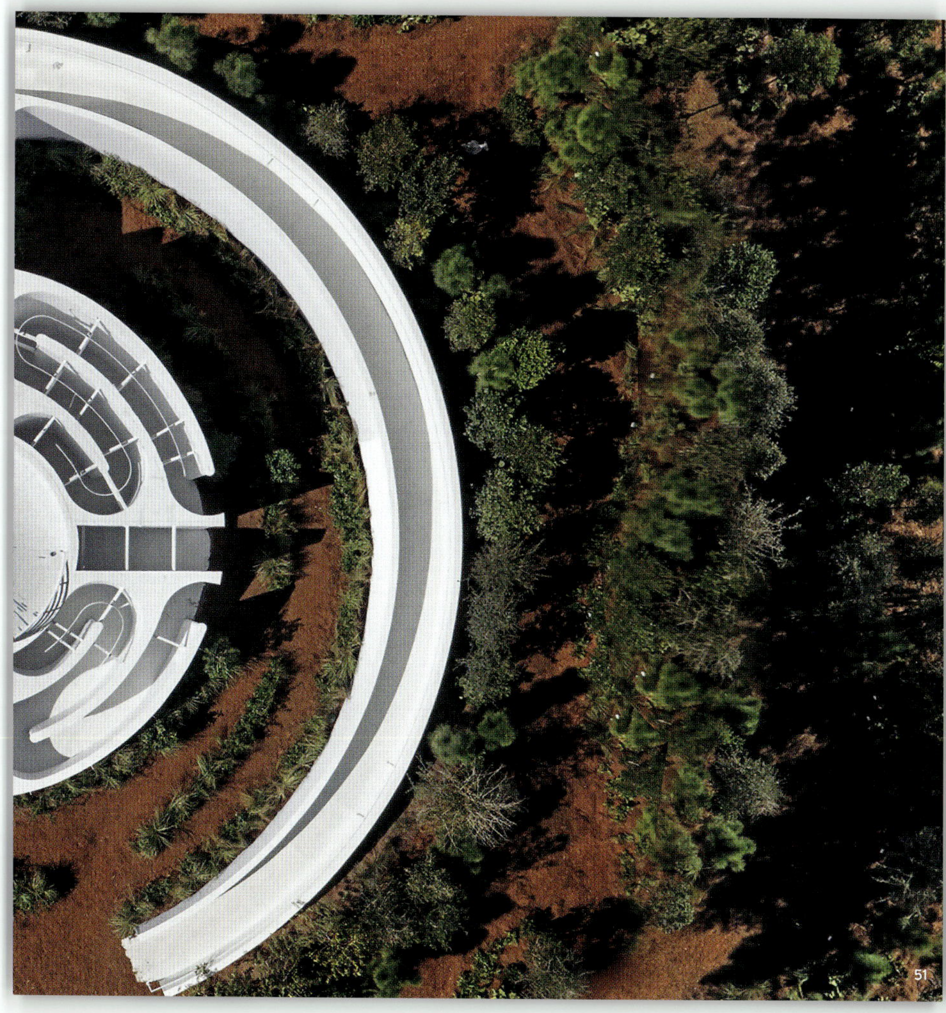

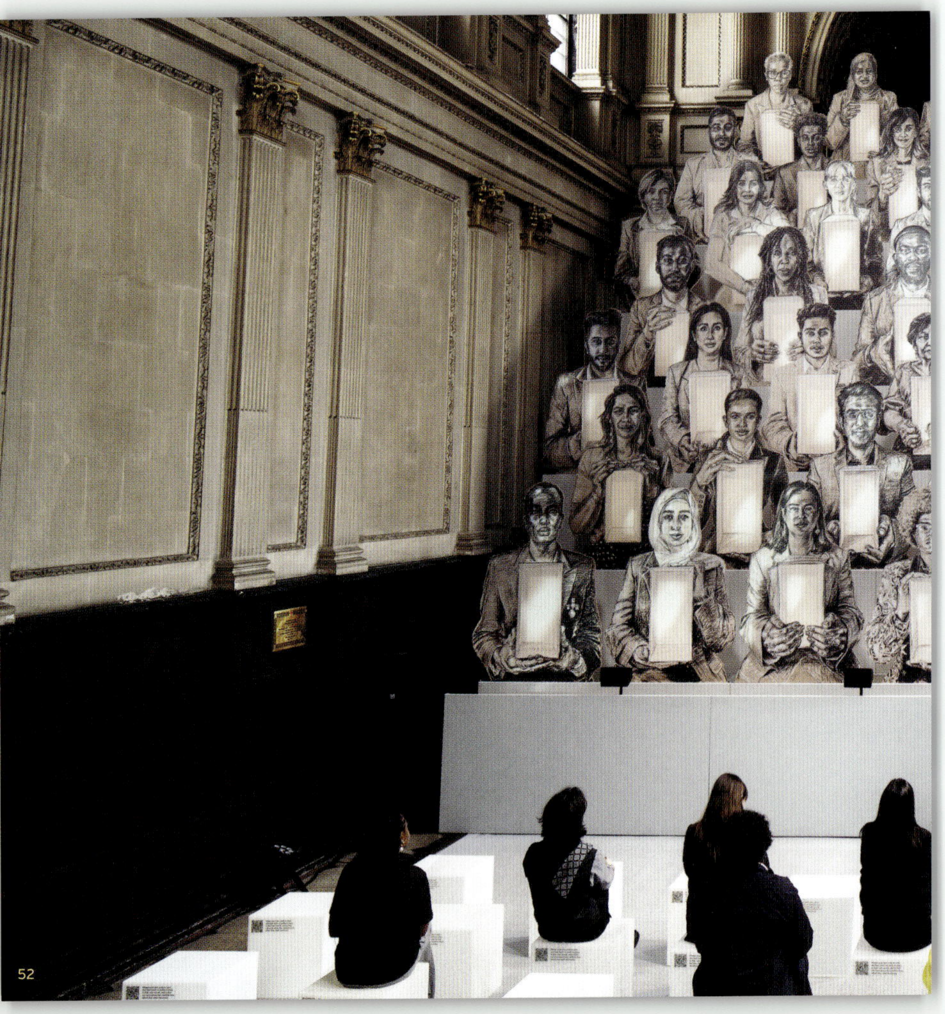

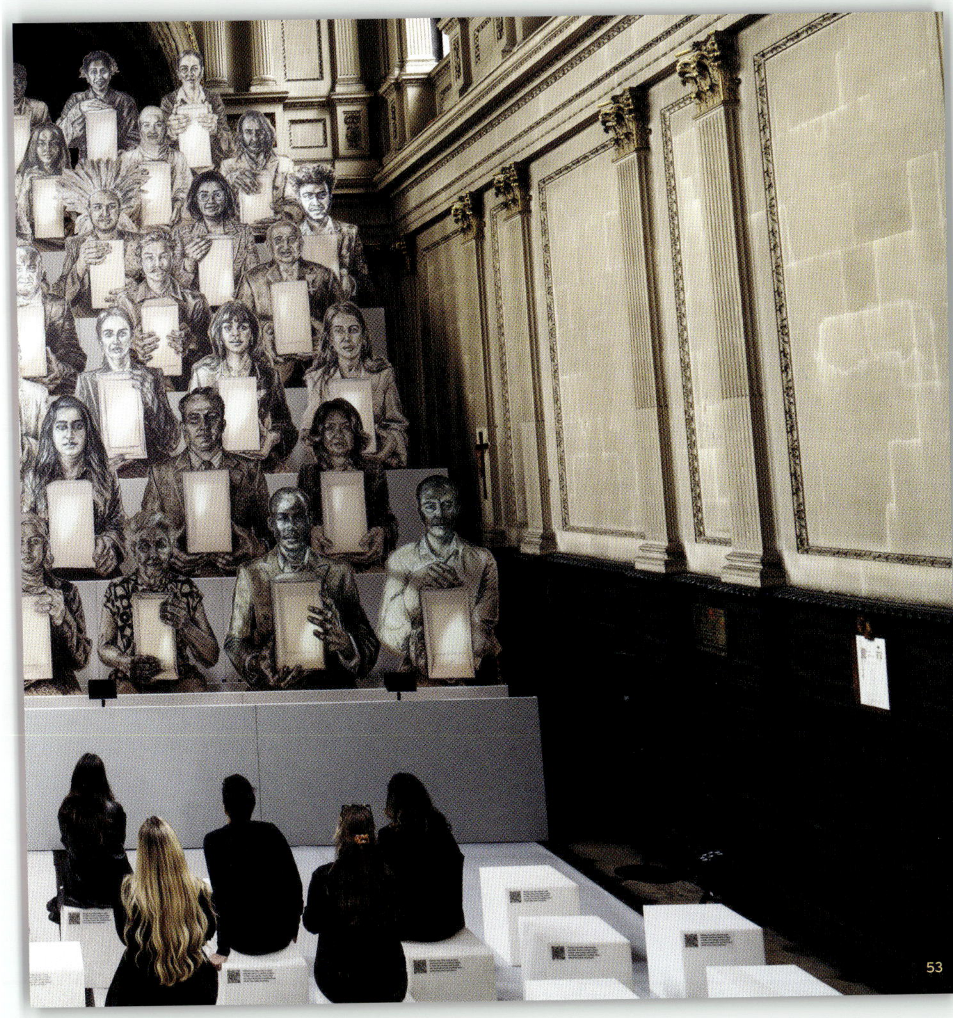

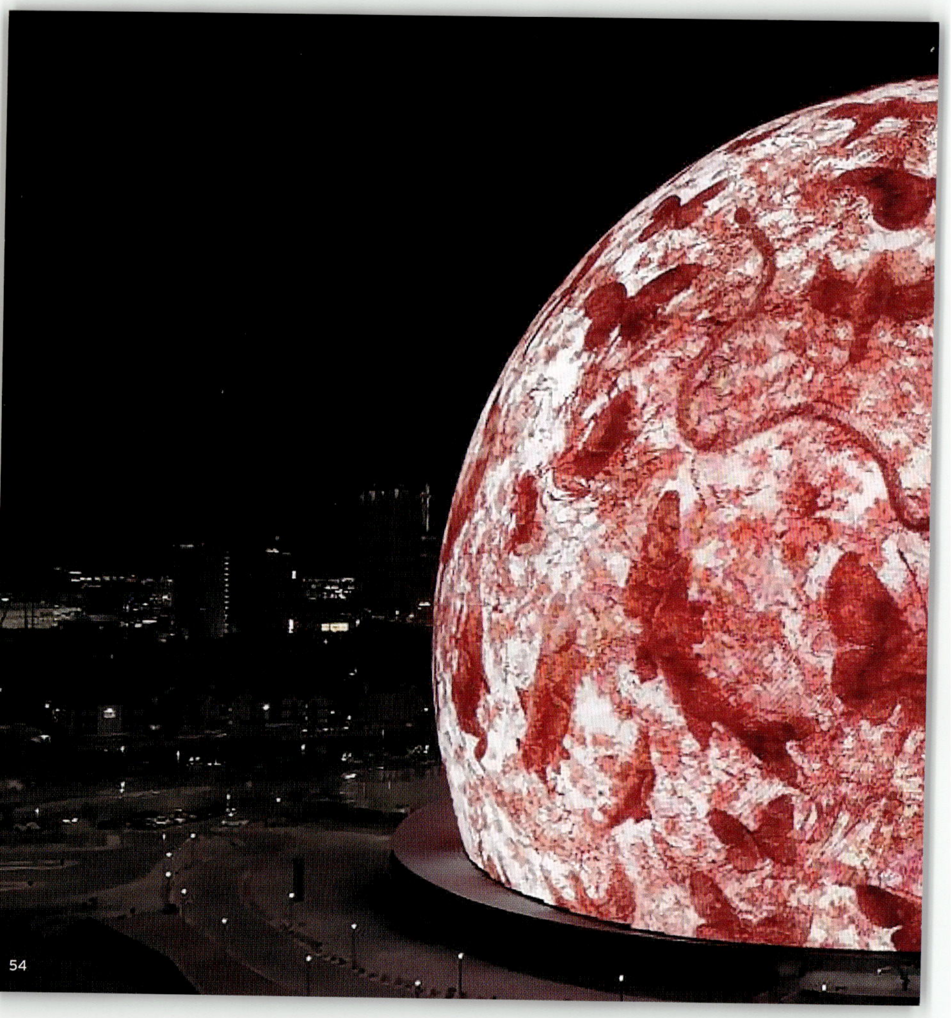

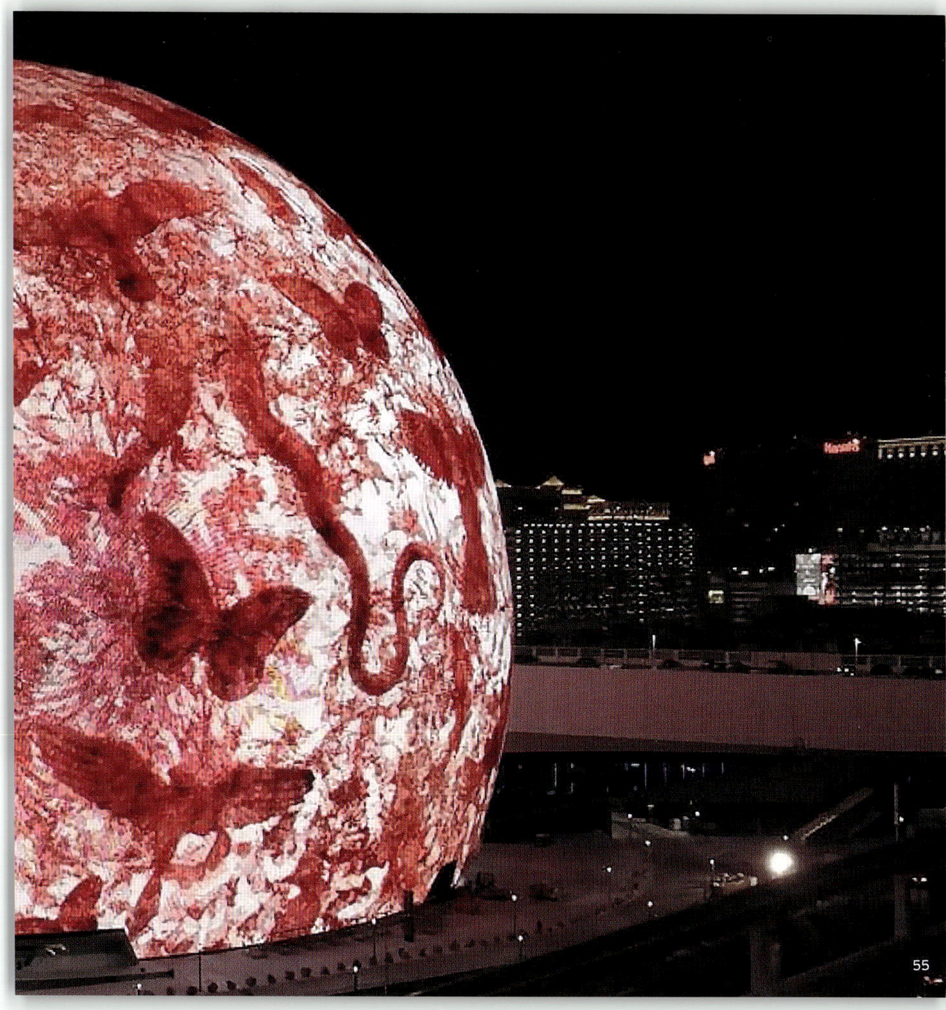

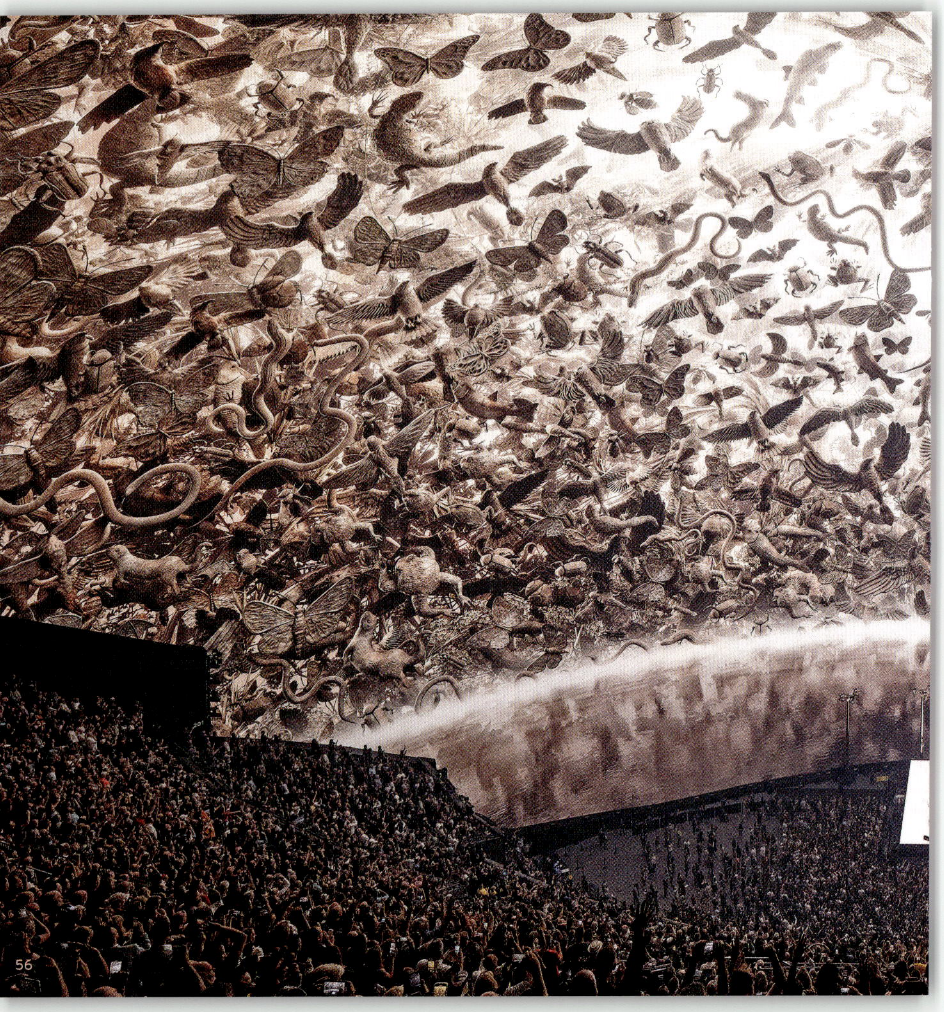

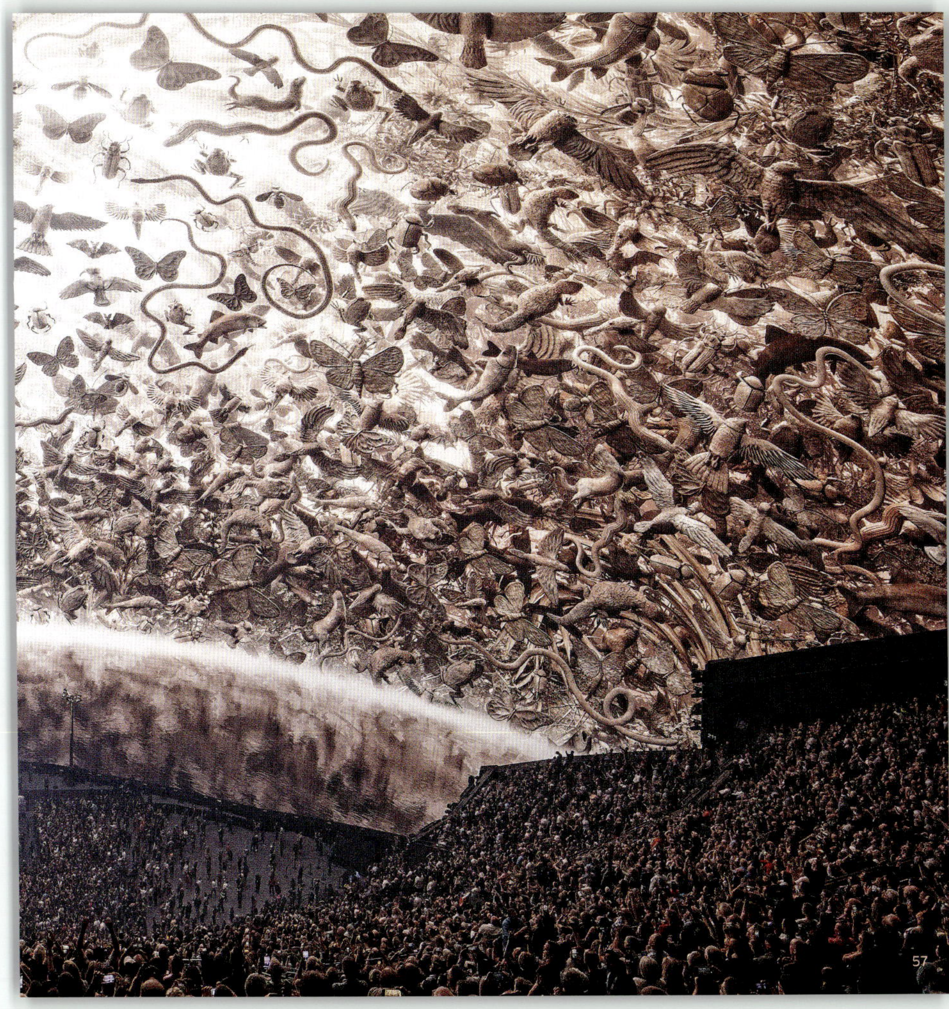

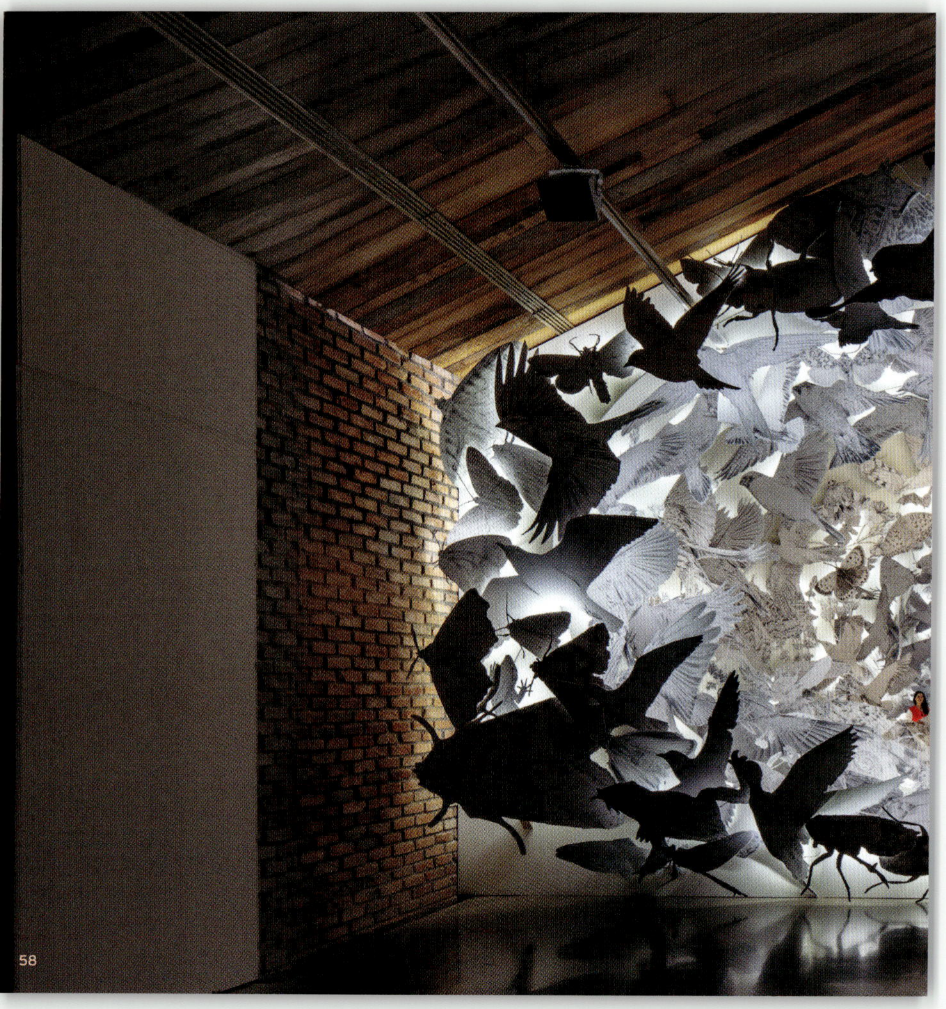

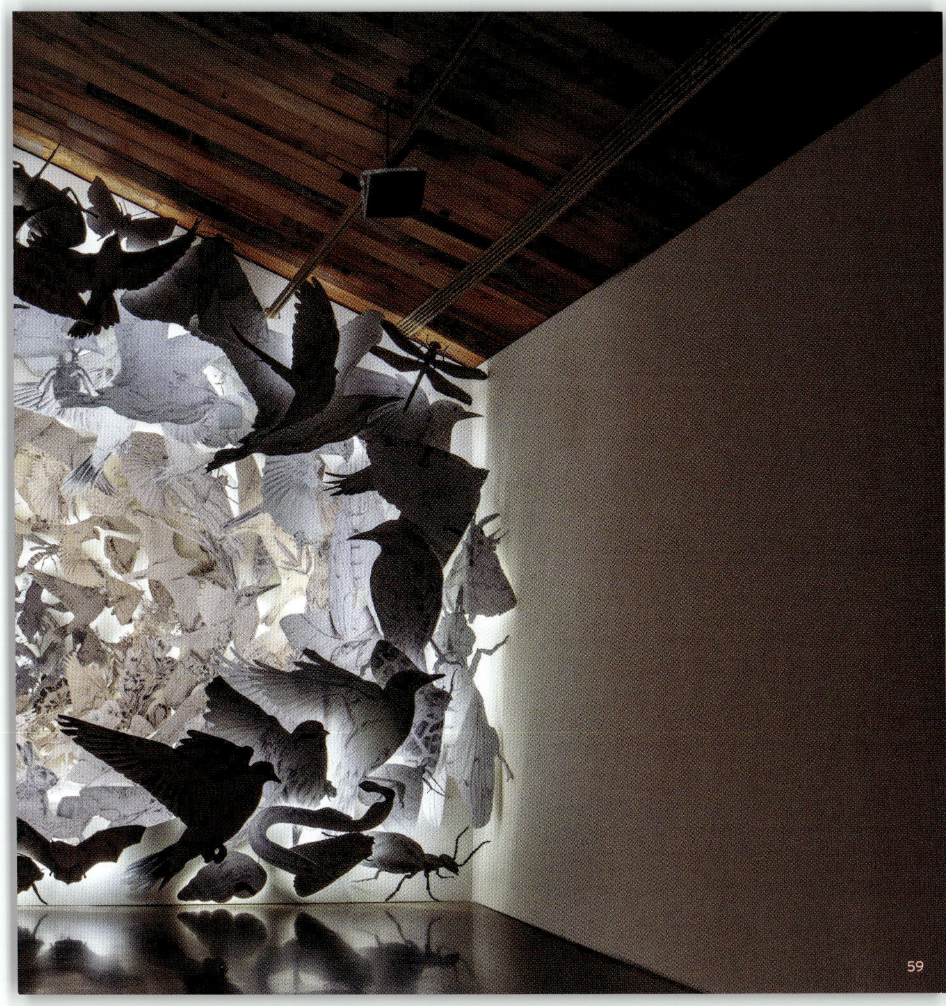

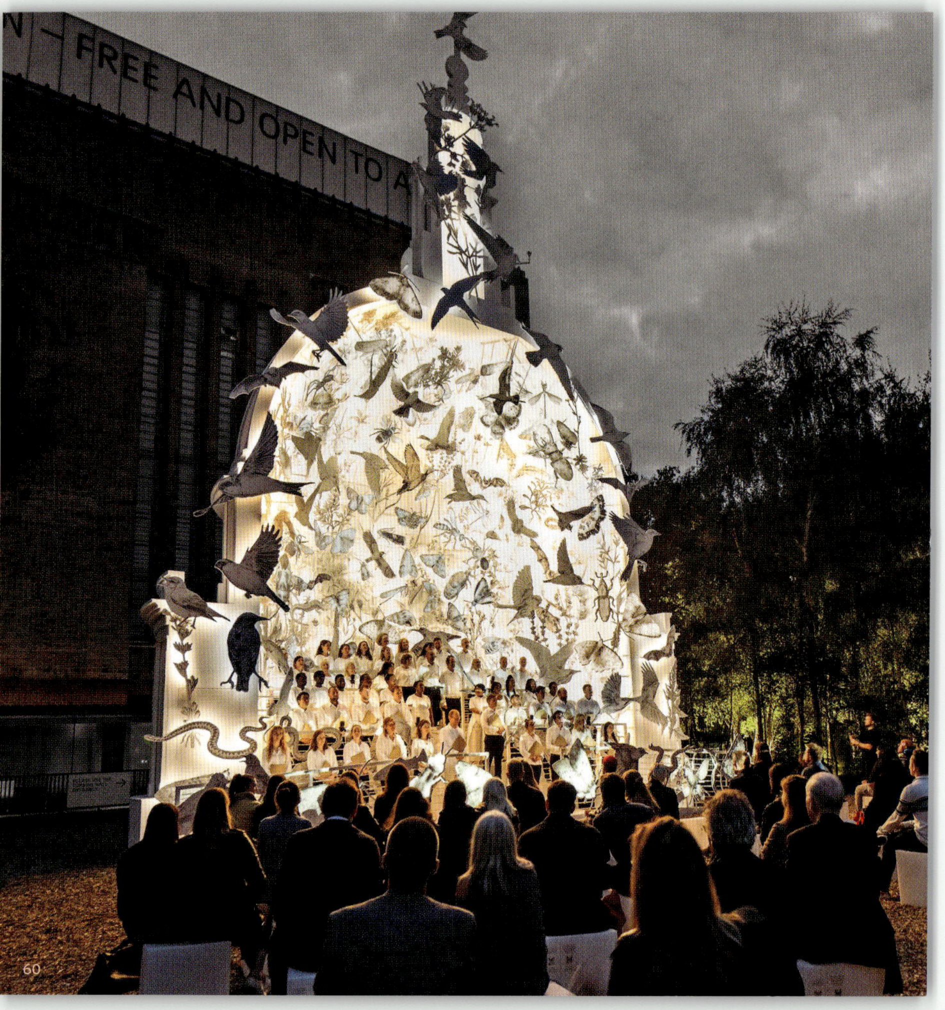
N – FREE AND OPEN TO A

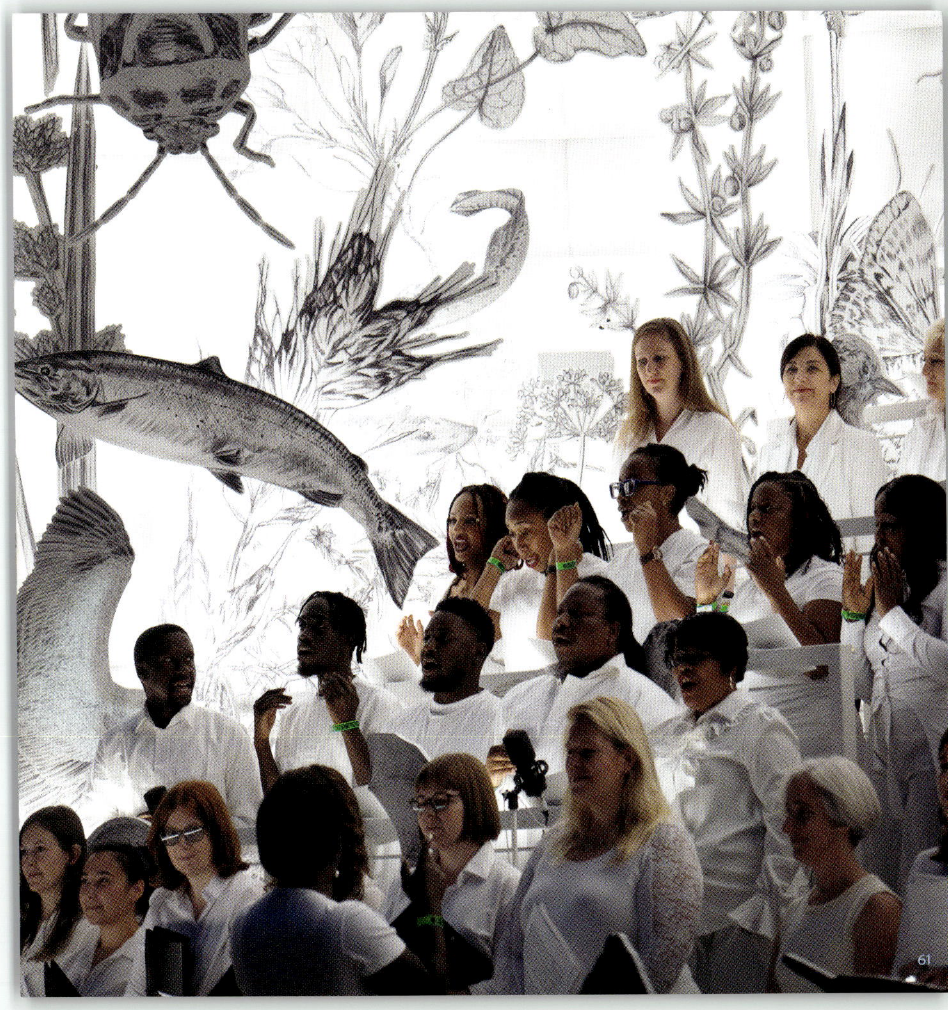

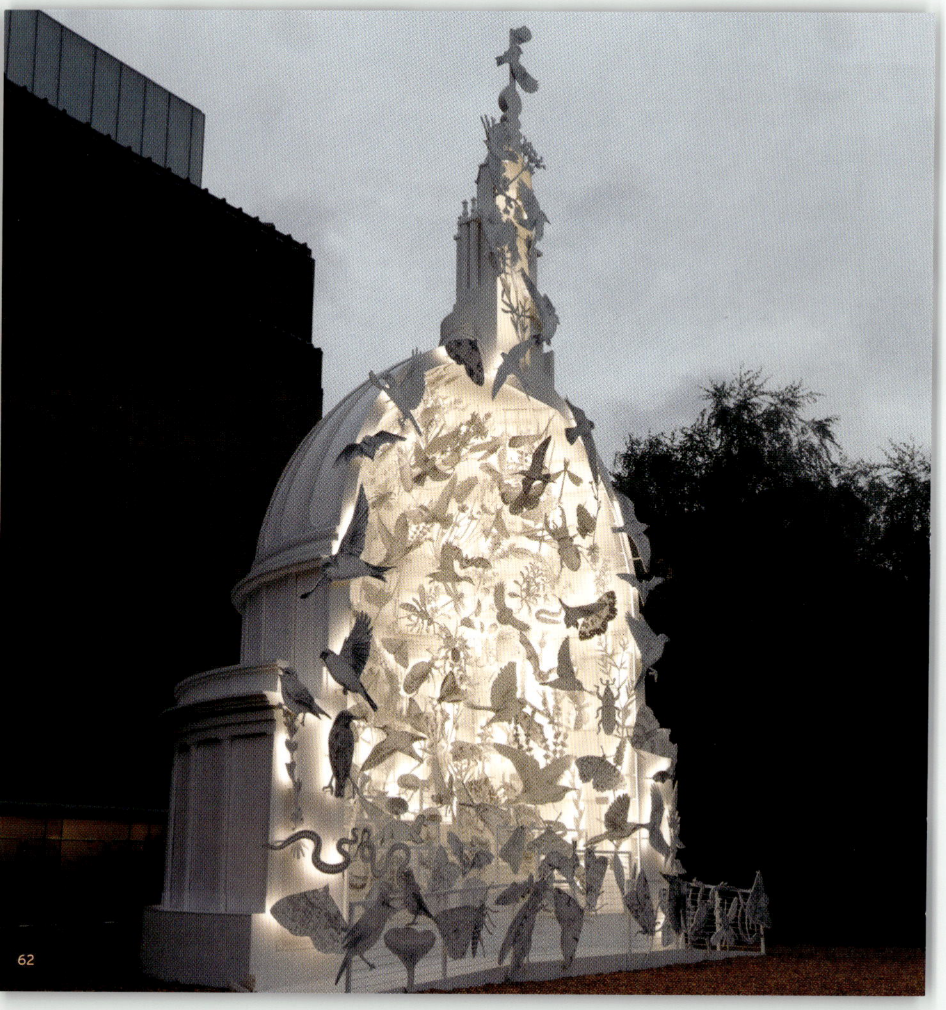

Be not afeard: the isle is full of noises,
Sounds, and sweet airs, that give delight, and hurt not.
Sometimes a thousand twangling instruments
Will hum about mine ears; and sometimes voices,
That, if I then had wak'd after long sleep,
Will make me sleep again: and then, in dreaming,
The clouds methought would open and show riches
Ready to drop upon me; that, when I wak'd,
I cried to dream again.

William Shakespeare, *The Tempest*

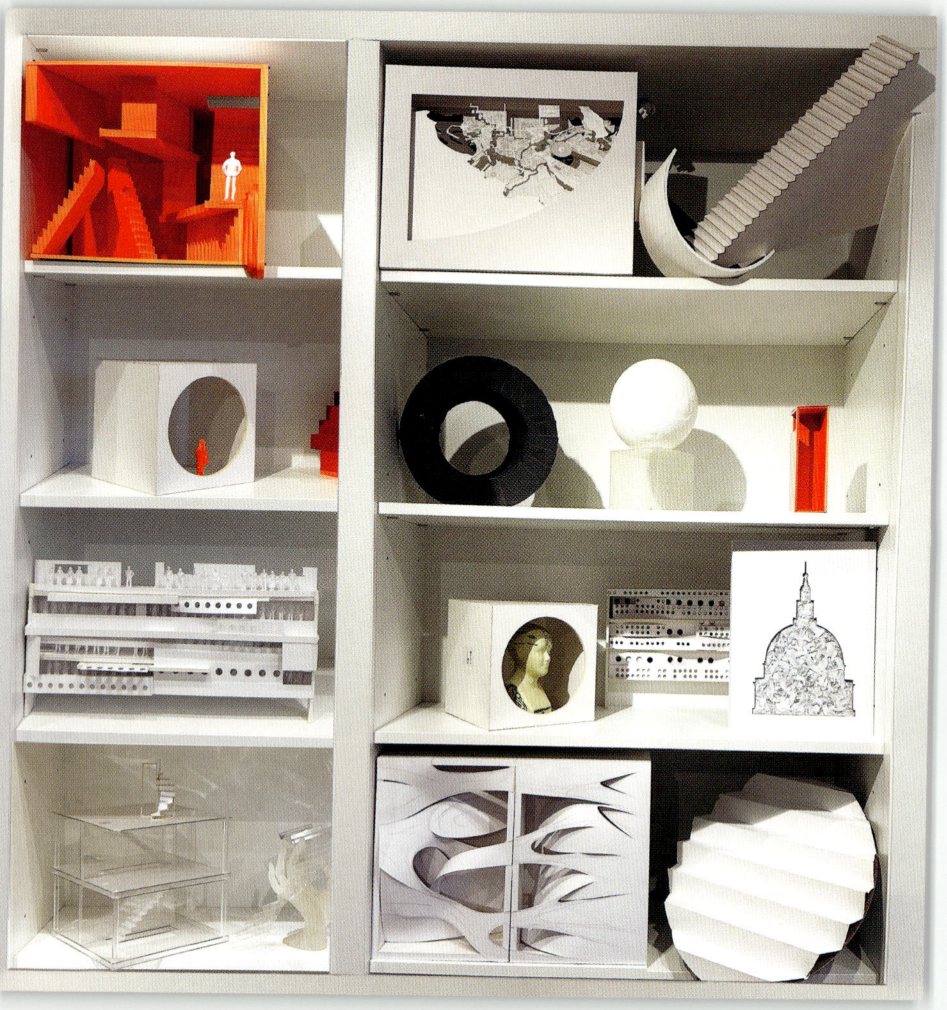

A NEW RENAISSANCE WOMAN

By Donatien Grau
Head of Contemporary Programmes at Musée du Louvre

Es Devlin's work is rooted at once in the intensity of the present and in the depth of time. She is a passionate reader of poetry and a consummate practitioner of drawing. At the same time, she works across the spectrum of contemporary culture and does not exclude any of its constituents. Every year comes with a new wealth of marks in the patterns of our world. As of today, her work encompasses installation, object design, stage design, sets for some of today's most prominent musicians, fashion shows, poetry, architecture, and, of course, drawing. There is hardly a field she does not touch, and, over the nearly thirty years of her life as a practising artist, she has contributed to major events in every sphere. Millions of people have – knowingly or unknowingly – felt the impact of her visions.

On the Stage of Life

Each of Es's works is specific and responds to a situation. The situation may be of many kinds: whether reading, watching, or listening, it is a reaction to an experience of the senses. There is no pre-existing rule for the origin or outcome of that experience, whether it originates in an intimate discovery or from an invitation. If it is Es Devlin's, it just is.

Her work has unfolded through several phases, from the drawings of her teenage years – a foundational moment – to the operatic, totally mastered extravaganzas of the present. One could attempt to decipher, across her work, an 'intimate moment', a 'theatrical moment', and then a 'public moment', in which she participates in the world through the setting of major events or the expansion of her own installations. However, these

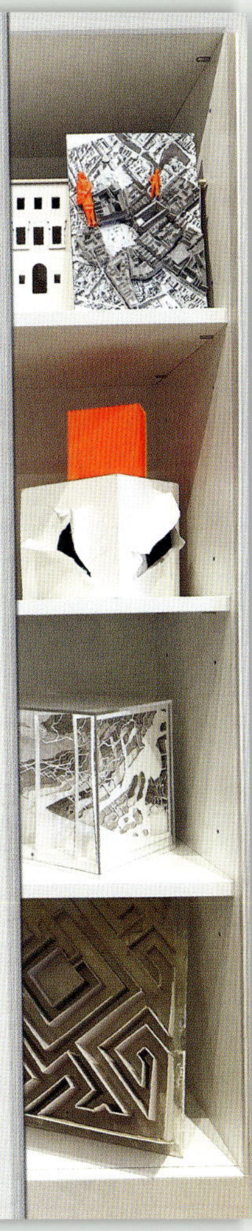

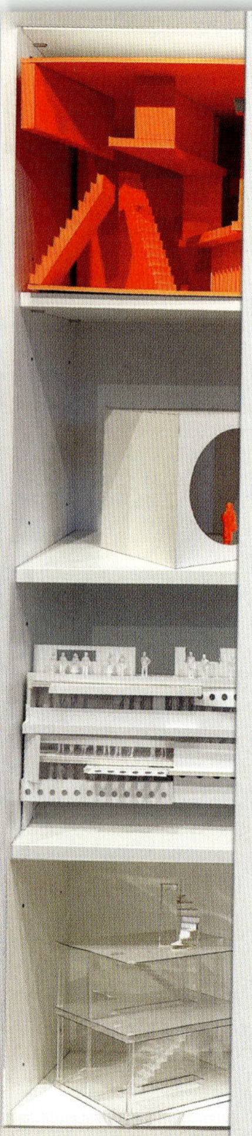

separations would soon appear very naïve. Today, as her work clearly comes across as participative, she continues to draw and write – as this very book bears witness. These moments are steps of a continuum.

In her many creations as a stage designer, she has manifested the importance of relation. It may well be for that reason that she turned to theatre in the first place. There is no better place for someone who likes to live in dreams, but who also wants to bring dreams into reality. In theatre, the design of the set is the very grounding of world-making. When we attend a play, we literally enter another world. In this world, as opposed to television, we are physically present. We may be separated from the action by the border of the stage, but we are all in. We are there.

Es's work as a theatre designer has been that of an unashamed dream-maker. She takes life, aspirations, longings – the most romantic and human of all – extremely seriously. Everything she has done in theatre facilitates the implementation of imagined possibilities in our world. Arguably, anything she has ever created participates in the experience of a higher, more poetic version of life. Poetry is not merely a form or a practice. It is the very synecdoche of making. Es Devlin's utopia is to have making and dreams coincide.

Poetry

In Ancient Greek, *poiein* merely means 'to make'. A poet is a maker. The many ways in which Es Devlin has been *making* things have amounted to world-making. Making is world-making. Every manifestation of that gesture contains every fragment of the world. There may be no better way of considering Es's work than to understand how, in every instance, it invokes everything else she has made and will ever make, as well as, perhaps, everything every human being – and, increasingly, every non-human being – has, in her mind, ever made. Making is a deeply personal action, but it is also a common one: everyone makes things, but not everyone is aware of it. Everyone makes things, but not everyone makes it into a self-reflexive action in which the entire world is involved.

Such an involvement may well be a fiction, but fictions have their own accuracies – as dreams do. Es Devlin inhabits that space of dreamlike, fictional accuracies.

The recurrence of poetry in her work pertains to the very origin of making. It also relates to everything poetry has been ever since. Poetry is line. It is the form one gives to feelings and the form one uses to depict what is on one's mind or in front of one. It is an image that appears from nothing, and some matter that is deposed on a sheet of paper – itself a fragile, transformed material. This may be the reason why the same word applies to a metric structure and the result of a gesture. Both address a way of making sense, of representing and altering reality – of changing and preserving it at the same time. This, too, speaks volumes on Es Devlin's practice.

In reciting the poem, rhythm will enable the voice to speak in a way that is different, to reach forces higher than ourselves. It is the pace of humanness turned towards its own transcendence. The same could be said, immanently, of Es Devlin's work. Whether in a performance, an exhibition, an installation, or any form she makes her own, time is of the essence. That is: not merely time, but the way it is played with, highlighted, showcased, tightened and expanded. Time is a material, for each of us to experience our own duration, our own take on it. The trituration of rhythms is an openness to many ways of living. The artist takes them all on in her journey.

The Classical and the Modern

Modernity asserted the power of the individual, first as a conduit for the universal, then as reason *per se*. Even though some of her works, such as drawings, may be placed in line with a purely personal practice, and others, such as sets for gigantic performances, may at first be considered to be entirely indebted to a pre-existing context, everything Es Devlin does relates to the situation, and is therefore never merely personal nor merely contextual. Her work pushes the boundaries of such separations, which may come across today as antiquated.

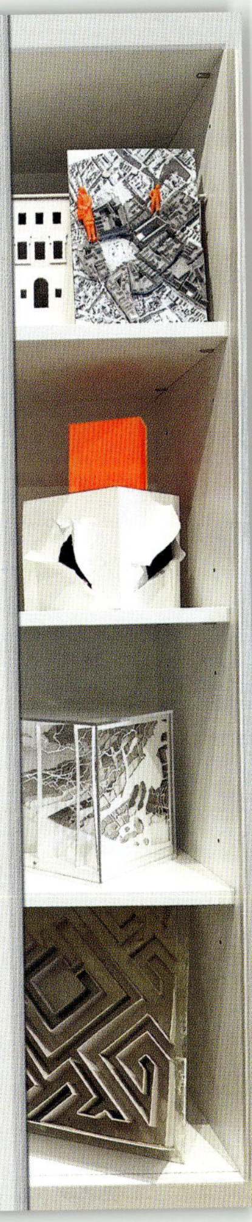

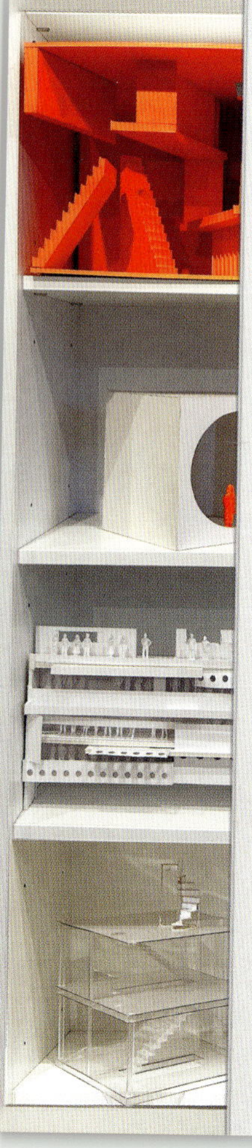

Whether we want it or not, our world is a nexus – it is a web of relations. Digital lives have done nothing but heighten what life was anyway, before them. Relationships make up our lives and limit our lives, but also protect them. In a concert, one can be part of a collective and fully exist at the same time. There is no need for a radical separation between the two. Being a hermit is more difficult than ever, and yet one may be no less lonely in the crowd than on one's own. Much of Es Devlin's work dwells on those apparent contradictions. She understands radically that this is our world – a place where artificial intelligence does not oppose drawing and writing as human activities, where being human in the highest sense does not mean we leave aside our environment.

Collaboration and relation are not the opposite of existence. They are the conditions for it. Es Devlin is a collaborator, and many other collaborators find themselves embedded within her work. In fact, we are all collaborators with the world, from the moment that we act within it in a position of openness and acceptance. Thus her stance is not merely creative; it is metaphysical. She sees herself, and everyone and everything in her art, as part of a greater collaboration.

Life is a constant collaboration, to the point that collaboration may be the other name of ecosystem. Culture is an ecosystem and, if seen aptly, it is a collaboration. Through her work, Es Devlin paves the way towards a greater understanding of and action in culture as a whole. We can live together. We can be together. There is no discrepancy between the Super Bowl and an intimate drawing. A tree is not the opposite of a dream.

Everything Es makes is located. It is an action within a field. Every set she has designed differs from every other; each drawing is different. There is no homogeneity in the multiplicity of her actions; but they are not disparate either. Looking at her work across mediums, times and contexts enables us to see the many threads that weave it all together. Everything can be itself and at the same time be included in a greater ensemble.

Her work is full of variation. Nonetheless, a number of traits appear, again and again, over her body of work: essential forms, circles in particular;

a taste for strong, direct colours, for powerful lights. Complexity and uniqueness meet. She works from a lexicon of forms shared across times and cultures. The culture to which she belongs and the collaborations she establishes are inherently part of the present. The forms she adopts are part of long traditions that she adjusts and transforms.

A book is a box. It is a container, but it is also a reality in itself. Everything that happens within the box reflects the outside world – like dreams in our head. But they are also the world outside of us, and reflecting on the box enables us to keep shaping dreams.

Renaissance Woman

Es Devlin stands on both sides of history. She was born in a time when modern sensitivities still mattered. Thus the role of the psyche, of personal feelings, are grounding principles for her. And yet, her drawing practice places her in a much larger chronological framework – the framework of everyone who has ever drawn. Her process of constant collaboration encounters a movement in art that developed in the 1990s, but it also converses with everyone who has ever designed a set for any event, be it political, ritualistic or social.

In making her work, she does not discriminate between the setting of her home, the grandest art institutions or pop venues. However, there is something at once essential and intimate in everything she does. Therein lies the most profound enigma of her work.

In order to elucidate it, one should probably remember that her time is a longer one. She does not merely conceive her art in a genealogy of fifty years, or a hundred years, but speaks to centuries of recent history. Such is the beauty of theatre – it brings all time periods together.

When the still-existing Accademia delle Arti del Disegno was founded in Florence in 1563, its purpose was to conceive decors for the upcoming ceremonies for Michelangelo's death. The master was soon to die, and Florence wanted to be ready to grant its greatest artist a national funeral.

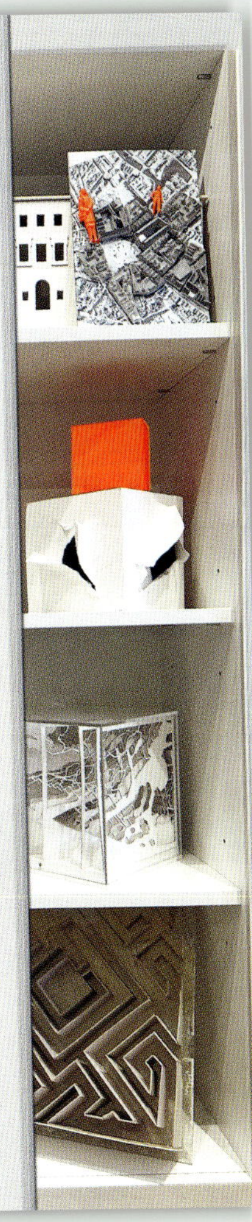

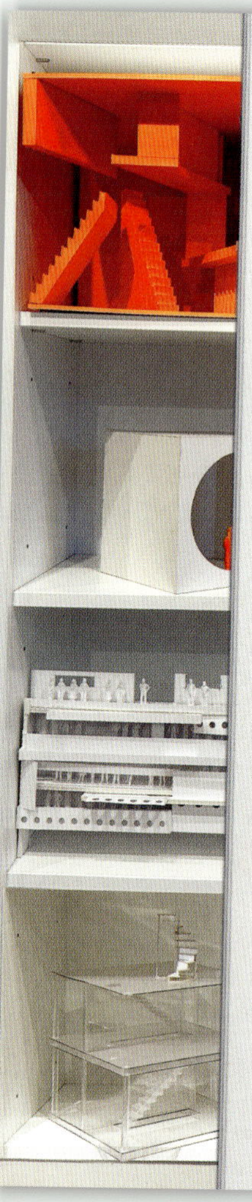

At that time, the word *disegno* signified at once 'drawing', 'design' and 'intent'. This semantic co-existence encapsulates the very spirit of the Renaissance. No separation is to be made between drawing – a 'cosa mentale', as Leonardo described painting; design – the making of objects and architectures; and intent – having a reason to do something. The depth of the self and the reality of objects coincide perfectly. That is the legacy Es Devlin brings forward.

The modern separation between 'use' (that is, design) and 'uselessness' (art) is an illusion. There never was such a thing as 'art for art's sake'. We now live in a world in which art and culture at large are often porous, and some have described art itself as an 'industry' – still holding to its symbolic capital to justify its value.

Es Devlin follows a path away from this crystallization, which otherwise leads to isolated, self-sustaining works. Looking at her work across a nearly thirty-year trajectory, one senses that she has been finding herself in and through all her works, while being open each time to other people and situations, and creating works that stated such openness. When working on the most populist occasions, she is no different than when she is conceiving a set for a Shakespeare play, an installation at the Tate, or a drawing from a vision. The legacy of the Renaissance gave birth to modernity. It is still present to and in her. She consistently manifests the power of *disegno* – intent, drawing, design – in her life and in contemporary culture, beyond any separation.

October 2023

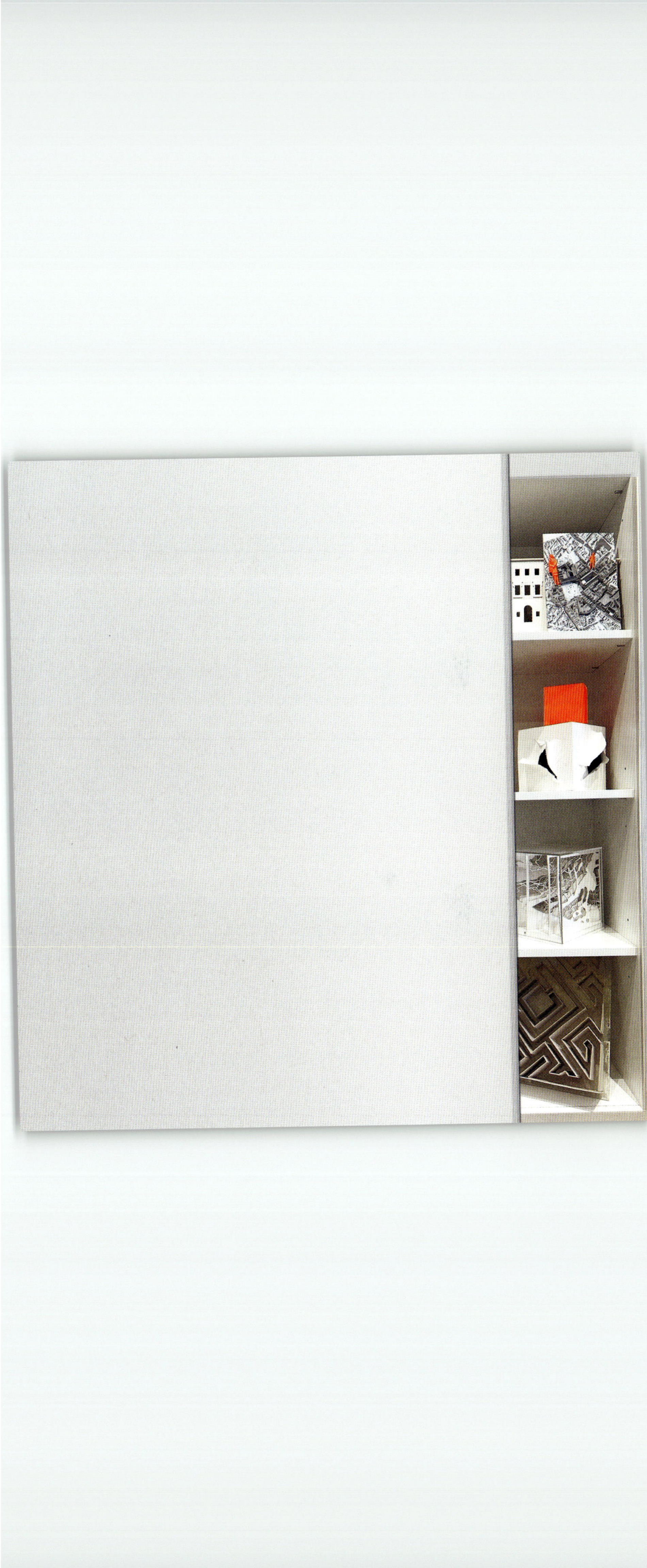

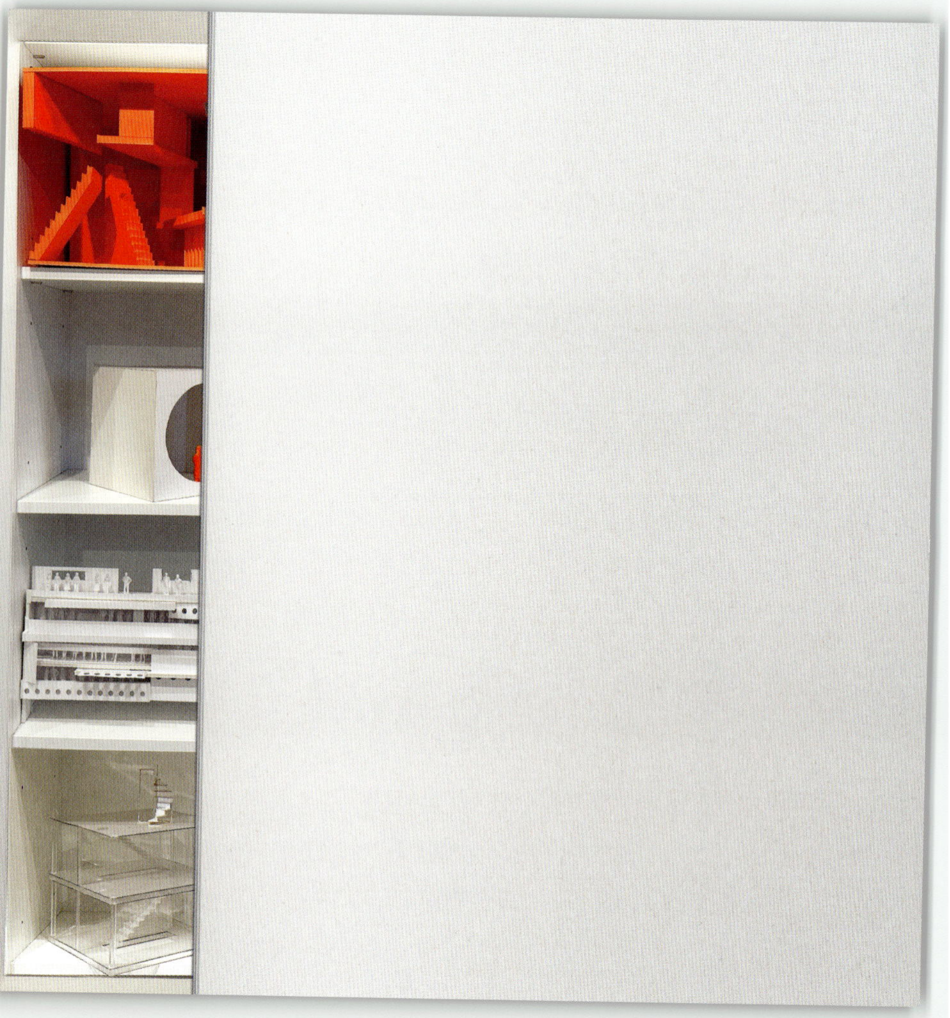

A CONVERSATION

With Hans Ulrich Obrist
Artistic Director at Serpentine Galleries

Hans Ulrich Obrist: I want to go back to the very beginning. Es, you are like superstring theory, at least 11 dimensions. It's extraordinary the many different fields you make great contributions to. It all began with your visionary theatre designs. You then went from theatre into music and invented a whole medium by conceiving these architectures for music shows. And you then went into art. Of course, you've always been an artist – these are, for you, parallel realities. Then once we saw your work in the art world, all of a sudden you were the architect of the UK Pavilion at the World Expo, and there are so many more dimensions. How did it all start? How did you come to theatre, art, architecture, design?

Es Devlin: I think I was probably looking for a tribe, looking for people who wanted to stay up all night in small dark spaces, finding and shaping light. Through various courses, I ended up in the small dark room above the Bush Theatre. And I learned that a group of tightly packed people could be greatly moved sitting together in the dark. That's probably where my practice really started.

HUO: Our dialogue and friendship began in 2016, when we met thanks to Jefferson Hack at his book launch at the Serpentine, and we started this collaboration for our Marathons. We have at the Serpentine this format called the 'Marathon' where we bring all disciplines together. It's the idea of bringing art together with architecture, music, literature, philosophy and science to break down the silos and

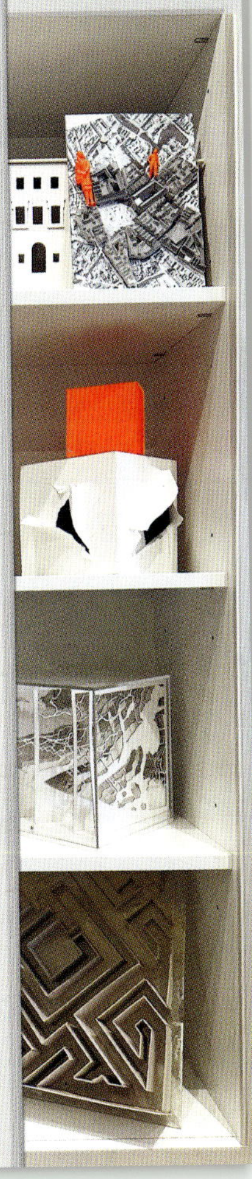

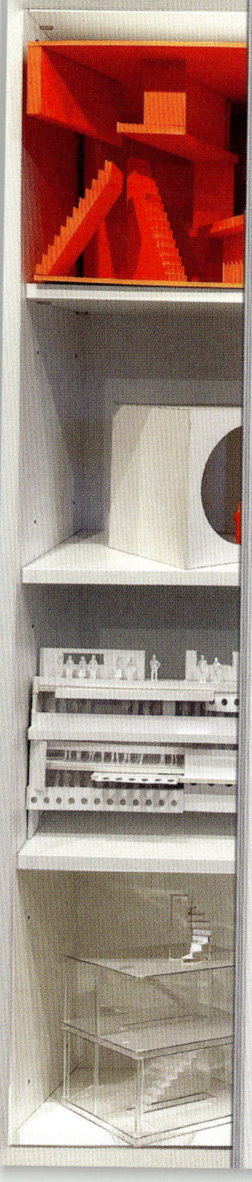

create more dialogue. The late poet Etel Adnan once said, 'The world needs togetherness, not separation. Love, not suspicion. A common future, not isolation.' This is the motto of these Marathons: to create togetherness. And you came up with the *Miracle Box*.

Es: I was immensely excited and nervous to speak at the Serpentine Gallery. I had visited the Felix Gonzalez-Torres exhibition there in 2000, which included a pile of shiny silver sweets that anyone could take. Its terms of engagement – between audience and art – fascinated me because everybody took a piece of the art away with them, which was what I was used to in the communal, collective spaces of theatres. So, invited to give a talk, I decided to make a performance. It was October 2016, and while I was talking about the origins of the mechanics of suspension of disbelief, I made a box [p.325]. It was a live act of construction, quite *Blue Peter* with Sellotape and string. And, once complete, the box started revolving and a film was projected onto it. The film was a self-portrait of my hands trying to penetrate different surfaces made from clay, paper and wood, to reach the light.

HUO: And then we enter the space of drawing and writing with the *PoemPortraits*, which is fascinating because, as Etel Adnan also said, 'writing is drawing, drawing is writing'.

Es: Francis Kéré was designing the Serpentine Pavilion that year. The invitation from you was to design something for the summer party. I was a bit confused because I didn't quite understand the terms of engagement. So I picked up on what I felt from the Gonzalez-Torres piece and said, 'What if everyone who comes to this party could contribute to a collective work of art?' It resulted in *PoemPortraits* [p.344], which is an ongoing collective poem still being composed online today. At the Serpentine, it was a mirrored photo booth. Each guest could sit inside it, donate a word, and receive a poem created in seconds by an algorithm trained on many millions of words of nineteenth-century poetry.

HUO: Yes, I had mentioned to you Joseph Beuys's theory of social sculpture. And in the 1960s, Billy Kluber had an idea for experiments in art and technology and brought artists together with Bell Laboratories, which was the leading tech company in the '60s. Artists like Robert Rauschenberg and Lillian Schwartz would collaborate with Bell Laboratories. And at the Serpentine we always thought, after these experiments in art and technology, we need *new* experiments in art and technology. Thus we instigate collaborations between artists and technologists in our time: *PoemPortraits* was a collaboration with Google Arts & Culture.

The year after, we asked you to create an architecture from music. Once one collaborates with Es, the collaboration is forever because it is so exciting. You've worked with some of the great musicians of our time – Beyoncé, Kendrick Lamar, The Weeknd. You created the Super Bowl halftime stage, sets which are kind of experiments. Obviously we couldn't do one of these very big sets at the Serpentine but one on a smaller scale, in a small space in the park. You created a pavilion for the summer party [p.400] and the structure rotated.

Es: The practice of making structures in which musicians sing is something like making musical instruments. They need to function, but they can also offer a visual counterpart to the music. In this case, time was a crucial factor. We had just finished painting this sculpture orange, and the performers danced on it while the paint was wet. I think they had orange paint all over their outfits.

HUO: And, of course, there is then the UK Pavilion for the World Expo. It really is extraordinary how in this fluid way you go from field to field. The *PoemPortraits* – this project that started on a very small scale at the Serpentine – developed into a very big, participatory poetry building. Normally artists make a contribution to one field, sometimes to two fields. That's already a lot. How all of a sudden did you manage to go into architecture?

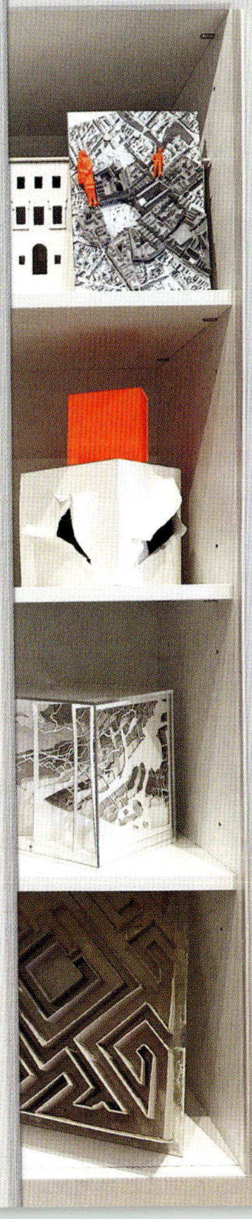

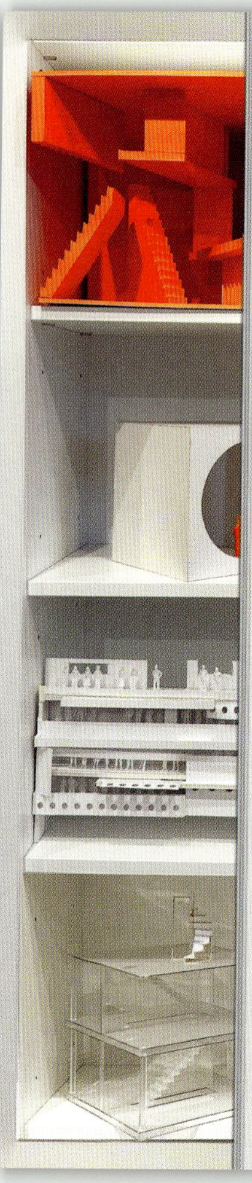

Es: It was an invitation to enter a competition. We went into it wanting to progress the collective poetry work we had been making. The pavilion [p.493] was a giant musical instrument, but of course the poetry algorithm had advanced. We worked with creative technologist Kyle McDonald and – very much aware of inherent biases – did a lot of work in training the AI with a diverse circle of poets. In the end, the AI felt perhaps more than human. It's an interesting collaborator. I believe 25 million people visited the Expo site and many of those people contributed a word. It was moving to stand in front of the pavilion's facade and read a new piece of poetry generated from people's words every 90 seconds by a 'more than human' creator.

HUO: And that's something Bruno Latour wrote a lot about – actor-network theory and this idea of different agencies. Bruno Latour also brings us to Timothy Morton. I want to talk about books. I remember many years ago you told me about Kate Raworth's *Doughnut Economics*. We also often discuss Timothy Morton and David Abram. Tell me about your literary inspirations.

Es: You gave me the Timothy Morton book *Hyperobjects* quite early on. I'd been working from primary texts for twenty years, and this and your other text recommendations helped guide the next part of my practice. You asked Timothy, 'What do you want artists to do in the face of the climate crisis?' And he said, 'It's not the role of artists to preach. The role of artists is to amaze people into changing their minds.' And more recently, the Director of Policy and Research of the London Wildlife Trust, Mathew Frith, said to me, 'We in conservation can help organize improvements in habitat for other species. But what we want artists to do is help to restructure the human imagination; to create habitats for species within the human imagination.' These statements have resonated with me.

It's easy to get overwhelmed by the enormity of the shifts we need to make in both perspective and behaviour. We sat around a table in my studio trying to remind ourselves of all the times throughout history in which human beings have changed their minds about something significant. We made a map of those shifts in human perspective, which became the *Memory Palace* [p.402] installed at Pitzhanger Manor gallery. It was a chapel of consolation. It located each of these moments of significant historical perspective shift onto the surface of the planet to create a new world map based on the human ability to change our minds and our world.

HUO: Your thinking was also greatly informed by David Abram's books *Becoming Animal* and *The Spell of the Sensuous*. Then there is Joanna Macy's *World as Lover, World as Self*. These are extraordinary books which are also a great inspiration for us at the Serpentine, for our *Back to Earth* project. The way you came to these books is quite interesting.

Es: I had been looking at Olafur Eliasson's Instagram because he very generously posts his current reading list. And the Amazon algorithm said to me: if you like those, then you might like *these*. And so the two most important books in my life that talk about consciousness of things that aren't human were recommended to me by the non-human.

David Abram is a sleight-of-hand magician and an eco-philosopher. He describes how you can shift perspective by penetrating the chinks in human cognitive armour using illusion, which interests me as I spend quite a lot of my practice working with magic and illusion.

And James Gleick's book *Chaos* – when you read it, you don't look at anything the same way again. It guides you to understand that there is pretty much one equation that governs all the underlying structures of our world: the way the veins in your hands are arranged or the way the branches of trees bifurcate or the way water droplets divide as they fall down a windscreen. You begin to understand that these phenomena are governed by the same maths, which led me to make bronchial tree drawings which coincided with your invitation, Hans Ulrich, to make a *do it* [p.466] during the lockdown.

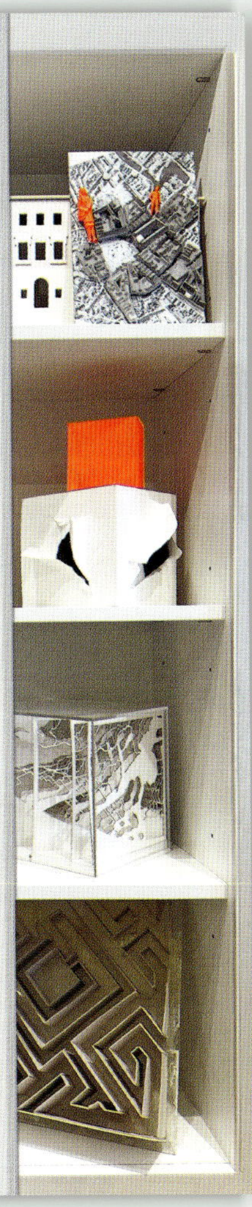

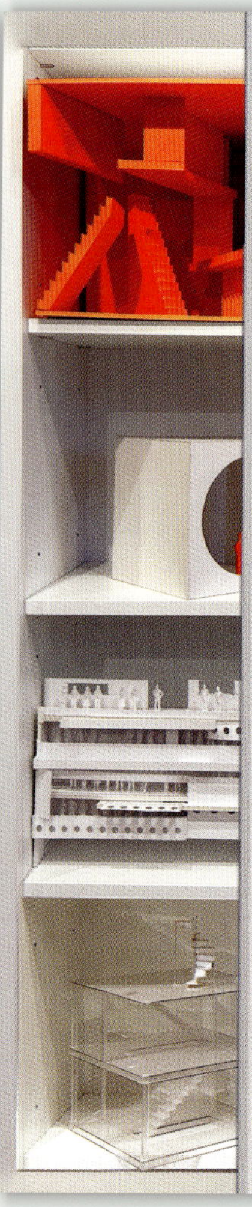

HUO: Exactly. During the lockdown, we reactivated the *do it* project that I started in 1993, where artists write instructions, recipes, all kinds of things one can do at home as participatory artworks. And we did it in relation to the environment and extinction crisis. You created a very beautiful piece.

Es: I was invited to write this during a difficult month in lockdown when my studio was empty, and when I read everybody else's contributions I saw so many of us were feeling the same way. I concluded my *do it* with a suggested action: 'If you have $8, go to www.institutoterra.org and plant a tree.'

The Instituto Terra is Sebastião Salgado's reforestation project in Brazil. The invitation to contribute to their project operates as a piece of activism at the end of a piece of meditation. So first it's an invitation to make a perspective shift, to make the connection between the trees inside and outside of our bodies, and then to try to translate that shift into a piece of action, the reforestation of an area in northeast Brazil. It's a physical as well as cognitive connection.

HUO: So let's all do it! And this leads to a whole body of your work that addresses the extinction crisis, which relates to the words of the poet Alexis Pauline Gumbs: 'We have the opportunity now, as a species fully in touch with each other, to unlearn and relearn our own patterns of thinking and storytelling in a way that allows us to be actually in communion with our environment as opposed to a dominating, colonialist separation from the environment.'

Es: Yes, and once I'd seen the visual connection between trees and lungs, I couldn't unsee it. So I thought it would be interesting if other people could experience that in quite a mass way. I'm used to large audiences, so I was keen for more people to make the connection I had made. I drew the bronchial branches as a maze and first made it in cardboard. Then it got extruded and constructed in Miami as *Forest of Us* [p.474], part of Pace Gallery's Superblue exhibition alongside a James Turrell piece. That led to a series of temporary forests: like Shakespearean forests of transformation, you enter in one state and you emerge transformed – *Five Echoes* [p.499] in Miami, *Forest for Change* [p.472] at Somerset House, and *Conference of the Trees* [p.483] at the Climate Change Conference in Glasgow for COP26.

HUO: It is about empathy. You quote Timothy Morton, who says, 'Don't bother preaching; amaze people.' And that's really what you do.

Es: That's certainly what we try to find the mechanics of doing.

HUO: Es, quickly explain about Kate Raworth. That's another book recommendation. Es and I are obsessed by this book, *Doughnut Economics*.

Es: She's an economist, and at the beginning of the book she says we are all entangled in economic systems designed to ensure systemic economic growth whether or not the population within the system thrives. What we should be doing is ensuring populations thrive, whether or not there's economic growth. This is the fundamental thing. And I shared this at the Google dinner you and I attended.

HUO: With the CEO, right.

Es: Yes. It went down like a cup of cold sick.

HUO: In our *140 Artists' Ideas for Planet Earth* book, Kate Raworth says, 'Be regenerative by design: work with and within the cycles of the living world. Be distributive by design: share opportunity and value with all who co-create it. Create economies that aim to thrive forever, rather than grow forever.'

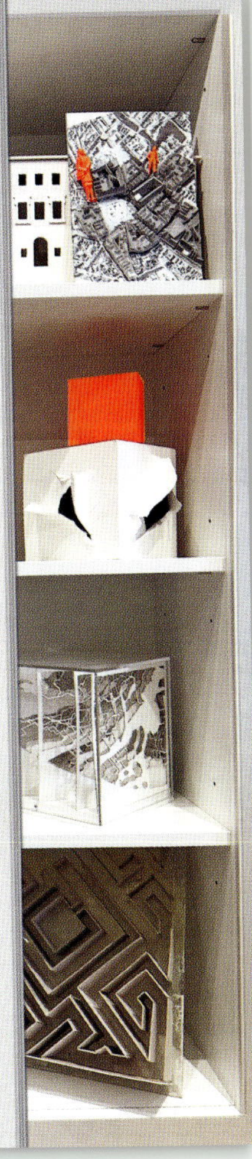

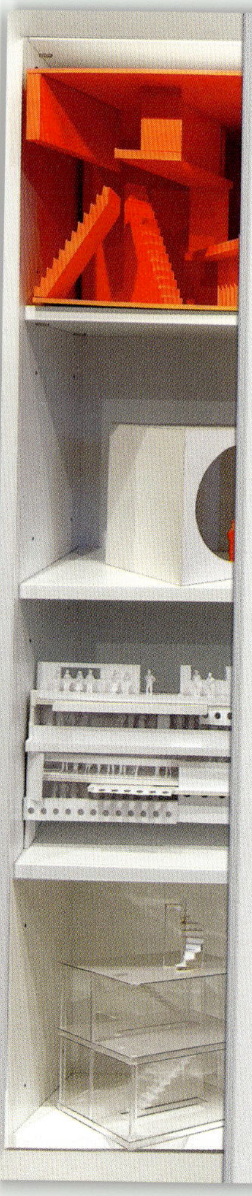

Es: The Amazon algorithm also recommended Joanna Macy's book. Her phrase, 'Now we can relinquish our separation. We can come home. We can come home again to our mutual belonging', provided the starting point for the sculpture outside Tate Modern called *Come Home Again* [p.519]. After a conversation with Dorothea von Hantelmann about the siloing of the arts that had once been combined in religious ritual – art, music, scent, poetry, light – we wanted to look for a way to reinvigorate that synaesthetic experience of ritual.

During research into St Paul's and Christopher Wren, I discovered Robert Hooke's phenomenally popular seventeenth-century book *Micrographia*. He and Wren were anatomists and astronomers before they were architects, and they amazed their readers with extremely minute creatures drawn through their microscope. I started to draw some of the 15,000 species of Londoners that aren't human.

HUO: And there's a very beautiful quote – you say that you made this work as an expression of a sensation that you began to feel at the edges of your hand as you created these 243 drawings of the most endangered birds, bats, fish, plants, amphibians, mammals; that, while drawing, you began to feel the resonance between the distribution of cells and arteries in your hand with the fish scales, the leaf veins, the bird feathers, and your non-human neighbours. Can you talk about this porosity that you felt, that's at the core of *Redraw the Edges of Your Self*?

Es: I had been drawing really intensively, sometimes 18 hours a day. One evening I got this email from you: 'Es, you have to do this poster for the *Back to Earth* exhibition at the Serpentine and we need to go to print tomorrow.' So I very quickly drew around my hand and cut out all of these animals that I'd been drawing and assembled them at the edges of my hand to try to express the interpenetration of edges that I was feeling between my hand and the species I was drawing. I think it was about 1 am and you needed it to print by 7 am.

So I quickly took a photo of the collage and that became one of the *Back to Earth* posters at the Serpentine. Later, when I was invited to make a piece for Frieze week in London, I developed the work into *Redraw the Edges of Your Self* [p.524].

HUO: One rarely speaks about books by artists. It's one of the most under-appreciated mediums in art, because when artists create books, they are important artworks that are quite democratic because they are accessible. Gerhard Richter told me he spends as much time on his artist books as on his paintings. So far you've done three extraordinary artist books. You did one for *Memory Palace*, one for *Forest of Us*, and one for *Come Home Again*. Tell us about the importance of these books, the books of Es Devlin.

Es: The books are especially important because they are small and I can make them in the studio on my own. So much of this large-scale work involves so many collaborators. But the nature of a book, the scale of a book, the fact that you can touch it and be in control of each page – for me that is very therapeutic. At the end of each very large project, I want to be able to contain it into one small world that I can hold in my hand. This is part of the process.

HUO: I have one last, recurrent question, which is to discuss unrealized projects. Tell us about works you haven't made yet.

Es: I would like to make *Come Home Again* in different cities. The process for me of drawing – four months of drawing so intensively – has become a meditation, and I want to learn about our non-human neighbours in different cities. It's the continued assault on my own ignorance, on my complete lack of knowledge of the design of these extraordinary creatures who aren't human, that will be the focus. As T. S. Eliot puts it: a raid on the inarticulate.

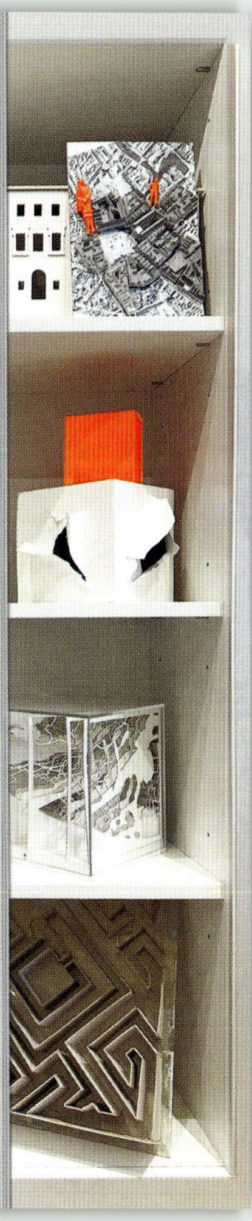

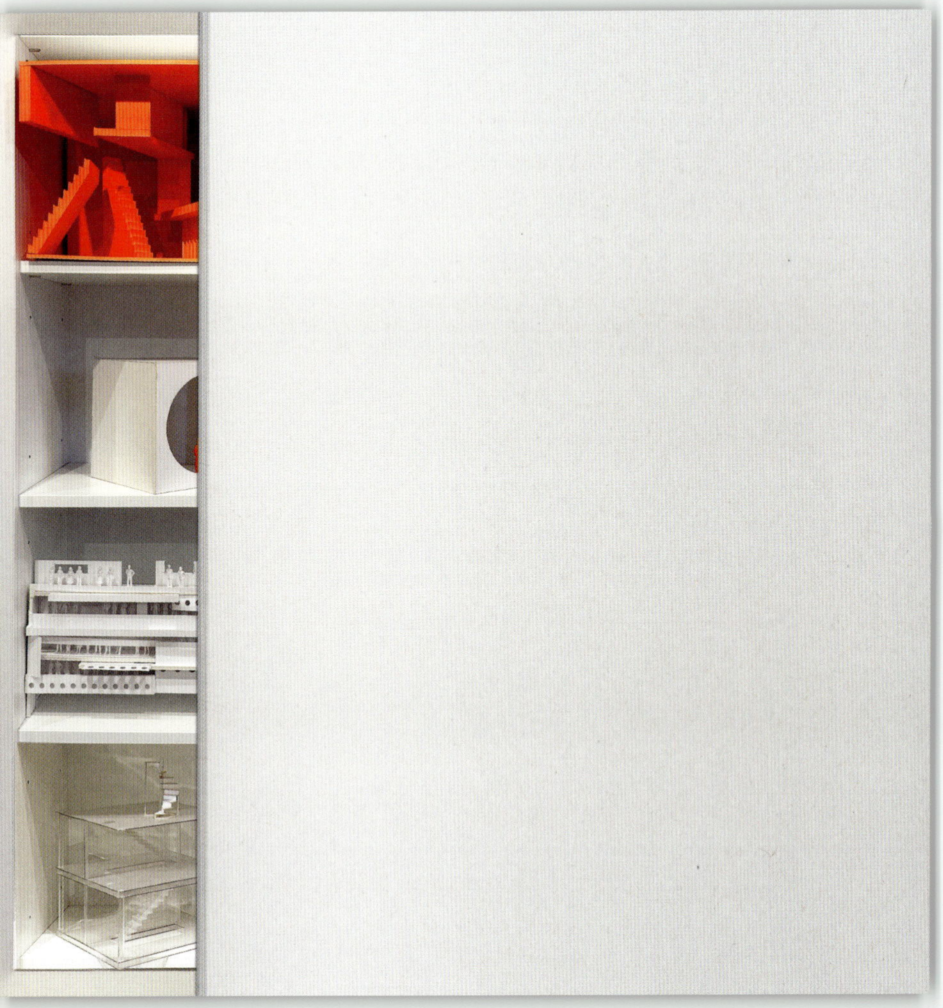

AN INFINITE ARCHIVE

By Andrea Lipps
Senior Curator of Visual Arts, Media, and Technology,
MIT Museum

There's a level at which words are spirit and paper is skin. That's the fascination of archives. There's still a bodily trace.

Susan Howe, *The Telepathy of Archives*

To visit Es Devlin's archive is to experience a kind of magic. Housed in an unassuming storage space in rural Kent, the relics of her 28-year practice form a skyline of towering boxes and bins stuffed with drawings, scale models, sketchbooks, photographs, notes and books. Against a wall, paintings lean like dominoes in rows twenty canvases deep.

Opening a box invites constant surprise. The sketchbooks are like sculptures, their pages collaged with gauzy fabrics, painted metal, colourful glass and miniature cogs. Models present jewel-like visions of designs for theatre, opera, stadium tours and immersive installations – among them delicate trees, mirrored mazes and a bloodied bathtub no bigger than a fingernail. Personal photo albums record her first travels abroad with the considered eye of someone memorising a place rather than documenting it, with photographs arranged in bands of colour, texture and light.

But it's through her drawings that one most closely approaches her thoughts, whether through meditative portraits and studies or urgent concepts rushed across sheets of music, scraps of newspaper, printed emails and set lists, or in the margins of scripts. She returns

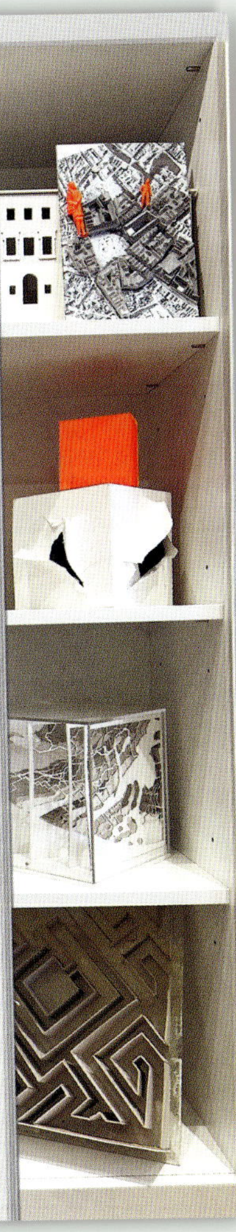

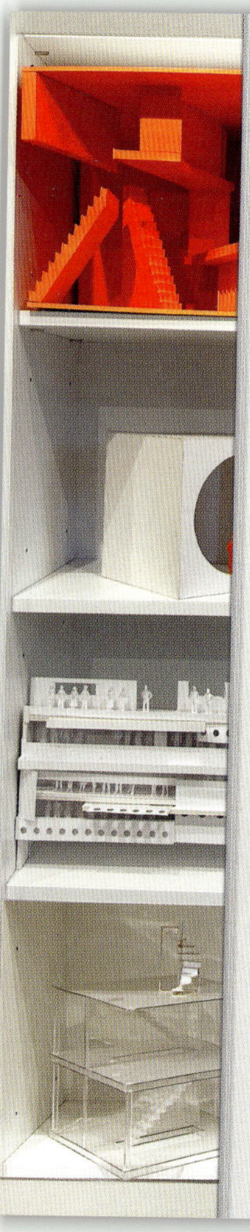

again and again to faces, figures and hands, layering materials and paint to suggest more under the surface. Bodies are confined and contorted into tiny boxes. Faces burst beyond the edge of the canvas. The content, dynamism and materiality are overflowing, suggesting a boundless creative mind.

Kneeling on the warehouse's cement floor in early November 2022, we pored over her process. I'd come from New York with our curatorial team to refine a list of objects to include in the forthcoming exhibition at Cooper Hewitt, Smithsonian Design Museum. The depth, richness and range of the work made choosing a challenge. We'd initially planned to spend a few days in the archive. We stayed for two weeks.

It is impossible to pin Es Devlin to a singular title, and perhaps it is defeating. She is polymathic. She is a storyteller, an artist, a designer, a director, a poet, a visionary, perhaps even a shaman, whose work razes through disciplinary boundaries. Her canvas is temporary space, her materials are as intangible as her work is ephemeral: breath, light, music, time, and anticipation. Her additive practice reveals a limitless curiosity. To be in her presence is to be transfixed with creative energy, poetry and a proliferation of ideas. She poses incisive questions of collaborators and immerses herself within texts. The result is the precise distillation of narrative in form: a merging of geometry, materials and words into an armature that holds the ritual of performance. And yet, as she points out, 'I do all this work and nothing physical remains. What I'm really designing are mental structures, as opposed to physical ones. Memories are solid, and that's what I'm trying to build.'

If this book is the physical evocation of the archive from a prolific career so far, it also points to the future of Es Devlin's practice. She is dedicating her craft as an experiential storyteller to elicit emotions from audiences, nudging us out of apathy and into action, to imagine our civilization's future and to act towards it every day, making concrete what is currently abstract. She examines the role of an artist in the face of civilizational crises and the importance of shared experiences, with clarified purpose around animism, regeneration, inclusivity and intention.

Language and Form
1995–2003

The threads and connections of geometries, forms, ideas and process that reverberate throughout Devlin's practice emerge in her archive. From her earliest theatre work beginning in 1995, there is a demonstrated devotion to an intensely rigorous process and an instinctive ingenuity, evidenced by the sheer volume of the archive's ever-expanding content – over 10,000 drawings, models, sketches and paintings to date. The success of the work is held up by the mountain of research, ideas and iterations beneath the surface.

A love and sophisticated understanding of literature grounds her forensic study of primary texts. Never one to think without a pencil, Devlin pores over scripts, jotting notes, sketching quick drawings to convey an idea, always working towards visual metaphor to unlock thought structures contained in the text. The process opens itself to a wide range of sources for each project: researching and reading, probing, and exploring with her collaborators. She interrogates a text, turning it on its side to reflect meaning that's not just on the page, but underneath it, above it, or bent around its corner, as though refracting it through a prism to transform an audience's perspective. Through diligent process, she identifies precise form. As theatre director and collaborator Lyndsey Turner describes, Devlin's mind is 'both forensic and associative'.

In her early proscenium-based work, we already see her engaging light as an evocative material – reaching for light, revealing or masking it, using it in acts of transformation. The line of light in *Howie the Rookie* [p.155] becomes the expanding horizon in *Four Scenes* [p.156], which is revisited in her staging of *I Remember Red* [p.167]. Luminosity imbues the *Betrayal* set [p.152] with memory. Kinetic blocks of brilliant, illuminated colour emulate a modulating sequence of stained-glass windows in *God's Plenty* [p.173].

Portraiture, long an interest from the early sketchbooks, begins to emerge as a central metaphor with the staging of *Powder Her Face* [p.165]. The performance unfolds through an over-scaled wedding portrait of the play's

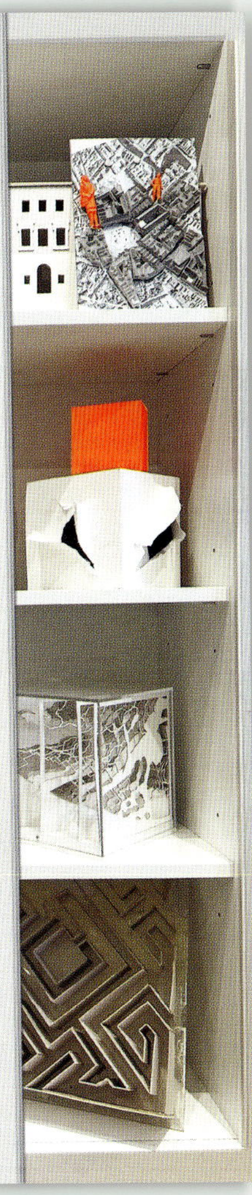

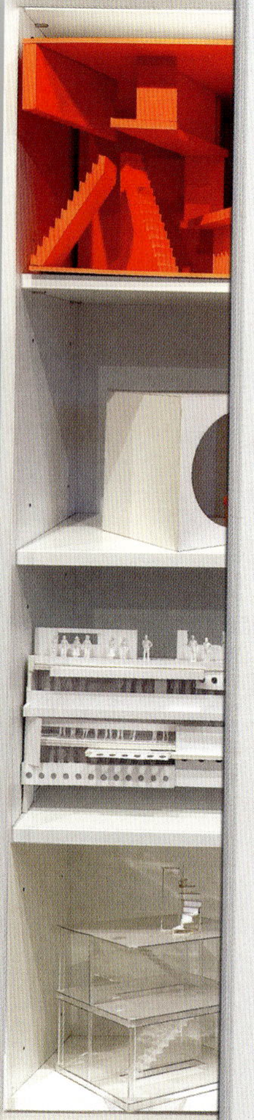

protagonist. Experimenting with the scale and framing of faces, Devlin draws on representation to suggest intimacy, a strategy she will apply across expanding terrains. As soon as she demonstrates an unrestrained instinct for world-building within theatre, she extends beyond the proscenium.

Form and Music
2003–2016

In 2003, she began penetrating new fields when music, which had consumed her early sketchbooks, entered her professional practice. That year, she collaborated with director Keith Warner on Ernest Bloch's *Macbeth* [p.182], her first European opera house production, in which a rotating perspective box delivered the play's illusions. Saturated red paintings of arterial systems, early explorations for *Macbeth*, mark a fascination to which she returns in later work. That same year, Alex Poots and Paul Smith invited Devlin to design the set for post-punk band Wire's farewell tour [p.174]. The minimal staging and attendant projections – four cubes, each containing a band member and overlaid with projections of an eye, ear, mouth or nose – not only signal the cube as a talisman in her practice but also present an abstracted portrait of a band in disarray. If her early stages had functioned as multi-layered narratives, they now began acting as instruments – every aspect serving sight, story and sound.

The design for Wire attracted the interest of Kanye West, beginning several years of collaboration [pp.179, 207, 245, 267, 274] and launching Devlin onto bigger stages with ever-larger audiences and additional artist collaborators, including U2 [pp.300, 384], Adele [pp.306, 487], Beyoncé [pp.314, 496], The Weeknd [pp.334, 374, 506], and Dr. Dre and Kendrick Lamar [p.488], among others. As the scale of performances increased, so did the degree of audience anticipation, which she moulded as a material. On stadium stages, she envisioned worlds in which performers became almost mythological – conduits to the multiple meanings fans ascribe to their songs. Portraiture became an often essential tool for calibrating energy within a stadium. Multi-storey sculptures project an artist as larger than life. Beyoncé emerges from a seven-storey monolith on which her monumental image is projected [p.665]; Miley Cyrus slides down a bright pink tongue protruding from the mouth of her over-scaled head [p.842]. Within these environments, performers often appear surprisingly vulnerable, offering at once a sense of spectacle and intimacy.

Narrative remains essential. Kinetic, layered environments tell the stories behind musicians' songs. Lyrics form fantastical or meditative landscapes. Crowds journey through concerts on a series of cresting and breaking waves. While arena tours can comprise an epic, the stages for televised performances present condensed, shorter stories. Devlin's designs for the BRITs [p.362] and MTV [p.410] present engaging visuals that function on both stage and screen – a constraint she explored in greater depth in her designs for Olympic ceremonies in London [p.258] and Rio [p.322]. If the proscenium arch restricts an audience's view, forcing the eye to a fixed vantage point, she masterfully focuses audience attention on monumental platforms, conceiving large-scale sculptures and activating light and colour such that the stage itself begins to dematerialize.

While a pop show tends to emphasize an individual, opera hinges on the power of collective voices. For Devlin, choral instruments often derive from a simple gesture or metaphor – Carmen throwing the cards that foretell her fate [p.349] or Parsifal's quest for compassion as a game of chess [p.248]. Through rigorous readings of texts and iterative process, she distills complex stories into simple forms. Circles and ellipses enter her lexicon [p.235]. A metaphorical landscape prioritizes the psychological story [p.294], and she deploys kinetic techniques in a continuous rhythm to propel a performance [p.370]. Objects rotate, revealing and concealing scenes. Dynamic projection-mapping creates movement within stillness, carefully timed to the beats and needs of the action. And the objects amplify music, projecting the voices of performers or arranging them in stacked staves [p.737] – a form that reappears in later work for Louis Vuitton.

Through her many collaborations, Devlin erodes and tears apart the seams between disciplines. The story of a song is equal to that of a play or a fashion collection or an opera. The more she experiments, the more she merges art forms to foster new modes of transformative performance.

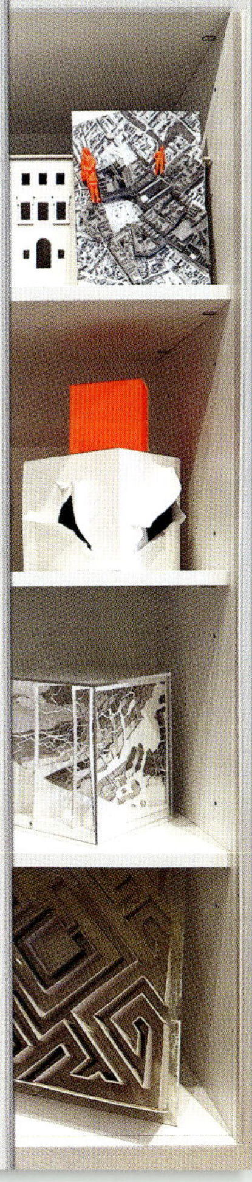

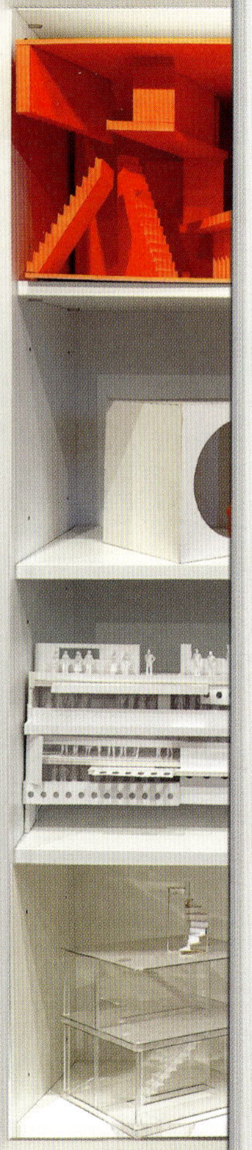

Immersions and Perspective Shifts
2016–present

In what would become a formative year, Devlin began moulding her craft to create ritual environments around her own texts in 2016. The genesis, as she tells it, was a misread email from a producer at *i-D* magazine. The message was, in fact, an invitation to suggest a film director and collaborate on a digital response to a Chanel perfume. Devlin, however, interpreted it as an invitation to create her first large-scale installation. *Mirror Maze* [p.326] was a decisive work, in which she eschewed the stage altogether. For the first time, she invited audiences to become the work's protagonists, changing the terms of engagement signalled with a hole in the introductory film. Audiences stepped through it to immerse themselves in a mirrored installation. This transformation of audience, from passive observer to a fully embodied, active participant, marks a profound shift in the practice.

That same year, she was invited by Hans Ulrich Obrist to participate as a speaker in the Serpentine's annual Marathon in London. In a testament to her rigour, Devlin used the opportunity to not just give a talk, but to create a work while on stage [p.325], aptly making a performance of her process.

Collectively, these works and the collaborations around them mark the beginning of her installation-based art practice. She had been dematerializing the stage, and it was only a matter of time before action and audience would coalesce in her art. After all, bastions fall in her presence. As her amphibious work encompasses more genres, it demonstrates the porosity and synchronicities that exist between fields of practice.

Like so many of us, Devlin has grown increasingly concerned, particularly in the last decade, about the climate and civilizational crises we face. The urgency to shift towards regenerative and harmonious ways of living with one another and the planet only continues to come into fuller relief with each IPCC report, extreme weather event, social justice movement and mass migration. Her attention centres on texts of eco-philosophy and economic transformation that will sustain a flourishing world. If humans currently confront climate facts with stasis, then perhaps it is through art and imagination that new perspectives will take root. Art provides a forum to synchronize collective thinking. It is here that form and purpose meet in the trajectory of the work, unifying her practice.

With each new commission, she dedicates her craft in service of narratives that will spark a shift in audiences: inviting contributions to collective poetry [pp.344, 357, 383, 493]; mapping locations of historical cognitive shifts [p.402]; bathing conference delegates in a forest of trees [p.483]; kindling awareness of underlying patterns in human and non-human arterial systems [p.474]; illuminating the beauty of linguistic diversity [p.510]; and celebrating endangered species [p.519]. Devlin often works with a quotational practice, collaging together extracts from devoured books to foreground these salient narratives, which she presents in immersive, sonic and spatial environments that are rigorously researched and realized.

Perhaps the best way to define Es Devlin is as a composer of space and narrative, a sculptor of time and engagement. She wields spectacle, scale and anticipation with an analytic and associative mind to extrude meaning and ritual. Her installation-based works invite all of us to participate and consider our connection to one another and to the planet, evoking emotions and advancing action towards our collective future. Her fearlessness in the face of boundaries releases her into a boundless practice.

The Archive

The poet Susan Howe suggests an archive is an 'empty theatre where a thought may surprise itself at the instant of seeing'. Each object awaits a potential audience. Each drawing, text, model or sketch reverberates with underlying meaning. The encounter surfaces the spontaneity and frisson of live performance. Intimate discoveries bend the arc of time when uncovering the inception of an idea, as evoked by the hand that pressed graphite on paper, leaving its bodily trace.

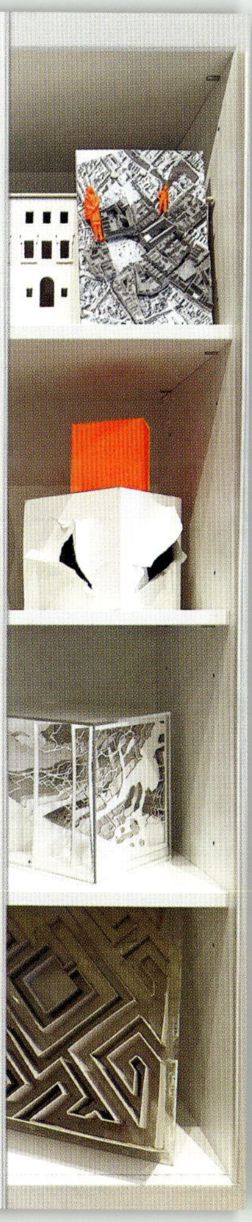

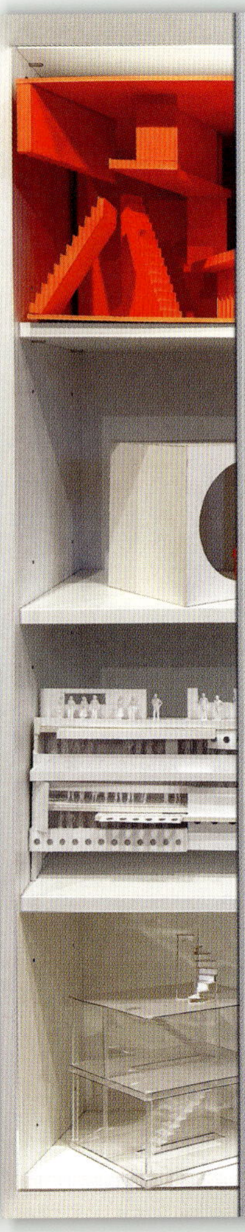

In our intimate experience encountering Devlin's archive, we uncovered connections, threads, stories and breadth in not just a body of work, but in a life. One can imagine each project and period forming a mental architecture that she temporarily inhabits; the archive, with its towering boxes, is a memory palace where they all simultaneously coexist, much like this book itself.

What begins with an initial sketch found in a box becomes a detailed rendering made with a community of collaborators, and finally manifests in a form experienced by thousands or hundreds of thousands. It's the expansion from the individual, with just a sheet of paper and pencil, out into the creative community, the audience and beyond. For Es Devlin, this is breath, this is life. It begins with one and leads to the infinite.

October 2023

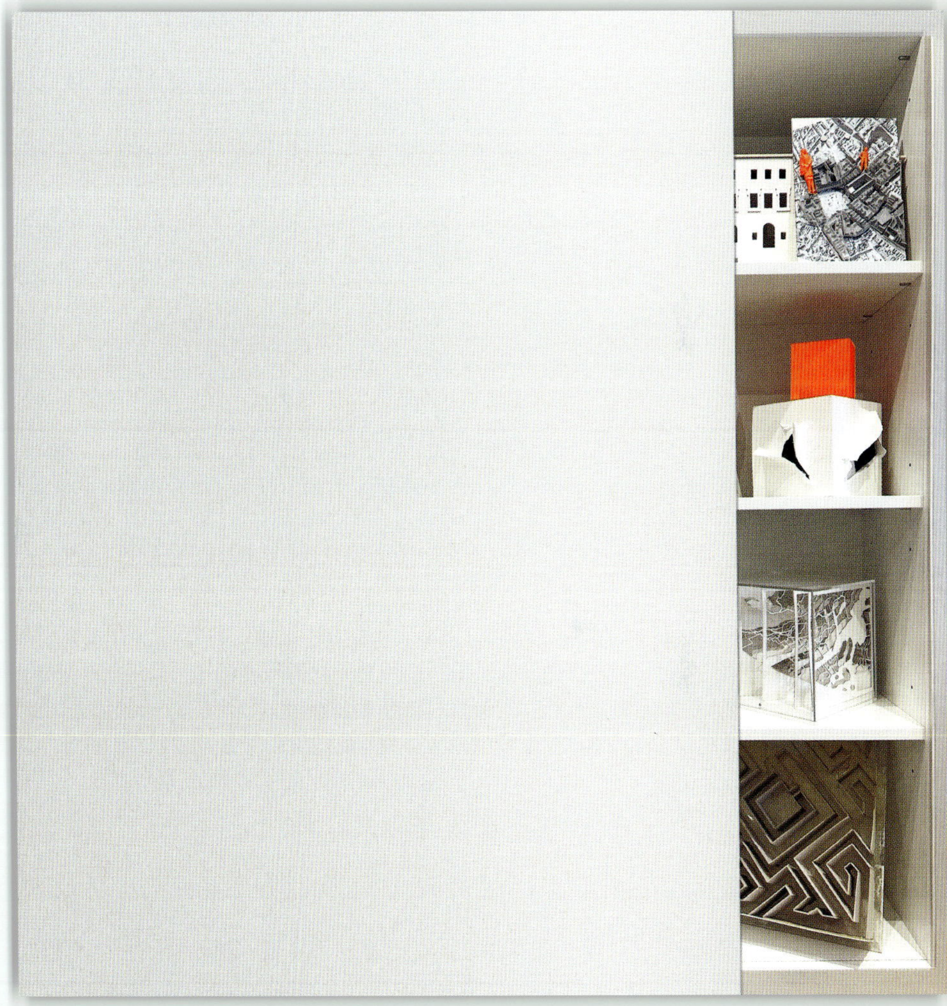

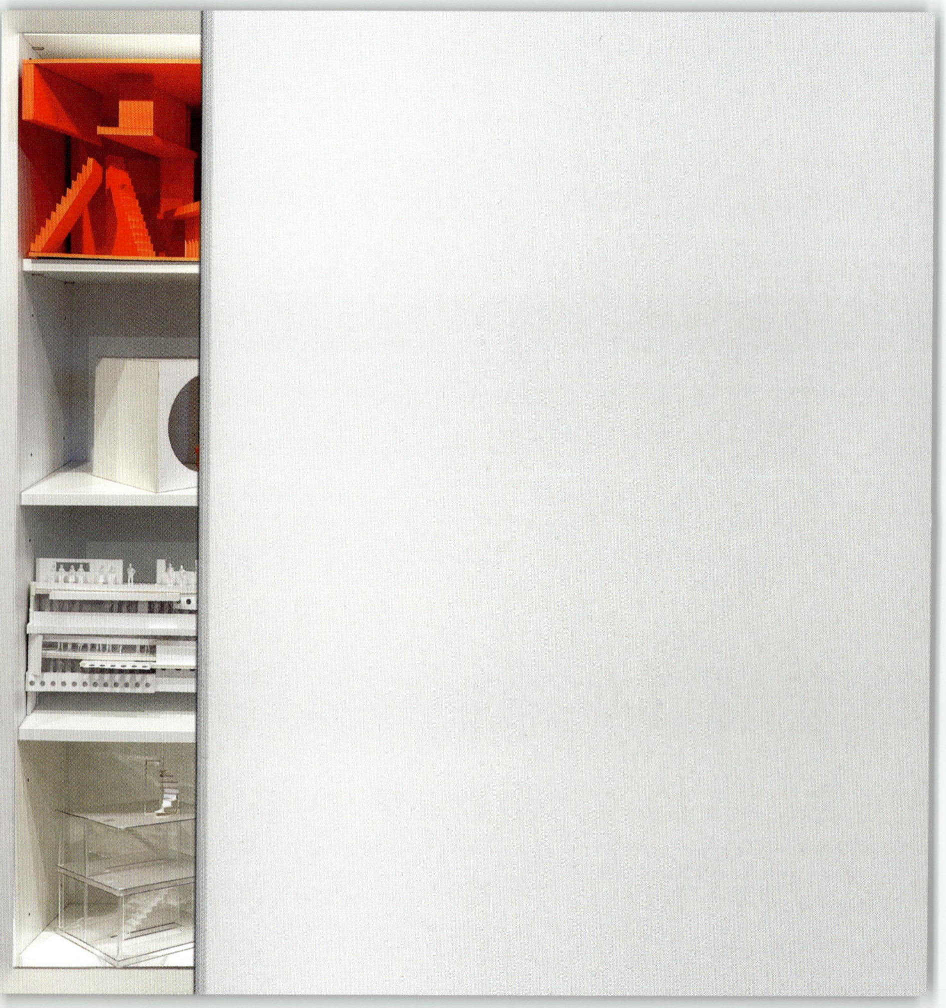

ART AS RITUAL

Johanna Agerman Ross

Conran Foundation Chief Curator, the Design Museum

Within the shapeshifting practice of Es Devlin, nothing is what it seems. What might at first suggest intimacy is instead revealed to be expansive. Walls are potential apertures into other worlds. Lines are new possibilities. Corridors are portals. Objects speak. Buildings move. Nothing is static.

For over thirty years, Devlin's practice has continuously evolved and expanded. The first edition of this book concluded with the 2022 installation *Come Home Again*, which Devlin structured as a mass in antiphony to St Paul's Cathedral. This new edition continues with her series of works that invite public gatherings, including *Congregation* [p.559], Devlin's 2024 installation composed of 50 portraits in the church of St Mary le Strand in London, and *Sou o Outro do Outro* [p.16 and p.58] which invited participants to make collective portraits each day at Cidade Matarazzo in São Paulo. *Surfacing* [p.555] gathered people at Art Basel's 2024 art fair in hourly ritual sequences, *Library of Light* [p.587] brought visitors to listen to Devlin's underscored voice within the courtyard of the Pinacoteca di Brera, Milan in 2025, and *Library of Us* [p.588] drew crowds to listen together to texts read aloud on the shores of the Atlantic Ocean in Miami. For Devlin, these installations and her ongoing performance works are instruments for creating temporary societies: the meeting of people who together navigate an artwork, play or performance, bonded momentarily by a focal point that inspires awe and wonder.

Here, Devlin's works reflect a very early function of art, namely that of ritual. As Walter Benjamin argues in his essay 'The Work of Art in the Age of Mechanical Reproduction' (originally published in German in 1935), works of art in the pre-industrial era were experienced through the social practices of rituals:

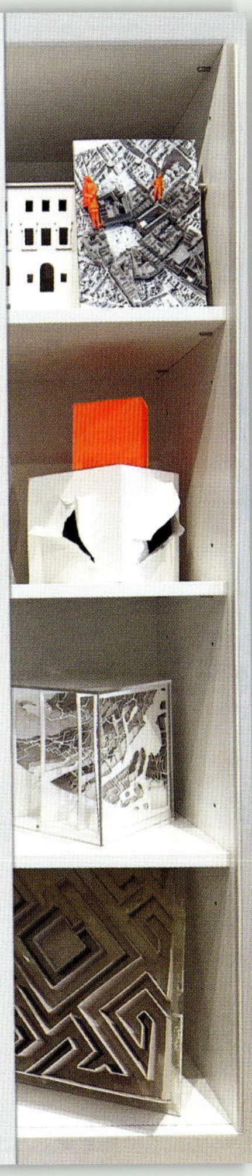

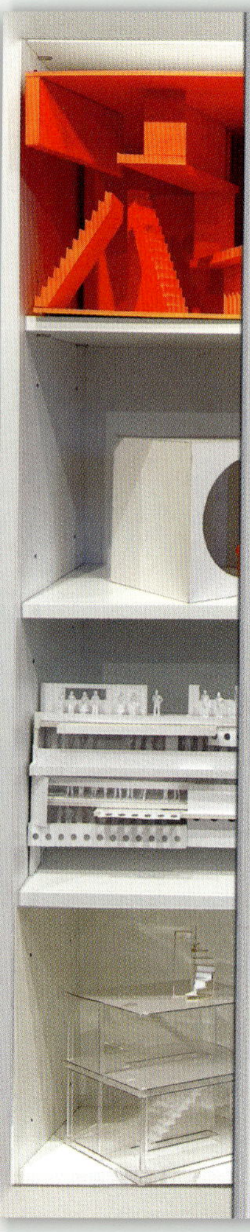

'... the earliest artworks originated in the service of rituals – first magical, then religious. And it is highly significant that the artwork's auratic mode of existence is never entirely severed from its ritual function. In other words: the unique value of the "authentic" work of art always has its basis in ritual.'

Benjamin refers to this sense of authenticity as the 'cult-value' of an artwork. Devlin's great-grandfather was an architect of altars, and it is perhaps not a coincidence that she attended the Catholic Church as a child, gaining first-hand experience of the 'cult-value' of objects Benjamin describes. 'My sister and I would chime a little bell at the end of the Latin phrases and we prepared the props: wine and wafers laid out behind a little curtain. We learned that the objects had voices, too,' remembers Devlin.

In the shift of artworks and objects from being the focal point of rituals to occupying a less worshipful status, however, Benjamin argues that they move from having 'cult-value' to 'exhibition-value', resulting in a different form of engagement:

'The masses are a matrix from which all customary behaviour toward works of art is today emerging newborn. Quantity has been transformed into quality: the greatly increased mass of participants has produced a different kind of participation. [...] The masses are criticized for seeking distraction in the work of art, whereas the art lover supposedly approaches it with concentration. In the case of the masses, the artwork is seen as a means of entertainment; in the case of the art lover, it is considered an object of devotion.'

Herein lies the duality and contradiction present in the appreciation of different modes of art. It also perfectly captures contradictions in Devlin's work, which simultaneously possesses 'cult' and 'exhibition' value, at once being the subject of ritual, devotion and deep concentration while also engaging with the art of entertainment. Her practice captivates and focuses audience attention, and over the years has increasingly moved from institutions connected with performance to those traditionally associated with display. Starting with her first monographic exhibition, *An Atlas of Es Devlin*, at Cooper Hewitt, Smithsonian Design Museum in New York in 2023, Devlin's work is now frequently the subject of monographic shows, with solo exhibitions at the Design Museum in London, Casa Bradesco in São Paulo, Futura Seoul, Powerhouse Parramatta in Sydney, and Singapore's ArtScience Museum. So, what occurs when her works, so carefully conceived for a specific place, are brought into the setting of a museum? How does this impact the cult-value and exhibition-value of the work? What new rules apply?

Exhibition-making around Devlin is an opportunity to explore the history of both the artist and her practice. This is true not only for an audience of exhibition-goers, but also for Devlin herself, who reflects: 'With over 350 productions and 15,000 pieces in the archive, it is really medicinal to thread them together and assemble who I have been.' And who she becomes.

The ritual of piecing together an archive, a person, has been the work of many curators in creating exhibitions of Devlin's work. It has involved retracing the steps of her practice, exploring her extensive archive, and discovering the alluring detritus of her creative output: drawings, models, photos and paper-cuttings. It is an act of recreating parts of an extraordinary oeuvre of experience and collaboration, and, in doing so, the boundaries of the work under consideration dissolve and refocus. To quote Benjamin again: '*The cathedral leaves its site to be received in the studio of an art lover; the choral work performed in an auditorium or in the open air is enjoyed in a private room.*' And while the purpose of the work on display has changed from its original function, it never lacks magic. Because within the shapeshifting practice of Es Devlin, nothing is what it seems.

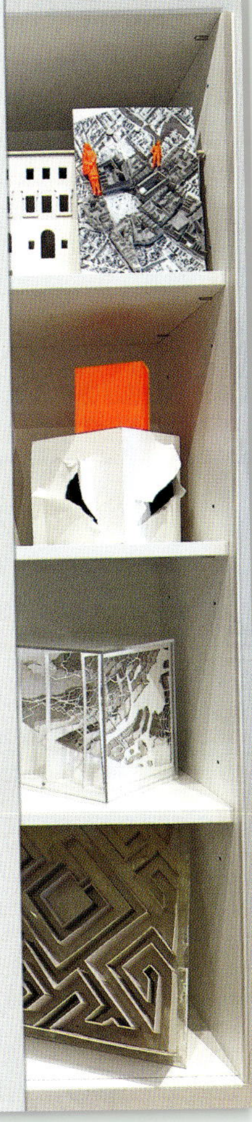

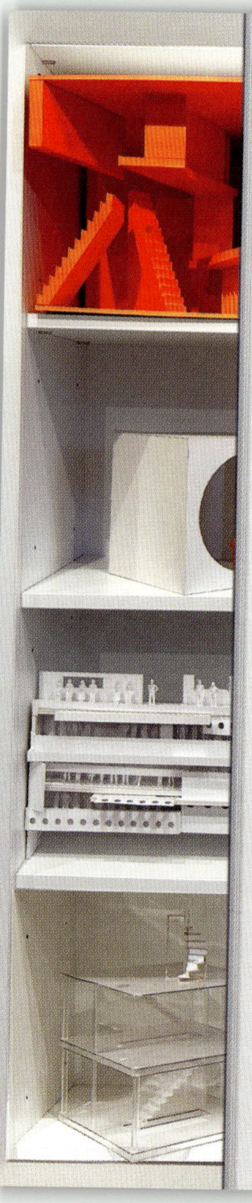

12 THINGS

1971–1985

I read The Memory Palace of Matteo Ricci *by Jonathan D. Spence as a teenager.*
It taught me to understand objects
as repositories of memory.
There are 12 objects that
I'd ask to give an account
of the first 14 years of my life.

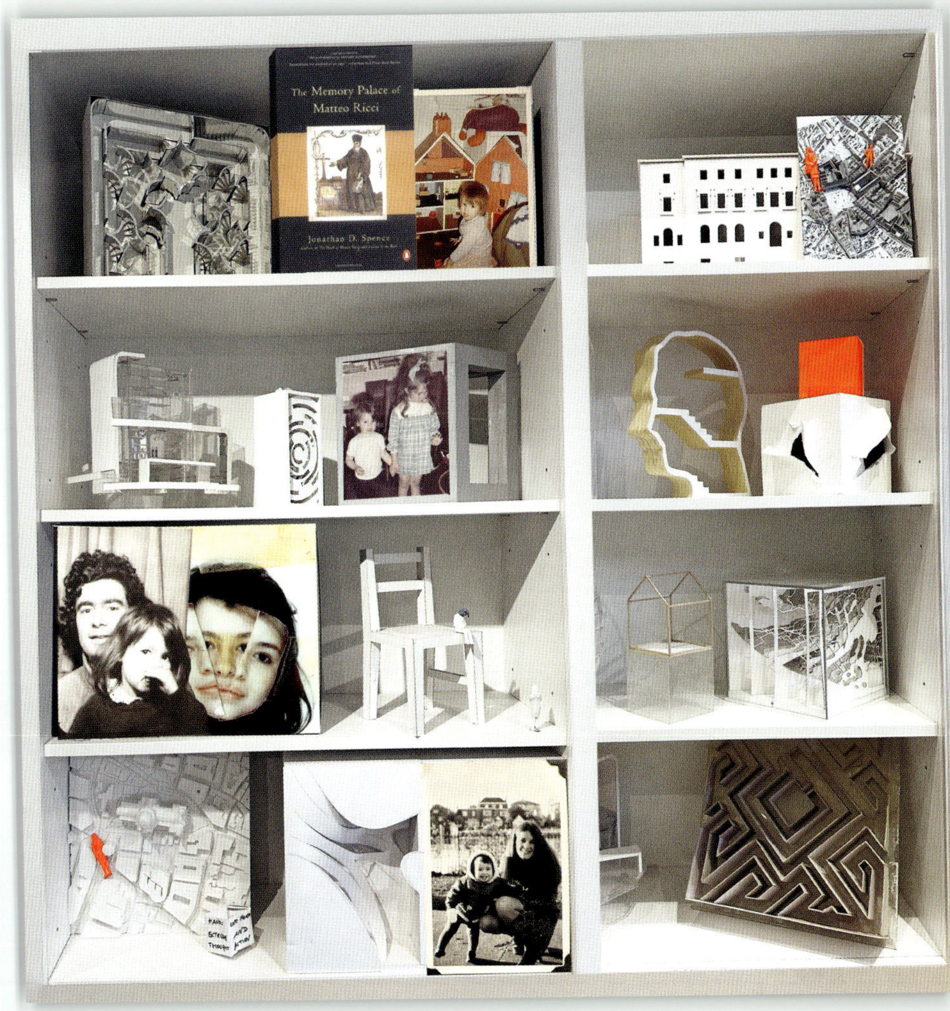
The Memory Palace of Matteo Ricci
Jonathan D. Spence

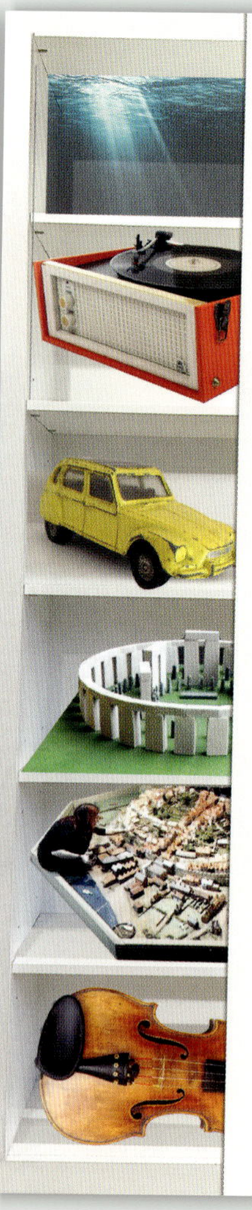

1. A LINE OF LIGHT
My earliest memory is a line of light through dark water. I was two or three years old. My dad had taken me and my baby brother to the River Thames near our house, and I fell in. I don't know how long I was under the water before he pulled me out. Perhaps it was only moments, but they are the first that I remember: voices and light penetrating a medium other than air.

2. A RED BOX
The first musical instrument I encountered was a red Bakelite record player. Stories and music emanated from the red box with a revolving black turntable: Richard Burton reading Dylan Thomas's *Under Milk Wood*, Prokofiev's *Peter and the Wolf*, The Beatles' *Red Album*, ABBA's *Arrival*.

3. A YELLOW CAR
We would lie in the back – seats removed, canvas roof rolled back – and look up at the speeding sky as our parents told us stories all the way to Wales and Wiltshire, where we visited our grandparents each summer. In my mind, it was the stories as much as the wheels which were propelling us through the countryside.

4. A STONE CIRCLE
We used to drive past Stonehenge and visit the stone circles at Avebury. On Sundays at the local Catholic church, we learned to count Hail Marys along rosary beads and followed the story of crucifixion and resurrection along carved wooden Stations of the Cross. We learned to understand objects as tellers of stories, whether they were wooden beads in our hands or stone monoliths towering above us.

5. A MINIATURE TOWN
My family moved to Rye in Sussex when I was six. There was a scale model of the town next to our house. The miniature buildings would glow and speak during a show, telling the town's stories and history. I felt at once larger than human scale – able to understand the pattern of the streets and their origins – and tiny enough to fit inside the miniature version of my glowing house as it spoke.

6. A VIOLIN
When I was seven, I started learning the violin. I drew pictures of my violin: this unnecessarily beautiful form that extended my body for hours every day, making music that had been composed long before my birth. I became an instrument, a time machine transmitting emotions from centuries ago. I learned the laborious process of practice, improving incrementally with each iteration. I played in orchestras and became part of something much greater than I could imagine alone.

7. A NUMBERED HAND
Between violin, and later clarinet and piano, there was a lot of annotation of musical staves, guiding fingers to press keys and strings, and feet to push pedals. Parts of the body became associated with numerical code. When I wasn't playing musical instruments, I was making games and gifts out of cardboard boxes. Cereal packets were printed with dotted lines and scissors: invitations to hands to intervene, to create change.

8. A CUPBOARD
There was a secret, dark, triangular space under the stairs in our house where my sister, brothers and I staged shows with a small red plastic projector and torches glowing through coloured sweet wrappers. Working crouched on the floor, we created our own worlds together, while the distant kitchen radio broadcast the BBC: the strikes, *The Archers*, the power cuts, *Desert Island Discs*, and Margaret Thatcher's 1987 message, 'There is no such thing as society, only the individual.'

9. A MAZE
At 11, I began taking music lessons on Saturday mornings at the Royal Academy of Music in London. I took the train then the tube, navigating the maze of underground tunnels using the brightly coloured linear tube map to emerge into the academy's labyrinthine stairs and corridors.

10. A MIRROR
On my way home through Charing Cross Station each Saturday, I used to visit the National Portrait Gallery, gazing at faces through centuries of paint. I started drawing people on the tube and used my mum's circular swivel magnifying mirror to document my changing face in a series of teenage self-portraits.

11. AN ALBUM COVER
At 13, I discovered Kate Bush's album *The Kick Inside* and painted a Japanese mural on my bedroom wall. I hoped that if my room looked like the Japanese-themed album cover, people who entered it might feel like I did when I listened to the music. Perhaps I was trying to play my room like an instrument.

12. A WINDOW
As teenagers, my cousin and I used to cycle to a small church in the village of Tudeley in Kent, whose stained-glass windows had been designed by the painter Marc Chagall. A local landowner had commissioned the windows to commemorate the loss of his 21-year-old daughter at sea. The story was told in coloured light – illuminated by the sun – which moved throughout the day across the church's paved stone floor.

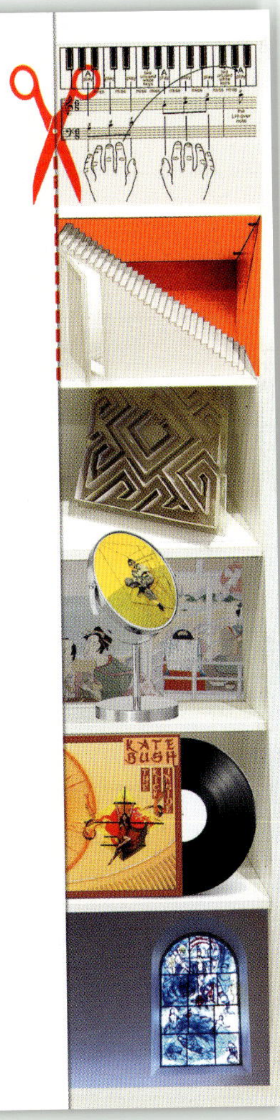

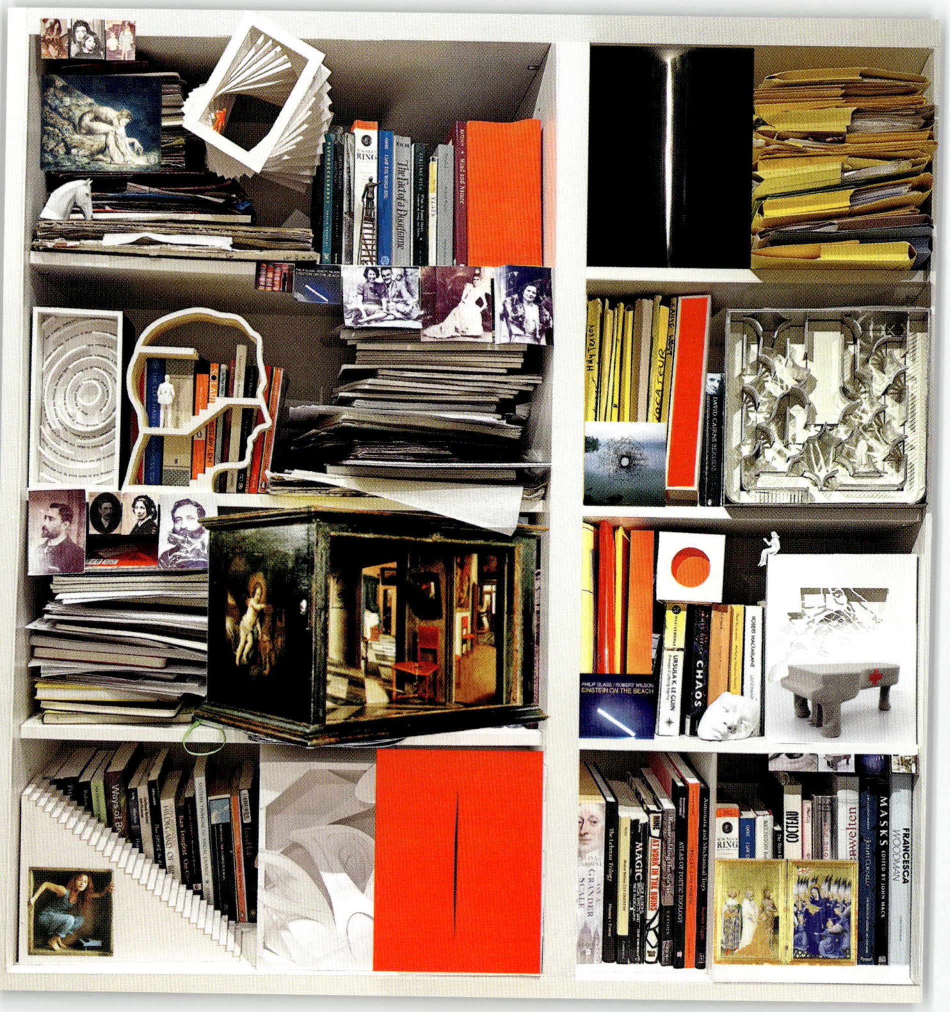
PHILIP GLASS / ROBERT WILSON
EINSTEIN ON THE BEACH
URSULA K. LE GUIN
CHAOS
ROBERT MACFARLANE
ON A GRANDER SCALE
The Lehman Trilogy
MAGIC
AT WORK IN THE RUINS
ATLAS OF POETIC ZOOLOGY
Automata and Mechanical Toys
COCTEAU
MASKS EDITED BY JOHN MACK
FRANCESCA WOODMAN

A STUDENT SKETCHBOOK

1985–1995

Our secondary school art teacher introduced us to the land art of Andy Goldsworthy and Richard Long, and took us into the local Kent forests to make sculptures with another land artist, Chris Drury. The class slept in a shelter we had made from fallen branches. We showed photographs of our work in the basement of the Tate Gallery and began making weekend pilgrimages to visit the Tate, Hayward and National galleries. In the hushed darkened print room at the Tate, I would study the visionary engravings of William Blake. I'd make my way slowly through the Turner galleries and the Pre-Raphaelites towards the slashed canvas portals of Lucio Fontana, Joseph Cornell's boxed infinities, Bruce Nauman's irreverent neon vocabularies, and the silenced grey-wool-clad piano of Joseph Beuys. At the National Gallery I was drawn to the illusory world within Samuel van Hoogstraten's seventeenth-century perspective box, and the framed luminosity of the fourteenth-century portable altarpiece, the *Wilton Diptych*.

My mother booked us the £5 seats, 'the gods', for the whole season at the English National Opera. I later learned that the creative teams behind these productions were influenced by works in German and Eastern European opera houses created by avant-garde auteur directors Ruth Berghaus, Erich Wonder and Achim Freyer. It was via these works that I accessed European theatre aesthetics, while deep sea divers drilled the heavily contested Channel Tunnel and fearful voices on the radio threatened rabies until the tunnel finally opened in 1994. I first left the UK when I was 12, on an East Sussex youth orchestra trip to Holland, by ferry and coach.

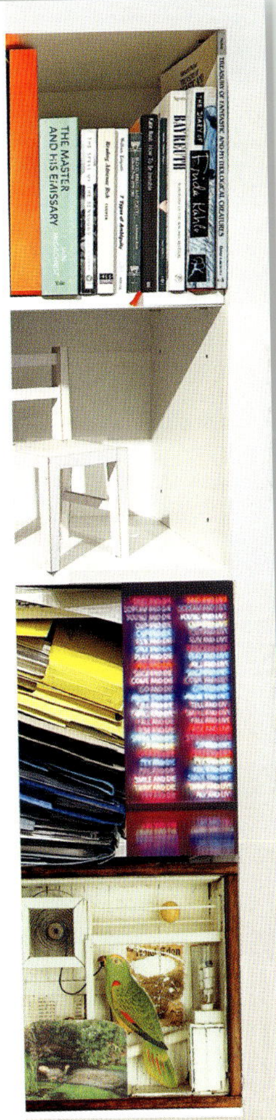

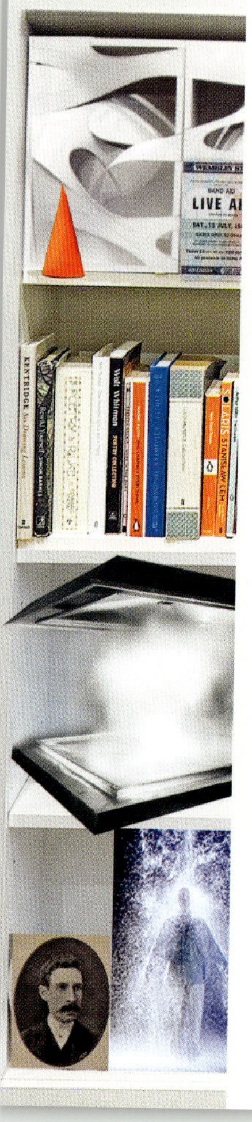

I played violin in local baroque chamber groups, while also spending my late teens and early twenties in recording studios listening to my sound-engineer boyfriend, Clive Martin, craft the layers of a track together. I watched his hands poised to edit the tape at a precise moment. I saw Bob Geldof and Bono ignite music with purpose through Live Aid in July 1985. The first concert I attended was The Boomtown Rats at Tunbridge Wells Assembly Hall later that year.

In 1989, I began a three-year treasure hunt through English literature at Bristol University – from Anglo-Saxon *Beowulf* through Chaucer and Shakespeare, focusing my final dissertation on cartography in the poetry of Adrienne Rich.

I moved to London in 1992 and found a job making stained-glass windows out of broken antique fragments at a shop on Portobello Road, while taking the Central Saint Martins Foundation Course in Art and Design. It was an intense period of drawing, painting, photography, printmaking, and looking at art: Bill Viola's *Nantes Triptych* and Cornelia Parker's *Cold Dark Matter* at the Tate; Rose Finn-Kelcey's untitled installation, a body of steam between two planes at the Chisenhale Gallery. Richard Wilson's *20:50* was at the Saatchi, along with the work of the Young British Artists. Rachel Whiteread's *House* was created and destroyed in situ in East London in 1993. These works still resonate through my practice today.

I assisted on the production of a Damien Hirst opera project at the Edinburgh Festival in summer 1994 and was set to carry on at Central Saint Martins that September, making layered prints and books. I'd picked out my spot in the beautiful empty white student studio spaces on the Southampton Row campus. But on the advice of various tutors, I visited a small red studio in the scene dock of the Theatre Royal Drury Lane, where ten quite feral-looking Motley Theatre Design Course students appeared to be living full-time.

They were making scale models, listening to opera, annotating texts, and eating Pot Noodles under the direction of the legendary 90-year-old theatre designer Percy Harris, the renowned theatre, opera and film designer Alison Chitty, and the ethereal artist and theatre designer Kandis Cook. The studio felt like a convergence of art, film and music as well as theatre. I walked in and didn't want to leave.

I had a sense that the empty white studio would still be there when I was ready for it, but for now, amid this noisy, red rag-and-bone shop, I had found my tribe.

These three powerful mentors taught me the importance of protecting the clarity of an idea while trusting the emergence of work through collective, collaborative process. They were also profoundly intolerant of anything that didn't contribute to the meaning and purpose of a primary text.

***

In the following pages, I have gathered sketches and paintings that I made between the ages of 14 and 21. They had been taped up in boxes in a storage unit in rural Sevenoaks until I began work on this book. As I revisited these student experiments for the first time in over thirty years, I was struck by how many of my current lines of enquiry were begun in these early studies. I include them here as a reminder that, however unrefined, the earliest marks that we make may prove to be helpful clues later, should we attempt to string our songs into an album.

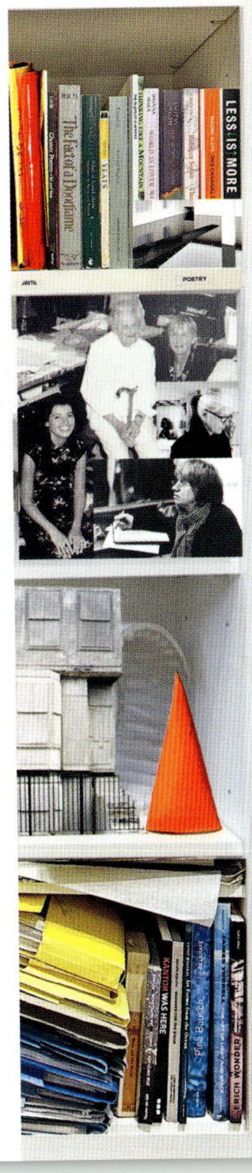

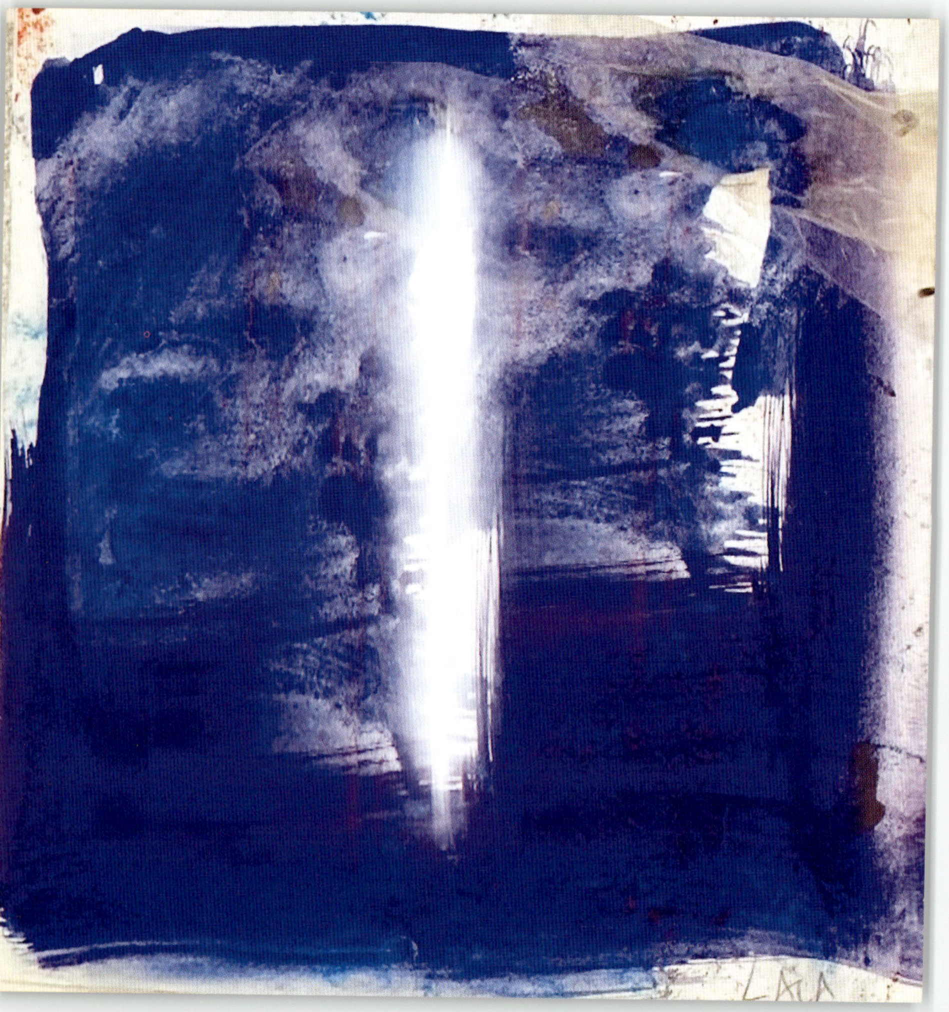

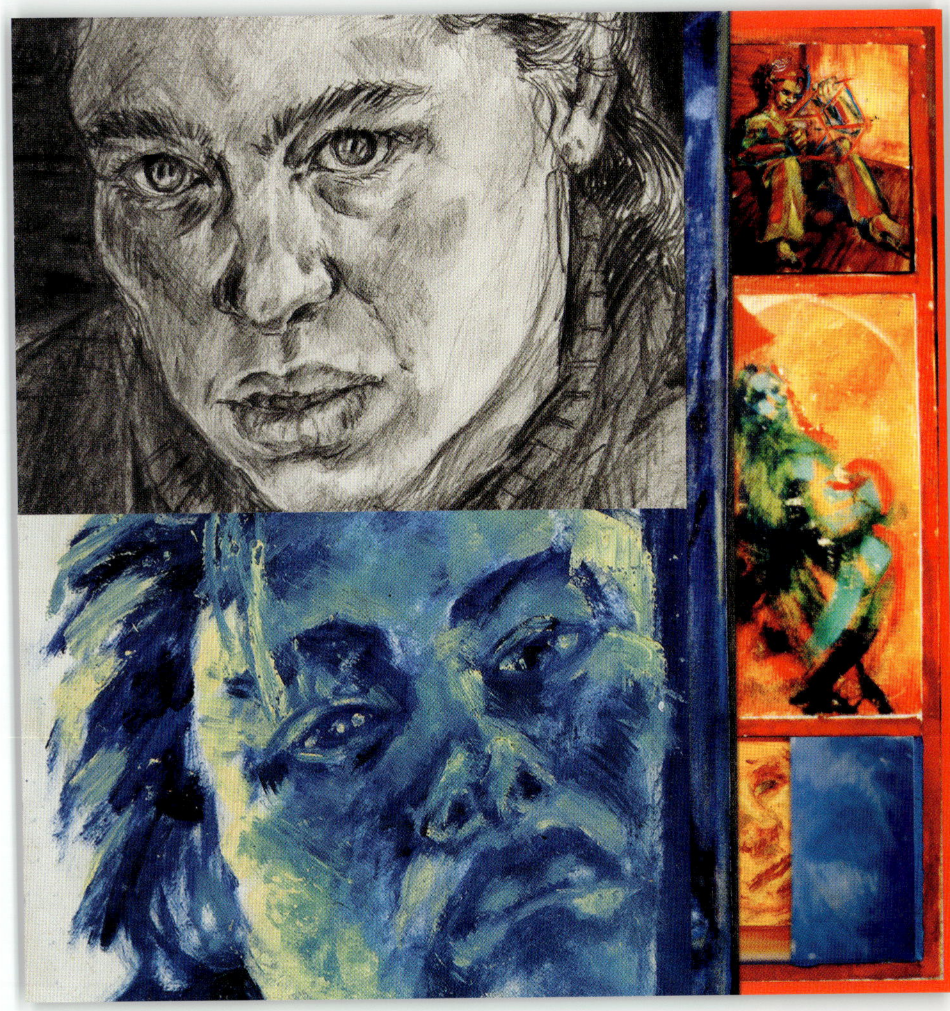

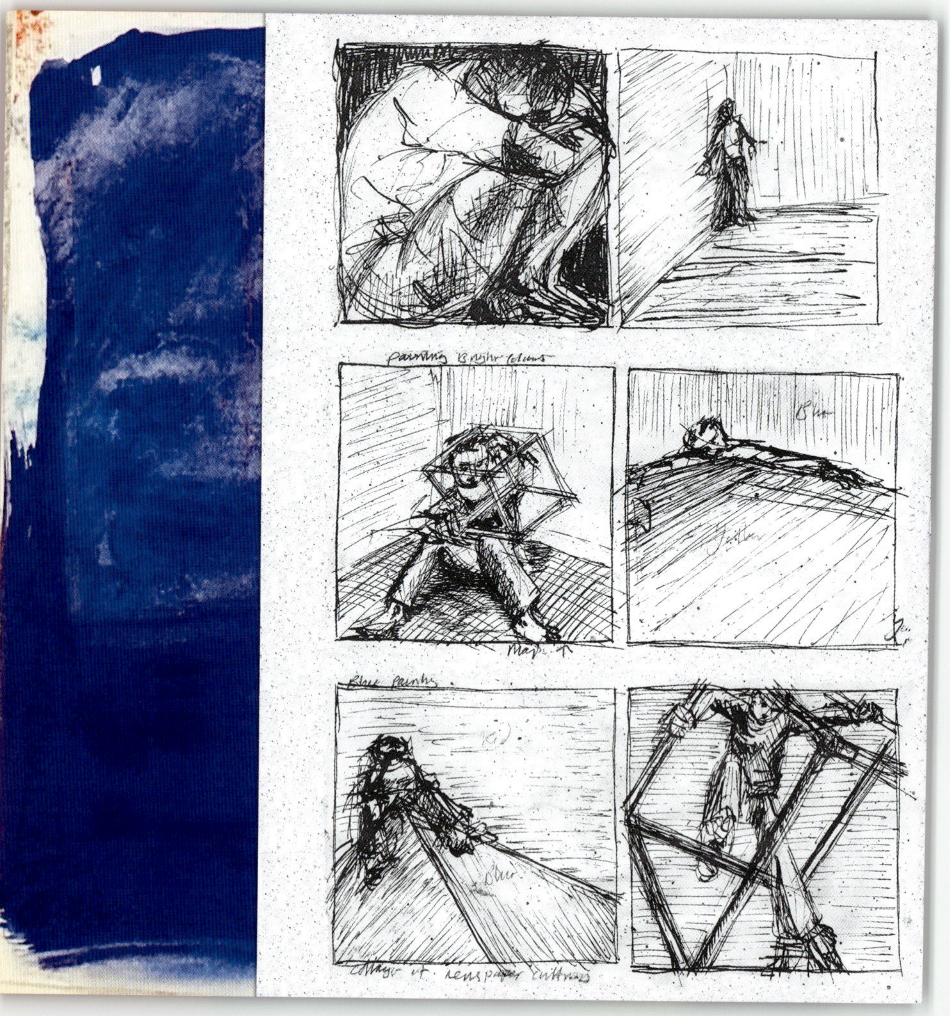

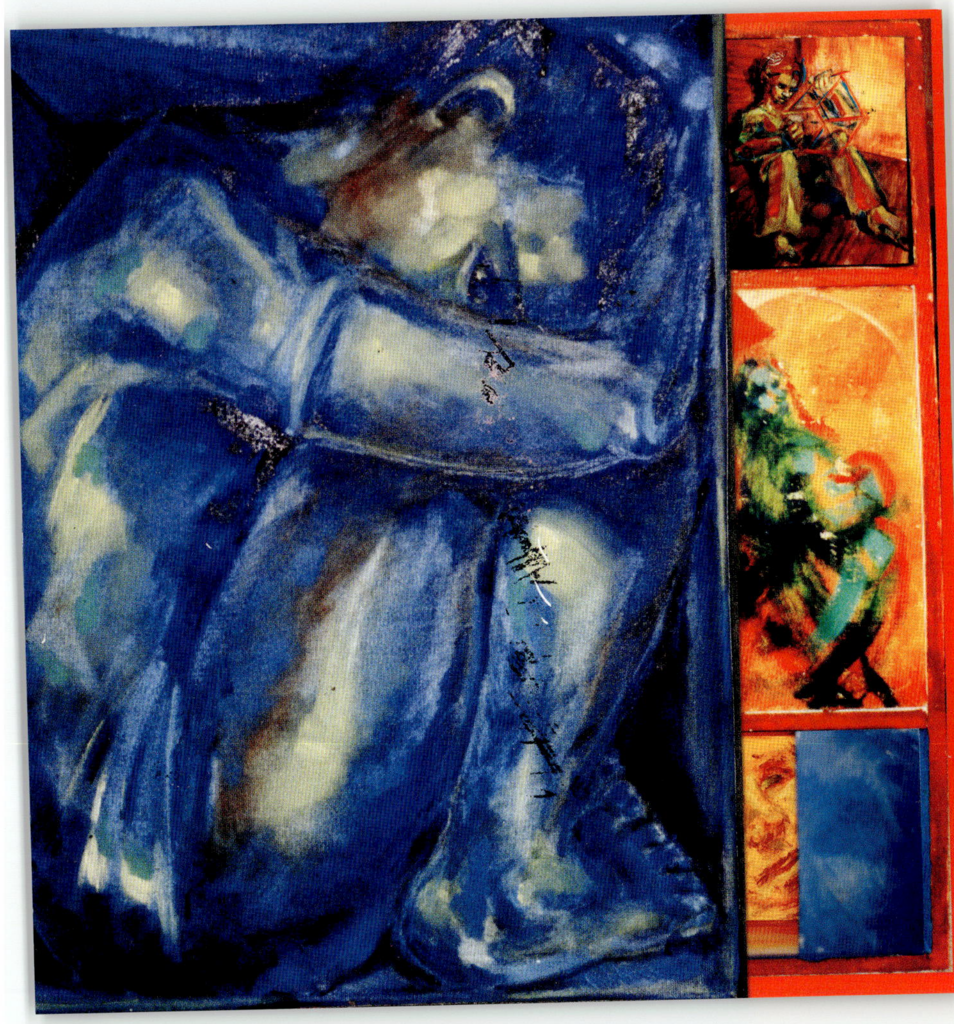

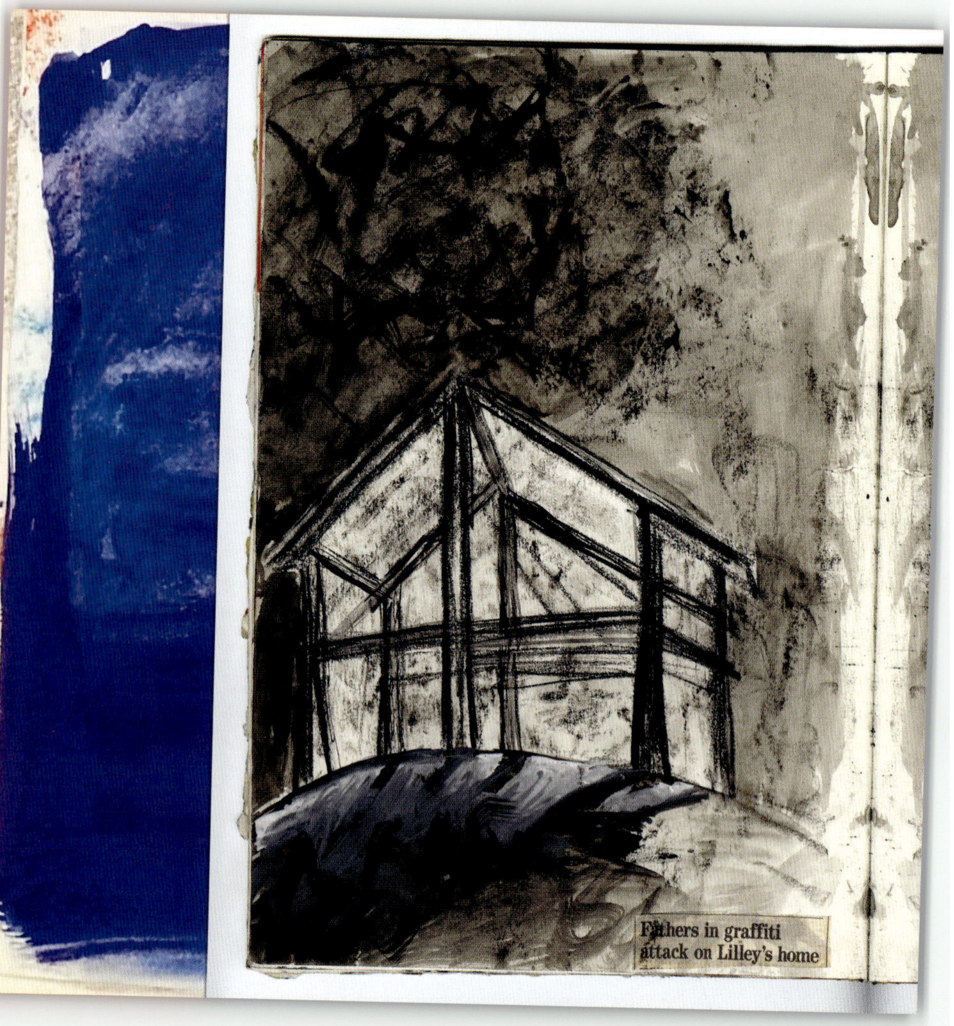
Fathers in graffiti
attack on Lilley's home

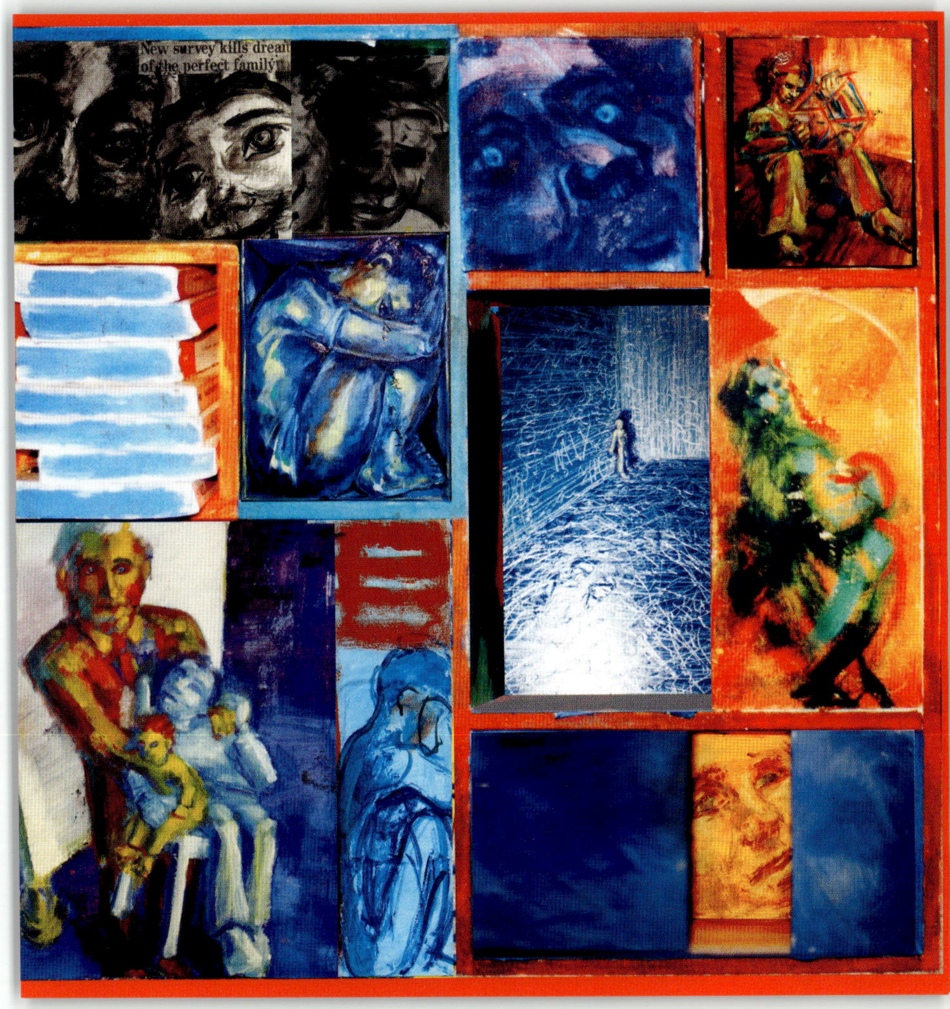
New survey kills dream
of the perfect family

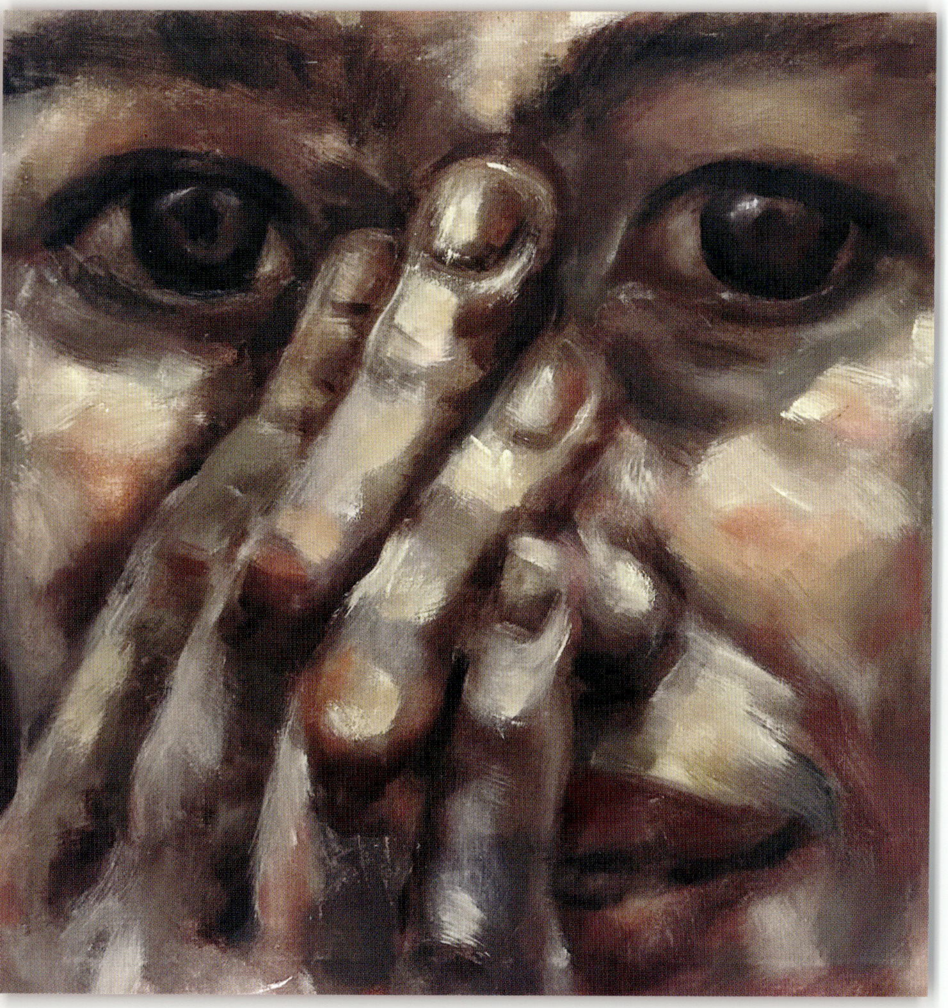

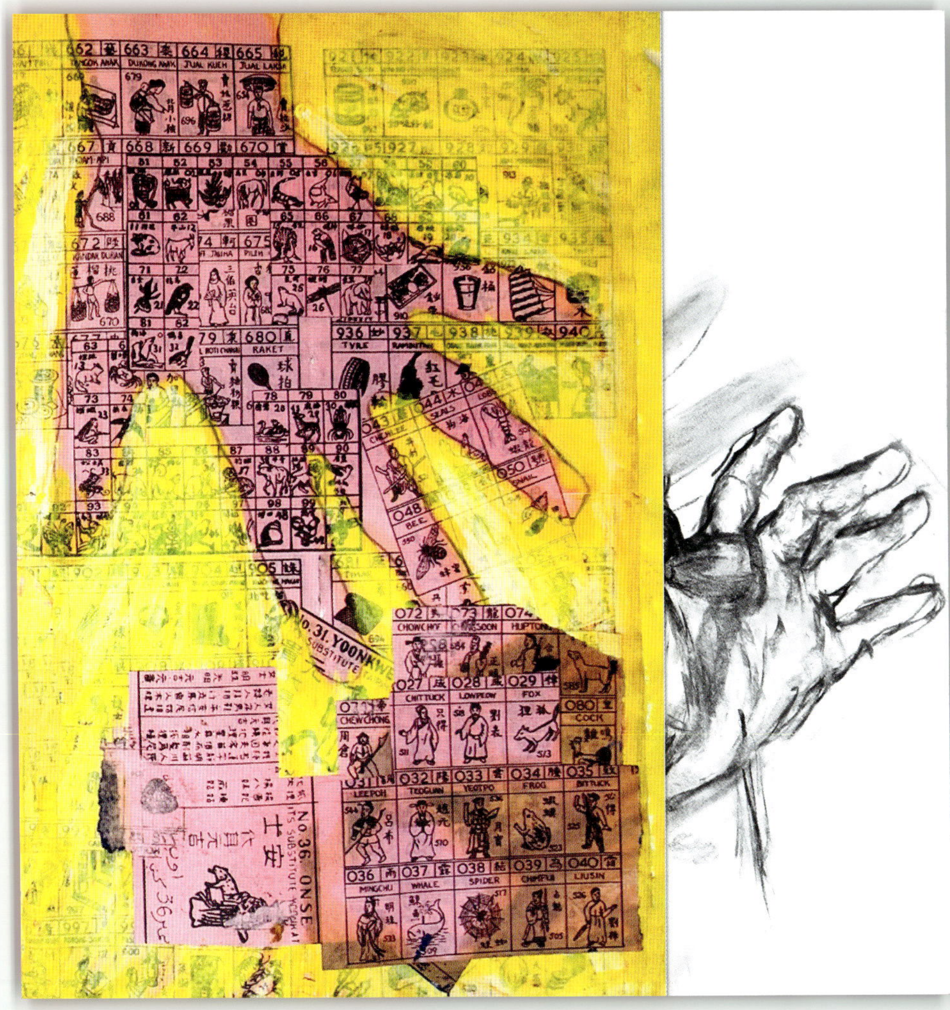

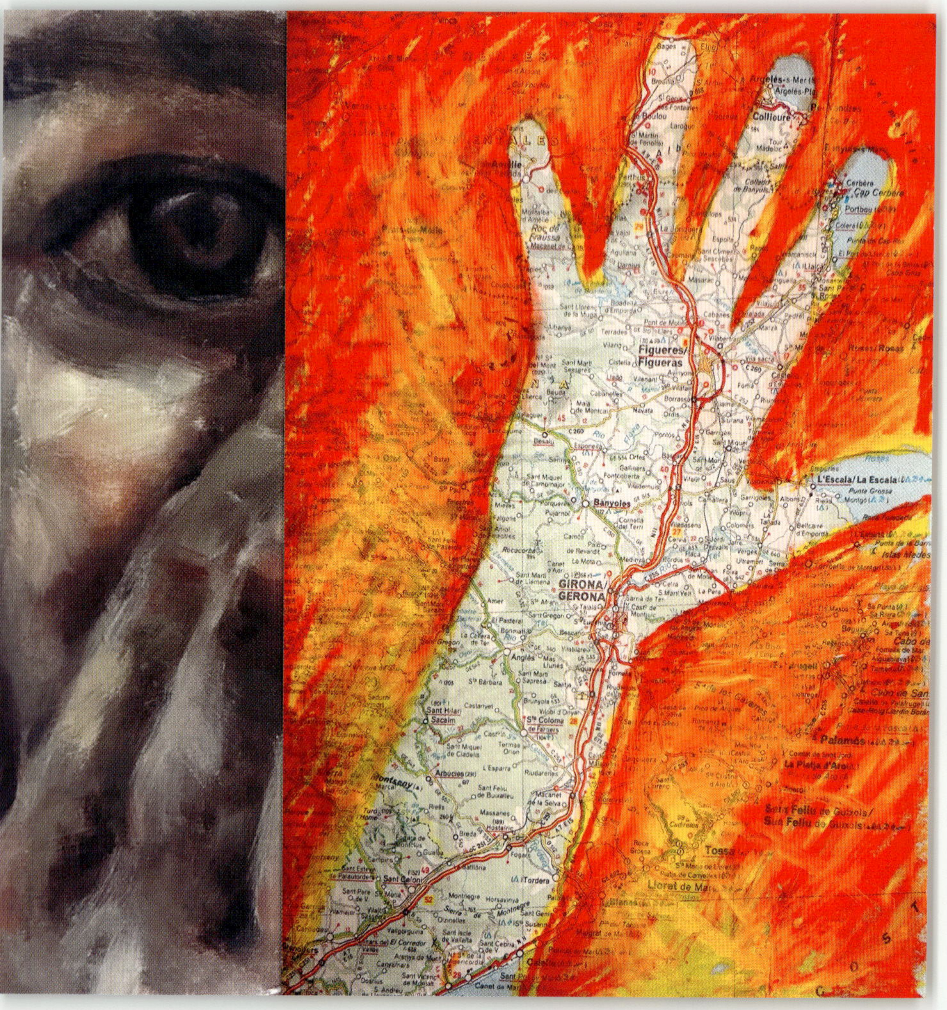
Collioure
Figueres
Figueras
L'Escala/La Escala
Banyoles
GIRONA
GERONA
Palamós

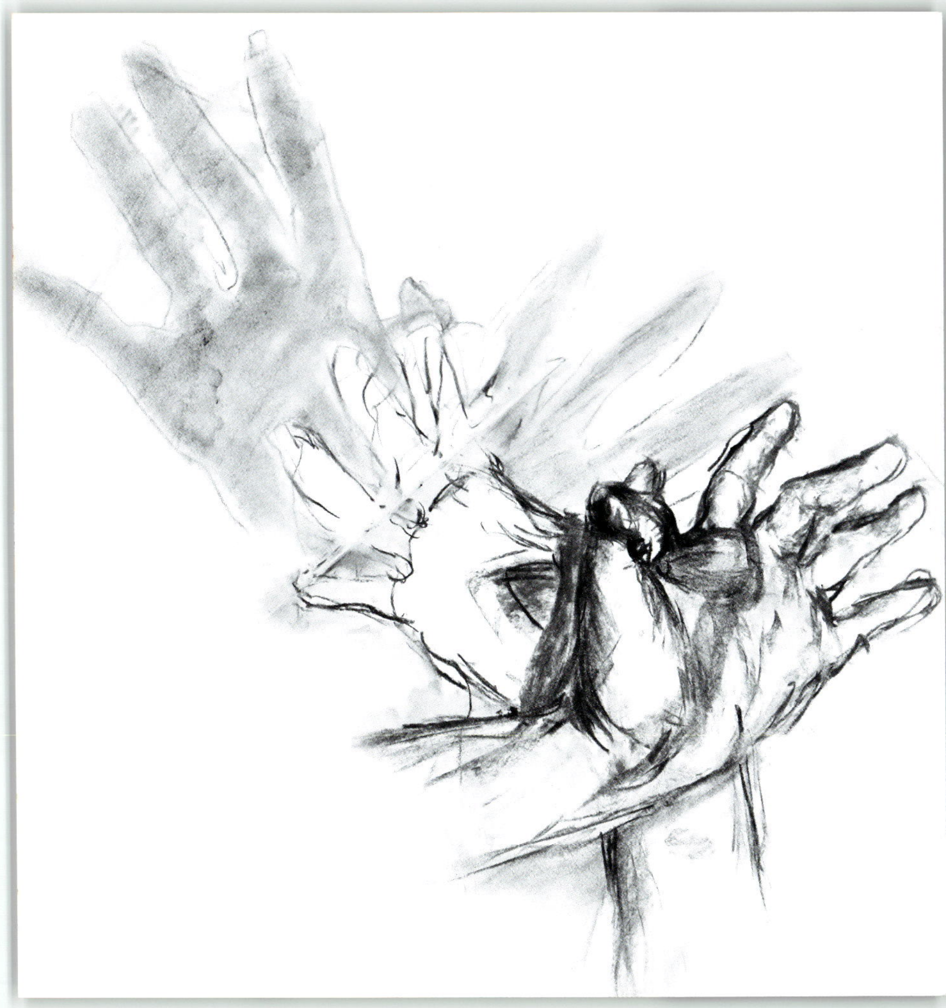

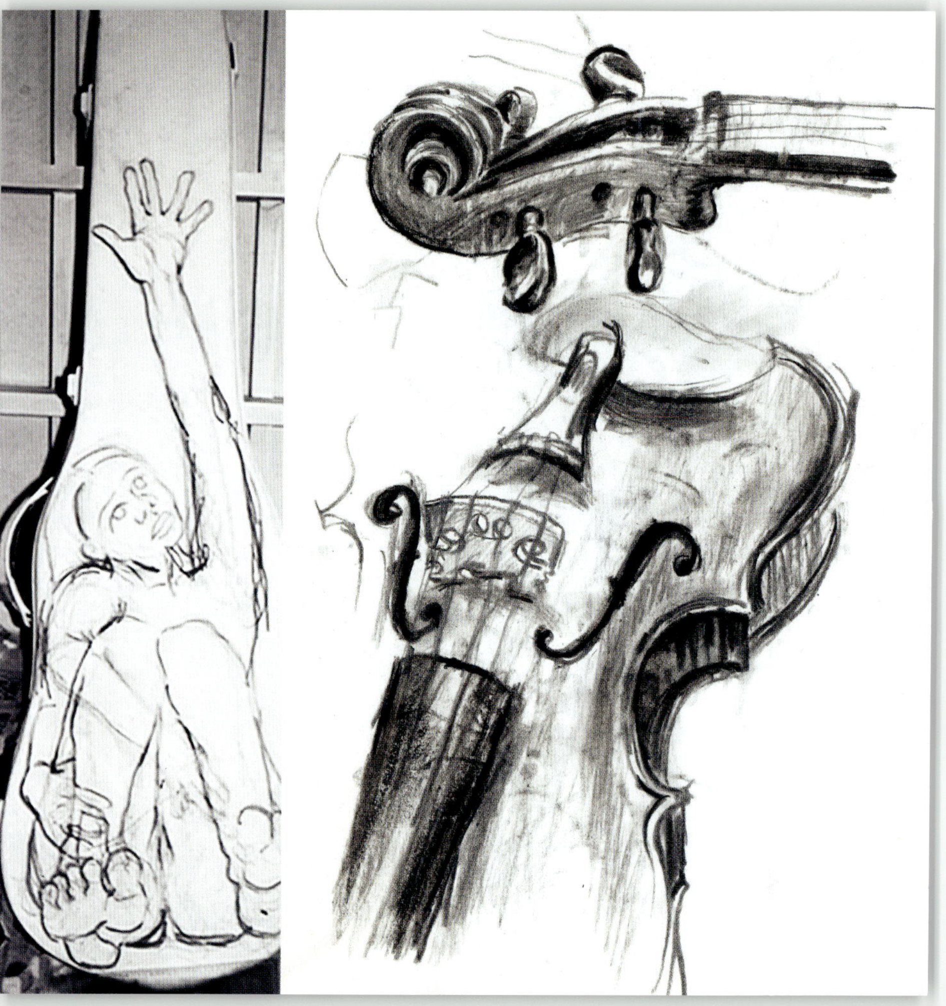

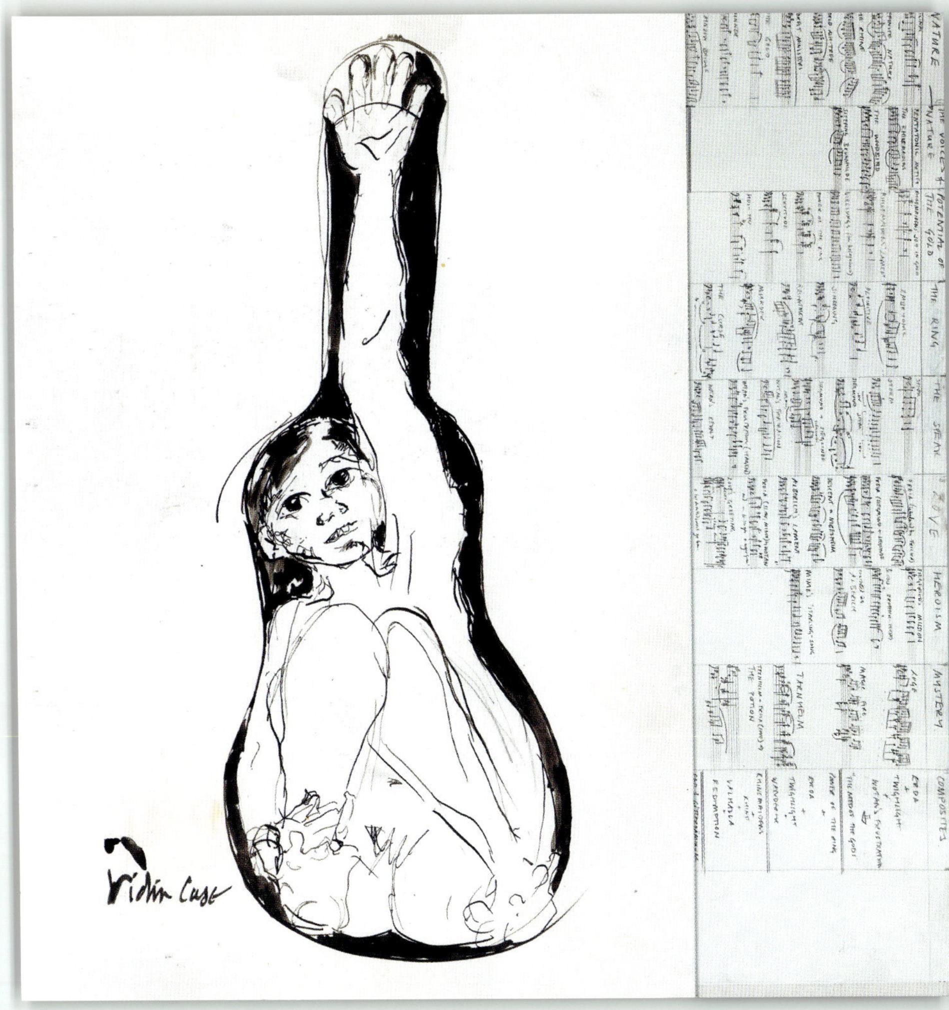
Violin Case

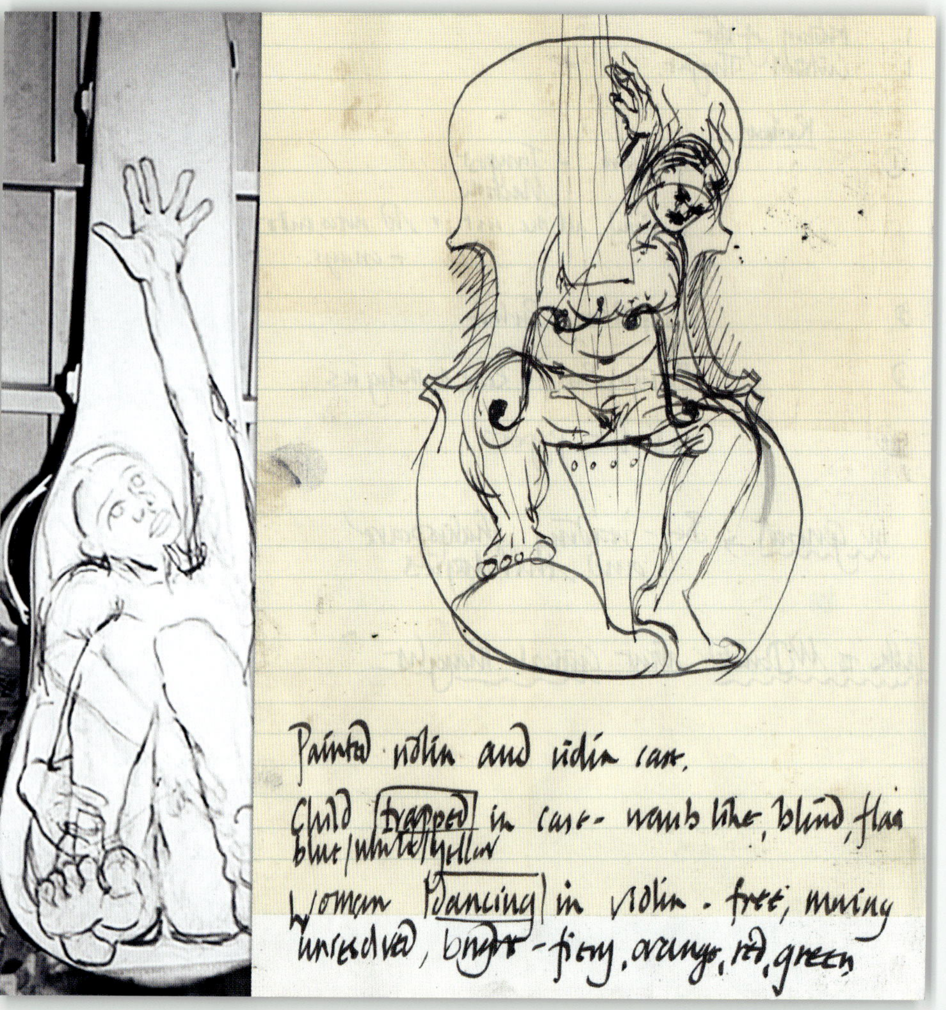
Painted violin and violin case.
Child trapped in case - womb like, blind, flat
blue/white/yellow
Woman dancing in violin - free, moving
unresolved, bright - fiery, orange, red, green

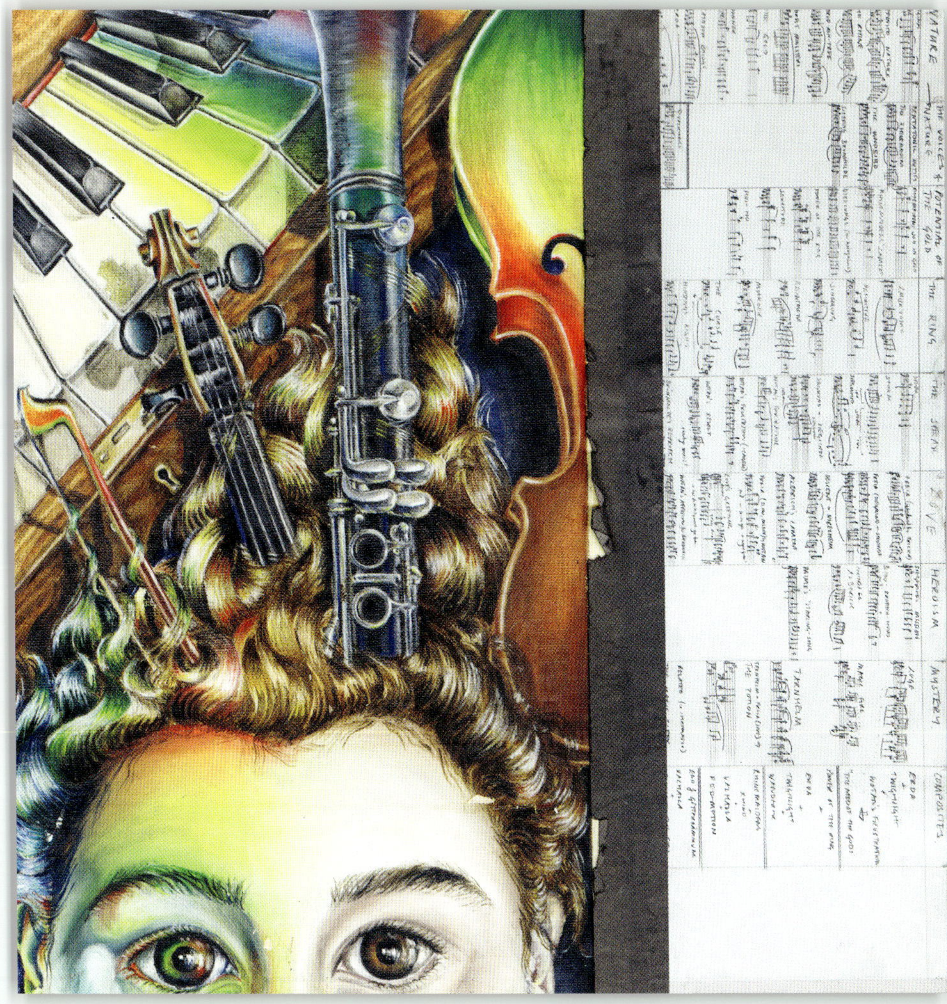
NATURE
THE RING
THE SPEAR
LOVE
HEROISM
MYSTERY
COMPOSITES

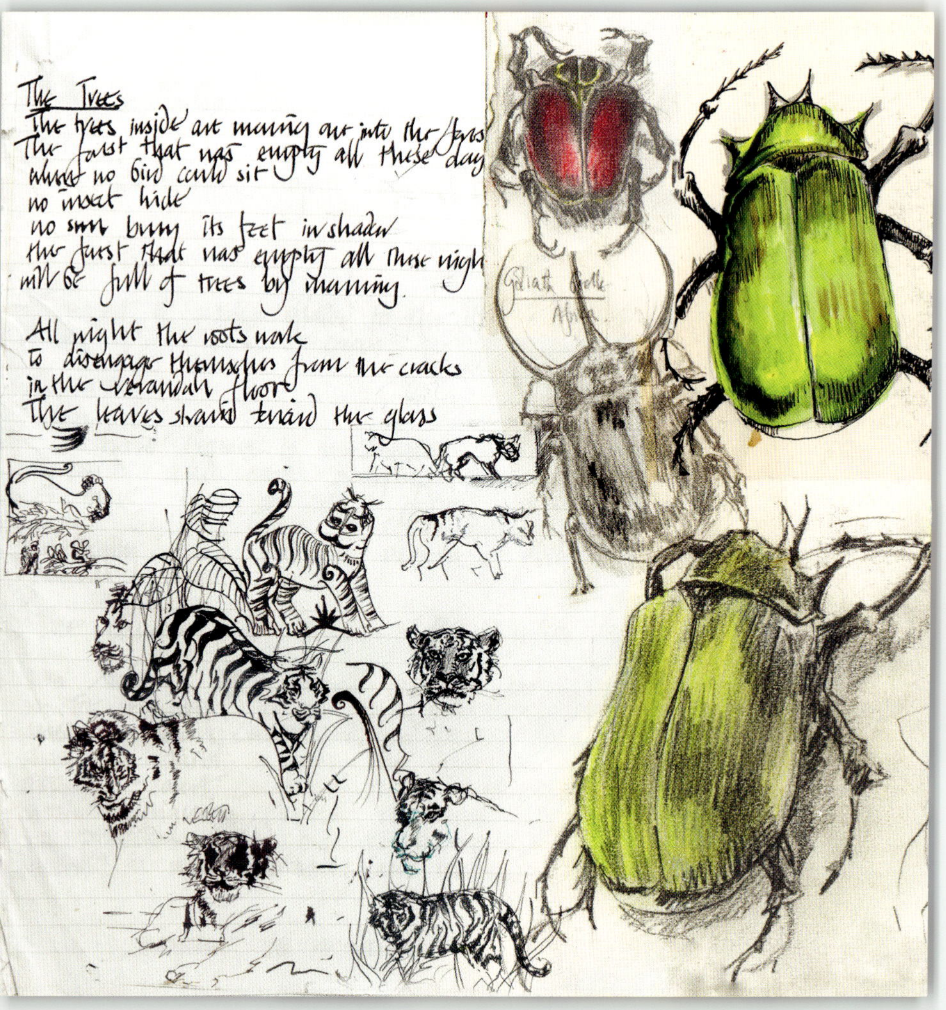
The Trees
The trees inside are moving out into the forest
the forest that was empty all these days
where no bird could sit
no insect hide
no sun bury its feet in shadow
the forest that was empty all these nights
will be full of trees by morning.
All night the roots work
to disengage themselves from the cracks
in the veranda floor
The leaves strain toward the glass
Goliath Beetle
Africa

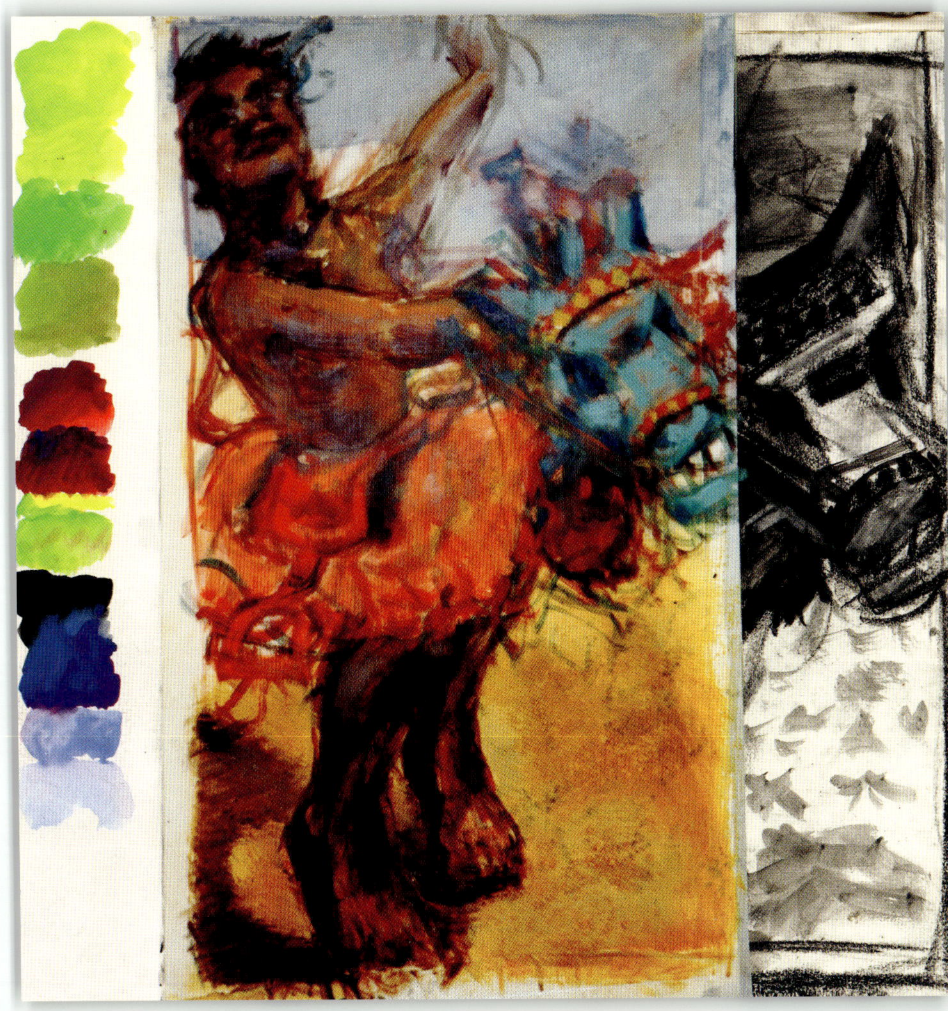

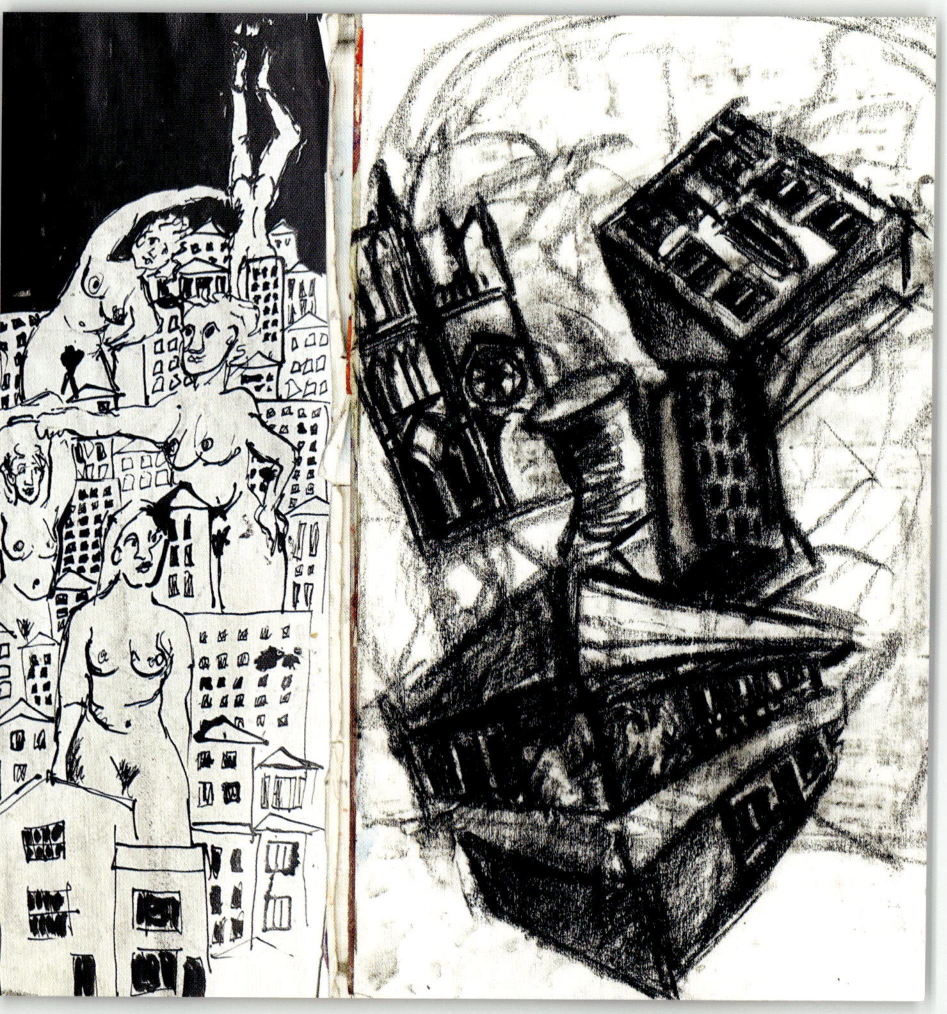

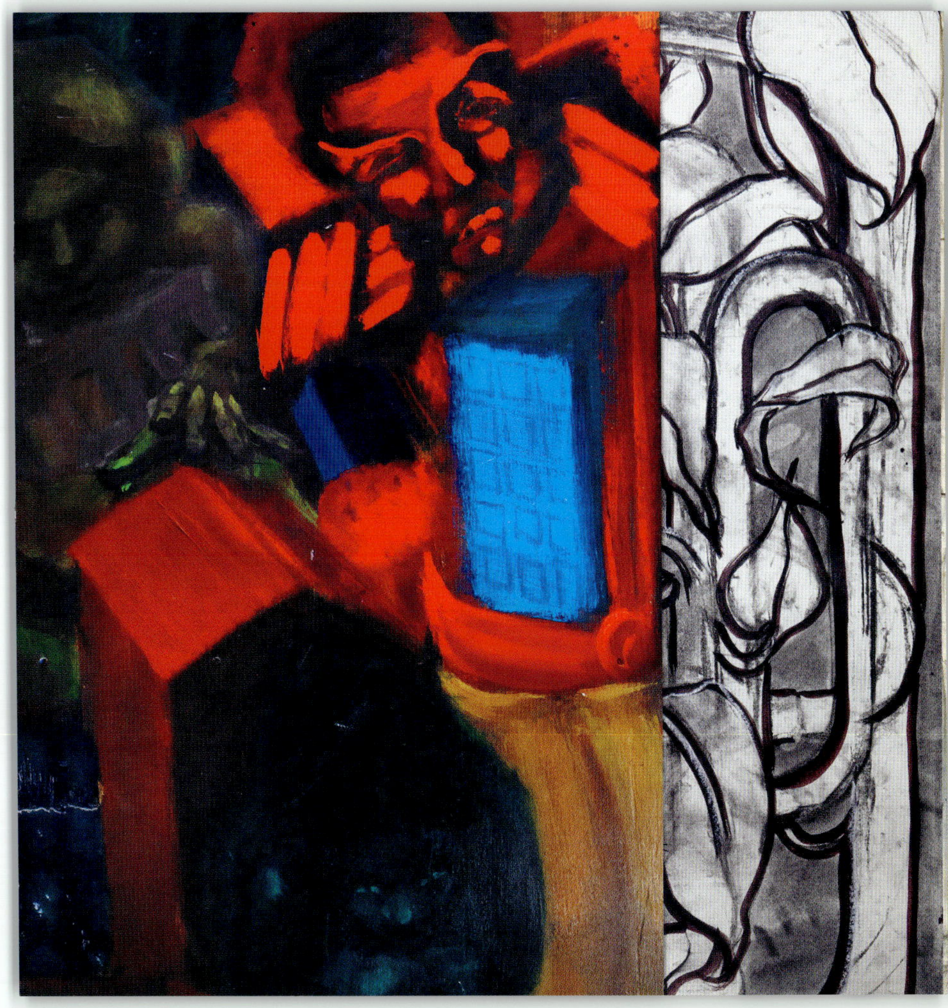

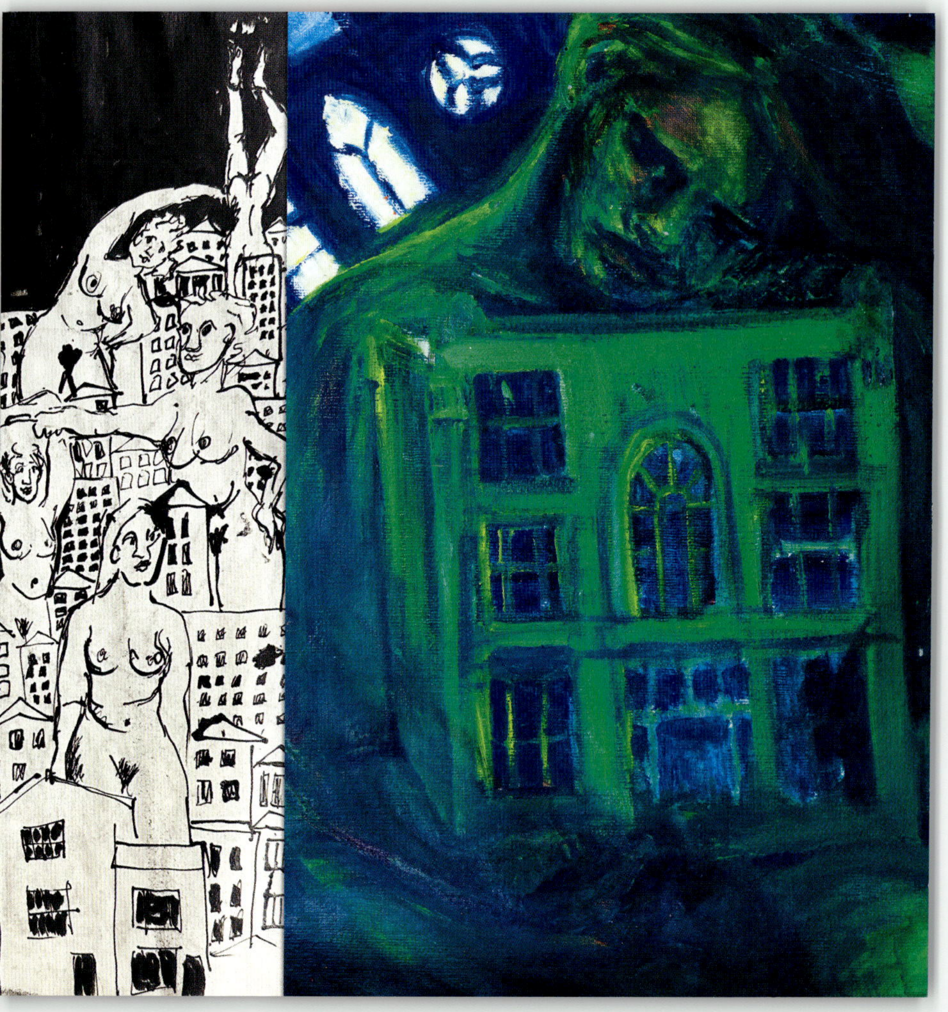

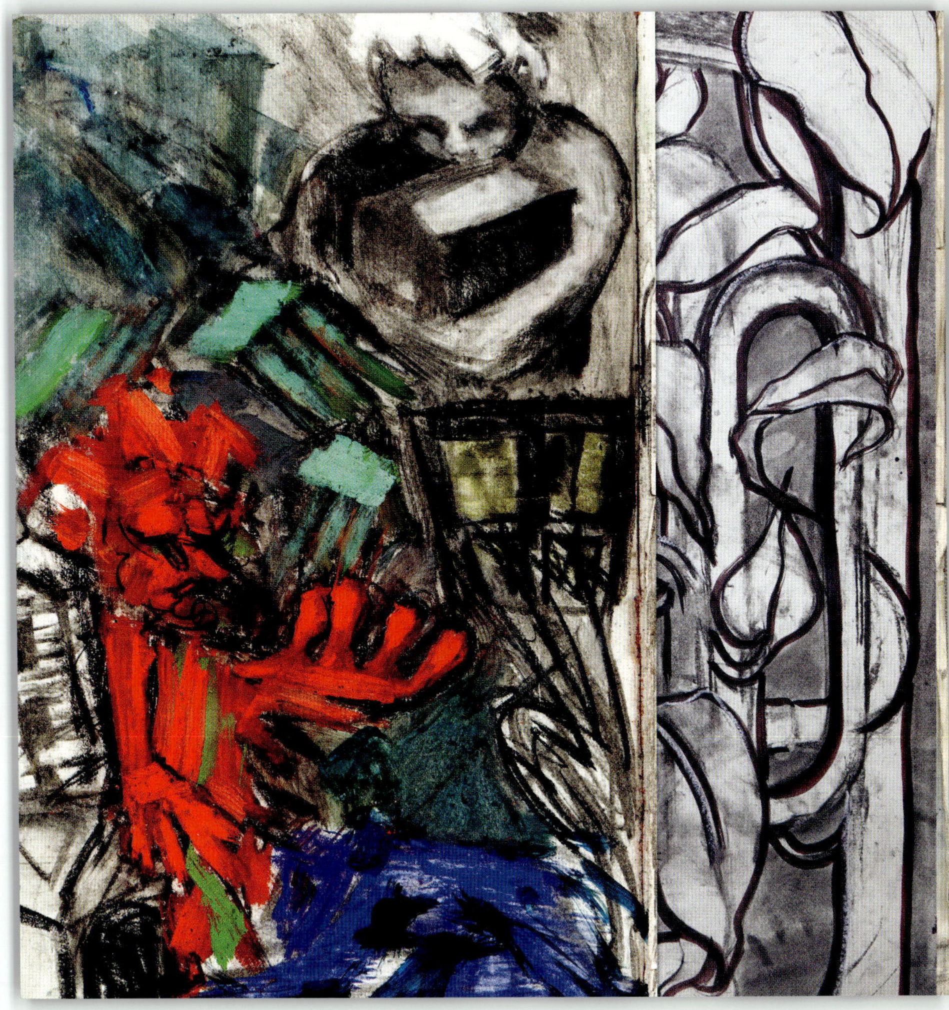

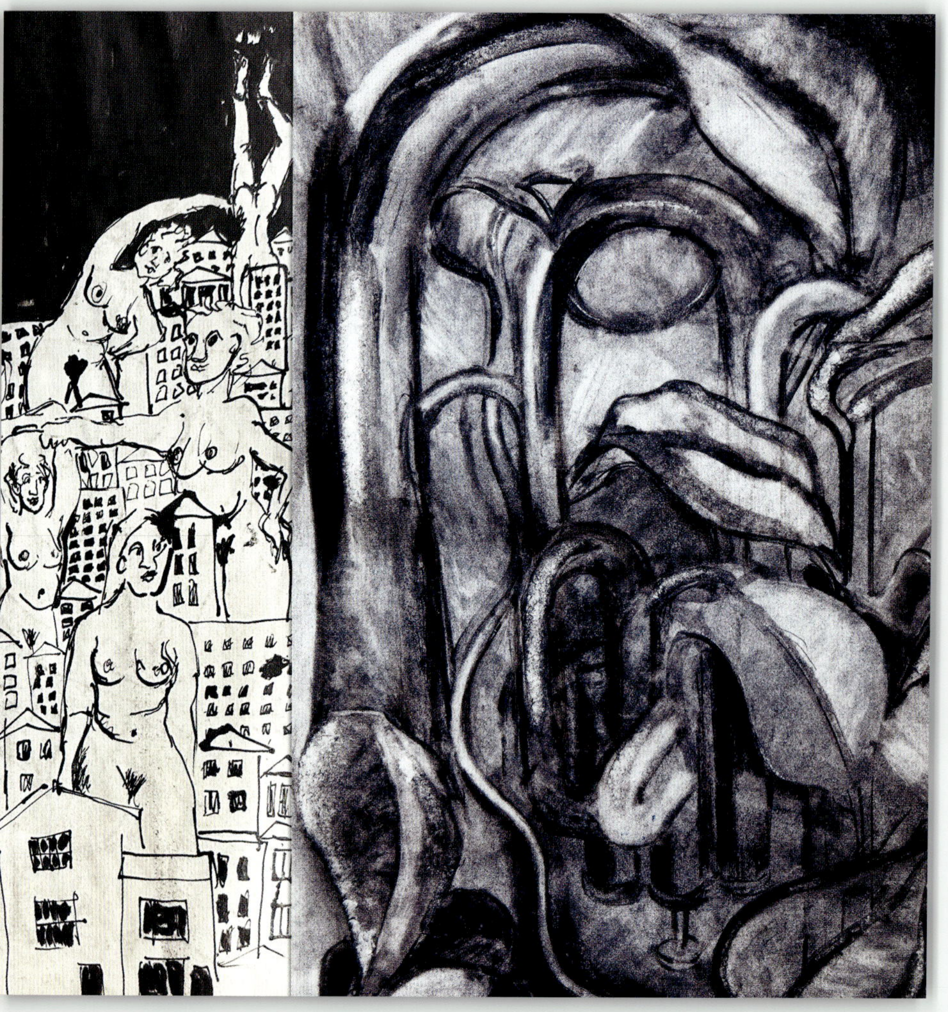

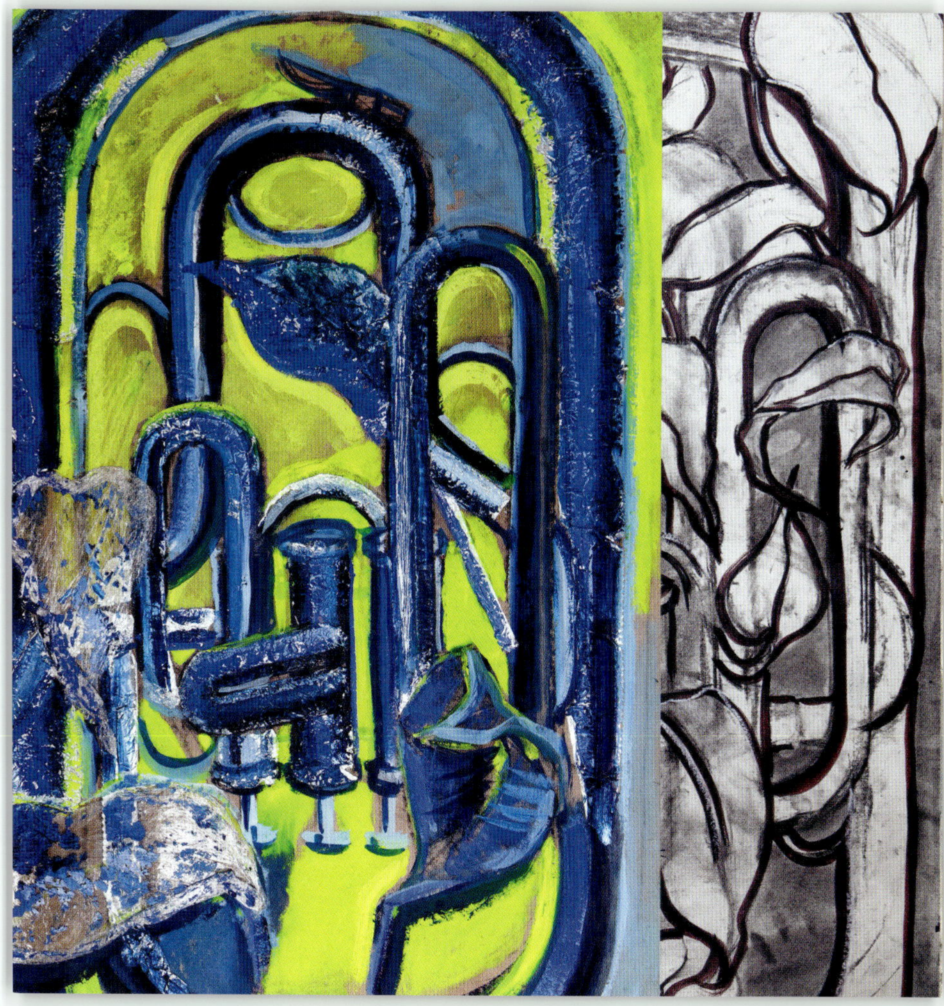

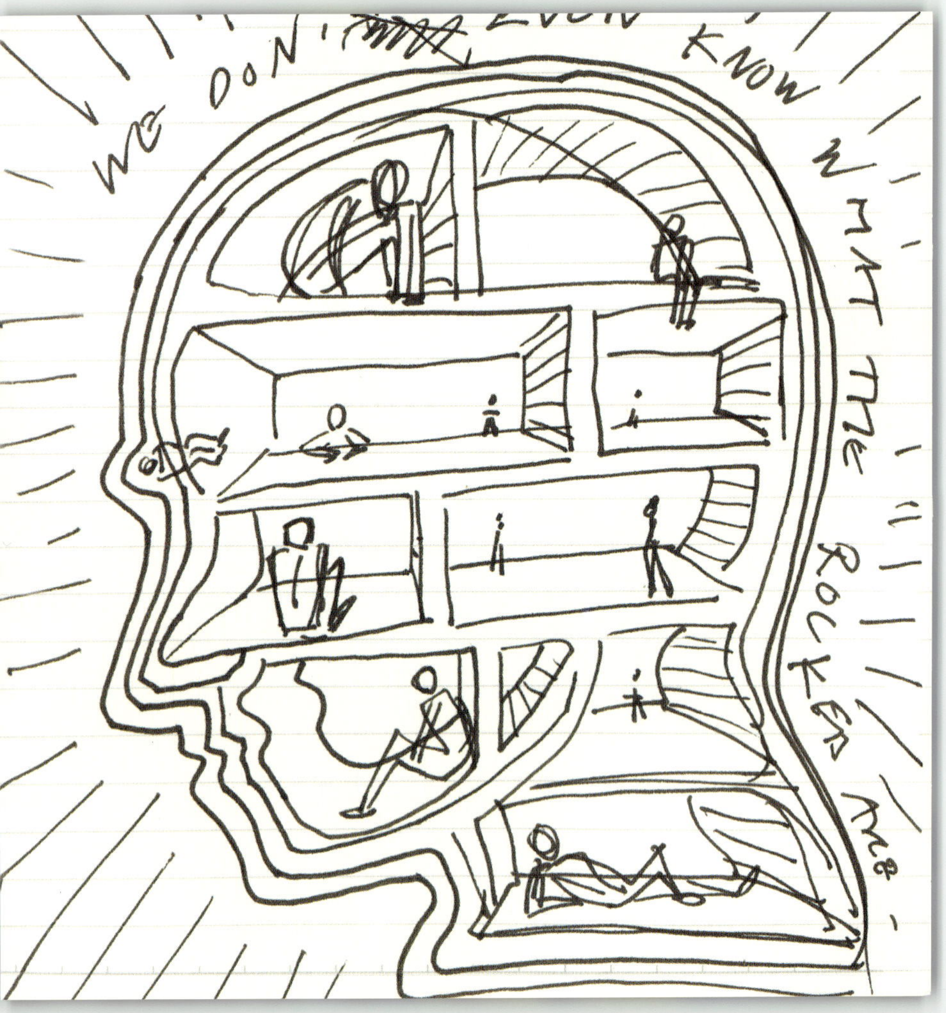
WE DON'T EVEN KNOW WHAT THE ROCKERS ARE -

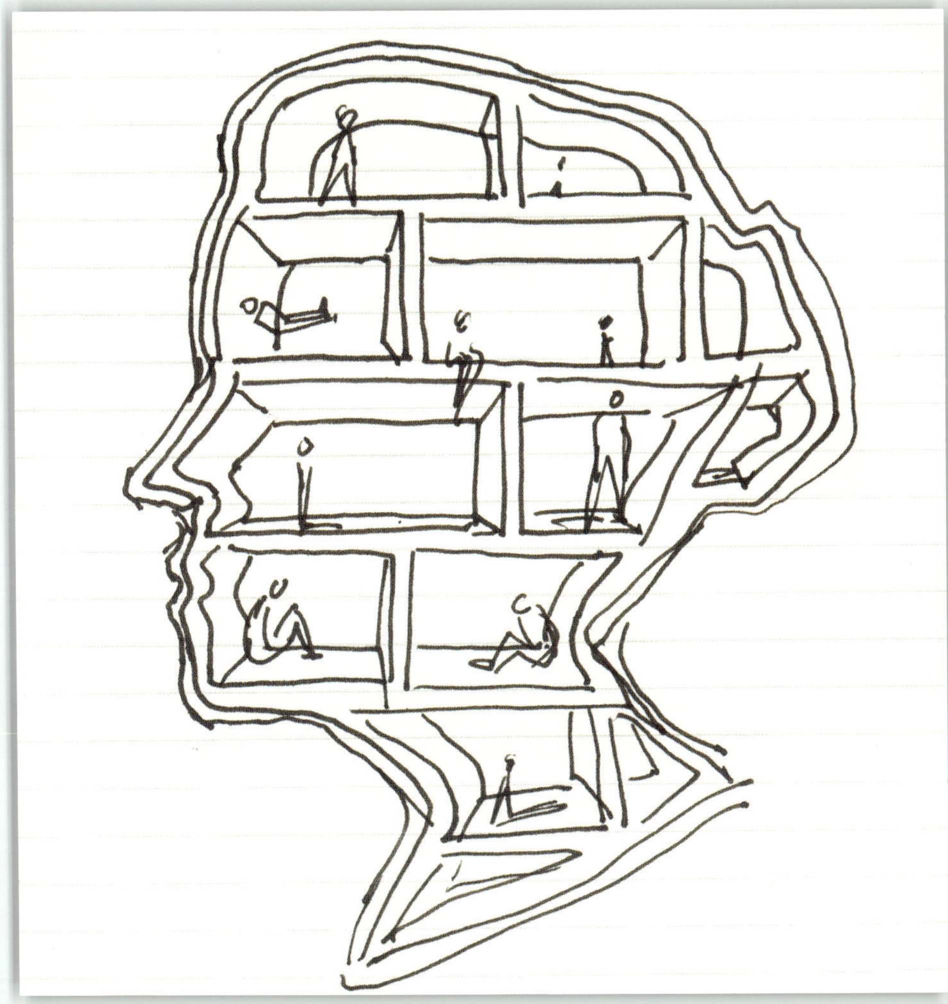

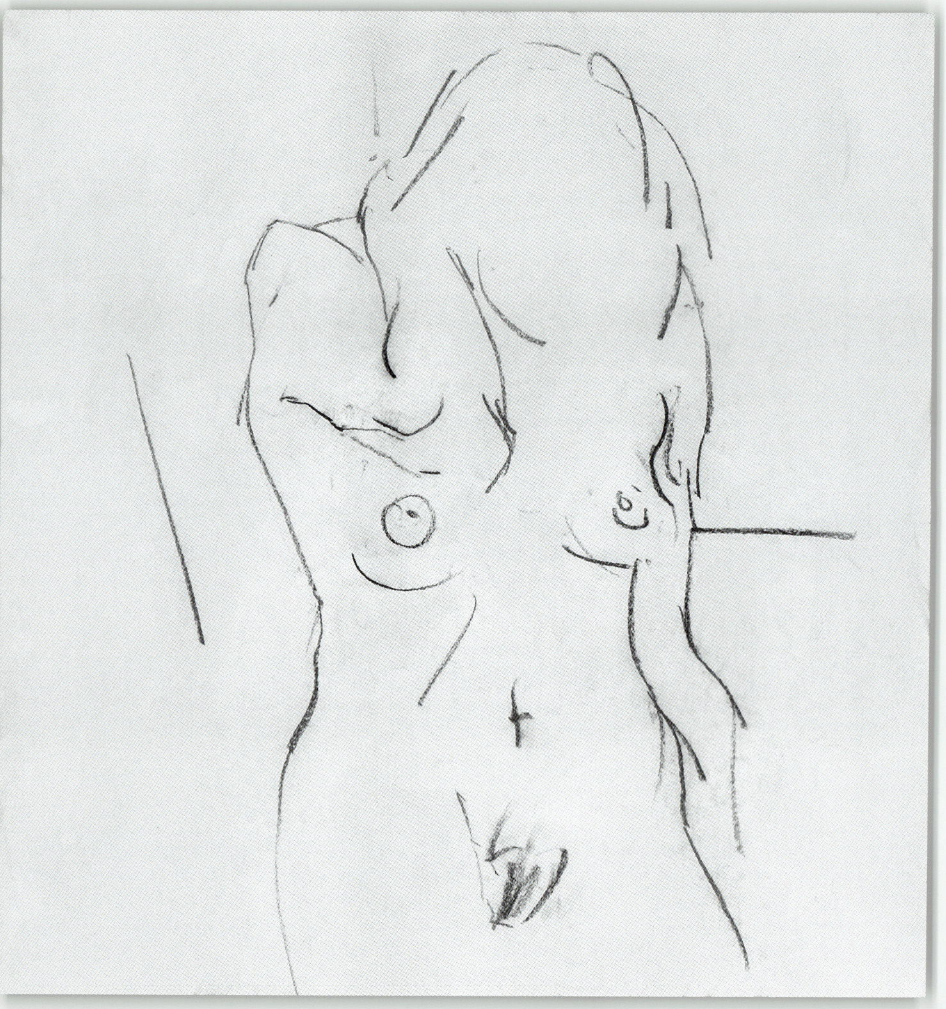

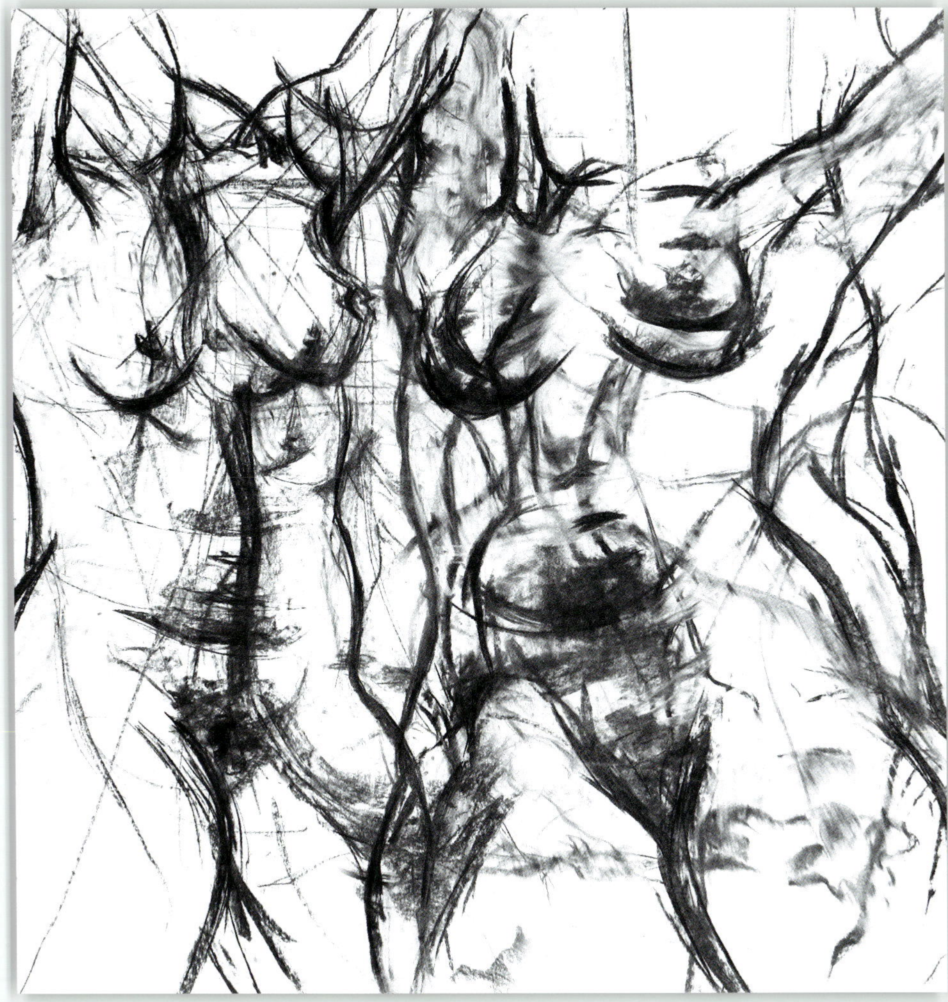

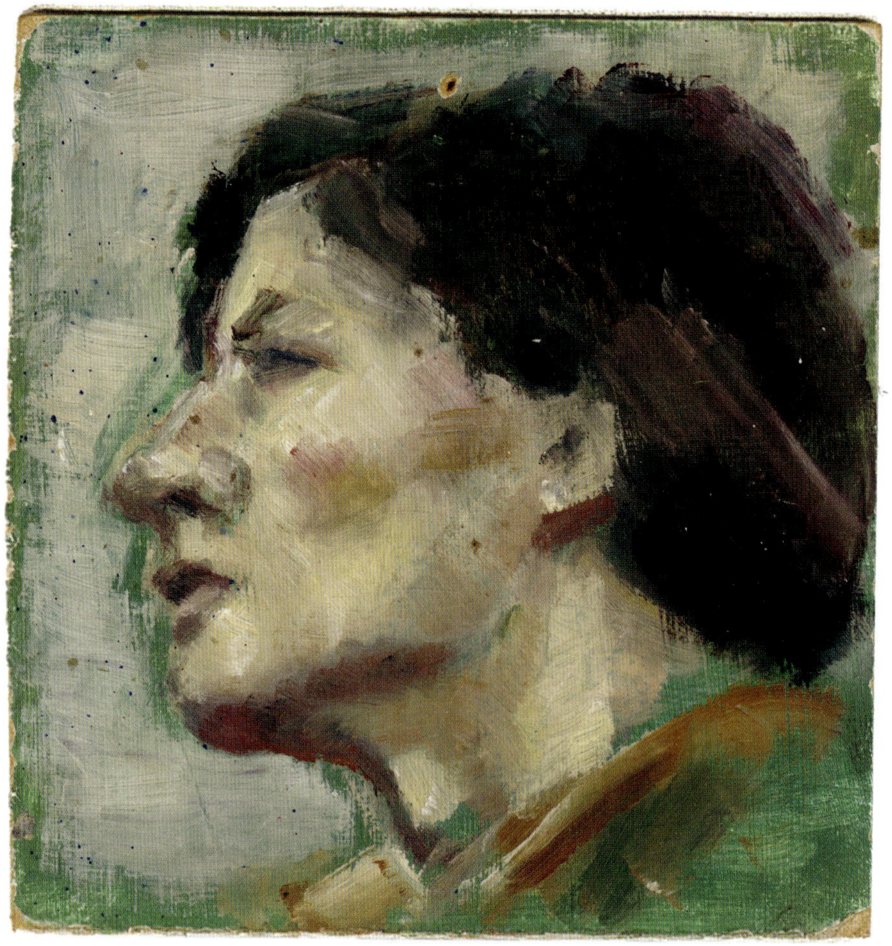

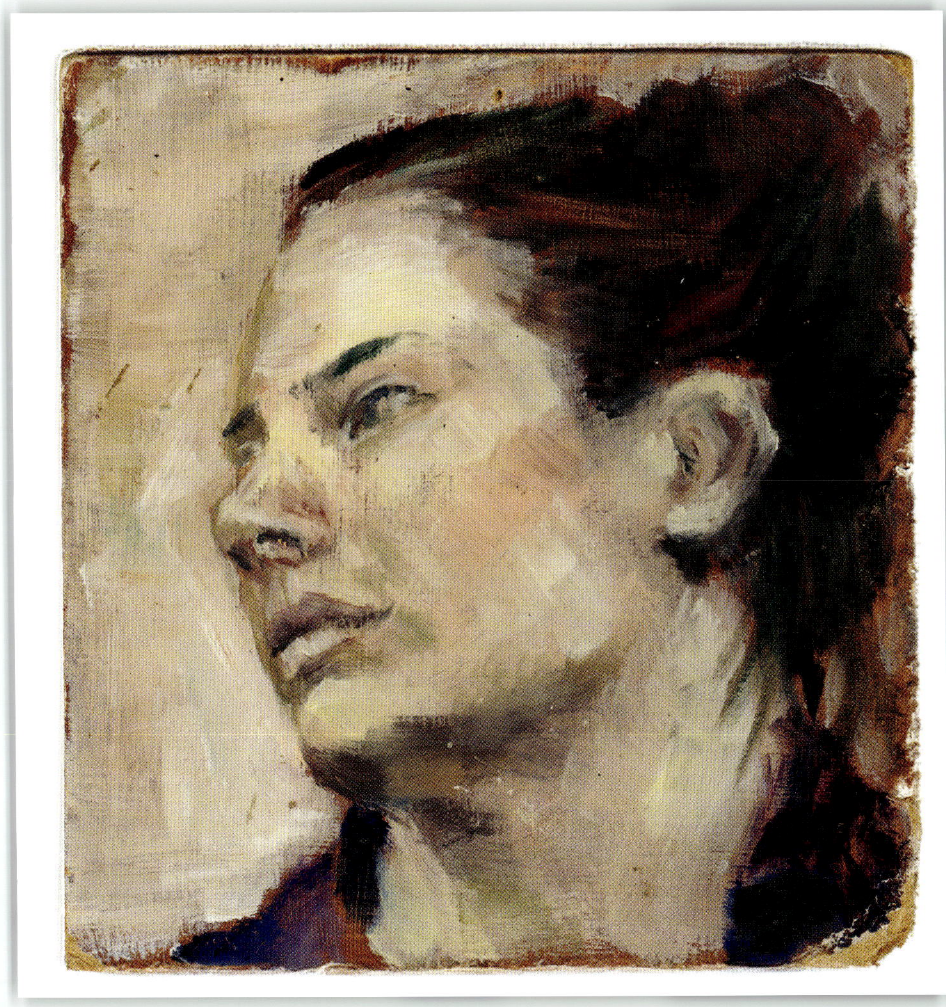

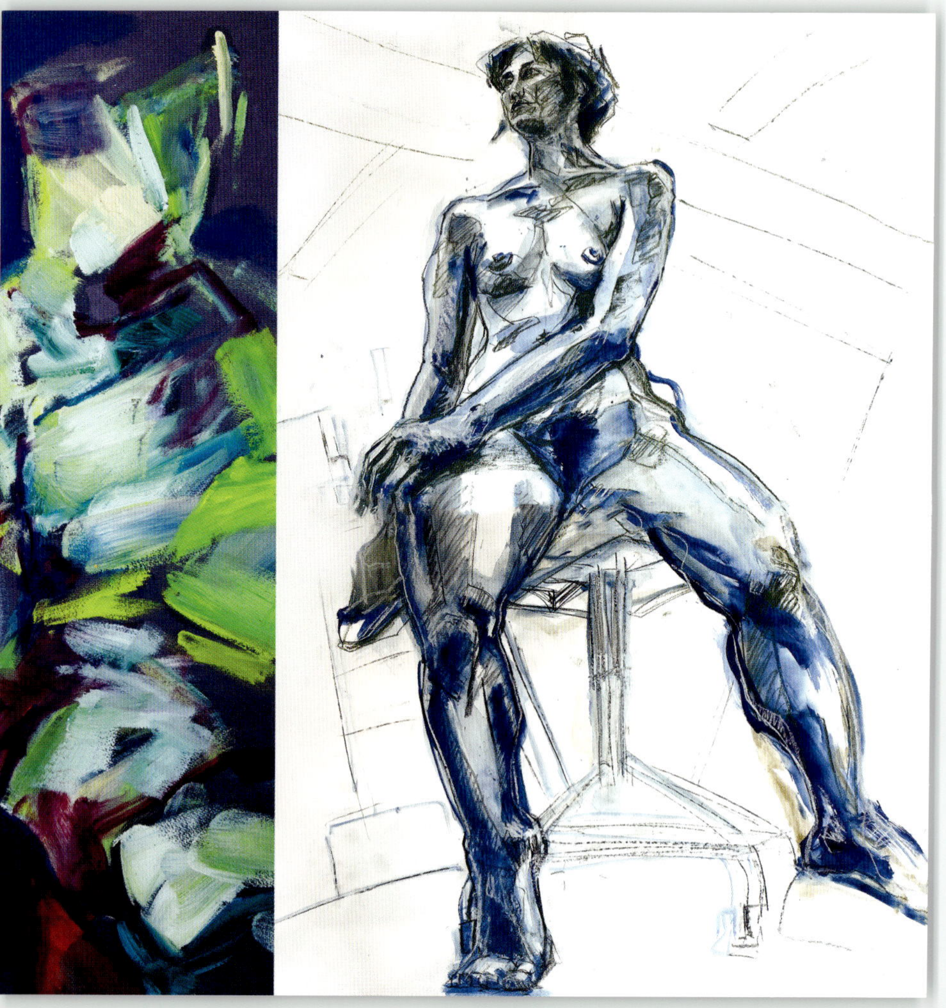

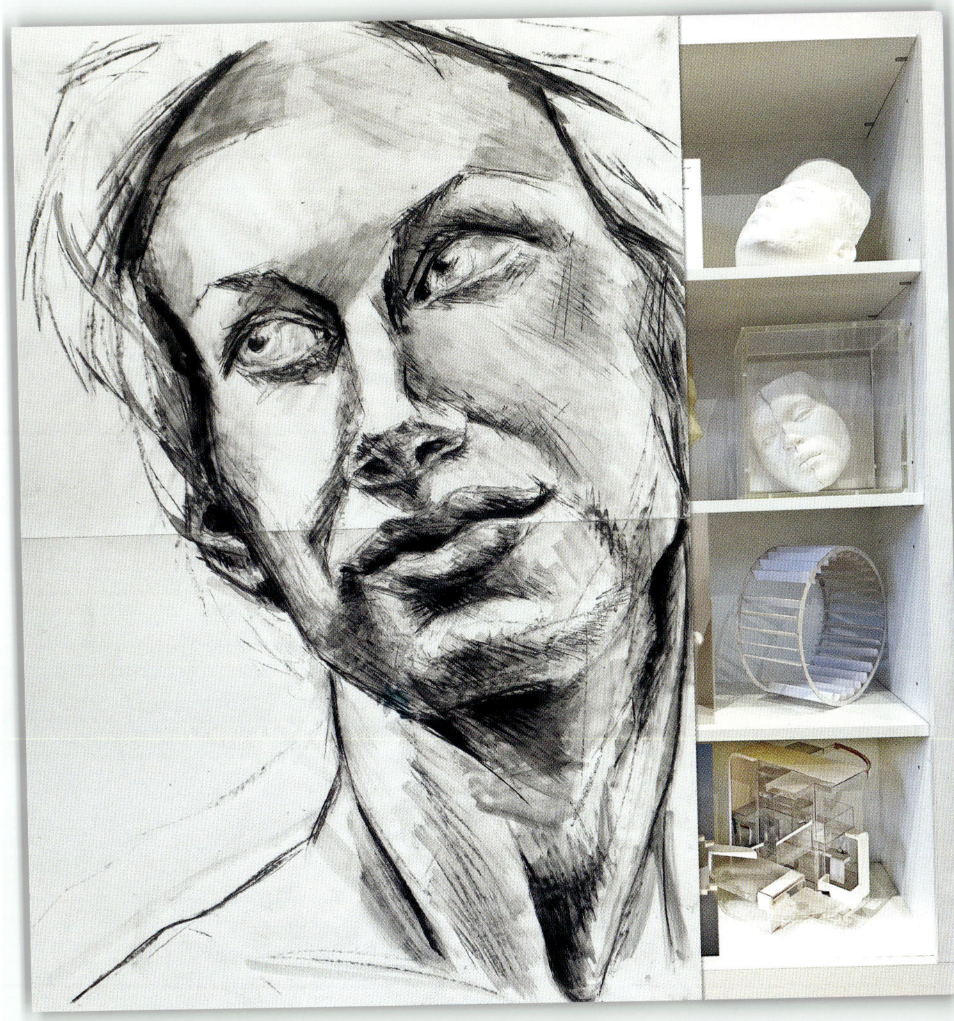

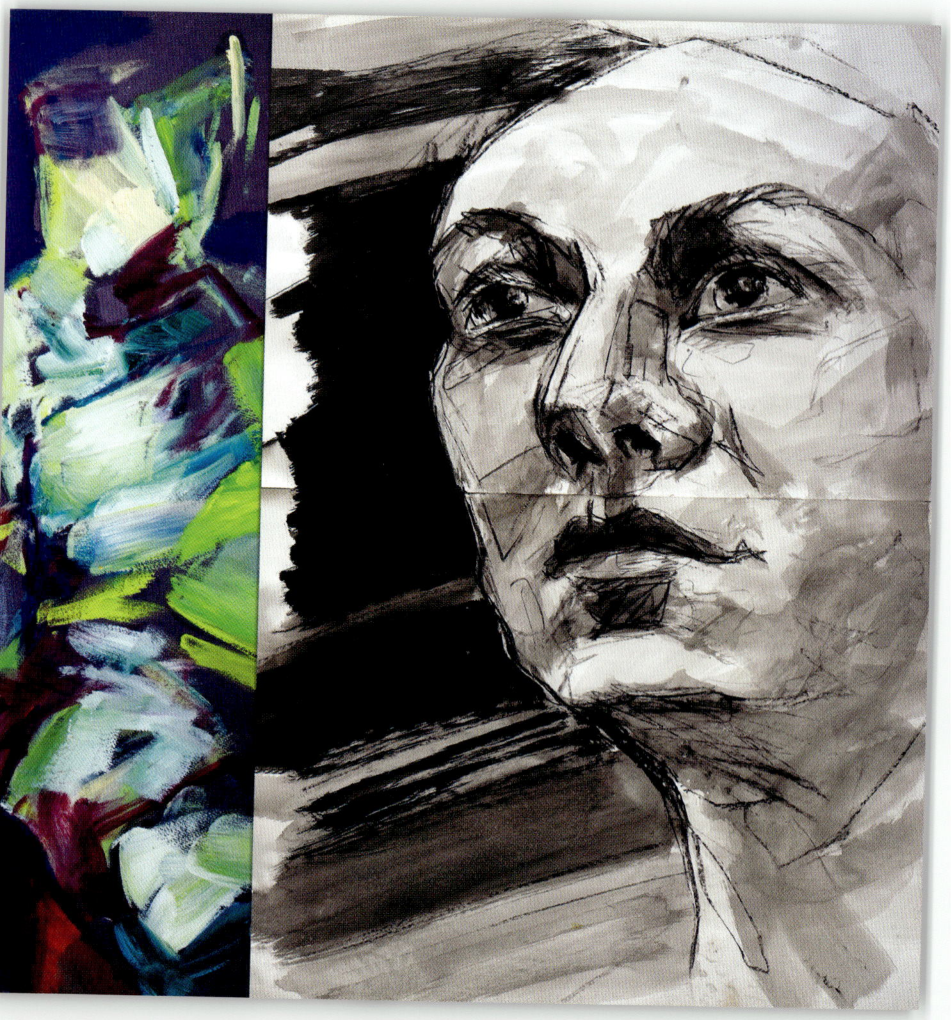

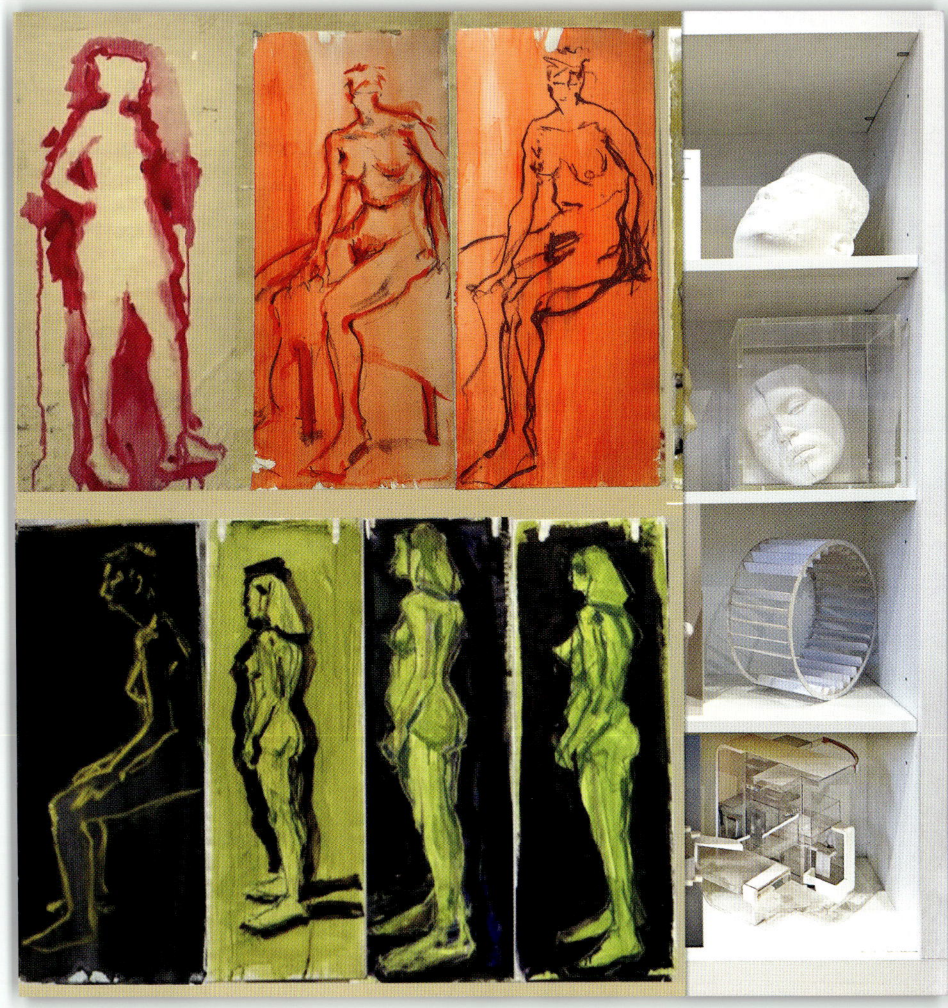

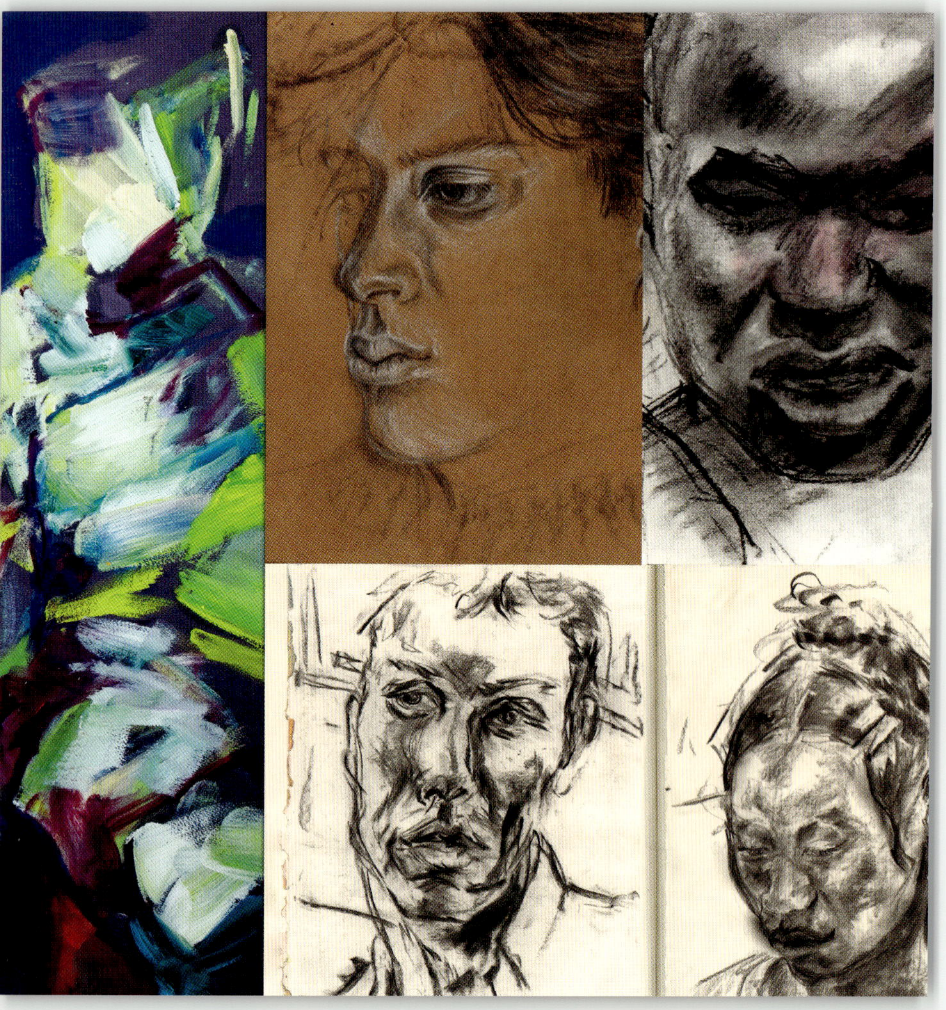

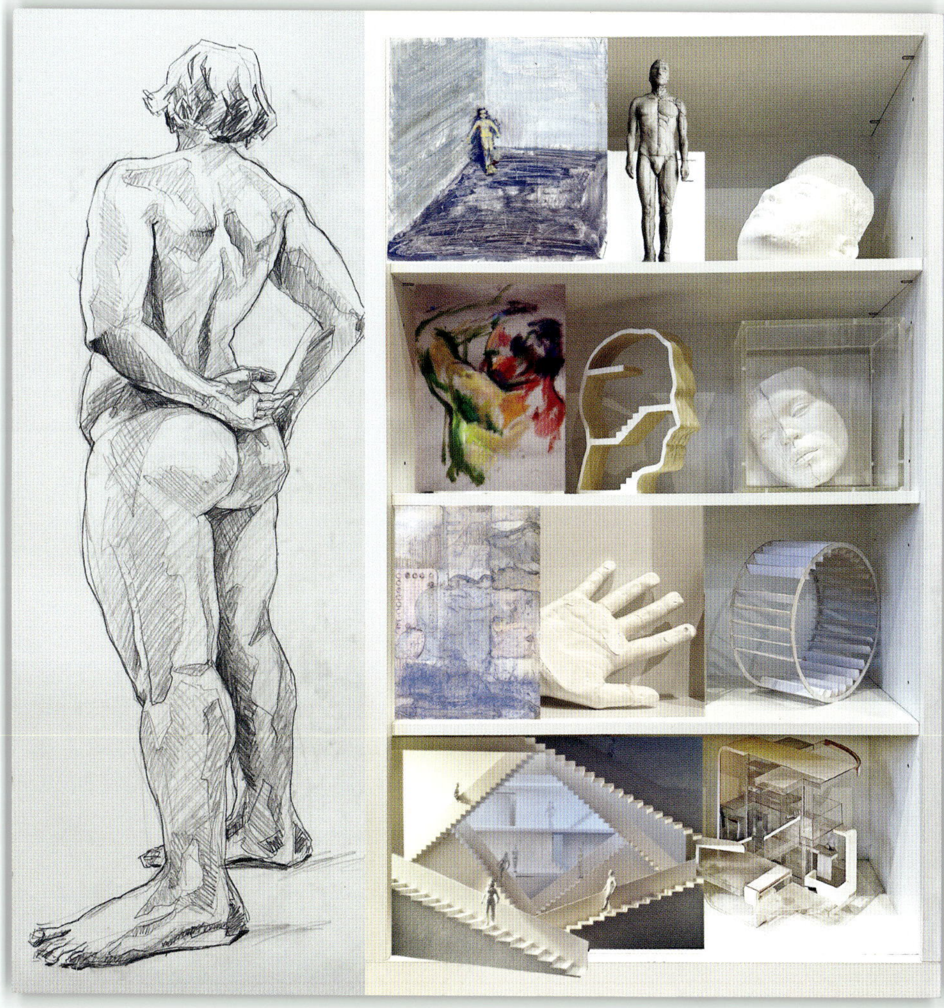

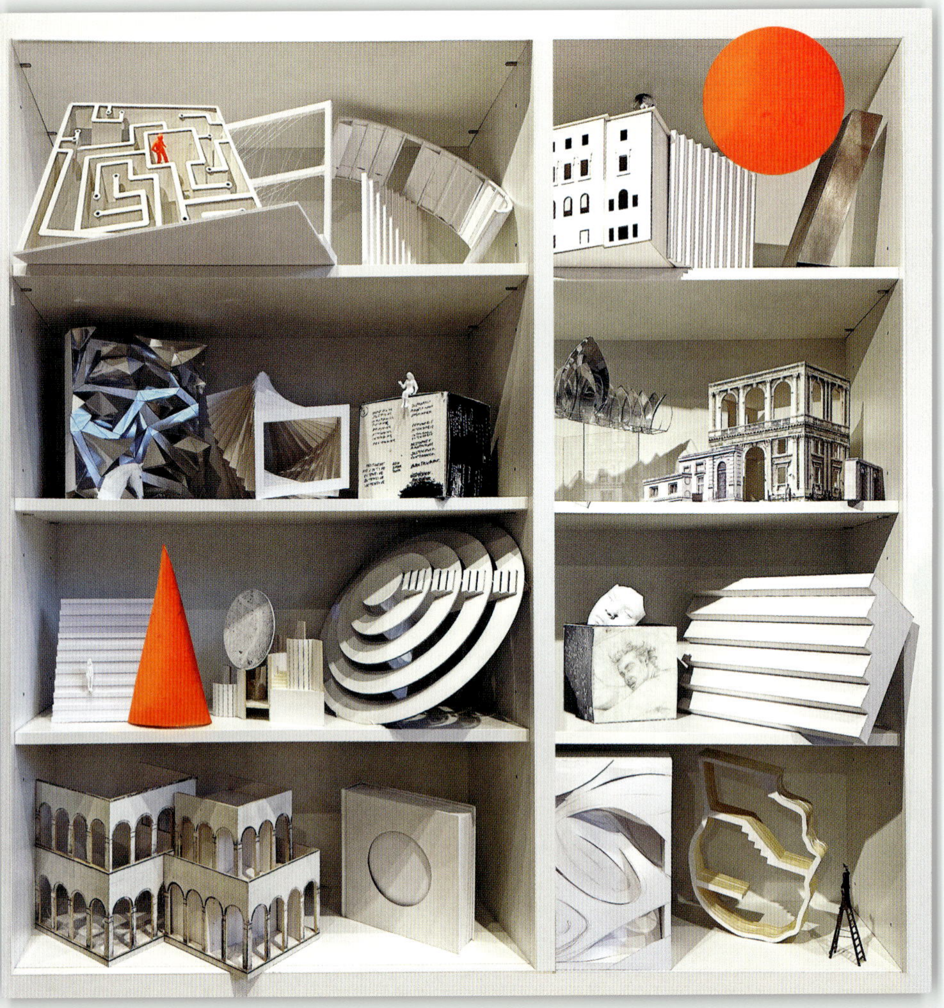

A 31-YEAR SKETCHBOOK

1995–2026

Every project I've made, whether staged in a theatre, arena, museum, art gallery or public space, is an ongoing conversation between place, light, music, text, people and objects. The process of drawing, painting and model-making runs in parallel to this dialogue, with multiple hands sketching while talking. Different types of drawings are produced at different stages. Fast 'thinking' drawings document the initial ideas. Annotations on primary texts, poems and opera libretti ensure we remember early instinctive reactions. Scale models and paintings articulate concepts in more detail. Quick sketches on the back of scripts and setlists illustrate ideas for video projections (often when the music is too loud to hear one another speak). Intricate diagrams produced by studio associates whose technical skills far eclipse my own are distributed to engineers and fabricators.

We have gathered fragments from the processes that have led to each sculptural installation and performance, and present them here as a continuous 31-year sketchbook. This series of fragile, small works on paper and cardboard sculptures has continuously paralleled the flow of large-scale temporary public architectures, and has, until recently, been stored unseen on shelves in the studio and archive. The archive contains over 15,000 drawings spanning 350 projects over 31 years. We selected 150 projects to include here, some of which remain unrealized. Nearly all are paired with photographic illustrations in the last two sections of the book – page numbers at the base of each commentary page will guide you to the corresponding photographs. As I've composed these commentaries, I've woven in references to events in Britain and beyond which have inevitably informed my practice, along with shifts in my more immediate personal orbit.

RAIDING PARADISE

First the air is blue and then
it is bluer and then green and then
black I am blacking out and yet
my mask is powerful
it pumps my blood with power
the sea is another story
the sea is not a question of power
I have to learn alone
to turn my body without force
in the deep element.

Adrienne Rich, 'Diving into the Wreck'

In July 1995, while still studying stage design, I made a series of masks for students at Rose Bruford College who had written a text exploring playwright Noël Coward's stay in Indonesia in the 1930s. Their play fused the Eastern and Western traditions of literal and psychological masks. Collaborating with the college students, we cast the performers' faces with canvas coated in plaster of paris and sculpted the mask features around the forms of their faces. I tried wearing a mask for a day, experiencing the way it worked as both protective shell and expressive instrument. The action alternated between texts spoken by human faces and texts spoken through face-like objects.

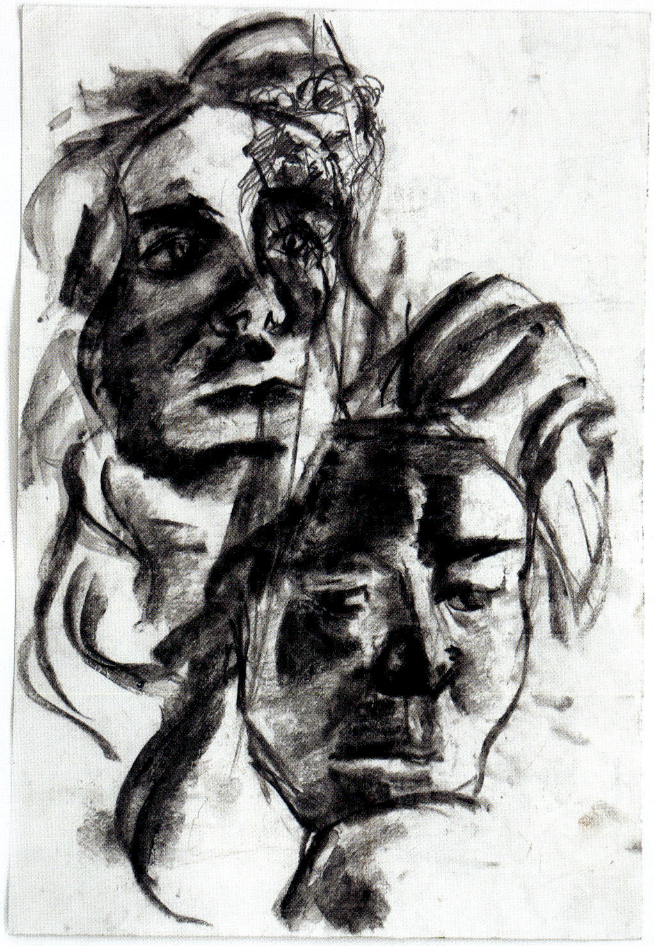

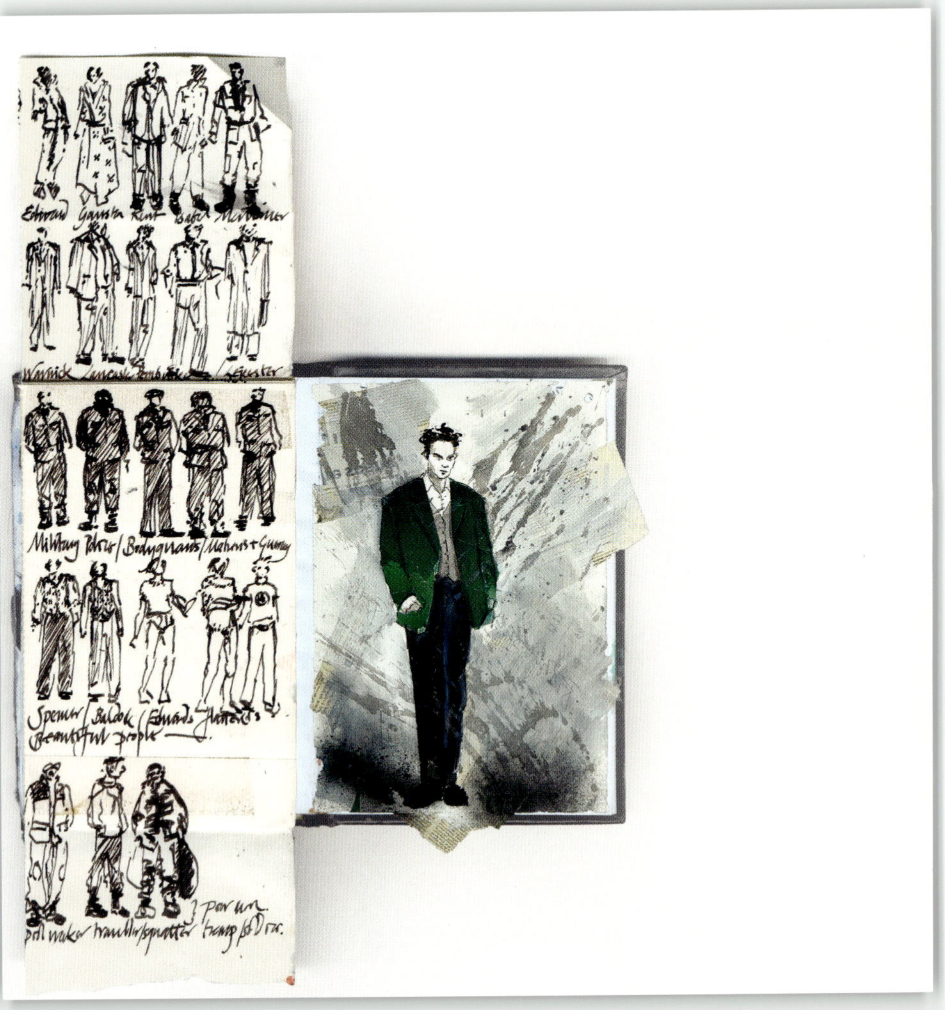
Edward
Kent
Warwick
Military Police / Bodyguards
Spencer / Baldock / Edwards
Beautiful people

EDWARD II

You must be proud, bold, pleasant, resolute,
And now and then stab as occasion serves.

Christopher Marlowe

Graduating in 1996, I entered the biannual Linbury Prize for Stage Design. The prize that year was to design Christopher Marlowe's 1592 play, *Edward II*, at the Octagon Theatre in Bolton.

We staged the piece in a drained swimming pool: the showers ran red, their tiles a foil for the torturous brutality of the text. I had spent years drawing the human form but was unprepared for the complexity of the encounter with actors in a costume fitting. Ink and charcoal drawings needed to become garments, which would operate as both an extension of character and a voice for the performer. The forms of clothes needed to work as a language in concert, as a collective. I drew and redrew the forms of the performers, their clothes and the spaces in between.

LOVE AND UNDERSTANDING

… there's something really thrilling about 3 people … the argument, the counter-argument and then the catalyst [or] … neutraliser. I'm really interested in the way people … form loyalties and then sabotage them and the best way to do that is with 3 people.

Joe Penhall

A lack of funding in the 1990s led new writers with ambitious film scripts into small-scale theatre productions at the Bush and Gate theatres. As designers, we conceived filmic transitions that would transport an audience of 75 from these small rooms above pubs to limitless locations.

Guided by playwright Joe Penhall and director Mike Bradwell, I visited each of the locations in the script: the Maudsley Hospital and the South London pub, flat and park bench. I then sat for hours in rehearsal drawing the actors and painting the environments around them, eventually distilling the sketches into two backlit translucent planes, windows. I suspended and illuminated – like X-rays – the interior workings of the specific objects observed during my research: bedsprings, a hospital fridge mechanism, the underside of shot glasses left on a bar.

The play opened at the Bush Theatre on 5 May 1997, a few days after the election that ended twenty years of Conservative government. It was a moment of euphoria and hope in Britain.

638

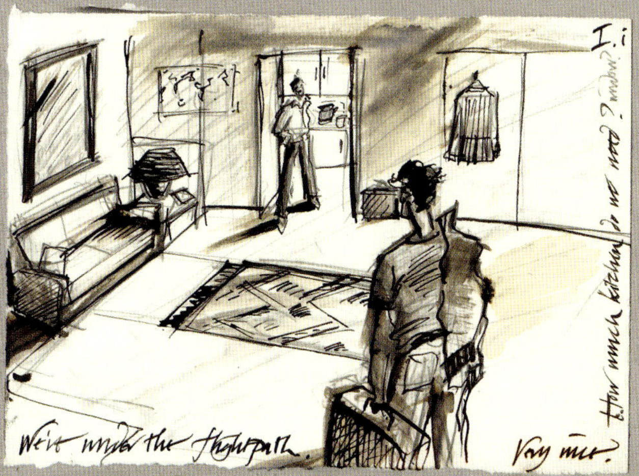
I.i
We're under the flightpath.
Very nice.

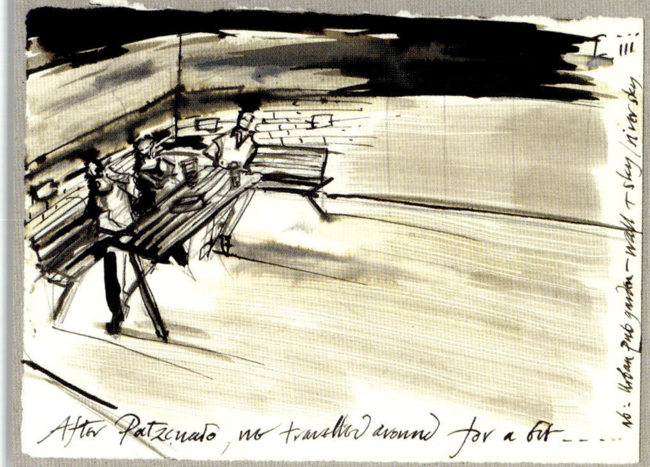
I.iii
After Patzcuaro, we travelled around for a bit....

an Anglican

LOVE AN

… there's somethin
the counter-argume
interested in the wa
and the best way to

A lack of funding in
scripts into small-s
theatres. As design
transport an audier
to limitless location

Guided by playwrig
visited each of the l
the South London
rehearsal drawing t
them, eventually dis
planes, windows. I
interior workings of
bedsprings, a hosp
of shot glasses left

The play opened at
the election that en
It was a moment of

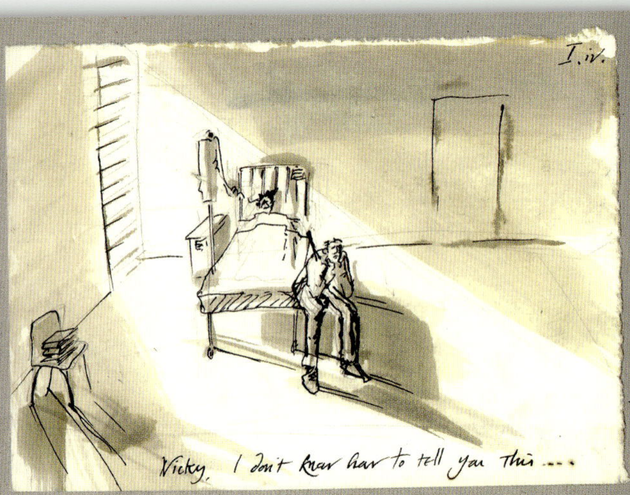

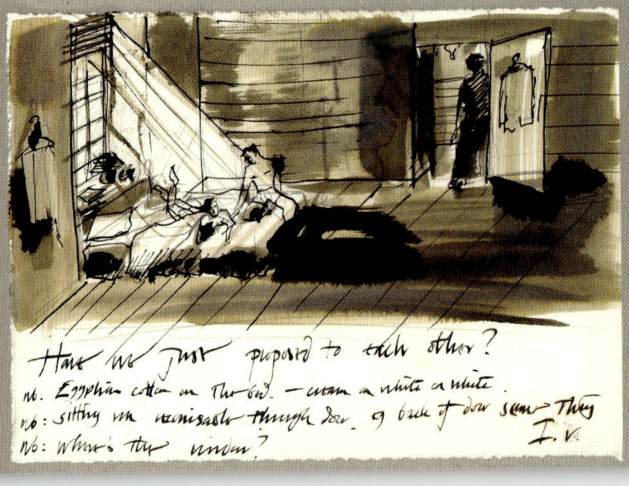

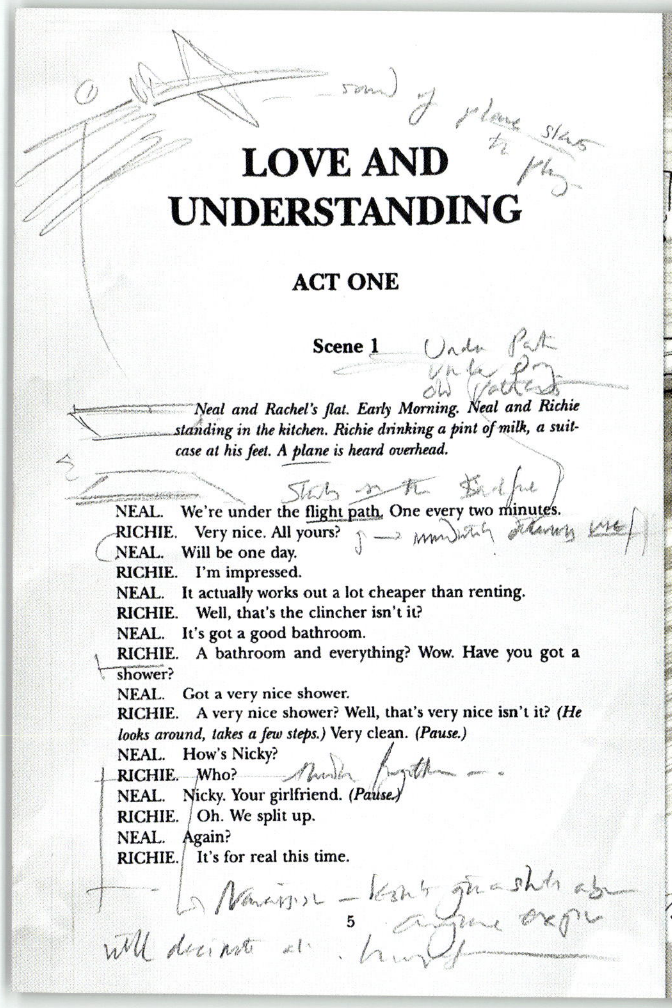

LOVE AND UNDERSTANDING

ACT ONE

Scene 1

Neal and Rachel's flat. Early Morning. Neal and Richie standing in the kitchen. Richie drinking a pint of milk, a suitcase at his feet. A plane is heard overhead.

NEAL. We're under the flight path. One every two minutes.
RICHIE. Very nice. All yours?
NEAL. Will be one day.
RICHIE. I'm impressed.
NEAL. It actually works out a lot cheaper than renting.
RICHIE. Well, that's the clincher isn't it?
NEAL. It's got a good bathroom.
RICHIE. A bathroom and everything? Wow. Have you got a shower?
NEAL. Got a very nice shower.
RICHIE. A very nice shower? Well, that's very nice isn't it? *(He looks around, takes a few steps.)* Very clean. *(Pause.)*
NEAL. How's Nicky?
RICHIE. Who?
NEAL. Nicky. Your girlfriend. *(Pause.)*
RICHIE. Oh. We split up.
NEAL. Again?
RICHIE. It's for real this time.

5

LOVE AN

… there's somethin
the counter-argume
interested in the wa
and the best way to

A lack of funding in
scripts into small-s
theatres. As design
transport an audien
to limitless location

Guided by playwrig
visited each of the
the South London
rehearsal drawing t
them, eventually di
planes, windows. I
interior workings of
bedsprings, a hosp
of shot glasses left

The play opened at
the election that en
It was a moment of

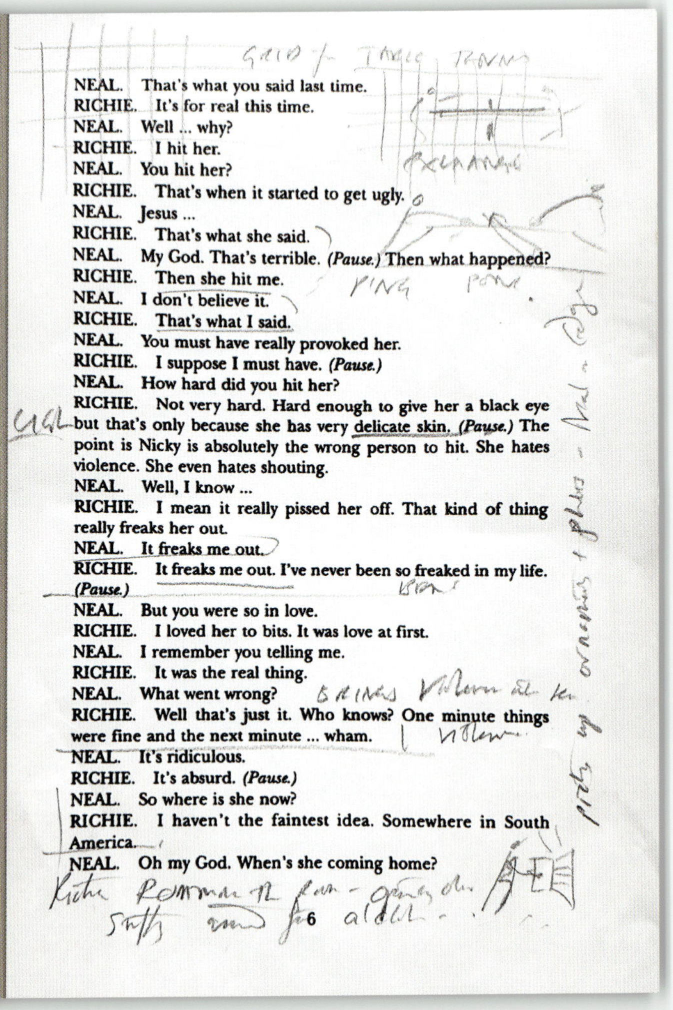

NEAL. That's what you said last time.
RICHIE. It's for real this time.
NEAL. Well ... why?
RICHIE. I hit her.
NEAL. You hit her?
RICHIE. That's when it started to get ugly.
NEAL. Jesus ...
RICHIE. That's what she said.
NEAL. My God. That's terrible. *(Pause.)* Then what happened?
RICHIE. Then she hit me.
NEAL. I don't believe it.
RICHIE. That's what I said.
NEAL. You must have really provoked her.
RICHIE. I suppose I must have. *(Pause.)*
NEAL. How hard did you hit her?
RICHIE. Not very hard. Hard enough to give her a black eye but that's only because she has very delicate skin. *(Pause.)* The point is Nicky is absolutely the wrong person to hit. She hates violence. She even hates shouting.
NEAL. Well, I know ...
RICHIE. I mean it really pissed her off. That kind of thing really freaks her out.
NEAL. It freaks me out.
RICHIE. It freaks me out. I've never been so freaked in my life. *(Pause.)*
NEAL. But you were so in love.
RICHIE. I loved her to bits. It was love at first.
NEAL. I remember you telling me.
RICHIE. It was the real thing.
NEAL. What went wrong?
RICHIE. Well that's just it. Who knows? One minute things were fine and the next minute ... wham.
NEAL. It's ridiculous.
RICHIE. It's absurd. *(Pause.)*
NEAL. So where is she now?
RICHIE. I haven't the faintest idea. Somewhere in South America.
NEAL. Oh my God. When's she coming home?

6

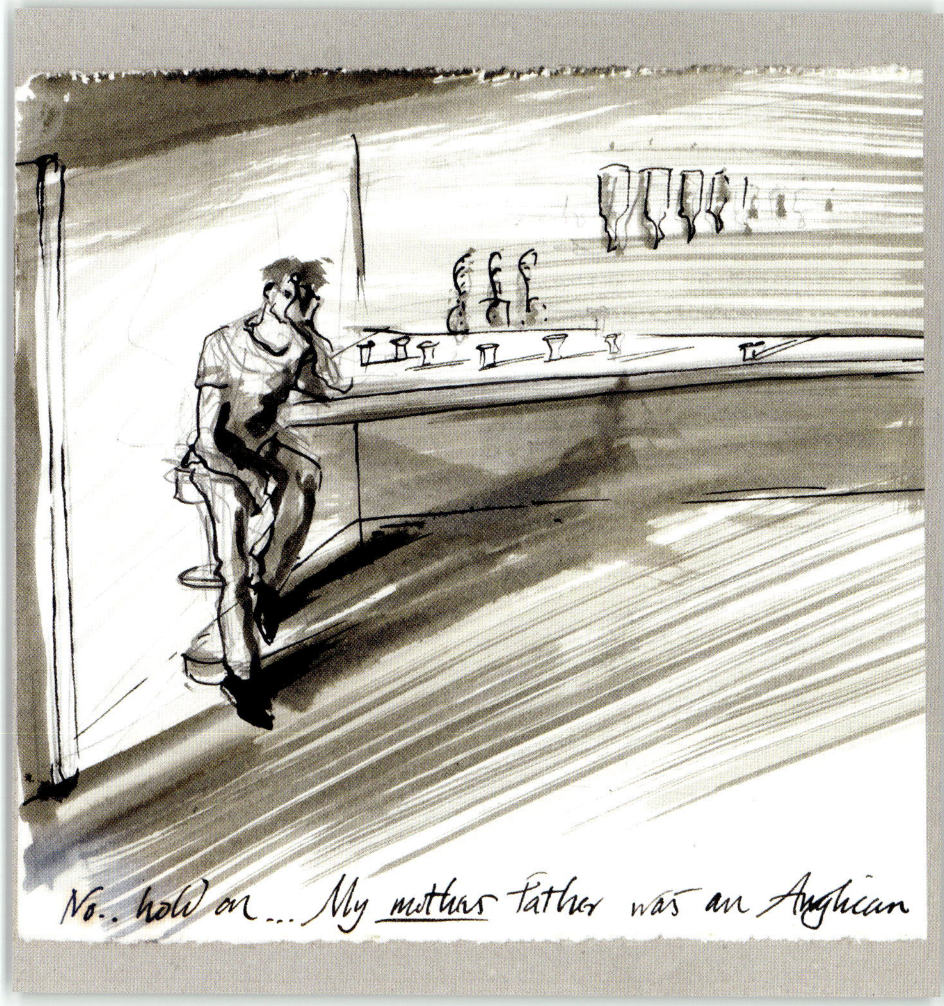
No.. hold on... My mothers father was an Anglican

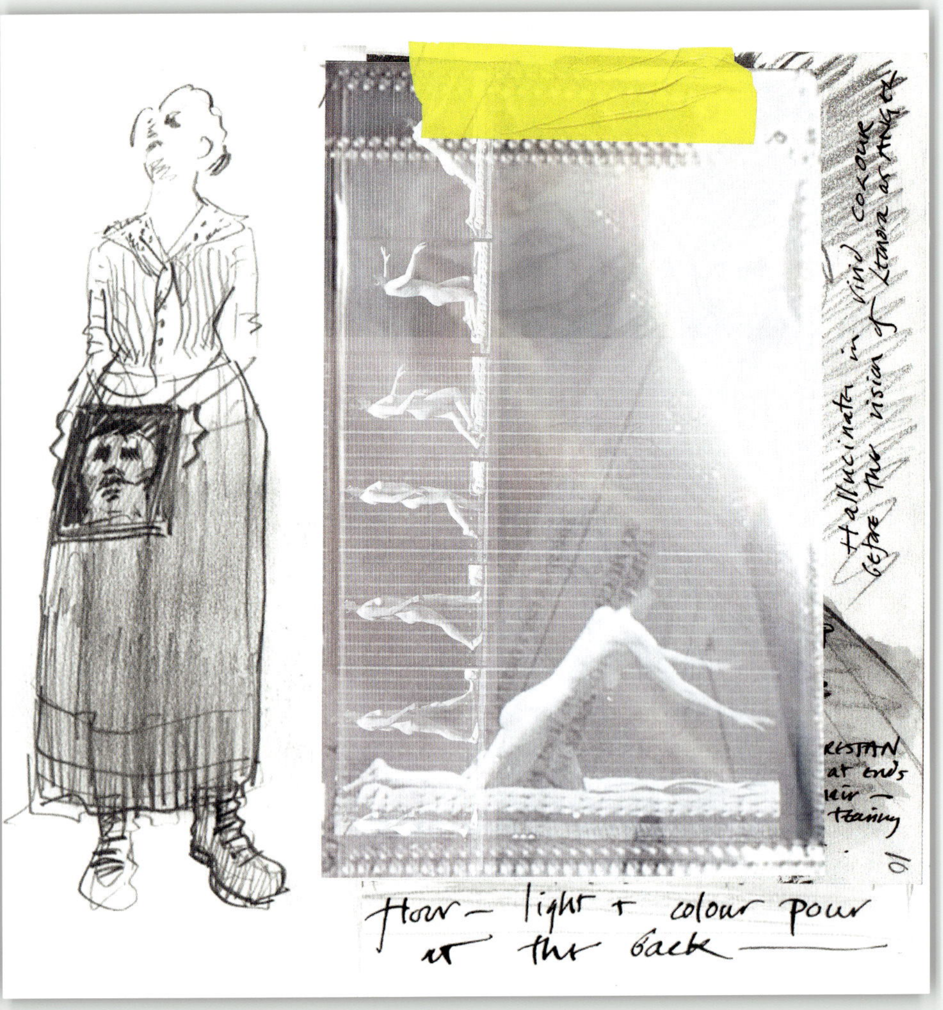
Hallucinates in vivid colour
before the vision of Leonora as angel
Floor – light + colour pour
at the back

FIDELIO

O what joy, in the open air / Freely to breathe again!
Only here, only here is life! / The dungeon is a grave.

Ludwig van Beethoven

Beethoven's only opera has been referred to as a mass. Its protagonist has to journey to a dark prison underworld, like Orpheus, to rescue her political-prisoner husband. In this March 1998 English Touring Opera production, we echoed newspaper images of women holding portraits of 'disappeared' Chilean political prisoners, ahead of the London arrest of Margaret Thatcher's military-dictator friend, Augusto Pinochet, later that year.

This was my third collaboration with the director Robert Chevara. We had spent 1997 working on student productions. I remember the night of 30 August 1997 particularly vividly. We wanted to project stills from Eadweard Muybridge's stop-frame sequence of a falling woman over a young singer presenting the 'Catalogue Aria' from Mozart's *Don Giovanni*. I managed to borrow a gigantic, large-format slide projector from the English National Opera and set about printing the big glass slides myself, with the help of my brother Fabian. As we sat in my boyfriend's basement flat in West London sellotaping printed transparencies between layers of glass through the night, we watched news of the death of Princess Diana unfold in slow motion on the TV. As dawn broke, we walked through Kensington Gardens where the grass was already covered with candles and flowers, as if in preparation for an open-air mass. It was the first time I had witnessed a people's spontaneous ritual take over the city.

635

BETRAYAL

... the real truth is that there never is any such thing as one truth to be found in dramatic art. There are many. These truths challenge each other, recoil from each other, reflect each other, ignore each other, tease each other, are blind to each other. Sometimes you feel you have the truth of a moment in your hand, then it slips through your fingers and is lost.

Harold Pinter

Having seen *Love and Understanding*, Trevor Nunn – then Artistic Director of the National Theatre – asked me to design Harold Pinter's *Betrayal* to open in November 1998. The play's nine scenes are set in reverse chronological order. I had visited Rachel Whiteread's monumental *House* sculpture in 1993, which seemed to cast time as a protagonist in concrete. The work had been demolished and, with Whiteread's permission, we responded to its spirit within the cast concrete of the National's Lyttelton Theatre. A single plaster plane held illuminated impressions of the play's five overlaid locations, as if the wall were actively remembering the time and place of each scene. Objects and furniture flowed through the remembered rooms, as projections of the characters' unseen children surfaced through the plaster between scenes. *Betrayal* is a precisely crafted play that isn't used to such an elaborate overlay. It works very well in a simple, neutral environment. Harold Pinter had seen many minimal productions and tolerated our baroque approach with wry humour, introducing me to his wife, the author Antonia Fraser, at the opening night, with the cryptic swipe, 'This is Es Devlin. She wrote the play.'

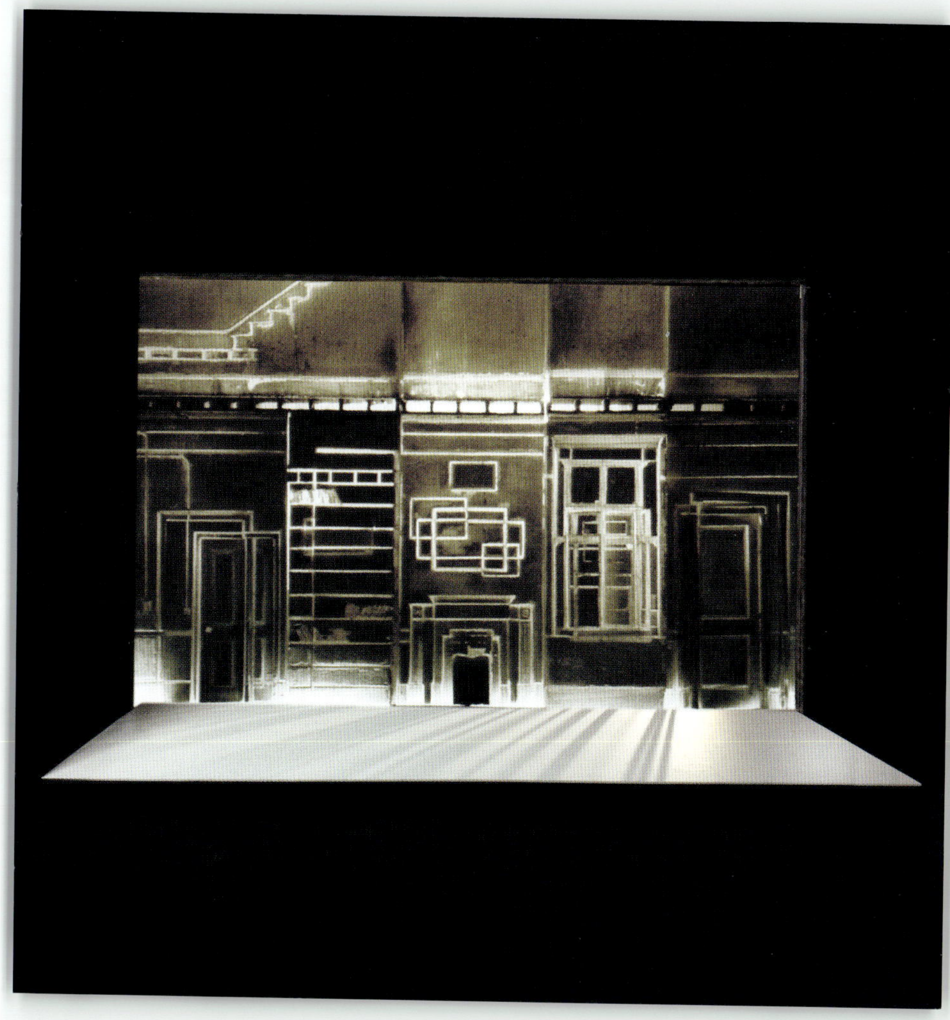

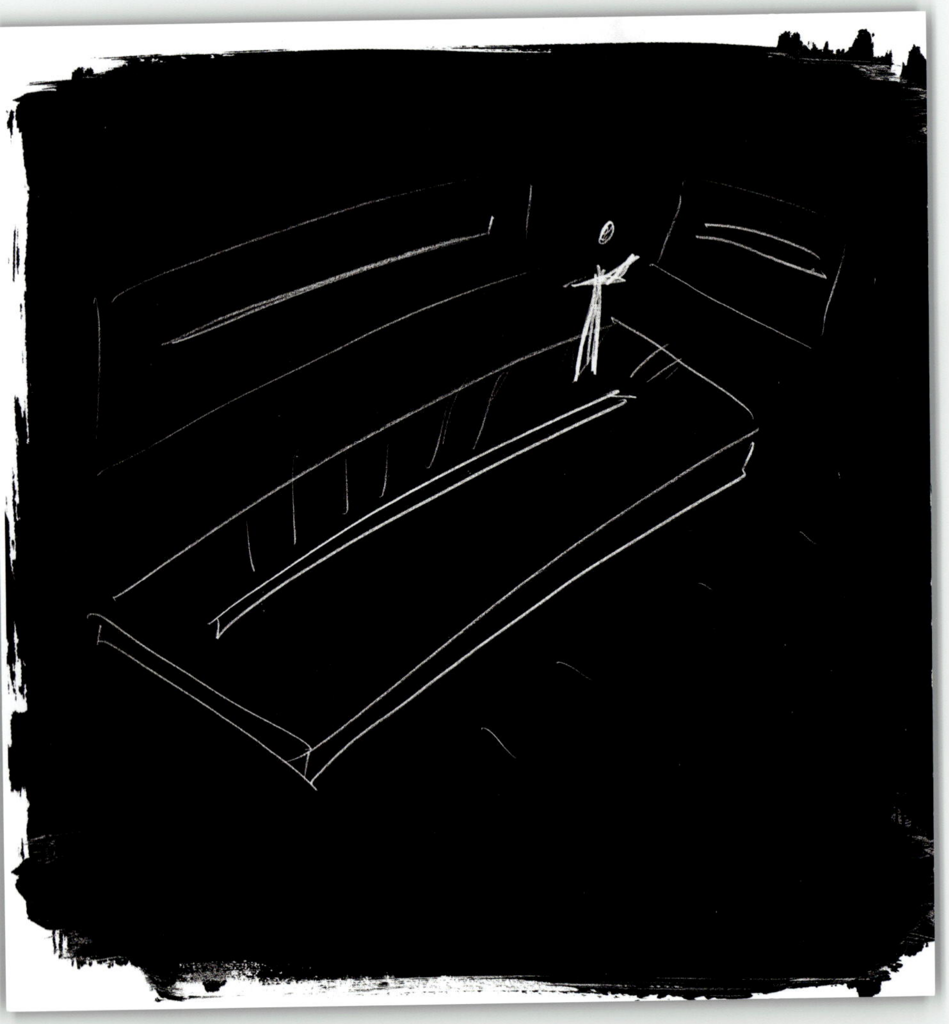

HOWIE THE ROOKIE

With a monologue there is just the story that you are telling; there is nothing that exists outside that, and you have to keep on moving forward, like a shark.

Mark O'Rowe

The Bush Theatre is about the size of a matchbox. What it was, was close-up magic. We created worlds in a very, very tiny space ... We were spending about four quid doing it out of junk and Es was working out how to do it, every single step of the way. She'd paint the set, she'd make the stuff, she'd weld.

Mike Bradwell

Mike Bradwell and I continued our collaboration at the Bush Theatre in February 1999. I was developing a relationship with this small room above a West London pub, transforming the three planes of the space into a distilled essence of the environment that we felt would most powerfully support and heighten each text.

Howie the Rookie by Mark O'Rowe is a pair of potent, visceral monologues set in the housing estates of Tallaght on the outskirts of Dublin. We perforated three dark concrete planes with lines of light, hovering over a plane of acid-lit grass. The text and sculptural context combined to evoke two perspectives: a line of burning fields on the horizon and the painted road-marking that heralded an exit along the Tallaght highway.

FOUR SCENES

The great thing about dance is the ambiguity. You can interpret it on many different levels, and it can speak to each individual member of the audience and have a different resonance.

Christopher Bruce

This was Rambert Dance Company's inaugural work in the newly remodelled Sadler's Wells Theatre in October 1998. The choreographer Christopher Bruce based the vocabulary on the animated movement of young children. I asked a friend's five-year-old son and his school friends to make drawings of what they would most like to see come to life in the new space. Their crayon sketches of dinosaurs, castles, birds and people were enlarged and painted in fluorescent white on translucent gauze, with an aperture revealing an expanding horizon of light through them.

This was my first encounter with dance. I tried to read the sculptural forms of the dancers as a kind of text. I painted over photographs of the dancers' formations in rehearsal and built up translucent layers of the children's scrawled pictures over them, creating a paper aperture that I could adjust to reveal slots of illuminated colour: a swelling light on the horizon. The dancers rehearsed wearing yellow hard hats as the new building was completed around us. The New Labour Prime Minister, Tony Blair, attended the opening night.

670

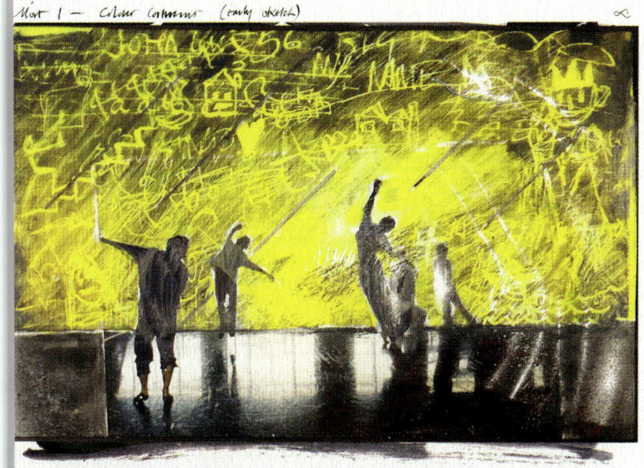

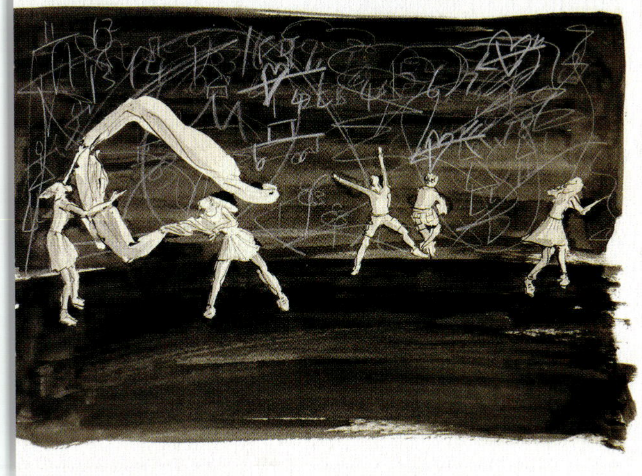

RA

William Shakespeare

istic Director of
ays in the early
l Shakespeare
espeare divides
s Egypt. As the play
ndenses into ever
a map made of
response to the
ompany engineers
expandable
It was impressive
got underway, it
vork in practice.
agments of the
creating a Nile
at each work is an
techniques won't
metimes need to be

FOUR SCE

The great thing about
many different levels,
the audience and have

This was Rambert Da
remodelled Sadler's W
rapher Christopher B
movement of young c
his school friends to r
see come to life in the
castles, birds and pe
white on translucent g
horizon of light throug

This was my first enc
forms of the dancers
the dancers' formatio
the children's scrawle
that I could adjust to
on the horizon. The d
the new building was
Minister, Tony Blair, a

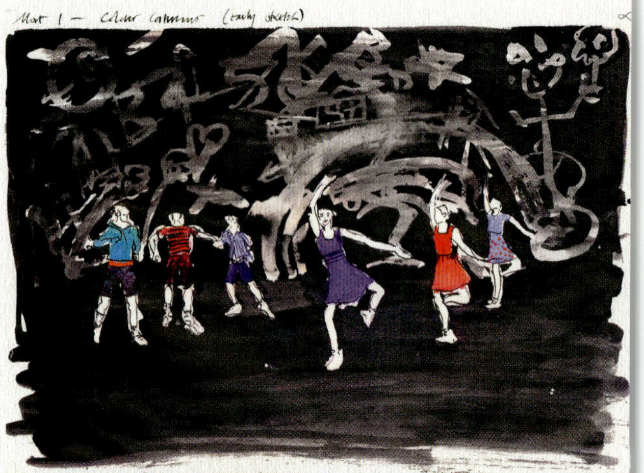

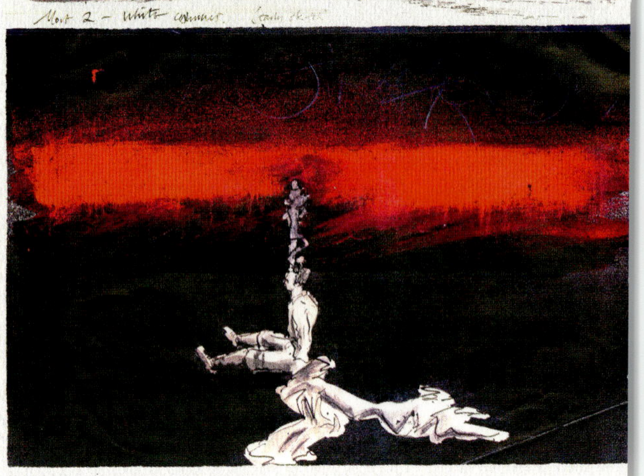

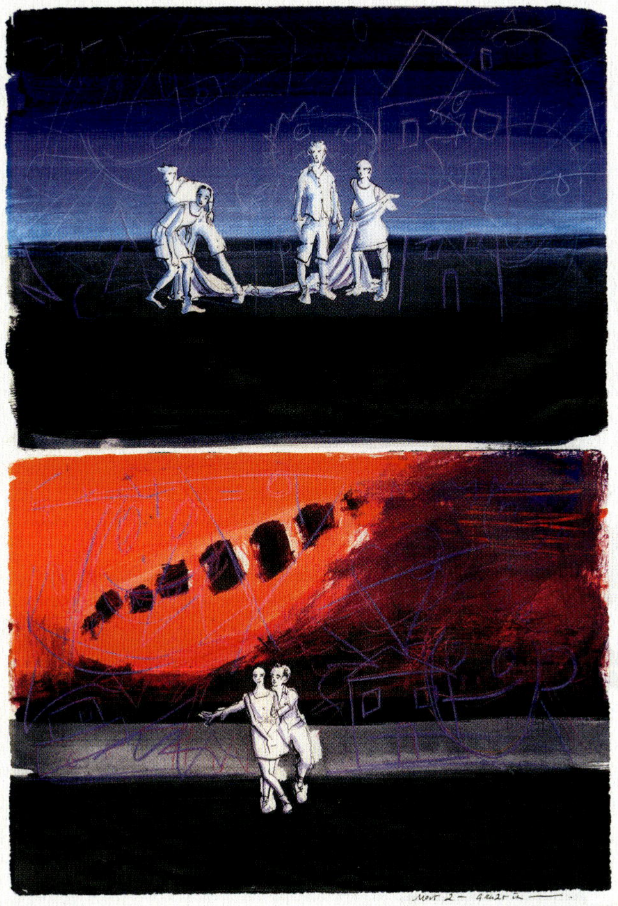

RA

William Shakespeare

istic Director of
ays in the early
l Shakespeare
espeare divides
s Egypt. As the play
ndenses into ever
a map made of
response to the
ompany engineers
expandable
It was impressive
got underway, it
vork in practice.
agments of the
creating a Nile
at each work is an
techniques won't
metimes need to be

FOUR SCE

The great thing about
many different levels,
the audience and have

This was Rambert Da
remodelled Sadler's
rapher Christopher B
movement of young
his school friends to
see come to life in th
castles, birds and pe
white on translucent
horizon of light throug

This was my first enc
forms of the dancers
the dancers' formatio
the children's scrawle
that I could adjust to
on the horizon. The d
the new building was
Minister, Tony Blair, a

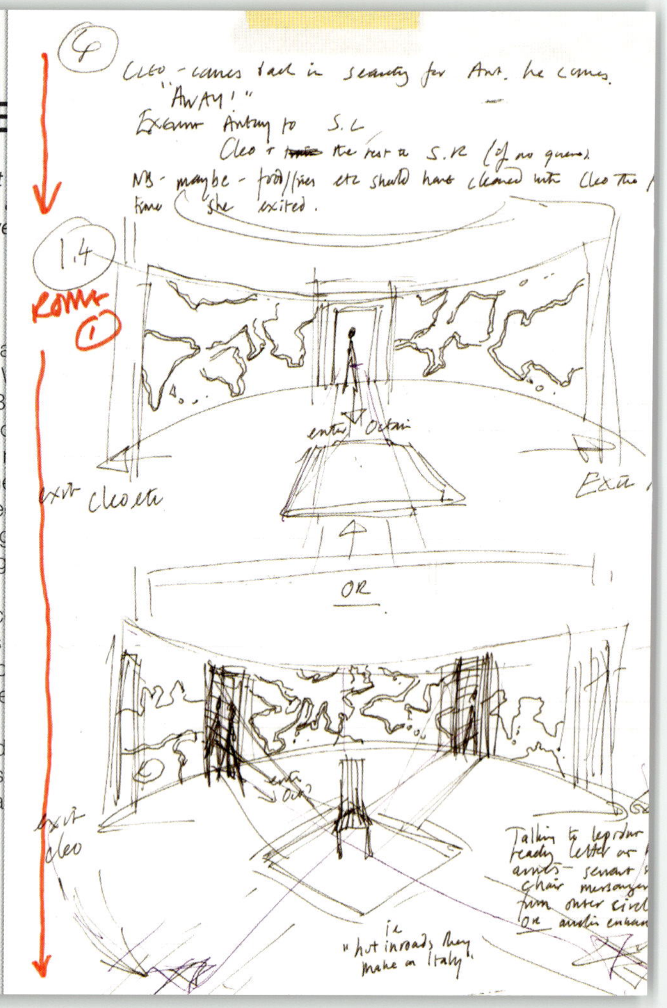

ANTONY AND CLEOPATRA

Let Rome in Tiber melt, and the wide arch
Of the ranged empire fall! Here is my space.

William Shakespeare

I collaborated with Michael Attenborough, then Artistic Director of the Royal Shakespeare Company, on a series of plays in the early 2000s, including *Antony and Cleopatra* at the Royal Shakespeare Theatre in Stratford-upon-Avon in April 2002. Shakespeare divides the action between Antony's Rome and Cleopatra's Egypt. As the play progresses, the vast map of the Roman Empire condenses into ever more pressured psychological spaces. I envisaged a map made of red earth that would slowly expand and contract in response to the text throughout the play. The Royal Shakespeare Company engineers developed an isokinetic mechanism, based on the expandable 'Hoberman sphere' toys I'd played with as a child. It was impressive and complex, but as the final technical installation got underway, it became clear that the design was never going to work in practice. With four days until the opening, we adapted the fragments of the map into a simple pair of planes, which split apart creating a Nile River-shaped aperture. I was beginning to learn that each work is an untested prototype: there is always a risk that new techniques won't succeed, and shifts to a new creative approach sometimes need to be adopted collectively, at speed, under pressure.

HAMLET

O God, I could be bounded in a nutshell, and count myself a king of infinite space, were it not that I have bad dreams.

William Shakespeare

At the Young Vic Theatre in April 1999, with an audience of 350 surrounding the performers, Shakespeare's text conjured the expansion and contraction of space. The costumes were carved from the dark in white canvas. A series of sliding black floor planes formed precipices from which Hamlet shared his soliloquies in the theatrical equivalent of a filmic close-up.

I had worked briefly at the Young Vic as an assistant during summer 1996. My first task had been to bring a pig's head from the local butcher into the rehearsal room to help the director, actors and costume designer find a visual language for *Beauty and the Beast*. I spent the day drawing the pig's head in charcoal on vast sheets of paper, which remained on the walls throughout the rehearsal process. I remember being struck by how much life could emerge from a day spent in close and careful observation of death. The drawings are now lost, but the memory of them returned to me as the actor Paul Rhys brought to life Hamlet's famous consideration of death. It was only much later I learned that this breeze-block building in which I have experienced so much collective life – both as theatre maker and as audience member – was constructed in 1970 from a former butcher's shop and a bomb site, on which 54 people were killed during the Blitz of 1941.

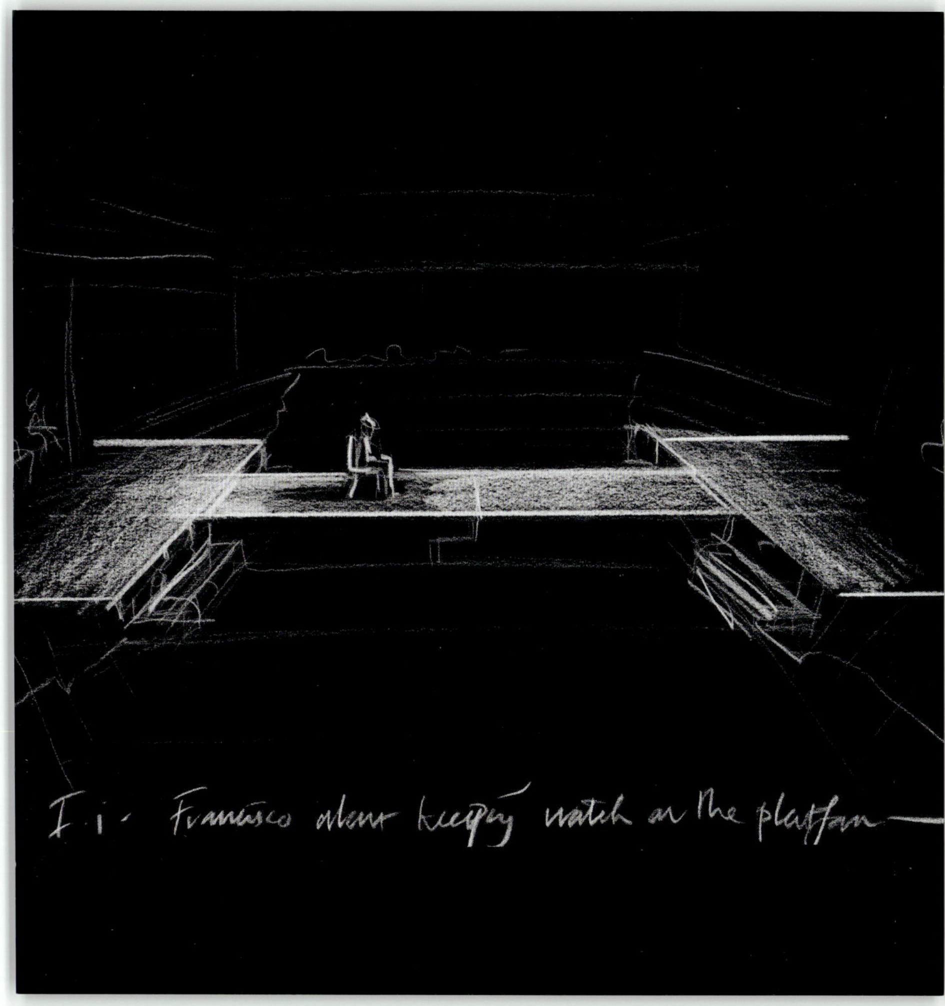
I.i - Francisco alone keeping watch on the platform —

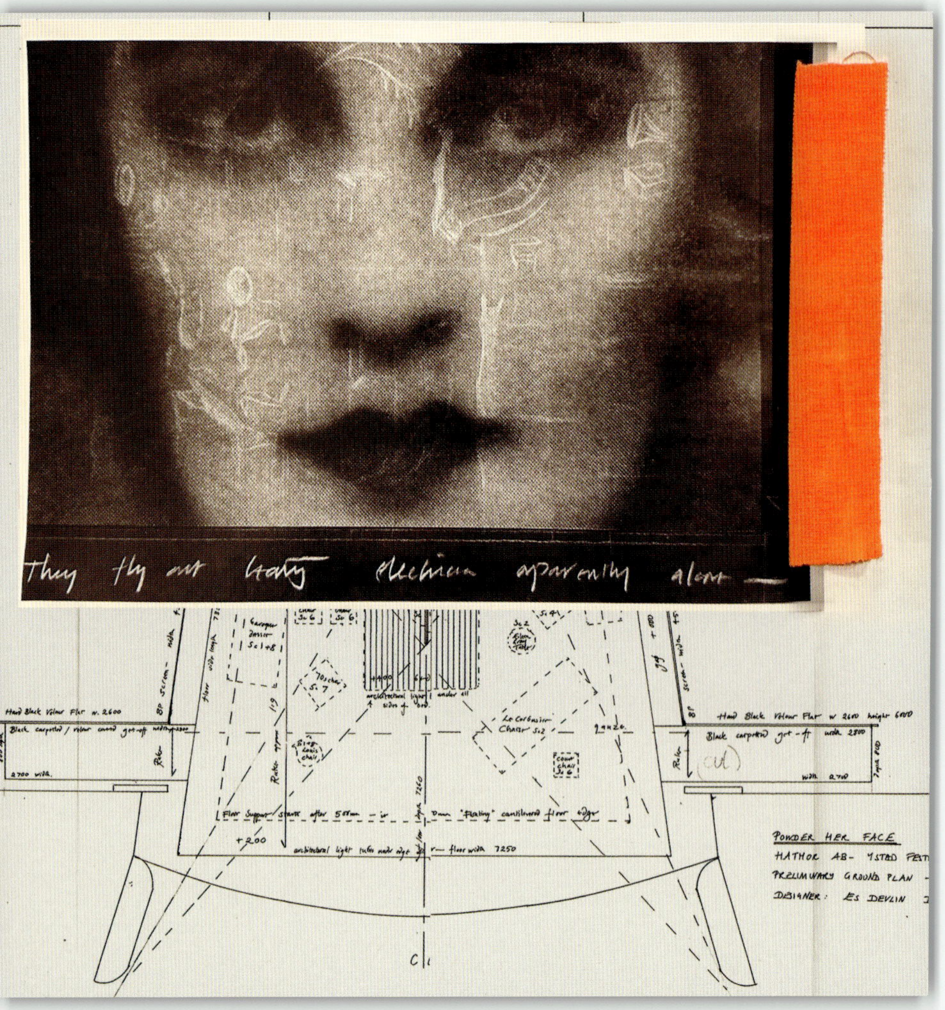
POWDER HER FACE
HATHOR AB- YSTAD FEST
PRELIMINARY GROUND PLAN -
DESIGNER: ES DEVLIN

POWDER HER FACE

... I do increasingly believe ... that there's a right version of the piece, a sort of master that exists outside of me somewhere ... It is almost like trying to be a radio receiver, though nobody is broadcasting this thing.

Thomas Adès

Performed at the small seaside opera festival at Ystad, Sweden, in July 1999, Thomas Adès's opera recounts the very public humiliation of Margaret, Duchess of Argyll. Her downfall was facilitated by explicit photographs she took in 1950 using the recently invented Polaroid camera. I zoomed into her face, treating it as a mask. I'd been moved by the power of large-scale projections I'd seen in the Bill Viola retrospective at the Whitney Museum in New York, but projectors were beyond the technical scope of the small nineteenth-century theatre, so I filled the proscenium with a painted reproduction of the photographic close-up. The entire opera took place through the lens of the painted face, objects and furniture flowing through the scenes as they had in *Betrayal*, but this time via the vertical axis of the theatre's flying system.

Like many theatre directors, Robert Chevara is highly attuned to shifts in atmosphere. When we met up the following year, I mentioned in passing that I'd started seeing the costume designer Jack Galloway. Robert gave me a quizzical look and said: 'I give it six weeks.' Sure enough a few weeks later he was helping me carry my suitcases into Jack's apartment as a new chapter in my life began.

790–791

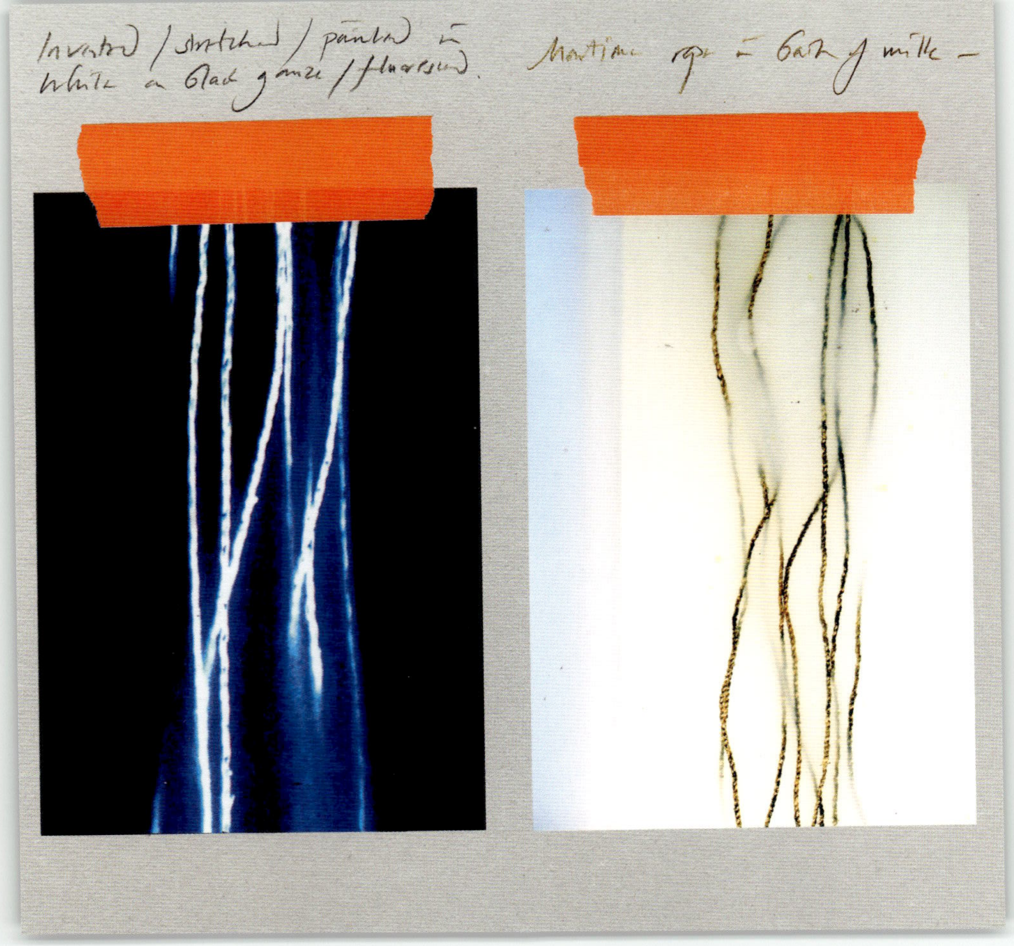
Inverted / stretched / painted in
white on black gauze / fluorescent.
Maritime rope in bath of milk –

I REMEMBER RED

The artist tries to show reason in experience and appearance – and lyric is the daily appearance, the commonplace dress, of reason. It shows us the rational. It makes the epic pattern human. It's the footprint on the pathway. In the epic-lyric the individual and particular are no longer isolated but are placed in a historical, social, human pattern. That's why there's a political way of cutting bread or wearing shoes.

Edward Bond, *The Activists Papers*

I met the choreographer Didy Veldman when she was performing with Rambert Dance Company in *Four Scenes*. We made a new work at Dansens Hus in Stockholm with Cullberg Ballet in November 2002, continuing to explore the relationship between a horizontal line of light and the kinetic text of dancers' bodies. We used translucent layers of gauzes and fluorescence, inverting photographs of rope strands suspended in a bath of milky water. We built two poles with fluorescent red-orange tops, which seemed to float amid the fluorescing waves like lifebuoys. I first used this luminous red-orange in a hypothetical student project on Edward Bond's drama, *Saved*. This was the first time I used it in action. The colour sang vividly against the dark Swedish winter afternoons. It seemed to me the colour of emergency.

Geo-political repercussions were playing out with ever-increasing urgency throughout 2002. Like most people, I can remember where I watched the 9/11 attacks unfold: hunched over a small TV at the Arts Theatre in Soho with the stage door manager and a bicycle courier, hands over our mouths in silence.

ESSENCE

Turning and turning in the widening gyre
The falcon cannot hear the falconer;
Things fall apart; the centre cannot hold;
Mere anarchy is loosed upon the world

W. B. Yeats, 'The Second Coming'

The choreographer Fin Walker and composer Ben Park created music and movement in response to 'The Second Coming' by W. B. Yeats, in preparation for performances at the Linbury Studio at the Royal Opera House in March 2005. The word 'choreography' literally means to draw or write with bodies. It fuses *chorus*, originally referring to a dancing group, and *graph*, originally meaning to describe in lines, to scratch lines in stone. Audiences are used to switching between two modes of reading in an opera house, shifting their focus between the suspended surtitle texts and the drama and song beneath them. In *The Spell of the Sensuous*, the geo-philosopher David Abram describes the evolution of the phonetic alphabet as a cognitive turning point, an unmooring of human language from its earthly points of reference. I wanted to encourage an audience to fuse their reading of bodies, light and text.

A horizontal line of musicians was seen and heard through translucent gauze; vertical and horizontal light lines moved through programmed sequences, converging and diverging to form and deform Yeats's phrases as the dancers moved between the layers, wearing silver costumes designed by Jack Galloway.

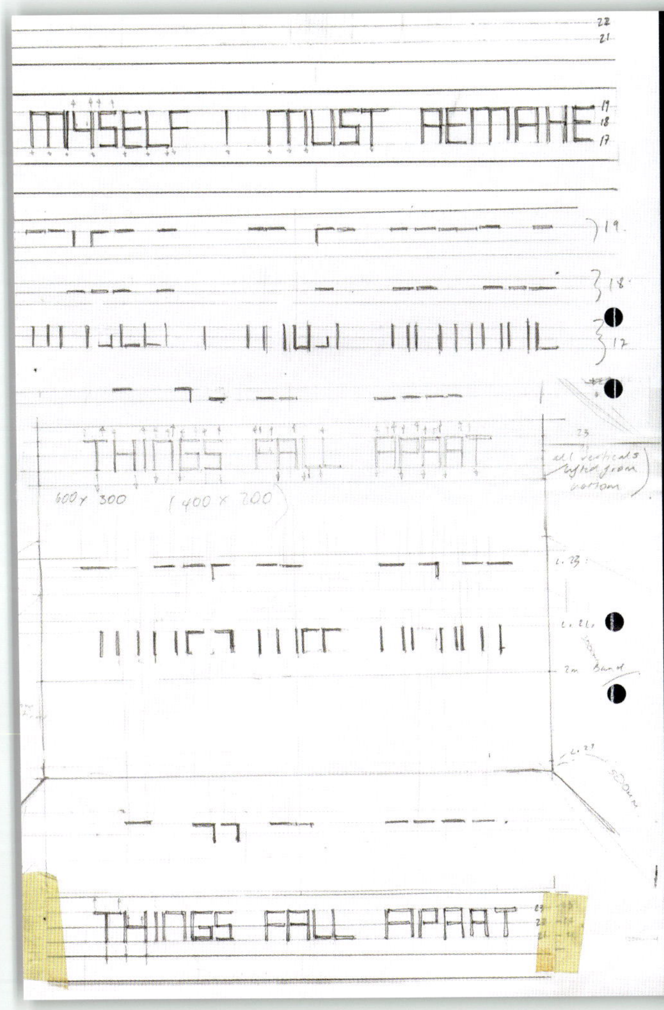

Canterbury Tales

ase. I took
ne to Ystad,
her Bruce's
n in September
s, torches and
eak I would find
er conceived *The*
ries within stories,
from fourteenth-
Cathedral from

onstantly shifting
be carefully
e wearing and
be fabricated
for. We often find
f coloured light

ESSENCE

Turning and turning in
The falcon cannot hea
Things fall apart; the c
Mere anarchy is loose

The choreographer Fi
and movement in resp
preparation for perfor
House in March 2005
or write with bodies. I
group, and *graph*, orig
lines in stone. Audien
reading in an opera h
surtitle texts and the
Sensuous, the geo-ph
of the phonetic alphab
of human language fr
encourage an audien

A horizontal line of m
gauze; vertical and h
sequences, convergi
phrases as the dance
costumes designed b

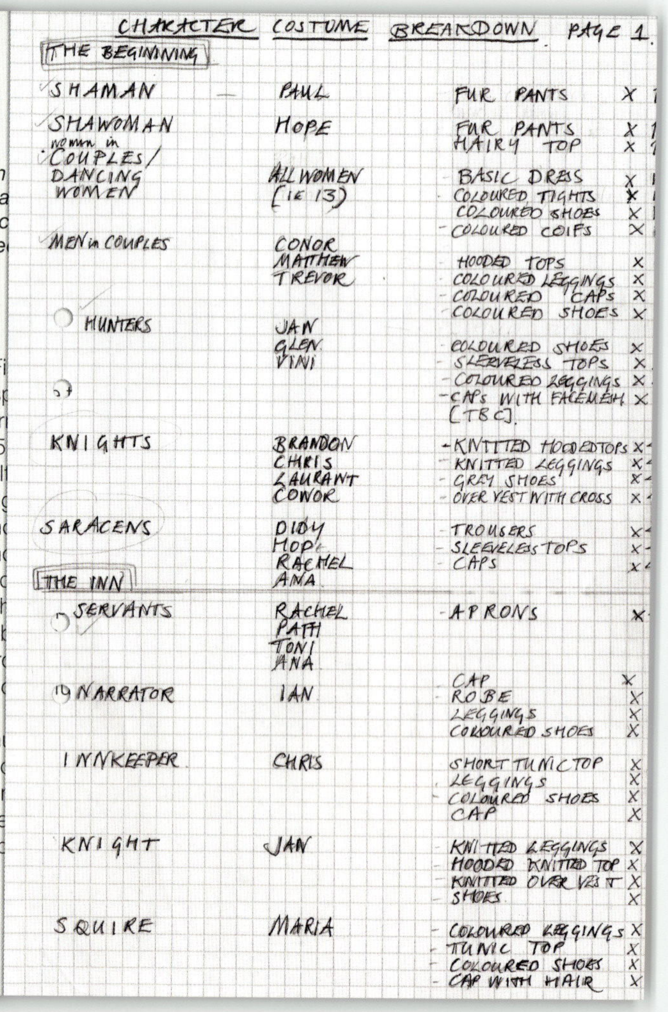

CHARACTER COSTUME BREAKDOWN PAGE 1.

THE BEGINNING

SHAMAN	PAUL	FUR PANTS	X
SHAWOMAN	HOPE	FUR PANTS	X
		HAIRY TOP	X
women in COUPLES/ DANCING WOMEN	ALL WOMEN (IE 13)	BASIC DRESS	X
		COLOURED TIGHTS	X
		COLOURED SHOES	X
		COLOURED COIFS	X
MEN in COUPLES	CONOR, MATTHEW, TREVOR	HOODED TOPS	X
		COLOURED LEGGINGS	X
		COLOURED CAPS	X
		COLOURED SHOES	X
HUNTERS	JAN, GLEN, VINI	COLOURED SHOES	X
		SLEEVELESS TOPS	X
		COLOURED LEGGINGS	X
		CAPS WITH FACEMESH [TBC]	X
KNIGHTS	BRANDON, CHRIS, LAURANT, CONOR	KNITTED HOODEDTOPS	X
		KNITTED LEGGINGS	X
		GREY SHOES	X
		OVER VEST WITH CROSS	X
SARACENS	DIDY, HOPE, RACHEL, ANA	TROUSERS	X
		SLEEVELESS TOPS	X
		CAPS	X

THE INN

SERVANTS	RACHEL, PATH, TONI, ANA	APRONS	X
NARRATOR	IAN	CAP	X
		ROBE	X
		LEGGINGS	X
		COLOURED SHOES	X
INNKEEPER	CHRIS	SHORT TUNIC TOP	X
		LEGGINGS	X
		COLOURED SHOES	X
		CAP	X
KNIGHT	JAN	KNITTED LEGGINGS	X
		HOODED KNITTED TOP	X
		KNITTED OVER VEST	X
		SHOES	X
SQUIRE	MARIA	COLOURED LEGGINGS	X
		TUNIC TOP	X
		COLOURED SHOES	X
		CAP WITH HAIR	X

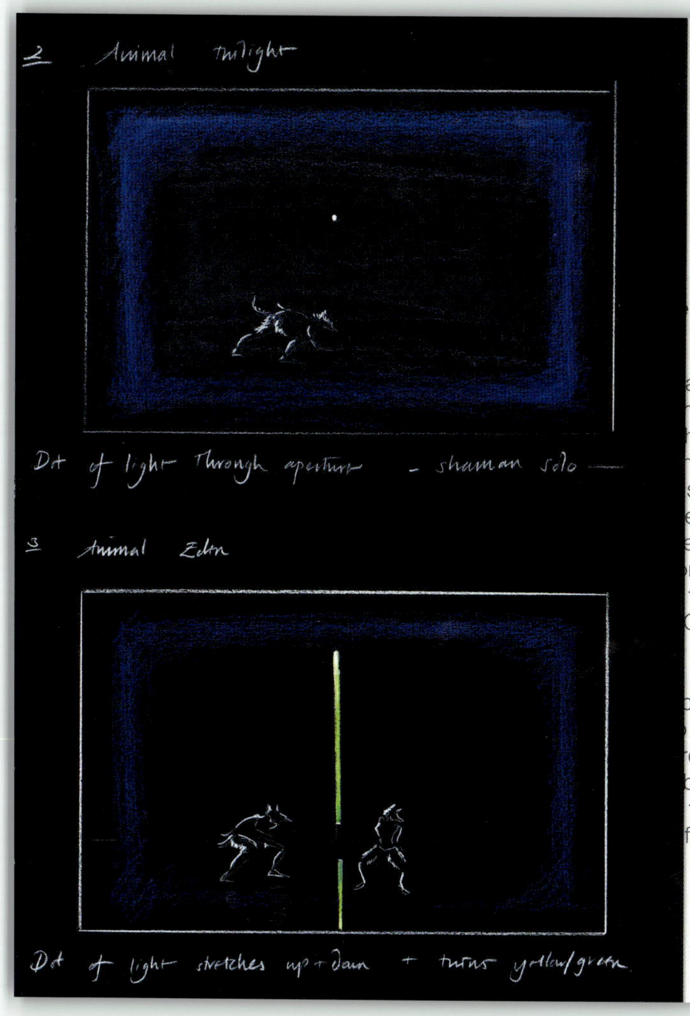

e Canterbury Tales

ase. I took
ne to Ystad,
her Bruce's
n in September
s, torches and
eak I would find
er conceived *The*
ries within stories,
from fourteenth-
Cathedral from

onstantly shifting
be carefully
re wearing and
be fabricated
for. We often find
f coloured light

ESSENC

Turning and turning
The falcon cannot h
Things fall apart; th
Mere anarchy is loo

The choreographe
and movement in r
preparation for per
House in March 20
or write with bodie
group, and *graph*,
lines in stone. Audi
reading in an opera
surtitle texts and th
Sensuous, the geo
of the phonetic alp
of human language
encourage an audi

A horizontal line of
gauze; vertical and
sequences, conve
phrases as the da
costumes designe

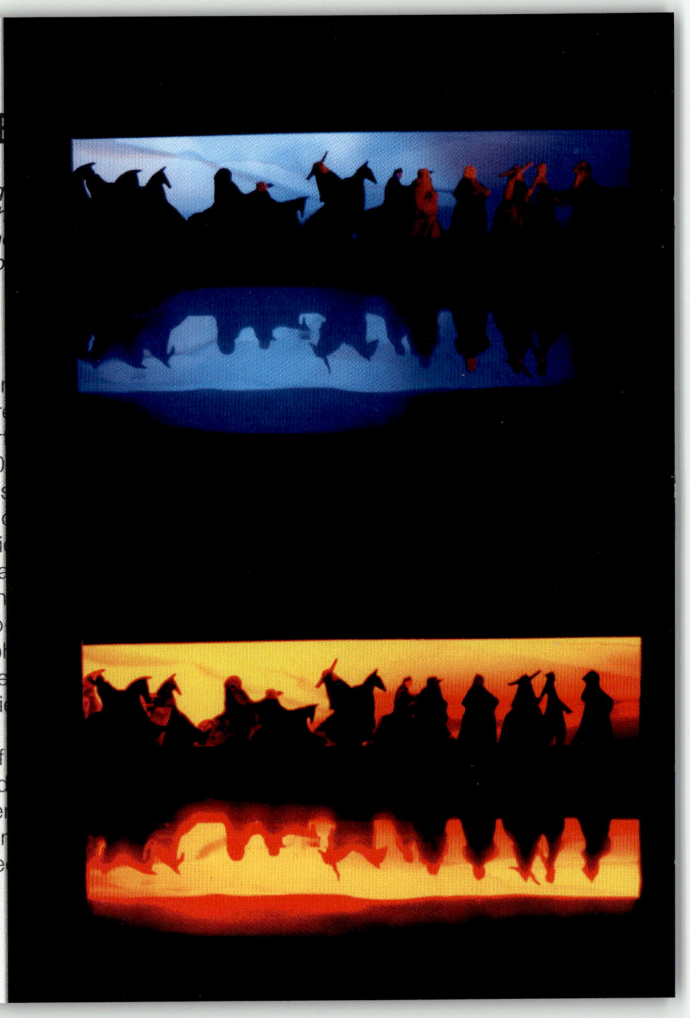

GOD'S PLENTY

When in April the sweet showers fall
And pierce the drought of March to the root, and all
The veins are bathed in liquor of such power
As brings about the engendering of the flower

Geoffrey Chaucer, *The Canterbury Tales*

The studio often had to be portable; a studio in a suitcase. I took a flatpack scale model of Sadler's Wells Theatre with me to Ystad, Sweden, to work on ideas for choreographer Christopher Bruce's exploration of *The Canterbury Tales*, which would open in September 1999. The suitcase was full of coloured translucent gels, torches and black card, and every time the opera singers took a break I would find a dark room, open up the case and start work. Chaucer conceived *The Canterbury Tales* as a series of portable narratives, stories within stories, told through multiple perspectives by pilgrim narrators from fourteenth-century society as they made their way to Canterbury Cathedral from the Tabard Inn in Southwark.

We created layers of coloured blocks of light within constantly shifting frames. Budgets for dance productions often need to be carefully balanced between the cost of what the performers are wearing and the cost of the space that frames them. Nothing can be fabricated until the price of every last shoe has been accounted for. We often find ourselves calibrating the cost of tights and the tone of coloured light within a single conversation.

630 632 634

FLAG : BURNING

In 2002 I had been given a Nokia 7650 – the first phone with a camera – to review for a magazine. The phone was also given to architect David Adjaye, *Wallpaper** magazine editor Tyler Brûlé and others. None of us grasped the revolution that camera phones would start. However, this first encounter tangentially led to a transformation within my practice, as the article was seen by the manager of the art punk band Wire and Alex Poots, director of the Only Connect festival at the Barbican, who invited me to design Wire's farewell performance in April 2003. I suggested we disrupt the habitual eight-legged, hump-backed silhouette of a four-piece band. The band members were open to being presented as a composite entity, using close-up photography of each element of their faces and ECG readings of their collective heartbeat. The four frames presented a combined portrait or mask.

Until this point, I had worked within theatres and opera houses, supported by the infrastructure of skilled stage managers who create technical cue sheets to orchestrate lighting and video. There was no such system in place here, just a band playing very loudly in the Barbican Hall with a lighting designer and a video operator awaiting instruction. So I made an illustrated cue sheet with timings, and the show went more or less to plan, although I hadn't considered how the band would leave their boxes at the end of the show. Velcro was beyond the scope of the very tight budget, so I had stapled the gauze covers onto the cubes once the four men were inside.

644–647

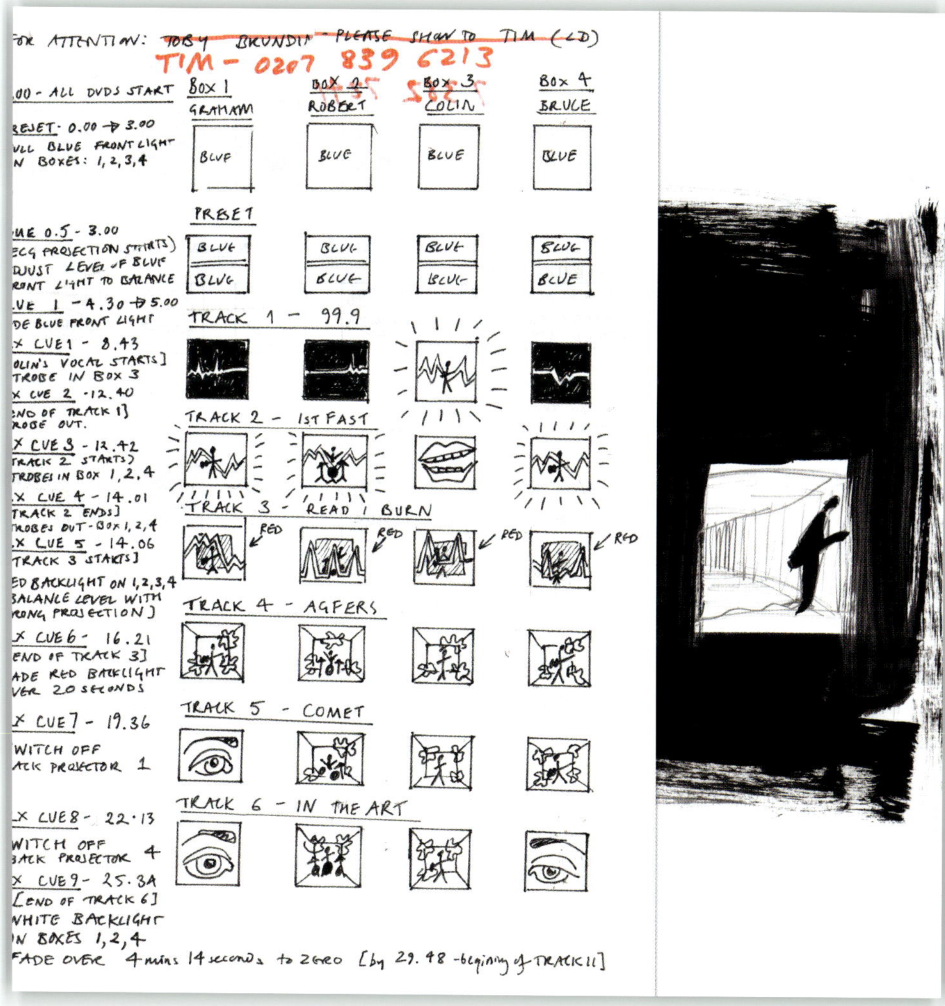
FOR ATTENTION: TOBY BRUNDIN - PLEASE SHOW TO TIM (LD)
TIM - 0207 839 6213
.00 - ALL DVDS START
BOX 1
GRAHAM
BOX 2
ROBERT
BOX 3
COLIN
BOX 4
BRUCE
RESET · 0.00 → 3.00
ULL BLUE FRONT LIGHT
N BOXES: 1, 2, 3, 4
BLUE
PRESET
UE 0.5 - 3.00
ECG PROJECTION STARTS)
DJUST LEVEL OF BLUE
RONT LIGHT TO BALANCE
UE 1 - 4.30 → 5.00
DE BLUE FRONT LIGHT
X CUE 1 - 8.43
OLIN'S VOCAL STARTS]
TROBE IN BOX 3
X CUE 2 - 12.40
END OF TRACK 1]
ROBE OUT.
X CUE 3 - 12.42
TRACK 2 STARTS)
TROBES IN BOX 1, 2, 4
X CUE 4 - 14.01
TRACK 2 ENDS]
TROBES OUT - BOX 1, 2, 4
X CUE 5 - 14.06
TRACK 3 STARTS]
ED BACKLIGHT ON 1, 2, 3, 4
BALANCE LEVEL WITH
RONG PROJECTION]
X CUE 6 - 16.21
END OF TRACK 3]
ADE RED BACKLIGHT
VER 20 SECONDS
X CUE 7 - 19.36
WITCH OFF
ACK PROJECTOR 1
X CUE 8 - 22·13
WITCH OFF
BACK PROJECTOR 4
X CUE 9 - 25·3A
[END OF TRACK 6]
WHITE BACKLIGHT
IN BOXES 1, 2, 4
FADE OVER 4 mins 14 seconds to ZERO [by 29. 48 - begining of TRACK 11]
TRACK 1 - 99.9
TRACK 2 - 1ST FAST
TRACK 3 - READ / BURN
RED
TRACK 4 - AGFERS
TRACK 5 - COMET
TRACK 6 - IN THE ART

FLAG : BU

In 2002 I had been g
camera – to review fo
architect David Adjay
others. None of us g
start. However, this f
within my practice, a
art punk band Wire a
festival at the Barbica
performance in April
eight-legged, hump-
band members were
using close-up photo
readings of their colle
combined portrait or

Until this point, I had
supported by the infr
technical cue sheets
no such system in pl
Barbican Hall with a
instruction. So I mad
show went more or l
the band would leave
was beyond the scop
gauze covers onto th

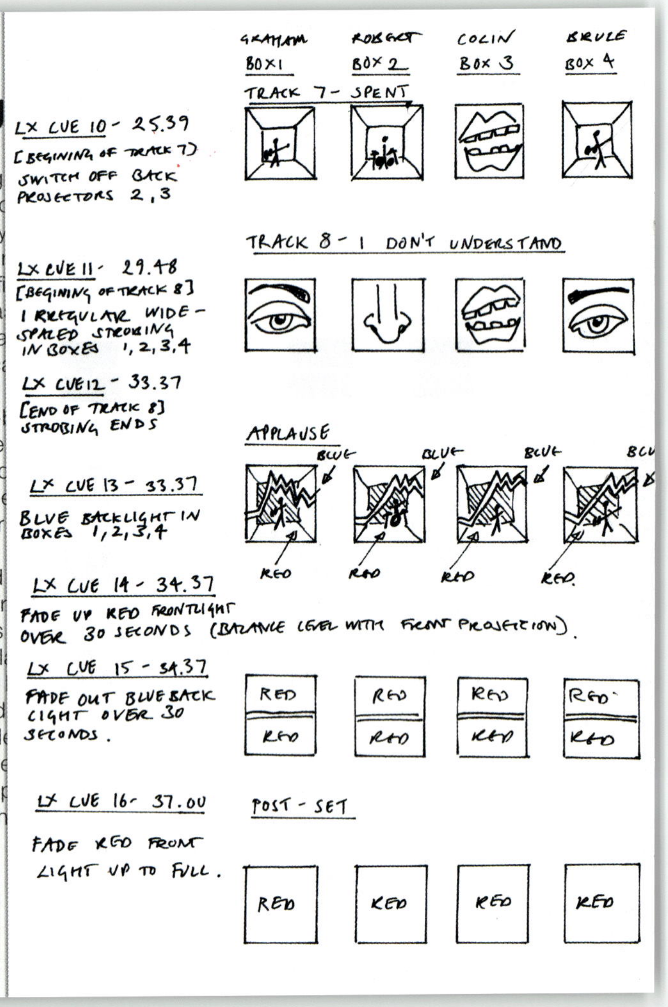

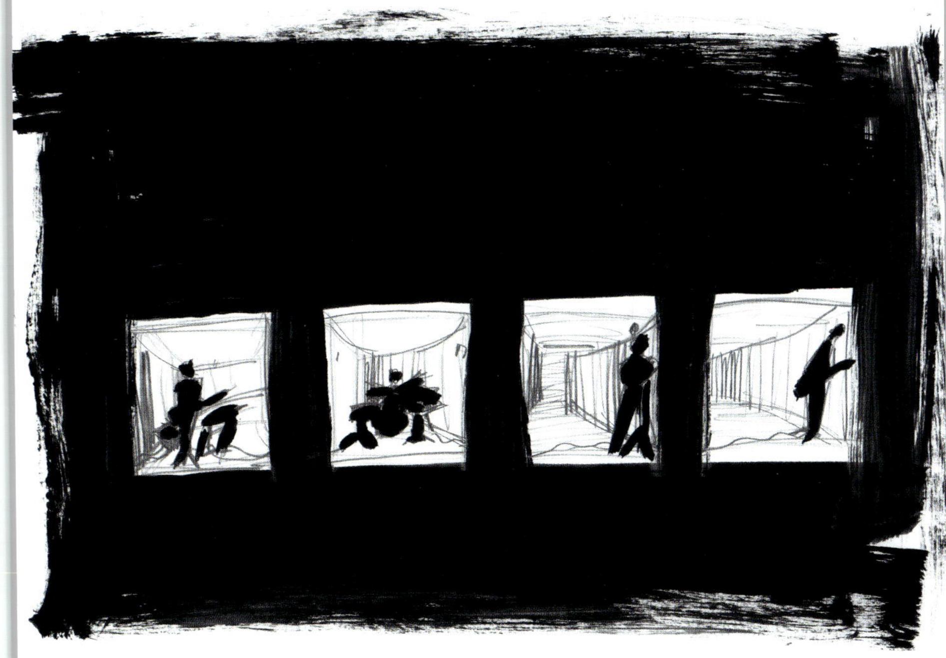

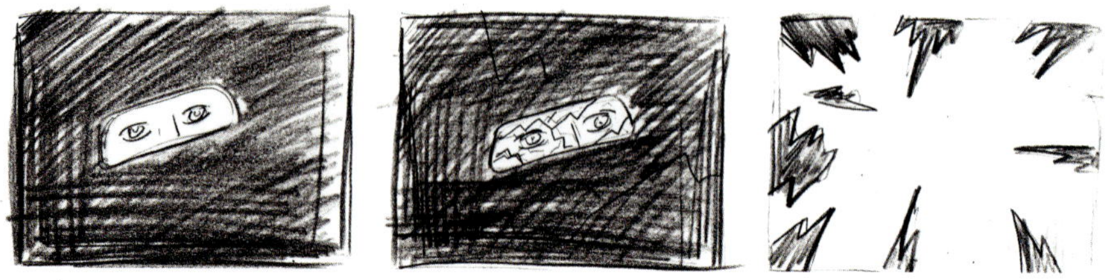

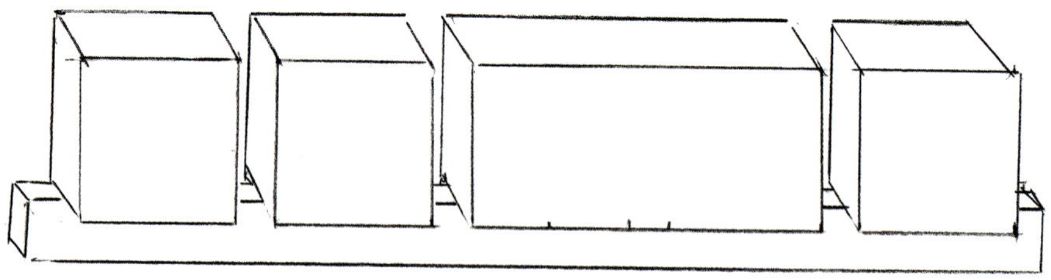

TOUCH THE SKY

Hey, Mama, you know I love you so, I never let you go
Wrote this song just so you know, no matter where you go my love is true

Kanye West, 'Hey Mama'

In late September 2005, I was having a birthday dinner with some friends when I received a phone call from Kanye West, who was looking for a new set designer for his tour opening in ten days. We agreed that I should start that evening, so I finished my tsatsiki, apologized to my friends, and headed to Heathrow. I filled two suitcases full of books so that we would be able to establish a frame of visual reference. I brought Ruth Berghaus, Achim Freyer, Erich Wonder and James Turrell, and took them to Kanye's hotel room in New York. I'd studied his lyrics on the plane. There were only two albums at this point, so it was quite manageable to read every line during a transatlantic crossing. On 11 October, the *Touch the Sky* tour opened at the University of Miami Convocation Center. A series of translucent boxes contained the band and an orchestra, seen only intermittently in shadows. The film projections were created during the final rehearsals. I asked Kanye's mum, Donda, who was his manager at the time, for old family photos. I went into the carpark with a video recorder and filmed car headlights flashing. I asked a local Miami hospital for images of a jaw wired up as Kanye's had been a few years earlier following a car crash. I remember sitting with Kanye on our own in the middle of the night with an operator programming the lights, and wandering the corridors of the empty arena looking for something to eat.

648–649

A MIDSUMMER NIGHT'S DREAM

Love looks not with the eyes, but with the mind,
And therefore is winged Cupid painted blind.

William Shakespeare

I researched the mechanics of dreaming and overlaid the stages of rapid eye movement onto Benjamin Britten's opera score for the 2006 Staatsoper Hamburg production of *A Midsummer Night's Dream*. Britten grafts a meditation on art, freedom and society onto Shakespeare's scheme of lovers, workers and spirits. I had experienced the idea of malleable neural architecture while reading Jonathan D. Spence's book *The Memory Palace of Matteo Ricci* in 1986 and watching Michel Gondry's film *Eternal Sunshine of the Spotless Mind* in 2004. We rendered the forest in which the lovers lose and ultimately find themselves as a disrupted arrangement of the oppressive domestic architecture from which they were trying to escape. Remembering Magritte's painting *La Carte Blanche*, in which layered slices of trees play tricks of perspective, we suspended the broken domestic elements on vertical cables that slid in layers across the stage as Oberon and Puck shift perspectives around the lovers lost in the forest. They scheme in sinuous music to alter the architecture of Titania's mind with orchid roots. These organic forms found their way into the ass's head that roots itself to the shoulders of Bottom, the weaver.

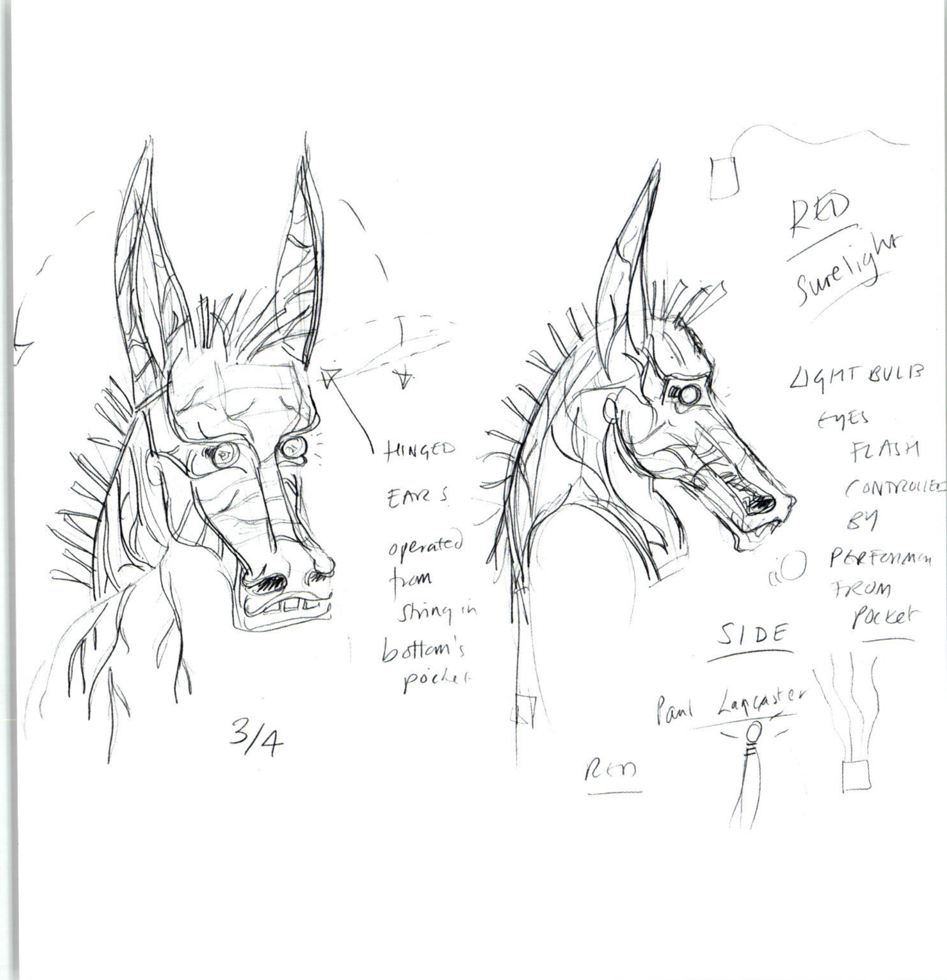
3/4
HINGED EARS operated from string in bottom's pocket
RED
Surelight
LIGHT BULB EYES FLASH CONTROLLED BY PERFORMER FROM Pocket
SIDE
Paul Lancaster
RED

MACBETH

To-morrow, and to-morrow, and to-morrow,
Creeps in this petty pace from day to day,
To the last syllable of recorded time

William Shakespeare

While preparing for the June 2003 production of Ernest Bloch's opera of *Macbeth* at Theater an der Wien in Vienna, I saw a petrified arterial system within a human hand at the *Body Worlds* exhibition in London, and read James Gleick's book *Chaos*. Gleick's revelation – that the bifurcations of human arteries are determined by the same maths as the bifurcating geometry of trees – intoxicated the early iterations of the design. This visual language linked Lady Macbeth's bloody hand and the trees of Birnam Wood, the final protagonists in the drama.

In close collaboration with the director Keith Warner, the design evolved into a rotating black perspective box. The revolutions framed Macbeth's churning conscience, conjuring scenes through smoke and mirrors. In the end, the box split to reveal an infinite Birnam Wood between two planes of mirror – a forest formed of people.

642–643

ROLOGUE

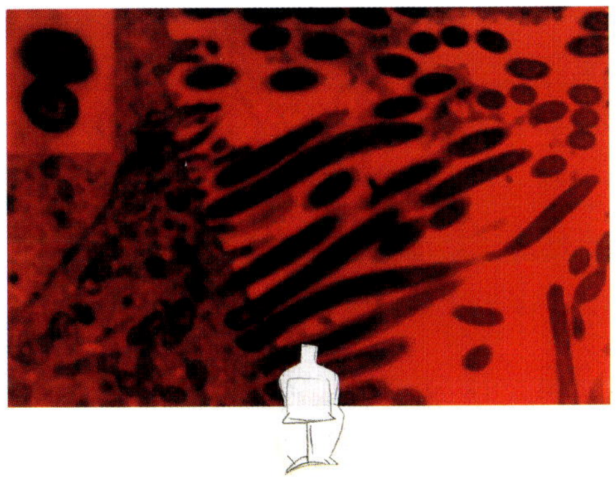

cells within arteries zooms out to . . . .

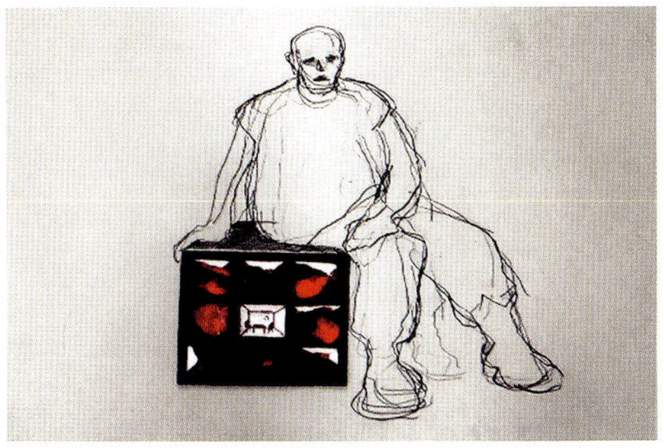

– All rooms full of bodies except central one – empty with ticking clock "Tomorrow and tomorrow and tomorrow creeps in this petty pace . . to the last syllable of recorded time"

l by Tony Harrison

of Iraq, a number
utility of war.
essa Redgrave
re Company's

sign a set for
horus clawed at
nts of their hands
dy Center in
collaboration with
atre of recently
nphitheatre at
ped levels using
shington and
r folds.

MACBET

To-morrow, and to-
Creeps in this petty
To the last syllable

While preparing for
of *Macbeth* at Thea
system within a hu
and read James G
bifurcations of hum
the bifurcating geo
the design. This vis
and the trees of Bi

In close collaborati
into a rotating black
churning conscienc
the end, the box sp
planes of mirror – a

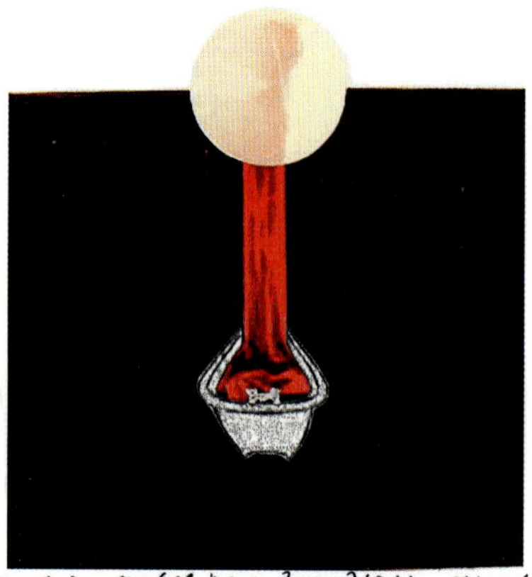

(27) Transition into Lady Macbeth "Out damned spot": Mirrors journey conc
mark + reveal Lady M in bath

III. Sc 2

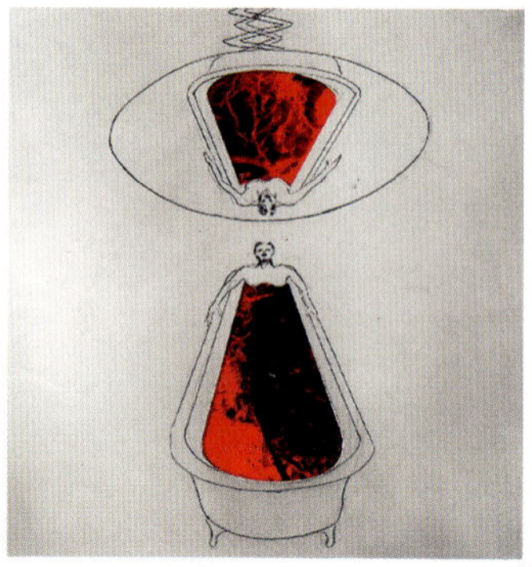

(28) "Yet here's a spot!" Lady M – still bloodsoaked clothed – can't get water – trying to wash in whatever the witches have chucked in.

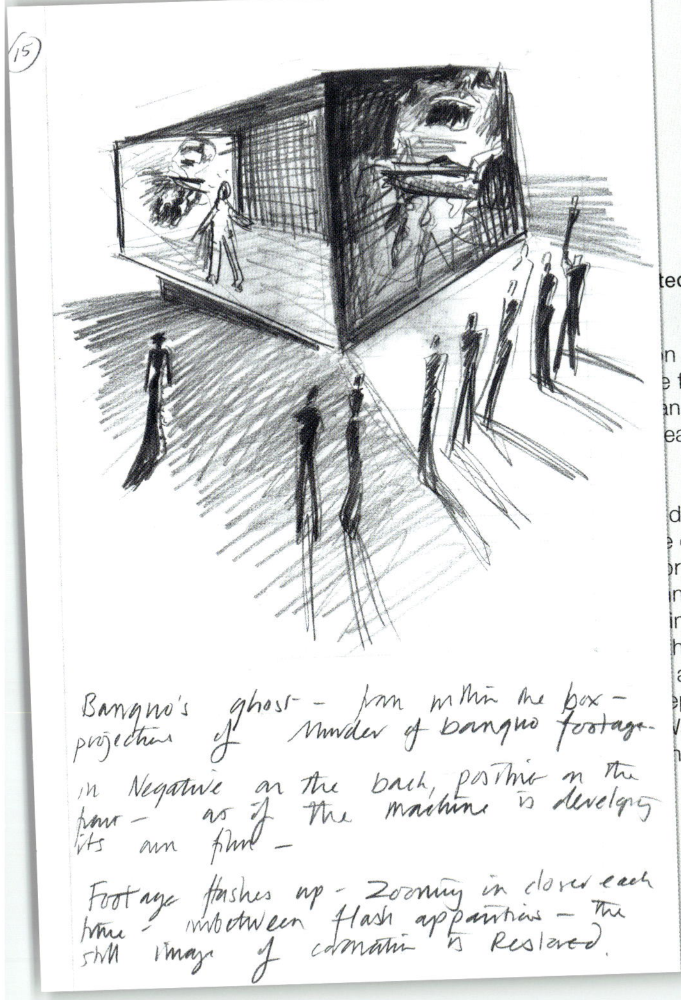

ted by Tony Harrison

n of Iraq, a number
e futility of war.
anessa Redgrave
eare Company's

design a set for
e chorus clawed at
prints of their hands
nedy Center in
in collaboration with
heatre of recently
amphitheatre at
epped levels using
Washington and
heir folds.

MACBET

To-morrow, and to-
Creeps in this petty
To the last syllable

While preparing fo
of *Macbeth* at The
system within a hu
and read James G
bifurcations of hum
the bifurcating geo
the design. This vi
and the trees of Bi

In close collaborati
into a rotating black
churning conscienc
the end, the box sp
planes of mirror – a

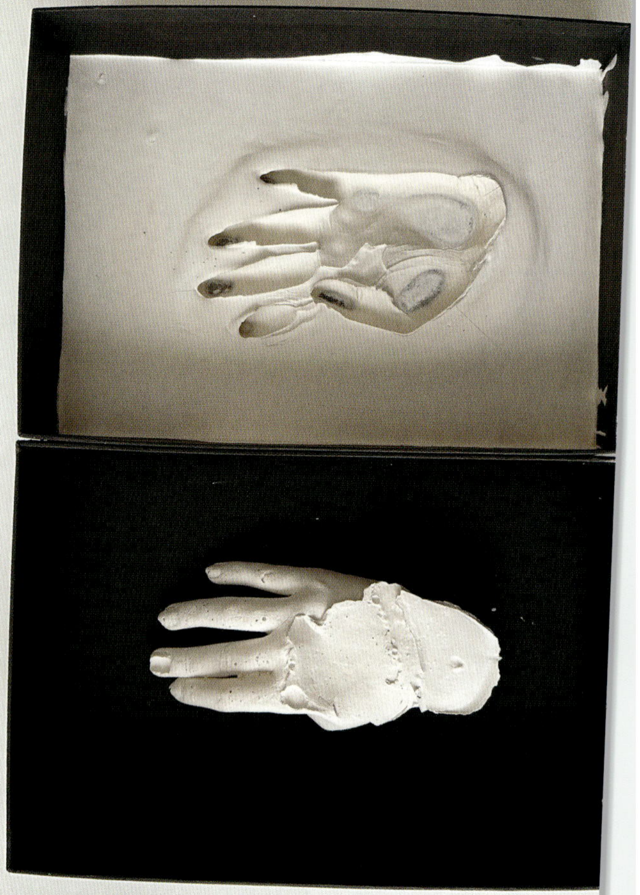

HECUBA

Earth, who gives birth
to dreams with black wings,
I refuse to believe
that night vision's true.

Euripides, translated by Tony Harrison

In the aftermath of the 2003 US- and UK-led invasion of Iraq, a number of theatres staged Euripides' tragic lesson on the futility of war. Having campaigned for peace and human rights, Vanessa Redgrave played the title role of Hecuba in the Royal Shakespeare Company's 2005 production in London.

The director, Laurence Boswell, said to me, 'Don't design a set for this play; create an altar.' At the Albery Theatre, the chorus clawed at cylindrical cardboard walls in grief, leaving clay imprints of their hands as they sang. When the play transferred to the Kennedy Center in Washington, DC, in May, I reconceived the design in collaboration with the poet Tony Harrison. We constructed an amphitheatre of recently used desert military tents. I had visited the ancient amphitheatre at Epidaurus the year before, and we recreated its stepped levels using tents that we bought from army surplus shops in Washington and Virginia. Some of them still held traces of sand in their folds.

FUNDAMENTAL

You're my nation / This is my application
Give me hope / Keep me sane
Give me / indefinite leave to remain

Pet Shop Boys, 'Indefinite Leave to Remain'

The neuropsychologist Paul Broks had invited me to observe a Wada test while collaborating on the dramatization of his book *Into the Silent Land* for Soho Theatre in 2005. During a cerebral angiogram, neurologists carried out language and memory tests on each half of the brain while the other half was anaesthetized. We watched black ink penetrating half the labyrinth of the brain. The X-ray image of the divided brain recurred to me while designing the Pet Shop Boys' *Fundamental* tour which would open in Norway in June 2006. For me it evoked the creative symbiosis between the two members of the band, and also, conversely, the cognitive dissonance each of us were feeling as our country remained deeply entangled in a war most of us didn't want. Neil Tennant and Chris Lowe were considered pop's most eloquent gazetteers of Thatcherism throughout the 1980s, and had initially been supportive of New Labour's arrival in 1997. But their 2006 album, *Fundamental*, now offered a blistering critique of Blair and Bush, the Iraq War, immigration policy, ID cards and the idea of an 'axis of evil'. The show was performed outside the Tower of London, complete with projected pink tanks for the anti-war extravaganza 'The Sodom and Gomorrah Show', and outsized sequinned cowboy hats for the lacerating Bush/Blair pantomime 'I'm with Stupid'.

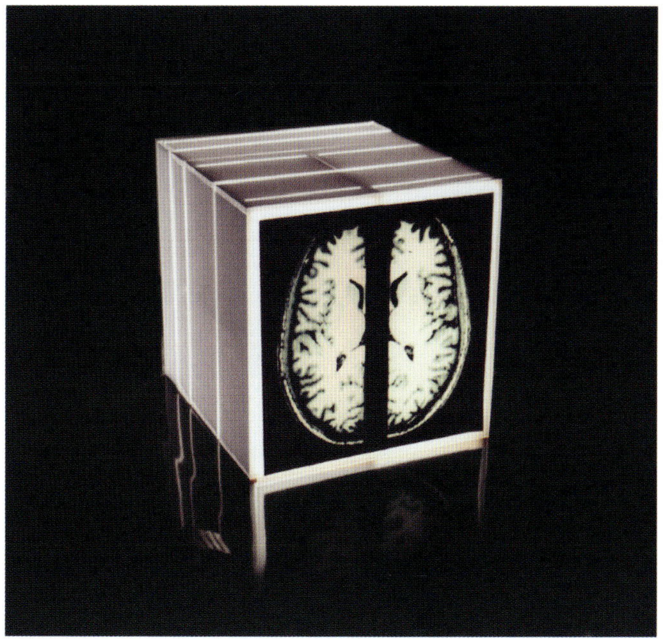

FUNDAMENTAL

You're my nation / This is my application
Give
Give

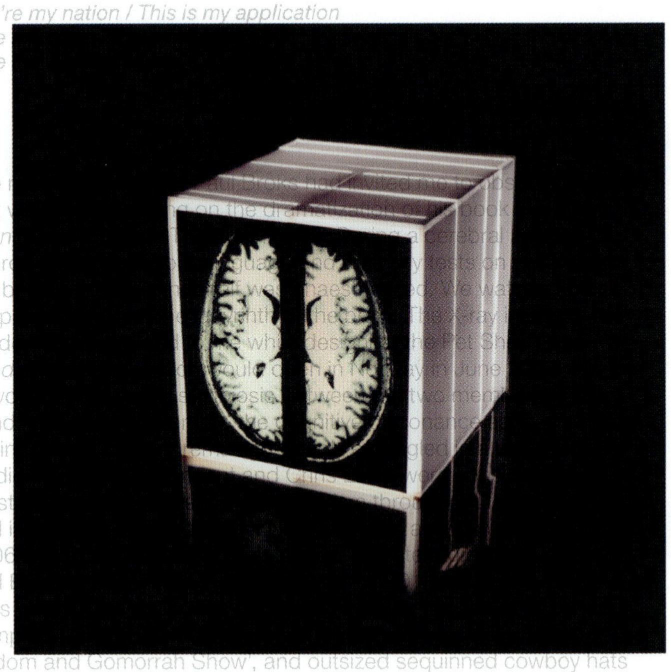

The
test
Silen
neuro
the b
ink p
divid
Fund
it evo
band
feelin
us di
most
had i
2006
and
'axis
comp
Sodom and Gomorrah Show', and outsized sequinned cowboy hats for the lacerating Bush/Blair pantomime 'I'm with Stupid'.

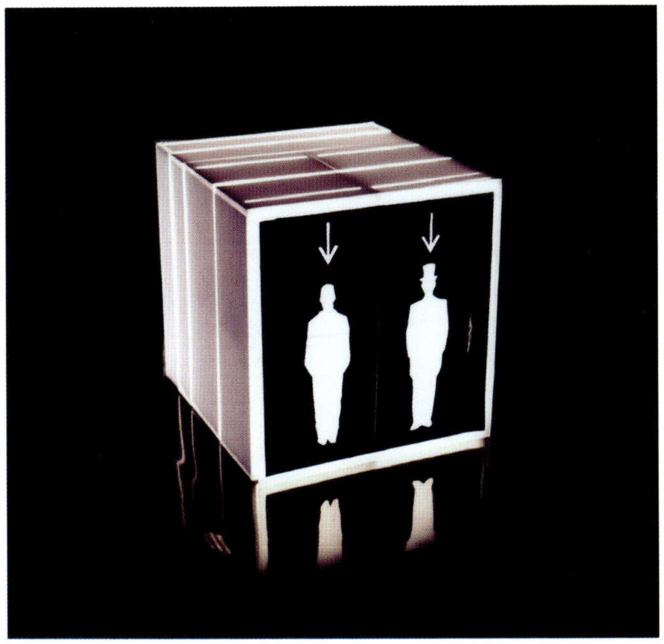

LA CLEMENZA DI TITO

Let my friend live, though he is faithless.
And if the world wants to accuse me of some failing,
let it accuse me of mercy.

Caterino Tommaso Mazzolà, after Pietro Metastasio

I had collaborated with the opera director Francisco Negrin on the Philip Glass/Jean Cocteau opera *Orphée* in 2005 at the Linbury Studio at the Royal Opera House. In preparation, we watched Cocteau's 1950 film in which horizontal water appears to be vertical glass mirror until the illusion is broken by the touch of actor Jean Marais's hand. Francisco and I continued to explore shifts between vertical and horizontal perspectives in the production of *La Clemenza di Tito* at El Liceu, Barcelona, in September 2006. Mozart wrote this *opera seria* in 1791 during the final months of his life. Commissioned for the coronation of Leopold II, the opera examines the possibility of empathy and compassion within an absolute monarch. In our design, Roman architectural ground plans behave as vertical, hierarchical front elevations at the start of the work. By the final act, restored to the horizontal axis, the plans slowly extrude plant-filled glass walls, as empathy pervades the structures of power.

666 742–745

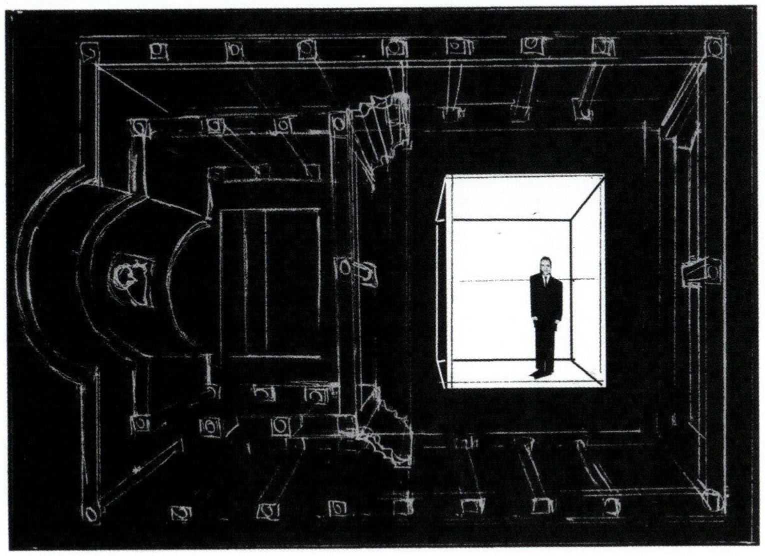

LA CLEMENZA DI TITO

Let my friend live, though he is faithless.
And if the world wants to accuse me of some failing,
let it accuse me of mercy.

Caterino Tommaso Mazzolà, after Pietro Metastasio

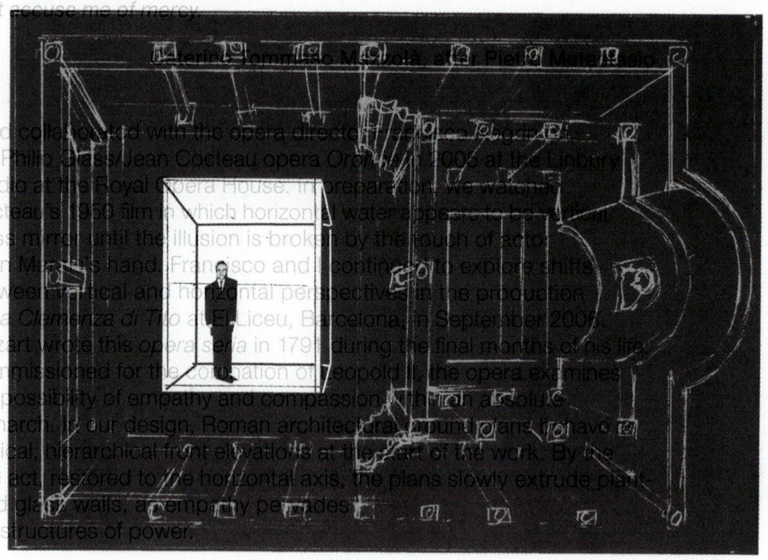

I had collaborated with the opera director Francisco Negrín on the Philip Glass/Jean Cocteau opera *Orphée* in 2005 at the Linbury Studio at the Royal Opera House. In preparation, we watched Cocteau's 1950 film in which horizontal water appears to be vertical glass mirror until the illusion is broken by the touch of actor Jean Marais's hand. Francisco and I continued to explore shifts between vertical and horizontal perspectives in the production of *La Clemenza di Tito* at El Liceu, Barcelona, in September 2005. Mozart wrote this *opera seria* in 1791 during the final months of his life. Commissioned for the coronation of Leopold II, the opera examines the possibility of empathy and compassion within an absolute monarch. In our design, Roman architectural ground plans behave as vertical, hierarchical front elevations at the start of the work. By the final act, restored to the horizontal axis, the plans slowly extrude plant-filled glass walls, as empathy pervades the structures of power.

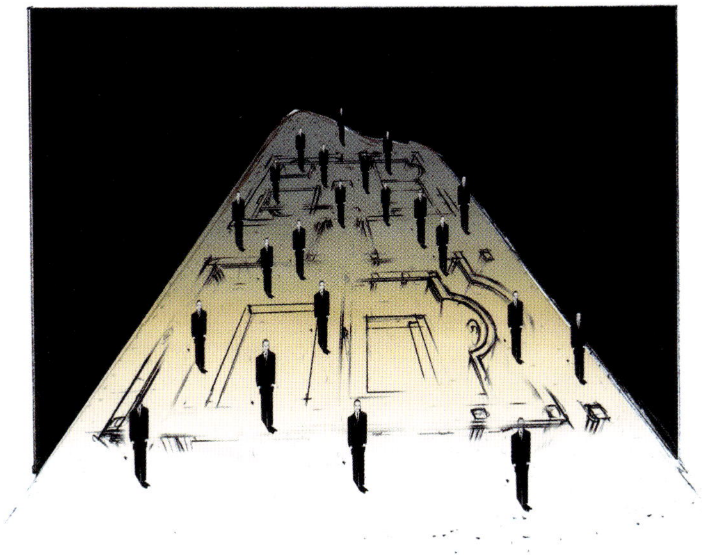

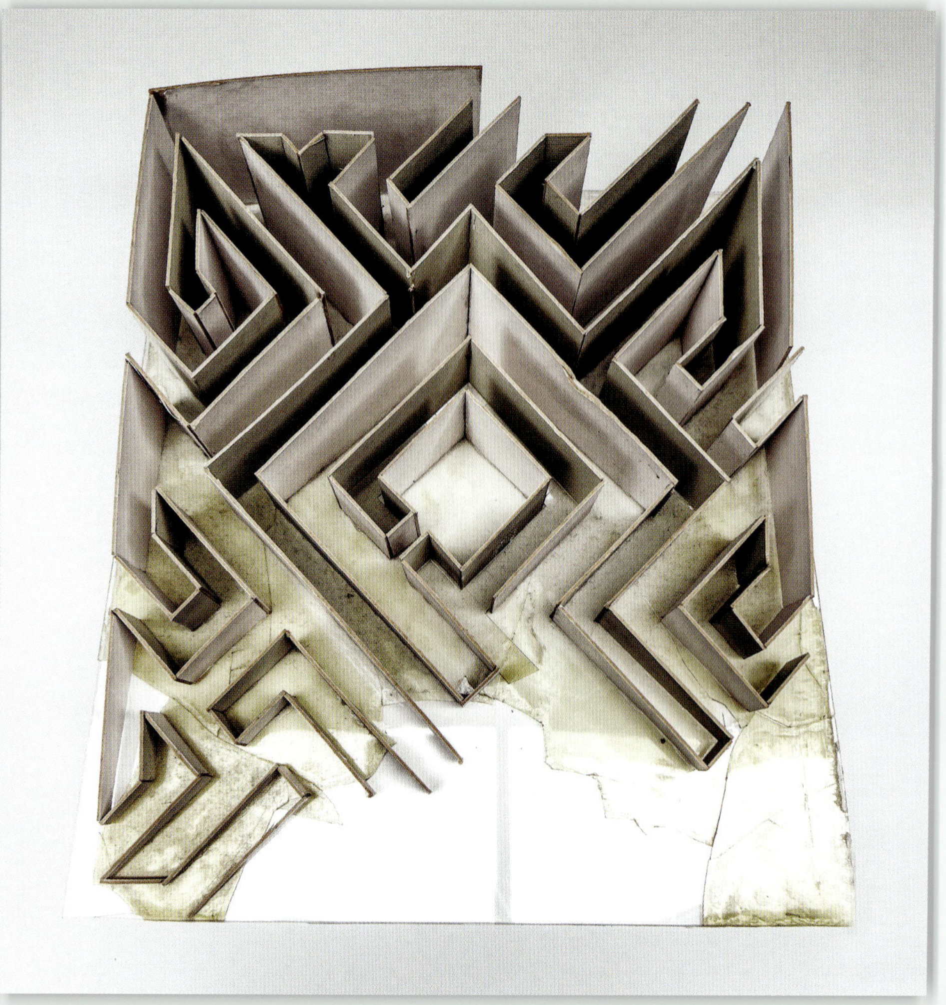

DON GIOVANNI

My head is whirling in confusion,
I no longer know what's happening.
A dreadful storm, oh Lord,
is thundering above me.

Lorenzo Da Ponte and Wolfgang Amadeus Mozart

Composed in 1787 on the eve of the French Revolution, Mozart's opera *Don Giovanni* explores conflicts between freedom and order, stability and chaos. For the Theater an der Wien production in July 2006, the director Keith Warner and I continued the experiments in kinetic architecture that we had begun on Bloch's *Macbeth* in 2003. We translated Don Giovanni's list of 1,003 lovers into a revolving, labyrinthine, neural network. We anticipated that corridors full of doors would serve the structure of the farce elements of the drama. A tilting mirror suspended above the labyrinth at the finale would offer the illusion of a gravity-defying release for the rest of the characters, while Don Giovanni remained trapped within. I had witnessed a similar illusion in 2003 when Québécois actor and director Robert Lepage appeared to float within a suspended mirror in *The Far Side of the Moon* at the Barbican.

My assistant Bronia and I stayed up for hours building the model – we didn't use computer modelling at the time. In the end, the labyrinth evolved into a series of simple hinged hotel corridors. The labour-intensive maze model remained on the shelf in the studio.

659

FLAMMEN

… around her, the air was sad, somehow. And behind the smile in her eyes, the Grief was a fresh, shining blue … Because of a Joe-shaped hole in the Universe.

Arundhati Roy, *The God of Small Things*

Erwin Schulhoff's opera *Flammen* is a 1932 reworking of the Don Juan legend from which *Don Giovanni* also originates. It was banned by the Nazis as *Entartete Kunst* (degenerate art). For the August 2006 Theater an der Wien production, I found newspapers of the period, copied them onto fabric, and used this to make the chorus costumes, walls and floor. The scenes took place around a series of apertures cut into the newspaper: a woman-shaped hole, a cross-shaped hole, a house-shaped hole. Arundhati Roy's 1997 description of a person-shaped hole in the universe remained lodged in my imagination.

I had been trying for three years to get pregnant. Just before arriving in Vienna, I had been told that my chances of conceiving were low. One evening after rehearsals I sat in the production office on a computer, researching adoption processes. A producer's boyfriend worked at the local IVF clinic. She phoned him and the next day I was on a train to the Hungarian border town of Sopron to buy low-cost IVF medication.

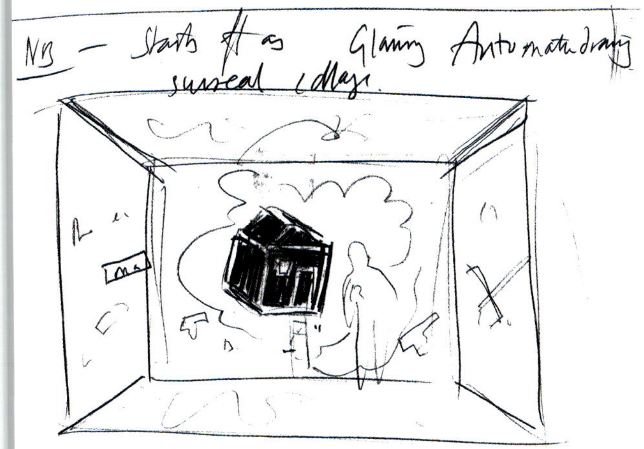

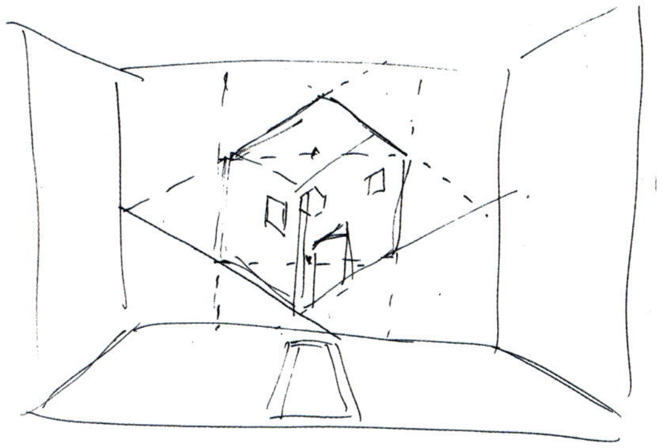

easure, while
ance

Georges Bizet

stage rehearsals for
era, *Carmen*, by
eeding and burping
the lead-up to the
We constructed
urveillance cameras,
tte factory worker,
ween Acts I and
n imprisoned in a
e. In 2007, Britain
led countries, with
people.

FLAMMEN

... around her, the air
eyes, the Grief was a f
in the Universe.

Erwin Schulhoff's ope
legend from which *D*
the Nazis as *Entartete*
Theater an der Wien
copied them onto fab
walls and floor. The s
cut into the newspap
a house-shaped hole
shaped hole in the u

I had been trying for
Vienna, I had been to
evening after rehears
researching adoption
local IVF clinic. She p
the Hungarian border

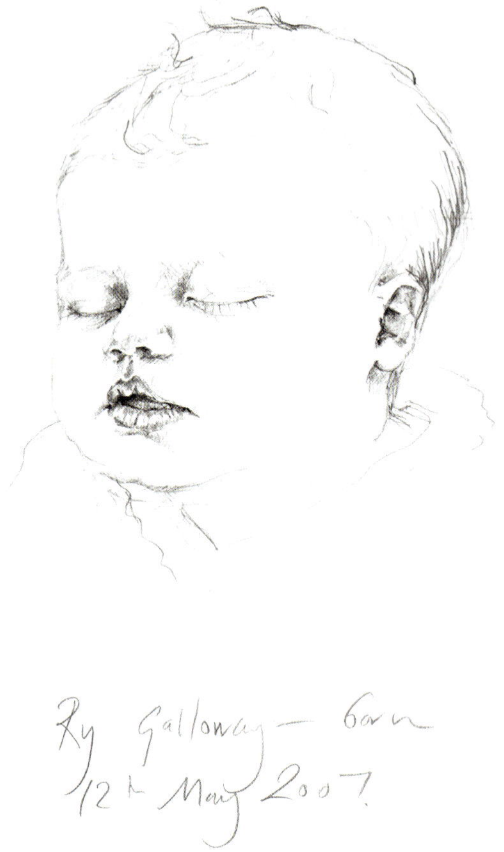

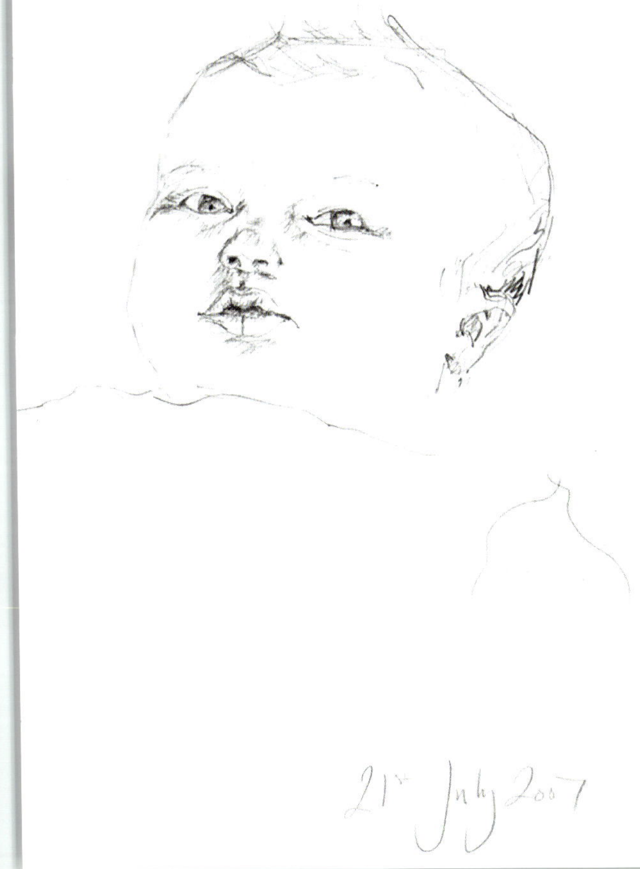

easure, while
ance

Georges Bizet

stage rehearsals for
era, *Carmen*, by
feeding and burping
the lead-up to the
We constructed
urveillance cameras,
tte factory worker,
ween Acts I and
n imprisoned in a
e. In 2007, Britain
led countries, with
people.

FLAMMEN

… around her, the air
eyes, the Grief was a f
in the Universe.

Erwin Schulhoff's ope
legend from which *Do*
the Nazis as *Entartete*
Theater an der Wien
copied them onto fab
walls and floor. The s
cut into the newspap
a house-shaped hole
shaped hole in the un

I had been trying for t
Vienna, I had been to
evening after rehears
researching adoption
local IVF clinic. She p
the Hungarian border

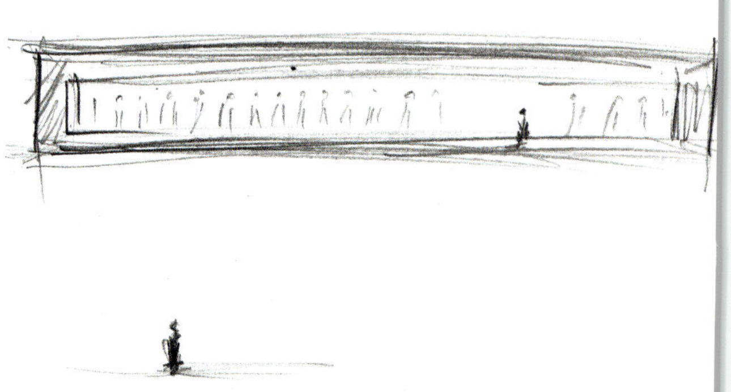

CARMEN

I have always read the ancient pagans with infinite pleasure, while in Christian writers I find only system, egoism, intolerance

Georges Bizet

My daughter Ry was five months old at the start of stage rehearsals for film director Sally Potter's production of the 1875 opera, *Carmen*, by Georges Bizet. I had a tiny, ornate room for breastfeeding and burping at the back of the stalls of the London Coliseum in the lead-up to the English National Opera premiere in October 2007. We constructed motorway overpasses and high walls topped with surveillance cameras, a military order to which Carmen, the gypsy cigarette factory worker, brought chromatic chaos. During the transition between Acts I and II, José, the soldier seduced by Carmen, was shown imprisoned in a small cell sliced within enlarged surveillance footage. In 2007, Britain was listed in the top ten of the world's most surveilled countries, with 4.2 million surveillance cameras – one for every 14 people.

640–641 672–673 762–763

SALOME

To live is the rarest thing in the world. Most people exist, that is all.

Oscar Wilde, 'The Soul of Man Under Socialism'

The director David McVicar introduced me to Pier Paolo Pasolini's 1975 film *Salò*. This visceral condemnation of fascism, consumerism, capitalism and corruption remains banned in several countries. The audience become passively complicit as they witness nauseating sequences that parallel a descent into Dante's *Inferno*. Similarly, Richard Strauss's opera of Oscar Wilde's drama, *Salome*, was banned in London until 1907. For the Royal Opera House production in February 2008, we constructed a basement environment in filthy, pale duck-eggshell blue-green, colour-matched to a scene from *Salò*. The Dance of the Seven Veils sequence became a descent through seven rooms. Each room accessed a disturbing memory from Salome's childhood, providing context for her sickening demand for the severed head of John the Baptist.

The South Bank Show was making a documentary about McVicar's process and broadcast a scene where he tore a delicately modelled staircase out of my cardboard scale model. The camera cut to my reaction: eight months pregnant, I appear to flinch very slightly, then carry on the conversation. Lebanese/British pop star Mika was impressed by this calm response to bracing critique, and recognized in it a potential suitability for the brutal world of stadium concert design. He immediately got in touch.

808–809

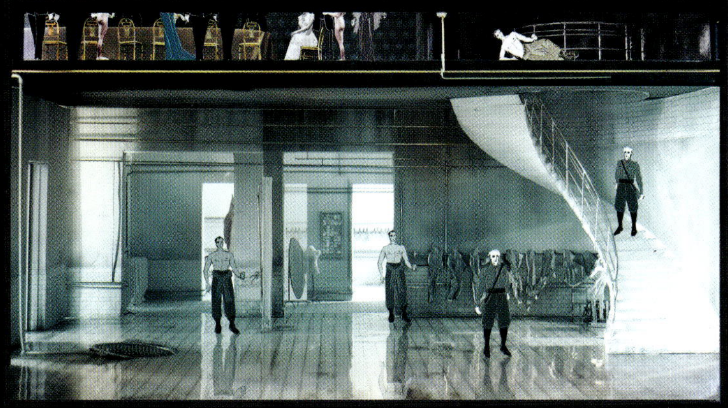

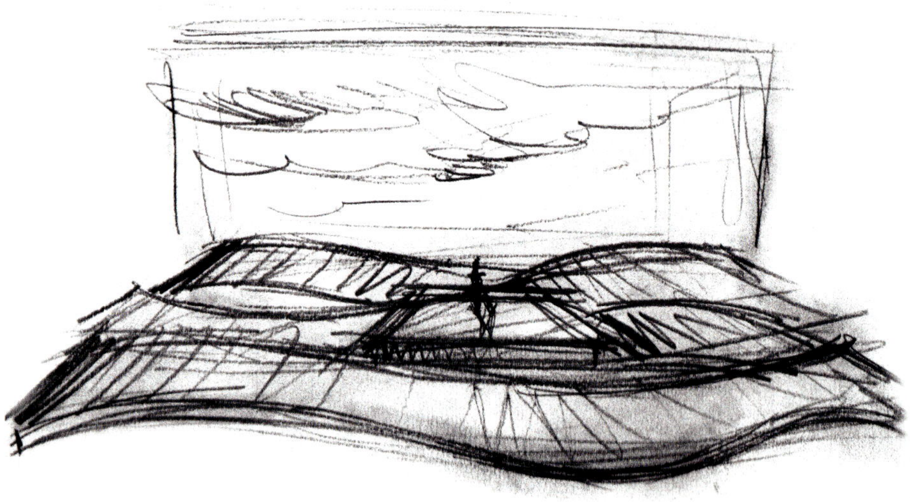

GLOW IN THE DARK

I'm exhausted, barely breathing
Holding on to what I believe in

Kanye West, 'Amazing'

Kanye came to the studio in Peckham to discuss the *Glow in the Dark* US arena tour that would open in Seattle in April 2008. We watched *Salome* at the Royal Opera House that February and replicated the orchestra pit, placing it beneath an undulating grass floor surface that echoed the organic Wagnerian opera stages of theatre designer Ralph Koltai and the grass-and-earth dance floors of choreographer Pina Bausch. Kanye selected footage of specific skies over terrestrial, Martian and lunar landscapes. The choral-layered resonance of the music seemed to require the full expanse of the biosphere. The production directors Martin Phillips and John McGuire navigated the design through rehearsals. Kanye wrote a narrative voiceover – a conversation between himself and a guiding female voice from another world. He was alone on stage facing a crowd of 20,000 throughout the show. At one point I asked whether the show's intention was to portray him as a boy lost on his own in space, to which he responded simply: 'Yes.'

SONGS FOR SORROW

The stage is my territory, my boxing ring. That's where I'm free.

Mika

I had seen photos of the huge, mask-like entrance to Luna Park in Sydney. I wanted Mika to be able to hide his character Billy Brown in plain sight in the vast stadium of Parc des Princes in Paris in July 2008. I drew a clown mask portrait with a huge open mouth surrounding the stage. I watched as Mika, who had quietly cooked me dinner in his basement flat a week earlier, radiated the energy of the vast crowd back to them, like a human mirror reflecting beams in every direction. I asked him afterwards, 'What does it feel like to have 50,000 people focus their gaze on you in a stadium?' He said, 'You become another person.'

Mika and his sisters Yasmine, Paloma and Zuleika are all talented artists, and we worked closely together on exuberantly toned costumes, puppets and props. I had my baby daughter Ry with me at the stadium and remember spoon-feeding her in the canteen surrounded by 300 male crew members all wearing identical blue overalls. With the help of my model-making assistant Machiko Weston, I made this layered paper-cut from some of the drawings for inclusion in Mika's 2009 *Songs for Sorrow* EP, alongside illustrations by Peter Blake, Walter Van Beirendonck and Paul Smith.

798–799

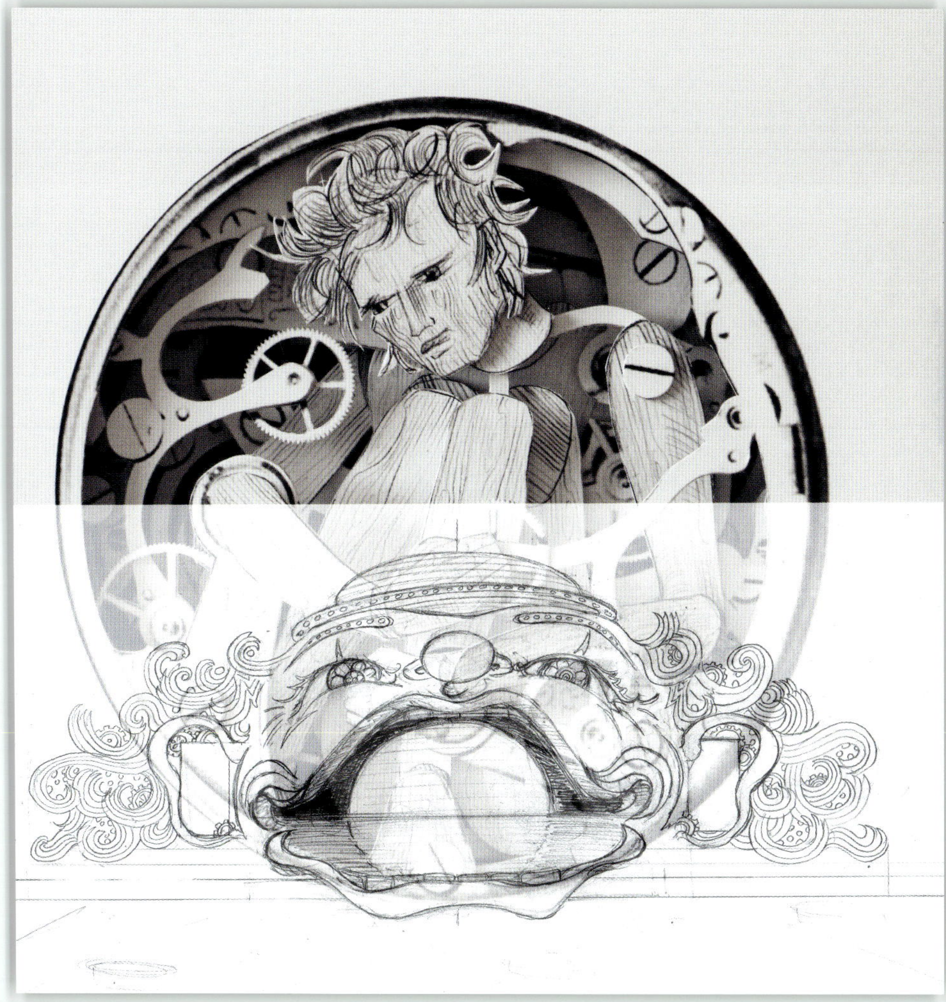

SONGS FOR SORROW

The stage is my territory, my boxing ring. That's where I'm free.

Mika

I had seen photos of the huge, mask-like entrance to Luna Park in Sydney. I wanted Mika to be able to hide his character Billy Brown in plain sight in the vast stadium of Parc des Princes in Paris in July 2008. I drew a clown mask portrait with a huge open mouth surrounding the stage. I watched as Mika, who had quietly cooked me dinner in his basement flat a week earlier, radiated the energy of the vast crowd back to them, like a human mirror reflecting beams in every direction. I asked him afterwards, 'What does it feel like to have 50,000 people focus their gaze on you in a stadium?' He said, 'You become another person.'

Mika and his sisters Yasmin[illegible] all talented artists, and we wo[illegible] on exube[illegible] costumes, [illegible]. I had my baby daughter [illegible] with me at the sta[illegible] surrou[illegible] ew me[illegible] identical [illegible] my mode[illegible] Machi[illegible] [illegible] cut [illegible] some of the drawings for inclusion in [illegible] *Songs* [illegible] alongside illustrations [illegible] Blake, [illegible] Smith.

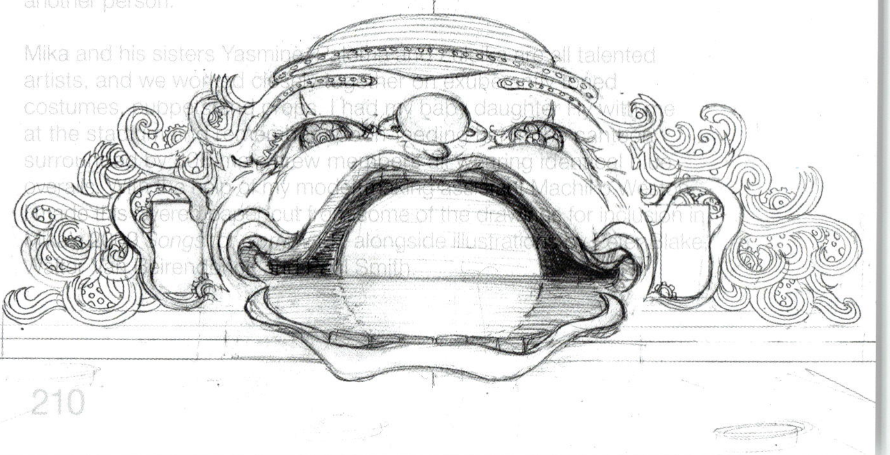

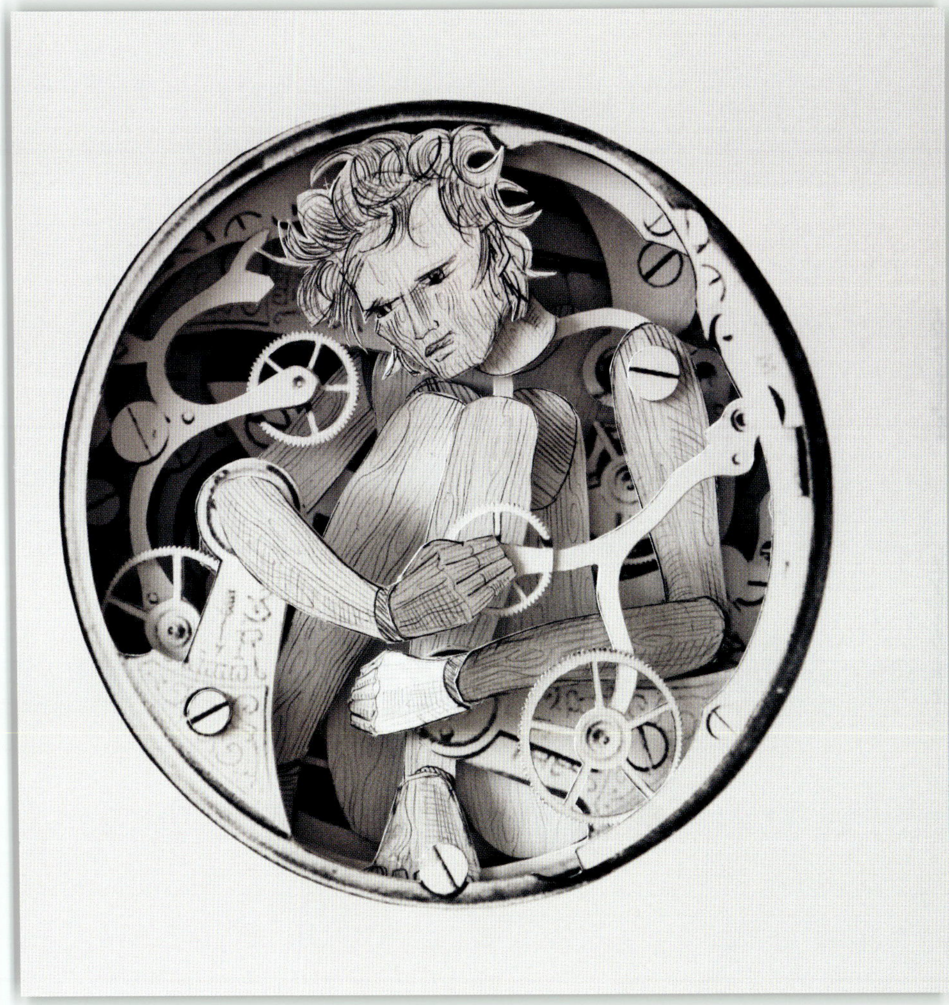

JEANNE D'ARC AU BÛCHER

Music is geometry in time.

Arthur Honegger, *I am a Composer*

Arthur Honegger's dramatic oratorio takes place in Joan of Arc's final minutes before being burned at the stake as a witch. The conductor Antonio Pappano commissioned a semi-staged production to open in October 2008 at the Renzo Piano-designed Accademia Nazionale di Santa Cecilia in Rome. It was my fifth collaboration with the director Keith Warner. Our giant chess-set version of Verdi's *Nabucco* remained unrealized, and we resumed this line of enquiry, envisaging Joan as a figure caught within the rules of a nonsensical game rigged against her. The French actress Romane Bohringer was to appear as a tiny lone protagonist suspended between heaven and earth on a giant chair surrounded by a storm of playing cards. Romane played the role with great sensitivity, but it became apparent at the start of rehearsals that she was six months pregnant and terrified of heights, so we cast a dancer as her alter ego.

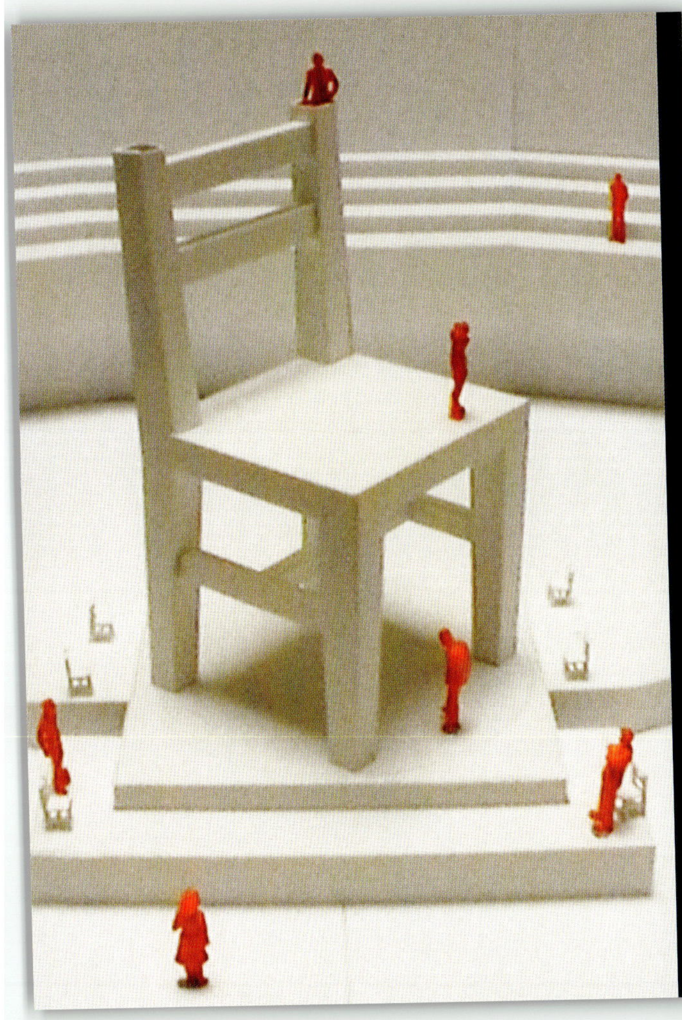

n

atty, 'Days of Fire'

e 7/7 London
Charles de
ing series of
t to life by the
ght through
sequence of

BFI IMAX cinema
out momentarily,
hormones in the
the Vietnamese
n slow motion
Around this time,
etrated my room
ravelling and
ly ritual, treating
global sun dial.

JEANNE D

Music is geometry in t

Arthur Honegger's dr
minutes before being
Antonio Pappano con
in October 2008 at th
di Santa Cecilia in Ro
Keith Warner. Our gia
unrealized, and we re
a figure caught within
her. The French actre
lone protagonist susp
chair surrounded by a
with great sensitivity,
that she was six mon
dancer as her alter eg

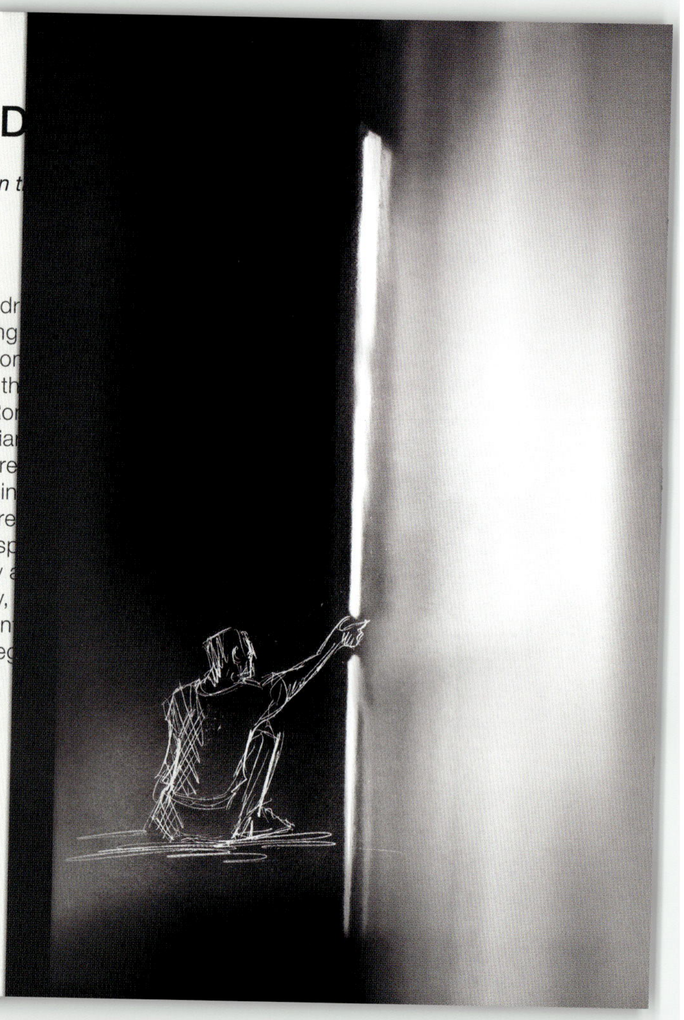

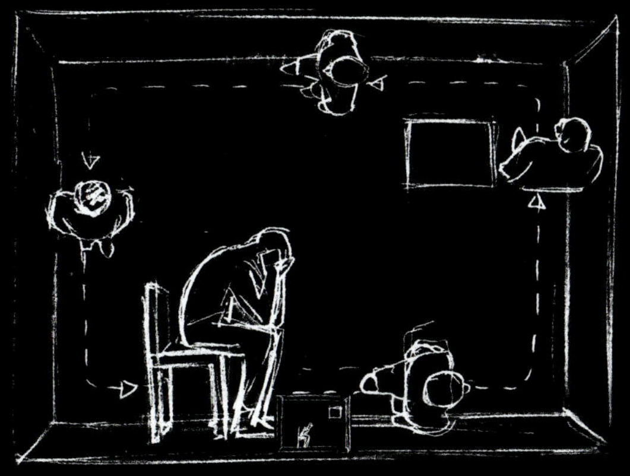

20. His thinking blocked, the dancer takes a break - gets up and paces around the edges of the room. [We've returned to filming the box horizontally] - the dancer appears to move freely in a dimension that obeys new rules.

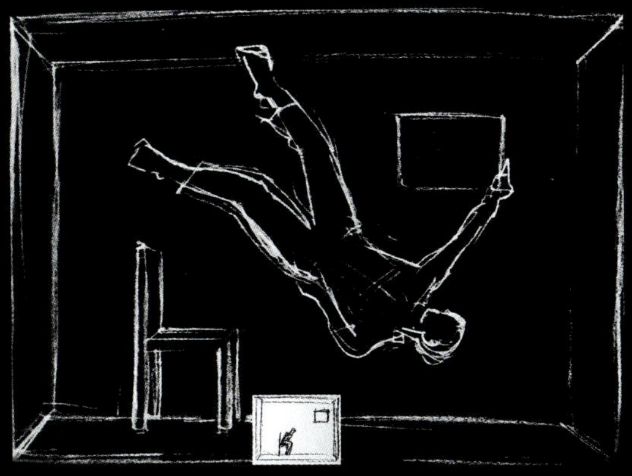

21. The seated dancer realises he's cracked it.. now follows a dance of free movement - ever revising the rules of gravity as we film the box now horizontally, now upside down, now on its side so the dancer appears to float and fly in thought.

n

atty, 'Days of Fire'

e 7/7 London
Charles de
ing series of
t to life by the
ght through
sequence of

BFI IMAX cinema
out momentarily,
hormones in the
the Vietnamese
n slow motion
Around this time,
etrated my room
ravelling and
ly ritual, treating
global sun dial.

JEANNE

Music is geometry i

Arthur Honegger's
minutes before bei
Antonio Pappano c
in October 2008 at
di Santa Cecilia in R
Keith Warner. Our g
unrealized, and we
a figure caught wit
her. The French ac
lone protagonist su
chair surrounded b
with great sensitivi
that she was six m
dancer as her alter

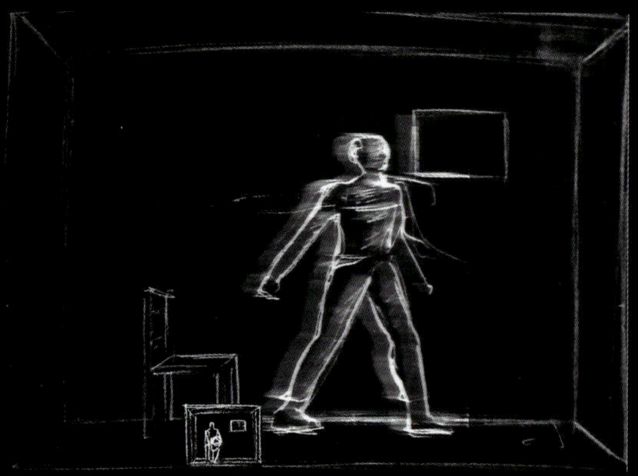

18. The dancer moves again. This time his movements appear to be straining to obey the normal rules of gravity. [This section is filmed with the box lying on its back so the dancer works with the idea of creating an impression of vertical movement while lying on the floor]

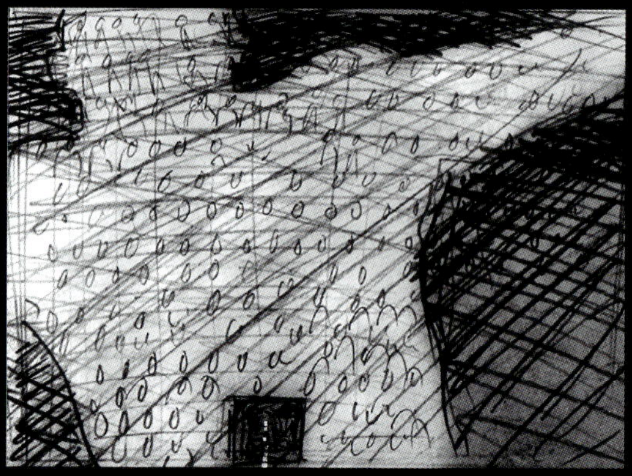

33. As the audience are leaving, the silhouetted dancing edges of the figure are filled with relayed film of the audience. The stage box contains a separate projection of a dotted vanishing line - a train of thought that invites the possibility of following it.

LONDON UNDERSOUND

First came the flash of lights then the sound of explosion
And we're still in slow motion, we're still in slow motion

Nitin Sawhney, featuring Natty, 'Days of Fire'

London Undersound is Nitin Sawhney's response to the 7/7 London bombings of 2005 and the wrongful shooting of Jean Charles de Menezes by police a few weeks later. I drew a modulating series of portraits of the city and its citizens, which were brought to life by the talented animator, Luke Halls. A hand sliced a line of light through the scene, perforating through the cinema screen to a sequence of perspectives on the city.

I stood at the back of the audience in the monumental BFI IMAX cinema watching the performance in November 2008. I crept out momentarily, at precisely 8:30 pm, to inject my daily dose of fertility hormones in the hope of conceiving my second child. I returned to see the Vietnamese choreographer and dancer, Dam Van Huynh, floating in slow motion above a chair on the immense 26-metre-wide screen. Around this time, I began photographing the vertical line of light that penetrated my room between the curtains each morning, especially when travelling and waking up in unfamiliar architecture. I continue this daily ritual, treating every room and window as a fragment of a composite global sun dial.

621 658

FIRST TRAIN HOME

Temporal dead zone where clocks are barely breathing
Yet no one cares to notice for all the yelling

Imogen Heap, 'First Train Home'

I made a series of drawings in response to 'First Train Home', the first single from Imogen Heap's 2009 album *Ellipse*. I'd met Imogen through her collaboration with Nitin Sawhney on *London Undersound*. She was living in an elliptically shaped house, which was also her recording studio. The house was her musical instrument and external memory device. Each night, she buried the hard drive containing the album in progress deep within the folds of the building for safekeeping. I sketched portraits of a female figure in motion at a series of different scales within a rotating zoetrope. Zoetropes – which combine the Greek *zoe*, meaning life, and *tropos*, or turning – are devices in which images seen through rotating slots seem to come to life. They are the precursors to the moving image, cinema, and all that followed. In the end, the animated music video we made was superseded by a more direct expression of the song filmed in Imogen's elliptical house itself. We went on to collaborate on the staging for her 2009 *Ellipse* world tour.

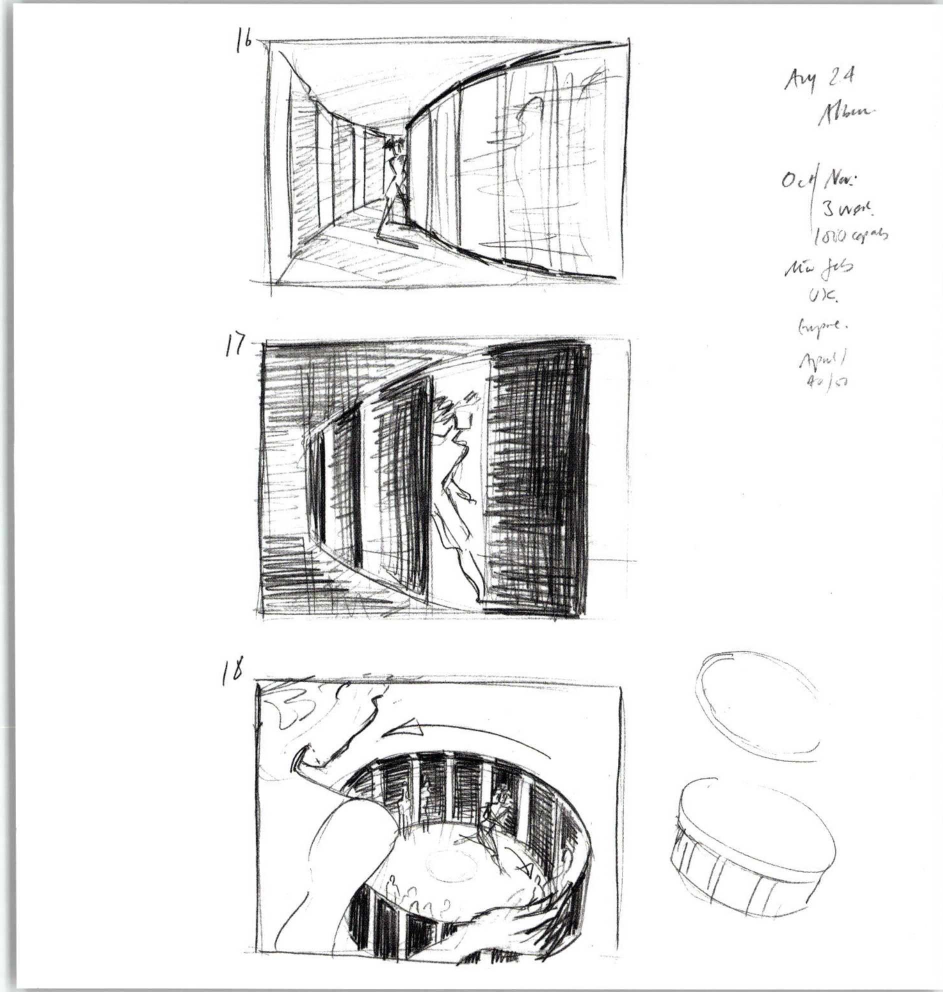
16
17
18
Aug 24
Album
Oct/Nov:
3 week
1000 copies
Mini Jobs
UK.
Europe.
April
40/50

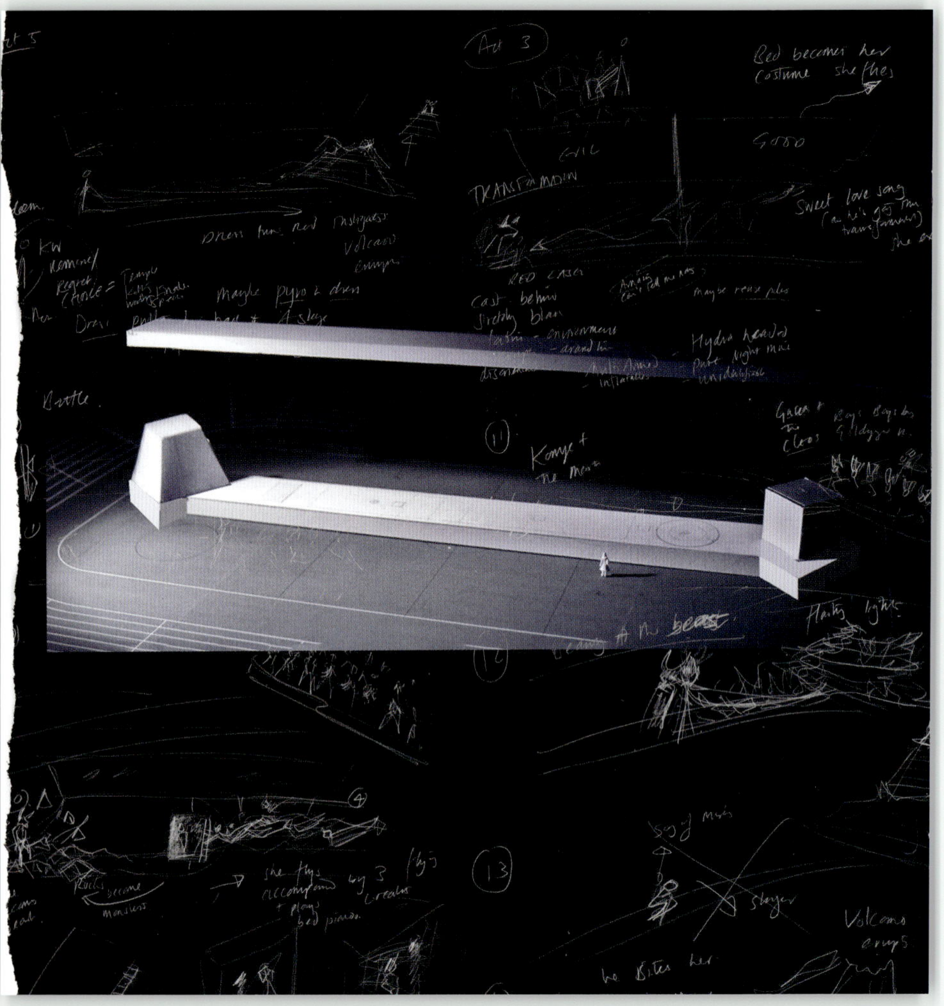
Act 3
Red becomes her costume
TRANSFORMATION
Sweet love song
RED CASES
Battle
Volcano erupts

FAME KILLS

When you make music or write or create, it's really your job to have mind-blowing, irresponsible, condom-less sex with whatever idea it is you're writing about at the time.

Lady Gaga

Kanye West and Lady Gaga envisaged a translation of their albums *808s & Heartbreak* and *The Fame Monster* into a continuous, joint opera. We conceived two sculptures with a runway between them that ran the full length of the arena. We set up a studio in Los Angeles with Kanye and Gaga, Matthew Williams (who was dating Gaga at the time) and designer Willo Perron sitting around a huge table sketching and making cardboard models. The tour got cancelled soon after Kanye's interruption of Taylor Swift's acceptance speech at the MTV Video Music Awards in September 2009.

PANDEMONIUM

You need more, you need more, you need more, you need more,
you need more, you need more

Pet Shop Boys, 'Love etc.'

The Pet Shop Boys' aesthetic is a bold combination of sophisticated electronic and homemade DIY. Their costume designer, Jeffrey Bryant, creates avant-garde sculptural outfits out of black drinking straws and IKEA plastic baskets. Their touring team pride themselves on squeezing elaborate staging elements into a single truck, while other bands might use twenty. The graphic designer Mark Farrow had based the new *Yes* album graphics on Gerhard Richter's pixelated stained-glass window at Cologne Cathedral. For the 2009 *Pandemonium* tour, I translated the pixels into 500 white projection-mapped cardboard boxes that could be flat-packed for touring. Jeffrey created dancing cardboard box costumes for the four dancers, and brightly coloured cardboard box heads for Neil Tennant and Chris Lowe. On the opening night at the Ice Palace in Saint Petersburg in June, Neil sang the first song through a cube head. Chris kept his on all night.

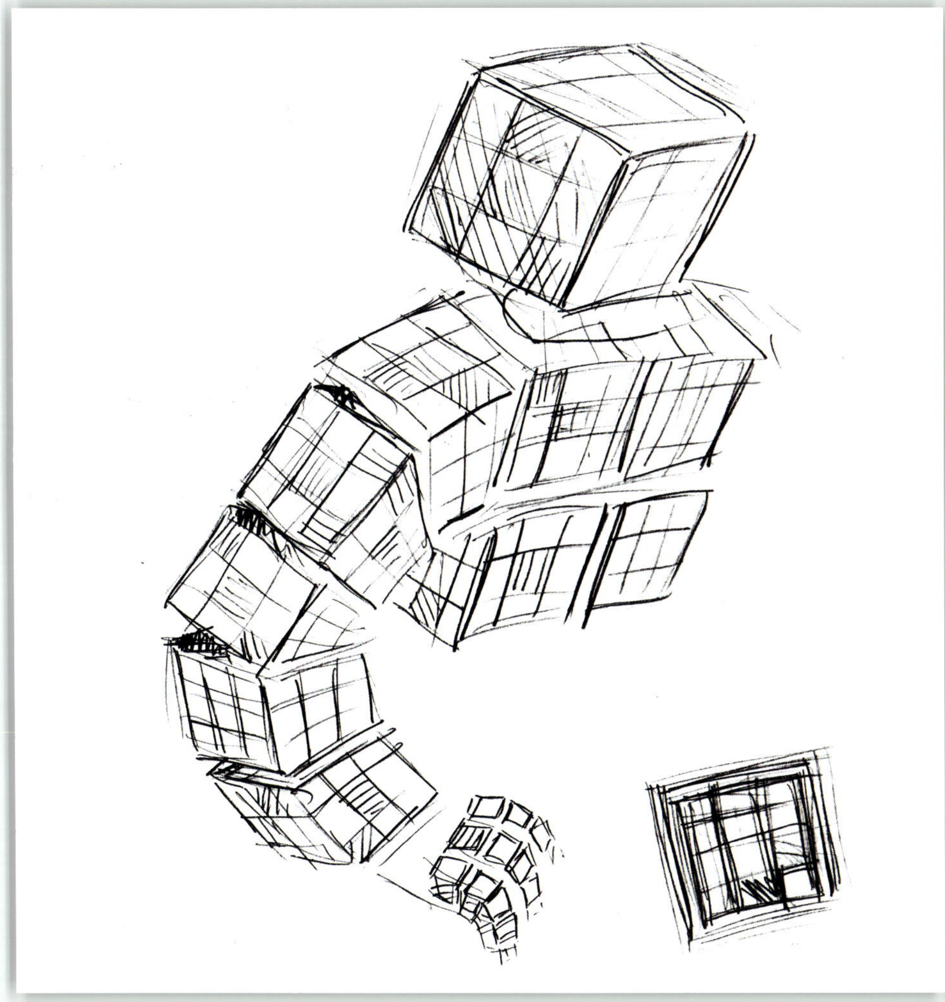

PROGRESS

We were holding back the flood
Learning how to dance the rain

Take That, 'The Flood'

A 20-metre-high, geometrically faceted male figure rising up from the stage and progressing across the stadium felt the most appropriate portrait of this five-piece band that had captivated British audiences with their televised odyssey back from oblivion. During the six-month period of design and fabrication, the ambitious kinetic sculpture seemed impossible, but then so did the re-emergence of this popular band, complete with Robbie Williams, after sixteen years apart. A number of fabricators declined to take it on, but the band, their director Kim Gavin, producer Chris Vaughan, and myself refused to be deterred. The brilliant, and much missed, engineer Andy Edwards conceived an ingenious mechanical truck that drove the giant straight from the motorway onto the football pitch. The size of its head was determined by the height of a motorway bridge in Hamburg, the lowest it would encounter on its European touring route. The *Progress* tour opened in May 2011 at the Stadium of Light in Sunderland. In July it travelled to London, where until recently it held the record for Wembley Stadium's longest residency, selling out eight consecutive nights.

804–805

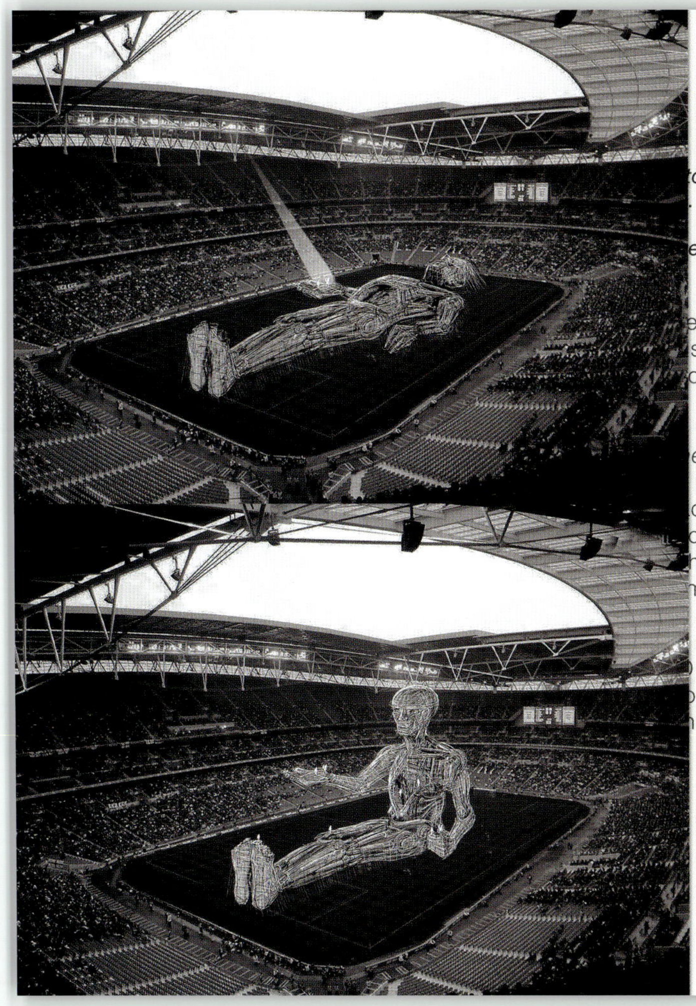

tory beliefs in
.

eteen Eighty-Four

en to the new
sunny spring
o's brutalist

eteen
Eileen Blair,
d been the
cled over and
he three kinetic
mber of the band.
band member
ascending and
structures
orridors and
nitectural

PROGRE

We were holding ba
Learning how to da

A 20-metre-high, g
stage and progress
portrait of this five-
with their televised
period of design an
impossible, but the
complete with Rob
of fabricators decli
Gavin, producer Cl
The brilliant, and m
an ingenious mech
motorway onto the
by the height of a r
encounter on its Eu
May 2011 at the St
London, where unt
longest residency,

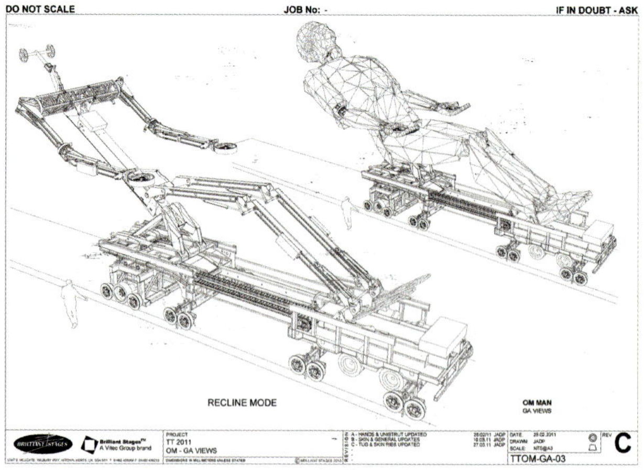

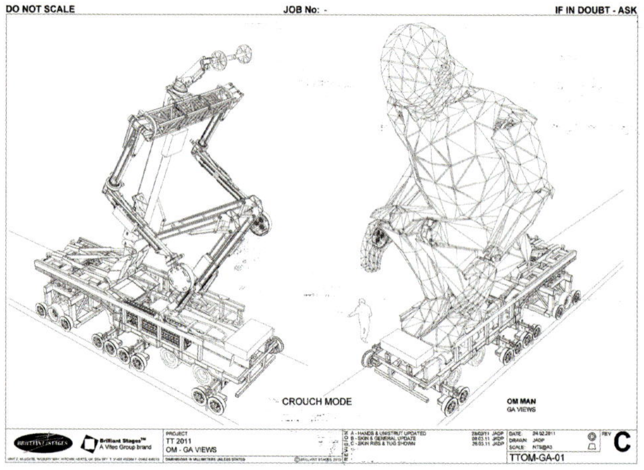

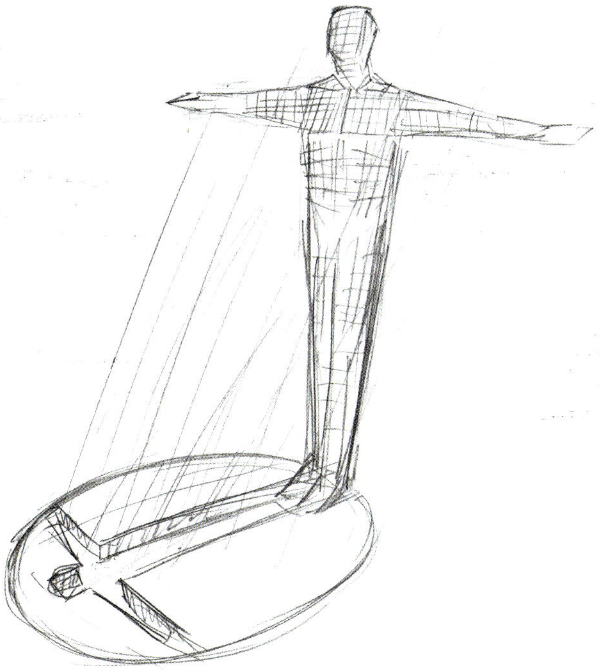

dictory beliefs in
em.

Nineteen Eighty-Four

isten to the new
a sunny spring
udio's brutalist

Nineteen
ife, Eileen Blair,
had been the
cycled over and
of the three kinetic
nember of the band.
ch band member
an ascending and
ED structures
corridors and
rchitectural

PROGRE

We were holding ba
Learning how to da

A 20-metre-high, g
stage and progres
portrait of this five-
with their televised
period of design an
impossible, but the
complete with Rob
of fabricators decli
Gavin, producer C
The brilliant, and m
an ingenious mech
motorway onto the
by the height of a r
encounter on its Eu
May 2011 at the St
London, where it s
residency, selling c

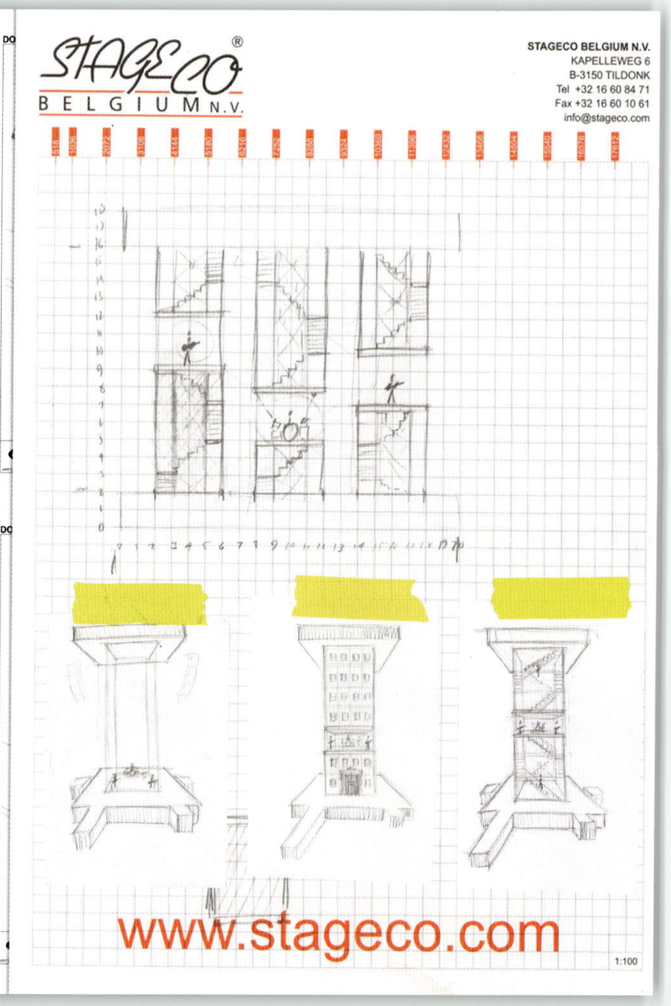

RESISTANCE

Doublethink means the power of holding two contradictory beliefs in one's mind simultaneously, and accepting both of them.

George Orwell, *Nineteen Eighty-Four*

I went to Studio Bellini near Lake Como to sit and listen to the new Muse album, *Resistance*, prior to its release. It was a sunny spring morning in an idyllic setting by the lake, and the studio's brutalist concrete walls firmly kept the outdoors out.

Resistance was rooted in George Orwell's book, *Nineteen Eighty-Four*. Matt Bellamy told me that Orwell's wife, Eileen Blair, worked at Senate House in London, and that this had been the architectural inspiration for the Ministry of Truth. I cycled over and took photographs of it to inform the architecture of the three kinetic ministries we created for the tour – one for each member of the band. The show opened in Helsinki in October 2009. Each band member was caught and compressed in the gap between an ascending and a descending tower. The film imagery within the LED structures presented populations endlessly queuing through corridors and stairs, and ultimately liberating themselves from architectural constraints to float in defiance of gravity.

MONSTER BALL 1.0

I hate the truth so much, I would prefer a giant dose of bullshit any day.

Lady Gaga

By the time we began rehearsals for Lady Gaga's *Monster Ball* tour in Los Angeles in November 2009, I was six months pregnant with my second child, Ludo. Gaga's music and aesthetic were evolving fast, as was her popularity. We had planned a lightproof white box for a modestly scaled theatre tour culminating in Radio City Music Hall. Tickets sold out in moments, so the tour shifted to much larger arenas in which the pure white box would seem tiny. Gaga took one look at it when she arrived at rehearsal and said, 'That's great, now puke on it.'

I went to the Culver City rubbish dump with a local fabricator, David Mendoza. We stuck whatever crap we could find onto a piece of truss, made the whole thing look as though it had been dipped in black oil, and strapped it to the front of the perfect white box. The film directors Nick Knight and Ruth Hogben projected Gaga in black gothic Alexander McQueen riding the trash truss as it descended. Gradually, as rehearsals progressed, we tore off the white walls to reveal truss, lights, drummers and guitarists, evolving the design to keep up with the speed of Gaga's maturing practice.

660–661

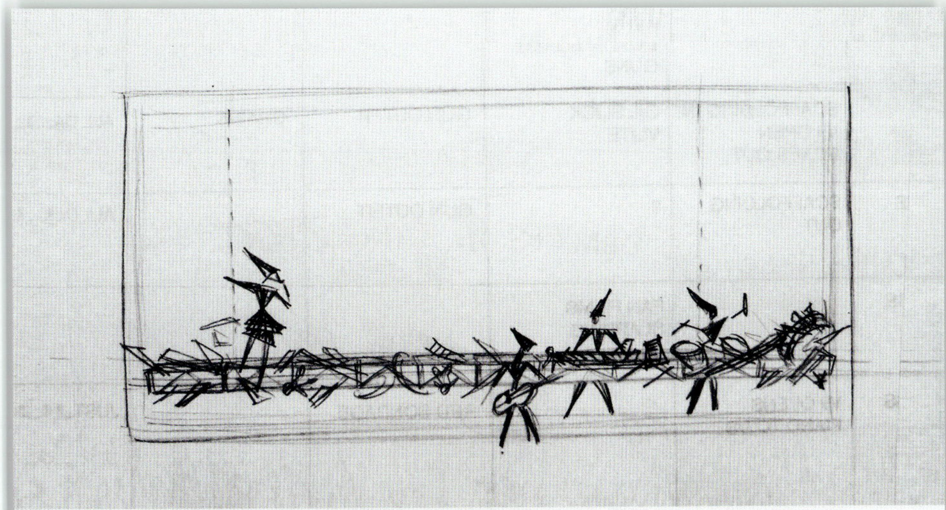

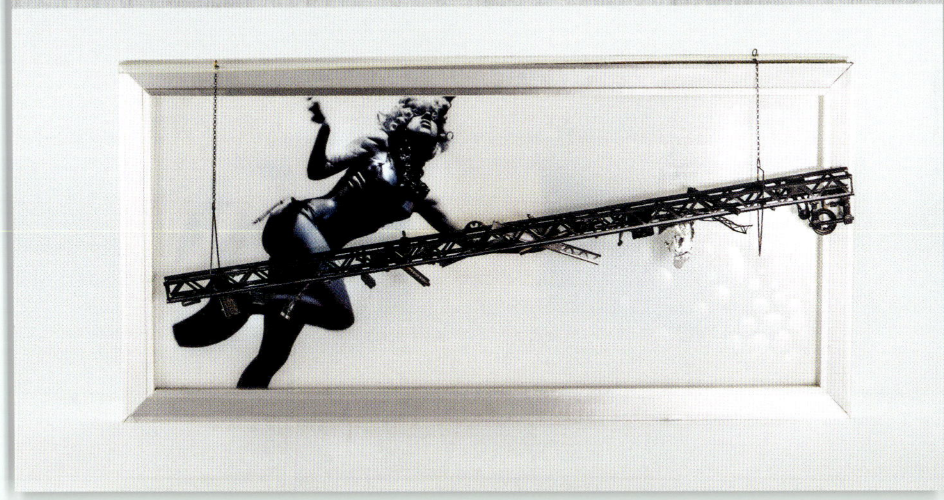

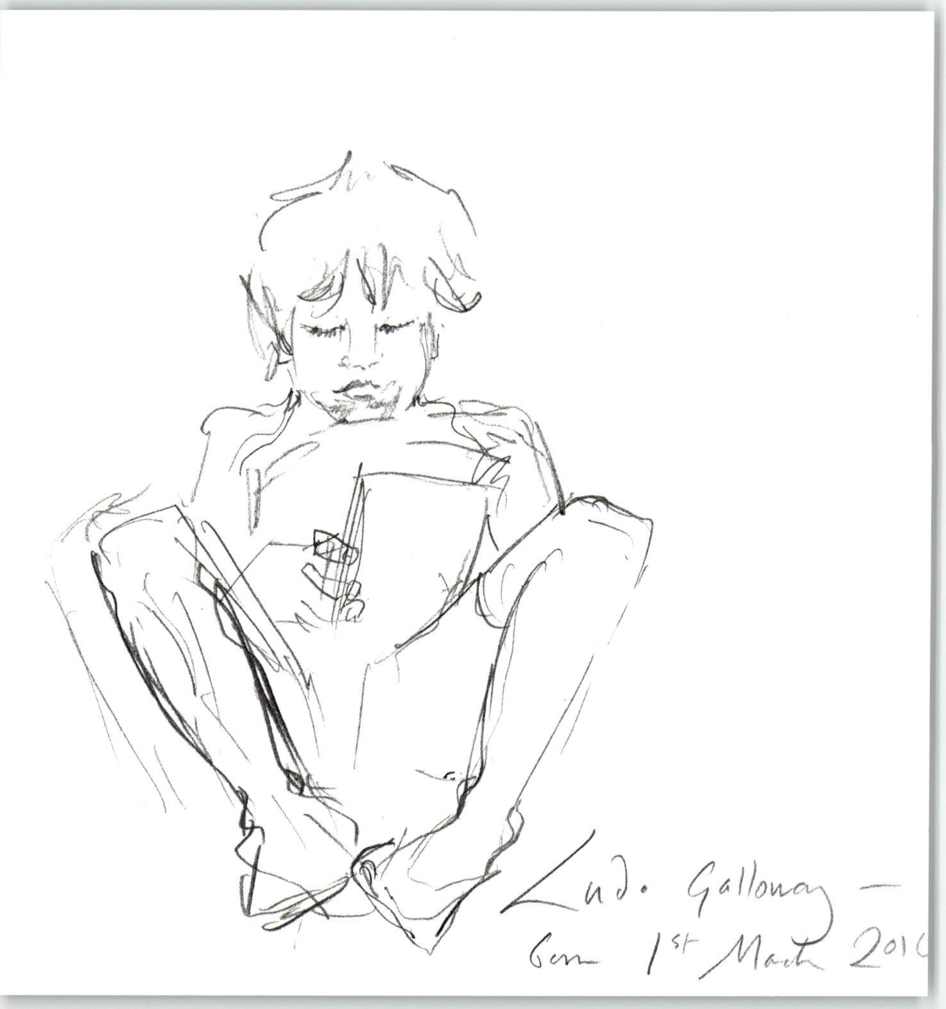
Ludo. Galloway —
1st March

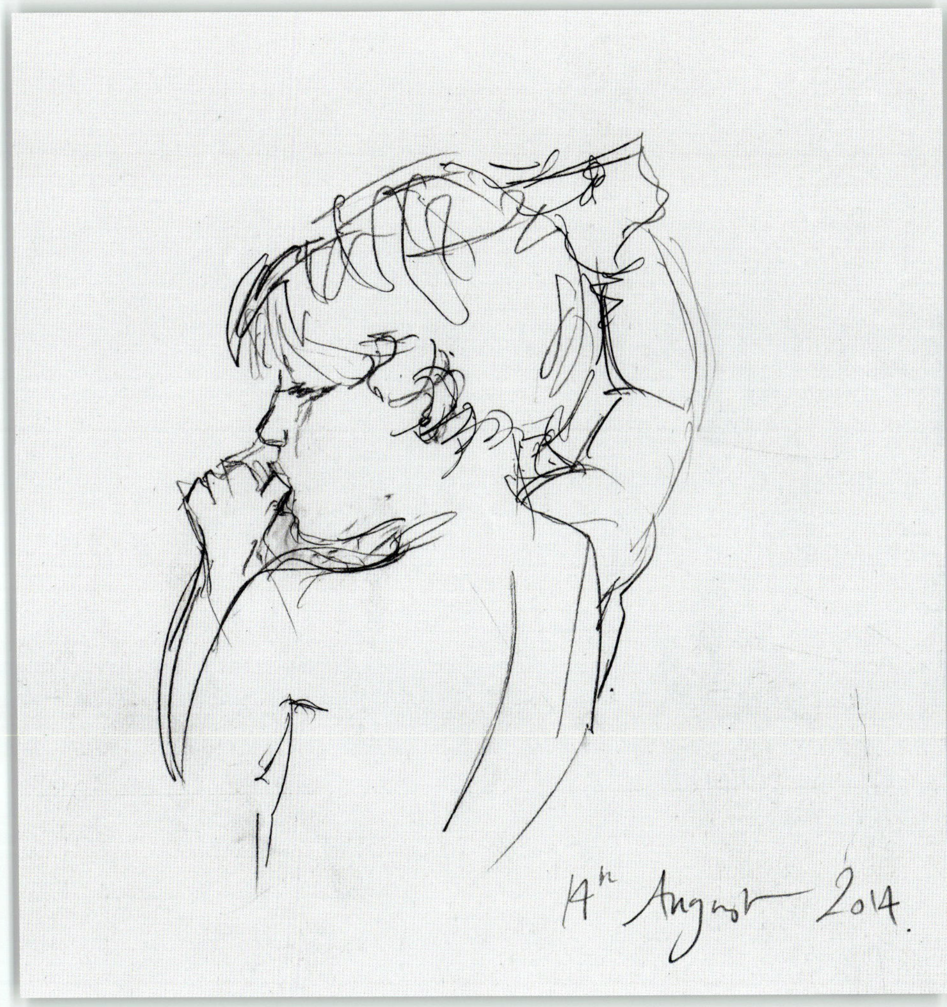
14th August 2014.

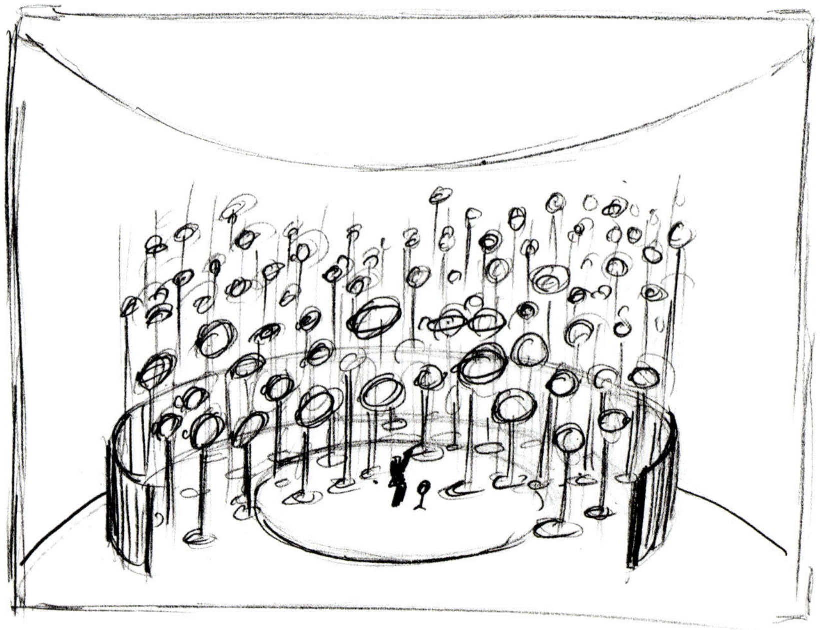

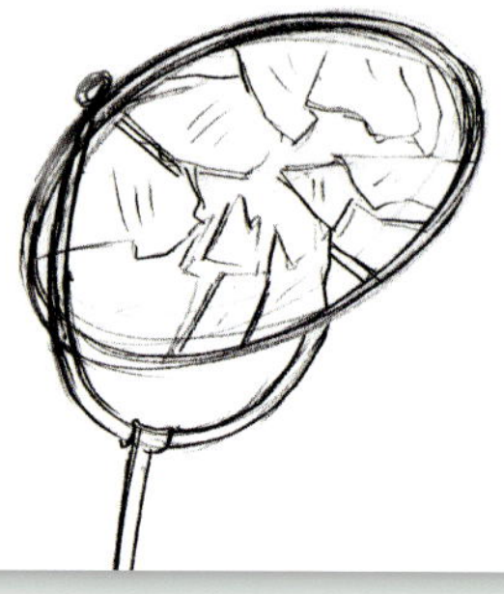

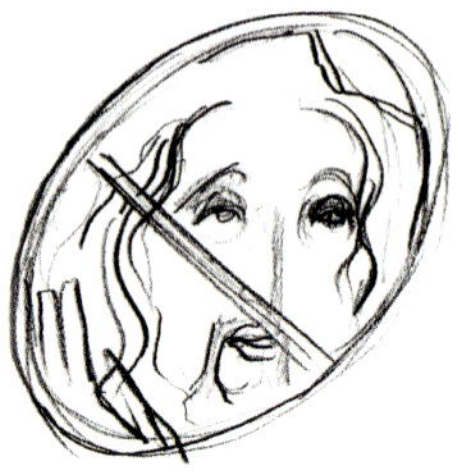

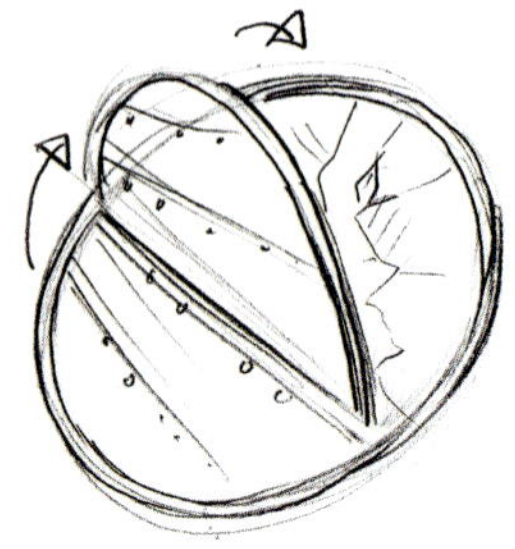

FAUST

... light and its absence are necessary to the production of colour ...
Colour itself is a degree of darkness ...

The highest goal that man can achieve is amazement.

Johann Wolfgang von Goethe, *Theory of Colours*

The opera director Keith Warner emerged from our Peckham studio bathroom with a circular rotating mirror and placed it in a black cardboard model zoetrope, which had been left over from the video shoot with Imogen Heap. We had read Johann Wolfgang von Goethe's *Theory of Colours* and his studies in optics, in preparation for the production of Charles Gounod's 1859 opera based on Goethe's 1808 drama. Both originate in the medieval legend of a doctor who sells his soul to the devil in exchange for knowledge and power.

In the opera's exuberant Act II waltz, we used concentric rotating zoetropes made of pivoting mirrored prisms to multiply the dancing, spectrum-coloured chorus. By the final act, a forest of circular mirrors reflected accusatory beams onto Faust's abandoned lover, Marguerite. The production opened at the Semperoper Dresden in June 2010 and I walked along the banks of the River Elbe between rehearsals, my three-month-old son Ludo strapped to my chest.

732–733

LA CAJA MÁGICA

I never know what day it is. Never, ever, ever.

Rihanna

The 2010 MTV Europe Music Awards took place at the Caja Mágica arena in Madrid. Echoing the venue's title, I imagined a 10-metre-high revolving box that could reveal a shapeshifting series of performances. It recalled my childhood toys: a Rubik's Cube, a Rubik's Snake, and a small black cube called Seven Uses, which transformed into a series of tools: ruler, compass, scissors, spirit level, penknife, set square, torch. The producers liked the idea but pointed out that there were eight performances and only four sides of a cube, and global superstars are not known for their enthusiasm for sharing.

Rihanna sang within a sea of red carnations pouring out of an iris of concentric irregular ovoids. Bon Jovi's performance was backlit through folded, perforated planes. Shakira and her dancers performed on cantilevered platforms within the cube. The talented young director Paul Shyvers brought enormous skill to what would very sadly be one of his last shows. I later revisited the revolving magic box in cardboard at the Serpentine Galleries in 2016, and as a 15-metre illuminated sculpture on the waters of the Persian Gulf in 2021.

714–715

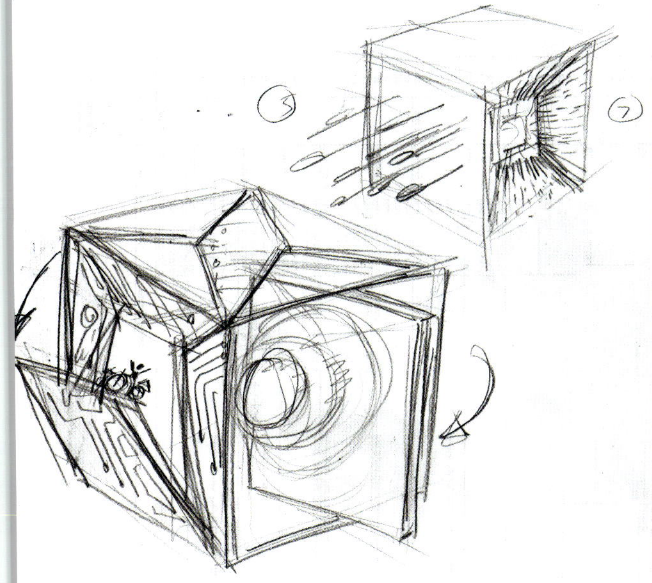

gold and Paul Schott

gang Korngold's
d with audiences
lhoff's *Flammen*,
ne in the 1940s.

olten on the
on, we framed the
ementos and relics
ealed a miniature
anically interlocking
d within his grief
this time is scored
My eight-month-
sheets of glass

LA CAJA M

I never know what day

The 2010 MTV Europ
arena in Madrid. Echo
revolving box that cou
It recalled my childho
small black cube calle
tools: ruler, compass,
The producers liked t
performances and or
not known for their er

Rihanna sang within a
of concentric irregula
through folded, perfo
on cantilevered platfo
Paul Shyvers brought
of his last shows. I lat
at the Serpentine Gal
sculpture on the wate

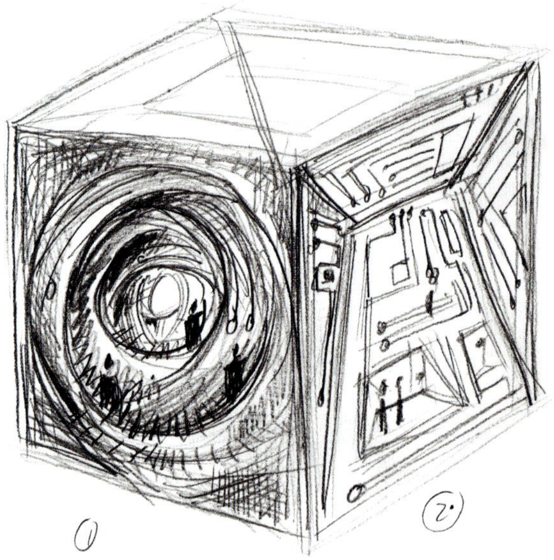

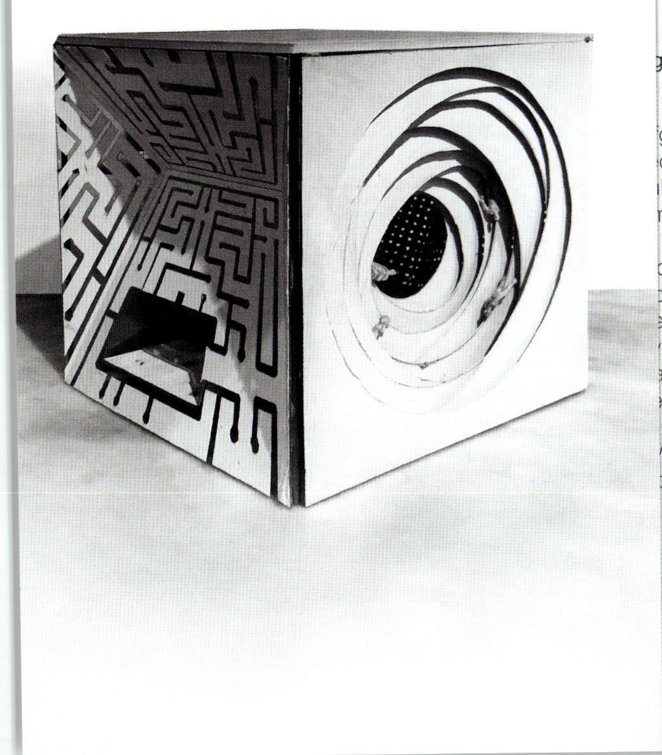

gold and Paul Schott

rgang Korngold's
d with audiences
lhoff's *Flammen*,
ne in the 1940s.

olten on the
on, we framed the
ementos and relics
vealed a miniature
anically interlocking
d within his grief
this time is scored
My eight-month-
t sheets of glass

LA CAJA M

I never know what day

The 2010 MTV Europ
arena in Madrid. Echo
revolving box that co
It recalled my childho
small black cube call
tools: ruler, compass,
The producers liked t
performances and or
not known for their e

Rihanna sang within a
of concentric irregula
through folded, perfo
on cantilevered platfo
Paul Shyvers brought
of his last shows. I lat
at the Serpentine Gal
sculpture on the wate

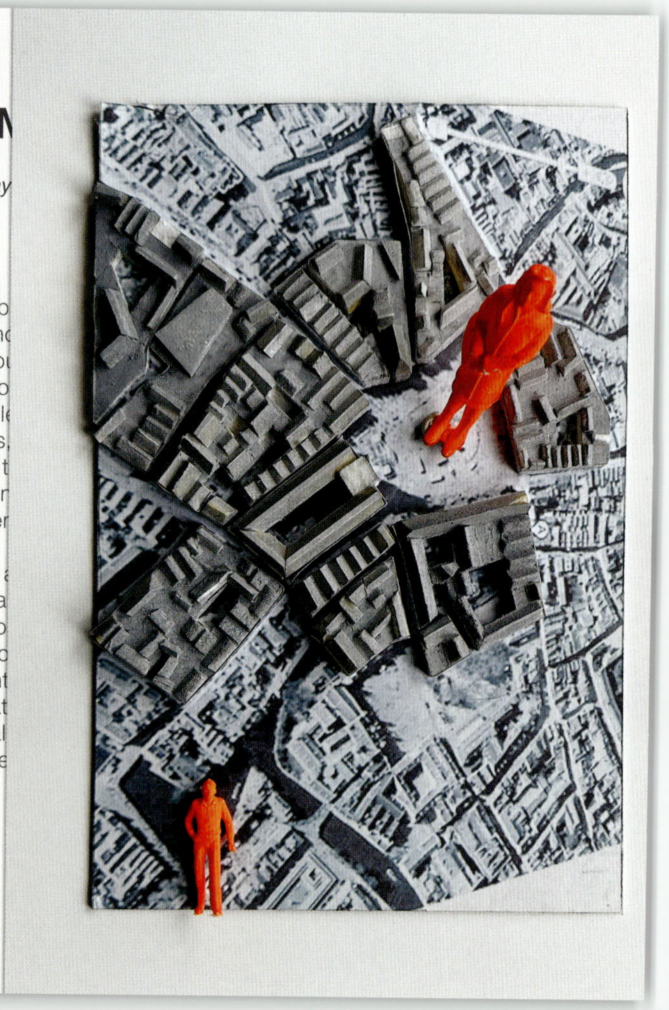

DIE TOTE STADT

Such dreams are sent us by our dead
If we live too much with and in them.
How far should we give way to grief,
How far dare we, without disaster?

Erich Wolfgang Korngold and Paul Schott

A meditation on grief for a lost loved one, Erich Wolfgang Korngold's 1920 opera *Die Tote Stadt* (The Dead City) resonated with audiences following the First World War, but, like Erwin Schulhoff's *Flammen*, it was banned as degenerate art by the Nazi regime in the 1940s.

Working closely with the Danish director Kasper Holten on the Finnish National Opera's November 2010 production, we framed the protagonist's grief within a memory palace full of mementos and relics arrayed on shelf-covered walls. A vast aperture revealed a miniature recreation of Bruges, with its brain-like maze of organically interlocking medieval streets. The protagonist appeared trapped within his grief with a conjured copy of his lost wife. My memory of this time is scored with the labyrinthine corridors of the opera house. My eight-month-old son Ludo crawled around in the huge foyer, vast sheets of glass between him and a sea of deep Helsinki snow.

BATMAN

Bruce Wayne: We all wear masks.

Lee Batchler, Janet Scott Batchler
and Akiva Goldsman, *Batman Forever*

In preparation for the *Batman Live* show, I read the vividly coloured 1939 Bob Kane illustrations for DC Comics. To me, they resembled a series of medieval illuminated manuscripts, or stained-glass windows, recounting the 'Bat-man' origin myth. An arena presentation of the fusion of animal and human in response to the tragic, premature death of parents seemed appropriate: once you get past the hotdogs and merch stands, the geometry of an arena echoes an ancient Greek amphitheatre. The initial concept mapped Gotham City in miniature throughout the arena, assigning each audience member a building to sit on, locating their seats not by row and number, but by street address. The show opened in Manchester in July 2011. The design had evolved and the audience arrived to see an illuminated model of Gotham City covering the stage.

The Joker manifested as an 8-metre-high painted mask whose eyes and teeth were formed of striped gymnasts. My husband Jack designed the costumes, and our children Ry, aged four, and Ludo, aged one, crawled around the model city between rehearsals.

706–707

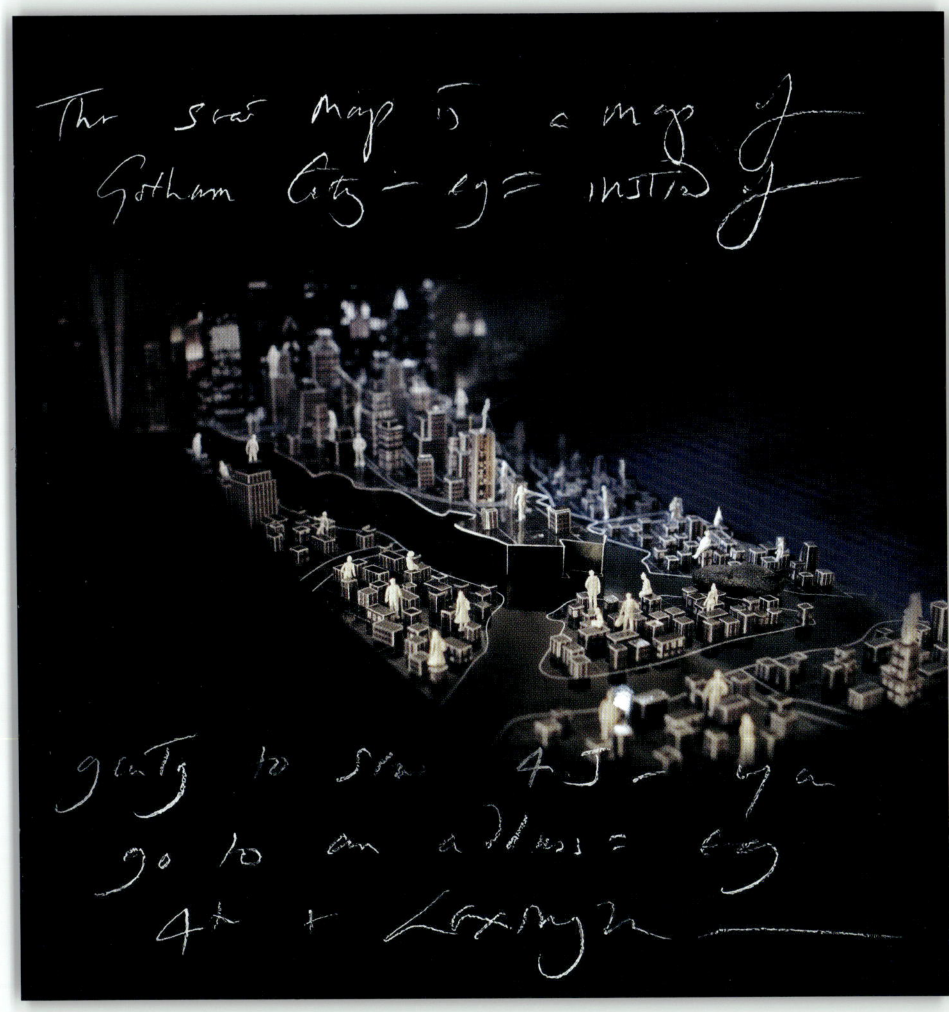
The star map is a map of
Gotham City – eg = instead of
going to star 45 – you
go to an address = eg
4th + Lexington

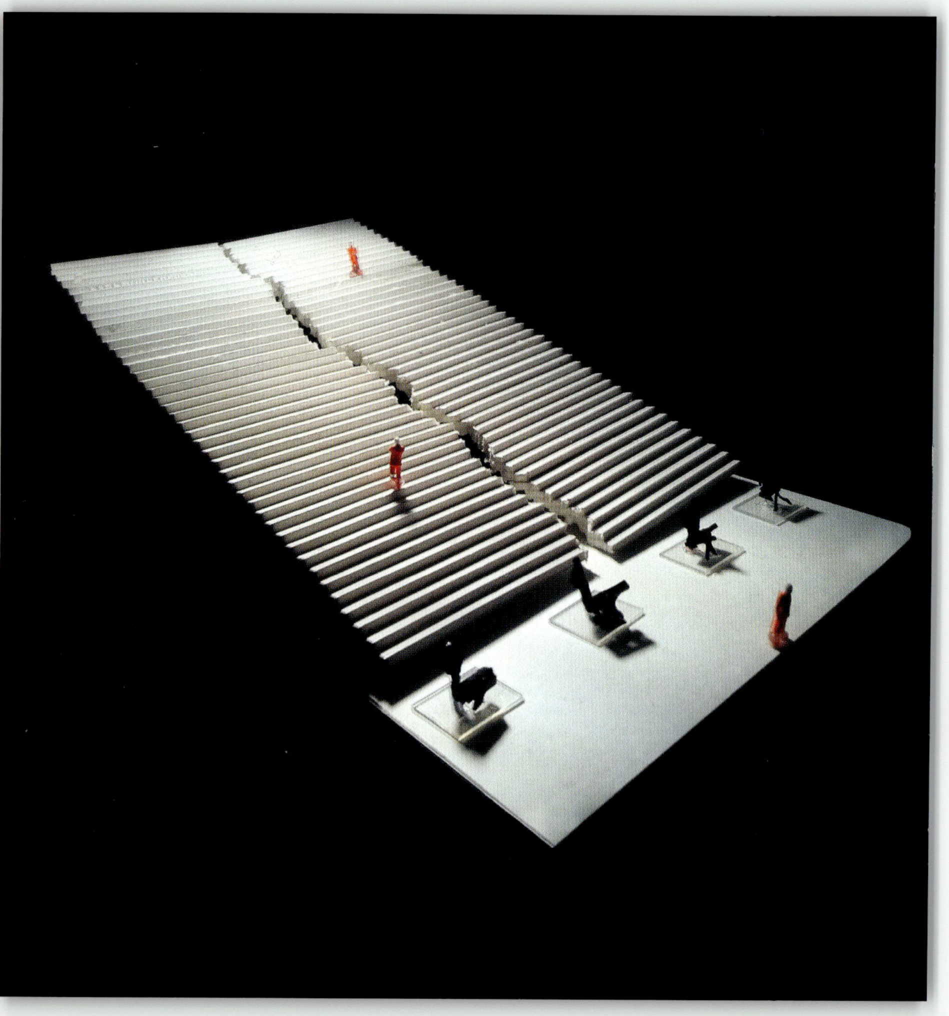

WATCH THE THRONE

What's a mob to a king? / What's a king to a God?
What's a God to a non-believer / Who don't believe in anything?

Jay-Z and Kanye West, featuring Frank Ocean, 'No Church in the Wild'

On 4 August 2011, Kanye West and Virgil Abloh arrived at my studio in Peckham to work on tour designs for the Kanye/Jay-Z joint album, *Watch the Throne*. It was the first day of the London Riots, which were instigated by a police shooting in Tottenham. London was literally burning – it wasn't safe to leave the studio – so we worked through the night. We listened to the album for the first time and played 'No Church in the Wild' on repeat. As Frank Ocean's plangent voice made its debut on a deserted South London side street, Kanye and Virgil made cardboard scale models with my team. Miniature Roman coliseum steps and stone tablets split apart and caught fire. The design evolved all summer. Kanye sent me an image of Keith Warner's Bregenz production of *Andrea Chénier* with the caption 'Make me an angel like this', and for a while an enormous angel sculpture filled the model arena. Jay-Z's designer, Bruce Rodgers, joined us and sensibly suggested we develop the kinetic LED cubes we had made with Muse a few years earlier. Two thrones, each a 5-metre cube on opposite sides of the arena, elevated each man, alone, above a crowd of 20,000 – at once powerful and vulnerable. Every lighting cue responded to a chord. The imagery filling the LED sculptures was mainly drawn from David Attenborough's BBC wildlife documentaries. The energy of wild sharks, tigers and falcons forced at the constraints of the orthogonal geometry.

652–653 680 806–807

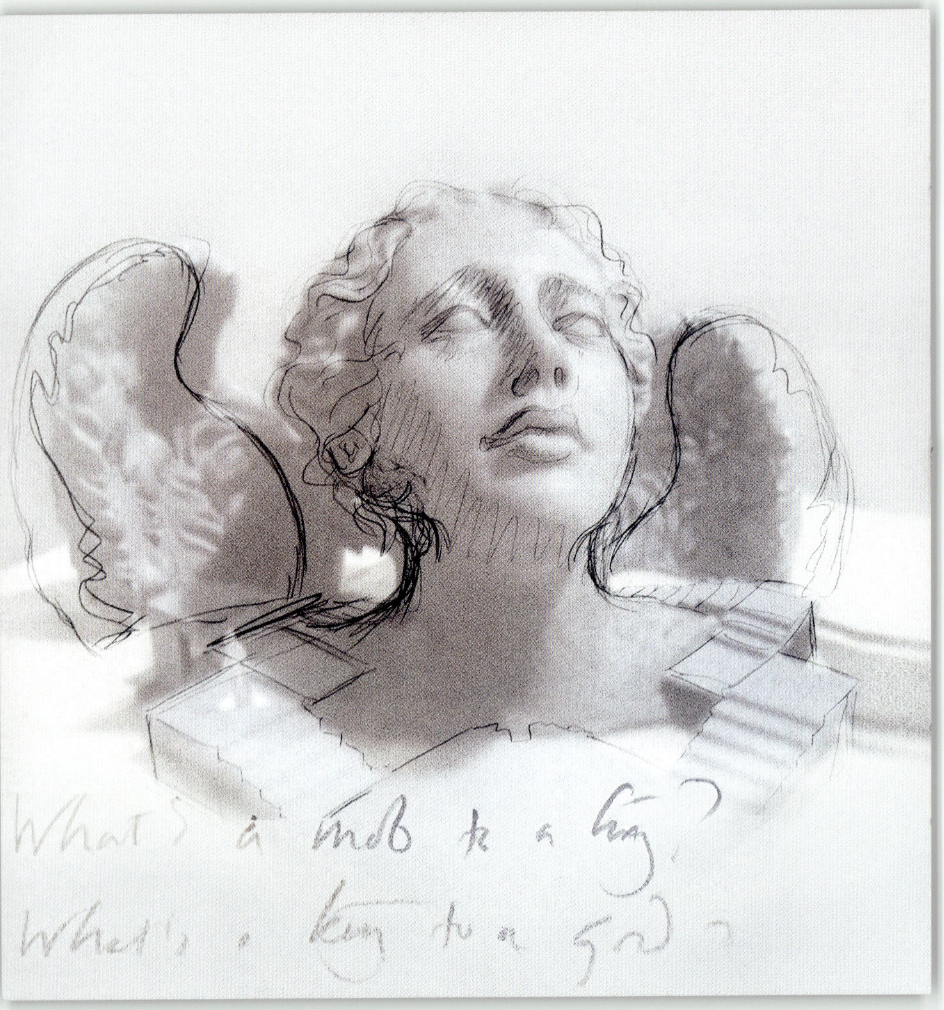
What's a mob to a king?
What's a king to a god?

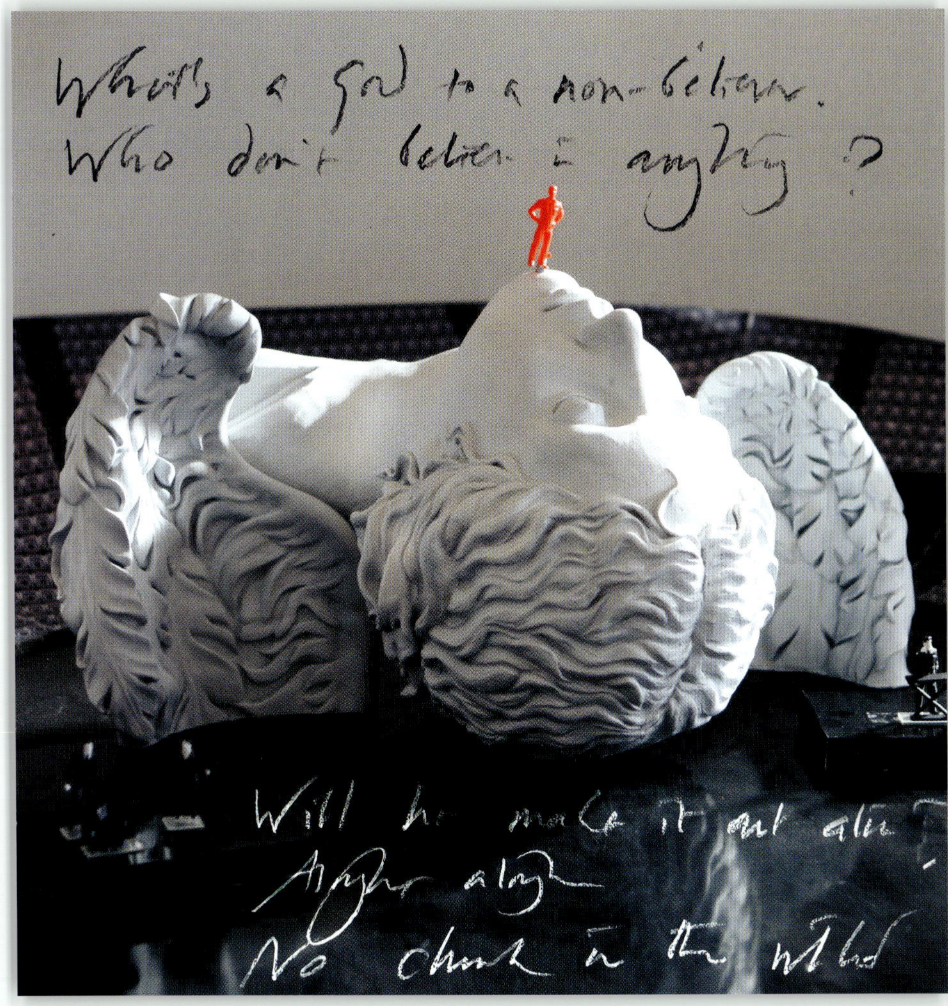
What's a god to a non-believer.
Who don't believe in anything?
Will he make it out alive?
No chance in the world

PARSIFAL

Parsifal: I hardly stir, and yet I move apace.
Gurnemanz: Thou seest, my son, here time is one with space.

Richard Wagner

Written in 1882, these lines in Richard Wagner's *Parsifal* suggest the unity of time and space two decades before Einstein. They also refer to the elaborate, mechanical, scenic transition between trees and mountains in Wagner's original Bayreuth production, which amazed the nineteenth-century, pre-cinema audience. Introduced to Buddhism by Arthur Schopenhauer, Wagner conceived his final work as a ritual mass for the consecration of a stage. Over four hours of largely static drama, the audience transcend time and space through a rite of compassion. For the Royal Danish Opera production in March 2012, the director Keith Warner and I conceived an enormous revolving rook chess-piece whose conical interior formed a new theatre within Copenhagen's opera house. We presented Parsifal's odyssey from naivety to wisdom as a resistance to the rules of an antiquated game. Ceramic tiles framed the ailing knights as residents of the Marienbad spa where Wagner first conceived the work. Before I arrived at rehearsals, Keith rang to say that the sculpture looked great and there were only two problems: no one could stand on its slippery angled floor, and no one could sing within its deafening tiled megaphone interior. Mercifully, the Danish team found solutions to both problems: a non-slip boat-deck soap and ear plugs for the male chorus.

718–720

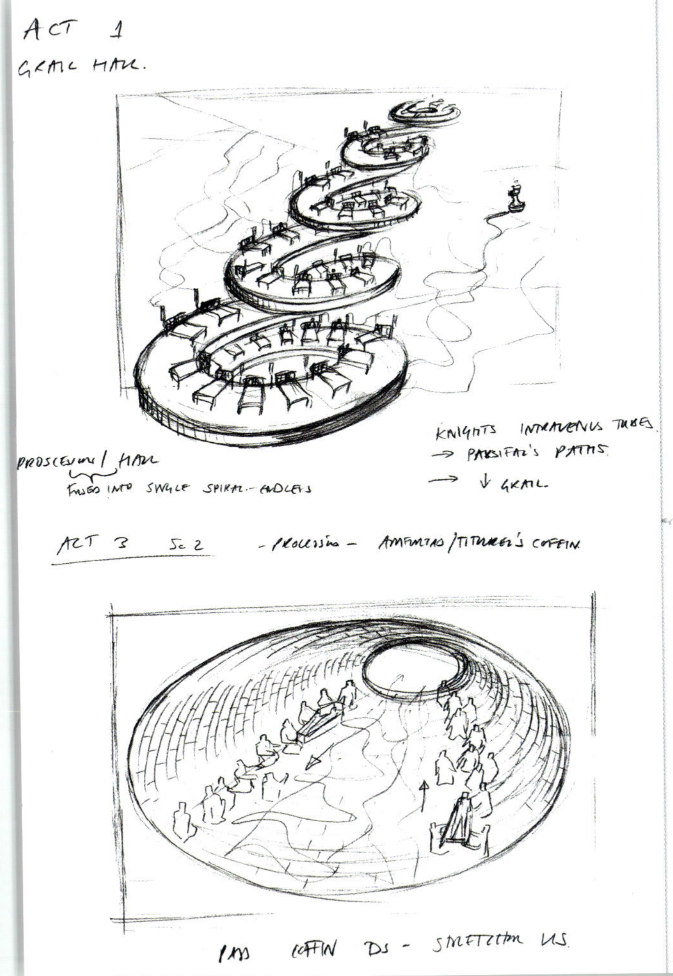

…RY

…nd others who …ew who go to …oth worlds

… Michael Ende

…dré Heller …9 fable, *The* …nfair Luna …el by Keith … Andy Warhol … After a short …n litigation …ee decades. …arallel world …eatened with …

…ng in his …point you will … We worked …ized production …ced a series of …André's Luna …2.

PARSIFAL

Parsifal: I hardly stir, a
Gurnemanz: Thou see

Written in 1882, these
unity of time and spa
to the elaborate, mec
mountains in Wagner
the nineteenth-centu
by Arthur Schopenha
mass for the consecr
drama, the audience
compassion. For the
the director Keith Wa
rook chess-piece wh
Copenhagen's opera
naivety to wisdom as
Ceramic tiles framed
spa where Wagner fi
rehearsals, Keith ran
were only two proble
floor, and no one cou
interior. Mercifully, the
a non-slip boat-deck

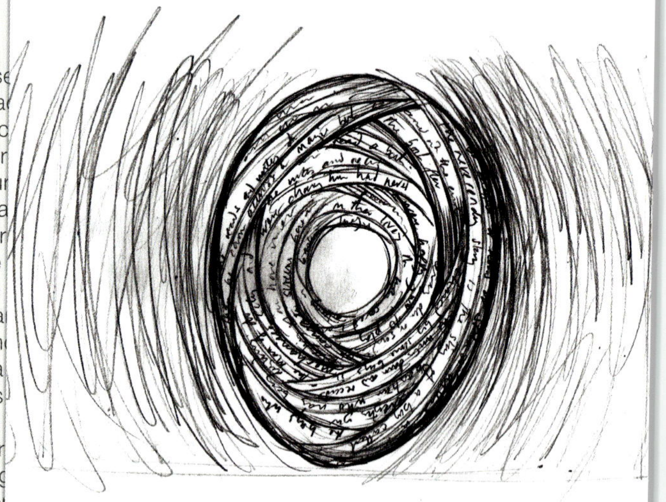

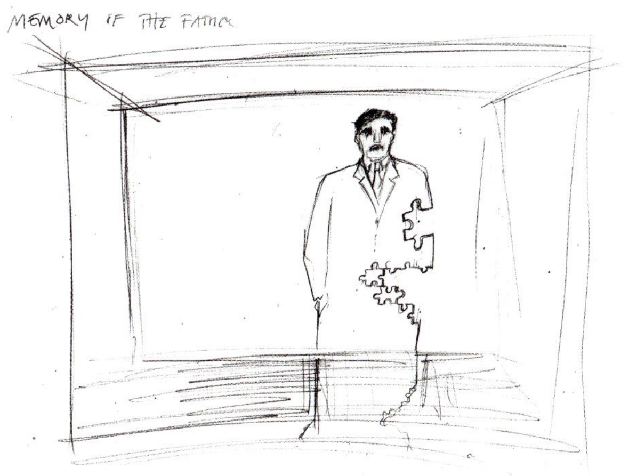

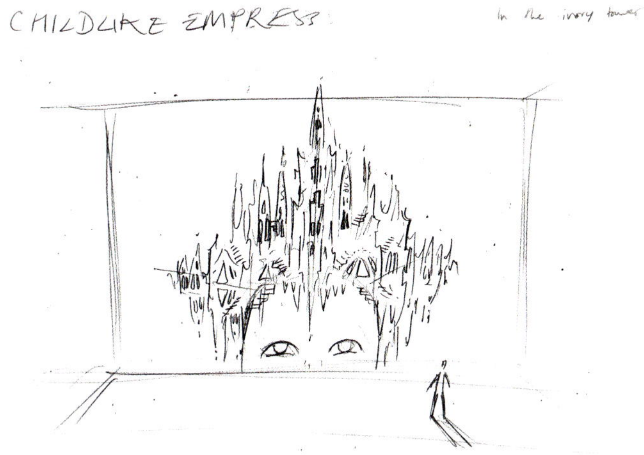

RY

ınd others who
ew who go to
ooth worlds

Michael Ende

dré Heller
9 fable, *The*
nfair Luna
el by Keith
Andy Warhol
After a short
n litigation
ee decades.
arallel world
eatened with
.

ng in his
point you will
We worked
ized production
ced a series of
André's Luna
2.

PARSIFAL

Parsifal: I hardly stir
Gurnemanz: Thou s

Written in 1882, the
unity of time and sp
to the elaborate, m
mountains in Wagn
the nineteenth-cen
by Arthur Schopen
mass for the conse
drama, the audienc
compassion. For th
the director Keith W
rook chess-piece w
Copenhagen's ope
naivety to wisdom
Ceramic tiles frame
spa where Wagner
rehearsals, Keith ra
were only two prob
floor, and no one c
interior. Mercifully,
a non-slip boat-dec

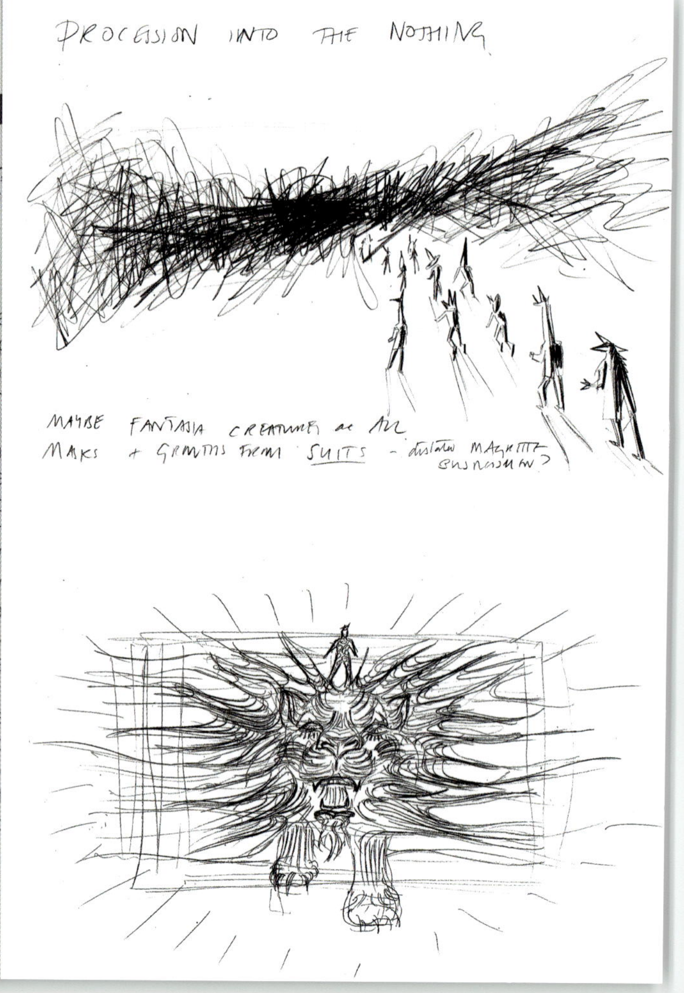

THE NEVERENDING STORY

There are people who can never go to Fantastica … and others who can, but who stay there forever. And there are just a few who go to Fantastica and come back. Like you. And they make both worlds well again.

Michael Ende

In 2012 I met the Austrian poet, musician and artist André Heller to discuss an adaptation of Michael Ende's potent 1979 fable, *The Neverending Story*. André had curated the 1987 art funfair Luna Luna, a 'travelling terrain of modern art' with a carousel by Keith Haring, a coloured glass maze by Roy Lichtenstein, an Andy Warhol photo booth and Jean-Michel Basquiat's Ferris wheel. After a short three-month run, André's luminous project got mired in litigation and was stored unseen in steel containers for over three decades. He seemed the ideal collaborator on a story about a parallel world called Fantastica ruled by a Childlike Empress and threatened with corrosion by a formless dark entity called The Nothing.

As we drank jasmine tea under a Georg Baselitz painting in his apartment in a Viennese palace, André said, 'At some point you will need to stop raping yourself: you are doing too much.' We worked together for a year on ideas, imagining an as yet unrealized production made entirely out of intricately cut white paper. I produced a series of drawings that I am still keen to develop as sculptures. André's Luna Luna finally emerged from its storage containers in 2022.

THE MASTER AND MARGARITA

Our talent for division, for seeing the parts, is of staggering importance – second only to our capacity to transcend it, in order to see the whole.

Iain McGilchrist, *The Master and His Emissary*

The writer and director Simon McBurney gave me Iain McGilchrist's book, *The Master and His Emissary: The Divided Brain and the Making of the Western World*, in preparation for our 2012 Théâtre de Complicité touring adaptation of Mikhail Bulgakov's novel, *The Master and Margarita*. During our first meeting, McBurney practised sonic magic using binaural headphones. His voice travelled from deep inside my left brain to my right. Bulgakov wrote his satirical critique of Soviet Russia between 1928 and 1940. Admired by Stalin but endlessly censored and never permitted to leave, Bulgakov knew the novel would remain unpublished in his lifetime.

I sketched a world of congested tramlines and a fake brick wall with blocked windows. The audience knew the brick was fake, but accepted it as real. They knew the blue skies were just projected light on brick, but still sensed summer air through the blind windows. When the show toured to the Palais des Papes in Avignon that summer, the thirteenth-century stone walls seemed to come crashing down; walls that had witnessed anti-popes in the fourteenth century, mass counter-revolutionary massacres during the French Revolution, and Napoleonic imprisonments. From the ruins rose a giant, projected galloping horse made from animated, fallen school chairs.

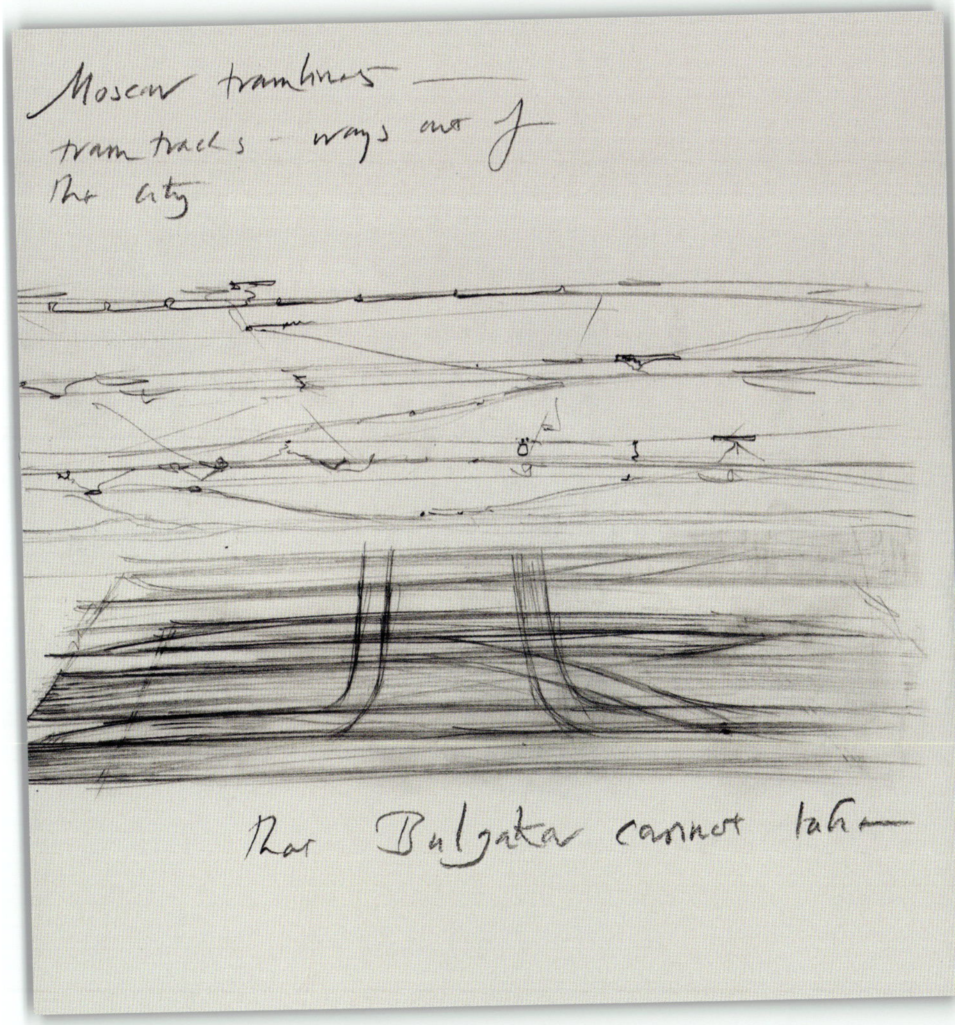
Moscow tramlines —
tram tracks – ways out of
the city
that Bulgakov cannot take —

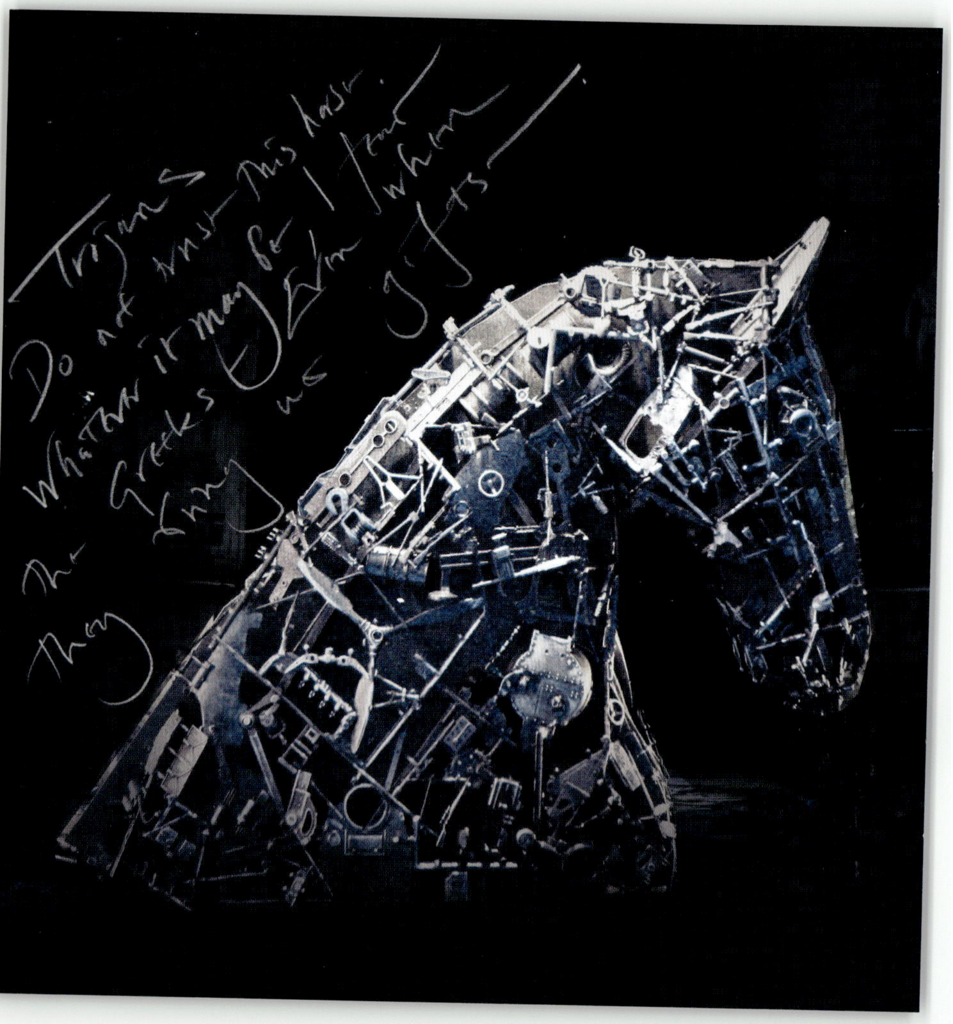
Trojans
Do not trust this horse.
Whatever it may be, I fear
the Greeks even when
they bring us gifts

LES TROYENS

Do not trust the horse, Trojans!
Whatever it is, I fear the Greeks, even when they bring gifts.

Virgil, *The Aeneid*

Hector Berlioz's two-part operatic work, first performed in 1890, 21 years after the composer's death, is based on Virgil's epic poem, *The Aeneid.* It presents war and peace as two sides of civilization constantly chasing one another in repeated cycles.

For David McVicar's June 2012 Royal Opera House production, I was interested in the huge Victorian industrial gas storage cylinders near my studio in South London. We treated the exterior of the revolving cylinder as Troy's steel defensive barricade, while revealing the inside as Virgil's vision of industrious humanity at peace, building the warm brick city of Carthage. Virgil was the son of a beekeeper, and Berlioz retained the simile of peaceful civilization as a functioning hive. The Trojan horse was a massive 7-metre horse-head sculpture formed of weapons. Its gesture of amnesty proved treacherous as its mane burst into flames.

786–789

LONDON OLYMPICS

Our house, in the middle of our street
Our house, in the middle of our …

Madness, 'Our House'

I considered the idea of setting the London 2012 Olympic Closing Ceremony on the UK flag to be nationalist and un-Olympic in spirit. I researched drawings made by King James I's flag designers and discovered an unedifying sequence of Scottish, Welsh and Irish flags being assimilated beneath the St George Cross. The most potent re-interpretation was Jamie Reid's, ripped and held together with safety pins on the cover of the Sex Pistols' *Anarchy in the UK* album, released during the Jubilee year of 1977. I asked Damien Hirst to contribute a 120-metre-wide celebratory Olympic spin painting in red, white and blue to manifest the centrifugal tensions inherent within the seams of the Union Jack flag. We expressed London as a model city wrapped in newspapers printed with British literature from Anglo-Saxon *Beowulf* to contemporary poet laureate Carol Ann Duffy.

During the 16 hours between Usain Bolt winning the final race and the start of the Closing Ceremony, one of the segments of the giant Hirst floorcloth got lost. It was found in a wheelie bin moments before the start of the show, confiscated by health and safety inspectors. As the TV cameras started broadcasting to a global audience of 750 million, my team and I were still pinning down its corners, our hands bleeding from dragging the canvas across the stadium.

46–47 822–823

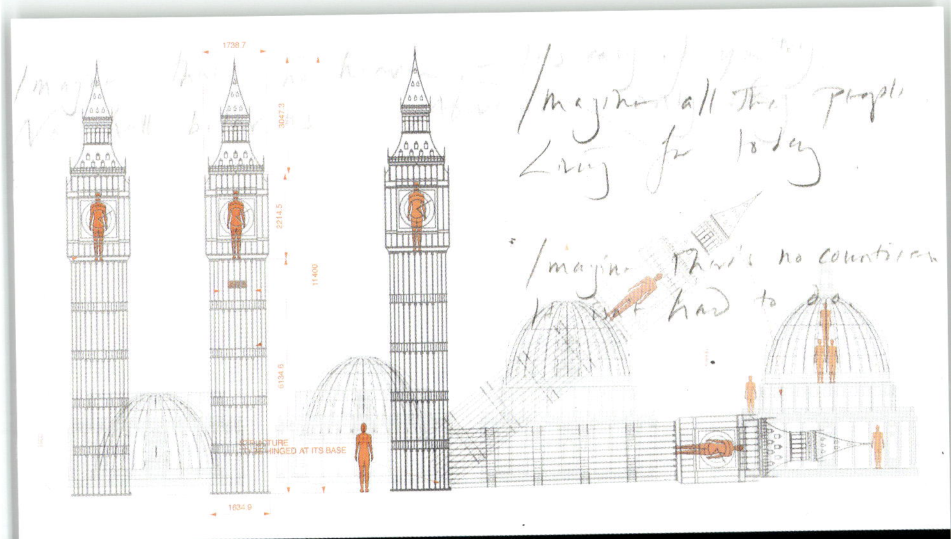
1738.7
3047.3
2214.5
11400
6134.6
1634.9
STRUCTURE
HINGED AT ITS BASE
Imagine all the people
Living for today
Imagine there's no countries
hard to do

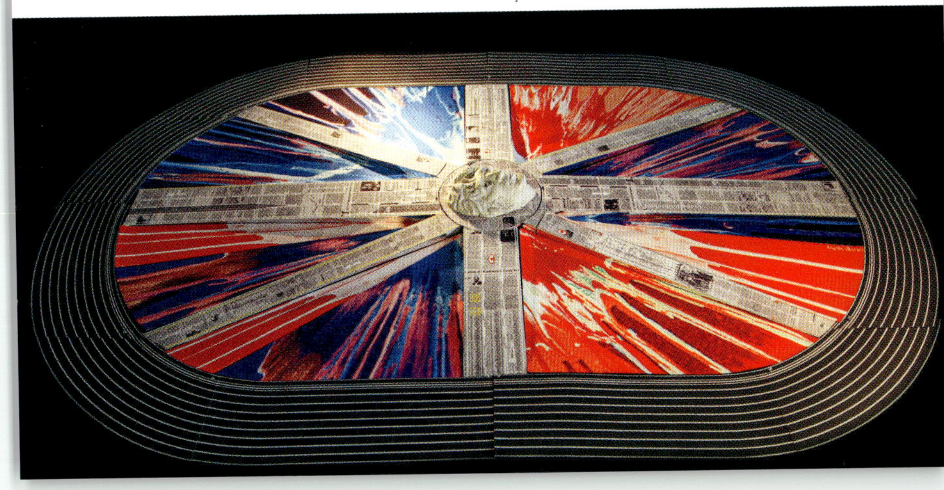

LONDON OLYMPICS

Our house, in the middle of our street
Our house, in the middle of our …

Madness, 'Our House'

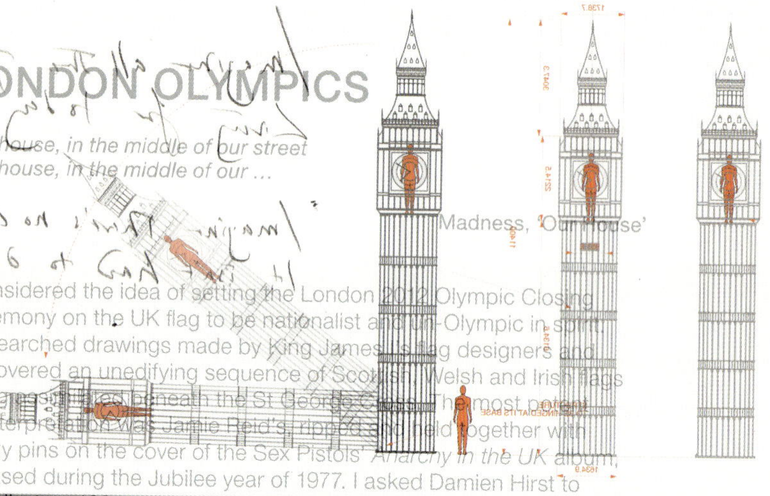

I considered the idea of setting the London 2012 Olympic Closing Ceremony on the UK flag to be nationalist and un-Olympic in spirit. I researched drawings made by King James I's flag designers and discovered an unedifying sequence of Scottish, Welsh and Irish flags being subsumed beneath the St George Cross. The most potent re-interpretation was Jamie Reid's, ripped and held together with safety pins on the cover of the Sex Pistols' *Anarchy in the UK* album, released during the Jubilee year of 1977. I asked Damien Hirst to contribute a 120-metre-wide celebratory Olympic spin painting in red, white and blue to manifest the centrifugal tensions inherent within the seams of the Union Jack flag. We expressed London as a model city wrapped in newspapers printed with British literature from Anglo-Saxon *Beowulf* to contemporary poet laureate Carol Ann Duffy.

During the 16 hours between Usain Bolt winning the final race and the start of the Closing Ceremony, one of the segments of the giant Hirst floorcloth got lost. It was found in a wheelie bin moments before the start of the show, confiscated by health and safety inspectors. As the TV cameras started broadcasting to a global audience of 750 million, my team and I were still pinning down its corners, our hands bleeding from dragging the canvas across the stadium.

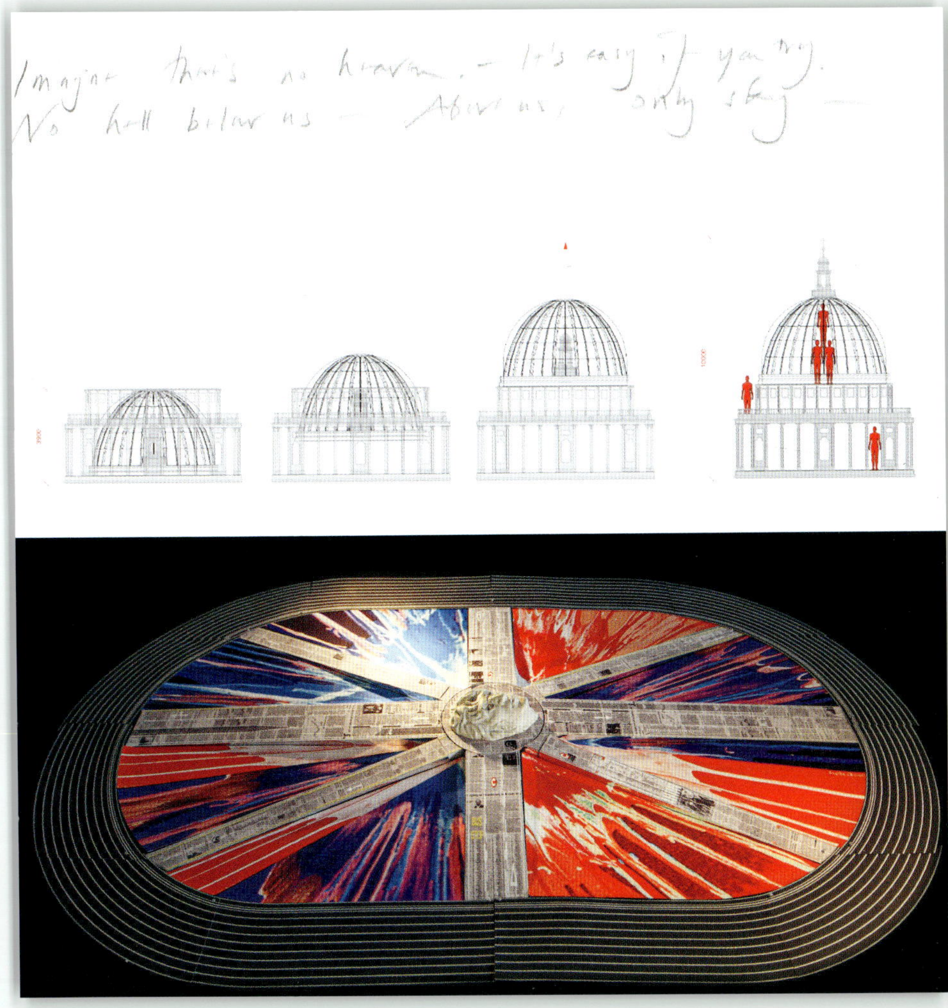
Imagine there's no heaven. – It's easy if you try.
No hell below us – Above us, only sky –

CHIMERICA

I hate any piece of art that delivers its ethics to you.

Lucy Kirkwood

Lucy Kirkwood's play *Chimerica* opens with Tank Man – Kirkwood's version of the unidentified Chinese man who was photographed standing in front of a column of tanks in Tiananmen Square, Beijing, after the massacre of protestors in June 1989. Over 39 scenes and three hours, we learn the Tank Man's identity and the story that led to this era-defining photograph. The play's other central protagonist is the fictional American war photographer who took the photo from his hotel window. The director Lyndsey Turner and I drew on the framing and shuttering mechanics of a single-lens reflex camera as we developed a rotating, sculptural device to propel the action through multiple locations and perspectives. My assistant Chiara Stephenson made an initial cardboard model for Lyndsey to test and study. Lyndsey's series of diagrams became the basis for mine, which in turn informed the next iteration of the model. We gave the series of illuminated model photographs to lighting and video designers as a canvas for their interventions. Our budget did not stretch to include encoders, which would have matched video to automation, so the projected images sometimes lagged behind or advanced ahead of the revolve, like an offset screen print.

654–655

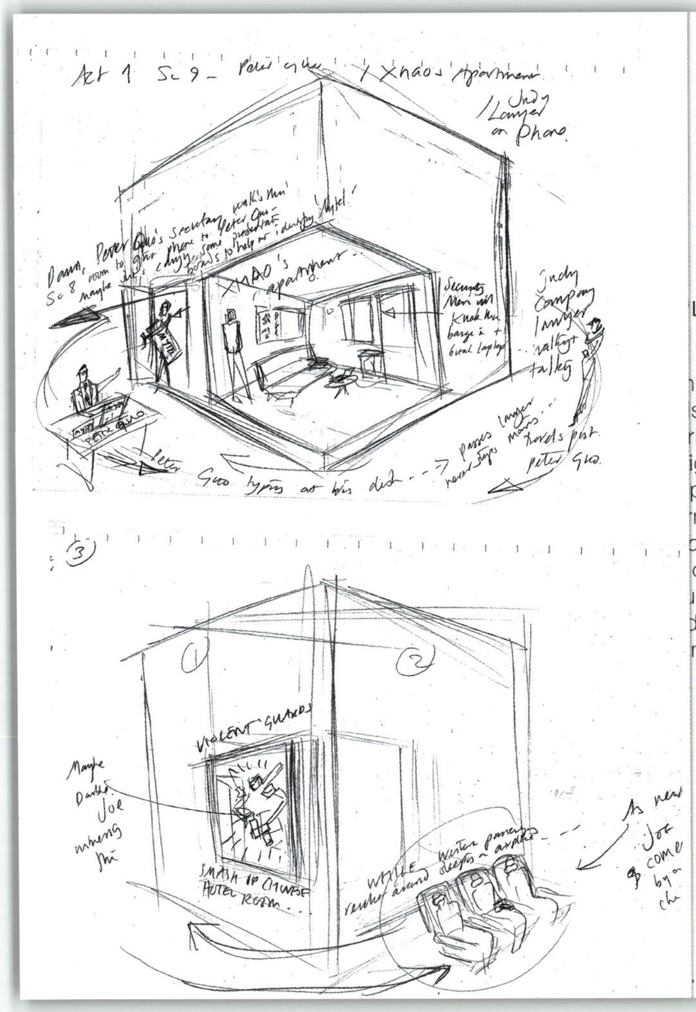

'Lost in the World'

hree-night
saged an
ries of paper
igure alone
proved
rned to the
orytellers
curated a
urfaces. For the
d and jewelled
n a paralyzed
over the walls of

CHIMERI

I hate any piece of a

Lucy Kirkwood's pl
version of the unid
standing in front of
after the massacre
three hours, we lea
this era-defining ph
fictional American
window. The direct
shuttering mechan
a rotating, sculptur
locations and pers
an initial cardboard
series of diagrams
the next iteration o
photographs to ligh
interventions. Our
would have matche
sometimes lagged
offset screen print.

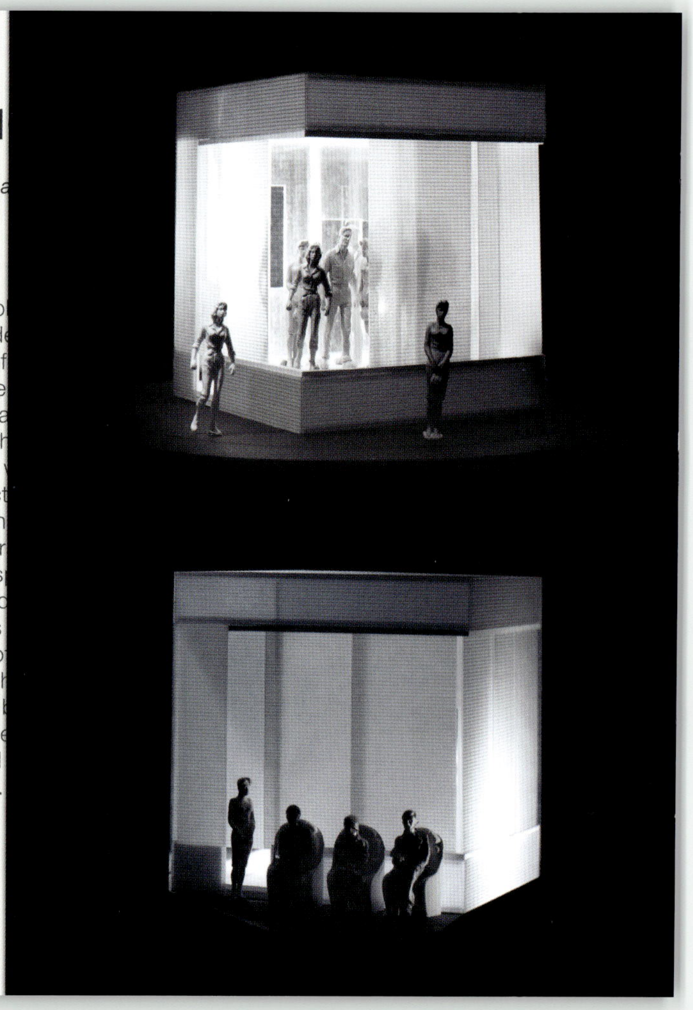

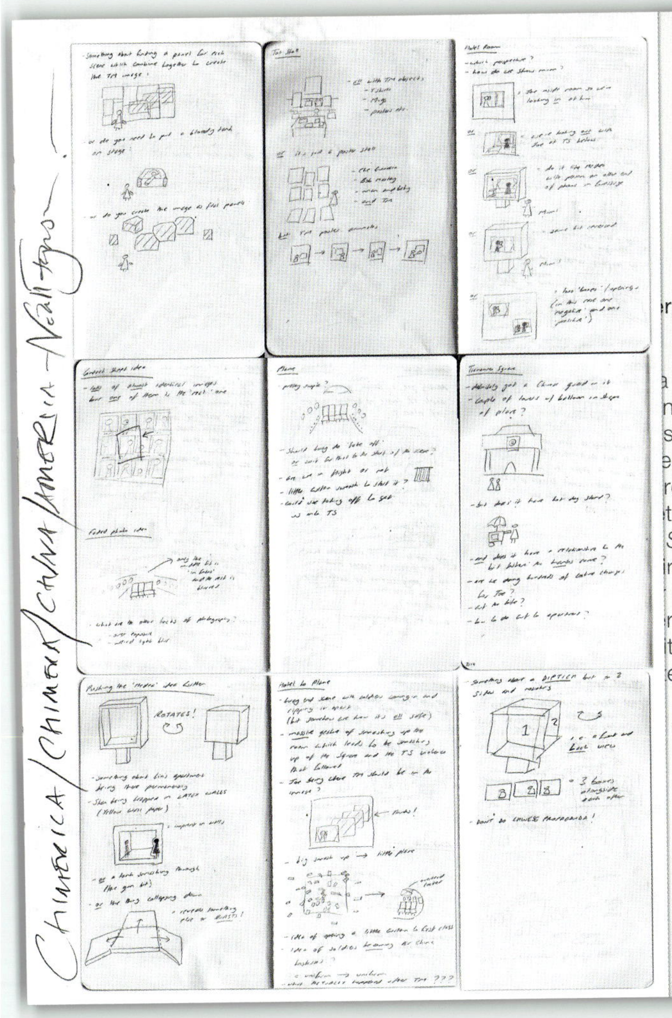

r, 'Lost in the World'

a three-night
nvisaged an
series of paper
el figure alone
re proved
turned to the
Storytellers
ire curated a
surfaces. For the
ered and jewelled
ithin a paralyzed
ed over the walls of

CHIMERI

I hate any piece of a

Lucy Kirkwood's p
version of the unid
standing in front of
after the massacre
three hours, we lea
this era-defining ph
fictional American
window. The direct
shuttering mechan
a rotating, sculptur
locations and pers
an initial cardboard
series of diagrams
the next iteration o
photographs to ligh
interventions. Our
would have matche
sometimes lagged
offset screen print.

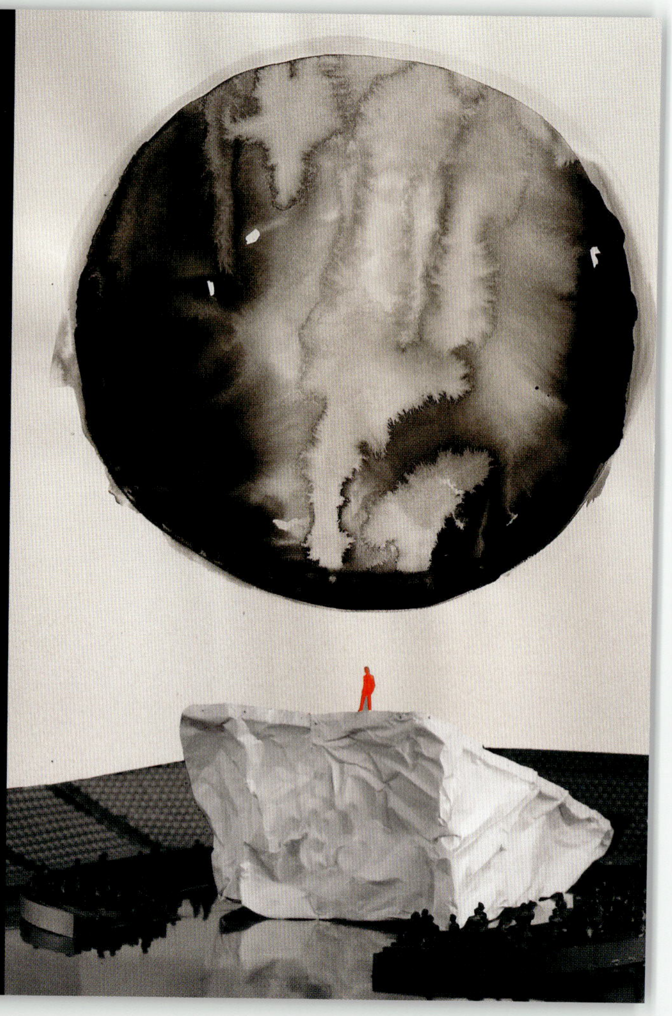

LOST IN THE WORLD

I'm up in the woods
I'm down on my mind
I'm building a still
To slow down the time

Kanye West, featuring Bon Iver, 'Lost in the World'

On 28 December 2012, Kanye West was to begin a three-night residency at the Revel theatre in Atlantic City. He envisaged an environment of monumental icebergs. We made a series of paper sculptures and photographed a small orange model figure alone amongst them. Building a physical iceberg sculpture proved unachievable in the lead-up to Christmas, so we returned to the two sculptural planes we had explored for his *VH1 Storytellers* performance in 2009. Virgil Abloh and John McGuire curated a series of arctic scenes that were projected on their surfaces. For the performance, Kanye wore a series of ornate feathered and jewelled masks by Maison Martin Margiela. Shaman-like, within a paralyzed glacial environment, his feathered face was projected over the walls of the theatre and the audience box seats.

812–813

THE CUNNING LITTLE VIXEN

The melodic curves of speech are an expression of the complete organism and of all phases of its spiritual activities ... The art of dramatic writing is to compose a melodic curve that will, as if by magic, reveal immediately a human being in one definite phase of his existence.

Leoš Janáček

In 1923, at the age of 70, the Czech composer Leoš Janáček transformed a newspaper comic into a philosophical meditation on the cyclical nature of life and death. His opera-ballet emulates the comic-strip structure with a flowing series of episodes featuring birds, animals and insects. It culminates in the merging of animal and human worlds, a radiant hymn to the symbiosis between all life forms within the biosphere, which the composer requested to be played at his funeral in 1928. For the December 2012 Royal Danish Opera production, we made every element out of paper. Remembering hours spent learning to make paper origami birds and animals, and responding to the traditional Moravian music woven into the score, I drew on Czech folk paper-cuts to express the environment, the animals and the humans: each species cut from the same paper. Luke Halls overlaid a luminescent spectrum of animation over cellular, internal human landscapes drawn from endoscopic photographs. The opera director Francisco Negrin is an avid scuba diver and we aimed to emulate the mesmerizing experience of diving amidst a coral reef.

268

738 830–831 858–859

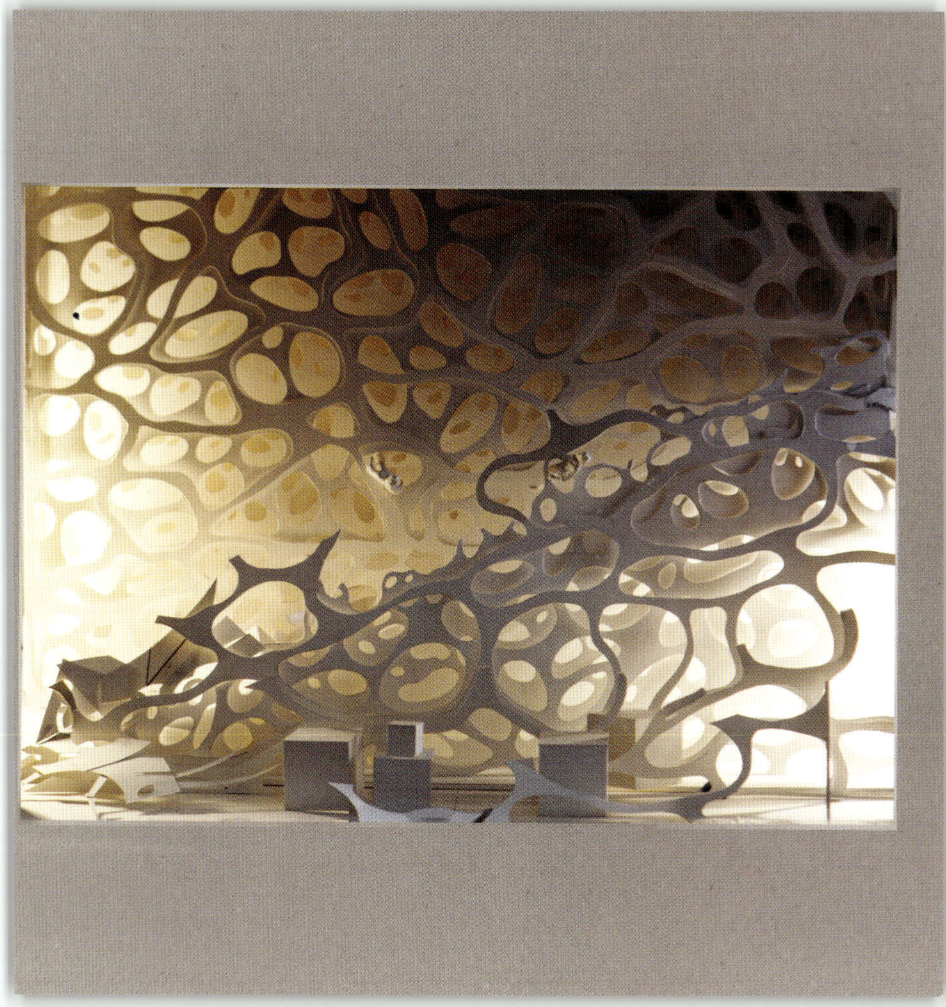

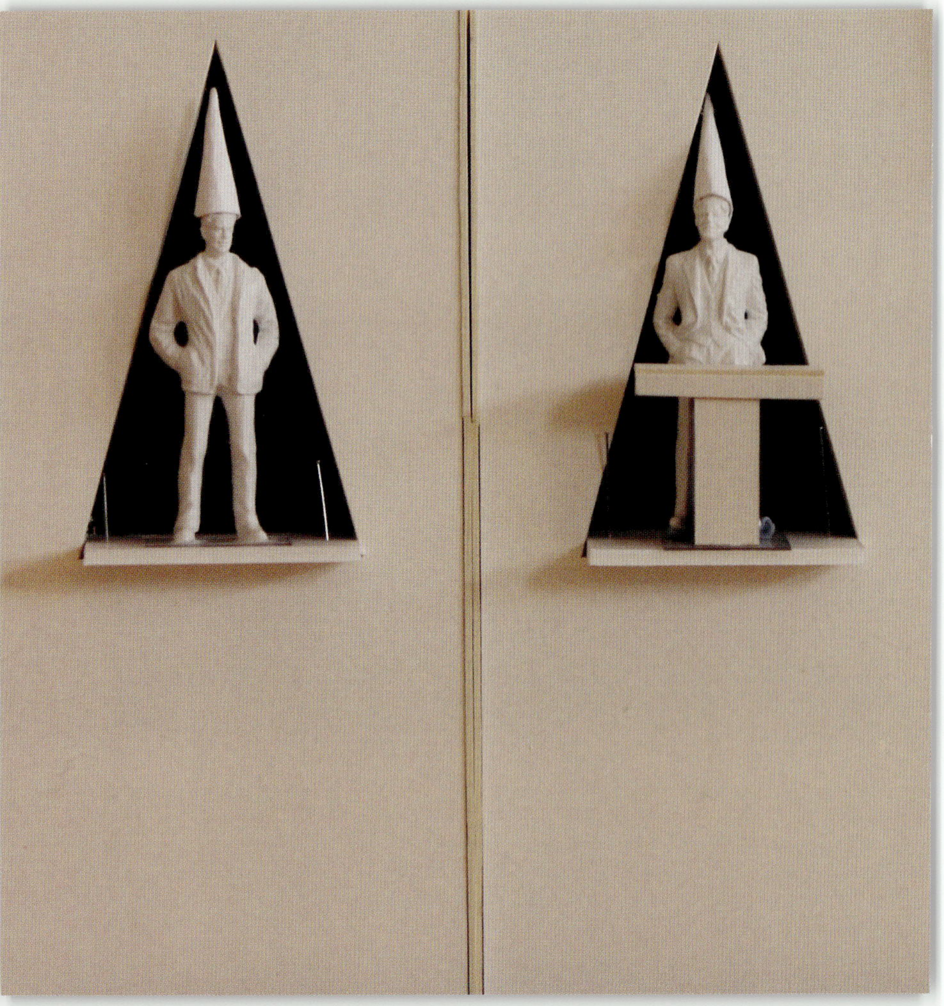

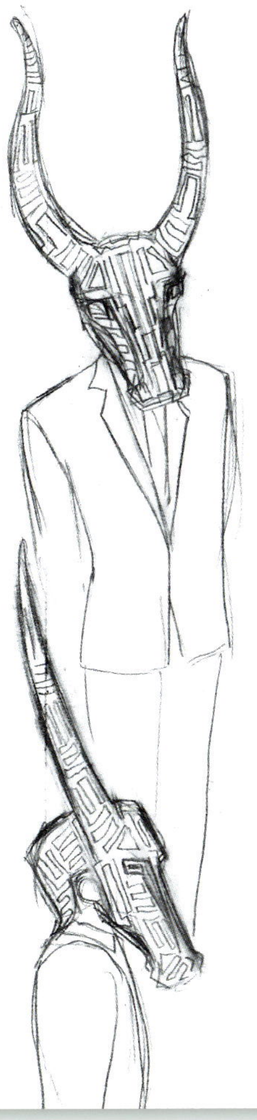

vent black
ces on our map

Bruce Springsteen, 'Last to Die'

e Pet Shop Boys, suggested
the presentation of their ecstatically
he *Electric* tour opened at the
in Saint Petersburg in June 2013.
arena crowd through a labyrinthine
Shop Boys' programmer and
he architecture of the printed circuit
s synthesizers. I made model mazes
try. Neil wore the maze etched into a
projected dancers wearing bone-and-
er him.

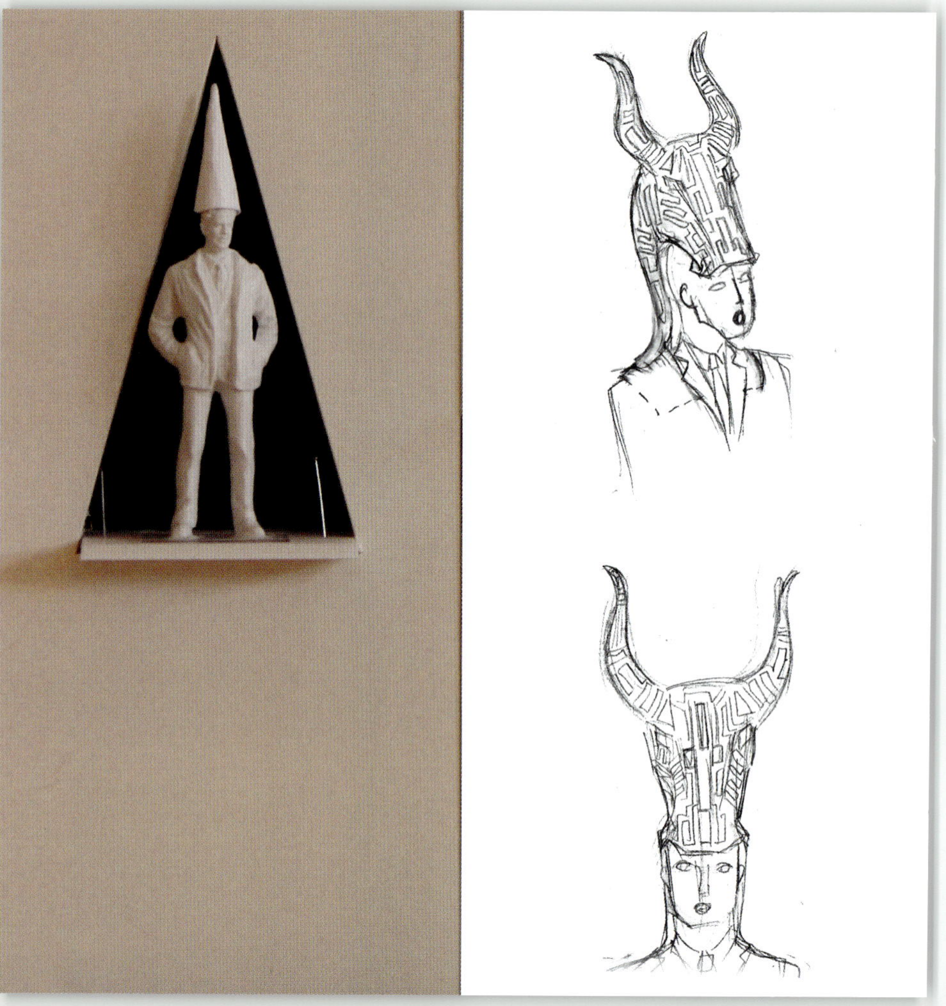

ELECTRIC

We took the highway till the road went black
We'd marked Truth Or Consequences on our map

Bruce Springsteen, 'Last to Die'

Neil Tennant and Chris Lowe, the Pet Shop Boys, suggested analogue chaos should pervade the presentation of their ecstatically electronic new album *Electric*. The *Electric* tour opened at the Oktyabrsky Grand Concert Hall in Saint Petersburg in June 2013. An orange ovoid tunnel led the arena crowd through a labyrinthine odyssey. Pete Gleadall, the Pet Shop Boys' programmer and producer, gave me a lesson in the architecture of the printed circuit boards at the heart of the band's synthesizers. I made model mazes based on this electronic geometry. Neil wore the maze etched into a laser-cut Minotaur head, while projected dancers wearing bone-and-hair Minotaur masks towered over him.

726 832–833

YEEZUS

I wear my heart on the sleeve
I know that we the new slaves
I see the blood on the leaves

Kanye West, 'New Slaves'

By July 2013, tickets had gone on sale for Kanye West's *Yeezus* world arena tour, based on a seating plan that would surround the performer with audience beneath an illuminated hemisphere. The form was influenced by Alejandro Jodorowsky's surrealist film *The Holy Mountain*. I was nervous about Kanye being surrounded by audience on all sides at this point in his practice: I felt his performance should be backed by the power of his imagery. We re-opened the design process – much to the promoter's exasperation – and altered the design and the seating plan to incorporate a vast 18-metre-diameter circular screen, suspended above a 15-metre-tall geometric mountain sculpture. Kanye gathered fragments of a carved model that John McGuire, Virgil Abloh, Vanessa Beecroft and myself had discarded, and pieced the final form together himself. Opening in October 2013 in Seattle, the show was conceived as a five-act ritual preceded by a prelude performed by Kendrick Lamar.

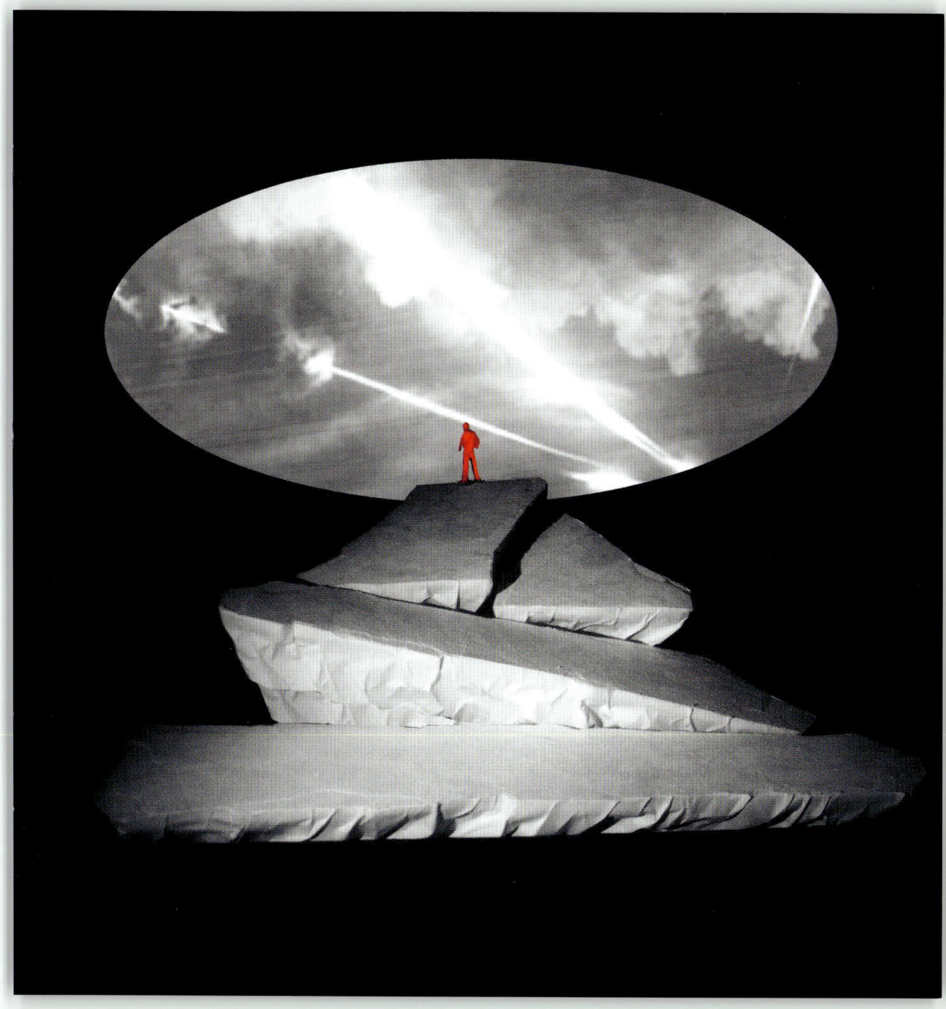

DON GIOVANNI

... death is the key which unlocks the door to our true happiness.

Wolfgang Amadeus Mozart

Works of art are like barometers: we return to them throughout our lives to check the weather conditions in our souls. I had first explored *Don Giovanni* in 2006 with the opera director Keith Warner within a series of labyrinthine hotel corridors. Now, in 2014, for the Royal Opera House production, I was re-cast under its spell with Kasper Holten. The first question any team asks when adventuring into this morality myth is: how will we present hell? Keith and I conjured a hell of infinite ageing, the extinction of death. Kasper and I determined that, if the ultimate expression of life is liberty and multi-directional exploration, then hell is the closing of doors and corridors, the end of choice and plurality. We materialized the multitudinous list of Giovanni's lovers into an often over-crowded, revolving, multi-storey structure full of stairs and corridors. The edifice closed its doors on Don Giovanni and left him alone on a bare stage at the end of the opera. The *Don Giovanni* set is now stored in silence in a warehouse in Aberdare in Wales. It's trucked out every few years for revivals or tours. The recipe for recreating the show is recorded in precise annotations to the score – each lighting and video cue, each beat and movement and intention of the staging – so that the entire three-hour sequence can be recreated with new performers.

276

656–657 740–741

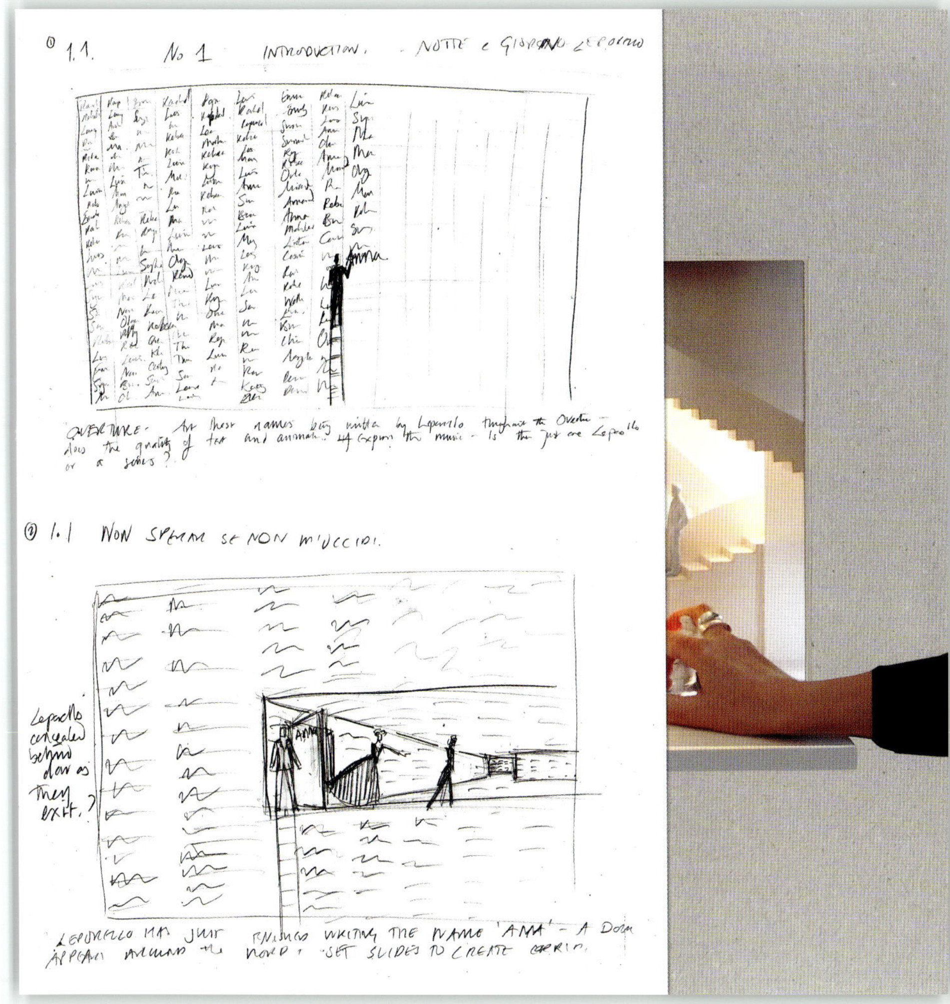
1.1. No 1 INTRODUCTION. - NOTTE E GIORNO
1.1 NON SPERAR SE NON M'UCCIDI.
Leporello concealed behind door as they exit?

… death is the key wh

Works of art are like b
lives to check the we
Don Giovanni in 2006
series of labyrinthine
House production, I v
The first question any
myth is: how will we p
ageing, the extinction
ultimate expression o
then hell is the closin
plurality. We materiali
an often over-crowde
and corridors. The ec
him alone on a bare s
set is now stored in s
It's trucked out every
recreating the show i
each lighting and vide
the staging – so that
with new performers.

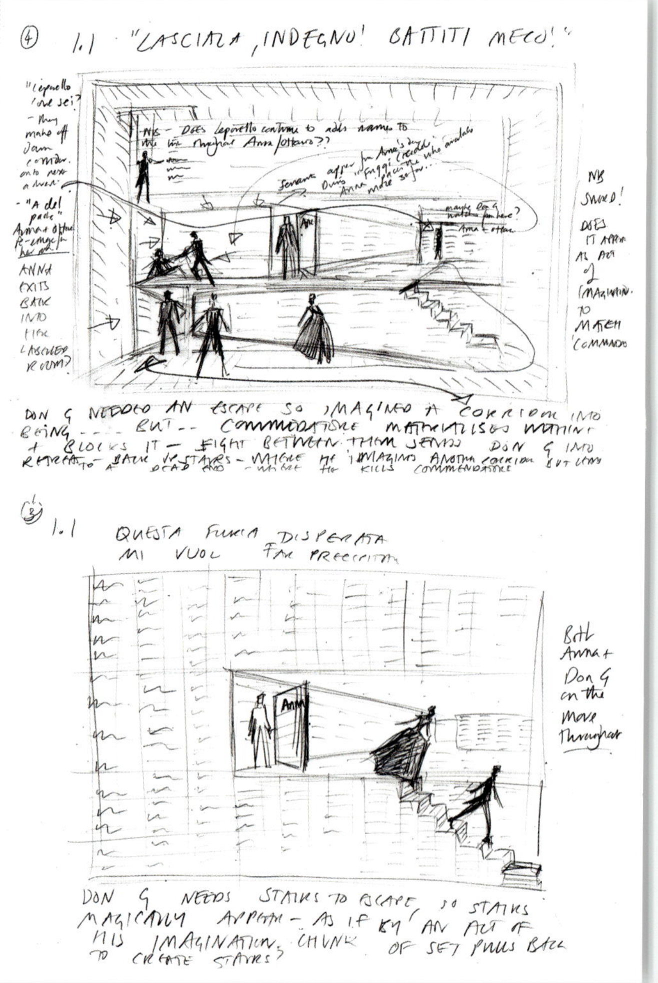

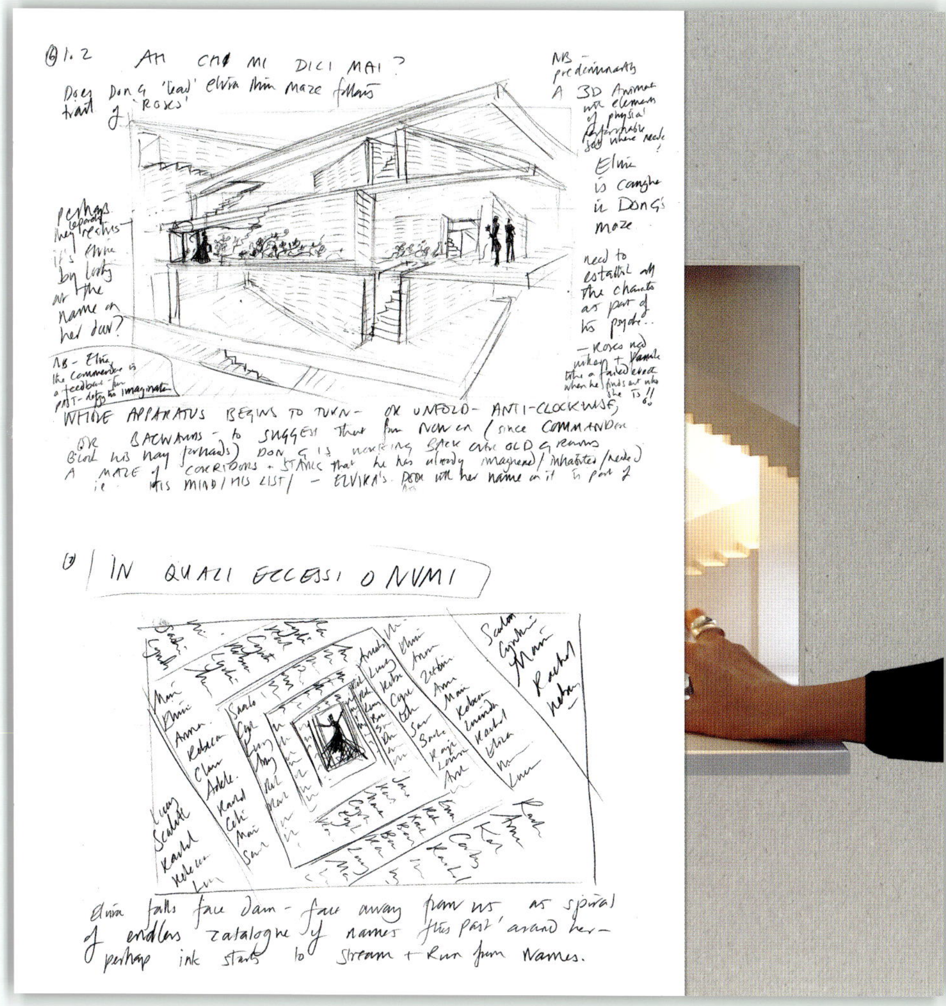

AH CHI MI DICI MAI?
Does Don G 'lead' Elvira thru maze follows trail of 'ROSES'
NB – predominantly A 3D Animation with elements of physical performable set where needed!
Elvira is caught in DONG's maze
perhaps he recognises it's Elvira by looking at the name on her door?
need to establish all the characters as part of his psyche...
WHOLE APPARATUS BEGINS TO TURN – OR UNFOLD – ANTI-CLOCKWISE,
OR BACKWARDS – to SUGGEST that from now on
IN QUALI ECCESSI O NUMI
Elvira falls face down – face away from us as spiral of endless catalogue of names flies past around her – perhaps ink starts to stream + run from names.

… death is the key whi

Works of art are like b
lives to check the wea
Don Giovanni in 2006
series of labyrinthine
House production, I w
The first question any
myth is: how will we p
ageing, the extinction
ultimate expression o
then hell is the closing
plurality. We materiali
an often over-crowde
and corridors. The ed
him alone on a bare s
set is now stored in s
It's trucked out every
recreating the show is
each lighting and vide
the staging – so that t
with new performers.

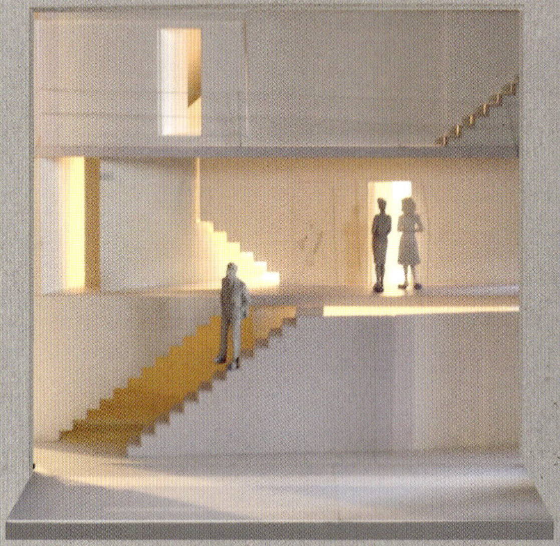

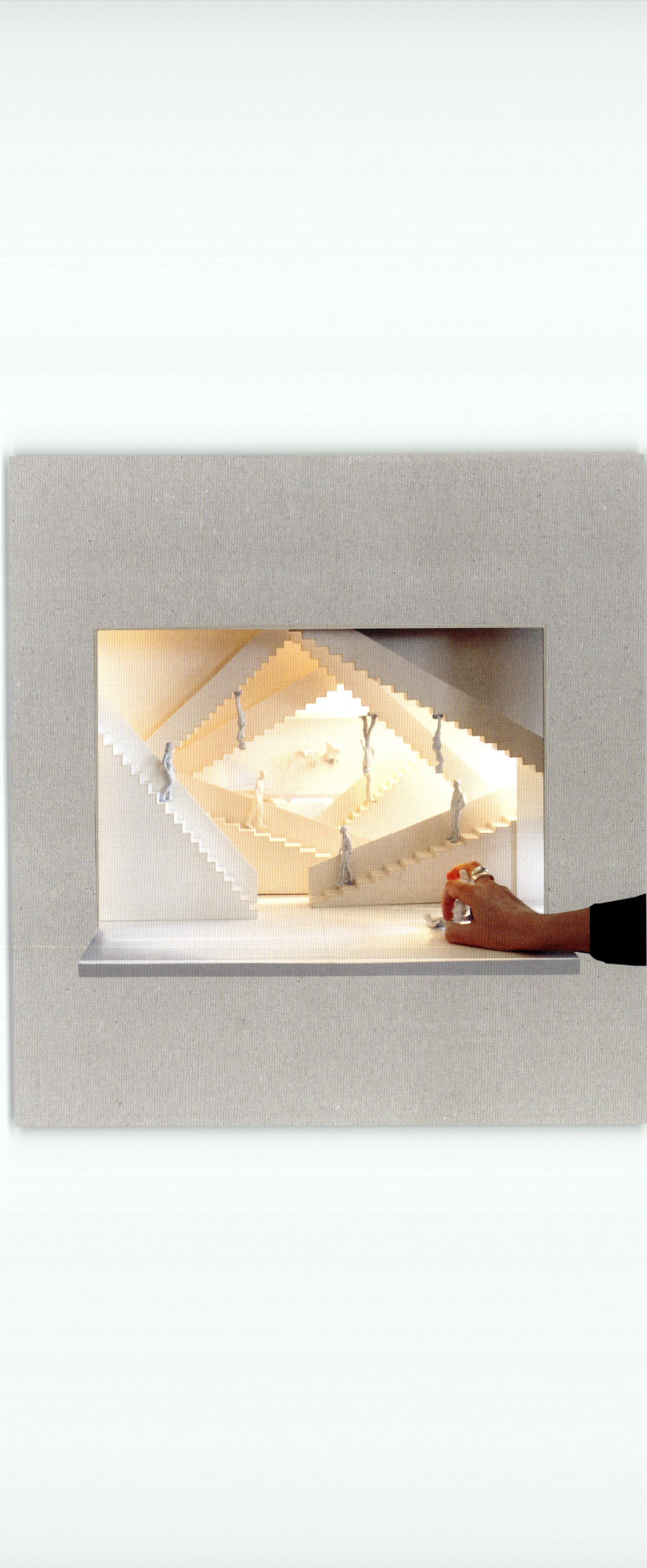

④ TIPS OF TREE CLUSTER ARE FLATTENED LIKE NAIL TOPS

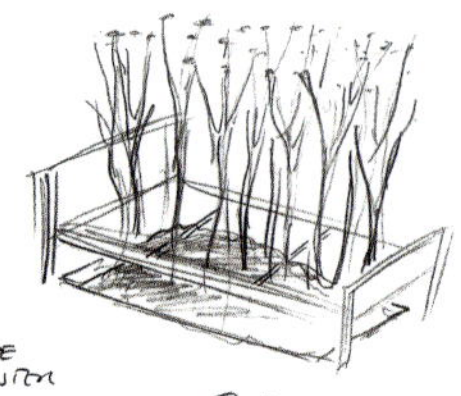

⑤ SO TREE CLUSTER CAN SUPPORT MATTRESS.

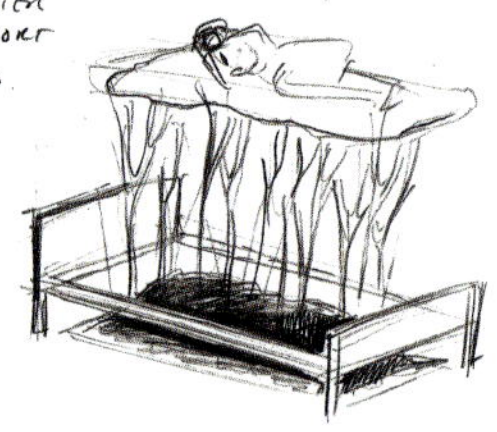

[MATTRESS IS AS LIGHTWEIGHT AS POSSIBLE: AIR BED WITH TWIN WALL RIGID BASE]

⑥ SHEET (CANOPY) HAS BEEN SET SO THAT IT IS BENEATH MATTRESS – BETWEEN TWINWALL MATTRESS BASE AND TREE CLUSTER.

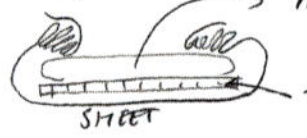

EXCESS MATERIAL IS FOLDED AND DRESSED AROUND PERFORMER SO THAT NONE OF IT IS BENEATH HER BODY CORNERS OF FABRIC ARE CLEARLY VISIBLE + ACCESSIBLE

⑬ ② – PUCK SPREADS OUT ARMS. PROJECTION EXTENDS then Tree Being Branches

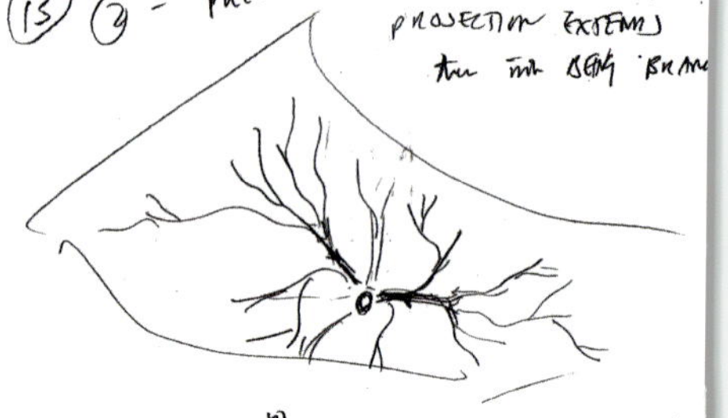

③ – Then his fingers extend to form trunk of tree.

FIREFLIES in Puja.

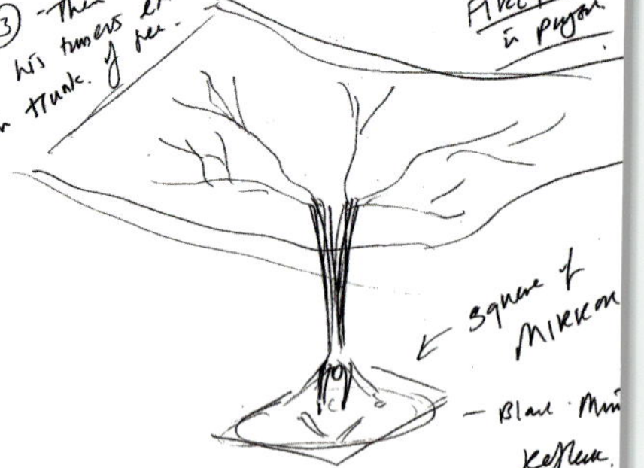

Black mirror could be square.

A MIDSUMMER NIGHT'S DREAM

Are you sure
That we are awake?
It seems to me
That yet we sleep, we dream.

William Shakespeare

The director Julie Taymor and I wondered if the whole of Shakespeare's *A Midsummer Night's Dream* could emerge from a small, single bed. As the audience arrived to see Theater for a New Audience's inaugural production at the new Polonsky Shakespeare Center in Brooklyn in October 2013, a bed was the only object on the stage. As the music began, the mechanicals hoisted ropes which magically spread the bed's sheet out over the entire theatre as a tree grew up beneath the mattress. The sheet became the membrane through which Kathryn Hunter as Puck could permeate, with elongated trouser-legs terminating in projected black ink roots. David Harewood's majestic Oberon conjured projected storms, and Julie sculpted dog heads from cardboard for a feral chorus of children. The domestic framework to which the lovers are propelled was here expressed as a miniature Palladian doll's house: less chaotic than the fragmented iteration in my earlier encounter with *A Midsummer Night's Dream* in 2006, but equally uninhabitable.

629 686–687 730–731

BANGERZ

I gotta open that door, oh yeah
... I'm part the way through, just like a robber
And smile for the camera

Miley Cyrus, 'On My Own'

When I met Miley Cyrus in preparation for her 2014 *Bangerz* arena tour, she was rapidly evolving away from her Disney child star Hannah Montana persona and being noisily criticized by various church groups and press for her 'twerking', tongue-protruding dance moves. In fact, her name had become almost synonymous with her tongue. So I suggested that, rather than resist the imposition of a new persona by the press, Miley should write the new character into her own story. We decided she should perform the entire show on her tongue. Working closely with the film director Diane Martel, we made a model of a giant Miley face with a tongue that became a stage filling the whole arena. The first iteration was deemed impractical, so we reduced the length of the tongue to a slide, down which Miley made her entrance – a sculptural portrait of a young woman rewriting her character and her script.

842–843

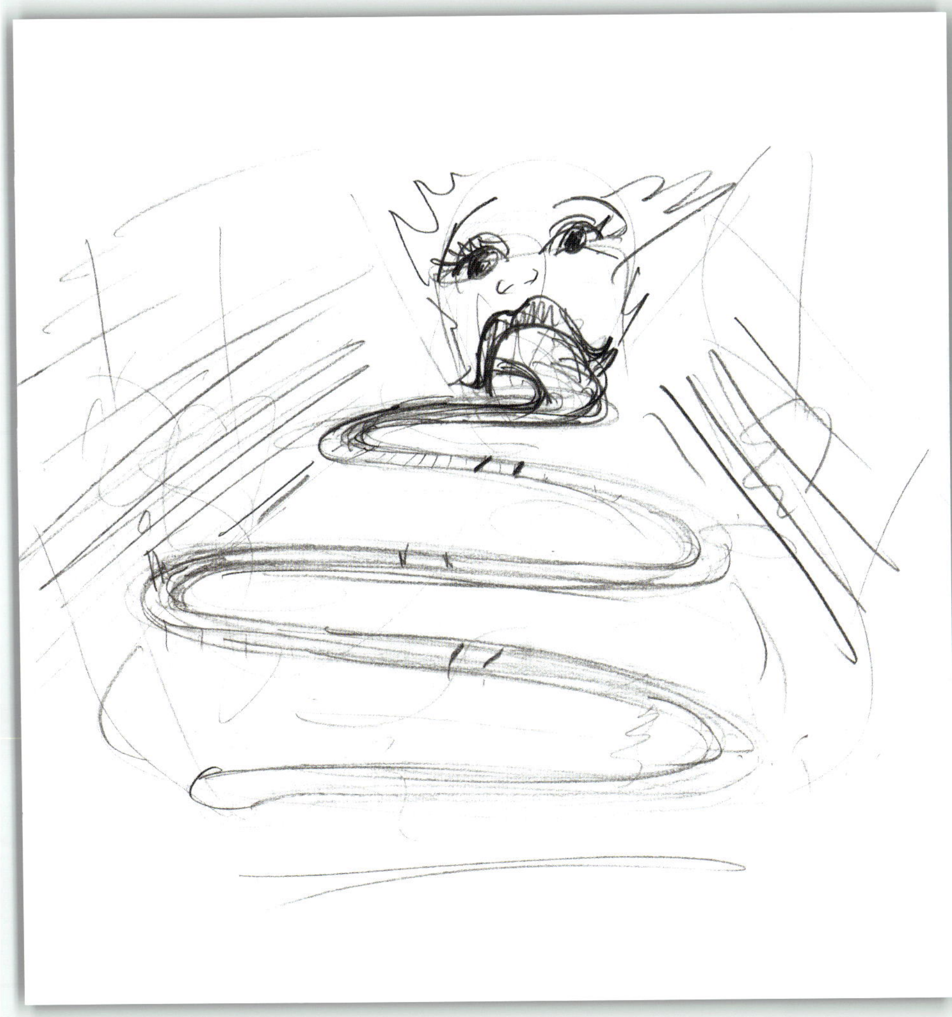

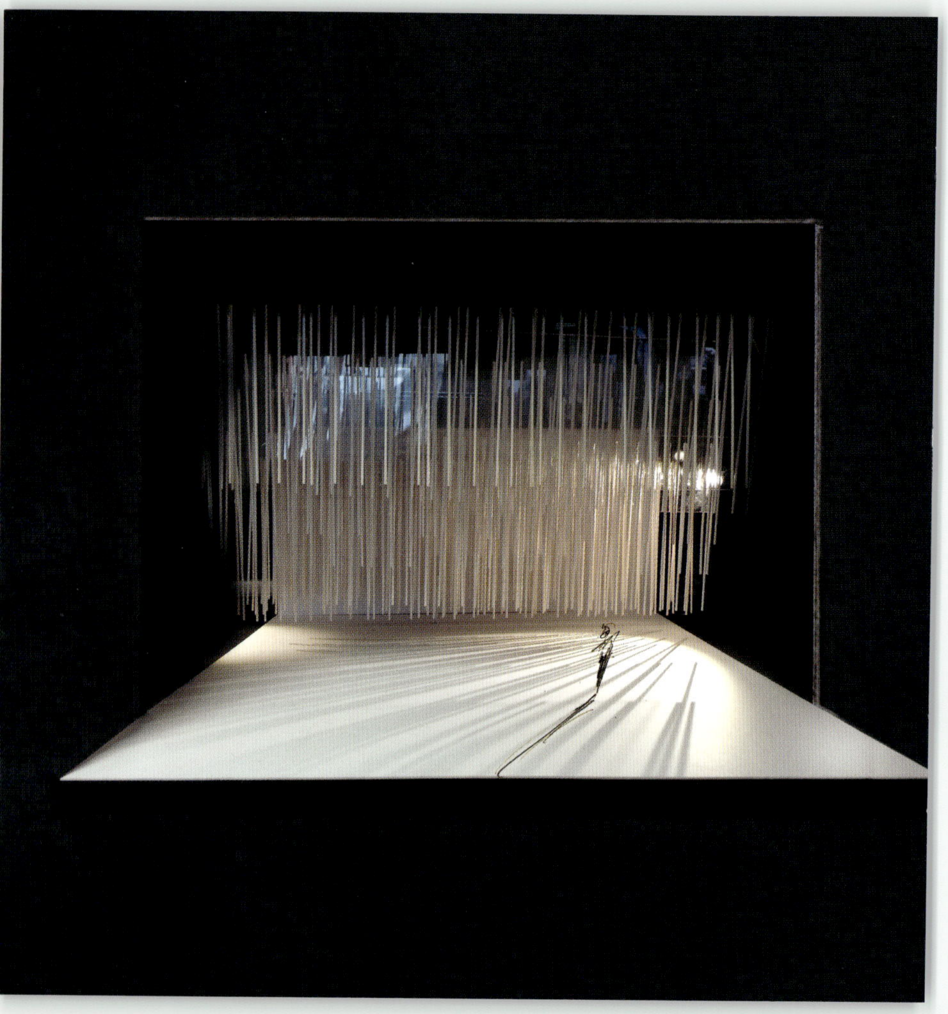

CONNECTOME

Unlike your genome, which is fixed from the moment of conception, your connectome changes throughout life … Neurons adjust, or 'reweight', their connections by strengthening or weakening them.

Sebastian Seung, *Connectome*

I was introduced to the 2009 Human Connectome Project by Muse singer Matt Bellamy. The cover of their 2012 album *The 2nd Law* featured striking MRI imagery, presenting the brain as brightly coloured interwoven strands – a technicolour counterpoint to the monochrome cerebral angiogram I had witnessed in 2005 while working with the neuropsychologist Paul Broks. I showed these images to the choreographer Alastair Marriott as we began conceiving a new work for the Royal Ballet to open in June 2014. On a limited budget, we were interested in expressing the extreme multiplicity and mutability of the forest of over 100 trillion neural connections inside a single human brain. We divided the £5,000 budget by the cost of the cheapest scenic element we could find – a single hanging white-painted scaffolding pole – and filled the available overhead rigging space with as many poles as we could afford. Dancing on the Royal Opera House electronic flying system, the forest of white lines became a canvas for video designer Luke Halls. Lighting designer Bruno Poet created a second light sculpture on the floor, fusing the choreography with kinetic overlaid shadows from the cloud of rods above.

628 735

OBSERVATORY

You need something that puts a little distance between what you really are and what you want to show; it's a shield, a protection.

Nicolas Ghesquière

The Frank Gehry-designed Fondation Louis Vuitton rises like a great glass ship above the trees of the Bois de Boulogne in Paris. Nicolas Ghesquière's Spring/Summer 2015 Women's runway show inaugurated the basement of the building, bewitching its roots with mirrors and holographic films materializing close-up portraits of each model as they intoned a futuristic inauguration ritual.

For the Autumn/Winter 2015 collection in March 2015, Nicolas proposed a giant glass bubble, an observatory at the side of the Fondation. We melded five enormous geodesic domes together like soap bubbles. Segments of their mirrored surface were peeled back to reveal brightly coloured triangular stepped seating. Initiated by Faye Mcleod and Ansel Thompson at the LV studio, I learned the labyrinthine logic of runway geometry. Sliced bright orange ribbed tops, upholstered mirrored bags and diagonal-seamed silver dresses emerged as the cameras flashed: Ghesquière crafted echoes of the dome structure into the collection. This was ephemeral architecture in the extreme – completed moments before the final rehearsal, and deconstructed and returned to its constituent parts by the end of show day.

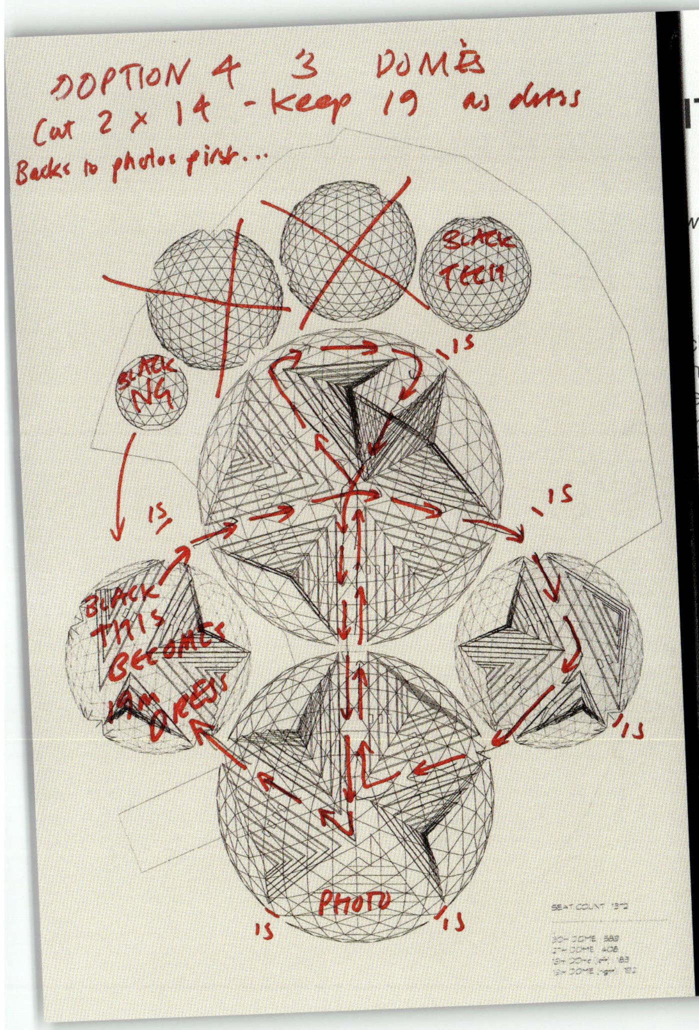

ITY

which to shape it.

Bertolt Brecht

cht and Kurt
nar Republic of
eipzig premiere
ra was banned
was familiar with
ed by The Doors
015 revival at the
dered how to
iftly rejected idea
est and see how
pond to a view

ne desert. We
stretched to
e stack of brightly
opera house
howing the web
ht and Weill's
ra house.

OBSERVAT

You need something
are and what you wan

The Frank Gehry-des
glass ship above the t
Ghesquière's Spring/S
the basement of the b
holographic films mat
intoned a futuristic ina

For the Autumn/Winte
a giant glass bubble, a
melded five enormous
Segments of their mir
coloured triangular ste
Thompson at the LV s
geometry. Sliced brigh
and diagonal-seamed
Ghesquière crafted ec
This was ephemeral a
before the final rehear
constituent parts by th

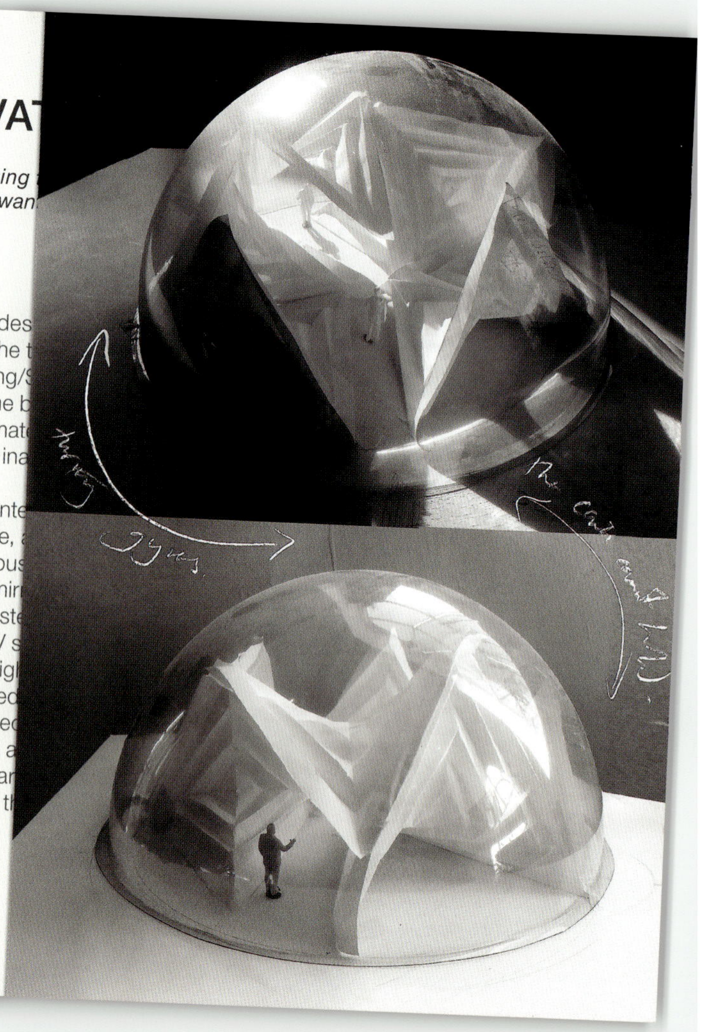

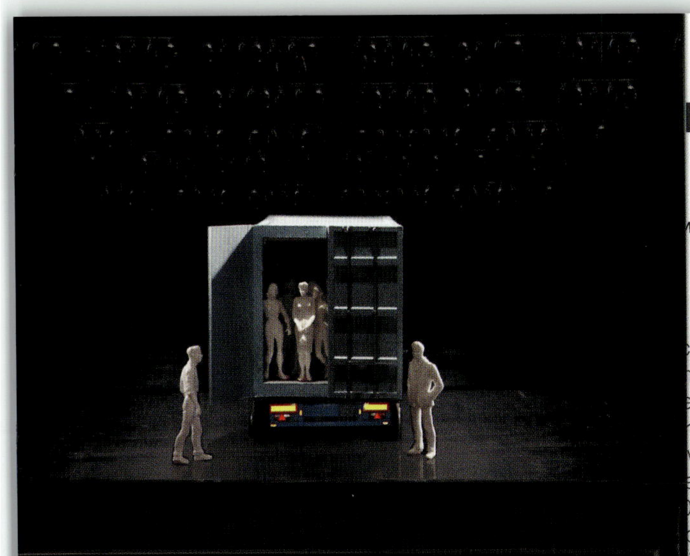

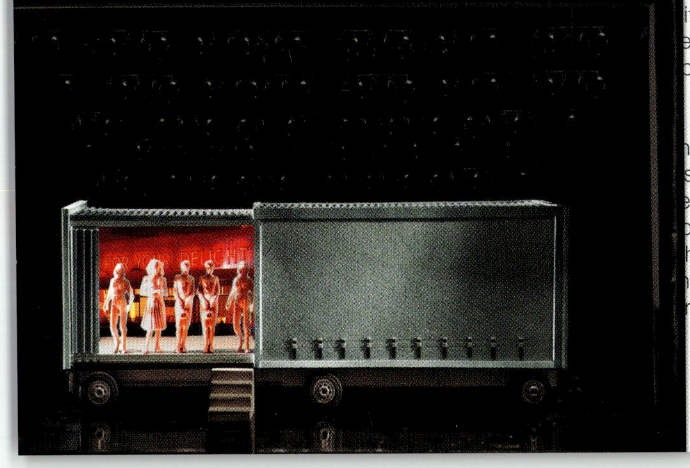

ITY

which to shape it.

Bertolt Brecht

cht and Kurt
nar Republic of
eipzig premiere
ra was banned
was familiar with
ed by The Doors
015 revival at the
dered how to
iftly rejected idea
est and see how
pond to a view

ne desert. We
stretched to
e stack of brightly
opera house
howing the web
ht and Weill's
ra house.

OBSERV

You need somethi
are and what you w

The Frank Gehry-
glass ship above th
Ghesquière's Sprin
the basement of th
holographic films m
intoned a futuristic

For the Autumn/Wi
a giant glass bubbl
melded five enorm
Segments of their r
coloured triangular
Thompson at the L
geometry. Sliced b
and diagonal-seam
Ghesquière crafted
This was ephemera
before the final reh
constituent parts b

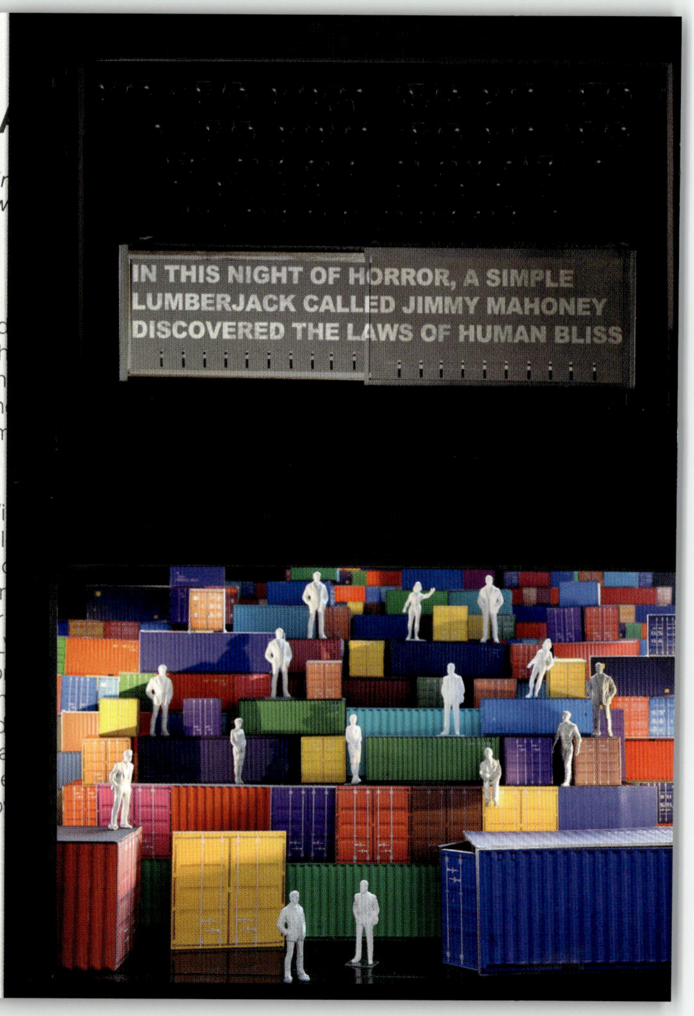

RISE AND FALL OF THE CITY OF MAHAGONNY

Art is not a mirror held up to reality but a hammer with which to shape it.

Bertolt Brecht

Rise and Fall of the City of Mahagonny is Bertolt Brecht and Kurt Weill's satirical critique of both America and the Weimar Republic of the 1920s. Amid looming economic crisis, its 1930 Leipzig premiere was disrupted by National Socialist riots and the opera was banned by the Nazis in 1933, resurfacing only in the 1960s. I was familiar with its haunting 'Alabama Song' through versions recorded by The Doors (in 1966) and David Bowie (in 1978). For the March 2015 revival at the Royal Opera House, the director John Fulljames wondered how to provoke a scandal equivalent to its premiere. One swiftly rejected idea was to swap the most expensive seats for the cheapest and see how the wealthiest Royal Opera House patrons would respond to a view from the gods.

The piece opens with a broken-down juggernaut in the desert. We made a revolving expandable container truck, which stretched to encompass the action, and proliferated into an infinite stack of brightly coloured shipping containers filling every inch of the opera house stage. The video designer Finn Ross overlaid maps showing the web of commodities revolving around the planet, as Brecht and Weill's 1930s vision of a carnivorous city consumed the opera house.

854–855

THE NETHER

... my mother ... said, The only way you hear the wind is if it has leaves to blow through.

Jennifer Haley

Performed at the Royal Court Theatre in July 2014, Jennifer Haley's play *The Nether* conjures a perfectly rendered verdant virtual world into which human minds can choose to migrate, leaving their bodies sustained by life support machines amidst the desiccated remains of planet Earth. An unflinching exploration of the ethics of online sexual encounters, the drama pivots between a 'real' grey windowless interrogation room and a series of idyllic tree-surrounded virtual interiors. The director Jeremy Herrin suggested that, rather than invoke a pixelated computer-generated world, we should construct exquisite naturalistic scenes, expressing the ever-increasing virtuosity of virtual world-building techniques.

Conjuring nature onstage is fraught with potential humiliation: sometimes fake trees with carefully painted silk leaves can appear more real in the heightened context of stage lighting than real trees gasping for life in a dark theatre, sustained by daytime doses of UV light. The luminous glass room we evoked was an illusion created by three flown white horizontal planes and a series of suspended domestic objects. As the play transferred into the Duke of York's Theatre, we discovered that a two-second delay to the mechanics delivering the illusion would over-expose the artifice and shatter the audience's suspension of disbelief.

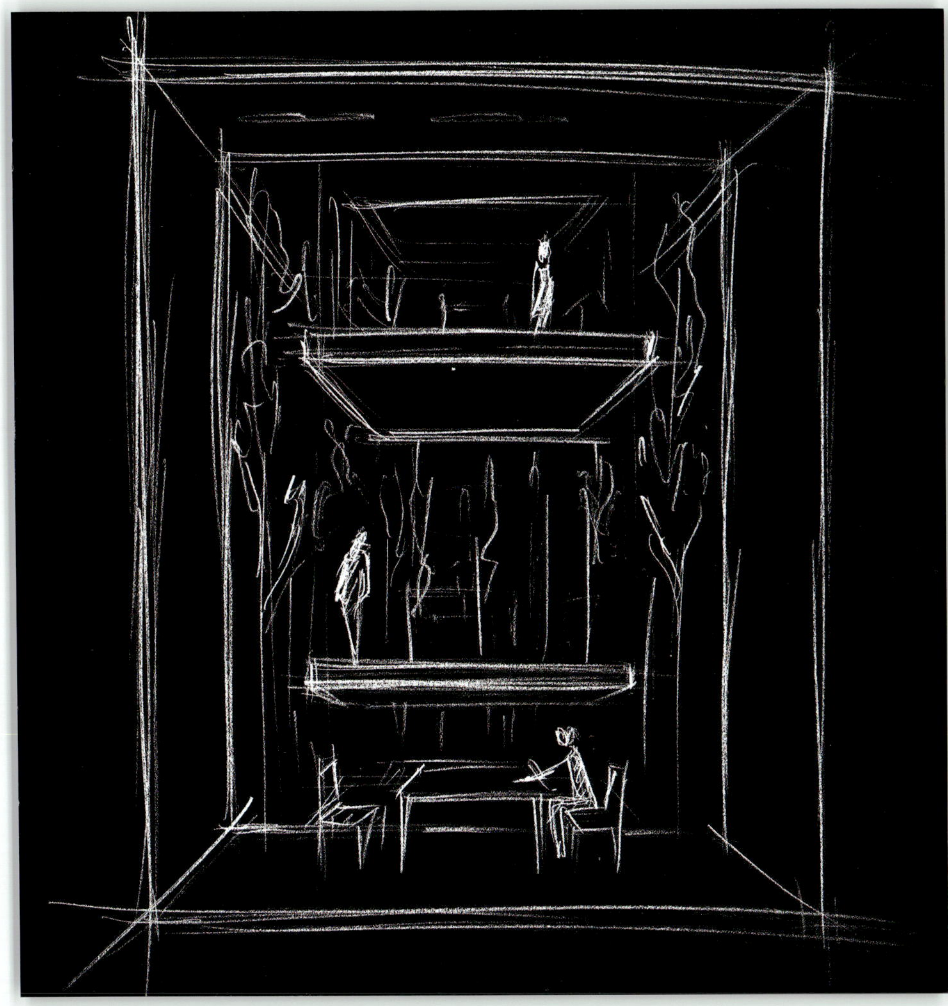

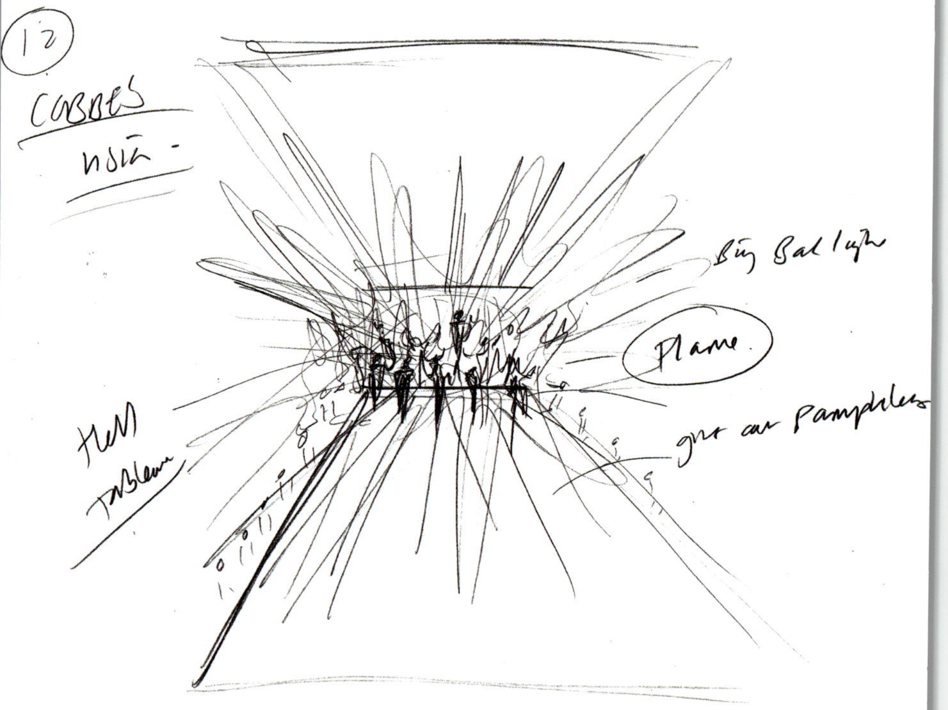
12
Big Bal light
Plame.

LIGHT SHINING IN BUCKINGHAMSHIRE

There's an even bigger mirror that we didn't break … You see your whole body at once. You see yourself standing in that room. They must know what they look like all the time. And now we do.

Caryl Churchill

These words are spoken by a seventeenth-century woman after seeing her full reflection for the first time in a ransacked manor house mirror. It's one of a series of piercing poetic images in Caryl Churchill's 1976 play *Light Shining in Buckinghamshire*. The piece is set during the English Civil War and charts the English revolution that never happened: the brief moment of imagining a future free from a tyrannical monarchy and a corrupt political system. At the first meeting in preparation for the April 2015 National Theatre production, the director Lyndsey Turner and I read the play aloud together before discussing how to shape an environment around the text. It's about the identity of our country and ourselves, and we were making it in the lead-up to the May 2015 UK general election. We imagined the stage as a giant dining table – first covered in silk and an elaborate dinner, then exposed as wooden planks beneath parliamentary debating benches. It was dismembered by a crowd of fifty community performers to reveal the mud of a civil war battlefield, and finally filled with a group of contemporary citizens standing in the rain, raising their voices in song.

633 690–691

HAMLET

There is a willow grows aslant the brook
That shows his hoar leaves in the glassy stream

William Shakespeare

It was through this August 2015 production with Benedict Cumberbatch playing Hamlet at the Barbican Theatre that I was led by the director Lyndsey Turner to the music of Jon Hopkins. Laertes and his sister Ophelia played a fragment of Hopkins's plangent track 'Abandon Window' as a duet on a grand piano in a stately hall during Act I. By the end of Act IV, the piano is partially swallowed by rising mounds of earth and bones. Laertes plays the left hand of the duet alone, as Ophelia picks her way through the surge of earth towards her watery suicide. The haunting asymmetry of the one-handed duet lands Hamlet's phrase, 'the time is out of joint', deep within the guts of the audience. We aimed to infect the production with the ghosts of not just Hamlet's father but a multitude of victims of his war-hungry generation, latent within the grave mounds that spewed through the doors and windows of the ever more suffocating hall.

637

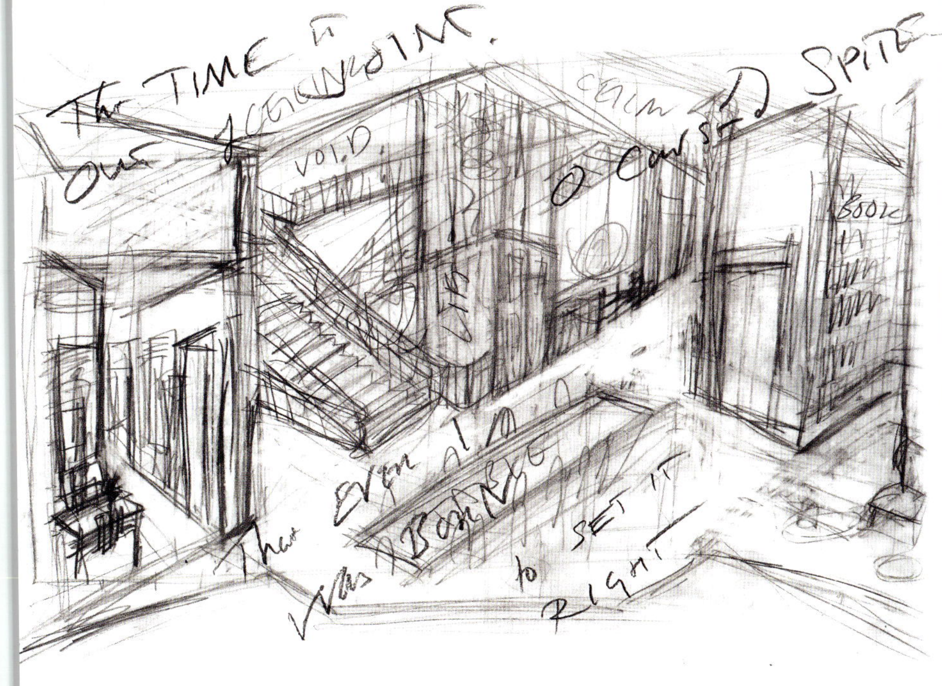
The TIME is
VOID
O CURSED SPITE
BOOKS
to SET IT
RIGHT

INNOCENCE + EXPERIENCE

I can't change the world / But I can change the world in me

U2, 'Rejoice' (1981)

Yes I can change the world … / But I can't change the world / In me

U2, 'Lucifer's Hands' (2014)

U2's 2015 *Innocence + Experience* tour charted the 33-year territory between these two song lyrics. The 1981 phrase described a teenager looking out of his bedroom window, feeling powerless in the face of the political instability of 'The Troubles' in 1980s Dublin, but able to alter his own psychological landscape. The 2014 lyric expressed the singer's discovery that, in fact, making some palpable change to the world – via the work of ONE.org and the (RED) campaign – turned out to be possible, while the inner struggles became more complex. The band, the director Willie Williams and I sought a sculpture that could operate as a temporal highway between U2's origins in Larry Mullen Jnr's kitchen and their contemporary practice as effective global activists. Dividing the crowd when lowered and unifying them when lifted, a block of transparent LED emerged through ink paintings during our meetings. Bono, The Edge, Adam Clayton and Larry Mullen Jnr inhabited Oliver Jeffers's chalk-drawn animations as protagonists among the pixels. Developed in collaboration with Ric Lipson from the architectural practice Stufish, the suspended luminous block pressured the four men like cornered wolves from above.

677 802–803

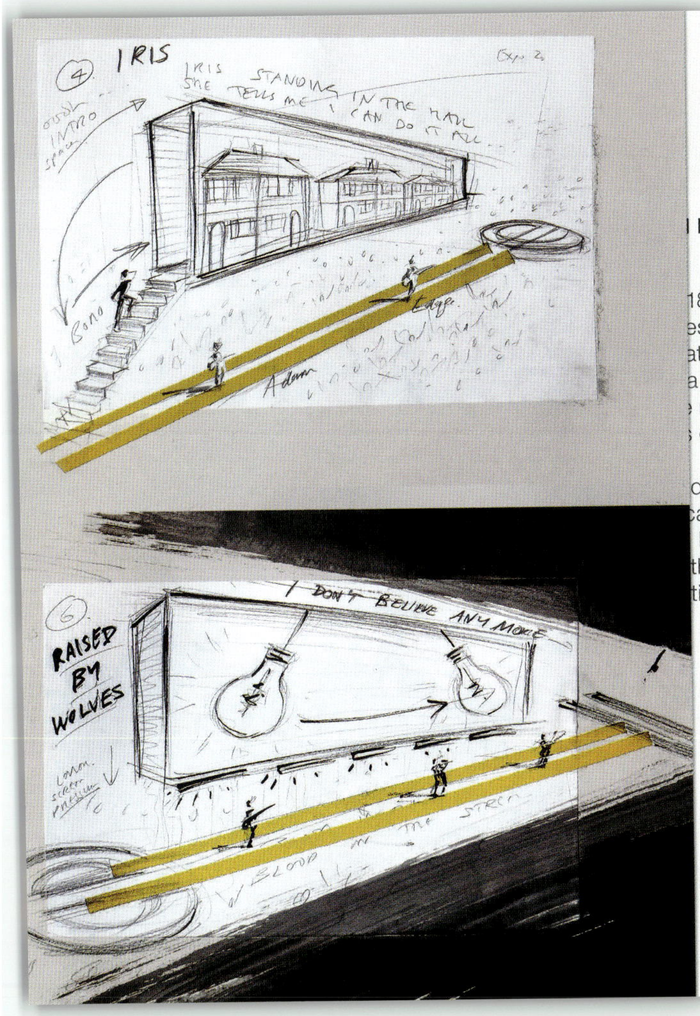

l Maria von Weber

1821 opera
es. The gun
ating again with
a production in
e revolving bullet
s of a clock.

d tools, whether
calibration of time
I remember
these instruments
tiful?'

INNOCEN

I can't change the w

Yes I can change th

U2's 2015 *Innocen*
between these two
looking out of his b
the political instabi
alter his own psych
singer's discovery
world – via the wor
out to be possible,
The band, the dire
could operate as a
Mullen Jnr's kitche
global activists. Di
when lifted, a bloc
during our meeting
Jnr inhabited Olive
among the pixels.
architectural practi
the four men like c

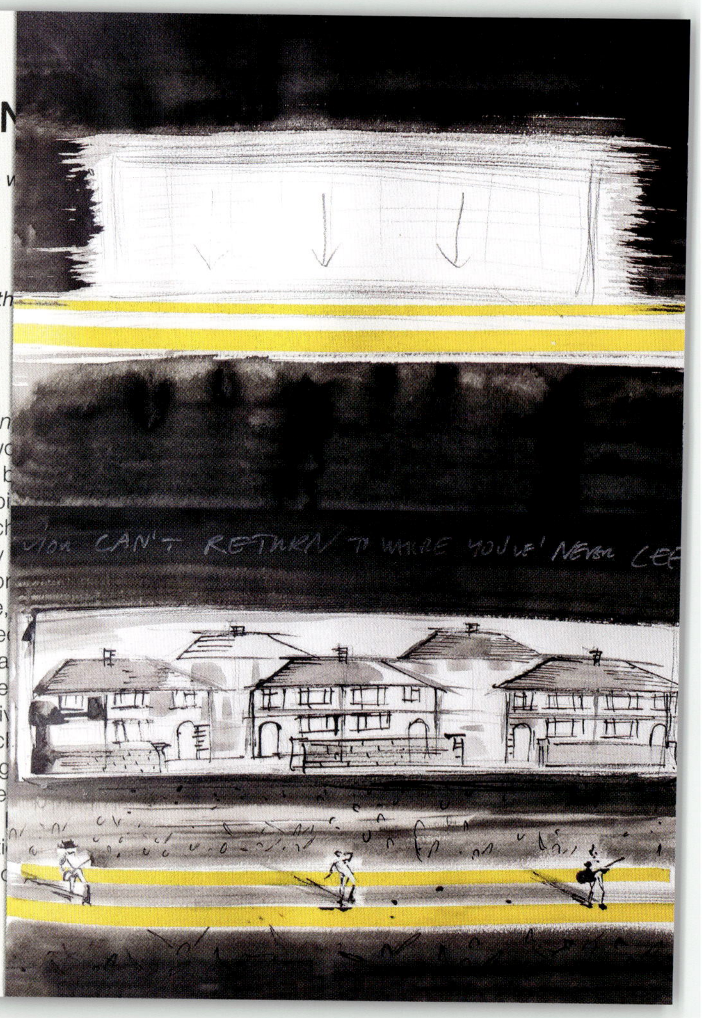

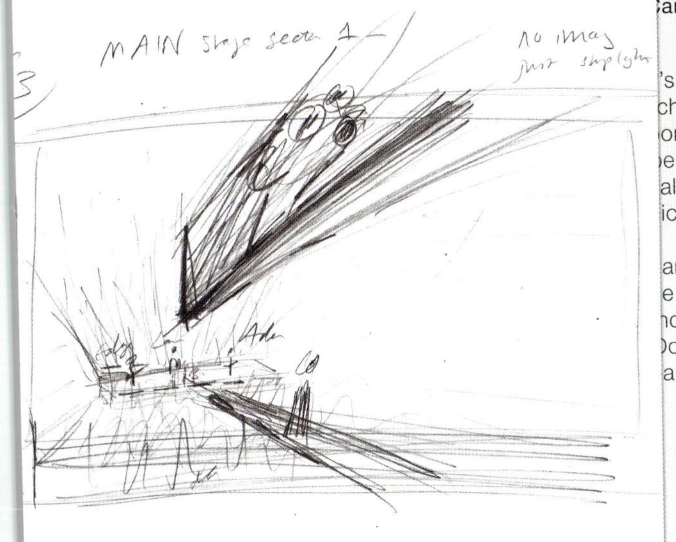

:arl Maria von Weber

’s 1821 opera
ches. The gun
orating again with
era production in
ale revolving bullet
ics of a clock.

and tools, whether
e calibration of time
nd. I remember
)o these instruments
autiful?’

INNOCEN

I can't change the w

Yes I can change th

U2's 2015 *Innocen*
between these two
looking out of his b
the political instabi
alter his own psych
singer's discovery
world – via the wor
out to be possible,
The band, the dire
could operate as a
Mullen Jnr's kitche
global activists. Div
when lifted, a bloc
during our meeting
Jnr inhabited Olive
among the pixels.
architectural practi
the four men like c

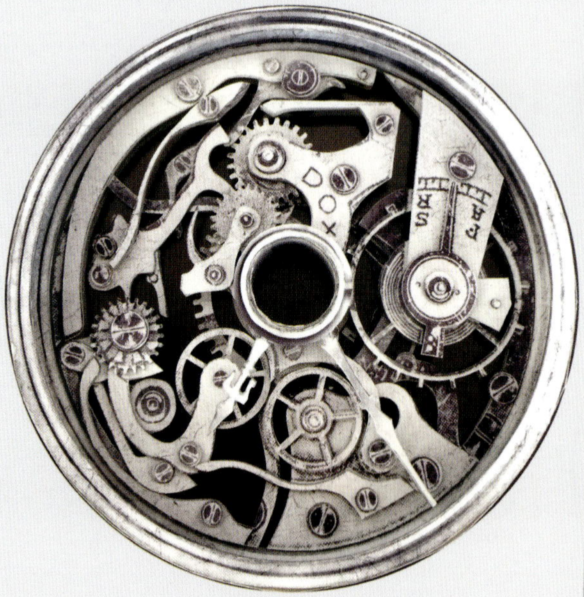

DER FREISCHÜTZ

An artist's sphere of influence is the world.

Carl Maria von Weber

Based on a German legend, Carl Maria von Weber's 1821 opera *Der Freischütz* centres on a series of shooting matches. The gun becomes one of the characters in the work. Collaborating again with the director Kasper Holten for the Royal Danish Opera production in November 2015, we filled the stage with a large-scale revolving bullet chamber which transformed into the inner mechanics of a clock.

I am often taken aback by the beauty of machines and tools, whether their purpose is the infliction of a fatal wound, or the calibration of time into seconds, or the conducting of breath into sound. I remember asking my violin and clarinet teachers as a child, 'Do these instruments have to look this beautiful in order to sound this beautiful?'

HELLO

I love hearing my audience breathe.

Adele

Adele arrived early for our first meeting at my Peckham studio. She was waiting patiently in her Mini on the South London street. I showed her pictures of Maria Callas and we talked about her make-up as a protective, expressive mask. We were planning her first tour in five years, which would open in Belfast in February 2016. She played me the blisteringly powerful new single, 'Hello'. We imagined an audience arriving to an arena filled with the sound of Adele asleep, breathing, her giant closed eyes filling one end of the arena. As the lights lowered to the opening chords of 'Hello', Adele would rise slowly into view, the enormous eyes opening as soon as she sang the first line. This arena tour and the subsequent stadium tour, as well as Adele's performances at Radio City Music Hall, the BBC, the BRITs and the Grammys were all studies in close-up portraiture. On 25 June 2016, the great eyes peered out from within the black hood of the famous Pyramid Stage at Glastonbury. Two hundred thousand people united in singing 'Someone Like You'. Many of us sang with tears pouring down our faces – we had never felt so disunited as a country. The Brexit vote had taken place two days earlier, with 52% voting to leave the European Union while 48% voted to remain.

699–703

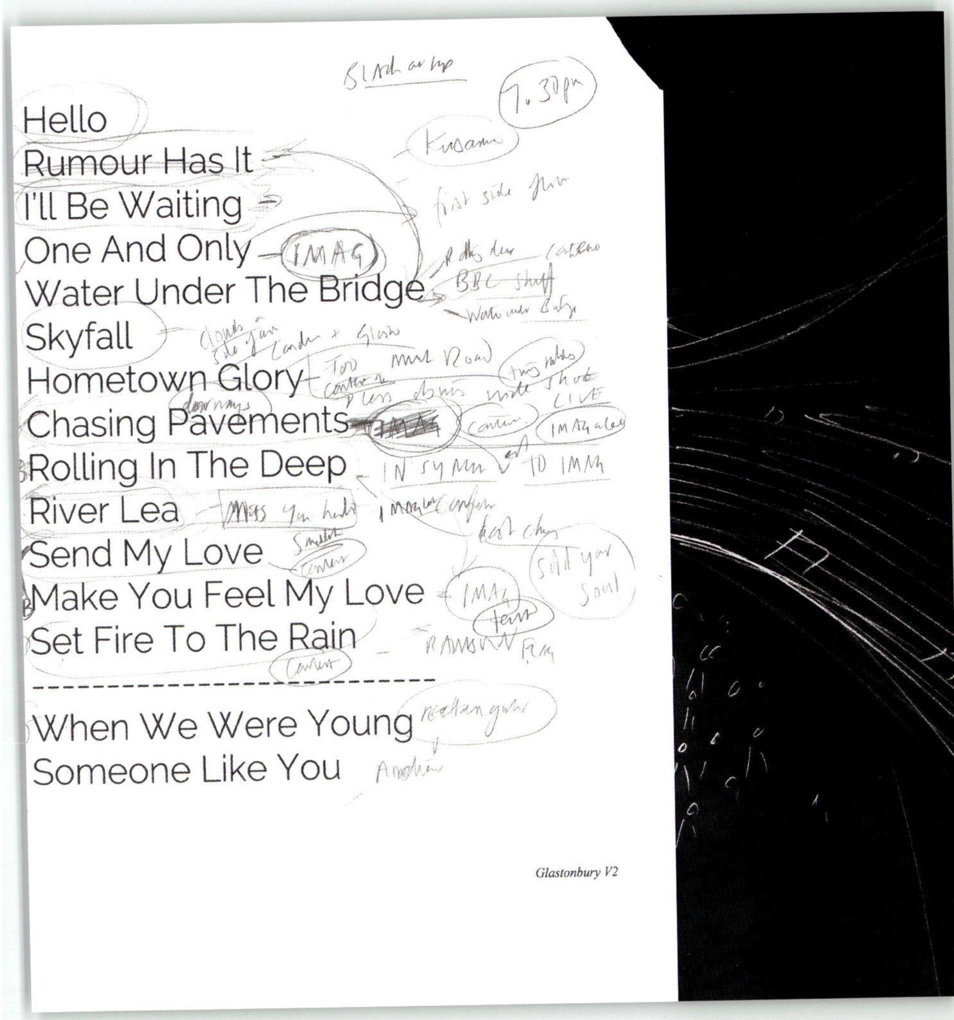

Hello
Rumour Has It
I'll Be Waiting
One And Only
Water Under The Bridge
Skyfall
Hometown Glory
Chasing Pavements
Rolling In The Deep
River Lea
Send My Love
Make You Feel My Love
Set Fire To The Rain

When We Were Young
Someone Like You

Glastonbury V2

HELLO

I love hearing my audi

Adele arrived early fo
She was waiting pati
I showed her pictures
make-up as a protec
tour in five years, whi
played me the bliste
an audience arriving
breathing, her giant
lights lowered to the
slowly into view, the
the first line. This are
well as Adele's perfo
BRITs and the Gramn
25 June 2016, the gr
of the famous Pyram
people united in sing
tears pouring down
country. The Brexit v
voting to leave the Eu

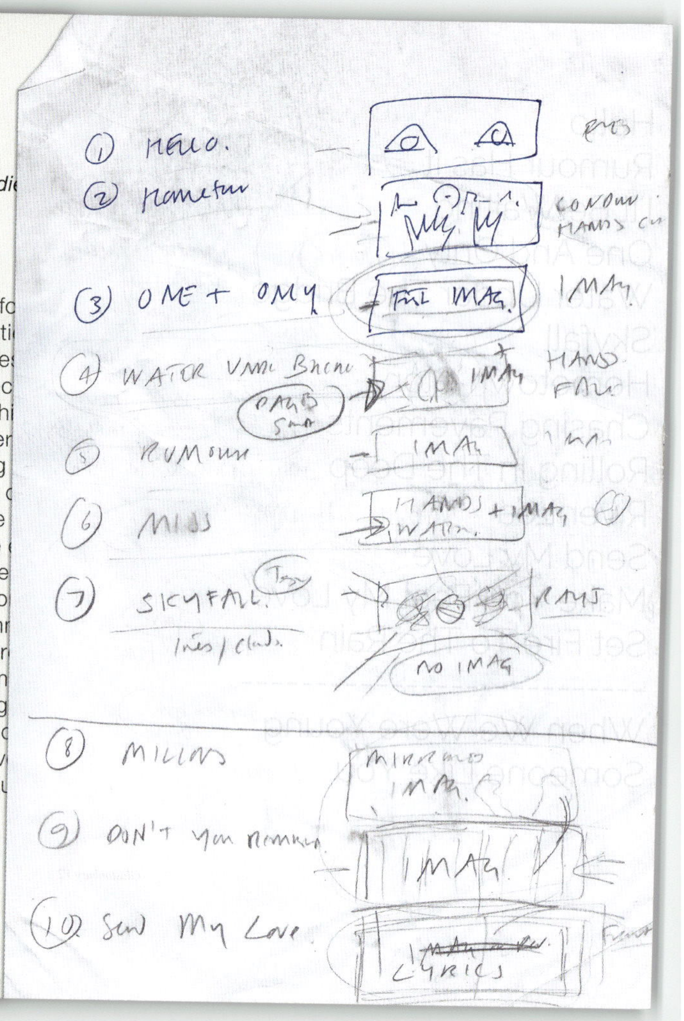

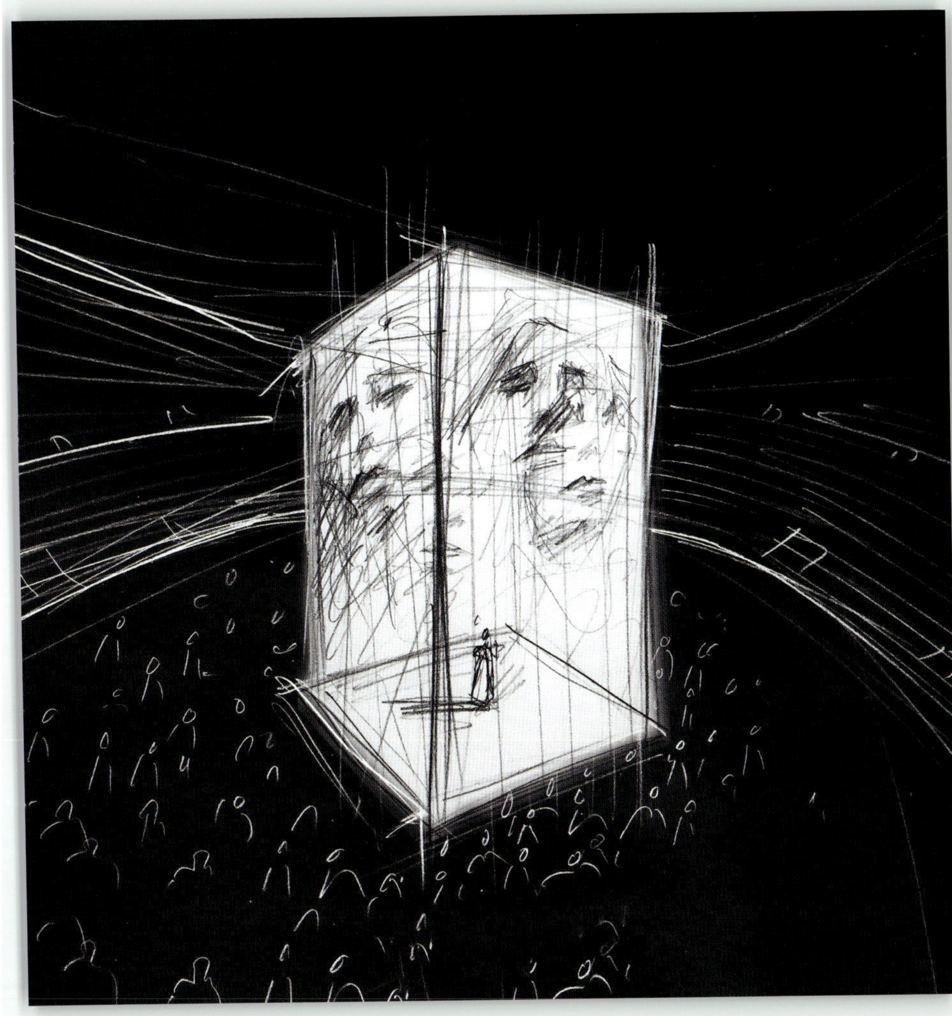

HELLO INTRO CHORD.

(1). CLOSED EYES – REM.

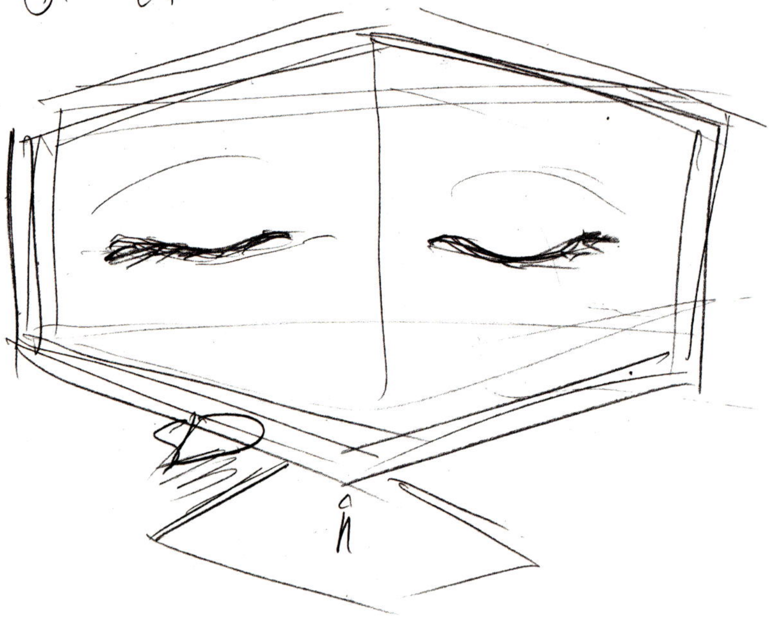

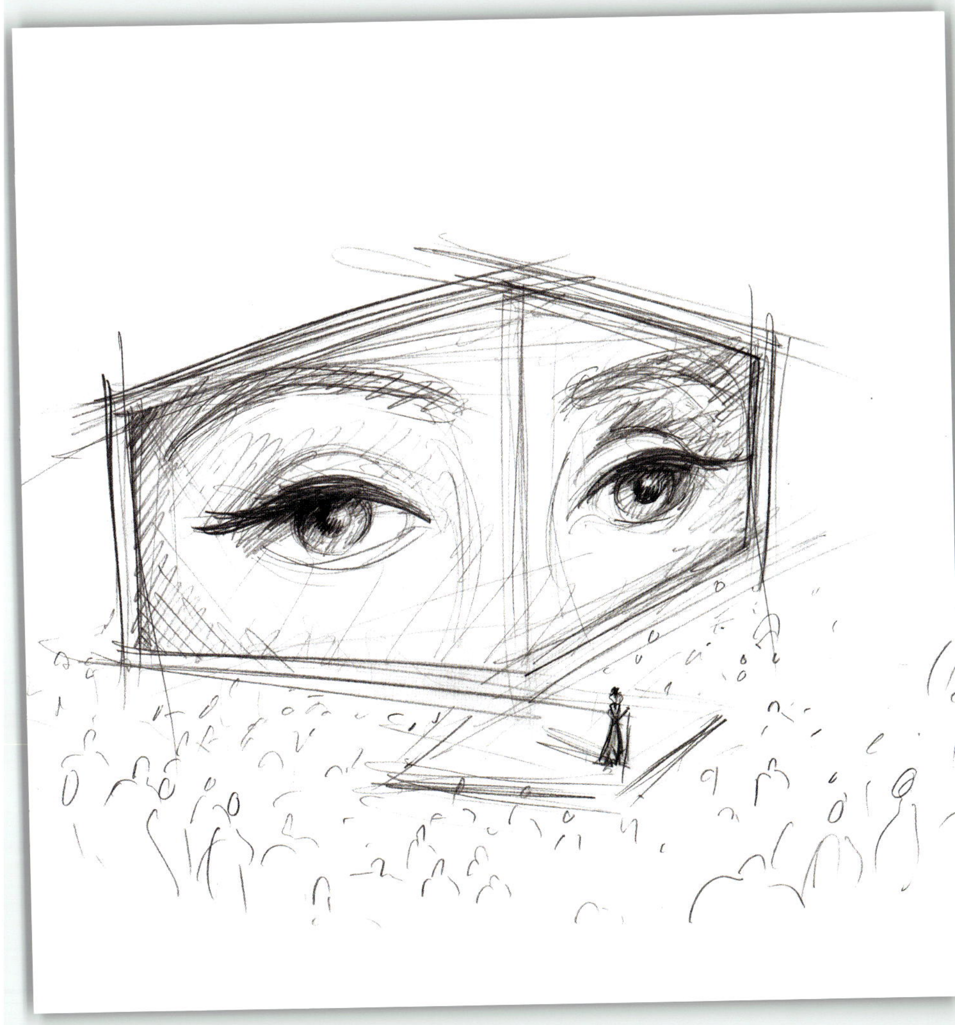

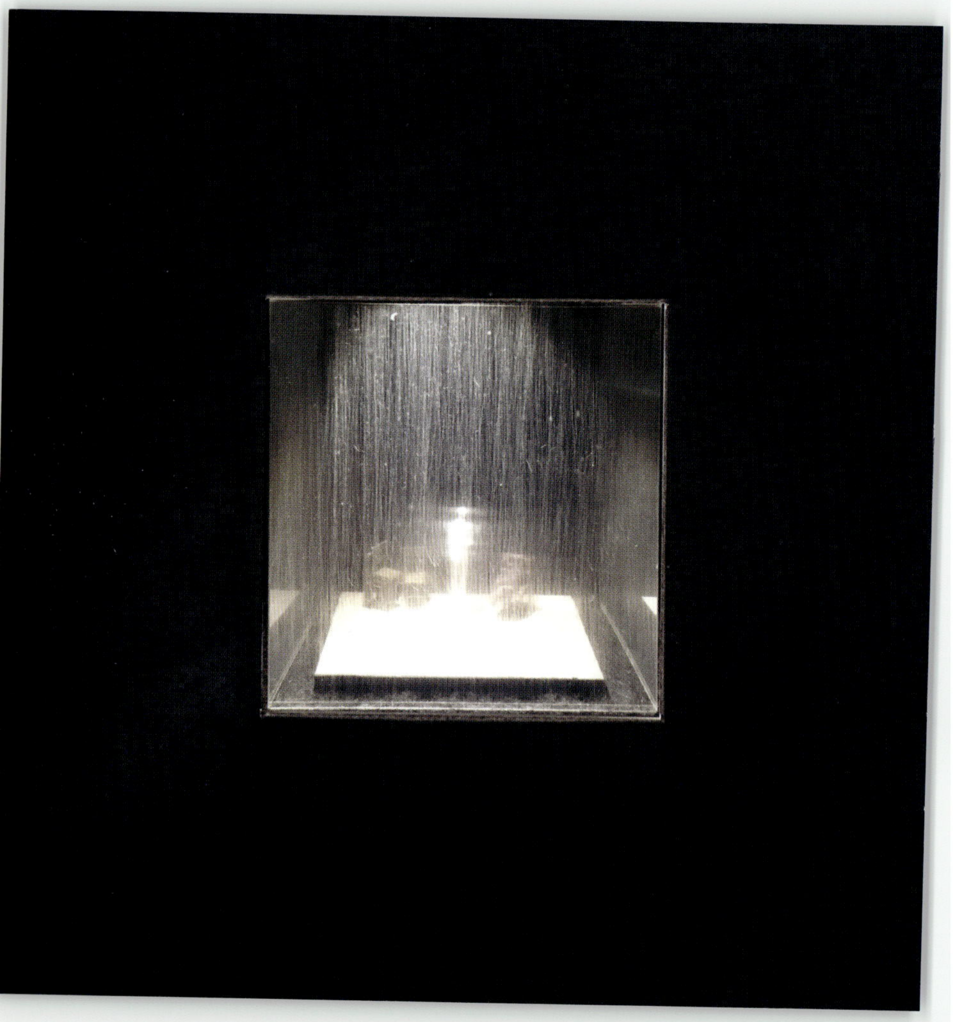

FAITH HEALER

Frank: … those were nights of exultation, of consummation … because the questions that undermined my life then became meaningless and because I knew that for those few hours I had become whole in myself, and perfect in myself

Brian Friel

Plays are like incanted spells. For our July 2016 staging of Brian Friel's 1979 play *Faith Healer* in the intimate Donmar Warehouse theatre, the director Lyndsey Turner and I crafted a series of close-up magic tricks aimed at subtly re-engineering the relationship between actors and audience. You could hear the crash and feel the chill of a cascading box of illuminated rain before you saw it. It silenced pre-show chat, as the congregation of visiting souls began to converge into a single audience before hearing the first line. The rain box was an invisibility cloak, revealing and concealing actors and objects at the start and end of a series of monologues. The mechanics of the illusion are simple: we expect rain to be transparent, and because we tend to look through the lens of our expectations, we believe that we are looking through rain to dark empty space beyond, when in fact there is a dark drape immediately behind the rain concealing the movement of scenery, actors and technicians. To aid the illusion, we calibrated the aperture of each individual eye in the audience using the nineteenth-century technique of shining a bright light straight at the audience whenever we wanted their irises to contract and perceive a deeper black, to erase any shadow of interstitial business.

FORMATION

I saw a TV preacher when I was scared, / at four or five, about bad dreams, / who promised he'd say a prayer / if I put my hand to the TV. / That's the first time I remember prayer, / an electric current humming through me. / You call me a singer, but I'm called to transform, / to suck up the grief, anxiety, and loss / of those who hear me into my song's form.

Beyoncé and Forrest Gander, 'Bey the Light'

I read this poem while researching for Beyoncé's April 2016 stadium tour, *Formation*. We made a revolving six-storey-high monolithic illuminated LED cuboid which behaved like Beyoncé's prayer-transmitting TV, conducting the waves of energy between artist and audience. It displayed a giant billboard-poster diva before splitting apart to reveal the bare forked creature within. Like the plywood boxes we had explored together for her 2015 'Made in America' performance in Philadelphia, the rotating sculpture operated as a magic trick, revealing and concealing Beyoncé at various scales of magnitude in relation to her dancers. The monolith developed its own character and became at times a dancing partner, at times an alter-ego for the protagonist – getting angry, spewing flames, turning its back on us, before slowly rotating through 180 degrees to grant us the power of its full beam.

662–665

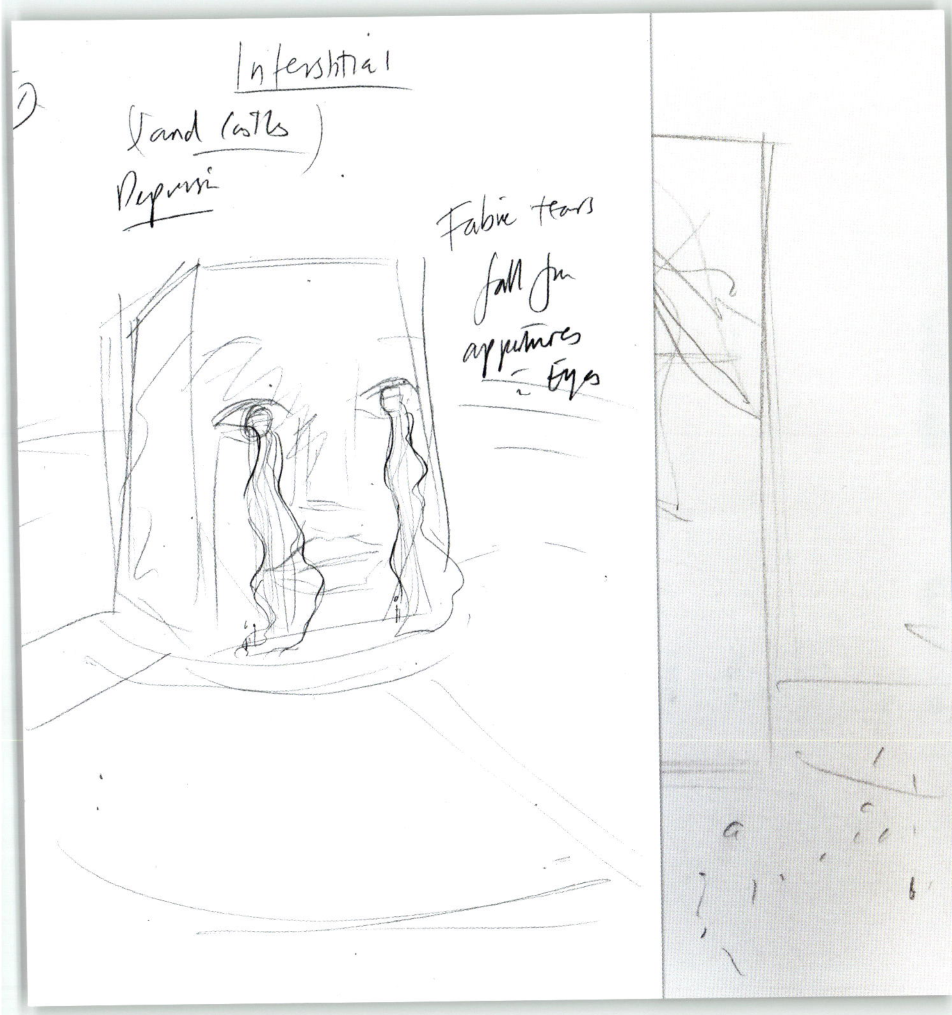
Interstitial
Sand castles
Fabric tears
fall
apertures
Eyes

FORMATIC

I saw a TV preacher w
dreams, / who promis
/ That's the first time I
through me. / You call
up the grief, anxiety, a

I read this poem while
tour, *Formation*. We r
illuminated LED cubo
transmitting TV, cond
audience. It displayed
apart to reveal the ba
boxes we had explor
performance in Phila
magic trick, revealing
magnitude in relation
character and becam
ego for the protagoni
back on us, before sl
the power of its full b

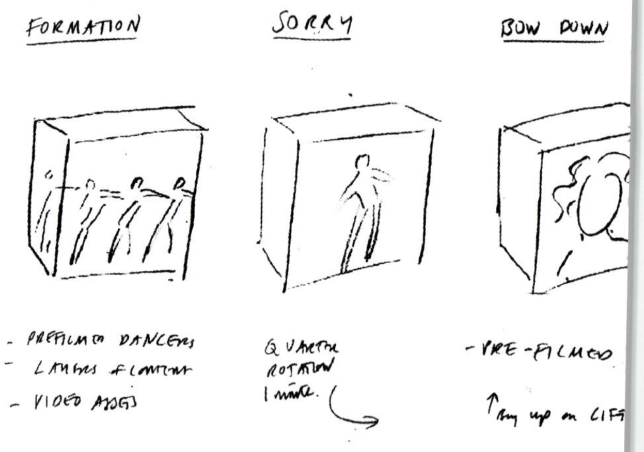

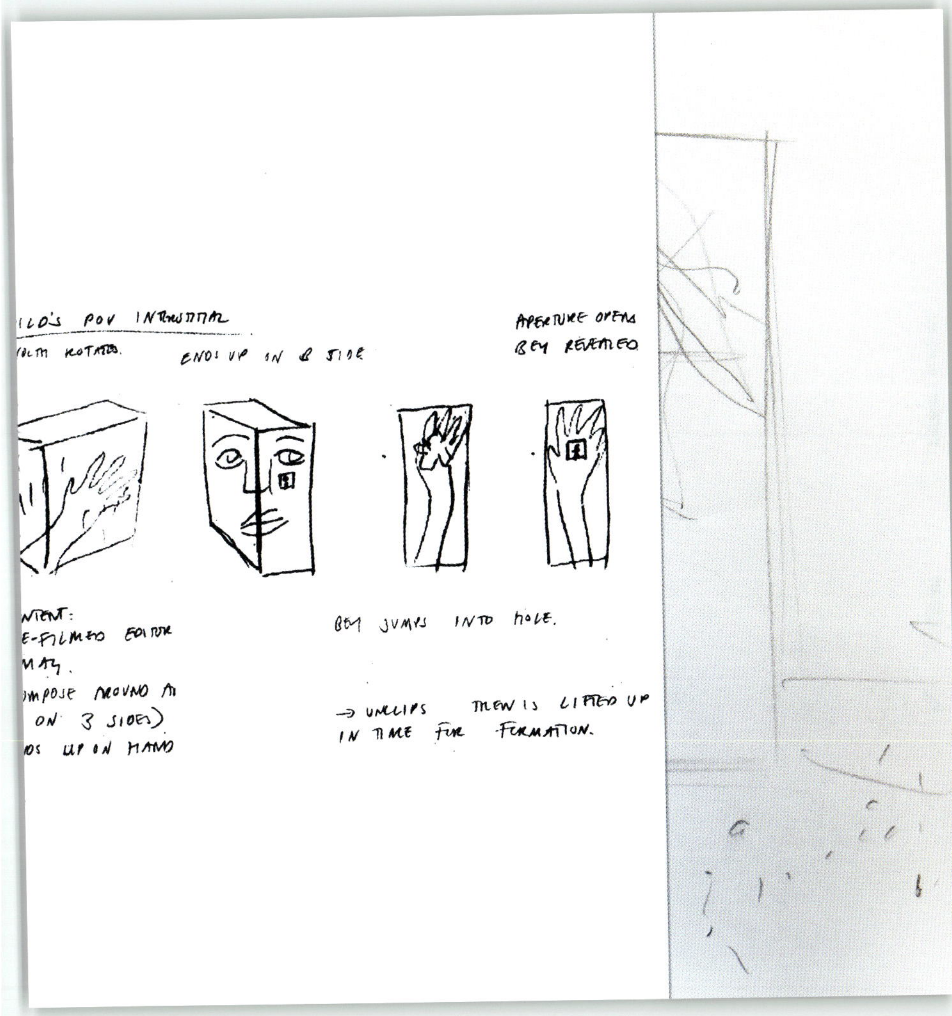
APERTURE OPENS
BEN JUMPS INTO HOLE.
ON 3 SIDES)
IN TIME FOR FORMATION.

FORMATIC

I saw a TV preacher w
dreams, / who promise
/ That's the first time I
through me. / You call
up the grief, anxiety, a

I read this poem while
tour, *Formation*. We r
illuminated LED cubo
transmitting TV, cond
audience. It displayed
apart to reveal the ba
boxes we had explor
performance in Phila
magic trick, revealing
magnitude in relation
character and becam
ego for the protagoni
back on us, before s
the power of its full b

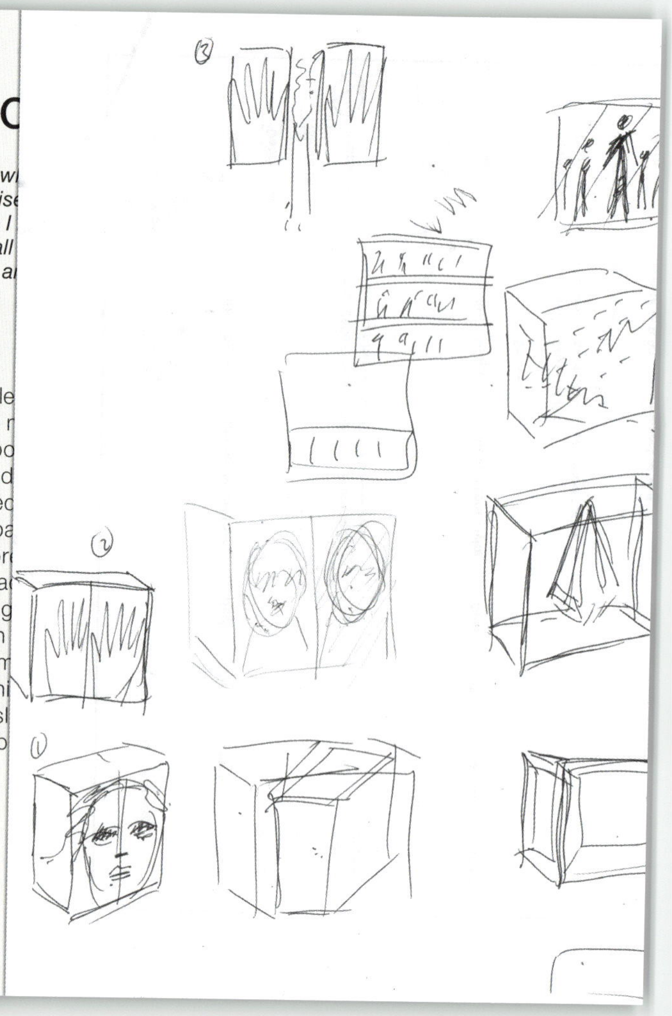

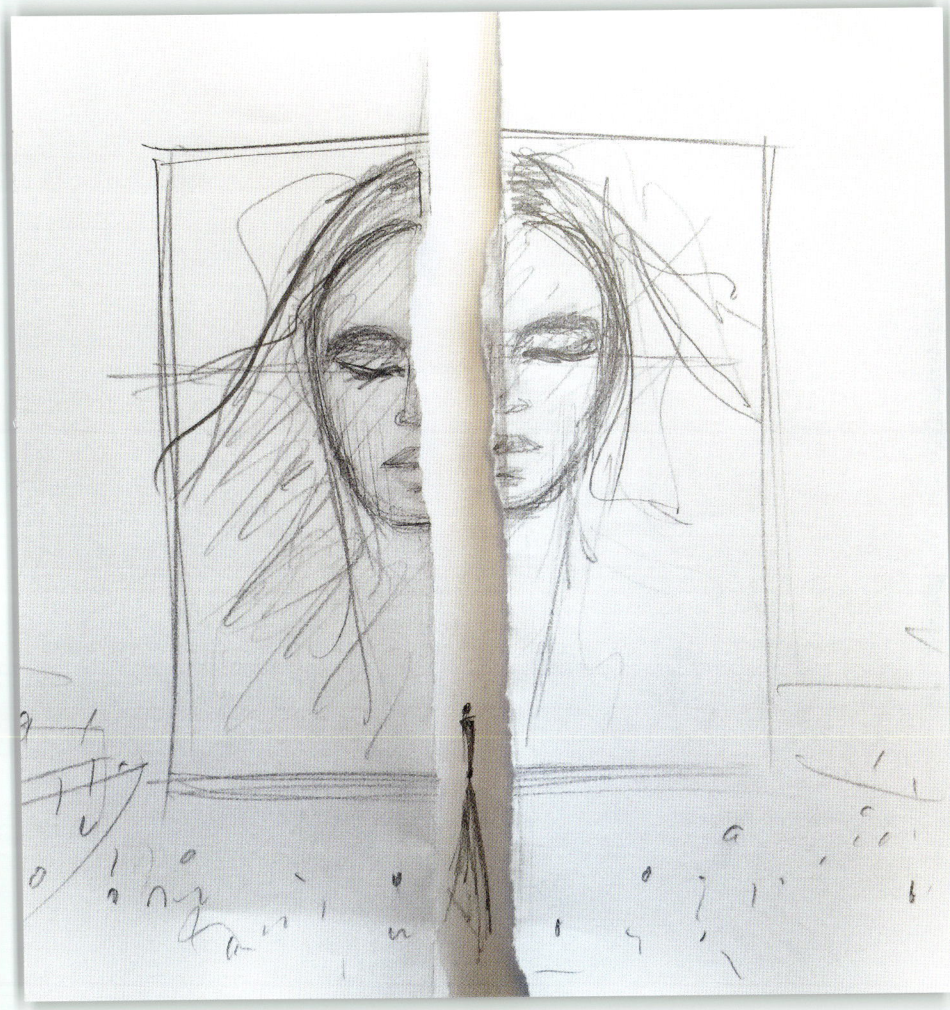

(2) BLOCK OF LIGHT AND POWER.
FILLS THE AIRSPACE
PHYSICAL / CHEMICAL EFFECT ON CROWD
THE MOST BLINDING TUNGSTEN LIGHT
AN INITIATION PROCESS FOR THE PEOPLE

VOICE OVER

SENSE OF HOVERING SPACECRAFT
WHY ?: OTHER SPECIES / OTHER PLANET

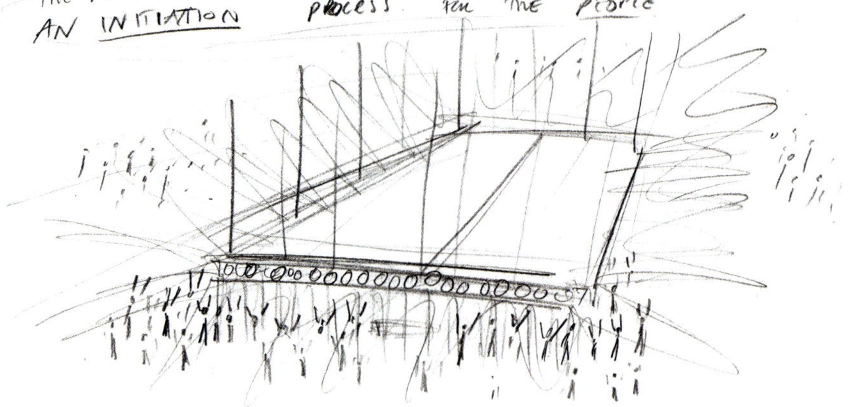

A BAPTISM IN LIGHT.
SET UP THE TERMS IF ENGAGEMENT WITH THE PEOPLE.
A PHYSICAL PHENOMENOLOGICAL. EVENT. / GOD DREAM
PHENOMENON OF ENERGY / SPIRIT – MANIFESTED IN. PHYSICAL / CHEMICAL
MECHANICAL LANGUAGE

PABLO STUDIES

When no one ain't around … I think I think too much …
Ain't nobody watchin' … I just fade away

Kanye West, 'Fade'

I (and many other designers) spent months sketching and modelling ideas for the tour that would accompany Kanye West's 2016 album, *The Life of Pablo*. Some of my sketches suggested that there would be no stage, just a vast kinetic ceiling of lights. Others imagined giant robots and spaceships. In a process that the creative director Virgil Abloh called 'torrentially circular', we explored at least a thousand ideas between us. Ultimately the production director John McGuire conducted the final design and execution for the 2016 *Saint Pablo* tour.

One of the most memorable ideation sessions took place at Karl Lagerfeld's famous bookshop, the Librairie 7L, in Paris. I sat at the side of the room sketching, surrounded by drawings on the floor. Kanye would comment every few minutes between takes during a seven-hour photoshoot on a bed in the middle of the library with Kim Kardashian. Karl looked on as I progressed ideas and said, 'It's good that you are drawing. Nobody draws anymore.'

RIO OLYMPICS

It was the drawing that led me to architecture, the search for light and astonishing forms.

Oscar Niemeyer

It has happened to me a few times that, having never visited a place, two separate invitations to encounter it arrive simultaneously. While studying Brazilian culture in preparation for the 2016 Rio Olympic ceremonies, I was invited by Nicolas Ghesquière to engage in a detailed study of Oscar Niemeyer's Contemporary Art Museum (MAC) in Niterói as the location for his Louis Vuitton 2017 Cruise Collection runway show in May 2016. Our intervention at the museum was a winding labyrinth of perforated, colourful, powder-coated steel seats. The serpentine pavement geometries of Roberto Burle Marx and the sinuous melodies of Gilberto Gil also threaded through the kinetic compositions of mass cast in the Olympic Opening Ceremony at the Maracanã Stadium in August 2016. Niemeyer attributed his love of floating curves to the female form, mountains and rivers of Brazil: these undulating geometries have infected my practice ever since these encounters.

818–819

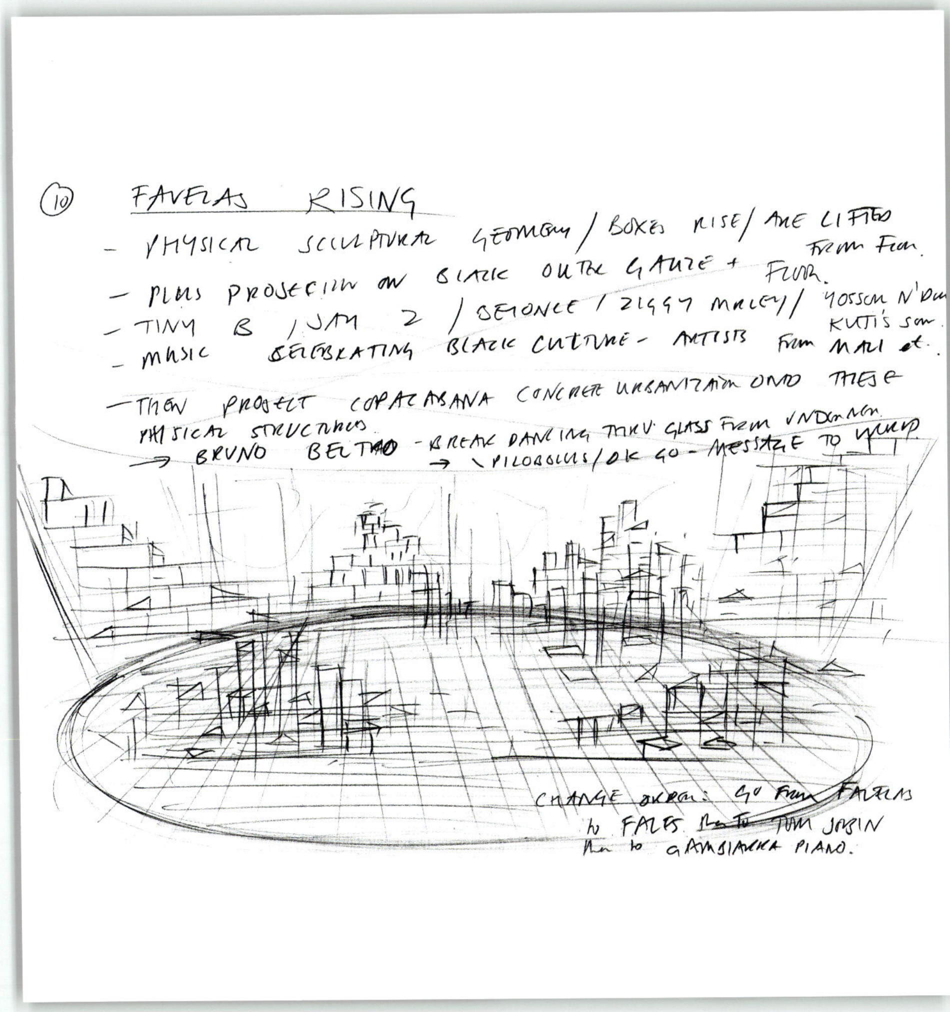
10
FAVELAS RISING
- PHYSICAL SCULPTURAL GEOMETRY / BOXES RISE / ARE LIFTED FROM FLOOR.
- PLUS PROJECTION ON BLACK OUTER GAUZE + FLOOR.
- TINY B / JAY Z / BEYONCE / ZIGGY MARLEY / YOUSSOU N'DOUR / KUTI'S SON
- MUSIC CELEBRATING BLACK CULTURE - ARTISTS FROM MALI etc.
- THEN PROJECT COPACABANA CONCRETE URBANIZATION ONTO THESE PHYSICAL STRUCTURES.
→ BRUNO BELTRAO - BREAK DANCING THRU GLASS FROM UNDERNEATH
→ PILOBOLUS / OK GO - MESSAGE TO WORLD
CHANGE SCREEN: GO FROM FAVELAS to FACES then to TOM JOBIM then to GAMBIARRA PIANO.

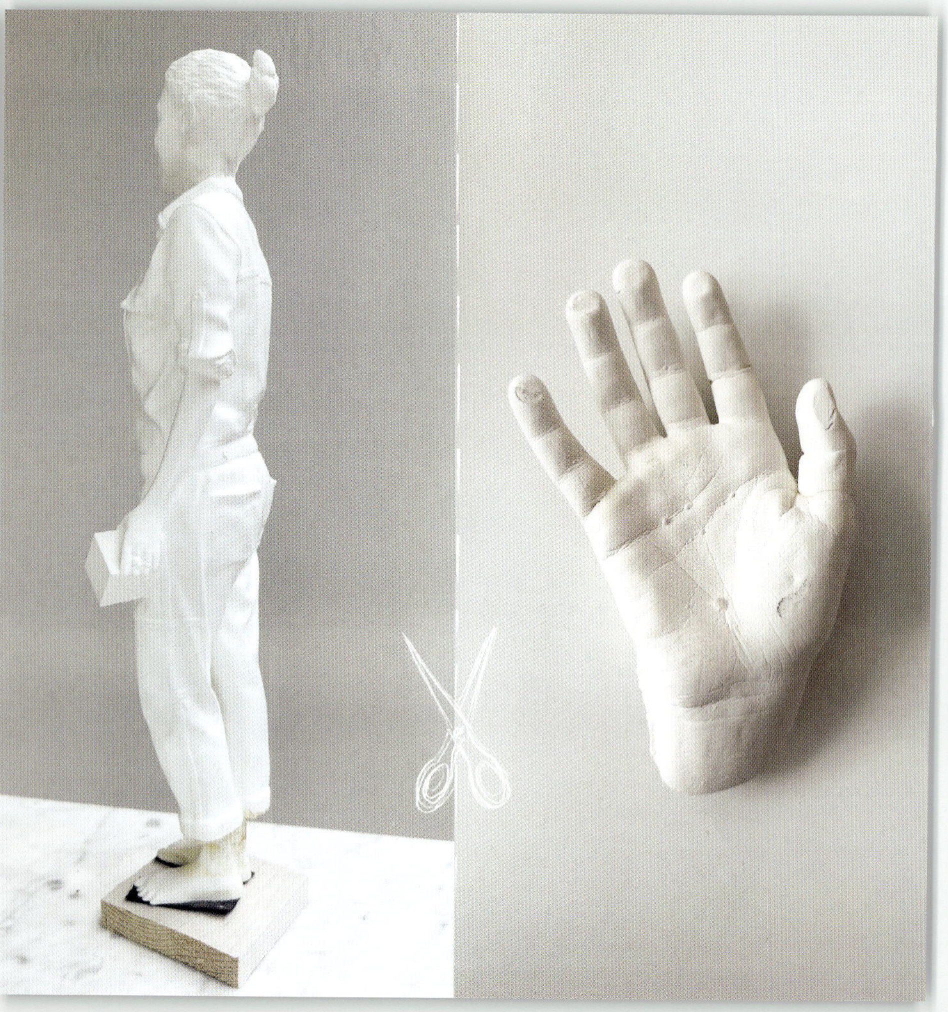

MIRACLE BOX

Because one has only learnt to get the better of words
For the thing one no longer has to say, or the way in which
One is no longer disposed to say it. And so each venture
Is a new beginning, a raid on the inarticulate,
With shabby equipment always deteriorating

T. S. Eliot, 'East Coker'

Asked by the author and poet Andrew O'Hagan to make a contribution to the October 2016 Miracle Marathon at the Serpentine Galleries in London, I offered a meditation on the origins and mechanics of the suspension of disbelief. I hypothesized on the earliest acts of collective imagination circa forty millennia ago, while constructing a sculptural self-portrait of my practice in the form of a revolving projection-mapped cardboard box. Each side of the box showed a film of my hands penetrating its surface to access a central light: one side clawing a hole through clay, another carefully slicing triangular apertures through mirror, another tearing a hole through paper, and one in which I cut a small doorway to reveal a printed model of a 3D scan of myself holding a copy of the box in my hand. The work was underscored by the track I had encountered through the director Lyndsey Turner on *Hamlet*: 'Abandon Window' by Jon Hopkins.

MIRROR MAZE

I emerged from watching the film *The Life of Pi* in 2012 both impressed by the extreme virtuosity of the animation and depressed by the limit of my own more analogue craft. I challenged myself as to what my twenty years building worlds in theatres, opera houses and arenas could add to an evening in the cinema. I decided I could most usefully contribute a hole, a perforation through the cinema screen, that would allow the audience to enter the film and become participants in its world.

In late 2015 I misread an email from *i-D* magazine about a digital perfume collaboration as an invitation to conceive my first solo art installation. The piece began as a film with an oval hole at its heart. The film was a kind of self-portrait, a pair of hands making a scale model of a mirrored maze overlaid with a meditation on naming, reason, the frontal cortex, and their rigid calibration of identity. As the film screen flooded with orange paint, the audience walked through the hole and entered the glimmering world that the film had foreshadowed. Installed in a Peckham, South London warehouse in September 2016, mirrored pathways either terminated in refracting cul-de-sacs or opened onto streaming spectrum-coloured vistas. These interruptions evoked the sensation I had of being transported in time, place and identity by the superhighway scent of a cupboard full of lavender: the ancient limbic system overwhelming the cerebral cortex. The work culminated in a field of vivid red-orange haze, infused with a new scent called Chanel SE15, composed by Olivier Polge, the 'nose' at Chanel, existing only for the five-day duration of the work.

14–15 850–851

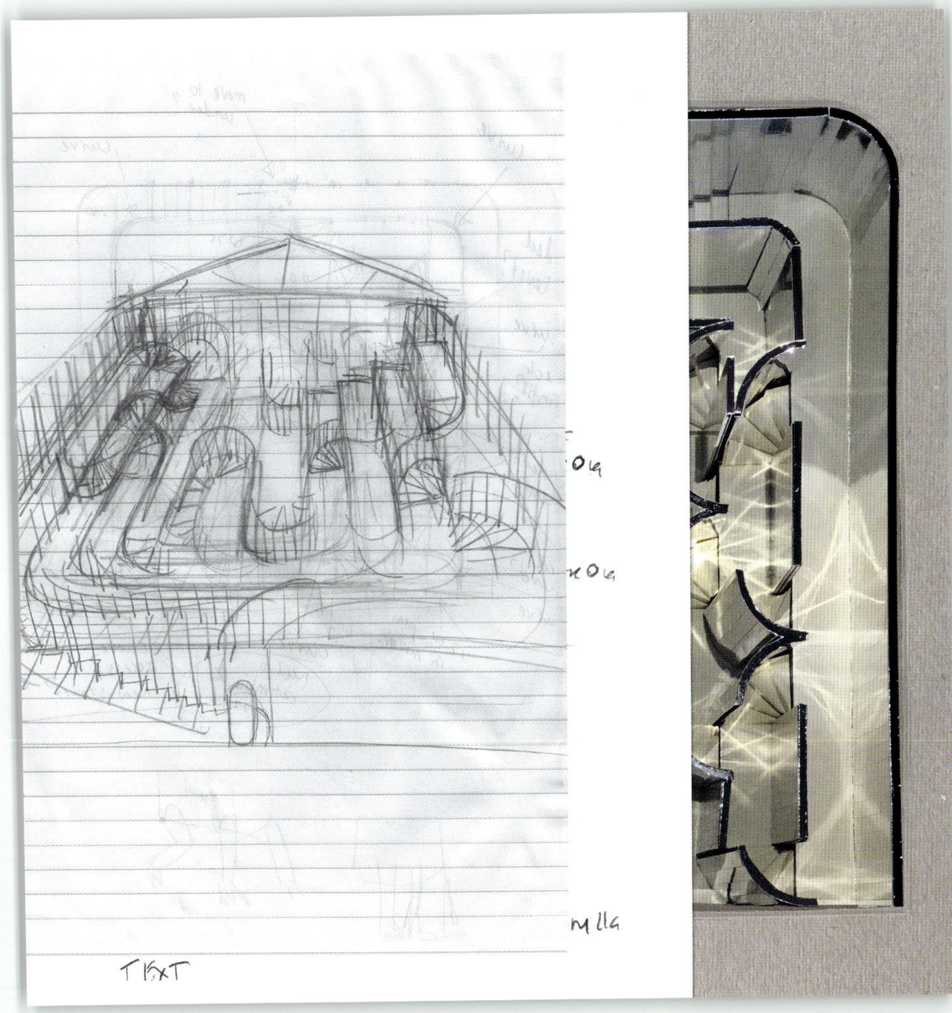
TEXT

MIRROR MAZE

I emerged from watching the fil
by the extreme virtuosity of the
my own more analogue craft. I
years building worlds in theatres
to an evening in the cinema. I de
a hole, a perforation through the
audience to enter the film and b

In late 2015 I misread an email
perfume collaboration as an inv
installation. The piece began as
The film was a kind of self-portr
model of a mirrored maze overl
reason, the frontal cortex, and
film screen flooded with orange
hole and entered the glimmerin
Installed in a Peckham, South L
mirrored pathways either termi
opened onto streaming spectru
evoked the sensation I had of b
identity by the superhighway s
ancient limbic system overwhel
culminated in a field of vivid red
called Chanel SE15, composed
existing only for the five-day du

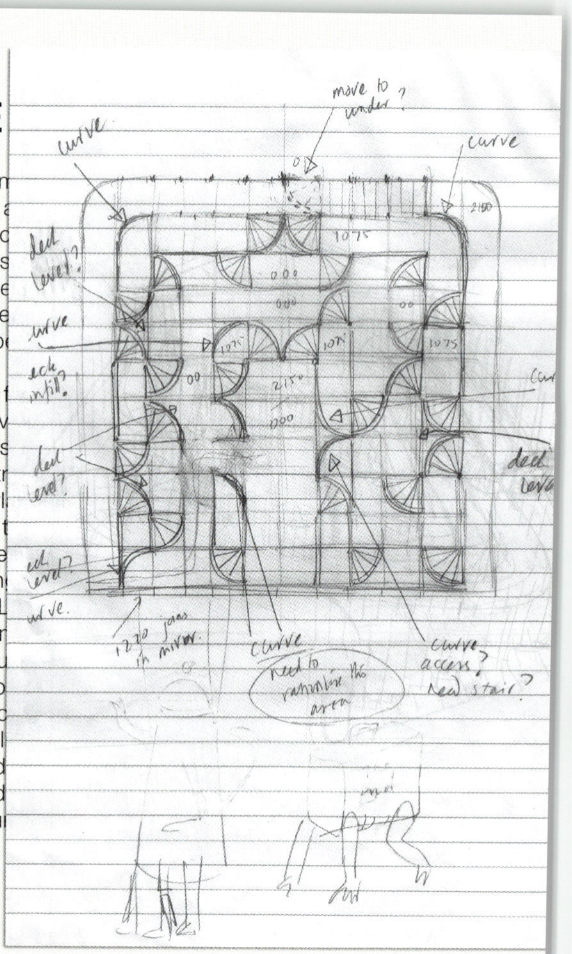

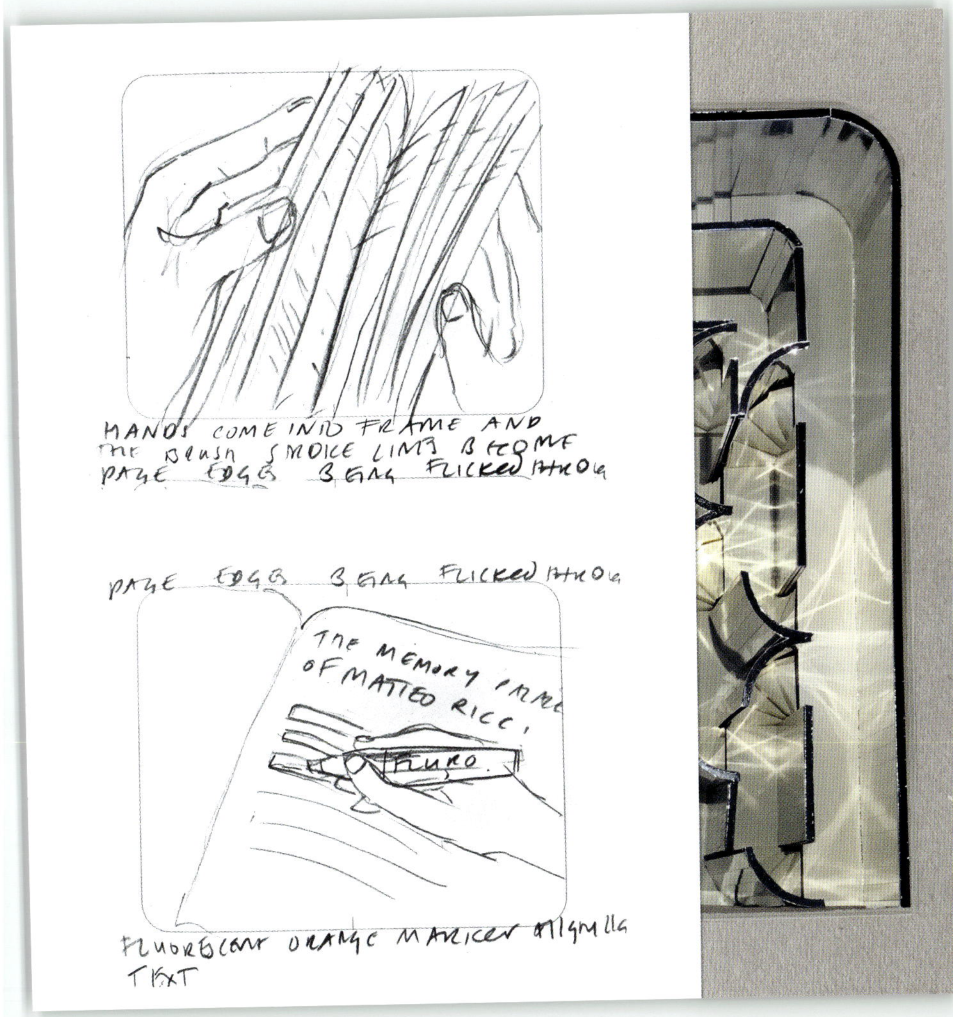
HANDS COME INTO FRAME AND
THE MEMORY
OF MATTEO RICC
FLURO.
TEXT

MIRROR

I emerged from wa
by the extreme virt
my own more analo
years building world
to an evening in the
a hole, a perforation
audience to enter th

In late 2015 I misre
perfume collaborat
installation. The pie
The film was a kind
model of a mirrored
reason, the frontal
film screen flooded
hole and entered th
Installed in a Peckh
mirrored pathways
opened onto strea
evoked the sensati
identity by the sup
ancient limbic syst
culminated in a fiel
called Chanel SE15
existing only for the

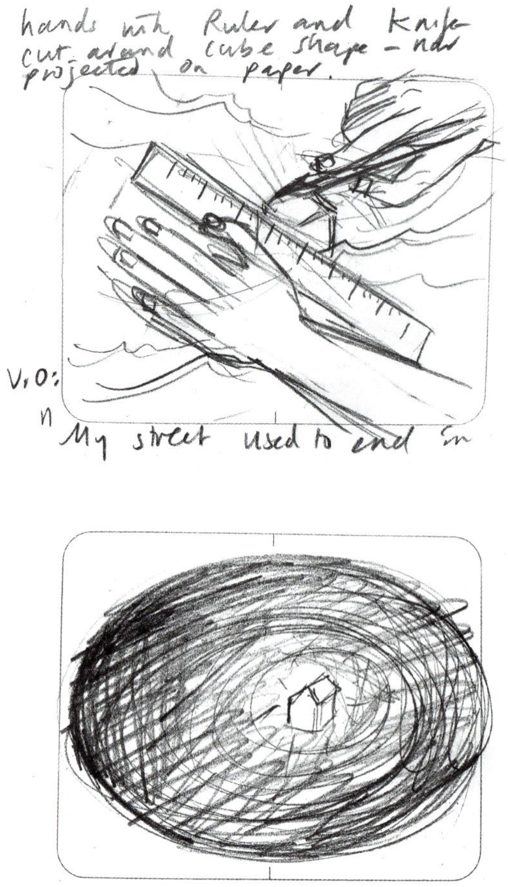

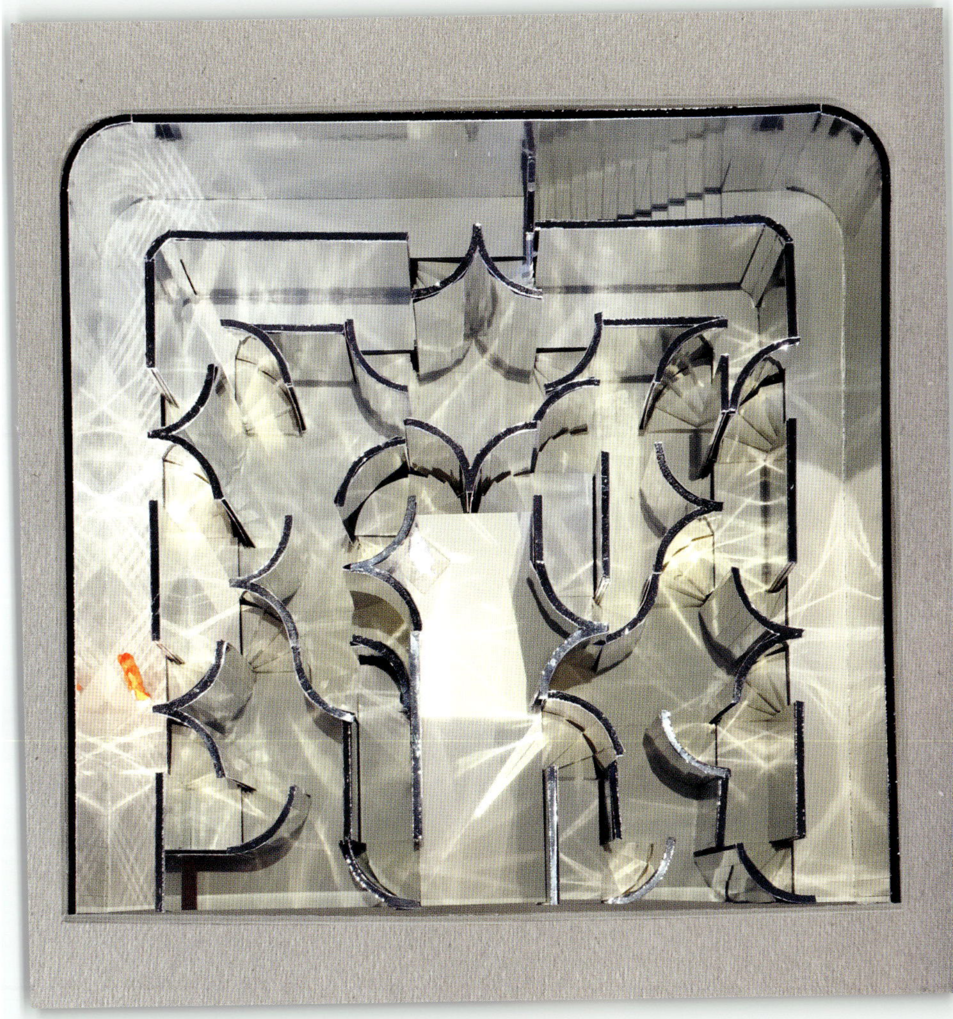

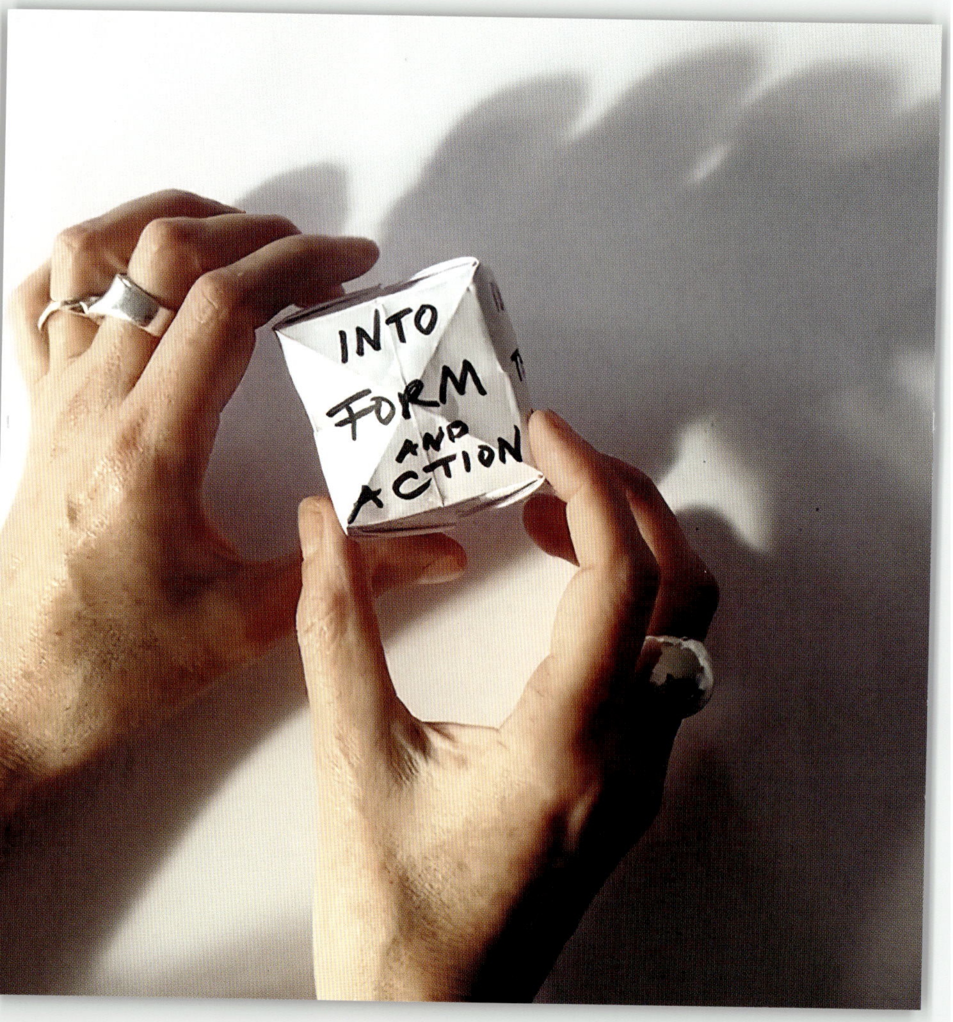
INTO
FORM
AND
ACTION

ORIGAMI POST-IT NOTE

Whatever you do, do something else.

Claire Fontaine, *do it*

While we were waiting backstage between talks at the Serpentine Galleries' Miracle Marathon on 8 October 2016, the galleries' artistic director Hans Ulrich Obrist gave me a Post-it note and asked me to quickly write a message on it for his Instagram. I was remarkably un-casual in my approach to this invitation. Hans Ulrich's Instagram collection of Post-it note messages is legendary. It includes pretty much every living artist and many of my heroes across the cultural, political and scientific spectrum. For the next two weeks I experimented and finally sent him a film of a white square of paper being origami-folded and inflated into a rotating box. After a number of rehearsals, I worked out how to write a scrambled message on the unfolded paper that would only make sense once the box was complete and revolving: 'Ideas in the mind / are like seeds in the earth / Hands extrude thought / into form and action'.

LEGEND OF THE FALL

Let me fall if I must fall.
The one I am becoming will catch me

Baal Shem Tov

Abel 'The Weeknd' Tesfaye proposed an intergalactic craft that would transport him and his audience into worlds beyond the arenas of his 2017 *Starboy: Legend of the Fall* tour. His creative director La Mar C Taylor, the TAIT Towers CEOs James 'Winky' Fairorth and Adam Davis and their engineering team, all watched as I folded a paper aeroplane in the lobby of the Mandarin Oriental hotel in New York in the autumn of 2016 to demonstrate how the suspended sculpture could function. We saw the pattern of the show as an aircraft flight path. The evening began with a lift-off: using the audience's pre-show anticipation as fuel, the vast triangular plane rose over the crowd's heads to reveal Abel beneath. There was an initial cruise during which the illuminated origami structure demonstrated its virtuosity, folding into a range of forms as the audience danced below. Mid-flight complications followed as parts of the structure came apart, culminating in a crash landing to mark the dark musical nadir of the setlist before the ship re-emerged from the ashes in a euphoric final sequence.

682–683 768–769

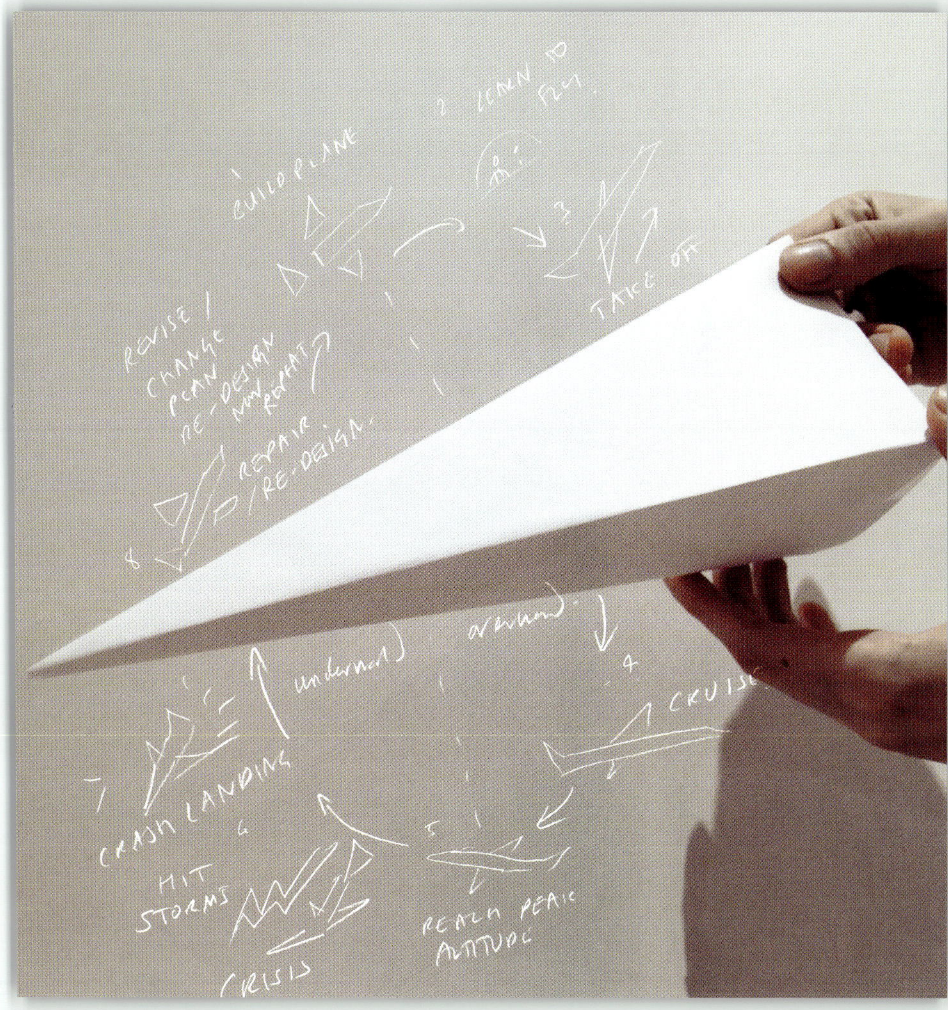
BUILD PLANE
2 LEARN TO FLY.
TAKE OFF
REVISE / CHANGE PLAN
RE-DESIGN
REPAIR / RE-DESIGN.
CRUISE
REACH PEAK ALTITUDE
HIT STORMS
CRISIS
CRASH LANDING

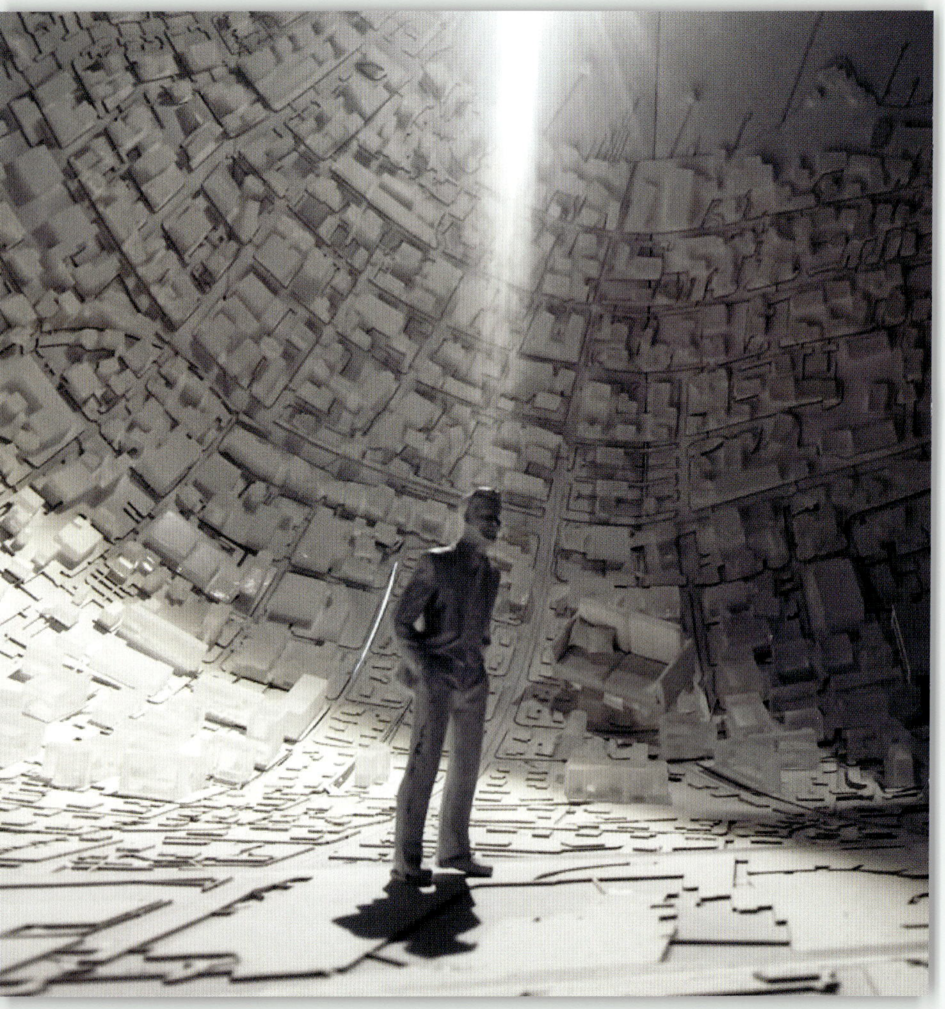

UGLY LIES THE BONE

Beauty is but skin deep, ugly lies the bone; beauty dies and fades away, but ugly holds its own.

Anonymous

Lindsey Ferrentino's play *Ugly Lies the Bone* centres on Jess, an ex-soldier who has returned from war in Afghanistan with debilitating burns and is offered VR therapy: pain relief via immersion in a virtual polar world. The action oscillates fast between the vast arctic virtual vistas she experiences within her VR headset and oppressive low-ceilinged domestic interiors. For the 2017 National Theatre production, the director Indhu Rubasingham and I proposed a bowl-shaped sculptural map of Jess's hometown, Titusville, Florida. Born of the national optimism of a now defunct space shuttle programme at Cape Canaveral, Titusville's low-rise breeze-block houses were constructed at speed to keep up with the escalating accommodation needs of the 1960s space race. The astronauts who studied the vastness of the cosmos slept beneath ceilings five feet from their faces. The National Theatre workshop team abseiled down the curved surface to apply each of the 2,000 buildings by hand. The video designer Luke Halls added luminous projected layers of depth and movement.

ROOM 2022

It might seem like a leap of imagination to extend this fantastical geometry from a single line of light, but is it really such a surprising feat, compared to what we all agree to believe, every time we stay in a hotel? That the room is ours, that the guests before us left no trace and the guests that follow us cast no shadow; that the walls between us are impenetrable, and that the chaos we leave behind us will be restored to order by invisible magic? It's a subtle act of strenuous imagination: to un-see the opposite version of the room through the wall; to un-draw the pipes that pass and beds that pair from one room to the next; to un-hear our many breaths cycling into synch across our multi-storey sleep.

During Miami Art Basel in December 2017, we invited visitors into a deceptively normal guest room at the EDITION hotel. The window became a cinema and the words quoted above are part of a script that I wrote to accompany the film. The final image was a single line of dawn light, which split apart to allow visitors to enter a series of maze-like hotel corridors. A flooded, video-saturated zoetrope behaved as the hippocampus/hippodrome of the hotel: fragments of remembered lives galloped along the walls in looped cycles. A vaulted elliptical mirror maze proposed what hotel corridors might look like had they drunk the combined imaginations of all of their occupants. Like many systems of civil organization, hotels work because everyone agrees each day to take part in invisible, heroic acts of collective imagination. The installation playfully explored what might happen if this combined imaginative force could be ingested by the system and reflected in its architecture.

852–853

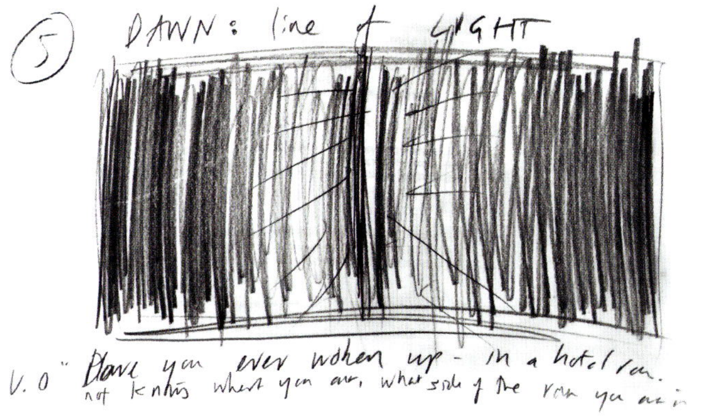

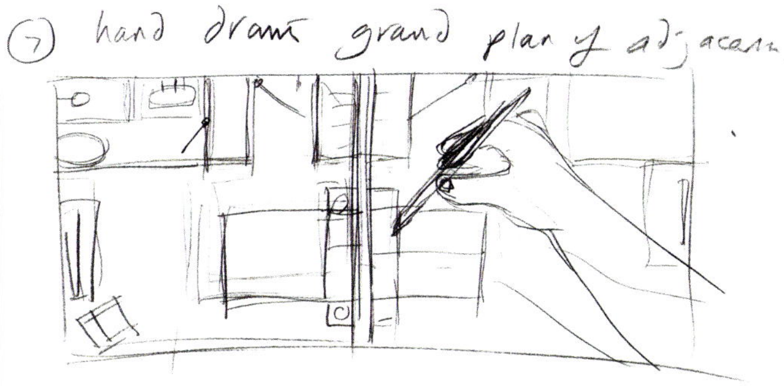

A

Lorde, 'Sober'

'ealand-born
iss room, an
e that would
enes described
wardly posed
glass walls,
ntents out in

ROOM 20

It might seem like a
from a single line of
what we all agree to
is ours, that the gue
cast no shadow; tha
chaos we leave beh
a subtle act of stren
the room through th
pair from one room
synch across our m

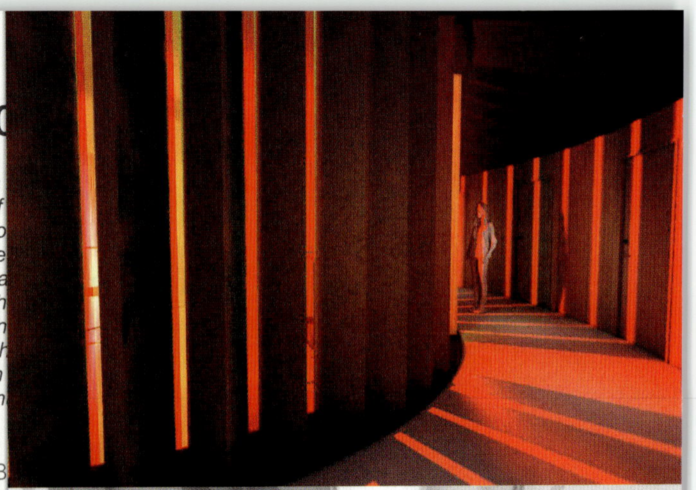

During Miami Art B
a deceptively norm
became a cinema
that I wrote to acco
dawn light, which s
like hotel corridors.
the hippocampus/h
lives galloped along
maze proposed wh
combined imaginat
civil organization, h
take part in invisible
playfully explored w
could be ingested b

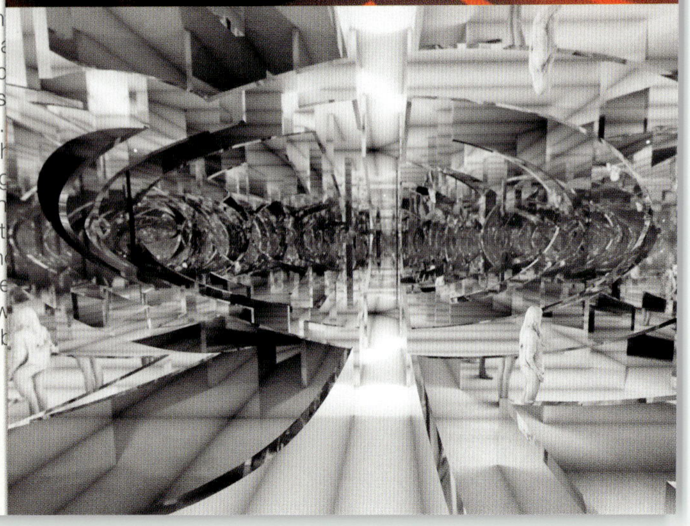

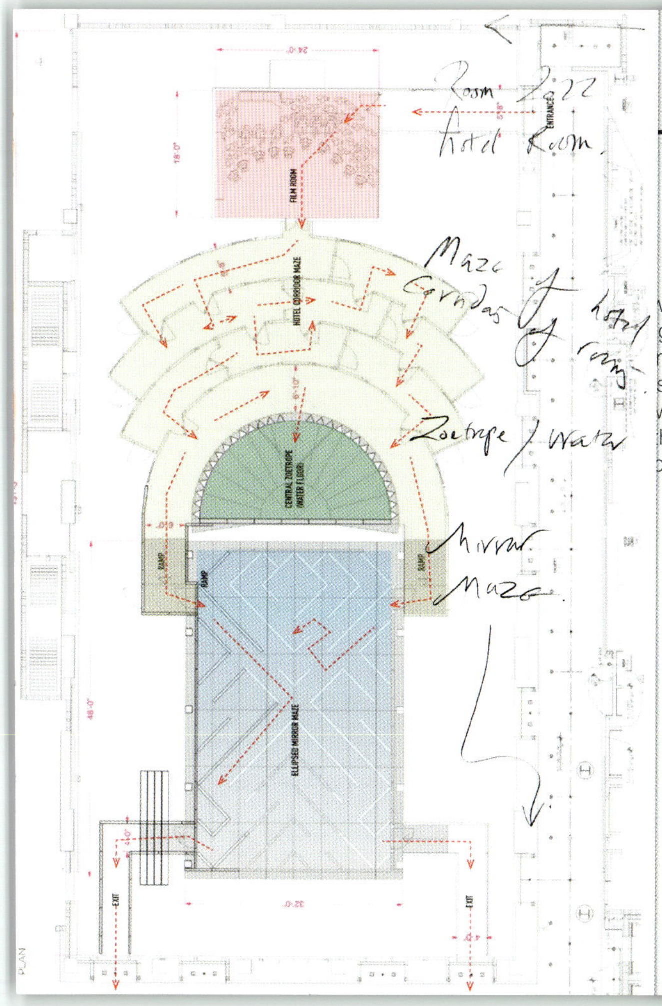

LA

Lorde, 'Sober'

v Zealand-born
glass room, an
nce that would
scenes described
wkwardly posed
the glass walls,
contents out in

ROOM 20

It might seem like a
from a single line of
what we all agree to
is ours, that the gue
cast no shadow; tha
chaos we leave beh
a subtle act of stren
the room through th
pair from one room
synch across our m

During Miami Art B
a deceptively norm
became a cinema a
that I wrote to acco
dawn light, which s
like hotel corridors.
the hippocampus/h
lives galloped along
maze proposed wh
combined imaginat
civil organization, h
take part in invisible
playfully explored w
could be ingested b

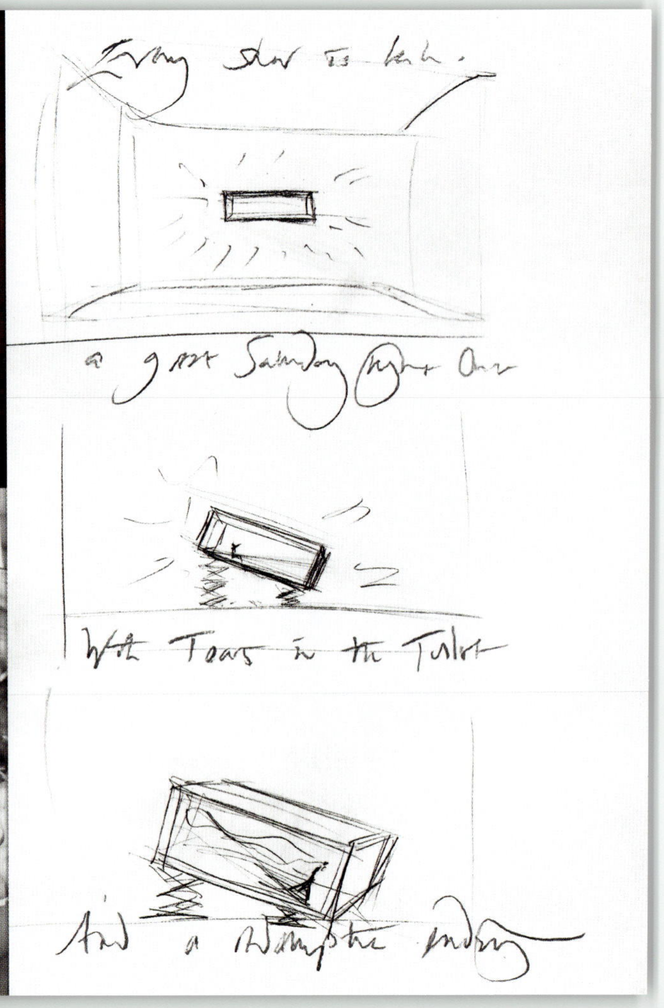

MELODRAMA COACHELLA

It's time we danced with the truth

Lorde, 'Sober'

For her April 2017 Coachella performance, the New Zealand-born singer-songwriter Lorde inhabited a fragile floating glass room, an enclosed world unmoored from gravity. In a sequence that would shape her 2017 *Melodrama* arena tour, a series of scenes described the course of an evening at a party: starting with awkwardly posed tableaux, erupting into waves of energy pounding the glass walls, and ending with the glass box spewing its human contents out in a lifeless heap.

667 814–815

POEMPORTRAITS

The instability of the human begins with the redesign of its own brain through the very act of thinking ... In redesigning itself, it redesigns the planet. But equally and simultaneously, the redesigned world redesigns the designing animal.

Beatriz Colomina and Mark Wigley, *Are We Human?*

Asked by Hans Ulrich Obrist and Yana Peel to make a temporary sculpture at the Serpentine Galleries Summer Party in London in June 2017, I sketched my intention as a spiral of text around the circular pavilion designed by Burkina Faso-born architect Francis Kéré. I took my lead from the Felix Gonzalez-Torres installation which heaped piles of silver sweets in the Serpentine Gallery in 2000 and invited visitors to take and eat the art. Each guest donated a word to a poetry-generating algorithm, which composed a cumulative collective poem, constantly retraining itself on each new donated word.

We collaborated with creative technologist Ross Goodwin at Google Arts & Culture, who developed a machine-learning algorithm trained on twenty million lines of nineteenth-century poetry. We built a mirrored photo booth which issued a printed portrait of each guest with the text of the collective poem saturating their skin. Using a new algorithm developed by Kyle McDonald, the collective poem is still being co-authored online today by the algorithm and the public.

860–861

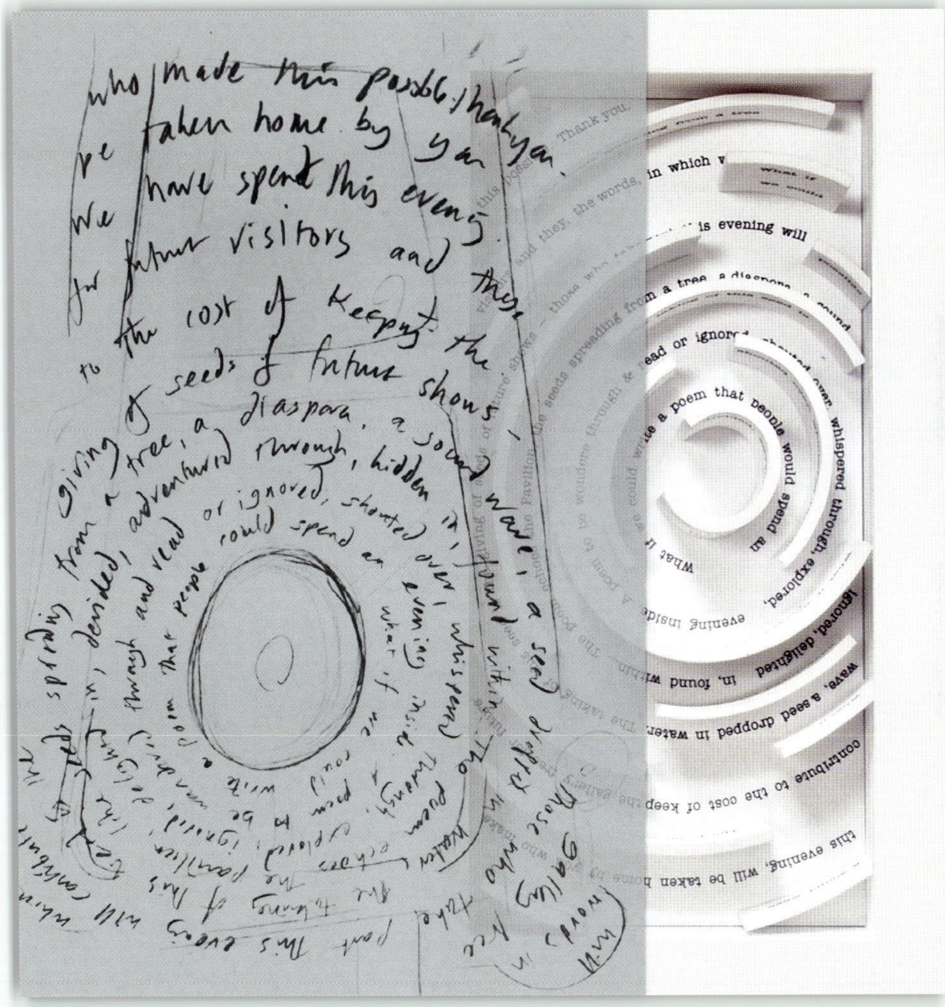
who made this possible. thank you.
be taken home by you
we have spent this evening.
for future visitors and those
to the cost of keeping the
giving of seeds of future shows
a tree, a diaspora, a sound
is evening will
contribute to the cost of keep
this evening, will be taken home

POEMPORTRAITS

The instability of the human begins with the redesign of its own brain through the very act of thinking … In redesigning itself, it redesigns the planet. But equally and simultaneously, the redesigned world redesigns the designing animal.

Beatriz Colomina and Mark Wigley, *Are We Human?*

Asked by Hans Ulrich Obrist and Yana Peel to make a temporary sculpture at the Serpentine Galleries Summer Party in London in June 2017, I sketched my intention as a spiral of text around the circular pavilion designed by Burkina Faso-born architect Francis Kéré. I took my lead from the Félix González-Torres installation which heaped piles of silver sweets in the Serpentine Gallery in 2000 and invited visitors to take and eat the art. Each guest donated a word to a poetry-generating algorithm, which composed a cumulative collective poem constantly retraining itself on each new donated word.

We collaborated with creative technologist Ross Goodwin at Google Arts & Culture, who developed a machine learning algorithm trained on twenty million lines of nineteenth-century poetry. We built a mirrored photo booth which issued a printed portrait of each guest with the text of the collective poem saturating their skin. Using a new algorithm developed by Kyle McDonald, the collective poem is still being co-authored online today by the algorithm and the public.

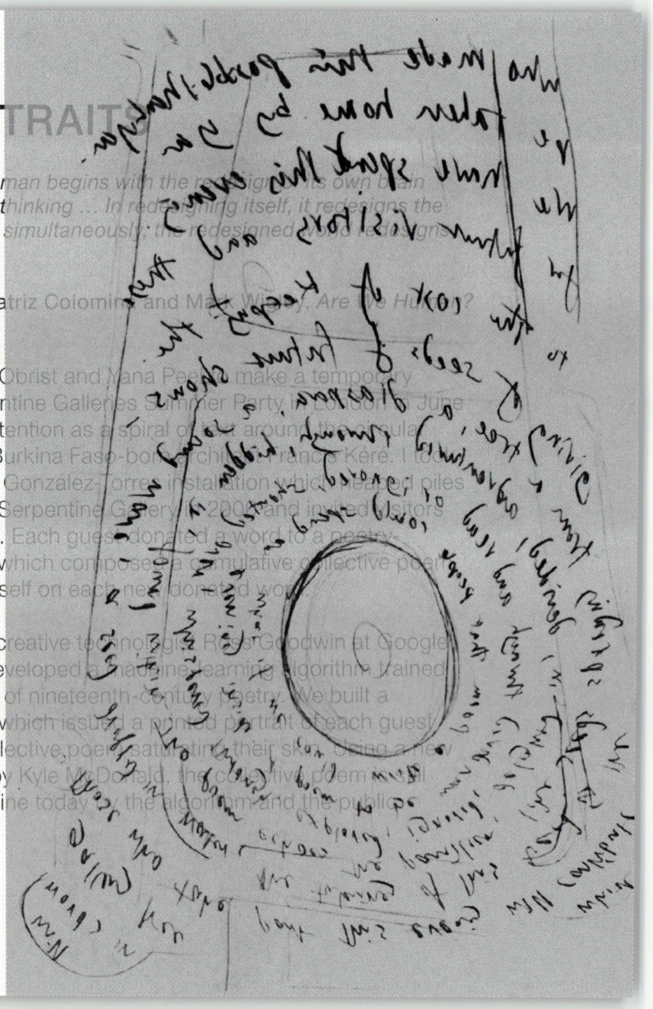

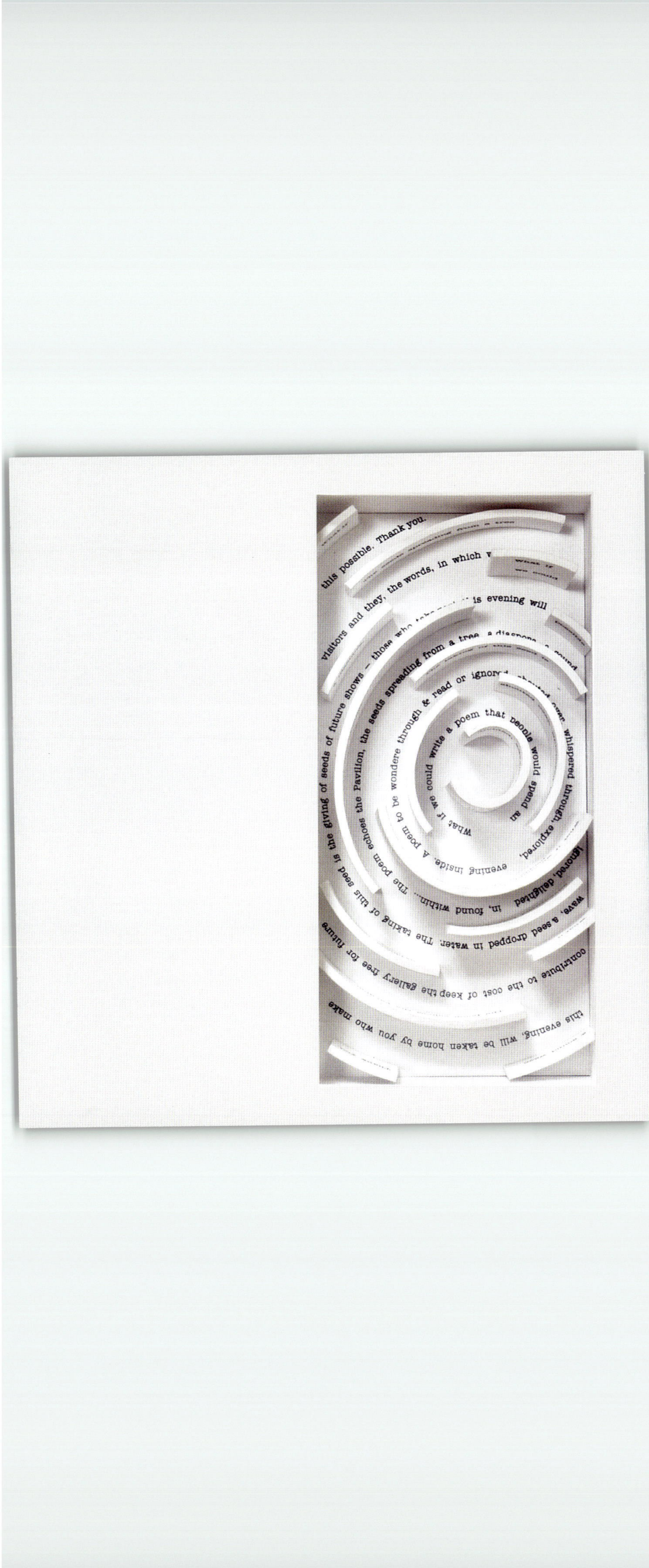
this possible. Thank you.
visitors and they, the words, in which
is evening will
the giving of seeds of future shows – those who
the seeds spreading from a tree
What if we could write a poem that people would spend an
to be wondere through & read or ignored
whispered through, explored,
evening inside.
ignored, delighted
in, found within.
wave, a seed dropped in water. The taking of this seed is
contribute to the cost of keep the gallery free for future
this evening, will be taken home by you who make

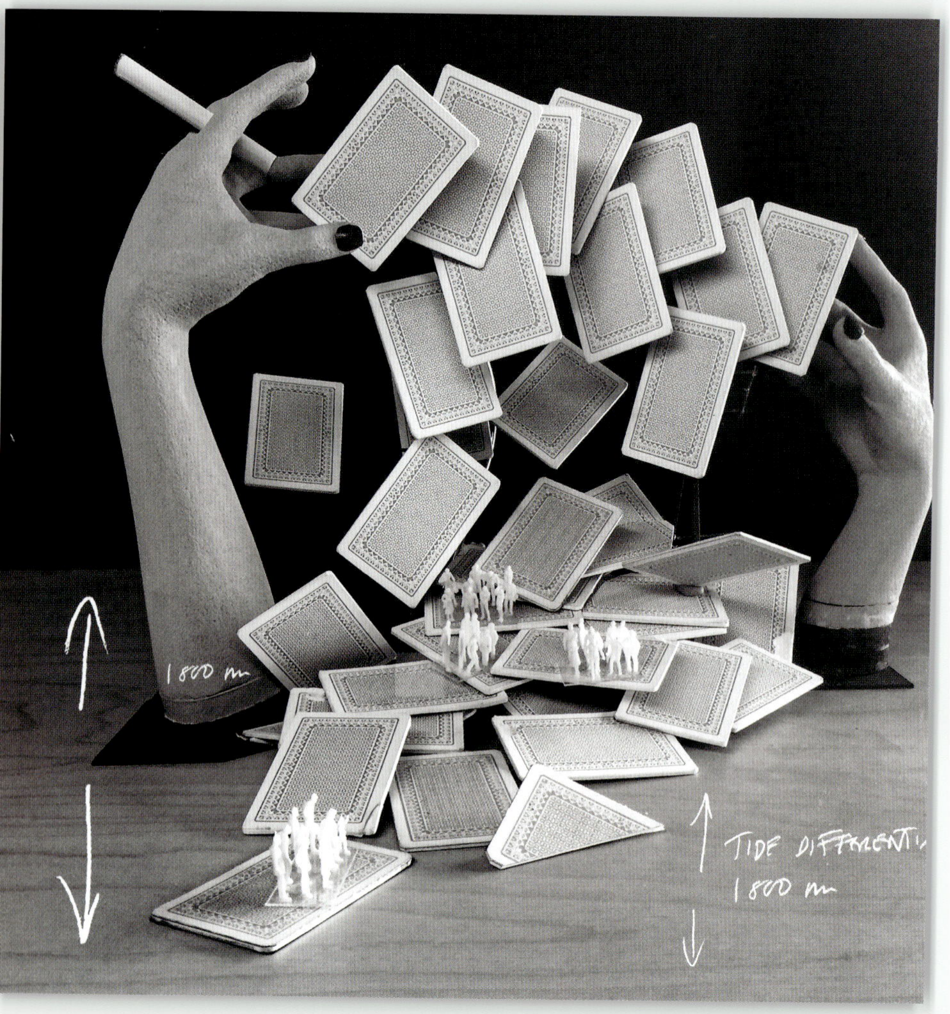
1800 m
TIDE DIFFERENTI
1800 m

CARMEN

In vain you shuffle,
nothing changes,
the cards are sincere
and never lie

Georges Bizet, Henri Meilhac and Ludovic Halévy

In 1945, Maria Wanda Milliore, a young Viennese painter and stage designer, arrived in the small West Austrian Swiss-border town of Bregenz on the shores of Lake Constance. She had been walking for days, following a wagon full of wounded soldiers, fleeing rape by Russian soldiers capturing Vienna. By 1946, the town's occupying officer was a French opera enthusiast who proposed a performance to celebrate the end of the war. The concert hall had been bombed, so Milliore, the set designer, needed to improvise. She suggested two barges on the lake: one for the orchestra, one for the singers – and so the most spectacular open-air floating opera was born, of necessity. Bregenz has since hosted some of the world's most breathtaking stage designs – all by men. My design for Kasper Holten's 2017–2018 production of Georges Bizet's opera *Carmen* was the first by a woman since Milliore's in 1946. Two 22-metre-high female hands emerged from the lake, throwing a pack of cards in the air. Suspended between sky and sea, projection made the cards dance during the performances, while concealed steel trusses held them in place through two years of high winds and snowstorms.

796–797

ZOETROPE

Zoetrope (n.): 'optical instrument which exhibits pictures as if alive and in action', 1867, literally 'wheel of life', from Greek zoe *'life'* + trope *'a turn'*

Online Etymology Dictionary

Our landscapes bear the traces of every successive historic transport system: the frequency of roadside inns was determined by the metabolism of a horse; the short-lived but industrially essential nineteenth-century canal network and arterial railways governed the expansion of towns; while the size of petrol tanks in twentieth-century fossil-fuel-powered cars specified the frequency of the global service station network. Commissioned by Design Indaba to make a pavilion outside the Zeitz Museum of Contemporary Art Africa in Cape Town, I conceived a solar-powered zoetrope based on the Japanese concept of Michi-no-Eki, which are roadside stations that offer local insights, performances and produce. Installed for a year from December 2018, the exterior panels of the zoetrope contained sand from 12 local sites. The interior enfolded a labyrinth of filmic haikus made by local South African filmmakers to express the geographic and demographic range of life within a 100-kilometre radius of the museum – from an underwater kelp forest and rooftop football match to choral groups and solar-power installers.

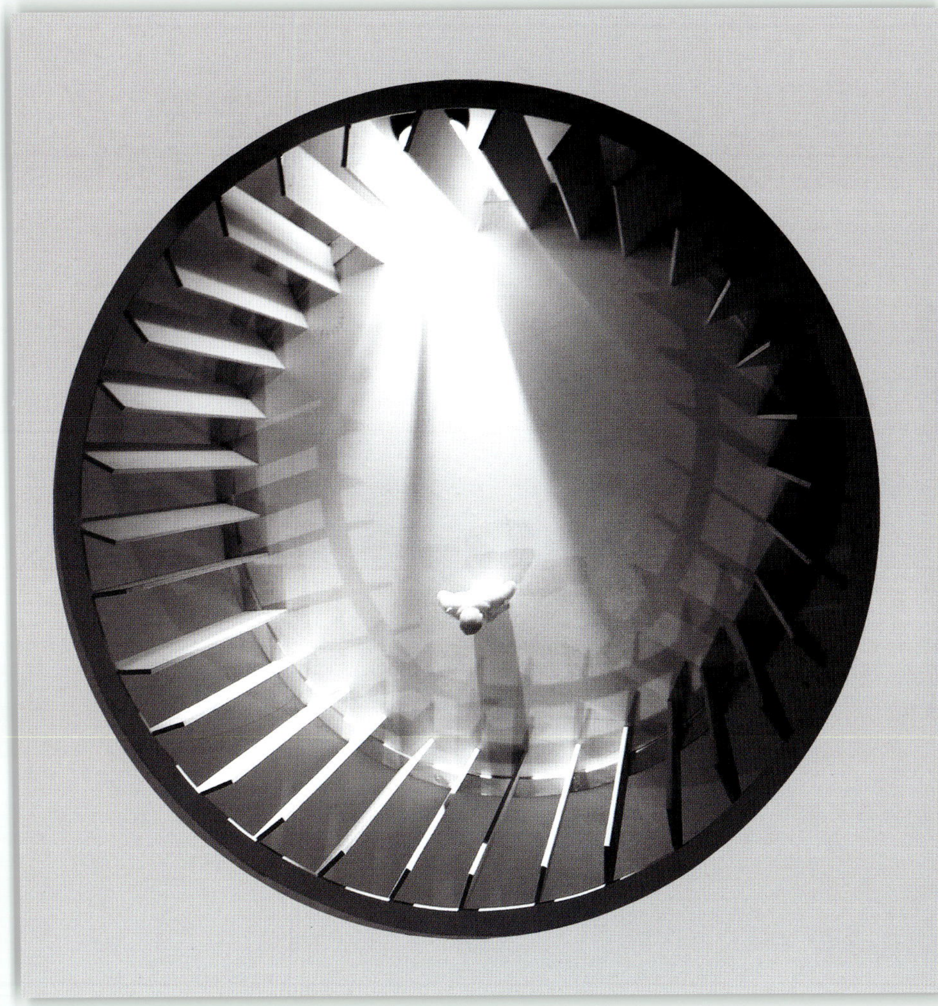

WITNESS

So comfortable, we're living in a bubble ...
So comfortable, we cannot see the trouble

Katy Perry, 'Chained to the Rhythm'

When my six-year-old son Ludo saw my ashen face as I woke and switched on the radio to hear the result of the 2016 US election on 9 November 2016, he quietly asked, 'What's wrong, Mum? Is it Donald Duck?' He recognized the same look that he'd seen six months earlier when we awoke to the news of the UK Brexit vote to leave the European Union. It was the look of someone who didn't recognize their own country, who realized they had been ignoring the perspective of 52% of the population.

Katy Perry had campaigned for Hillary Clinton and wrote 'Chained to the Rhythm' in response to a parallel realization about the Trump victory. We collaborated on her 2017 Grammys performance within a Norman Rockwell white-picket-fenced house that exploded into mirrored fragments and finally culminated as protest placards displaying the text of the US Constitution. In early studies for her 2017 *Witness* arena tour, we explored the form of the megaphone, the hand of the activist, and the cerebral architecture of an evolving consciousness.

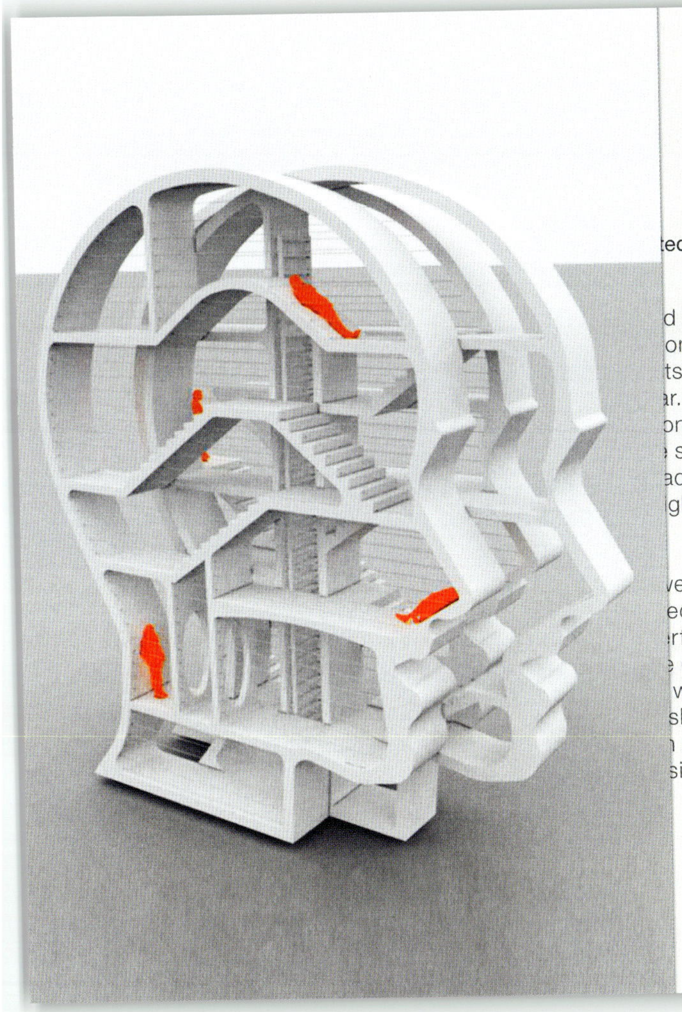

ted by Ludo Galloway

d real fir trees
on the medieval
ts and designers
ar. Queen Victoria's
oncept of the
sixteenth-century
added candles
ghting of stars

ve revisited Ross
ed each museum
erful projectors in
donated words
wooden strips
shaped cloud.
and synthesized
sing along with us

WITNESS

So comfortable, we're
So comfortable, we ca

When my six-year-old
switched on the radio
9 November 2016, he
Donald Duck?' He rec
earlier when we awok
European Union. It wa
own country, who rea
52% of the population

Katy Perry had campa
Rhythm' in response t
We collaborated on h
Rockwell white-picket
fragments and finally c
of the US Constitution
we explored the form
the cerebral architectu

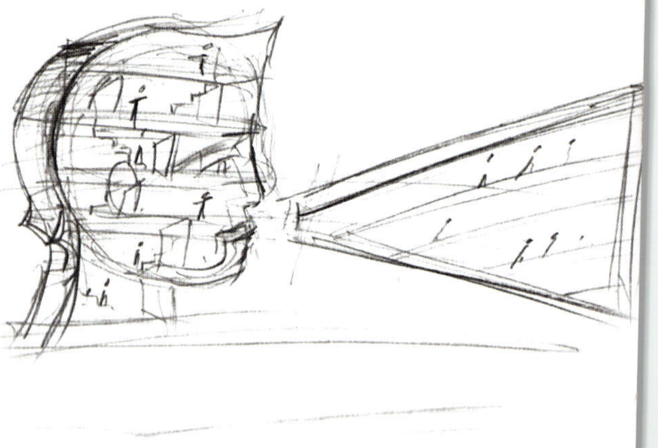

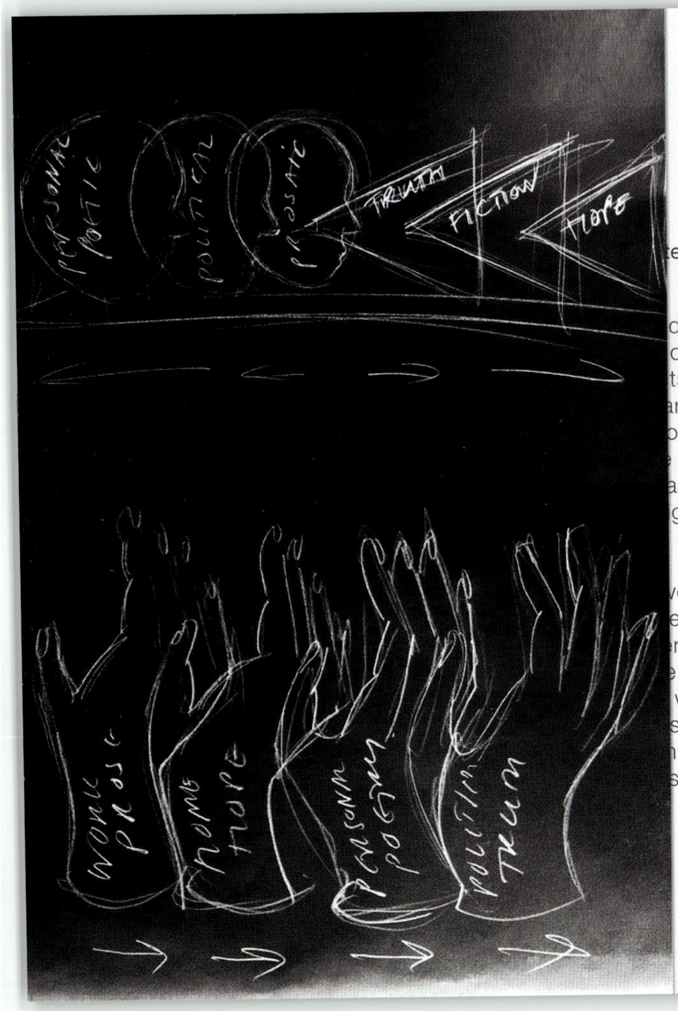

ted by Ludo Galloway

d real fir trees
on the medieval
ts and designers
ar. Queen Victoria's
oncept of the
e sixteenth-century
added candles
ghting of stars

ve revisited Ross
ed each museum
erful projectors in
e donated words
wooden strips
shaped cloud.
n and synthesized
sing along with us

WITNESS

So comfortable, we're
So comfortable, we ca

When my six-year-old
switched on the radio
9 November 2016, he
Donald Duck?' He rec
earlier when we awok
European Union. It wa
own country, who rea
52% of the population

Katy Perry had campa
Rhythm' in response t
We collaborated on h
Rockwell white-picket
fragments and finally
of the US Constitution
we explored the form
the cerebral architectu

THE SINGING TREE

A carol of the sunset shades of the sea:
a love of light and silence

The Singing Tree AI, based on a word contributed by Ludo Galloway

Ever since the Victoria and Albert Museum banned real fir trees due to the havoc their attendant insects wreaked on the medieval tapestry collection, they have commissioned artists and designers to create a new synthetic Christmas tree each year. Queen Victoria's husband Prince Albert popularized the German concept of the decorated Christmas tree in England in 1848. The sixteenth-century Protestant reformer Martin Luther is said to have added candles to the traditional Yuletide branch to recreate his sighting of stars between the trees on a winter evening walk.

For the 2017 V&A installation *The Singing Tree*, we revisited Ross Goodwin's poetry-generating algorithm and invited each museum visitor to donate a word. We perched eight powerful projectors in the rafters of the V&A entrance hall to project the donated words from over eight million visitors onto 7-centimetre wooden strips that we had suspended to form a luminous tree-shaped cloud. The tree sang a collective carol formed of human and synthesized voices – it was an invitation for our machines to sing along with us at Christmas.

40 753

GIRLS & BOYS

There are only two characters in this play: the actor and the audience. You risk running the audience out of the play when it gets hard.

Dennis Kelly

Girls & Boys, Dennis Kelly's searing exploration of male violence, opened at the Royal Court Theatre in February 2018. The 2006 #MeToo movement had been remobilized in October 2017 to expose the extent of sexual assaults worldwide, echoing the eighty women who emerged one by one to accuse the Hollywood film producer Harvey Weinstein. Kelly's play was written prior to this, and asks why 90% of murderers are male, specifically focusing on a gut-wrenching case of family annihilation by a father. The play is a monologue, performed by Carey Mulligan as she interacts with her two invisible children. The director Lyndsey Turner and I constructed a detailed domestic environment around the character: we determined that it would be easier for the audience to believe in an invisible child in the context of a solid chair and spoon. During initial design meetings we took turns reading the monologue, using some of my children's brightly coloured Lego and soft toys as props: a few of them ended up in the show. We painted the rest of the room and its entire contents a single shade of pale duck-eggshell blue and, in each transition, a momentary flash of projection unbleached every surface and object in the room, returning them to their remembered colours. It was as if the room were emulating the mother's ritual of remembering each scene with her children while trying to erase the memory of their father.

810–811

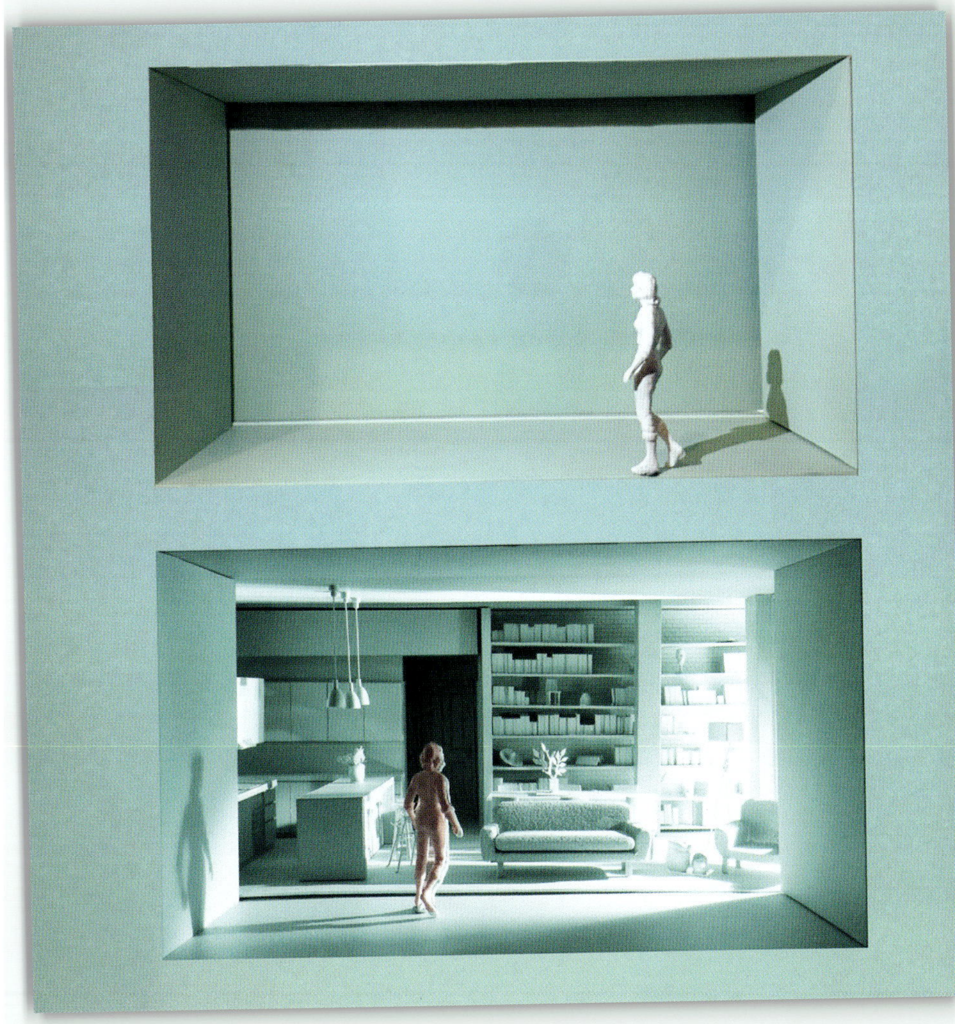

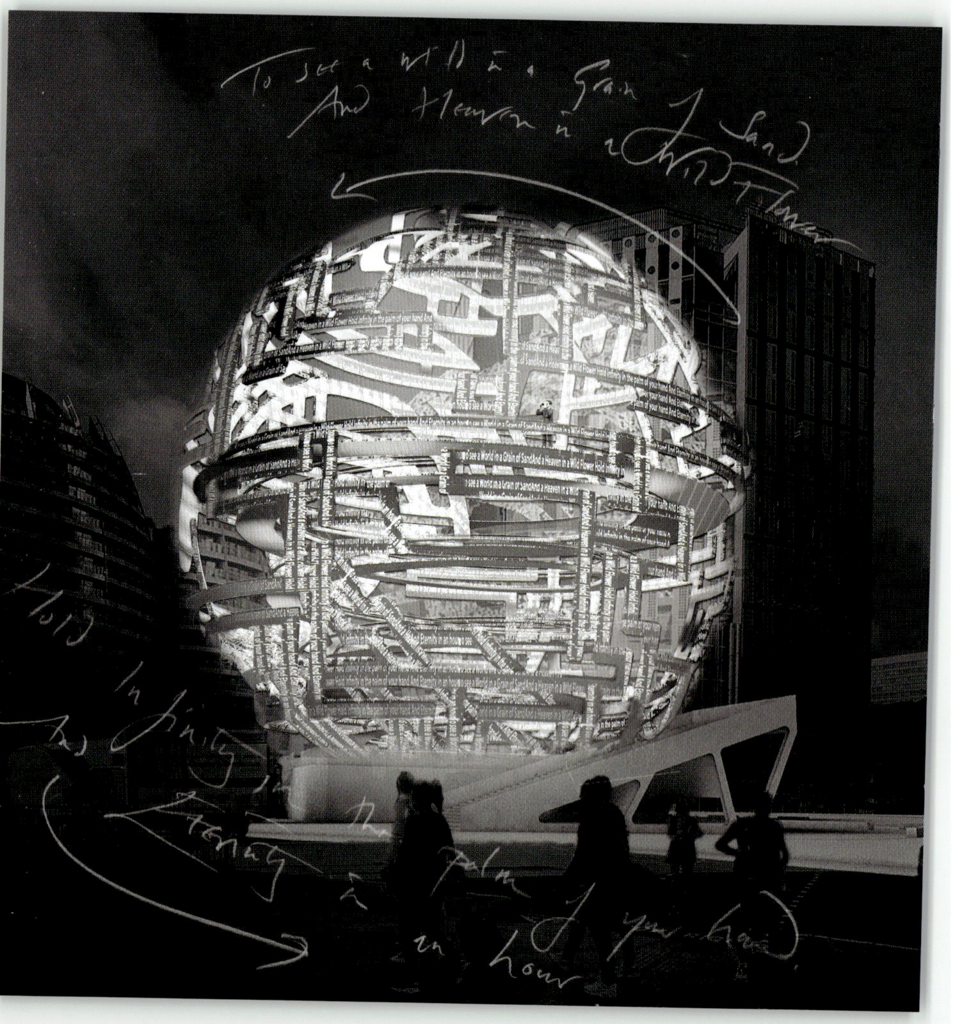

THE INFINITE LIBRARY

To see a World in a Grain of Sand
And a Heaven in a Wild Flower
Hold Infinity in the palm of your hand
And Eternity in an hour

William Blake, 'Auguries of Innocence'

I have spent hours not finding people I planned to meet at the labyrinthine underground station beneath London's Old Street roundabout, where the entrances are named using a combination of cardinal point initials and numbers. For a competition to redesign the roundabout in February 2018, my studio team and I imagined a library, not least because we would rather say 'meet me in Anthropology' or 'meet me in Neuroscience' than 'meet me at Entrance 3 SW' or 'Entrance 4 NE'. Developing our recent experiments with poetry-generating algorithms, we conceived a spherical, labyrinthine sculpture that would display a collective poem generated from words donated by everyone who passed through the roundabout. We planned to invite artists, musicians, scientists and poets to compile reading lists each week: a kind of 'portrait of the artist as a bookshelf'. Within the space of the infinite open-air library, we wanted passengers to be able to read every book ever written. The proposal was inspired by the visionary work of William Blake, who is buried nearby at Bunhill Fields Burial Ground.

BLINDED BY YOUR GRACE

Yo, Theresa May where's that money for Grenfell? What, you thought we just forgot about Grenfell? You're criminals, and you got the cheek to call us savages? You should do some jail time, you should pay some damages. We should burn your house down and see if you can manage this.

Stormzy

In the early hours of 14 June 2017, a fridge-freezer caught fire in Flat 16 on the fourth floor of Grenfell Tower, a 24-storey council-housing block in North Kensington in London. The building had recently been renovated by its owners, the Royal Borough of Kensington and Chelsea, the wealthiest local authority in London. Their contractors had reduced costs by using highly flammable cladding, which rapidly spread the flames into an uncontrollable inferno, killing 72 people in Britain's most lethal domestic fire in over a century. Images immediately proliferated of the burnt-out shell of the tower block set against luxury apartments a few streets away. The extremes of inequality in the UK – the growing gulf between Britain's rich and poor – could not have been more clearly articulated. By the time I met Stormzy in late 2017 to plan his BRIT Awards performance in February 2018, the public outrage against governmental inaction in response to the tragedy was mounting, and he composed a rapped text to incite urgency. He opened with 'Blinded By Your Grace, Pt. 2', a redemptive song. The choir was set within a reworking of the Last Supper tableau seen through Stormzy's South London lens. The rap quoted above shattered the hymn like a grenade lobbed through a church window, and rain cascaded over his performance, bringing an urgency it is impossible to rehearse, magnifying each word and gesture.

737

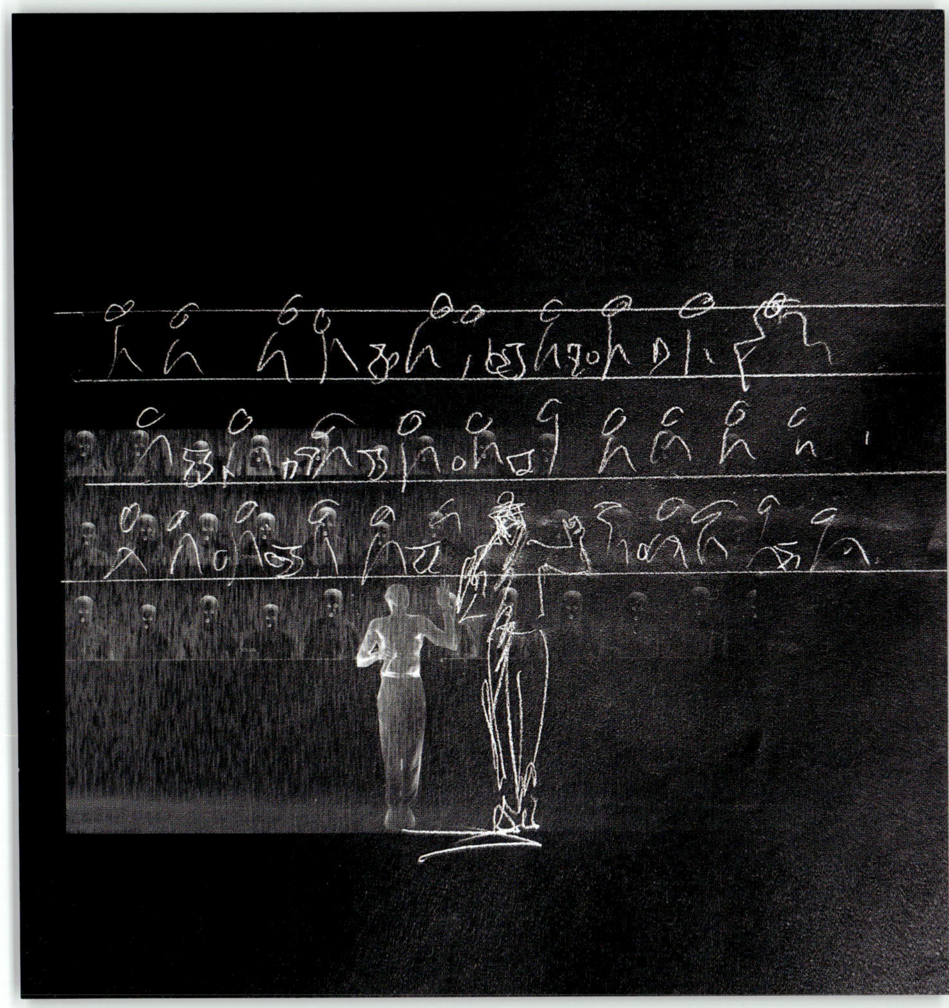

MASK

We all wear masks, and the time comes when we cannot remove them without removing some of our own skin.

André Berthiaume, *Contretemps: Nouvelles*

I made a mask-shaped, semi-ovoid concave clay form, sculpturally imprinted with the geometry of Central London and showed it at the Photo London fair at Somerset House in May 2018. A filmed infusion of black ink along the River Thames divided the map, recalling the X-rayed brain imagery that I'd witnessed over a decade earlier. Projected hands peeled at the map's surface and mined through layers of paper, clay and mirror, before washing their stained fingers in black ink until it clarified into water. The film played on a loop, rinsing and repeating. The work considered the range of scales of time and space that we simultaneously perceive and choose to remain blind to, as we calibrate our position within the period that we have begun to call 'The Anthropocene'. Through an ink-river divided city recalling an X-rayed divided brain, I aimed to evoke my daily cognitive dissonance – aware of the climate impact of each of my actions while still entangled in the systems I knew needed to change.

The hands were relayed six times larger than life, like the hands of a giant, trying to draw eyes on its own blind, oval mask. The city was presented as remote aerial cartography: geometry extruded from earth by unremembered generations of builders using their distant, 1:1500-scale hands. The two scales were held together, unreconciled in the work.

722–723

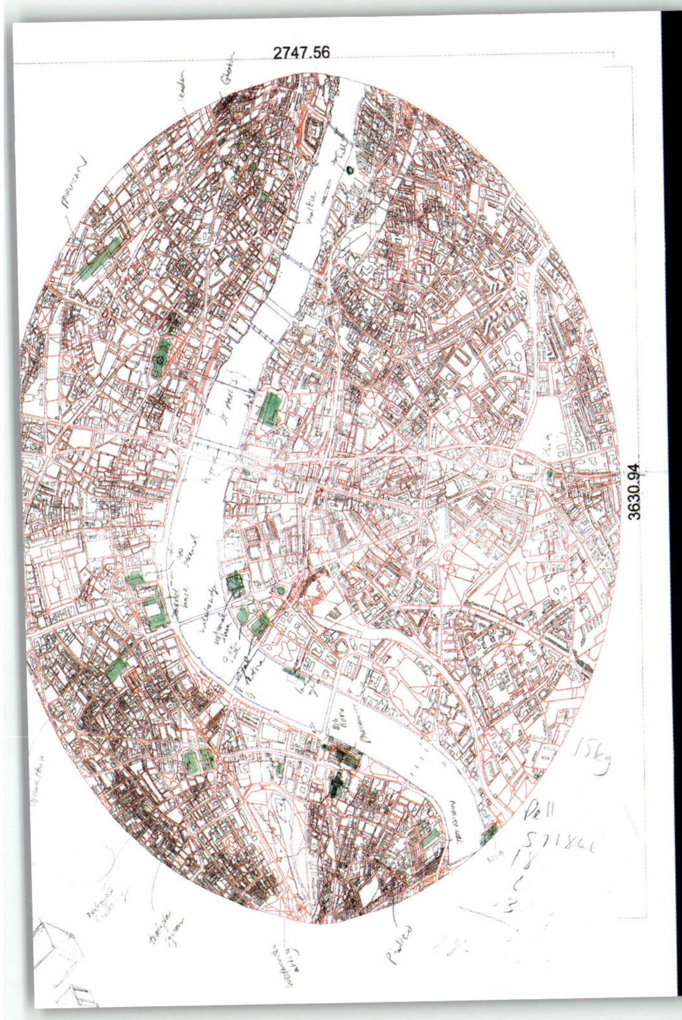

Steinem, 'Lemon'

rding studios
017 to discuss
D. album
ely critical of the
grant rhetoric,
o incite political
ir muscles via
os as a series
uel Knight as 'a
he world?'

cking human
ouldn't afford
title of our (as
re-show, on-site
centric cylinders
nth would lift
he previously
an audience, but
tive ritual.

MASK

We all wear masks, an
without removing som

I made a mask-shape
imprinted with the geo
Photo London fair at S
of black ink along the
X-rayed brain imagery
hands peeled at the m
clay and mirror, before
it clarified into water. T
The work considered
we simultaneously pe
calibrate our position
Anthropocene'. Throu
divided brain, I aimed
of the climate impact
systems I knew neede

The hands were relaye
giant, trying to draw ey
presented as remote a
unremembered genera
hands. The two scales

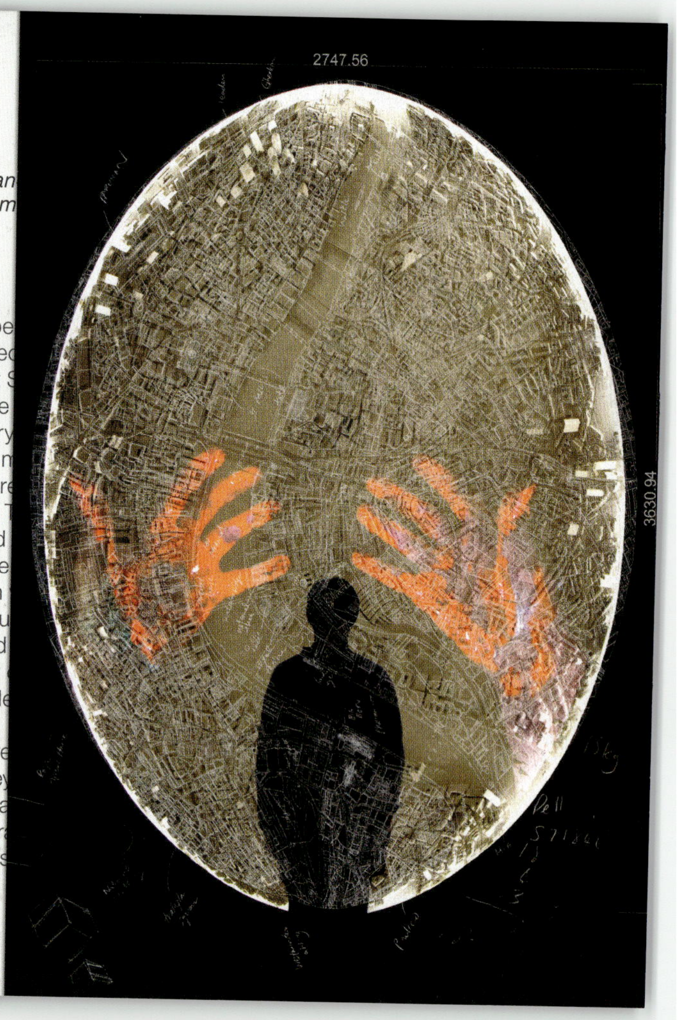

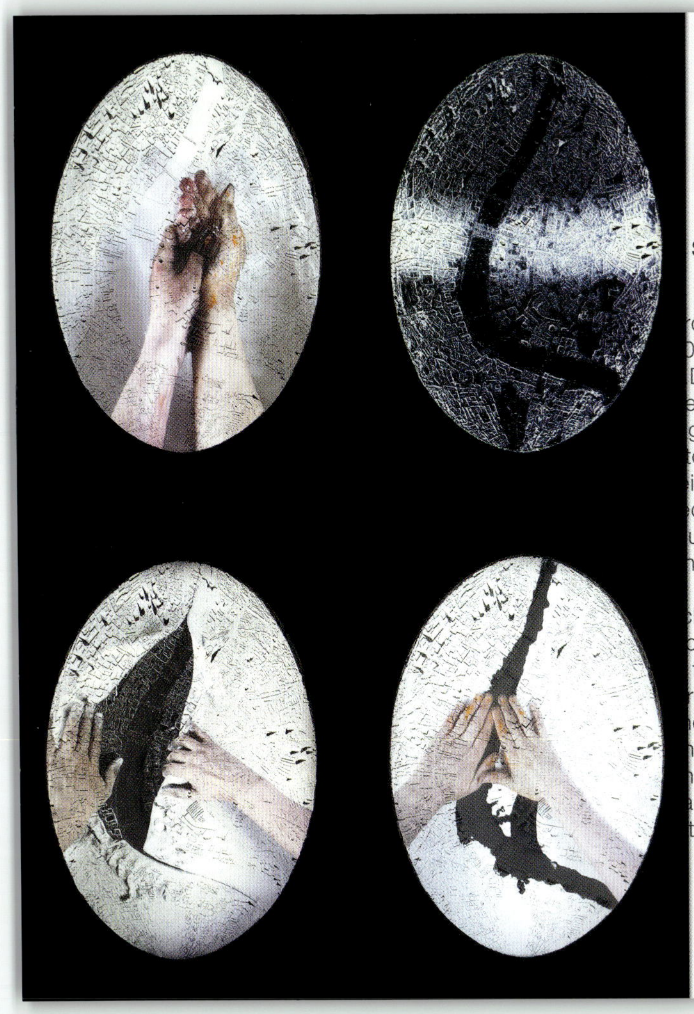

Steinem, 'Lemon'

rding studios
017 to discuss
D. album
ely critical of the
grant rhetoric,
to incite political
ir muscles via
os as a series
uel Knight as 'a
ne world?'

cking human
ouldn't afford
title of our (as
re-show, on-site
centric cylinders
nth would lift
ne previously
an audience, but
tive ritual.

MASK

We all wear masks,
without removing s

I made a mask-sha
imprinted with the g
Photo London fair a
of black ink along t
X-rayed brain imag
hands peeled at th
clay and mirror, bef
it clarified into wate
The work consider
we simultaneously
calibrate our positi
Anthropocene'. Thr
divided brain, I aim
of the climate impa
systems I knew ne

The hands were rel
giant, trying to draw
presented as remot
unremembered ger
hands. The two sca

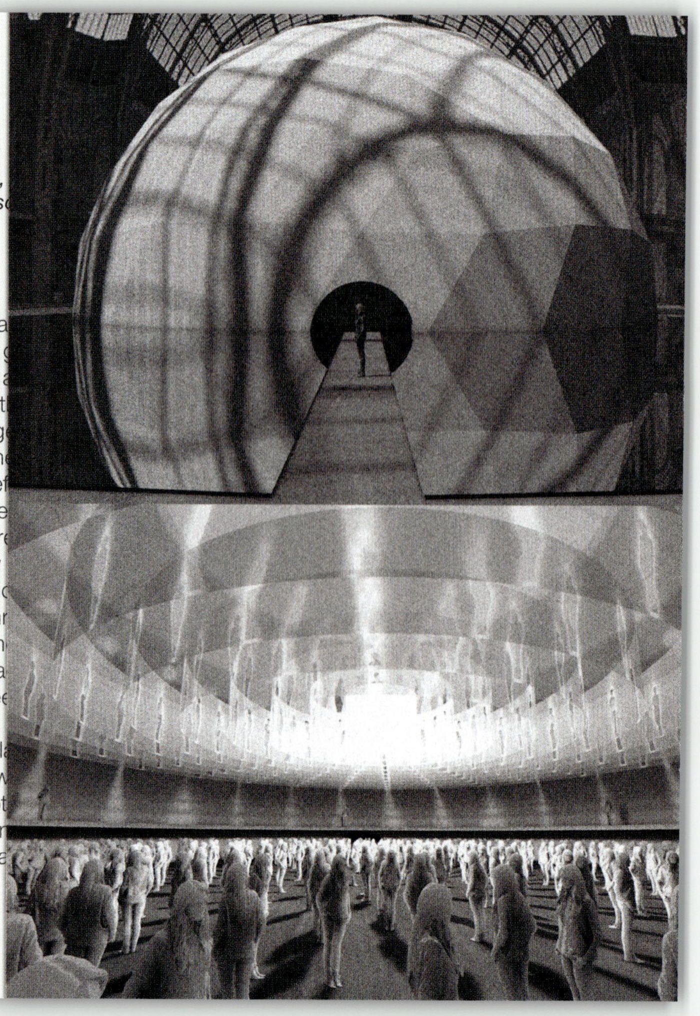

YOU

The truth will set you free
But first, it'll piss you off

N.E.R.D. featuring Rihanna, quoting Gloria Steinem, 'Lemon'

Pharrell Williams and I met a number of times in recording studios and on phone calls between July 2016 and August 2017 to discuss ideas for performances of the December 2017 N.E.R.D. album *No_One Ever Really Dies*. The album lyrics were fiercely critical of the recently elected Donald Trump, Republican anti-immigrant rhetoric, and systemic racist police brutality. Pharrell wanted to incite political awareness in his audience, to instil his lyrics into their muscles via memorized dance moves. He treated the music videos as a series of dance tutorials, described by choreographer JaQuel Knight as 'a healing source – how can we use dance to change the world?'

We conceived a camouflage pattern featuring interlocking human forms, and planned DIY tutorials so that those who couldn't afford to buy the merch could make their own. The working title of our (as yet unrealized) show was 'YOU', and we envisaged pre-show, on-site dance tutorials inside a labyrinthine installation of concentric cylinders perforated with human-shaped apertures. The labyrinth would lift above the crowd's heads at show time, connecting the previously segregated visitors and conjoining them, not just as an audience, but as costumed, choreographed participants in a collective ritual.

THE LEHMAN TRILOGY

An audience will travel with you all the way to Hell, as long as it says 'Hell' on the front of the bus.

Sam Mendes

Written by Stefano Massini and adapted by Ben Power for the National Theatre's April 2018 production, *The Lehman Trilogy* is a three-hour parable charting the inexorable rise and periodic crashes of Western capitalism, told through three generations of the Lehman family by three actors, a pianist and a revolving glass box. Like an unstoppable musical toy, the skeletal glass-and-steel structure propels the action from the expansive cotton fields of rural Alabama to the rising towers of New York City. At the start of our first design meeting, the director Sam Mendes took a black marker and a large sheet of card and wrote down five precepts that formed the basis of our design process, and much of my practice ever since. They remain stuck on the studio wall where he left them nine years ago. We explored a range of visual languages, and the cardboard bankers' boxes from our earliest versions remained an important part of the vocabulary. The more we invested the boxes with meaning and metaphor, the more poignant the revelation that those containers of cotton, coffee and coal would become containers of digits and dreams, ultimately revealing themselves to contain nothing at all. As the show worked its spell on the audience, their heads began to understand – through the feeling in their guts – that we are all walkers on the precarious tightrope of ever more complex and unsustainable human systems.

678–679

1. animate the idea.

2. make concrete the shape of history...

3. understand the order present in chaos.

4. understand in your head...

   ... because you can feel it in your gut.

5. Reveal the simple human needs

   behind the creation of complex human systems.

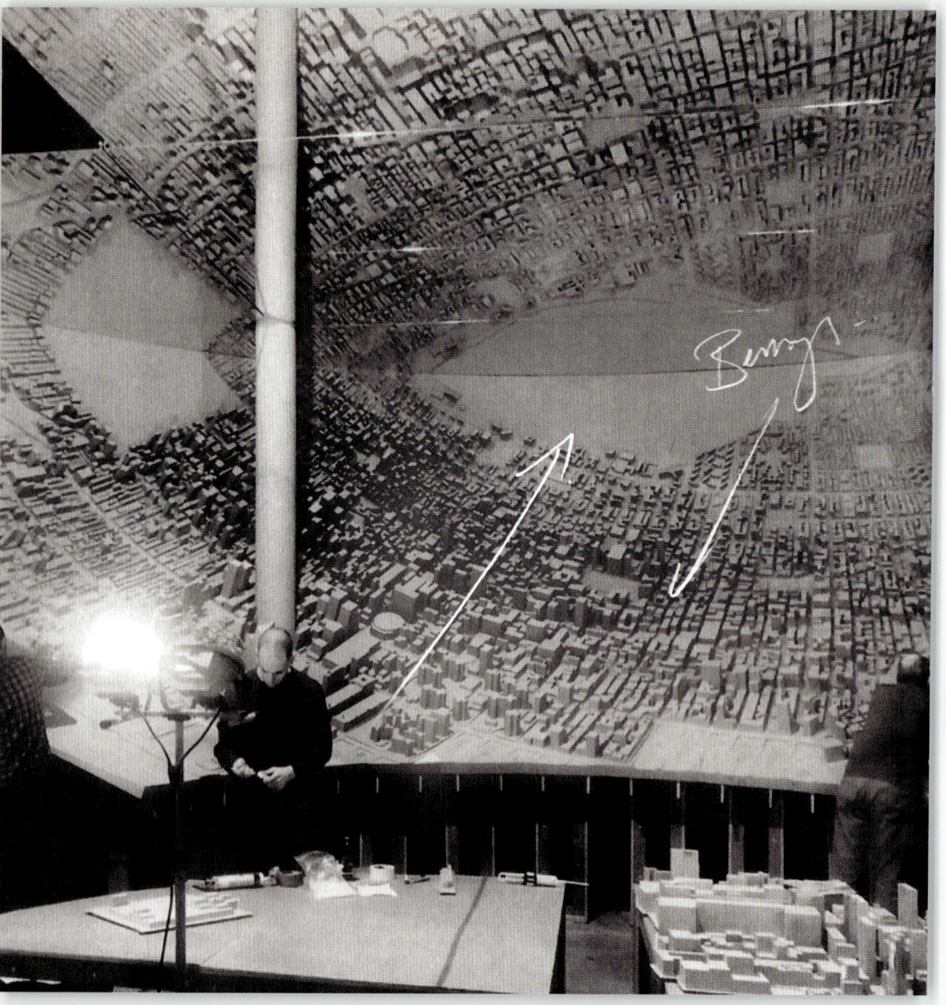

EGG

Architects have to become designers of ecosystems. Not just designers of beautiful facades or beautiful sculptures, but systems of economy and ecology, where we channel the flow not only of people, but also the flow of resources through our cities and buildings.

Bjarke Ingels

In April 2018 I made a series of sculptures to contextualize the Danish architect Bjarke Ingels's design for a new pair of residential towers on the shores of the Hudson River, near the High Line in New York City. Collaborating with skilled New York architectural model makers, we translated a distorted map of part of the city into a 10-metre-diameter, concave, elliptical hemisphere. The semi-ovoid form terminated in a horizontal plane of mirrored ceiling, presenting an illusion of completion in its reflection. The city was at once recognizable and abstracted into an organic symmetrical form, like a primeval world egg or a mysterious oyster – a brain within an elliptical shell. Each facet of its sculpted surface formed a canvas for projections that treated the city as a shapeshifting organism, composed of infinite, individual stories. A projected hand met an imagined world, as if the architect's hand were extruding thought into form. It was a through-the-looking-glass version of Manhattan, expressing the act of an architect showing the city to itself.

38–39 727–729

ABEL'S MASK

You need a hero? Look in the mirror, there go your hero

The Weeknd and Kendrick Lamar, 'Pray For Me'

Abel 'The Weeknd' Tesfaye, his creative director La Mar C Taylor and I were preparing designs for The Weeknd's April 2018 Coachella performance in parallel to the release of the 2018 Marvel film *Black Panther*, for which The Weeknd and Kendrick Lamar had composed the track 'Pray For Me'. The film's costume designer, Ruth Carter, the first Black woman to win two Oscars, drew patterns from what she described as 'the sacred geometry of Africa', including shapes based on Maasai, Ndebele and Himba tribal designs.

Abel's parents emigrated from Ethiopia to Toronto before he was born. For this performance we researched the linear, scarred inscriptions on Ethiopian masks and incorporated them into a 3D scan of Abel's head. We worked closely with engineers to construct an 8-metre-high sculptural mask that could be installed within Coachella's frequently windy conditions. Illuminated in vivid reds and blues – like the red and blue illusion and reality pills in the film *The Matrix* that Abel, an extreme cinephile, refers to in his lyrics – the giant mask seemed to emanate sound as well as light over an entranced, dancing crowd of 125,000.

770–771 824–825

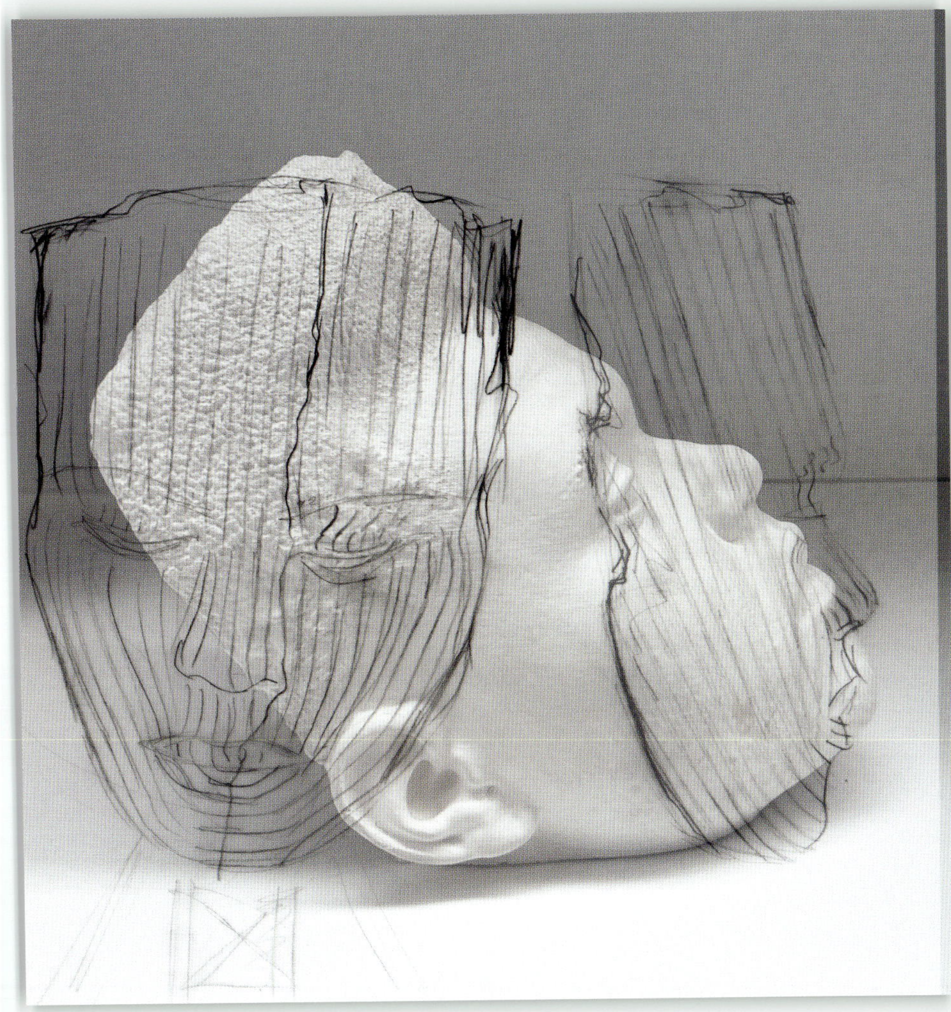

ABEL'S MASK

You need a hero? Look in the mirror, there go your hero

The Weeknd and Kendrick Lamar, 'Pray For Me'

Abel 'The Weeknd' Tesfaye, his creative director La Mar C Taylor and I were preparing designs for The Weeknd's April 2018 Coachella performance in parallel to the release of the 2018 Marvel film *Black Panther*, for which The Weeknd and Kendrick Lamar had composed the track 'Pray For Me'. The film's costume designer, Ruth Carter, the first Black woman to win two Oscars, drew patterns from what she described as 'the sacred geometry of Africa', including shapes based on Maasai, Ndebele and Himba tribal designs.

Abel's parents emigrated from Ethiopia to Toronto before he was born. For this performance we researched the linear, scarred inscriptions on Ethiopian masks and incorporated them into a 3D scan of Abel's head. We worked closely with engineers to construct an 8-metre-high sculptural mask that could be installed within Coachella's frequently windy conditions. Illuminated in vivid reds and blues – like the red and blue illusion and reality pills in the film *The Matrix* that Abel, an extreme cinephile, refers to in his lyrics – the giant mask seemed to emanate sound as well as light over an entranced, dancing crowd of 125,000.

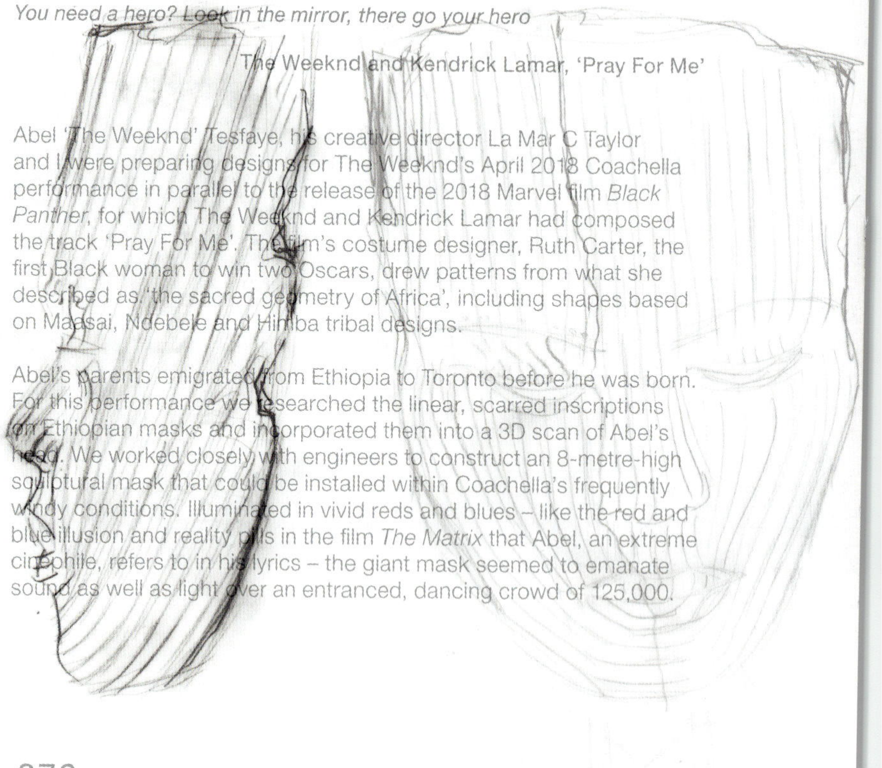

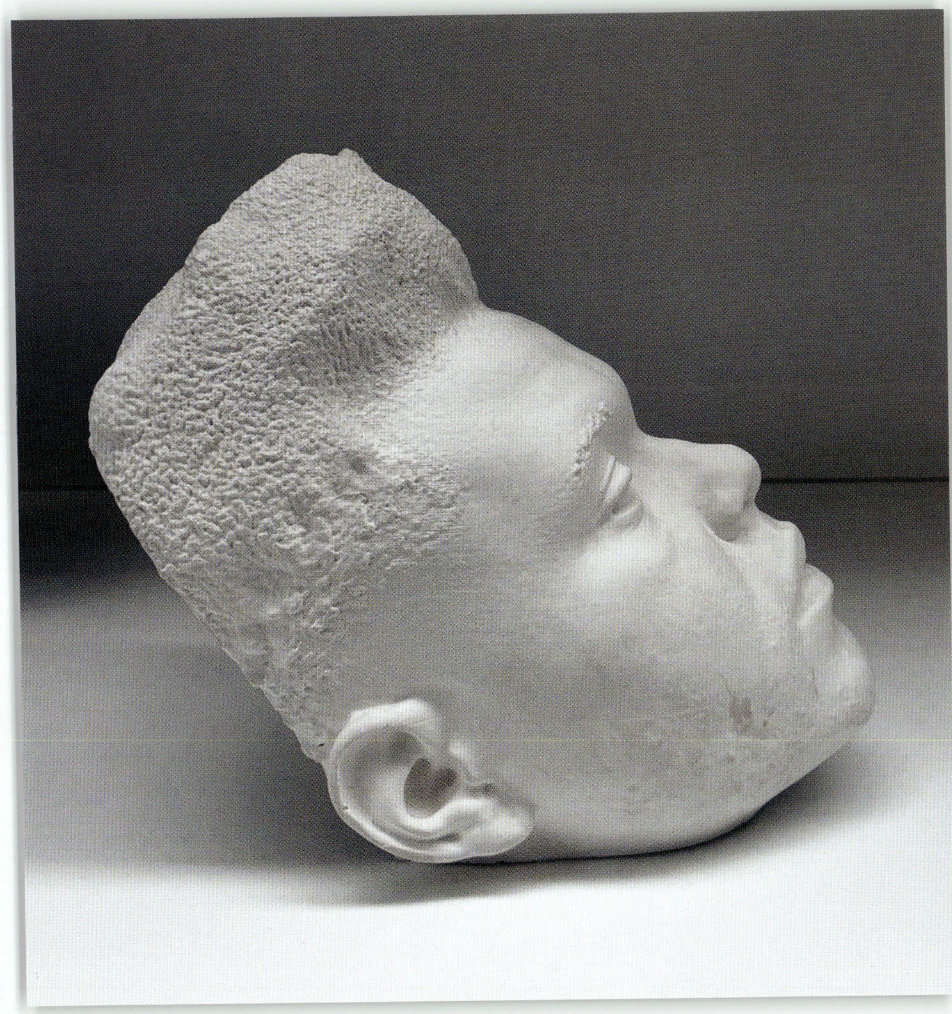

VOYAGE STUDIES

Walking through an empty house, tears in my eyes
Here is where the story ends, this is goodbye ...
In these old familiar rooms, children would play
Now there's only emptiness, nothing to say

ABBA, 'Knowing Me, Knowing You'

I worked with Benny Andersson and Björn Ulvaeus from ABBA between November 2016 and February 2019 to develop ideas for their virtual concert residency *Voyage*, which eventually opened (with an evolved creative concept and new team) in London in May 2022. The band were constructing computer-generated models of themselves pixel by pixel and were interested in the philosophical and psychological questions that this technologically virtuosic endeavour raised about digital immortality, physical ageing and death. During an early meeting in their 150-year-old warehouse studio overlooking the waters of Stockholm, I asked Benny and Björn if we could make a choir of Frida and Agnetha using recordings from different decades, as if they were a choral group of women of multiple ages singing together in one present moment. Benny immediately sat at the piano and played exquisite chromatic chords beneath a sextet of the overlaid voices of Frida and Agnetha aged 21, 31 and 68. It sounded ethereal and very moving. During these early studies we were exploring the avatars emerging from the hands of their human creators to exert their own agency and write their origin myths within four kinetic, fragmenting, sculptural memory palaces in the form of the band's silhouetted heads.

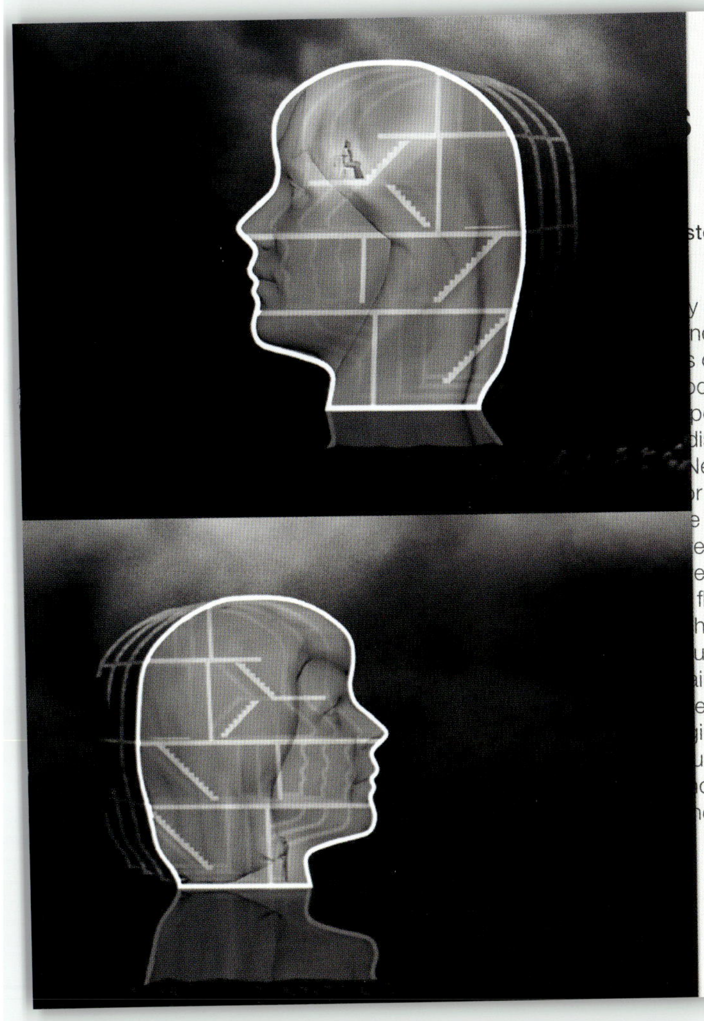

ster, *Howards End*

y in Trafalgar
nd celebrations
s clashes
oody Sunday
people gather
disarmament to
New Year's Eve
r the London
e of these lions
e still raging daily
ere asked to
fluorescent red-
he originals. They
umn. We used the
ined on millions
em was therefore
inal bronze lions
und national
oped that people
e power of the

VOYAGE

Walking through an
Here is where the s
In these old familiar
Now there's only en

I worked with Benn
November 2016 an
concert residency
creative concept ar
constructing comp
and were interested
that this technologi
immortality, physica
150-year-old wareh
I asked Benny and
using recordings fr
of women of multip
Benny immediately
chords beneath a s
aged 21, 31 and 68
early studies we we
of their human crea
myths within four k
form of the band's

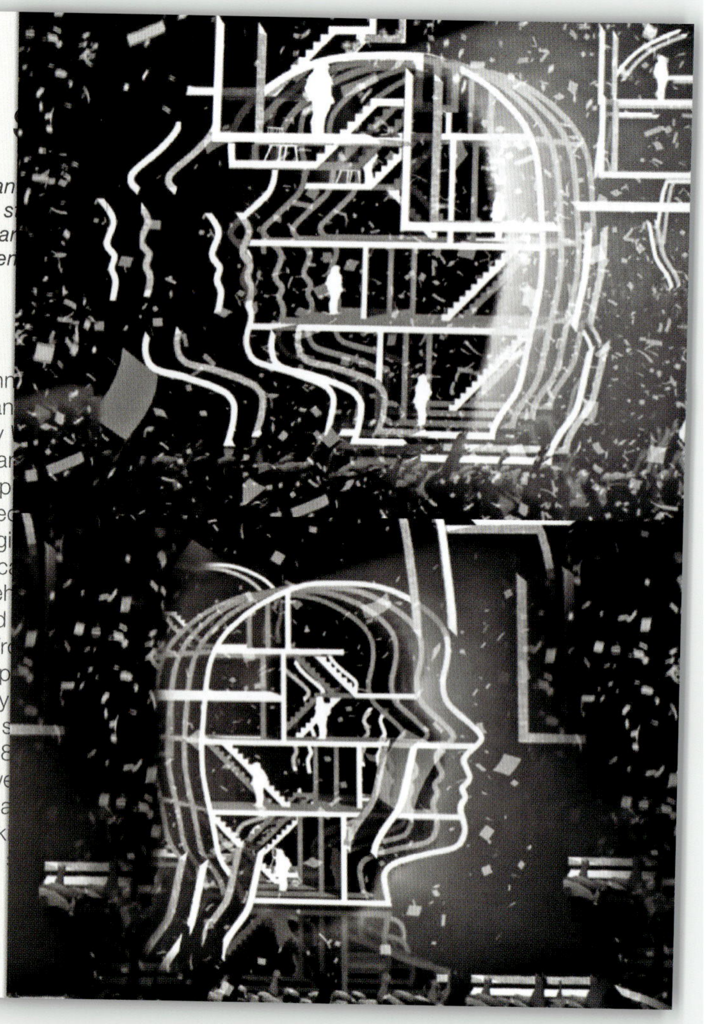

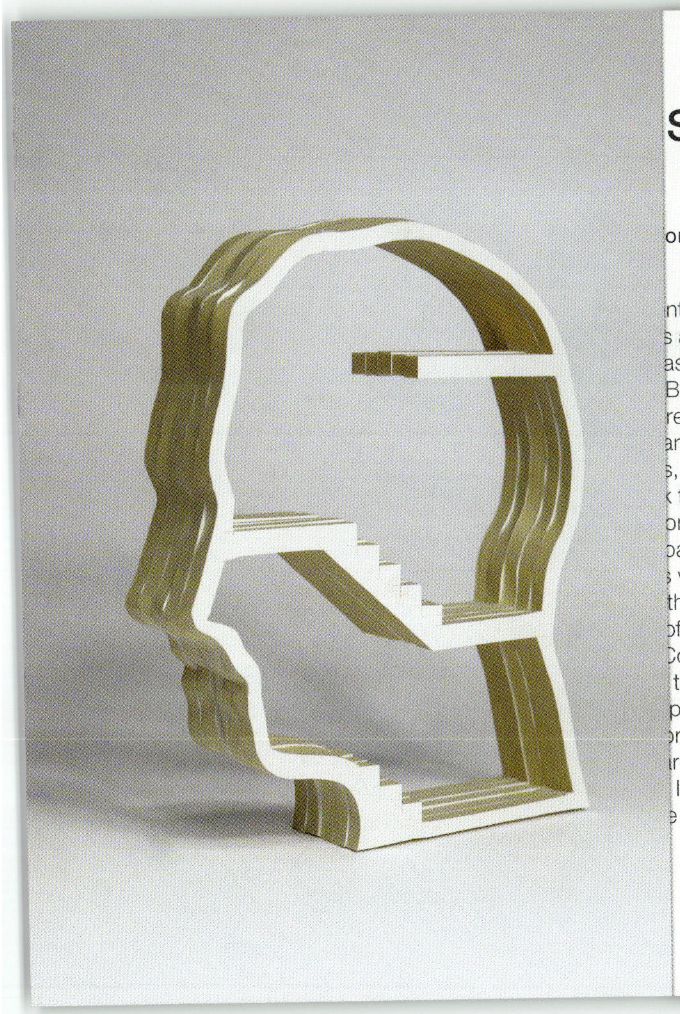

s

orster, *Howards End*

ntly in Trafalgar
s and celebrations
ass clashes
Bloody Sunday
re people gather
ar disarmament to
s, New Year's Eve
x for the London
one of these lions
pate still raging daily
s were asked to
th, fluorescent red-
of the originals. They
Column. We used the
trained on millions
poem was therefore
original bronze lions
round national
I hoped that people
e the power of the

VOYAGE

Walking through an
Here is where the s
In these old familiar
Now there's only em

I worked with Benn
November 2016 an
concert residency
creative concept a
constructing comp
and were intereste
that this technolog
immortality, physic
150-year-old wareh
I asked Benny and
using recordings fr
of women of multip
Benny immediately
chords beneath a s
aged 21, 31 and 68
early studies we we
of their human crea
myths within four k
form of the band's

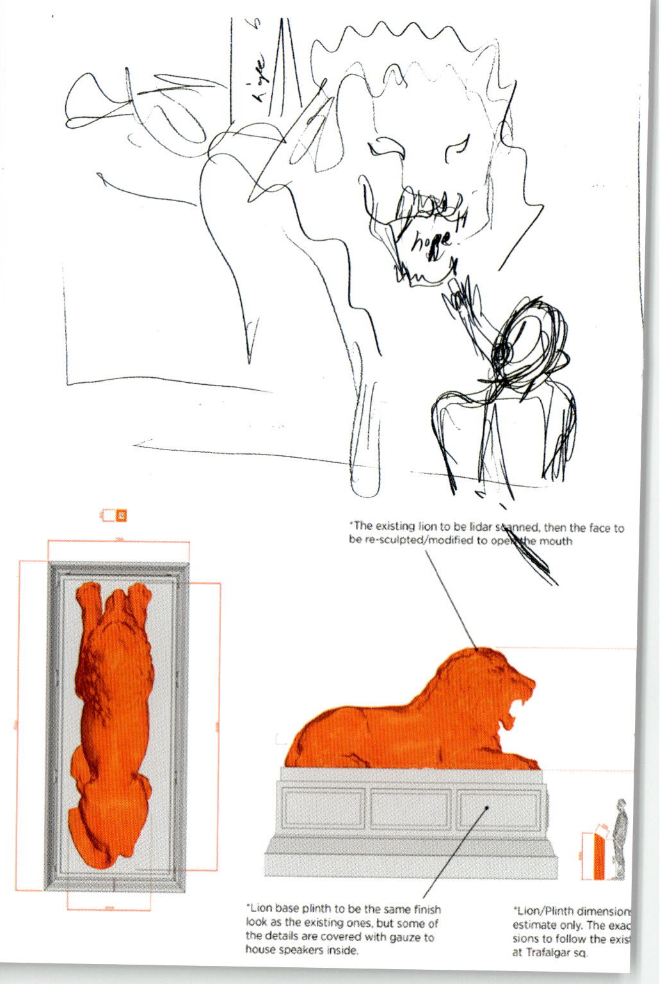

PLEASE FEED THE LIONS

Only connect! … Live in fragments no longer.

E. M. Forster, *Howards End*

Cast in 1867, four bronze lions have been sitting silently in Trafalgar Square, mute witnesses to protests, demonstrations and celebrations for over 150 years. The site of nineteenth-century class clashes culminating in the violent military intervention of the Bloody Sunday protests in November 1887, Trafalgar Square is where people gather to have their voices heard on everything from nuclear disarmament to war and climate change, and to celebrate Christmas, New Year's Eve and Pride. Asked by Sir John Sorrell to make a work for the London Design Biennale in September 2018, I wondered: if one of these lions could open its mouth and speak, with the Brexit debate still raging daily through a divided nation, what would it say? Visitors were asked to 'feed' their chosen word into the mouth of a new, fifth, fluorescent red-orange lion, which we had cast from a scan of one of the originals. They watched as their poem was projected up Nelson's Column. We used the same algorithm as we had in previous experiments, trained on millions of lines of nineteenth-century poetry. The collective poem was therefore based on choices made by poets writing while the original bronze lions were being cast 150 years ago. The public debate around national identity in 2018 was often both divisive and prosaic: I hoped that people who took part in *Please Feed the Lions* would sense the power of the collective poetic.

41 780–781

EXPERIENCE + INNOCENCE

Now you're at the other end of the telescope / Seven billion stars in her eyes / So many stars / So many ways of seeing / Hey this is no time not to be alive

U2, 'Love Is All We Have Left'

U2's 2018 *Experience + Innocence* tour was the second part of a diptych which began in 2015 with the *Innocence + Experience* tour. The physical elements of the design for both shows were conceived by the band, the director Willie Williams, Stufish architect Ric Lipson and myself. Taking the lyric quoted above as its lodestar, events of the past were now seen through 'the other end of the telescope'. Already heightened by a serious bike accident in 2014, Bono's perspective on mortality had significantly shifted following heart surgery in 2016. The show began with an augmented-reality sequence that preceded the band's arrival. Viewed through an AR app on phones, the experience recast the 30-metre-wide sculptural block that divided the crowd as a monumental iceberg, gradually melting and eventually flooding the floor of the arena. The virtual deluge engulfed the audience, prefiguring the cataclysm of the 'tsunami' at the mid-point of the show. The block then lifted to reveal Bono encompassed within a gigantic AR avatar that loomed magically over the audience. Echoing the 1813 William Blake engraving, *The Soul Hovering over the Body Reluctantly Parting with Life*, the ethereal blue form radiated the singer's movements into the most distant depths of the crowd.

674 676 685

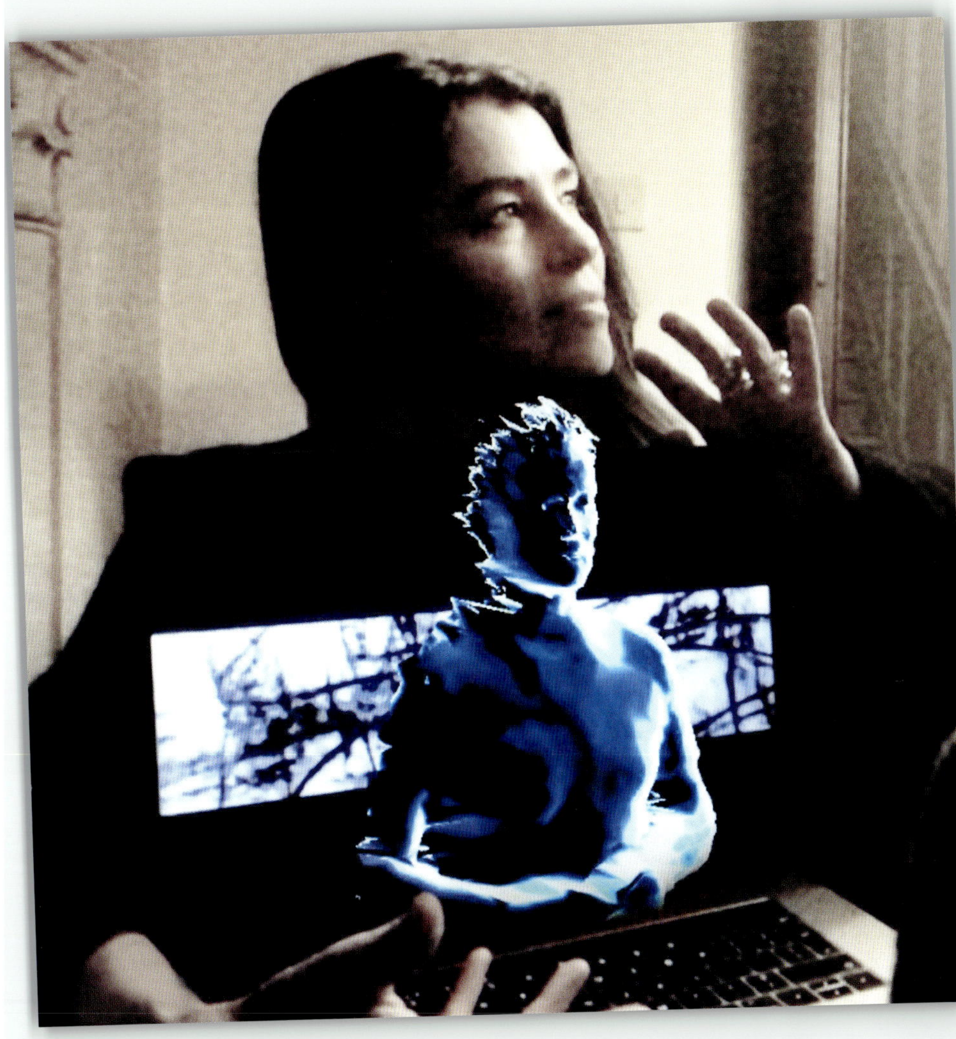

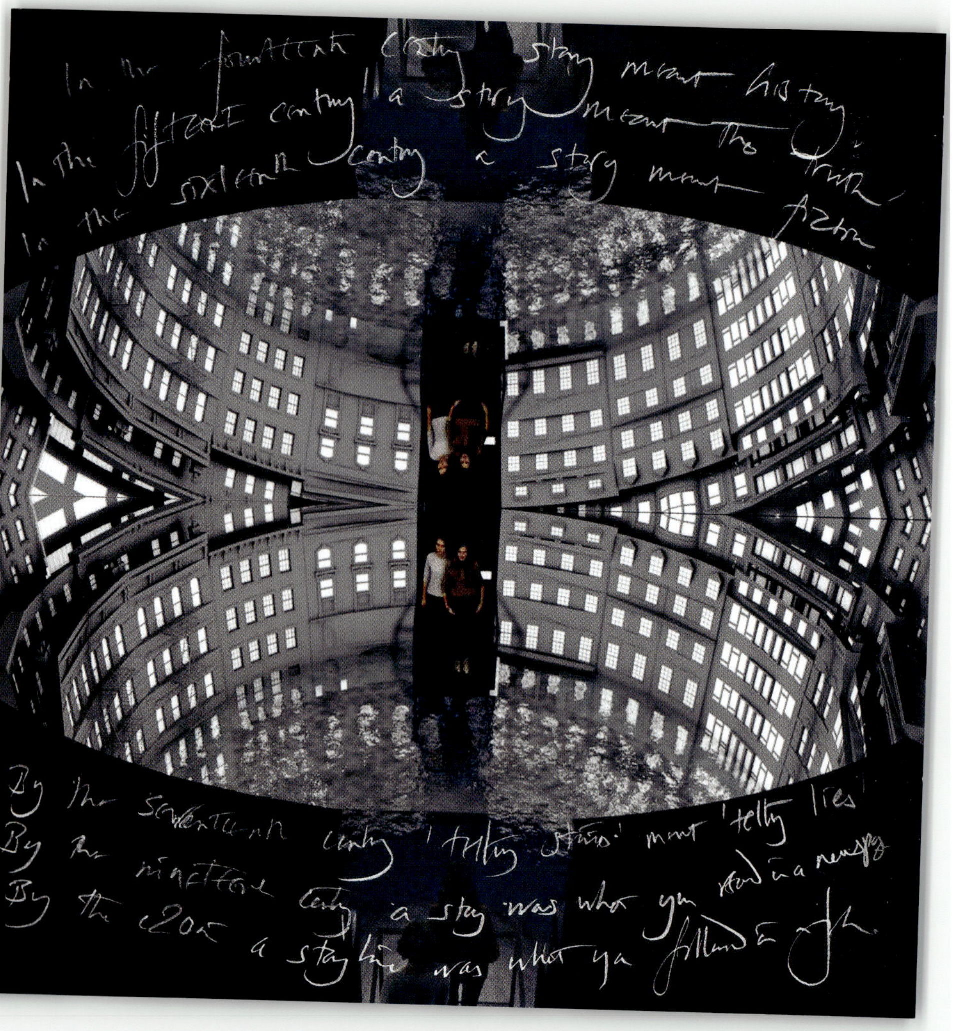
In the fourteenth century story meant history
In the fifteenth century a story meant the truth
In the sixteenth century a story meant fiction
By the seventeenth century 'telling stories' meant 'telling lies'
By the nineteenth century a story was what you read in a newspaper
By the c20th a storyline was what you followed

MULTI-STOREY

In the fourteenth century, story meant 'history'. In the fifteenth century, a story meant 'the truth'. In the sixteenth century, a story meant 'fiction'. By the seventeenth century, telling stories meant 'telling lies'. By the nineteenth century, a story was what we read in a newspaper. By the twentieth century, a storyline was what we followed in a film. In the twenty-first century, stories are what we scroll through in the palms of our hands, our own merging with others; a third of the world, sharing their stories; unindexed, unsorted. Stories of celebration, devastation, discovery, recovery; first steps, last wishes; appetite, famine; design, detail, and decoration; destruction, despair, and deterioration; cake, comic, car, cartoon; lunch, lounge, launch; diver, driver, digger, danger; environmentalists, soldiers, shooters, protesters. Will these multi-storey streams of fact and fiction add up to our history?

For an installation within the Instagram area at the Festival of Ideas in Cannes in June 2018, I asked the question above, my voice reverberating within the sculpture, which was a water-flooded cylinder whose walls were lined with multi-storey layers of buildings. A few months earlier, the Pulitzer Prize-nominated journalist Carole Cadwalladr had exposed the Cambridge Analytica scandal, detailing the influence of Instagram's owner, Facebook, on both the Brexit referendum and the US election of Donald Trump. The words 'storey' (of a house) and 'story' (as a narrative) share a common etymology: the piece explored architectural and narrative structures as parallel societal forces.

THE ORDER OF TIME

... we are time. We are this space, this clearing opened by the traces of memory inside the connections between our neurons.

Carlo Rovelli

Originally conceived as part of a model city sculpture in New York (illustrated here), *The Order of Time* was eventually presented at Bold Tendencies in September 2018 with 2,000 people gathered in collective reading on the roof of a multi-storey car park in Peckham, South London. Anxious that I no longer read books as I used to – my attention constantly fragmented by the cries of my devices – I observed that my reading was most concentrated during long Wagner operas in German, which required up to four uninterrupted hours reading English surtitles. I decided to eliminate the opera, install a 40-metre-wide surtitles screen, and present a compelling text for an audience to read together. The curator Hannah Barry and I chose *The Order of Time* by the Italian theoretical physicist Carlo Rovelli, read by Benedict Cumberbatch and accompanied by a solo violin amidst a layered soundscape. Carlo explains that our perception of time is determined by the shape of our brains, our limited perspective, and layers of ancient errors of understanding. Segments of the text were interwoven with treated footage of swarms of mayflies: an emblem to poets since Aristotle of the ephemerality of life, mayflies' 24-hour adult lifespan earned them the name 'dayflies'. The illuminated text did not always align with the spoken word, playing on our ability to read and learn, listen and watch, in a range of registers simultaneously.

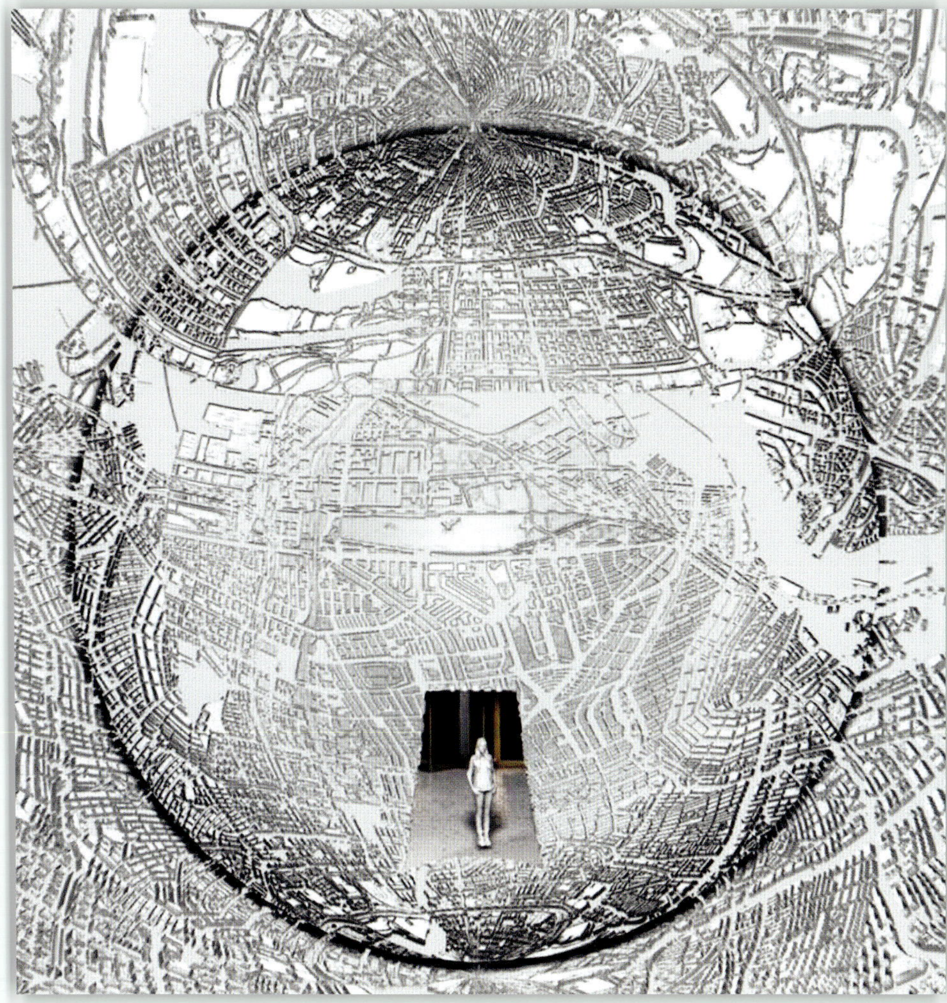

ZOETROPE MALAWI

We lose the people we love, we become poets. We fight battles no one knows about, we use the blood to write poetry.

Xara Hlupekile, 'Loss'

Advised by Benny Dembitzer, the octogenarian economist specializing in sub-Saharan Africa, I donated the fee from the 2017 Zoetrope pavilion in Cape Town to Support Malawi, a rural schools project near Blantyre, Malawi. A former pupil, Chisangalalo Ntonio, interviewed the local communities and determined that a girls' boarding house was a priority to enable 45 of the most at-risk girls to stay on each year to complete their secondary school studies and avoid teenage marriage and pregnancy. We began construction in 2019 and opened the boarding house in November 2020. The next priority was a skills centre: many of the local community wanted to learn car and bike mechanics, welding, plumbing, bricklaying, sewing, and sustainable farming and reforestation techniques. The skills centre was completed in October 2022. We based its design on the original Zoetrope pavilion and painted it entirely bright red-orange – a luminous beacon and a gathering place for the community. Both buildings provided temporary shelter during Cyclone Freddy in March 2023, which devastated local homes and harvests, displacing 500,000 and killing 1,200, its increased force a direct result of the climate crisis.

784–785

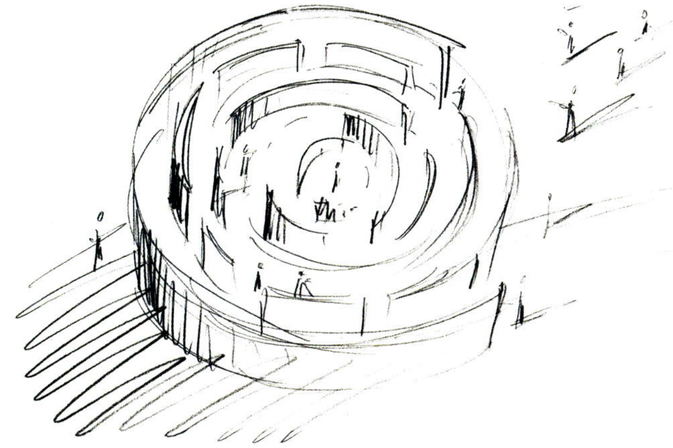

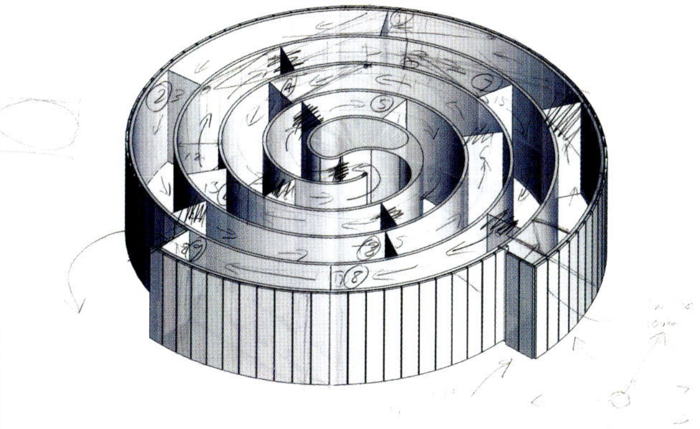

The Robber Bride

Marianelli and I
Ballet to premiere
gramme marking
hotographer
close-up portraits
in Afghanistan in
itain's longest-
before his death
n describing the
l 20-year-old
old faces. In early
in each projected
oped in initial
9.

ZOETROI

We lose the people
no one knows abou

Advised by Benny
in sub-Saharan Afr
pavilion in Cape To
Blantyre, Malawi. A
the local communit
was a priority to en
year to complete th
marriage and preg
the boarding house
centre: many of the
mechanics, weldin
farming and refores
in October 2022. W
and painted it entir
gathering place for
shelter during Cycl
local homes and ha
increased force a c

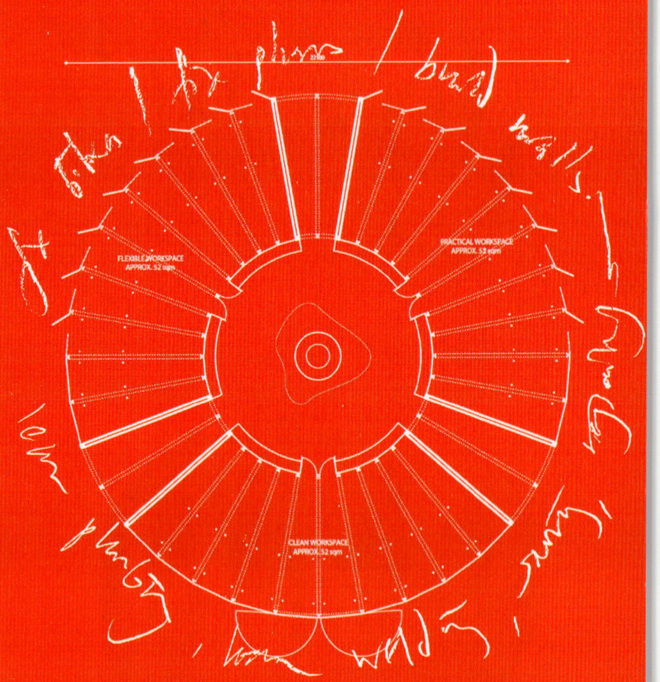

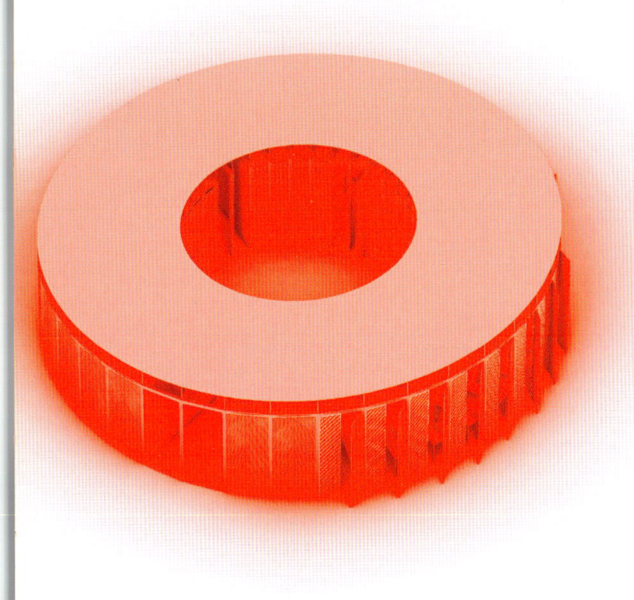

R

d, *The Robber Bride*

io Marianelli and I
yal Ballet to premiere
ogramme marking
l photographer
ad, close-up portraits
ce in Afghanistan in
Britain's longest-
11 before his death
ton describing the
ed 20-year-old
ar-old faces. In early
ithin each projected
eloped in initial
019.

ZOETROI

We lose the people
no one knows abou

Advised by Benny
in sub-Saharan Afr
pavilion in Cape To
Blantyre, Malawi. A
the local communit
was a priority to en
year to complete th
marriage and preg
the boarding house
centre: many of the
mechanics, weldin
farming and refores
in October 2022. W
and painted it entir
gathering place for
shelter during Cycl
local homes and ha
increased force a c

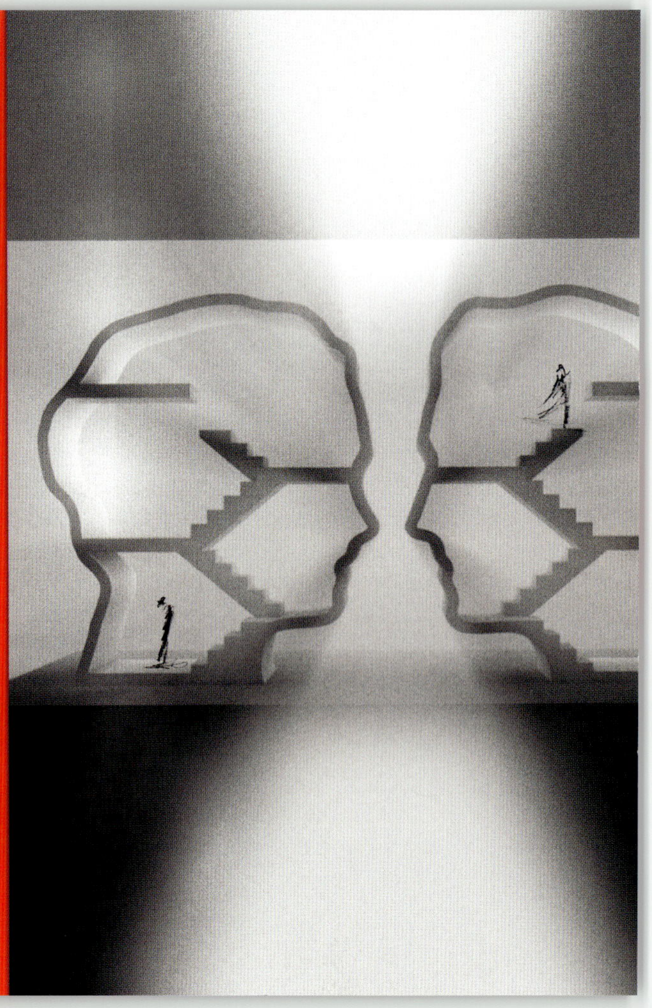

THE UNKNOWN SOLDIER

War is what happens when language fails.

Margaret Atwood, *The Robber Bride*

The choreographer Alastair Marriott, composer Dario Marianelli and I were commissioned to make a new work for the Royal Ballet to premiere in November 2018 as part of the 14–18 NOW arts programme marking the centenary of the end of World War I. We studied photographer Lalage Snow's haunting series, *We Are The Not Dead*, close-up portraits of soldiers taken before, during and after their service in Afghanistan in 2011. We projected portrait footage of Harry Patch, Britain's longest-surviving World War I veteran, interviewed at age 111 before his death in 2009, as well as the centenarian Florence Billington describing the death of her beloved in battle. The audience watched 20-year-old dancers through translucent projections of 100-year-old faces. In early sketches, we explored multi-storey architectures within each projected portrait, continuing to evolve the forms we had developed in initial ideas for *Witness* and *Voyage* between 2017 and 2019.

ATLAS

I work in between the cracks, where the voice starts dancing, where the body starts singing, where theatre becomes cinema.

Curiosity is a great antidote to fear.

Meredith Monk

Meredith Monk's transcendent wordless opera charting the spiritual growth of the nineteenth-century explorer Alexandra David-Néel was first performed at Houston Grand Opera in 1991. Yuval Sharon directed this June 2019 LA Philharmonic production at the Frank Gehry-designed Walt Disney Concert Hall in Los Angeles. It was the first time Monk, the avant-garde composer/director/designer/choreographer had entrusted her work to another director.

The young girl's encounters with travel companions and spirit guides were revealed through tableaux within a 12-metre-diameter sphere, scored with webs of international trade and travel routes. Journeying through ice, desert and tropics, challenged by ordeals and temptations including the frenzied seduction of one of the companions into an autocratic, technocratic world order, the work culminates in the hypnotic, meditative sequence 'Invisible Light: Earth Seen from Above'. Singers positioned around the auditorium passed batons of light and ululated sounds to one another, encompassing the audience in Monk's radiant vision of a possible alternative to the current world order.

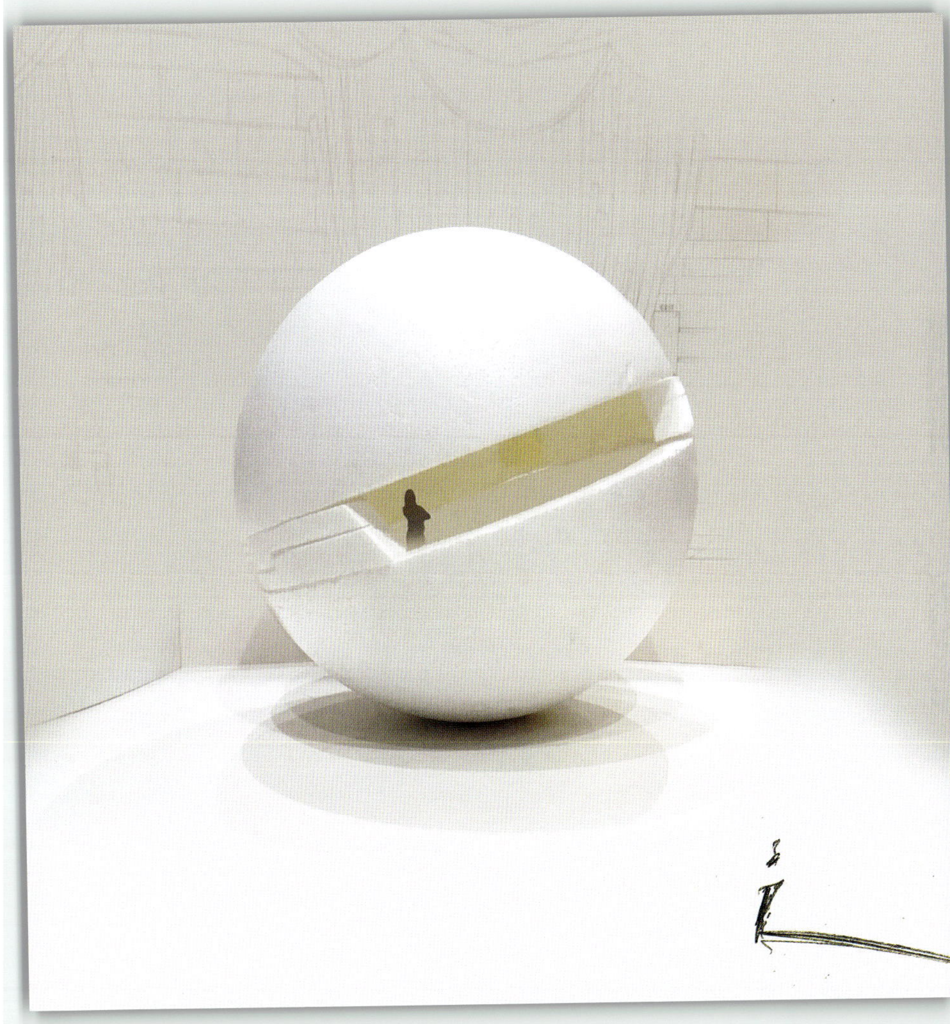

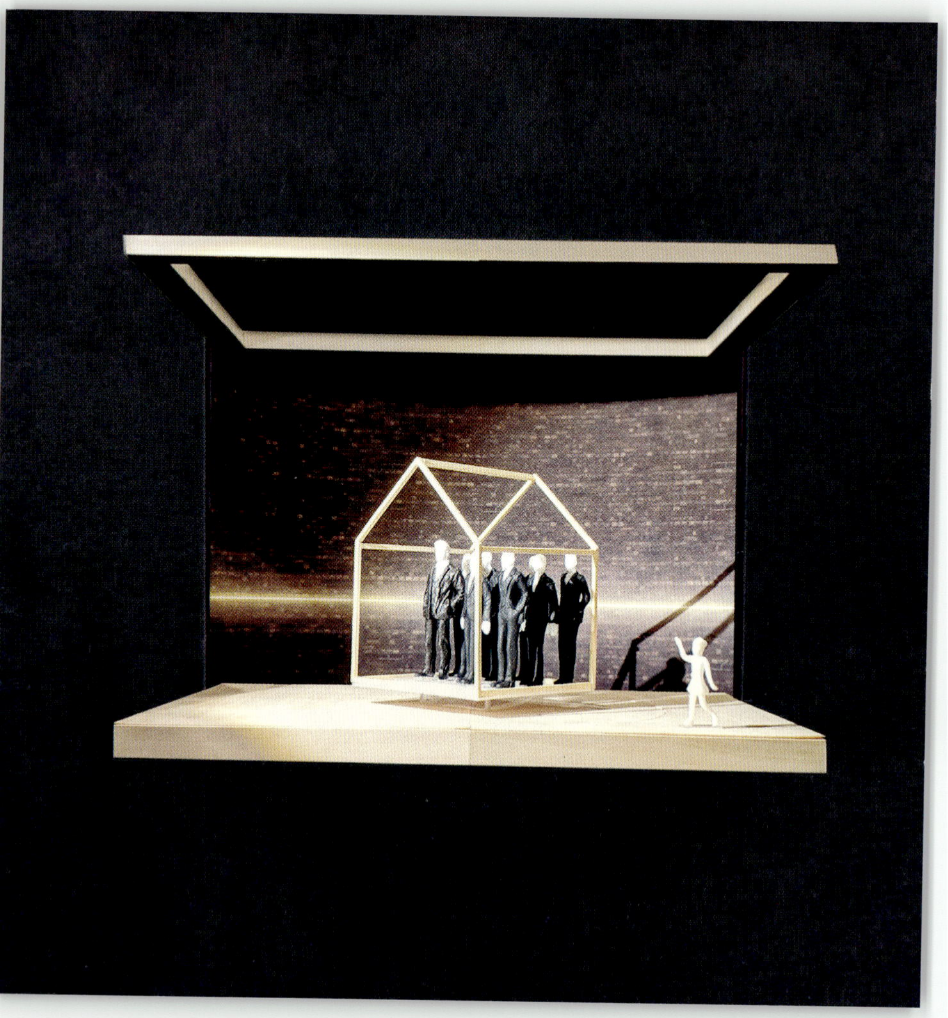

THE HUNT

Hilde: We are a small community. The happiness of our children is everything. Our hopes and dreams rest in these tiny souls.

David Farr

I first saw one of René Magritte's *Empire of Light* paintings at the Guggenheim Museum in New York in my 20s, having studied them in books since I was a teenager. In these works, a warm light glows through domestic windows within a night-time forest beneath a paradoxically bright daylight blue sky. I used to think of them when I saw golden, illuminated windows pierce the trees as I walked home through evening forests in Kent as a teenager. To me they expressed the illusory idyll of other people's homes.

A simple child's drawing of a home expressed in Scandinavian IKEA-pine occupied the stage for David Farr's adaptation of Thomas Vinterberg's film *The Hunt* in this June 2019 Almeida Theatre production. Fabricated in 'smart glass', which becomes opaque with electric current, the rotating house operated like a magician's box under Rupert Goold's direction and Botis Seva's choreography. At times it conjured the warmth of a home, at others it encased the protagonist in his ostracization from the small-town community. Sometimes its glass surface condensed the breaths of the entire community in a claustrophobic church. Occasionally the fragile glass was threatened with fracture by the pounding masculine drinking rituals in a forest den. Towards the play's ambiguous close, the glass house revealed the fugitive hero's sighting of a hunted deer between the trees.

ORANGE CUBE

Everything I do is somehow connected to velocity.

Hans Ulrich Obrist

The 2019 Serpentine Pavilion designed by Japanese architect Junya Ishigami focused on the essence of a home: a shelter, a roof. A cloud of scattered slate seemed to emerge from the Serpentine lawn, combining the weighty certainty of the grey rock with a billowing form that appeared provisional, ready to blow away. Ishigami chose slate for its global ubiquity as a roofing material, expressing the idea of home and shelter for a multitude of cultures and countries. Commissioned by the Serpentine for the third year to create a stage for the June 2019 summer gala performance, I proposed a rotating fluorescent red-orange pavilion: an illuminated compass that beamed centrifugal light. The piece revolved throughout the evening, inhabited by DJ and producer Mura Masa – named after the mythical Japanese swordsmith – and danced in by singer Olly Alexander, whose iridescent diamanté jumpsuit emerged tinged with orange paint.

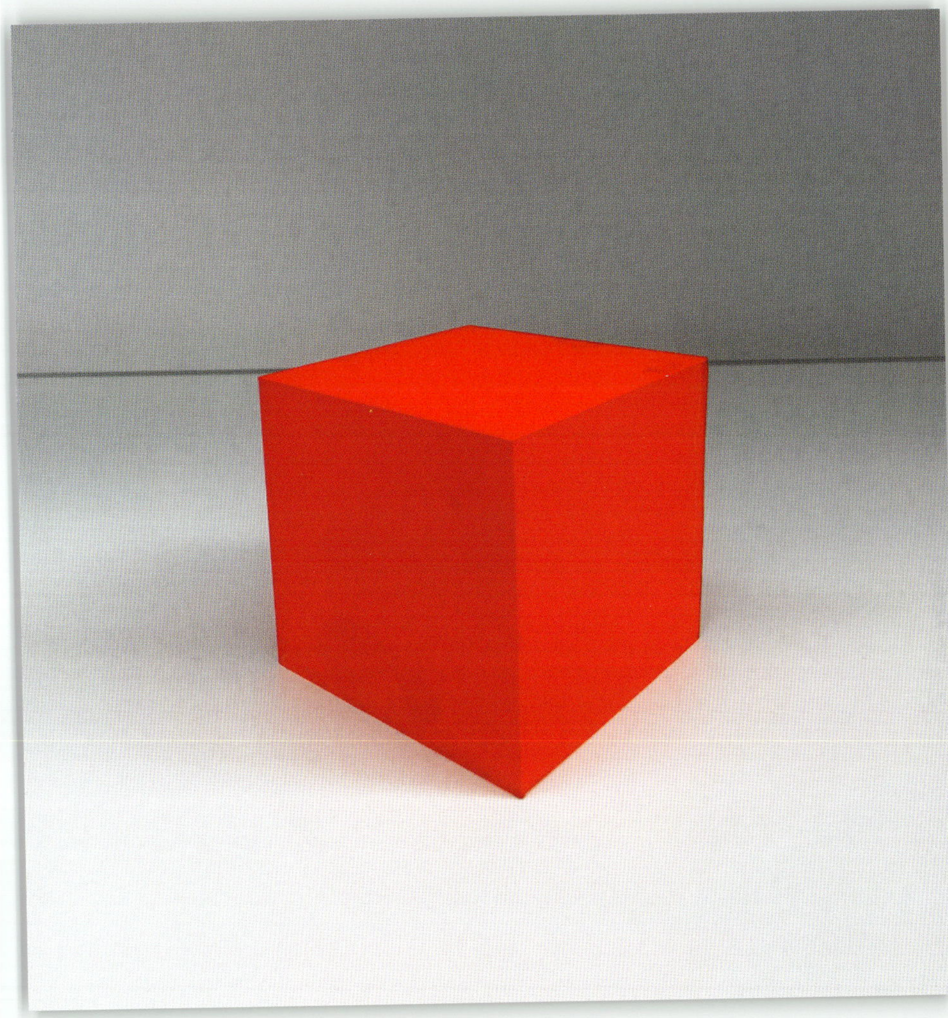

MEMORY PALACE

While the agricultural revolution took centuries, and the industrial revolution took generations, this ecological revolution has to happen within a matter of a few years.

Joanna Macy and Molly Brown, *Coming Back to Life*

In response to climate scientists' alarming 2018 Intergovernmental Panel on Climate Change report, my studio and I sought historical precedents for the major cognitive shifts that would be necessary to limit impending climate catastrophe. Drawing on classical mnemonic 'memory palace' techniques that suggest ideas are most memorable when spatially located, we constructed a vast model atlas featuring the tower in Frombork, Poland, where Copernicus taught us the Earth's true position within the solar system; the railings in Parliament Square where Emmeline Pankhurst changed minds about women's rights; the street in Montgomery, Alabama, where Rosa Parks shifted views on civil rights; and 70 more instances of major shifts in human perspective over 75 millennia. I had recently read the philosopher Timothy Morton's invitation to artists to amaze rather than preach, and, as visitors stood within the ovoid globe at Pitzhanger Manor Gallery in September 2019, we hoped that, emulating the wizardry of Renaissance memory architecture, the model rooms, streets and mountains would help restructure thought and action.

36–37

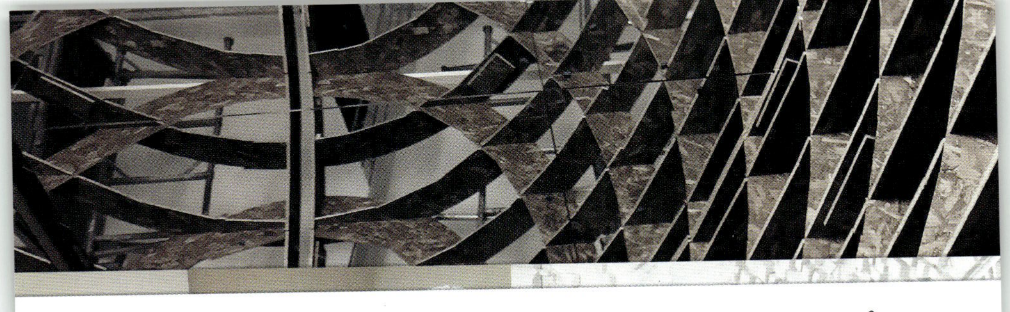

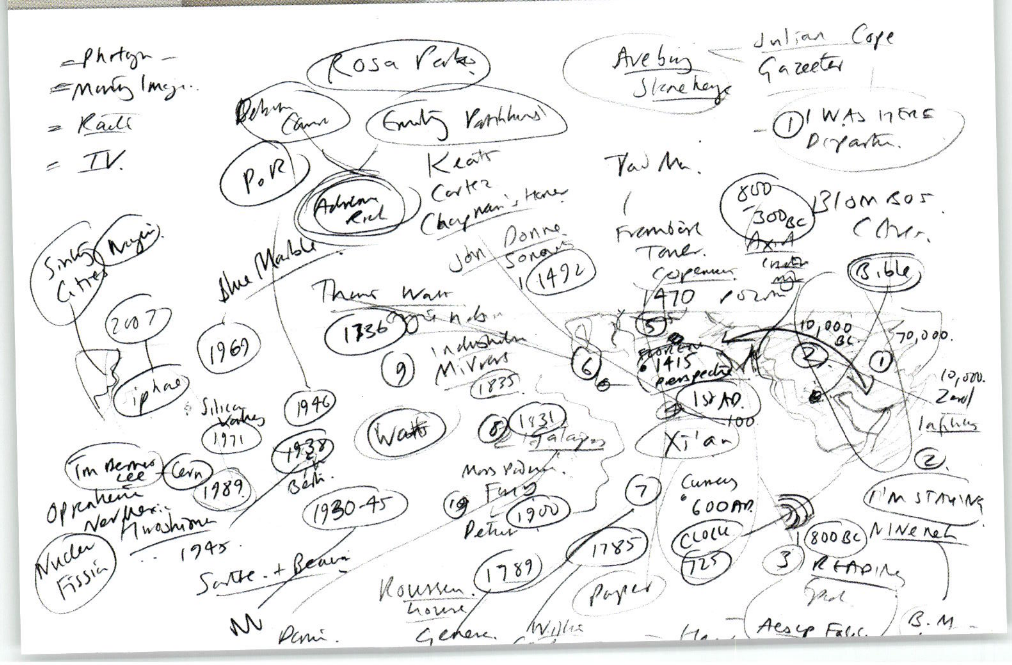
Rosa Parks
Emily Pankhurst
Keats
John Donne
1492
Avebury
Stonehenge
Julian Cope
Gazeteer
I WAS HERE
Bible
1789
1785
Xi'an
Watts
1969
2007
1946
1989
1930-45
1945
Nuclear Fission

MEMORY

While the agricultural r
revolution took genera
within a matter of a fe

Jo

In response to climat
Panel on Climate Cha
precedents for the m
limit impending clima
'memory palace' tech
when spatially locate
tower in Frombork, P
true position within th
where Emmeline Pan
street in Montgomery
civil rights; and 70 m
over 75 millennia. I ha
invitation to artists to
within the ovoid glob
2019, we hoped that,
architecture, the mod
restructure thought a

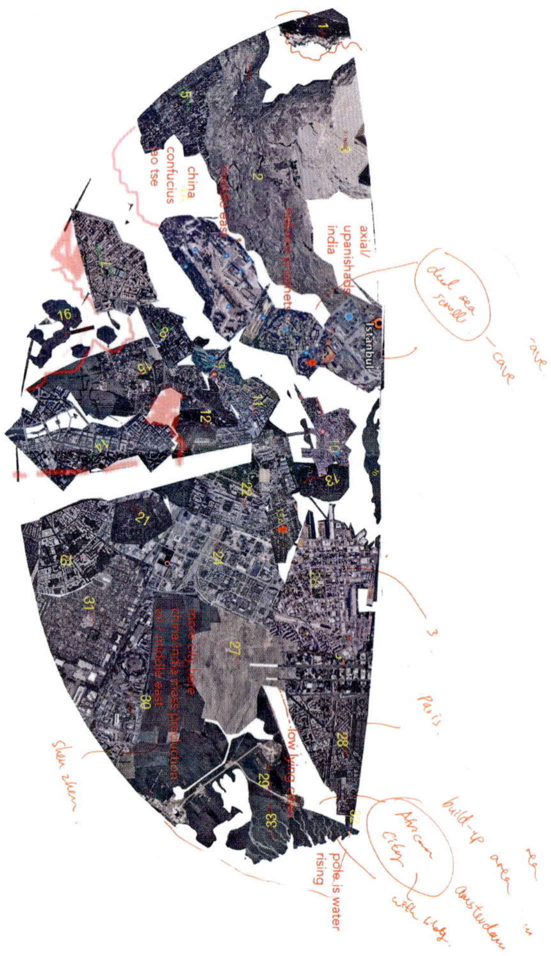

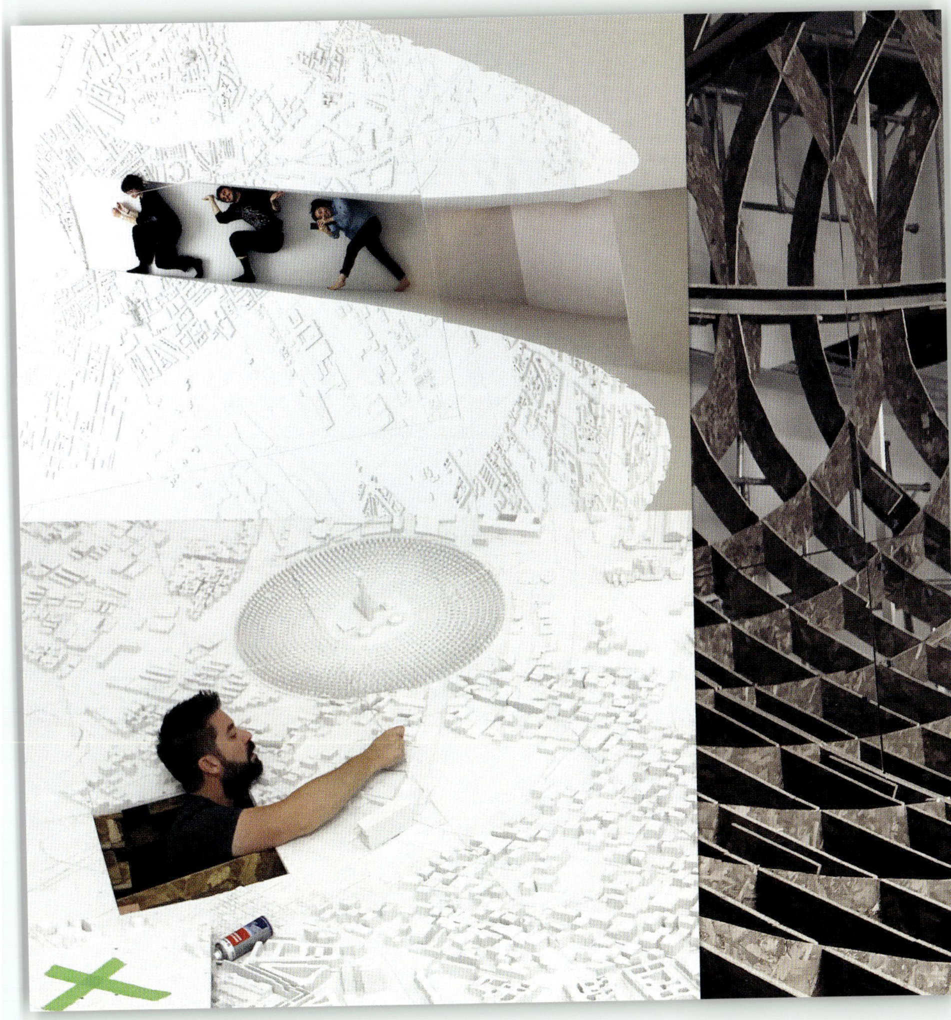

MEMORY

While the agricultur
revolution took gen
within a matter of a

In response to clim
Panel on Climate C
precedents for the
limit impending clim
'memory palace' te
when spatially loca
tower in Frombork,
true position within
where Emmeline P
street in Montgome
civil rights; and 70
over 75 millennia. I
invitation to artists
within the ovoid glo
2019, we hoped th
architecture, the m
restructure though

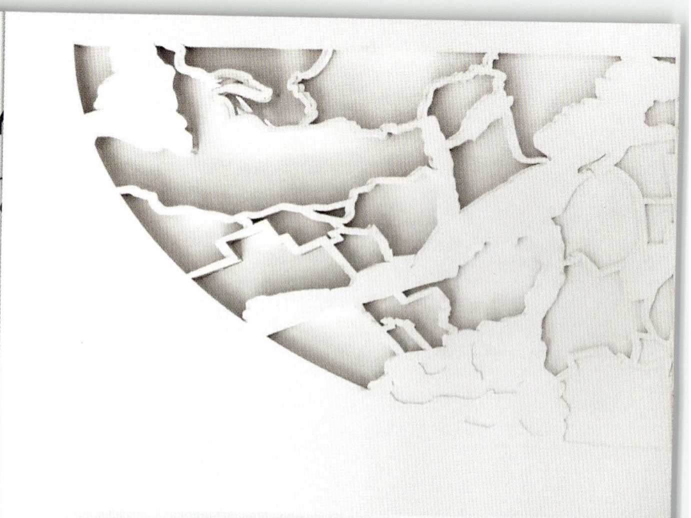

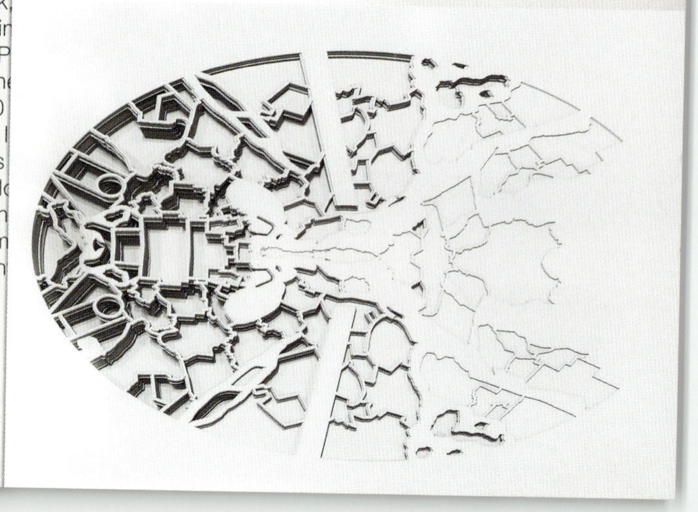

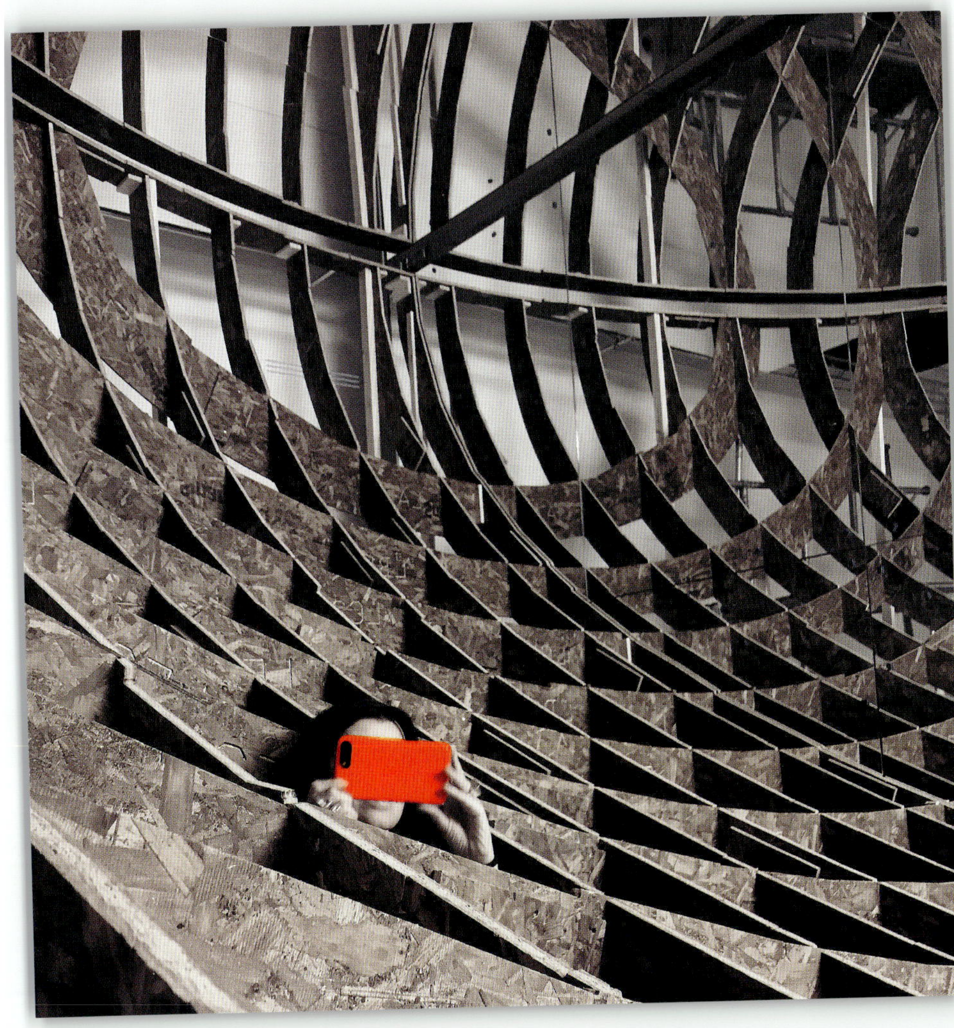

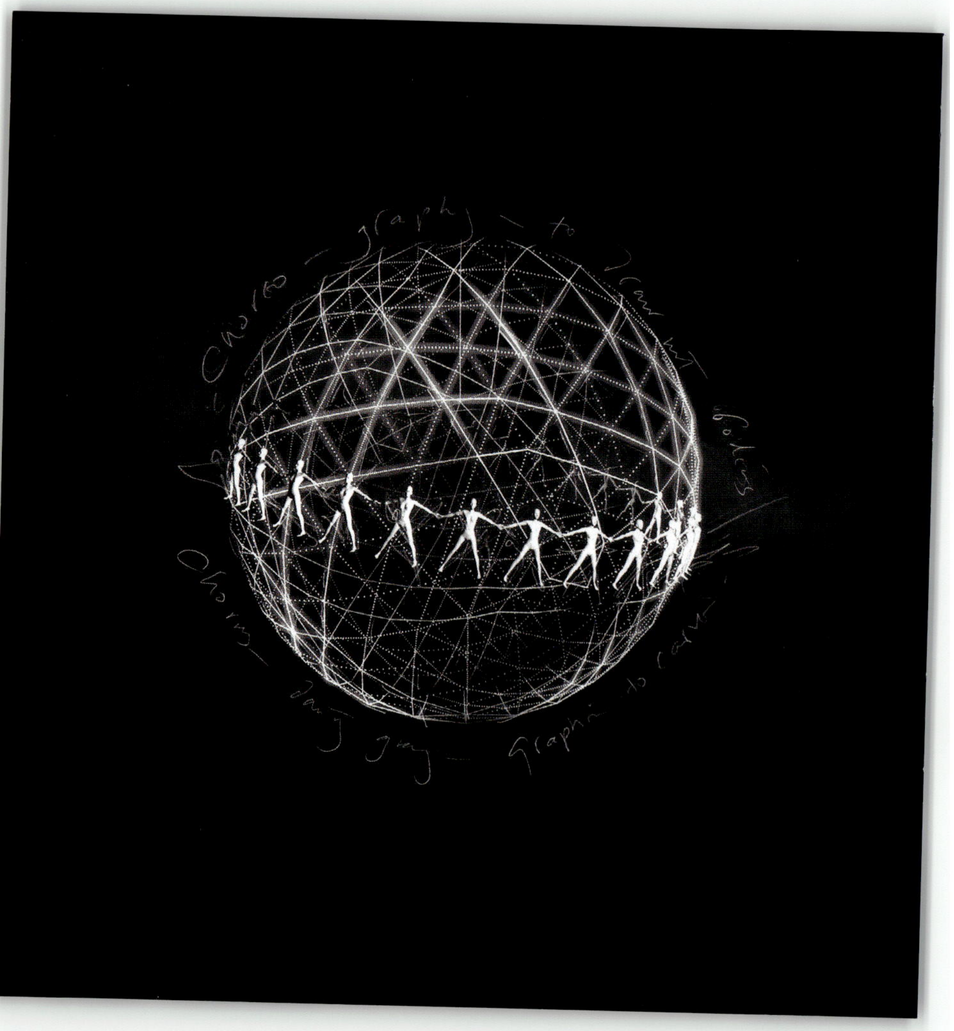
Choreo — graphy — to

THE LINE

Choreography is very much a process of physical thinking.

Wayne McGregor

In December 2018, the choreographer and director Wayne McGregor, fashion designer Gareth Pugh and I watched The Rockettes' Christmas show at Radio City Music Hall in New York. Wayne comes from Manchester and explained to us the origins of precision dancing in the nineteenth-century Mancunian dance troupe, the Tiller Girls. He envisaged a re-imagined geometric dance form that would be proportionally representative of the multiple ethnicities of the population of New York City. We worked for two years on concepts for a show which remains unrealized, but was originally planned to inaugurate the vast new spherical venue in Las Vegas called 'The Sphere'. A few years later we would begin work with U2 on their inaugural Sphere show, this time filling it, like a vast ark, with the more-than-human geometries of Nevada's endangered species.

IN YELLOW

I see the moon … when you're looking at the sun
I see in blue … when you see everything in red

Dua Lipa, 'Be the One'

For her November 2019 MTV Europe Music Awards performance in Seville, the British-born Kosovan/Albanian artist Dua Lipa and I proposed to the choreographer Charm La'Donna a vivid canvas peopled with fifty dancers all dressed in the same primary yellow. Charm took each of Dua's movements and echoed them through each dancer. The camera director Liz Clare committed to a static shot – a rare and bold choice that resisted the peripatetic orthodoxy of live music television. The result was a mesmerizing, moving human painting in luminous colour.

800–801

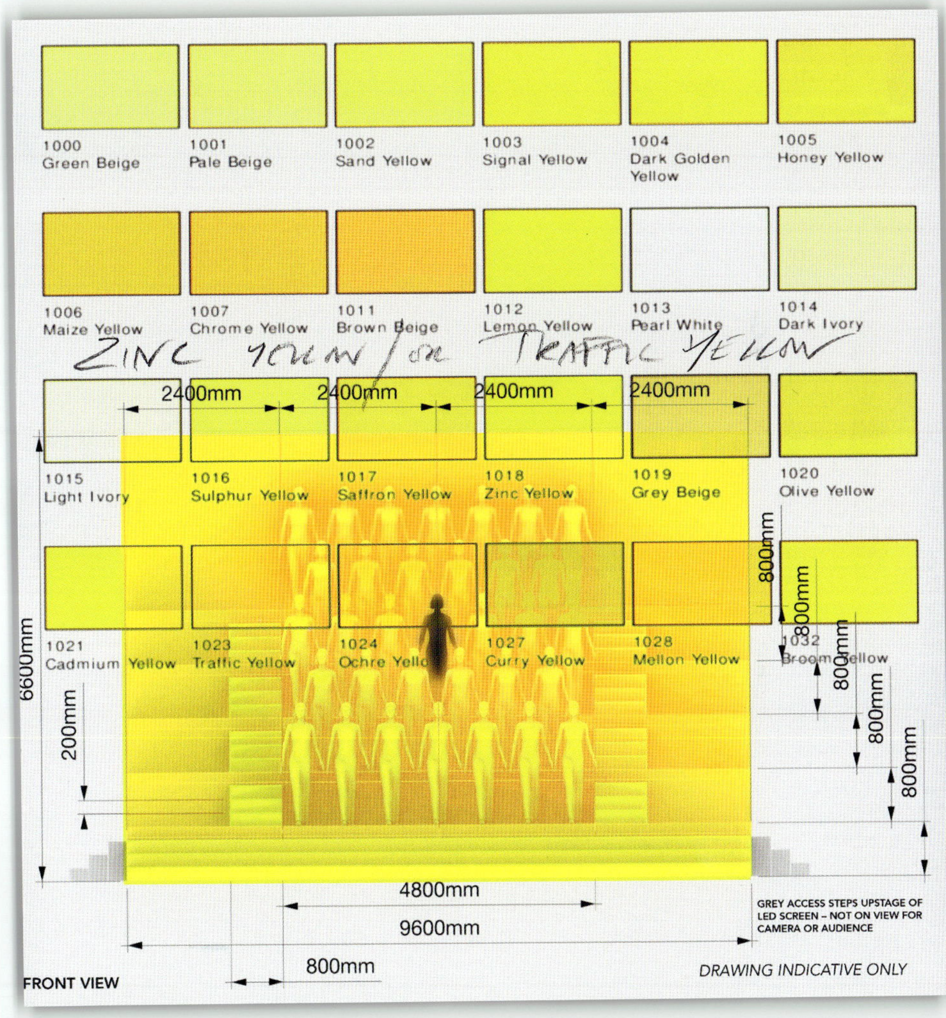

1000
Green Beige
1001
Pale Beige
1002
Sand Yellow
1003
Signal Yellow
1004
Dark Golden Yellow
1005
Honey Yellow
1006
Maize Yellow
1007
Chrome Yellow
1011
Brown Beige
1012
Lemon Yellow
1013
Pearl White
1014
Dark Ivory
ZINC YELLOW / OR TRAFFIC YELLOW
2400mm
2400mm
2400mm
2400mm
1015
Light Ivory
1016
Sulphur Yellow
1017
Saffron Yellow
1018
Zinc Yellow
1019
Grey Beige
1020
Olive Yellow
1021
Cadmium Yellow
1023
Traffic Yellow
1024
1027
Curry Yellow
1028
Mellon Yellow
1032
6600mm
200mm
800mm
800mm
800mm
800mm
800mm
4800mm
9600mm
800mm
GREY ACCESS STEPS UPSTAGE OF LED SCREEN – NOT ON VIEW FOR CAMERA OR AUDIENCE
FRONT VIEW
DRAWING INDICATIVE ONLY

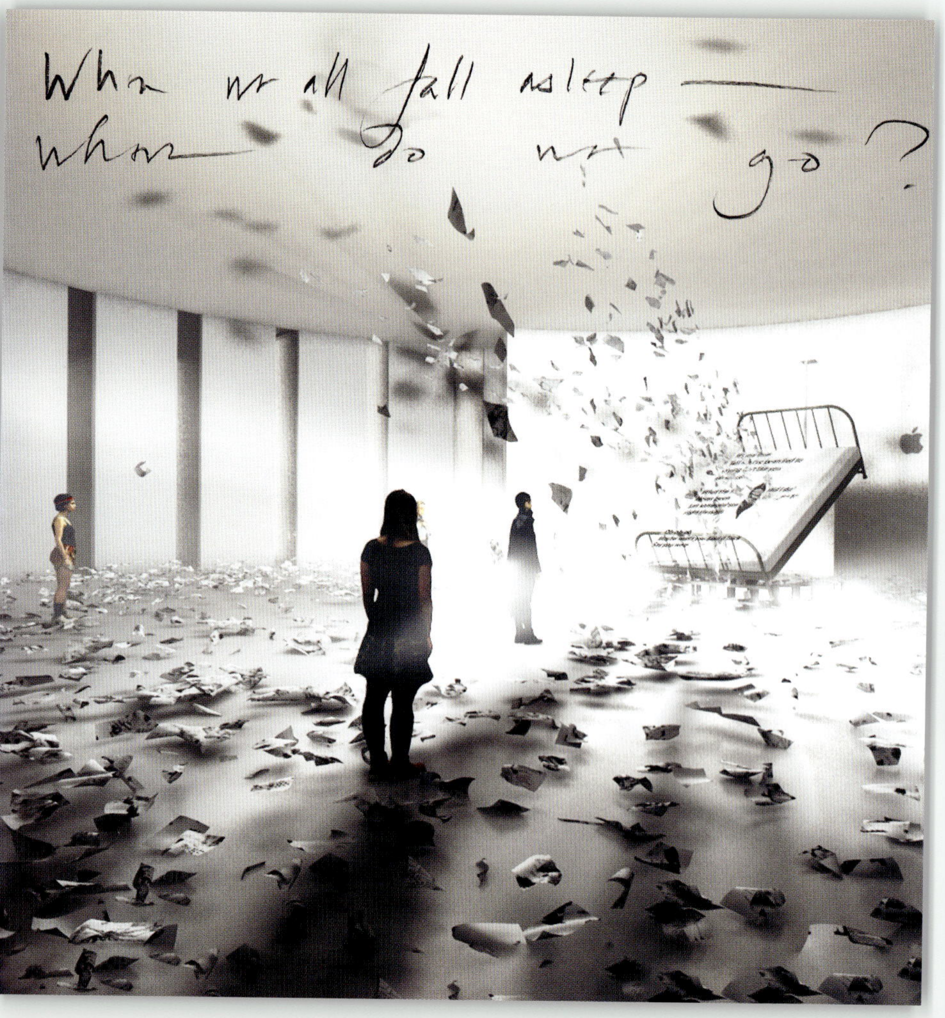
When we all fall asleep —
where do we go?

IN THE FOREST

I'm in love
With my future
Can't wait to meet her

Billie Eilish, 'My Future'

Early in 2019, my 12-year-old daughter Ry introduced me to the work of the 17-year-old artist Billie Eilish through her concert at the small Shepherd's Bush Empire theatre in London. It felt like a church of 2,000 early teenage girls singing so loudly you could barely hear Billie and her brother Finneas on stage. Ry showed me the annual interviews that Billie carries out with her future self, and I was struck by this young artist's instinct for long-term thinking. Asked to collaborate with Billie on her December 2019 performance at the Steve Jobs Theater at Apple's headquarters in Cupertino, California, I suggested we bring the arboretum that surrounds Norman Foster's circular glass building onto the stage. The theatre had only ever been used for Apple device launches: the whole complex was exceptionally white and clean, and I felt it would benefit from a messy intrusion of dark earth and trees. We filled the spotless white 'hands-on' area where tech journalists normally try out new iPhones with a replica of Billie's bed, its mattress slashed open and belching clouds of haze and handwritten, torn paper lyrics.

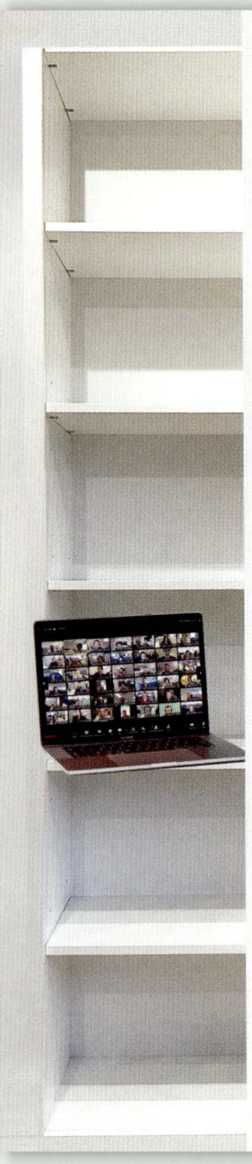

AN INTERVAL: LOCKDOWN CONVERSATIONS

March 2020–March 2021

On 23 March 2020, we tuned into the BBC to watch the Prime Minister's instruction to the nation to stay at home in order to prevent the spread of coronavirus. Each of my studio team packed up their computers and left. For the first time in two decades, I found myself alone in the studio. Over the coming weeks, one by one, all of our projects were cancelled. Mass gatherings became temporarily extinct.

Over the course of the lockdown, we found ourselves meeting in digital rooms, in the multi-storey, multi-windowed architecture of Zoom. We couldn't gather in theatres or stadia, we couldn't sing together, but we could still reflect and imagine worlds together. This collective imagining became a vital means of holding our communities together at a time when we were full of fear and tentative hope about a post-COVID future.

I recorded many of the Zoom conversations with colleagues and friends. Andrea Lipps, the editor of this book, joined me on many of the calls and we have gathered fragments from the hours of transcripts here. In a way, the lockdown years of 2020–2021 merged into a single Zoom conversation between many collaborators and peers exploring the concept of suspension of disbelief.

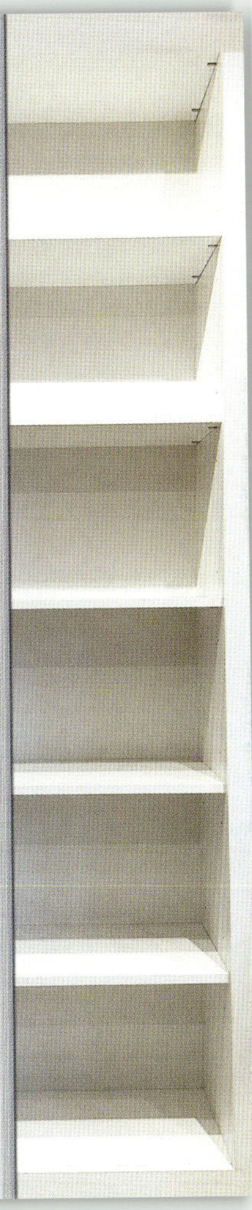

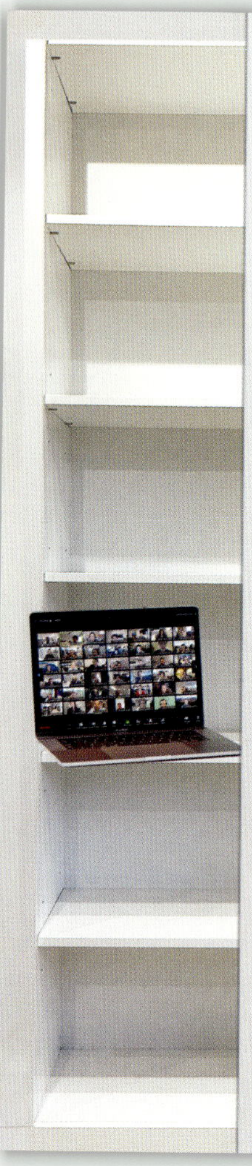

Brian Eno and Fraser T Smith

3 March 2021

Fraser: Just how are you both?

Brian: As impostors go, I'm feeling fine. Do you ever have impostor syndrome, Es?

Es: Of course. I mean, every good impostor has to see the impostor in the mirror. There is no courage without vulnerability, no wholeness without recognizing the hollowness within the shell. I can't imagine an honest artist who doesn't feel the dissonance between the outward, resonating bell that we try to be and the inward hollowness that a bell needs in order to resonate. Isn't that the way many musical instruments work, that they need a hollowness within in order to resonate in some way?

Brian: Yes. It's a body of air inside an instrument that's making the vibration make the sound. So there's a sort of absence, a vacuum that possibly exists inside everybody, and that's a malleable space, something that you can change the shape of. I think what artists are doing generally is shape changing. They're inventing other worlds and other people to be in that world and saying, come on, see what this world is like, see how it feels. Art says, here's another possible world, it deals with our vocabulary, our repertoire of feelings. It instigates emotions in an imagined new world that might be useful in our current world. Imagining is a way of creating in your mind a place that doesn't exist yet.

Es: Yes, utopias can be thought exercises to help us shift perspective. When I was a kid, extinction was something that referred to dinosaurs and dodos. When I saw a sign saying: 'Extinction Rebellion', that choice of vocabulary felt very radical. We now refer to the extinction of ourselves in the future tense in a way we wouldn't have done even five years ago. We have realized we can't shape any kind of utopia without first recognizing our current trajectory towards extinction.

We still use the word 'horizontal' to describe a straight light, even though we have learned that the horizon, the edge of the Earth, is curved. We have learned to hold multiple dissonant beliefs at once: I feel like I'm walking on flat ground, the horizon looks straight, but I know that the Earth is actually a sphere: both of these experiences can co-exist. Our language won't catch up. Our language is the archaeology of what we used to think.

Brian: Yes, one way of thinking about the evolution of the human mind is as a process of gradually realizing that we are not at the centre of things. Think of the shock of Copernicus revealing that the Earth wasn't the centre of the universe. In fact, it wasn't the centre of anything. It was at the edge of a solar system that was not at the centre of a not very large galaxy that was not at the centre of the universe. We were just a little bit of dust on the edges somewhere. The next huge shock was Darwin showing that we weren't at the centre of creation. Apart from not being at the centre of the universe, we weren't even particularly at the centre of life as we saw it. We've been going through this gradual process of de-centring, and that has led us to an ecological consciousness of seeing that we are connected with everything.

Fraser: When working with megastars like David Bowie and Abel from The Weeknd, are you able to talk to them in that way? One can imagine it would be very hard for Abel to understand that he isn't at the centre of the universe after an incredible performance at the Super Bowl, or David Bowie after releasing *Hunky Dory*. How do you calm that kind of ego, which is necessary for these kinds of artists to push themselves forward into these situations, when you're working with them?

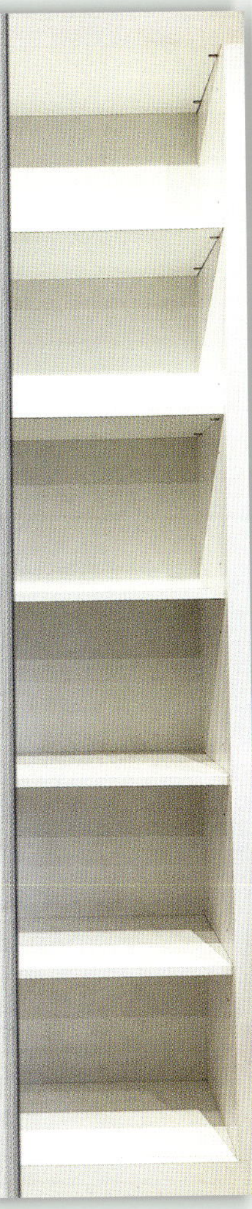

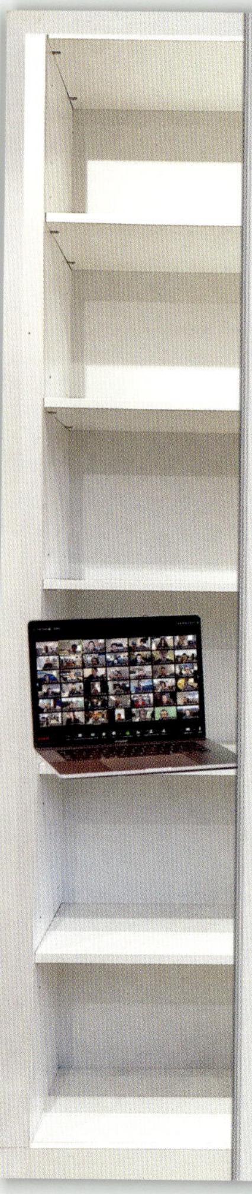

Es: I feel fortunate in that the collaborators I'm lucky enough to share ideas with are generally conscious that they are assuming a character. They know that it's like putting on a costume. And the healthier they are, the more they are aware of the delineation between themselves and their investiture. The character is armour as well. It's protection because if you don't draw a line, you'll be vulnerable. And the artists I've worked with who have been most vulnerable and have made themselves a bit unwell, their armour, their character, just wasn't quite complete. They weren't fully protected and they weren't able to use their mask in a resonant way and then take it off and be a bare forked creature at the end of the night. Brian, what's your experience?

Brian: My experience is I wish I'd had you as the psychologist on a few of the projects I've been involved with. I think that's very much the process that's going on and I think people generally do it intuitively without that much awareness of what it is that's happening.

Es: Brian, what's happened with your choir during lockdown? We were talking a while ago about the oxytocin that's released when you sing together and the hormonal and health benefits of choral singing. And during this pandemic, singing has become toxic. Singing has become an instrument of mass destruction. Have you been holding the choir on Zoom?

Brian: It doesn't work. We tried it. The most important thing about singing together is singing *together*, losing yourself in a bigger sound. I think in certain activities that we humans love doing – sex, drugs, art, religion – we deliberately create situations in which we go back to that condition of being part of something, of not being separate or separated. I call that surrender.

14 September 2020

Es: I've seen you get into character before a performance. Standing next to you in Glasgow, you started shivering, wrapped your jacket around you, and became the character who'd written the song you were about to perform.

Bono: Was it Oscar Wilde who said, 'give the man a mask and he'll reveal his true self'? I only had one character for a long time, a character who wanted to be believed as authentic, as real. I objected to the distance between the stage and the audience. My favourite performers were Iggy Pop, Patti Smith, Mark Rylance, those who you felt might get off the stage and follow you home. They might mug you, they might make love to you, they might set your taxi on fire. It was more an emotional landscape I was sketching. I wanted to break down the fourth wall, to jump off stage and be carried by the audience. If the audience moved out of the way, I'd fall flat on my face, but I believed they'd carry me. That's faith. I wanted to be in the audience. I've been bitten and have bitten back. It's like a lover's tangle. It's very physical.

In the '90s I started developing properly contrived characters, and I was relieved – I didn't have to be authentic! It was fucking brilliant! U2 could be licentious, we could be flirtatious, we could be assholes. The mechanisms for breaking down the fourth wall became technological innovations and staging, which brought our audience into the stories. It was wonderful to find these masks and be more playful.

Willie Williams had started it by always looking to the text for meaning. Es, you extend this. You're very narrative-based: 'What's the story you're trying to tell? The rest is unimportant.' Our last shows, the *Innocence + Experience* and *Experience + Innocence* tours, were as theatrical and narrative-based as we've ever been,

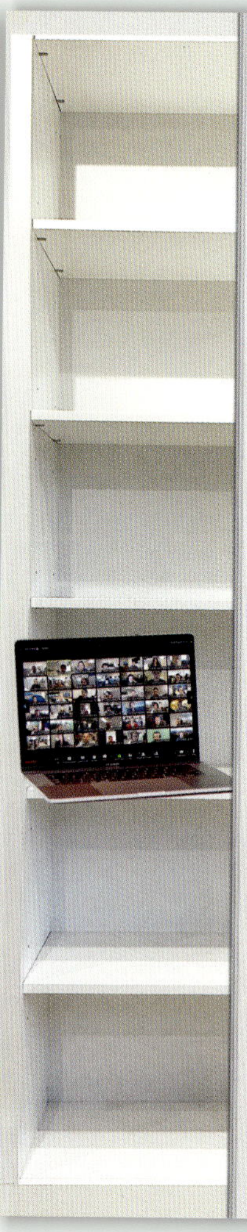

driven by David Bentley Hart's idea that 'wisdom is the recovery of innocence at the far end of experience'.

Es: We were all intolerant of anything that lacked meaning, which, when faced with the brutal logistical parameters of touring, is the only way to operate.

Bono: Within our team, the relationships are very horizontal – same as being in the band, same as my marriage, same as my friends. We don't like verticals, we like everybody to be looking creatively across at each other, and it really works. The idea is boss.

Why do we allow ourselves to be transported by an artist or an experience? Suspension of time is part of it, finding the eternal in the instant. The humbling thing is that you go to all the trouble to build a frame for the songs and the band, and then realize that the audience is the largest part of the show. Their connections to the songs are already very visual and internal. You can build anything you want, but it won't be as intense as the meaning that each person brings – the loss of a loved one, the time they went out with their friends in a different country.

In a way, you have more opportunity for narrative in the liminal spaces between songs. The edges of emotions are where we do our best work.

5 November 2020

Pharrell: Some people go into character and they turn the thing on, but I don't know that Es has an on/off switch. I think she was just born on.

Es: At the moment I feel we've all been reborn – into a different world – entirely changed since we last met.

Pharrell: Yes, now everyone has a personal assistant – it's called your phone and it has never told you no. It tells you yes for everything, making us incredibly dependent on the word 'yes'. And because of that, we become opportunistic. We no longer search for which of the grapes is sweet on the vine. We search for the sweetness we want to hear in our slants, no matter what they are politically, racially, religiously, socially. Our phones are changing the way that we see ourselves as a species, and I think now, for the first time, mankind is seeing its reflection in the waters of the Internet.

Yana: Es, can you give us a glimpse into 'Children of the Internet', the track you've just made with Fraser T Smith and Dave.

Es: My contribution to it is a meditation based on my reading of Beatriz Colomina and Mark Wigley on the feedback loop between objects and humans. Humans design an object, the object redesigns the human. The redesigned human designs a new object, the new object redesigns the human again. And we constantly live in this feedback loop between ourselves and the things we design. Exactly as you were describing about the smartphone.

Yana: Es, you have this uncanny ability to always look at things in 360 degrees. Did you always look at things this way or was there a specific turning point?

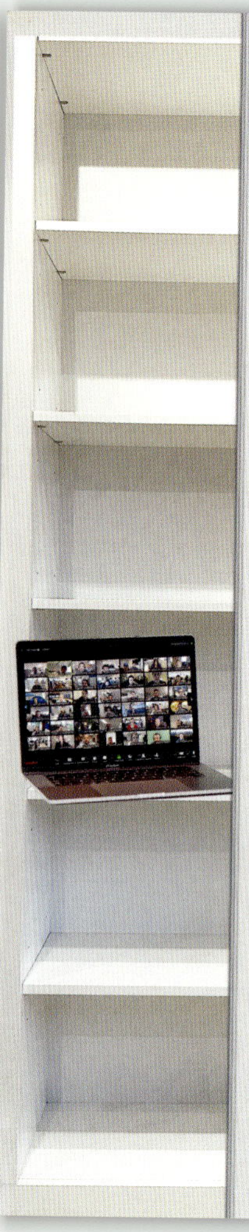

Pharrell: Can I just say something? You asked about her turning point? And I just want to say that I think anyone that's ever worked with Es realizes that Es *is* a turning point. When you meet with her, with her perspective, she literally turns things around. She's a walking turning point for anyone that she interacts with.

Yana: It's true! It reminds me of Zaha Hadid's beautiful saying: 'there should be no end to experimentation'.

You both have children. How is their childhood different from yours, creatively?

Es: Anything that I've tried to project into my own children's upbringing that relates to mine, it's ended with me sitting there on my own with a cereal packet and scissors and them going off because they're not interested. So I've tried to enter their world and I spent quite a lot of time at the beginning of the lockdown in Fortnite with my son, just trying to see it from his perspective, to try and understand, what does a ten-year-old see? Why does he love this? As I began to enter into his world, I realized that he is associating memories with this virtual landscape the way that I associate memories with physical landscape. I plant my memories in places and my son is planting memories in virtual places. I've got to learn because this is where he's native and I'm not.

Pharrell: I think I second that. Rocket is the Mars generation and then the triplets are … man, I don't even know. But Es is correct, our memories are more offline and geographical and our children's memories are often online, which is a beautiful thing, right? The technology continues to evolve. We are forever changed as a species. We always were, right? In the 1970s, we were already forever changed. But this is different. This is 'The Matrix' full on.

Es: Pharrell, back in 2015 you already had the sense of people mobilizing online. You gave them pre-concert tutorials. This was before TikTok. You wanted people to learn the steps, make their costumes, participate in a mass ritual, to be a participant and not a consumer. One of the things I'm interested in is a game that will seduce and entrance my son as much as Fortnite does, but instead of just keeping him enchanted by the pixels, can we lead him back out into the planet? Is there a game that takes me in through a screen but magically leads me out the other side of the computer? Back to the trees, back to the sea, back to the stars, back to Mars, back to the grass, back to the sand, back to the things we can touch because we've still got a body. This is the inconvenient thing: the pace of evolution of our minds is fast, but we've still got these inconvenient bodies stuck to our brains, right? They don't seem to be evaporating. They're still here, these weird appendages called bodies.

Pharrell: So you just witnessed the turning point. That was the turning point in action.

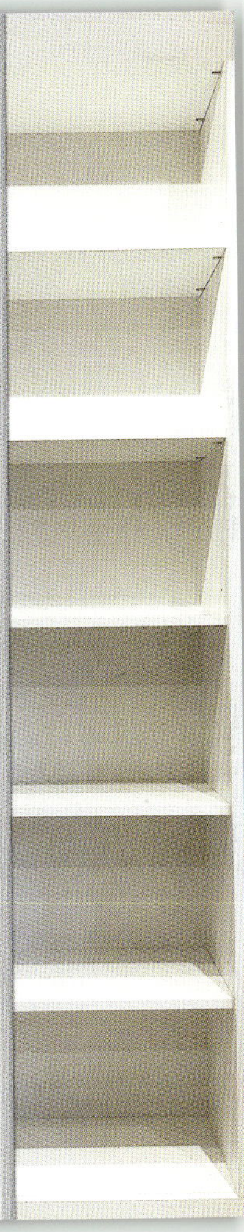

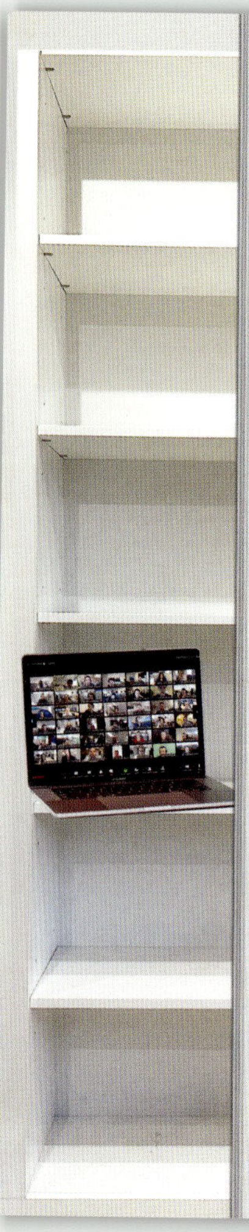

Akram Khan

20 June 2020

Akram: I haven't found many people who can see the importance and hone the craft equally in different genres. Es is one of very few artists who does that.

Es: I wonder if the generation that follows us will feel much more comfortably polymathic.

Akram: I hope so. Collaboration has really changed over the years. All of us are usually in the same environment, having the same conversation to the point where you wouldn't know who's leading it. It's not a vertical hierarchy, it's more horizontal. The story becomes bigger than any individual and we all become its authors.

Es: It's like open-source software, able to be co-authored. One almost thinks of a virus – it mutates from person to person in the most culturally creative way, each of us anticipating evolutions in the patterns we perceive.

Akram: In modern civilization, we are educated to only believe what we can see, yet there's so much in between that we cannot see – feeling, emotion, your mother telling you a story when you're a child and your imagination that spins out from that. What art, what theatre, and what Es does is take from the book and open it out ...

On stage and off, there is a very big shift in time – what happens in real time and what happens in stage time ... Before I step on stage, I'm in a different time zone – the past. I'm thinking of all the mistakes I made. And then I'm in the future, projecting about all the things that could go wrong. But once you're on stage you click into the present. You move at Kairos' time, which is a much slower, thick and serene time. The stage suspends clock time, which is Westernized, Christianized, masculine, economic, financial time. Stage time is nature time, horizontal time, life and death time, spiritual time, ritualistic time, magical time. So we shift from the vertical masculine into a more horizontal, deep ocean time. And the moment the audience claps, you suddenly return to clock time. What the stage does to an audience as well as an artist is to take us from our reality not just in imagination but in time. It elongates time.

Es: That is such a profound insight. When the audience and performers breathe at the same pace and in the same time, there is a place-ness, a presence, a stability in the shared breath. Our collective breath reaffirms life.

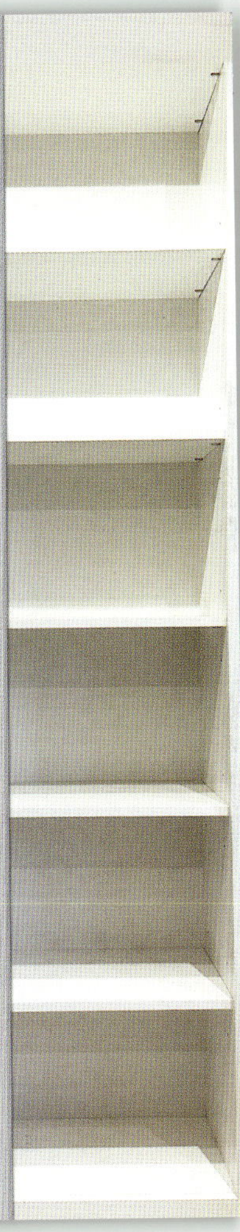

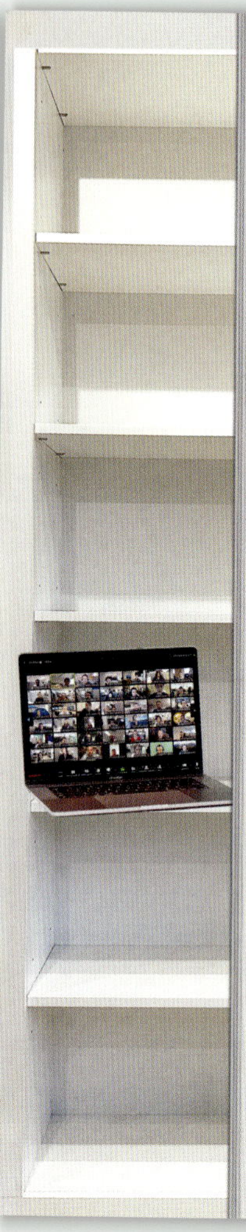

Carlo Rovelli

27 May 2020

Es: I often think of your analogy between the perception of time and the perception of music. You liken it to the suspension we hold between memory of the note we've just heard and anticipation of the note we are about to hear. In a way, this moment of mass lockdown, this suspension, invites a global act of imagination.

Carlo: There is a subtle game played in music: the musical phrase we've just heard allows us to anticipate the sound that is coming next. Yet, over and over again, we do not really hear what we expect. Music plays with us. It tricks us into expectation that it may not meet, which forces us into openness. What really has meaning for us is not what we expect, but what we did not expect. We have to believe and at the same time be ready not to believe.

Perhaps this is how our mind works all the time. We always know what we believe, don't we? And yet what's interesting is what doesn't fit. Without our beliefs we would be lost, but they are also the traps from which we want to escape.

Es: The other big influence on my thinking is your suggestion that artists perceive patterns often in parallel to, or before, scientists.

Carlo: Artists and scientists use very different methods. But we do the same thing, ultimately: we both develop and search for novel ways of looking at the world. Our worldview is not fixed. It evolves continuously with new images, new understanding, new conceptualizations, new perspectives, new ways of looking. In their own ways, artists and scientists keep enlarging or modifying our view of the world, and this in turn changes the world ...

The evening of our collaboration on the Peckham rooftop was magic. I was astonished and so happy. It was cold, wet and miserable; I had been travelling and was tired and knew almost no one. And then we gathered and your lights and sounds started and everything was suddenly dramatically intense, and, with the voice of Benedict Cumberbatch, the words took an absolute power that I did not expect. It was such a strange and strong experience for me, seeing that so much depth could be built upon words I had written. And then the unaccompanied violin of the Missa Solemnis 'Benedictus' amazed me. I am in love with that melody, which I mention at the end of my book, and I had always suffered to barely hear it over the full orchestra. You took it out and had it singing freely. For me, it was a moment of paradise ...

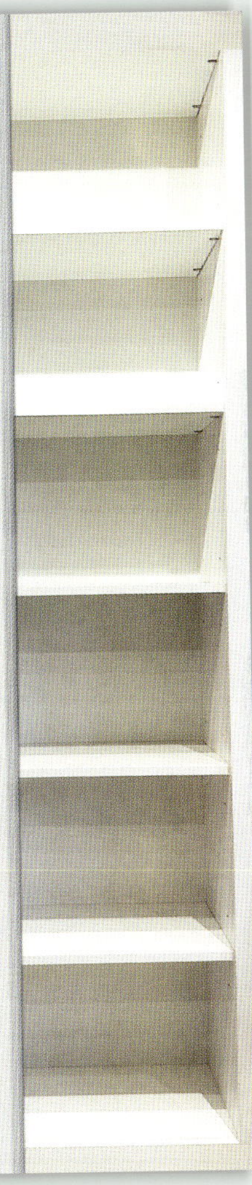

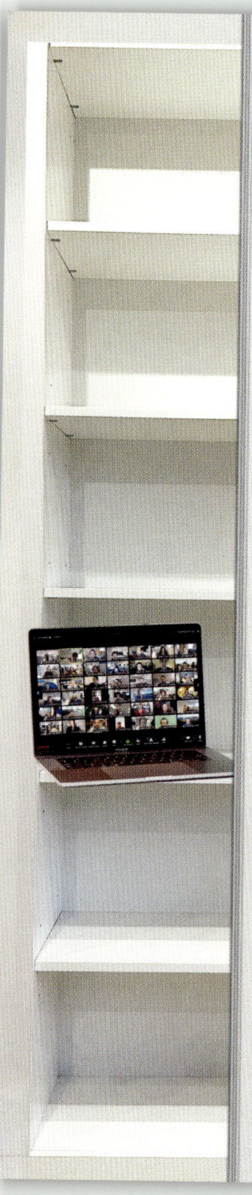

Benedict Cumberbatch

26 May 2020

Benedict: Carlo Rovelli is a real linguist. It's fantastically poetic language that offers a condensed explanation of some of the most complex ideas about our existence. I had to read the passages eight or ten times in order to follow the logic. I found Carlo to be a very gentle, loving soul, an incredible empath and super bright. He's a massive star – the Stephen Hawking of Italy. His writing helps us understand why we are so addicted to pattern-finding and story-telling. Most narratives are some form of pattern; they're some form of structure. We're hardwired for narrative. We're desperate to make some sense or order out of the chaos and give meaning to what can, at times, feel like a cruel and heartless universe. What is it to be alive? What is it to love? What is it that makes all this valuable? Pattern-finding enables us to begin to understand. It helps us to inhabit the questions and embrace uncertainty.

Es: Yes, Hamlet seeks order in the chaos we pile around him. What did the space we designed for the play at the Barbican feel like, from the inside?

Benedict: The extraordinary thing about it is the scale. You're enveloped by a visual poetry that enhances everything about Shakespeare's four-hundred-odd-year-old words. It's an outward expression of the interior landscape, this high-ceilinged, high-doored world that feels claustrophobic despite its scale. This rumination bursts in the form of rage and bile and darkness and disorder and chaos, which is everything that the play pushes towards in its climactic ending, with recrimination and death. The set breathes with the piece.

Sets are strange things. We all, as an organism of people, have to adapt to this environment. It's a living, breathing thing, and it becomes your home for the story-telling of that world.

Es's design of *Hamlet* – the richness of texture, especially in colour and detail and the daring nature of angle and scale and drama – was nearly operatic. The Barbican is a wide stage. To cover that with a light that draws you into a sudden intimate moment with this man's mind, into his dilemma and the human condition, it's paramount to the audience's journey. But it also involved feasts, battles, and a huge pile of earth bursting through massive doors. It required all these varying landscapes and a place that was both outside landscapes and within them. It did a lot.

I know the audience thought they'd seen one of the most beautiful productions of *Hamlet* ever. We wanted something generous, didn't we, Es? The director, Lyndsey Turner, Es and I wanted something bold and still timeless … There was a palpable connection to what happens in *Hamlet*, a trans-generational trauma that seeps up through the earth, almost like Baader-Meinhof playgrounds built over Jewish mass graves in Germany – that idea of violence.

It's always about finding a balance between verisimilitude and something abstract, something more imagined. When you're dealing with an examination of the human condition, you want to have a little bit of all of that: the fakery in which we're knowingly participating in order to achieve truth. Obviously, theatre audiences go in with empathy for the creative process. They're willing to lean in. But there's an element now in culture as a whole whereby we sit back with folded arms and wait to be transported. We want to be impressed by the blockbuster effect of it all, but what usually undoes us is the quieter poetry, the intimate detail.

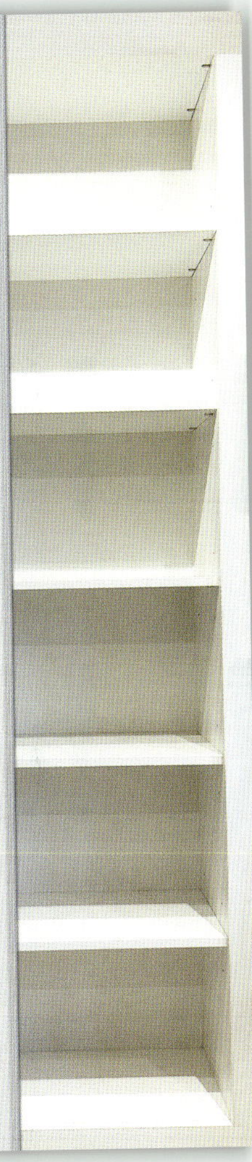

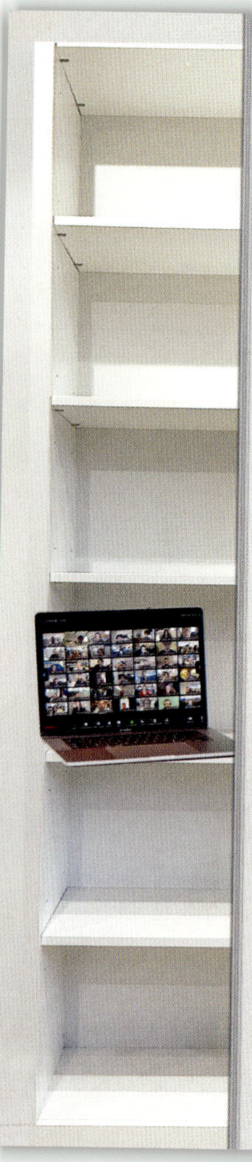

Lyndsey Turner

8 May 2020

Lyndsey: I believe *Chimerica* was the first time we met inside a piece of work, wasn't it? It was a phenomenally demanding piece of writing and a real challenge to stage, but I secretly enjoyed the fact that we got to meet inside a riddle. Lucy Kirkwood is an astounding writer who loaded the play with images. We made sure to invite her into the design process, so the last draft and a half of Lucy's play was imagined into Es's design.

What I cherish most about that project is it felt like the first time in my career where I'd been involved in a piece of work in which you couldn't get a cigarette paper between the design and the performers, the performers and the writing, the writing and the sound, the sound and the projection. The audience had no idea which department was leading on which moment of stage action. It really felt like we'd made a complete piece of theatre.

Andrea: What led to the box of rain that surrounds Brian Friel's *Faith Healer*?

Lyndsey: I found it difficult to imagine any of the three characters in *Faith Healer* either walking onto a stage or walking off a stage, and that's all I said to Es. For me, it began as a failure of imagination.

Es: The piece is an incantation. It's a ritual, a spell.

Lyndsey: It was also about trying to make the space unsafe for the audience. Occasionally at the Donmar, you'll see an audience member or two crossing the stage to take their seat. So I was excited to do something that rigged the deck in the play's favour and made the stage a 'no go' area for anything other than the actors. In the best possible way, the design cowed the audience slightly so that when a man emerged through that curtain of rain, even though he was one body in a tatty suit, he dominated the space right from the start of the piece. Ultimately, with any production, there is a point at which Es and I step away, leaving only the performers. They have to be at the centre of it.

Es: We try to facilitate the performers' as well as the audience's suspension of disbelief. We aim to create a place that the performer can believe in, so that they can transmit this faith to the audience.

Lyndsey: That's the magic of theatre. It's so unlike any other art form because for it to work we, on stage, have to pretend that you, the audience, are not there and then you, the audience, have to pretend that you're not there, and then we all agree to do that at exactly 7:30. It's a collective fantasy. It's sustained by cobwebs of our imagination, by each of us retracting our ego and stilling our bodies for the general good. Theatre holds itself up through the collective.

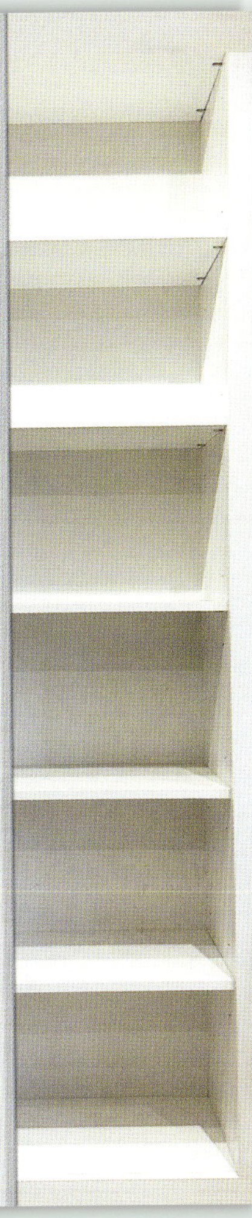

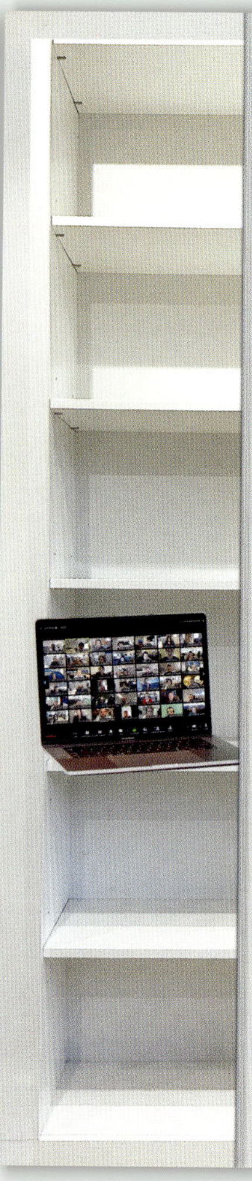

Neil Tennant

14 May 2020

Es: The writer Chris Heath says the Pet Shop Boys' world is so complete you need a visa to enter it. When we first met, you described the anatomy of a pop concert to me as a great Saturday night out with tears in the toilet and a redemptive ending.

Neil: You've got to suspend your disbelief about Chris [Lowe] and me being pop stars, really. Right from the beginning, Chris and I set out to create our own world where we didn't compete with anything other than ourselves. We're like the artist Charles Avery, who's creating a world on a mythical island by just adding more and more stuff to it. With the Pet Shop Boys, we're creating a Pet Shop Boys world where we add people to it like Es Devlin or Liza Minnelli. And it's all part of this giant artwork. So in that way perhaps you don't have to suspend disbelief because you know these two guys are the Pet Shop Boys and therefore only their rules apply to them. And then you get a rock critic who comes in and says, 'Oh, Neil Tennant's got the charisma of a tax collector.' I know what they mean, but then how come everyone's going berserk at the end of a show?

There's a certain amount of marshalling of the forces of the audience. In a rock or a dance show, you're trying to get these waves of energy that crash everywhere and then build up to another wave of energy that crashes and the whole audience gets the surge. We're orchestrating waves of energy.

4 June 2020

Wayne: The great thing about collaborations is the fact that they weave; they move. Our time thinking together has affected the way I've been making work since. The collection of decisions that you make at the end of the process are only a tiny part of the richness. For *The Line*, we were exploring the basic Bauhaus principles of drawing – point, line, plane – in relationship to bodies and architecture. How can you blend the technologies of bodies and stage design to create a hybrid, live piece? I'm not only choreographing with individuals, looking at their personal physical signatures. I zoom out and work with bodies as architectural objects. I'm thinking of architectural forces and dynamism, not the personal or the personality. That creates a different physical geometry and force. Es, your design process is very choreographic, isn't it?

Es: Yes, we fit the negative space around the human form like a kinetic costume. Actually it's taught me to look where humans aren't: to view the biosphere as the protagonist, with human-shaped holes, rather than humanity surrounded by environment.

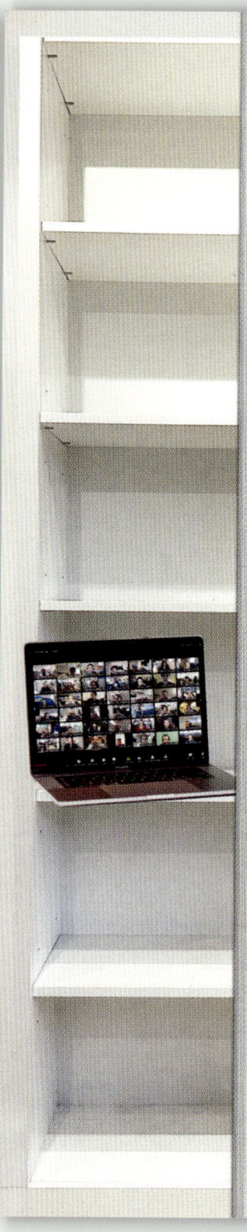

Bjarke Ingels

18 May 2020

Bjarke: In any aspect of architecture and design, there is an expectation about what the outcome will be. The potential lies in how you navigate that expectation – how you play with it, how you accommodate it, how you contradict it or expand it or cross-breed it with other things. It's important to remember that the standard solution did not become the standard solution by being bad. It became the standard by being incredibly good at delivering a certain outcome within a given set of parameters.

The only way to beat the standard is to expand on those parameters, to make the problem more difficult so you actually make it easier to solve in an interesting way. Evolutionary leaps happen when you are forced to give up on your first trajectory and explore something else. Even in nature, evolutionary leaps happened when the fish was forced out of the water onto land; it was when the ape was forced out of the jungle into the savannah that it became a human. When you have to escape because the road is blocked, that's when new trajectories emerge.

Es: We often use the phrase 'the art of the just-about possible'. If it feels barely possible from the perspective of each parameter, if it almost breaks the boundaries of every parameter but just doesn't quite break them, then you're probably on the way to the solution somehow.

Bjarke: Yes, and Es, your work evolves its technology. You find seamless, non-disruptive ways to navigate incredible leaps of scale in performances. And you meaningfully integrate the performers with images at front and back of the arena. Bringing all of those elements into more of a *Gesamtkunstwerk* in a Wagnerian way, identifying that there are new capabilities rather than just reproducing the old answers.

Es: You and I were both moved by Andri Snær Magnason's obituary of the first Icelandic glacier lost to climate change.

Bjarke: Yes. Why are humans incapable of taking action in the face of climate change? After all, we are great at making very large, very ambitious plans and executing them. My favourite examples from architecture are the cathedrals. The great cathedral in Cologne took 632 years to build. The Catalans have been building the Sagrada Família for 137 years. How can they do this? Because they have a blueprint, a master plan. When the first architect died, the next one picked it up, and then the next one. But with climate change, we haven't made a master plan for the whole planet. Our lifestyle has an impact at the scale of the planet. We have the tools and technologies to observe the planet at a planetary scale. We can understand the systems holistically at the planetary scale. We need a master plan. We need to take care of the Earth not just out of responsibility for the species or the planet in the abstract. No, no, no: we need to care for it because we are connected in the most intimate way imaginable.

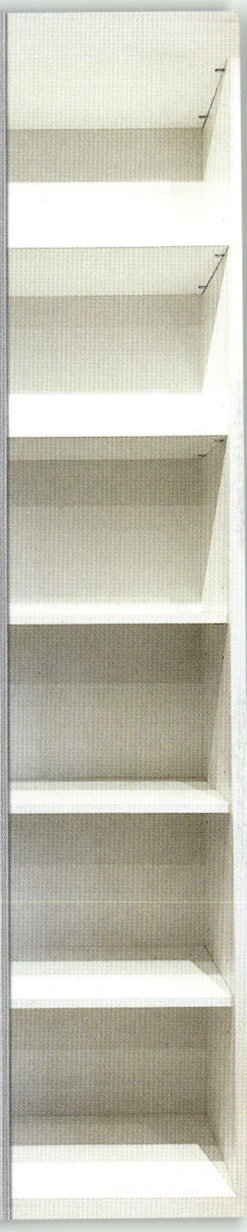

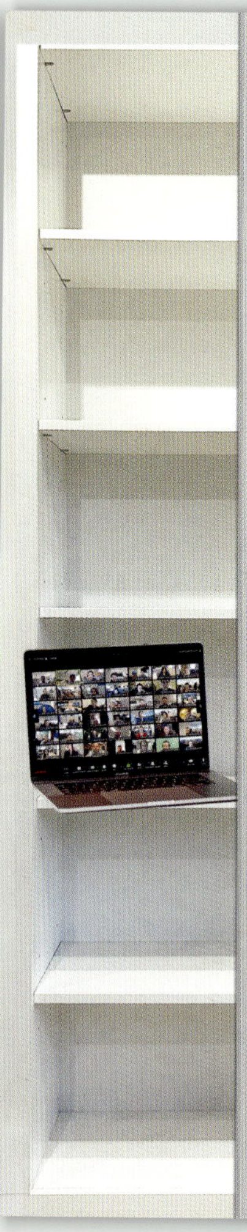

Nicolas Ghesquière

9 February 2021

Es: I was trying to understand the medium of a fashion show, seeking where I could graft my process onto yours. I remember asking you, who is this character whose house we're conjuring in Palm Springs? And you explained, she lives in here, she's got a telescope, she walks down these stairs in the morning. I had never understood clothes like that before: that the reason I put something on in a shop is because you imagined me putting it on.

Nicolas: It's really about utopia. We need that utopia for the 15-minute duration of the show to establish the character who's going to evolve in the season. When we build these landscapes together, these atmospheres, including the music, it's like a short movie with not much dialogue but a lot of messages – in the clothes, the character of the woman, and the life that goes with it. Each world is there just for a moment, and evokes a crucial combination of familiarity and novelty.

Kyle McDonald

10 June 2020

Kyle: We are in the process of creating this algorithm: it's a kind of fascist artwork. This is not a neutral connective tissue.

Es: Yes, you've had to fiercely shepherd this poetry-generating AI away from morose poetry.

Kyle: Morose, offensive, violent, suggestive, religious, discriminatory ... This is an algorithm, so you have to be incredibly precise with your descriptions of what you do and don't want.

Es: I'm looking up the etymology of 'fascist' ... The Italian *fascismo* is derived from *fascio*, meaning a bundle of sticks. So we're calling it a fascist artwork because, by its very nature, however inclusive we aim to be, we are still a bundle of people ...

Kyle: ... organized into this one direction. And that's what art does a lot of the time! It forces people into these systems, and as artists we often think, 'I'm just putting this thing out into the world and letting people experience it', but that's not really true. Artwork is a kind of violence, in that it's forcing people to see things from our perspective or to put themselves into a situation we've constructed for them. The problem of utopia is the idea that we can get away with a kind of neutrality or with a kind of pure anarchy, but there's always some kind of structure, some kind of power dynamic. I think designing those in a way that is optimistic, which encourages the behaviours we want from each other, that's our work as artists and as humans.

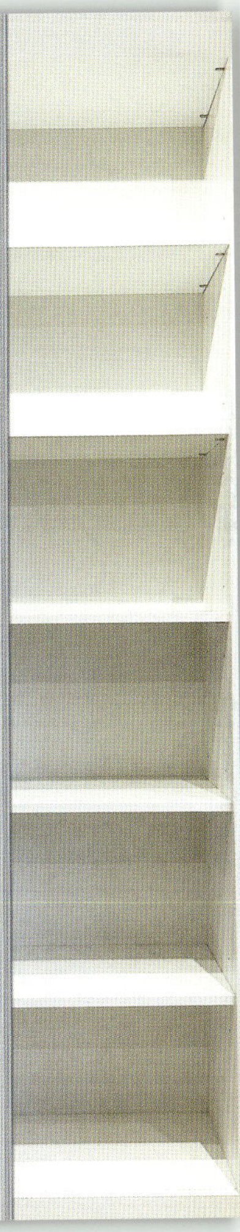

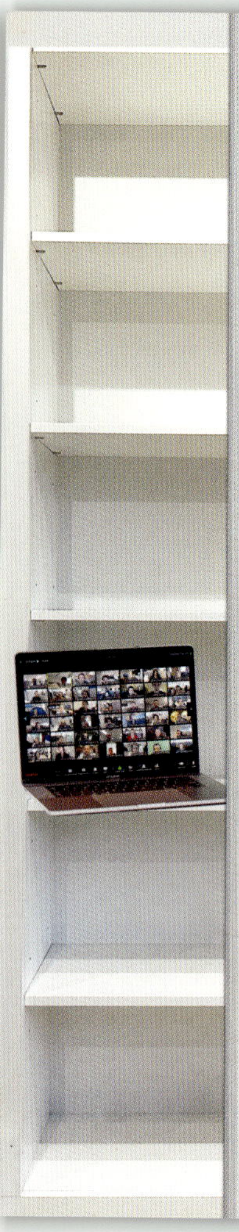

Abel 'The Weeknd' Tesfaye and La Mar C Taylor

19 May 2020

Andrea: Whether it's a broadcast performance such as SNL or a tour, how does your collaborative process work?

Abel: Honestly, it's me coming up with the most ambitious and craziest idea and giving it to Es and Es saying, 'We can do it.' And then La Mar gets nervous because, with Es, there's no 'No'. I come up with crazy non-linear concepts and Es makes a story out of it to create something cohesive. With Es, it's not about doing more, it's about doing less and making it look massive from home. She's so good at creating a universe.

> **Es:** Isn't it ironic, Abel, that we were talking before COVID about your relationship to the audience becoming more cinematic? Social distancing was already part of our concept for the tour.

Abel: Very ironic. The album was actually supposed to be called *Alone Together*. That was the original title of the record.

> **Es:** You were prescient. I think artists see patterns of events before they happen, so I'm not surprised by this. When you listen to the album, almost every lyric is about being alone; it's a study of the art of being alone. And for the tour, we'd been planning to present how Abel suspended in his own disbelief, immersed in his own world, separated from the audience.

Abel: With the *After Hours* tour, I want to perform like an actor playing the character that I've been portraying in the music videos and short films. I want to wear the same outfit and the bloodied-up makeup. We want to bring the audience into the *After Hours* universe. We created this fictional Las Vegas world, this extended performance with the character going through a linear, *Jacob's Ladder*-like storyline, where he confronts the demons within himself.

Es: My understanding of this character is it's an expression of you opening the book of your life and getting stuck in one night.

Abel: Yeah, that's why I wanted to continue the story, which we've done with the 'Blinding Lights' video and the Jimmy Kimmel performance. I wanted to do that with this tour as well. How do we make this feel like it's all part of one night?

Es: Yes, and how do we sustain this narrative while giving the audience what they crave, which is intimacy with you, or their version of you.

La Mar: Es, we've learned to keep the audience's eyes focused on the show and the performer on stage, rather than looking at him through VR goggles or on a screen.

Es: Yes, it's an act of portraiture. I think this clash between what the audience wants, which is to touch you, and what you want, which is to express yourself, is always in tension. We're always going to fail at both and succeed somewhere in the middle. This clash of expectation, we just need to embrace it.

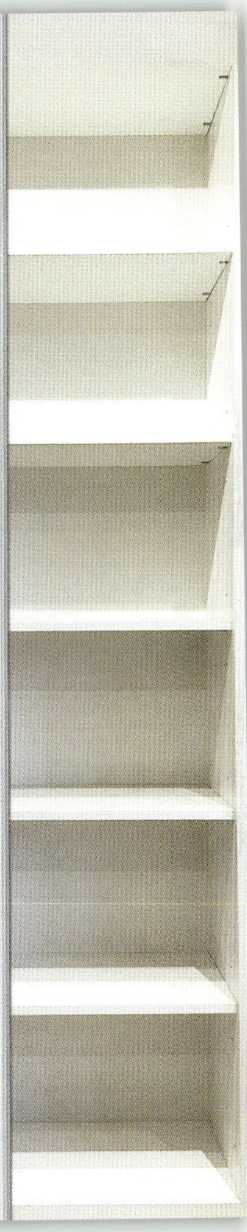

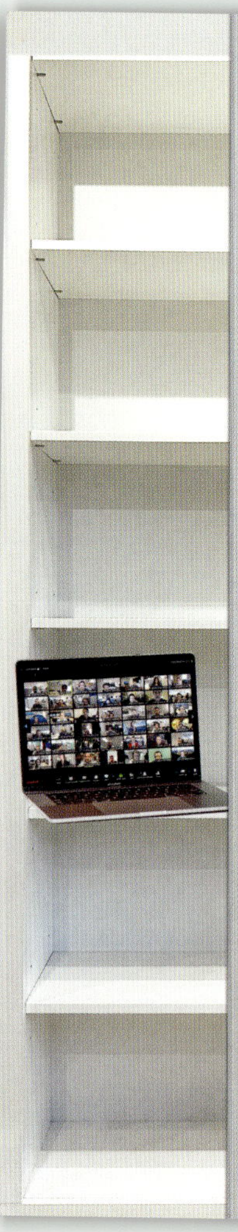

Chris Heath

14 May 2020

Andrea: Brian Eno said that pop music is about the creation of a new, imaginary world, which beckons the listener to enter it.

Chris: I think that's true as an ambition. But the interesting thing is how impossible creating an imaginary world is, based on the collision between trying to do that and the impossibility of doing it. Part of it is purely pragmatic. Es knows better than me that the literal pragmatics of putting together a pop performance are like watching ten thousand things fighting against whatever pure idea has been envisaged.

Es: That's such an understatement. Only ten thousand …

Chris: There you go! And there are two other actors also fighting against it, even though they're the ones who benefit the most: the artist and the audience. To be a nuts-and-bolts, jamming-in-a-garage group is just as much a fantasy, an imaginary world, as creating the most high-tech, complex, world-within-a-world vision.

Then there's the audience. When people talk about the shows they've seen, the greatest moments they articulate are being transported into something completely outside their quotidian experience. Yet, at the same time, the audience is resistant to the imaginary world. People's favourite bit is when the artist breaks through that and says, 'Goodnight Birmingham', or makes some stupid joke. Part of the sabotage from the audience is that on a basic level what they want, even if it's only an illusion, is a connection with the real person that they've projected all this stuff onto. So there's an incredible tension or collision between trying to create the imaginary world, and everyone, the audience and the artist, fighting against it.

Es: 'Collision' is a really interesting word in this collaborative sphere because we say collaboration, but often it's collision. We're turning things that have no matter associated with them – music, breath, and vibration – into these intransigent lumps of tour-able concrete and steel and brute materials.

Andrea: Is there a collision between an artist and their audience? What is their relationship?

Chris: Everyone's got a different idea of it. The people involved don't have the best understanding of what they want in it. I don't think the audience understands what entertains them best. The performer doesn't always understand both what entertains best and what makes them feel artistically satisfied. There are all kinds of contradictions and collisions happening. So one of the many things that goes into creating a world that's staged is managing that messed-up dialogue between them. It feels almost like a peace treaty where you give each side something that not just satisfies them, but thrills them. There's a structural compromise built into this in order to make it work.

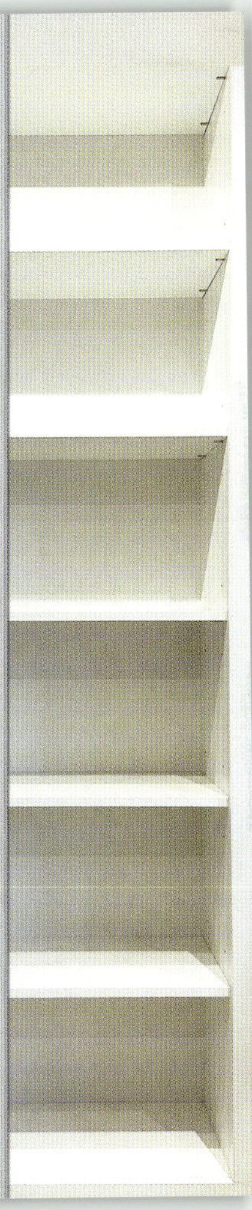

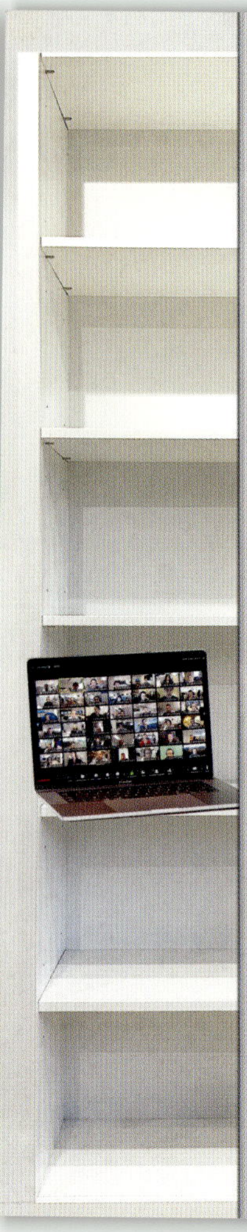

Virgil Abloh

29 May 2020

Es: What you can't tell over Zoom is that Virgil is literally twice my height. When I initially met Virgil, he was sitting in a corner just beyond Kanye, furiously doing Photoshop. I thought it was out of politeness to my shortness that you didn't stand up to meet me. It was only the third time I met you that I realized you were twice my height.

Virgil: That was the era of working at an impolite pace. We were all working so hard that we wouldn't even get up and shake someone's hand to meet. Kanye had given us an unbelievable passion pitch, and Es and I were the fingers and hands behind these inconceivable ideas. We were a motley crew, different talents put in a room because Kanye knew that all the people combined would make something greater than any of us individually.

Es: I have a strong memory of you and Kanye coming around to my studio the night of the 2011 London Riots. You could hardly cross London because it wasn't safe. Then finally you came and you played the new album, *Watch the Throne*, on repeat all night.

Virgil: You get into a room and by the time you leave the room you need to have a concrete idea. You don't leave the room until the epiphany happens. It's starting in quicksand, because the process is torrentially circular. That, to me, is the most defining moment of all of us trying to inject performance art into the veins of pop culture.

Kanye and I would work on laptops in a car, in a plane. The world was our studio. I'd be in Economy and he would come back from First Class and ask the person who was sitting next to me, 'Hey, do you want to sit in my seat up front?' It'd be like three in the morning with all the lights down and we'd be on Illustrator or

Photoshop. And we always called Es from our satellite lounges. Your approach was much more singular and focused on the history of theatre.

When we would go to your studio, those were the best work sessions because we had at our fingertips staff who could make models and articulate and add to the ideas of the process work. Working with models was something that we never did – we hadn't invested in that way of making – but I appreciated how foamcore and a piece of clay could illustrate an idea in a way that's more exciting than looking at it on a computer. Working those images into the right compositions expressed the way Kanye wanted the fans to feel. The staging had to be emotive. The ambition of the work was to try to raise the taste level above the status quo. Culture deserves more, not less. In theatre and art there is such a high level of intellect happening, and it can be the same if it's happening on MTV or at the Revel theatre. If we do good work, we expose some kid who's never going to go to the Royal Opera House to this level. That's important.

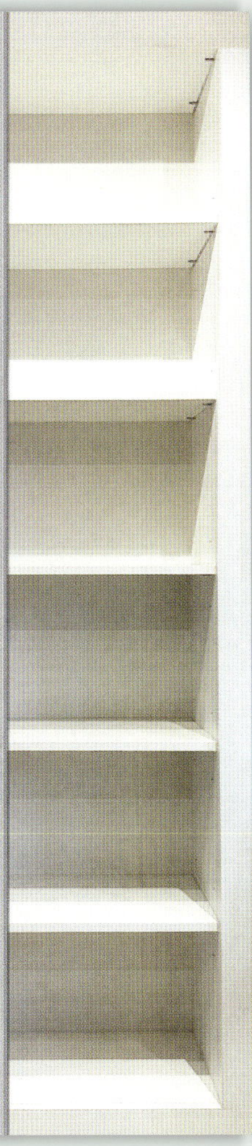

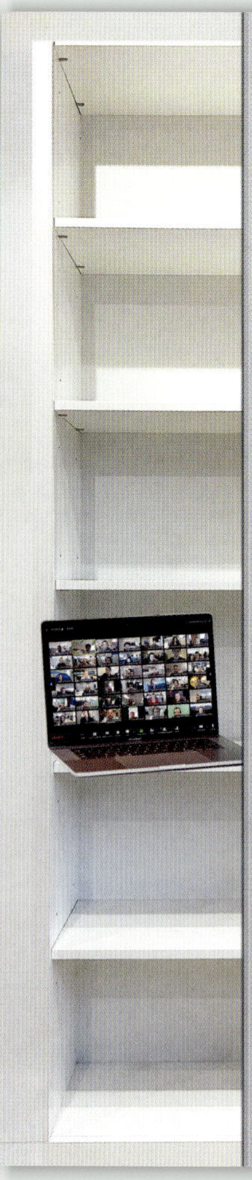

Keith Warner

5 May 2020

Es: Each collaborator arrives at a new project through the lens of whatever they've just been making, and whatever is colouring their cultural perspective at that moment. Collaborating is like picking up the threads of someone else's imagination and continuing the stitching.

Keith: Andrea, Es is the most driven person I have met in my life: her imagination is so driven it needs its own chauffeur.

If you've got somebody you can hold hands with and jump, it's fantastic. When we work on a design, the very weedy practical things often happen very late, like where to put the door. You first need the big world in which you want this thing to come alive because, without that, you're always just moving furniture around.

Es: And everyone collides with the text at a different moment. With *Macbeth*, there was one meeting when I'd made these big red paintings. They were strewn around the room when you walked in. And you said, 'This is all wonderful, but I think somewhere in the excitement you've forgotten that we're trying to do *Macbeth*.'

Keith: That sounds rude enough to be me.

12 May 2020

Andrea: Alice, how do you situate the practice of set design within the broader design landscape?

Alice: It's an interesting question because it has changed dramatically in recent years, and Es has had a big role to play in that change. Traditionally, set and stage design was seen as much more part of the theatre or the film industry than the design community. Yet there are historically wonderful examples. Es, I think you trained with the Motley Theatre Design Course? It's one of the great lesbian sagas of early twentieth-century London. These three women commissioned Marcel Breuer – when he and fellow Bauhausers were temporarily in London, having fled Nazi Germany – to design a theatre for them that had a hugely influential theatre school.

Yet in conventional historic retrospectives of modern design, set design is rarely mentioned. That's because so many areas of design, particularly when they're intensely gendered, have been marginalized for misogynistic or homophobic reasons. Just as interior design has rarely been taken seriously within critical design discourse, which I think has to do with so many women and gay men being prominent in that field, exactly the same happened in set design.

Es: Yes, I think the word 'set' is part of the problem. It would be like describing a choreographer as a 'step designer'.

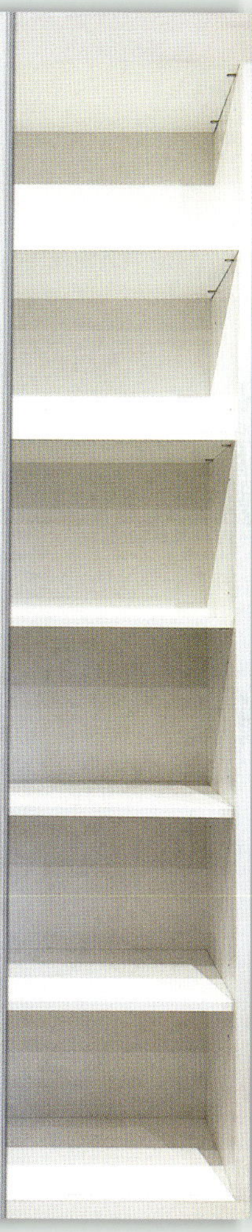

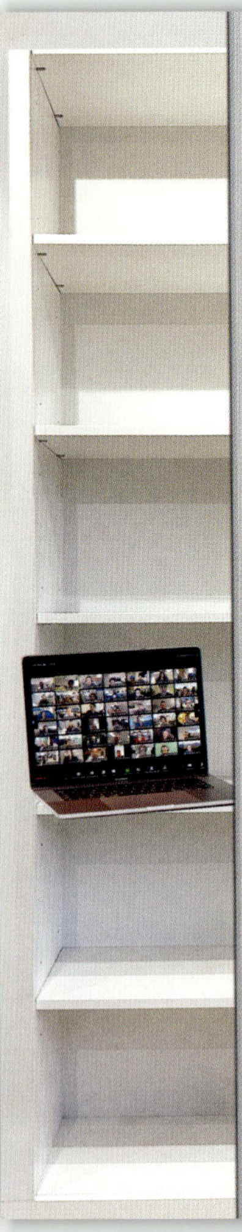

Sam Mendes

27 May 2020

Es: Sam, the list of five precepts that you wrote during our first design meeting is still on our studio wall. It has been the compass for us in everything ever since.

Sam: Early on, I wanted to make clear that I was working outside of the literal. That's what the list was about: to release you back into your world where you feel and continue to be a world leader. What struck me when I walked into your studio was that you'd created a model of the set in white cardstock. You'd put together the cube with its epic landscape. The way the curve of the screen sat with the strict functionality of the cube, the two things coexisted: that was the genius of it.

With *The Lehman Trilogy*, we needed to guide an audience through a simple shape into a very complex world. The obvious precedents to *Lehman* in Es's work were at the forefront of my mind. *Chimerica* was one of them, which was an endlessly changing, revolving cube of a very different sort. And another was the revolving rectangle of *Machinal* that she designed on Broadway. Those two examples depended on the effect of constantly changing elements – ceiling height, the narrowness of the stage, the way it was dressed, the way it was occupied. Within both of those plays there was a simple governing idea that made me feel a sense of unity and purpose moment-to-moment. In other people's design hands, those plays can seem bitty and fragmented, fractured even. But somehow, I was made to feel that there was a single unified intelligence behind it.

When you're searching for a good design, it's similar to getting an idea to rise like a hot air balloon. A good designer finds ways to throw the sandbags over so the balloon rises. Every time we threw a sandbag, the balloon went up a little more, and it got to this shape that felt just perfectly itself.

With the cube, you're deliberately repeating patterns like a dance, but the meanings change each time. So, deliberately, the organization of bodies becomes a pattern – the audience who watches it doesn't know that they're watching the same pattern, but they feel it. Unconsciously, in the way that you do with music, you feel that, 'Yes, I'm back in that world again but something subtle has shifted.' It's the shape of history: you understand it.

Es: You are ambidextrous between film and theatre. What is the correlation between the kinetic aspect of a dance with a camera and a dance with a moving environment?

Sam: I wouldn't have been able to make *1917* without having done *Lehman Trilogy*, and I think part of it is the kinetic element, in that you're constantly shifting perspective. Movement is very important. If the audience feels there's always the possibility of movement, then once things start to move there's a sense that you're being led. You're not going to get stuck.

But also with *Lehman*, we'd set ourselves a task: here are the tools we have to tell this story and we can't move outside of these tools. There is an immense freedom when the audience understands what the rules are. Once you open the door to what Christopher Marlowe called 'infinite riches in a little room', then new and interesting ideas will emerge within the language you've created ... That's one of the things I admire most about Es's work – the economy of means. The determination to find something both simple and epic. Something that expresses scale on a magnitude of what you're trying to do but at the same time is so simple, you think, 'Of course, why didn't I think of that?'

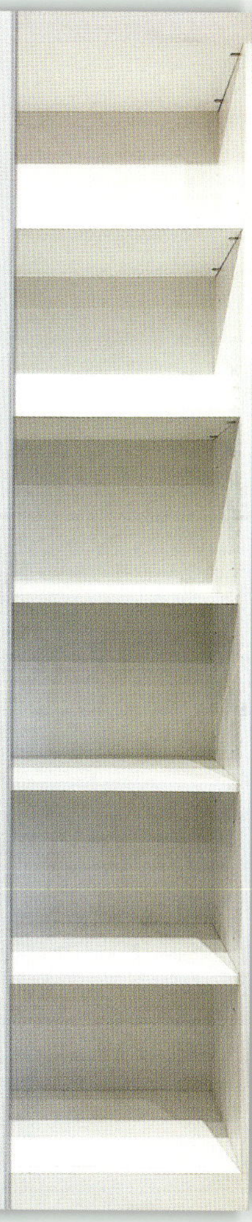

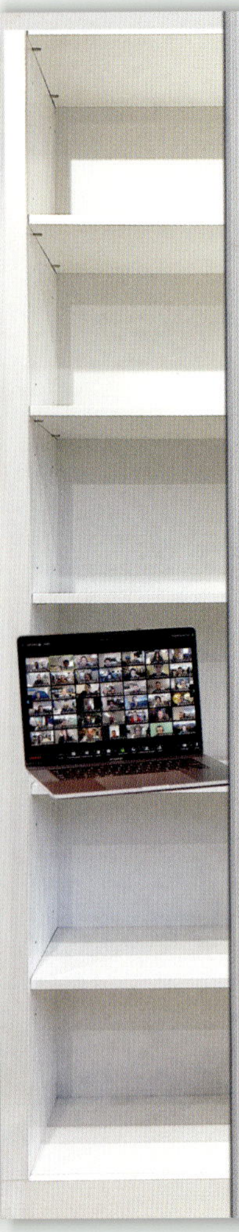

Alex Poots

30 June 2020

Es: Alex, when we first met you ran a festival called 'Only Connect', and since then I have witnessed you constantly connecting makers who would not normally collaborate, in roles they might not normally inhabit.

Alex: You know, I did my dissertation at university on the idea that seemingly different art forms can have a shared essence. It came to me when I was in Indonesia and I heard a certain piece of Gamelan music. It completely shocked me how much it sounded like an aspect of Miles Davis's *In a Silent Way*, which is one of his most important, transformational works. It's not about mashing things up, it's about recognizing two things that might be compatible.

It's important to embrace the magic of the arts. If you think of them as magical, in the deeply spiritual sense of the word, they can be transcendent. Like the magic of Bach, who was a great wizard and could make you feel differently through dots on a page. When people are in their dying moments, some of the things they'll value most in their lives are how they felt when they heard a particular piece of music or saw a play or attended a concert.

Es: Charm, I witnessed a Harry Potter-like phenomenon where your body seemed to enter into Rosalía’s movement. I’d never seen two artists morph into each other in that way.

Charm: I know it sounds crazy, but we talk about having a sense that our energy, our spirits, are intertwined. I think it’s why I’m sometimes very exhausted. It’s more than choreography what I do. Even when I’m performing next to Kendrick, everyone always says, ‘You guys look like one. How are you doing that?’ I don’t know how to explain it.

Es: I think there is a kind of magic in your work. It’s like an incantation; it transports us.

Charm: It’s through dance that I can emote. It’s something that’s in me. To create, I take what is given to me and how I feel. I believe that everything that comes, comes from the ancestors. Once I take what’s given and blend that with who the artists are, the movement transforms to another realm. There is no way I could have made the performances with Dua, Rosalía, Kendrick, or any artist I work with without having something bigger than me driving me.

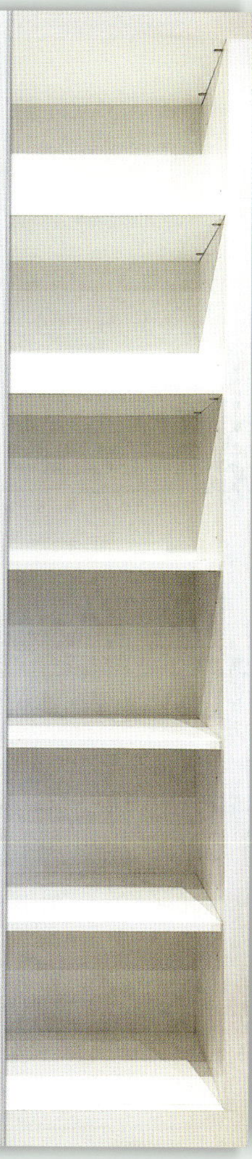

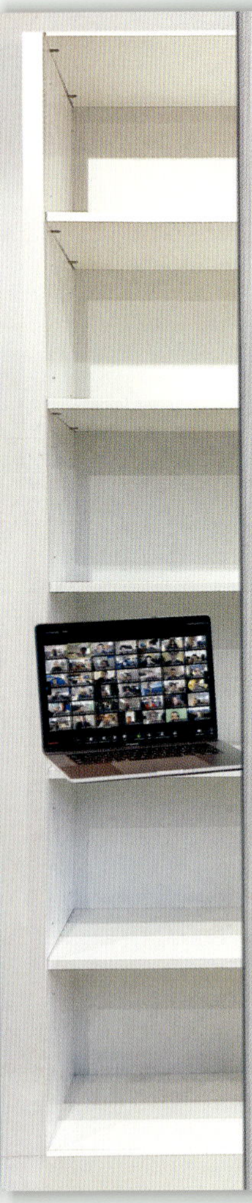

Kasper Holten

9 June 2020

Kasper: I think for opera to work it needs to be rooted in the personal and emotional. But at the same time opera is a cynical, practical art form where the lead singer might be replaced at a moment's notice and all the work you poured into details and psychology is lost. That psychological precision, which is so important to make opera work, needs to be visible as a bold gesture. It needs to be translated into something that survives even if you replace the main character. This is what Es is so brilliant at doing at any scale. She takes something very intimate and turns it into something extremely visible, which communicates clearly with the audience. She makes the internal external. We try to show what the world looks like from the inside, which is often very different from the world as it is.

Opera is ridiculous to start with. There's an orchestra playing, everyone is singing to each other, there's a man waving his arms in the front. The whole thing is so obviously artificial. Yet there's a great freedom in that. You don't have to try and convince people that this is credible or natural.

Es: When I'm asked which of all the different media I work in is the one I couldn't live without, it's always opera. It's surprising, but through this extreme artifice you can access profound truth.

Kasper: Yes. Opera is about the tectonic plate shifts. It's about the big, big echoes in the human soul, and it will always feel current because the stories it tells – about love, hate, betrayal, loneliness, death, lust – will always resonate.

Willie Williams

1 June 2020

Willie: The concert-touring world is remarkably small because there are so few people who are prepared to put up with it. It takes over your entire life. As a show designer, I always say my job is like making someone else's wedding dress: it doesn't matter what I think about it. It's about creating for this extraordinary person – the person who does the magic – an environment in which they can flourish. And each time you start with a new artist you're entering an entirely new universe that has its own rules and physics. Obviously as designers we have our own agenda, we want to further the form. But to be that portal between the music and the audience, it's not a normal thing.

Es, you came to us from opera, which is unafraid of scale, and is based on narrative rather than on equipment.

Es: Yes, the logistics of large-scale tours are brutal. The current emphasis is on efficient portable instruments and structures that can relay the performer with maximum luminosity to the back of a stadium within 48 hours of arriving tightly packed in trucks. Like giant Meccano sets, lighting, video and staging elements return to inventory and are reused. The largest element of a tour's climate impact is the CO_2 emitted by the audience travelling to the venue. As well as improving public transport and making every aspect of touring circular and sustainable, I think the fundamental question we need to ask of any mass gathering is: is it societally and culturally worth the inevitable planetary impact, or not. Stadium tours will eventually use the sound, lighting and video equipment permanently installed in each venue. The real event is what's happening between singer, audience and the setting sun.

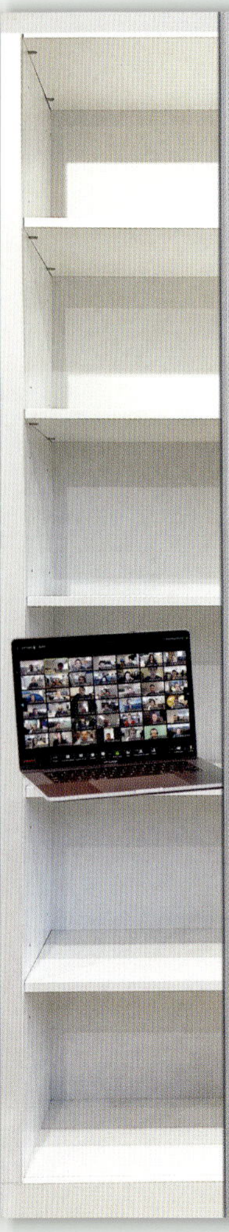

Conrad Shawcross

11 June 2020

Es: I remember feeling very emotional when I held one of the small *Schism* sculptures that was on your studio shelf. It felt like an unhealable, infinite wound.

Conrad: The *Schism* pieces investigate the tetrahedron, which is incredibly ordered. It's made of four equilateral triangles. When you start putting them together, you would expect them to form a bigger tetrahedron – like when you put nine cubes of the same size together, they form a bigger cube. You'd expect there to be a rational, almost fractional, nature to it, but by some quirk of nature, the tetrahedron does not tessellate with itself. It forms these weird cracks and fissures and failed geometries. It never heals, it never seals itself. It's quite dystopic. It implies there is a sort of godless universe or that there is a platonic ideal that is not happening – it will never be resolved. As with any piece of conceptual art, it's not really up to me to see what the resonance is, but it is quite disturbing. Yet maybe in a different time it will feel optimistic, that this thing is healing and coming together at the moment when it feels like it's falling apart.

8 June 2020

Es: In 2016, Beyoncé paused the *Formation* concert in Scotland for a one-minute silence in the wake of the shooting of Alton Sterling and Philando Castile in the US. She filled the monolith with their names along with many others who died as a result of police brutality. Then she sang 'Freedom'.

JaQuel: At one stretch, it seemed that every day we would wake up to see another killing of a Black man by the police. Go to sleep, there was another name; go to sleep, another name; go to sleep, another. Four deaths and we were so heavy. 'Freedom' was this moment in our show, a release, a cry out. We were dancing in water, kicking and throwing it around. It was a beautiful, powerful number, one of my favourites and one of the simplest, too. This process of being fearless is very much like that of a child. Kids don't know anything is wrong until you tell them, 'Don't do that.' I try to attain that fearlessness and openness through movement. There's no gravity, there's no floor, there's no wrong. There's beauty within that.

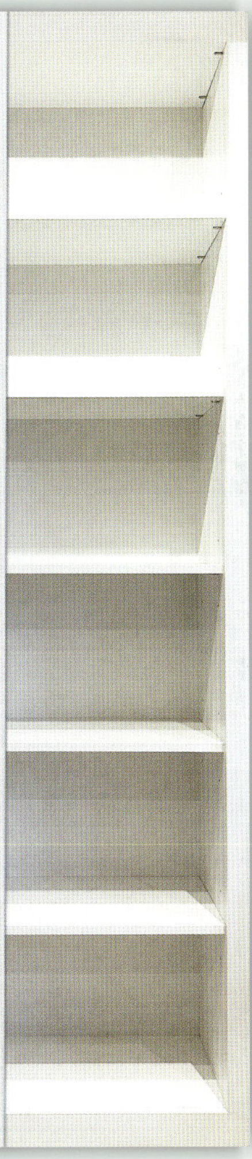

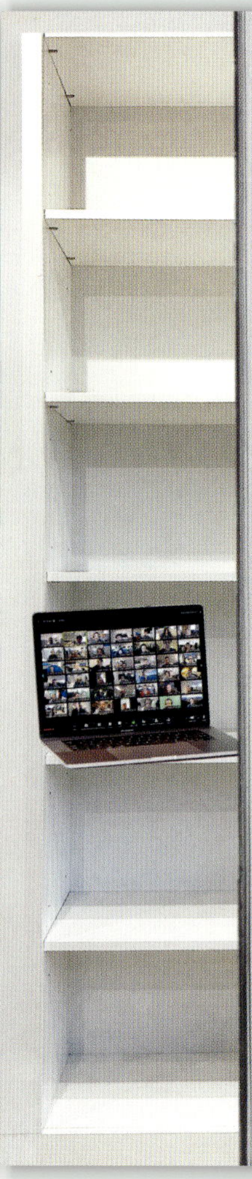

Hannah Barry

15 May 2020

Es: Hannah, it was thanks to you that I found the Peckham warehouse where we made my first art installation, *Mirror Maze*, in 2016.

Hannah: Es, you are fearless about whether or not things are popular. That certainly comes from the broad experience you've had across a range of fields. You can be very genre-specific and also manage to entwine disciplines. When I talk about the collective reading work that we did with Carlo Rovelli and Benedict Cumberbatch at Bold Tendencies, it's a piece that almost defies genre.

You are defining another way of doing things that is reverent to speaking and acting and performing and exhibiting, but has no discipline yet attached to it to describe it. That's a very, very interesting area to operate in, and it's there that the audience and participation become much more available.

I think it's possible to be many people and many things, and in order to do that one has to be as free as possible. And being constrained by questions – Is it art? Is it theatre design? Is it pop music? – is short-sighted. When you allow them to inhabit each other, it's a special thing. I'm glad you had that decisive year in 2016, Es. Sometimes you remember who you are, and sometimes you are able to forget who you are, and in doing that you are able to do more.

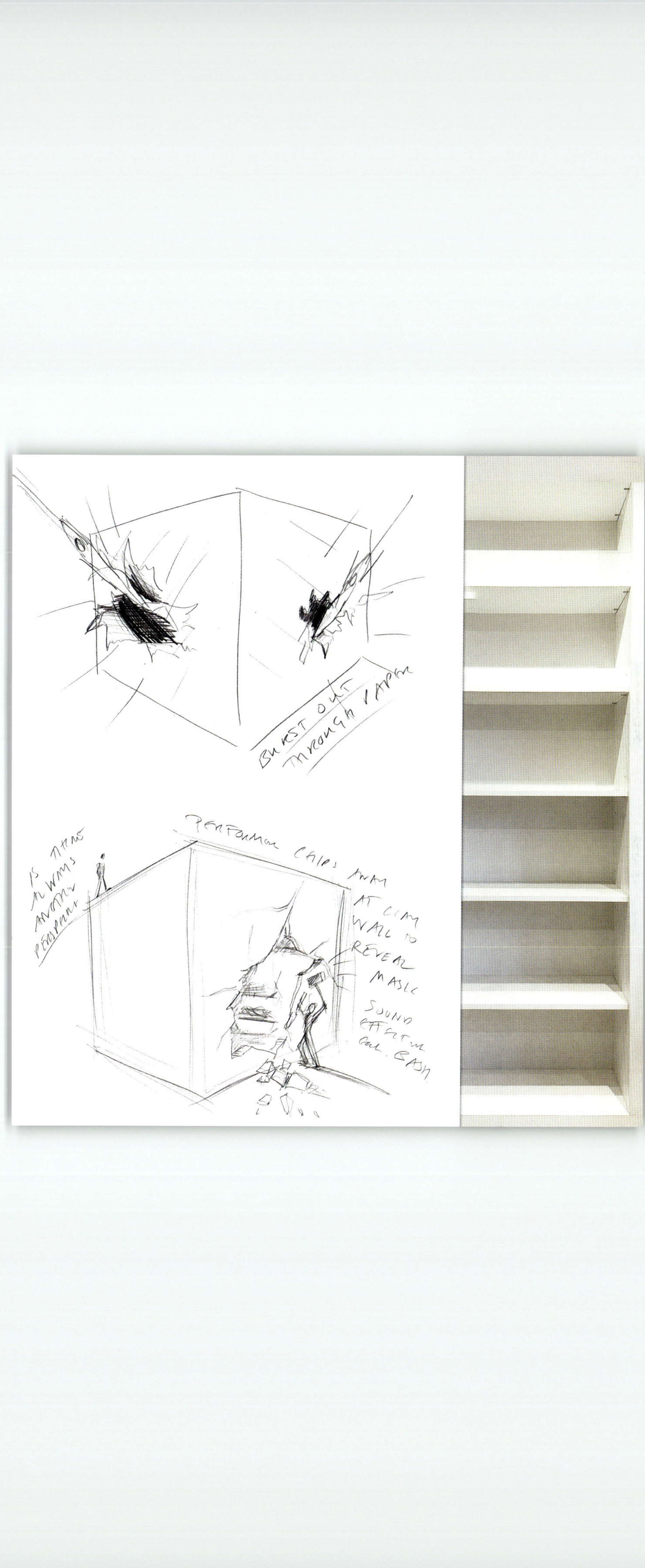
BURST OUT THROUGH PAPER

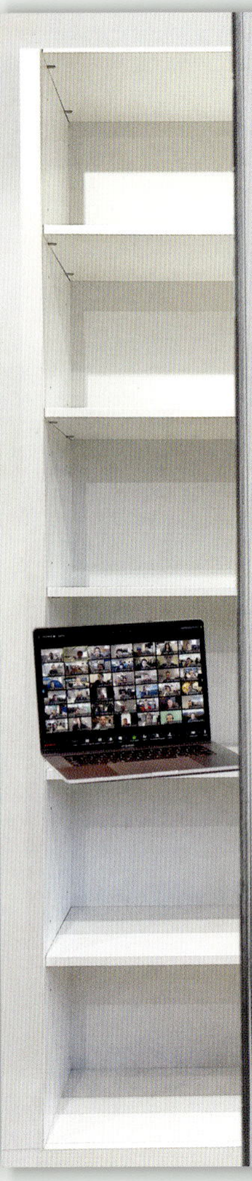

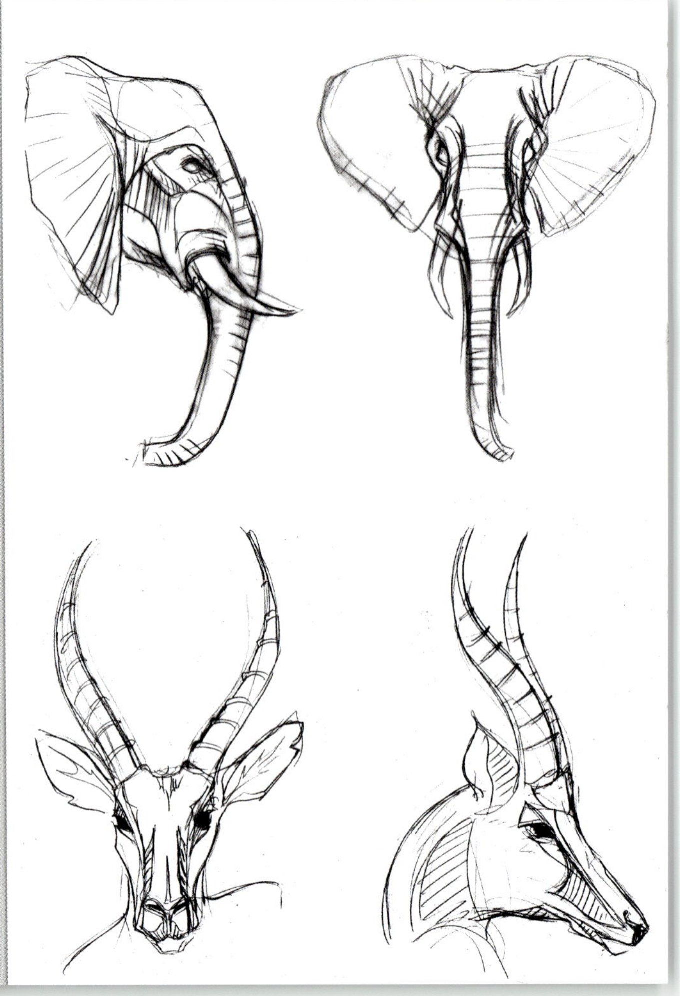

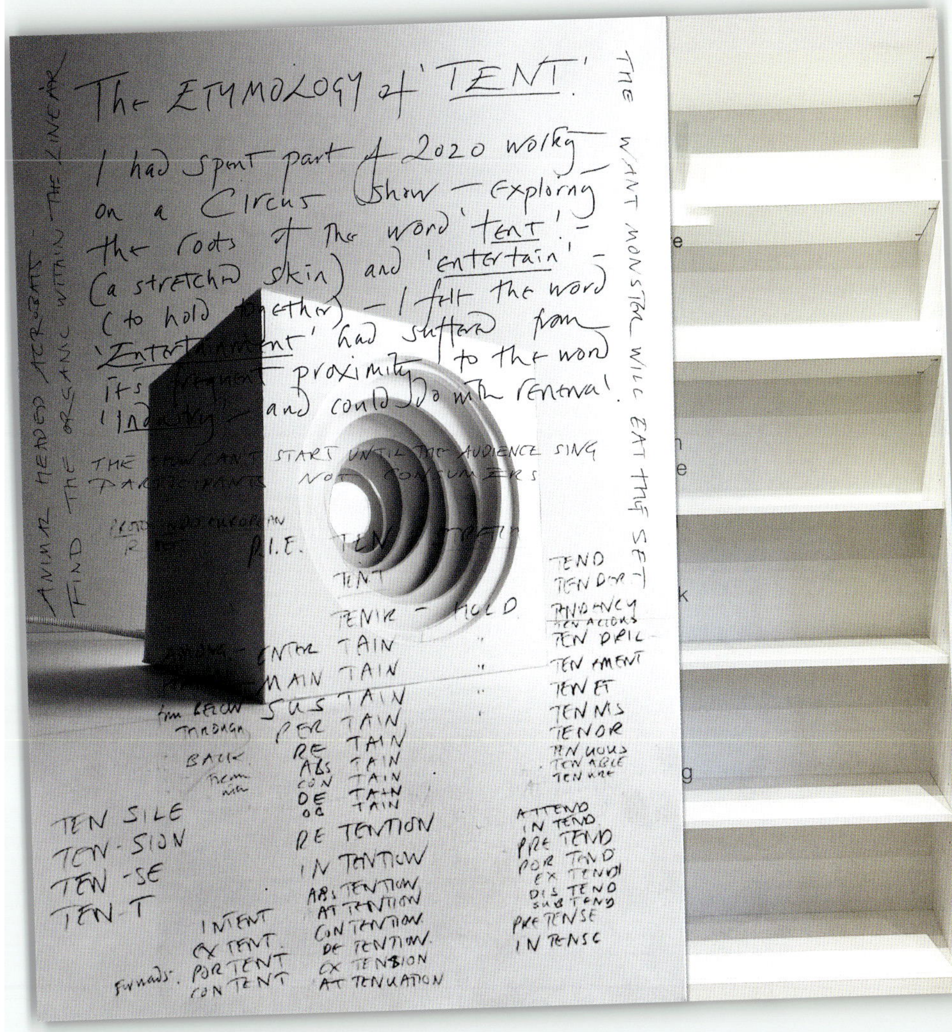
The ETYMOLOGY of 'TENT'
I had spent part of 2020 working on a Circus show – exploring the roots of the word 'tent' – (a stretched skin) and 'entertain' – (to hold together) – I felt the word 'Entertainment' had suffered from its frequent proximity to the word 'Industry' – and could do with renewal.
THE SHOW CAN'T START UNTIL THE AUDIENCE SING
PARTICIPANTS NOT CONSUMERS
THE WANT MONSTER WILL EAT THE SET
ANIMAL HEADED ACROBATS
FIND THE ORGANIC WITHIN THE LINEAR
P.I.E.
TENT
TENIR – HOLD
TEND
TENDER
TENDENCY
TEN SILE
TEN-SION
TEN-SE
TEN-T
RE TENTION
IN TENTION
INTENT
EX TENT
POR TENT
CON TENT
ATTEND
PRE TEND
PRETENSE
IN TENSE

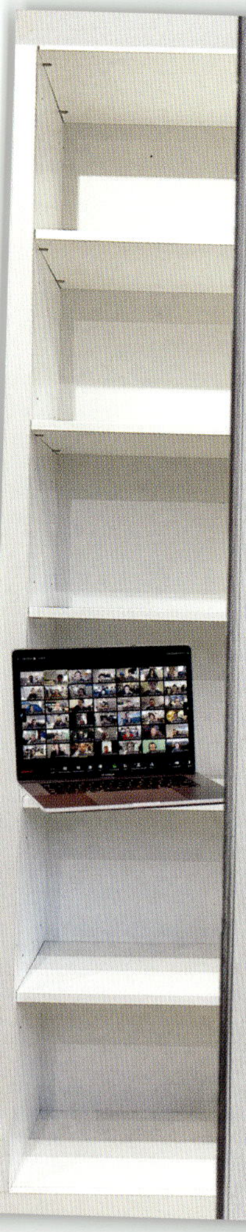

Ha

Ha
po
ha
an
the
Be
aln

Yo
sp
dis
int
an

I th
or
co
po
ea
yea
so
yo

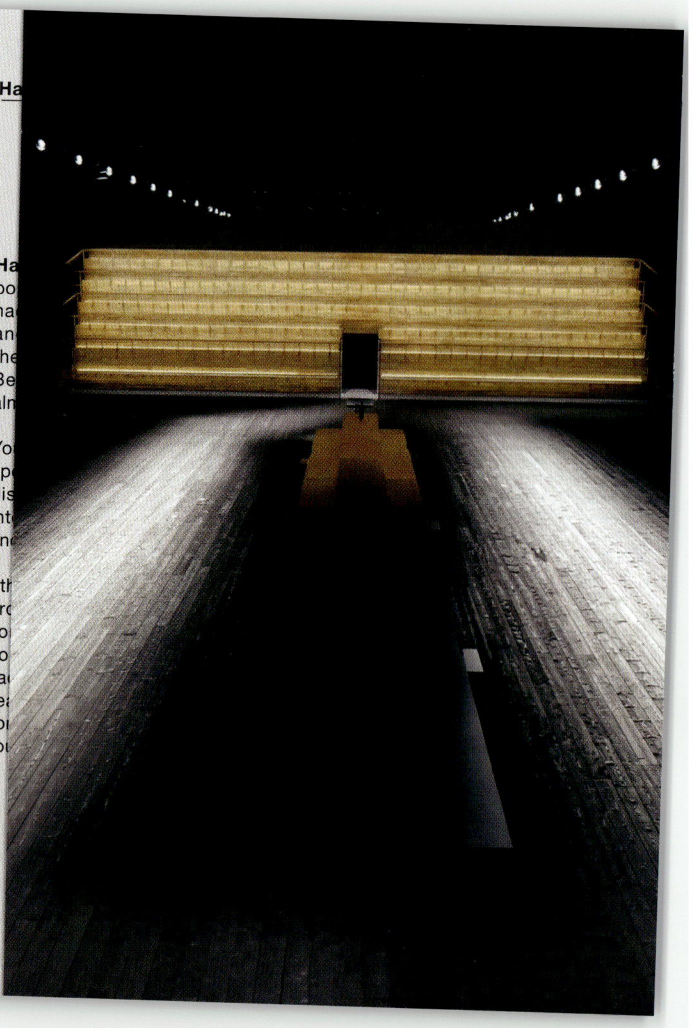

SILENCED CHOIR

I want to be a witness of my time.

Nicolas Ghesquière

The very last piece I worked on before gatherings and performances became temporarily extinct during the coronavirus lockdowns was 'Collisions of Time', the Louis Vuitton Fall/Winter 2020 Women's runway show at the Louvre Museum in Paris on 7 March 2020. Working in concert with the Metropolitan Museum's costume exhibition *About Time*, which would explore the evolution of the female form through fashion over centuries, Nicolas Ghesquière and I envisaged a 200-strong choir in period dress spanning half a millennium, paralleling the portraits in the Louvre collection. The costumes were designed by Milena Canonero, who frequently collaborated with Stanley Kubrick on films that stretch across centuries. The haunting choral music – a composition by Woodkid and Bryce Dessner of The National – reworked a theme by Bach's contemporary Nicolas de Grigny, who died at 30, never having played at the Louvre. Choirs were becoming mass spreading events at the time: many of the singers, as well as the opera director Francisco Negrin who staged them, left Paris taking the virus with them.

IDEAS TO FORMS

The work is not so much an end in itself but a kind of recording process ... the crumbs that you're leaving to remind yourself later when you look back at this piece, who you were when you made it and how you've changed since you made it.

These words refer to the series of small paper sculptures that I made during lockdown – alone in the studio, re-engaged in the practice of thinking with my fingers, bypassing the brain. During the pandemic, I was spending hours each day on Zoom conferences with colleagues in theatre, pop music, fashion, activism and art. Each community was filled with a combination of fear and curiosity: fearful that the structures that had informed our practices were crumbling, curious about ways to re-invent them.

In mid-May 2020, I was asked by the BBC to self-film a masterclass for their programme *Culture in Quarantine*, encouraging creativity for those locked down at home. I watched Antony Gormley's masterclass and Paul Smith's, then cleared my studio back to its white bones to film my own. Using paper, scissors and glue, I guided viewers through the process of translating an idea – through research, sketching and making – into a series of forms. The resultant projection-mapped paper sculptures formed the basis of the *Forest of Us* installation that would open a year later in Miami.

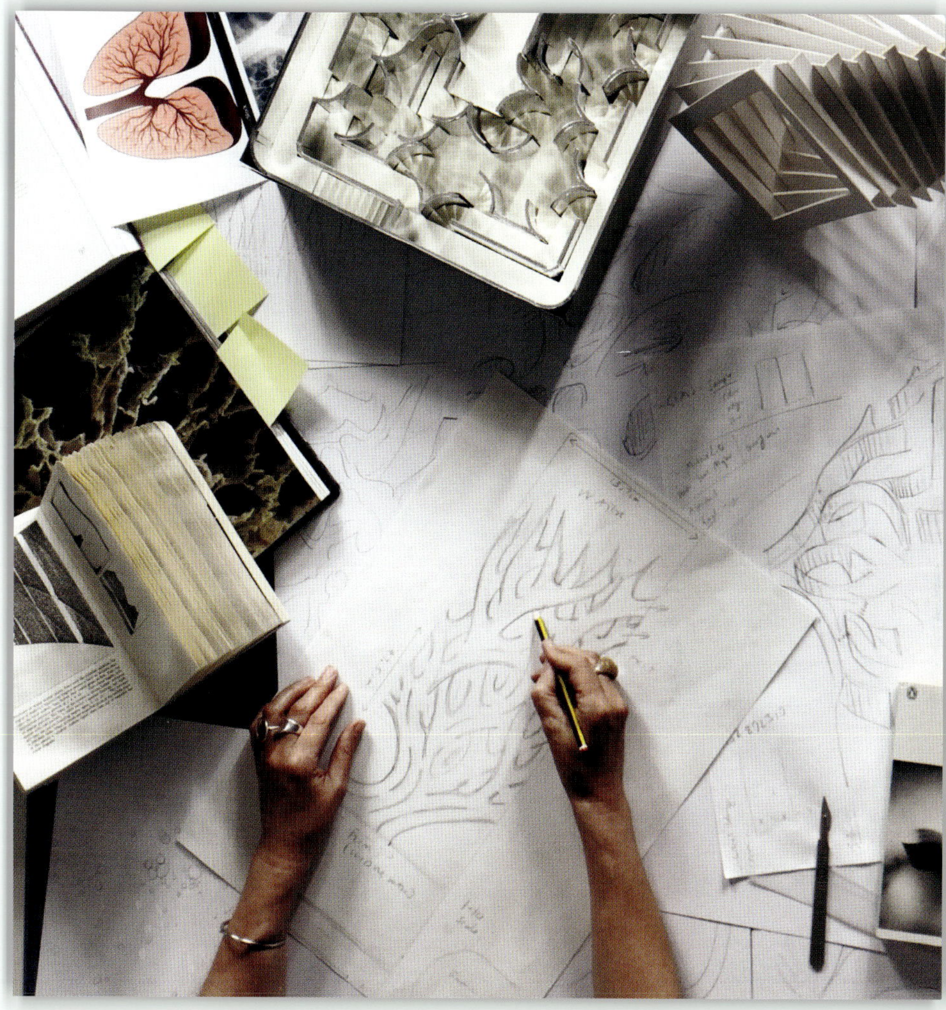

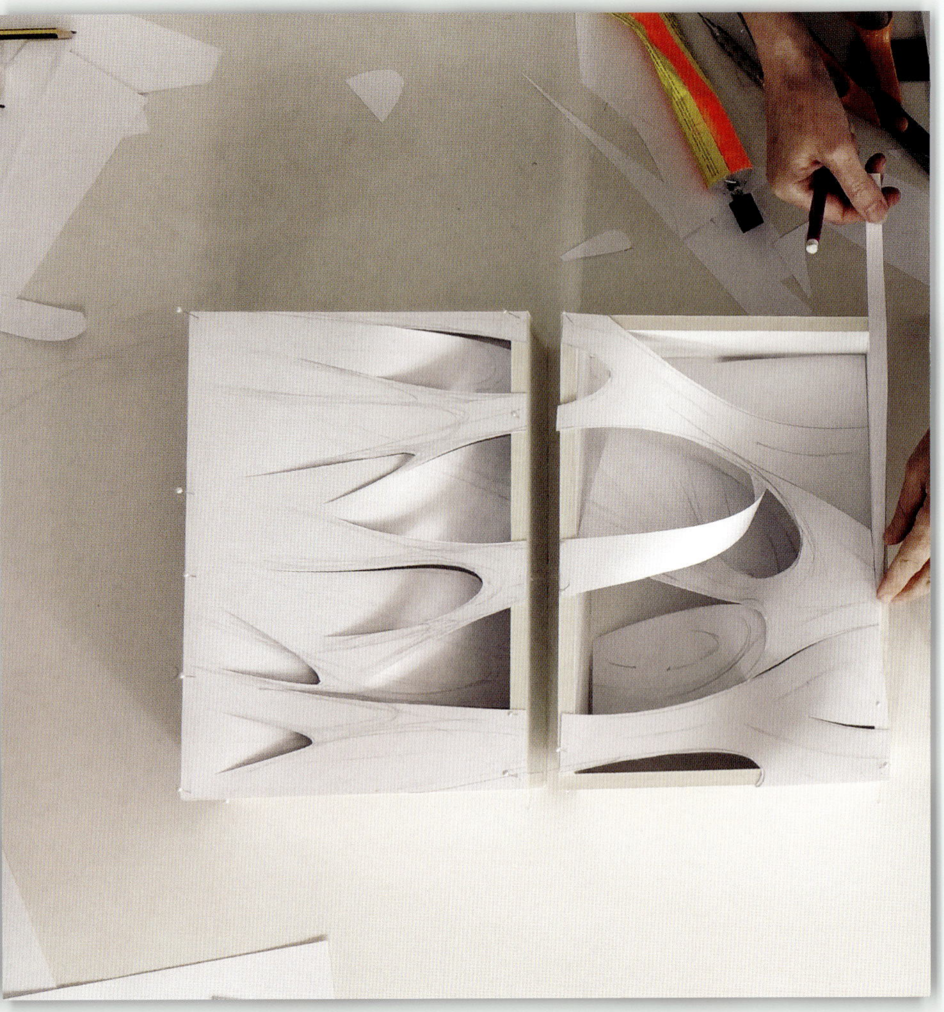

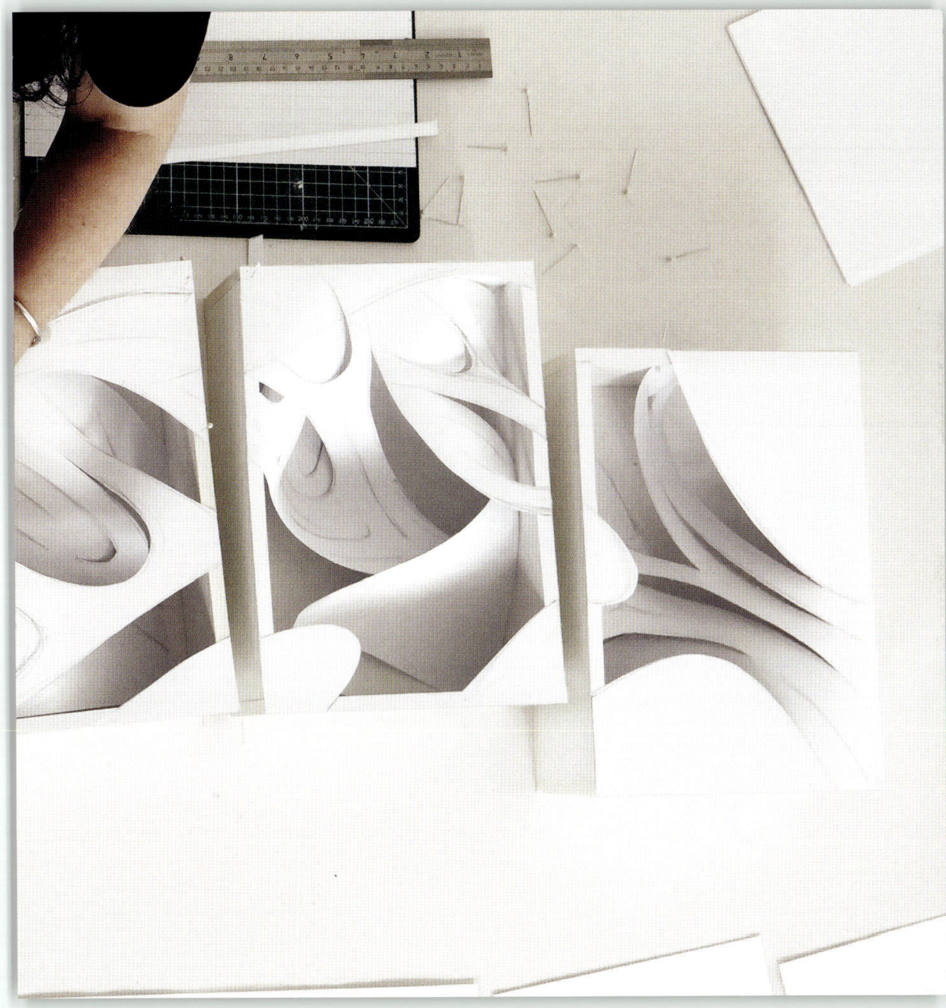

I SAW THE WORLD END

The unleashed power of the atom has changed everything save our modes of thinking and we thus drift toward unparalleled catastrophe.

Albert Einstein

To mark the 75th anniversary of the bombings of Hiroshima and Nagasaki, the Imperial War Museums commissioned a new work to be shown on the largest single digital screen in Europe, at Piccadilly Circus in London on 6 and 9 August 2020. Working with my Japanese studio colleague Machiko Weston, we created a 45-metre-wide illuminated collective reading. Locked down in separate studios, we carried out our research in separate languages. Half of the text – read by me in English – spanned over 75 years and traced the origination of the atomic bomb in fiction by H. G. Wells, the translation directly from fiction to physics by Leo Szilard, and the aspiration, rationale and rehearsal by the leading protagonists of the Manhattan Project. The other half of the text was read in Japanese by Machiko – all from accounts of the moments the atomic bombs landed on Hiroshima and Nagasaki. A screen-splitting line expressed at once the potential for division: splitting the screen, splitting the atom, the division between fiction and fact, race divisions, the division between humans and the planet; and also the possibility of reconnection, as the reader moves their gaze from one side of the line to the other, repairing the schism. Part of the binaural score featured a cello line extracted from Wagner's opera, *Parsifal* – a reference to Deryck Cooke's seminal work on Wagner which inspired the title.

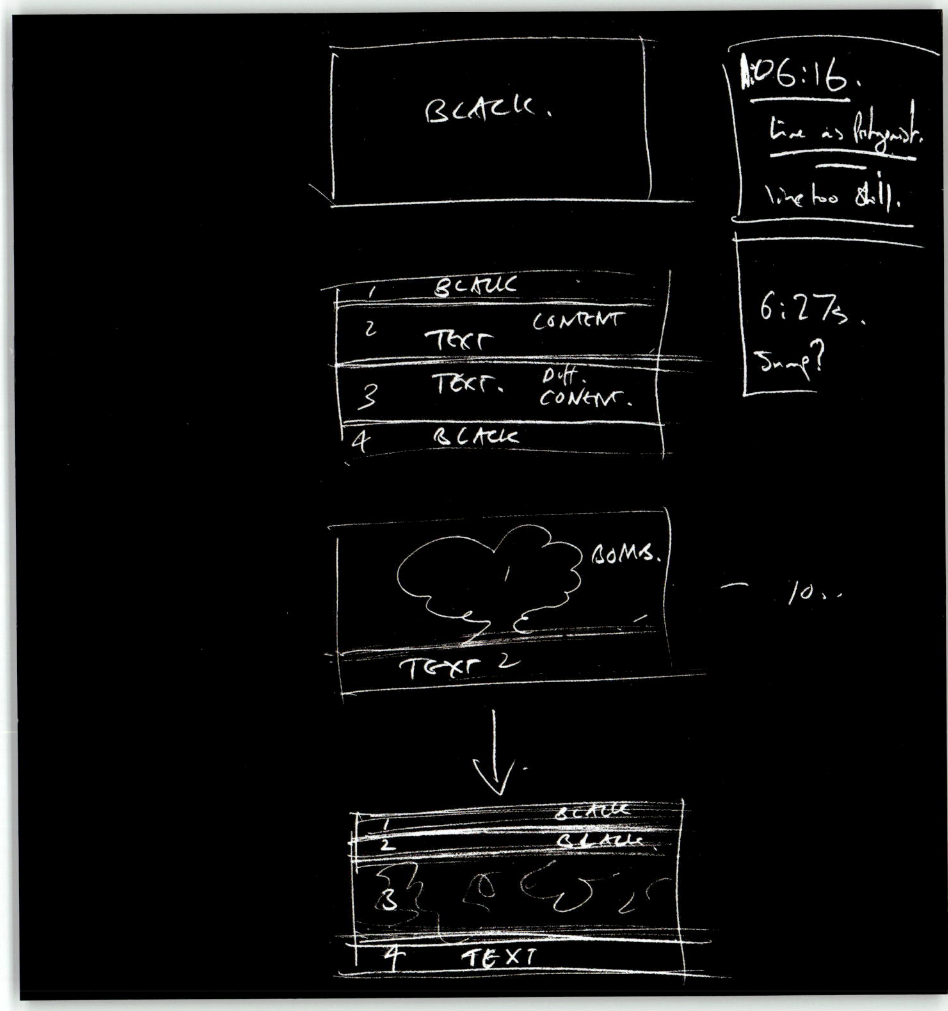
BLACK.
06:16.
1 BLACK
2 TEXT CONTENT
3 TEXT. Diff. CONTENT.
4 BLACK
6:27s.
BOMB.
TEXT 2
1 BLACK
2 BLACK
3
4 TEXT

DO IT

Find a hill it has to be a steep hill …
Roll down hill yelling
'i am not my body, i am the universe' …
Repeat until dizzy, spinning falling spiraling

Precious Okoyomon, *do it*

During the 2020 lockdown, curator Hans Ulrich Obrist invited a group of artists, poets, philosophers and scientists to make new works for his *do it* exhibition, the world's longest-running 'exhibition in progress', which began in Paris in 1993 as a conversation between Hans Ulrich and the artists Christian Boltanski and Bertrand Lavier. A *do it* is a score or written instruction by an artist to be interpreted and re-enacted by the reader. Aiming to encourage people to make their own works of art while locked down in their homes, Hans Ulrich relaunched the series as *do it (home)*. Yoko Ono, Olafur Eliasson, Tracey Emin, Marina Abramović, Tomás Saraceno and more contributed thought experiments, recipes, gardening ideas, poems and personal revolutions, which were published in June 2021 as *140 Artists' Ideas for Planet Earth*. Although each contributor was writing in isolation, many converged on themes of symbiosis between humans and the rest of the biosphere. My *do it* was an invitation to the reader to observe and draw both the bronchial trees within our lungs which facilitate our breathing, and the parallel structures of trees which render the air breathable. I continued to contemplate and study these human and more-than-human structures throughout the lockdown, alone in my studio, as I prepared initial ideas for the Miami installation, *Forest of Us*.

DEVLIN, Es
(2020)

Find a photograph of two trees.

Find an x-ray image of the two bronchial trees
within a pair of human lungs.

Trace over both.

Overlay the two tracings.

Contemplate the visual connection:

the bifurcating geometry that defines both:

the structures inside us that allow us to breathe;

the structures outside us that make the air breathable.

As you breathe in, visualise the 600 million alveoli, like
leaves on the branches of the bronchial trees within your lungs

As you breathe out, visualise the stomata on the leaves
of the 3 trillion trees which make your breathing possible

If you have $8 go to www.institutoterra.org and plant a tree
Think of it growing as you breathe.

ABOUT TIME

Time is how you spend your love.

Nick Laird, 'The Last Saturday in Ulster'

The costume collection at the Metropolitan Museum in New York City documents one and a half centuries of socio-political history through the shifting architecture of the female form. It is intriguing that the body parts subjected to the wildest architectural extremities are those that relate to childbearing: the hips, the bust, the belly. Perhaps our ever-shifting relationship to the female form is an expression of our evolving attitude to our own propagation, our future survival. The October 2020 *About Time* exhibition, curated by Andrew Bolton, held the visitor securely within a grandfather-clock-like interior with a central brass pendulum steadily ticking from 1850 to 1914. At 1914, the clock stopped abruptly and visitors entered a dark No Man's Land and emerged in a space fragmented by sliced glass and mirror. As if a smashed clock had reconstituted itself into a glimmering, quivering new timepiece, the linear narrative was disrupted by shards of reflection and refraction. The visitor had to work harder to stay on course, to keep their eyes from being drawn in every direction. The clock ticked faster, with seconds calibrated into nanoseconds. The title 'About Time' was also an admonition and invitation to consider the circular design principles which the fashion industry urgently needs to adopt to keep the Earth habitable by humans.

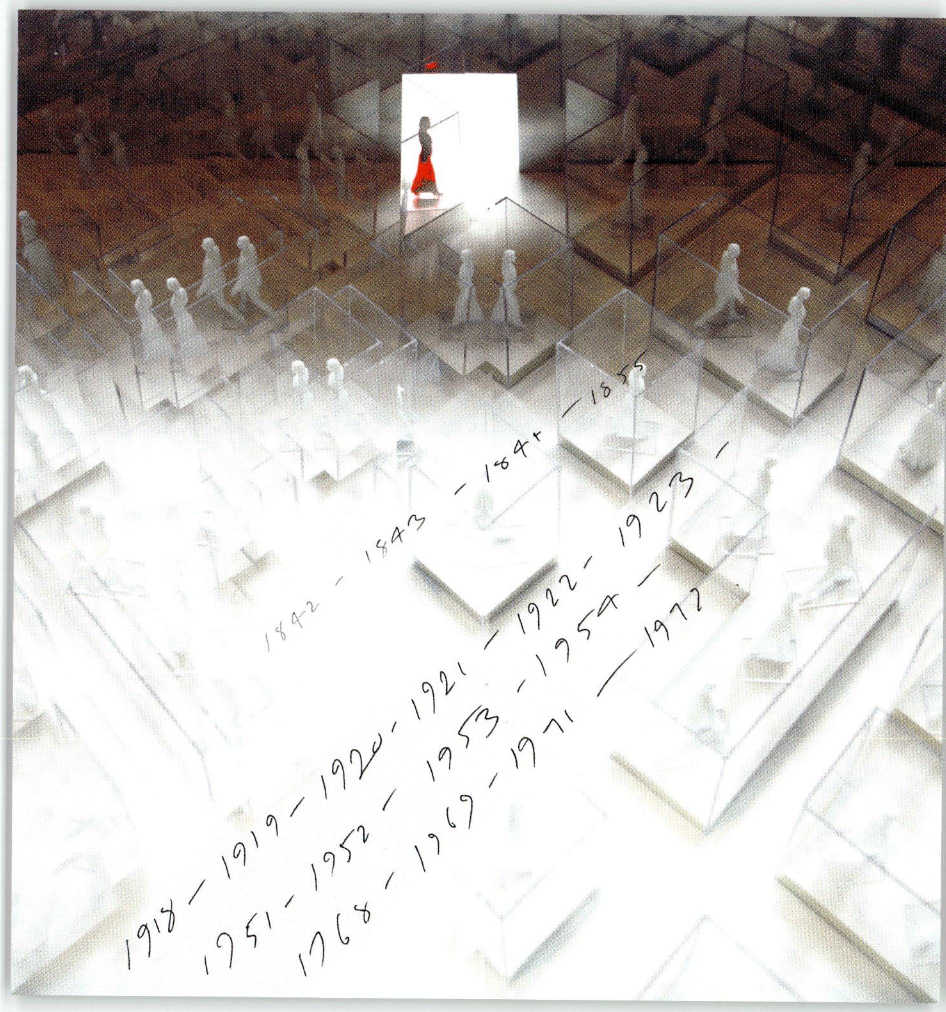
1842 – 1843 – 1844 – 1855
1918 – 1919 – 1920 – 1921 – 1922 – 1923 –
1951 – 1952 – 1953 – 1954 –
1968 – 1969 – 1971 – 1972

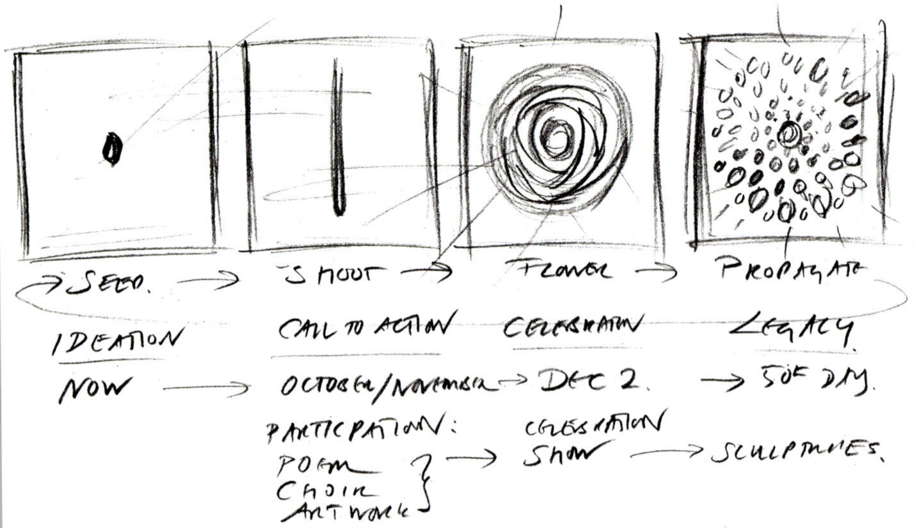
SEED.
SHOOT
FLOWER
PROPAGATE
IDEATION
CALL TO ACTION
CELEBRATION
LEGACY.
NOW
OCTOBER/NOVEMBER
DEC 2.
PARTICIPATION:
POEM
CHOIR
ARTWORK
CELEBRATION SHOW
SCULPTURES.

THE SEED

If there are no mangroves, then the sea will have no meaning. It's like a tree with no roots, for the mangroves are the roots of the sea.

Mad-Ha Ranwasii

I worked closely with a group of predominantly female Emirati artists, poets and researchers on *The Seed*, a 15-metre-high 'floating', revolving sculpture on the waters within the Jubail Mangrove Park near Abu Dhabi. The sides of the cube were inscribed with illuminated apertures whose forms were based on the life cycle of a mangrove plant, from single seed to shoot, flower, and finally disseminated seeds. Known as the 'rainforests of the sea', this amphibious species sequesters up to five times more carbon than other forest ecosystems while acting as a defensive frontline against coastal soil erosion, and the country was embarking on a quest to plant 100 million mangroves by 2030. The sculpture formed the canvas for a performance that took place on 2 December 2020, the UAE's annual celebration. It was brought to life by projected interviews with Bangladeshi, Filipino, Sri Lankan and Indian doctors, nurses, teachers, builders, scientists and drivers who help make up 90% of the country's population, and who had formed the country's frontline defences through the past nine months of the coronavirus pandemic. This was prior to the advent of readily available vaccines, and the work was extremely complex to produce within the logistical parameters of highly restricted international travel, closed borders, stringent social distancing and daily COVID testing. Each of our team spent two weeks in hotel-room quarantine before arriving on site in the turquoise shallows of the Persian Gulf.

34–35

FOREST FOR CHANGE

I tried to discover, in the rumour of forests and waves, words that other men could not hear, and I pricked up my ears to listen to the revelation of their harmony.

Gustave Flaubert, *November*

When Somerset House director Jonathan Reekie mentioned that the Enlightenment principles on which the building was founded specifically forbade trees in the courtyard, I resolved to plant a temporary forest there for the June 2021 London Design Biennale. In Shakespeare and the Brothers Grimm, forests are often places where protagonists get lost in the wilderness, encounter ordeals, and emerge transformed. Working with the team at Project Everyone, which makes people aware of the 17 UN Sustainable Development Goals, we wanted visitors to emerge from our forest more informed about the goals and how they could contribute to the world achieving them by 2030. Brian Eno's compilation of birdsong animated the forest, aligning specific bird calls to each hour of the day. An illuminated, polychrome, mirrored sculpture at the heart of the forest introduced visitors to the 17 brightly coloured UN Global Goals and invited them to add their voices to a collective audio message, which was played at the COP26 Climate Change Conference in Glasgow later that year. The 400 trees were replanted in parks in Islington and Southwark at the end of the Biennale.

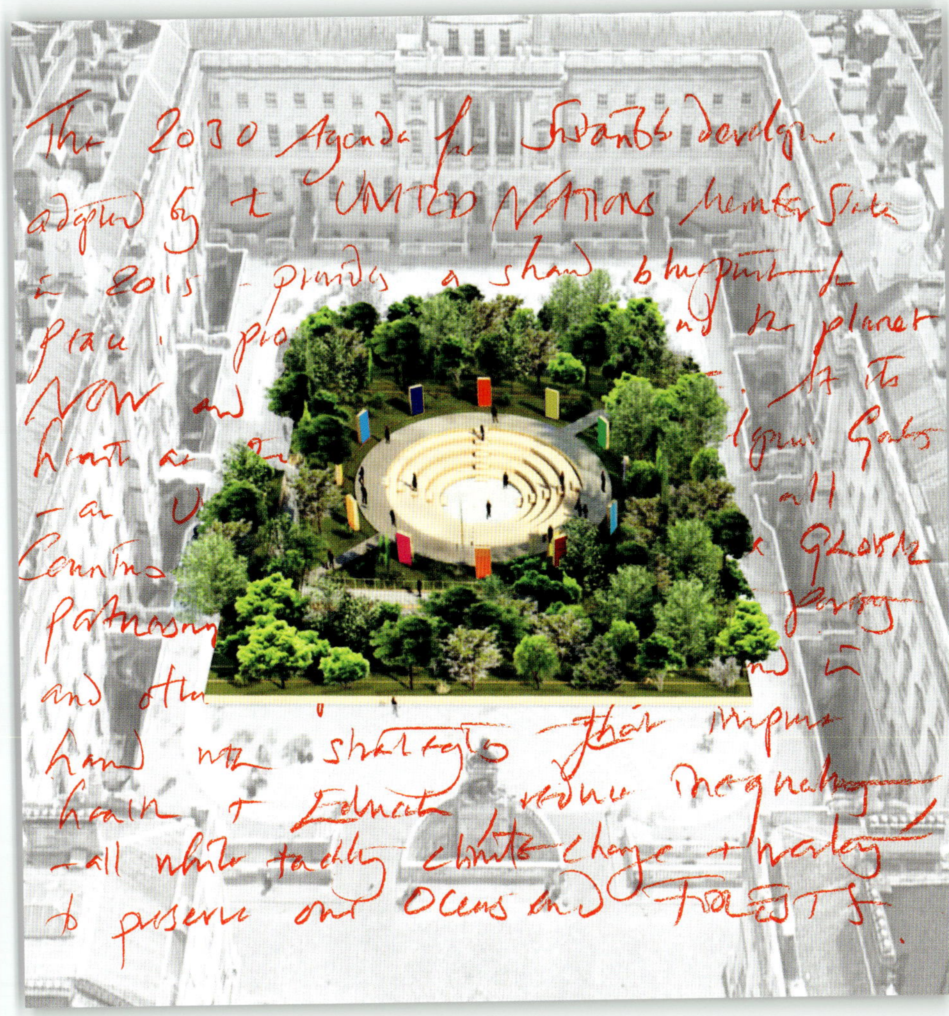
The 2030 Agenda
UNITED NATIONS
2015
planet
NOW and
all
GLOBAL
and
climate change
to preserve our Oceans and FORESTS.

FOREST OF US

[In] the phonetic writing system … the word beta doesn't mean house. It doesn't mean anything except the letter itself, which just refers you back to your own face. So, the letters begin functioning as mirrors … just referring the human back to itself.

David Abram

Forest of Us opened in March 2021 as part of Pace Gallery's inaugural Superblue Miami exhibition alongside a luminous new installation by James Turrell (I had to pinch myself when I saw the wall signs with my name next to his). It starts with a film that considers the visual symmetries between lungs and trees. The film breaks apart to reveal a glimmering mirror maze, which splices viewers' reflections together as they penetrate the film's surface. Although I had been working with mirror mazes since 2016, I had only recently discovered their resonance within geo-philosophical discourse through reading David Abram's *The Spell of the Sensuous*. Abram locates the origins of human dislocation from the rest of the biosphere in the inception of the Greek phonetic alphabet around 3,000 years ago, in which written language was no longer an ideographic pictorial link to natural phenomena but a veil of self-reflexive code – a hall of mirrors between humans and the biosphere. *Forest of Us* culminates in a flood across which people perceive branching forms within their own digital shadows. Invoking the music of trees flowing through our breath as we walk oblivious through the shimmering maze, it suggests a clue to the way out of the self-reflexive loop – through perception of the symmetries between human and more-than-human geometries.

18–21 820–821

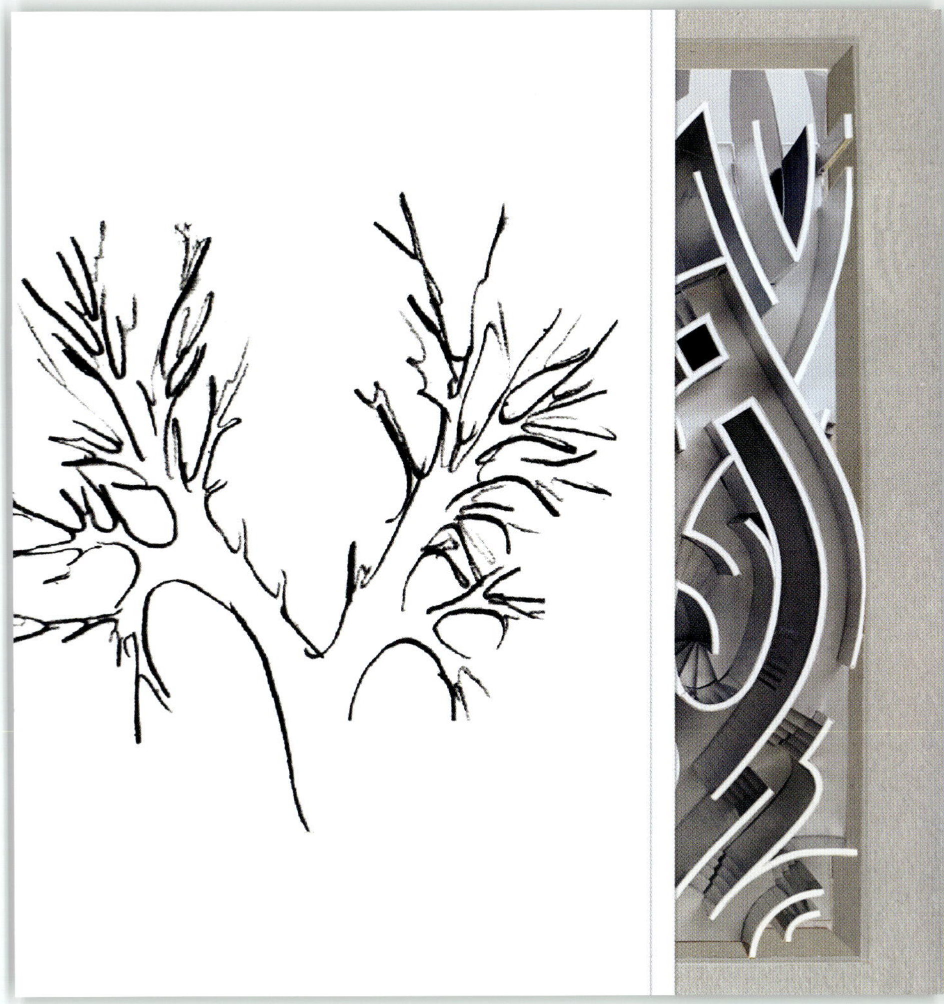

FOREST O

[In] the phonetic writin
It doesn't mean anythi
back to your own face,
just referring the huma

Forest of Us opened i
Superblue Miami exh
James Turrell (I had t
my name next to his).
symmetries between
a glimmering mirror m
as they penetrate the
mirror mazes since 20
within geo-philosophi
The Spell of the Sens
dislocation from the r
phonetic alphabet ar
was no longer an ide
a veil of self-reflexive
the biosphere. *Forest*
perceive branching fo
music of trees flowing
the shimmering maze
reflexive loop – throug
and more-than-huma

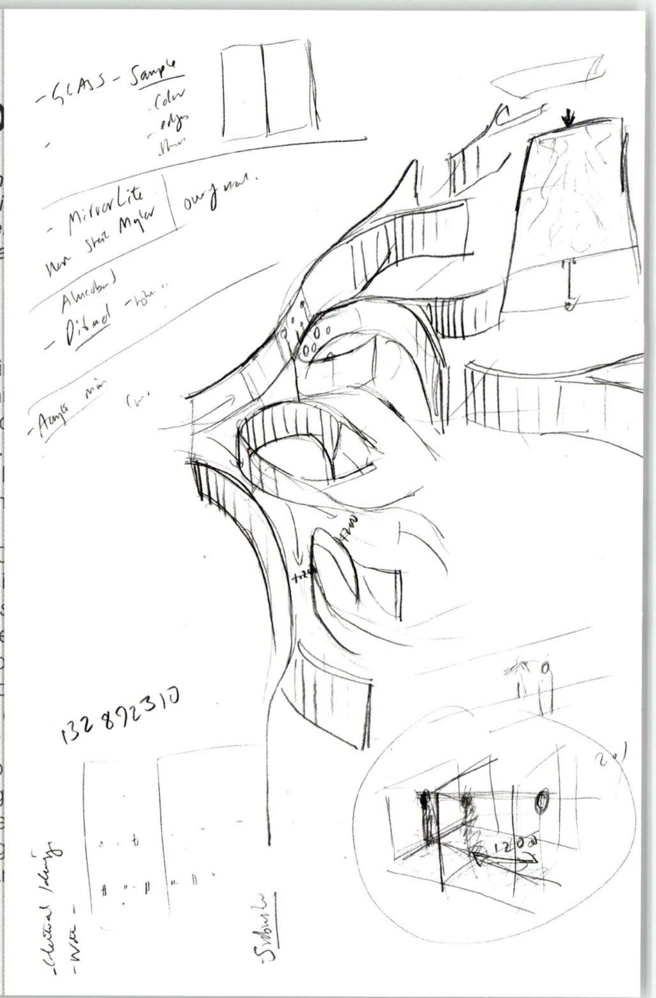

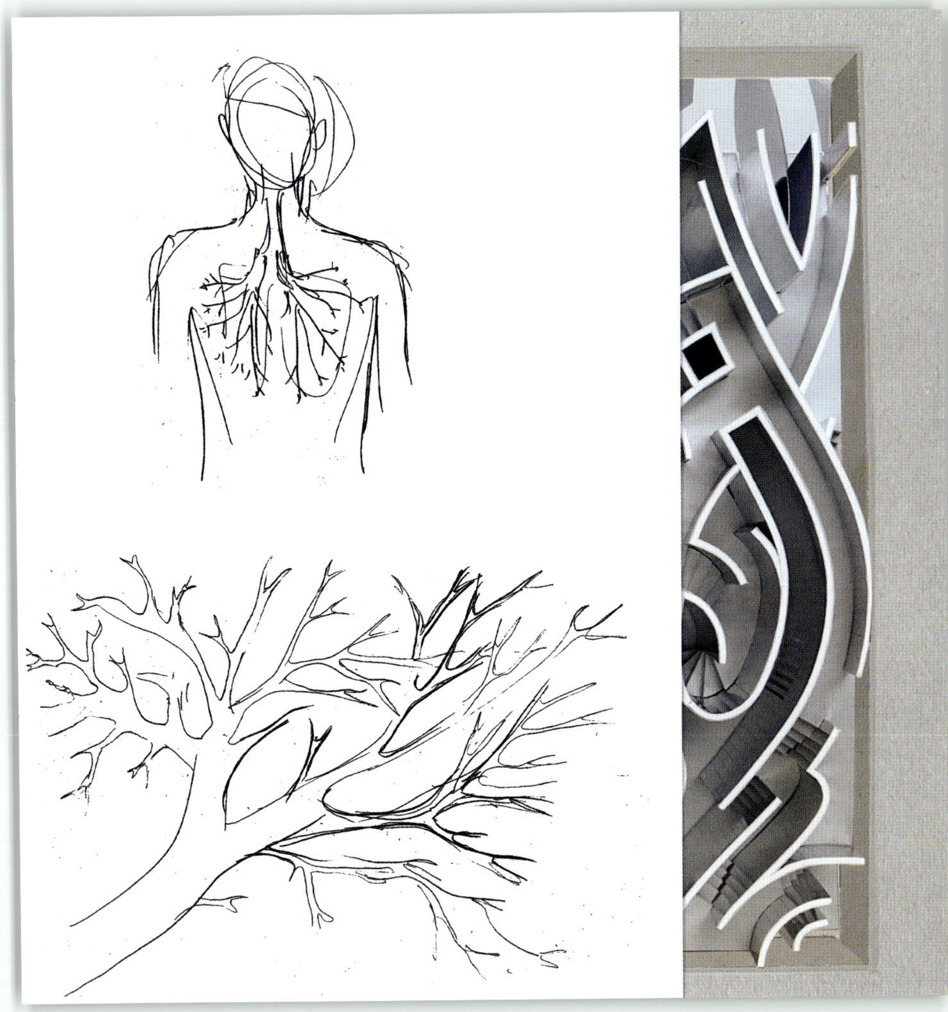

FOREST

[In] the phonetic wr
It doesn't mean any
back to your own fa
just referring the hu

Forest of Us opene
Superblue Miami e
James Turrell (I had
my name next to h
symmetries betwee
a glimmering mirror
as they penetrate th
mirror mazes since
within geo-philosop
The Spell of the Se
dislocation from the
phonetic alphabet a
was no longer an ic
a veil of self-reflexiv
the biosphere. *Fore*
perceive branching
music of trees flowi
the shimmering ma
reflexive loop – thro
and more-than-hum

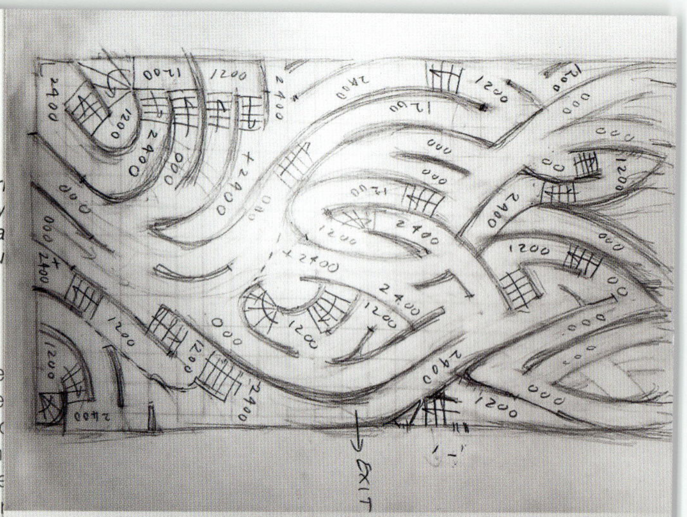

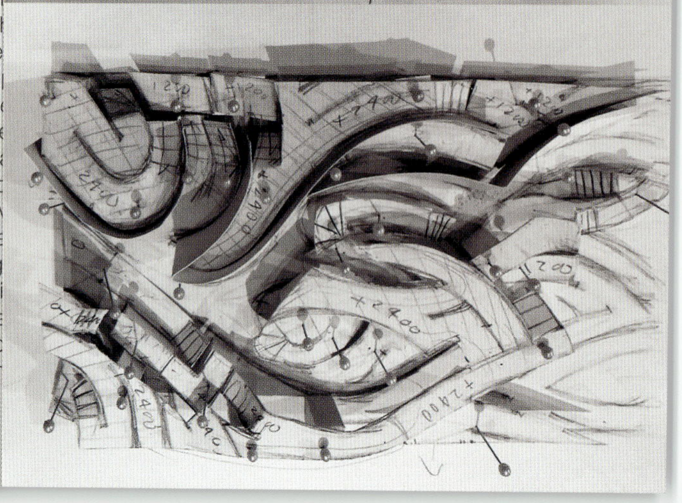

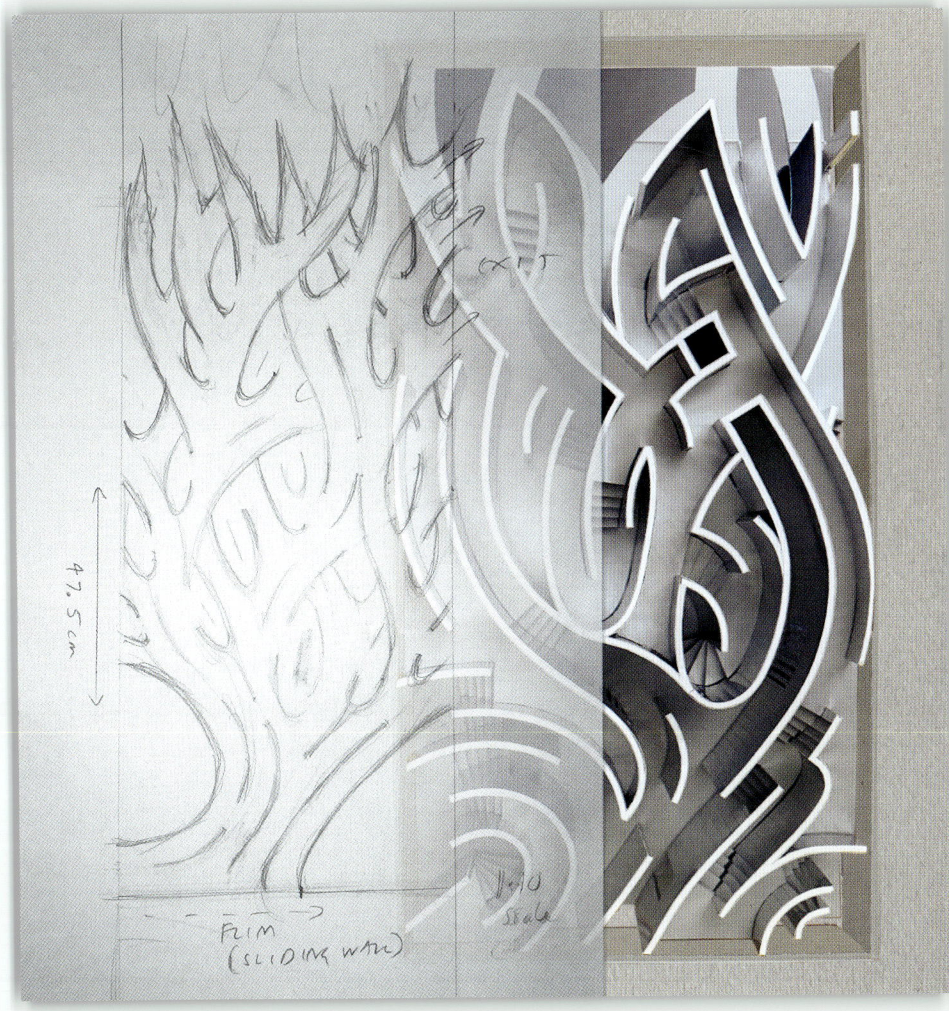
EXIT
47.5cm
FLIM
(SLIDING WALL)
1:10
Scale

FOREST

[In] the phonetic wri
It doesn't mean any
back to your own fa
just referring the hu

Forest of Us opene
Superblue Miami e
James Turrell (I had
my name next to h
symmetries betwee
a glimmering mirror
as they penetrate th
mirror mazes since
within geo-philosop
The Spell of the Se
dislocation from the
phonetic alphabet a
was no longer an ic
a veil of self-reflexiv
the biosphere. *Fore*
perceive branching
music of trees flowi
the shimmering ma
reflexive loop – thro
and more-than-hum

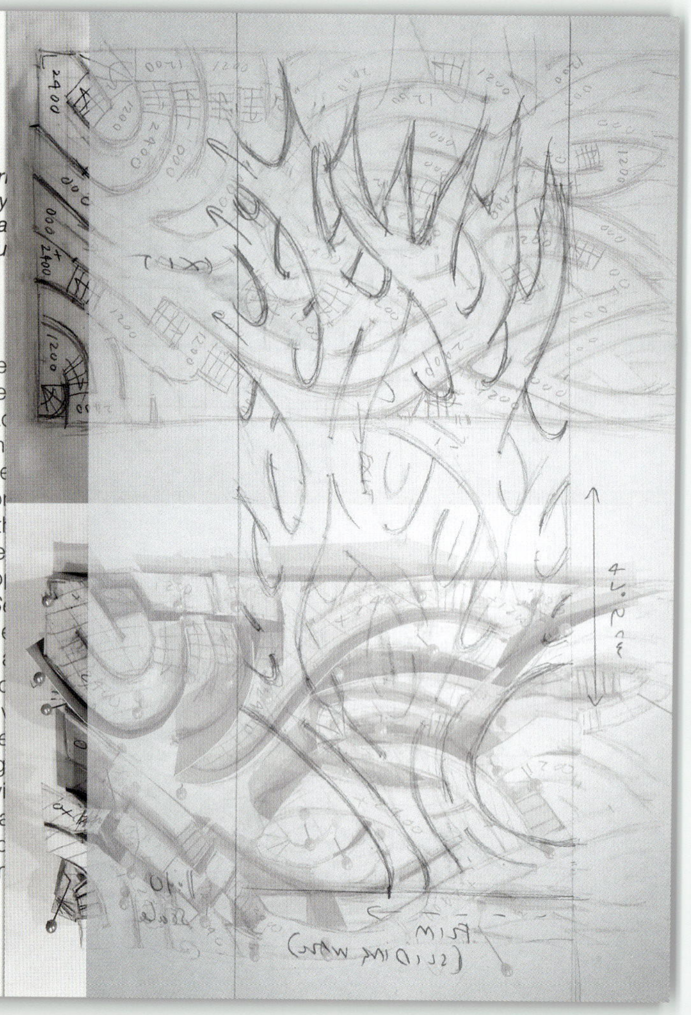

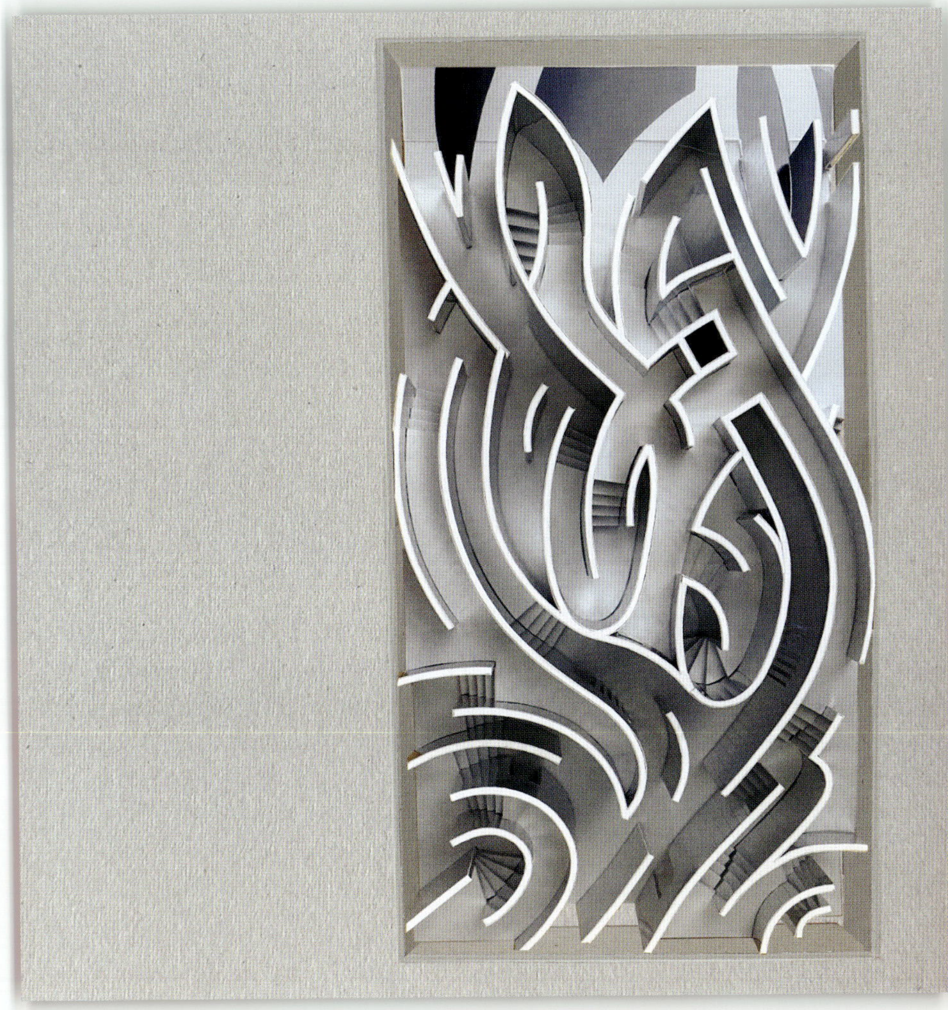

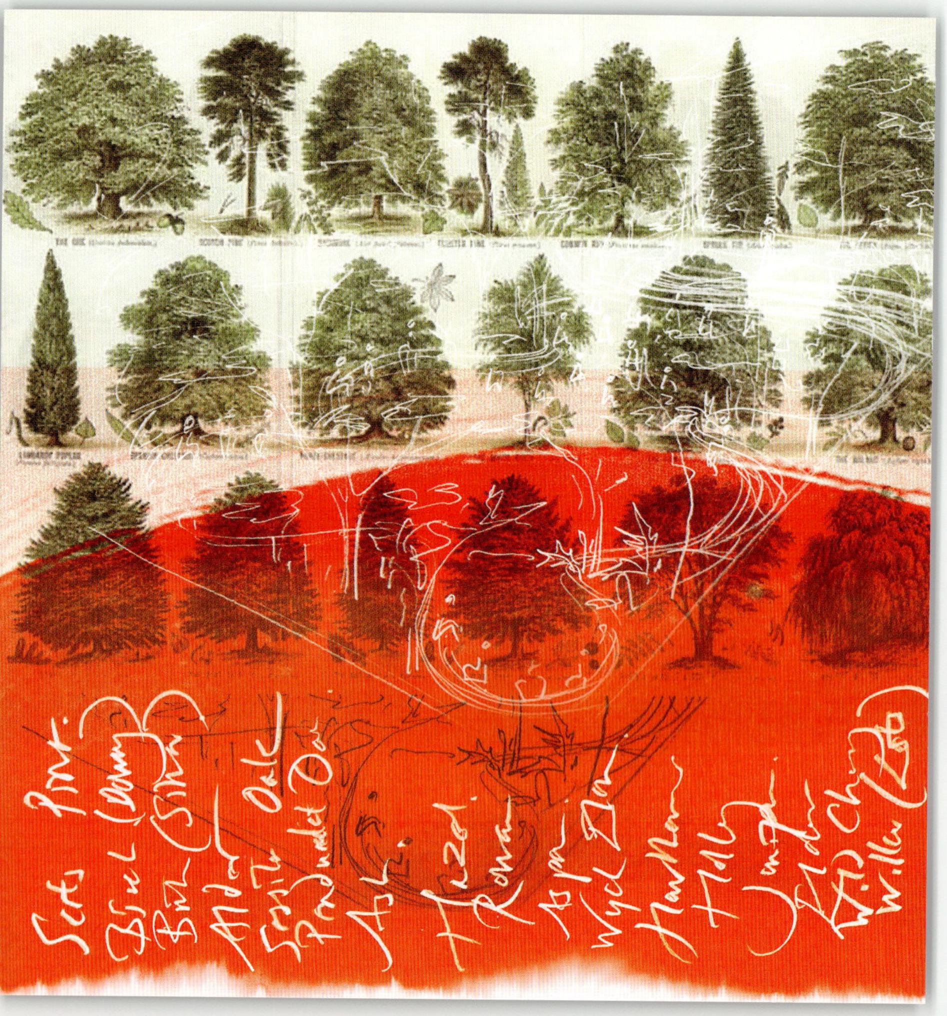

CONFERENCE OF THE TREES

To be human is to confuse a satisfying story with a meaningful one, and to mistake life for something huge with two legs ... This is not our world with trees in it. It's a world of trees, where humans have just arrived.

Richard Powers, *The Overstory*

In November 2021, the 197 parties who signed the 2015 Paris Agreement met in Glasgow at COP26, the United Nations' climate summit. We proposed a parallel conference of 197 trees. Emulating Richard Powers's Pulitzer Prize-winning novel, *The Overstory*, in which the trees are the lead protagonists while the humans form the subplot, *Conference of the Trees* invited the trees to bear witness to the progress that the humans might or might not make during the negotiations which many viewed as our species' last chance to avert extreme climate catastrophe. We installed our temporary forest of 197 trees at the SWG3 arts centre in Glasgow. A series of talks was held by *The New York Times*, with leading climate activists including Al Gore, Vanessa Nakate and Greta Thunberg all speaking from a stage among the trees. A plethora of recent studies suggest that humans' health and mood are improved by exposure to phytoncides secreted by trees. Conferences typically take place in large, rectilinear, fluorescent-lit boxes: this work proposed that an arboreal environment might have a positive effect on the quality of ideation and conversation. The trees were all replanted in a new local park once the conference was over.

BLUESKYWHITE

I had a dream, which was not all a dream.
The bright sun was extinguish'd, and the stars
Did wander darkling in the eternal space

Lord Byron, 'Darkness'

Commissioned by 180 Studios for their October 2021 group show *LUX: New Wave of Contemporary Art*, I made *BlueSkyWhite* after I'd read solar-engineering proposals to 'dim the sun' in order to counter global heating. In Part I, visitors passed through a 24-metre-long luminous red tunnel surrounded by the sound of me reading Byron's 1816 poem 'Darkness'. The desolate text was written during the cold, damp 'Year Without a Summer', in which the 18-year-old Mary Shelley conceived the story of Frankenstein during a nightmare, and painters J. M. W. Turner and Caspar David Friedrich recorded intense red sunsets. Much later, scientists attributed the bleak global weather conditions to the eruption of Mount Tambora, in Indonesia, in April 1815, which released over 100 million tonnes of gas and fine particles into the atmosphere, perceptibly dimming the sun and reducing the Earth's temperature by around 3 degrees Celsius. Part II was an audio-visual collage of geo-engineering proposals documented by writer Elizabeth Kolbert and others. The geo-engineers suggest that suspending a haze of diamond or sulphur particles in the stratosphere might soon become necessary in order to reduce global temperatures to pre-industrial levels. Such extreme measures could potentially turn our skies permanently white. Sunsets would be spectacular, but the blue skies we associate with infinite possibility would become extinct.

758–759 848–849

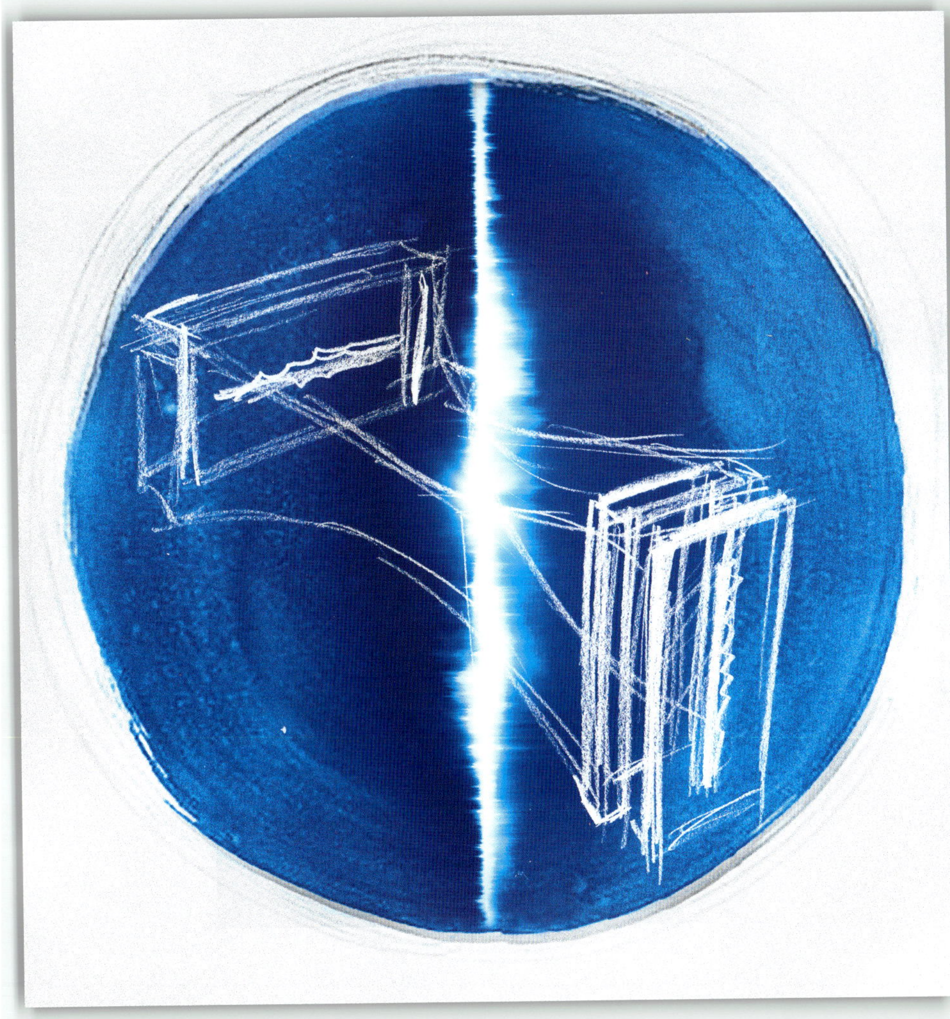

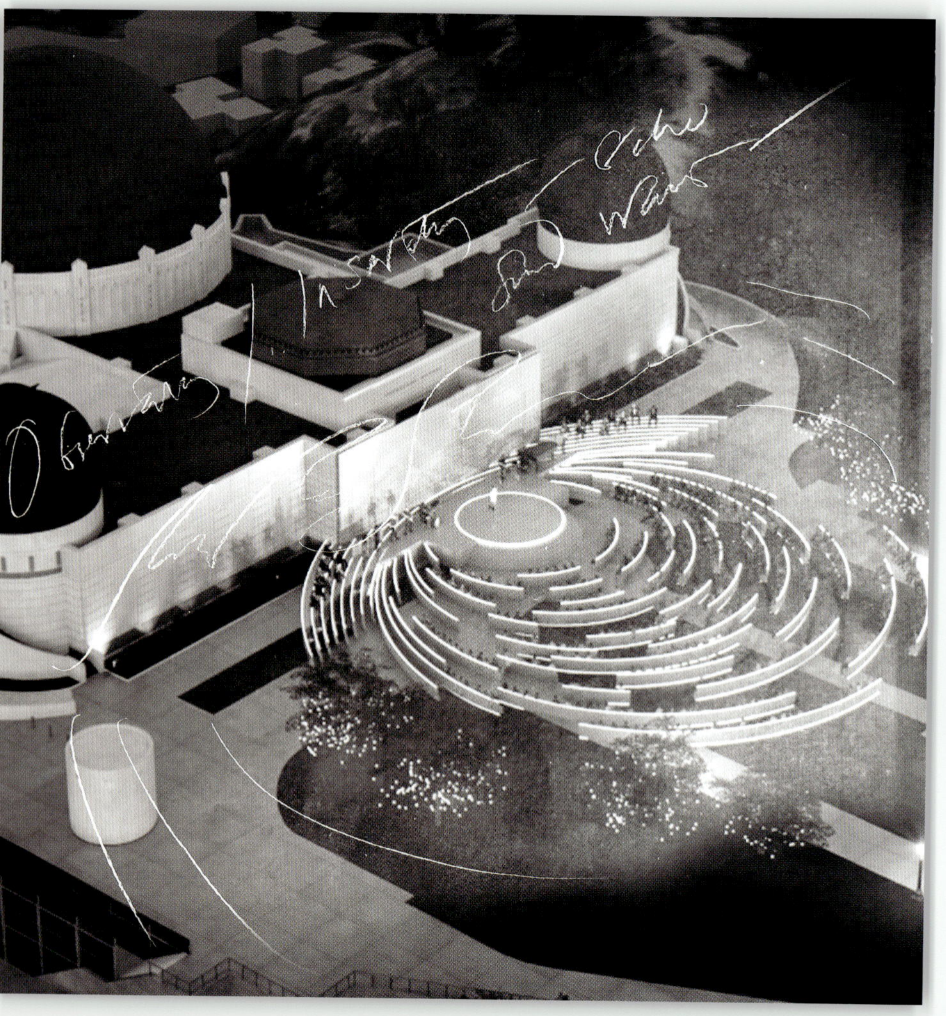

GRIFFITH OBSERVATORY

Then I hit my Saturn return … When that comes, it can rock your life … Who am I? What do I want to do? What makes me truly happy? All those things.

Adele

A Saturn return … occurs when the planet Saturn returns to the place in the sky that it was in when a person was born … a major developmental stage, marking the final passage into adulthood … from the age of 27 to 30.

The Astrology Dictionary

Interested in the connections between planetary motions and seismic human emotional shifts, Adele chose the Griffith Observatory on the southern slope of Mount Hollywood, Los Angeles, for the first filmed performance of her new album, *30*. As the aerial cameras captured the November 2021 sunset, Adele's voice reverberated across the Santa Monica Mountains. We mapped concentric, illuminated orbits of audience around her and pounded projections of the Pacific Ocean across the observatory facade. Six stone figures silently witnessed the concert from the Astronomers Monument across the lawn – Hipparchus, Copernicus, Galileo, Kepler, Newton and Herschel, the scientists responsible for some of the most seismic perception shifts in Western human history.

COMPTON SUPER BOWL

I be hangin' out at Tam's, I be on Stockton
I don't do it for the 'Gram, I do it for Compton

Kendrick Lamar, 'ELEMENT.'

As we prepared for the February 2022 Super Bowl halftime show, Dr. Dre and I proposed that Compton become another protagonist in the work: we would etch a map of the city onto the global Super Bowl stage in Los Angeles's new SoFi Stadium. Having watched *Straight Outta Compton* and listened to Kendrick Lamar's album *Good Kid M.A.A.D City*, I understood the recording studio was the enzyme that transformed painful experience on the streets into music, poetry, and a future. With Kendrick's school friend Tremeal as our guide, we visited Compton and cast a series of buildings as protagonists within the work, including the Martin Luther King memorial designed by one of California's first registered Black architects. We crafted a narrative which led us through Snoop Dogg's house to 50 Cent in the 'Eve After Dark' club to Eminem breaking out of the city jail. The story culminated in the familiar LA sound of a helicopter above a fallen Mary J. Blige and an army of men bent low in a grid of cardboard boxes – at once an apt evocation of LA in 2022 and, with 'Dre Day' branded on each box, a tribute from Kendrick to the generation that preceded him. As the map of Compton coursed through his hand, Dre played the stadium as he plays his recording desk, transposing lived experience from a very specific place into music which touches a global audience.

838–839

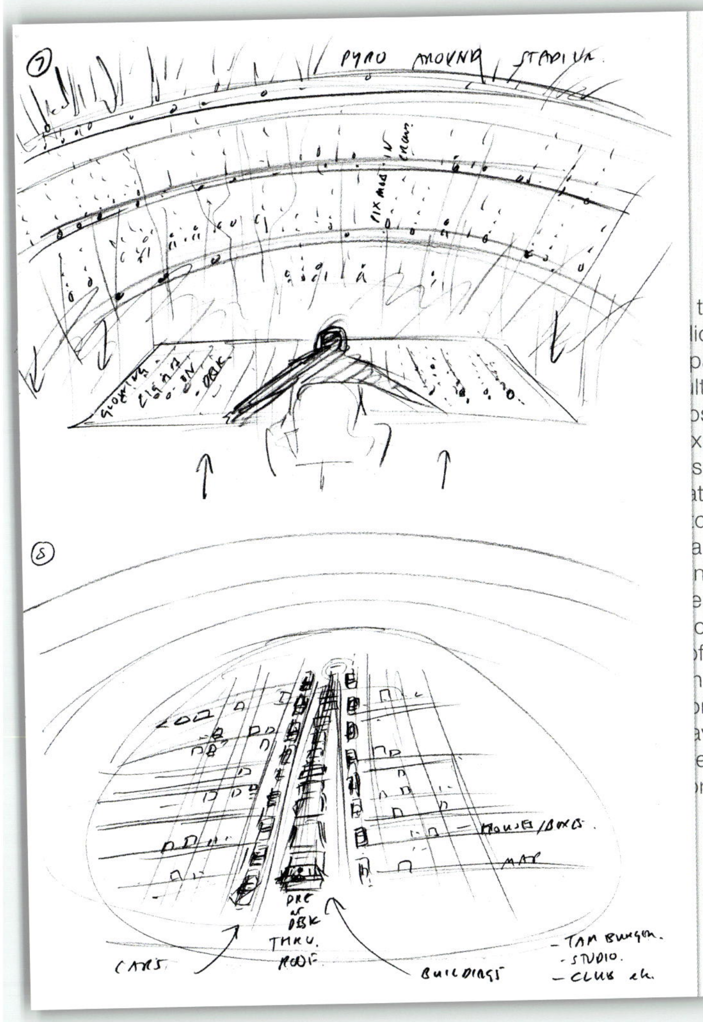

Plato

the more
lion a musical
pan in a single
lture, and all
osity. My studio
xpo 2020 Dubai
ssed the breaths
t its heart, and
tors through
a cumulative
ng, LED-laced
esigned by a
onceived the
f the UK's recent
n was a feat of
om sustainably
avilion's cross-
ere engineered
orithm was

COMPTO

I be hangin' out at T
I don't do it for the

As we prepared fo
Dr. Dre and I propo
the work: we woul
stage in Los Ange
Outta Compton ar
M.A.A.D City, I und
transformed painfu
and a future. With
visited Compton a
the work, including
of California's first
which led us throu
After Dark' club to
culminated in the f
Mary J. Blige and
boxes – at once ar
branded on each b
preceded him. As
Dre played the sta
lived experience fr
a global audience.

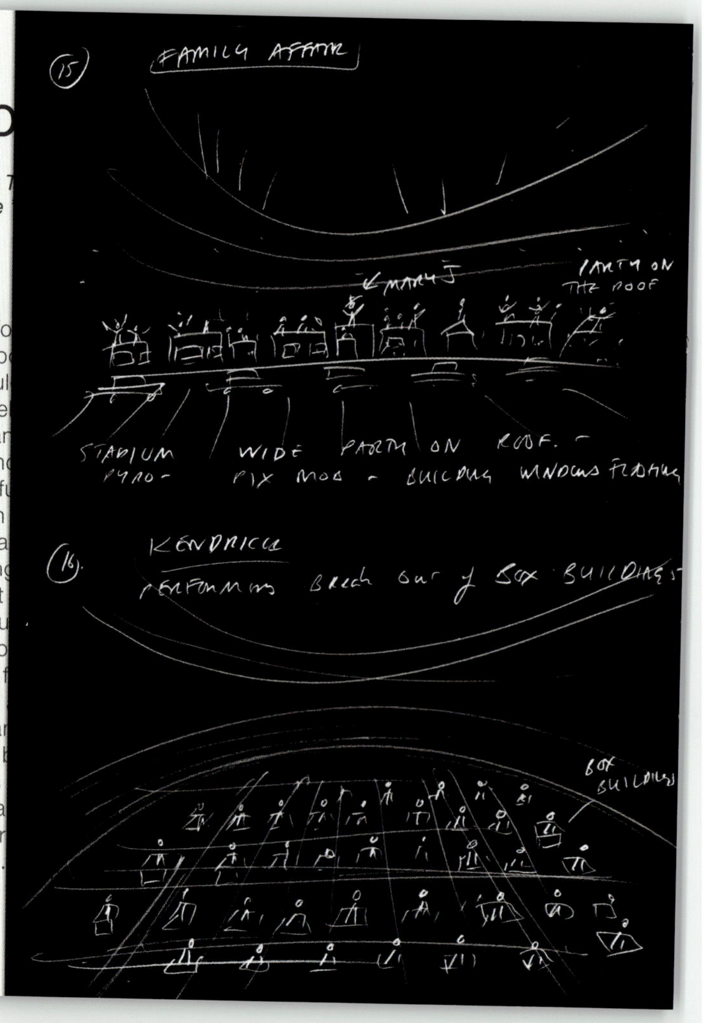

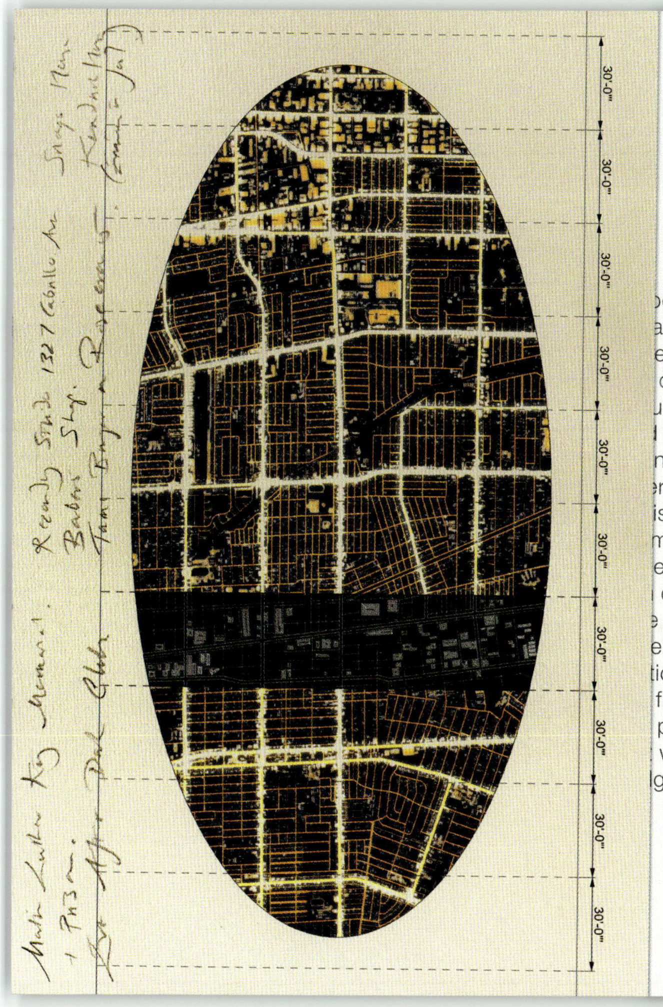

oo, the more
avilion a musical
espan in a single
culture, and all
uriosity. My studio
d Expo 2020 Dubai
nessed the breaths
er at its heart, and
isitors through
m a cumulative
ering, LED-laced
designed by a
e conceived the
e of the UK's recent
tion was a feat of
from sustainably
pavilion's cross-
were engineered
lgorithm was

COMPTO

I be hangin' out at T
I don't do it for the

As we prepared fo
Dr. Dre and I propo
the work: we woul
stage in Los Ange
Outta Compton an
M.A.A.D City, I und
transformed painfu
and a future. With
visited Compton a
the work, including
of California's first
which led us throu
After Dark' club to
culminated in the f
Mary J. Blige and
boxes – at once ar
branded on each b
preceded him. As
Dre played the sta
lived experience fr
a global audience.

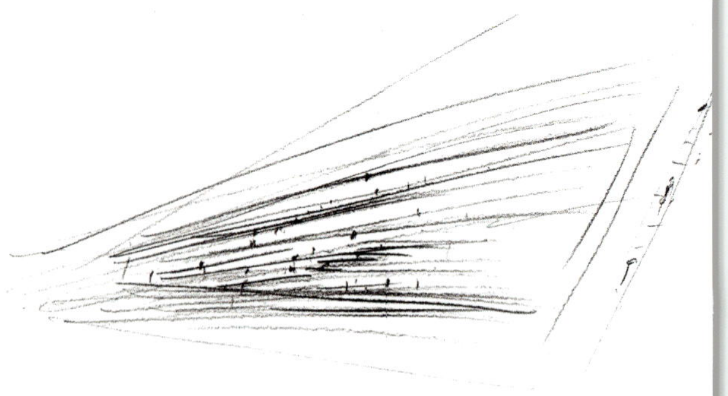

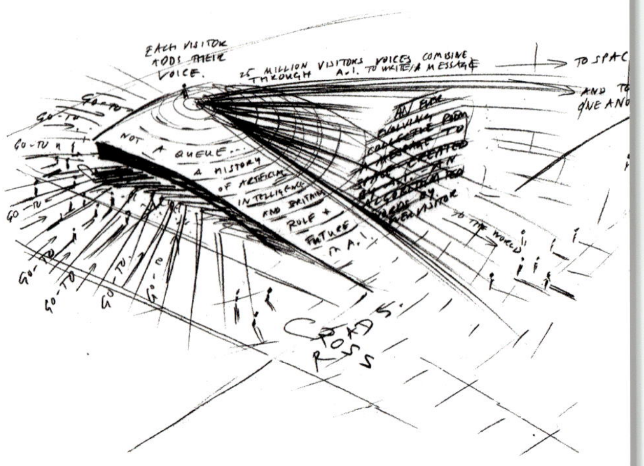

POEM PAVILION

Poetry is nearer to vital truth than history.

Plato

The more I researched the history of the World Expo, the more I perceived it as an architectural orchestra: each pavilion a musical instrument communicating beyond its six-month lifespan in a single place, each singing a solo born of its specific local culture, and all joining in concert to express global concern and curiosity. My studio team and I conceived the UK Pavilion for the World Expo 2020 Dubai as a giant, conical, wooden wind instrument. It harnessed the breaths of UK multicultural choirs within the choral chamber at its heart, and gathered words donated by each of its 25 million visitors through a GPT-2-based machine-learning algorithm to beam a cumulative collective poem from its 20-metre-diameter, glimmering, LED-laced facade. It was the first time a UK pavilion had been designed by a woman since the inception of the Expo in 1851. We conceived the work as an expression of cultural inclusivity, in spite of the UK's recent departure from the European Union, and its execution was a feat of European and international collaboration. Sourced from sustainably managed European forests in Austria and Italy, the pavilion's cross-laminated timber was crafted around LED tiles that were engineered in Belgium and manufactured in China, while the algorithm was developed by creative technologists in California.

48–49

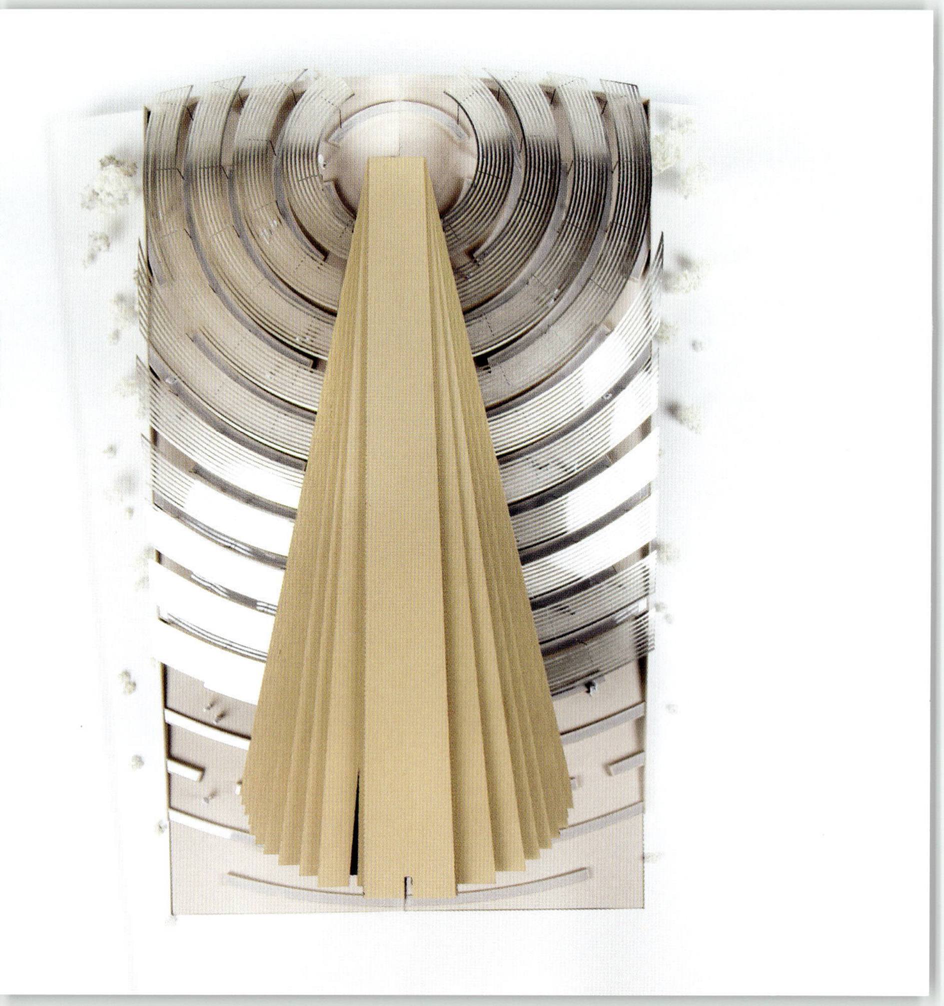

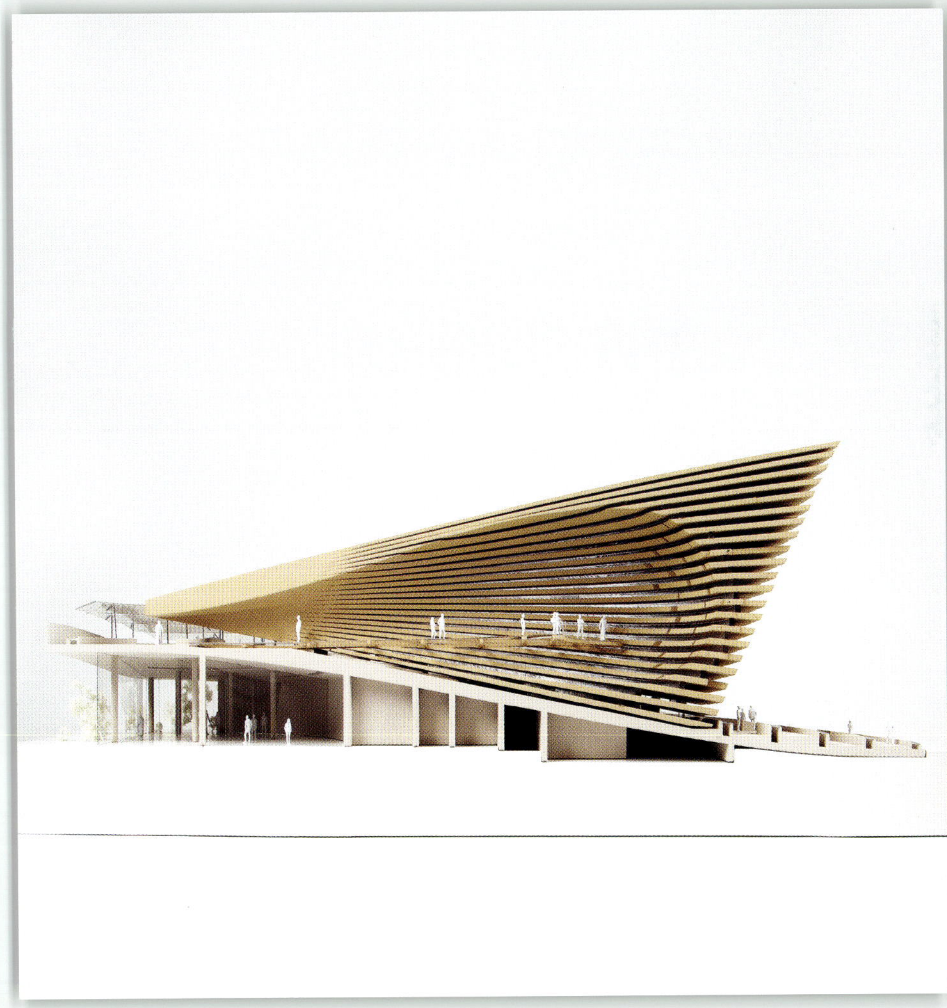

RENAISSANCE

… poetry is not a luxury. It is a vital necessity of our existence. It forms the quality of the light within which we predicate our hopes and dreams toward survival and change, first made into language, then into idea, then into more tangible action … The Black mother within each of us – the poet – whispers in our dreams: I feel, therefore I can be free. Poetry coins the language to express and charter this revolutionary demand the implementation of that freedom.

Audre Lorde, 'Poetry Is Not a Luxury'

Beyoncé's LA studio reminds me of Andy Warhol's Factory: her endlessly curious creative team are there all year round, helping Beyoncé translate her poetry and sketches into films and artworks. We had meetings at the studio and on Zoom between September 2021 and March 2023 to shape ideas for the *Renaissance* world stadium tour which opened in Stockholm in May 2023. As Beyoncé read her poetic lockdown film scripts to us, the show's three-hour, six-act structure began to emerge. Her range of reference was broad: redlining (the denial of financial services such as mortgages in Black residential areas); reclamation of rodeo culture by Black Americans; and the echo chambers of surveillance capitalism – all shot through with the silver-sequinned joy, liberty and luminosity of LGBTQ+ Ball culture. Working closely with the architects from Stufish, we envisaged a stadium-sized film with a hole. Ed Burke and Andrew Makadsi from Beyoncé's Parkwood team curated the vast, perforated LED sculpture into a euphoric three-hour kinetic painting made of light.

844–847

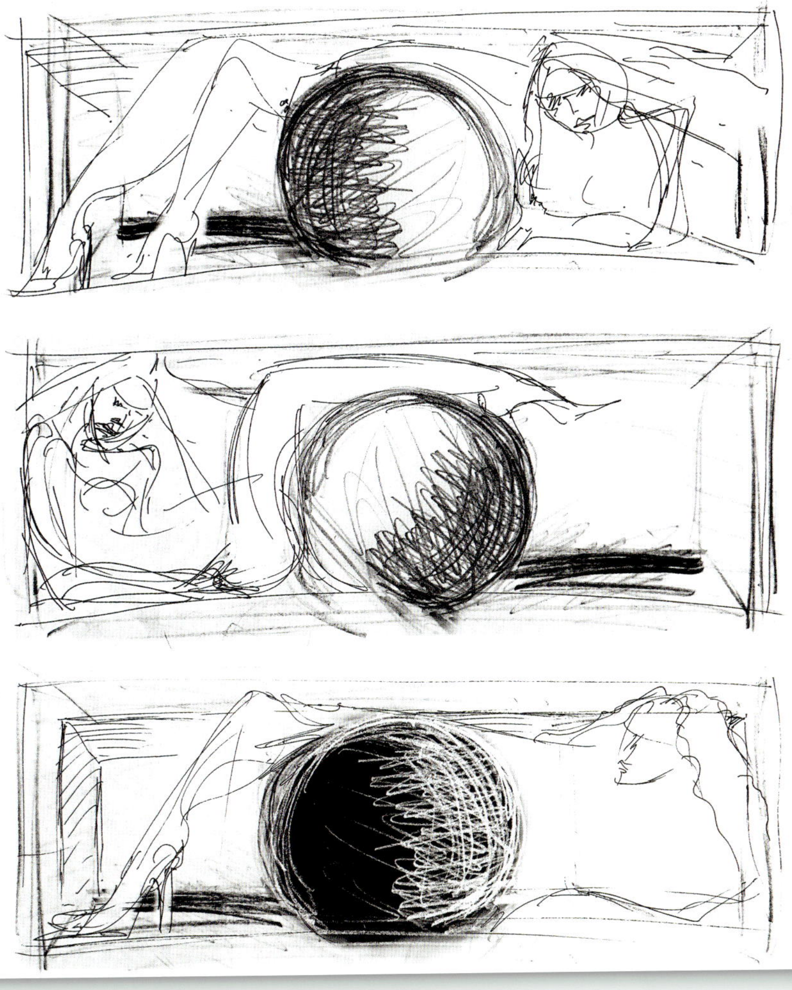

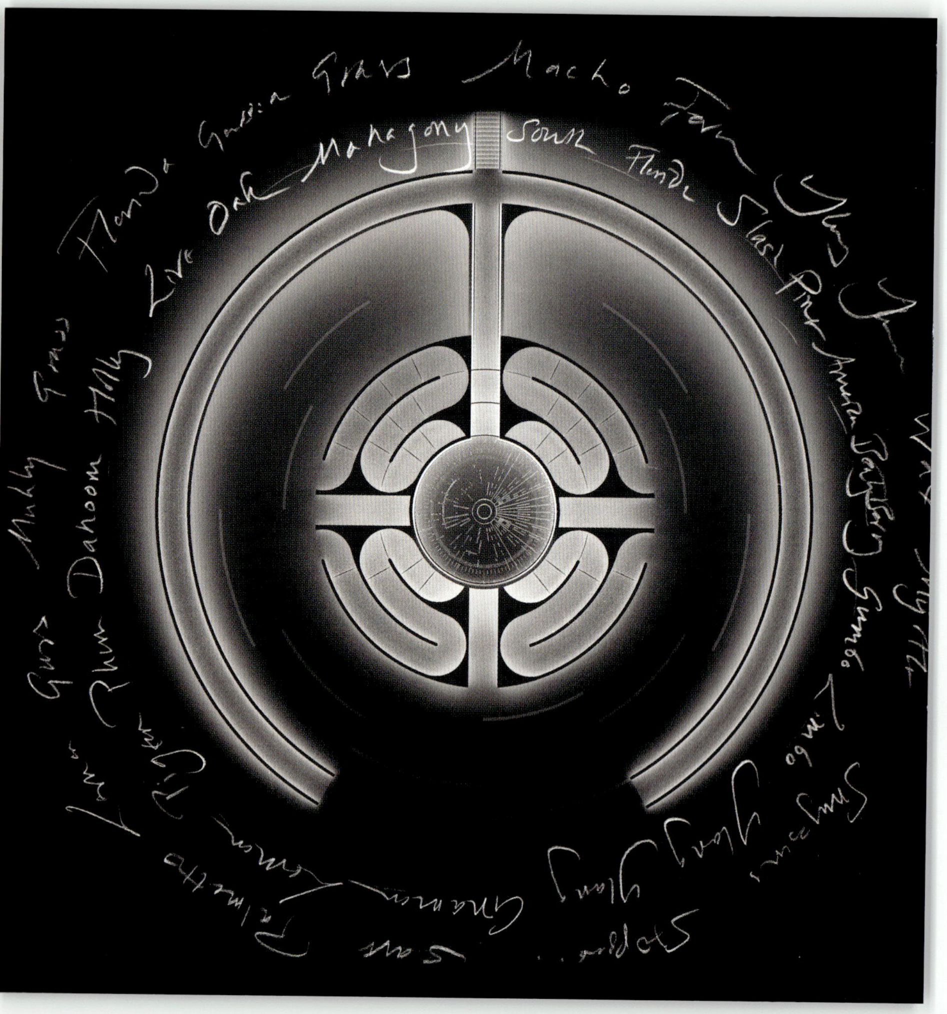
Macho Fern
Mahogany
Live Oak
Holly
Dahoon
Muhly Grass
Gumbo Limbo

FIVE ECHOES

The worst labyrinth is not that intricate form that can entrap us forever, but a single and precise straight line.

Jorge Luis Borges, *Labyrinths*

The word 'labyrinth' was used by the ancient Greek philosopher Plutarch nearly 2,000 years ago to describe circuitous ritual dances. Medieval labyrinth pavements, like the thirteenth-century stone floor of Chartres Cathedral, were laid as guided prayer paths for those who could not manage the pilgrimage to Jerusalem: they could accomplish the same spiritual journey by prayerfully walking the enfolded paths within their local cathedral. For *Five Echoes*, commissioned by Chanel for Miami Art Basel in December 2021, I reduced the eleven circuits of the Chartres design to five. We surrounded the illuminated 15-metre-diameter labyrinthine sculpture with a temporary forest and immersed walkers within the sound of each species' name, labelling all the trees and plants with their names and a memorable story in the hope that visitors would be able to greet each species by its name in the future. The stretched fabric and sustainably sourced wood that formed the piece were later reused by local theatre groups. The trees and plants were replanted by the Million Trees Miami charity, whose mission is to increase Miami's urban tree canopy cover to 30% to reduce urban temperatures and sequester carbon.

50–51 711

HERE NOT HERE

I want to talk about the inside from the inside, I do not want to leave it
I am so happy in the silky damp dark of the labyrinth and there is no thread

Hélène Cixous, *The Book of Promethea*

I had long admired Maxine Doyle's narrative choreography through her work with Felix Barrett and their immersive theatre company Punchdrunk, and was intrigued when she suggested we conceive a new work to take over the whole of the GöteborgsOperan building in southwestern Sweden in January 2022 – backstage, understage, convoluted corridors and all. Incidentally I had first experienced Punchdrunk's *Faust* in spring 2007 when I was nine months pregnant with my daughter, Ry: its seven-storey labyrinthine odyssey in pitch black with no exit signs felt like an appropriate rehearsal for the adventure of labour and birth. Three years later Felix and I had some of our most fruitful meetings in preparation for our collaboration with the Colombian singer Shakira in the waiting room at King's College Hospital in South London when I was about to give birth to my son, Ludo. By 2021, Maxine and I both had teenage children and the installation we conceived together originated in memories of our own teenage bedrooms and their importance to our emerging identities. The work was co-created with the Göteborg dancers, who each brought in posters remembered from their teenage bedroom walls. We painted them into the sculpture within layers of luminous red-orange paint. As they made their way through the belly of the building, the audience discovered a fragment of the same red in a child's lost balloon within a shimmering glass maze.

636 675 754 760–761

real. It's dreaming

urchill, *A Dream Play*

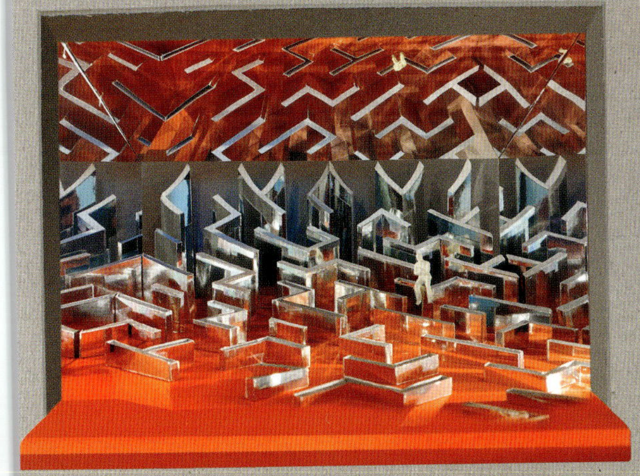

ill's 2002 play,
, each cloned
entirely distinct
characteristics and
e changes and a
ner choreographed
magic within a
he clones' father,
ch item that entered
s replicated second
ed by the original
meeting a third
the third clone's

ny other person.
e. We've got thirty
up at all? I love

HERE NOT

I want to talk about the
I am so happy in the si

I had long admired Ma
work with Felix Barret
and was intrigued wh
take over the whole o
Sweden in January 2
and all. Incidentally I h
2007 when I was nine
storey labyrinthine od
appropriate rehearsal
later Felix and I had s
our collaboration with
at King's College Hos
birth to my son, Ludo
and the installation w
own teenage bedroo
The work was co-cre
in posters remember
them into the sculptu
made their way throu
a fragment of the sam
glass maze.

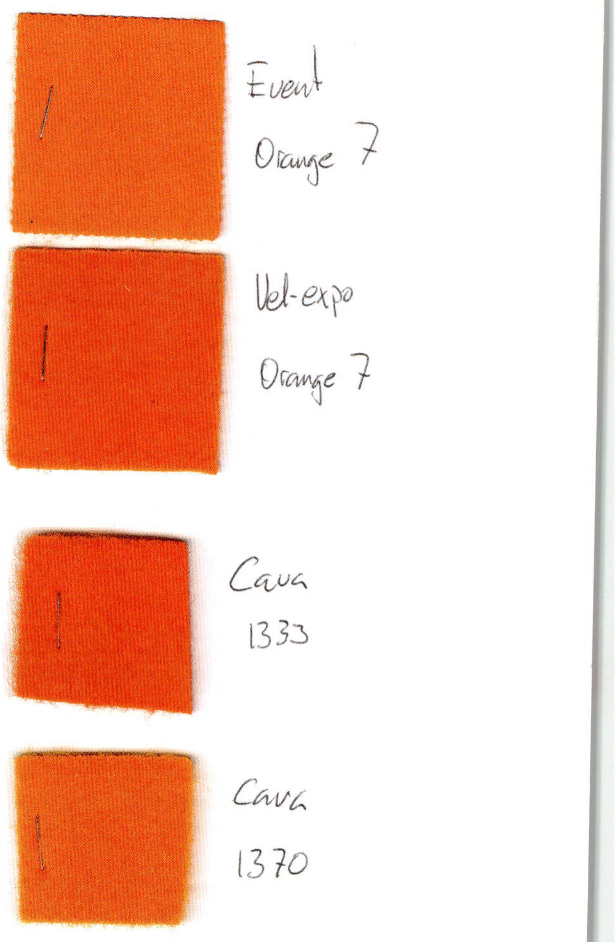

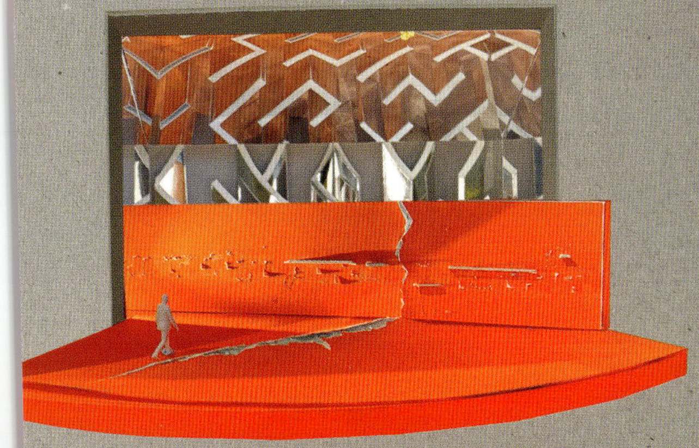

real. It's dreaming

urchill, *A Dream Play*

ill's 2002 play,
, each cloned
n entirely distinct
characteristics and
e changes and a
ner choreographed
magic within a
he clones' father,
ch item that entered
s replicated second
ed by the original
meeting a third
the third clone's

ny other person.
e. We've got thirty
up at all? I love

HERE NOT

I want to talk about the
I am so happy in the si

I had long admired Ma
work with Felix Barret
and was intrigued wh
take over the whole o
Sweden in January 2
and all. Incidentally I h
2007 when I was nine
storey labyrinthine od
appropriate rehearsal
later Felix and I had s
our collaboration with
at King's College Hos
birth to my son, Ludo.
and the installation we
own teenage bedroon
The work was co-crea
in posters remembere
them into the sculptur
made their way throug
a fragment of the sam
glass maze.

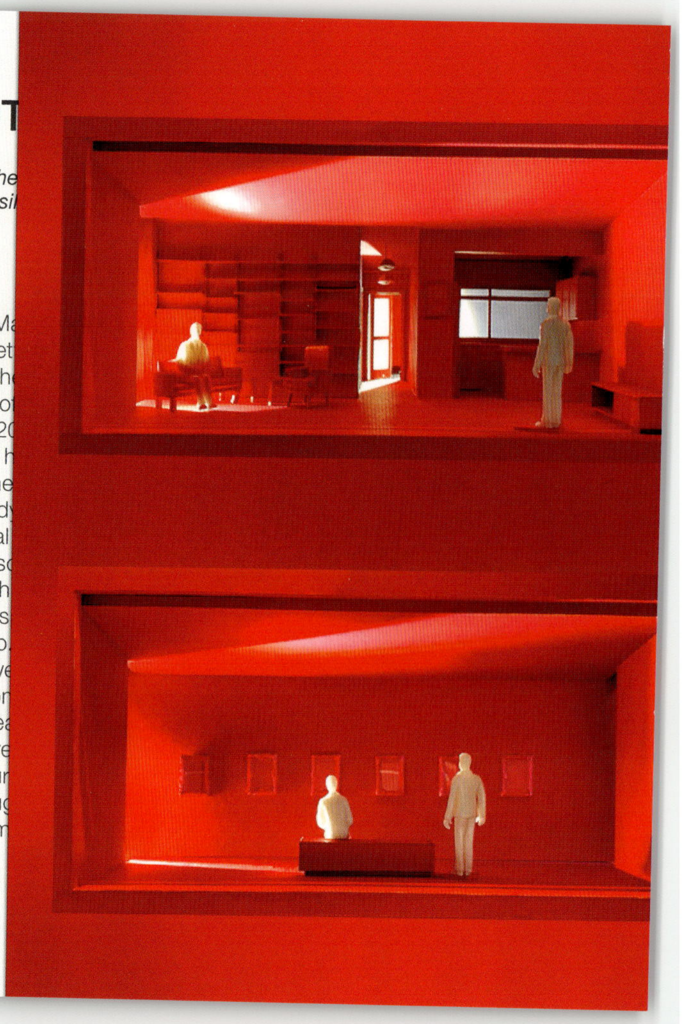

A NUMBER

What's poetry? It's not real but maybe it's more than real. It's dreaming while you're awake.

Caryl Churchill, *A Dream Play*

In the January 2022 Old Vic revival of Caryl Churchill's 2002 play, *A Number*, Paapa Essiedu played three characters, each cloned from the same genetic information but brought up in entirely distinct circumstances and manifesting completely different characteristics and intentions. Using a body double, very quick costume changes and a frame of blinding LED light, the director Lyndsey Turner choreographed the genetic replicas to replace one another as if by magic within a luminous red-orange room. Lennie James played the clones' father, pedantic and controlling about the orientation of each item that entered the monochrome domestic space. When the father's replicated second son – whom he has loved and cared for – is murdered by the original son he abused and abandoned, he seeks solace in meeting a third cloned son for the first time. The meeting ends with the third clone's chilling rejection of his biological father:

We've got ninety-nine per cent the same genes as any other person. We've got ninety per cent the same as a chimpanzee. We've got thirty per cent the same as a lettuce. Does that cheer you up at all? I love about the lettuce. It makes me feel I belong.

766–767

AFTER HOURS TIL DAWN

... somehow his heart had come open at this chapter of his life and he didn't have the strength to shut it.

Saul Bellow, *Herzog*

In his January 2020 'Blinding Lights' video, Abel 'The Weeknd' Tesfaye appeared as a character on a chaotic night out in Vegas in a red jacket with a bloodied, bruised face. He continued to appear in the same outfit for a year – an act of durational performance art, unusual in the context of some of his celebrated peers' addiction to novelty. The character originated in Tesfaye's Las Vegas arrest in January 2015. He describes that night in a Nevada police cell as a critical personal crossroads, a choice between oblivion or growth. For his February 2021 Super Bowl halftime show in Tampa, we created a chaotic maze of lightbulb-scorched mirrors populated with fifty bandaged-faced, red-jacketed Abel doubles – as if his life had cracked open at this specific chapter, playing on infinite, distorted repeat. By the time his pandemic-postponed world stadium tour began in July 2022, Abel had completed a new album, *The Dawn*, and we staged it within a science-fictional stadium sandcastle city beneath a giant scorched red moon. Abel and his creative director La Mar C Taylor's choice of red-veiled female performers staged against a dystopian desert city seemed to acquire extended resonance with the overturning of Roe v. Wade in the US in June 2022, curtailing women's access to abortion, and with the death of 22-year-old Mahsa Amini after removing her veil in Iran later that year.

716 772–773 840–841

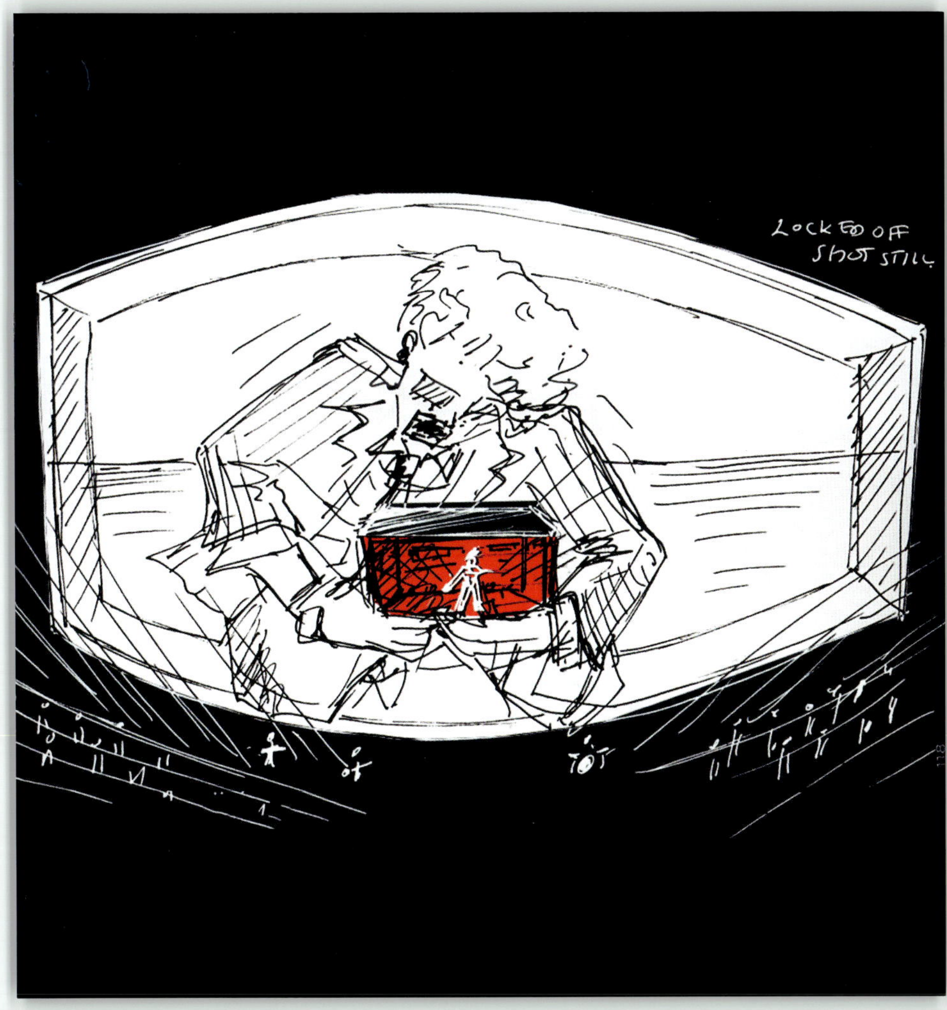
LOCKED OFF
SHOT STILL
118

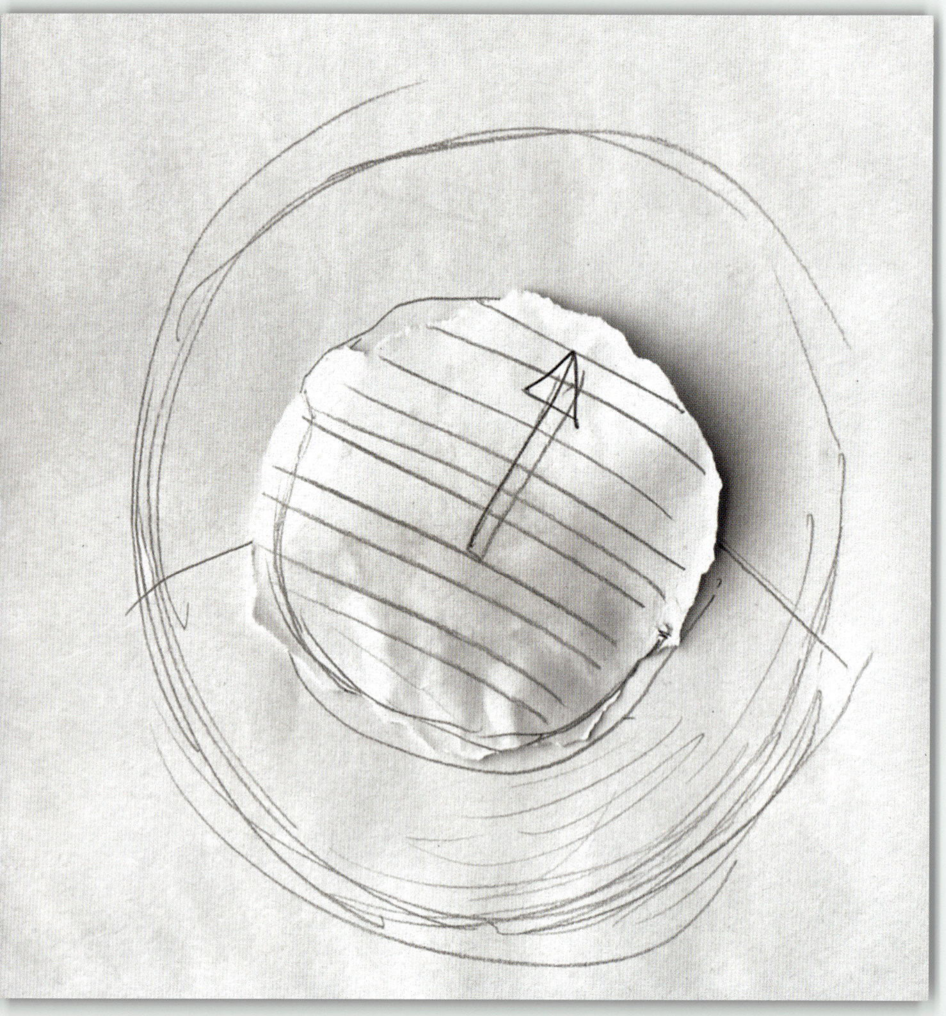

DESERT MOON

... we get to think of life as an inexhaustible well. Yet everything happens only a certain number of times, and a very small number, really. How many more times will you remember a certain afternoon of your childhood, some afternoon that's so deeply a part of your being that you can't even conceive of your life without it? Perhaps four or five times more. Perhaps not even. How many more times will you watch the full moon rise? Perhaps twenty. And yet it all seems limitless.

Paul Bowles, *The Sheltering Sky*

I underlined these words in my copy of Paul Bowles's haunting novel as I read it during my first visit to Morocco aged 18, and they have come to my mind each time I have seen a full moon ever since. The phrases resurfaced as we prepared proposals for Anthony Vaccarello's Saint Laurent Spring/Summer 2023 Men's show to take place near Marrakech in July 2022. I drew a ring of light hovering in haze above a circular pool in the fierce heat of the Agafay Desert: it was Anthony who suggested the glowing ring should be absent at the start of the show and only emerge from the water during the finale. He proposed that by the time the 15-minute show had ended, the ring would have sunk back out of view, as if the audience had collectively hallucinated it.

YOUR VOICES

Every language is an old-growth forest of the mind, a watershed of thought, an ecosystem of spiritual possibilities.

Wade Davis

I was introduced to the Endangered Language Alliance by Brian Eno. He also showed me a copy of the *Ethnologue*, an encyclopaedia of all 7,151 living languages, which highlights the world's most endangered languages and marks the moment when the last remaining speaker of each dies. Every language is a vast library of cultural, historical and biological knowledge gathered over centuries, and we are losing languages as fast as we are losing species. New York is the most linguistically diverse city on the planet, with 637 languages currently spoken by its inhabitants. *Your Voices* was an illuminated kinetic sculpture installed at Lincoln Center Plaza in New York City in December 2022 to celebrate this diversity. Like a giant revolving harp, it was formed of 637 glowing cords tensioned between a series of structural arcs, enveloping visitors and local choral groups within its illuminated web as it rotated, compass-like, through a multilingual choral soundscape that interwove languages drawn from all over the city: from Algerian, Arabic, Alsatian, Azeri and Ashanti to Zapotec, Zarma and Zulu. The viewer's perspective was spliced and framed by its shifting strands, as our perspectives are shaped by tasting the linguistic structures of others when we learn to speak through their voice. The soundscape translated an adapted extract from E. M. Forster's 1910 novel *Howards End* into multiple overlaid languages: 'Only connect … and live in fragments no longer'.

510

746–747

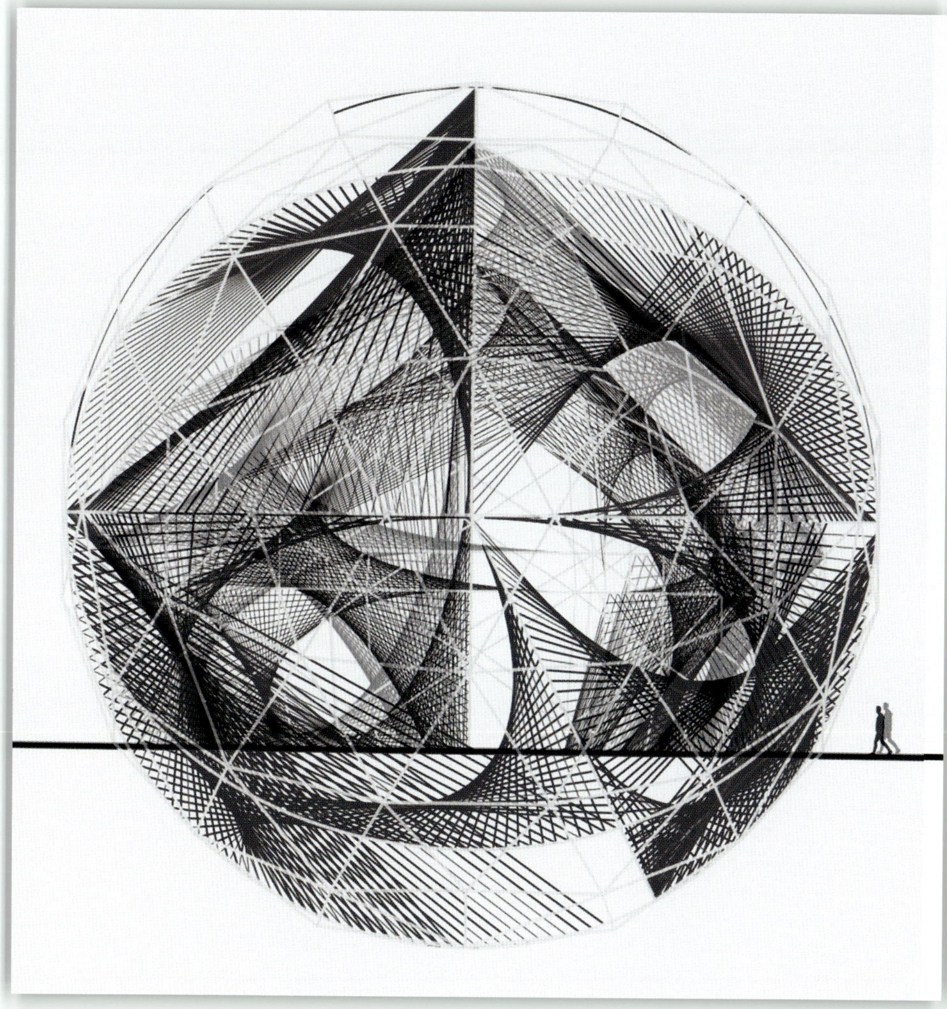

YOUR VOICES

Every language is an old-growth forest of [illegible] watershed of thought, an ecosystem of spiritual possibilities.

[illegible] Davis

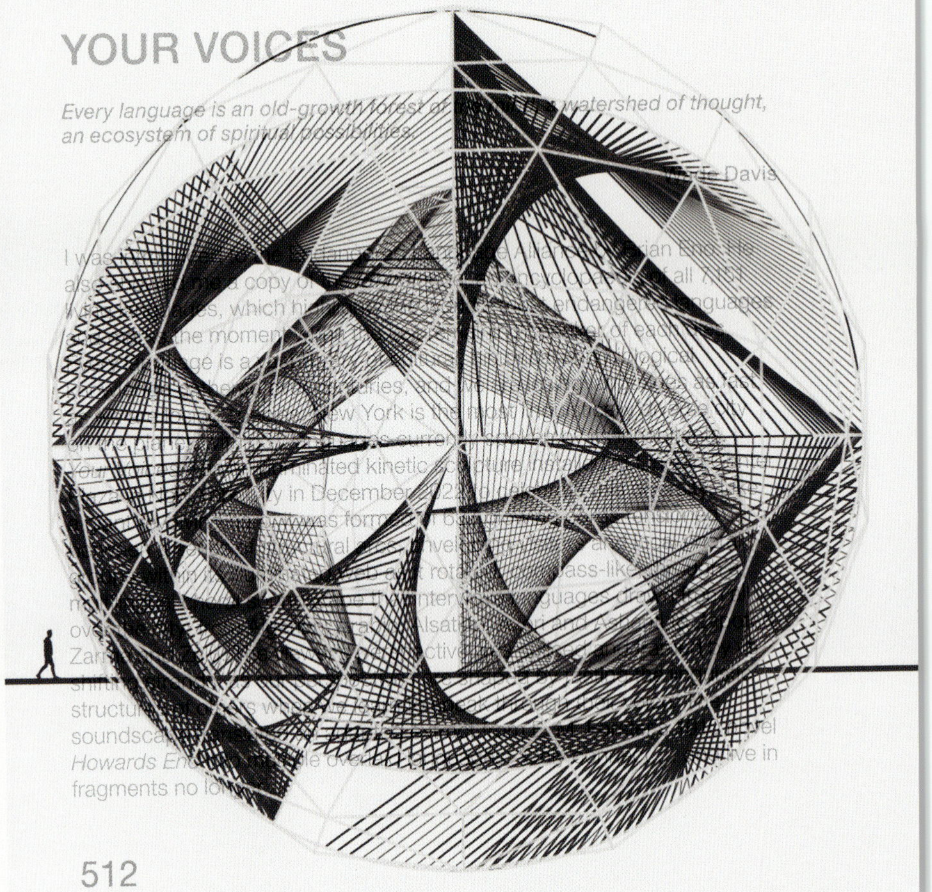

I was [illegible] Brian [illegible] also [illegible] a copy of [illegible] encyclopaedia of all [illegible] [illegible] es, which hi [illegible] endangered languages [illegible] he moment [illegible] of each [illegible] age is a [illegible] logical [illegible] dries, and [illegible] ew York is the most [illegible] [illegible] inated kinetic sculpture [illegible] y in December [illegible] was form [illegible] ral [illegible] nvel [illegible] rotat [illegible] ass-like [illegible] interv [illegible] guages [illegible] Alsati [illegible] activel [illegible] structu [illegible] soundsca [illegible] el *Howards En* [illegible] le over [illegible] ive in fragments no lo [illegible]

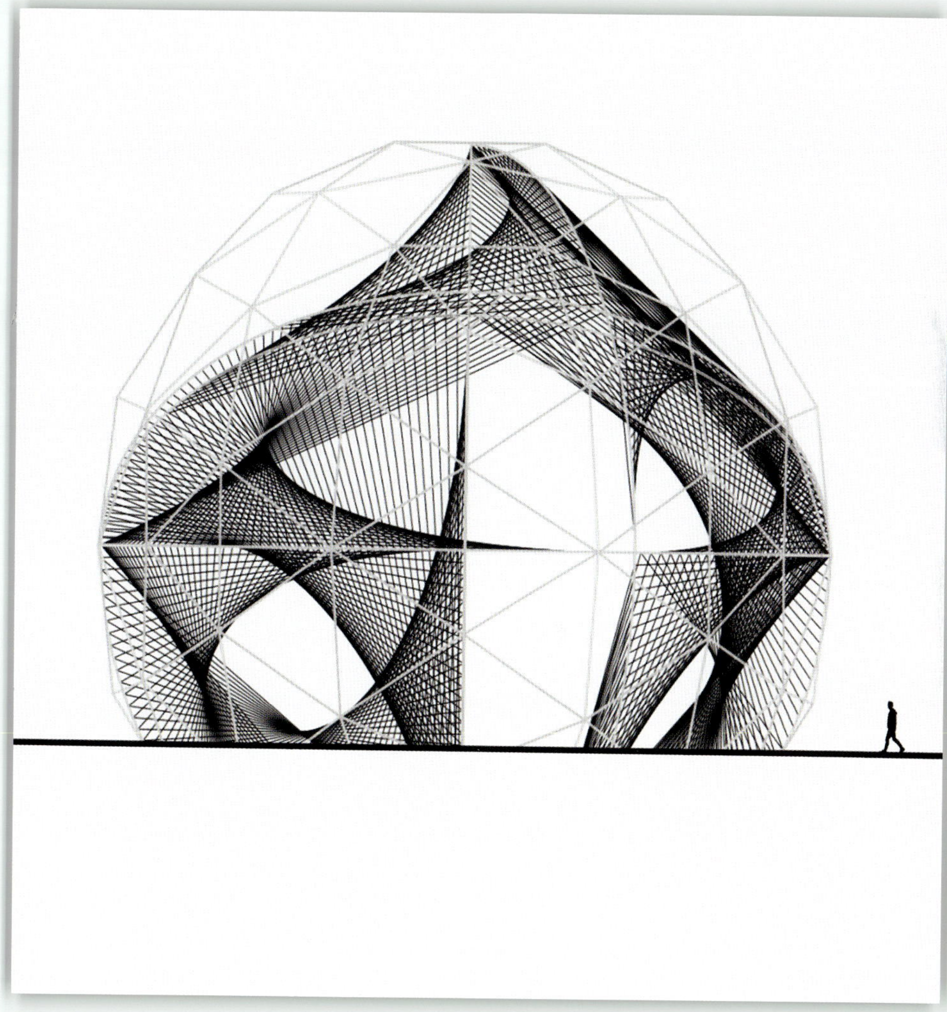

THE CRUCIBLE

The very impulse to write springs from an inner chaos, a crying for order, for meaning

Arthur Miller

As the audience entered the Olivier Theatre in September 2022 for Lyndsey Turner's National Theatre revival of Arthur Miller's 1953 play, *The Crucible*, they were met with cascading sheets of rain around the stage, violently hushing any pre-show chit-chat. As the auditorium lights dimmed, the glowing torrents were perforated by the sight and sound of a twenty-strong congregation fervently singing a choral hymn by the Pulitzer Prize-winning composer Caroline Shaw. By the time the actors spoke the first lines of the text, they met the audience already one foot through the play's door. Miller was compelled to conjure this community ravaged by the chaotic hysteria of the seventeenth-century Salem witch trials as a fierce, urgent critique of Senator Joseph McCarthy's 1950s witch-hunt for communists among public figures, which had already blacklisted Albert Einstein and Orson Welles along with tens of thousands of others. The play needed no translation into contemporary costume for an audience to be chilled by its resonance with today's online cancel culture.

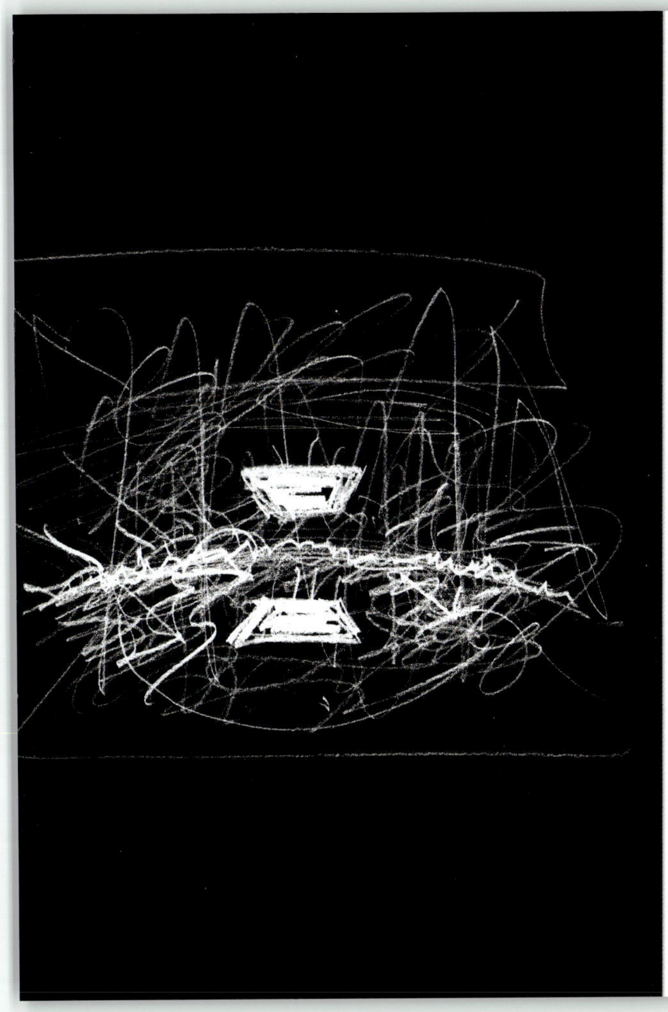

As we relinquish
e home to our

over, World as Self

n *dem-* (home).
gh Latin
vas drawn by
thedral and, in
ca of the dome of
cathedral across
ngs made over
uman species
f extinction. The
nmental activist
e its separation
ier and made in
t diasporic choirs
the non-human
invited to learn
nake a habitat for
Queen Elizabeth II
five miles along
work as they lined

THE CRUC

The very impulse to w
for meaning

As the audience ente
Lyndsey Turner's Nati
The Crucible, they we
stage, violently hushi
lights dimmed, the gl
sound of a twenty-str
by the Pulitzer Prize-
actors spoke the first
one foot through the
community ravaged b
Salem witch trials as
McCarthy's 1950s wi
which had already bla
with tens of thousand
contemporary costum
with today's online ca

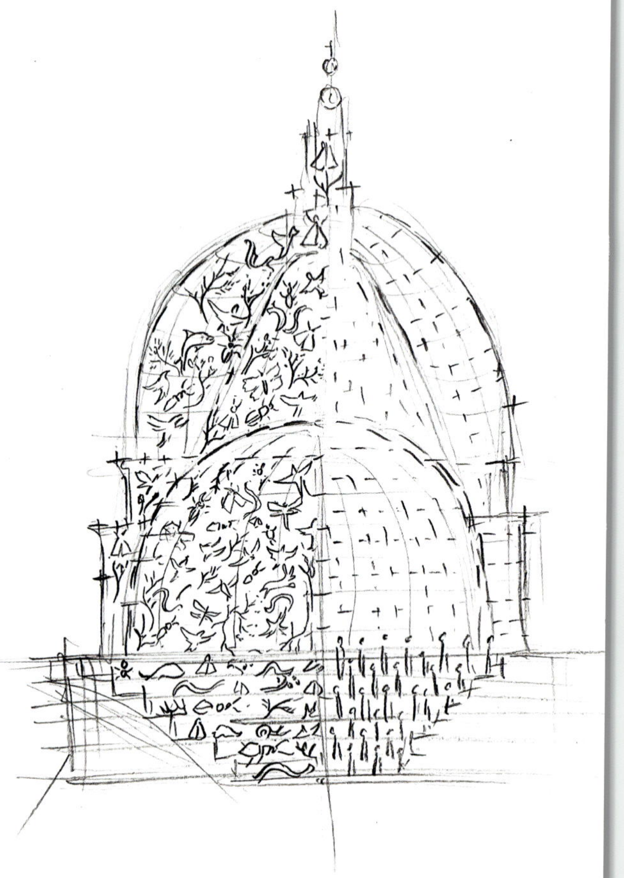

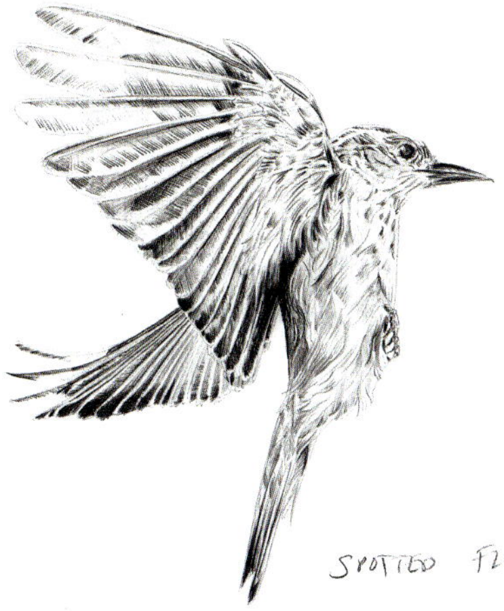

SPOTTED FLY CATCHER

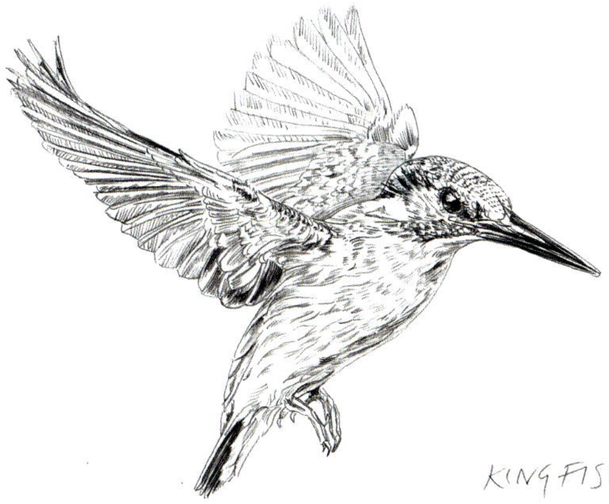

KINGFISHER.

As we relinquish
e home to our

over, World as Self

m *dem-* (home).
gh Latin
was drawn by
thedral and, in
ca of the dome of
cathedral across
ngs made over
uman species
of extinction. The
onmental activist
e its separation
ier and made in
t diasporic choirs
the non-human
invited to learn
nake a habitat for
Queen Elizabeth II
five miles along
work as they lined

THE CRU

The very impulse to
for meaning

As the audience en
Lyndsey Turner's N
The Crucible, they
stage, violently hus
lights dimmed, the
sound of a twenty-
by the Pulitzer Priz
actors spoke the fi
one foot through th
community ravage
Salem witch trials a
McCarthy's 1950s
which had already
with tens of thousa
contemporary cos
with today's online

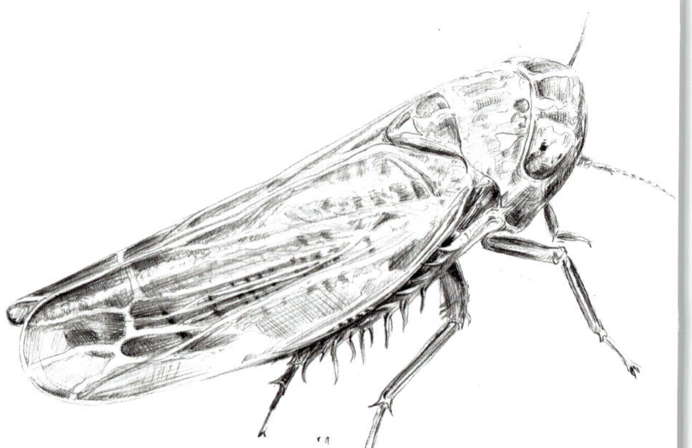

SEA WORMWOOD LEAFHOPPER.

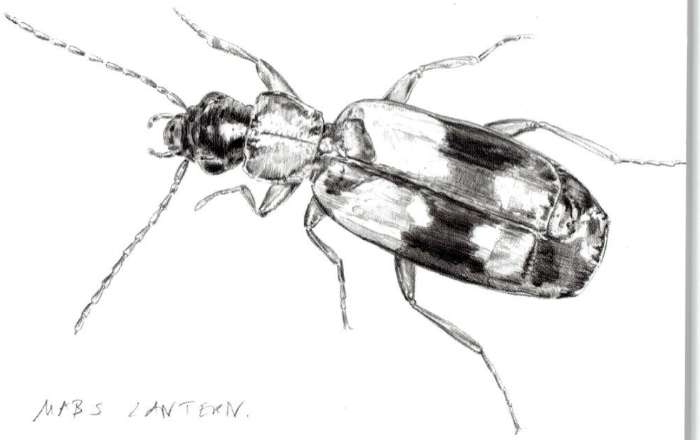

MABS LANTERN.

COME HOME AGAIN

Now it can dawn on us: we are the world knowing itself. As we relinquish our isolation, we can come home again … we can come home to our mutual belonging.

Joanna Macy, *World as Lover, World as Self*

The word 'dome' originates in the proto-European stem *dem-* (home). The word 'danger' shares these roots: it evolved through Latin *domus* (home) via *dominarium* (the power of a lord). I was drawn by these etymological enquiries to London's St Paul's Cathedral and, in September 2022, I constructed a one-third-scale replica of the dome of St Paul's on the lawn outside Tate Modern, facing the cathedral across the river. I filled the dome with my observational drawings made over the preceding four months of 243 of the 15,000 non-human species which call London home: the Londoners most at risk of extinction. The title of the work was drawn from the 93-year-old environmental activist Joanna Macy's exhortation to our species to renounce its separation from the rest of the biosphere. Commissioned by Cartier and made in collaboration with the London Wildlife Trust, each night diasporic choirs sang within the structure accompanying the voices of the non-human Londoners, and each day visitors sat within the work, invited to learn the names of their more-than-human neighbours, to make a habitat for them within their imaginations. Following the death of Queen Elizabeth II on 8 September 2022, a 24-hour queue stretched for five miles along the Thames, with 250,000 mourners walking past the work as they lined up to pay their respects at Westminster Hall.

60–62 752 864–865

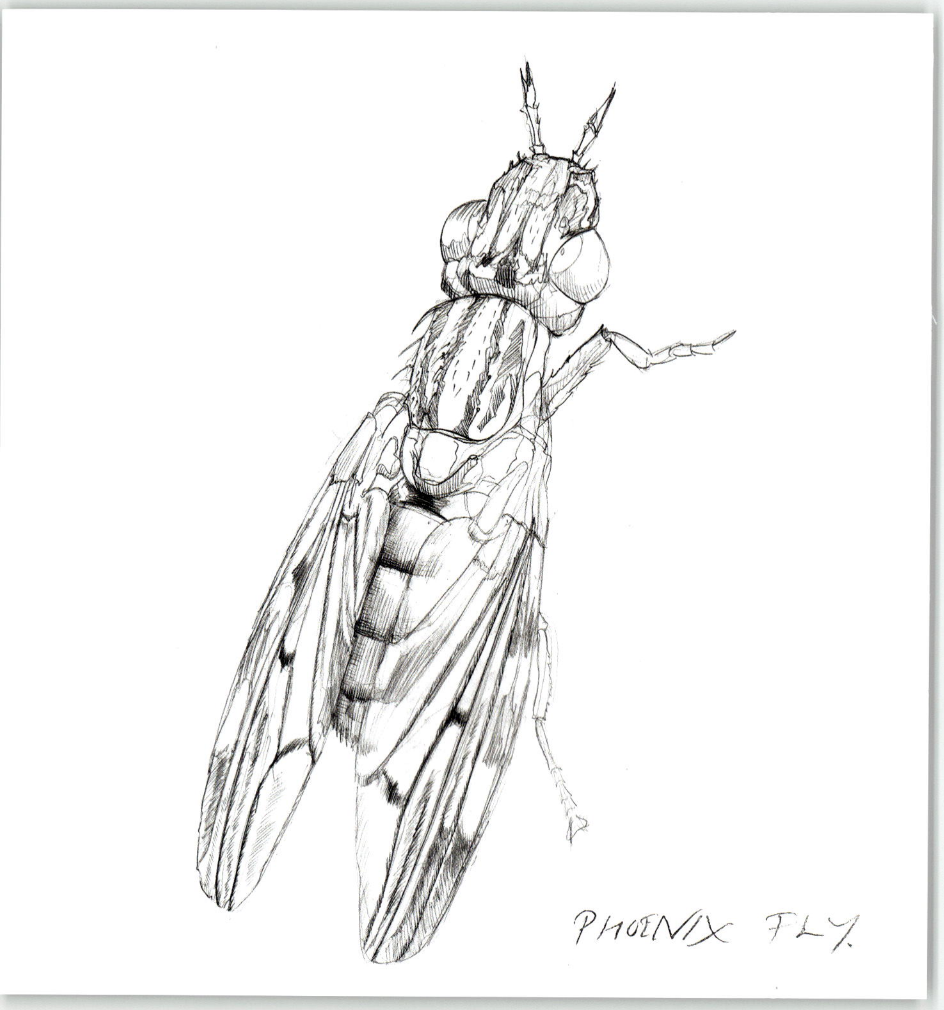
PHOENIX FLY.

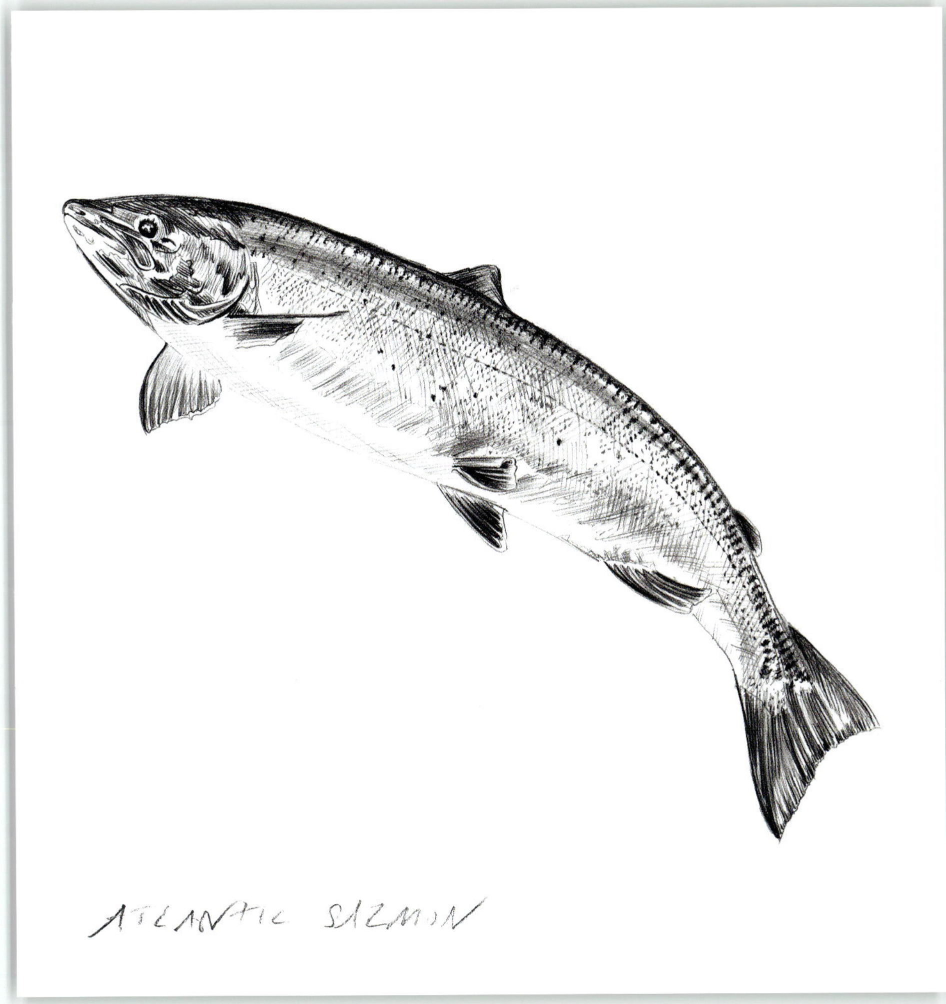
ATLANTIC SALMON

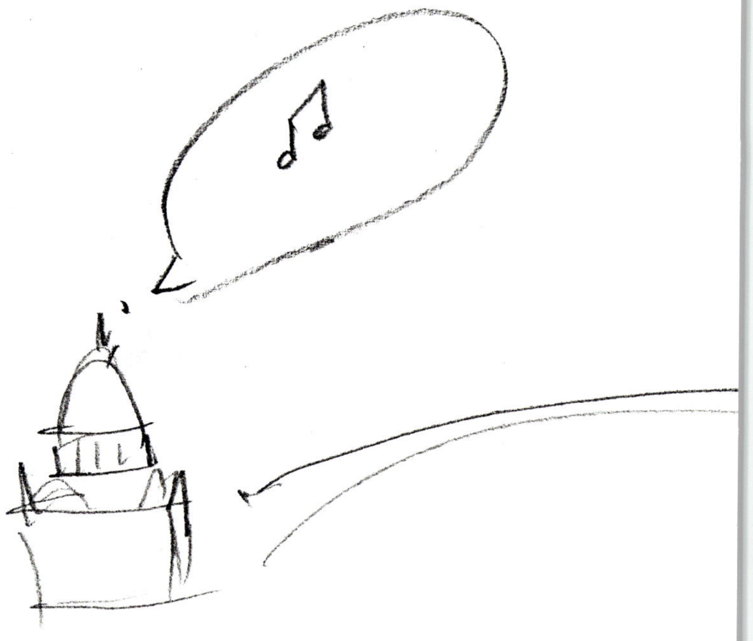

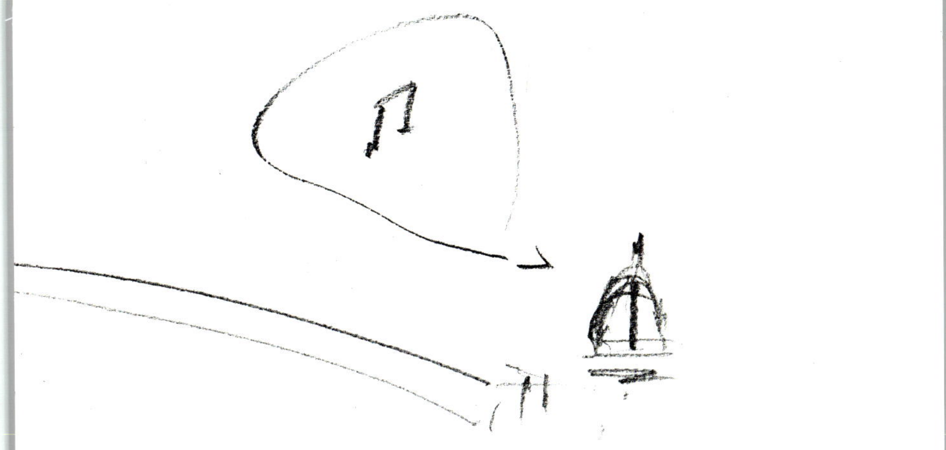

REDRAW THE EDGES OF YOUR SELF

I am the breeze that nurtures all things green …
I am the rain coming from the dew
that causes the grasses to laugh with the joy of life.

Hildegard of Bingen

This 3-metre by 2-metre illuminated bas-relief in pencil, charcoal and ink on plywood is based on a small paper collage that I made late one night in June 2022, which became part of a series of artists' posters in the Serpentine Galleries' *Back to Earth* exhibition. I had been making observational drawings of London's endangered species every day for a few months in preparation for *Come Home Again*. I would barely leave my desk, drawing insects, mammals, fish, birds, amphibians, fungi and plants from the moment I woke up until the time I went to sleep, usually listening to stories about them on podcasts while drawing. My encounter with the non-human species continued in my sleep: I had begun dreaming about them. I was shocked and a bit ashamed to realize how little the more-than-human world had featured in my dreams until I started devoting hours each day to observing it. I made *Redraw the Edges of Your Self* to mark this awakening at the edges of my hand and mind. In the way people get a tattoo to mark a significant personal shift, I made this piece like a giant paper and ink tattoo let loose beyond the boundaries of my skin.

August 2022

A CONVERSATION

With Dorothea von Hantelmann
Professor of Art and Society at Bard College Berlin

Es Devlin: I really enjoyed the sustained act of paying close attention to 243 non-human Londoners, drawing for sometimes 18 hours each day over the last few months. It's made me want to return to self-portraiture, to draw my reflection and my own drawing hand, to try to sustain this act of observational continuity – paying attention to the feathery antennae of a moth, the scale of a lizard, then to the eyelash or wrinkle on the skin, and recognizing the continuity between myself and the biospherical network, the expanded self, which sustains me.

Dorothea von Hantelmann: Your description reminds me of the German biologist and philosopher Andreas Weber, who once wrote in a book about erotic ecology, 'No biological description is complete unless it is laid out as a biology of love.'

In the early days of modern science, drawing was an important practice to approach and understand all these new phenomena discovered in the world. Involving the mind and the hand, the practice of drawing creates a connection to the studied object that is not only rational, but also physical, emotional and affective. You give something of yourself. In addition, drawing imbues these objects that are studied with time, which was an important factor in the early days of experiencing art in museums. Goethe, for example, spent hours, days and months in museums, looking, writing and drawing.

Es: That is such a valuable way into this conversation, to talk about it as an act of Eros, as an act of love.

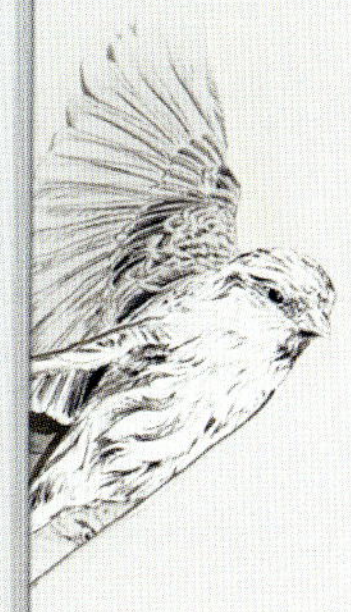

REDR/

I am the breez
I am the rain c
that causes th

This 3-metre
ink on plywo(
night in June
the Serpenti(
observationa
for a few mo(
leave my des
fungi and pla
to sleep, usu
drawing. My
sleep: I had b
ashamed to r
in my dreams
I made *Redra*
edges of my
significant pe
tattoo let loo

Dorothea: Yes, and – again with Weber – it's going beyond the limited and limiting modern notion of love to capture Eros as a desire of all beings, human and non-human, to unfold, to realize, to expand beyond one's self. Touch and material penetration are fundamental forces of reality. Perhaps we can understand your drawings in this way – as a form of material penetration and, by extension, of love. This leads me to something else I was thinking in relation to *Come Home Again*: how it, as a monument to these endangered species, reminds us of our own vulnerability and fragility. Modernity has been obsessed with the idea of abolishing death. But it is in the acknowledgement of death, of our mortality and vulnerability, that we can celebrate life and perhaps be as alive as possible.

I wonder what, for you, is the specific potential of a project like this one, where you have the possibility to create everything: the form, the content and the ritual. This is very different from your stage design works.

Es: Yes. I think that's the daunting thing but also an opportunity, having developed a practice which, for the past twenty years, has responded to primary texts – whether Shakespeare, opera libretti or more contemporary texts like a pop song. In 2016, I had the opportunity to write and design for my own text. Interestingly, the processes are not so different. Because the practice has always been creating environments for ritual, what I've tended to do in the work I'm now authoring is to still make the ritual, but just draw the threads together myself. A lot of text is drawn from those whom I admire, read and would like to communicate with audiences more broadly, such as Joanna Macy, David Abram, Timothy Morton and Rebecca Solnit. But I'm selecting my own collage of those texts, my own synthesis from work I think is incredibly important. I do the same with music, so the ritual becomes a concert of voices – Bulgarian folk songs, African folk songs, some sacred music.

Every time I tried to make a piece that wasn't a total ritual artwork,

I felt somewhat unsatisfied. So the process is still trying to achieve what I feel when I'm in a stadium of 100,000 people, or a theatre, or a concert – where I often feel part of a temporary community, a sort of rehearsal society – but trying to take that energy out into the planet, where elements of it can be more precisely crafted to what I feel is most urgent to say.

Dorothea: This idea of creating something holistic – which works in different artistic registers, which addresses multiple senses simultaneously – goes beyond a modern understanding of art, which is so much connected to a modern impetus, a modern modality of separation. The modern separation of art corresponds to a logic of separation that permeates all areas of society: from the way modern societies are fundamentally organized, based on separation of powers as well as separation of state and church; to the organization of economy and production based on division of labour; to the division of knowledge, dividing wisdom into academic disciplines that bring forth such things as medical specializations according to individual parts or organs. Ritual forms are divided into different artistic disciplines to which, again following a division of labour, different sense organs are assigned – visual art for the eyes, music for the ears, dance for the body.

This general model of separation, differentiation and specialization could initially and over a long period of time achieve great wealth and welfare effects. Yet the effects become progressively smaller over time and, moreover, the consequential damages grow, be they of an ecological or psychosocial nature. These have to be included, and can only be addressed with difficulty by this culture of specialization. The principle of separation has prevailed to a degree where the lack of ability to think of the whole becomes more apparent than the need for further forms of specialization. From today's perspective, where the social, ecological, economic and psychological consequences of this attitude of separation press irrefutably into consciousness, where people are sickened by

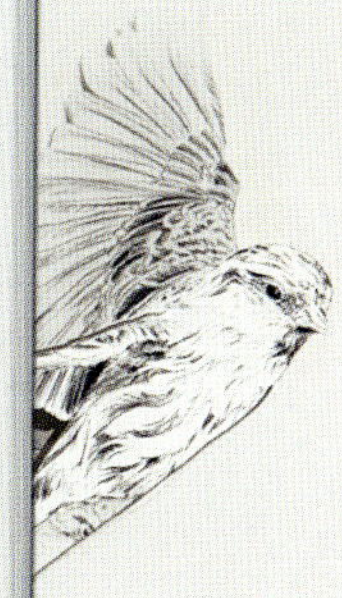

REDR/

I am the bree
I am the rain
that causes t

This 3-metre
ink on plywo
night in June
the Serpenti
observationa
for a few mo
leave my des
fungi and pla
to sleep, usu
drawing. My
sleep: I had
ashamed to
in my dream
I made *Redr*
edges of my
significant p
tattoo let loo

their inability to envision wholeness, we become increasingly aware of the limitations of a culture that no longer knows any form, practice or ritual for wholeness.

Es: As I've gone through this process, I ask myself where this practice is leading and what I'm going to do next. What I've realized is that what I'm most interested in, what I'm making, is not actually the resultant drawing. The drawing is a means to something else.

While I've been drawing, I've been filming the process – and as an artefact, I think that the film is the real work. Because ultimately what I want to express is the continuity that I experienced having done this practice of 243 drawings, one after the other, in a concentrated period. As I've done it, I've bounced between the veins of a leaf and the veins on a bat's wing, between the scales on a fish and the scales on the back of an insect. That is what I want to really communicate. Because – and I'm reminded of the James Gleick book, *Chaos* – these morphologies are ultimately governed by the same laws, the same fractal equations.

Dorothea: It's beautiful to understand art as a medium to create, to manifest, to experience these kinds of correspondences between animate and inanimate beings – between us and everything that surrounds us. Art can capture how we are part of an ecology of living things, and in that sense it can ground us.

Es: And I think, in addition, I've always been concerned that any work I create should not only draw attention to these phenomena, but should offer first some kind of consolation, and some kind of instruction, as a tool to help us take the next step forward. I hope with the ritual offered by *Come Home Again* we have this clarity of instruction.

Each day, the invitation to the visitor is to come and sit where the choir will sit that evening. The choir won't turn up till sunset and

528

will be there only for an hour. But for the rest of the day, you're invited to come and sit in the choir stalls. There's a hymn book on the back of each stall with text about the project, and a QR code which takes you to a microsite explaining a story about every animal. Some of these stories are really beautiful. The swift, for example, flies the equivalent distance to the moon and back seven times in its lifetime; it flies non-stop for ten months. Its life is so unique, so extraordinary, and it is at risk of extinction. The London Wildlife Trust, who are collaborators on this project, try to protect these species through building codes and by rigorously documenting numbers. They are excited by the work because, in their words, it encourages people to create a place in their imaginations for these species to exist.

I cannot tell you the shift that happened in my mind just these last months. I hadn't seen a tiger moth since I was a child; there used to be quite a lot of them when I was a kid in the countryside. But suddenly my daughter spotted one in our house and it has since been sitting above where I'm drawing. Maybe it's because my family is now paying attention. Or maybe it is paying more attention to us.

Dorothea: Naming it gives it an identity and creates a connection, a relation.

Es: Yes, which is why I have also spent a long time recording the names of these animals so that when you go into the piece during the day, you will hear their names being read and these little pieces of information about each animal.

I have found that some of the most interesting species are those that have ten different names, because names embody the history of human connection to the plant or animal. To have many names suggests a duration of a connection between humans and this species. By inviting people to learn the names, the work tries to open these histories, too.

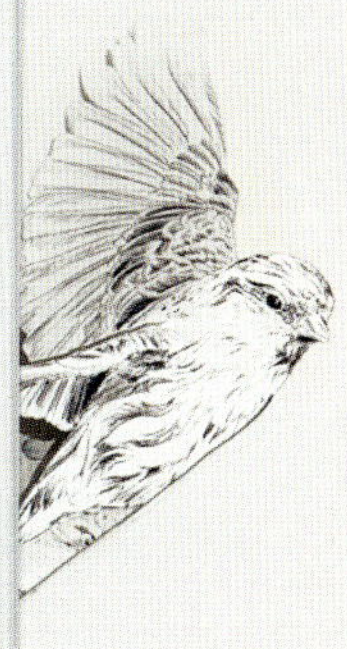

REDR

I am the bree
I am the rain
that causes t

This 3-metre
ink on plywo
night in June
the Serpenti
observationa
for a few mo
leave my des
fungi and pla
to sleep, usu
drawing. My
sleep: I had
ashamed to
in my dream
I made *Redr*
edges of my
significant pe
tattoo let loo

Dorothea: It's interesting how your project combines this aspect of grounding, of connecting us to the species around us, with an uplifting moment that introduces higher frequencies. I'm referring to the singing choirs. The choir is a very powerful medium. In general, hearing connects us more directly with the environment, while the eye is a distancing sense, as sociologist Georg Simmel puts it. The choir is interesting because it has this power to produce these emotional energies that Émile Durkheim called 'effervescence' and that create this feeling of being part of something transcendent. It's a form of singing that seems to come from a different time and place.

Es: I agree. As Joanna Macy says, 'We are our world knowing itself', and sound seems to have the capacity to make this more obvious to us. That's how you feel when you engage with choral song. It's the world knowing itself, the world singing itself. If we could recognize this, realize the beauty in some aspects of human culture despite how badly we have treated other aspects of our environment, we would go a long way towards finding balance with the biosphere and our place in it.

Dorothea: Speaking of balance, I'd like to hear your thoughts on concepts of the active and passive in art and to speak a little bit about participation. The Evensongs that are part of *Come Home Again* are songs where the audience gets to be involved, as far as I understand. They can join in. Theatres and museums conceptualize the partaker primarily as a recipient, as a passive viewer or spectator. A significant question to me seems to be how a new ritual can be based on a more active conception of the partaker. How it will – as in traditional rituals, and along with contemporary knowledge and creative societies – conceptualize the partaker as a participant who can freely choose to be or not be active, and thus can both actively and passively contribute to the outcome of the ritual.

Es: Shortly after COVID restrictions eased, I went to the theatre for a production which I didn't enjoy, but I completely loved the audience. I sat down and the lights dimmed and there was this hush of absolute concentration and generosity. That was my favourite part of the whole night – before it started. I just so enjoyed the beauty of how dedicated the audience was. And because I hadn't been to the theatre for a while, there was a kind of absolute contrast with what the world online had become during lockdown. This group of people were so giving of their entire being to this moment. There is so much potential in that.

Dorothea: You're absolutely right. We could think of theatre this way, not primarily as the production of a piece, but as a gathering of people, willing to give their time and attention to something that addresses them with all their senses and all their capacities – body, mind and soul. This would connect the idea of participation to forms of wholeness.

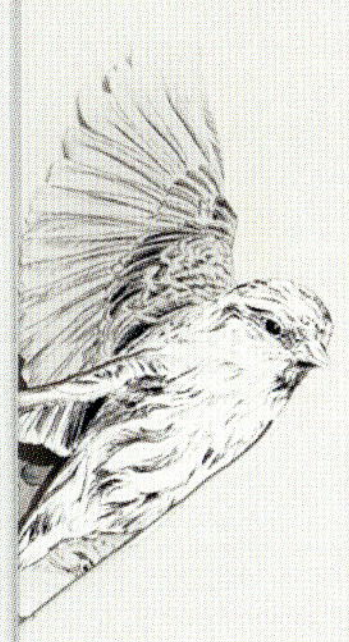

Es: It's interesting to consider Tate Modern. When I've been examining why I chose this place, I think it relates ultimately to the society I grew up with and its relationship to wholeness.

I grew up in England during the '80s, when one might say the dogma of the twenty years under Margaret Thatcher was that there is no such thing as society, only the individual. Now, with the reading I'm doing, people like Joanna Macy are essentially saying there is no such thing as the individual, only the biosphere. I see the trajectory of my own practice as a journey between those two statements; and I see Tate Modern as a pivotal place in the middle, this kind of balancing point on that journey.

In 1997, lots changed in the UK. The country changed its government. It was a year when the nation responded in a very unexpected way to the death of Princess Diana. And, quite significantly from my perspective, it was the year Tate Modern opened with a whole new attitude towards the art gallery. Here was a centre of industrial power: Bankside power station on the banks of the River Thames –

an arterial, natural, planetary force – which had always sat opposite St Paul's Cathedral, a seat of ecclesiastical power. With the opening of Tate Modern, it seemed to unite or reconcile these varying forces into a new whole, into a profound statement of cultural power.

I think the urgency with which I wanted to place something outside Tate Modern, outside this space, singing back across the river to re-forge that resonance with the church, has something to do with a desire to bring together these different ways of looking at the world.

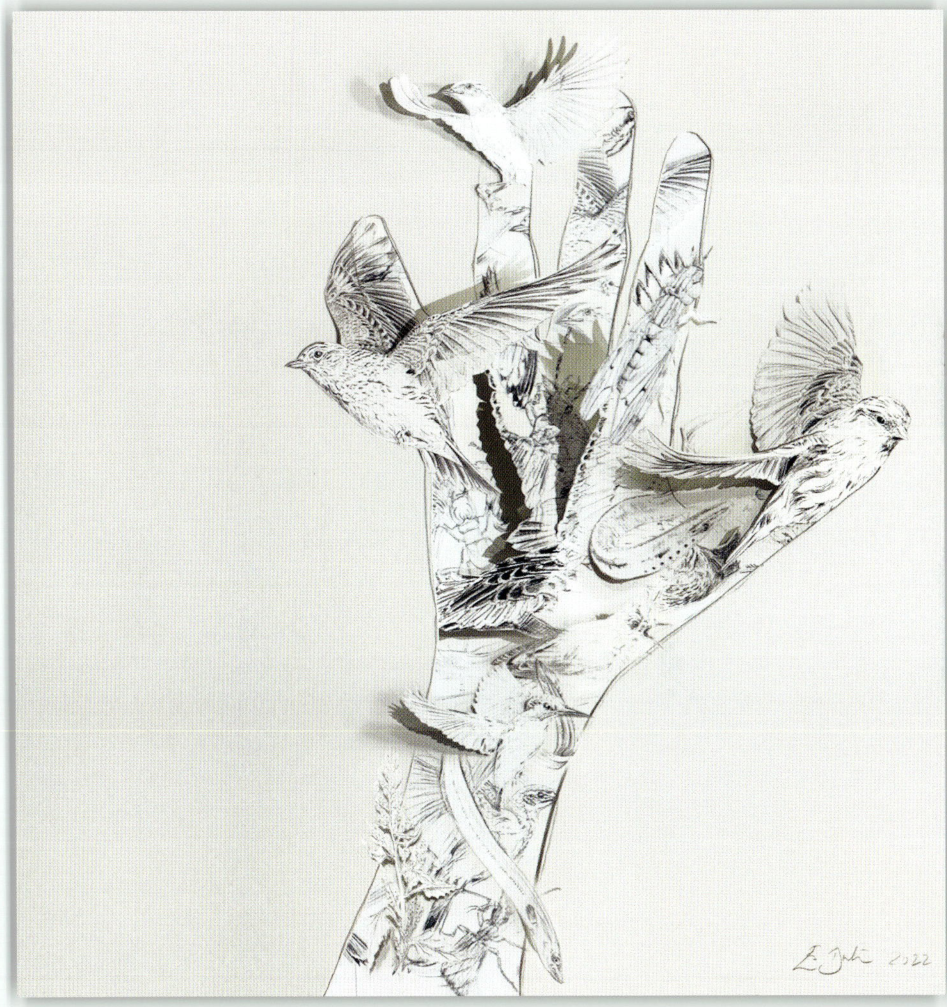

NEVADA ARK

After the flood all the colours came out.

U2, 'Beautiful Day'

In September 2023, U2 inaugurated the newly constructed Sphere in Las Vegas with their canon of contemporary hymns, envisaging the building as an illuminated cathedral in the desert. Together with the band, Willie Williams, Ric Lipson and other creative counsellors, we conceived a group art show formed of 256 million LED pixels pierced by 167,000 speakers. We made the Sphere a protagonist of the work, first formed of concrete, then splitting, melting and unfolding to reveal a series of glimmering digital worlds, the last of which was called *Nevada Ark*: a domed alabaster ceiling carved with the illuminated forms of Nevada's endangered species. The choral introduction to U2's song 'Beautiful Day' suffused the bleached creaturely forms with colour. The audience emerged to find the Sphere's exterior broadcasting out to space the song of the species we had started in *Come Home Again* outside Tate Modern the previous year.

On the opening night, Bono observed across the stalls to Paul McCartney that, with its fusion of sound and image, the Sphere's singing LED skin offers the most advanced medicine yet in response to The Beatles' first stadium show at Shea Stadium in 1965 – in which the band were largely invisible and inaudible over their audience's 131-decibel screams.

534

54–57 862–863

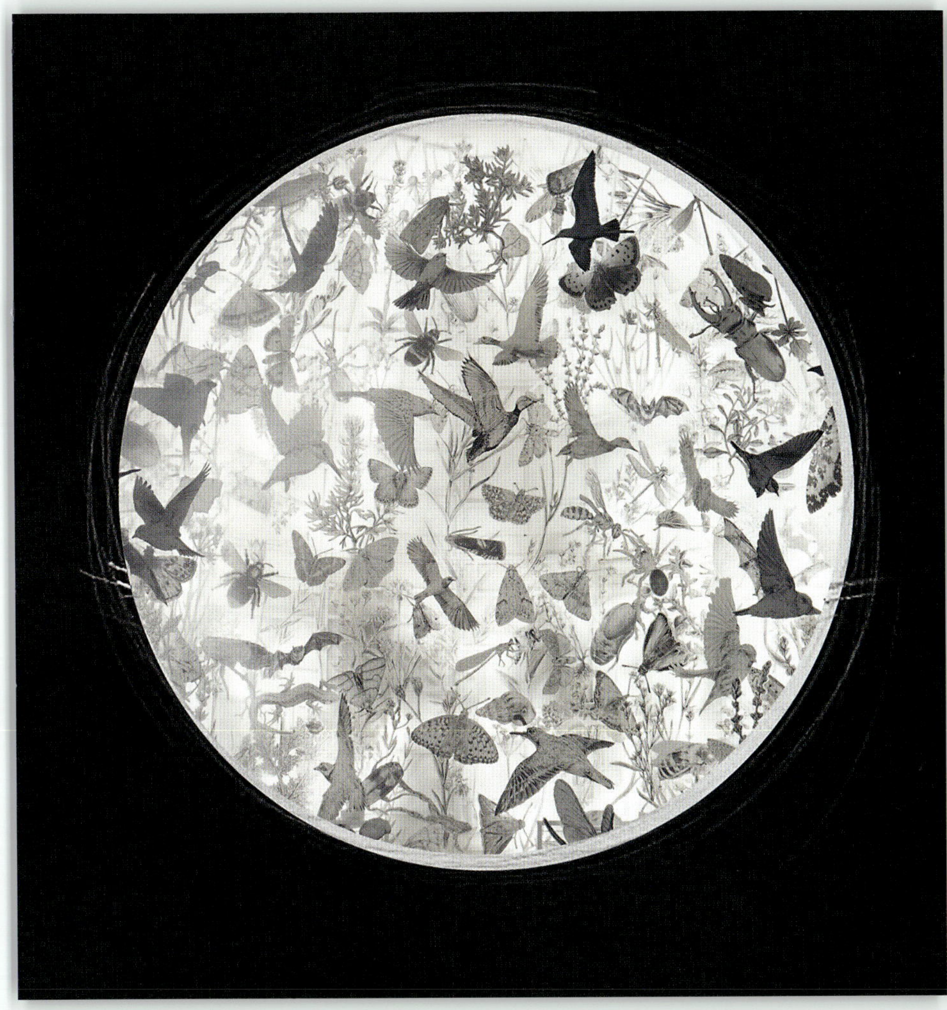

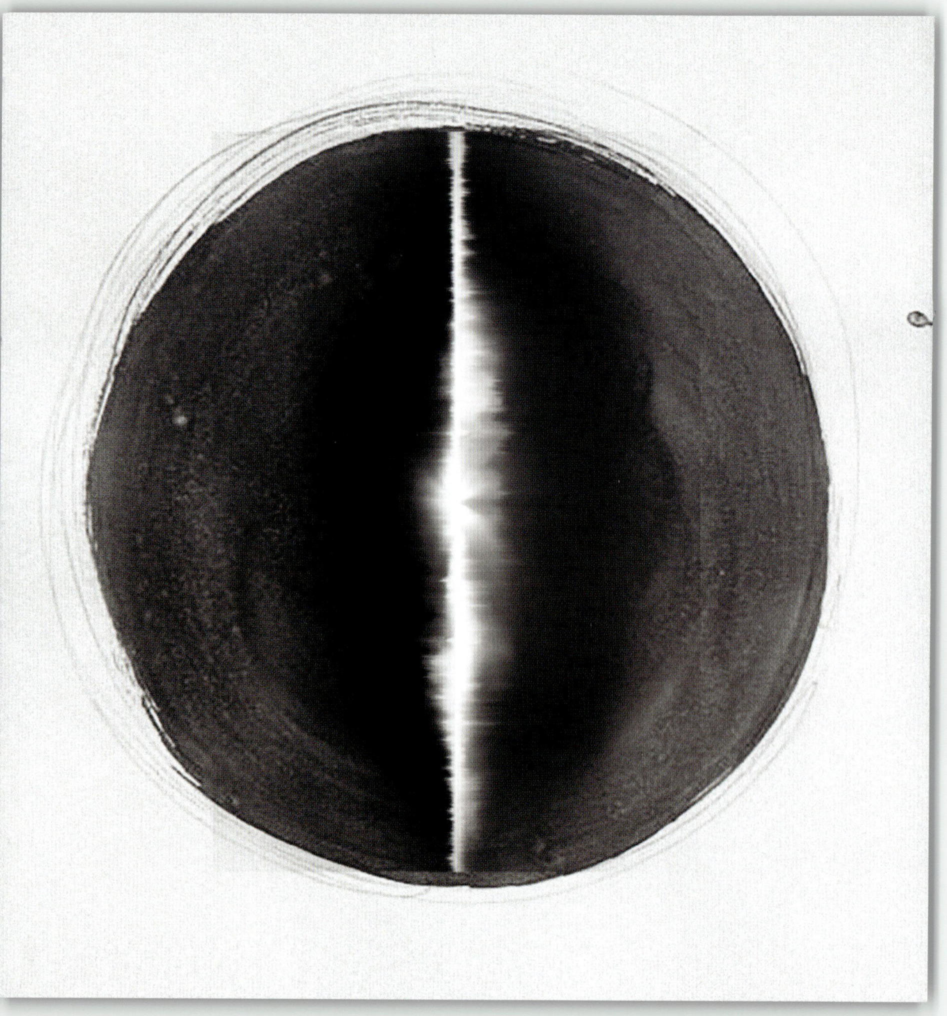

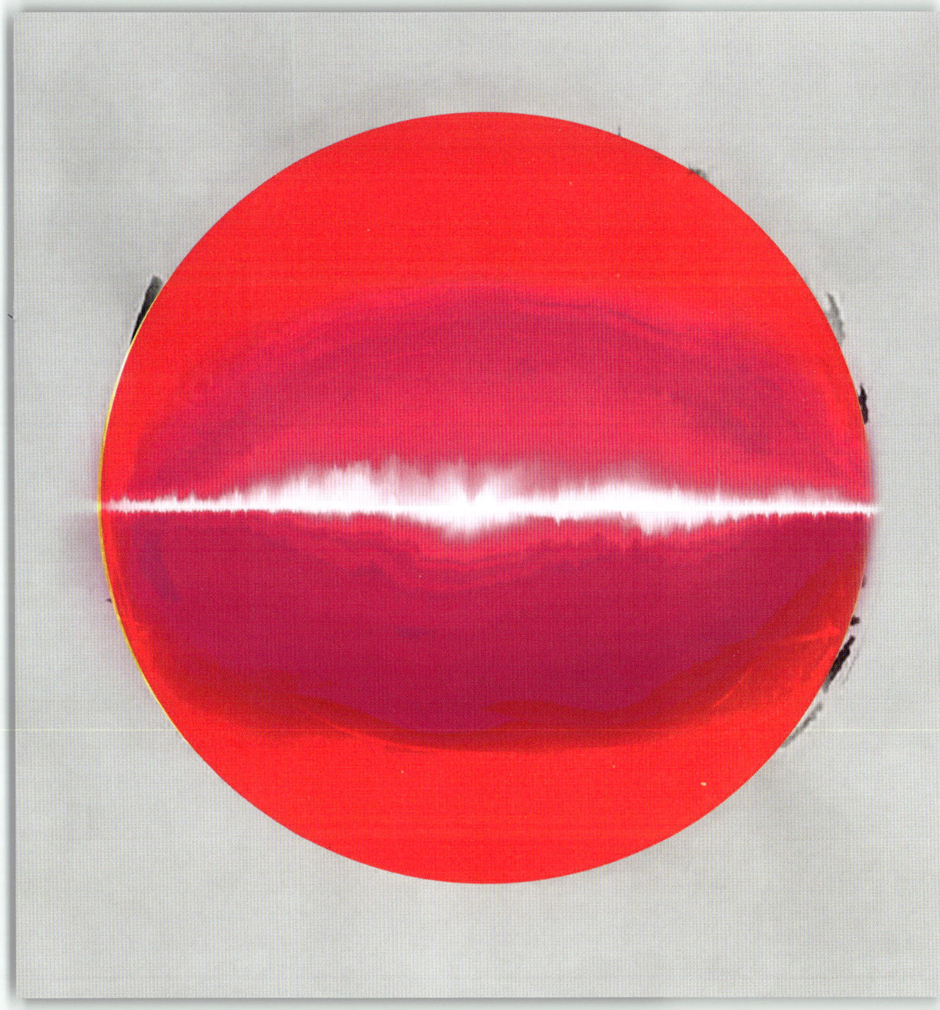

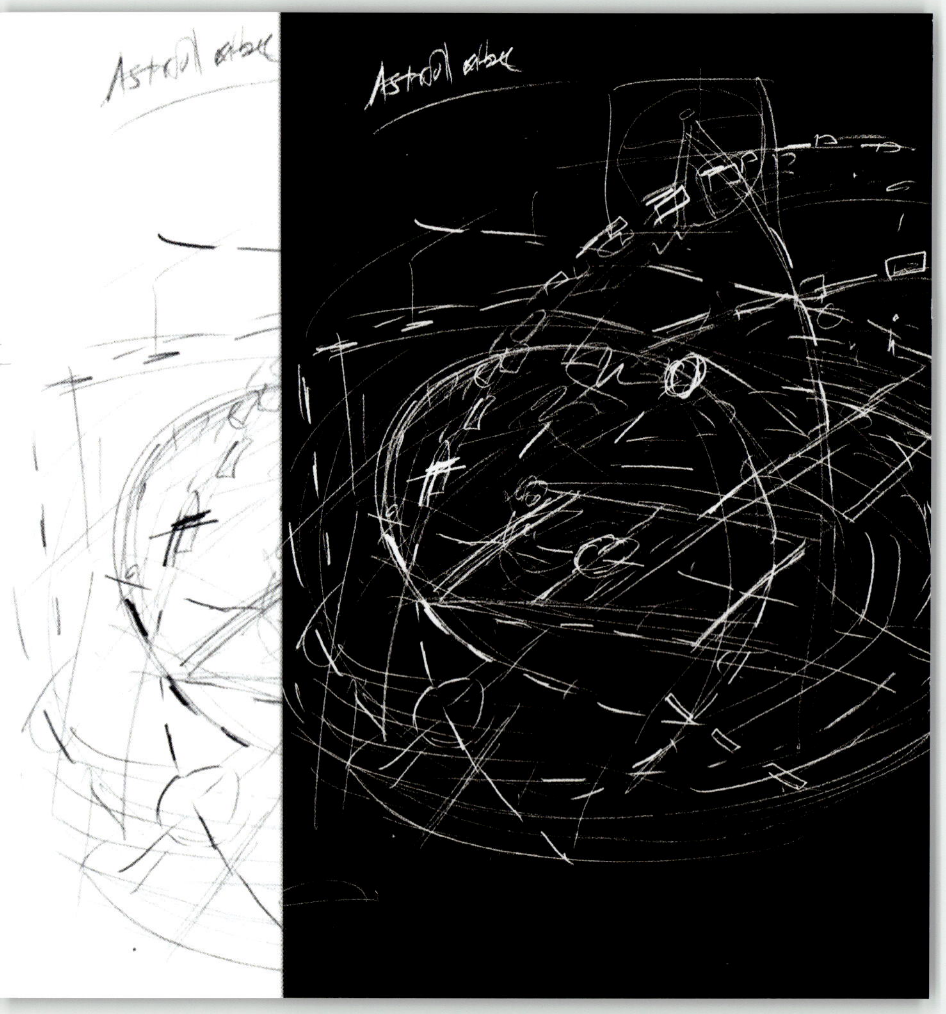

DEAR ENGLAND

What England has to learn, Gareth … it's not how to win. It's how to lose …

James Graham, *Dear England*

James Graham's *Dear England* premiered at the Olivier Theatre in June 2023. The play invokes Britain's nostalgia for England's 1966 World Cup win, and explores the nature of the country's misplaced exceptionalism through the lens of the England football team's historic failure to win a match on penalties. We staged the scenes within a ballet of boxes on three concentric revolving rings, between an illuminated circular floor and kinetic halo, to invoke locker rooms, streets and stadia.

The audience was a 50:50 mix of theatre lovers who don't know much about football, and football fans who don't normally go to the theatre. Every evening they took their seats as a split community, a politely tolerant microcosm of a divided nation. By the end of each show, the entire audience was singing 'Sweet Caroline' together – a temporary society if only for a night, resounding the civic optimism cemented into the amphitheatre's concrete seams.

712–713

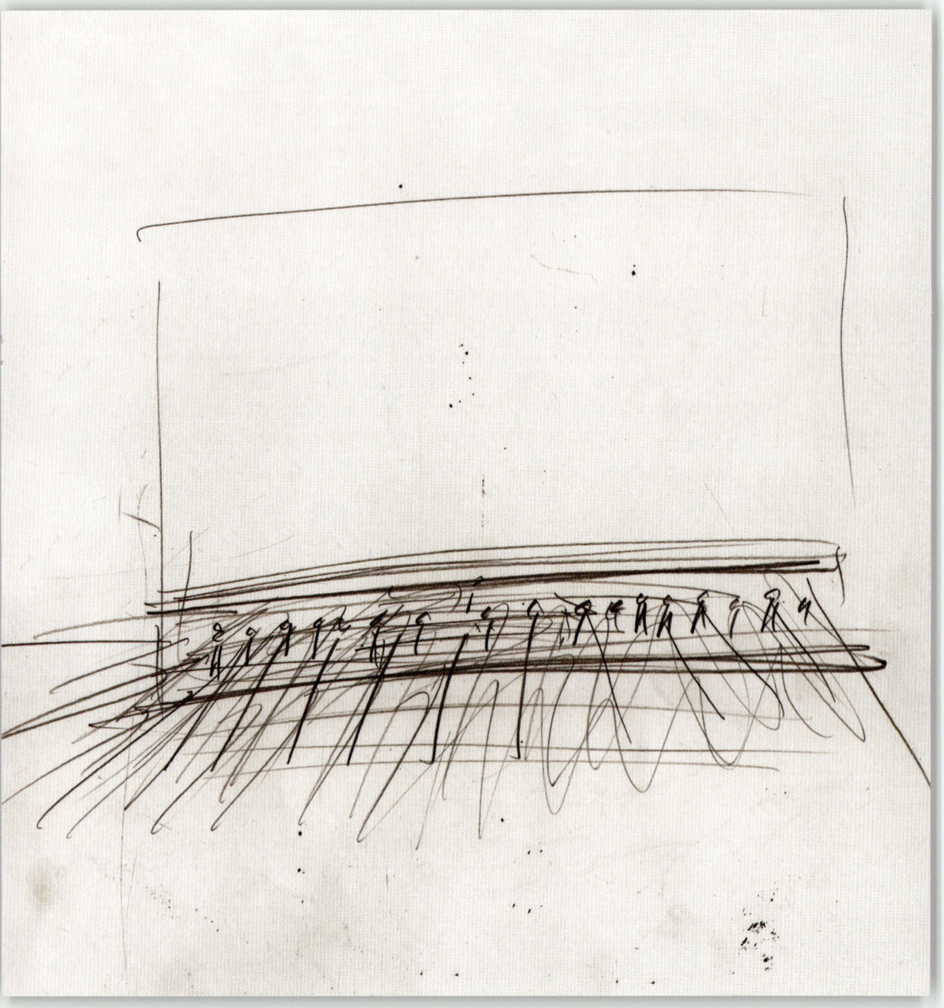

FREE YOUR MIND

I can only show you the door. You're the one that has to walk through it … You have to let it all go, Neo. Fear, doubt, and disbelief. Free your mind.

Lana Wachowski, *The Matrix*

Based on the Wachowski sisters' prescient 1999 film, *The Matrix,* Danny Boyle conceived *Free Your Mind* as a tightly drilled mass choreographic work with Boy Blue, the London 2012 Olympic Opening Ceremony choreographers. The show inaugurated Factory International in Manchester in October 2023. It is one of Europe's most ambitious new art centres, and the UK's largest investment in a cultural project since Tate Modern in 2000.

We gave the audience red and blue tickets on arrival, to emulate the central choice in *The Matrix* between a red pill and a blue pill; between reality or simulation. A lecture by Alan Turing rooted the show's exploration of contemporary tech-enslavement in the punch cards of Manchester's industrial past. We led the audience from the hall into a vast warehouse where we had installed an all-encompassing white cyclorama to conjure the film's white placeless 'construct' scene. Here, red ticket holders watched from one side of a luminous 50-metre-wide traverse stage, blue ticket holders from the other.

42–43

AN ATLAS OF ES DEVLIN

I came to explore the wreck. The words are purposes. The words are maps.

Adrienne Rich, 'Diving into the Wreck'

I had begun compiling a book about my practice in 2017. I envisaged it as a sculptural object, perforated by apertures. I struggled for years to find a way of organizing my archive that would be nourishing to a reader, rather than exhausting.

It was only when curator and editor Andrea Lipps, designer Daniel Devlin and I separated the works into sketches, illuminated forms, and sequences of a coloured spectrum, that the broad range of elements started to find a palatable order. Meanwhile, Andrea and her colleagues spent weeks at my studio archive selecting objects, sculptures and sketches to show at an exhibition, and my composer colleagues Polyphonia (Jade Pybus and Andy Theakstone) gathered together the music they had written to underscore our installations and public sculptures.

An Atlas of Es Devlin became the title I gave to these reflections on my decades-long practice: the first edition of this book, an album of underscored texts, and a monographic exhibition. We launched the book at the Serpentine Galleries in October 2023 and the exhibition at Cooper Hewitt, Smithsonian Design Museum a month later. Luke Halls assembled elements from our video installations on a 50-metre-wide LED sculpture at Factory International in Manchester to debut the album.

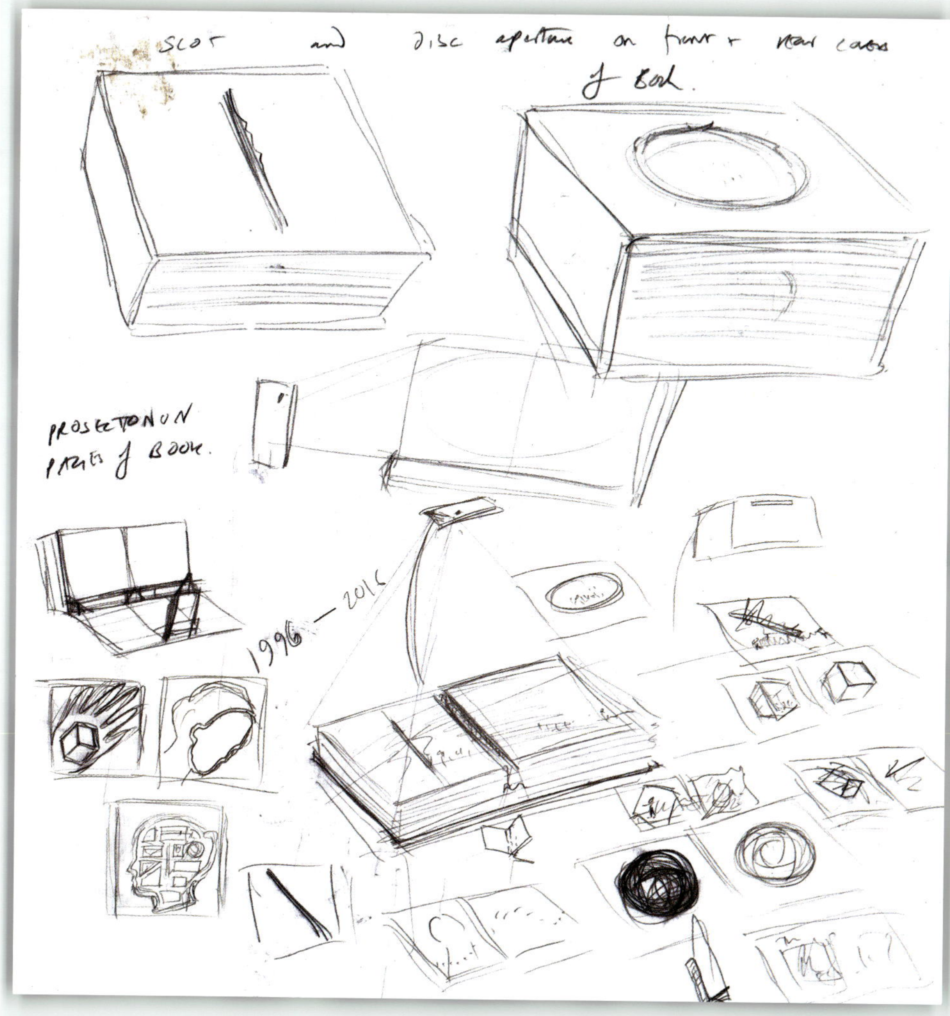
slot and disc aperture on front + rear covers of book.
PROJECTION ON PAGES of BOOK.
1996 — 2016

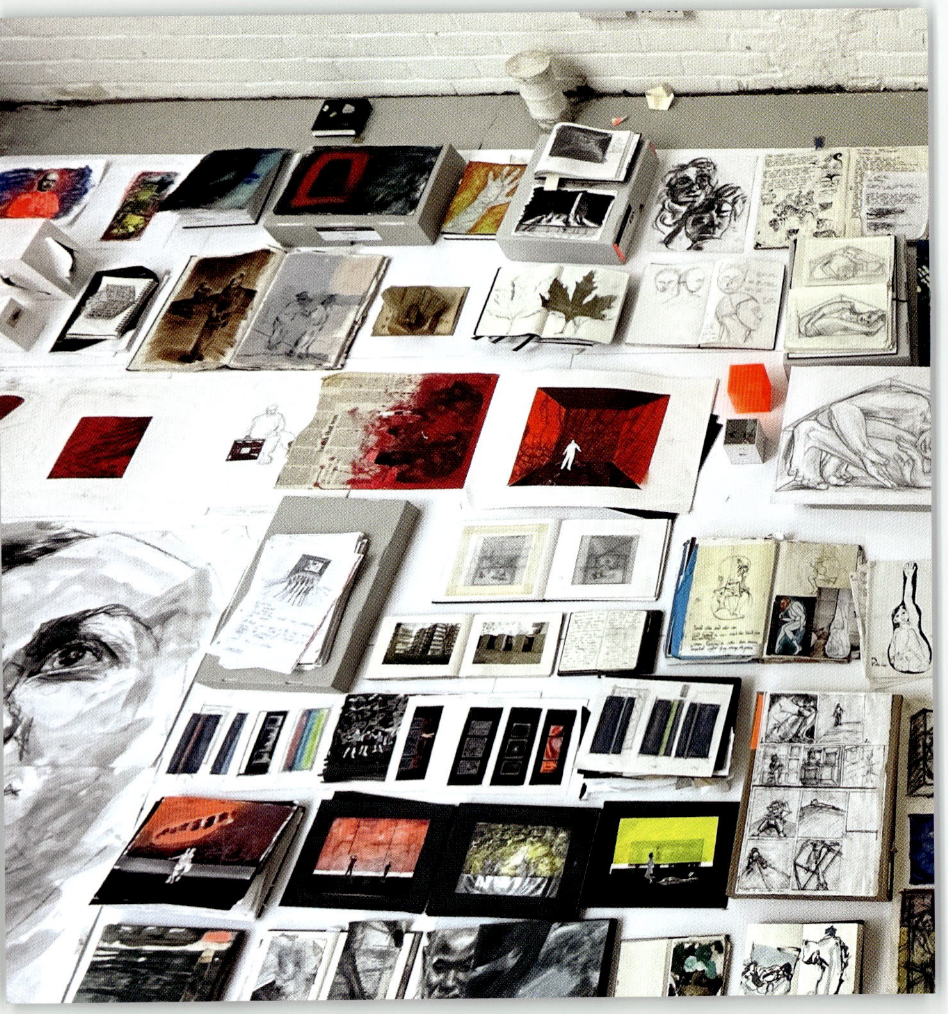

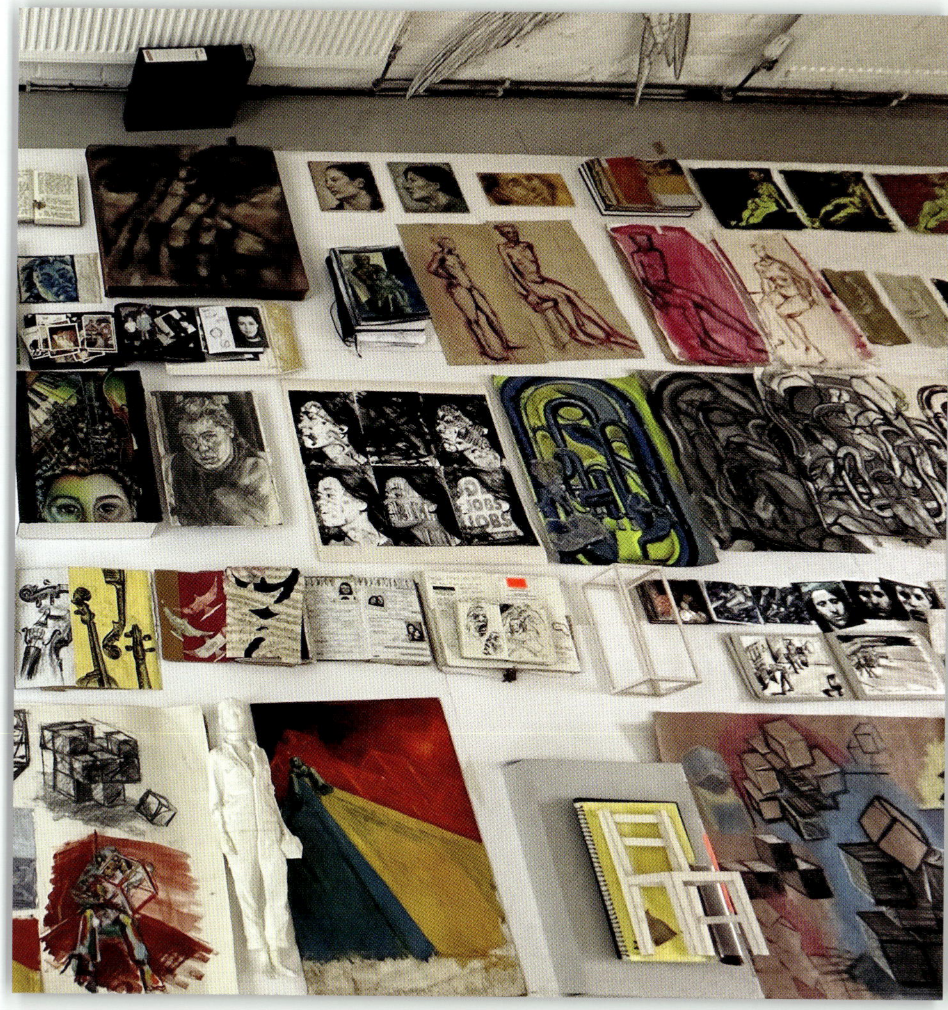

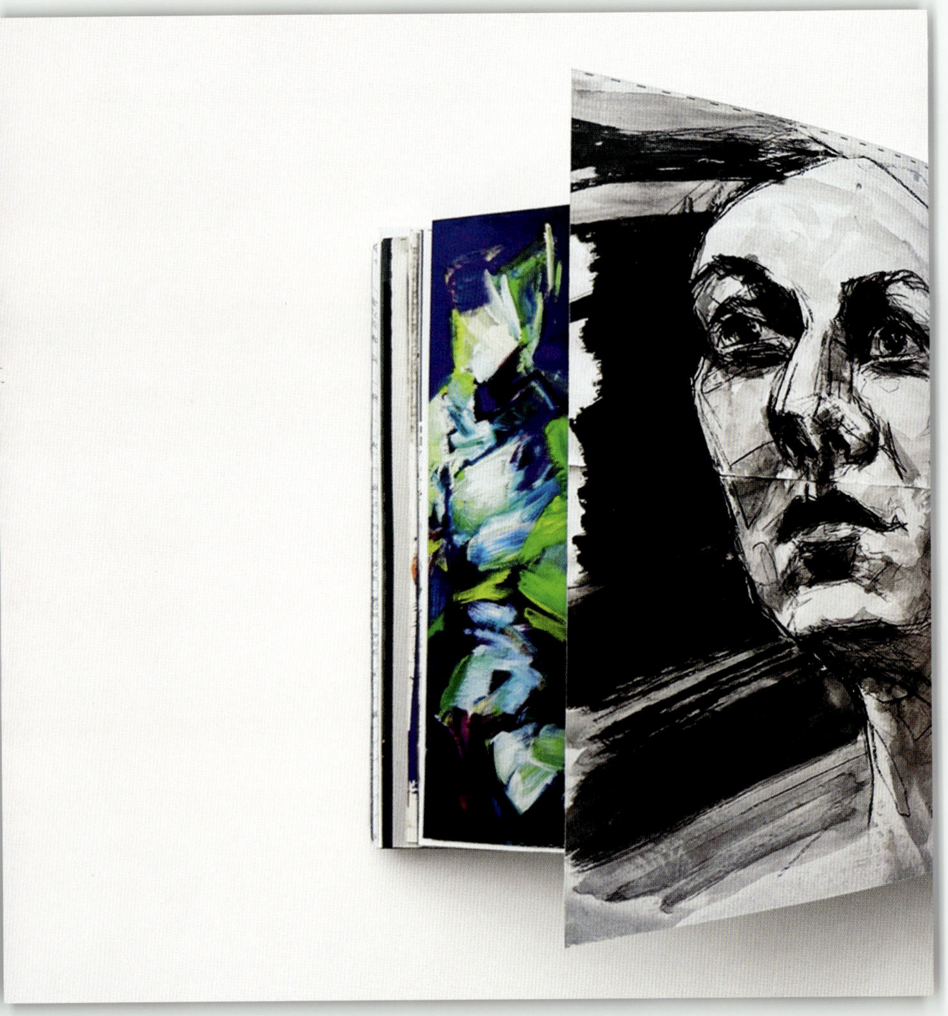

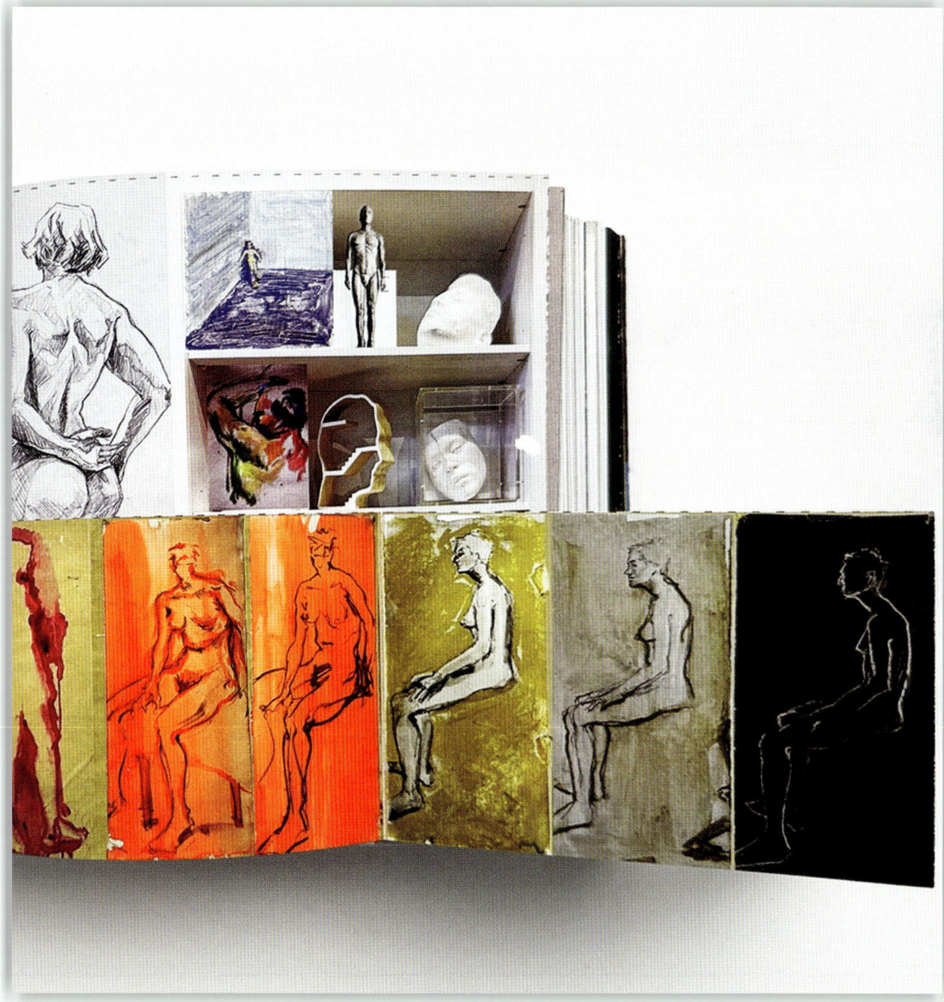

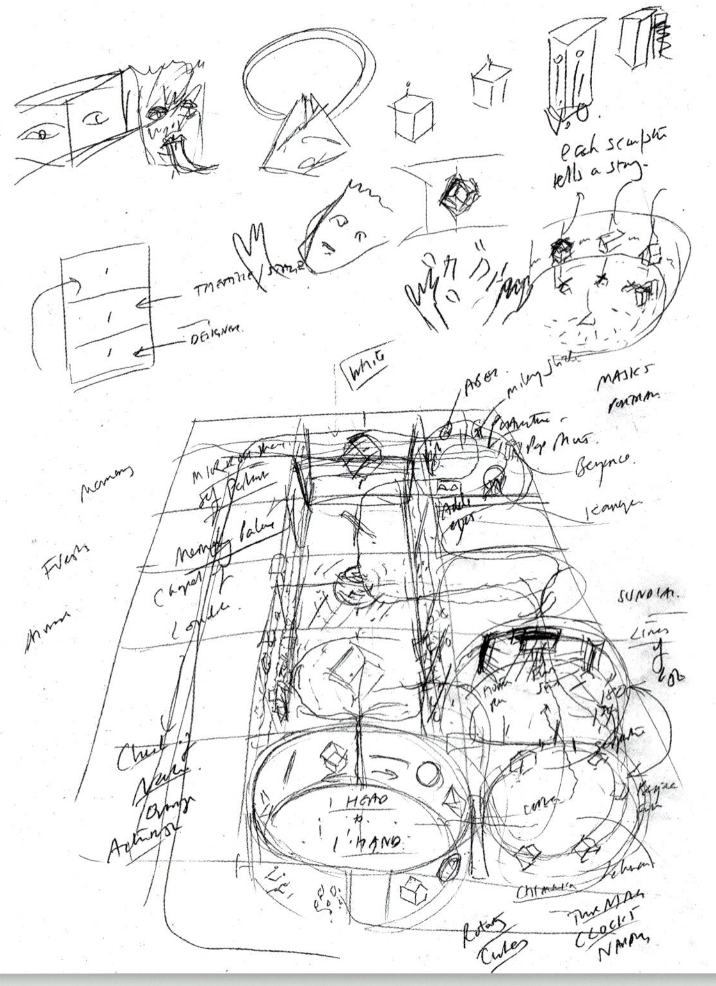
each sculpture tells a story.
WHITE
MASKS
SUNDIAL
1 HEAD
1 HAND

AN ATLAS OF ES DEVLIN

A map tells you where you've been, where you are, and where you're going – in a sense it's three tenses in one.

Peter Greenaway

In November 2023, visitors entered a replica of my London studio on the top floor of Cooper Hewitt, Smithsonian Design Museum in New York. They sat at my desk, surrounded by sketches, paper sculptures, works in progress. A radio played snatches of the three decades of music and news bulletins that have underscored my working life. The objects on the shelves and table came to life, animated with projection-mapped drawings, film clips and my recorded voice. I invited the audience to co-imagine the studio wall splitting apart, so they could walk through it and enter this first monographic museum exhibition in which curator Andrea Lipps brought together over 300 original objects that hold the roots of my practice.

The studio replica from this exhibition is now being prepared for re-creation at solo shows over the coming years at the Design Museum in London, Casa Bradesco in São Paulo, Futura Seoul, Powerhouse Parramatta in Sydney, and ArtScience Museum in Singapore. In each of these places, visitors will sit among the fragile pencil and paper origins of everything I have made.

SCREENSHARE

Above all else, it is about leaving a mark that I existed: I was here. I was hungry. I was defeated. I was happy. I was sad. I was in love. I was afraid. I was hopeful. I had an idea and I had a good purpose and that's why I made works of art.

Felix Gonzalez-Torres

In May 2024, I contributed to *REVERB*, a 180 Studios group show. My response to the commission was a cinema screen which consisted of 365 sketchbooks. Each sketchbook contained replicas of drawings I had made over 35 years – sketches of London species, studies of my children, process drawings, traces of me trying to work out ideas or share them with collaborators. We projected an eight-minute film, an anthology of my earlier cinematic explorations, onto this 'sketchbook' screen. At the end of the film, a text emerged on the screen inviting each member of the audience to take a piece of the cinema screen – a single sketch – away with them.

The work draws on my experience of Felix Gonzalez-Torres's seminal 1991 sculpture *Untitled (Portrait of Ross in L.A.)*, which I first saw in 2000 at the Serpentine in London. Visitors were invited to take coloured sweets from a vast pile that gallery staff replenished daily, always maintaining 'an endless supply'. Staff only replaced the sketchbooks in *Screenshare* every three months. I would visit the work occasionally throughout its ten-month run. At times its surface was almost fully depleted – a screen made of torn edges. I had a visceral reaction to it, as if seeing my own skin plucked of feathers.

782–783

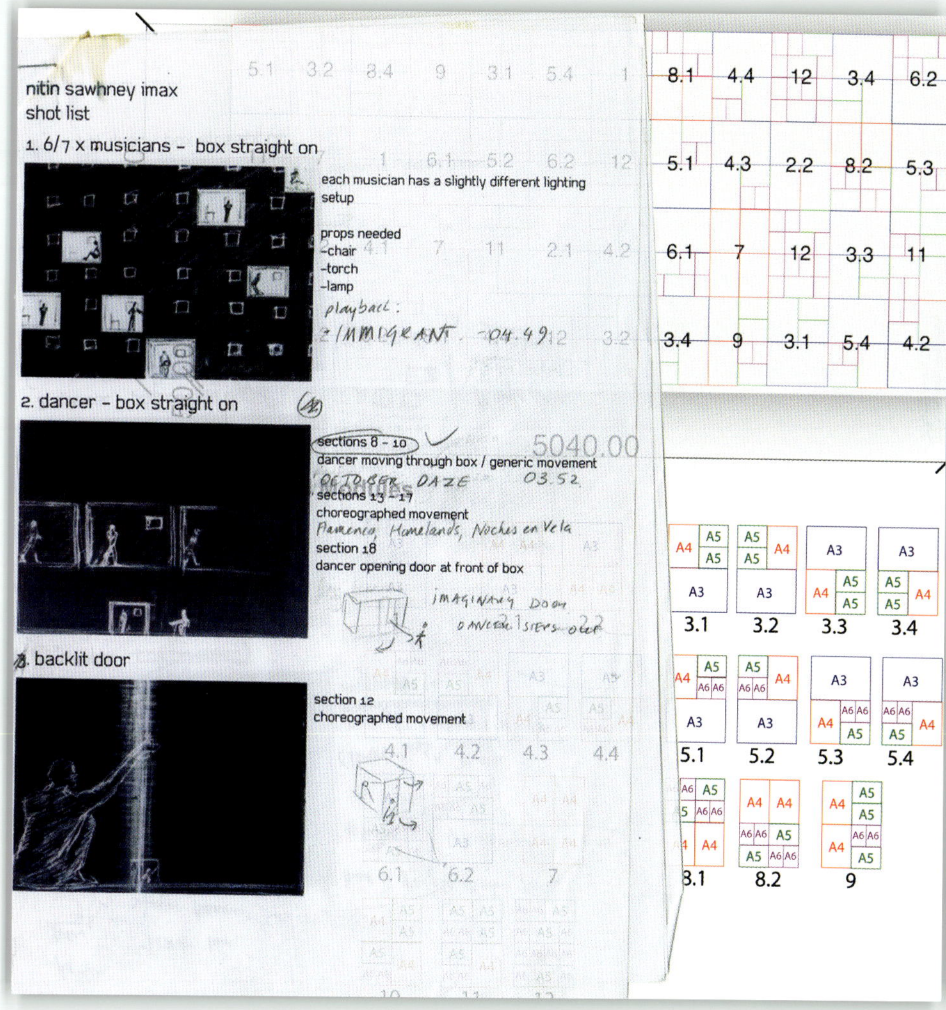
nitin sawhney imax
shot list
1. 6/7 x musicians - box straight on
each musician has a slightly different lighting setup
props needed
-chair
-torch
-lamp
playback:
IMMIGRANT 04.49
2. dancer - box straight on
sections 8 - 10
dancer moving through box / generic movement
OCTOBER DAZE 03.52
sections 13 - 17
choreographed movement
Flamenco, Homelands, Noches en Vela
section 18
dancer opening door at front of box
IMAGINARY DOOR
3. backlit door
section 12
choreographed movement
5040.00

GUCCI COSMOS

Those who think that objects aren't alive are eluding a great truth, however mysterious it may seem.

Alessandro Michele

Throughout 2023 and 2024, I became immersed in the Gucci archive in Florence. We made the *Gucci Cosmos* exhibition in Shanghai, London and Kyoto as a sequence of sculptural installations which expressed emblems of the Italian fashion house.

I traced Gucci's origin myth to the first electric lift in London at the Savoy Hotel in 1889. The elevator took seven minutes to reach the top floor. Some guests found the experience alarming and claustrophobic, so the theatre impresario and hotel owner Richard D'Oyly Carte painted it bright red and called it 'The Ascending Room'. A young Italian intern was installed to entertain guests during the slow ascent. He discussed horses, cars and British country pursuits with the guests. The world's luggage cycled inch by inch up and and down the storeys with the young Italian all day. By the time he returned to Florence he knew all he needed to know about human life and every detail of its luggage. The Italian intern immediately started work to expand his family saddle-making business. His name was Guccio Gucci.

I elided the mythic red elevator with the pulsing heart that Gucci's creative directors Alessandro Michele and Sabato De Sarno sought within the archive. A monumental deep red cabinet revolved as its drawers breathed open and closed, revealing glimmering glimpses of the Gucci archive within.

748–751 764–765

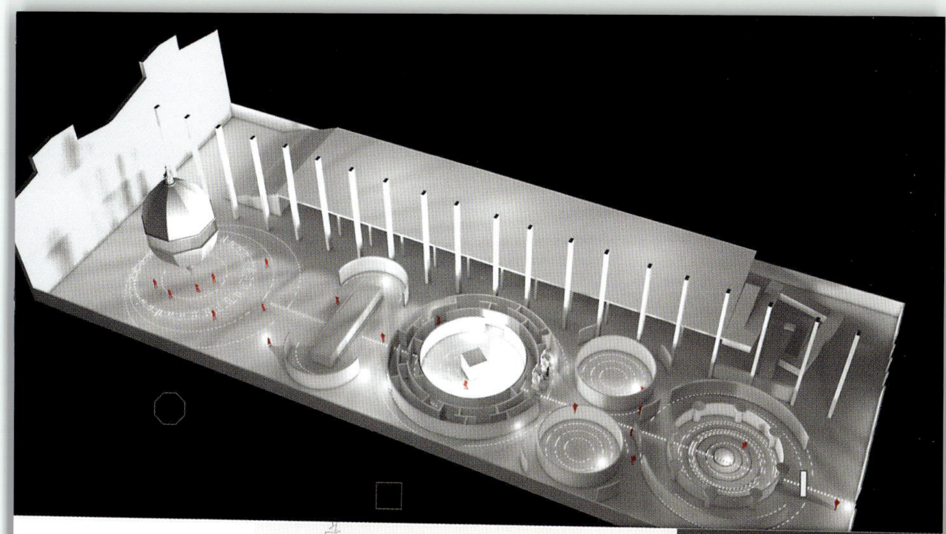

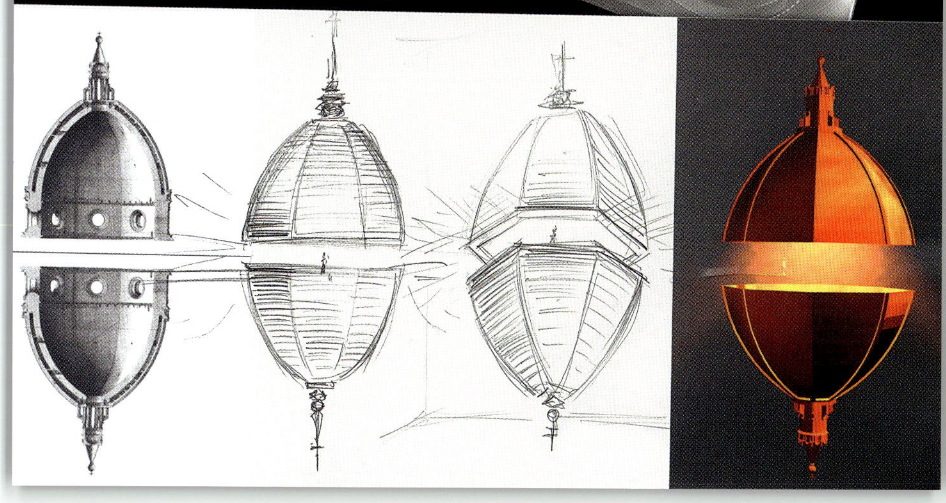

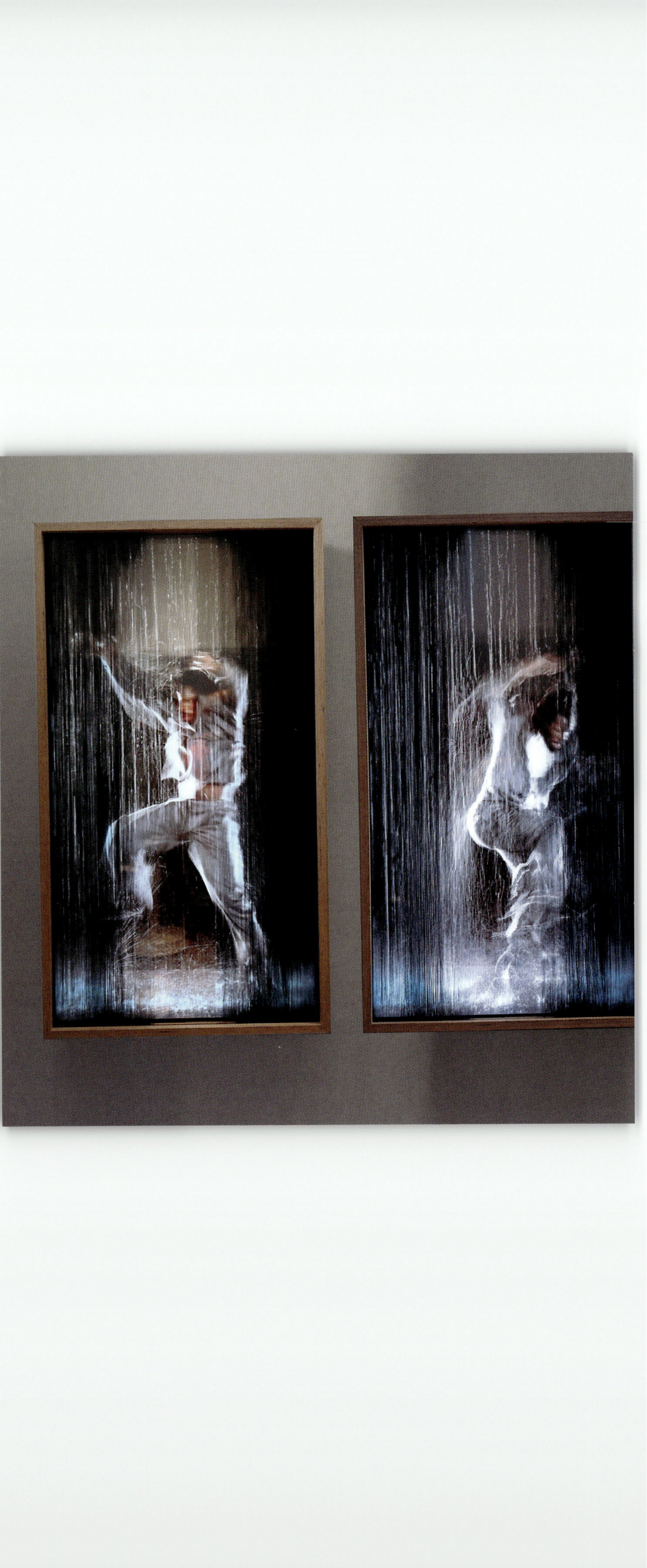

SURFACING

I don't want to see the choreography, I want to see the magic.
... I'm asking [the dancers] to be naked from the inside.
I want to see them. I don't want to see anything else.

Sharon Eyal

Between the two painted televisions that you see in this image, overlaying paint onto the pixels of slow-motion footage of a dancer through rain, we installed a four-metre-tall cuboid of constantly falling water in a booth at Art Basel, Switzerland, in June 2024. Every half an hour a small audience would gather around the work for 20 minutes and witness five dancers materialize within it. I had been drawn to philosopher Byung-Chul Han's suggestion that 'ritual is what makes time habitable' – and a commercial art fair like Art Basel is an unlikely environment for establishing a sustained engagement in ritual or performance, which is why we were keen to make this experiment.

Using a nineteenth-century magician's technique, we blinded the audience momentarily, causing their irises to contract so they perceived a darkness deep enough to conjure five human bodies, as if by magic, through the illuminated rain. I think the shock of the illusion destabilized viewers' expectations and engaged them more intently with the work. The Jerusalem-born choreographer Sharon Eyal and I did not discuss the deadly attacks by Hamas on Israeli citizens on 7 October 2023, nor the brutal reprisals against Gazan civilians by the Israeli Defence Force. We made a piece of work together about the recalibration of time through ritual and magic, and we wept together as we watched it.

696–697 834–835

THERE IS NO OTHER

We trace and cut the outlines of each other from the sea, the city, the clouds, the trash, the trees.

These words form part of a poem I wrote to underscore a film in miniature cinema on the shores of the Mediterranean Sea in Cannes in June 2024. Every 20 minutes the audience filled the seats and watched a six-minute dance film in portrait format. The film was choreographed by Botis Seva and performed by seven dancers within the boundaries of a series of wooden boxes. Their movements responded to reflections I had written and recorded about the porous boundaries between myself and others:

Every portrait is a self-portrait: a daily act of remembering what we keep forgetting: that we can see through the frame of a single singing form, the conjoined pattern of all of us, extending through time.

As the film concluded, the screen ascended to reveal a mirror image of the audience. After about two seconds the audience realized that in fact they were not looking at a mirror, but an entirely new audience, who had been watching the film from the opposite side of the screen. In a way the work really took place in those two seconds, when, for a very fleeting moment, a group of people cast on one another the gaze they would normally reserve for their own reflection.

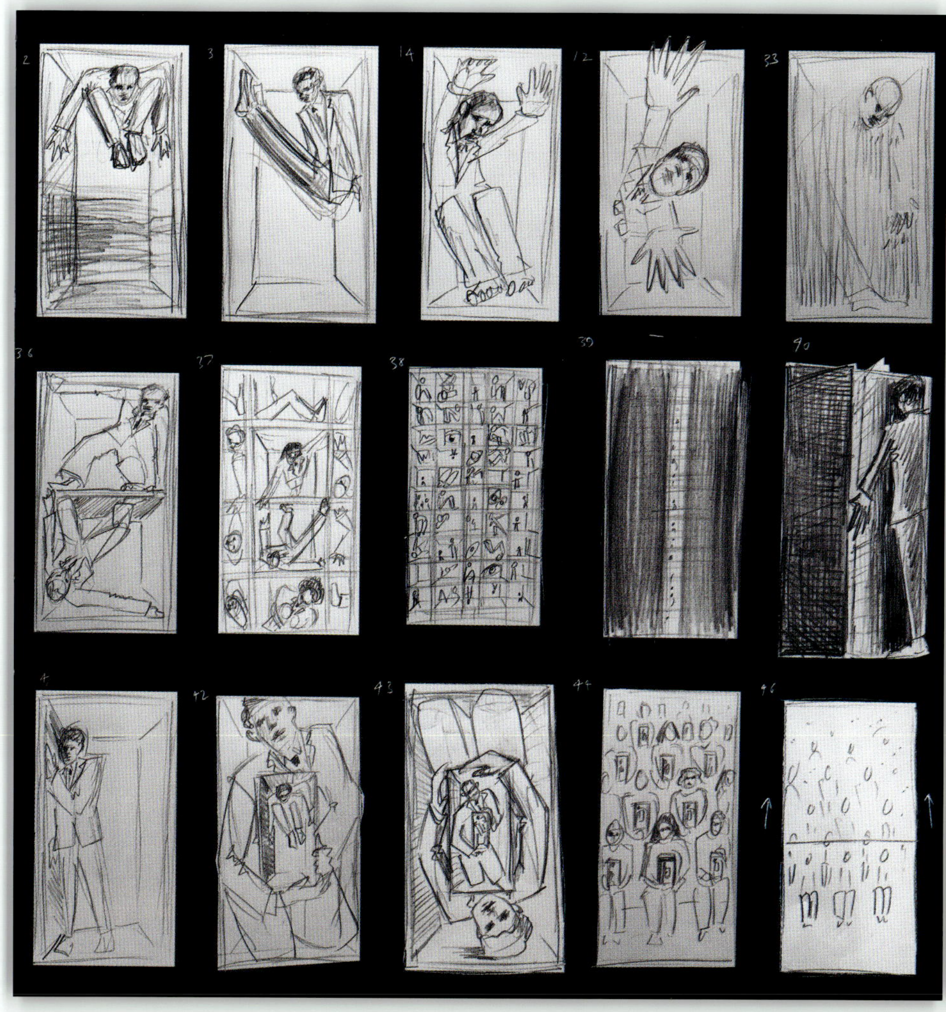

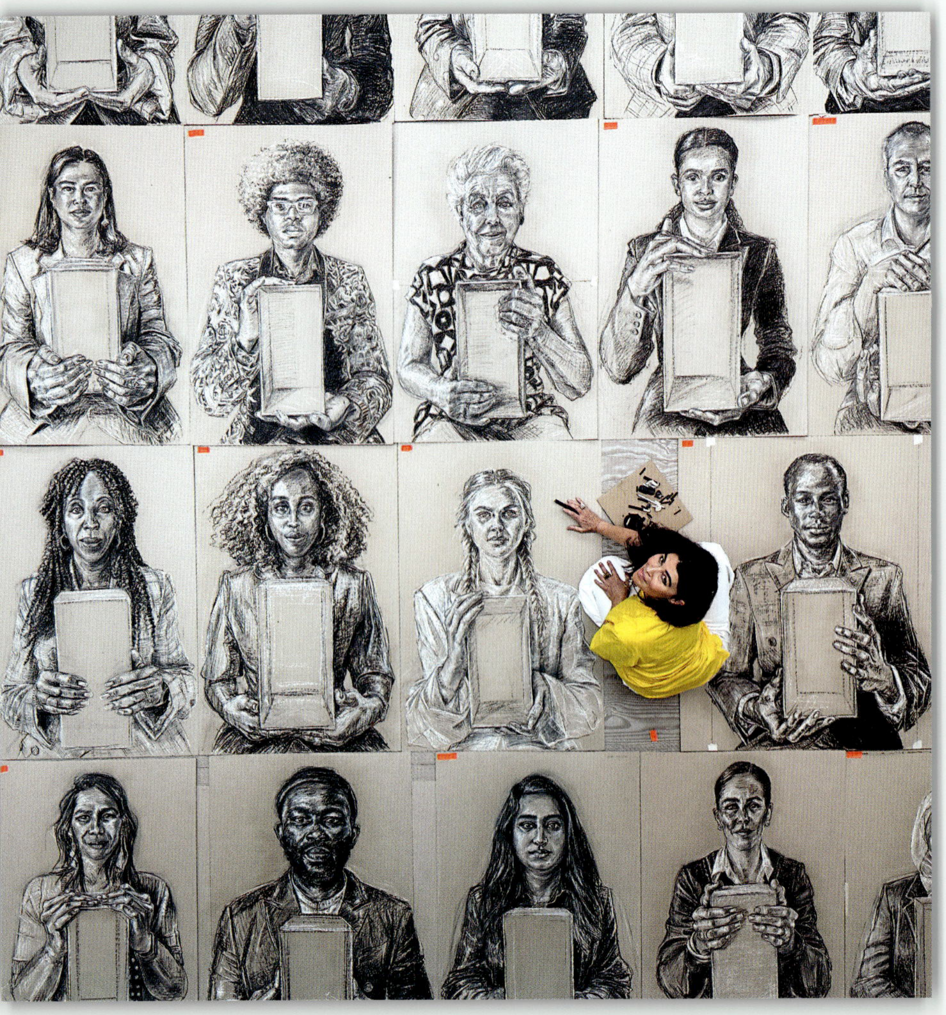

CONGREGATION

You told me of your journey here: sometimes decades ago as a small child, sometimes months ago on a small boat.

These lines form part of a poem I wrote to underscore *Congregation,* a portrait installation conceived at the start of Russia's invasion of Ukraine in 2022. I witnessed the UK's compassion for Ukrainian refugees and wanted to understand why it didn't extend to those seeking asylum from other conflicts. I sought guidance from the United Nations High Commissioner for Refugees, who, between April and August 2024, introduced me to 50 Londoners who became my *Congregation* co-authors. One at a time, each of these Londoners arrived at my studio in southeast London. I knew only their first names and that they had come to London at some point in their lives seeking refuge from one of 28 different conflict zones.

I drew their portraits in chalk and charcoal for 45 minutes, as we listened to music without speaking. I encountered my own crude overlays, associations and biases like layers of static interference. Then each described their lives and journeys, the gifts they bring to their new home. I wove strands of their recorded voices into a choral tiered projection-mapped installation of portraits in London's St Mary le Strand church in October 2024. 'Those who bring their gifts to London' feels like a more apposite term than 'refugee' for this resplendent, resilient community.

52–53

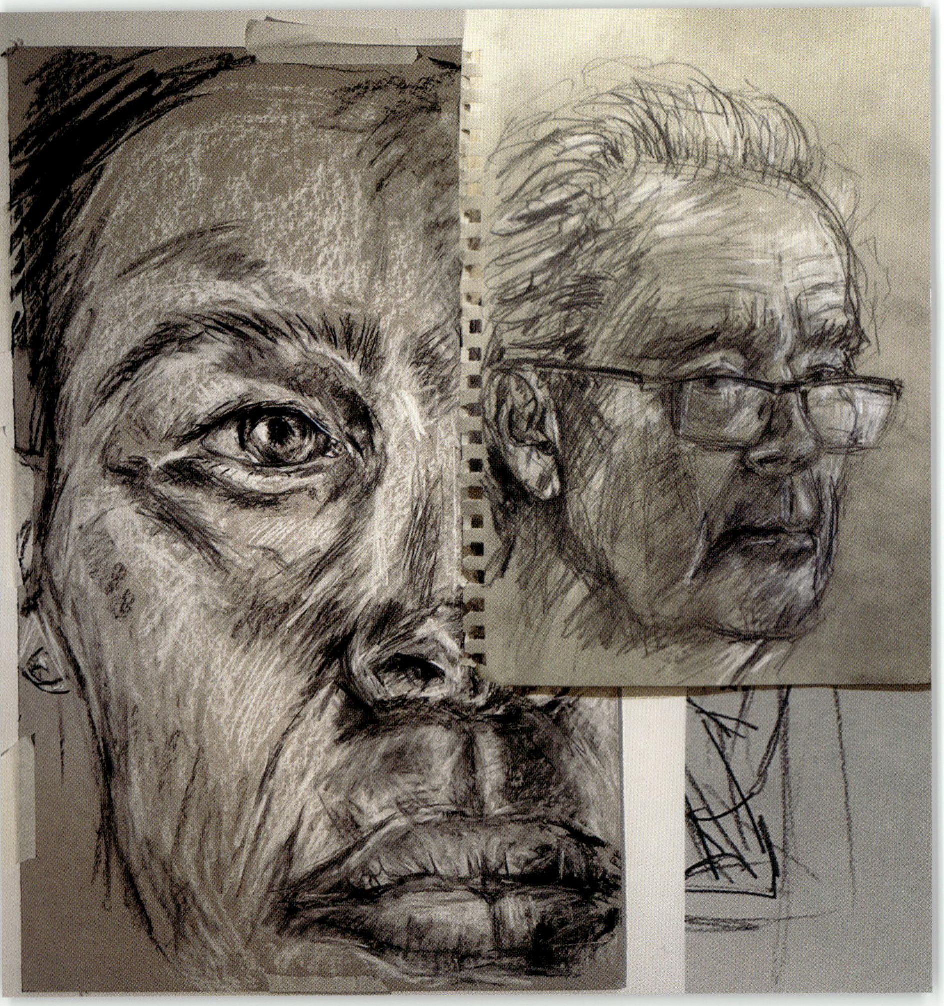

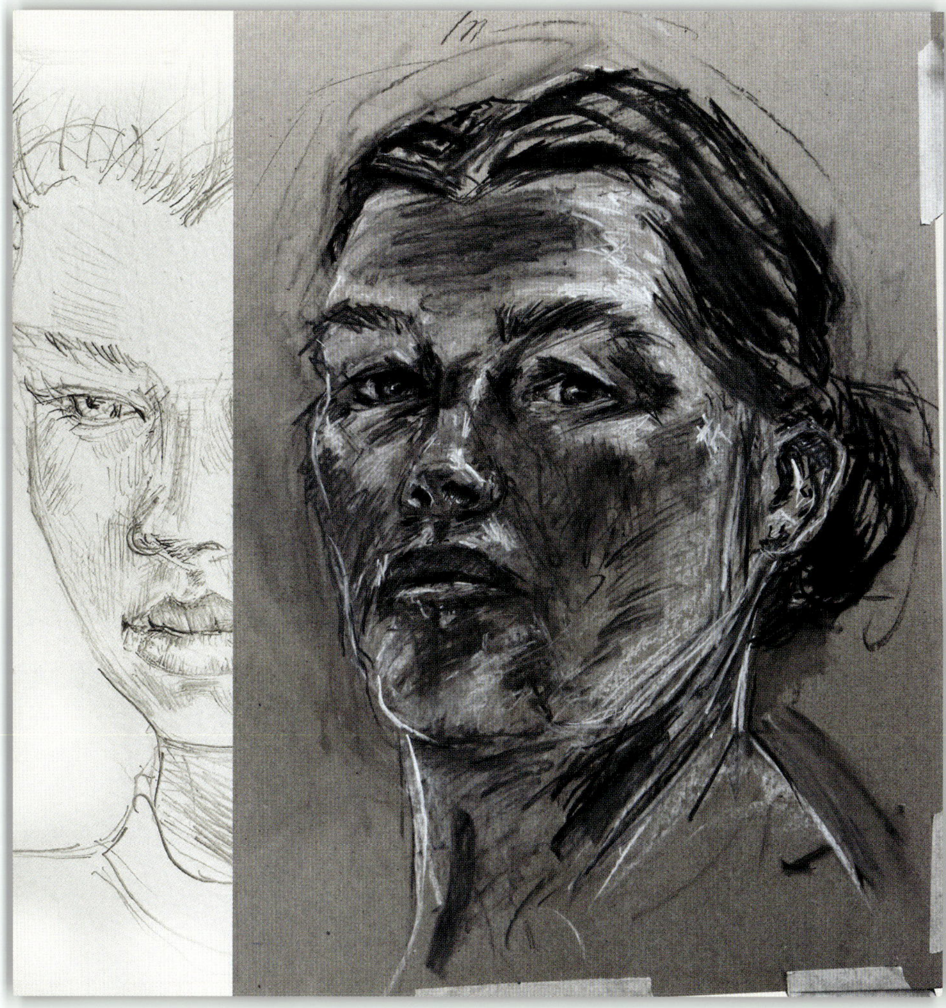

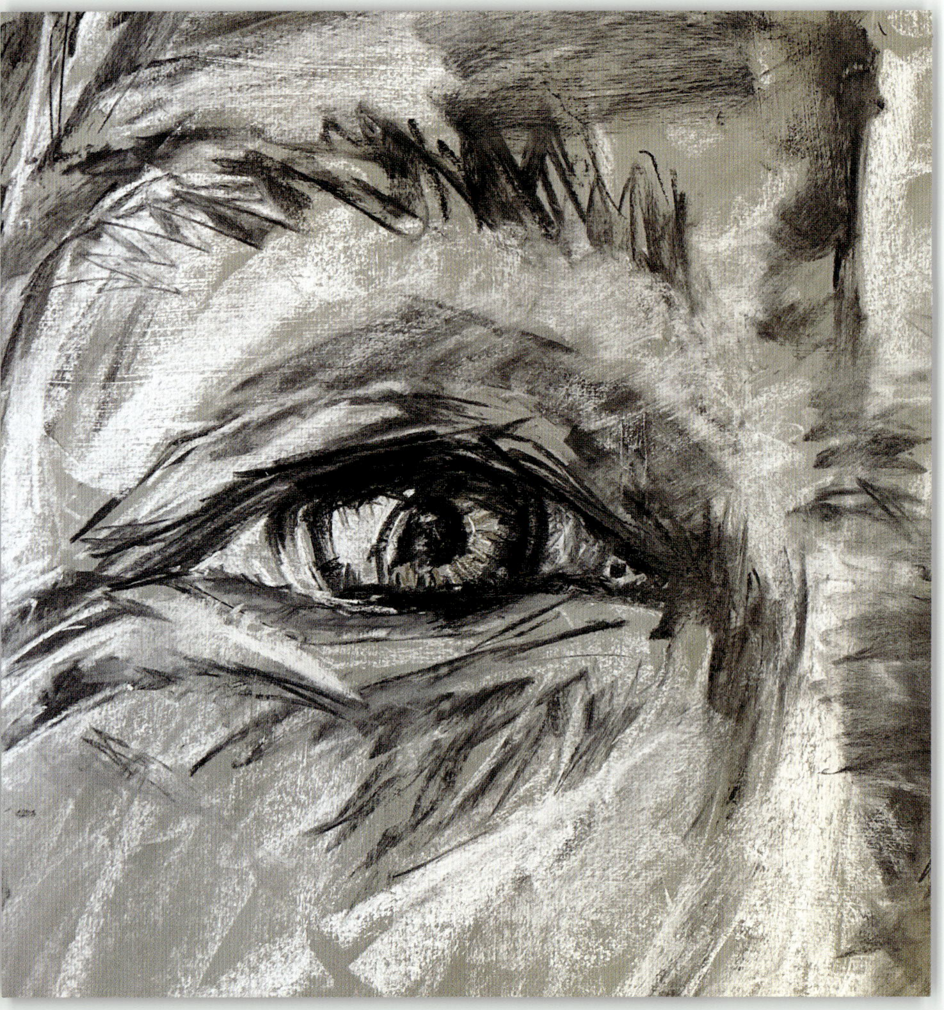

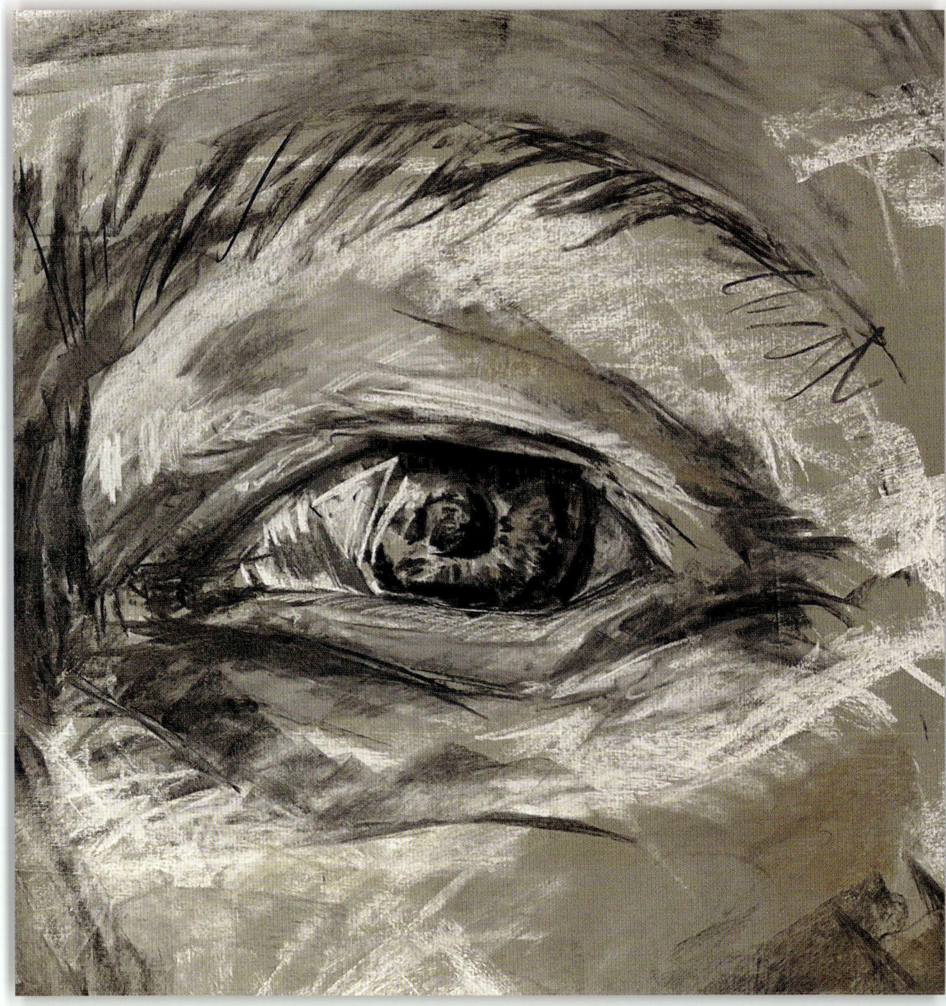

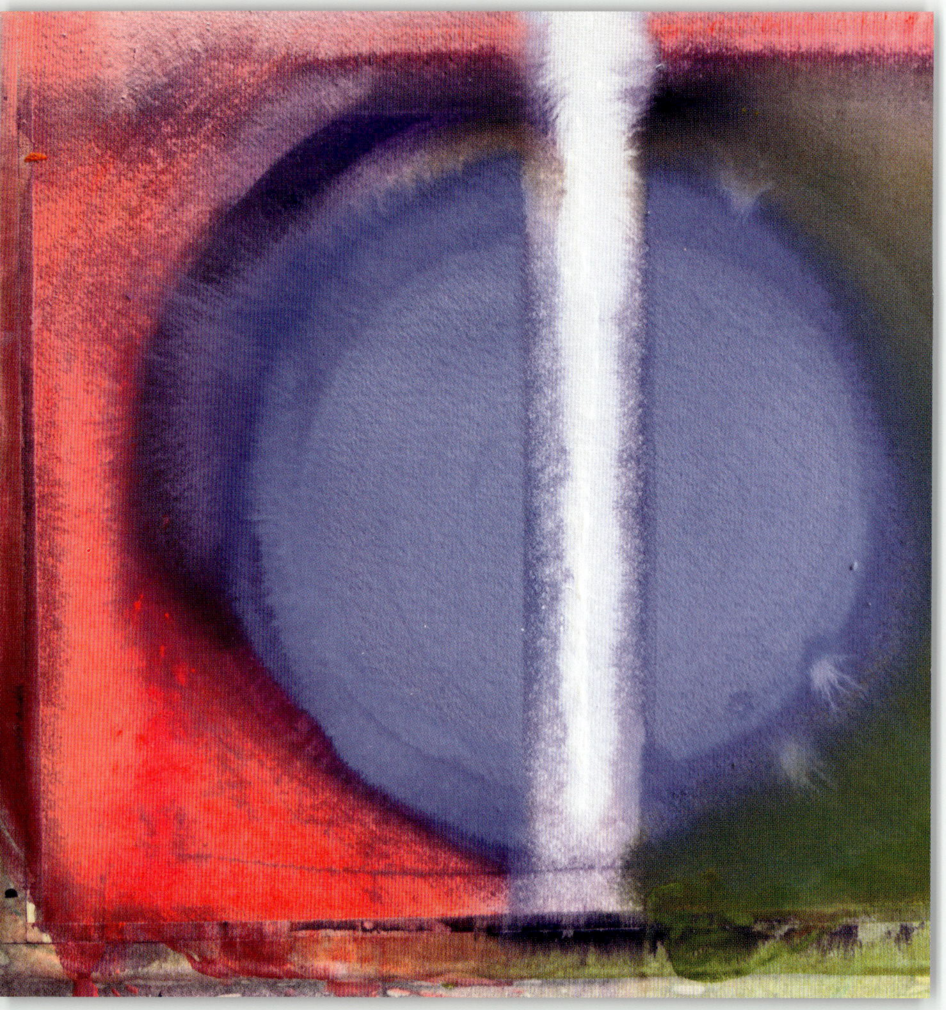

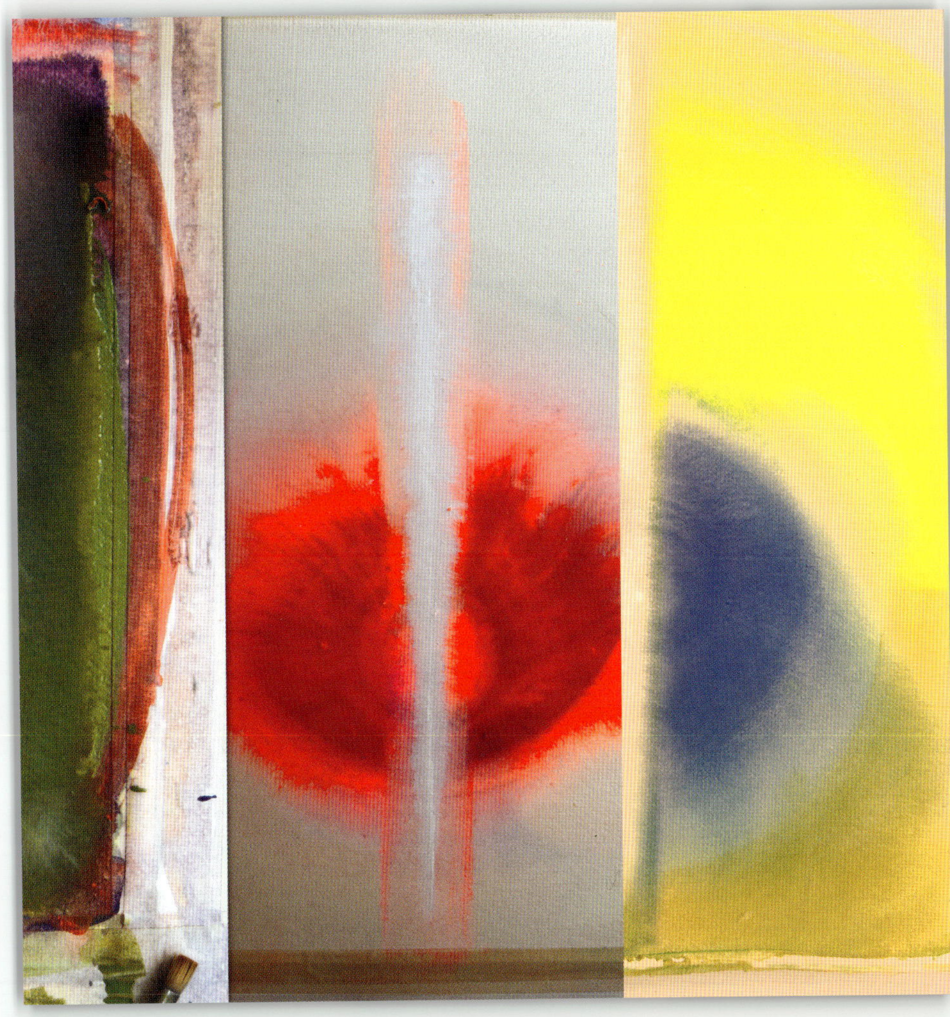

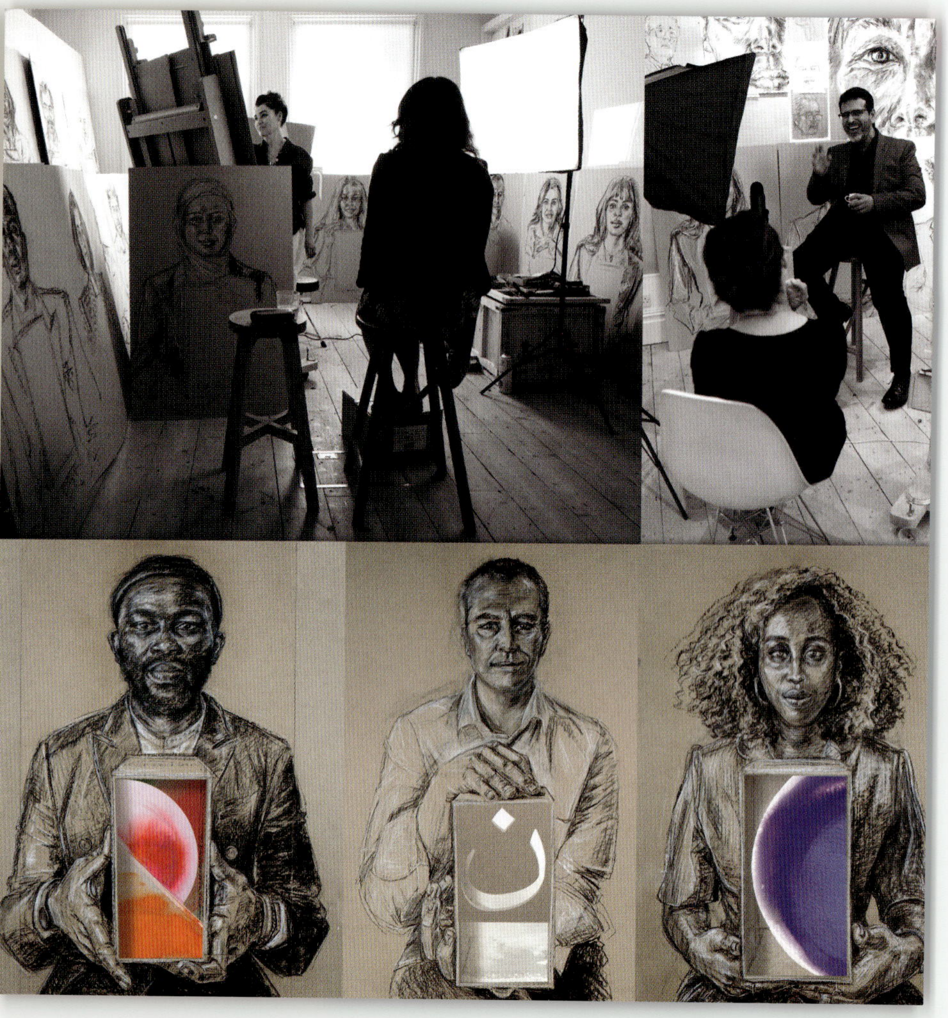
ن

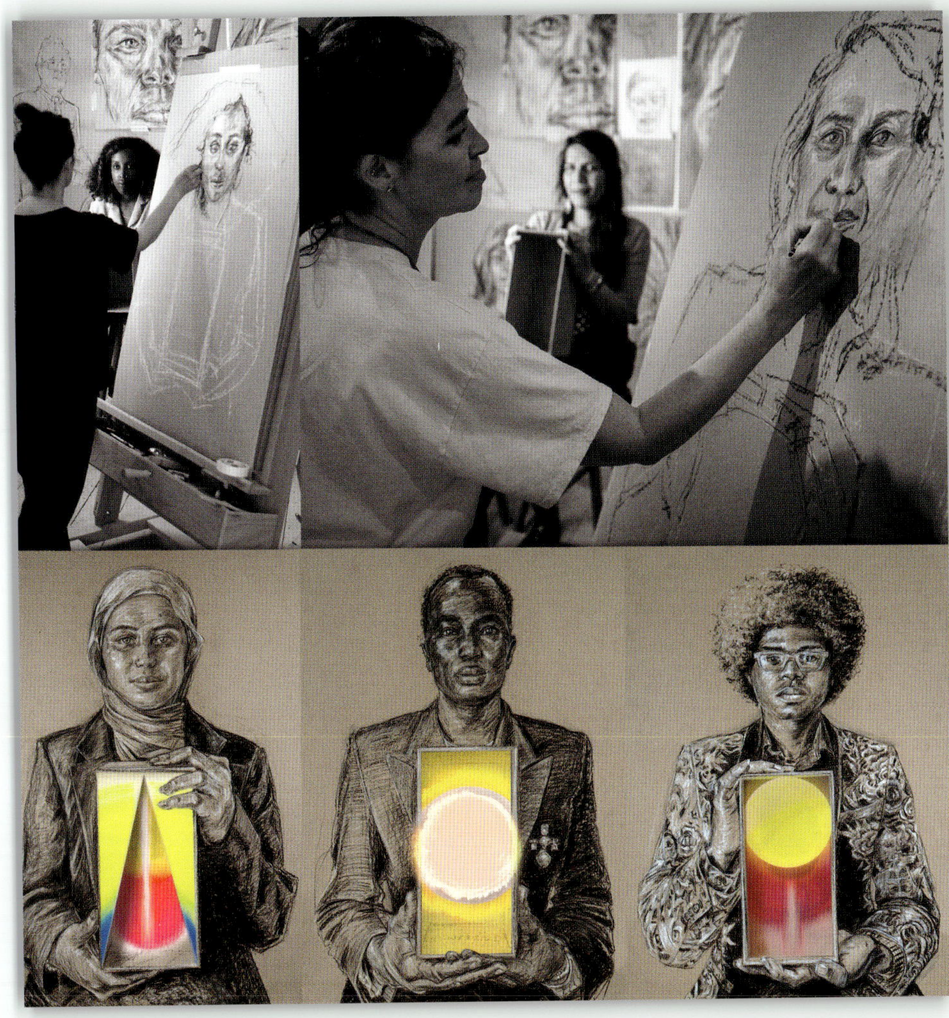

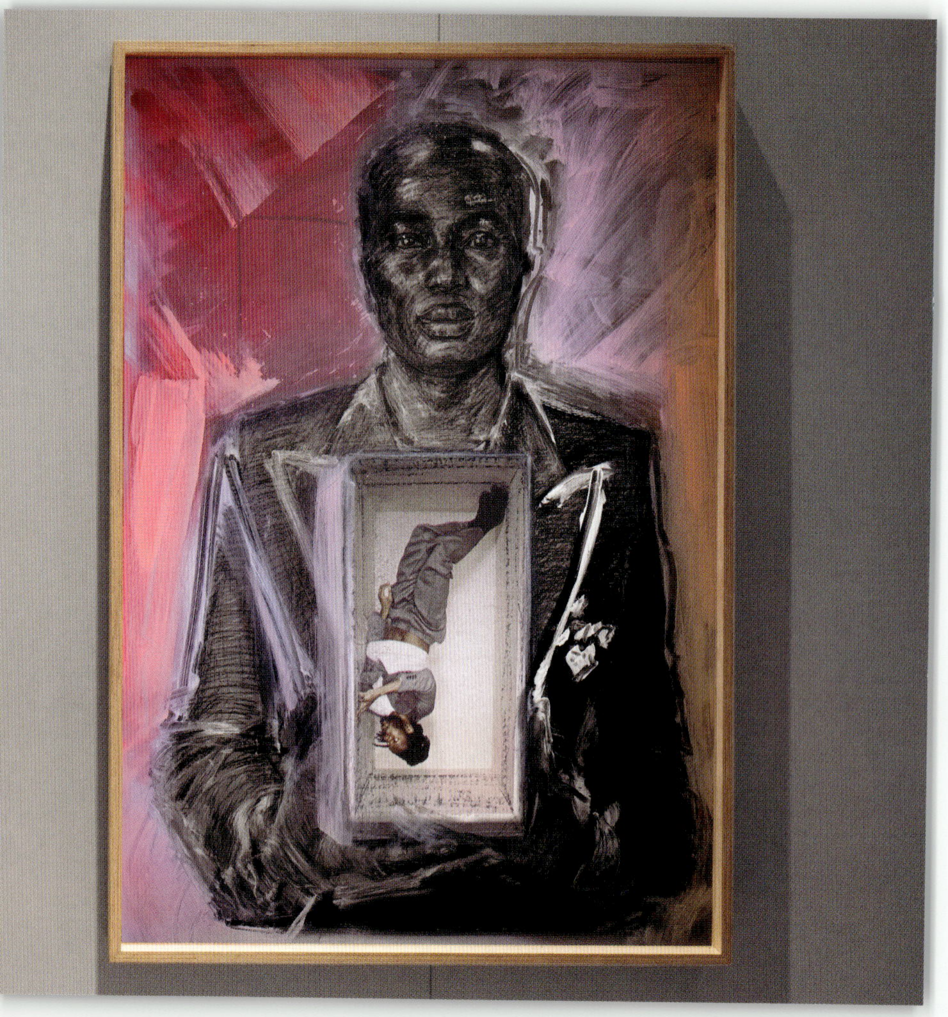

FACE TO FACE

The idea of infinity ... is concretely produced in the form of a relation with the face ... this is the epiphany that occurs as a face.

Emmanuel Lévinas, *Totality and Infinity*

In November 2024, the exhibition *Face to Face: 50 Portraits of Strangers* at London's Somerset House presented the portraits I had made of Londoners for my earlier installation, *Congregation*. I reworked some of the portraits, adding luminous paint gestures and projected footage of a dancer on layers of glass. I aimed to express some of the weather that passed between each sitter and me as we co-authored the works.

I initiated a new edition of *Face to Face* during my Eugene McDermott Award artist's residency at the Massachusetts Institute of Technology (MIT) in May 2025. Students, faculty members, cleaners, technicians, security guards, professors and other members of the university community became the portraitists, encountering one another as strangers to make drawings without speaking.

During the residency, I discussed Dr Iain McGilchrist's *The Master and His Emissary: The Divided Brain and the Making of the Western World* with a number of MIT neuroscientists. McGilchrist suggests that our times are textured by a growing imbalance between the modes of attention of right and left brain hemispheres. The team at MIT made a scan of my brain, clearly showing the corpus callosum that bridges the two sides of my brain: it is probably my favourite of any portrait that has been made of me.

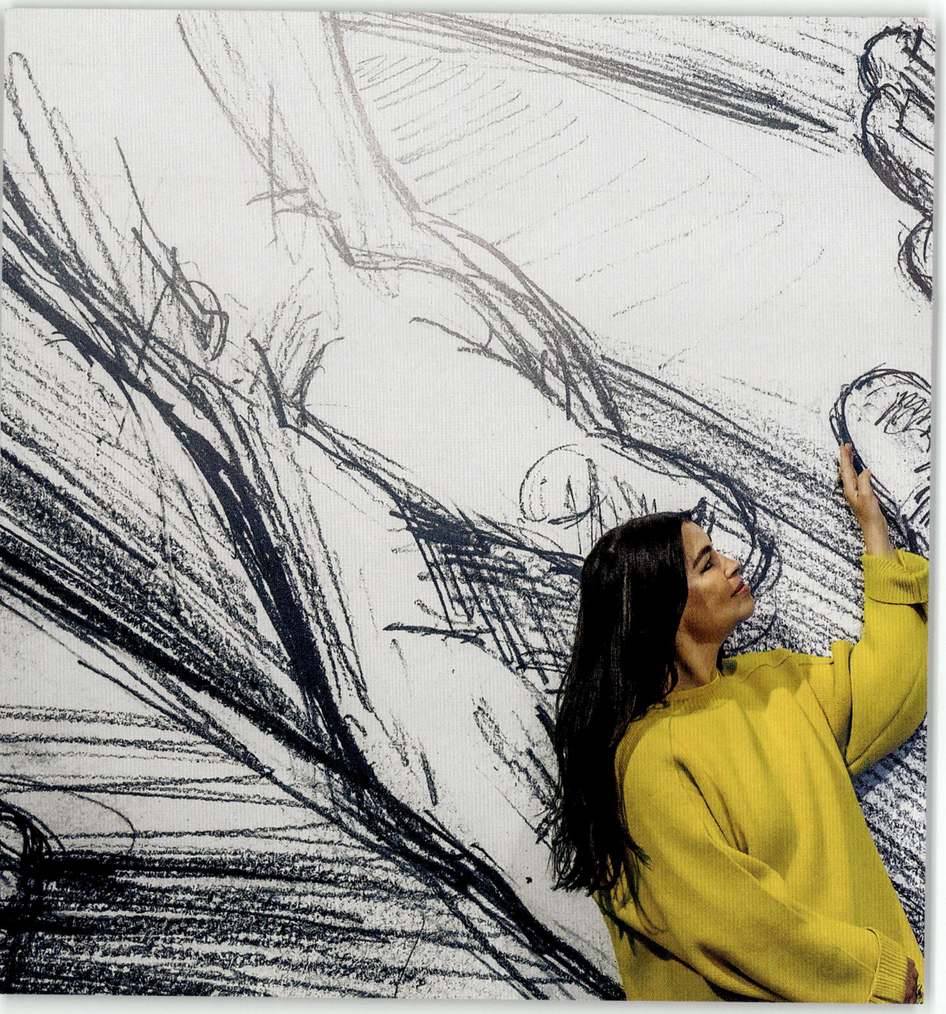

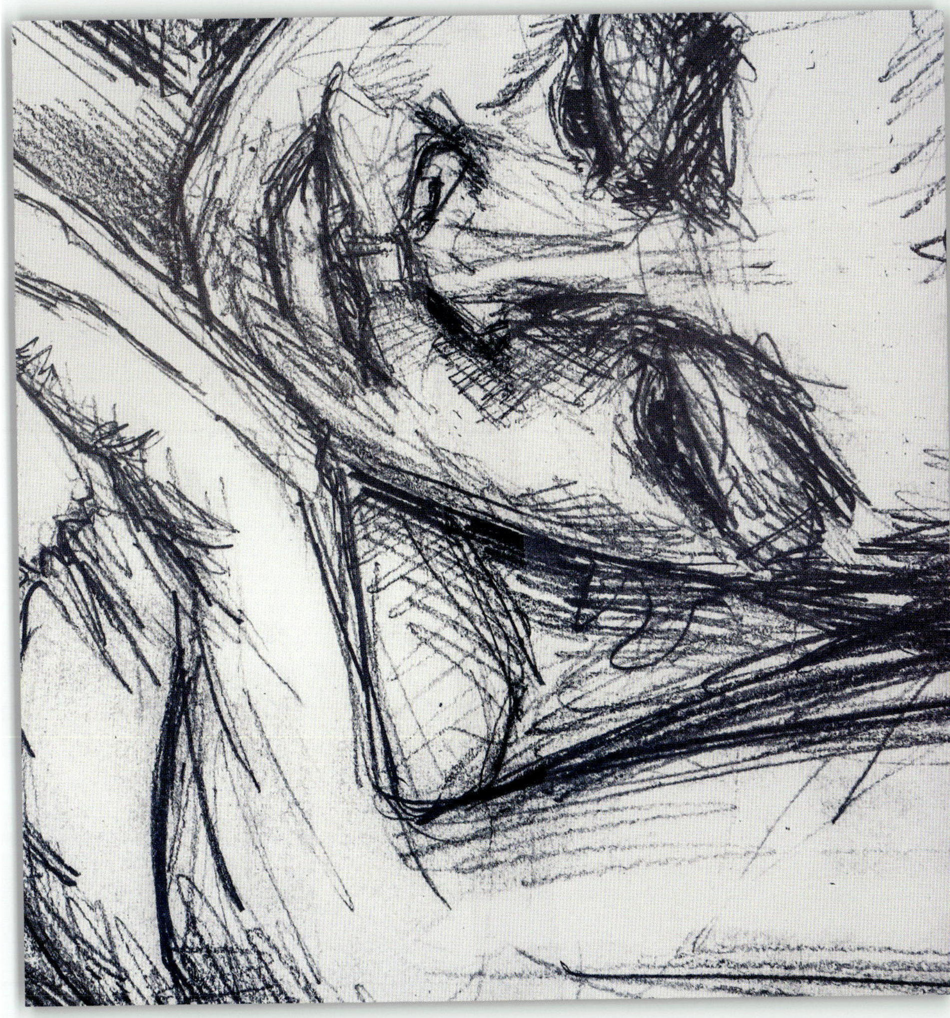

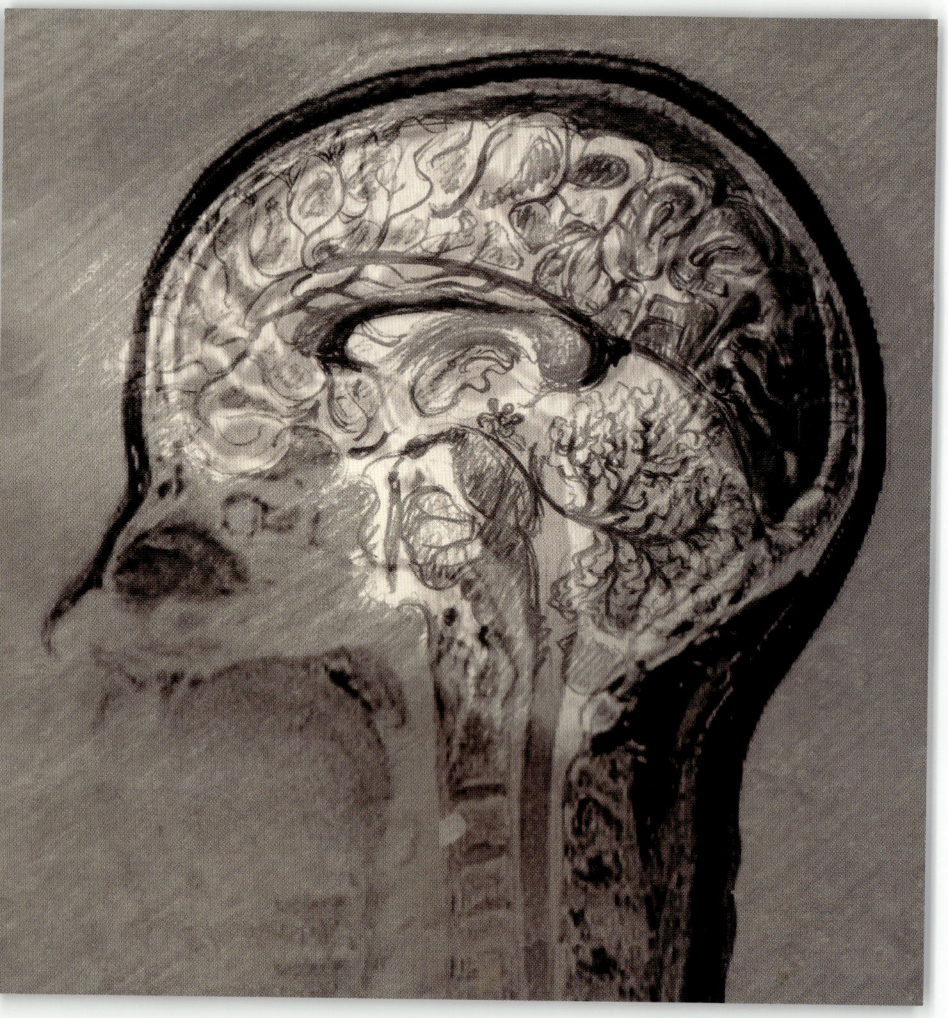

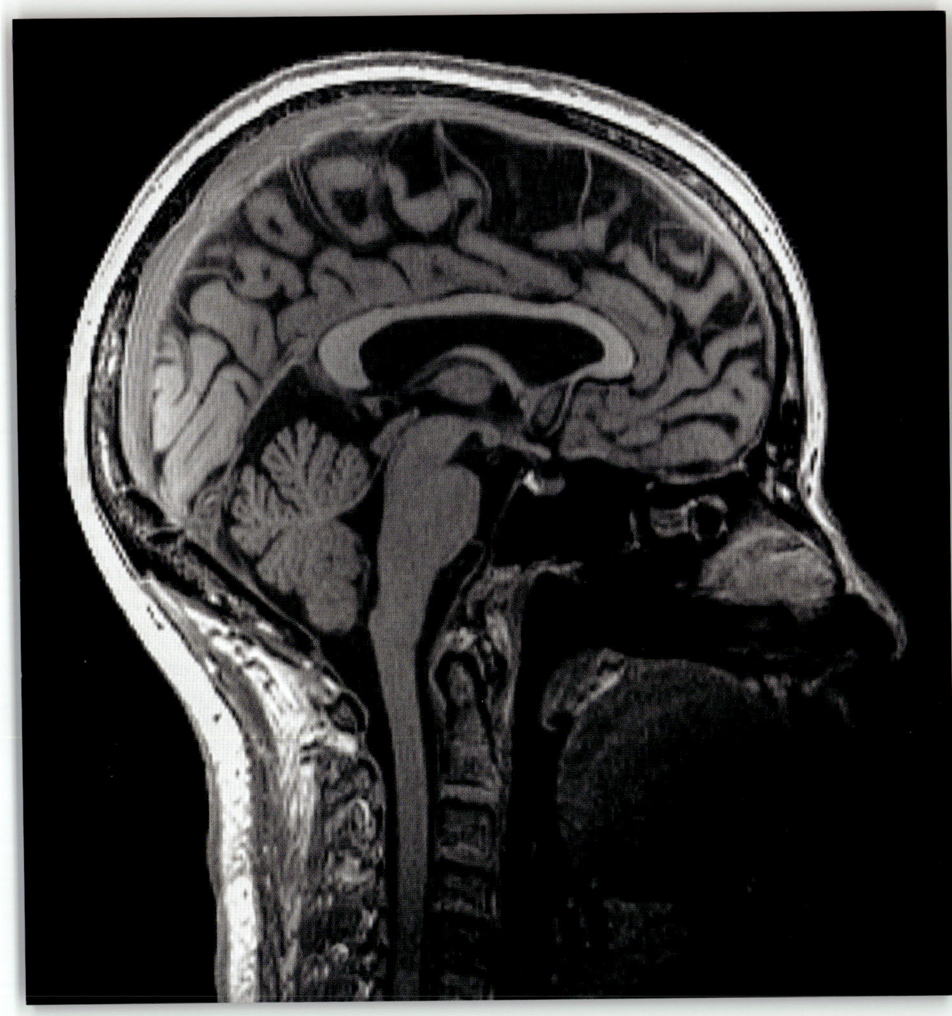

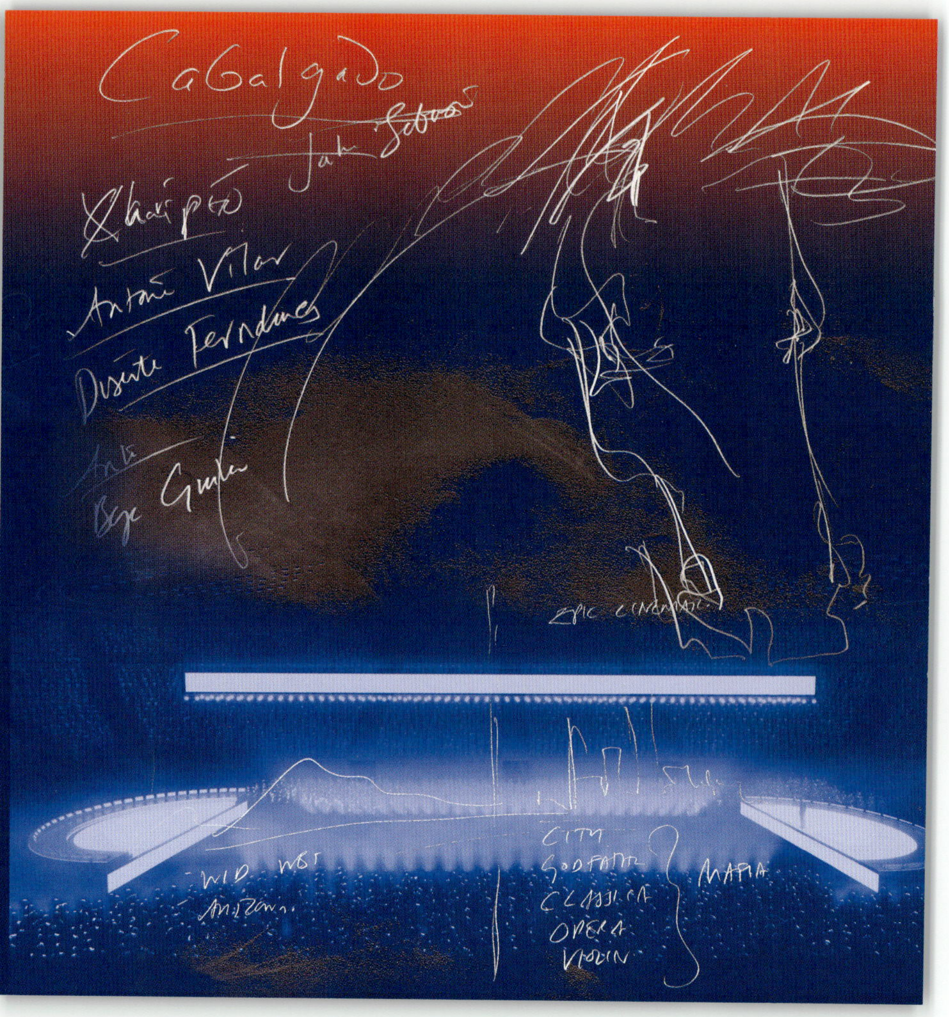
Cabalgado
CITY
OPERA
VIOLIN
MAFIA

MOST WANTED

Baila sin miedo, ama sin miedo: Dance without fear, love without fear.

Bad Bunny

On 21 February 2024, Benito Antonio Martínez Ocasio – also known as Bad Bunny – launched his *Most Wanted* tour in Salt Lake City. He conceived of the show as a bridge: between the city and the plains, between a symphony orchestra and a reggaeton band, and between the Americas. We created a stage at each end of the arena, with no apparent means of connection between them. The show began with a ten-minute cinematic overture performed by a 24-piece symphonic ensemble. Bad Bunny appeared on the opposite stage and eventually rode a luminous 25-metre rotating bridge that descended and brought him face to face with his fans at multiple heights. He made his way back into the arena for the start of the second act on horseback. The 20,000-strong audience on the opening night danced with such vibrant force that every rivet and beam of the Delta Center in Salt Lake City seemed to shake and shimmer.

The tour made its final stop in San Juan, Puerto Rico, on 9 June 2024.

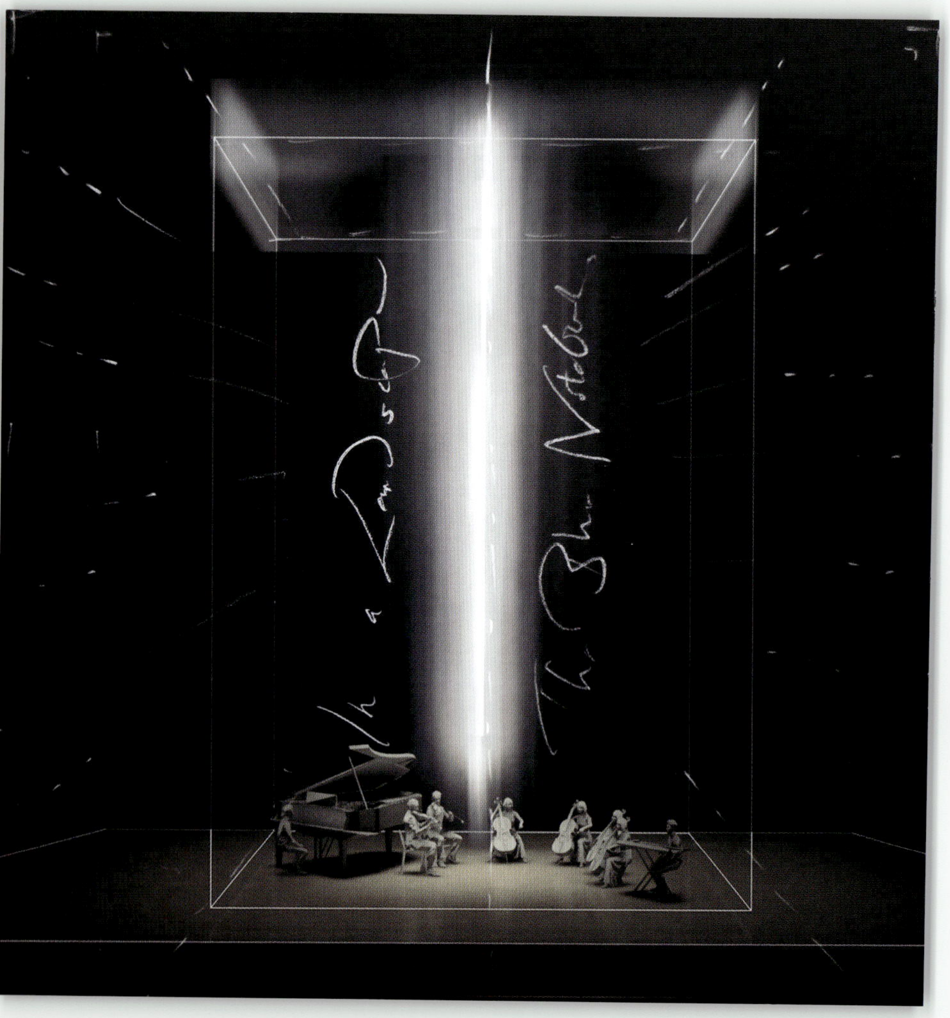

IN A LANDSCAPE

Everyone carries a room about inside him … the rattling of a mirror not quite firmly fastened to the wall.

Franz Kafka

Contemporary composer Max Richter began his first world tour in September 2024. In the first act Richter and his ensemble performed his new album *In a Landscape*, which he describes as 'a memoir of the present moment' and an attempt to 'reconcile polarities' – the electronic and the acoustic, the human and the biosphere. It was the first album composed at Studio Richter Mahr in rural Oxfordshire in southeast England and emanates a sense of being deeply rooted in place. The concert's second act presented Richter's 2004 work *The Blue Notebooks*, which explores the lead-up to the 2003 Iraq war that Richter strongly opposed. The composition includes texts by Franz Kafka and Czesław Miłosz, read by the British actress Tilda Swinton.

Richter has said: *'I'm always looking for ways to get to the essence of things, to get to the simplest version of everything.'* I adopted a parallel approach, offering a single vertical light as tall as a cresting wave that served as a visual counterpoint to the music. Its light swelled and diminished with the currents of the score as the ensemble played on a simple, exposed stage. We materialized the vertical light with a powerful and versatile lighting instrument – the JDC Line – which I had begun to incorporate in several artworks, including *Surfacing* at Art Basel a few months earlier.

626–627

CORIOLANUS

... thus I turn my back: There is a world elsewhere.

William Shakespeare, *Coriolanus*

As we approached *Coriolanus* with the actor David Oyelowo – to open in September 2024 – the director Lyndsey Turner and I sought a world in which Shakespeare's imagining of civic uprising in Rome would resonate with a contemporary audience. In January that year, protestors threw yellow pumpkin soup at the *Mona Lisa* in the Louvre Museum as an expression of agricultural, social and environmental rage. Our production at the Olivier Theatre opened with Shakespeare's grain-starved Roman plebeians hurling orange soup at a statue of Romulus and Remus in a contemporary museum. Artefacts on museum plinths served as props for the flow of domestic, civic and military scenes. We conjured a democratic object layout emulating architects Diller Scofidio + Renfro's designs for the Victoria and Albert Museum's collections at its new V&A East Storehouse that would open the following spring. A cubic mass of concrete slices echoing architect Denys Lasdun's National Theatre exteriors filled the Olivier stage. They slowly rose and fell to reveal and conceal a series of architectural configurations, like a magician's box, hovering weightily above the action. At the end of the play, the pillars descended like a concrete mausoleum, enclosing Coriolanus within one of the museum's display plinths, viewed briefly by a schoolboy on a museum tour before the lights went out.

704–705

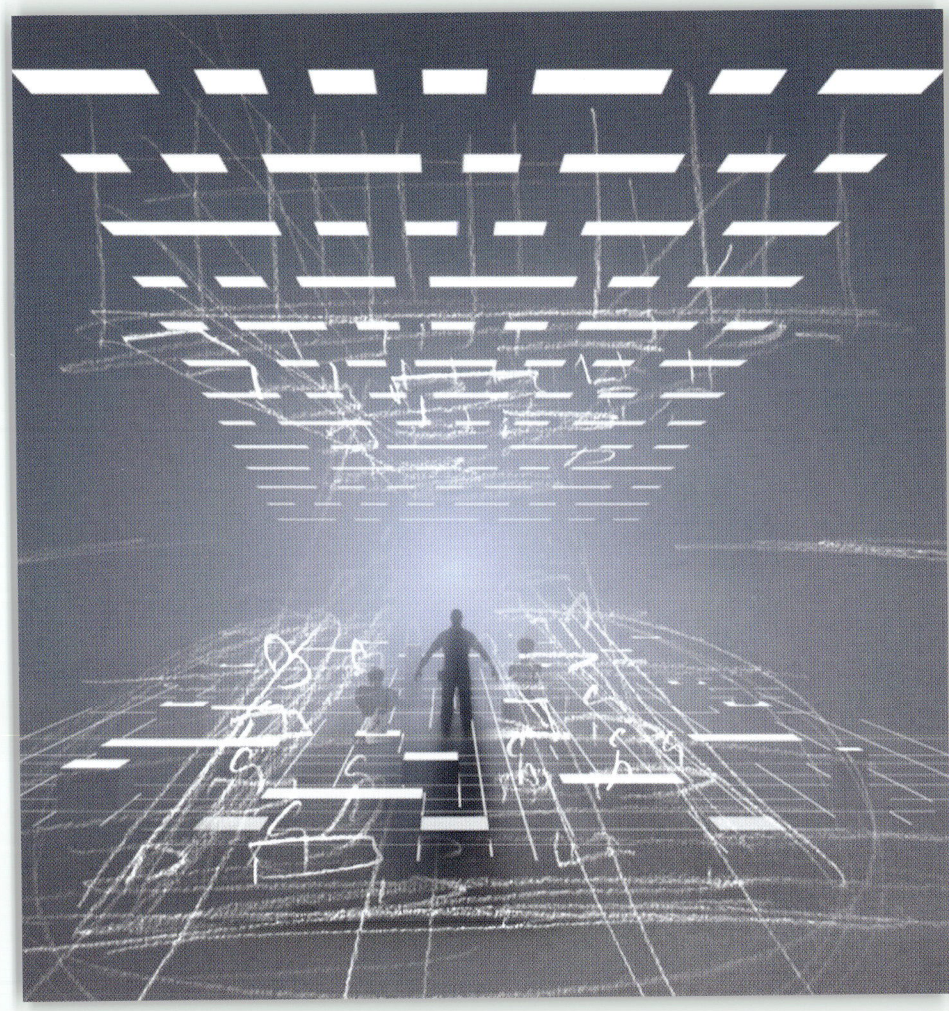

HAMLET

The time is out of joint: O cursed spite,
That ever I was born to set it right!

William Shakespeare, *Hamlet*

In February 2025, at the Royal Shakespeare Company (RSC) in Stratford-upon-Avon, the director Rupert Goold and I opened a new production of *Hamlet* with the actor Luke Thallon in the lead role. Rupert envisaged the foundational idea for the production in a dream. He imagined the 2 hours 40 minutes of Shakespeare's most famous play transposed over the 2 hours 40 minutes that it took the *Titanic*, the 'unsinkable' luxury British ocean liner, to sink in April 1912. With the expertise of the RSC engineers, we created a 14-metre-long tilting wooden stage deck that eventually reached an extreme 45-degree angle, sending performers sliding overboard as it lurched. The action was surrounded by a cyclorama screen of ever more vertiginous projections of the sea.

This was my third encounter with the play, and the unstable, out-of-kilter floor rendered the stage itself 'out of joint'. While researching the play in relation to the sinking of the *Titanic*, I was reading Iain McGilchrist's *The Matter with Things*. McGilchrist suggests that the mode of attention of our brains' left hemispheres has come to dominate that of our right, rendering our times 'out of joint', with our experience of language lurching out of contact with our bodily experience of the planet. This research informed the physically destabilizing choice of design.

692–693

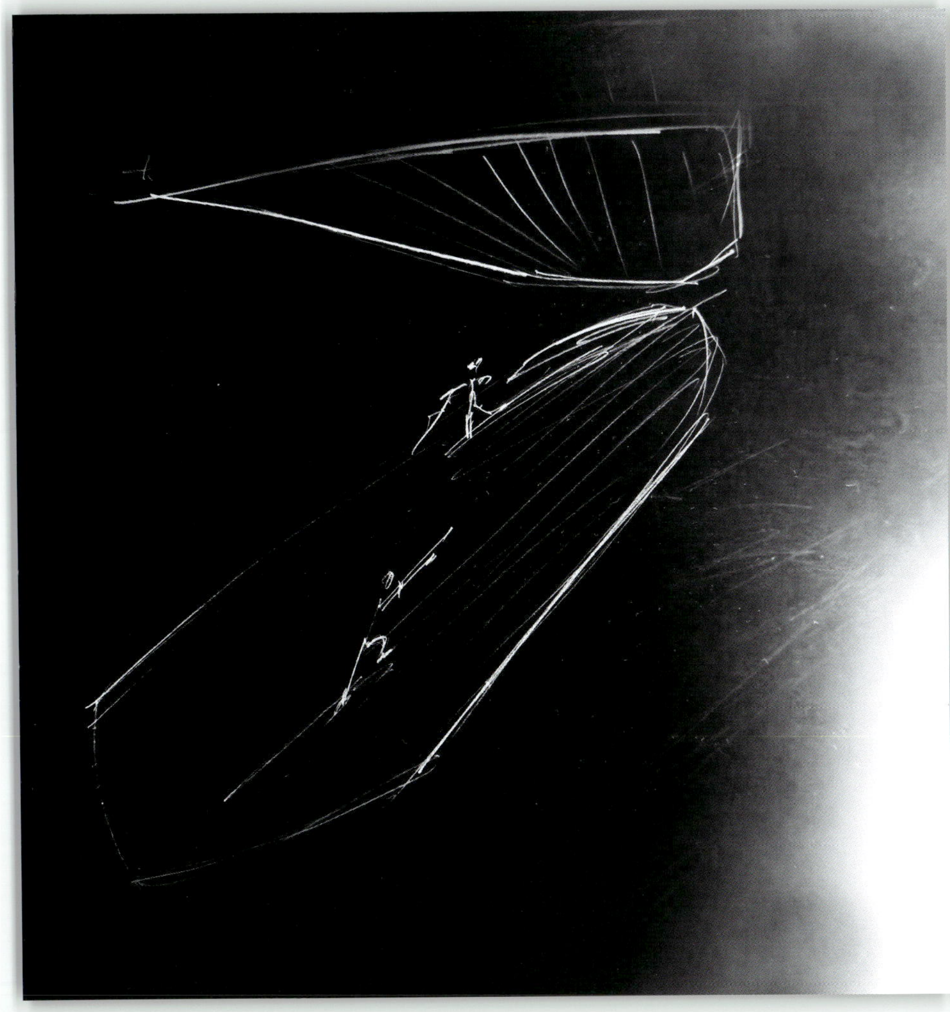

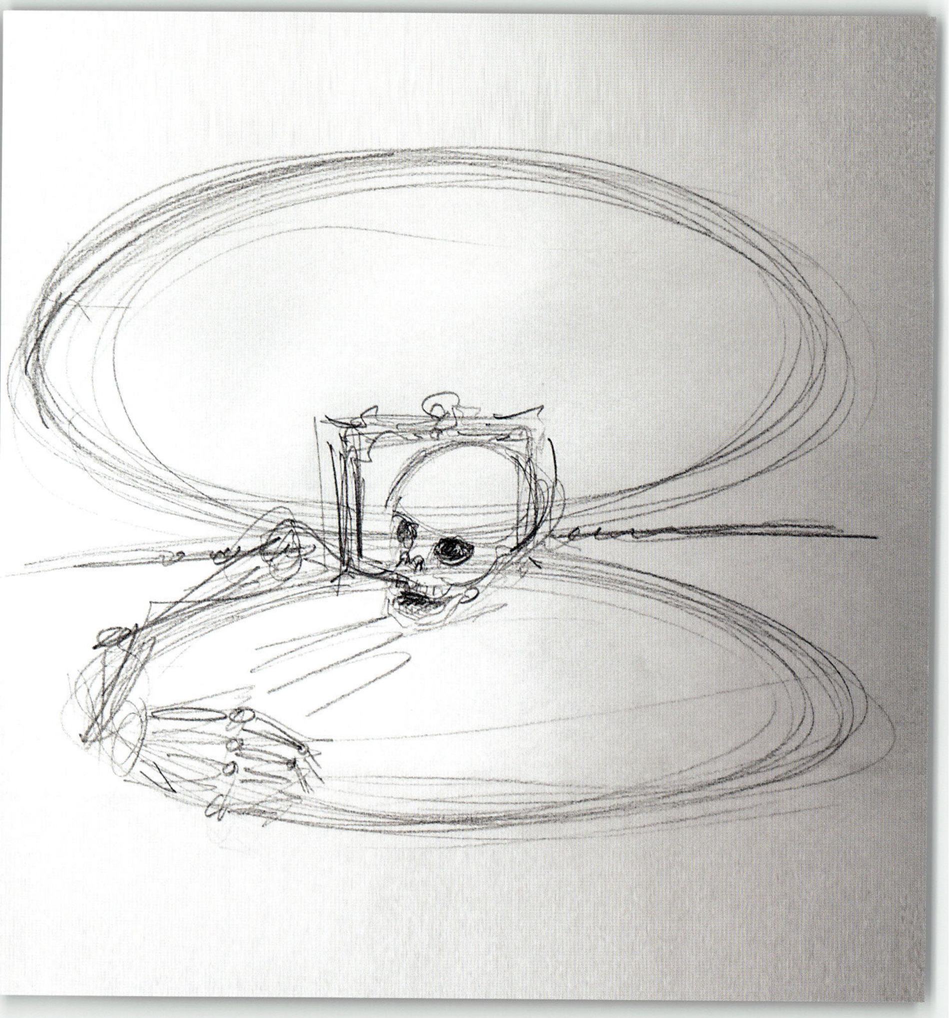

THE MAYHEM BALL

To not know any peace is the great nightmare for us all.
To wake and feel unsettled in a house that has no walls.

Lady Gaga, *Mayhem Manifesto*

On 11 April 2025, Lady Gaga performed within a distorted replica of the Palais Garnier opera house in the desert plains of the Coachella festival. While developing ideas for this performance, we observed the seismic cultural shifts since our last collaboration in 2010. Gaga had just made a speech in support of the LGBTQ+ community in response to more than 600 proposed state legislature bills across the United States that sought to restrict the rights of LGBTQ+: 70 would become law in 22 states. We discussed a passage from journalist Charlotte Beradt's collection of German citizens' dreams in 1930s Berlin: *'I was about to relax on the sofa with a book ... the walls of my room, of my whole apartment, suddenly disappeared. I looked around in horror and saw that none of the apartments as far as the eye could see had any walls left.'*

Gaga's team transported our stage to South America, and she performed *The Art of Personal Chaos* on Copacabana Beach in Rio de Janeiro on 5 May, reaching a live audience of 2.5 million, the largest ever for a female performer. We refined the Coachella opera house design for a world tour, and *The Mayhem Ball* arena tour opened in Las Vegas in July 2025.

WOMEN'S PAVILION

Over and over, we begin again.

Banana Yoshimoto, *Kitchen*

The second edition of the Cartier Women's Pavilion opened at the World Expo Osaka in May 2025. Architect Yuko Nagayama recycled her modular facade from the Japan Pavilion at Expo 2020, while artist Fujiko Nakaya reprised her Expo Osaka 1970 installation to envelop the building in clouds at its October closing.

My studio team and I conceived three routes through the pavilion to allow visitors to walk in the shoes of three extraordinary women: Japanese novelist Banana Yoshimoto, Sudanese American poet Emtithal Mahmoud, and Mexican climate activist Xiye Bastida. Visitors watched a short film about each protagonist on a curved cinema screen. The women opened oval apertures between their filmed hands and each guest heard their name called to enter via one of the three openings. As we walked along the corridors of their narratives, we read manga comics through the broken glasses of the teenage Banana Yoshimoto, we peered up from under the bed of the 9-year-old Emi Mahmoud at soldiers running through smoke, we gazed through the flooding rain from Xiye Bastida's forest hut. After a pause in a skylit ovoid 'Ma' – or 'interval' space – guests emerged into a wooden cabinet with sliding drawers revealing screens full of data. In 2025, the World Economic Forum ranked Japan 118th out of 148 countries on the path towards gender equality, 69 places behind the UAE, site of the first edition of the Cartier Women's Pavilion in 2020.

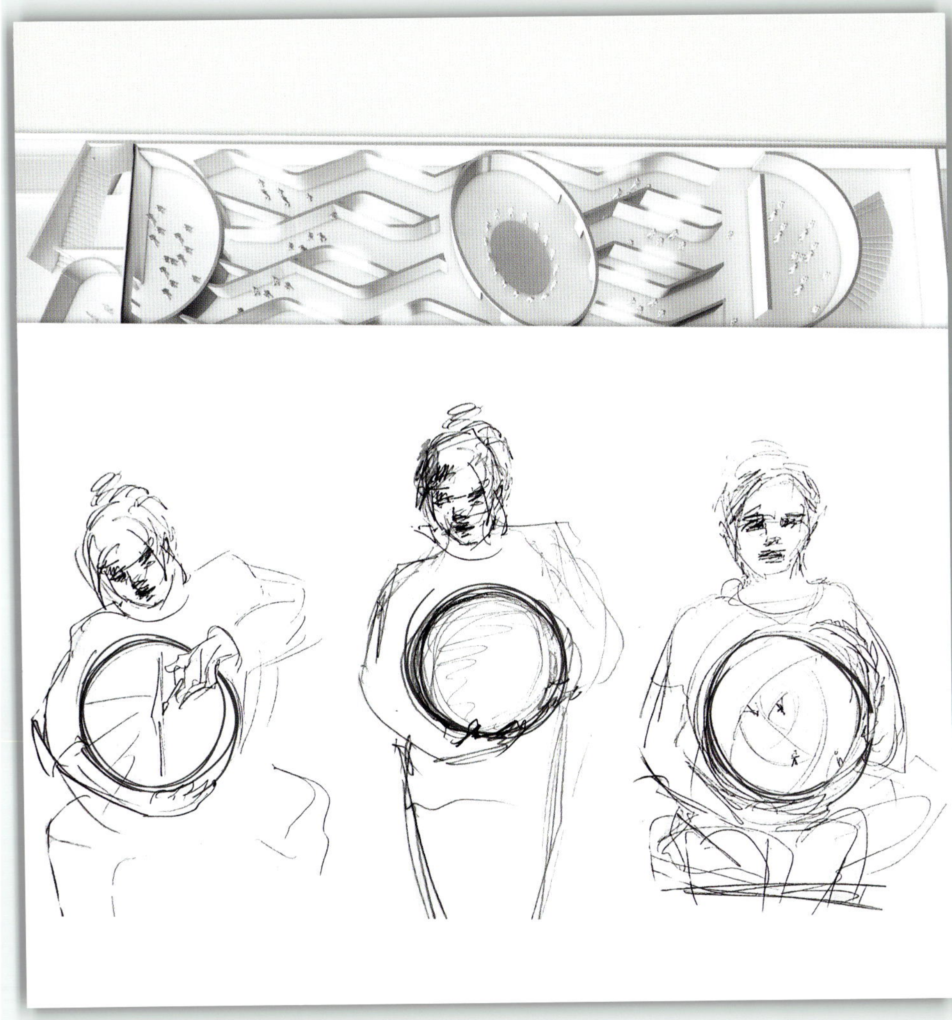

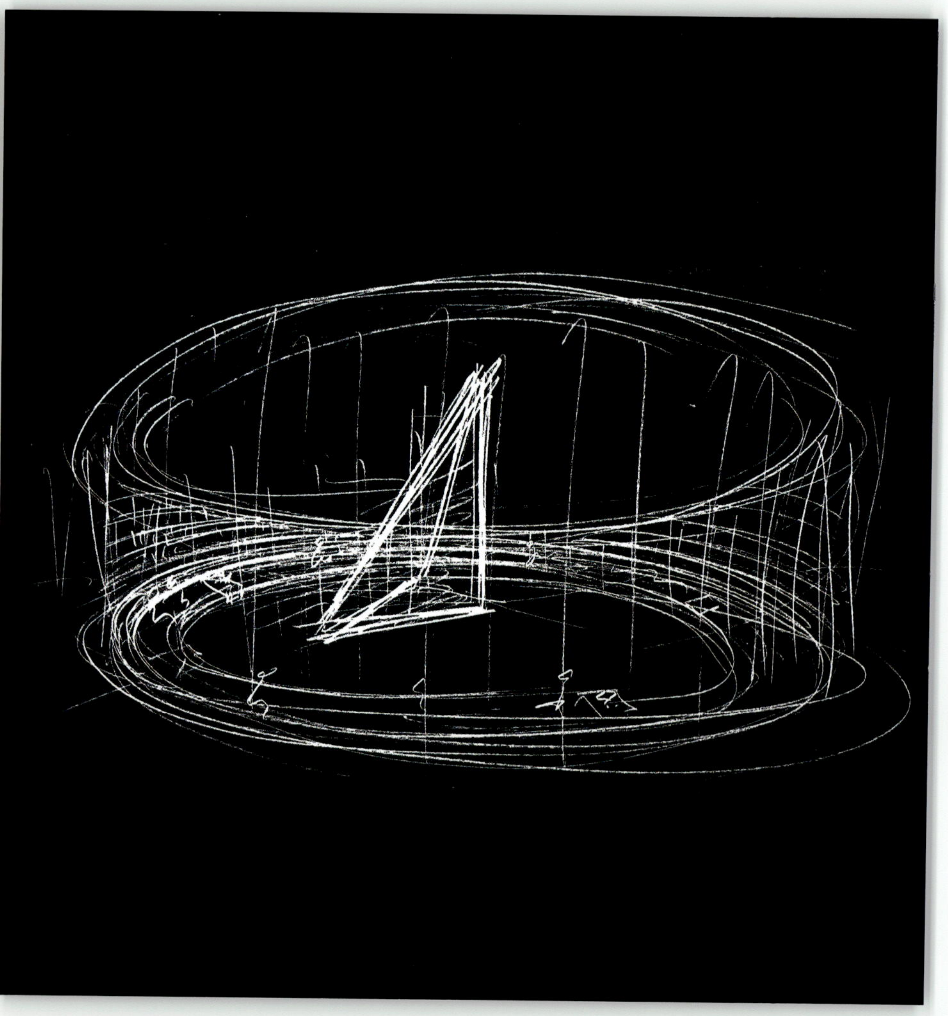

LIBRARY OF LIGHT

I am not sure that I exist, actually. I am all the writers I have read, all the people I have met, all the women I have loved; all the cities I have visited, all my ancestors.

Jorge Luis Borges

I created a revolving library sculpture in the seventeenth-century courtyard of the Pinacoteca di Brera museum in Milan, commissioned by the producers of Salone del Mobile, the international design fair, in April 2025. I conceived the work as a response to a question I am asked regularly by students and interviewers: 'Where do your ideas come from?' The library contained 2,500 books that have most influenced my thinking. As it slowly rotated, the structure read aloud – in my recorded voice – 250 phrases from the books on the shelves, each of which has guided my life and practice. You could call it a 'portrait of the artist as a bookshelf'.

The sculpture's circular form drew on the work of the only woman within the courtyard's statues of Enlightenment academics: Maria Gaetana Agnesi. She was a renowned eighteenth-century mathematician and mystic, whose diagram of a cubic plane curve was mistranslated from 'curve' to 'witch'.

Each evening a revolving violinist played a composition by British composers Polyphonia, to underscore the words of Agnesi and the Italian quantum physicist Carlo Rovelli on the nature of time. Five hundred thousand people visited *Library of Light* during its month at the Pinacoteca. We donated the books to Milan public libraries after it ended.

28–29

LIBRARY OF US

You think your pain and your heartbreak are unprecedented in the history of the world, but then you read. It was books that taught me that the things that tormented me most were the very things that connected me with all the people who were alive, or who had ever been alive.

James Baldwin

The revolving triangular form of *Library of Us* echoed Umberto Eco's description of his library as a 'compass of the mind'. Four thousand books filled the rotating bookshelf of this Faena Art commission on the public beach during Miami Art Week in December 2025. Strangers encountered one another through shared texts as they revolved around the circular reading table. An LED strip within the shelf broadcast texts by Toni Morrison, Octavia E. Butler, Margaret Atwood, and many others. I discovered during the install period that many of their books had been banned in Florida schools and libraries.

It was unsettling to see shelves of fragile paper books in such close proximity to the waters of the installation's reflecting pool and the tides of the Atlantic. The community in the Miami Beach area are acutely tuned to the daily possibility of flooding, which has increased by 400% since 2006, driven by regional sea-level rise. When the installation ended, we donated the books to Miami Dade county libraries, salted by their time on the beach.

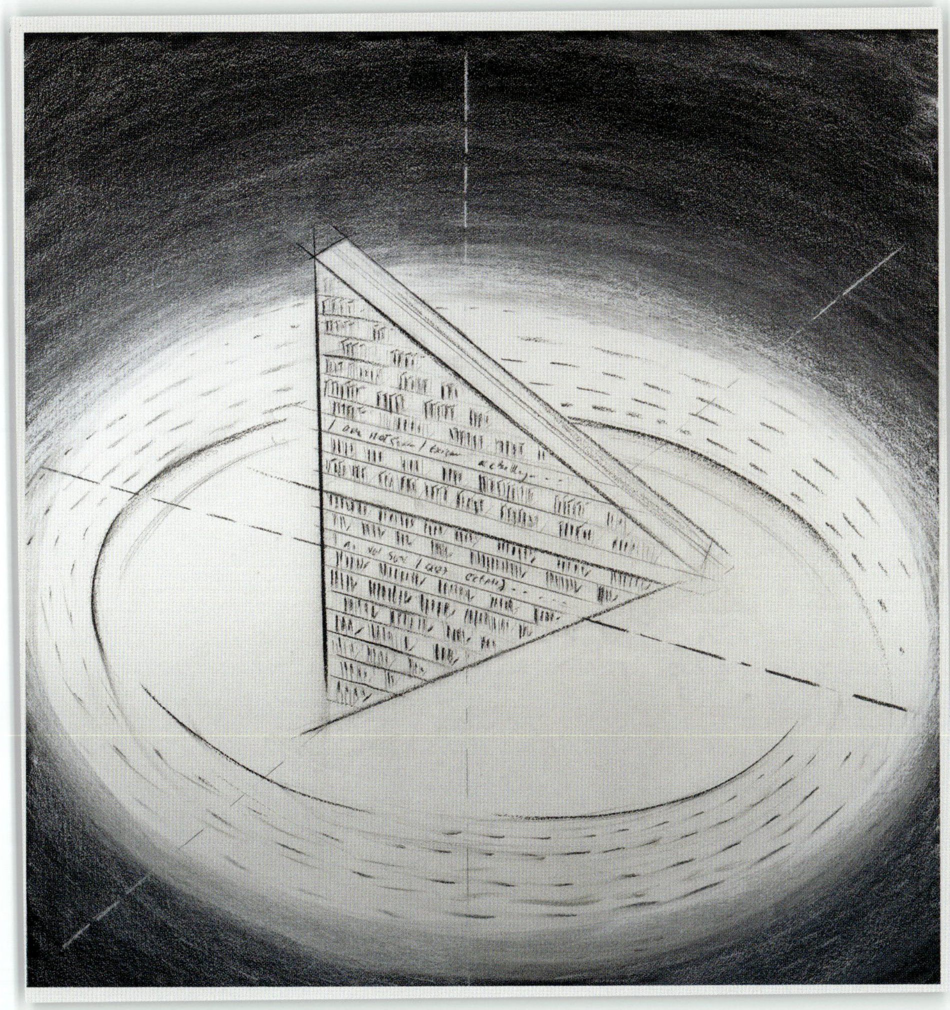

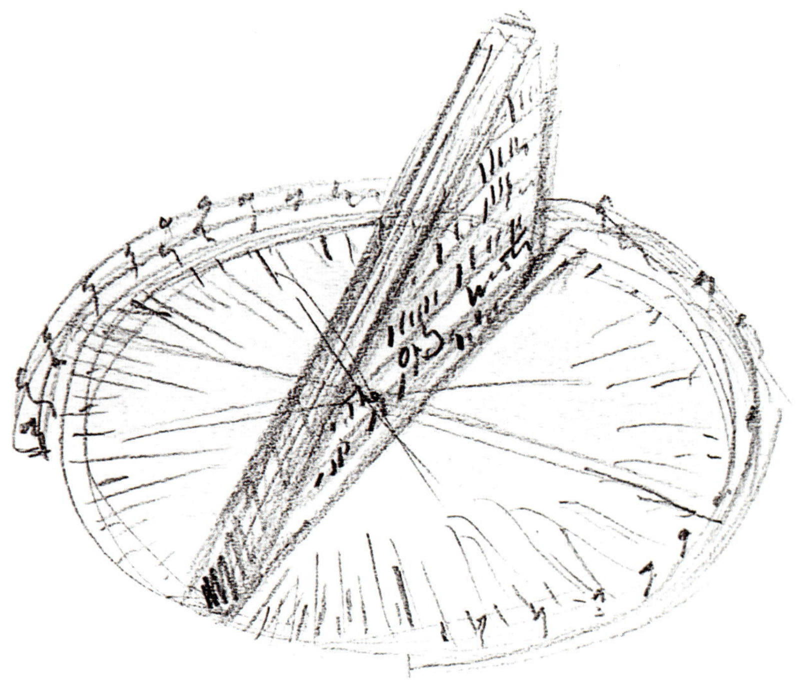

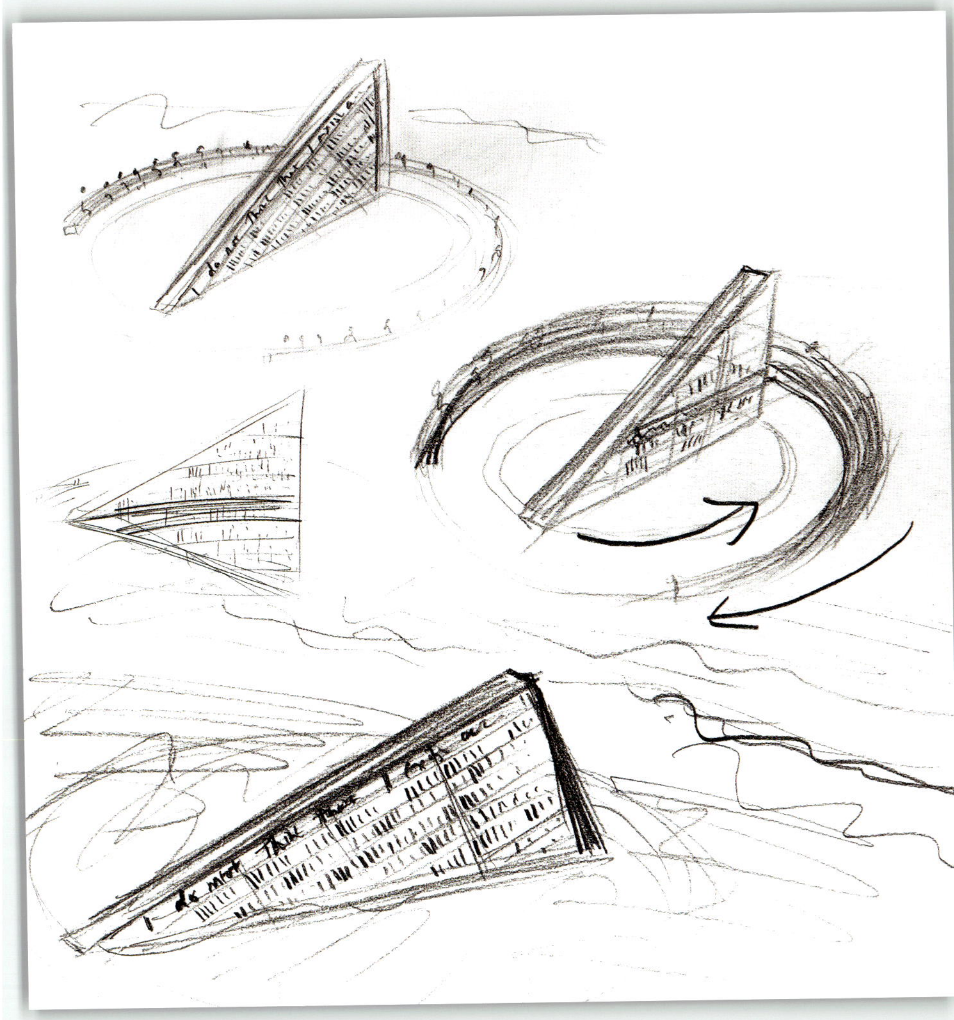

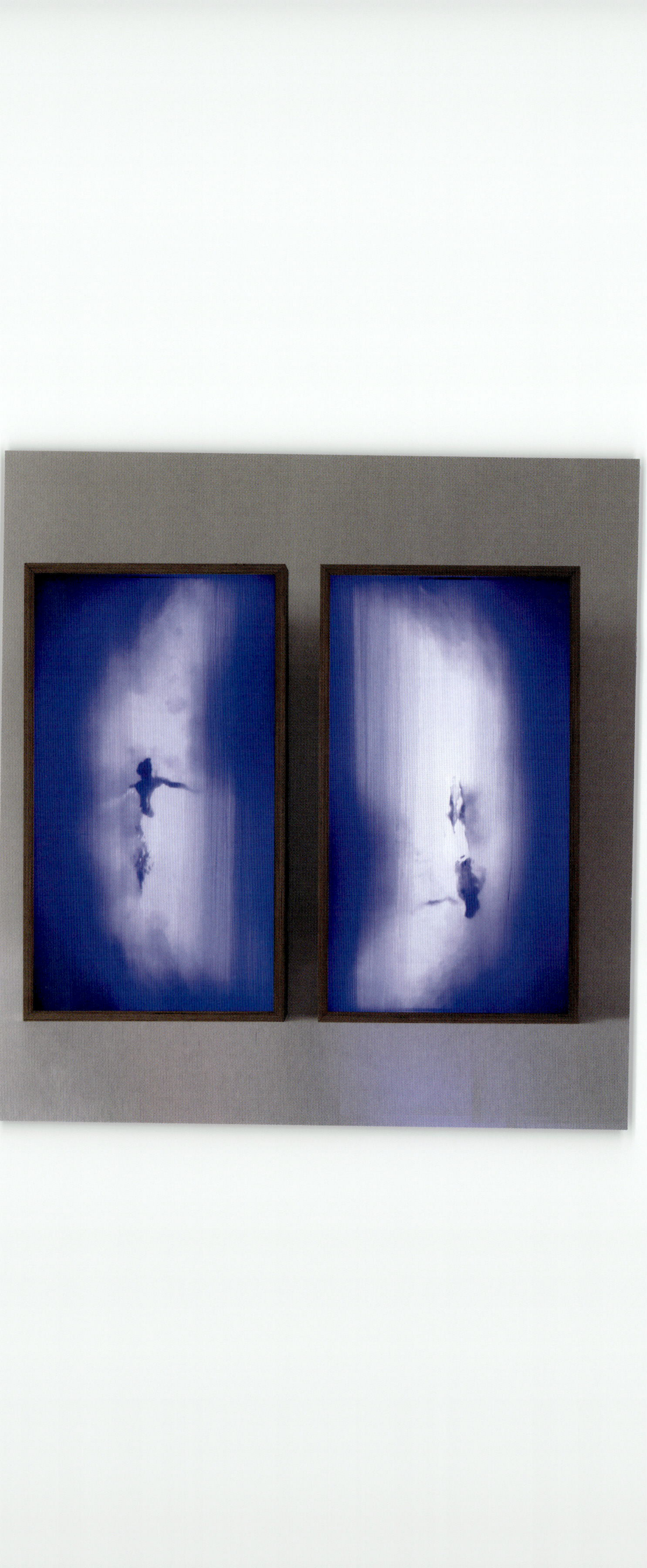

TRACING TIME

Drawing takes time. A line has time in it.

David Hockney

In parallel with the large-scale works that involve myriad collaborators, I have maintained a personal practice of drawing and assembling small sculptures alone in the studio, choosing dimensions and materials that are manageable with my own hands. *Tracing Time* was an exhibition at the Faena Art Project Room in Miami from December 2025 to February 2026 of my painted television screens, boxed cardboard drawings, and layered glass paintings.

I applied paint to layers of Perspex over portrait-oriented television screens that relayed slow-motion footage of my son Ludo swimming, as well as a figure dancing in the rain. Within painted layers of glass, I set cardboard cut-out ink-wash drawings of a dancing figure in the rain. I scrawled onto an oil-paint portrait on layered glass a transcendent oceanic phrase chosen by the curator Ekow Eshun from Melville's *Moby Dick*. I am interested in the ways paint, pixels and water hold the traces of time. Perhaps I am still drawing on my earliest memory of almost drowning in the River Thames at the age of two or three. I can't be sure.

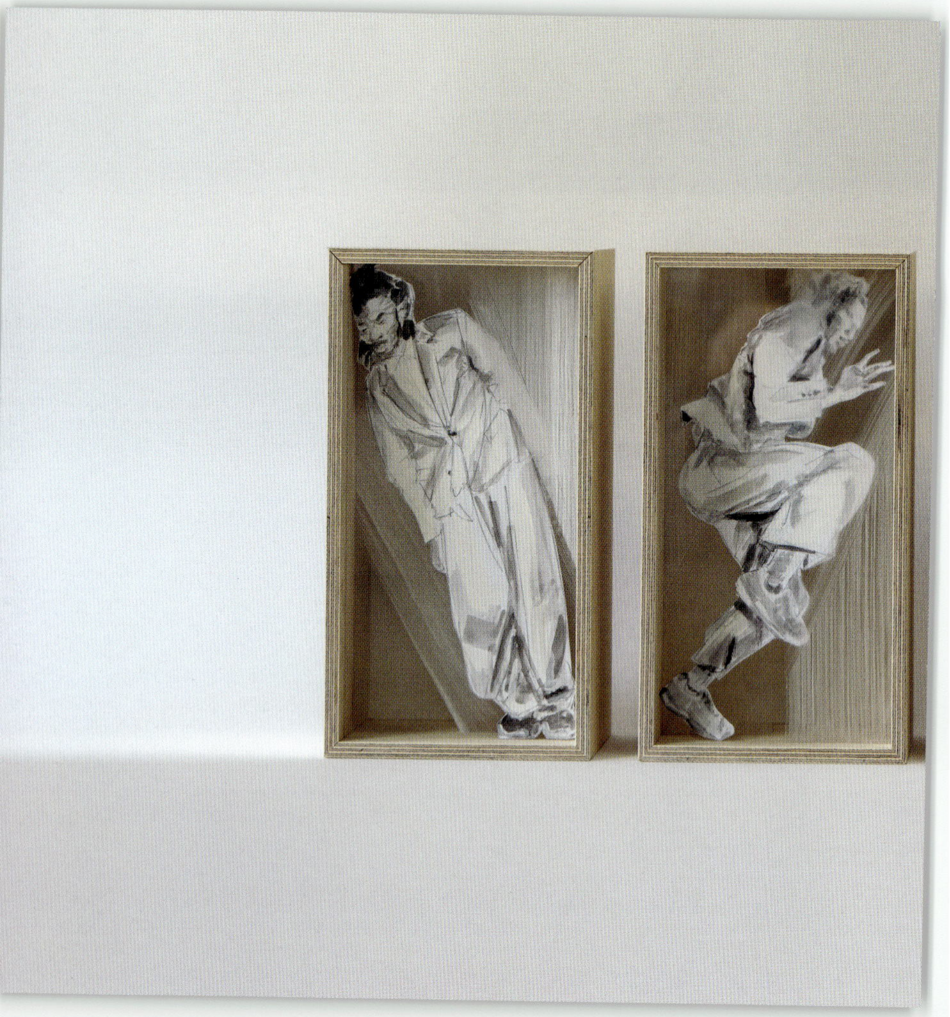

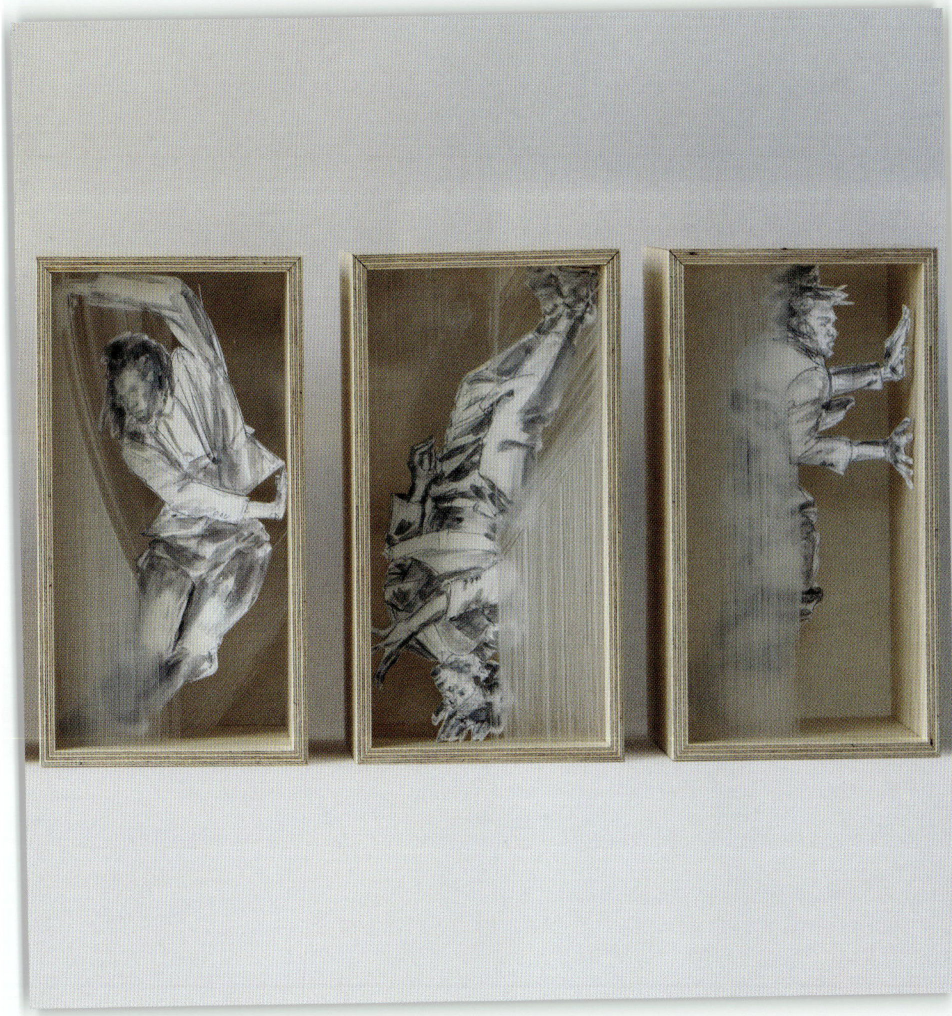

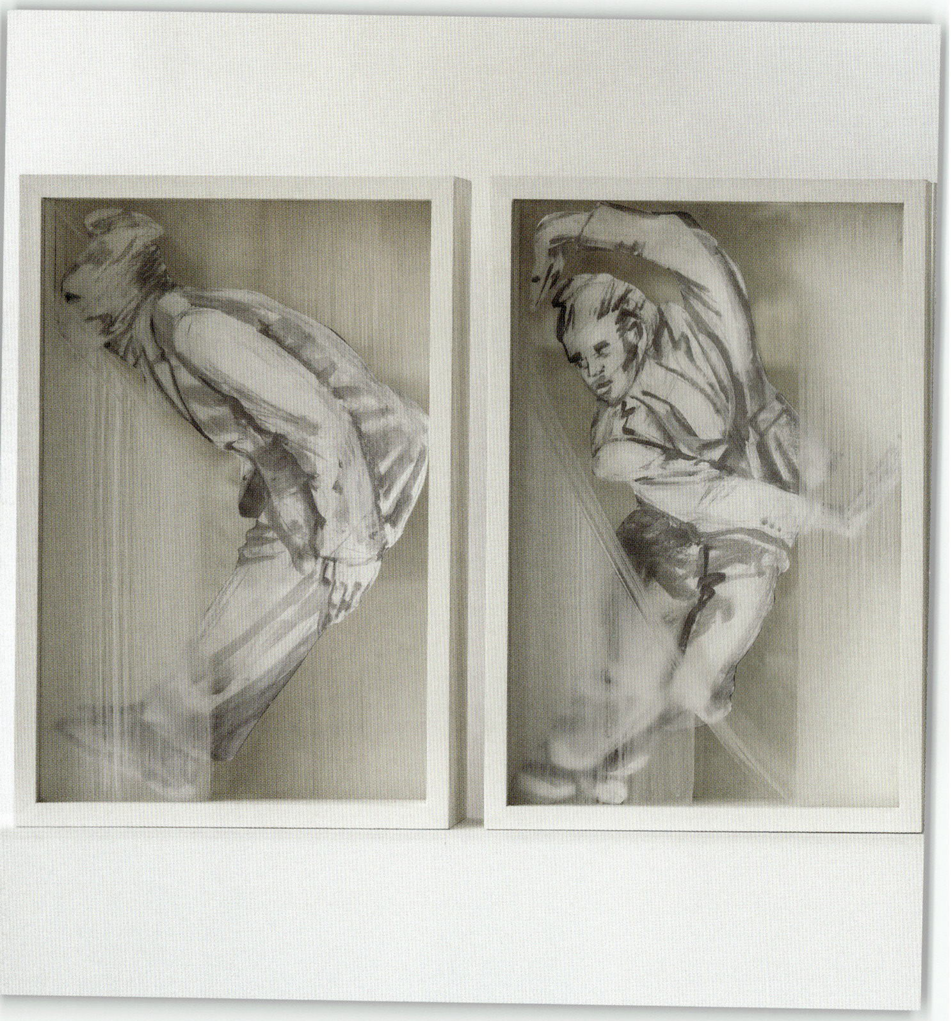

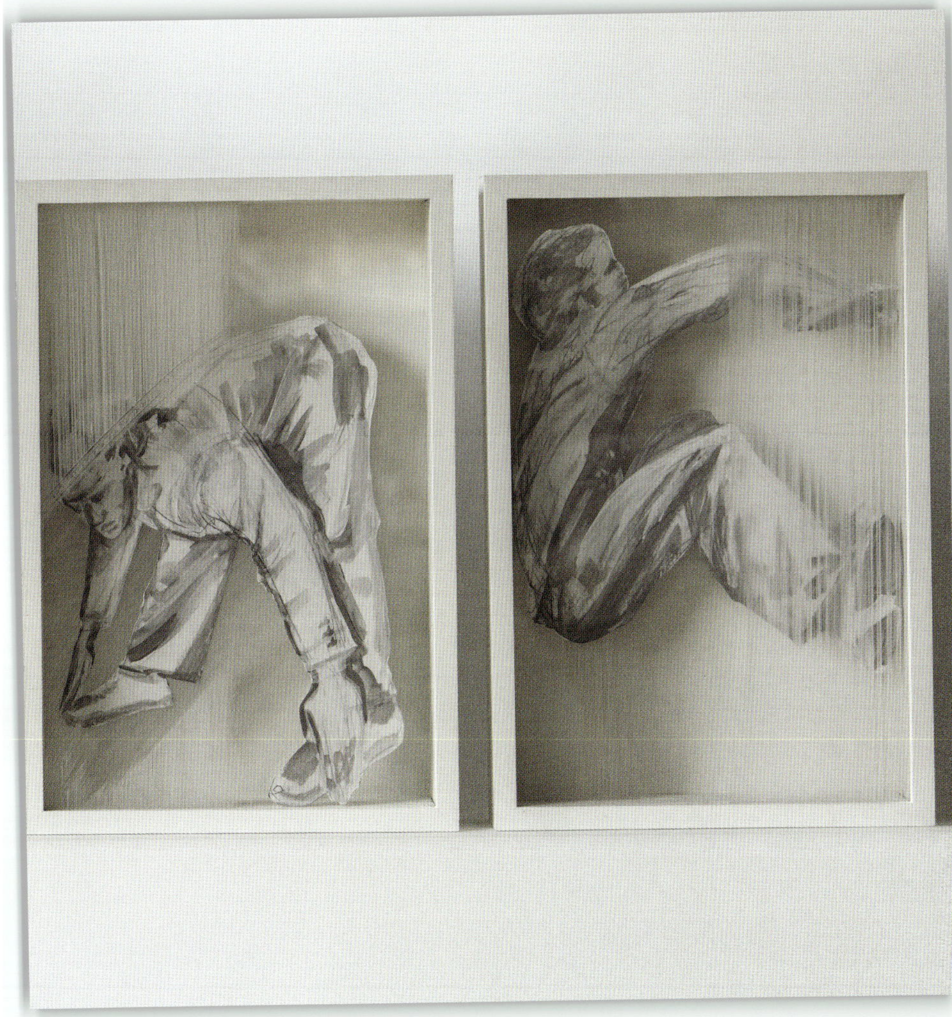

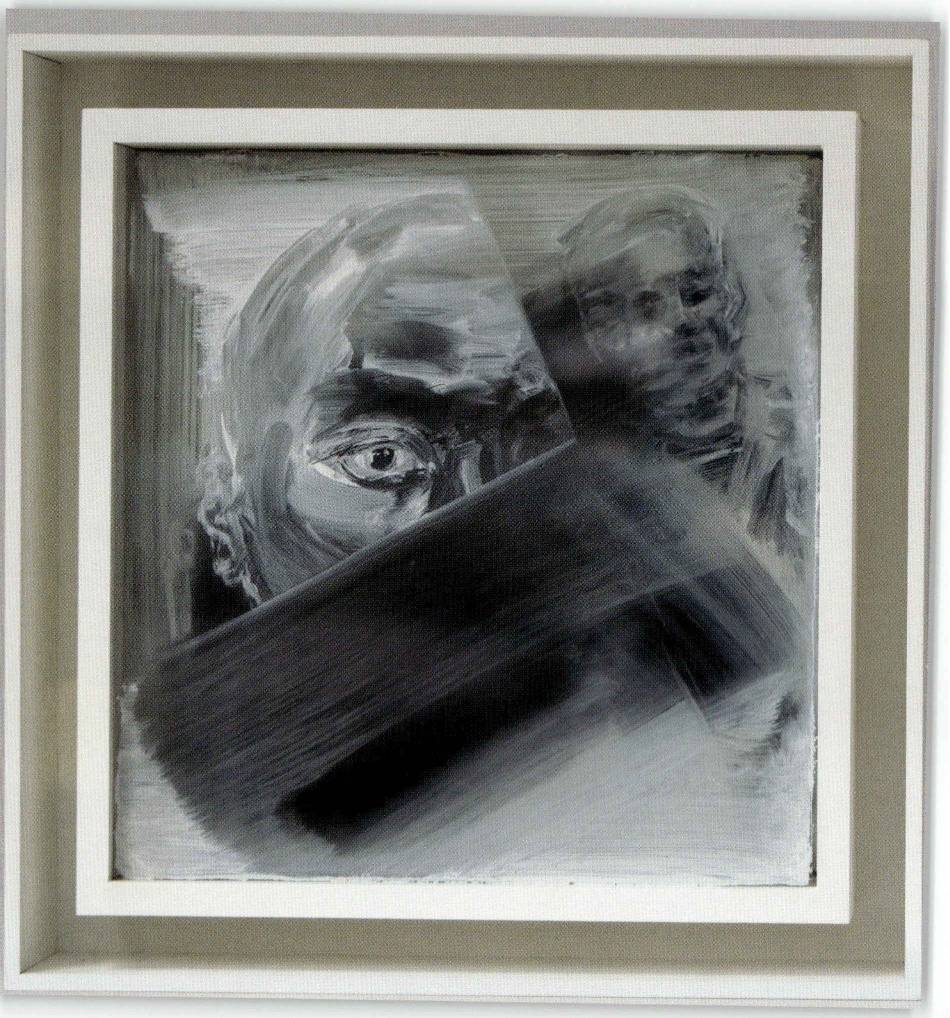

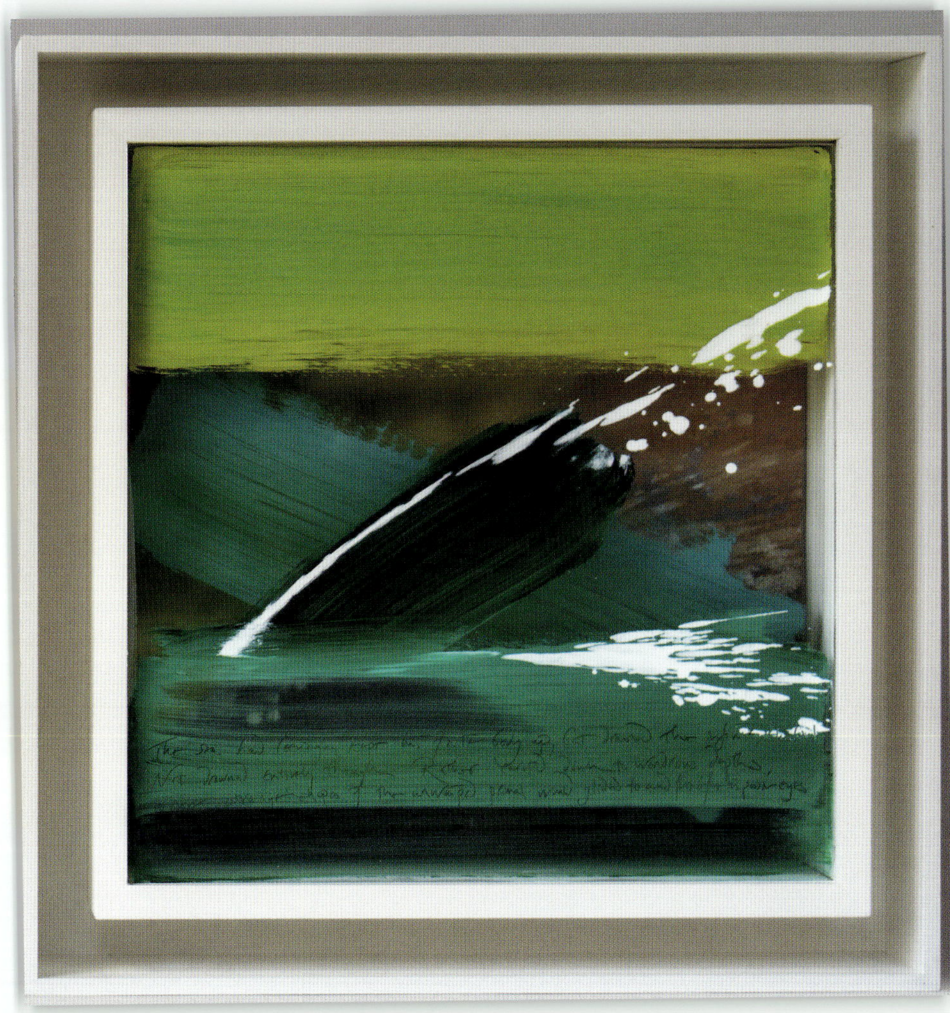

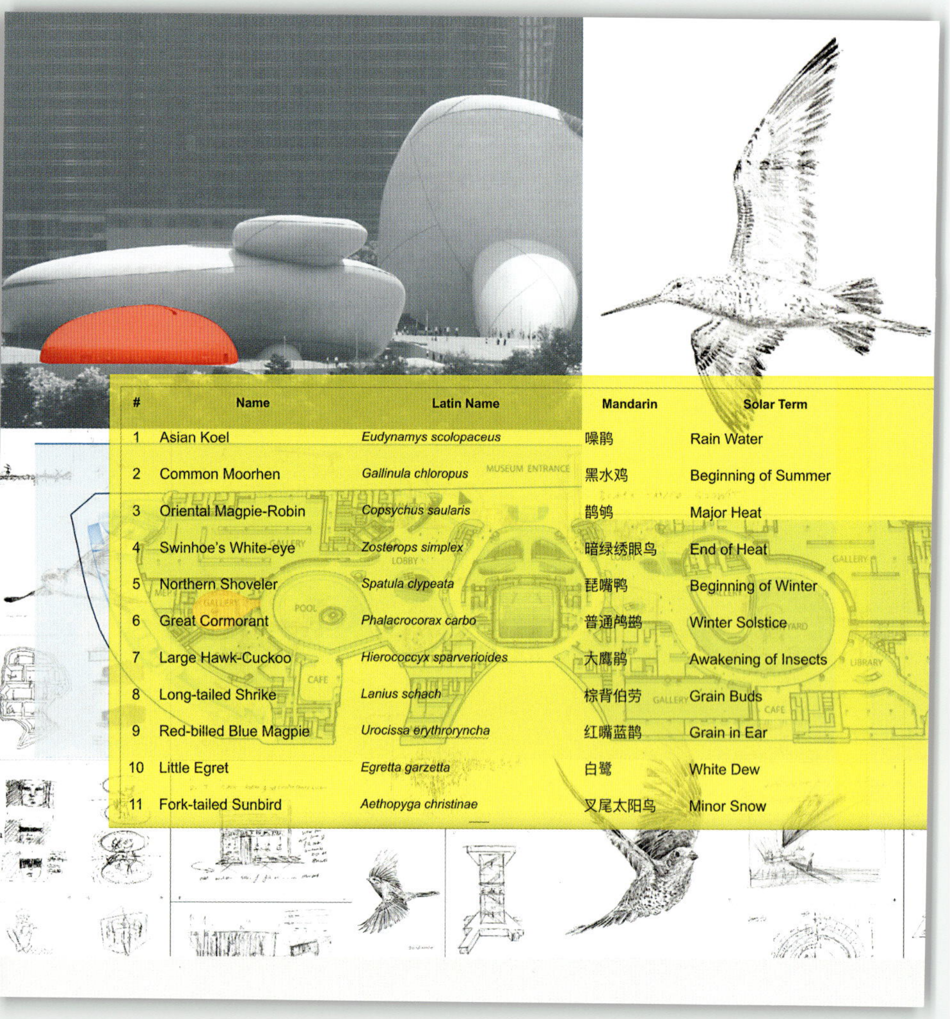

#	Name	Latin Name	Mandarin	Solar Term
1	Asian Koel	*Eudynamys scolopaceus*	噪鹃	Rain Water
2	Common Moorhen	*Gallinula chloropus*	黑水鸡	Beginning of Summer
3	Oriental Magpie-Robin	*Copsychus saularis*	鹊鸲	Major Heat
4	Swinhoe's White-eye	*Zosterops simplex*	暗绿绣眼鸟	End of Heat
5	Northern Shoveler	*Spatula clypeata*	琵嘴鸭	Beginning of Winter
6	Great Cormorant	*Phalacrocorax carbo*	普通鸬鹚	Winter Solstice
7	Large Hawk-Cuckoo	*Hierococcyx sparverioides*	大鹰鹃	Awakening of Insects
8	Long-tailed Shrike	*Lanius schach*	棕背伯劳	Grain Buds
9	Red-billed Blue Magpie	*Urocissa erythroryncha*	红嘴蓝鹊	Grain in Ear
10	Little Egret	*Egretta garzetta*	白鹭	White Dew
11	Fork-tailed Sunbird	*Aethopyga christinae*	叉尾太阳鸟	Minor Snow

TAKE ME HOME

Everything is always in motion, everything is always migrating: the Earth, her continents, mountains, her magnetic charge, and her birds, especially here, at the midpoint of the Great East Asia–Australasia Flyway.

These words are drawn from a poem I wrote as part of *Take Me Home*, an inaugural commission for the permanent collection of the new Shenzhen Bay Culture Park in China, which opened in December 2025. Envisioned as a contemporary cave painting, the work inscribes traces of my hand on every interior surface of Chinese architect Ma Yansong's Floating Stone Gallery, which feels simultaneously ancient and futuristic. As visitors enter the two-storey chapel-like space, they are surrounded by 2,000 replicas of my sketchbooks, including drawings of many of the migratory bird species that score Shenzhen's skies. A narrow, horizontal LED strip bisects the wall of drawings, beaming out phrases in Mandarin that I had read aloud in *Library of Us* a few weeks earlier in Miami. The Chinese censor auditing the installation questioned our inclusion of the same authors that are banned in some schools and libraries in Florida. We removed the authors' names and retained their words. Every five minutes, the LED text invites viewers to take one sketch from the wall home with them. Visitors ascend a curved stair to discover a vast domed ceiling, illuminated with AI-assisted animations of my sketches of the bar-tailed godwit, a bird that flies 10,000 kilometres from Siberia to New Zealand via Shenzhen in 10 days. The film is a meditation on migration: of birds and humans between mountains and magnetic poles, conceived to catalyse the paper sketch that visitors hold in their hands from souvenir to invitation to look up at the airborne migrants, wanderers and residents that also call Shenzhen home.

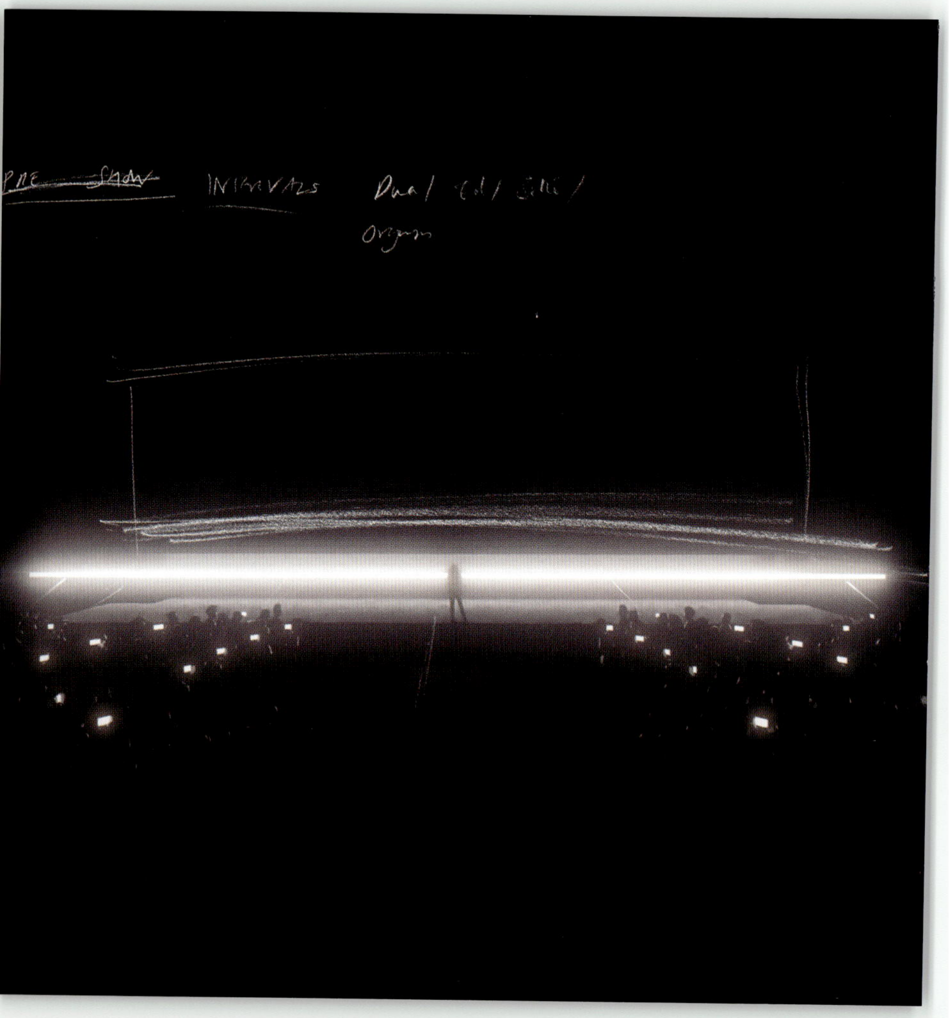
PRE SHOW
INTERVALS
Dual /

LULLABY

Yamma mweyl el hawa, Yamma mweyl el hawa, Oh, sing for me, mama. Mama, sing to the wind, I wish my bones could form a bridge, and carry you to the other side.

Based on a traditional song, additional words from Mahmoud Darwish and Peter Gabriel

In June 2025, I joined an artists' retreat at the late Vietnamese Zen master Thich Nhat Hanh's monastery in rural France, Plum Village. We were 80 artists learning from 70 Buddhist monks. A number of choral singers taught us to sing in harmony, and we offered a choral lullaby for an artist's friend, a mother trapped in Gaza trying to help her two very hungry and frightened children get to sleep during the desperate depths of the war.

I returned to London and the director Amir Nizar Zuabi, whose portrait I had drawn as part of *Congregation* in 2024, invited me to work with the painter Malak Mattar on *Together for Palestine*, a concert to raise funds for Gazan charities. We filled a simple horizontal screen with paintings by Palestinian artists, and pierced the darkness between songs with a 20-metre-wide line of light. I suggested releasing a choral lullaby rooted in a traditional Arabic song with the aim of reaching the Christmas number 1 spot in the charts to raise additional funds to support those affected by the war. Led by the singer Nai Barghouti and composer Kieran Brunt, a new choral interpretation of *Yamma mweyl el hawa* made it to number 5 in the UK charts by 25 December 2025, the highest position ever for a song in Arabic.

AMERICAN PSYCHO

Surface, surface, surface, was all that anyone found meaning in …
this was civilization as I saw it, colossal and jagged …

Bret Easton Ellis, *American Psycho*

In January 2026, the director Rupert Goold and I revisited our 2013 production of *American Psycho* at London's Almeida Theatre. Patrick Bateman, the psychopathic solipsist at the heart of Bret Easton Ellis's prescient 1991 novel, is obsessed with Donald Trump. There are 37 references to Trump in the novel. Back in 2013 this didn't seem particularly significant, and the 2013 version of the script included only one brief allusion to Trump. By the time the play transferred to Broadway in 2016, three more mentions of Trump had crept into the script. And by 2026, Trump had physically made his way onto the stage as a character with his own lines.

Writer Aron Solomon noted perceptively about the novel: 'American Psycho *was never about murder. It was about what happens when surface replaces substance, when accountability becomes optional, when cruelty is indistinguishable from confidence. We were supposed to recognize the monster before he learned how to govern. Instead, we taught him the language of applause and handed him the microphone.*'

In 2026 we felt our 2013 design, a gleaming white box, could no longer contain the 'monster with a microphone'. We released the action out onto an LED catwalk stage that appeared to emerge into the audience from a vast hold in the Almeida's distinctive curved brick wall.

778–779

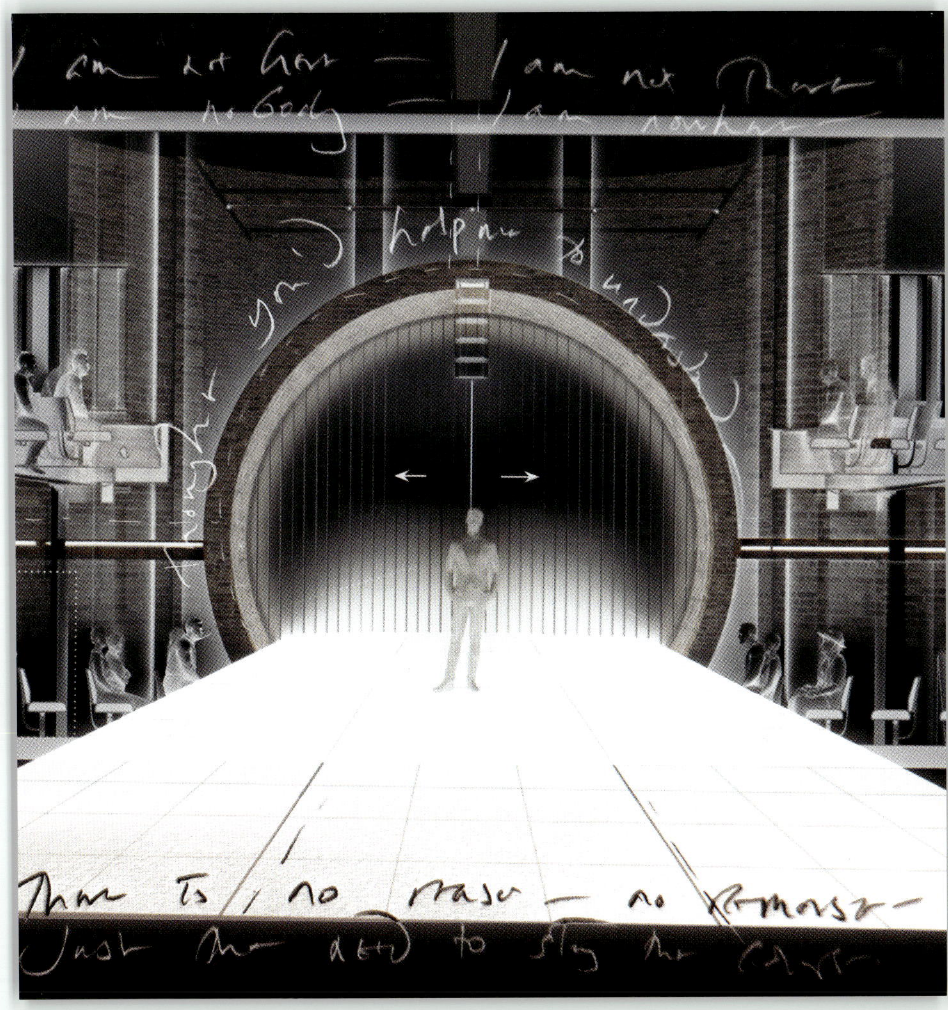
I am not here — I am not there
I am nobody — I am nowhere —
There is no reason — no remorse —

TRISTAN UND ISOLDE

Treat a work of art like a prince: let it speak to you first.

Arthur Schopenhauer

The Metropolitan Opera in New York has a perfectly square gilded proscenium opening. At nearly 16 metres, it's the tallest in any opera house and towers above the performers. Tristan and Isolde are known as the 'Mount Everest' of operatic roles, requiring barely achievable feats of vocal power and stamina. The first production in 1860 was abandoned after 70 rehearsals as 'unperformable'. In our March 2026 interpretation, directed by Yuval Sharon, the soprano Lise Davidsen and tenor Michael Spyres walk onto the stage before the music starts, dressed in contemporary clothes: two ordinary humans, about to take on the monumental challenge of producing four hours of some of the most transcendent music ever composed. The tools they require to tell the mythic story are laid out before them on a table: a knife, a jug, a bottle. As they lift each object, it is relayed cinematically onto a vast projected surface that fills the entire gilded frame. The water they pour into a simple jug transforms into a tempestuous ocean. As Isolde lifts a knife from the table it becomes a vast angled performance space for the singers within the projected film, a freeze frame of her fateful decision not to kill Tristan. The sculpture is a kind of musical instrument: each performance area is designed to amplify the singers' voices. Act III, the most challenging for the tenor, is designed as a megaphone-shaped tunnel; a metaphor for the space between life and death that Tristan inhabits during this final act, and a practical means of giving his voice additional volume over the orchestra.

622–625 794–795 828–829

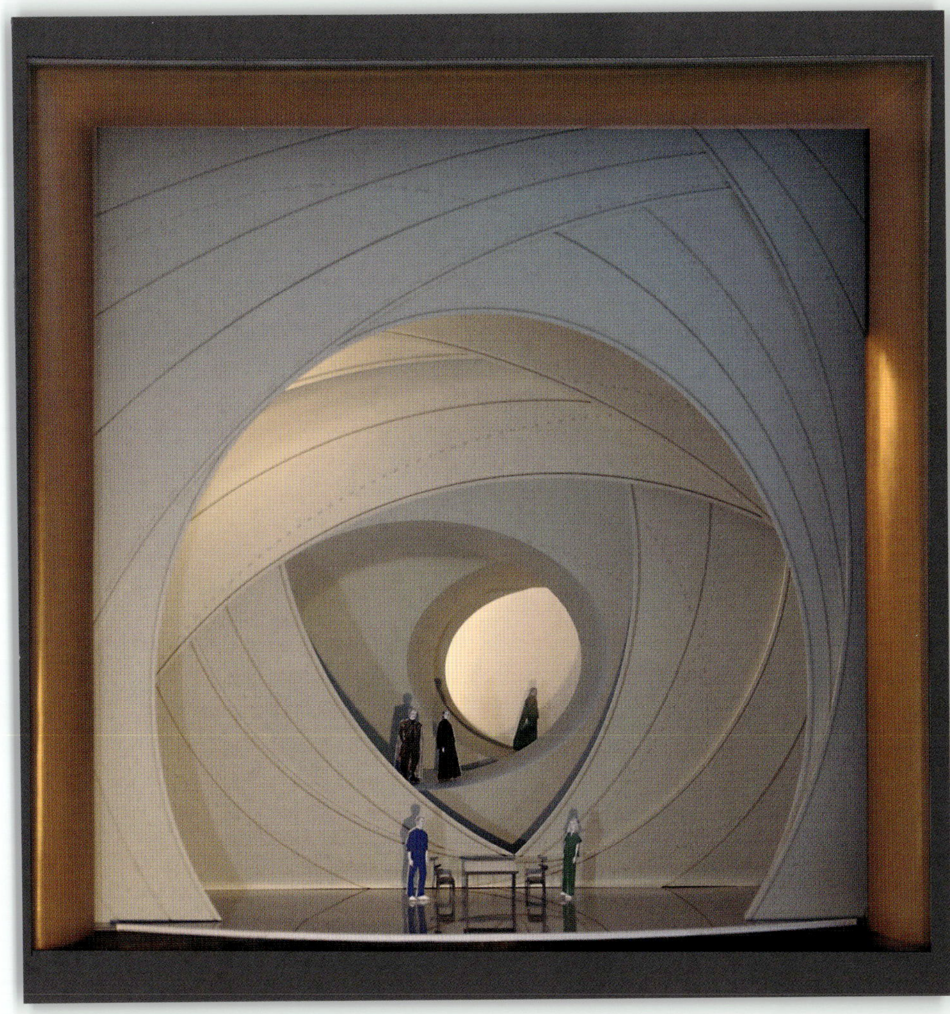

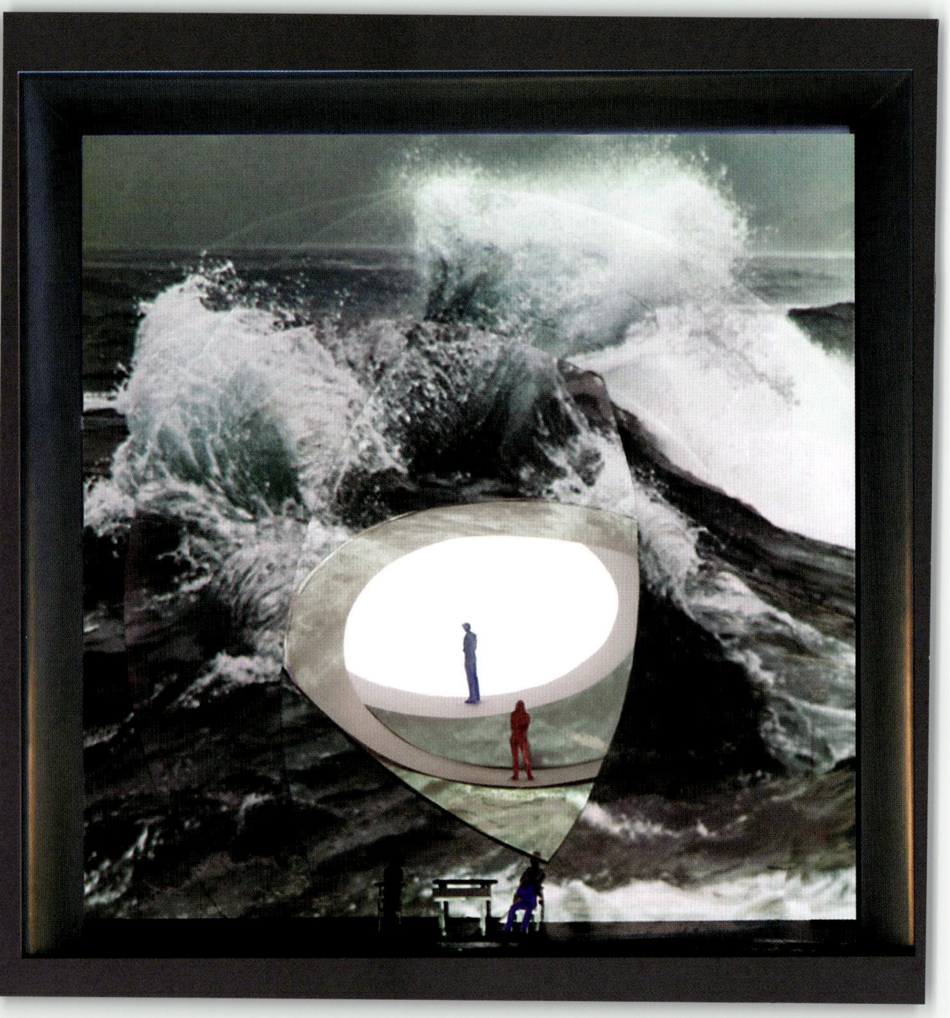

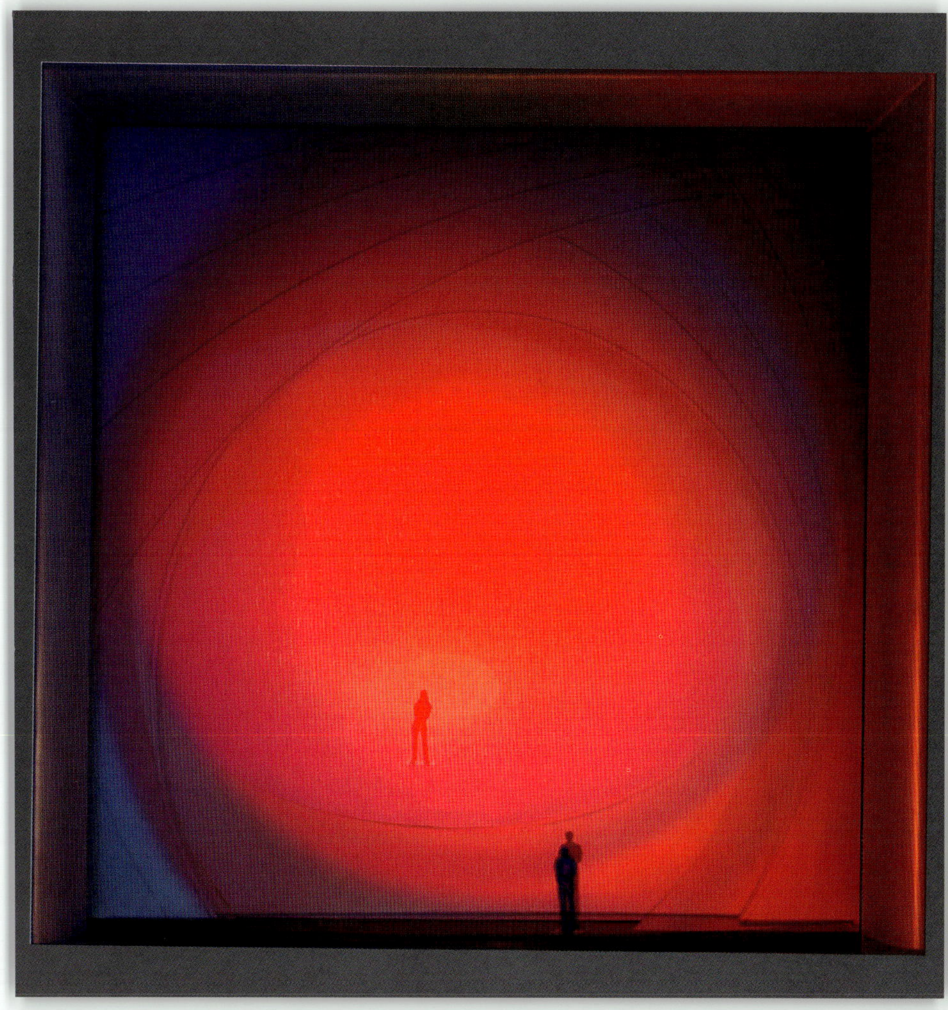

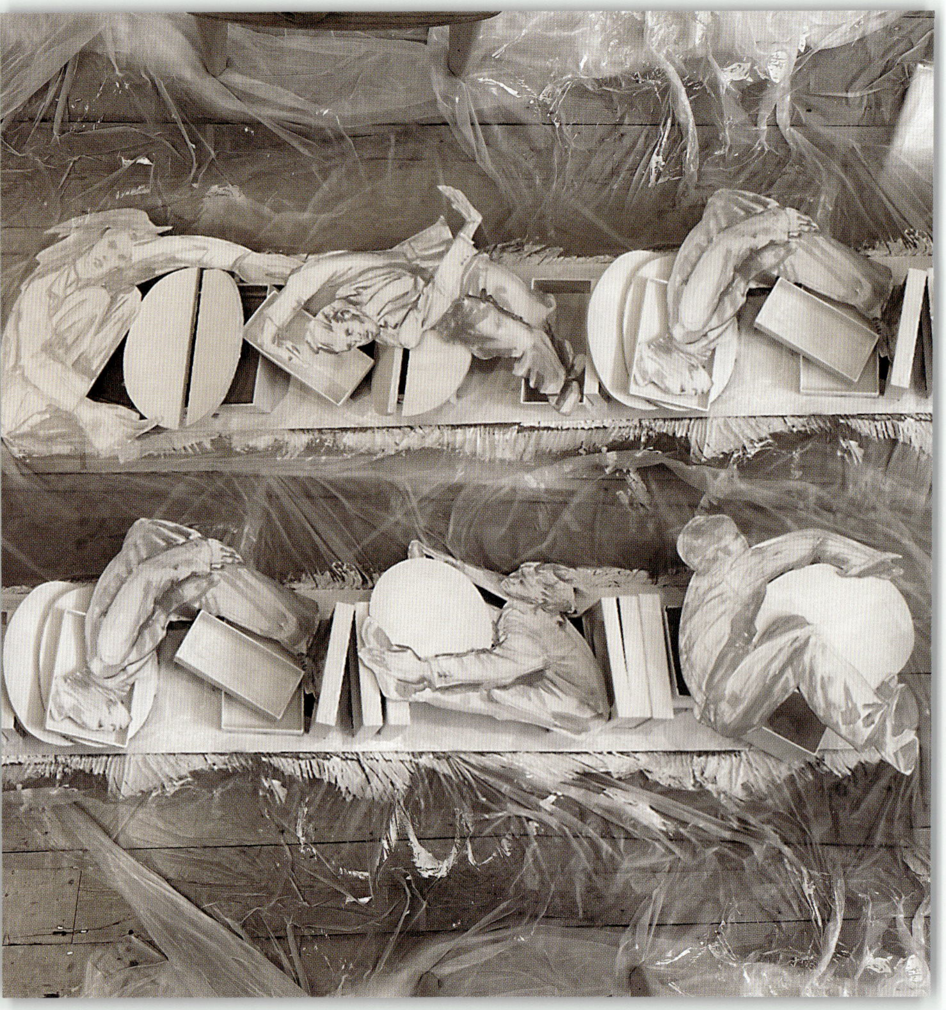

THE EVERYTHINGISTS

The future is behind us ...
Art for life and even more – life for art! We exclaim: the whole brilliant style of modern times – our trousers, jackets, shoes, trolleys, cars, airplanes, railways, grandiose steamships – is fascinating, is a great epoch, one that has known no equal in the entire history of the world.

Mikhail Larionov and Natalia Goncharova, *The Rayonist Manifesto*

In April 2026, I made an artwork – commissioned by London's V&A East Storehouse – in response to the early twentieth-century Russian artist Natalia Goncharova's vast painted cityscape backdrop for Stravinsky's 1926 *Firebird* ballet, which is held in the V&A's collection. The term 'Everythingism' (*vsechestvo* in Russian) was coined to describe Goncharova's wildly inclusive practice: painting, theatre design, fashion, cinema, interior design and performance art. She studied flowers, birds and angels, as well as soldiers and cities. I made *The Everythingists,* a 10-metre-wide, painted plywood sculpture depicting a dancing, falling figure in a sequence of five positions, caught between enlarged iPhone packaging boxes and split oval forms. I also projected a sequence of videos I had shot from moving car windows alongside drawings of East London species that I had made in my studio in southeast London. The V&A's Youth Collective guided me away from an earlier iteration of the work in which the figures were contained within the enlarged iPhone boxes. Invoking Goncharova's costuming of the lead dancer as half-woman, half-bird, the work draws on the distinction between centaurs (humans empowered by machines) and reverse-centaurs (machines empowered by humans).

THE LUNAR CHRONICLES

Mirrors have an uncanny way of telling the truth.

Marissa Meyer, *Cinder*

I researched the origins of animation as I began work on the production design concepts for the Warner Bros. animated films of Marissa Meyer's *The Lunar Chronicles* novel series. I discovered that Lotte Reiniger, the 'mother of animation', was educated in the early twentieth century at Berlin's Charlottenburger Waldschule, the first entirely outdoor school, conceived to give children maximum access to sunlight. It was in the forest school that Reiniger encountered the 2,000-year-old Chinese art of shadow puppetry. She spent her life telling stories through the intricate crafting of light and shadow, created the first full-length animation in 1926, and invented the multi-plane animation camera long before Walt Disney patented it.

The Lunar Chronicles is a science-fiction retelling of classic fairytales in which Cinderella and Rapunzel are redrawn, respectively, as a highly skilled mechanic and an advanced coder. The director Nöelle Raffaele's storyboards focus on the female characters' virtuosic hands in action, echoing Reiniger's 1922 animation *Aschenputtel*, in which Cinderella is shown being cut from black paper by the director's scissored hands.

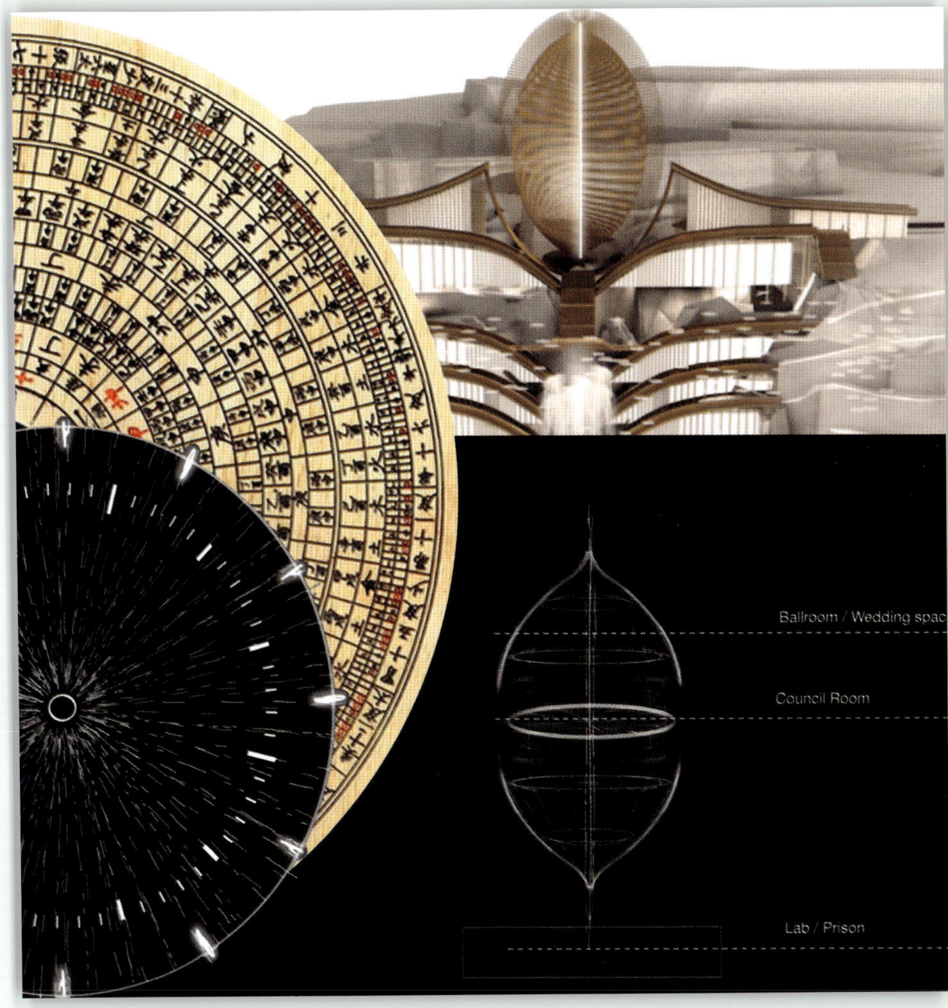
Ballroom / Wedding spac
Council Room
Lab / Prison

A NATIONAL PORTRAIT

... this little world, This precious stone set in the silver sea ...
This blessed plot, this earth, this realm, this England.

William Shakespeare, *Richard II*

In May 2026, we installed *A National Portrait* at the National Portrait Gallery in London. It is a perpetual digital drawing of as many of the United Kingdom's 69 million inhabitants as want to take part. The algorithm that produces the drawing has been trained for two years by the team at Google Arts & Culture on all the chalk and charcoal portraits I have made. We made *A National Portrait* as an invitation to everyone in the country to become a co-author of an ever-evolving, monumental collective portrait. You do not have to be physically at the gallery to participate. Wherever you are in the UK, whether citizen, resident or visitor, you can contribute your face and watch as your portrait etches itself, combined with countless others, onto the sculpture. Each participant can ask the algorithm to redraw their portrait until they are happy with it, and each receives a unique digital edition.

UK Prime Minister Keir Starmer warned the country, in a July 2025 speech, that it risked becoming 'an island of strangers'. By 2026, members of the UK's far right Reform UK party proposed that the adjective 'English' should only be applied to people whose grandparents were born in England. As a counterpoint, this work frames national identity as a continuous, always fragile process of collective authorship, shaped by participation, visibility and mutual recognition.

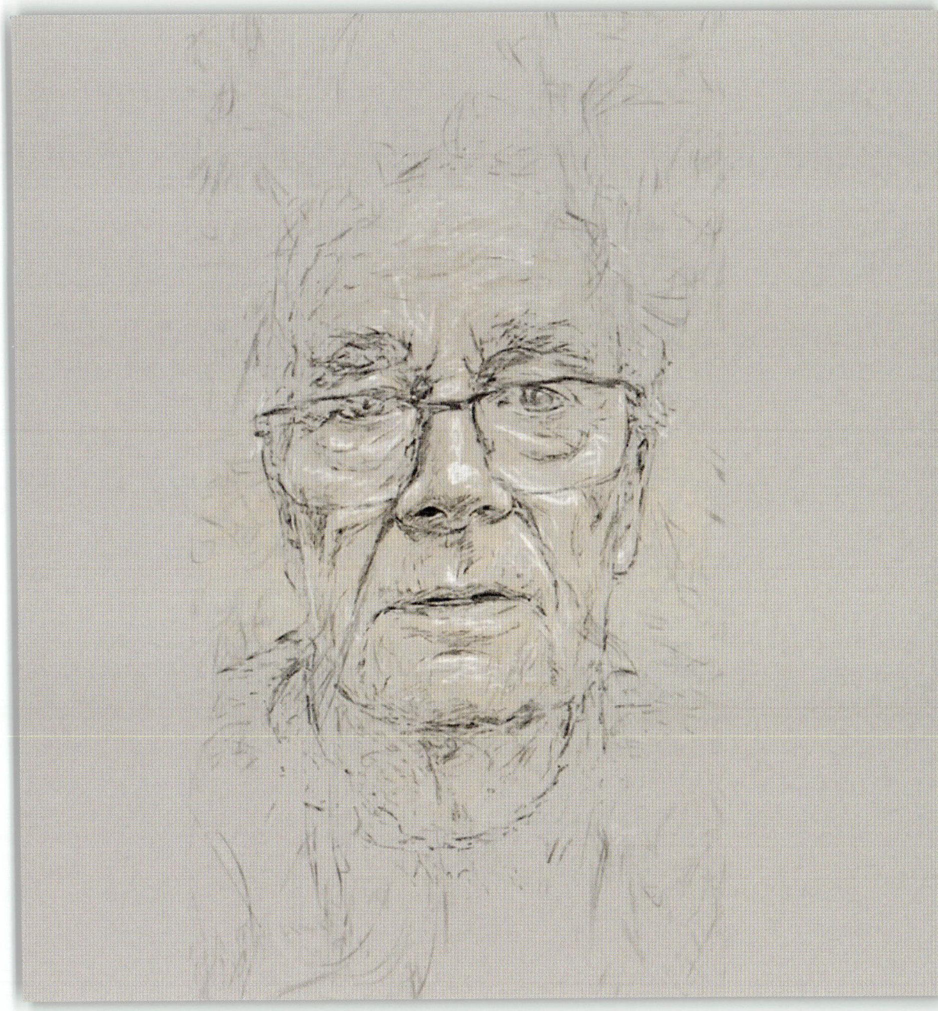

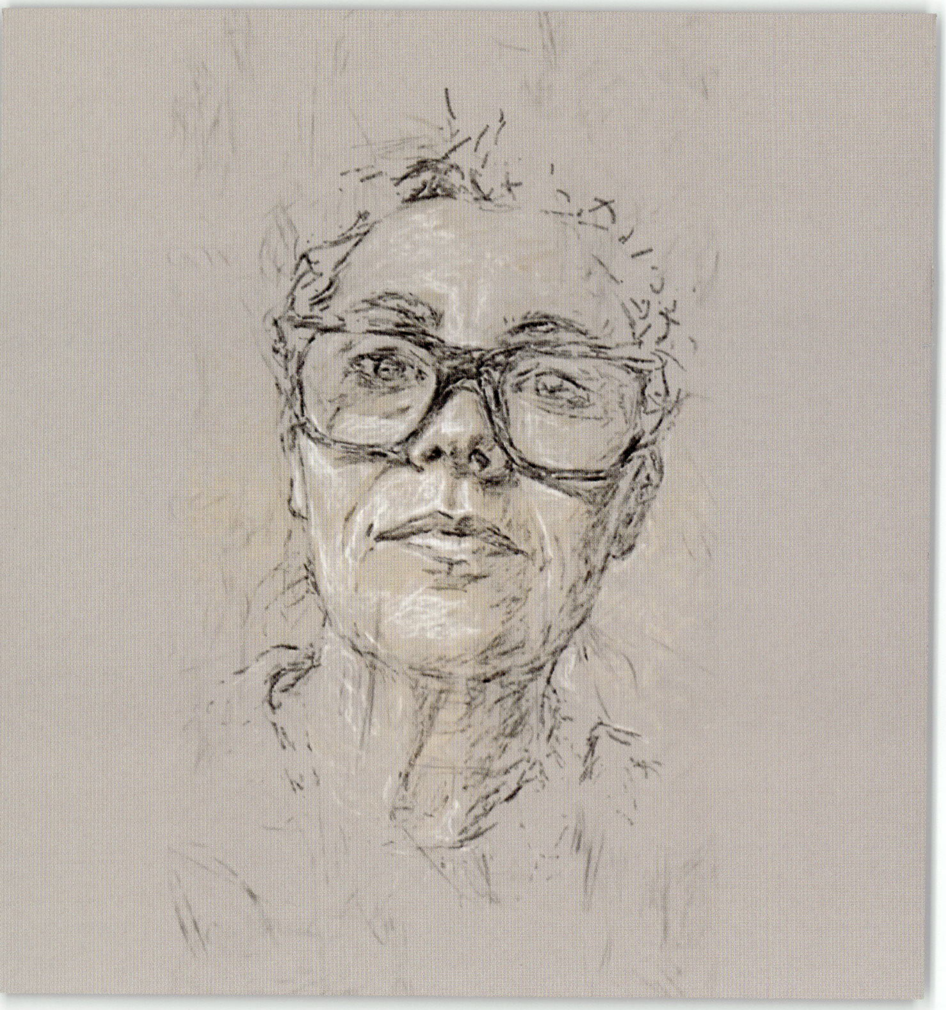

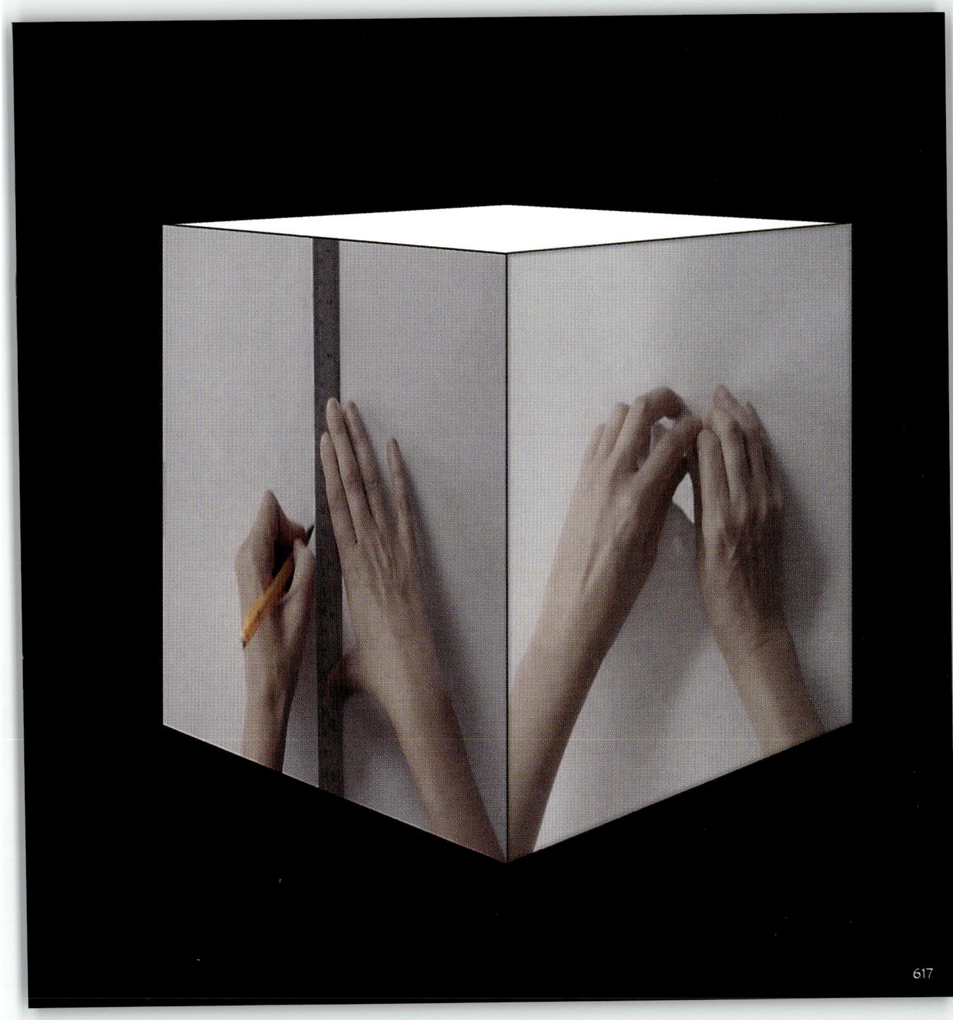

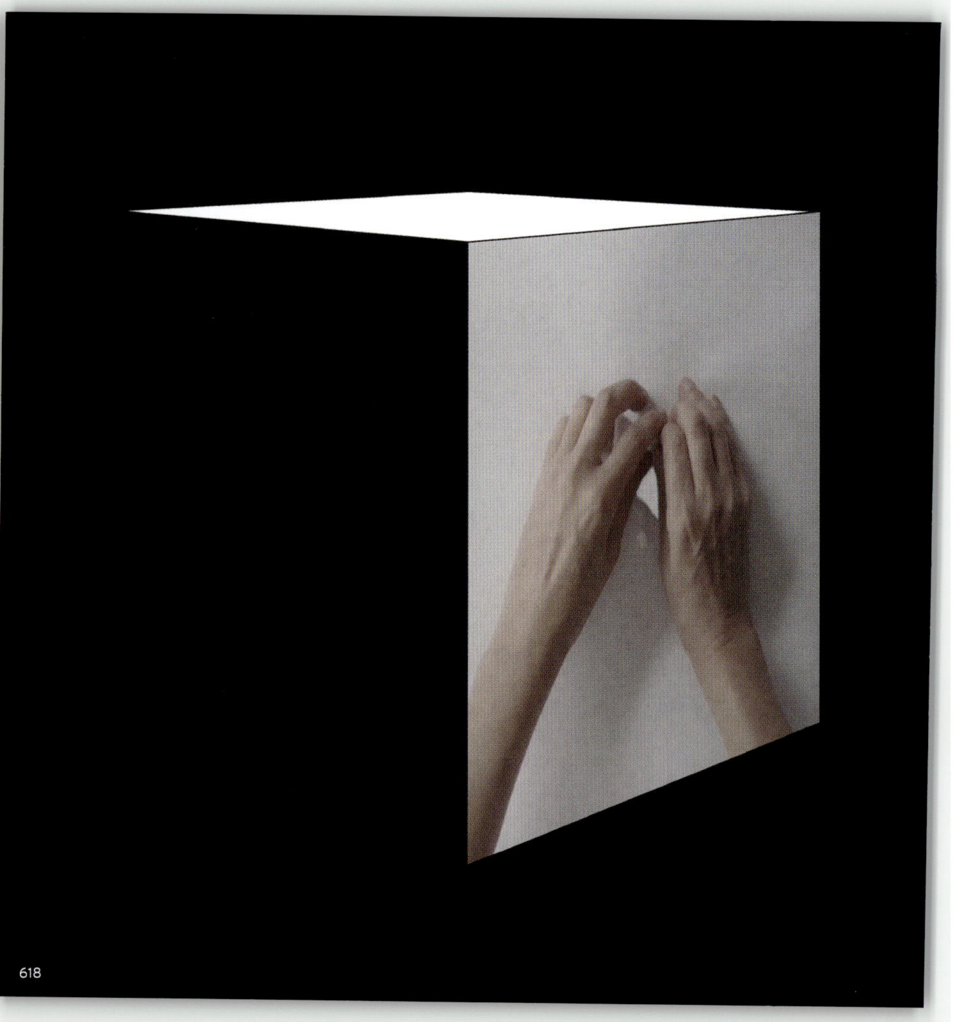

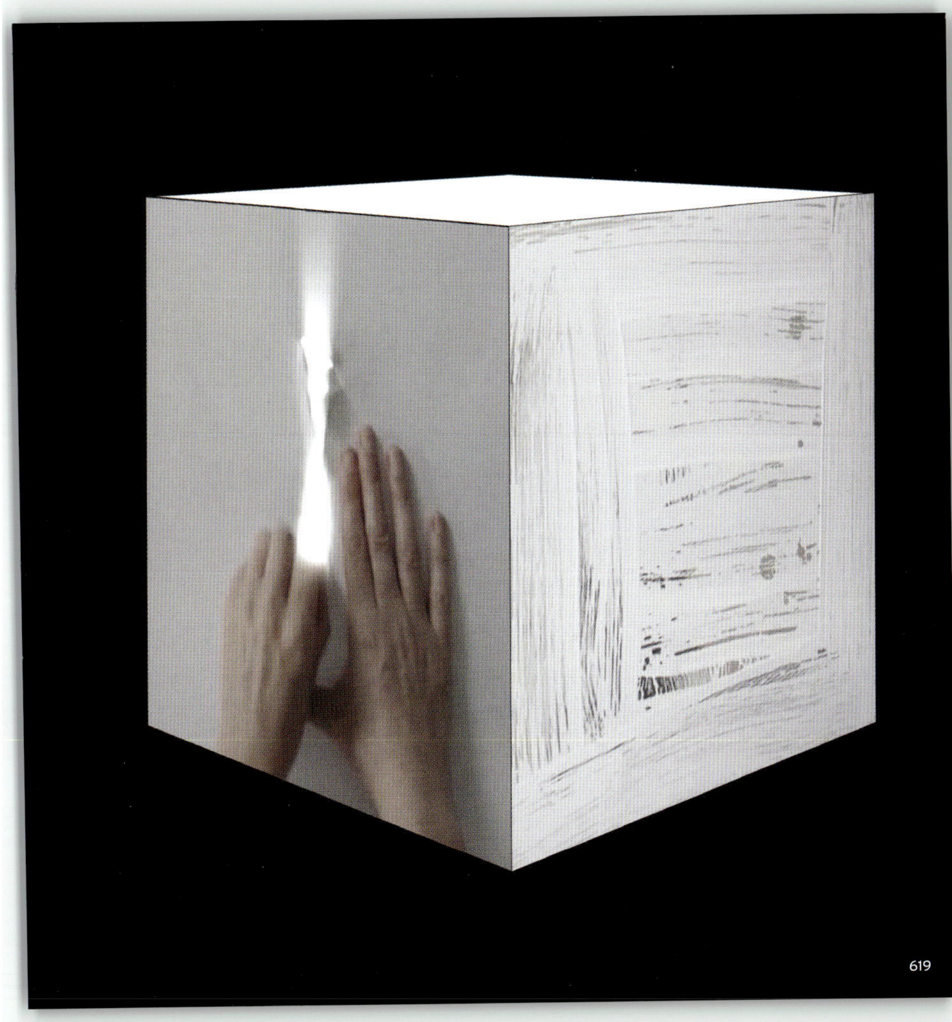

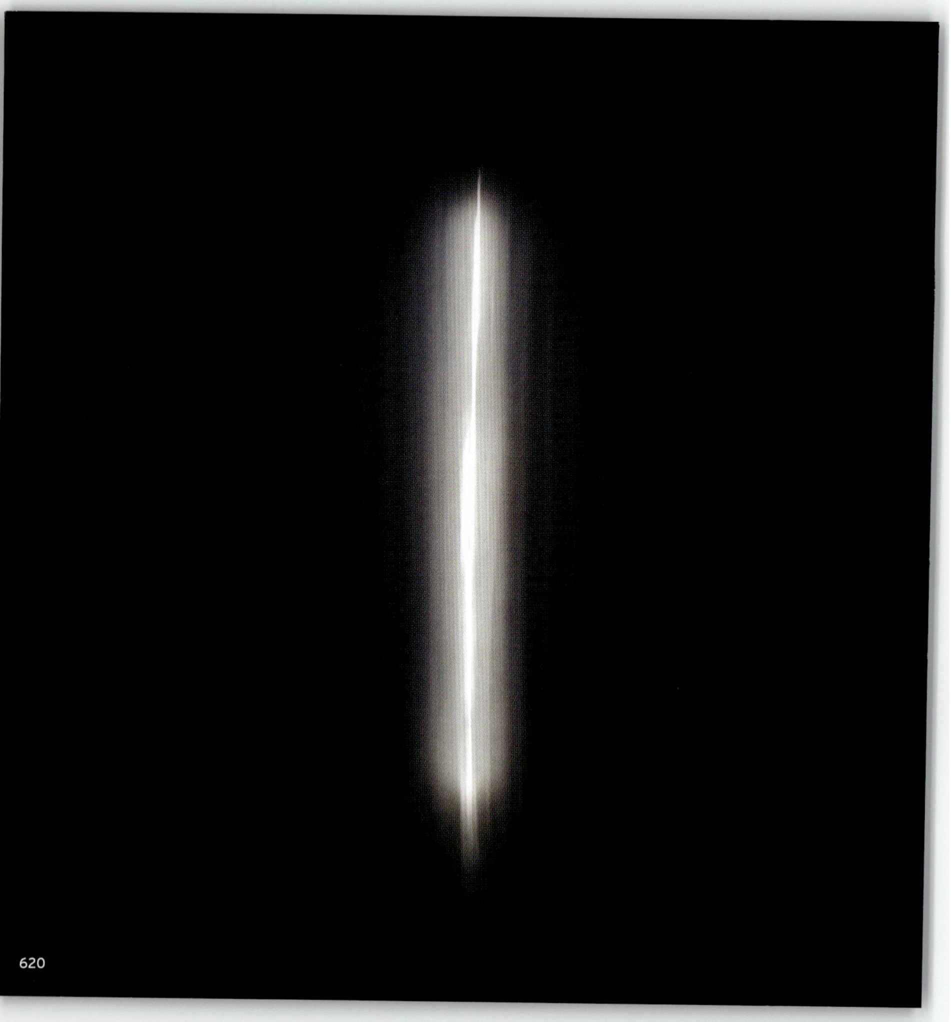

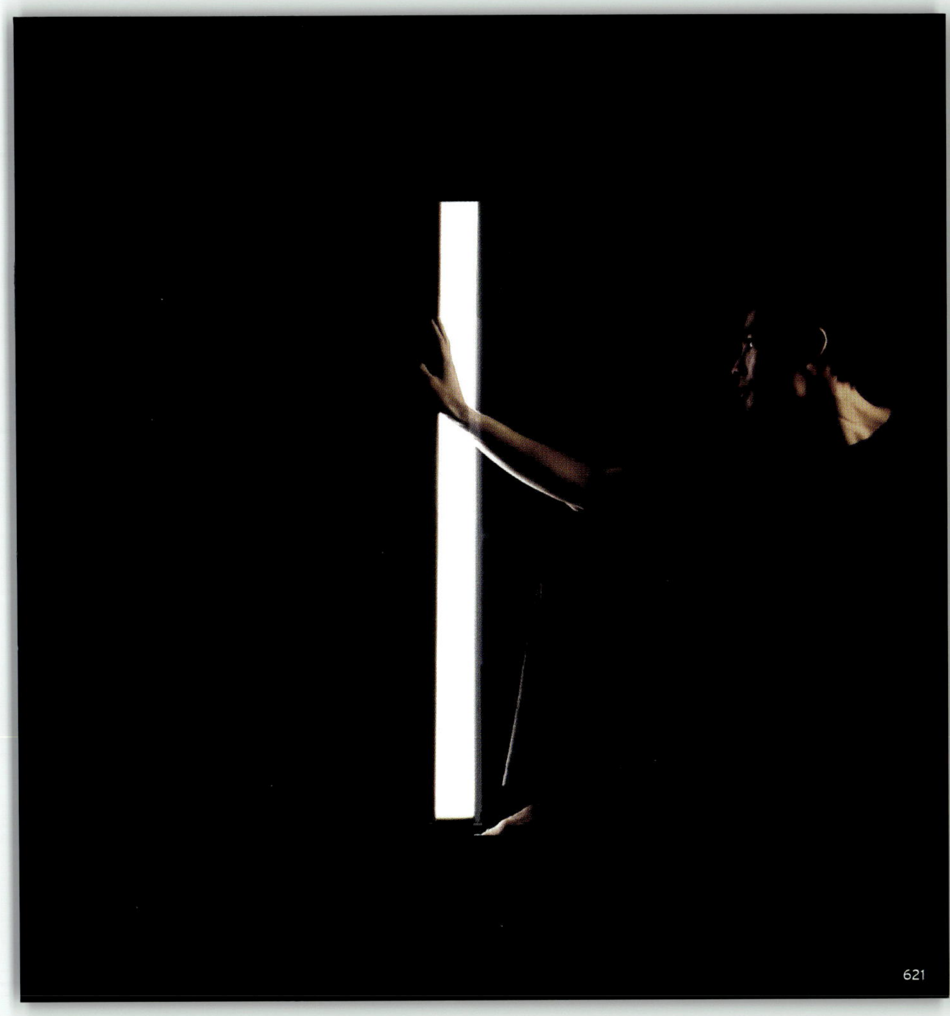

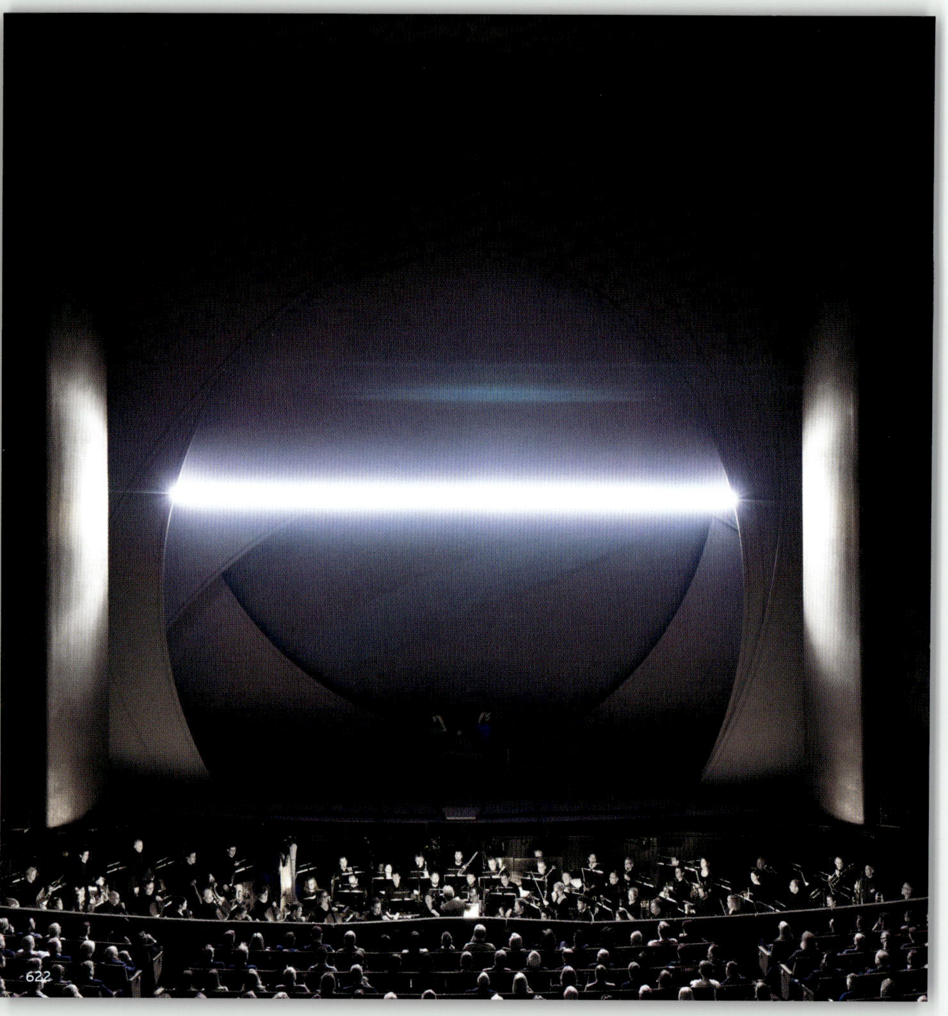

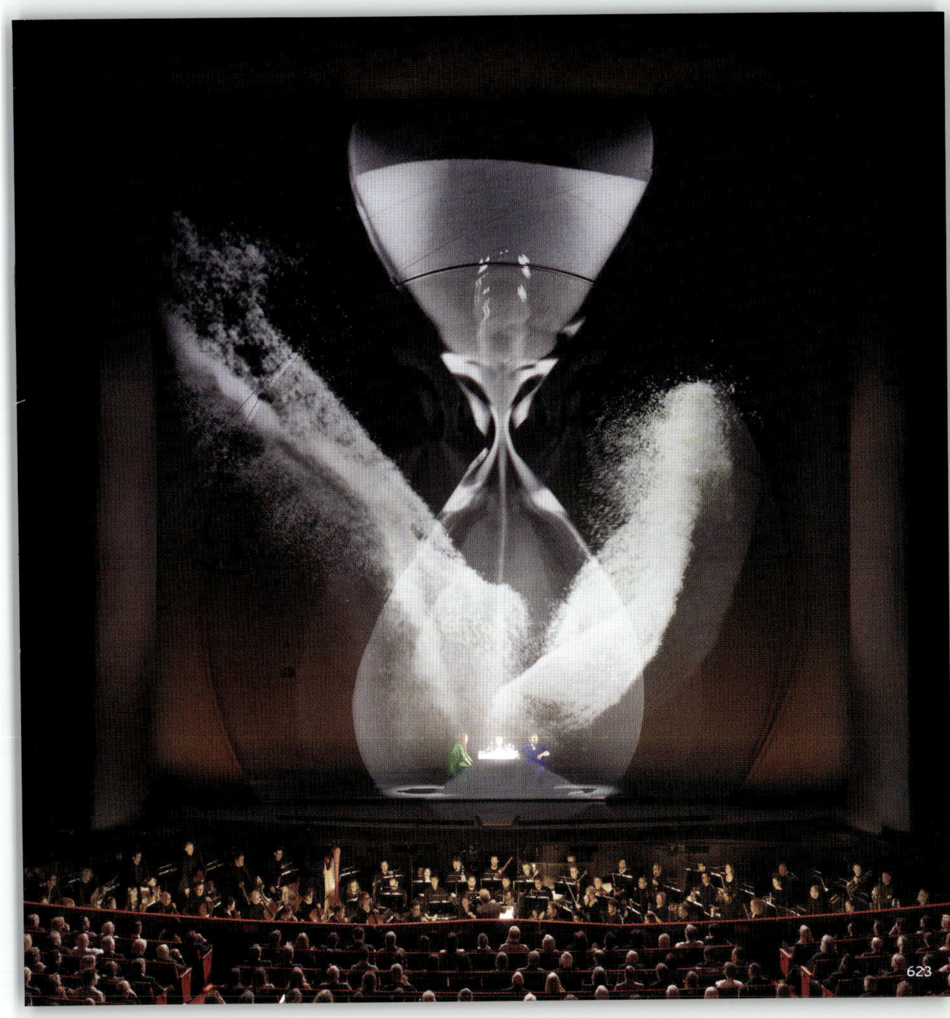

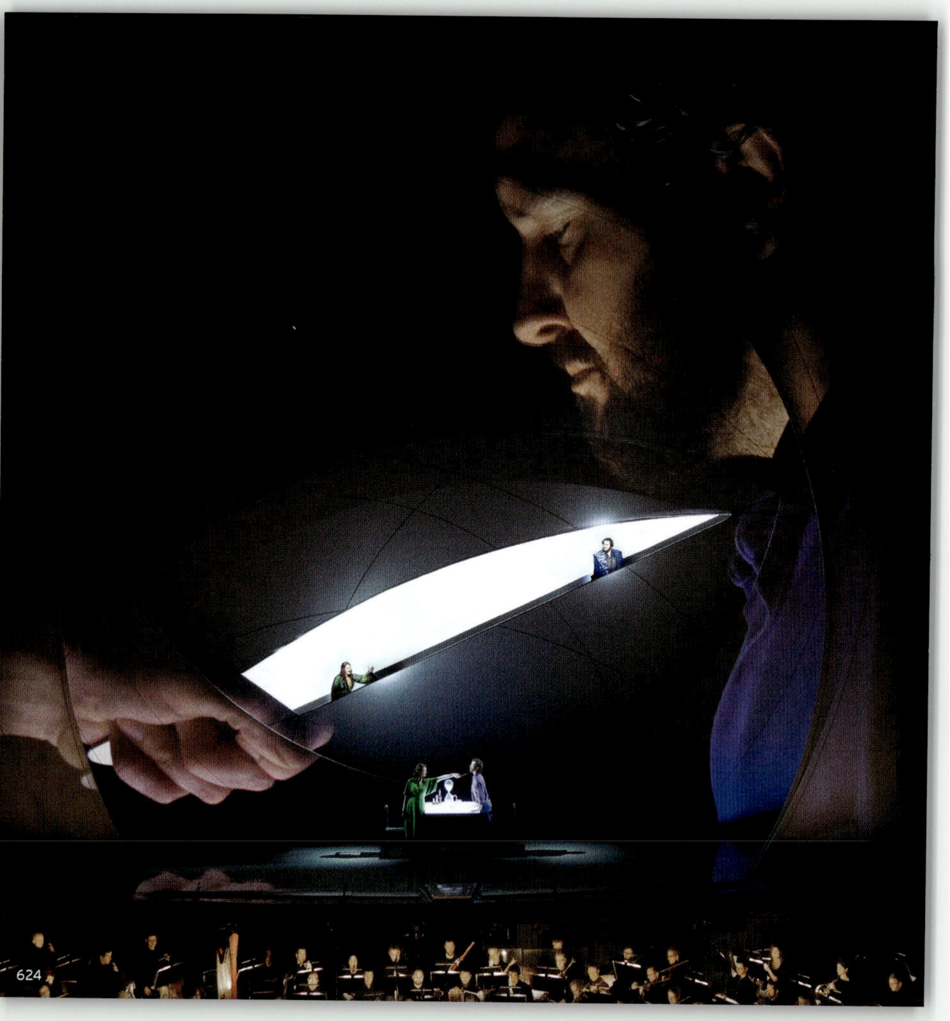

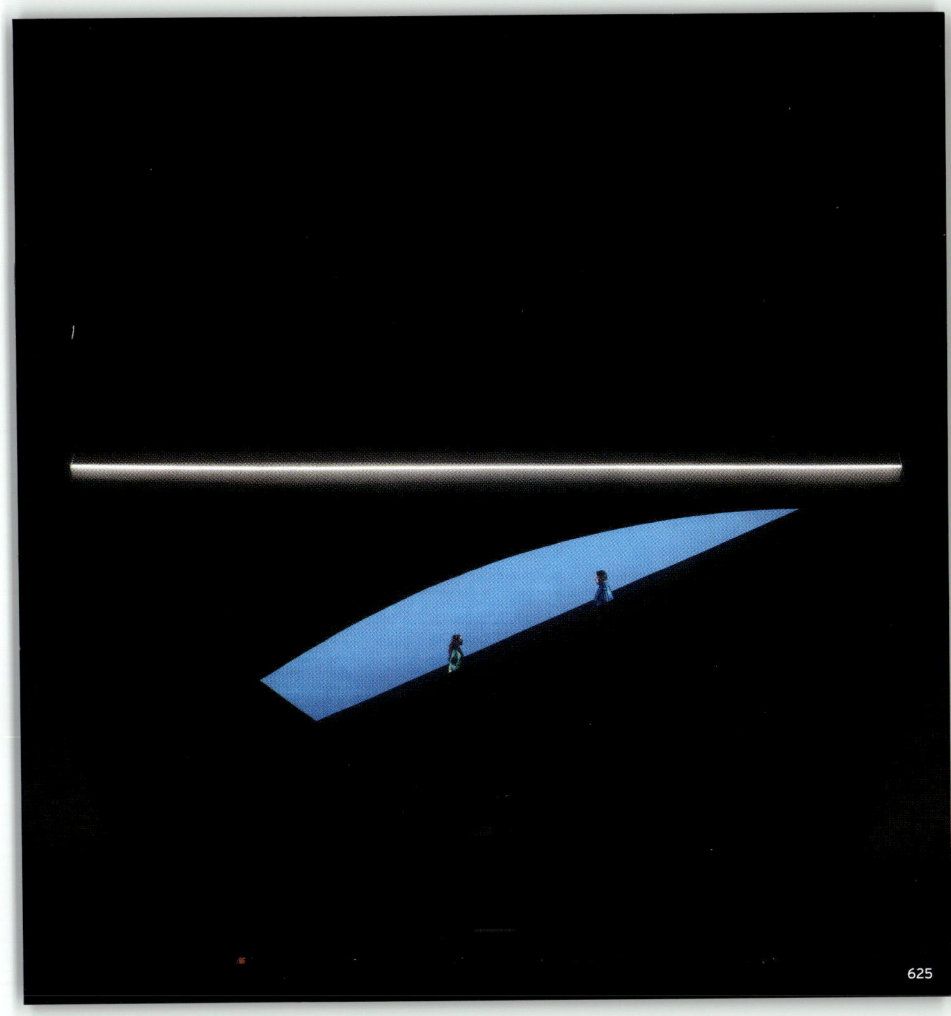

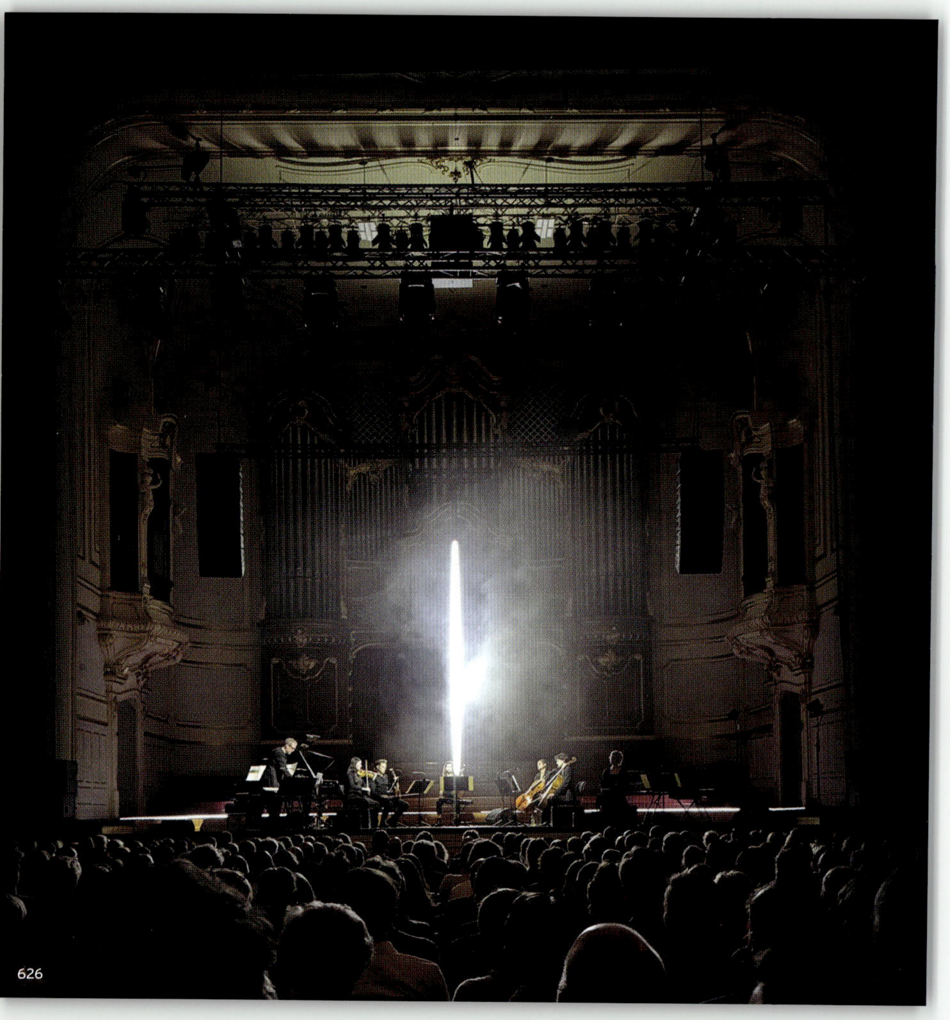

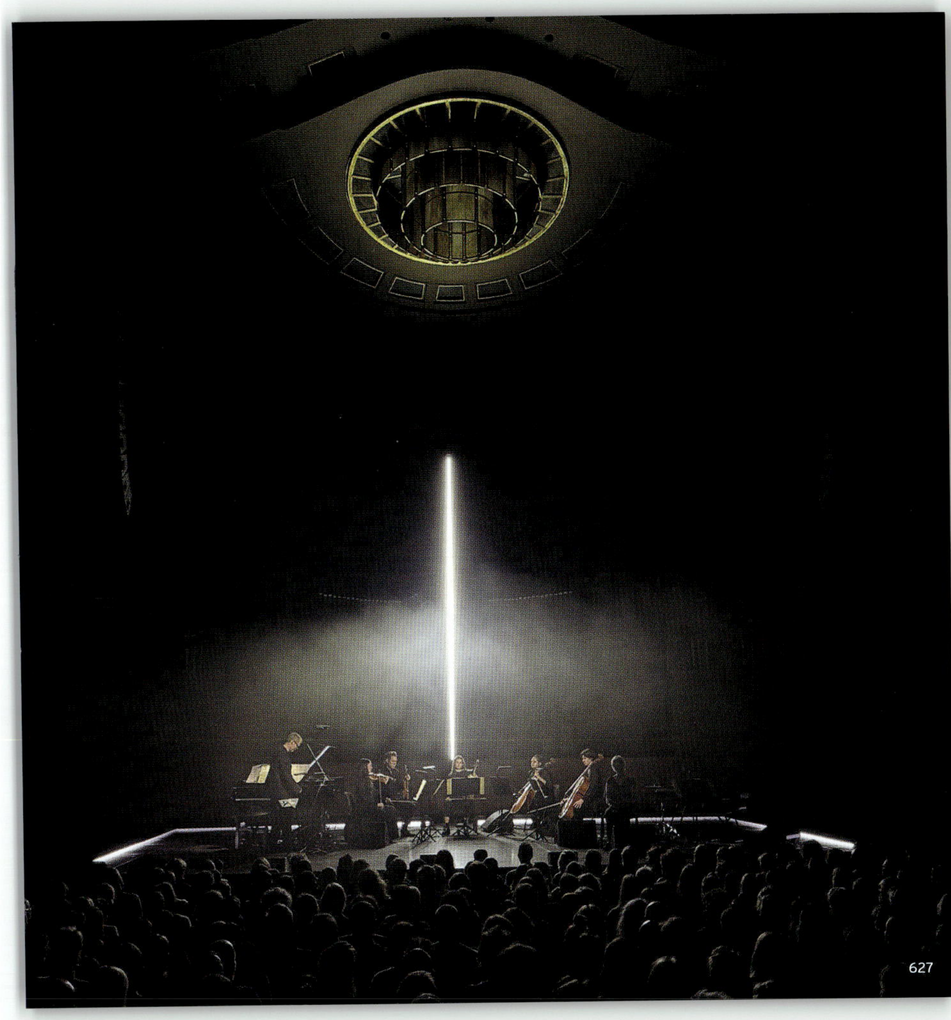

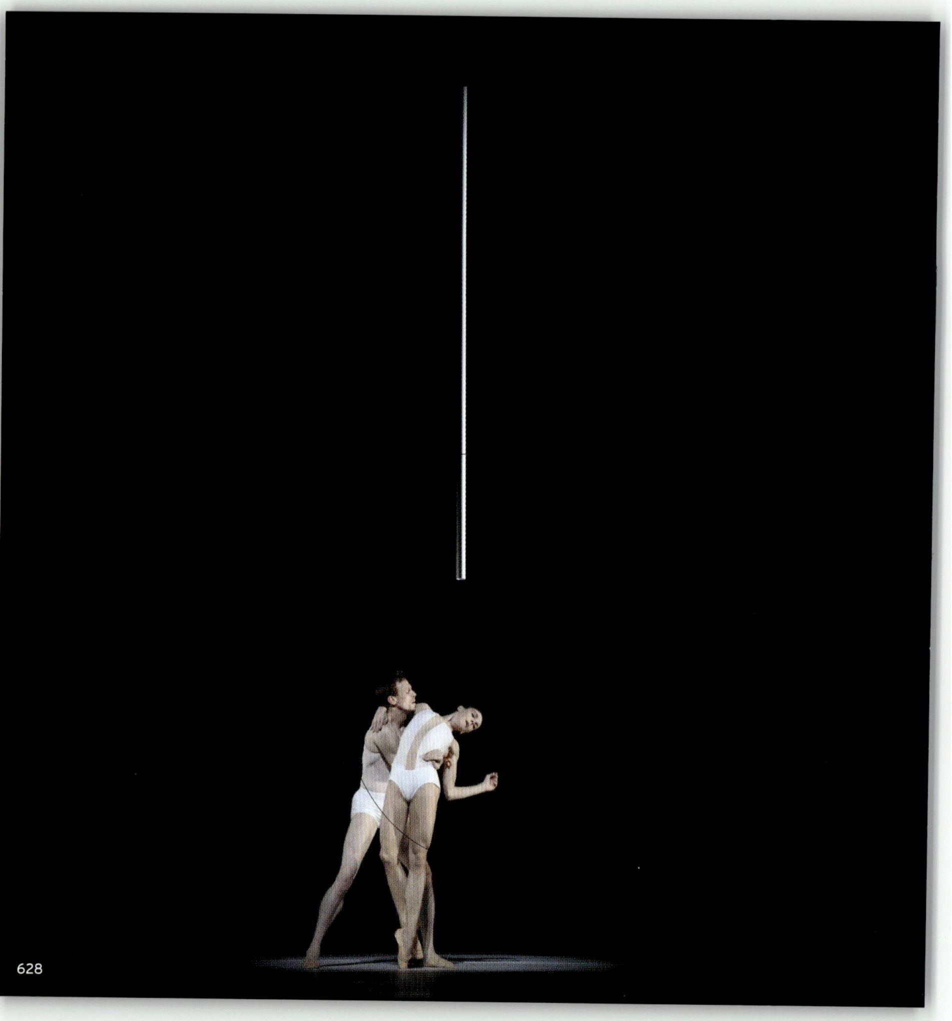

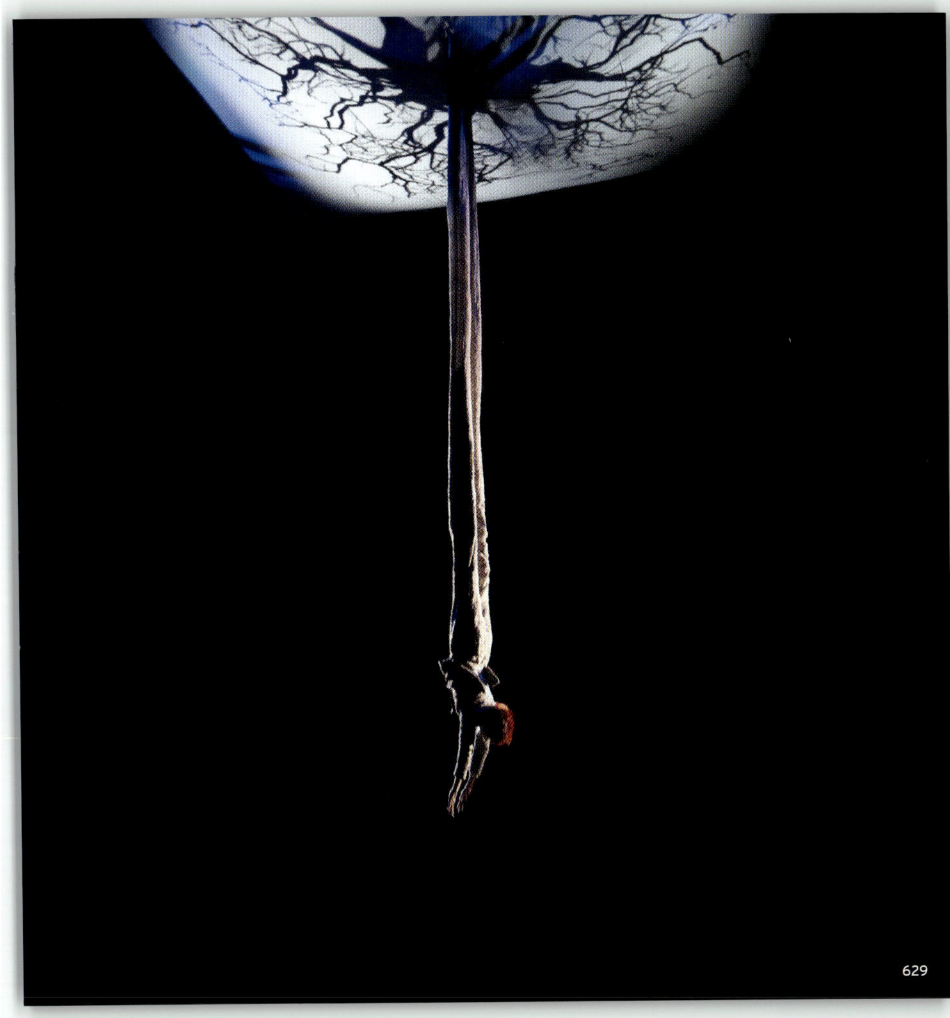

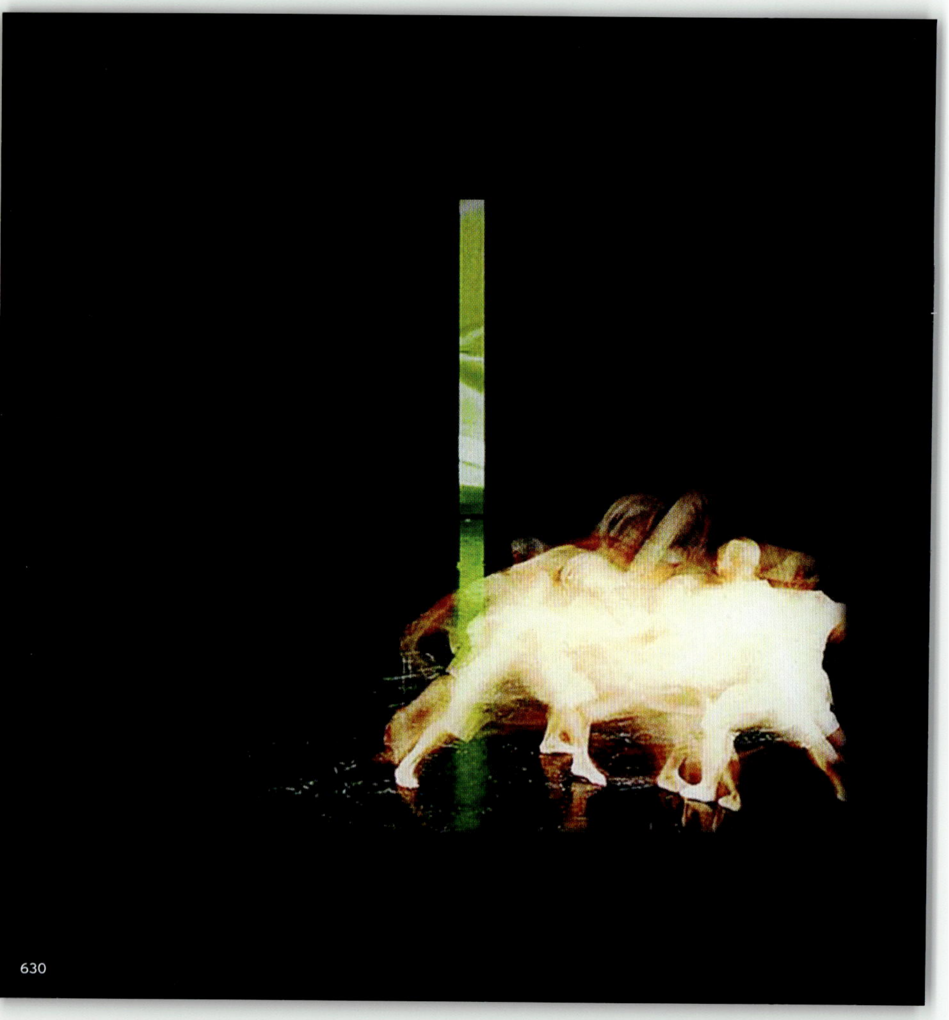

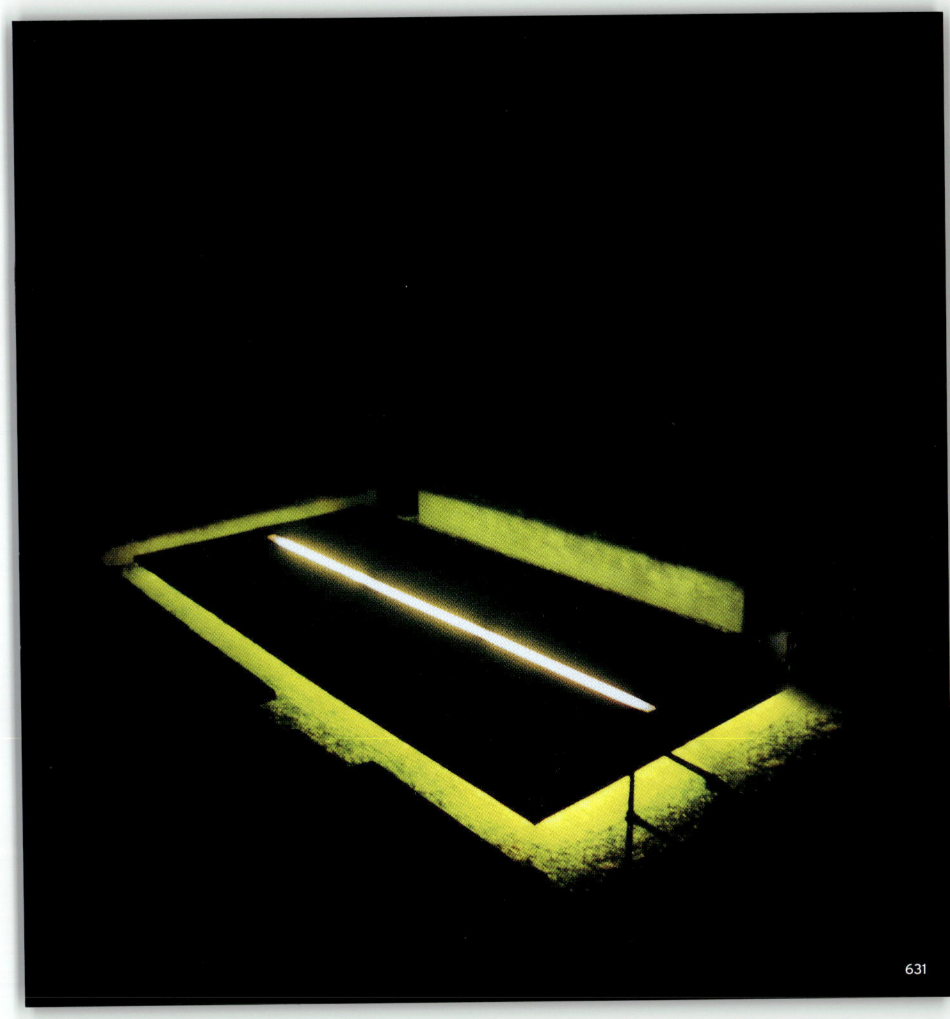

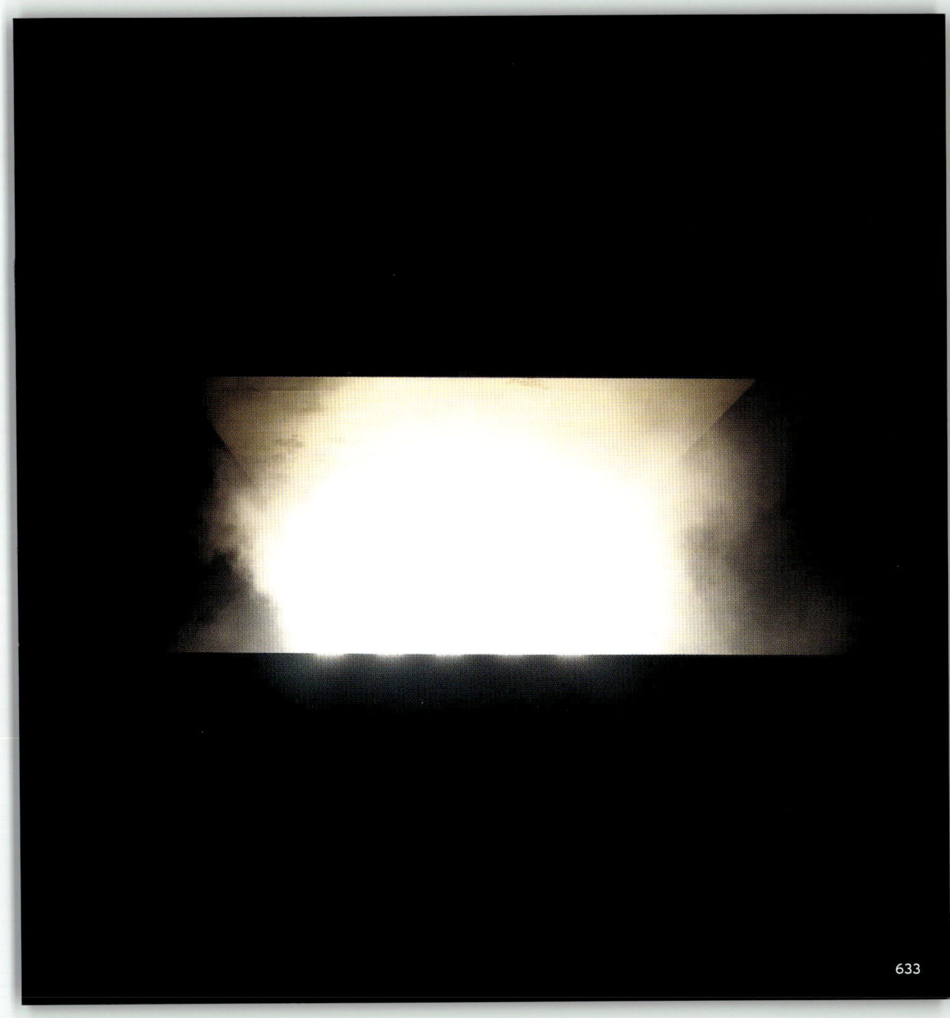

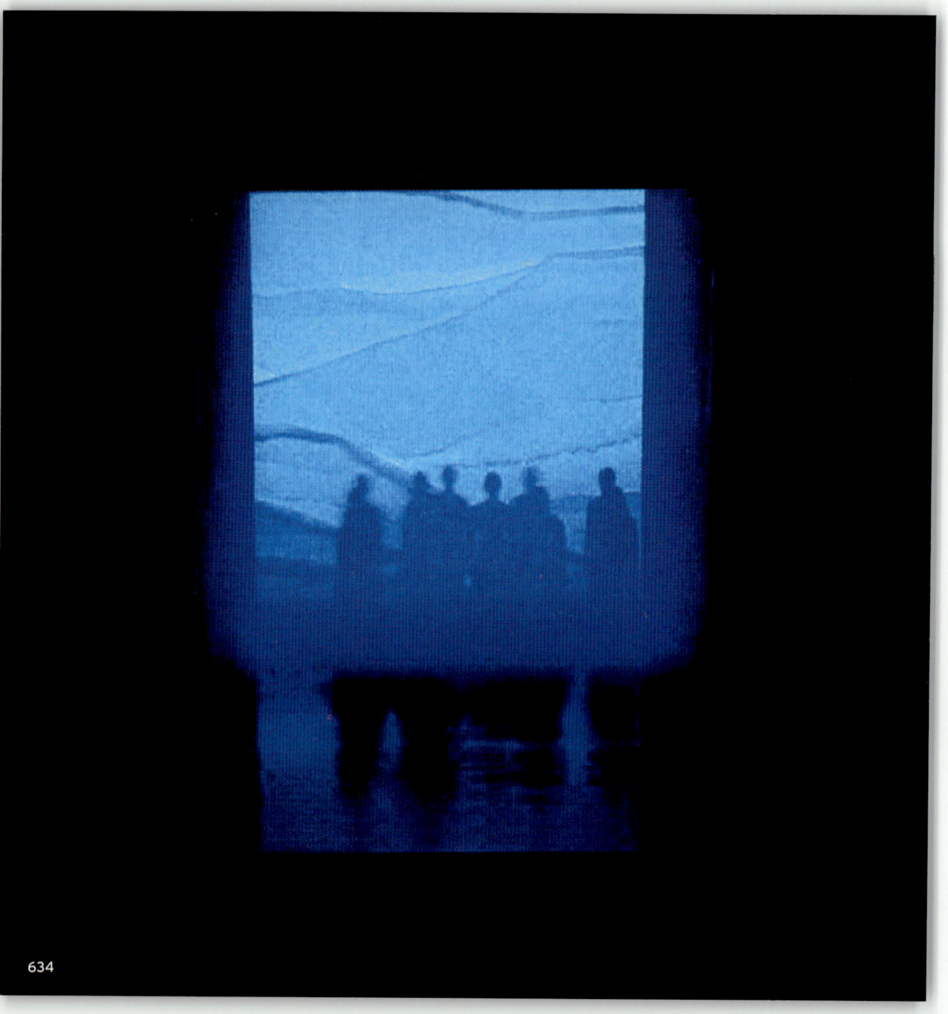

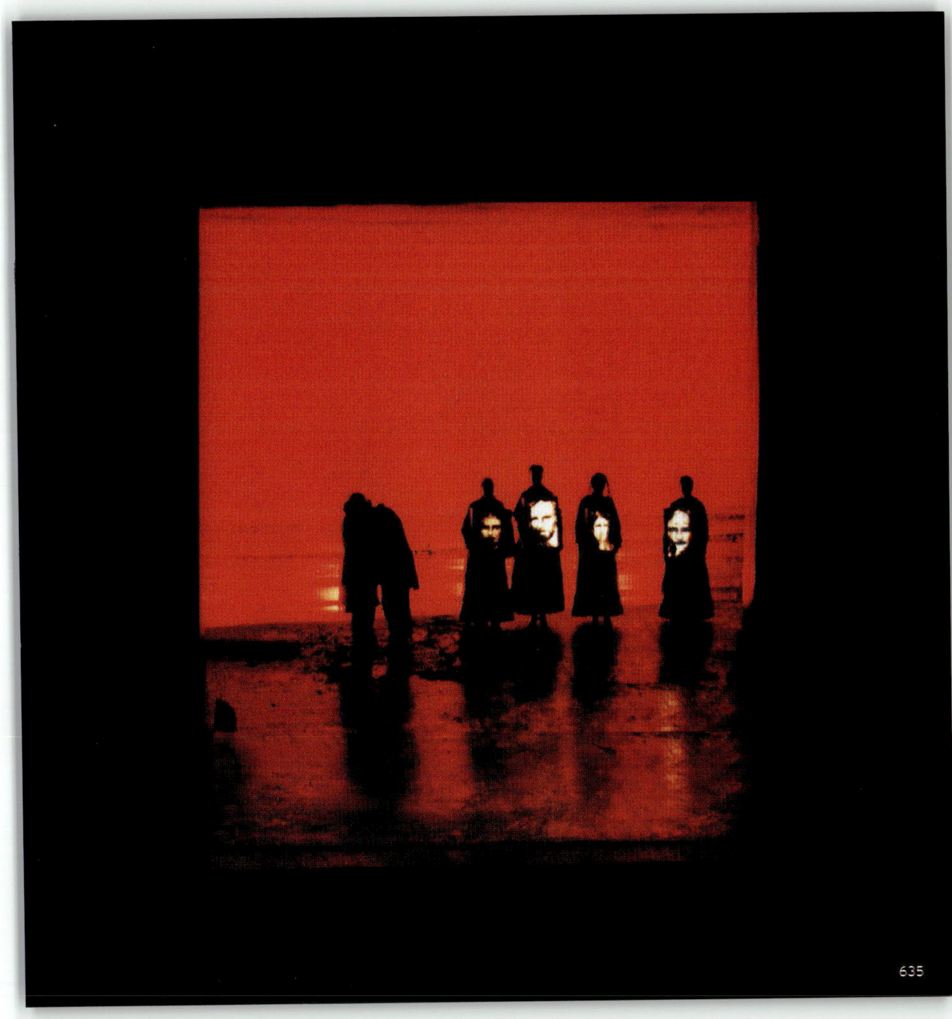

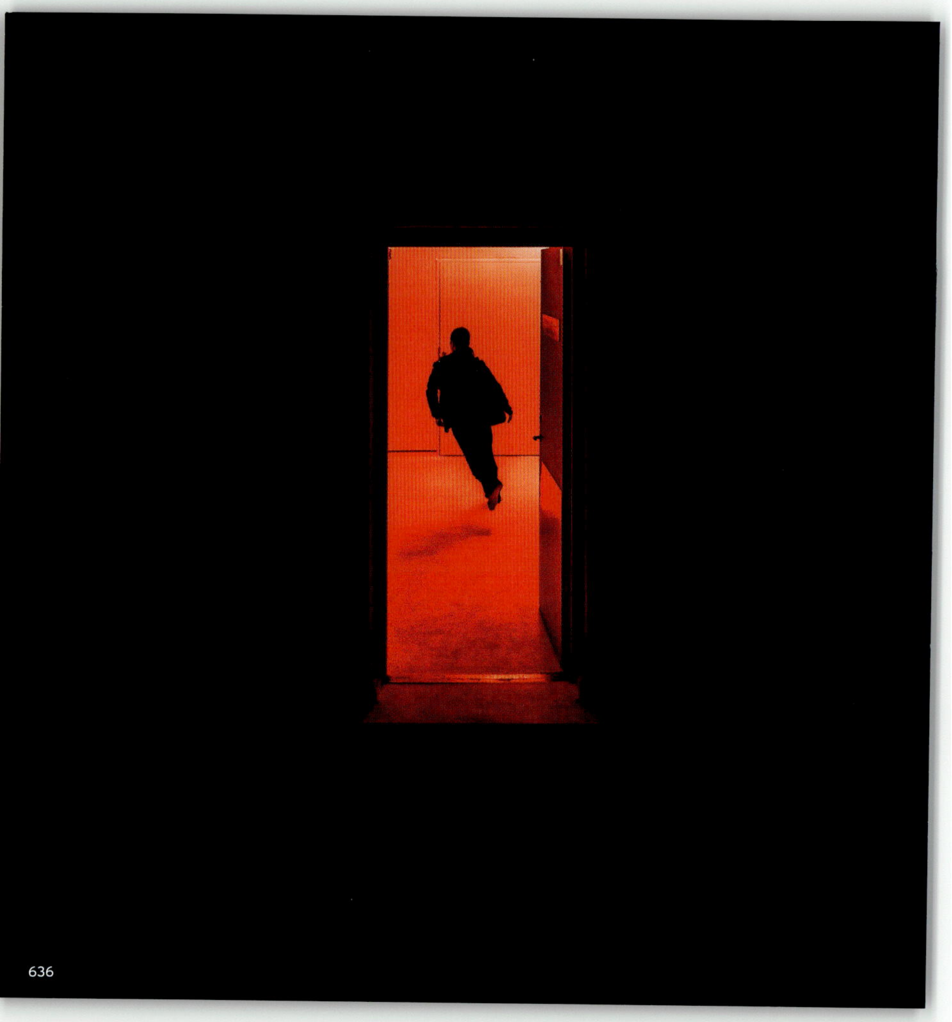

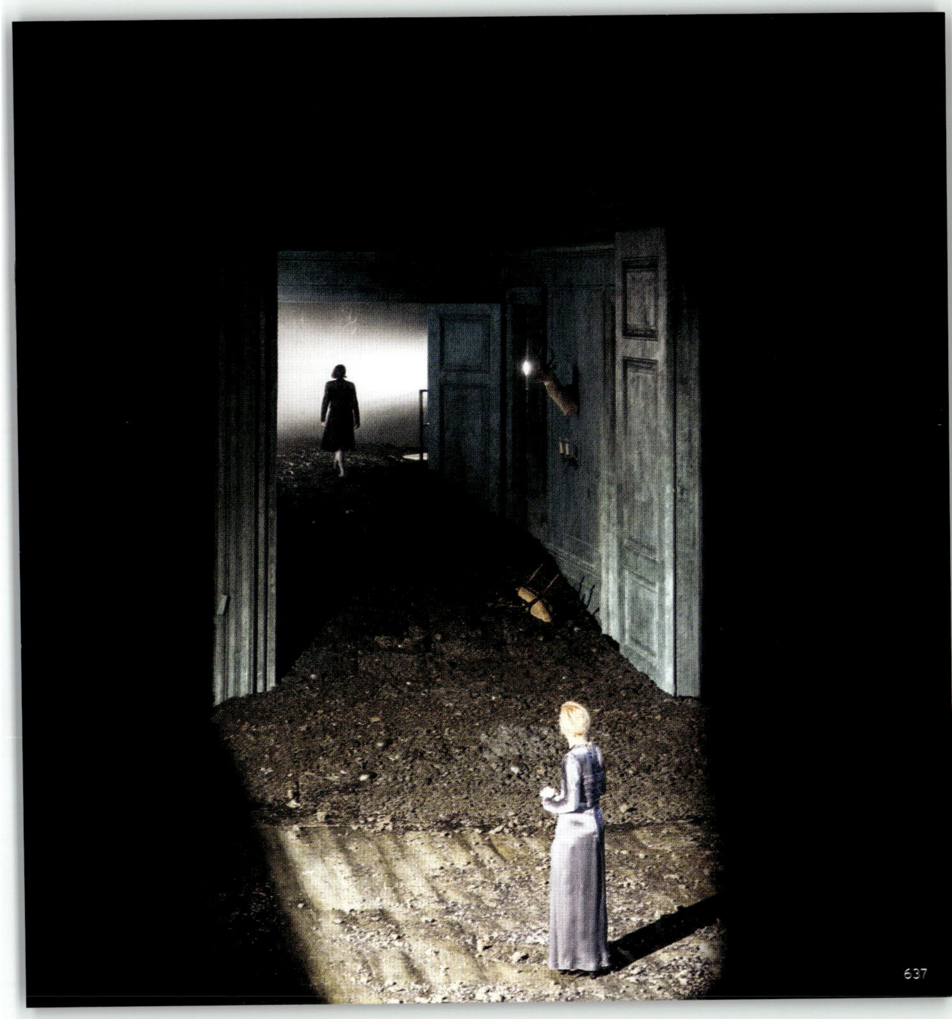

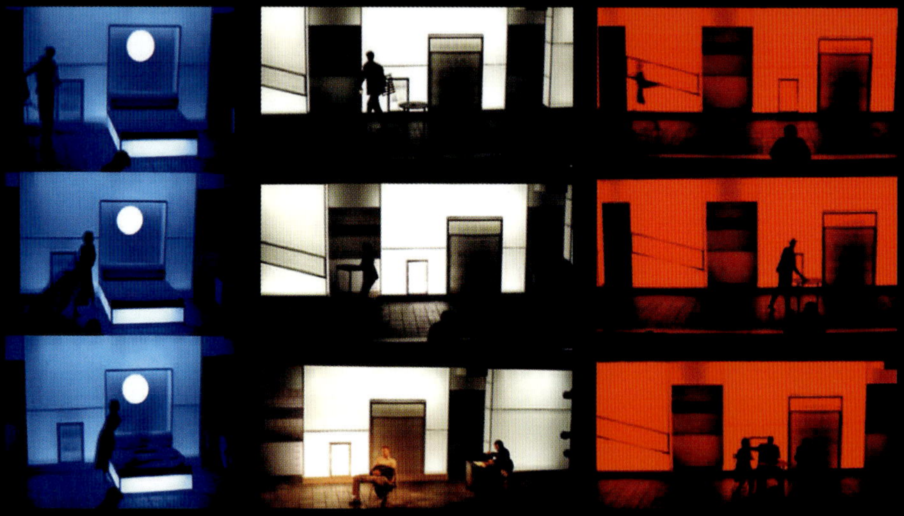

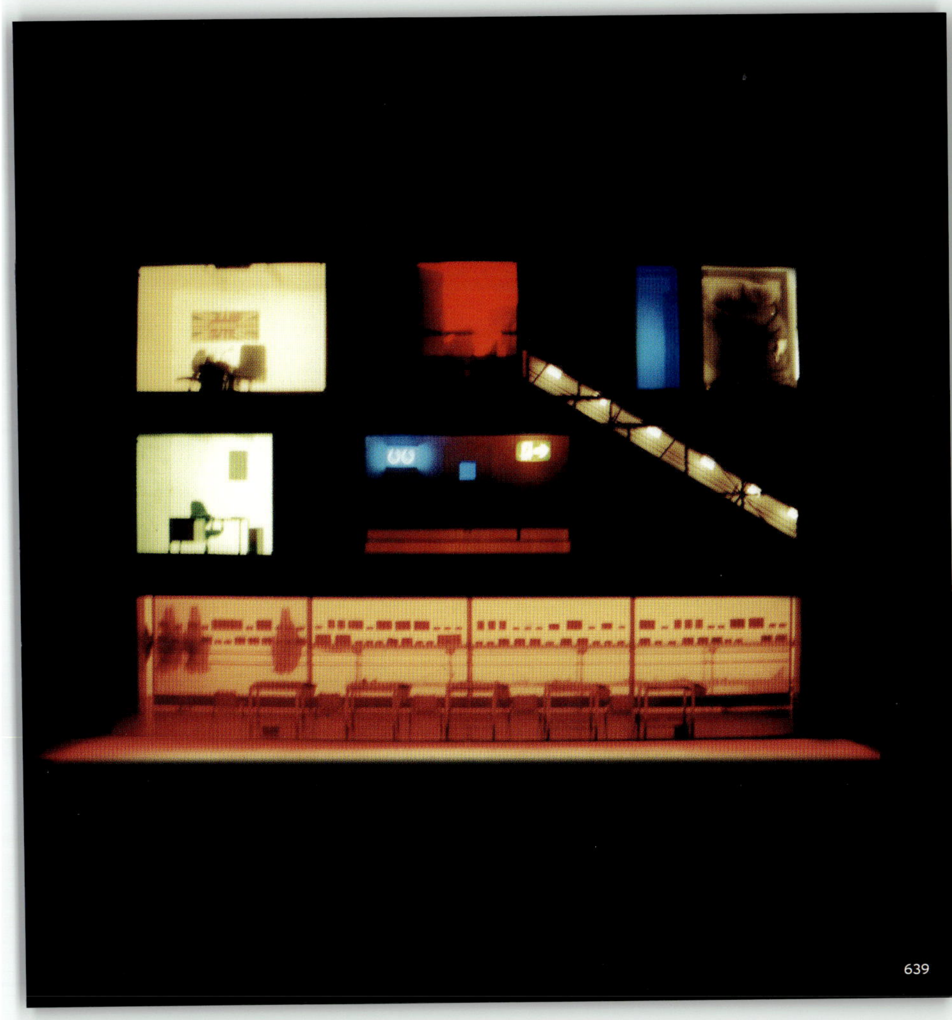

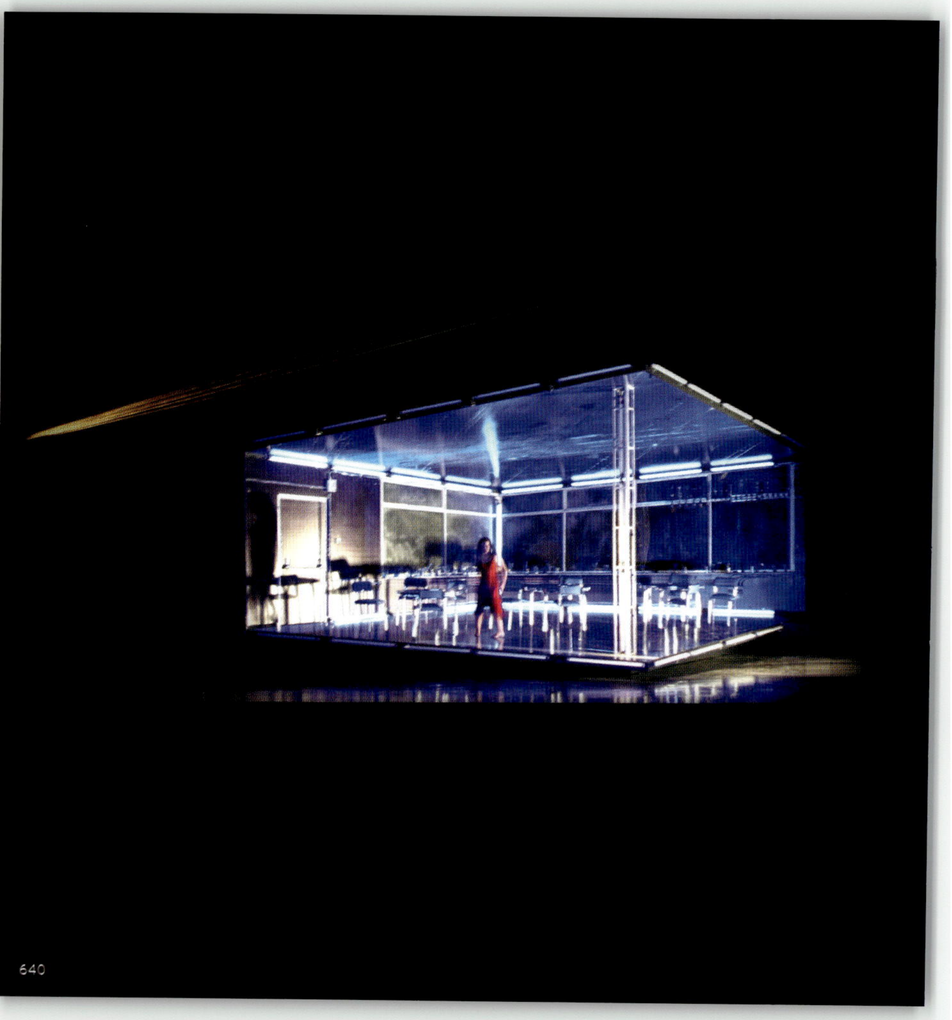

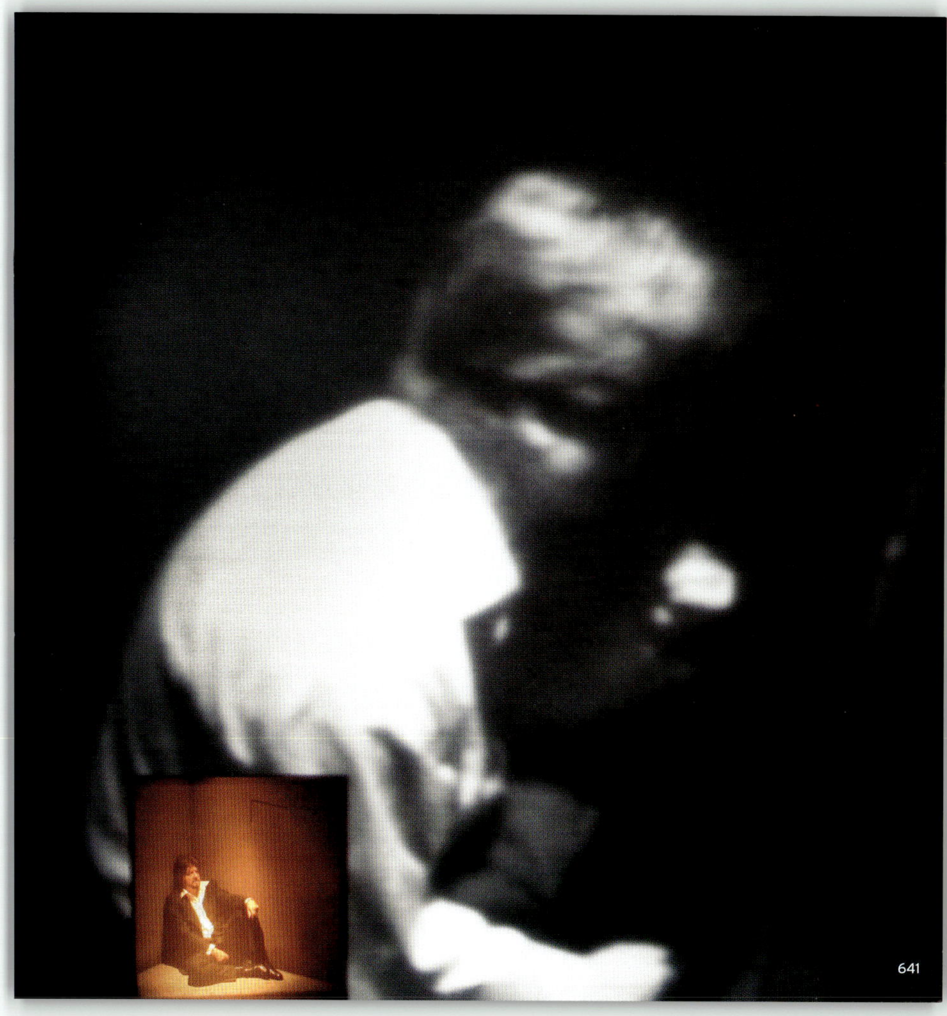

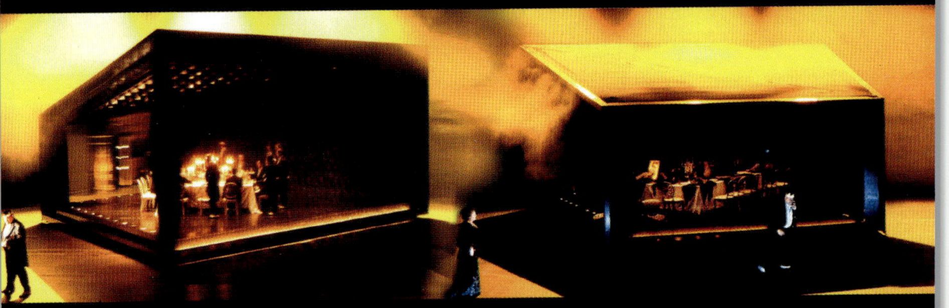

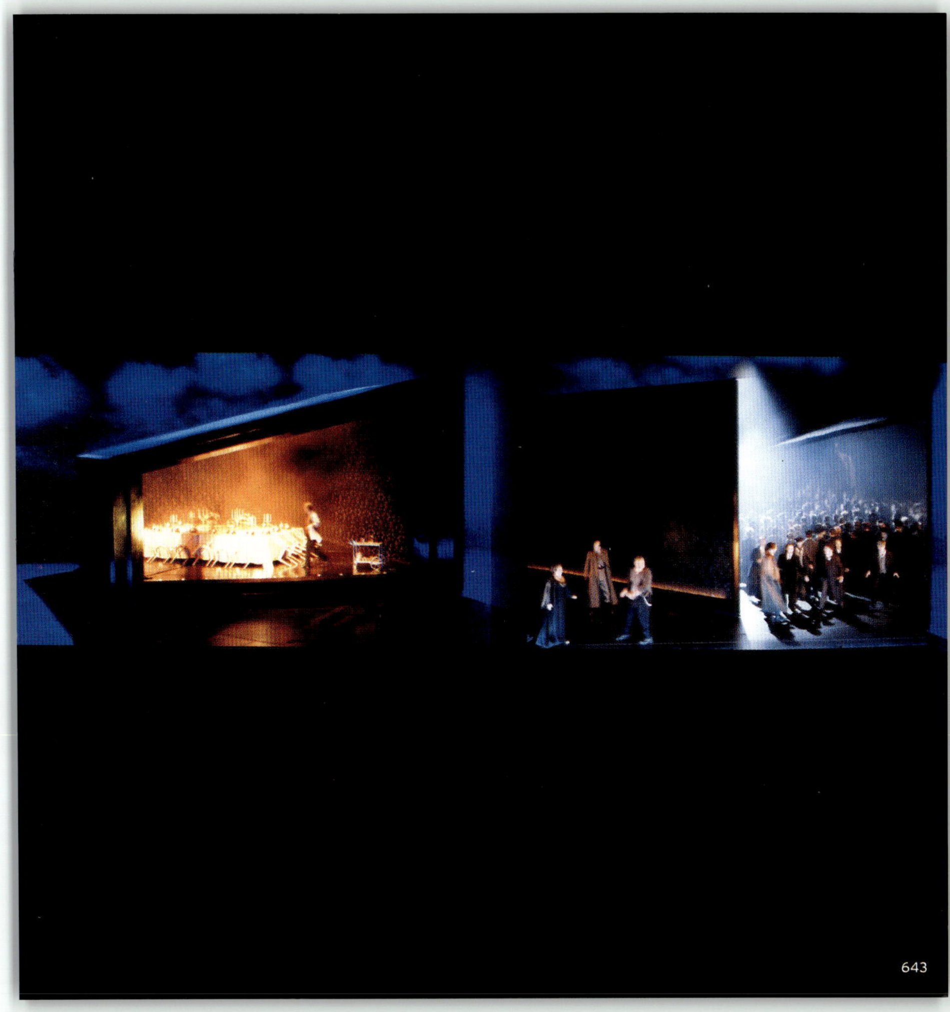

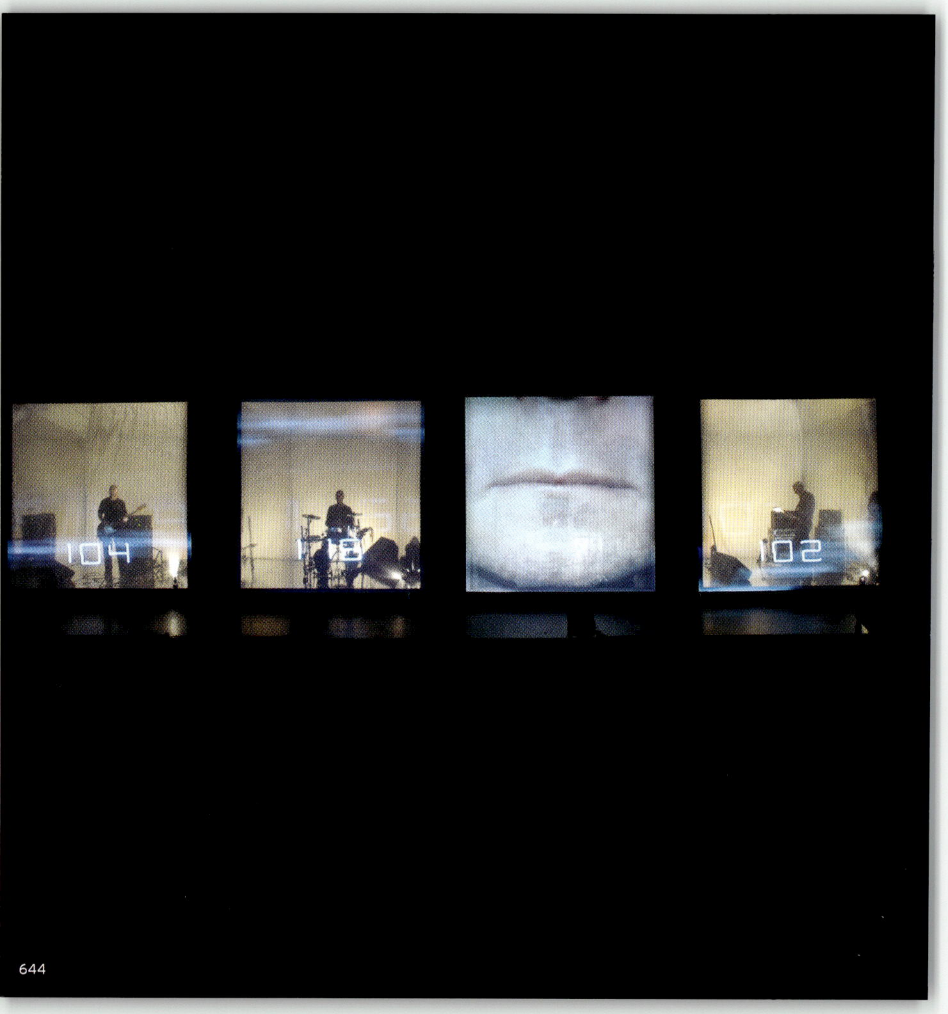
104
102

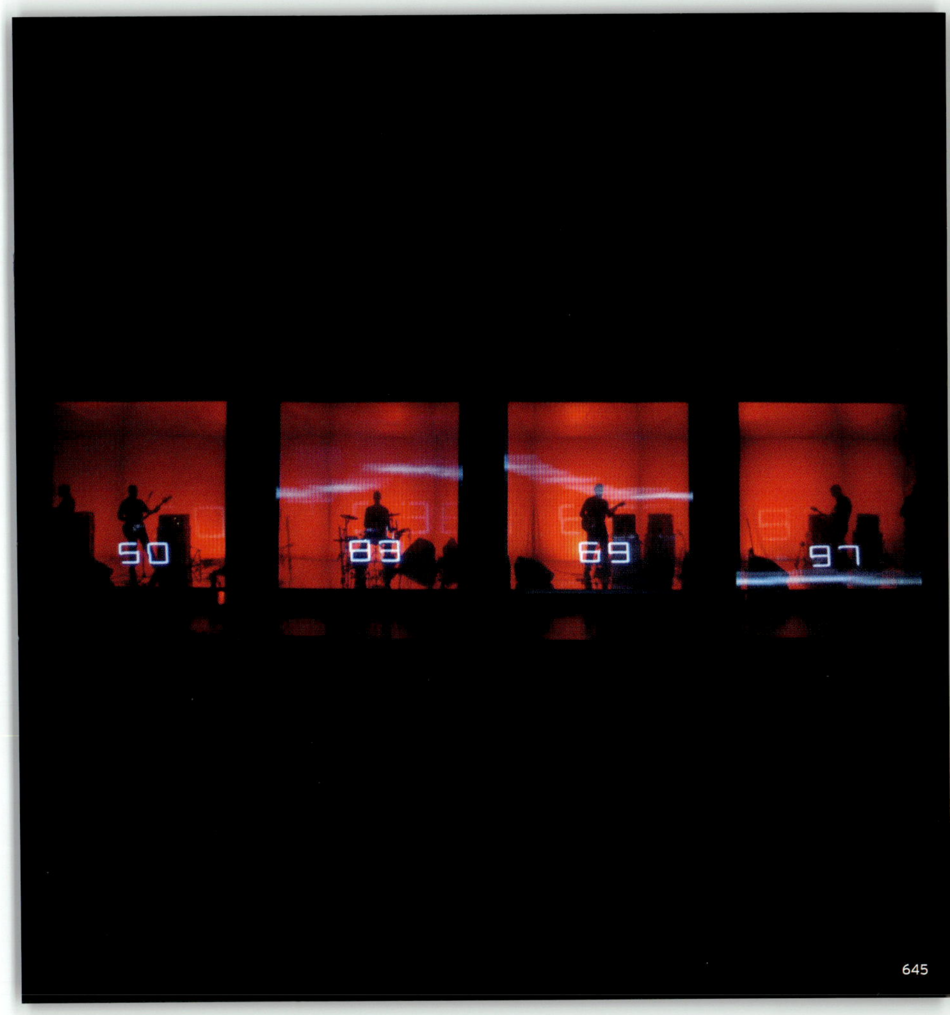
50
88
69
97

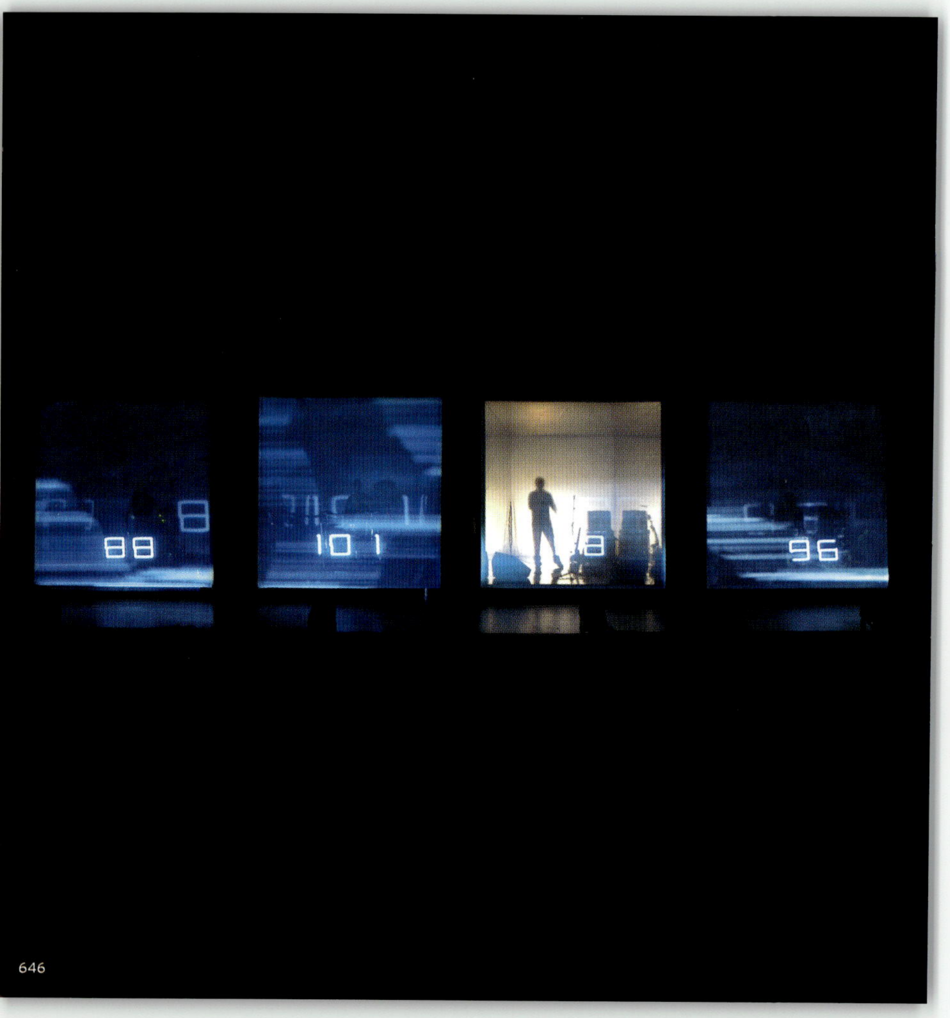
88
101
96

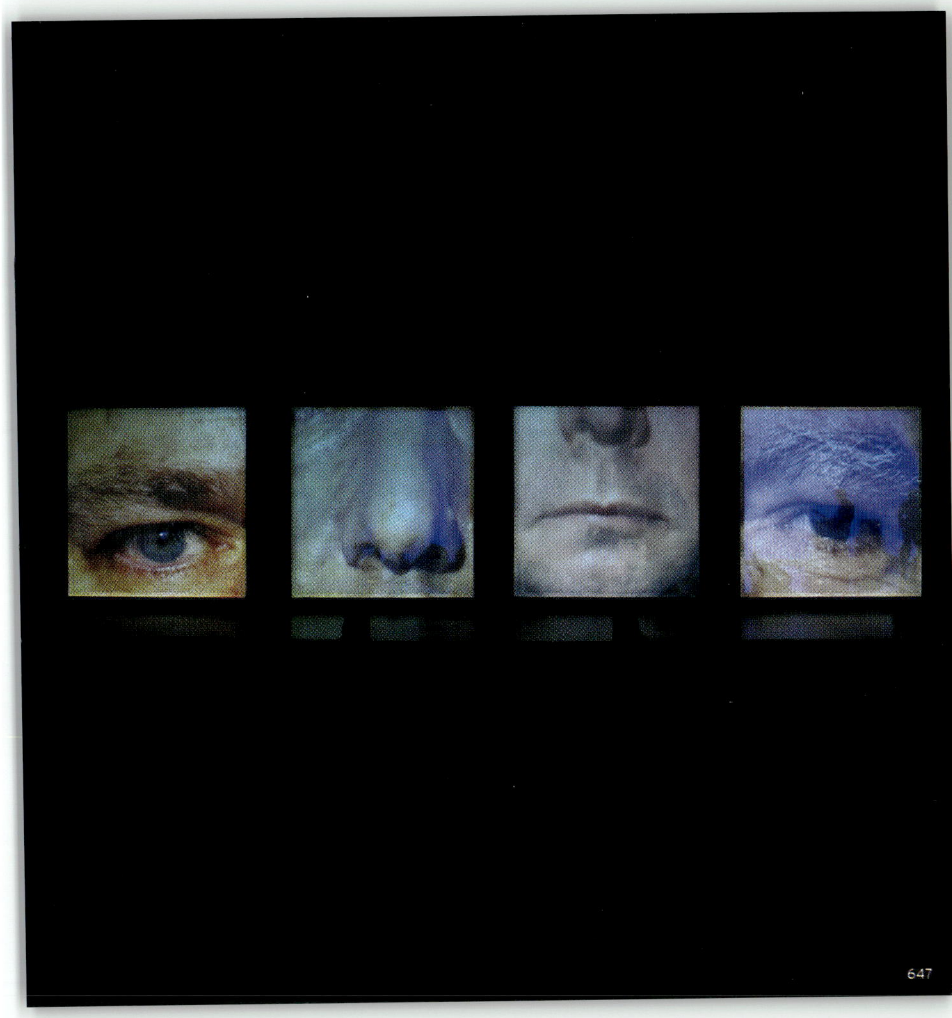

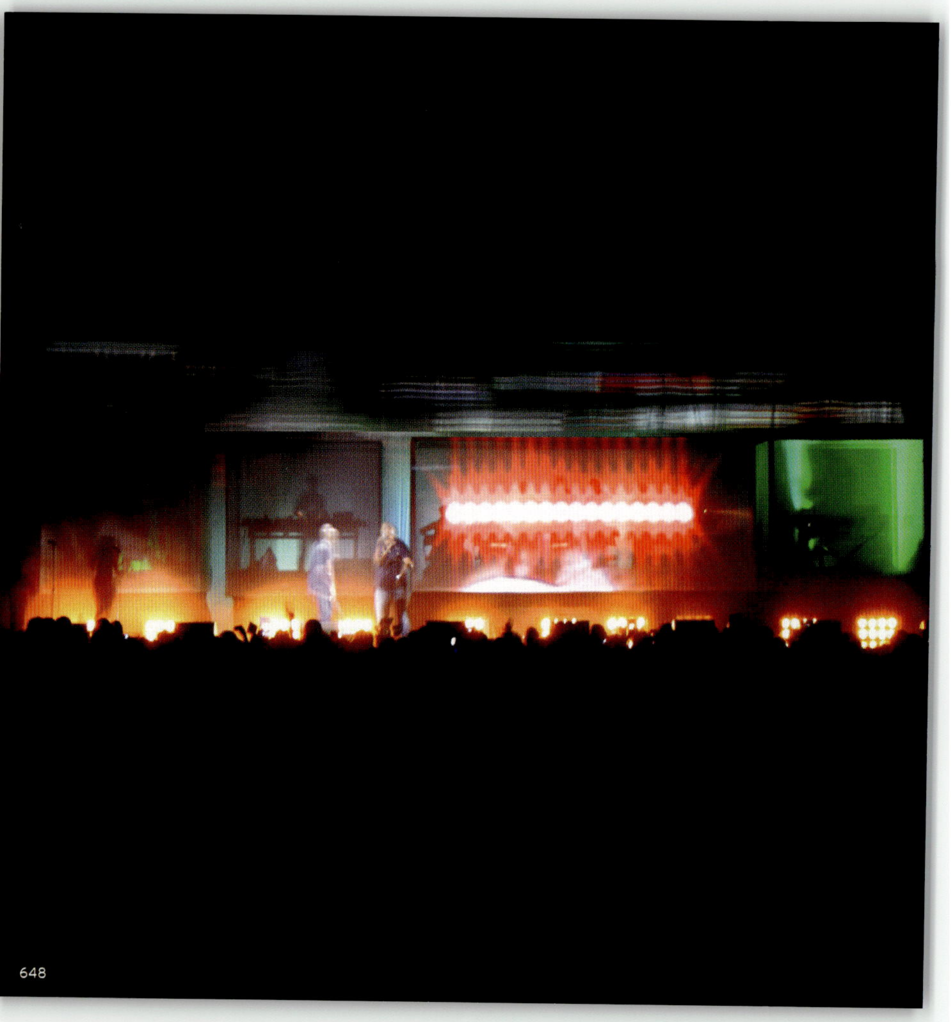

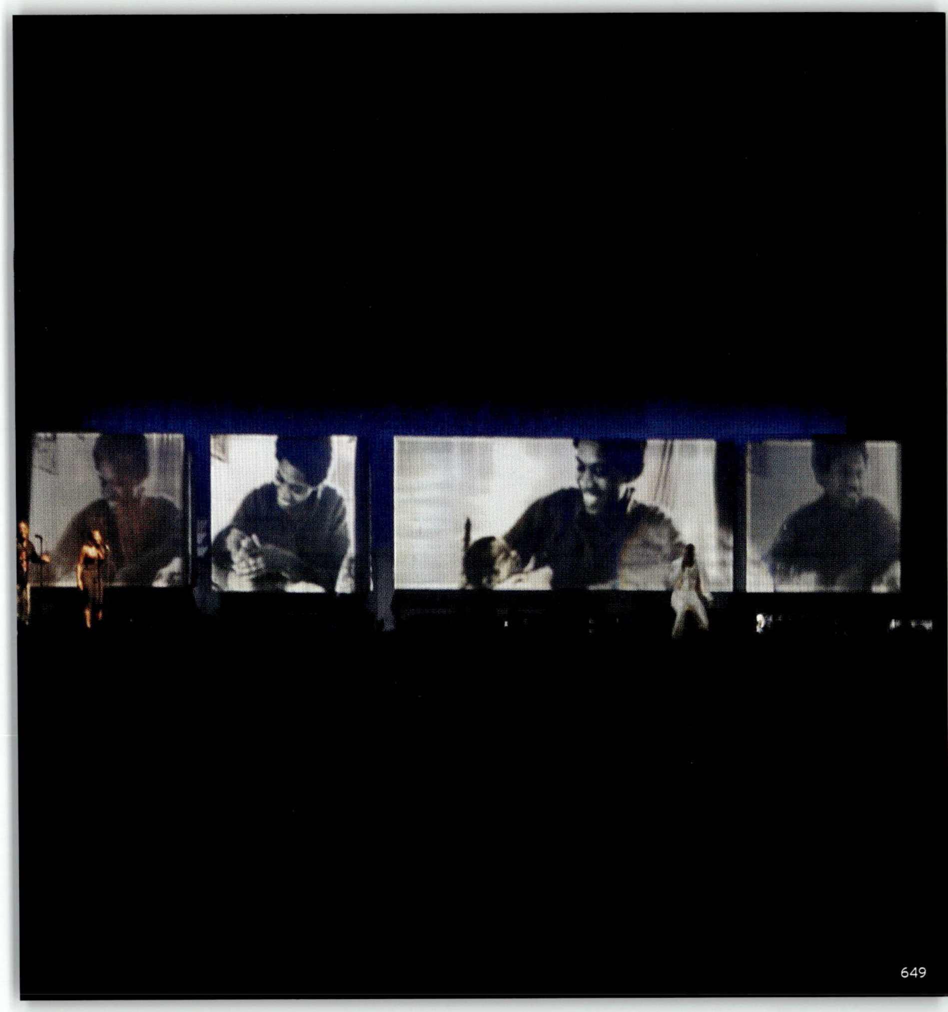

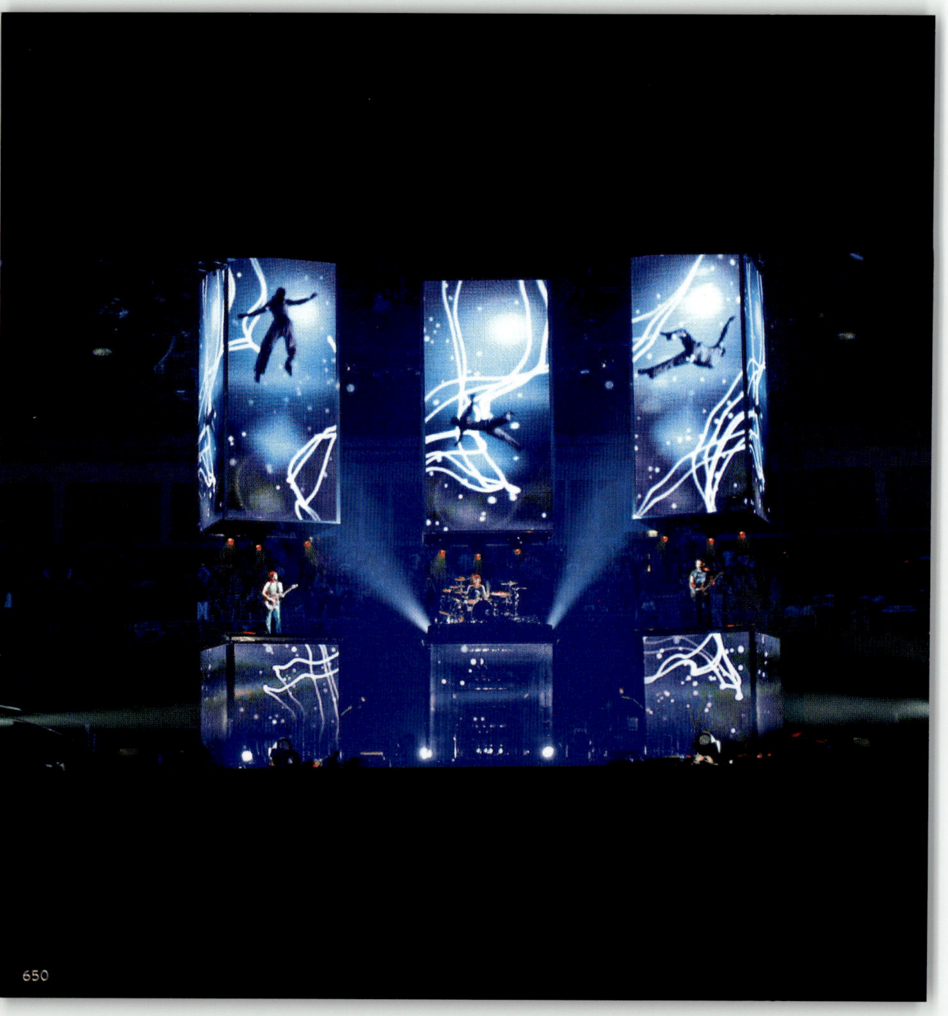

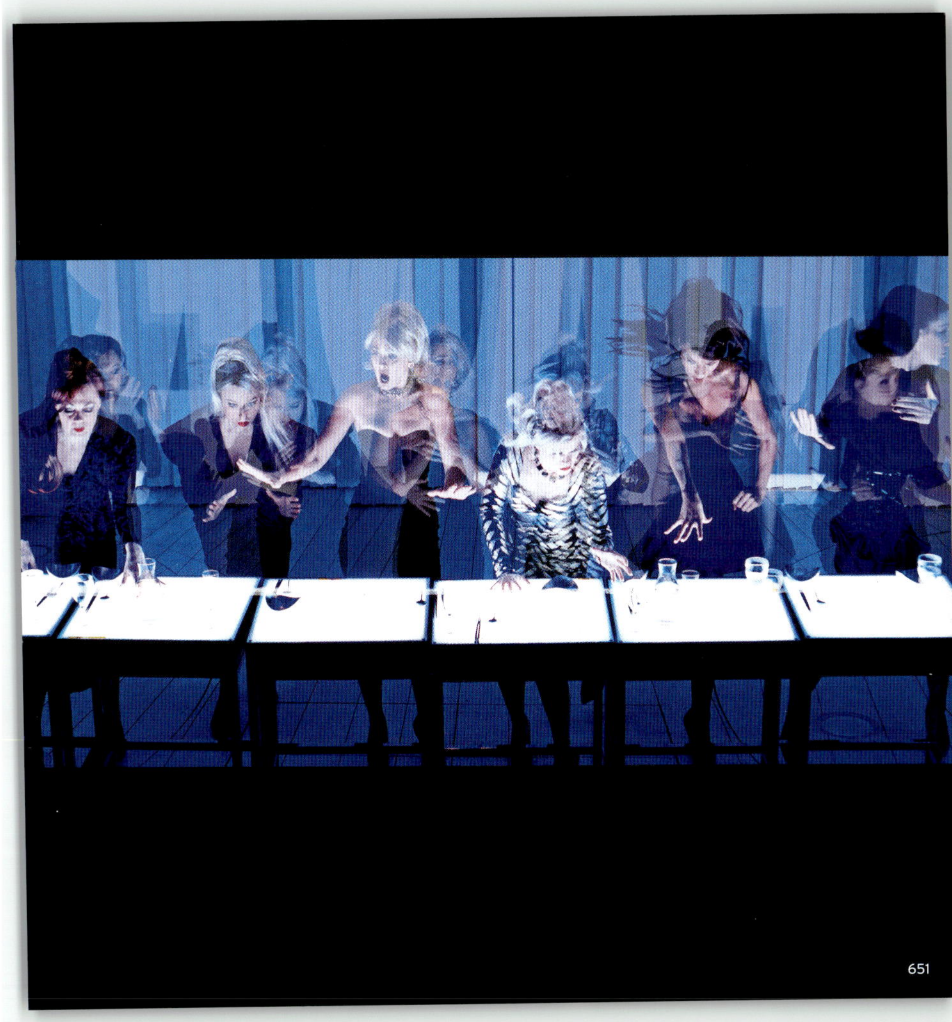

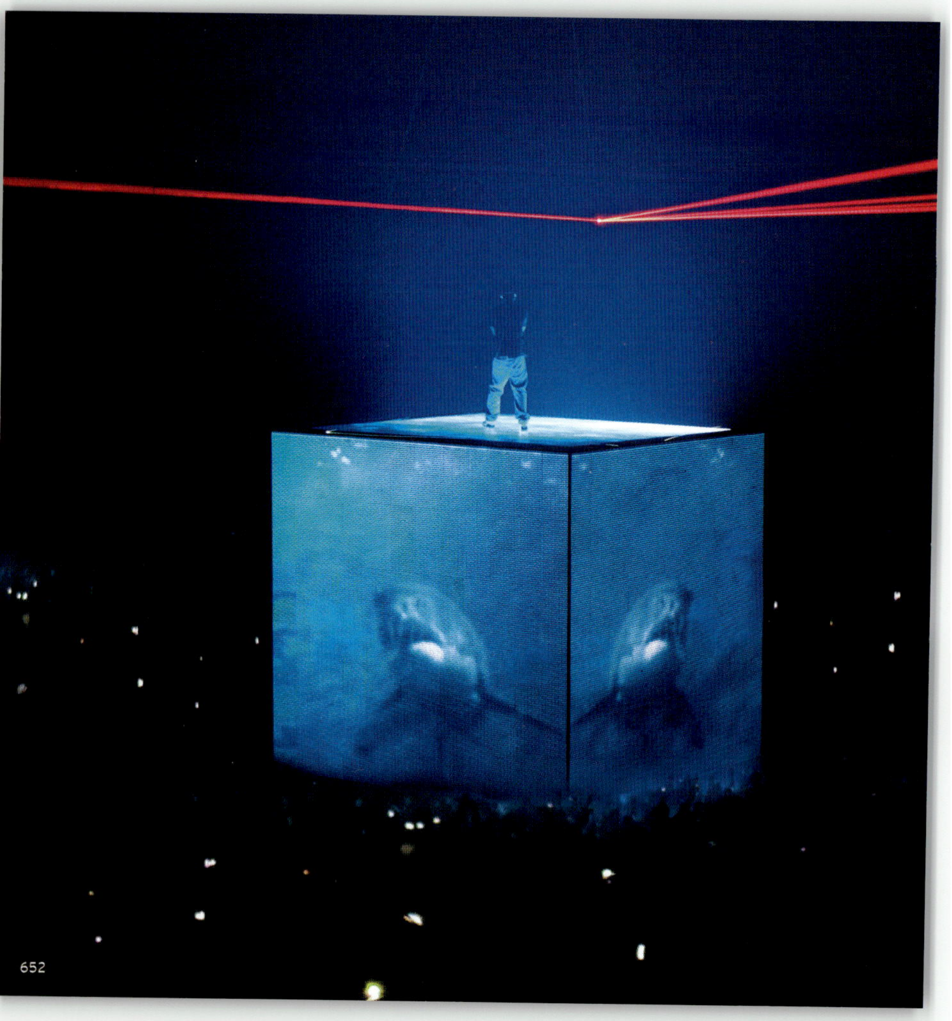

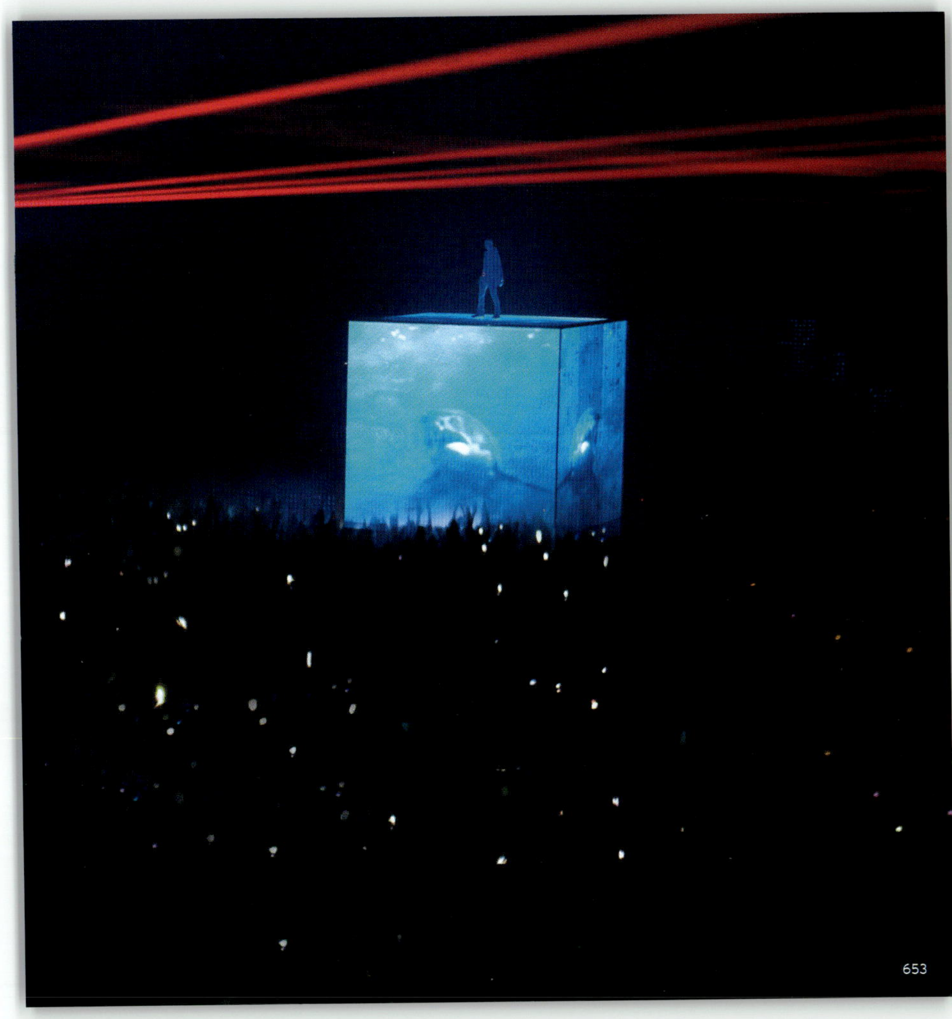

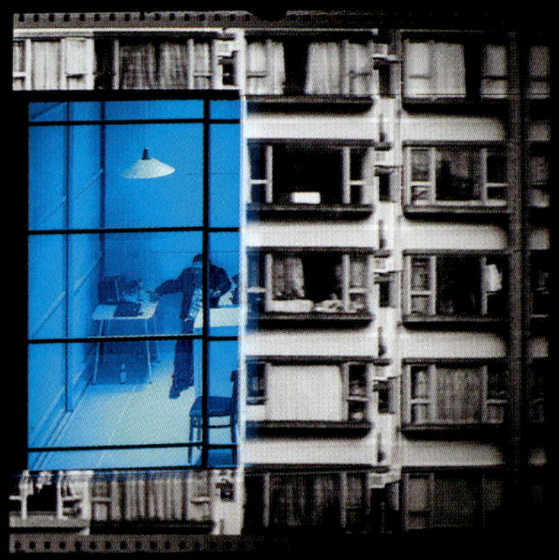

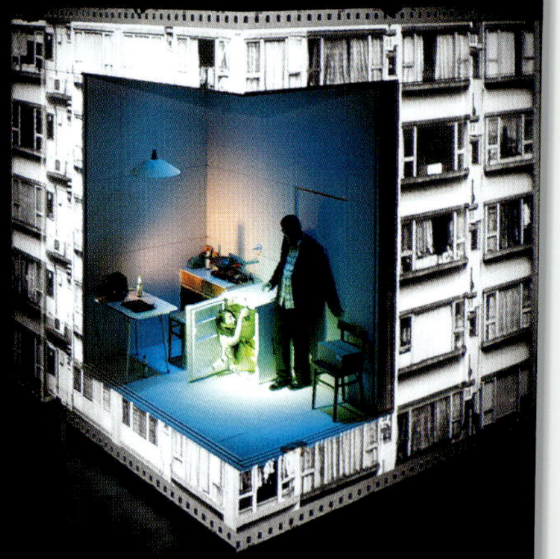

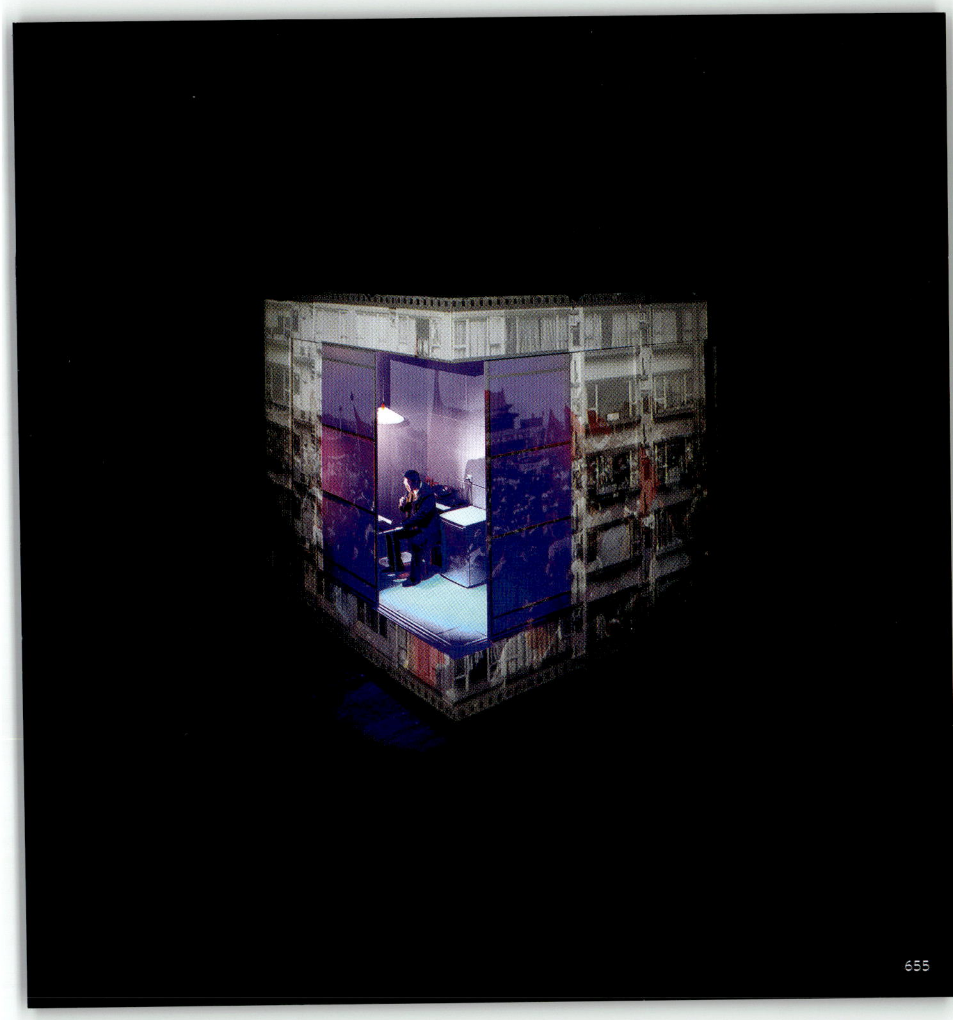

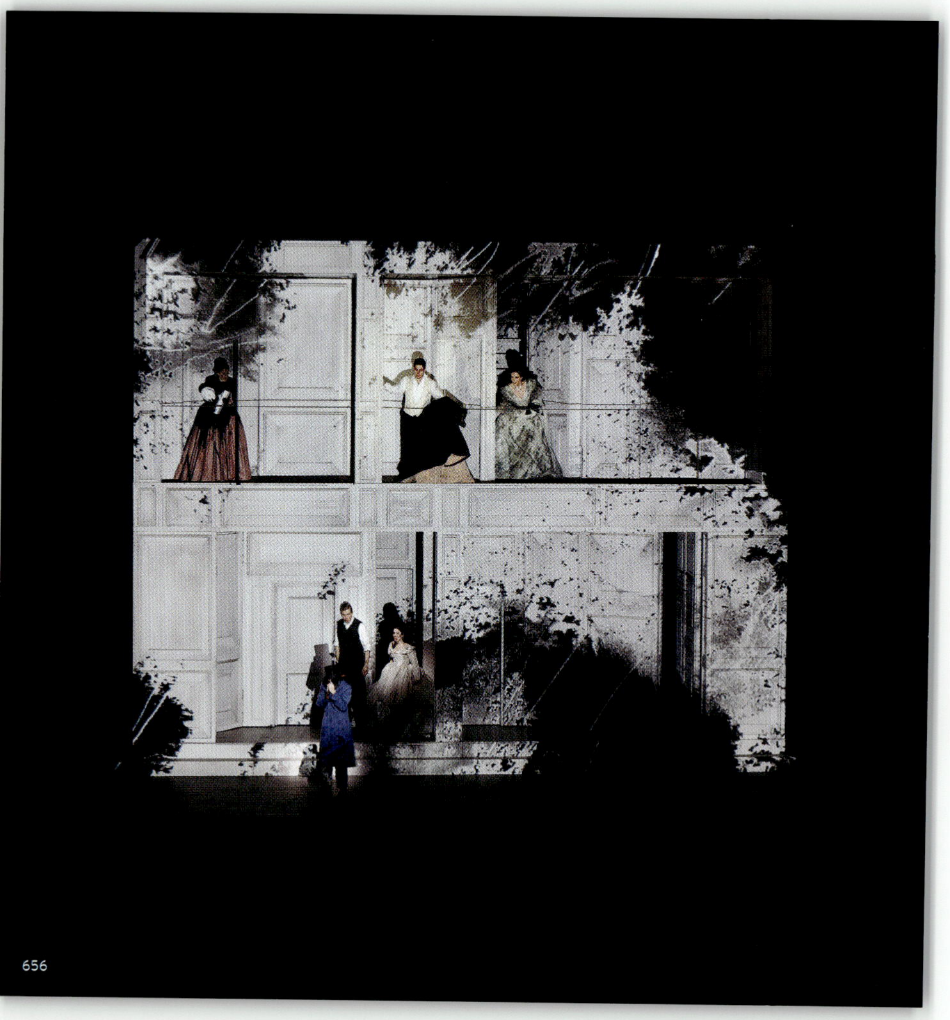

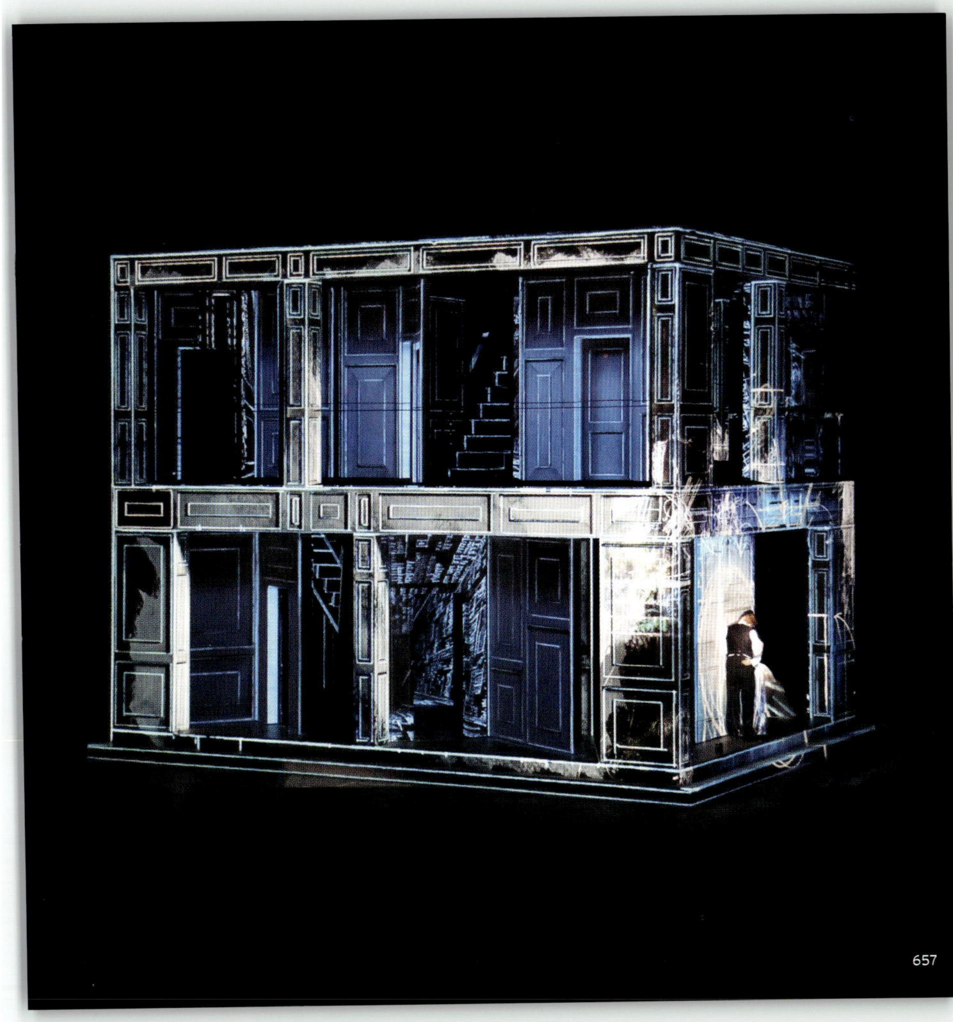

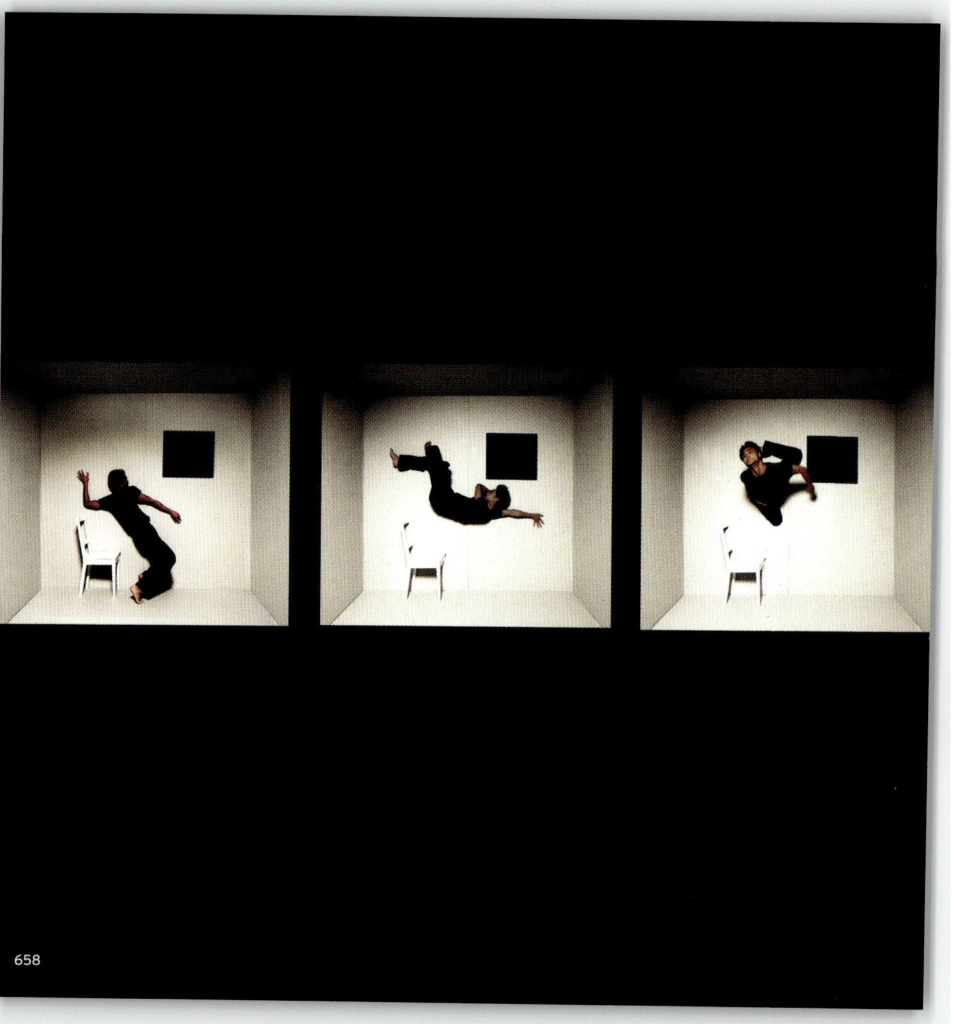

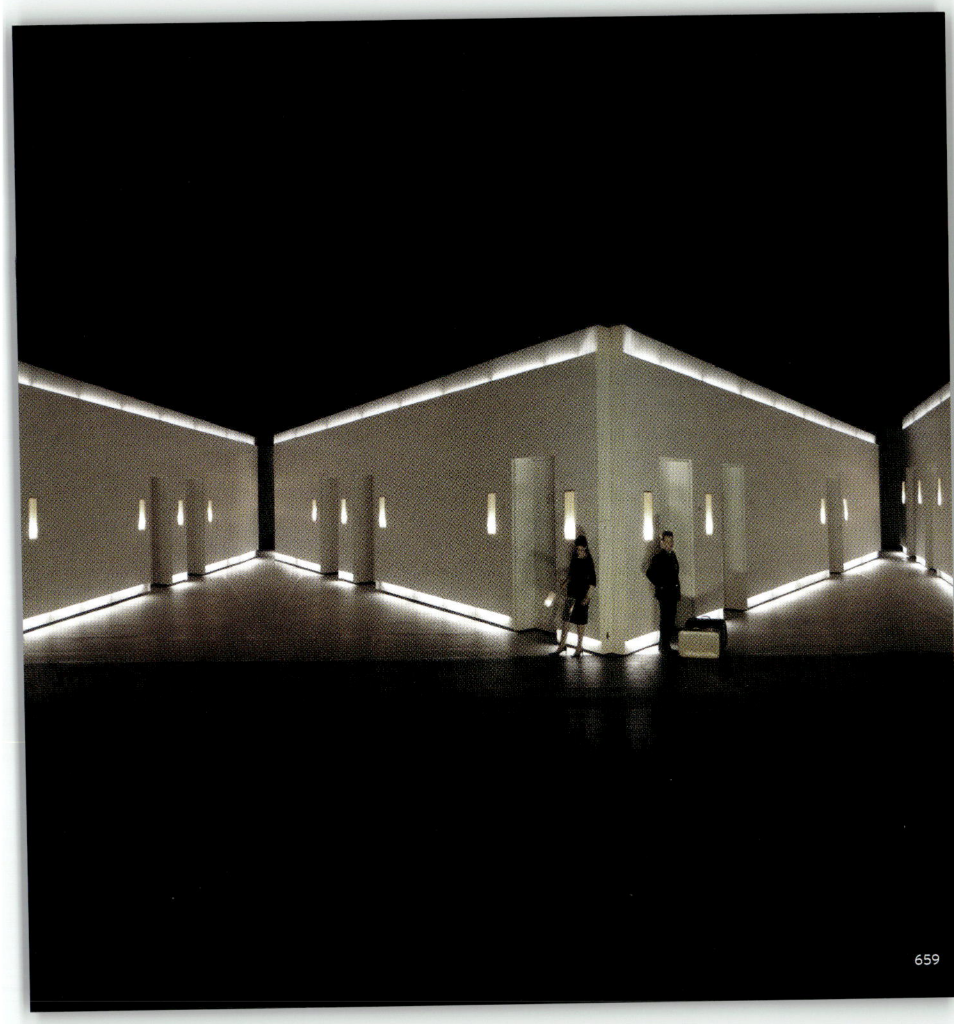

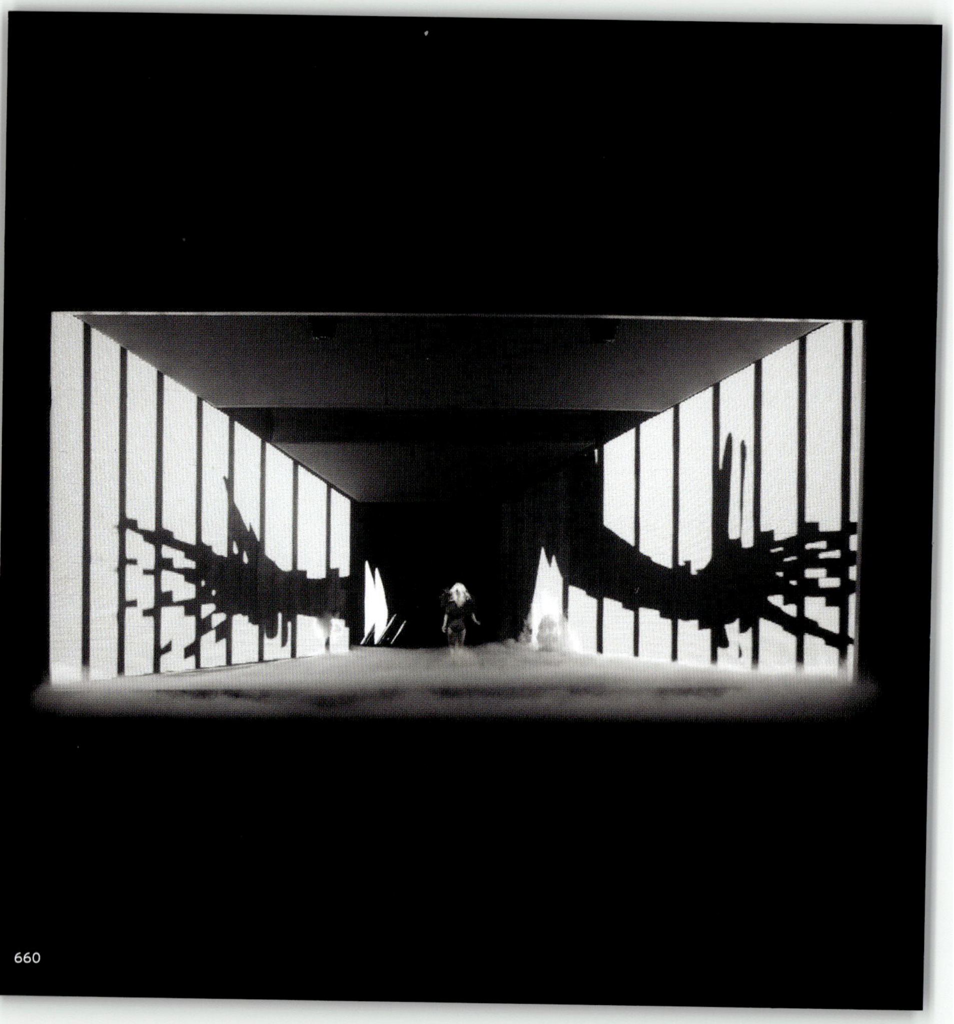

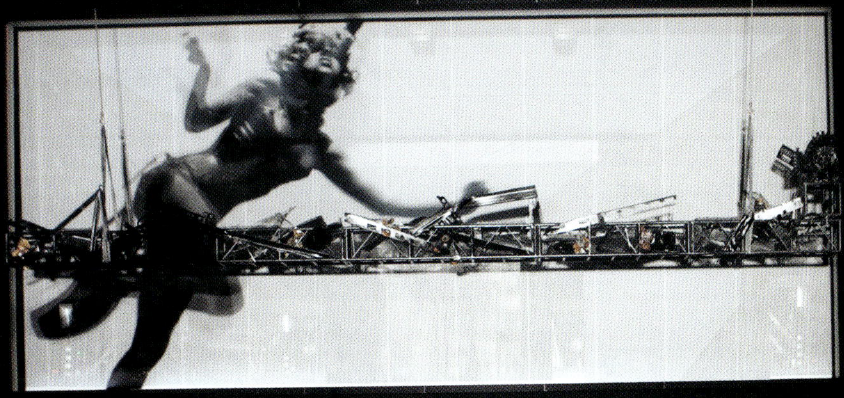

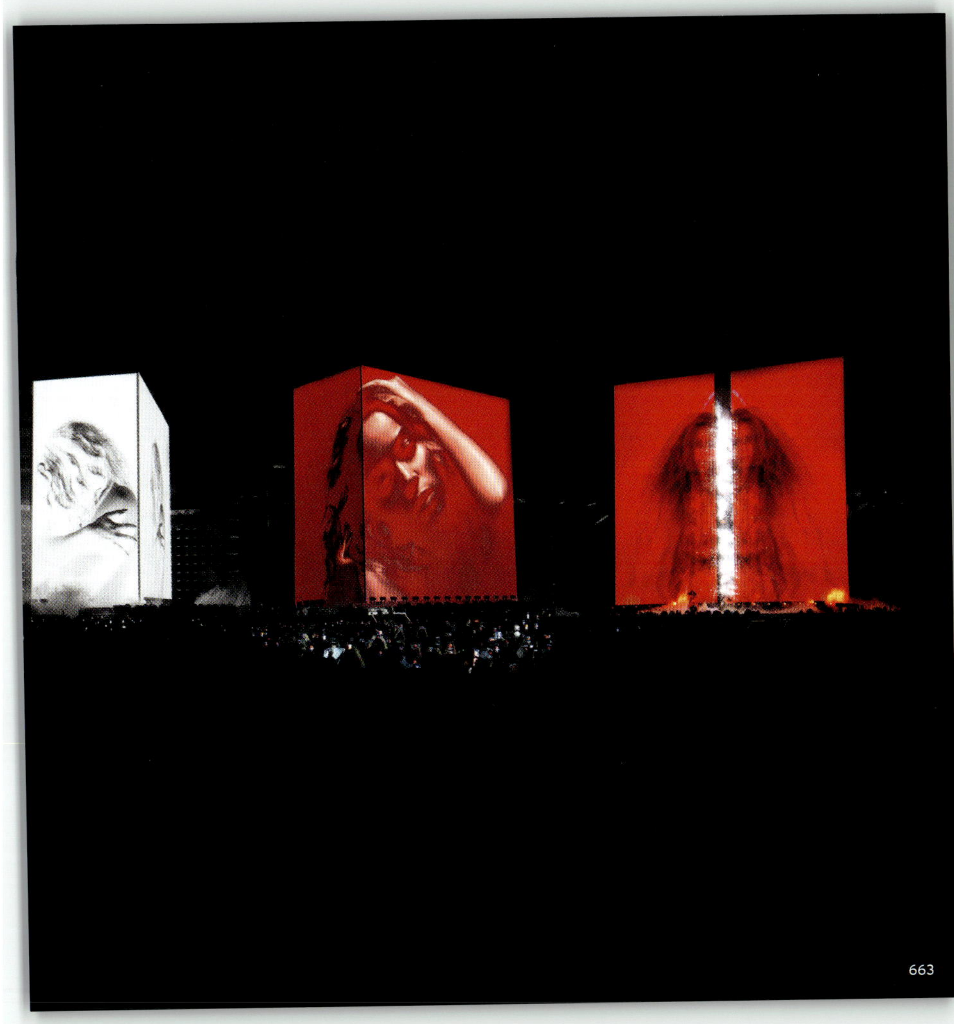

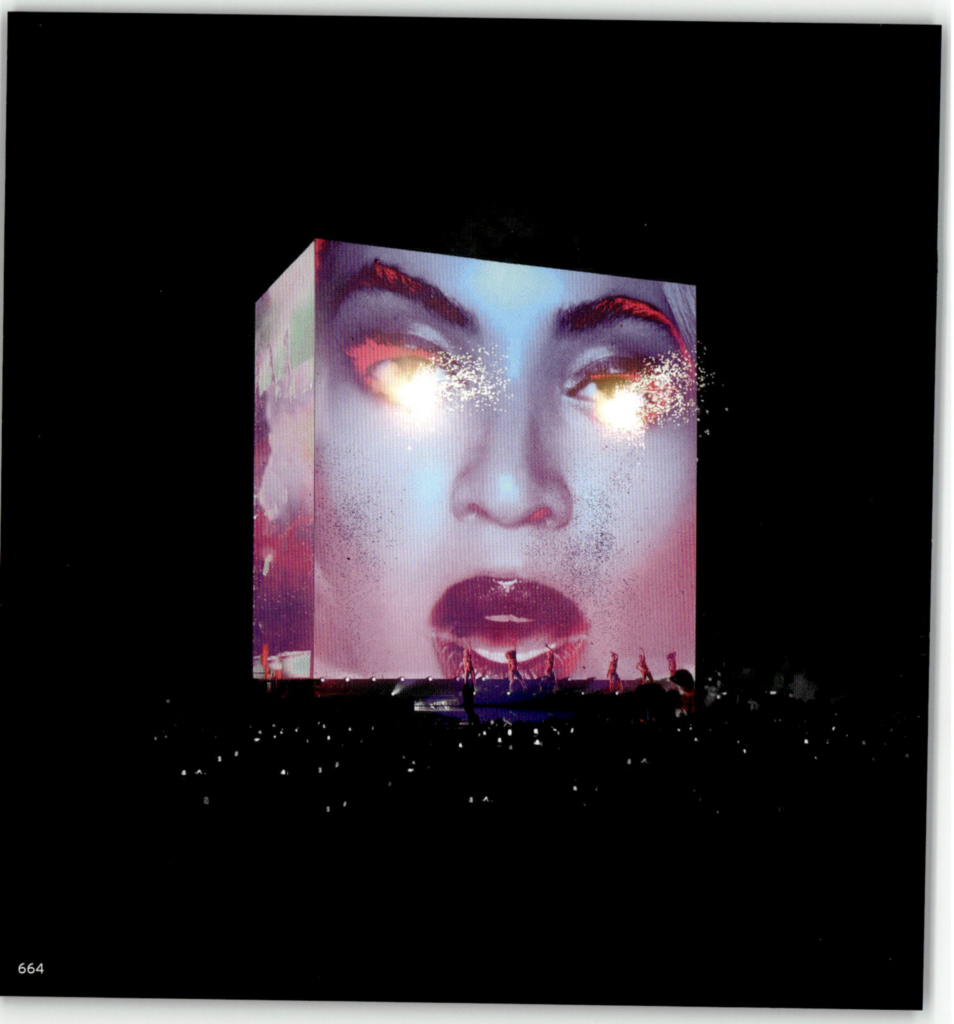

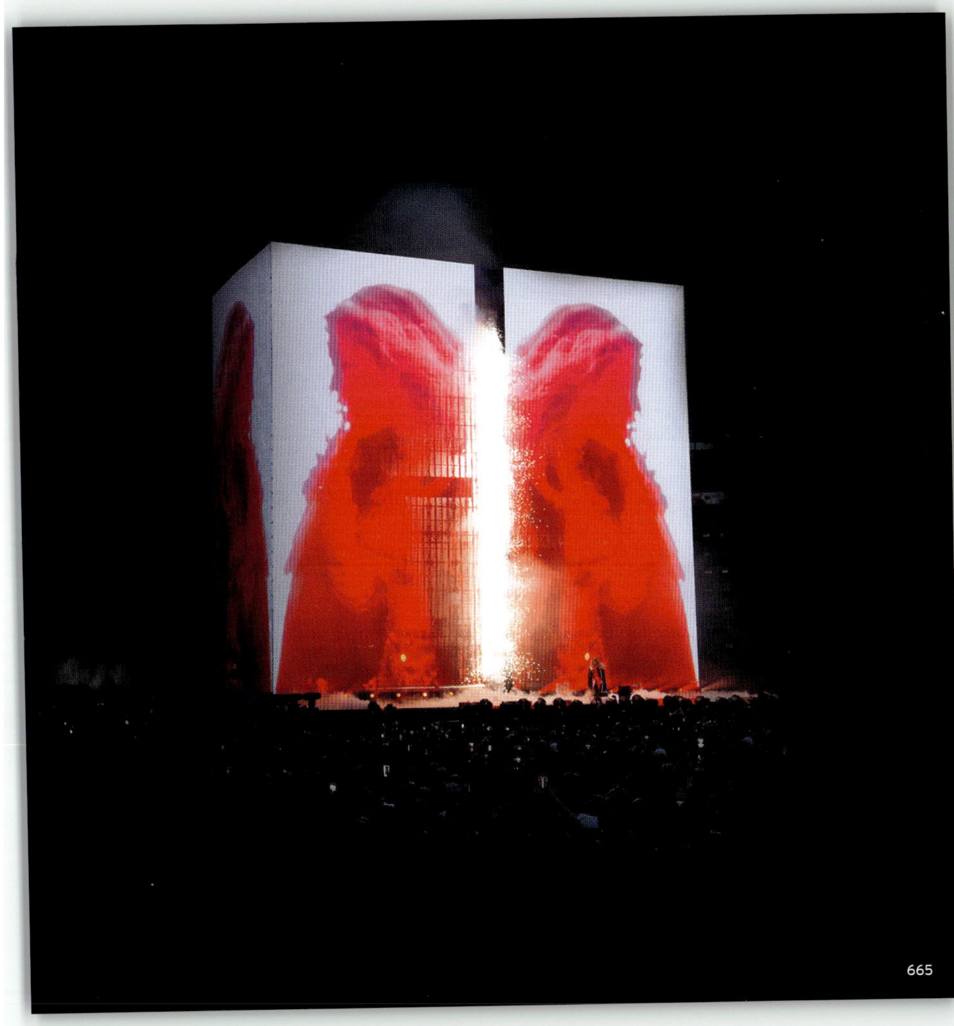

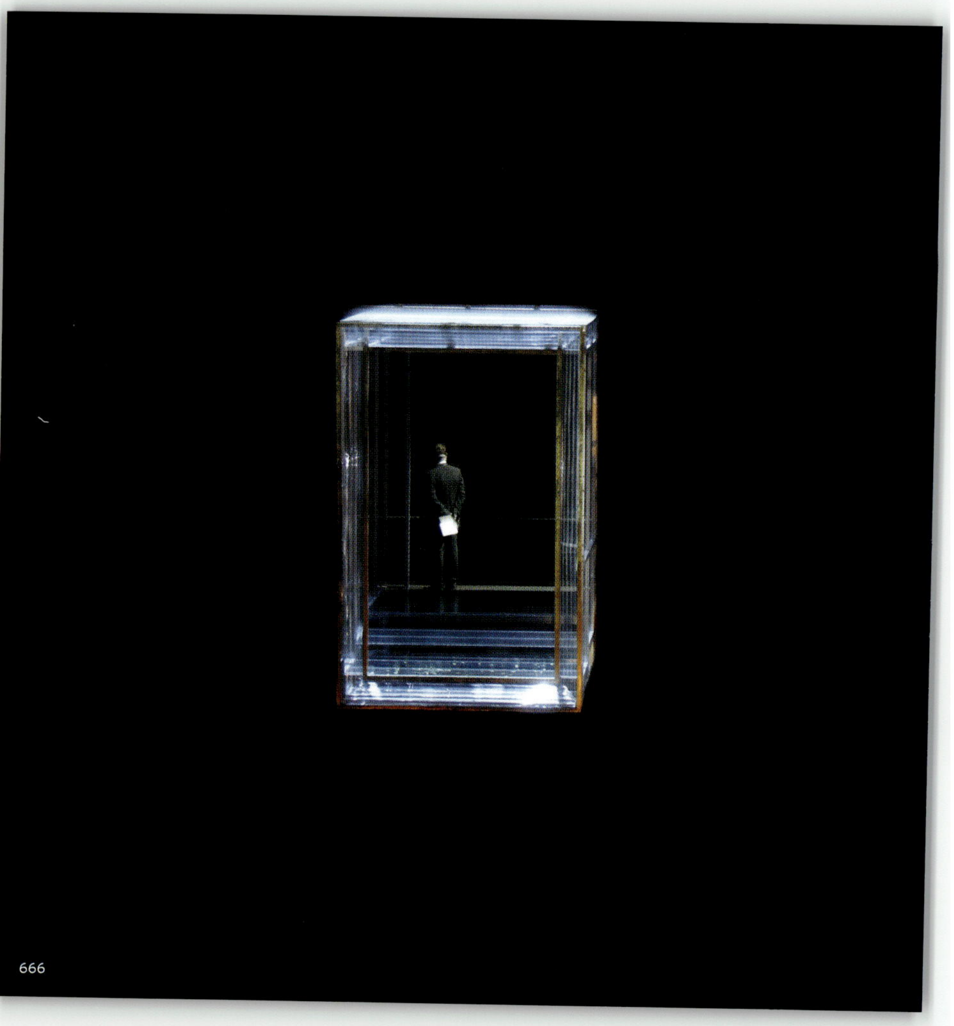

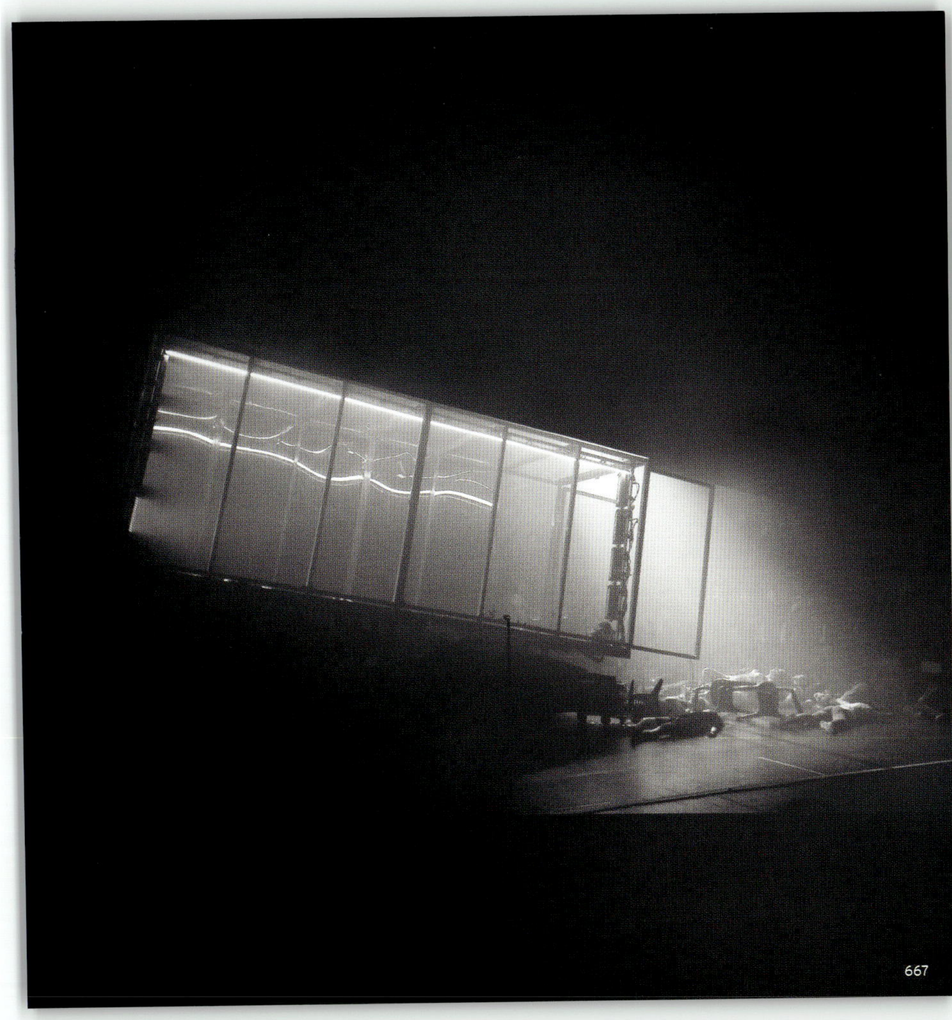

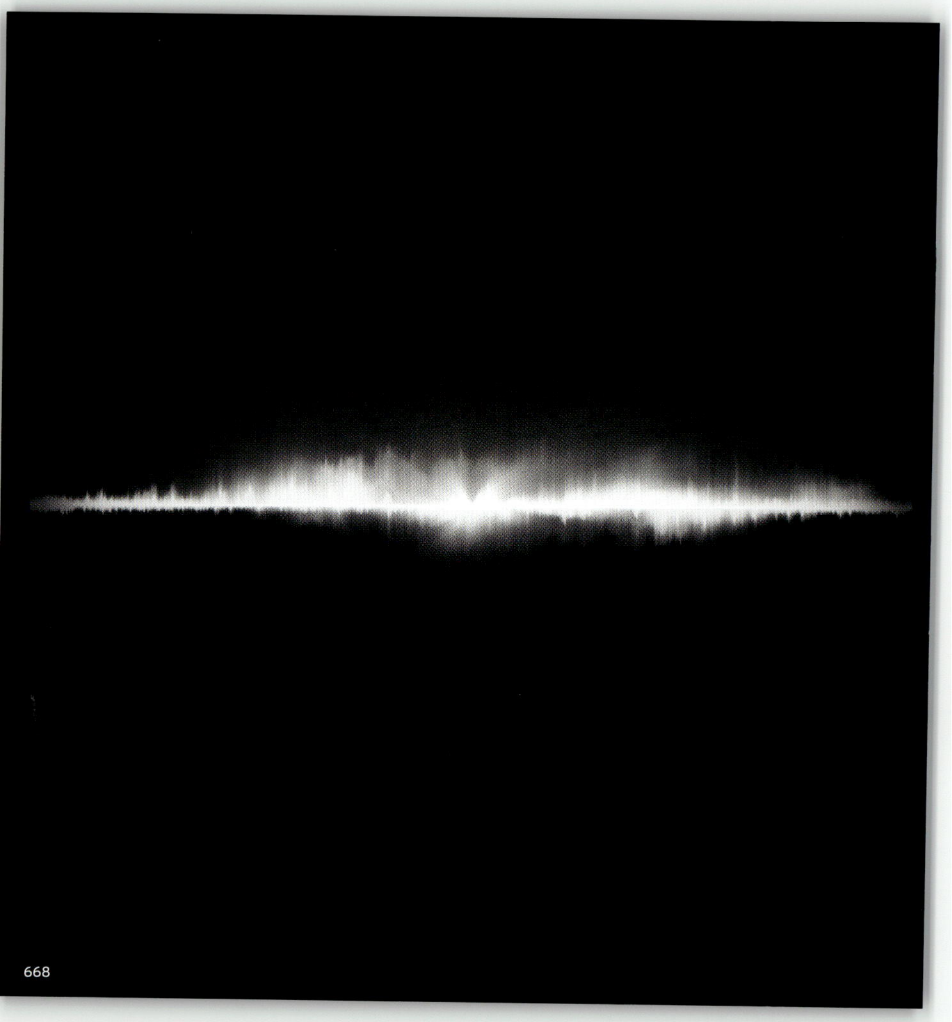

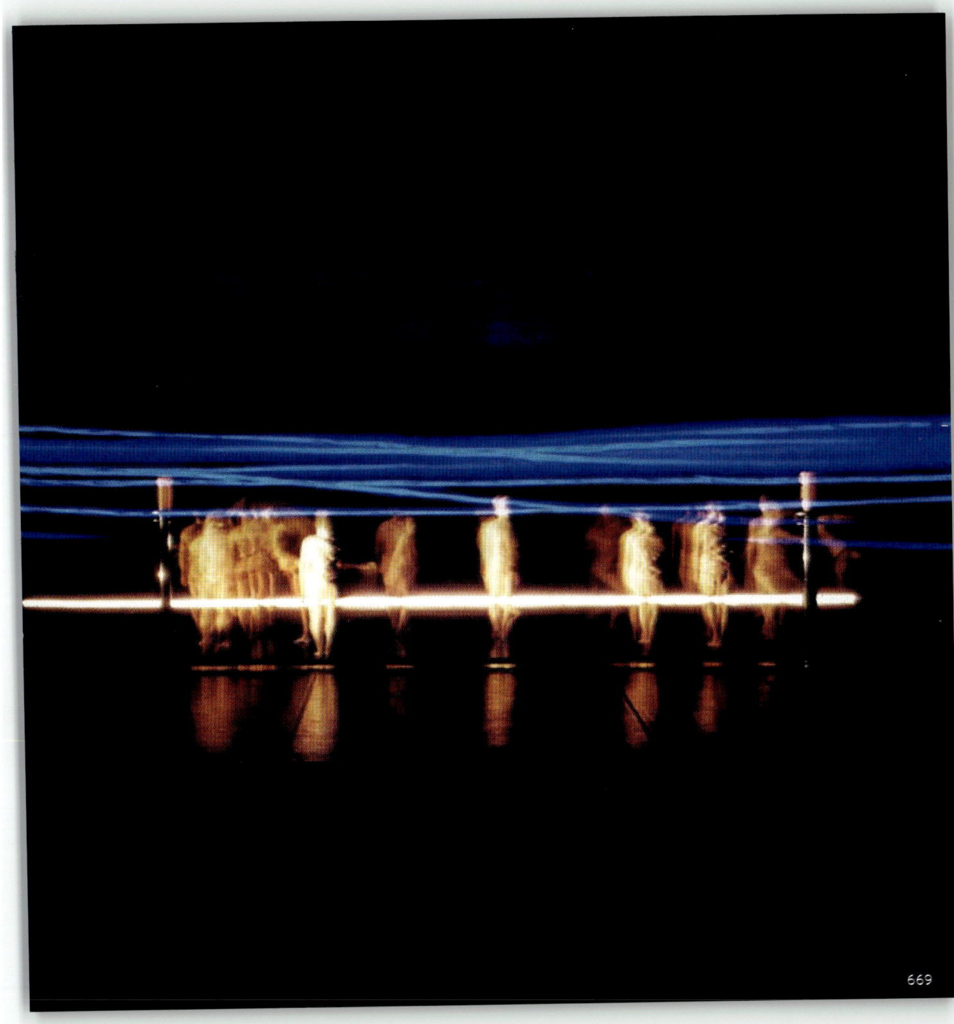

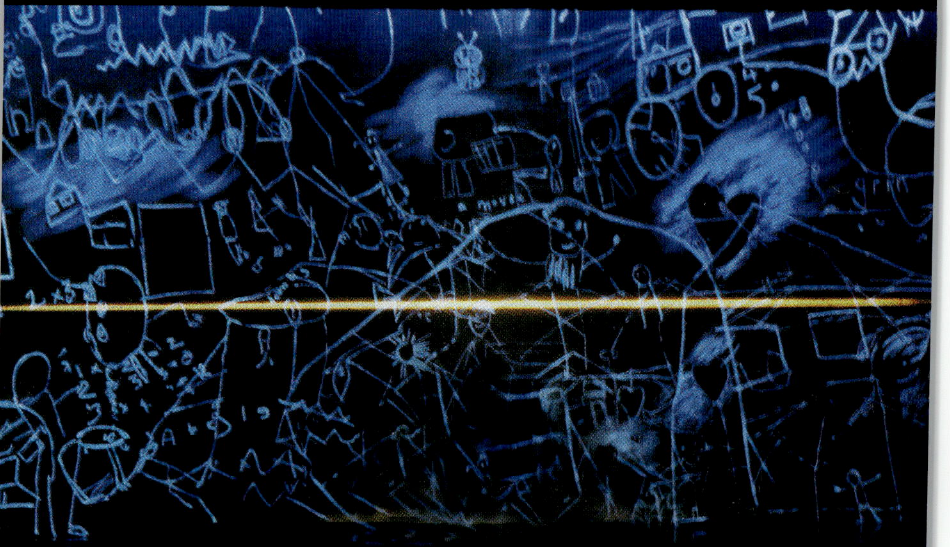

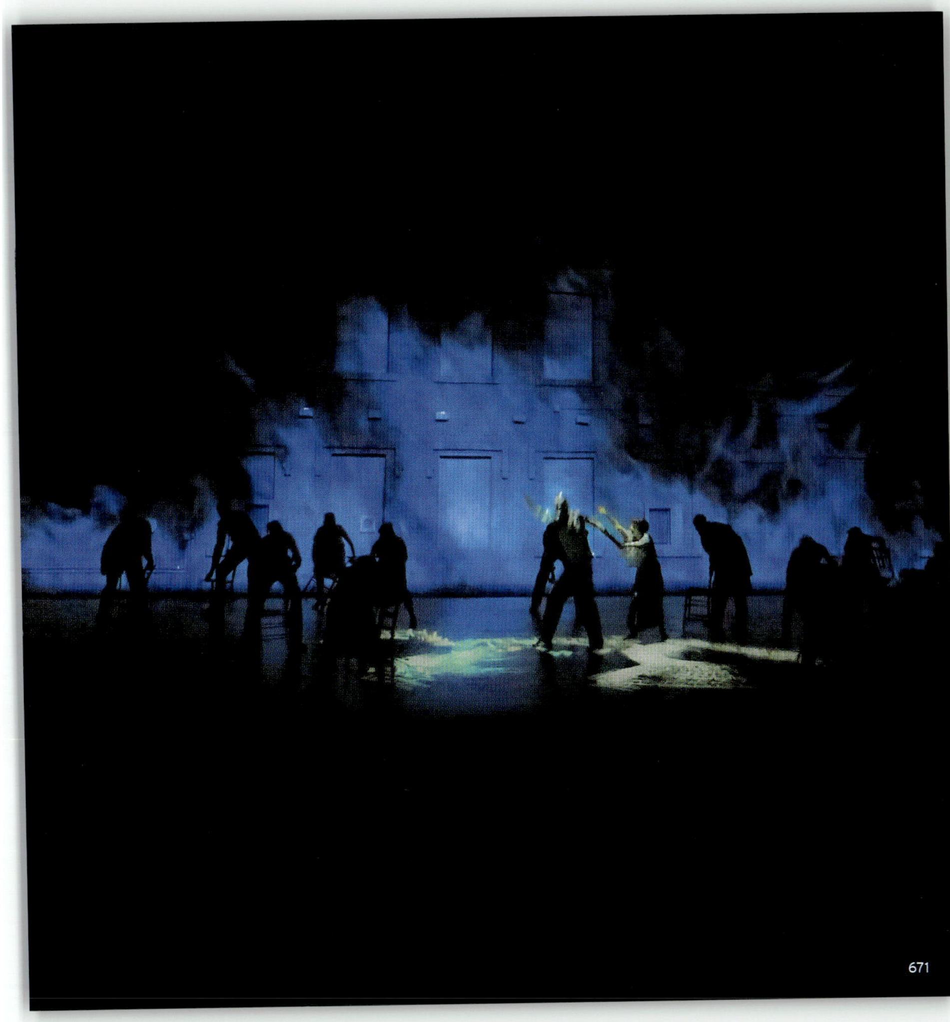

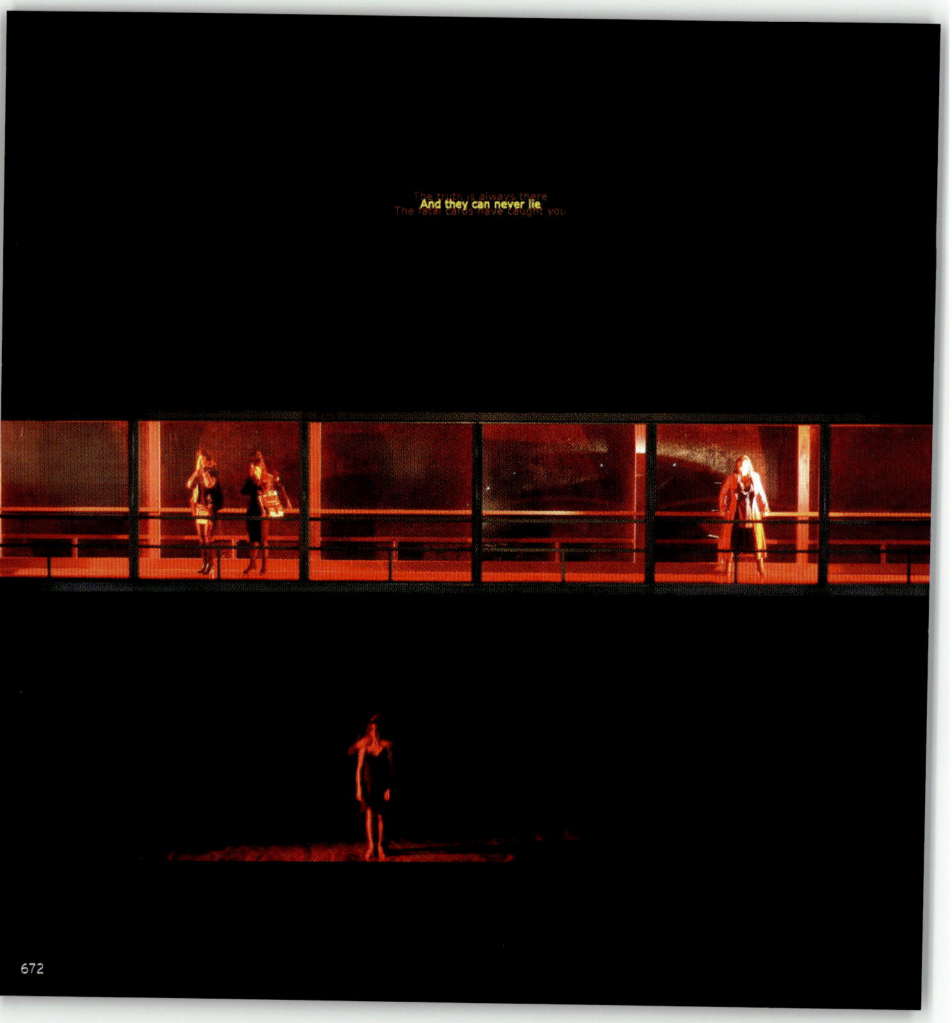
The truth is always there
And they can never lie

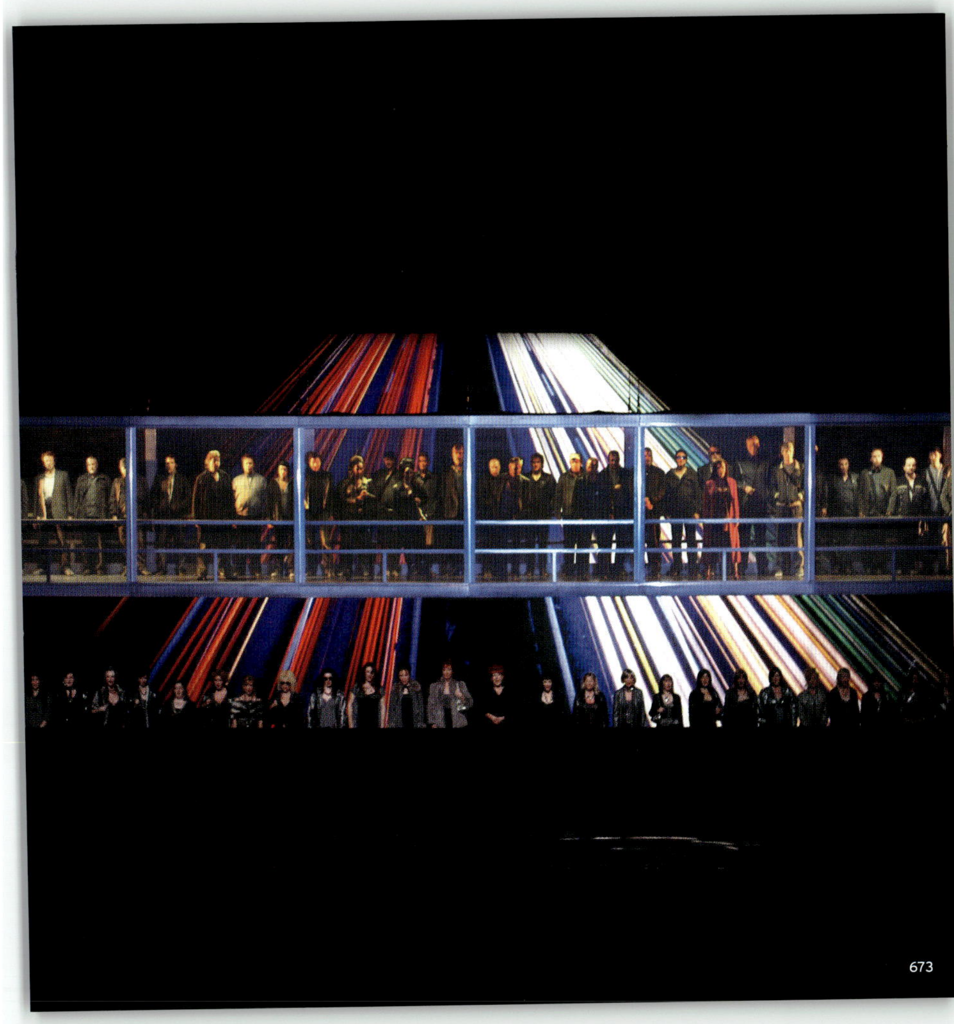

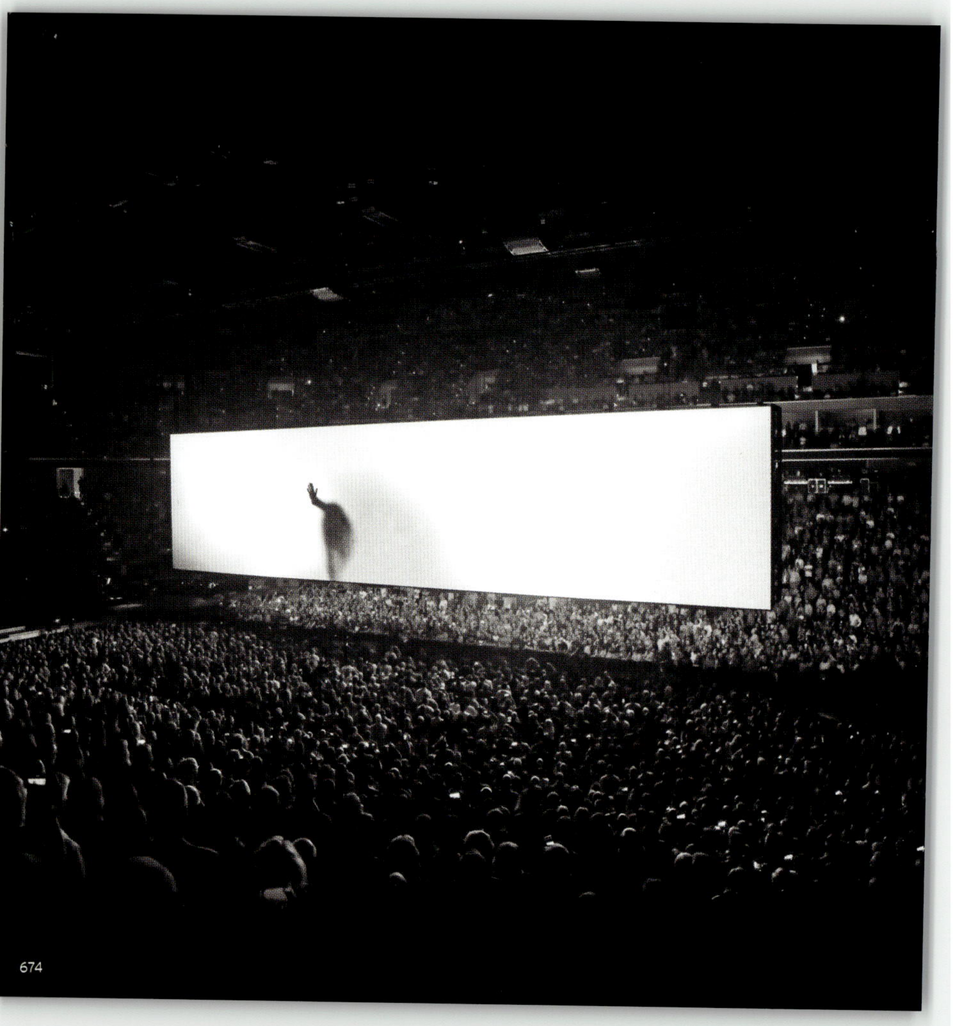

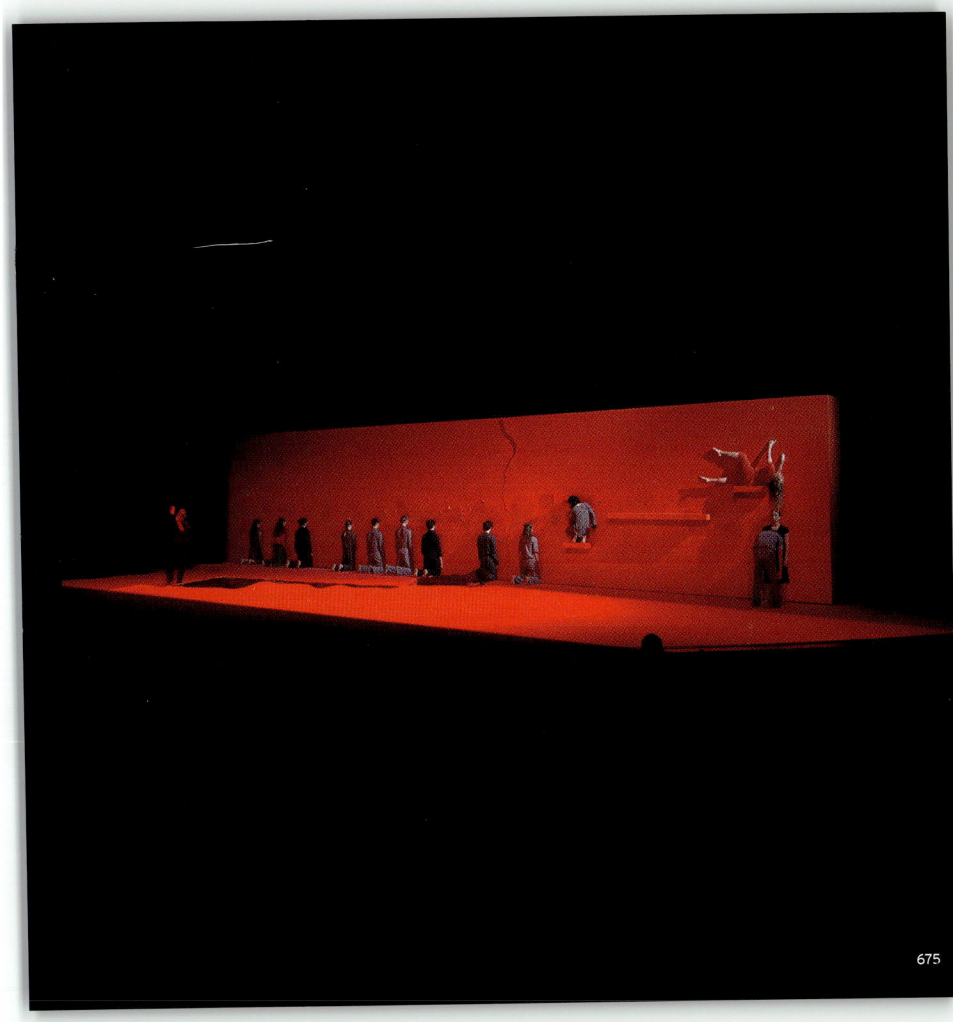

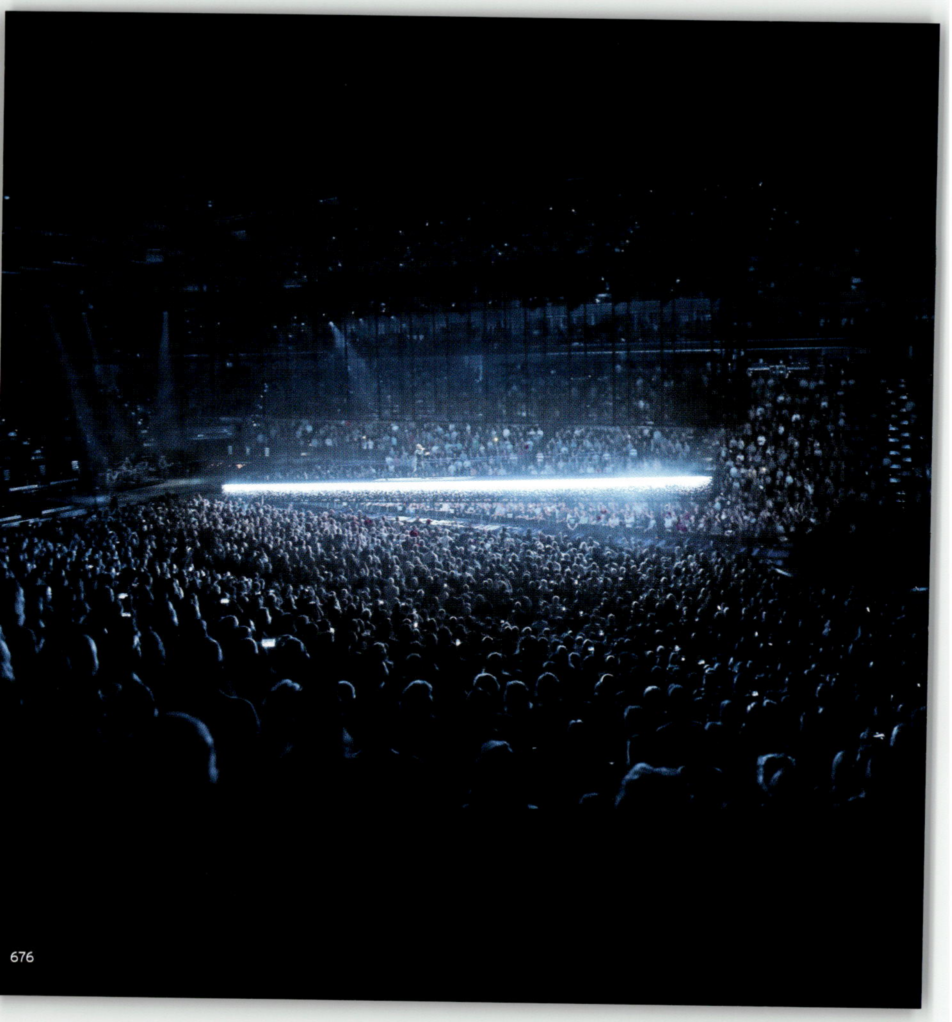

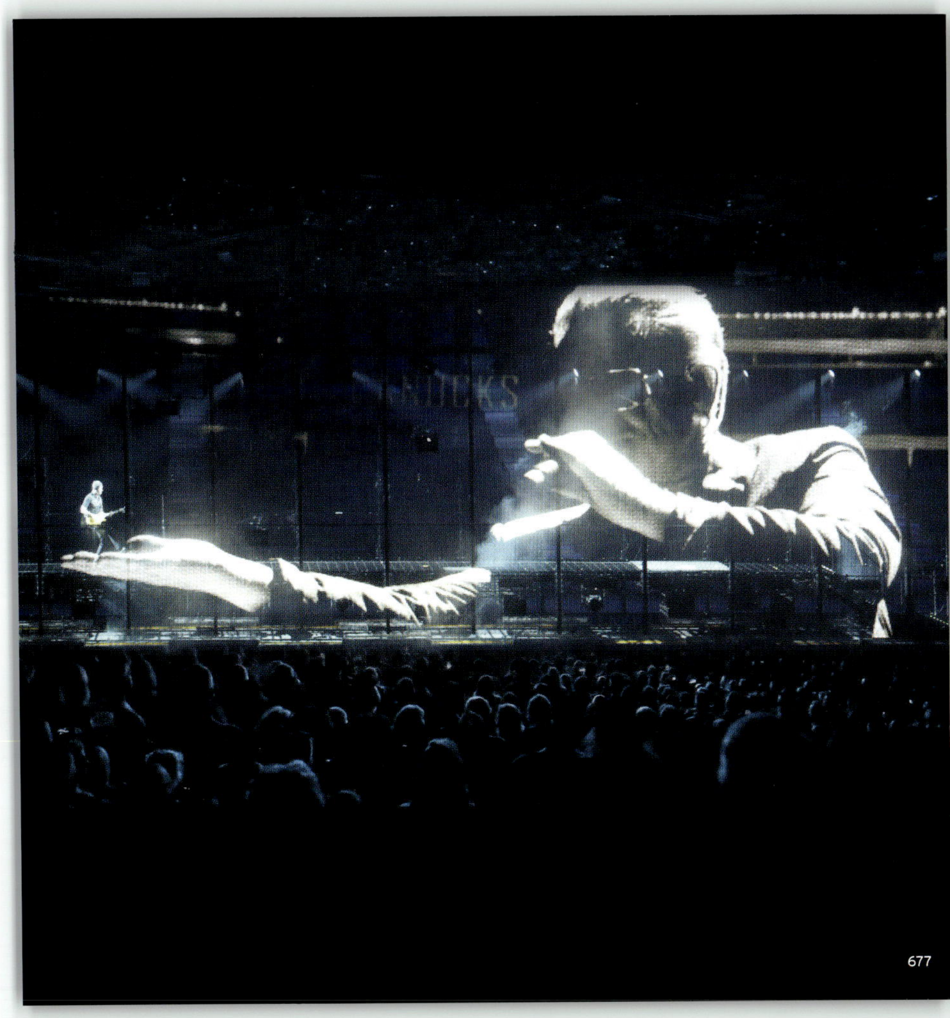

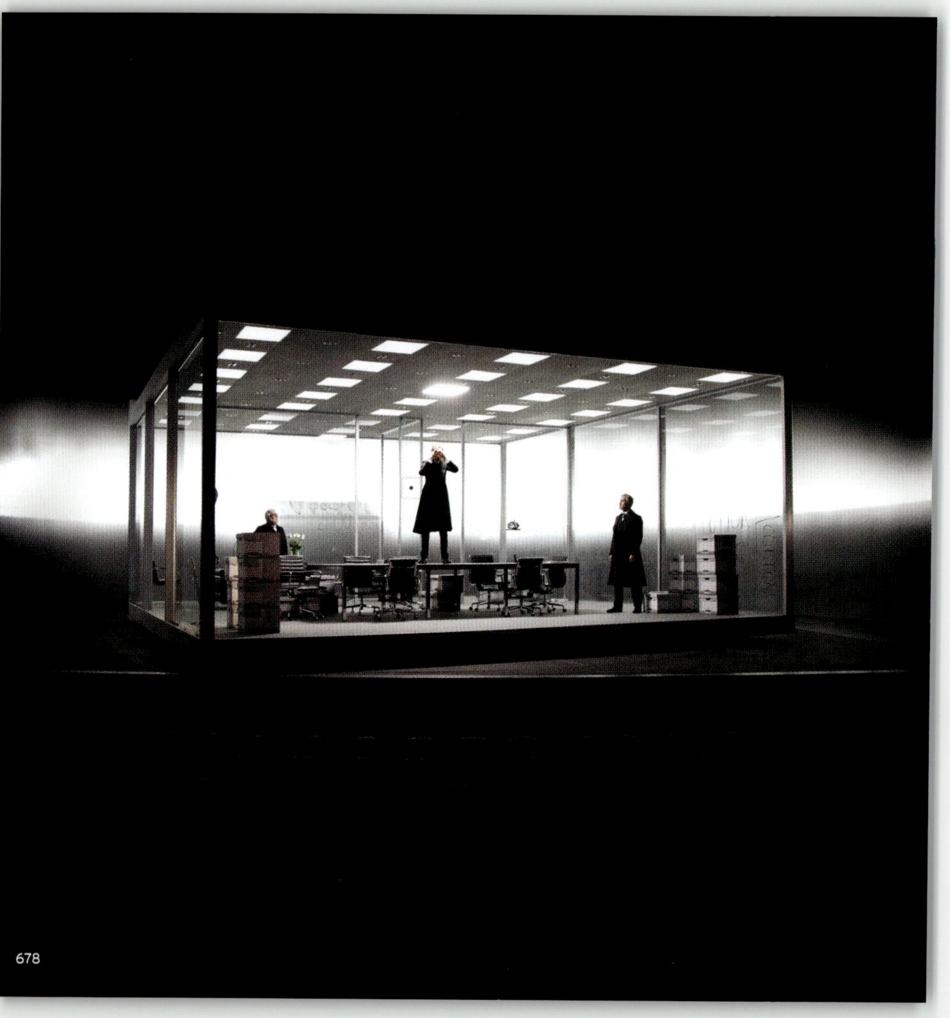

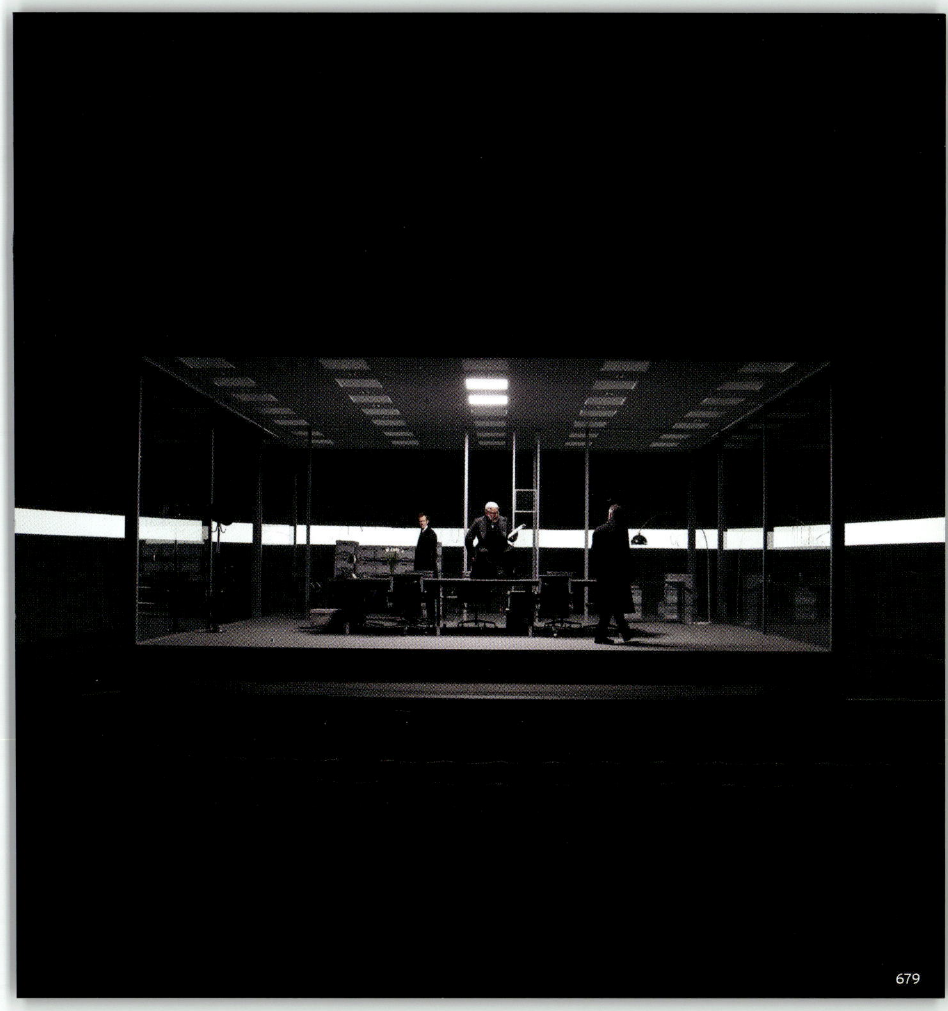

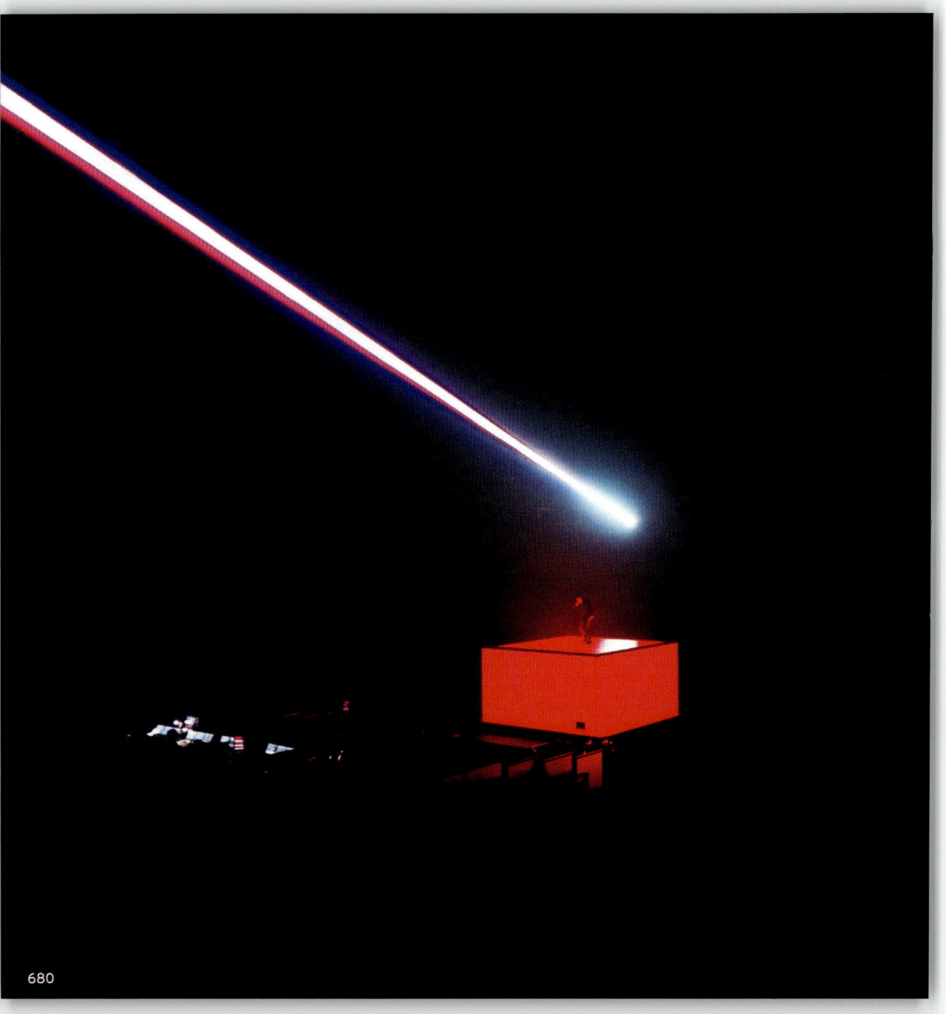

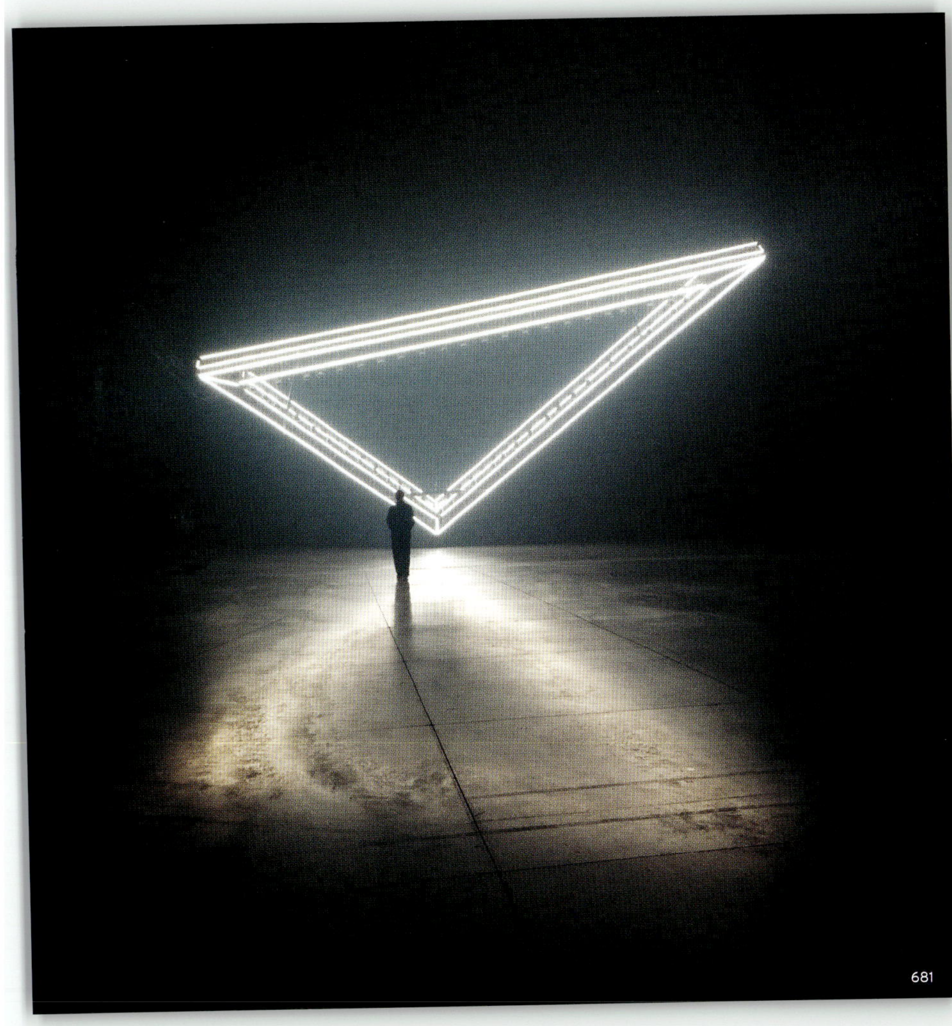

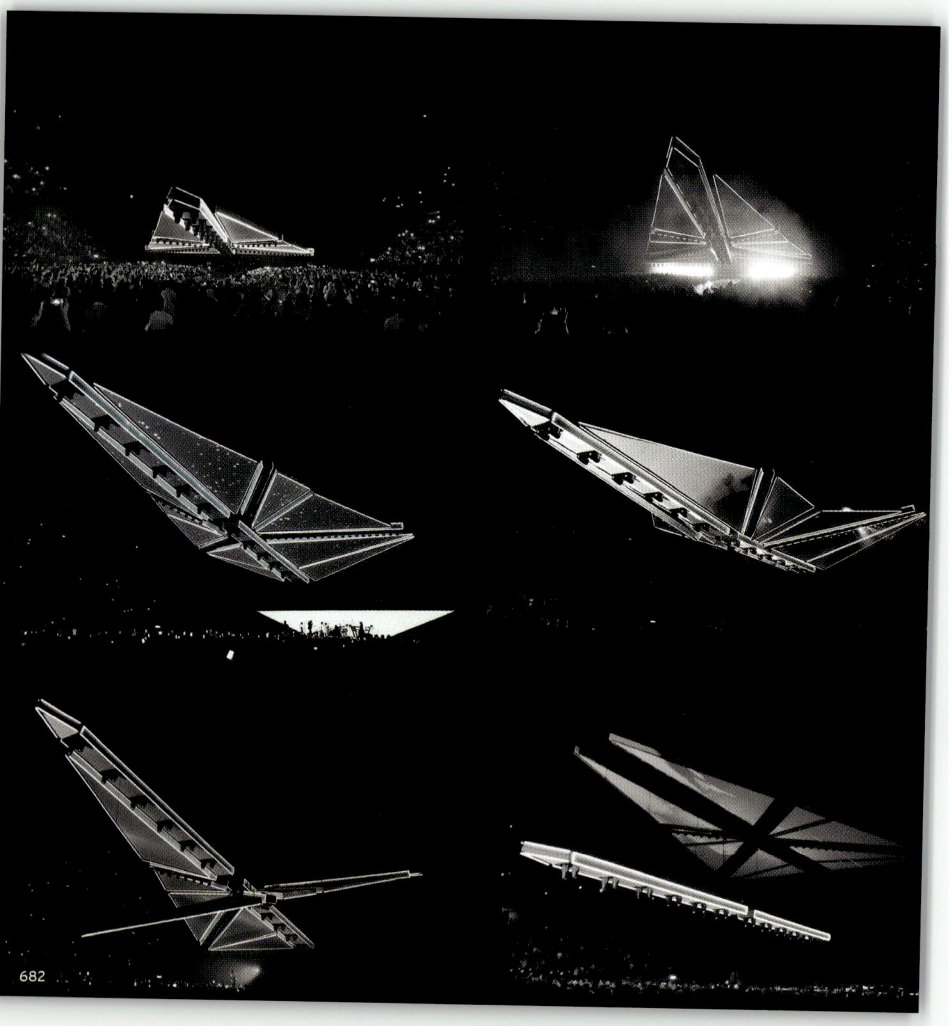

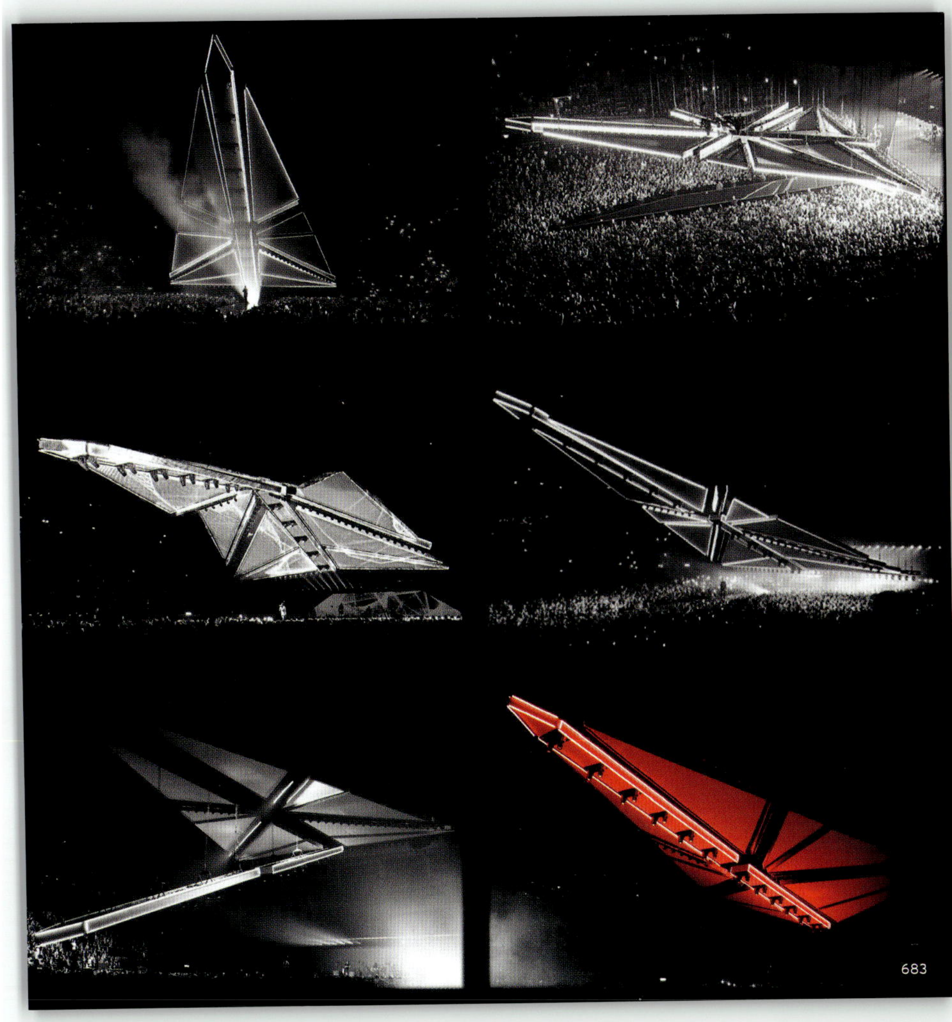

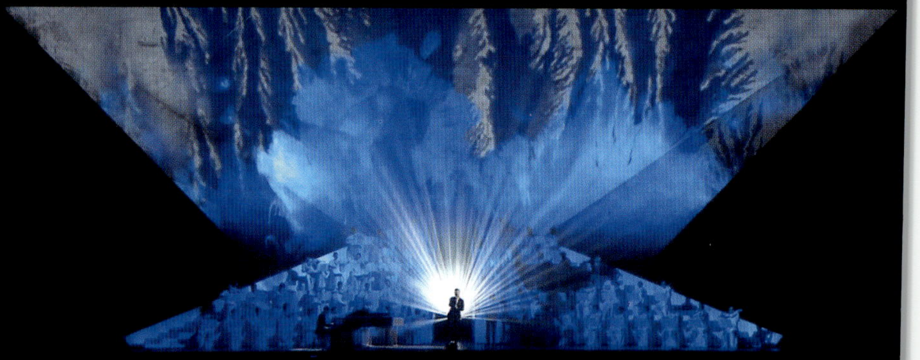

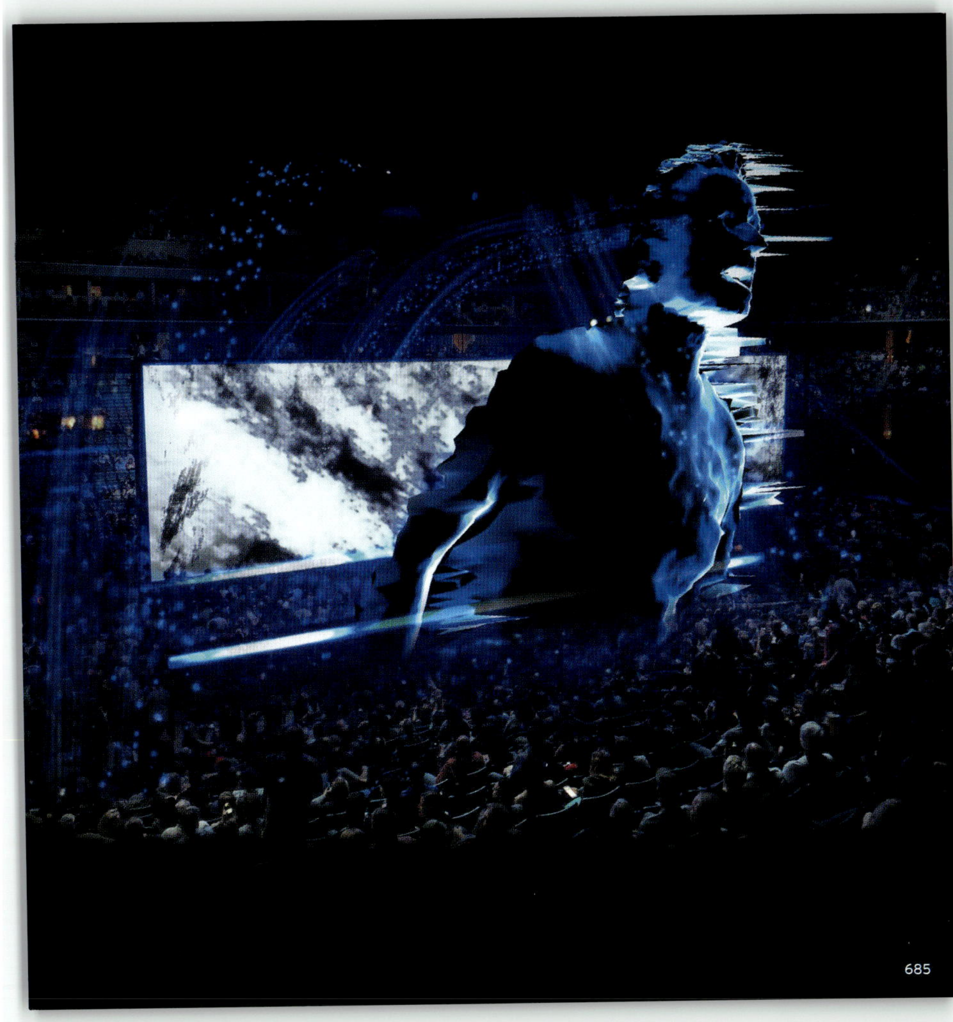

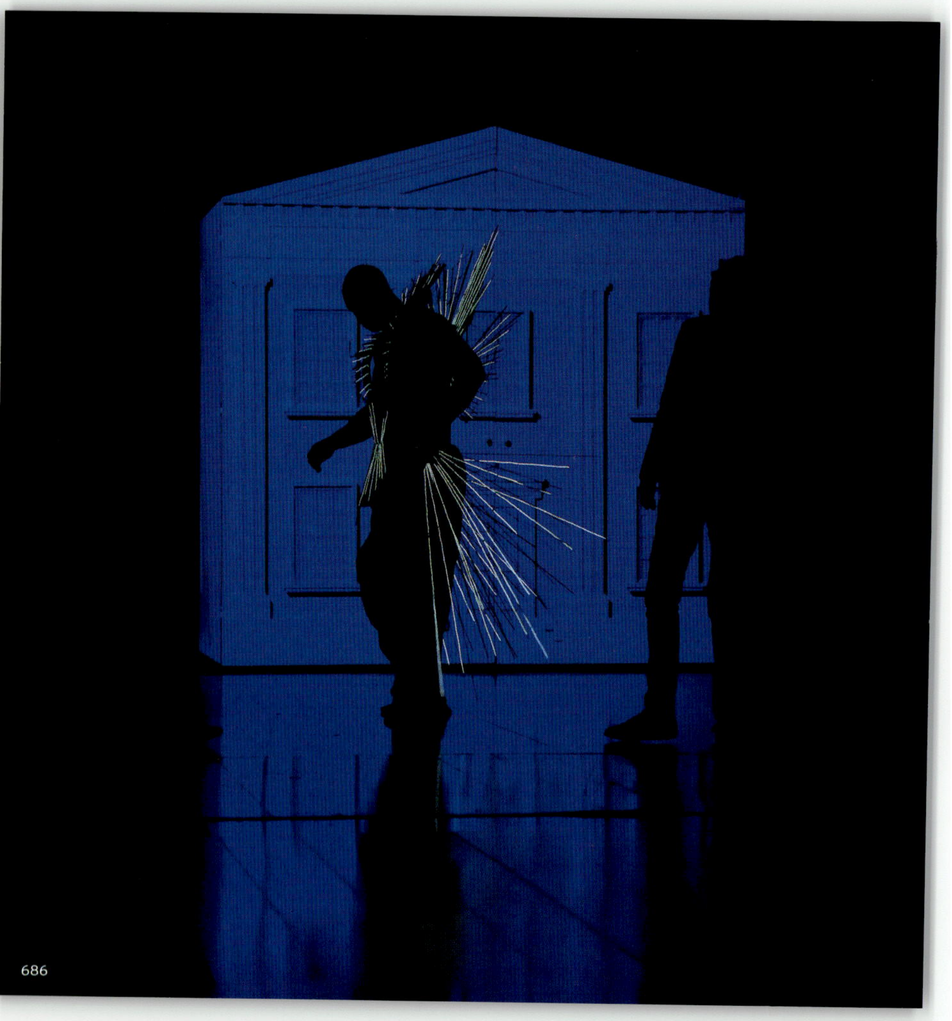

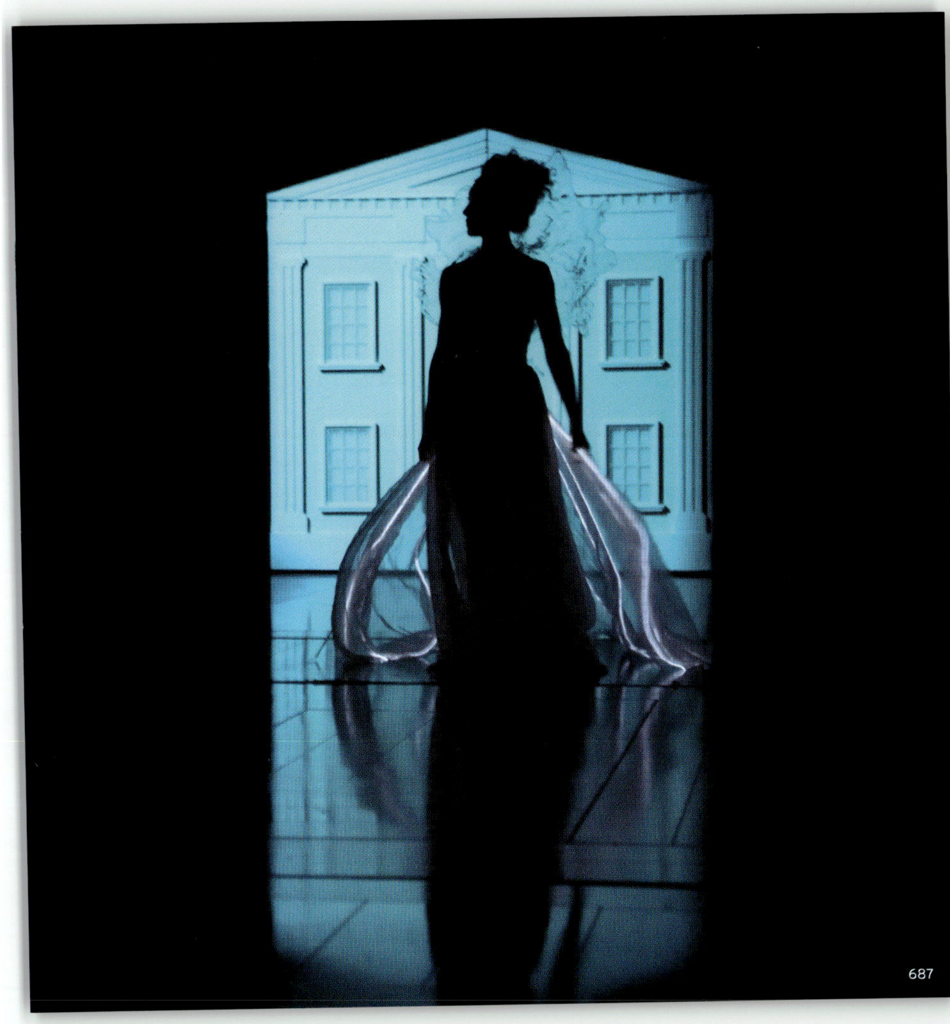

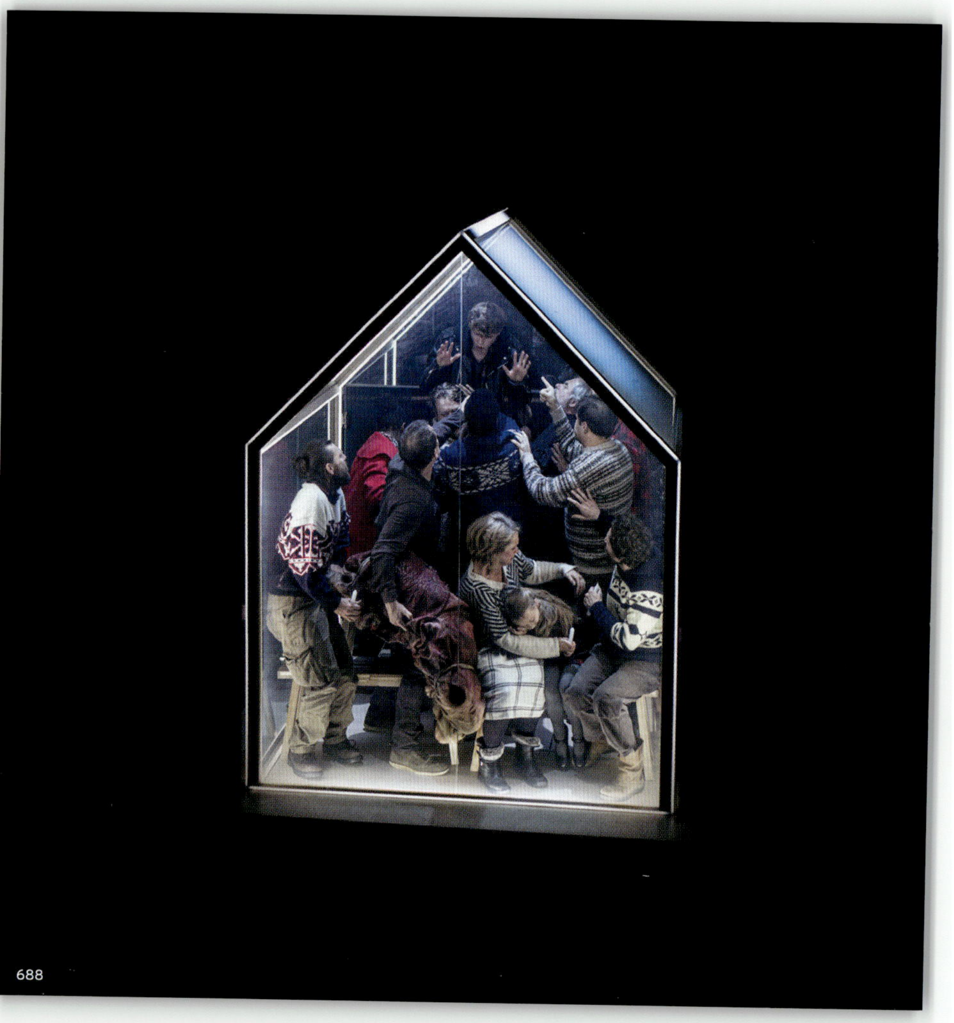

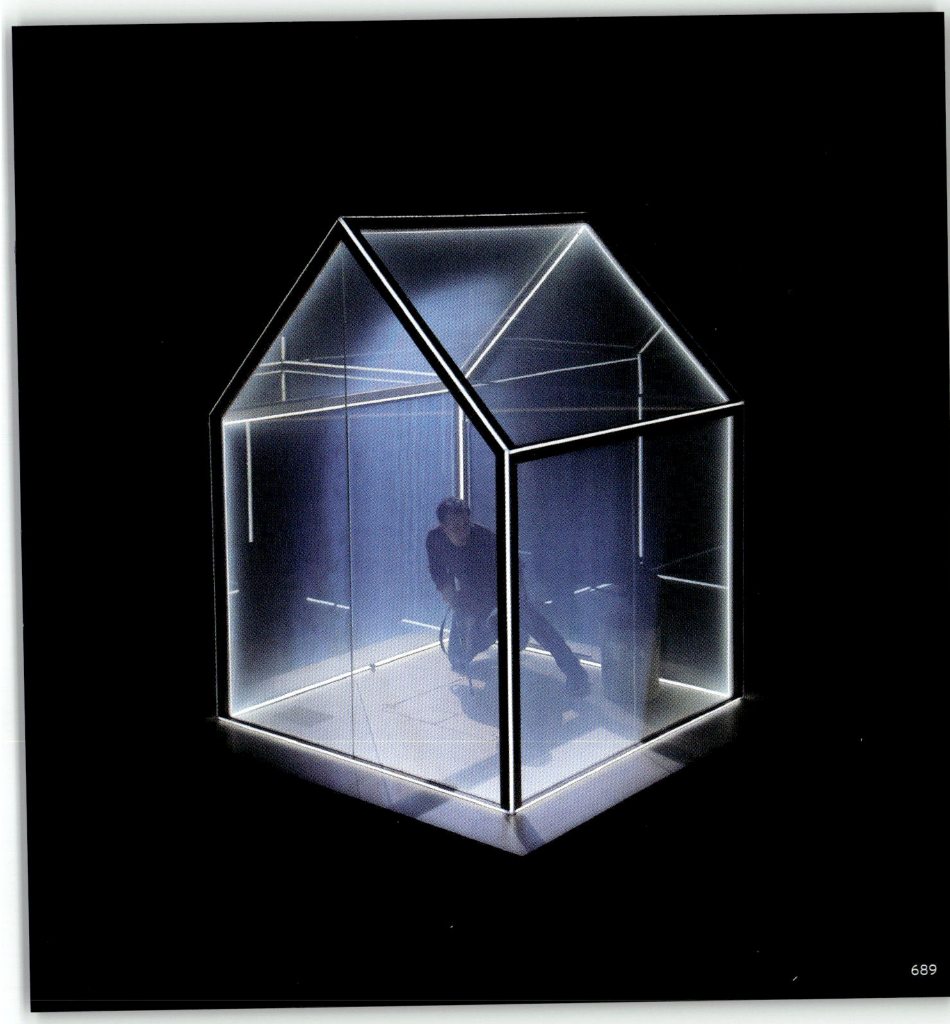

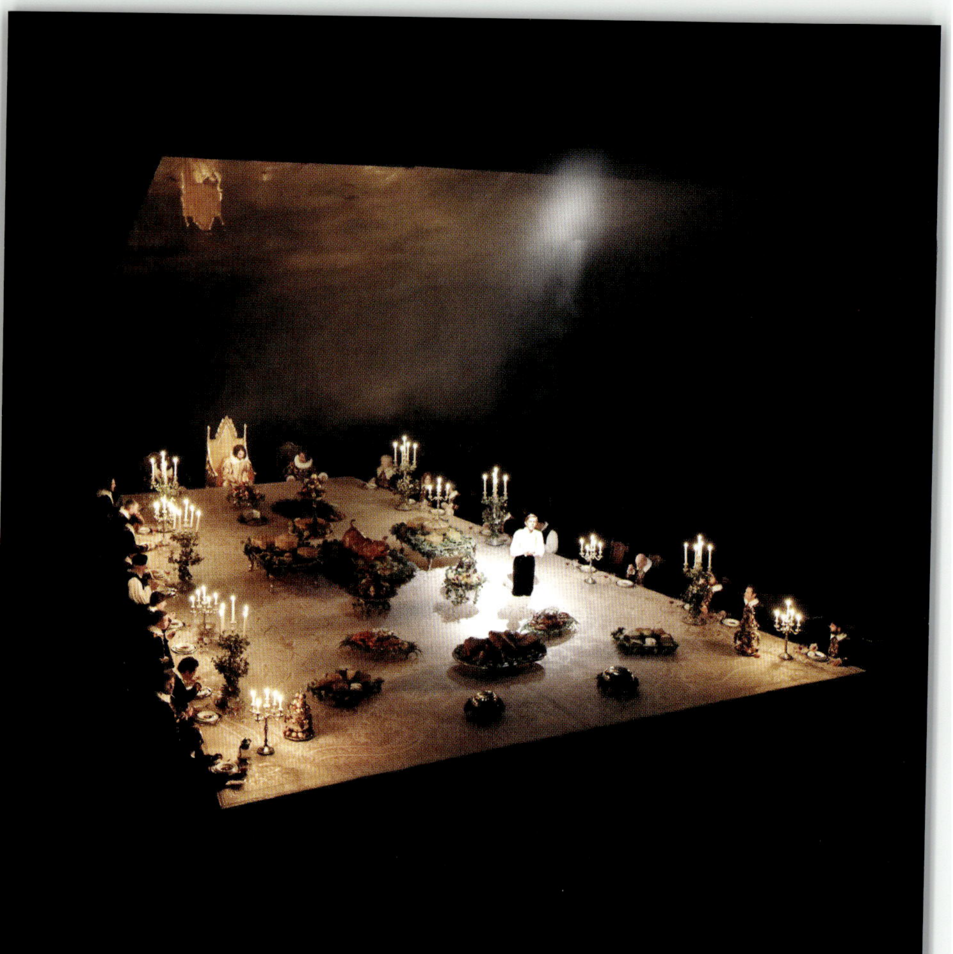

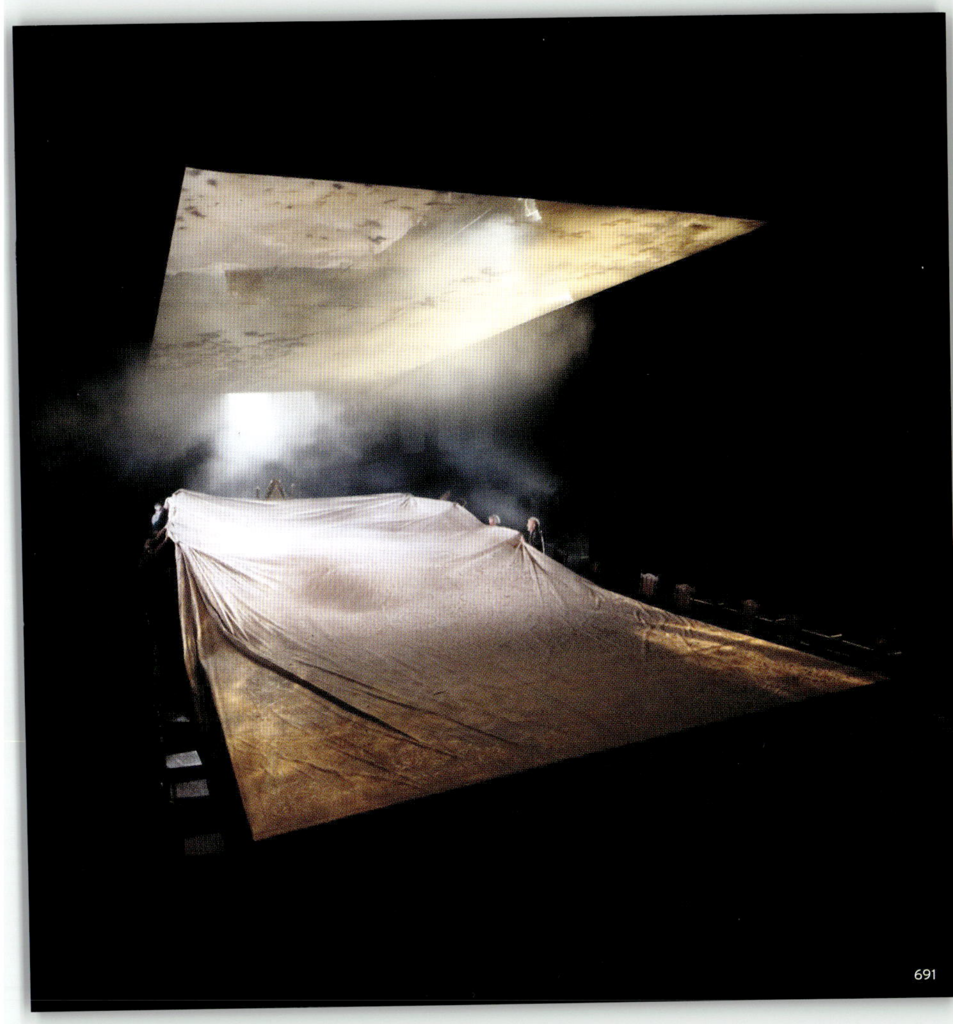

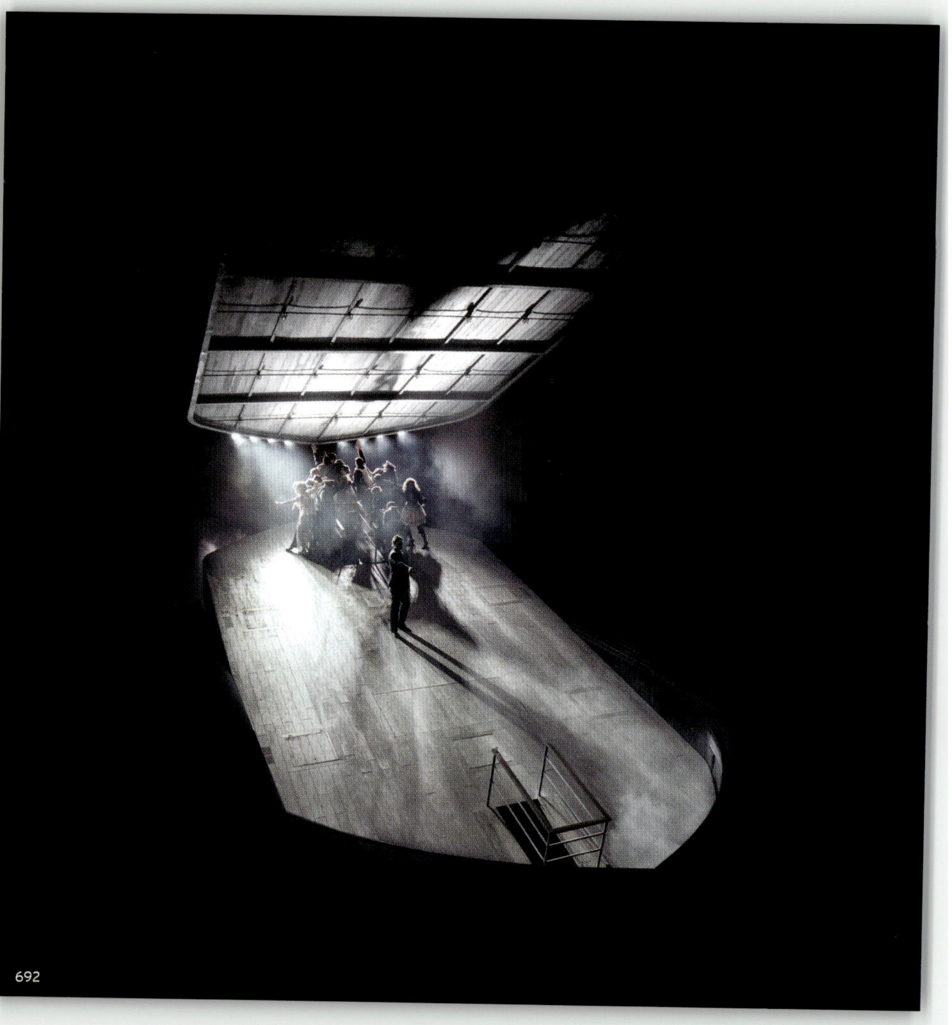

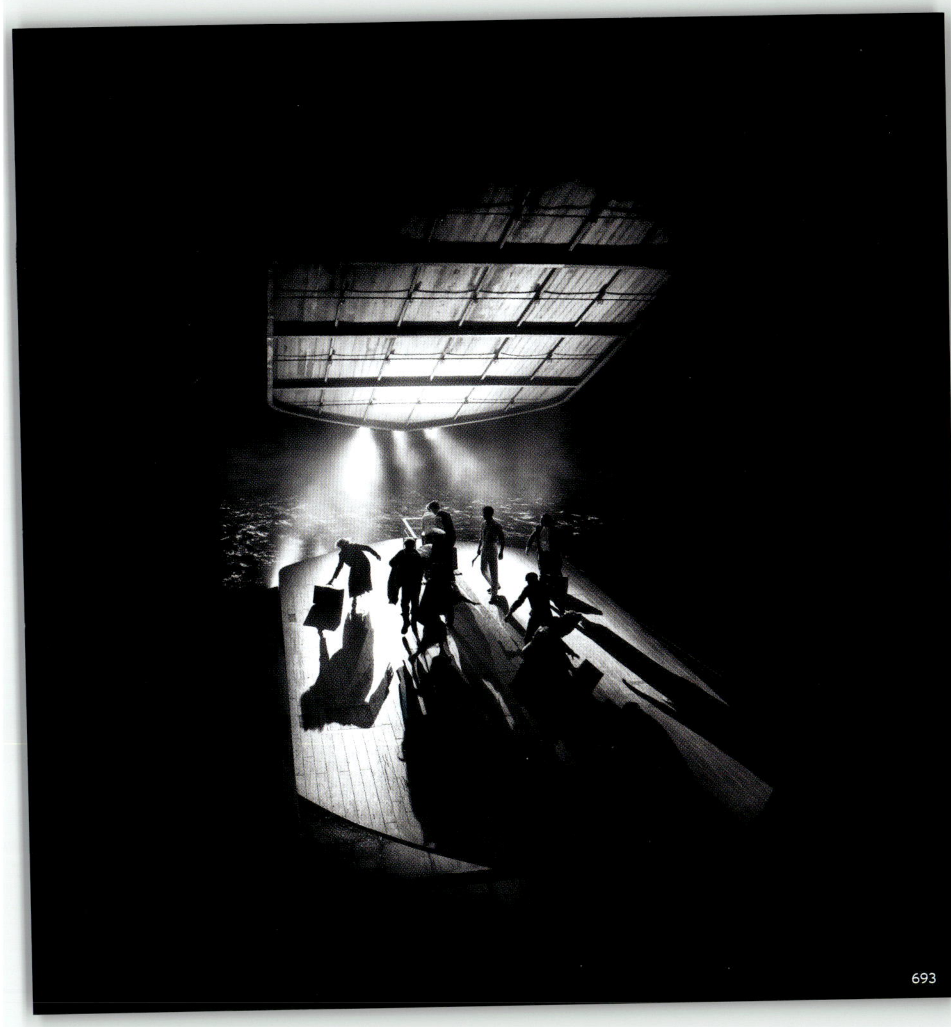

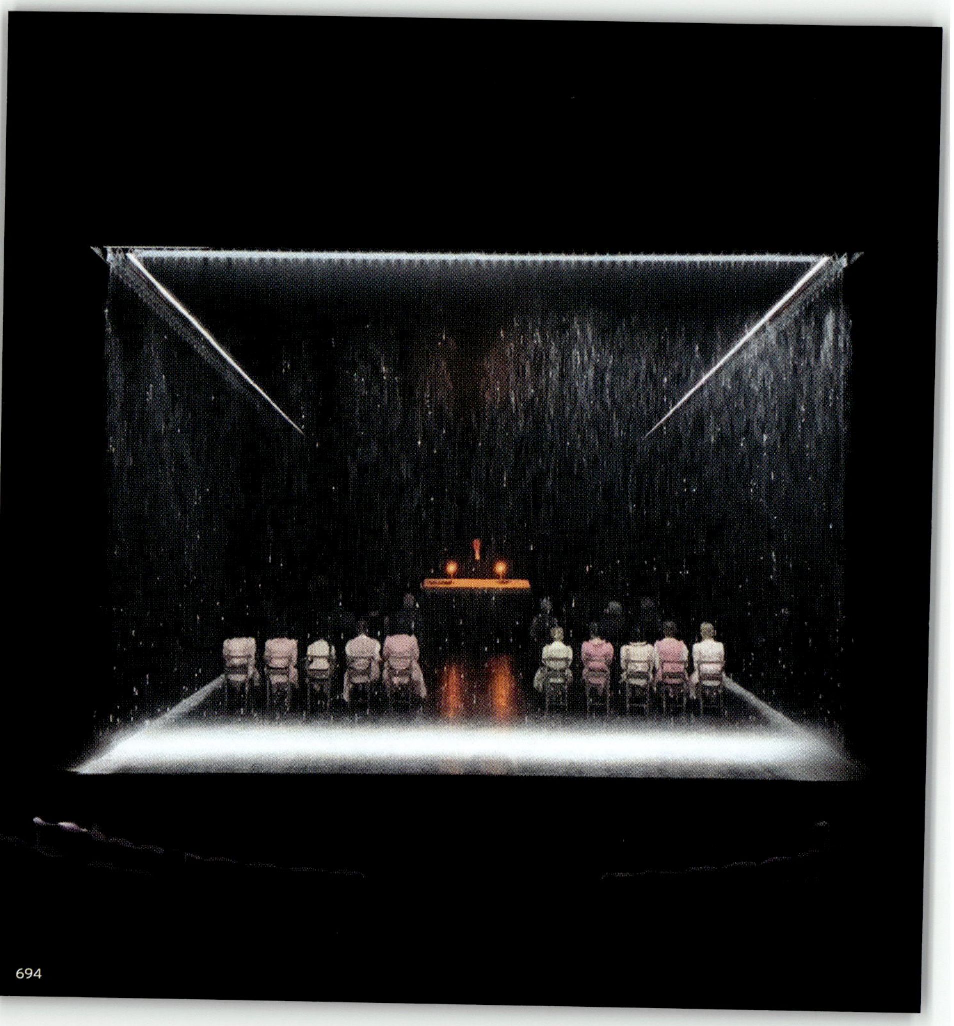

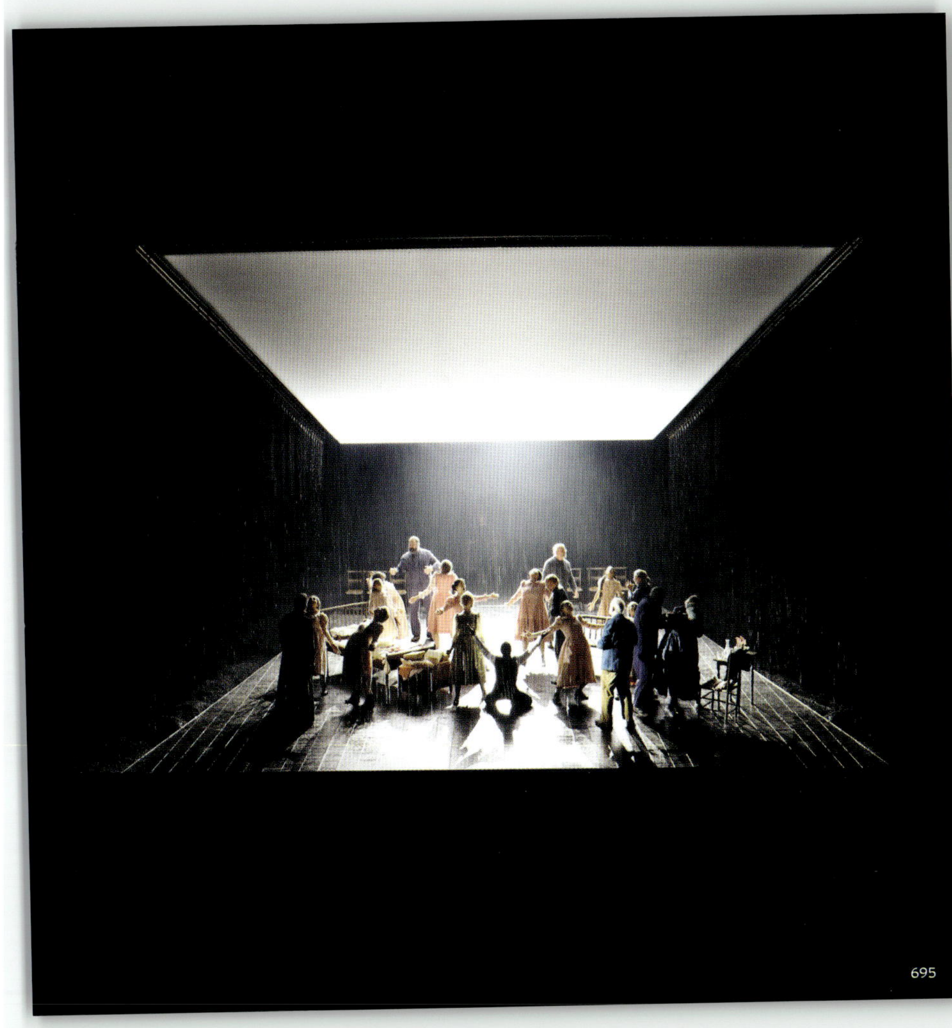

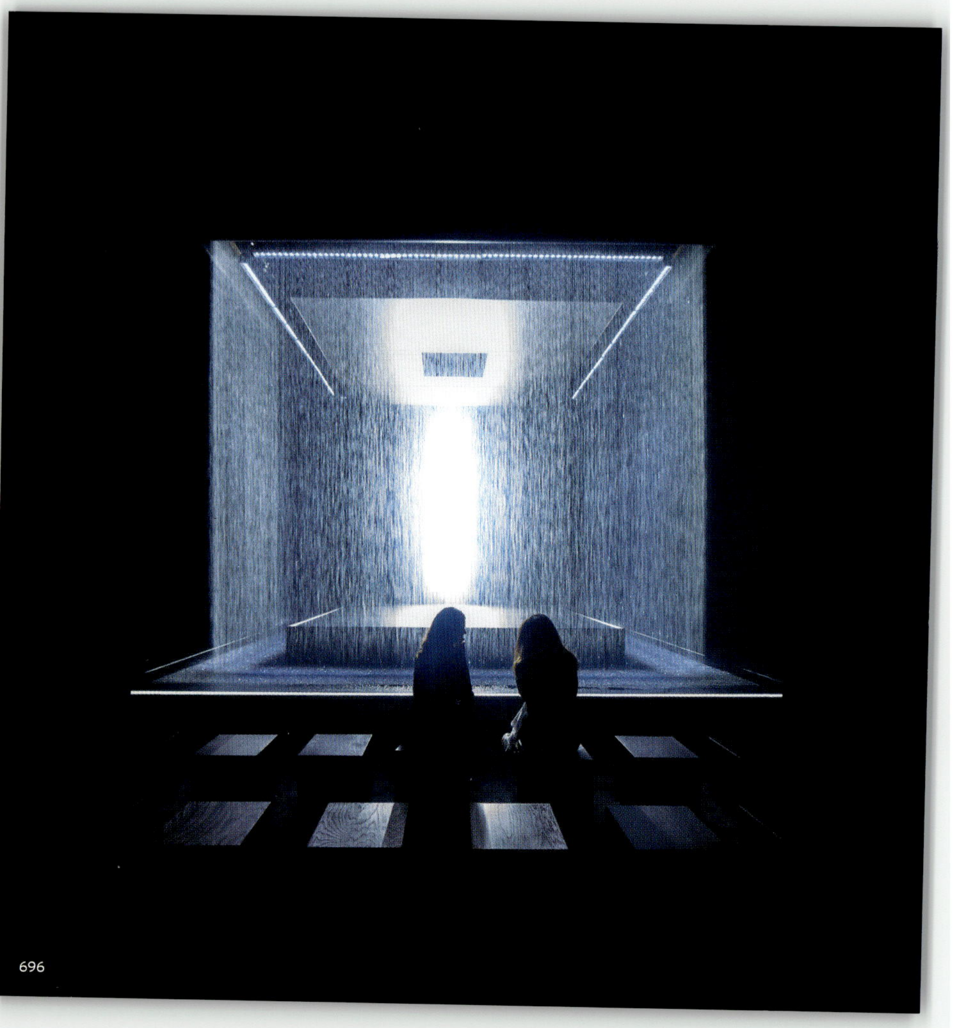

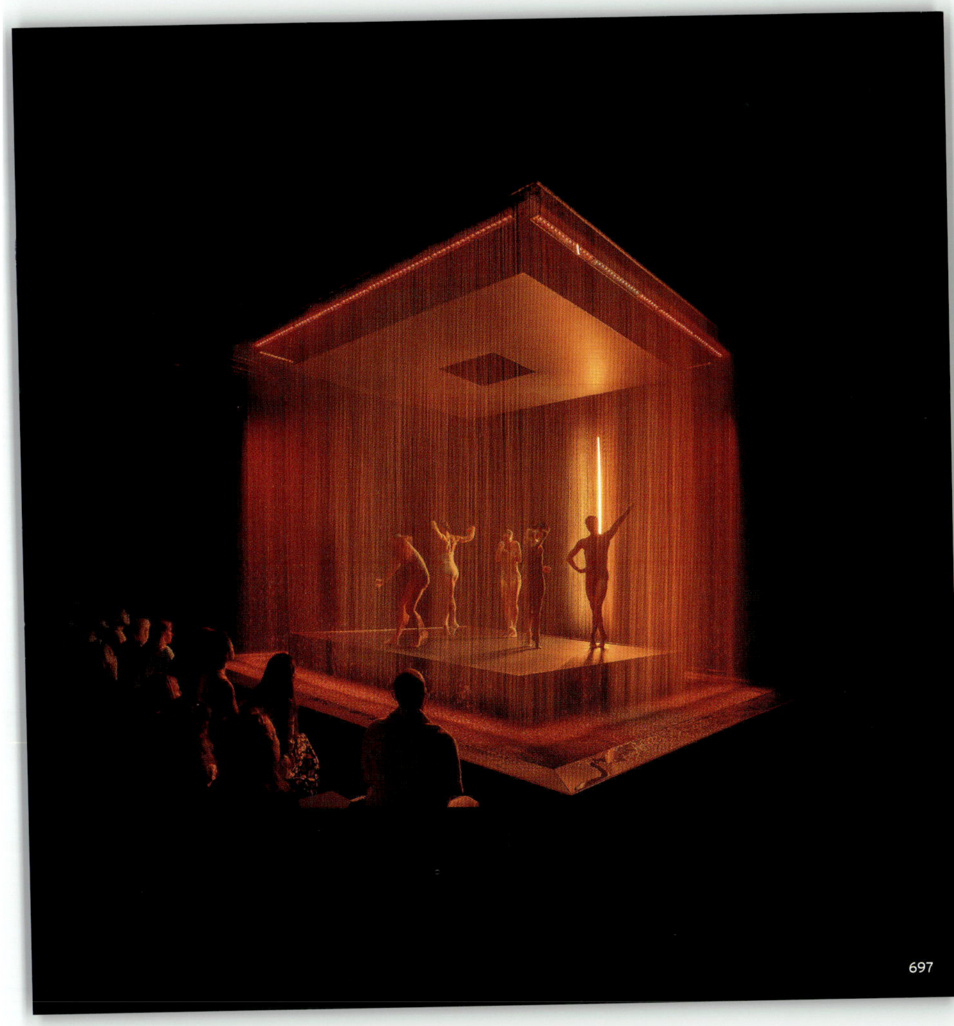

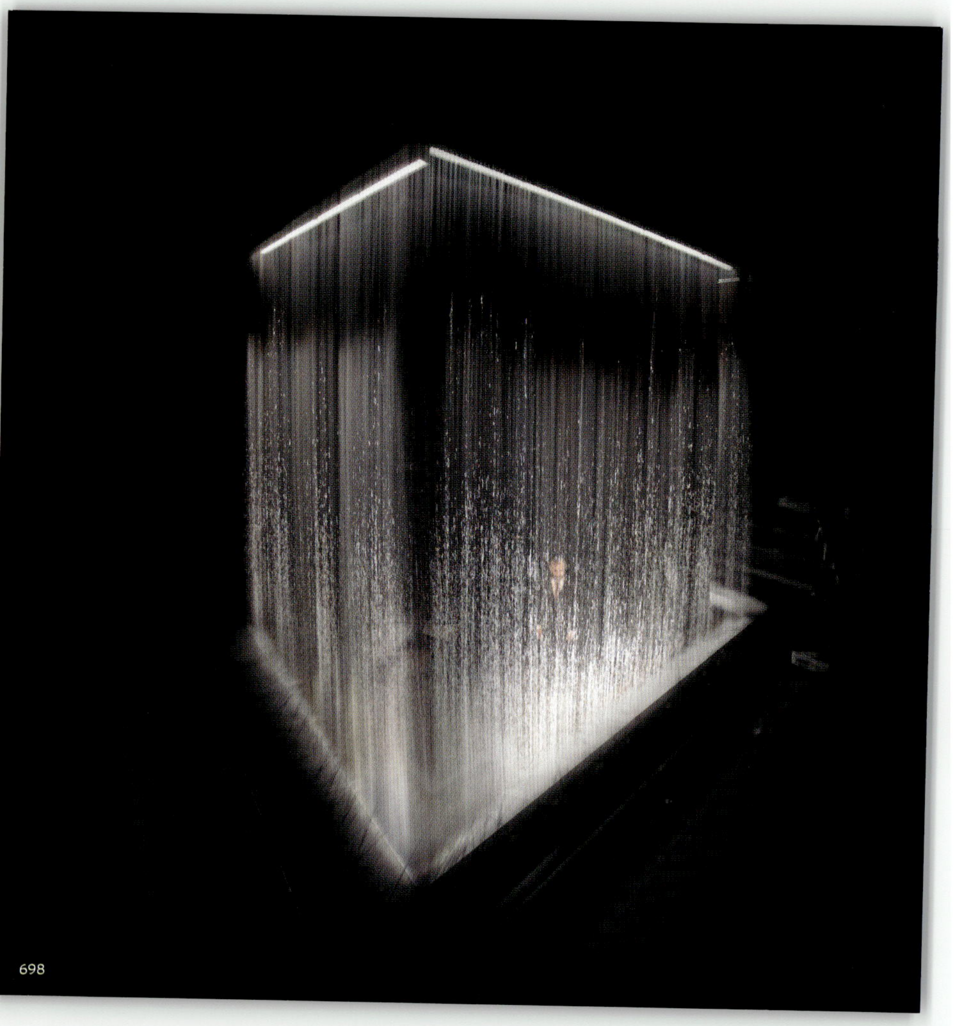

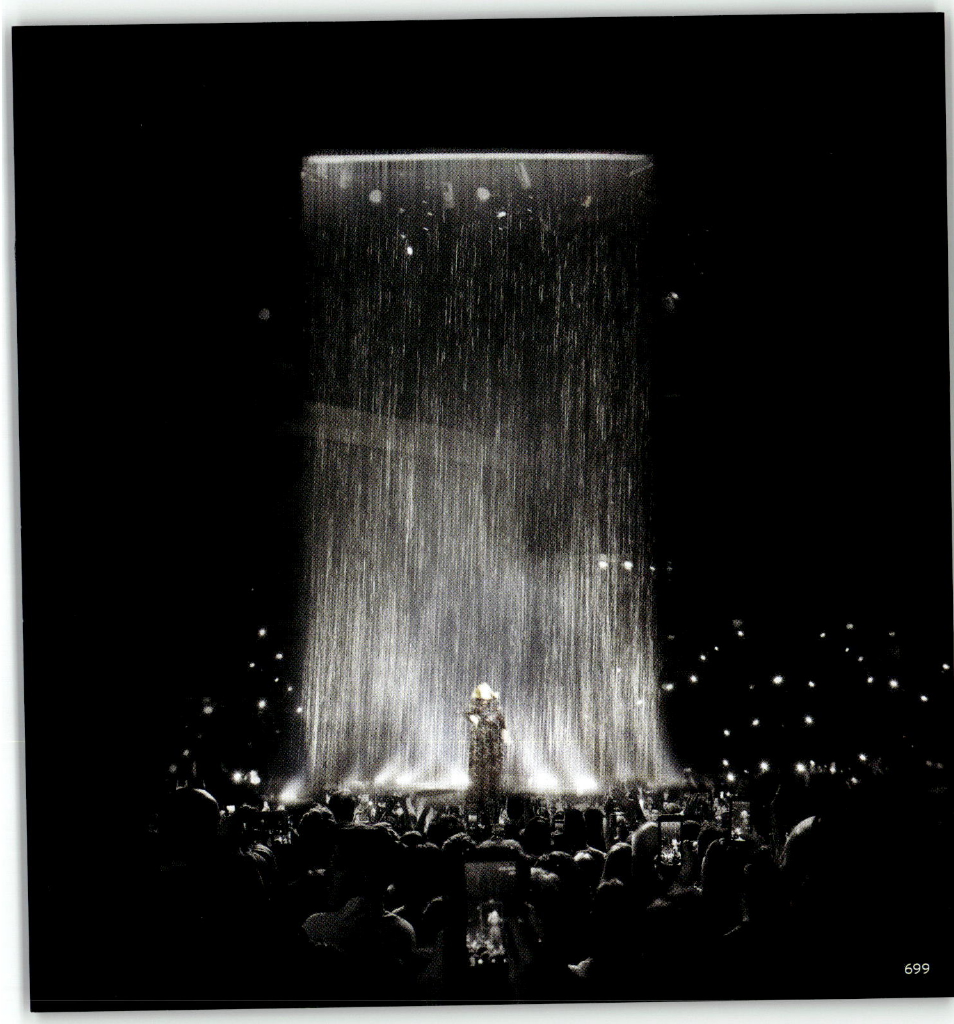

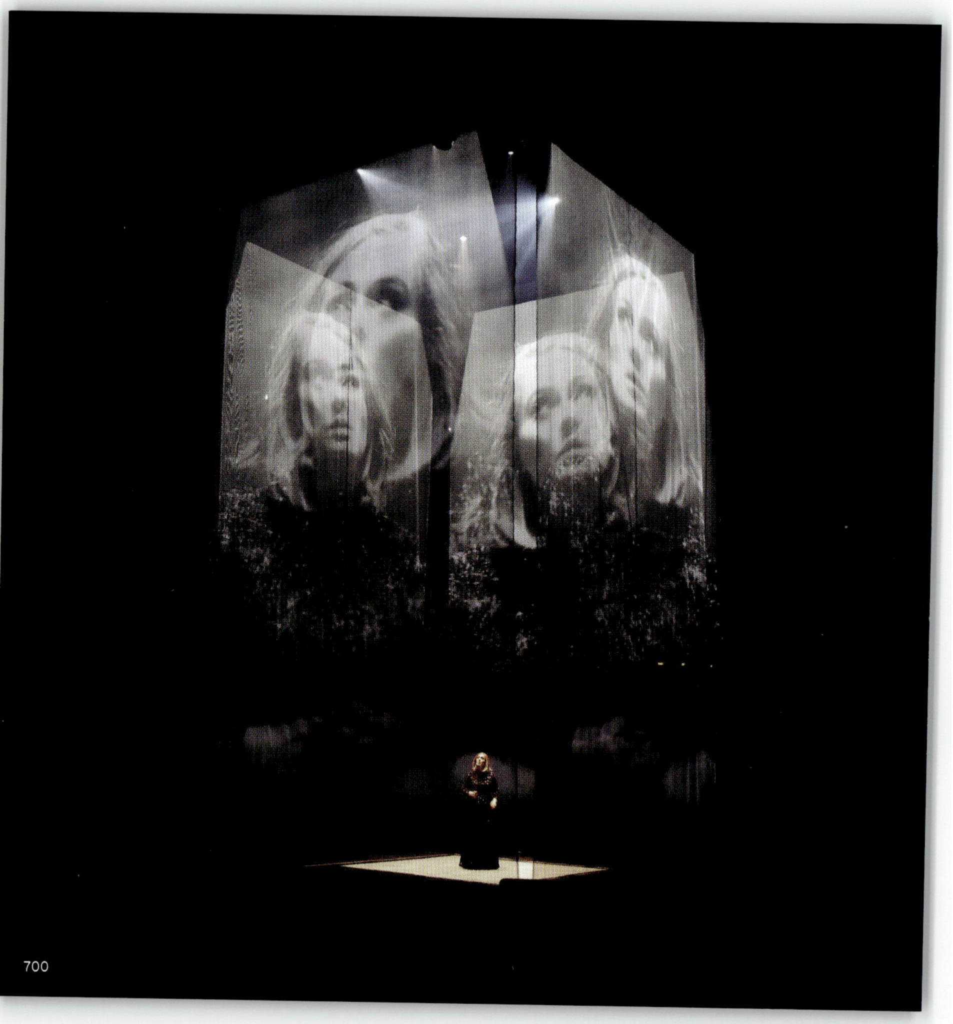

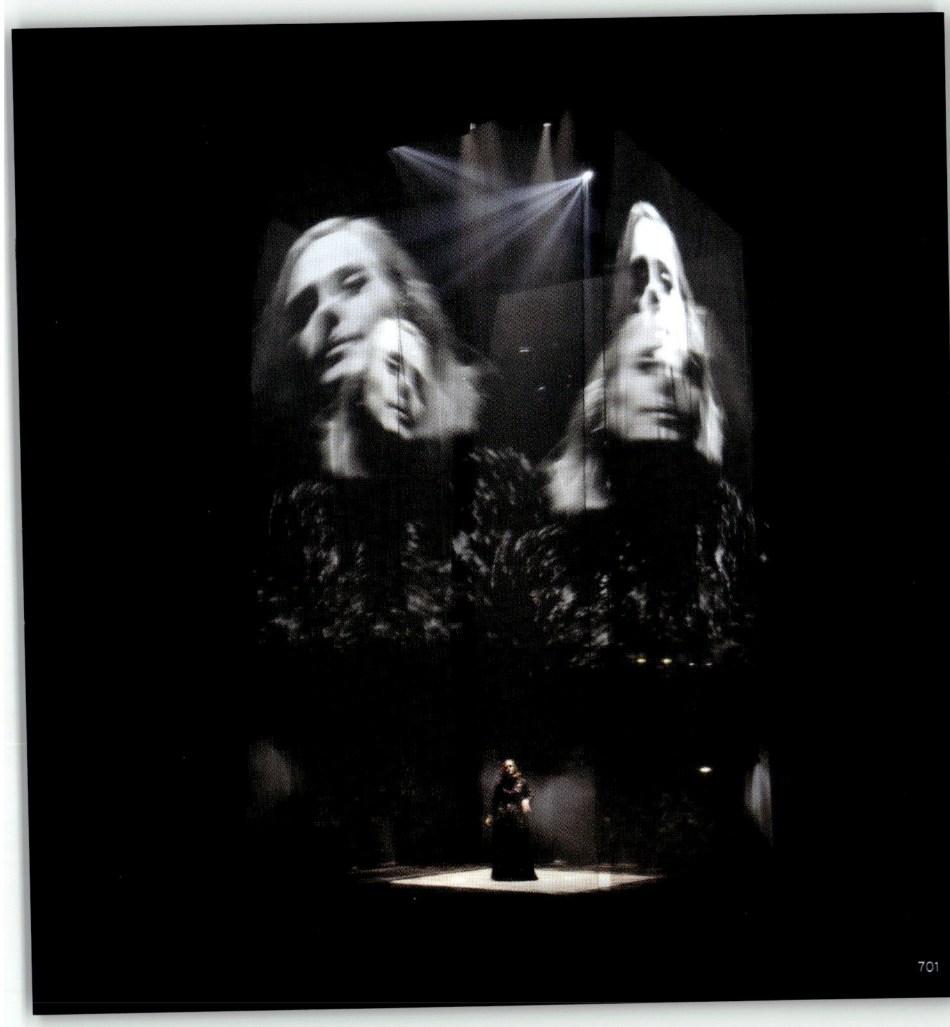

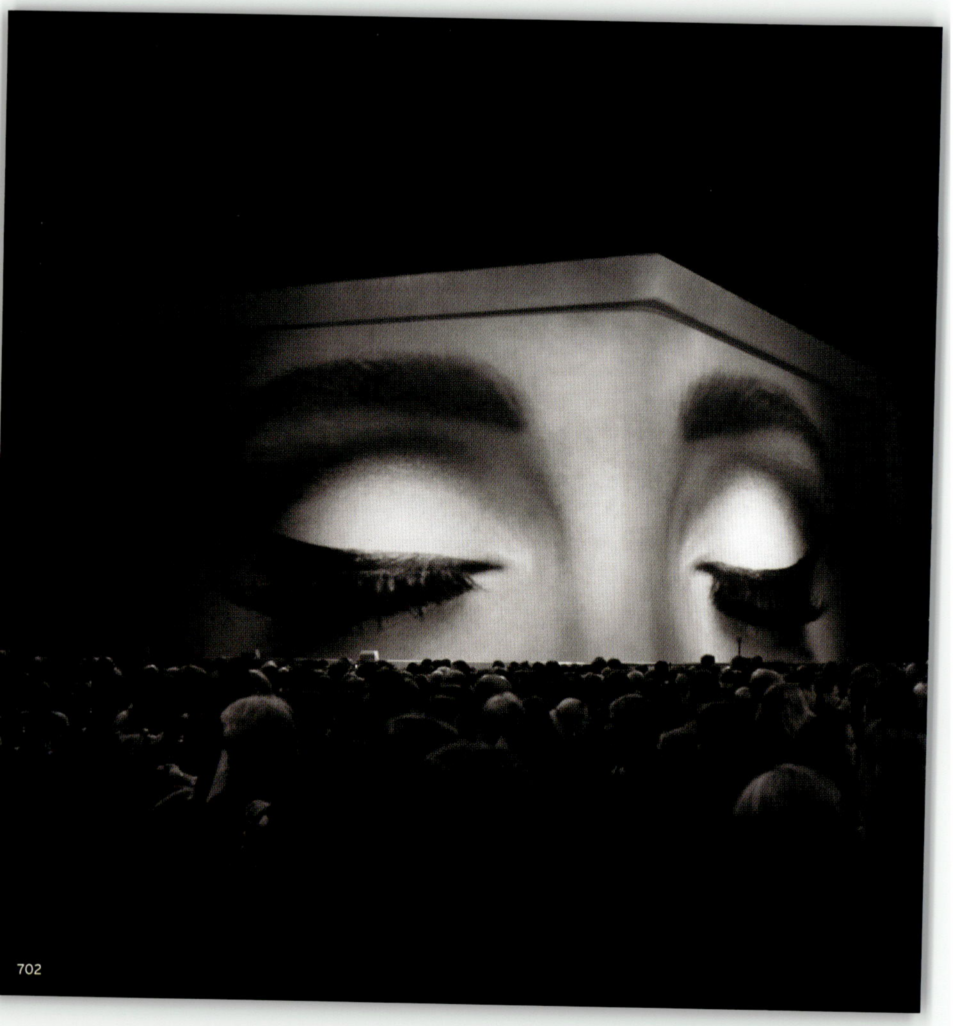

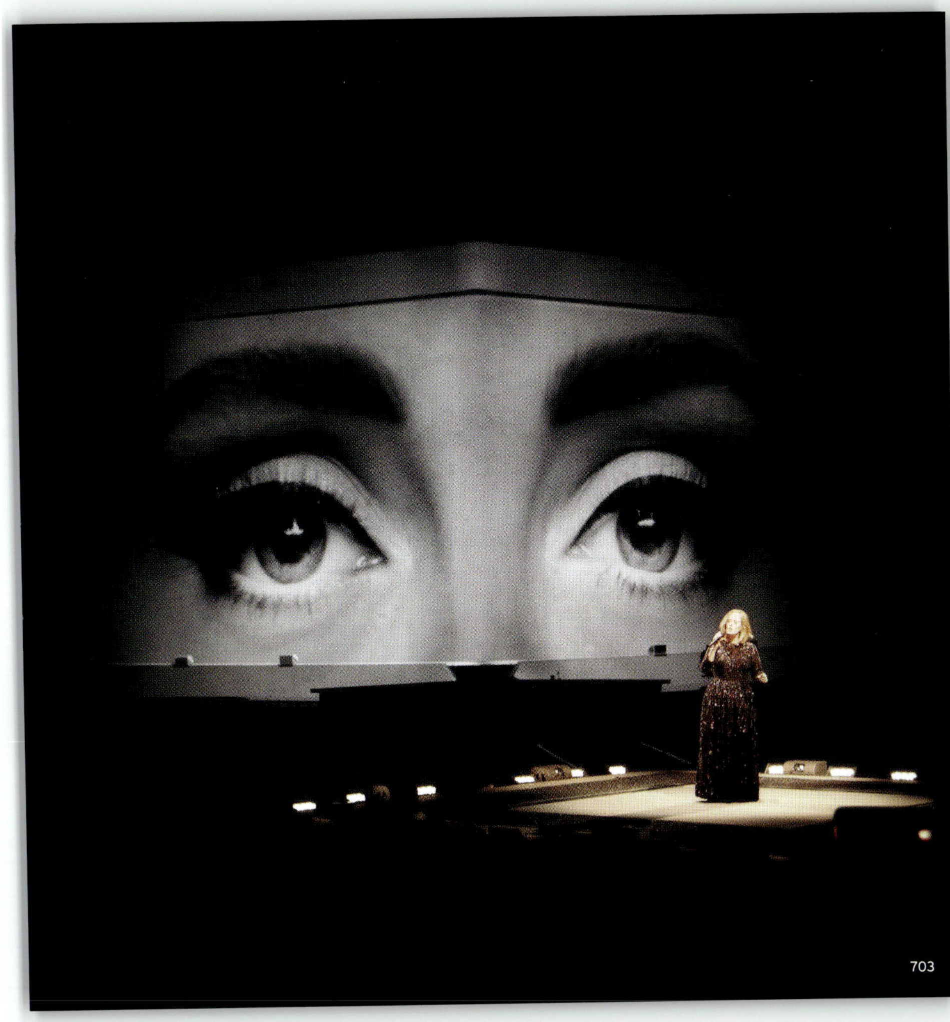

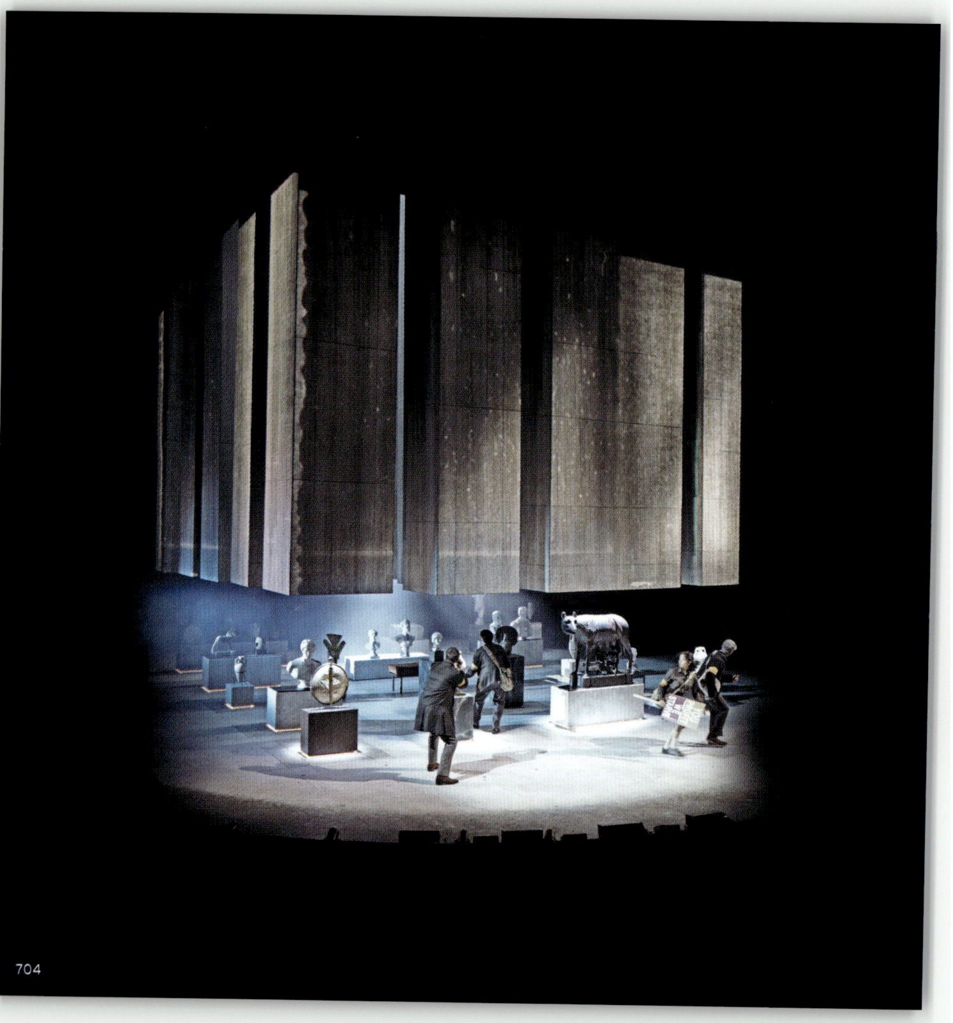

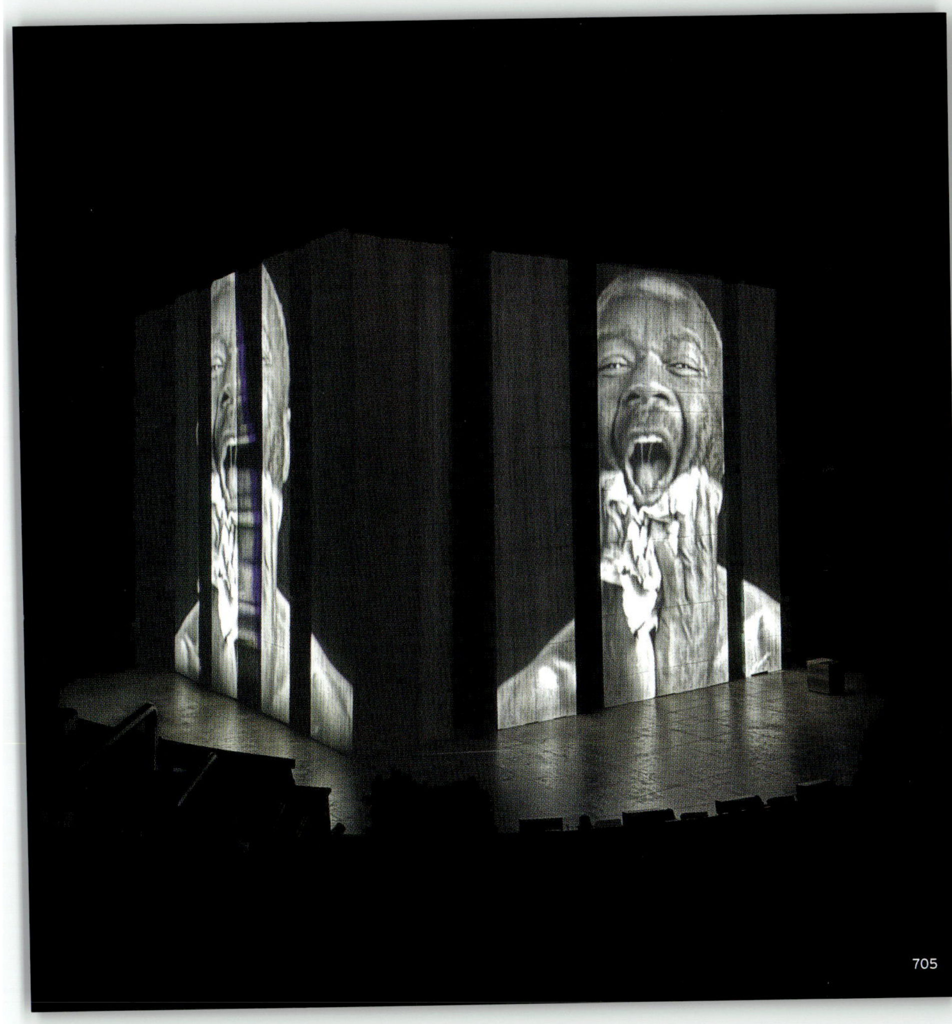

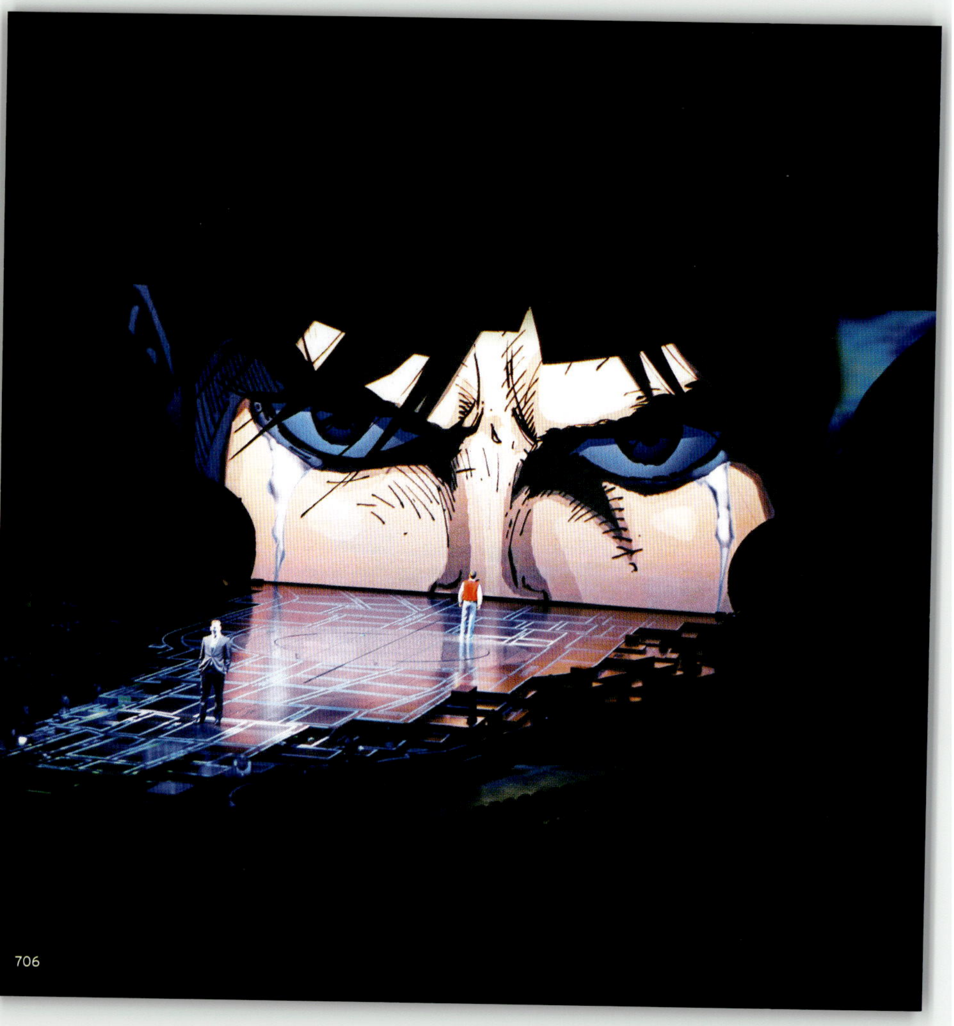

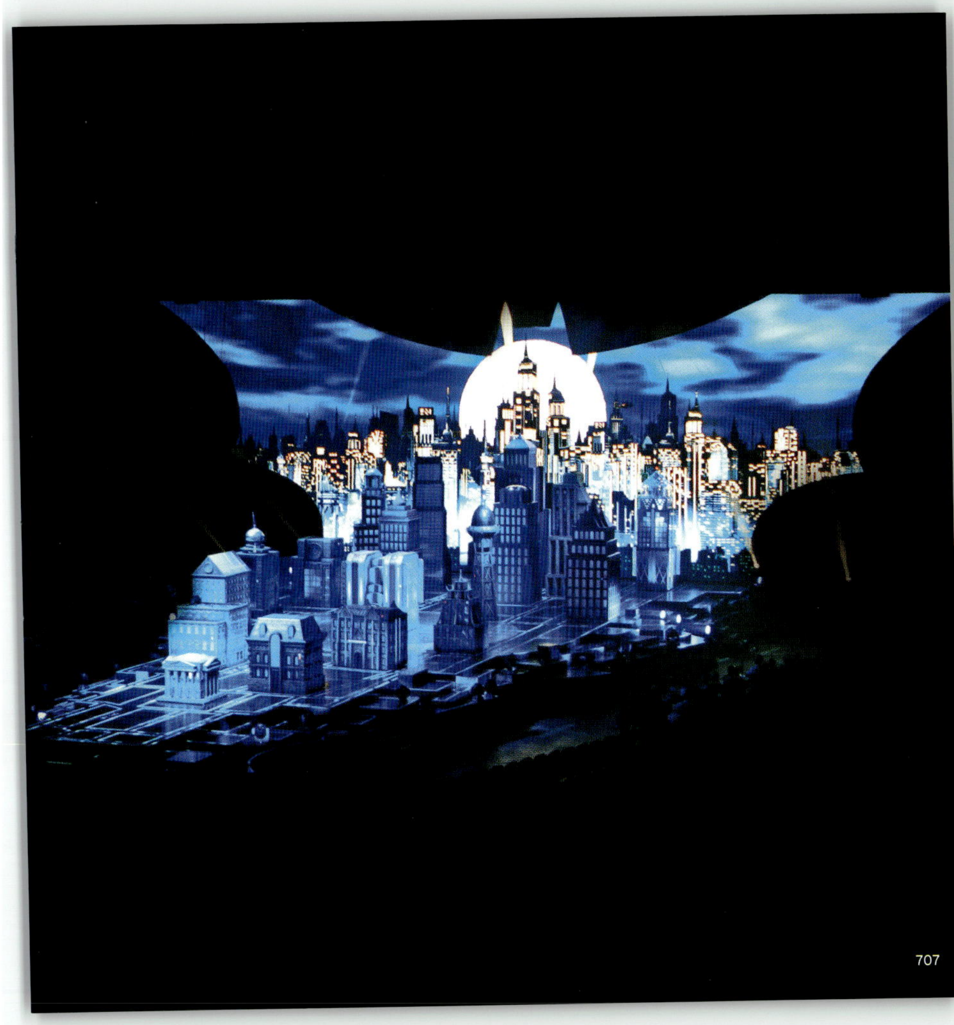

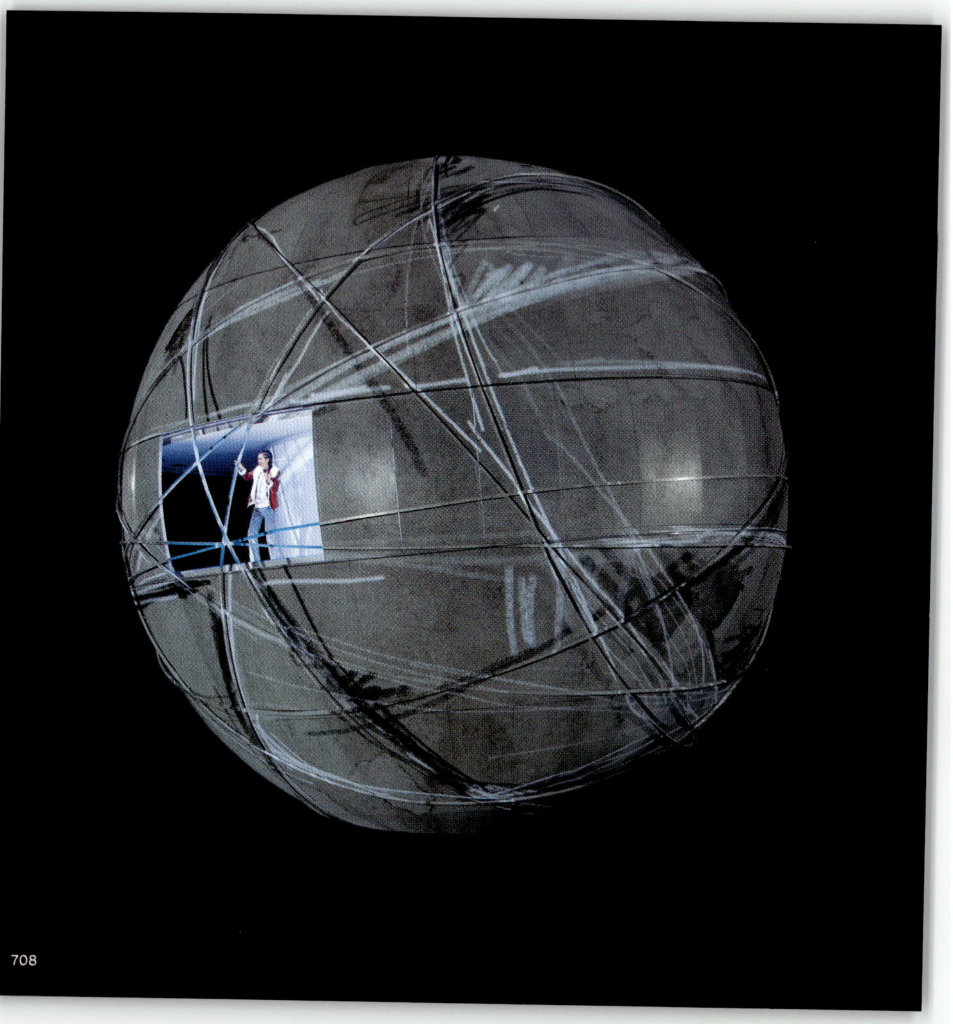

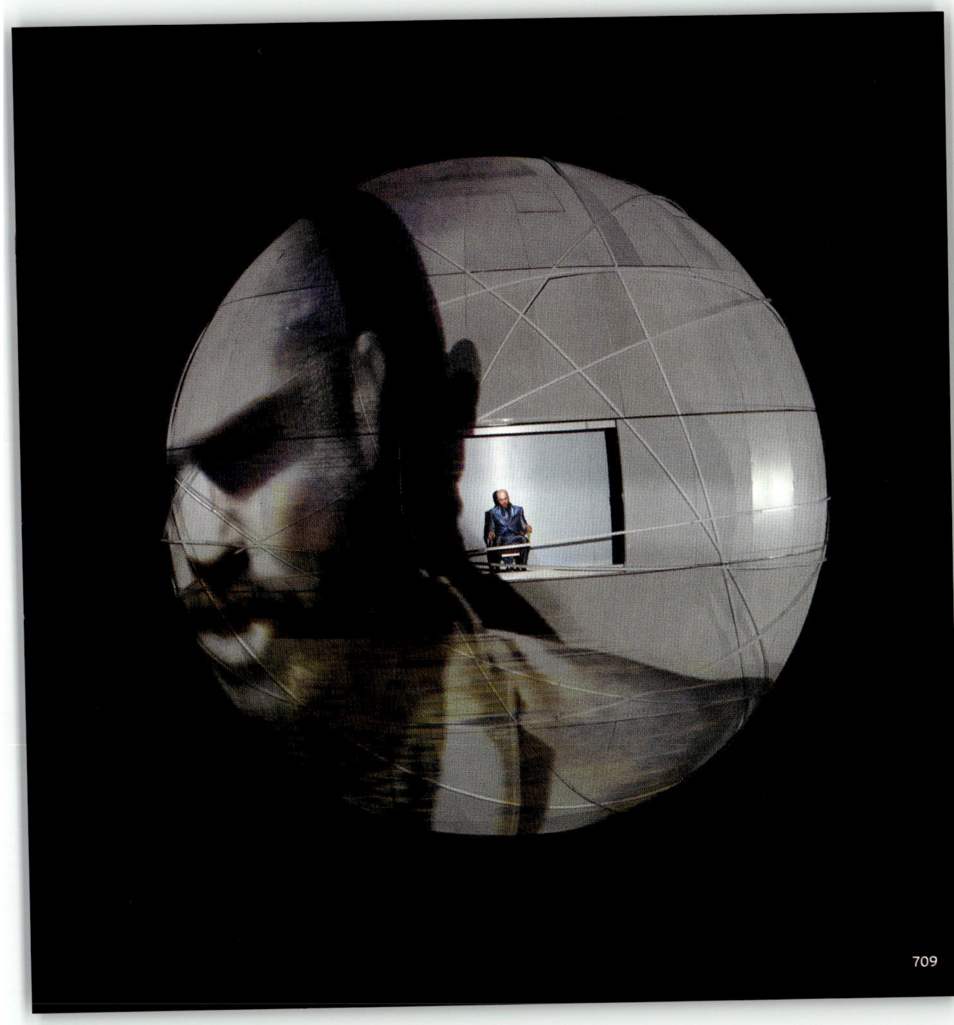

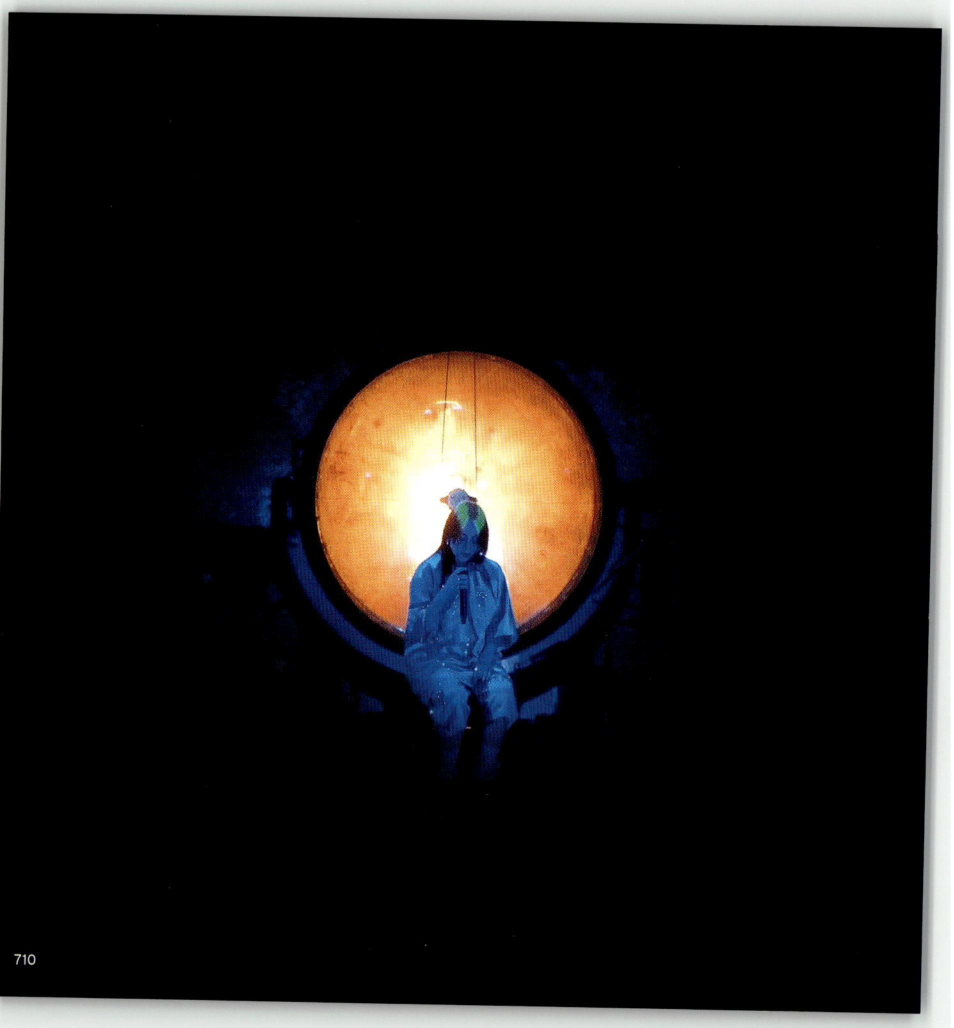

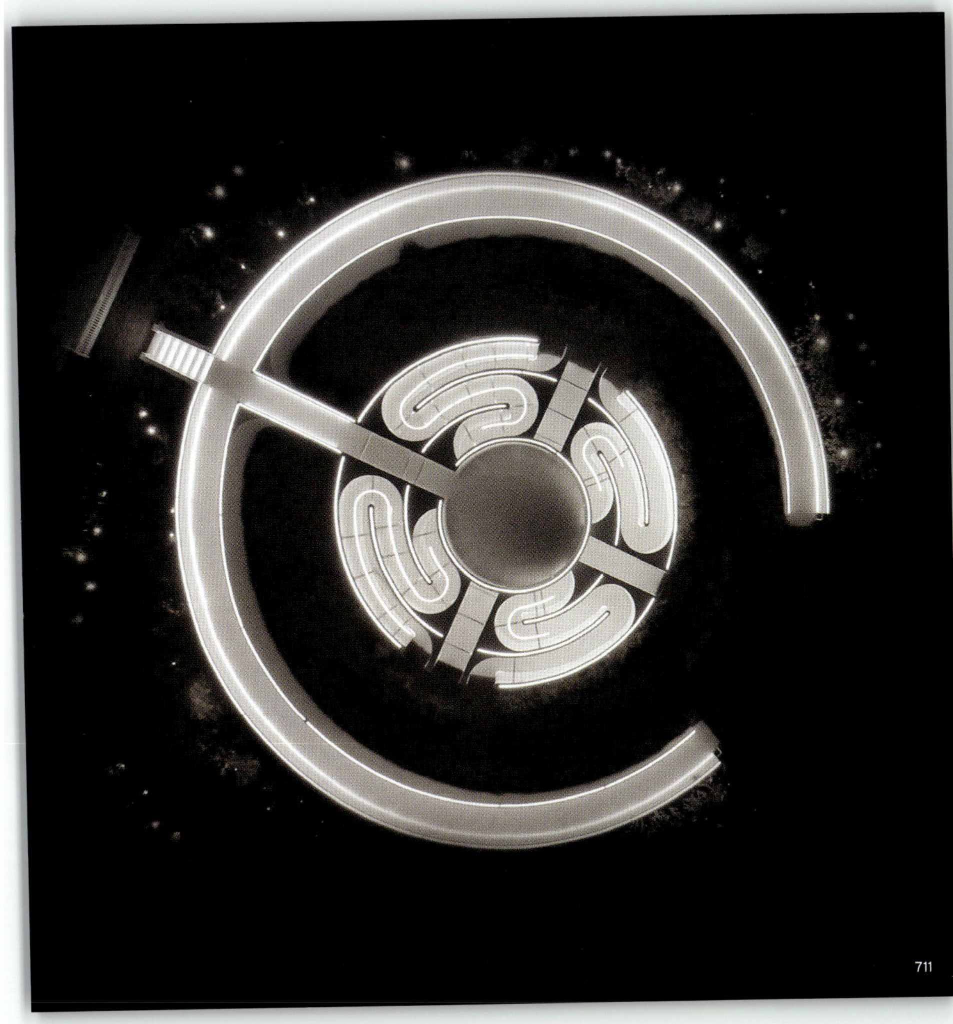

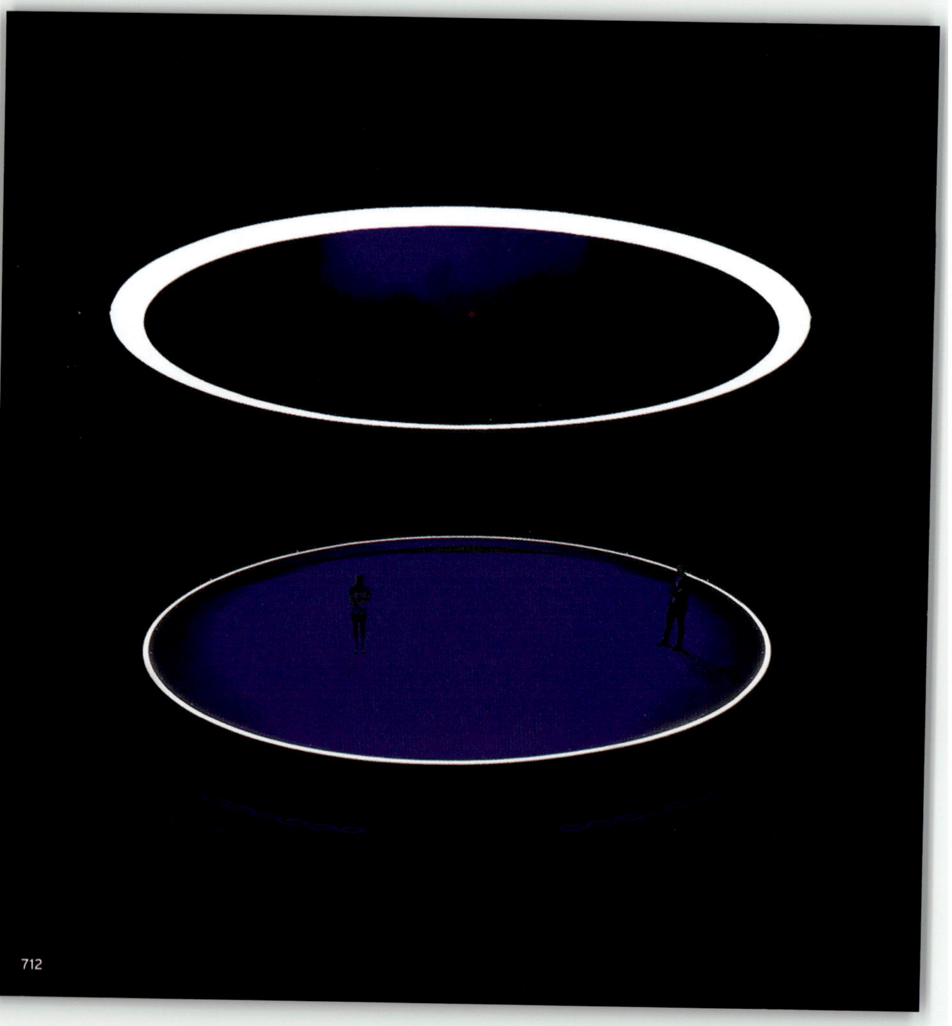

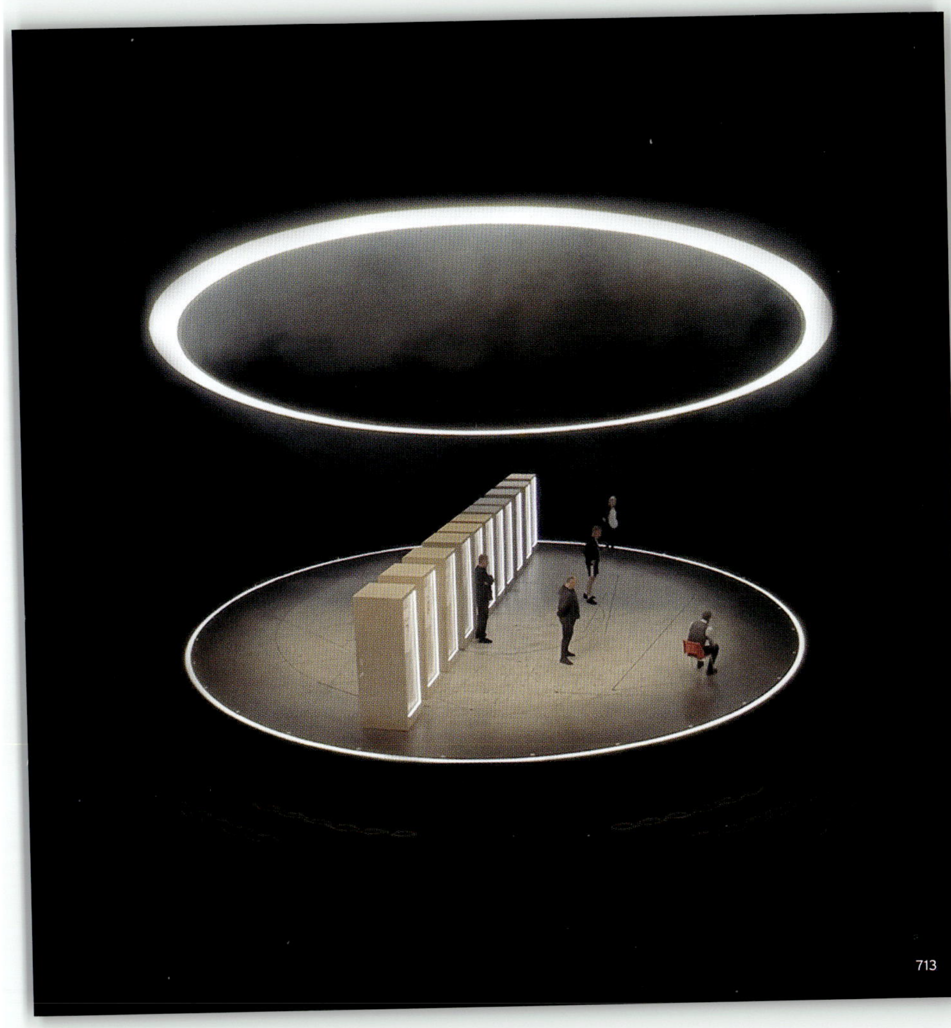

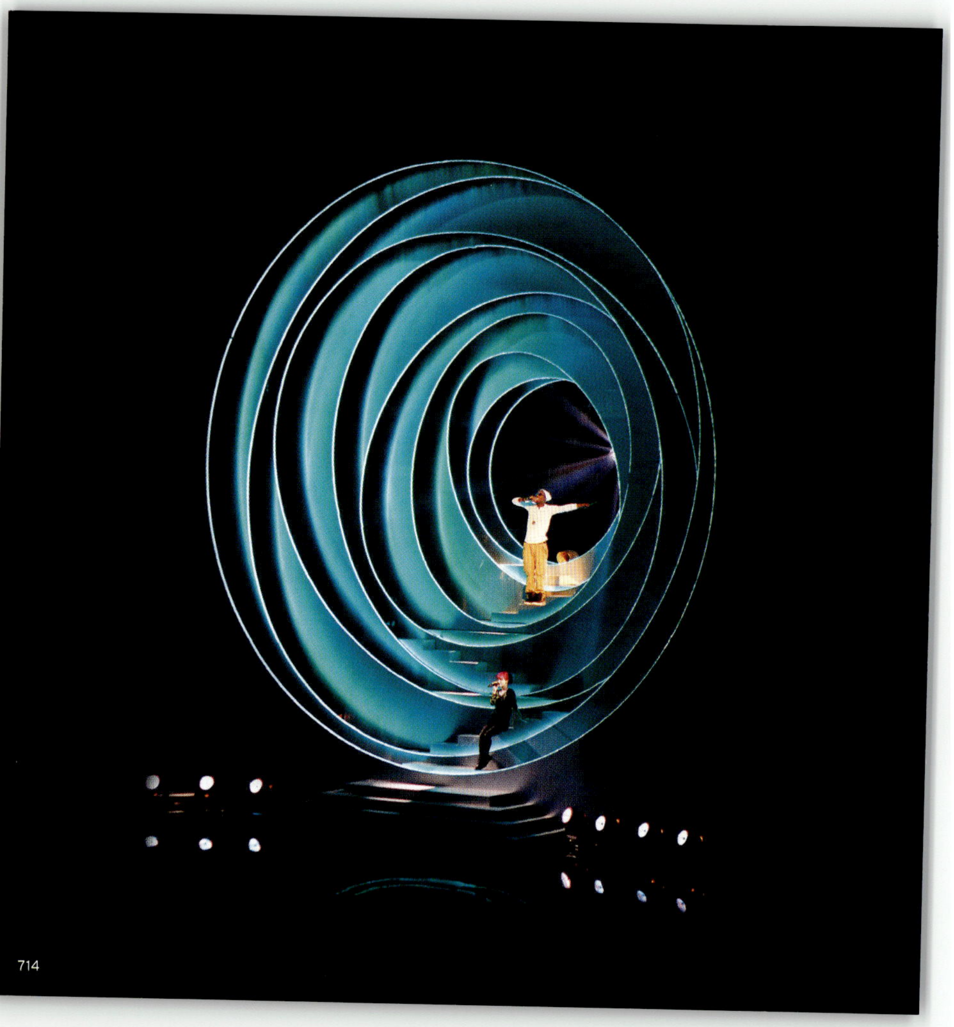

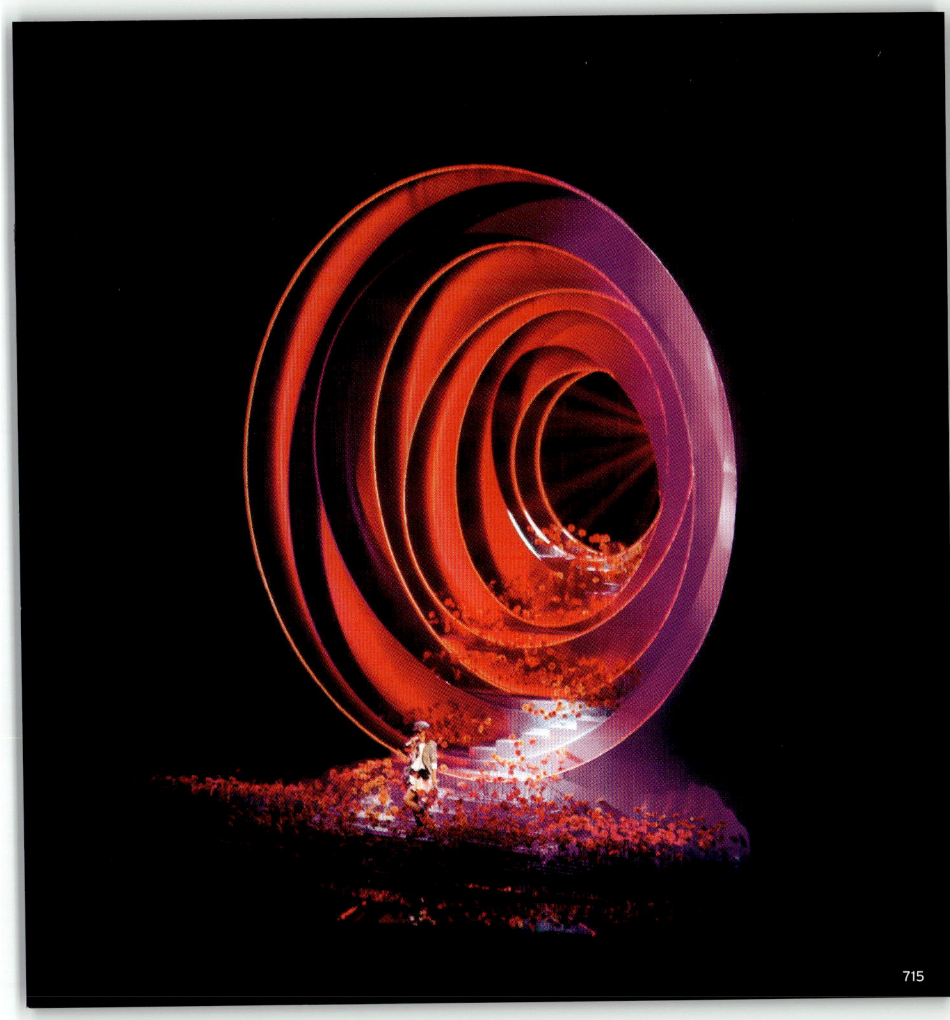

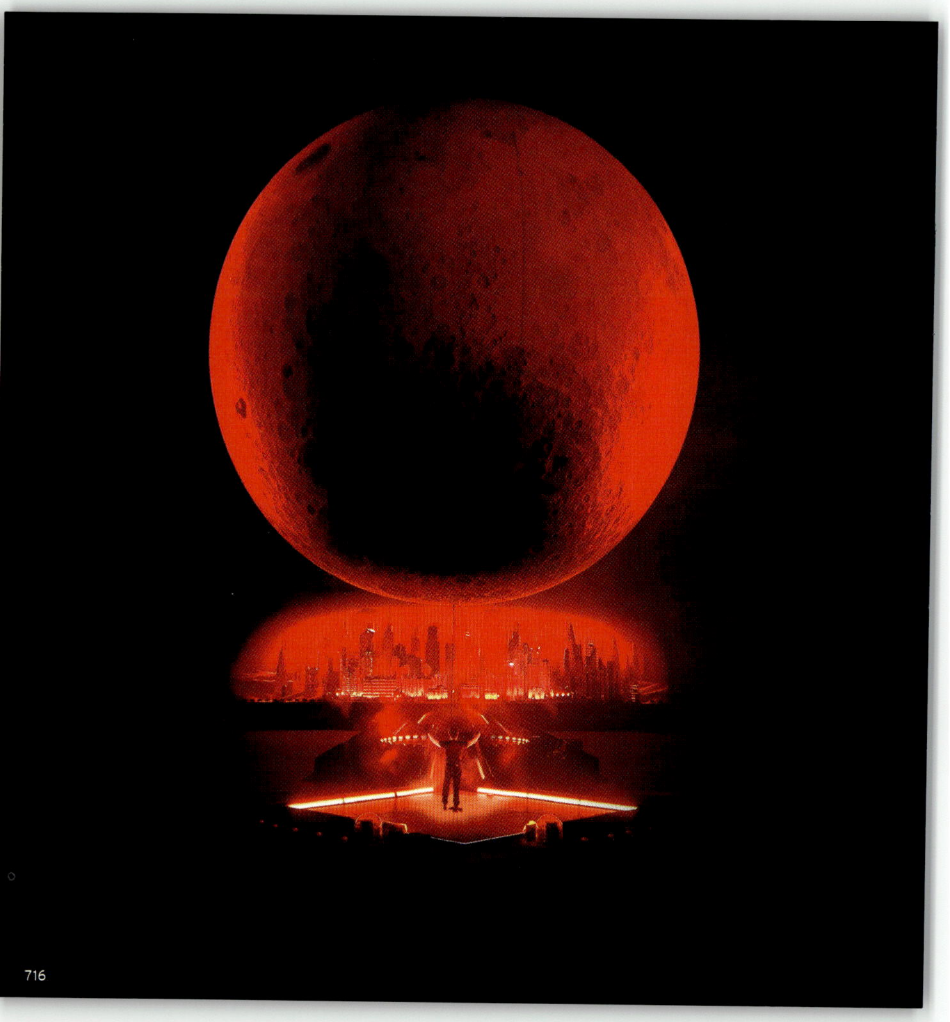

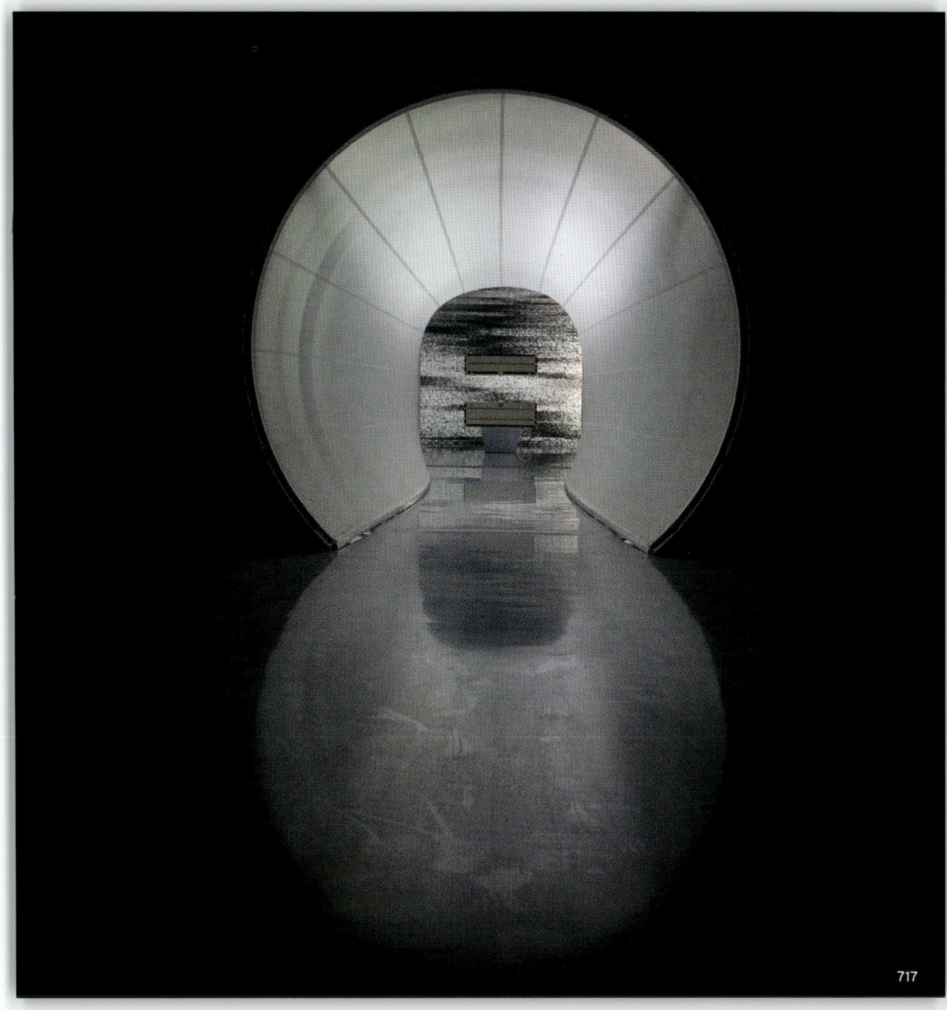

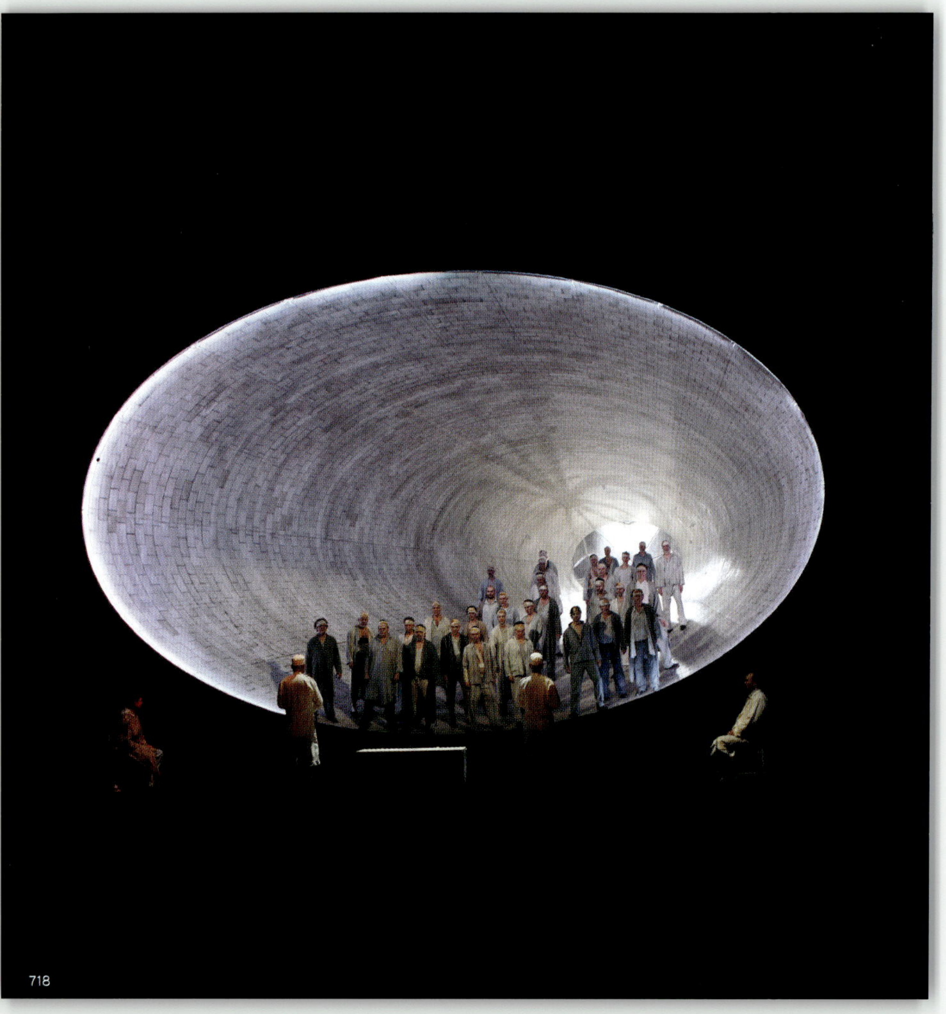

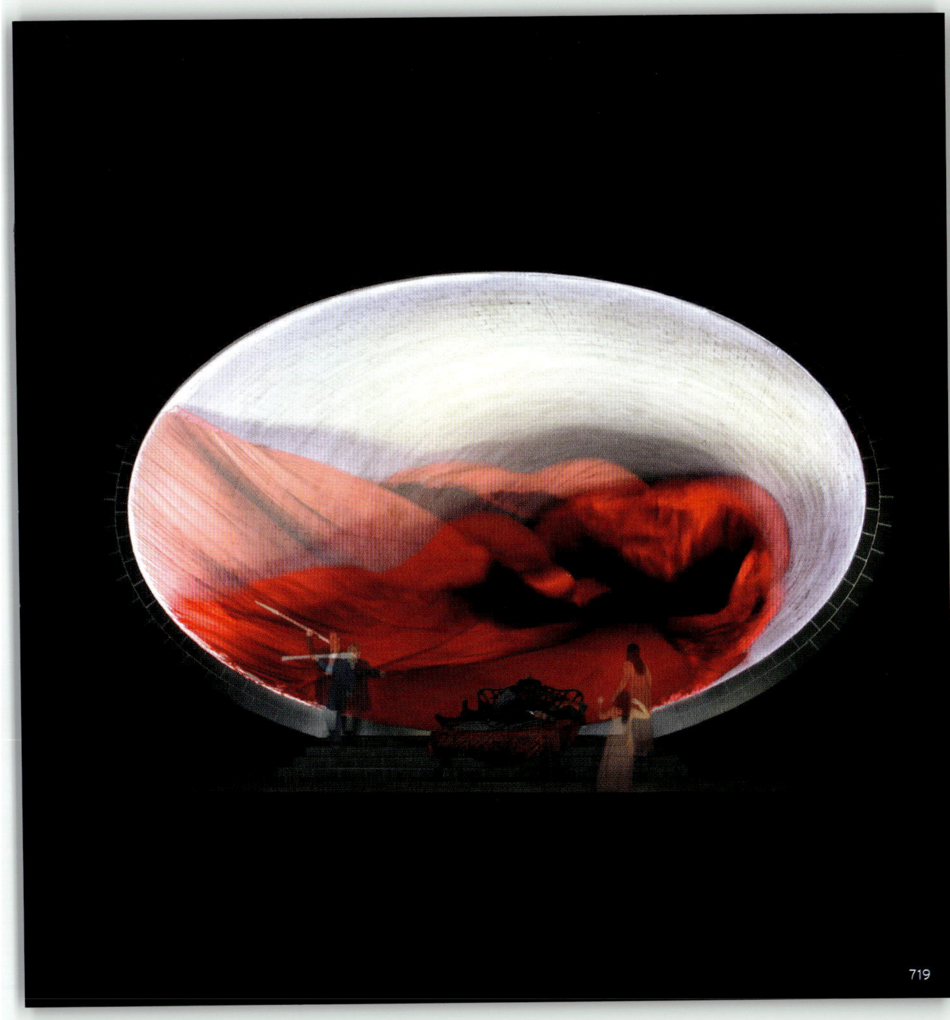

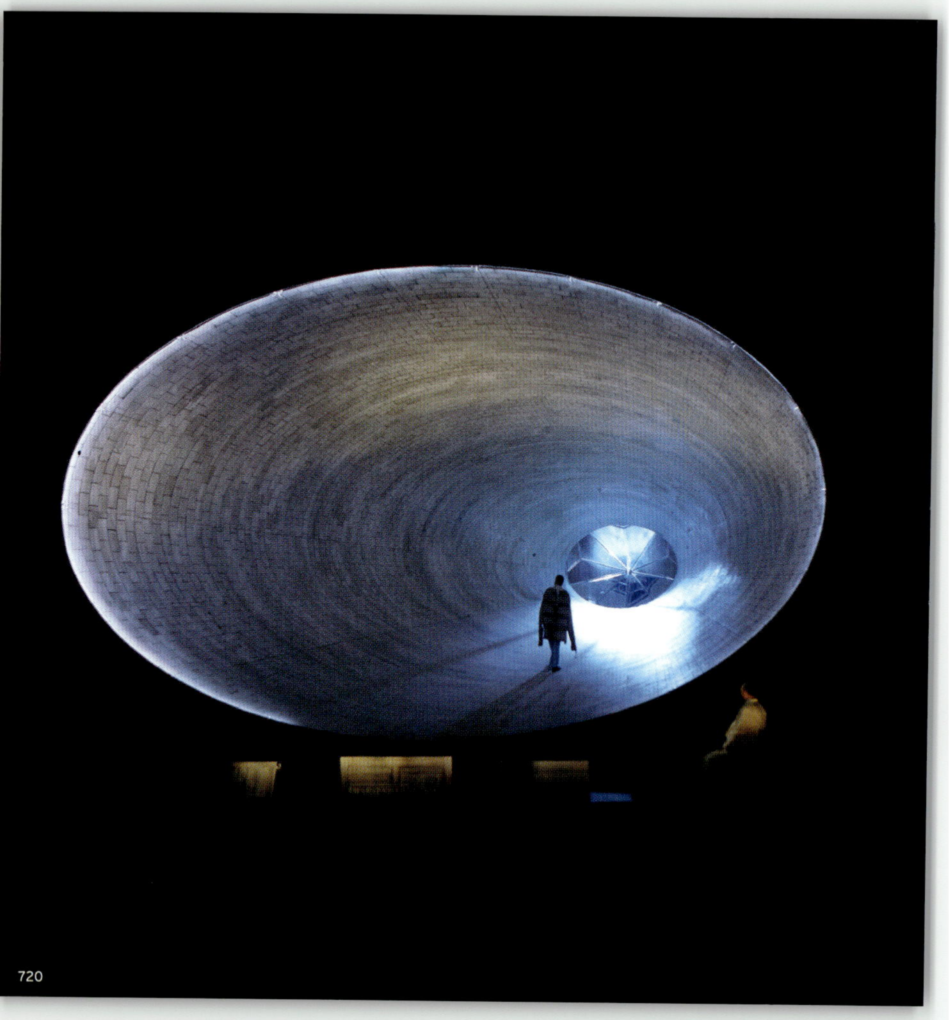

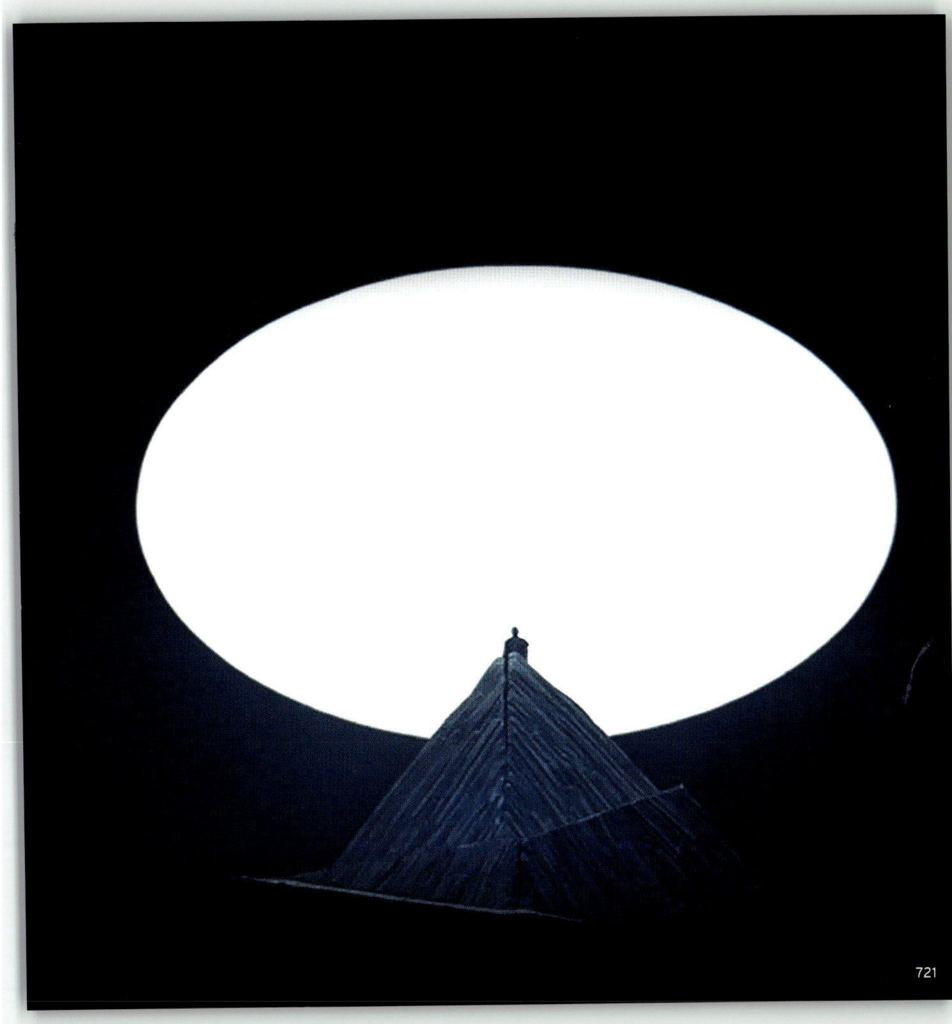

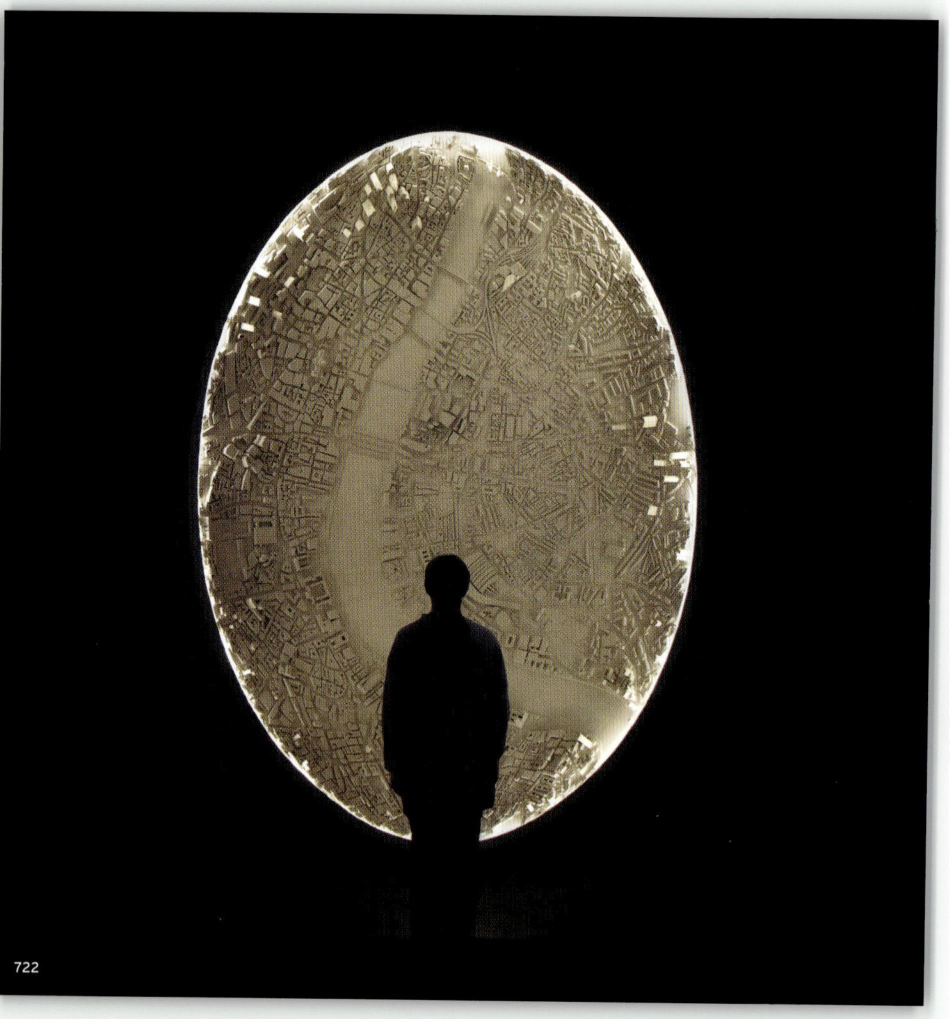

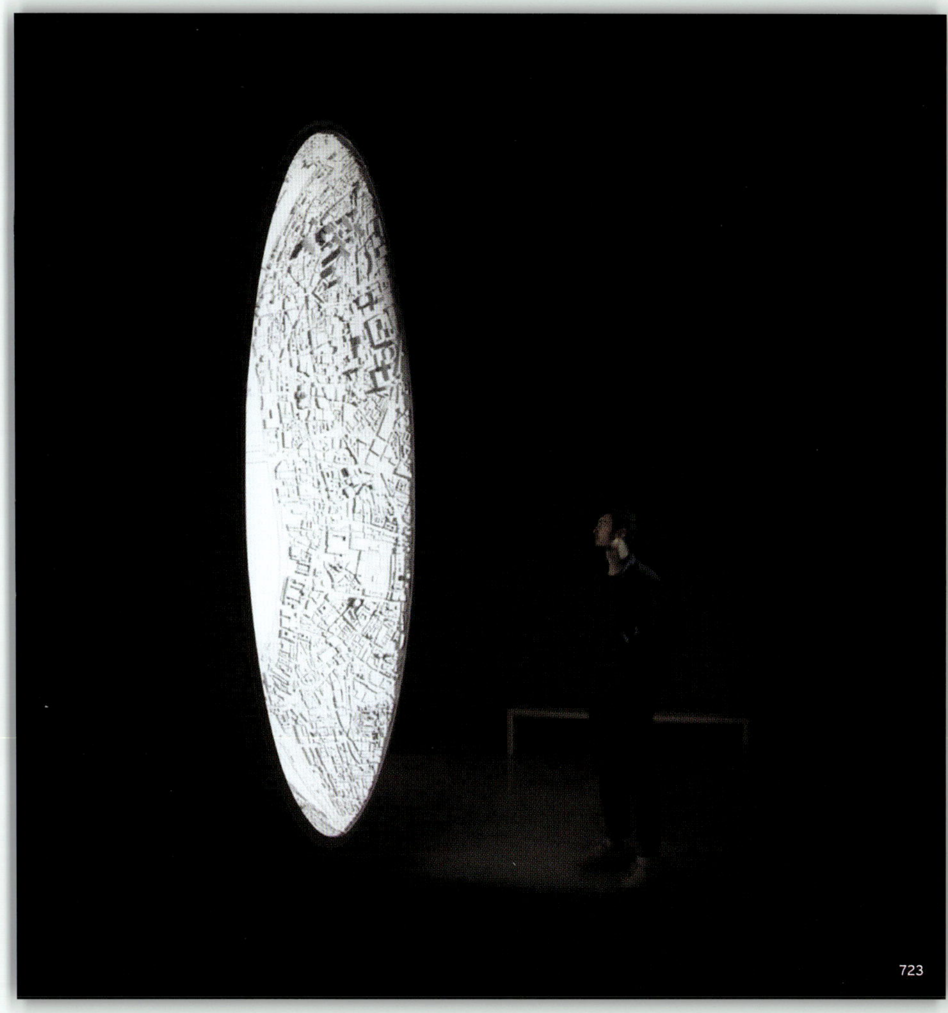

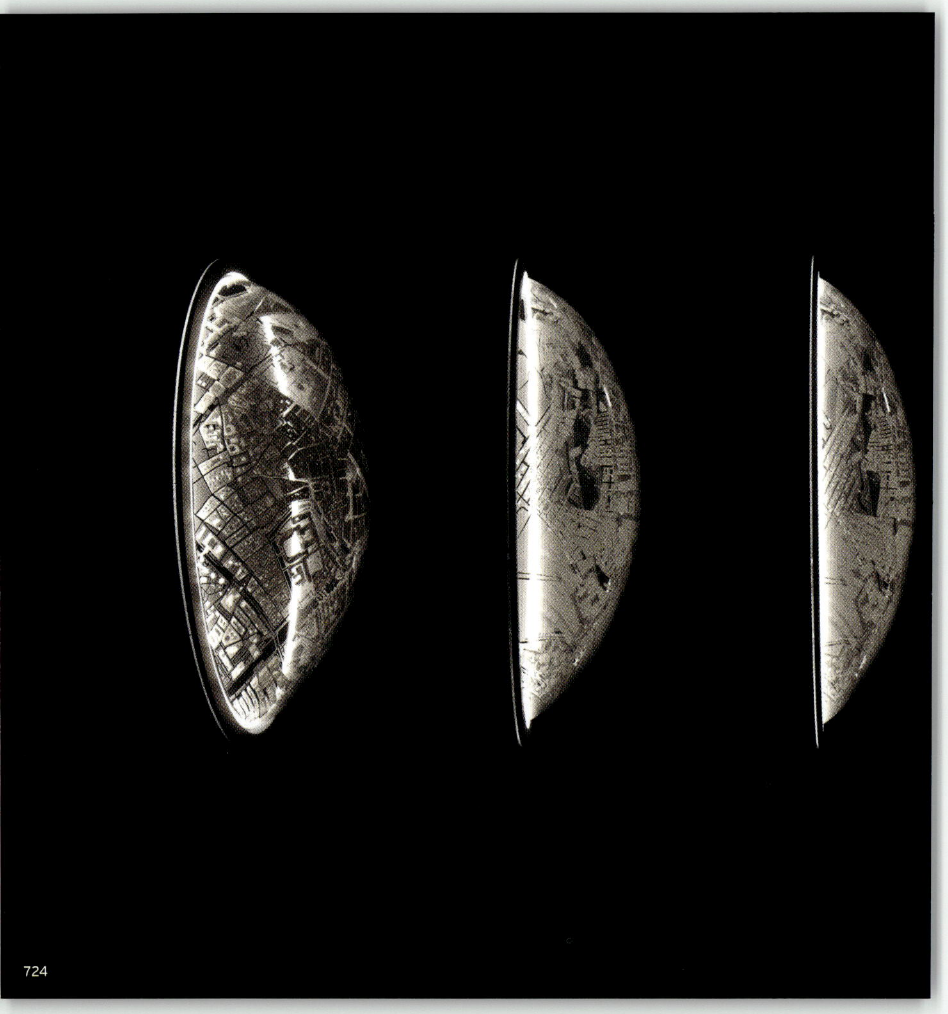

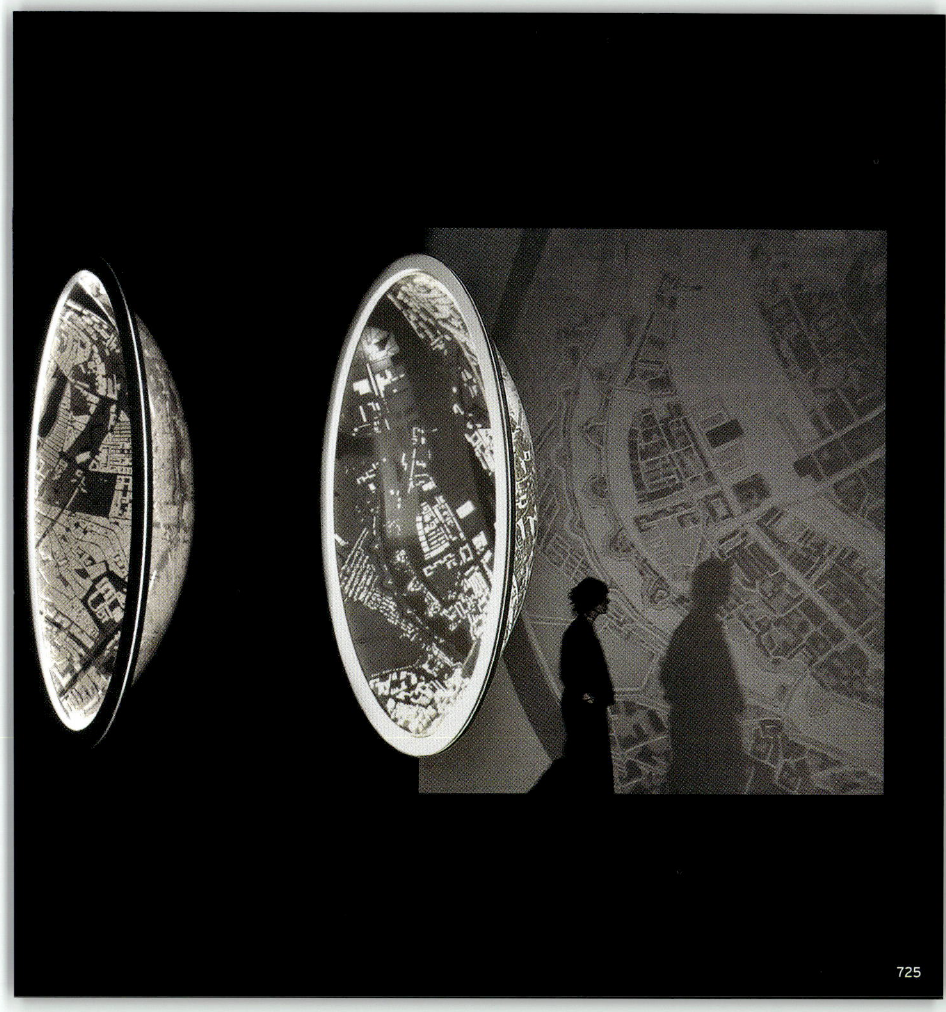

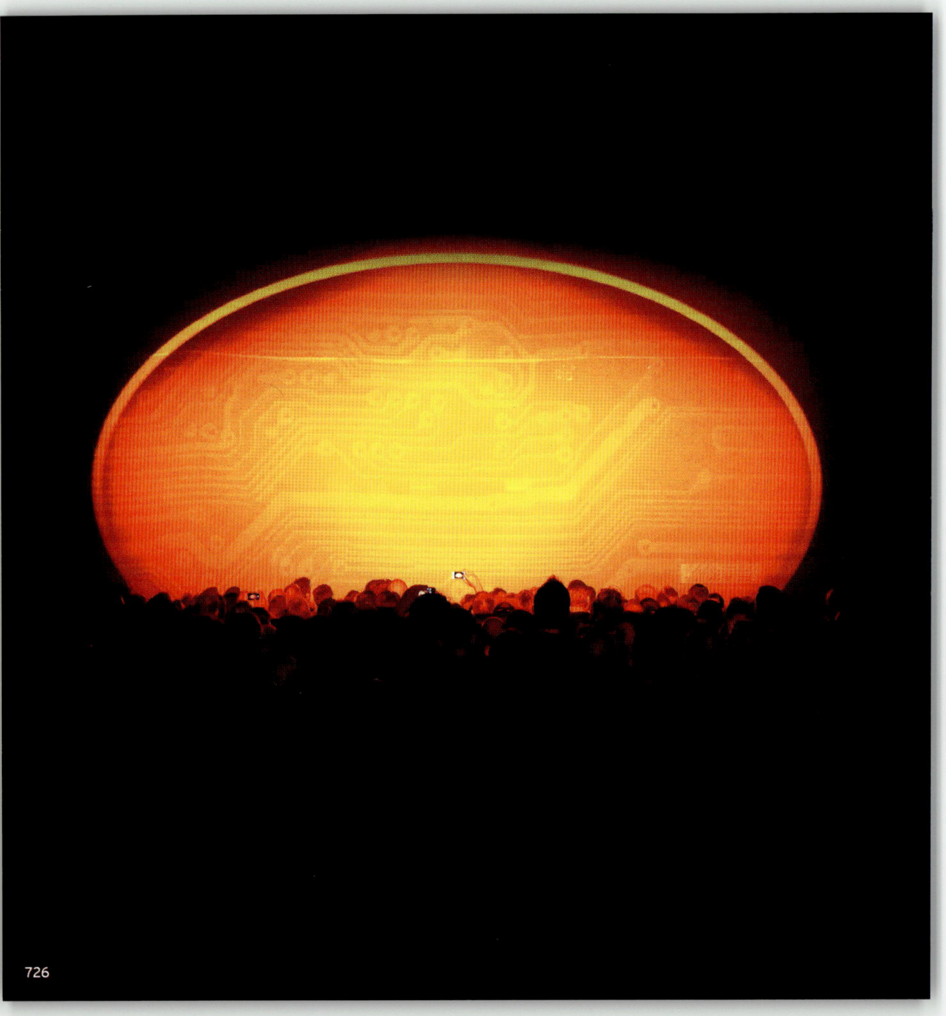

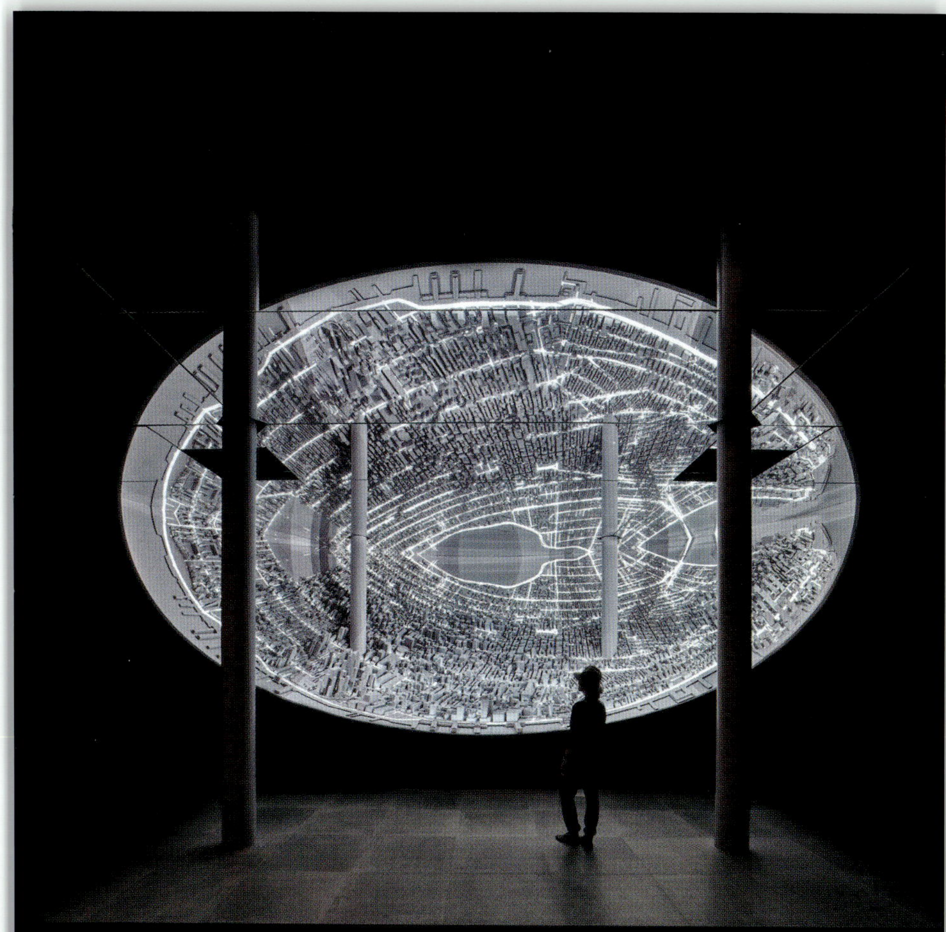

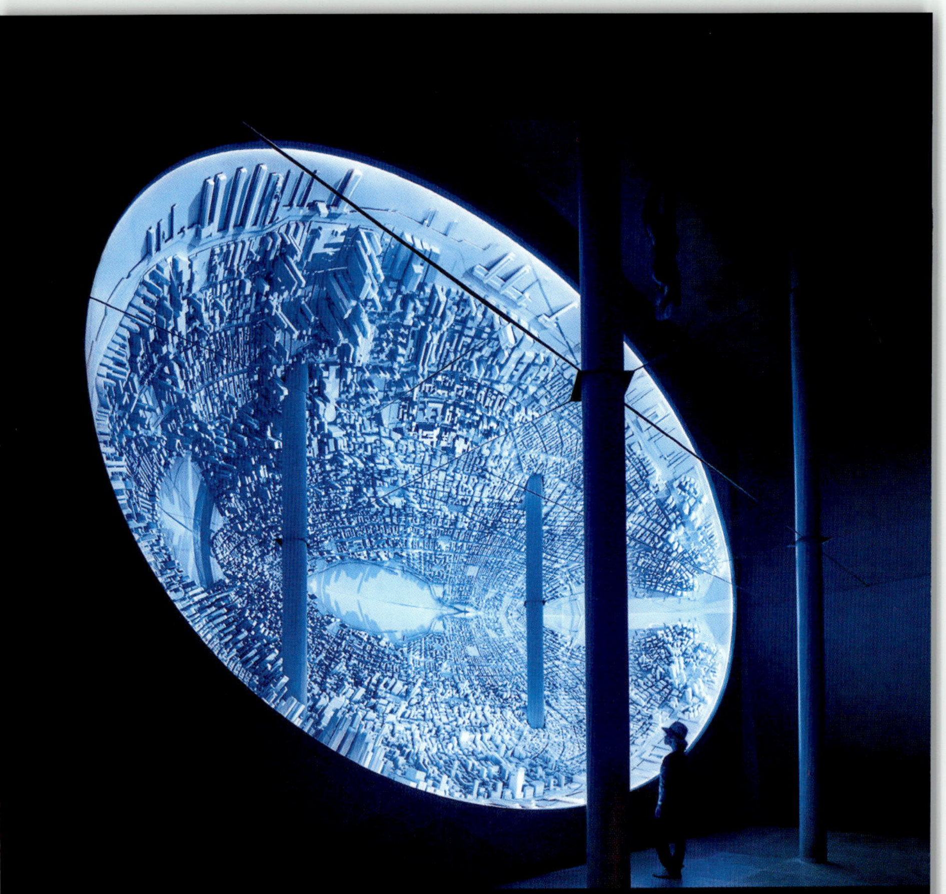

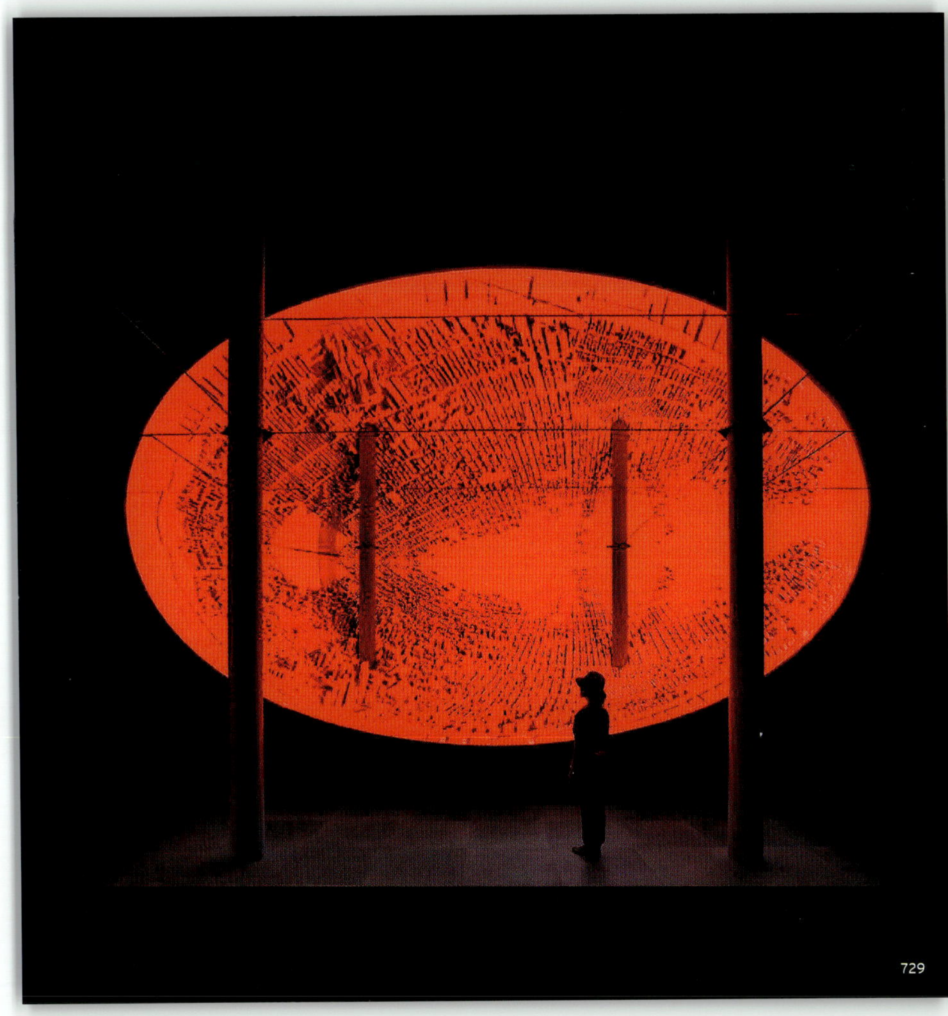

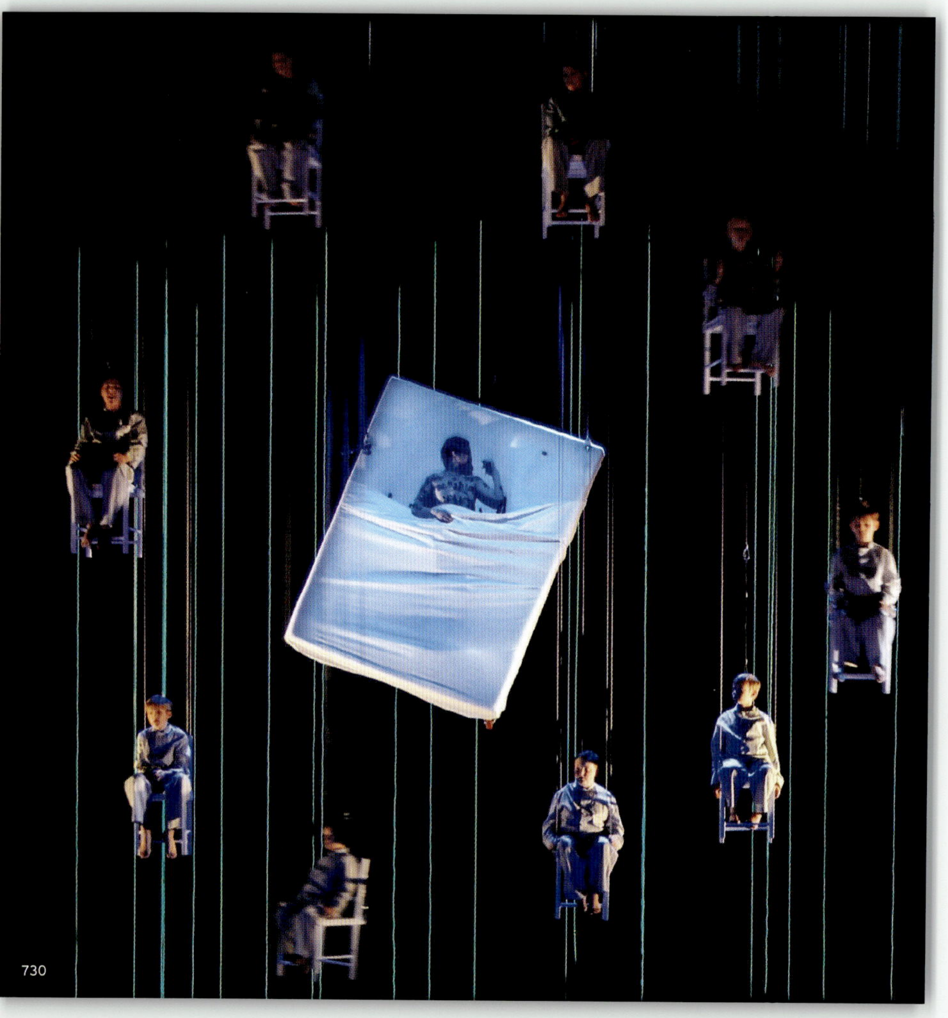

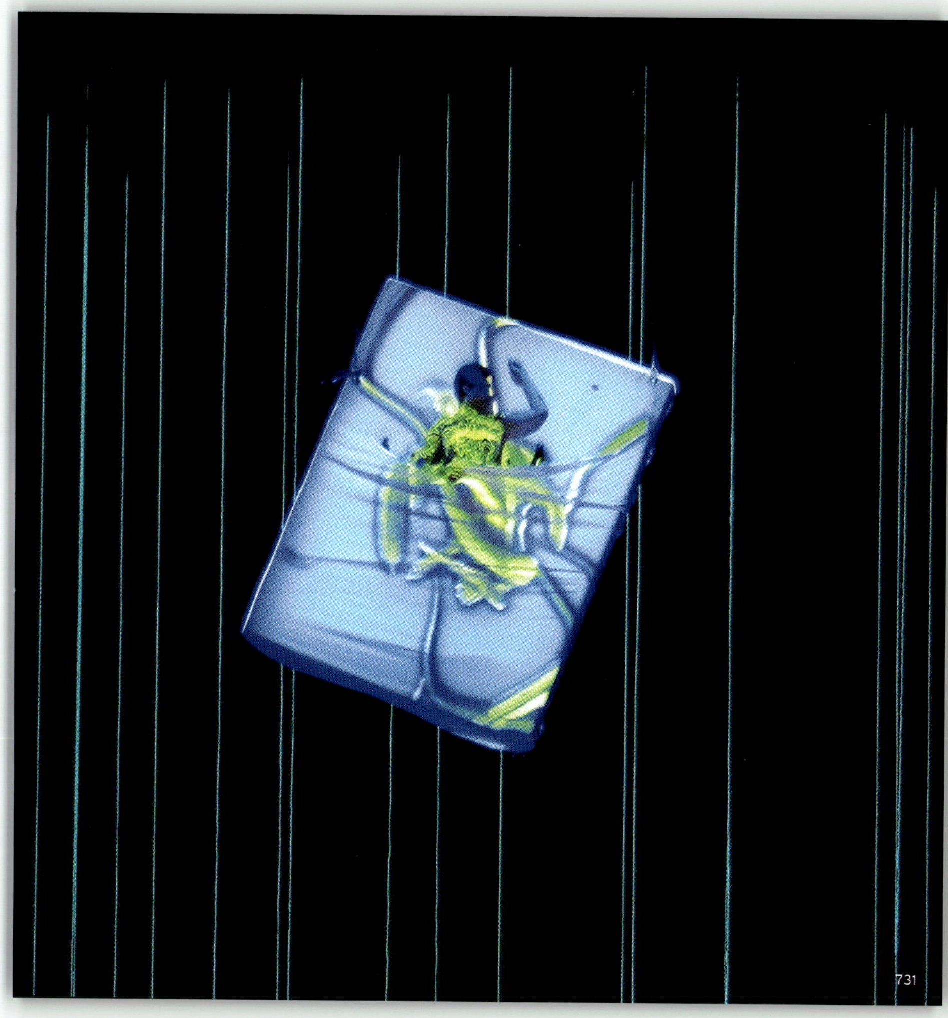

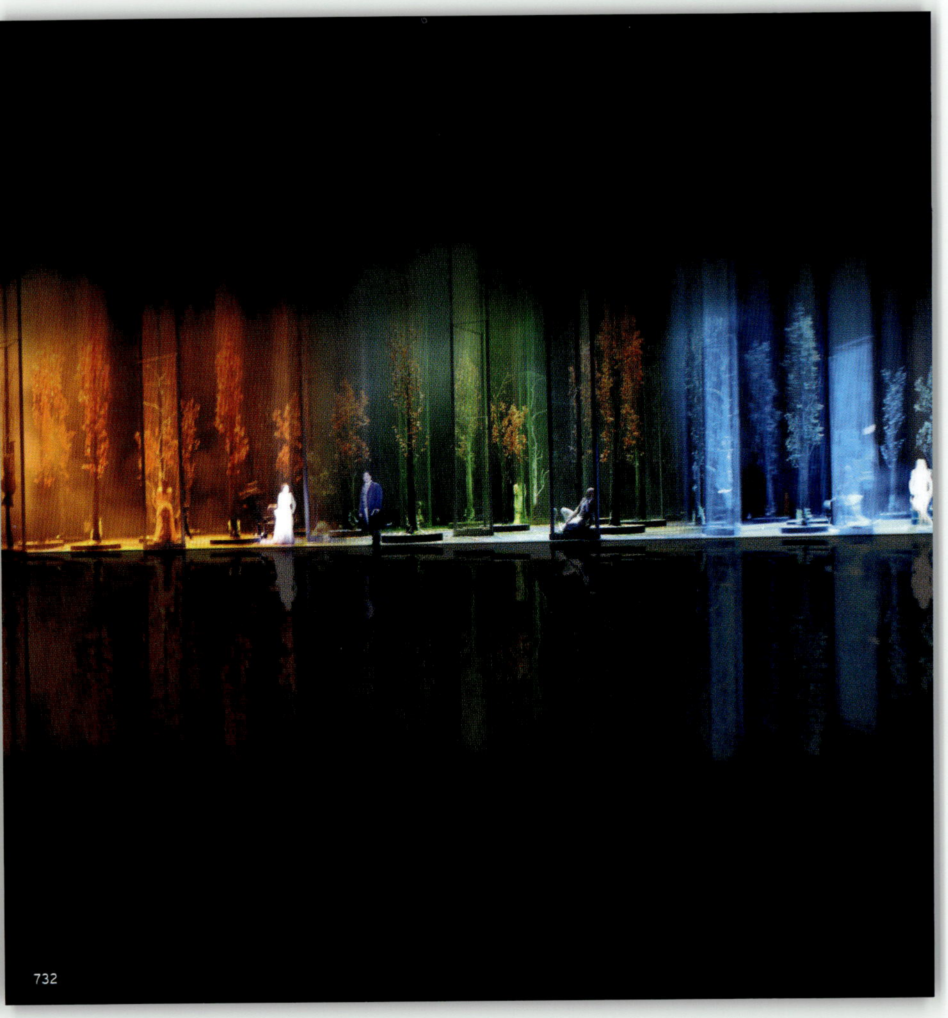

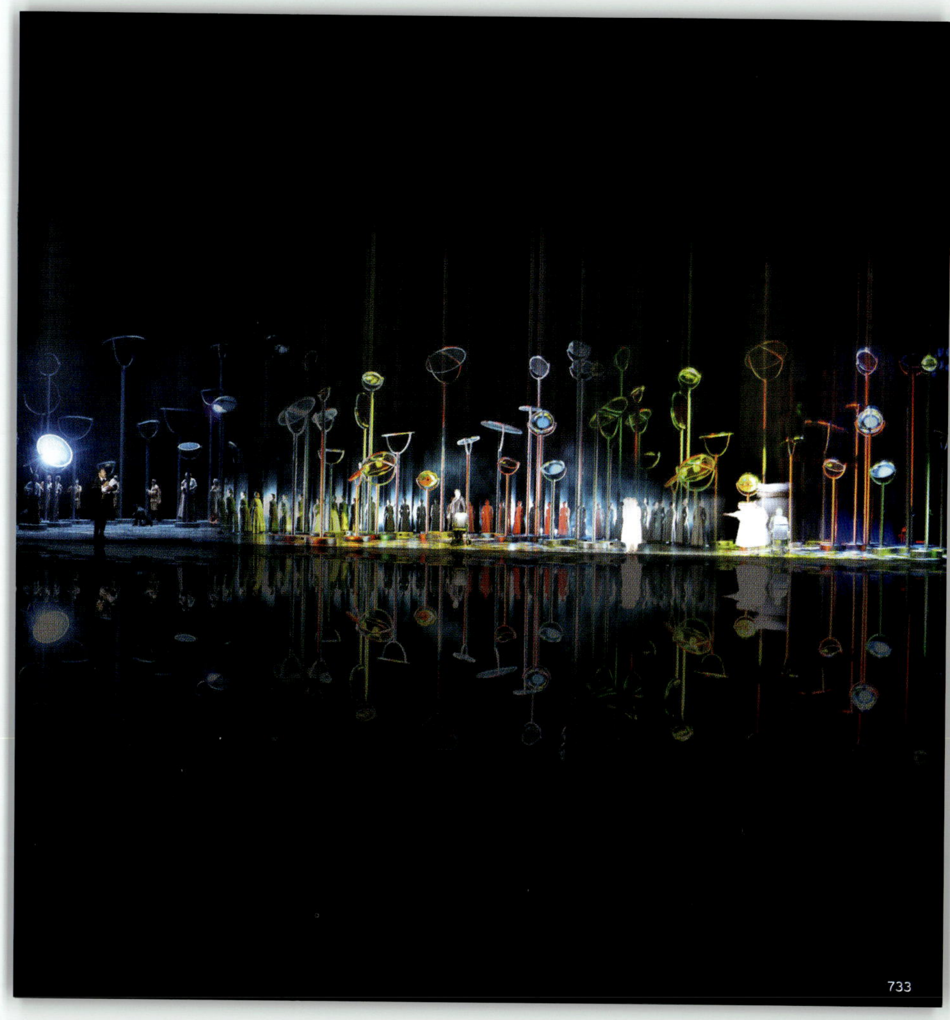

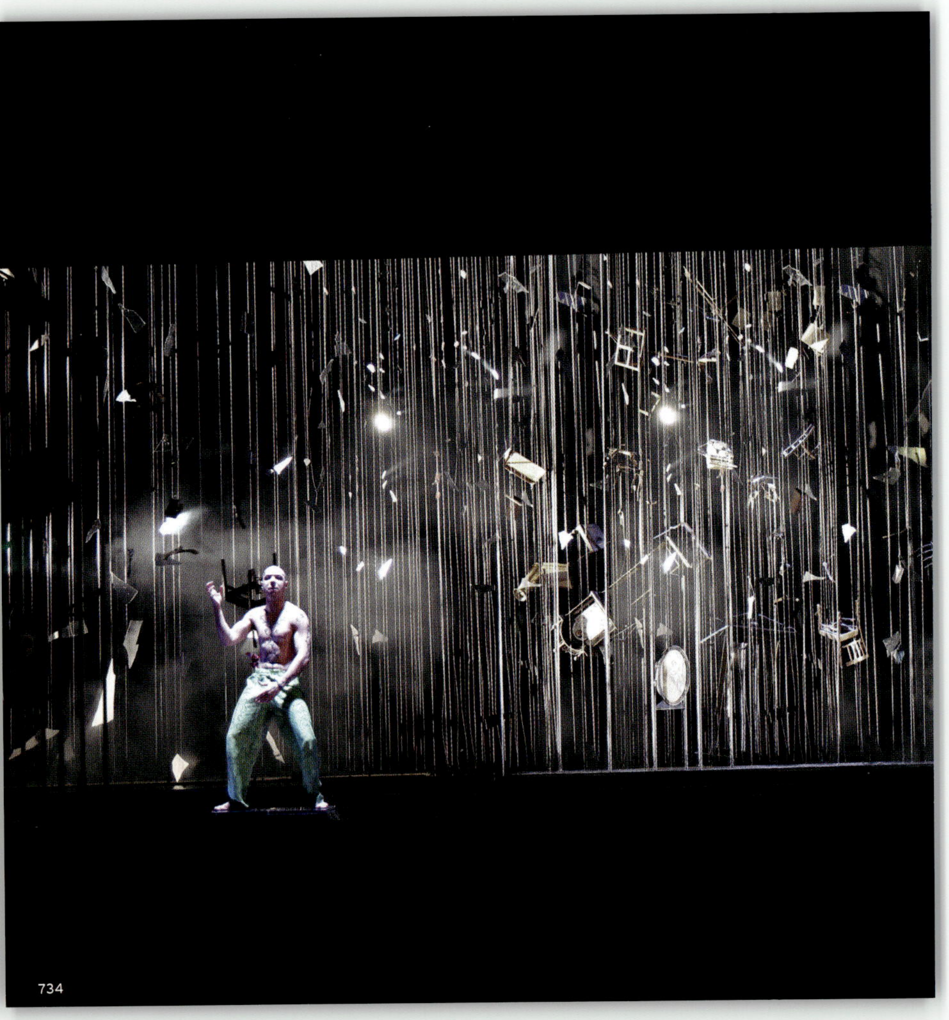

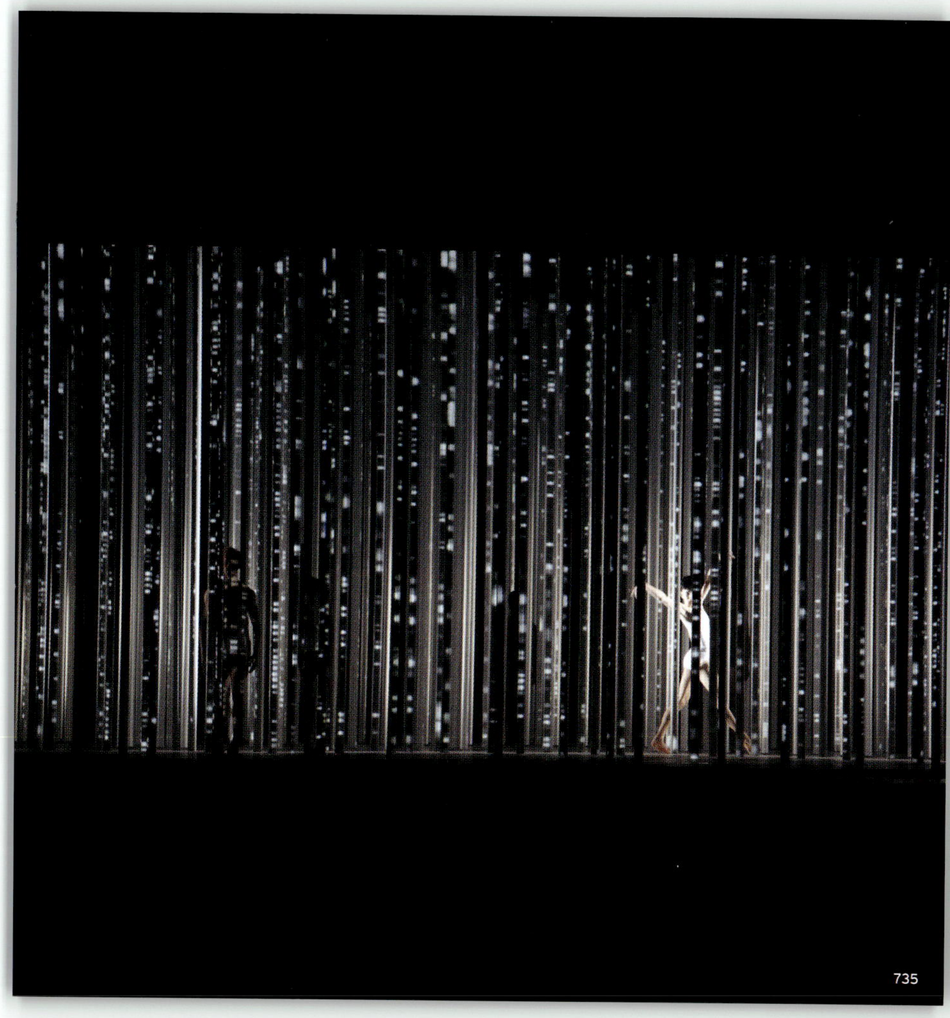

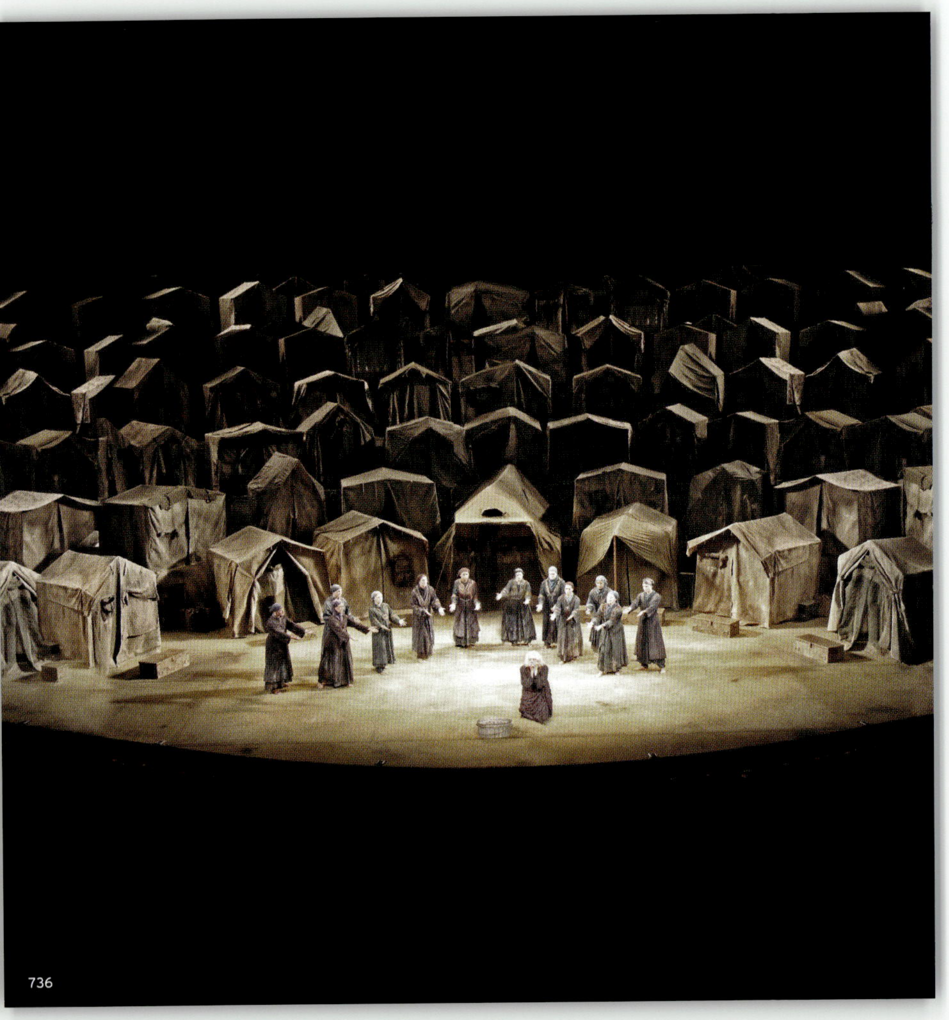

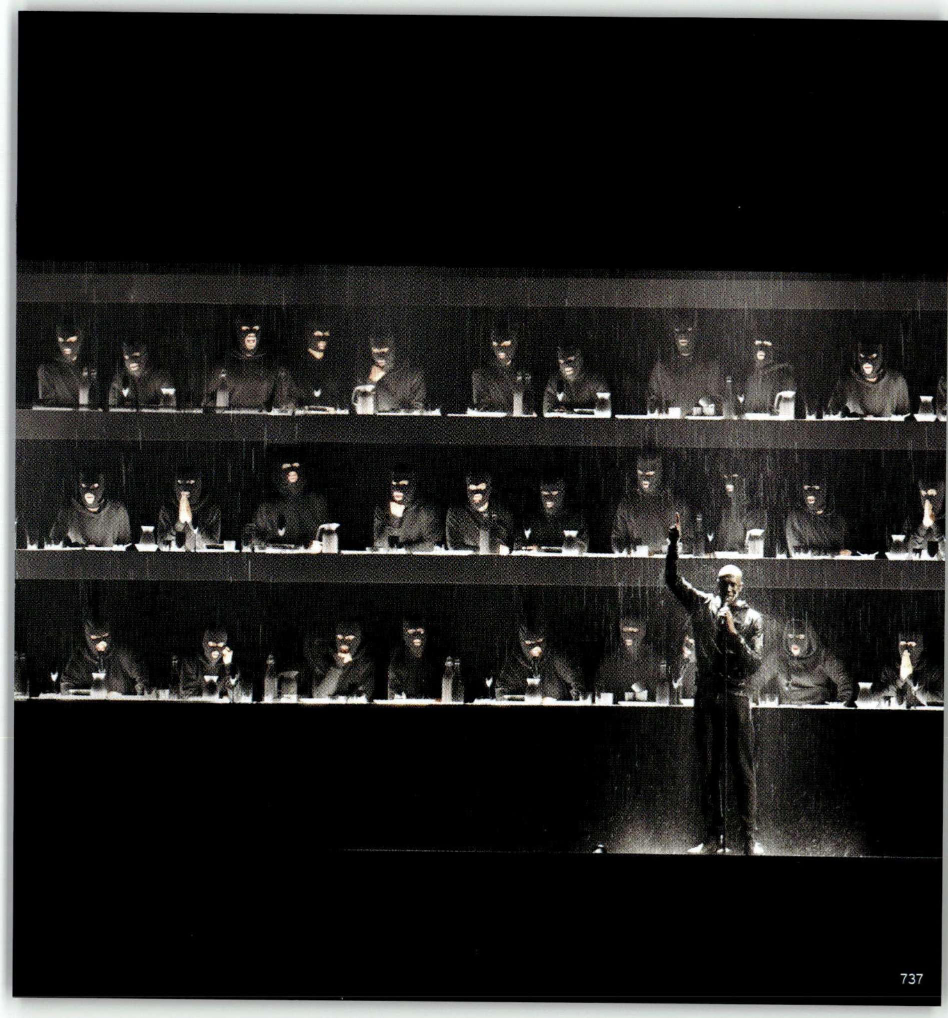

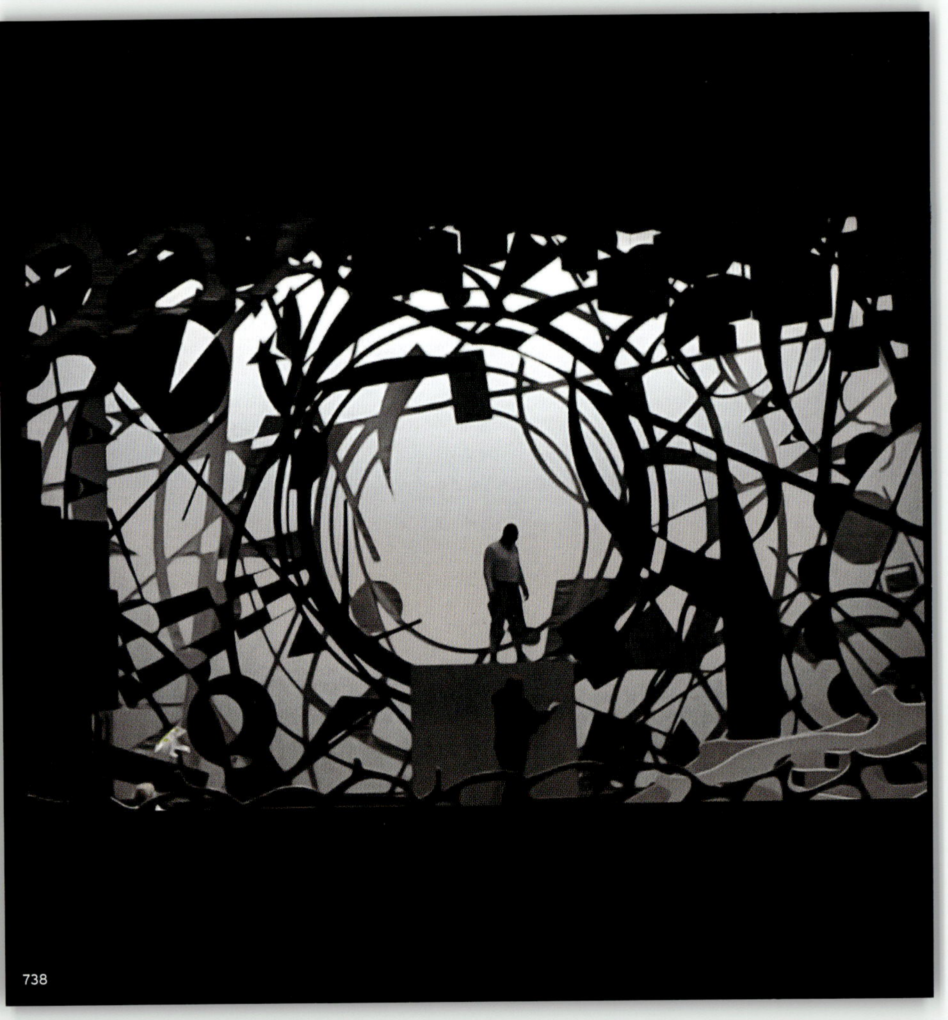

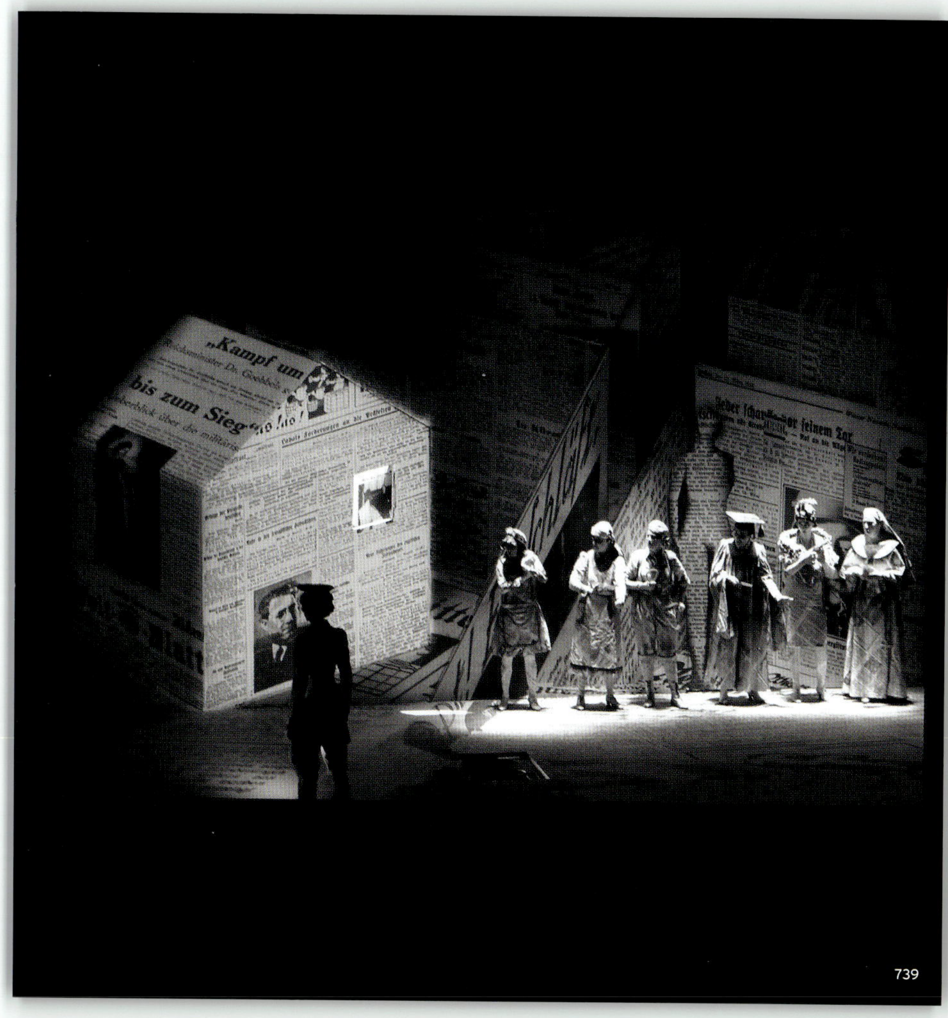
„Kampf um
bis zum Sieg

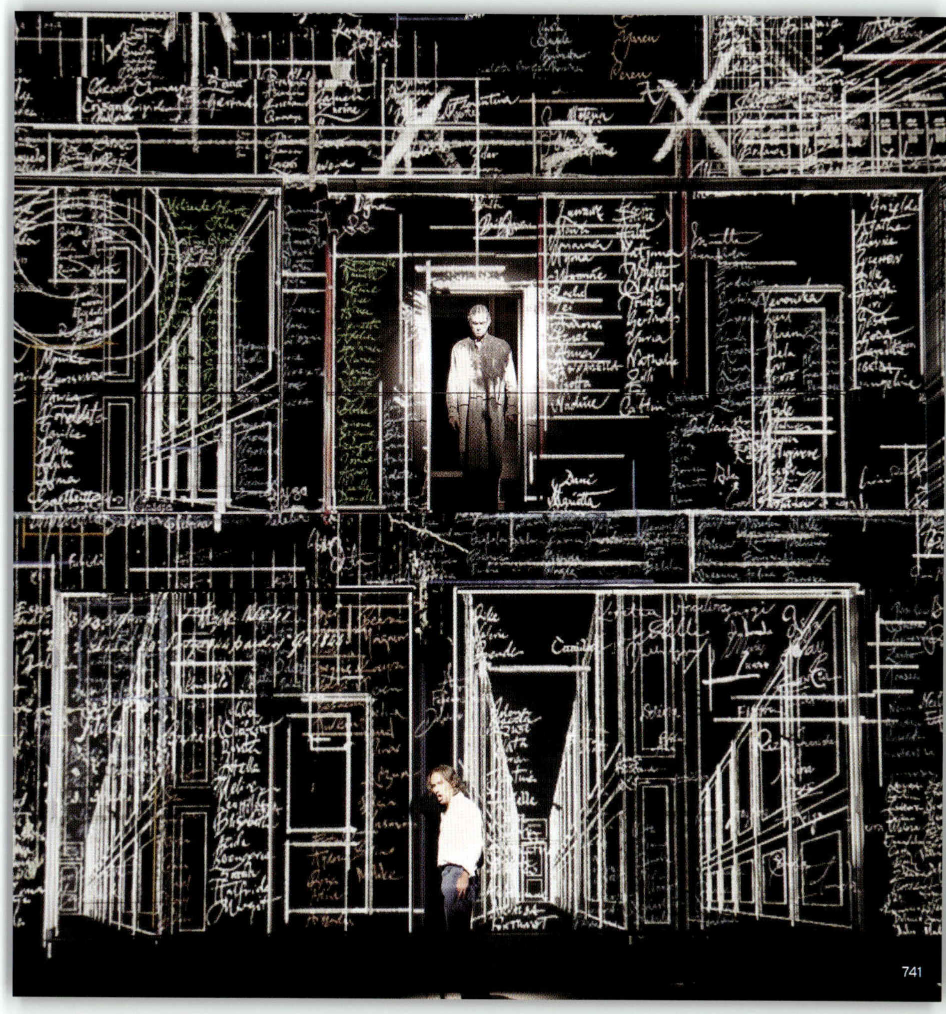

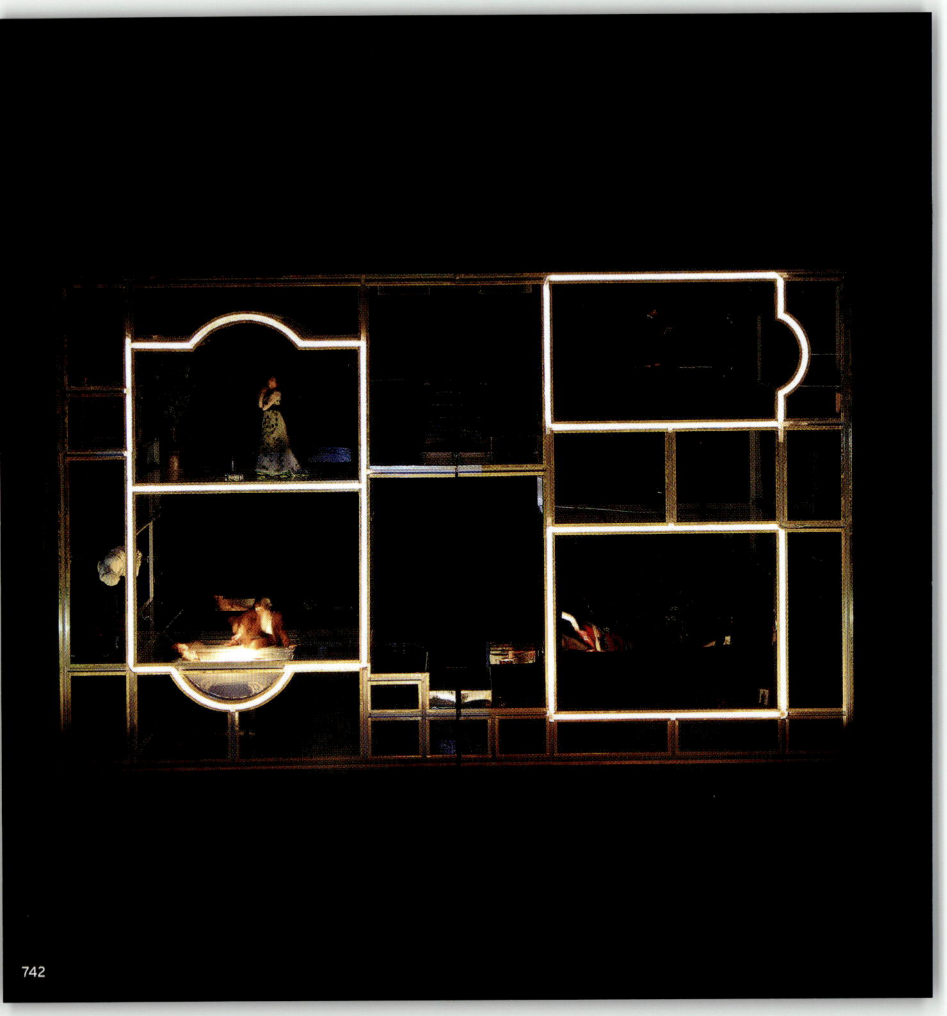

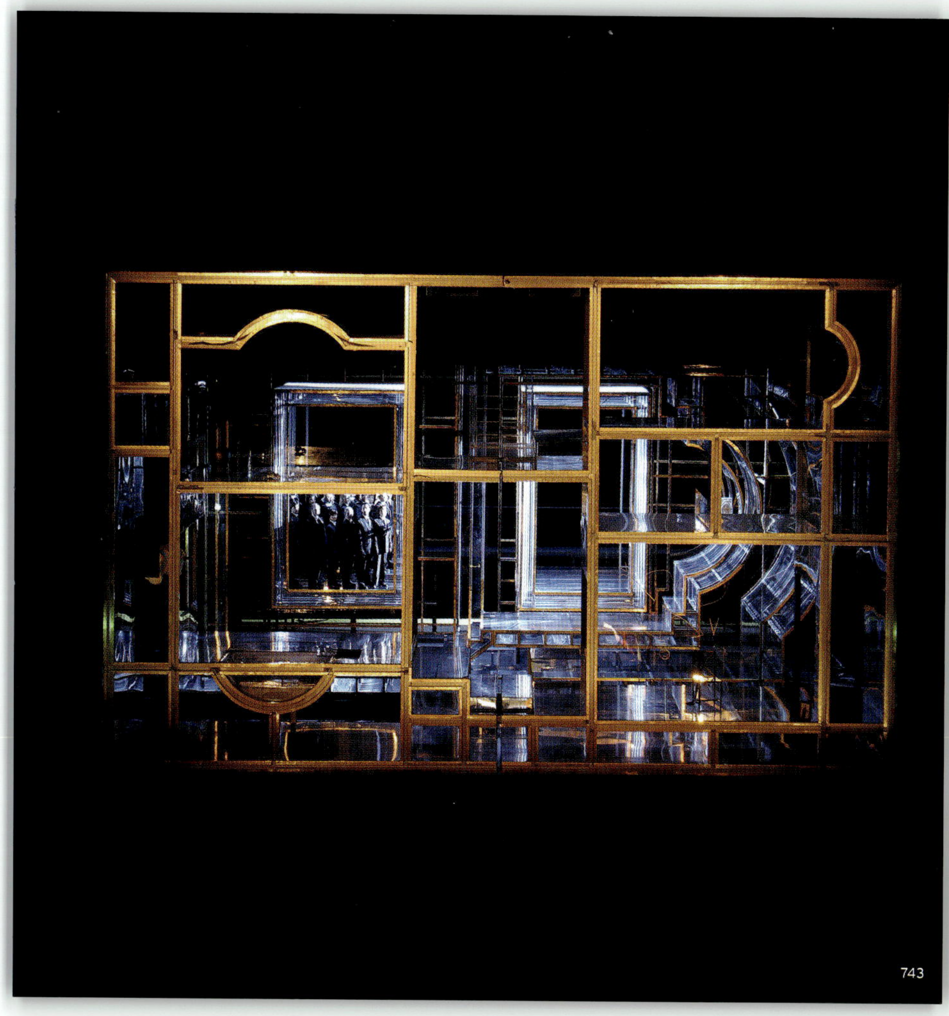

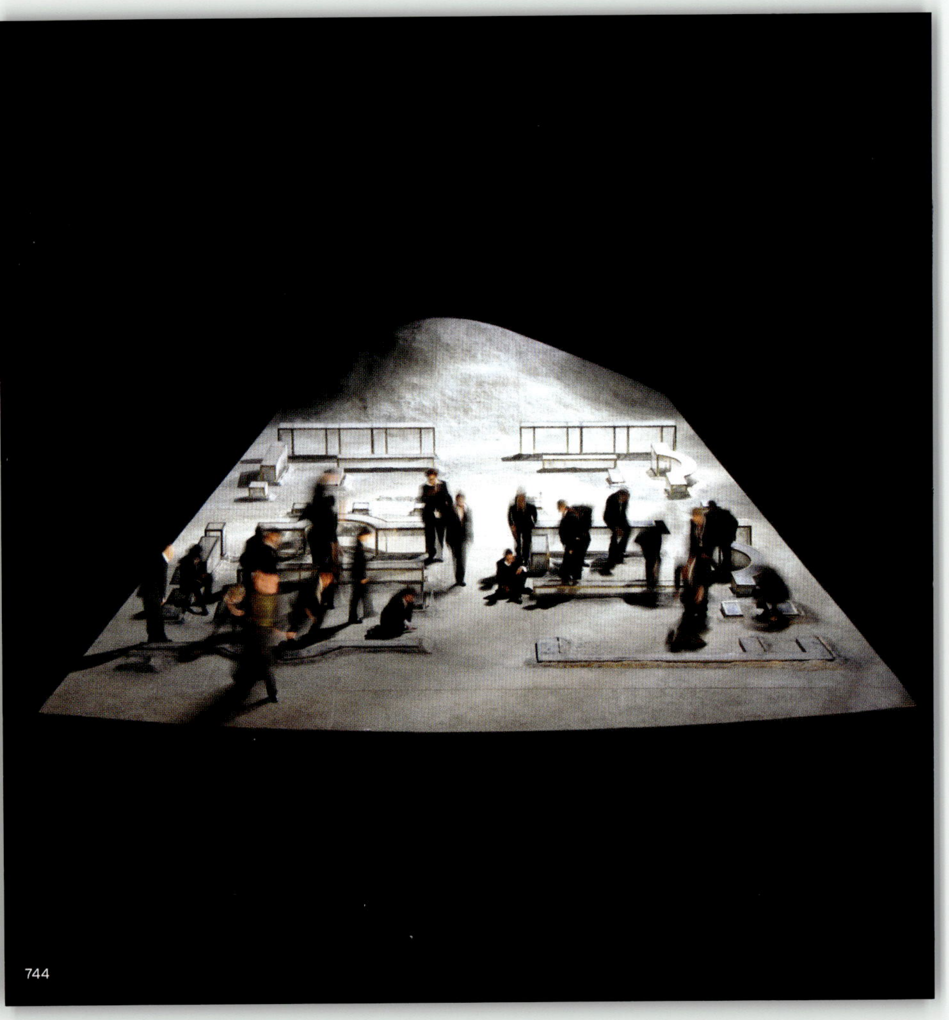

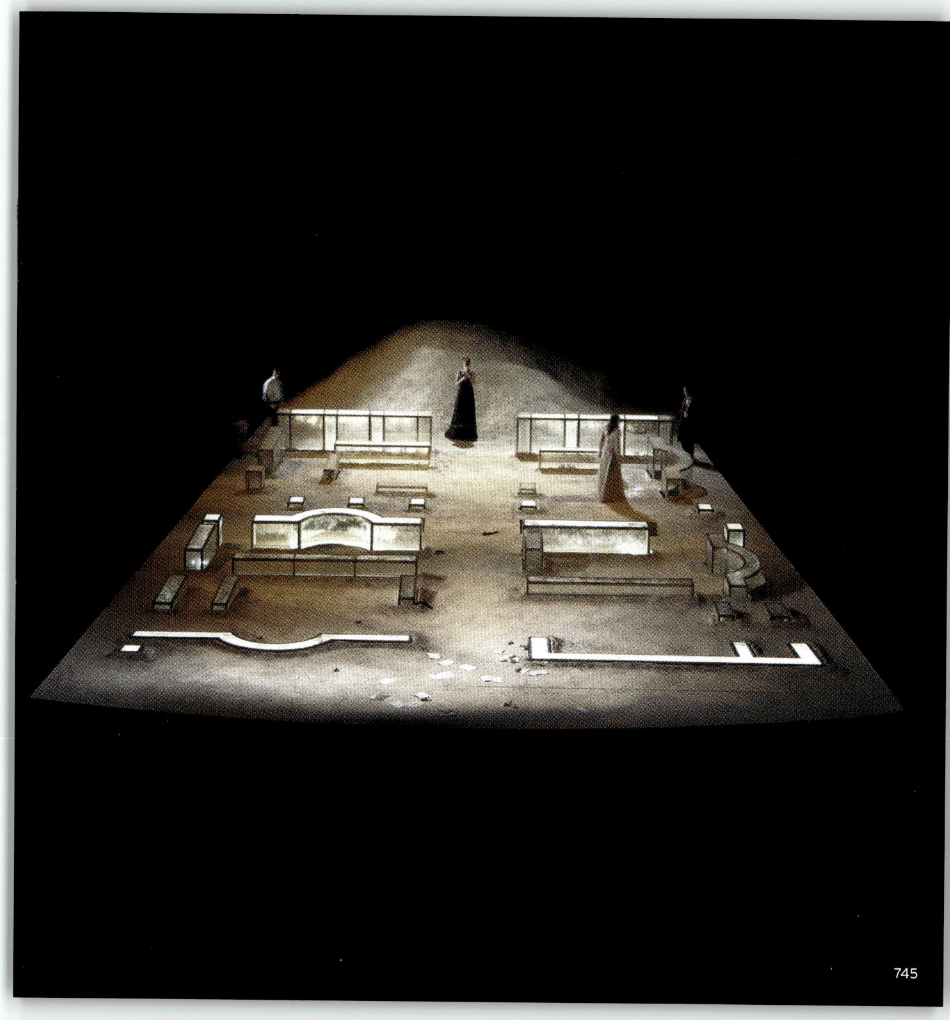

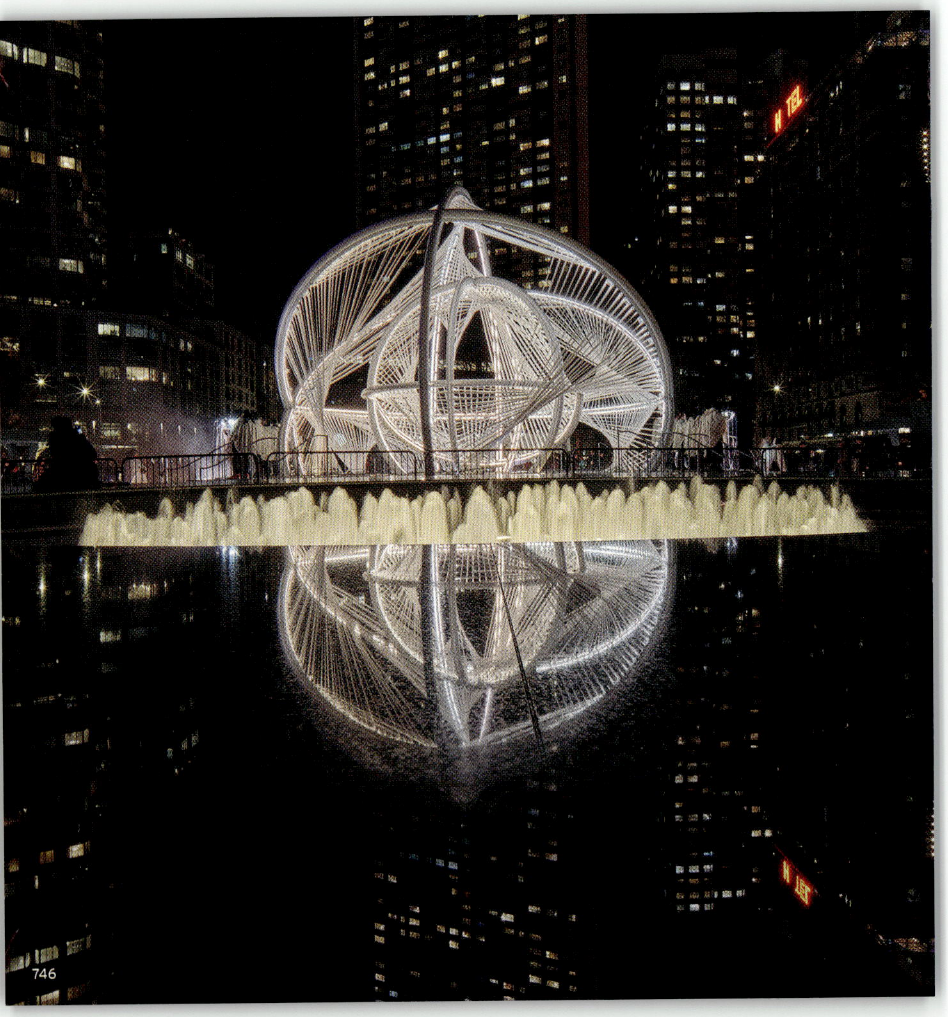

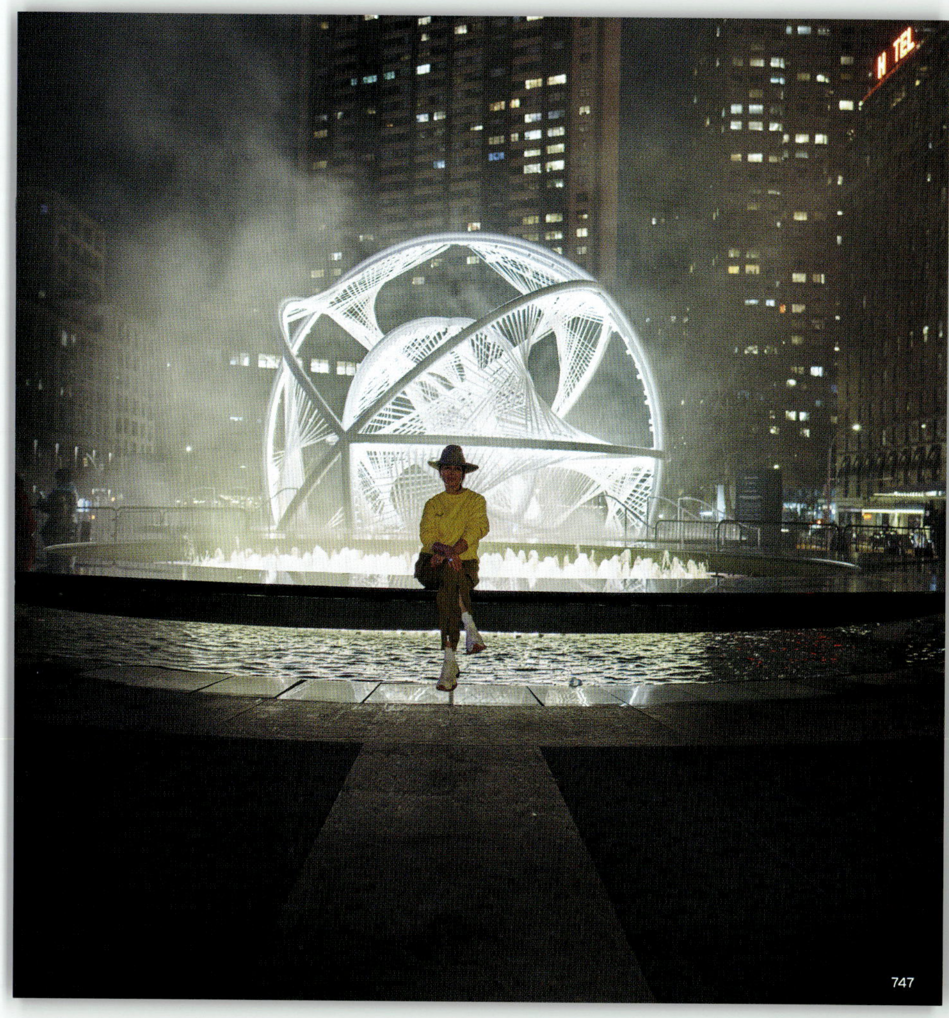

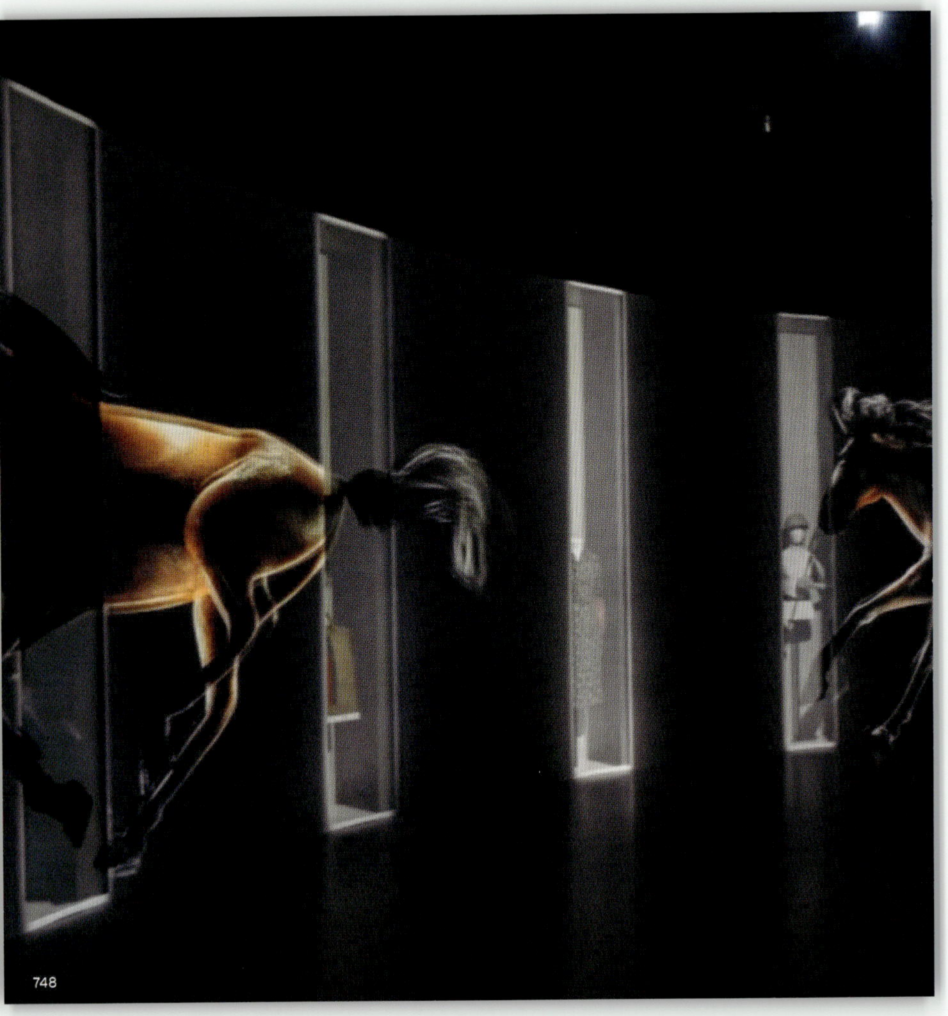

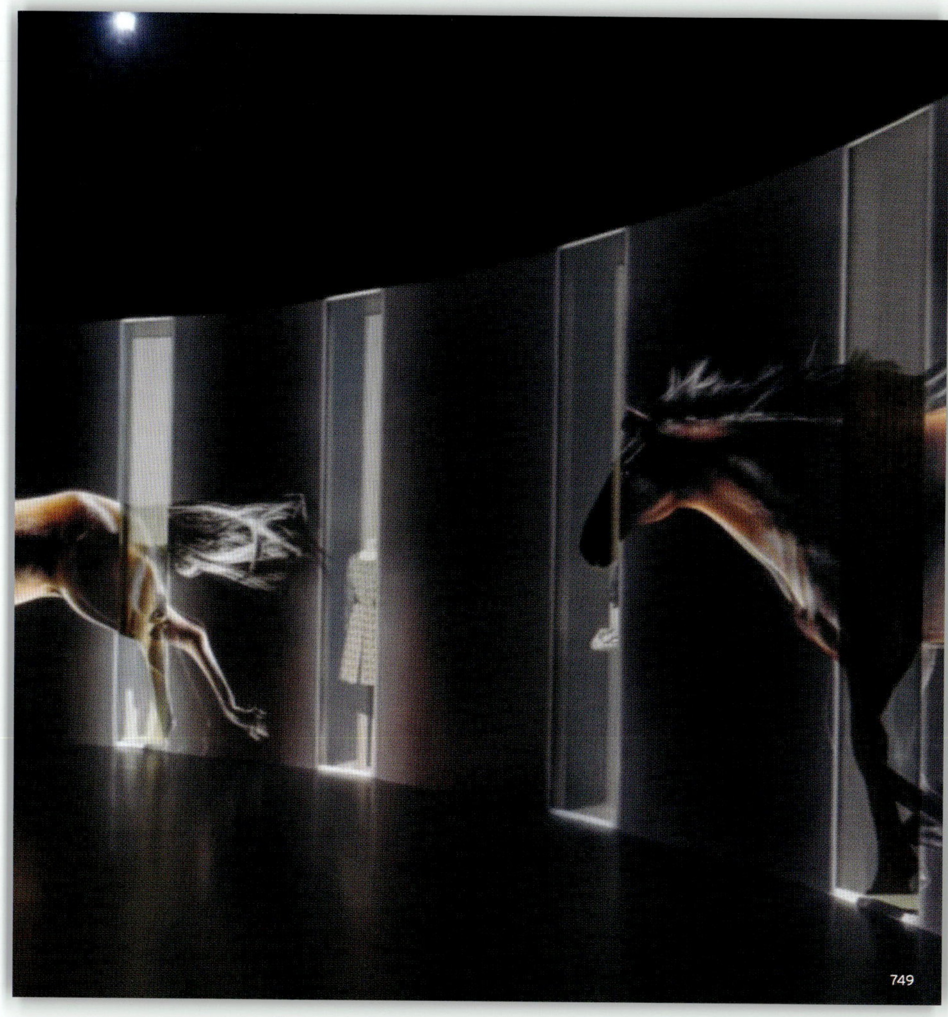

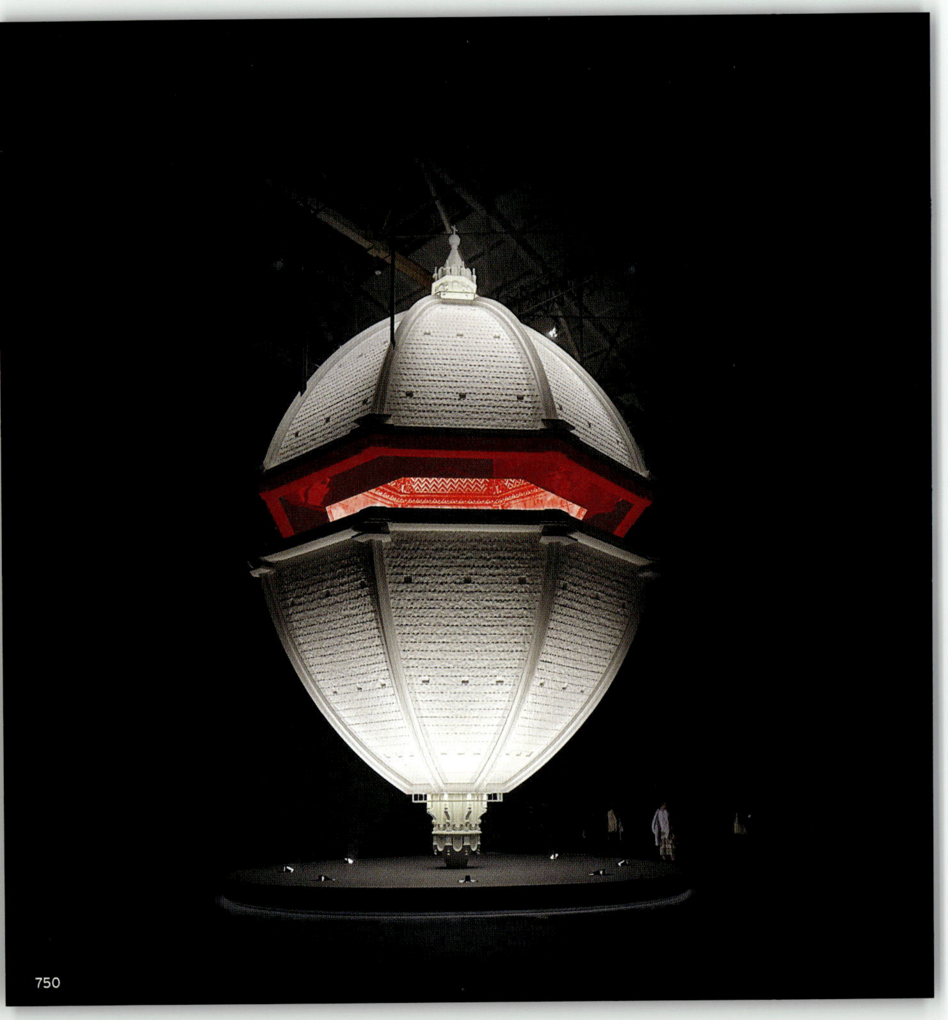

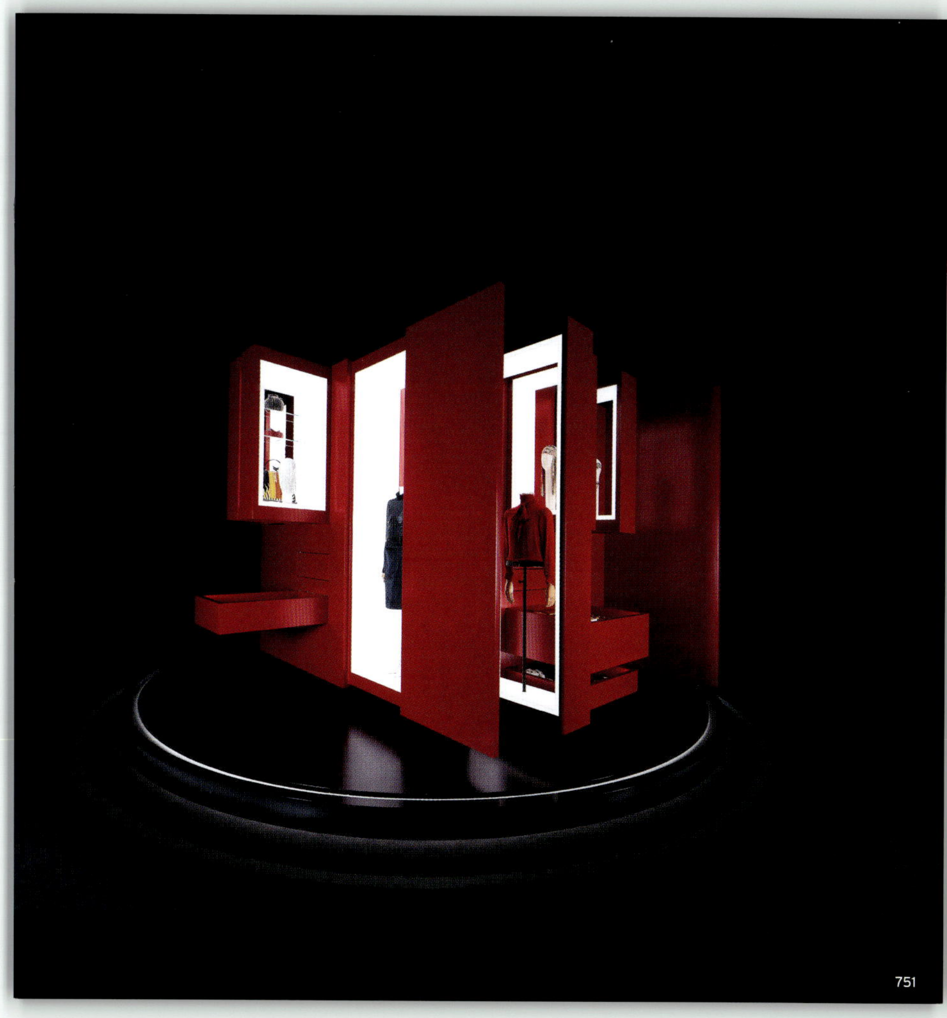

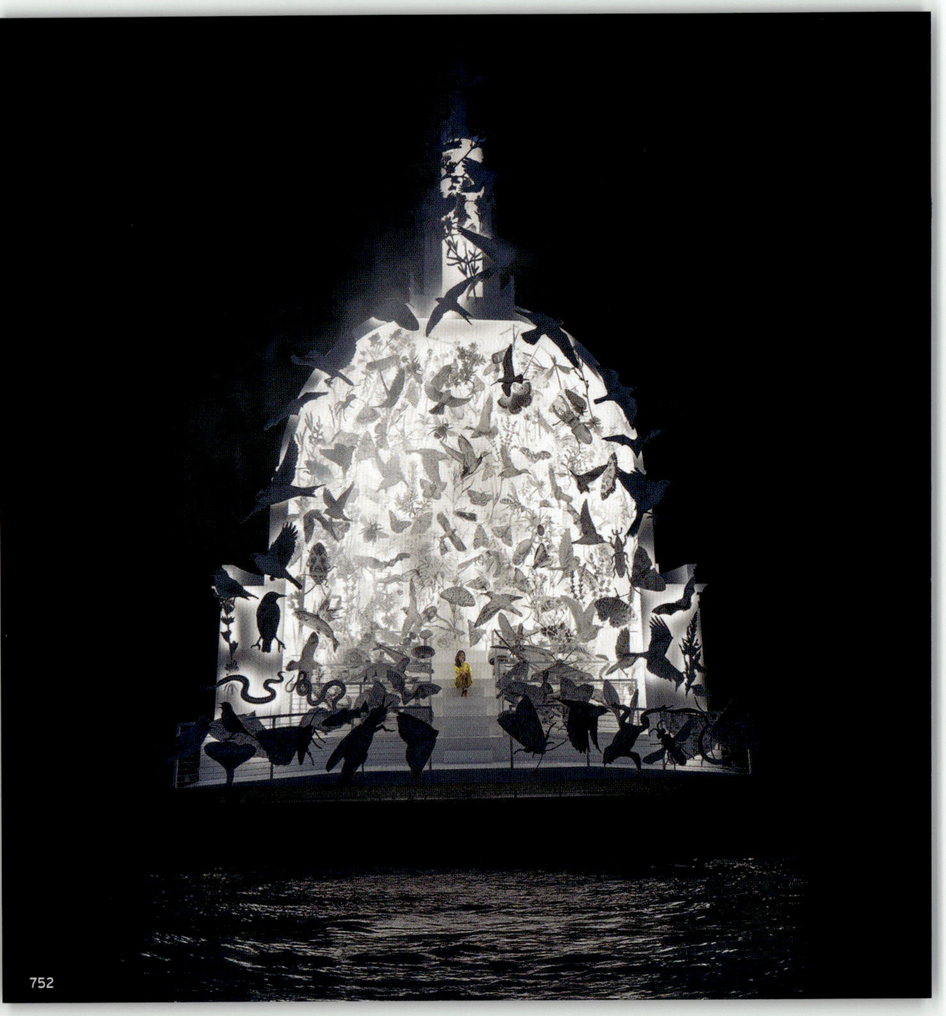

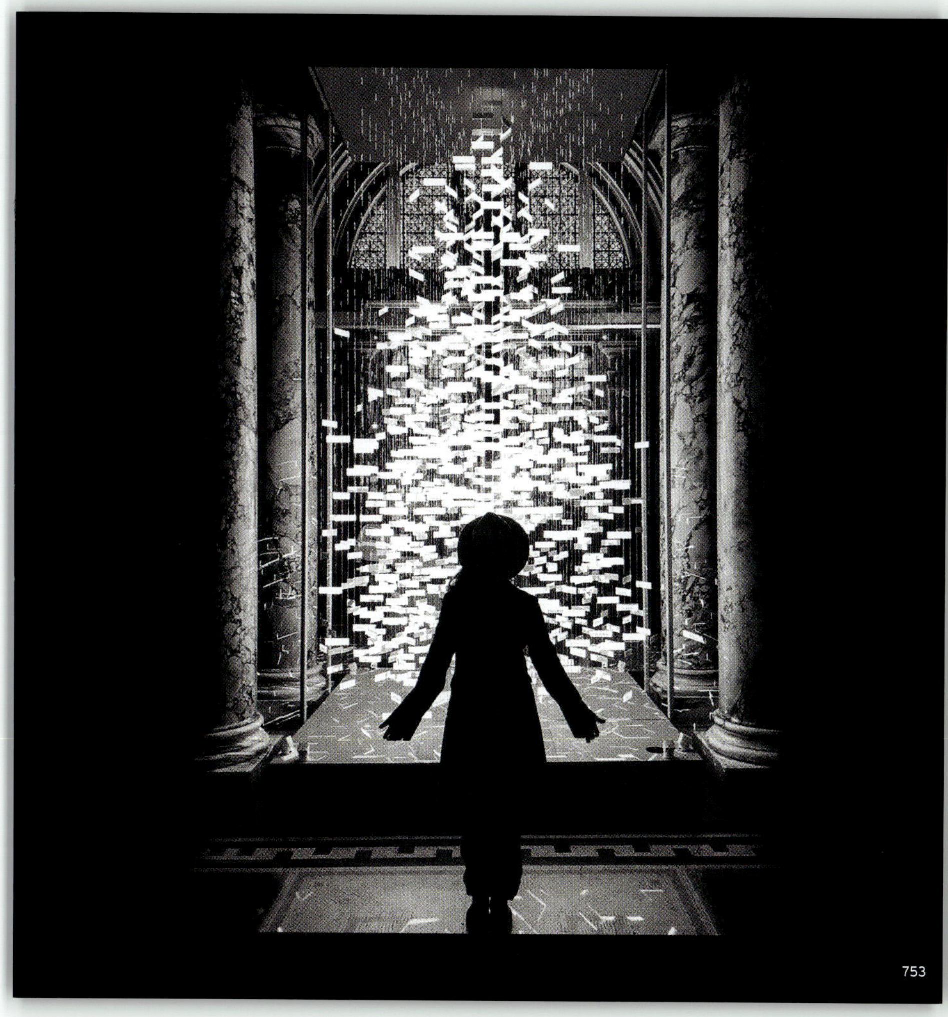

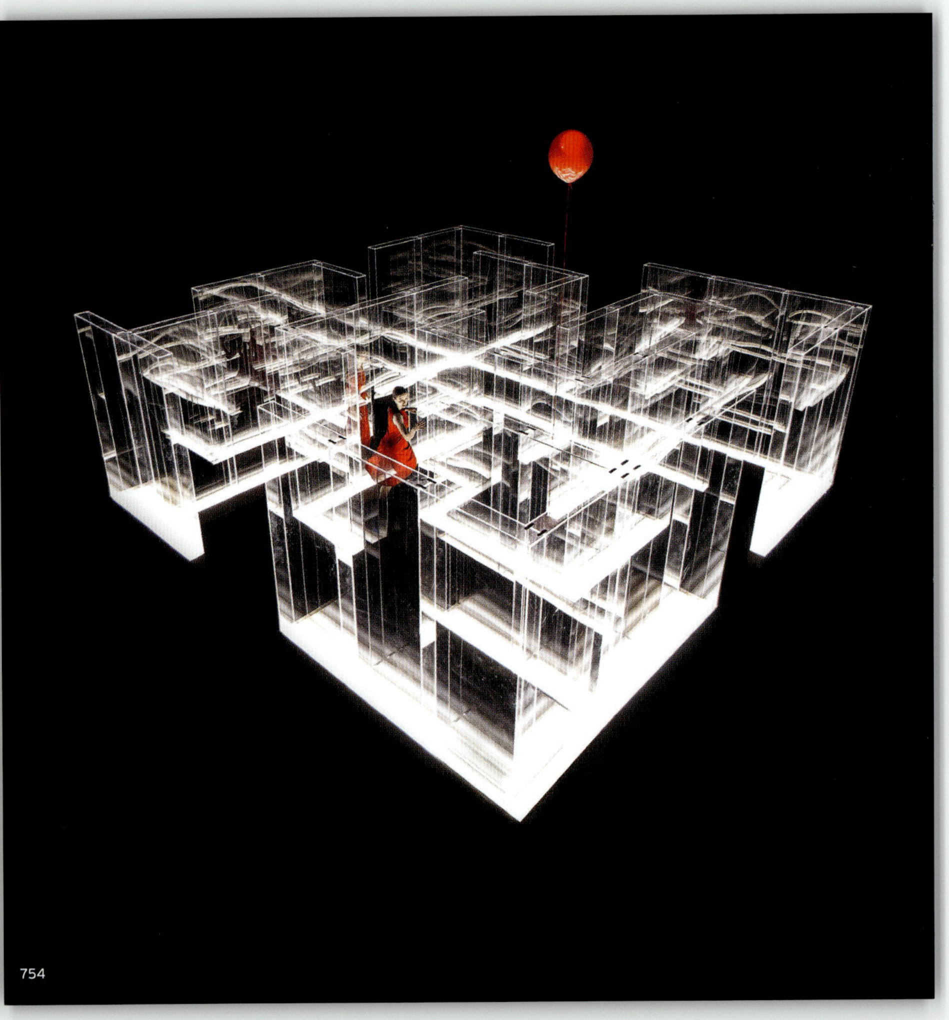

A SEQUENCE IN COLOURED LIGHT

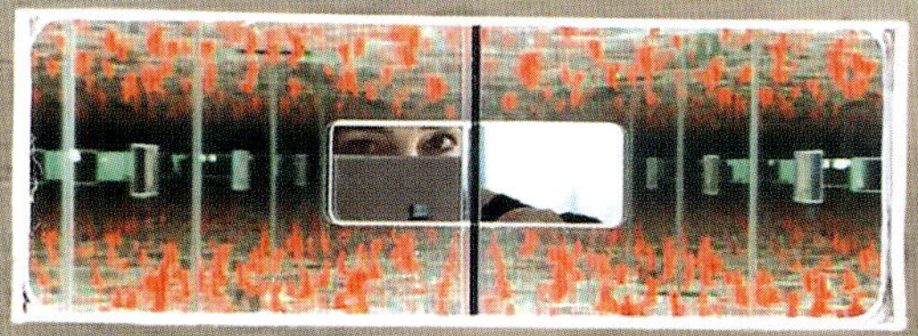

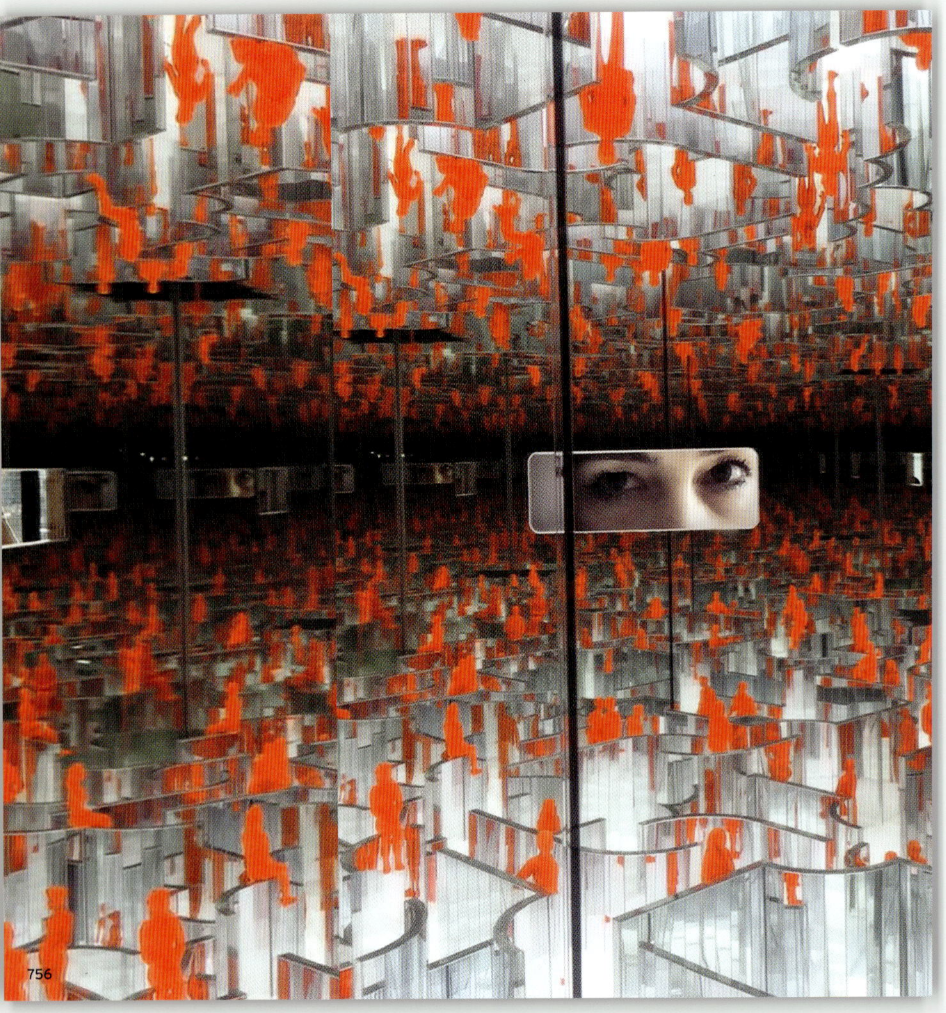

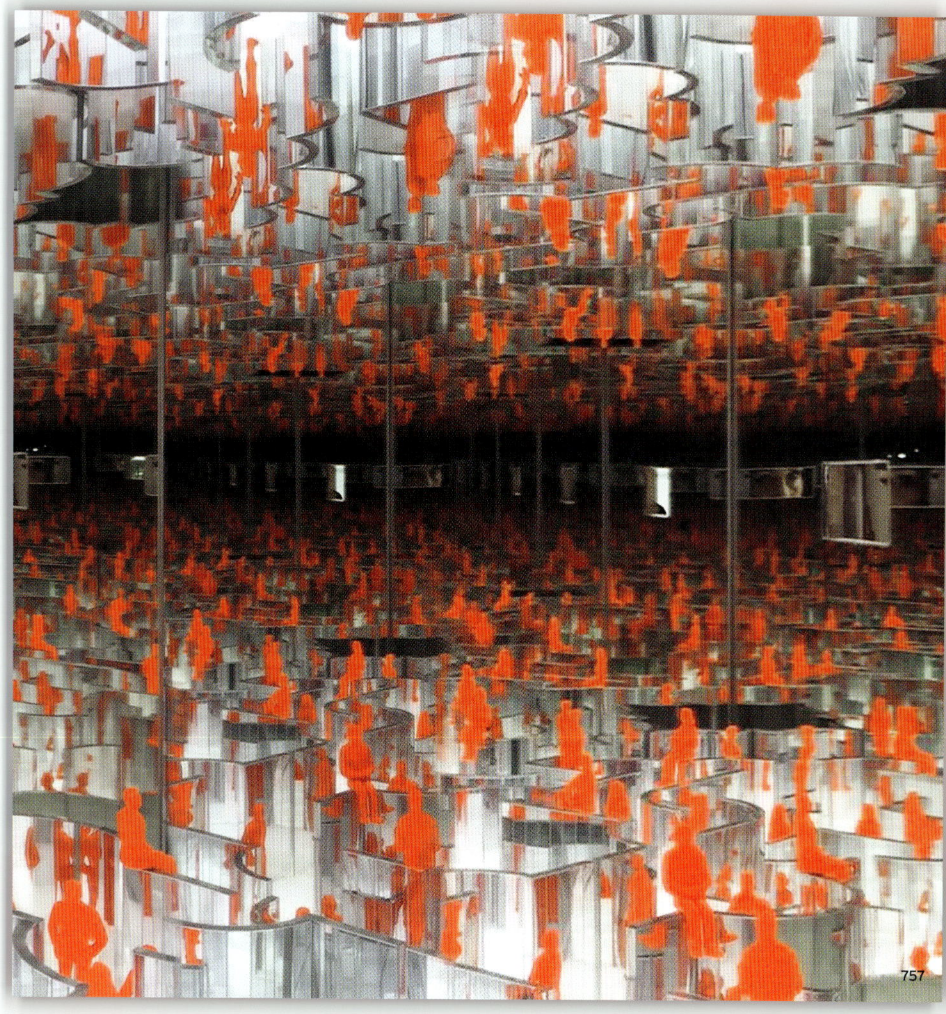

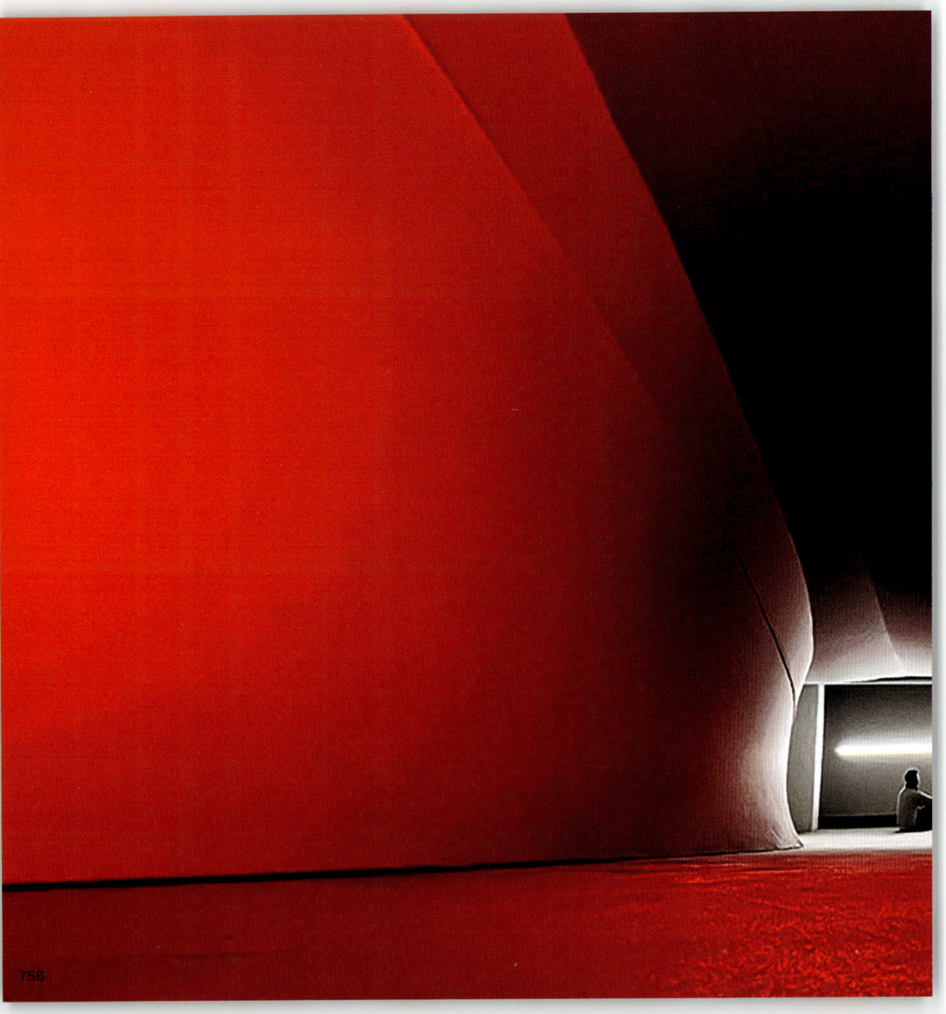

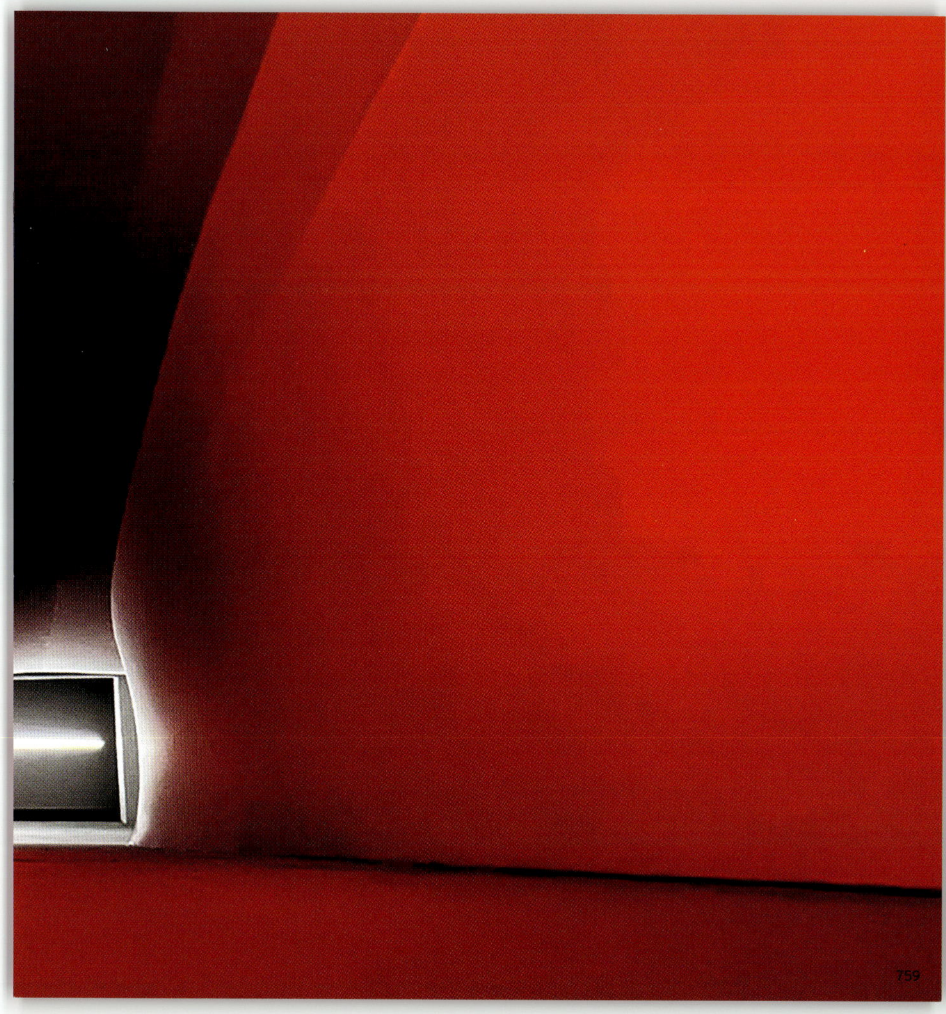

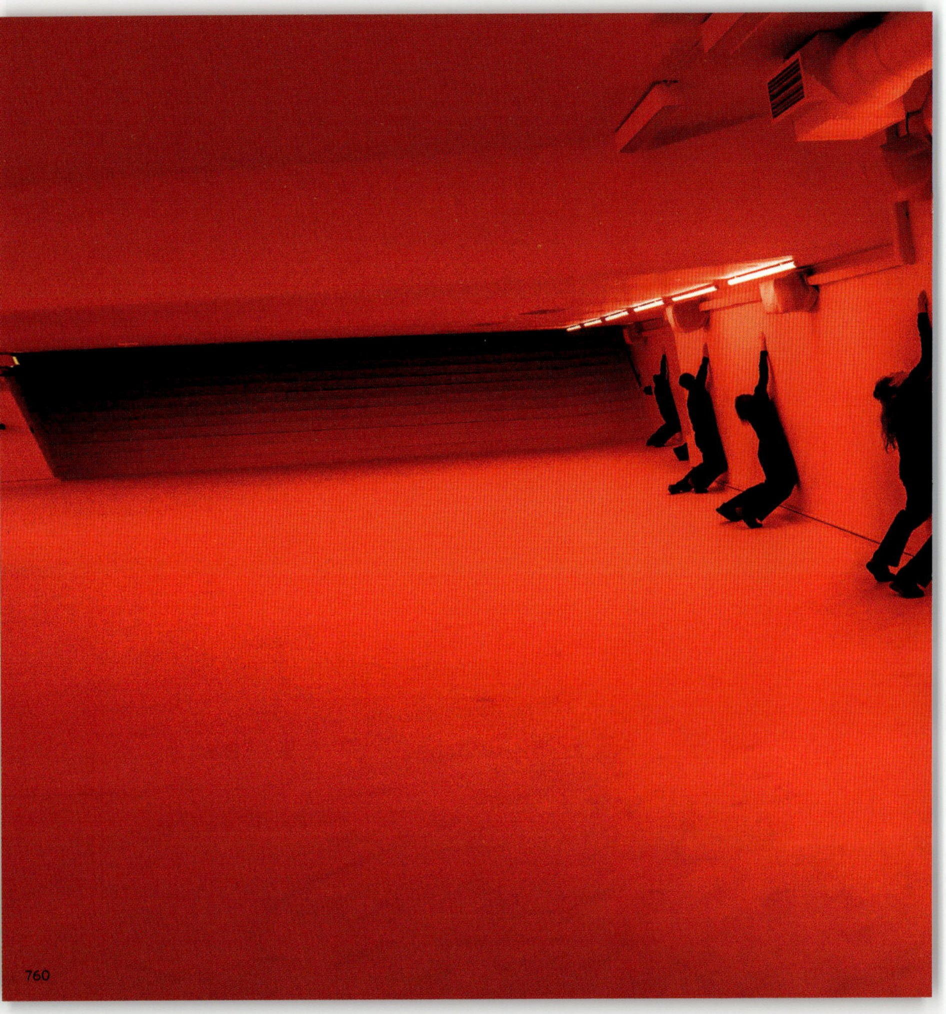

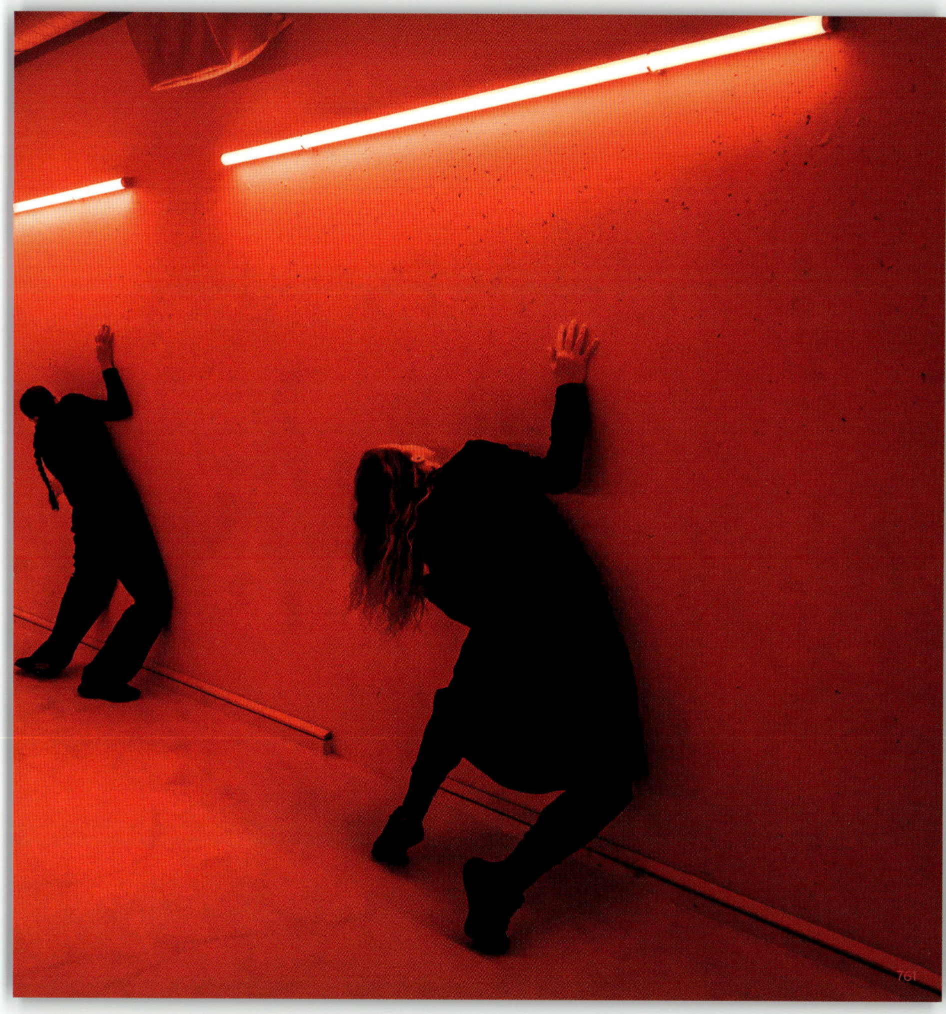

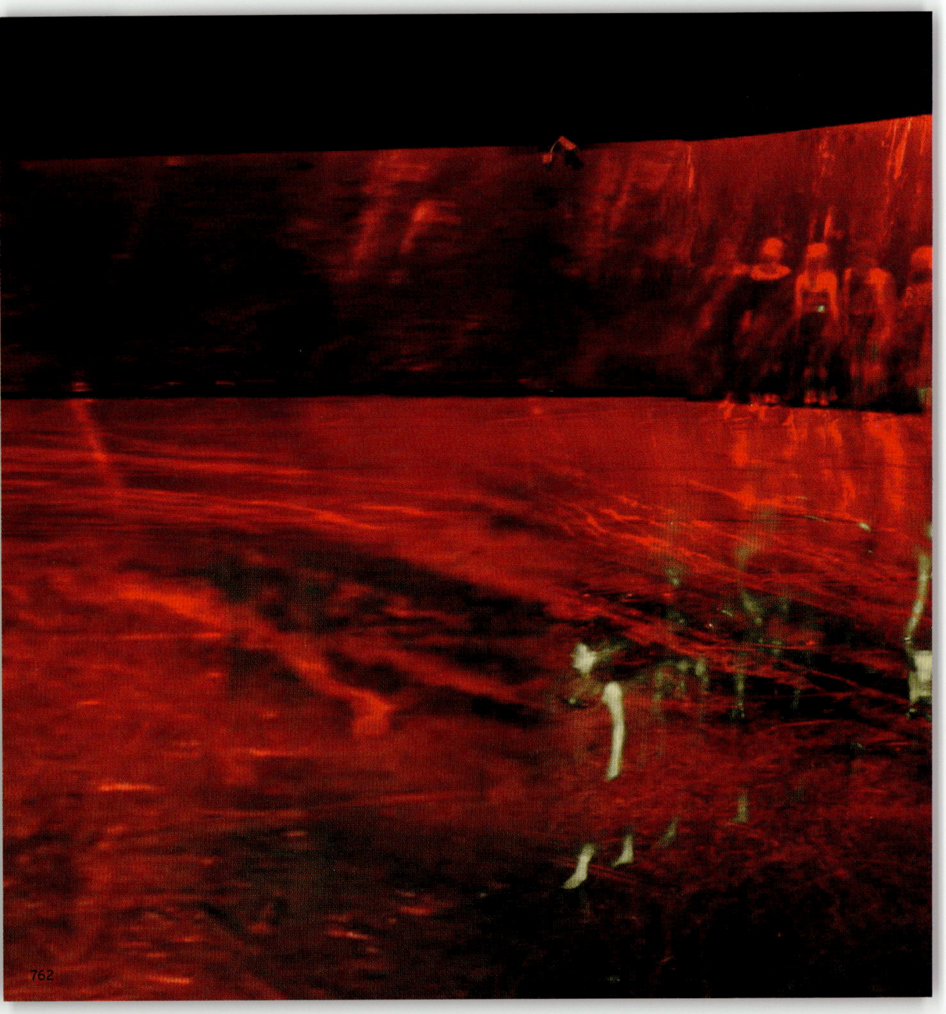

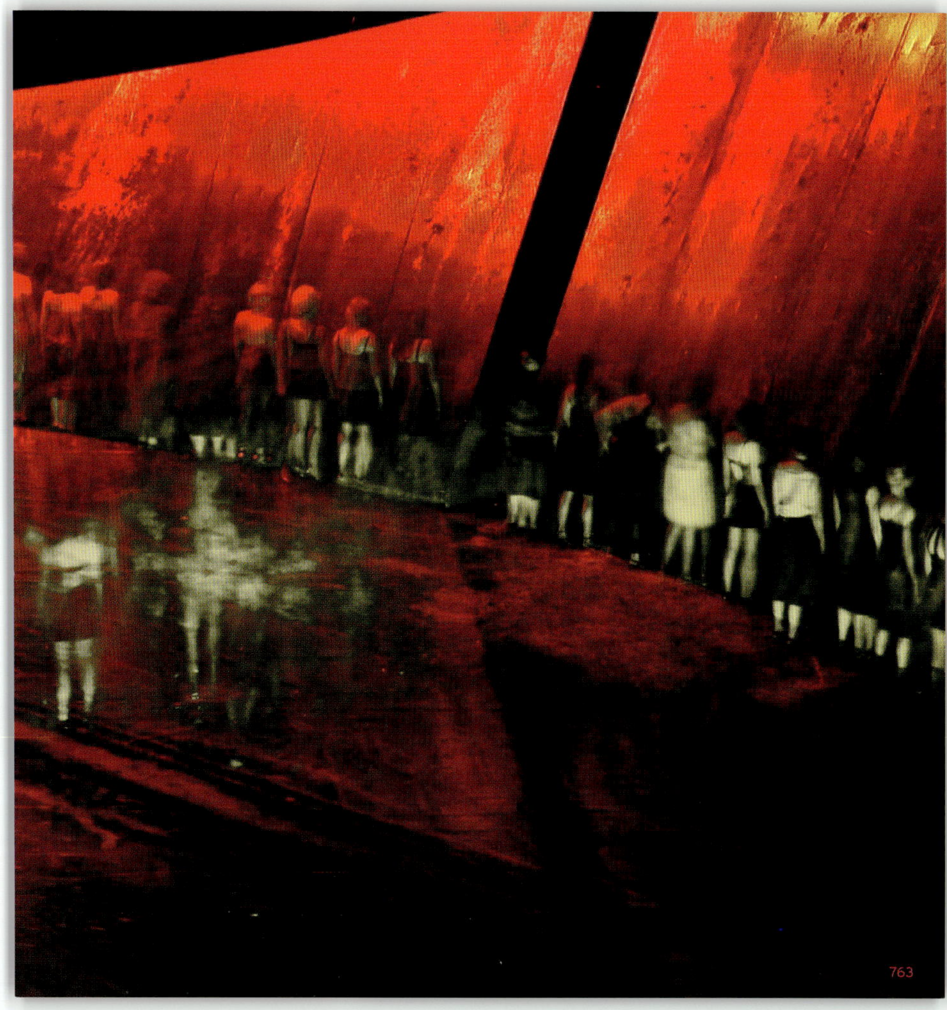

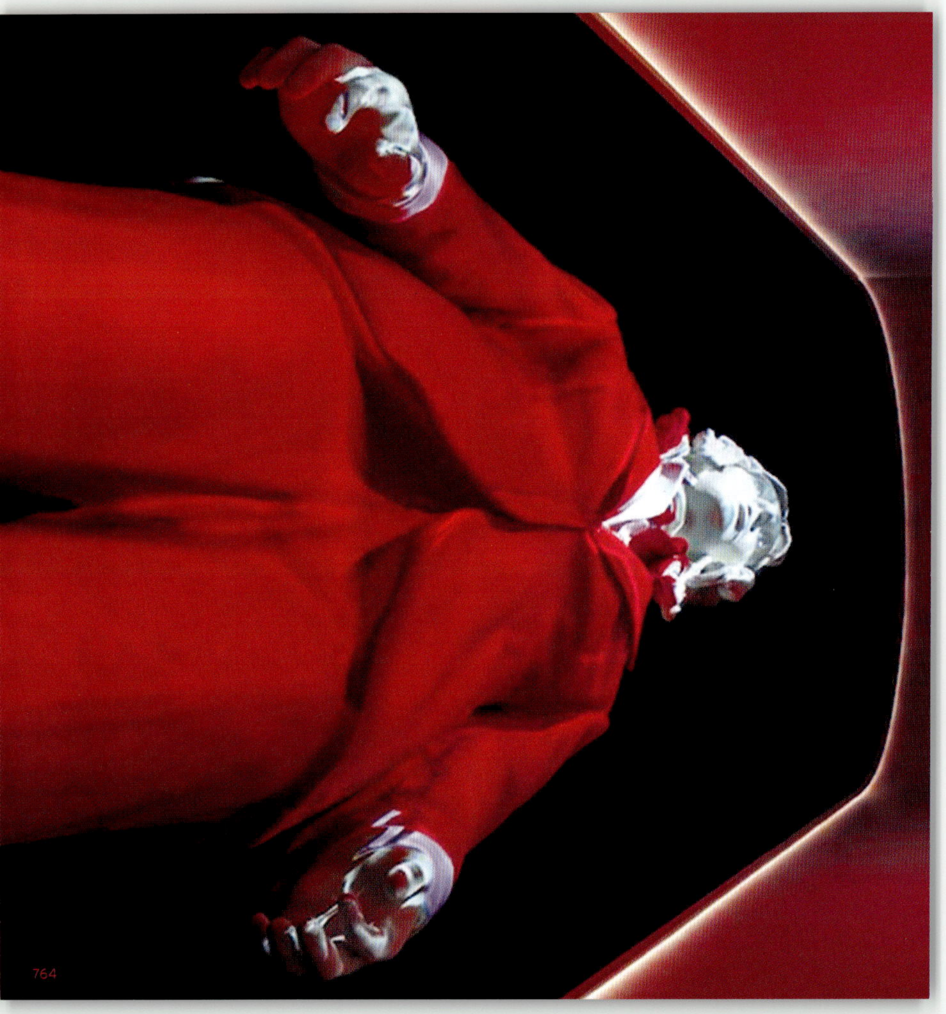

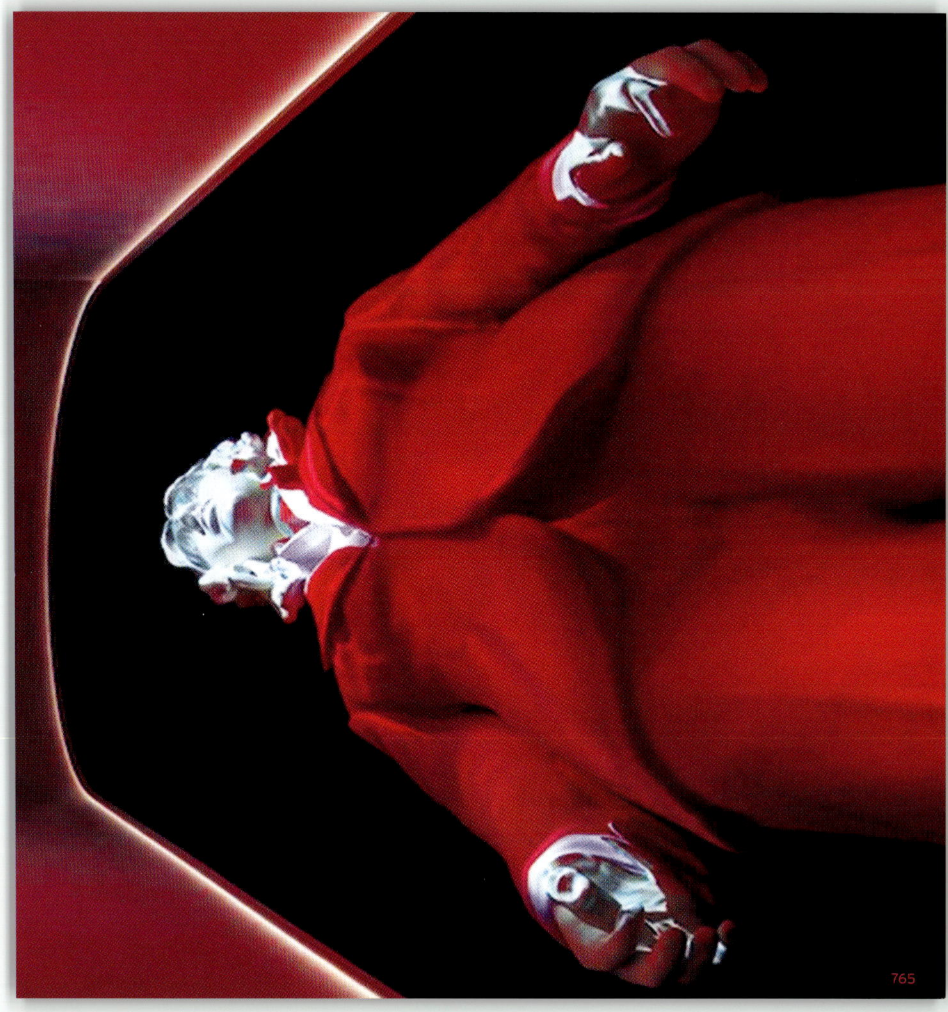

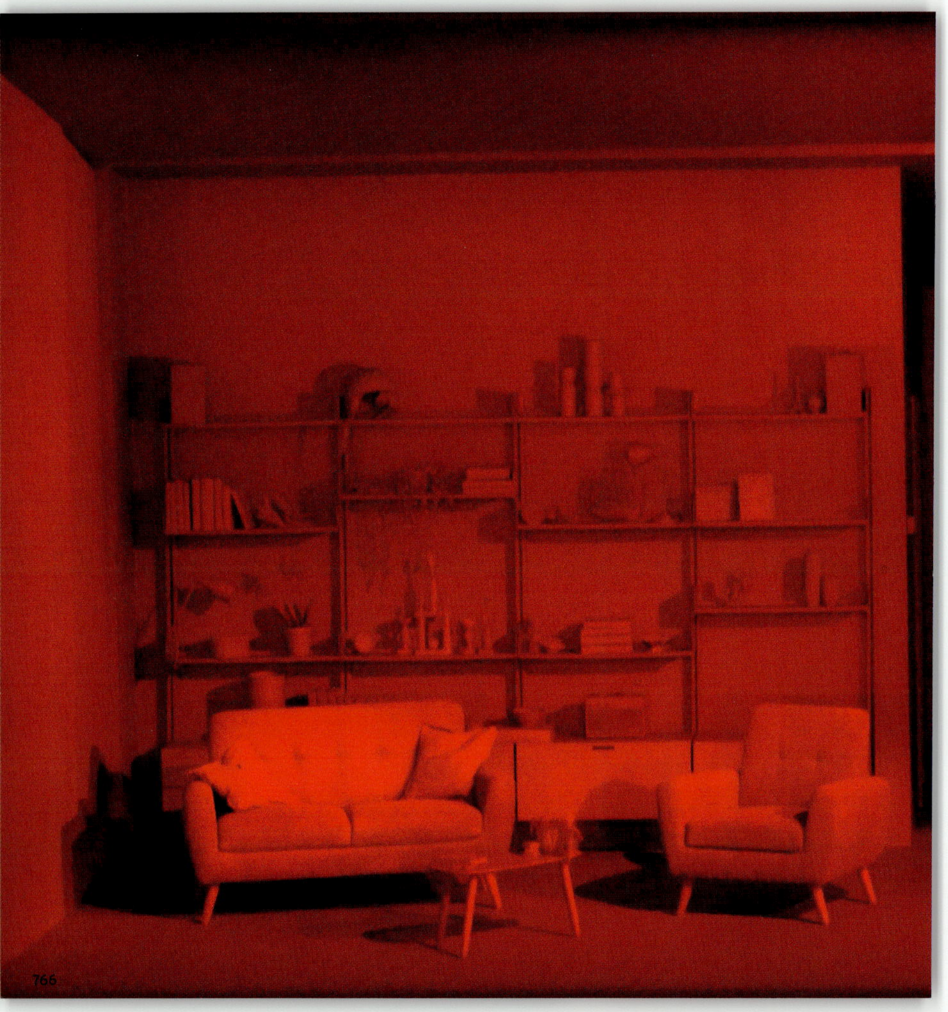

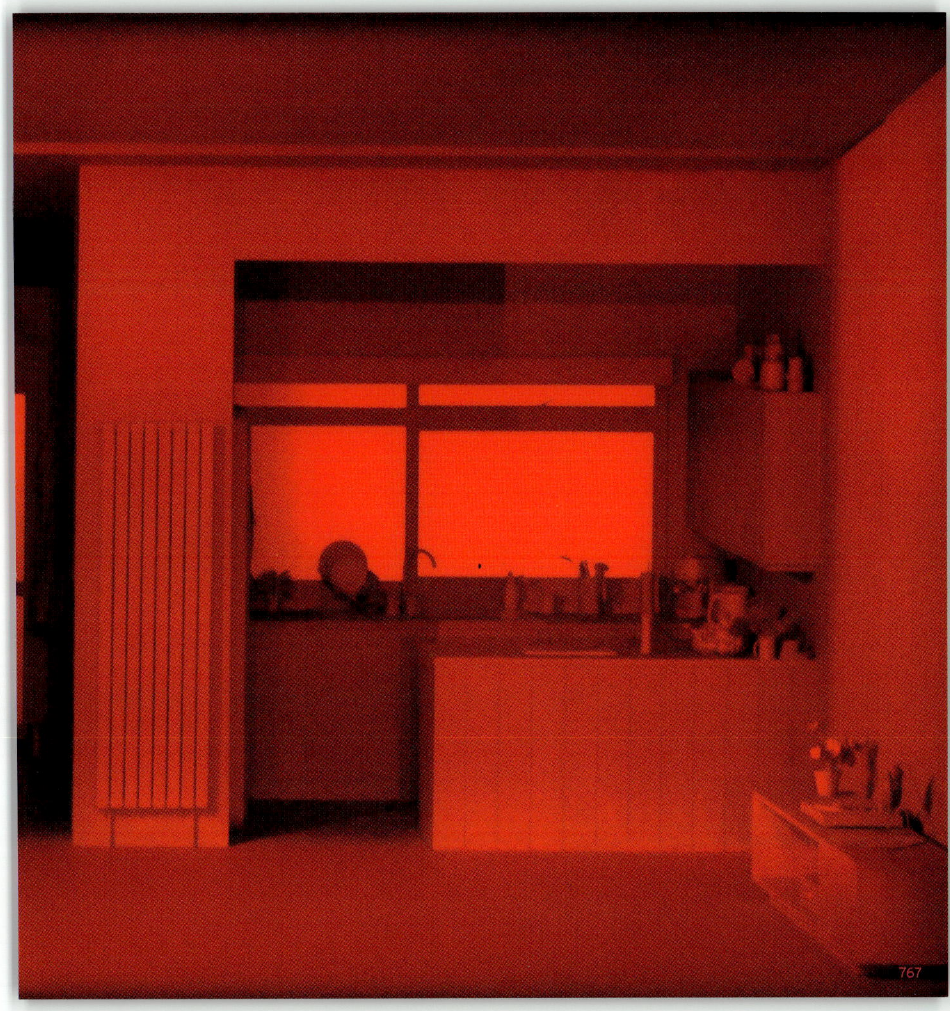

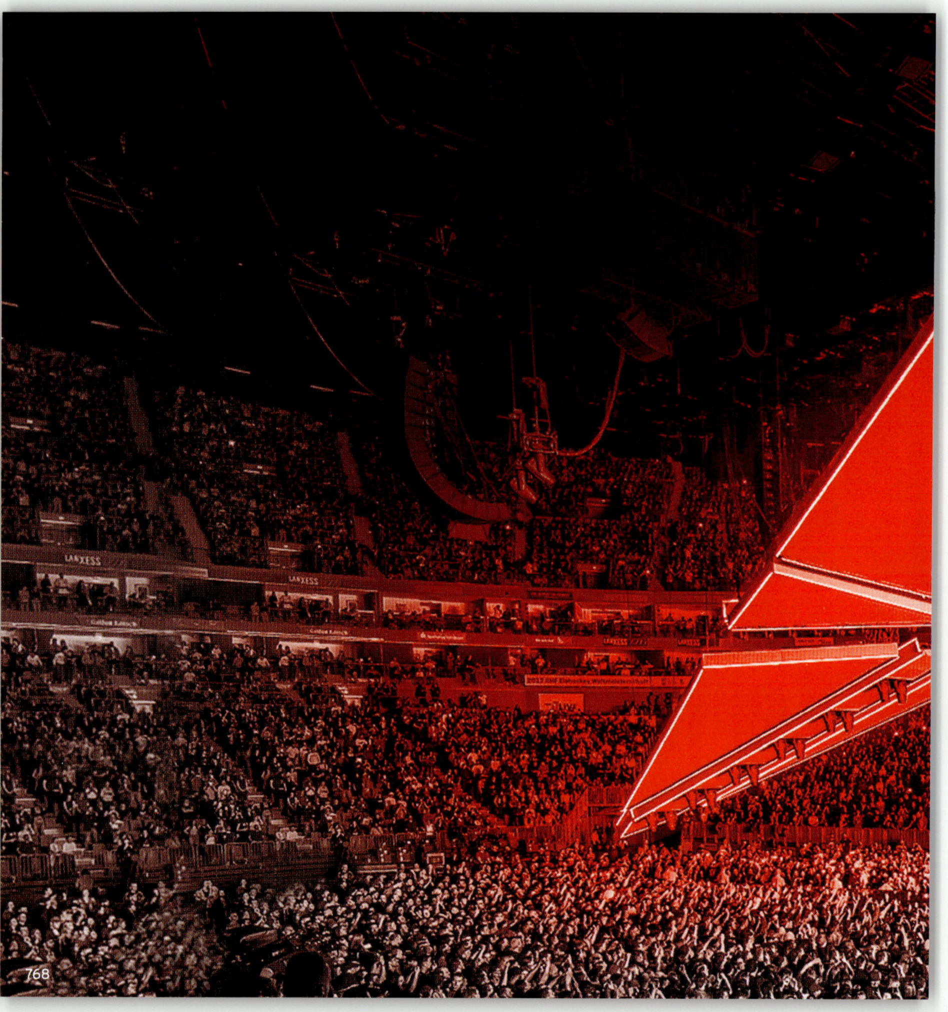
LANXESS
LANXESS

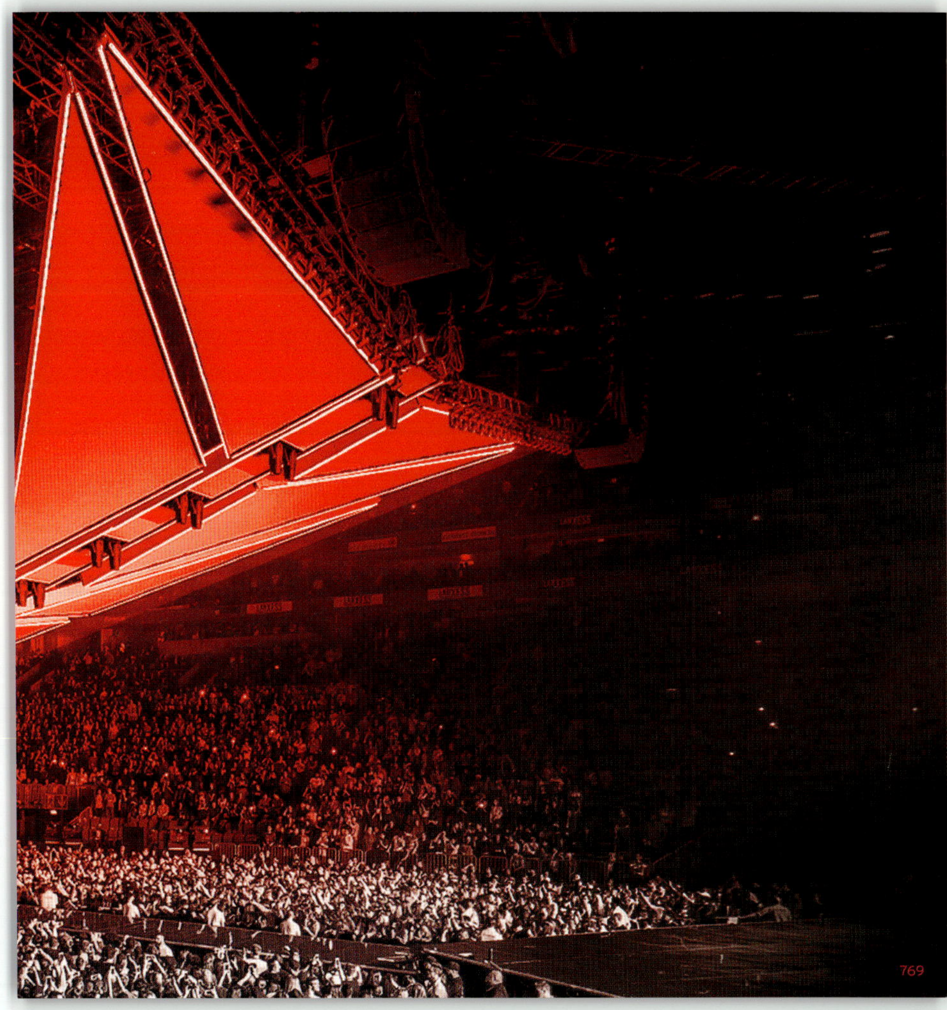

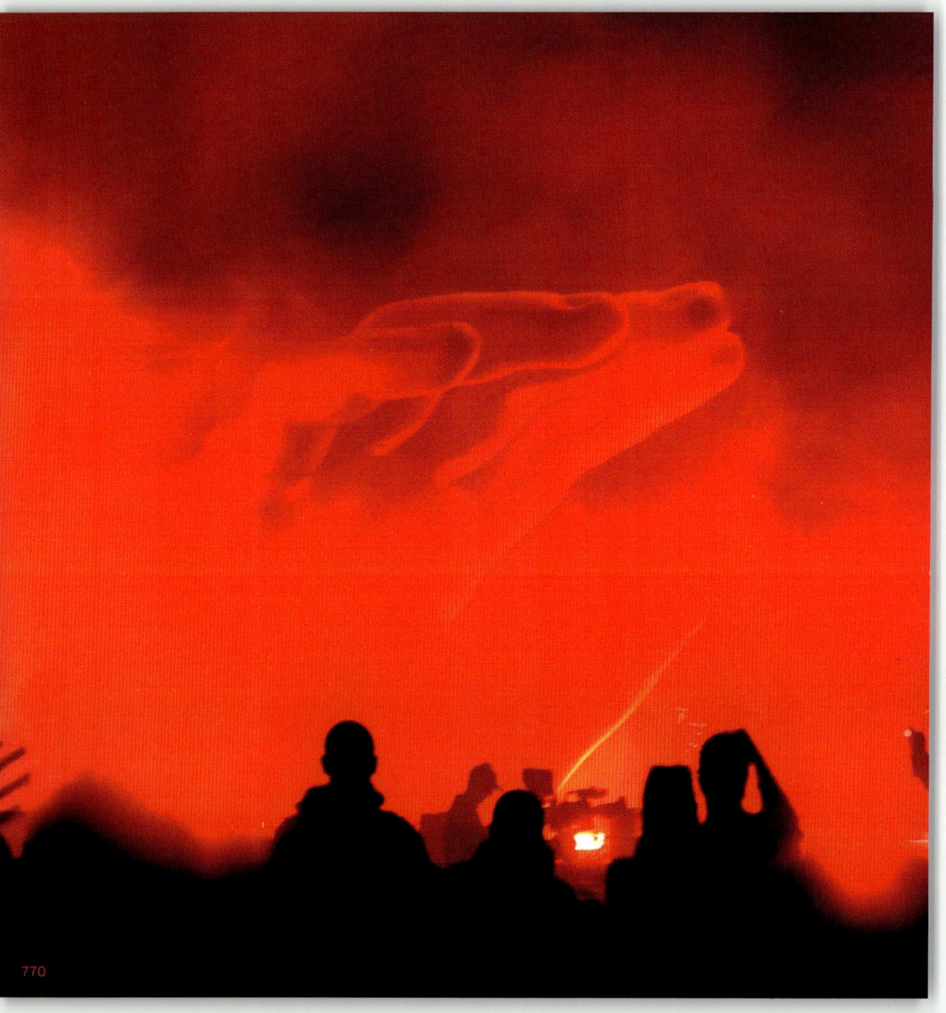

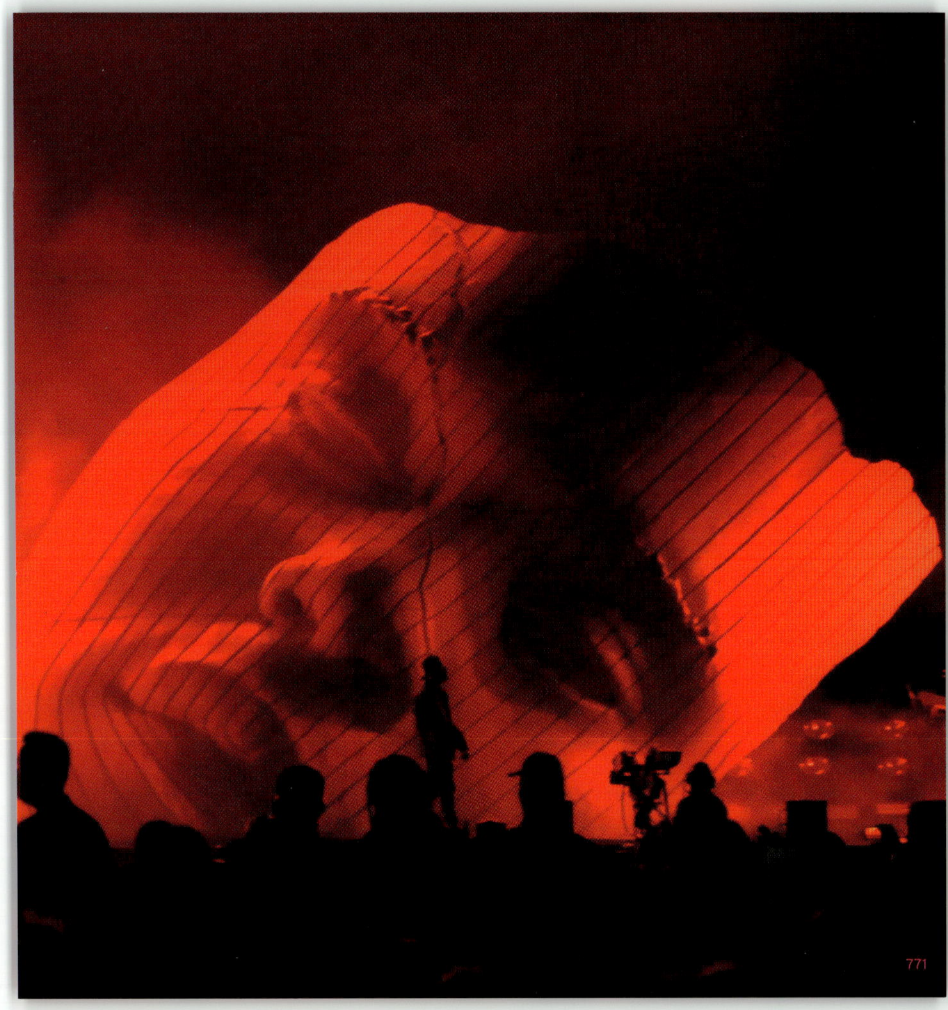

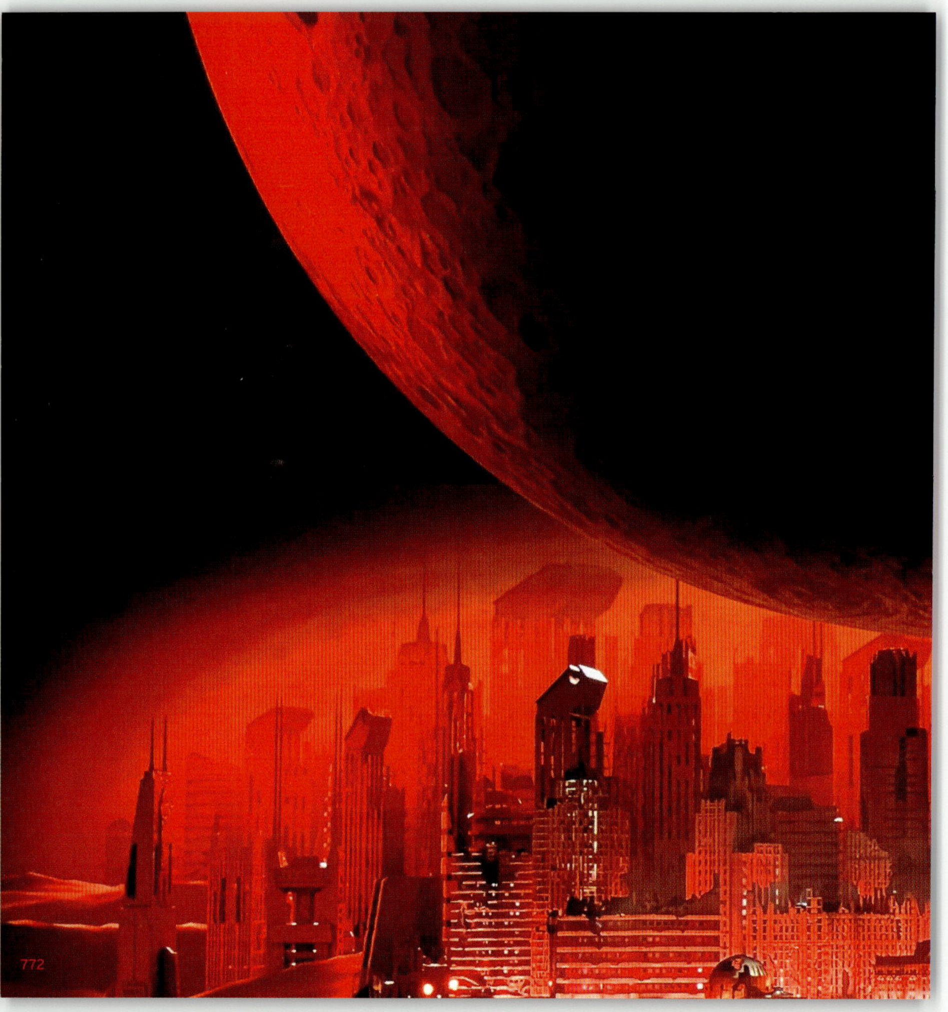

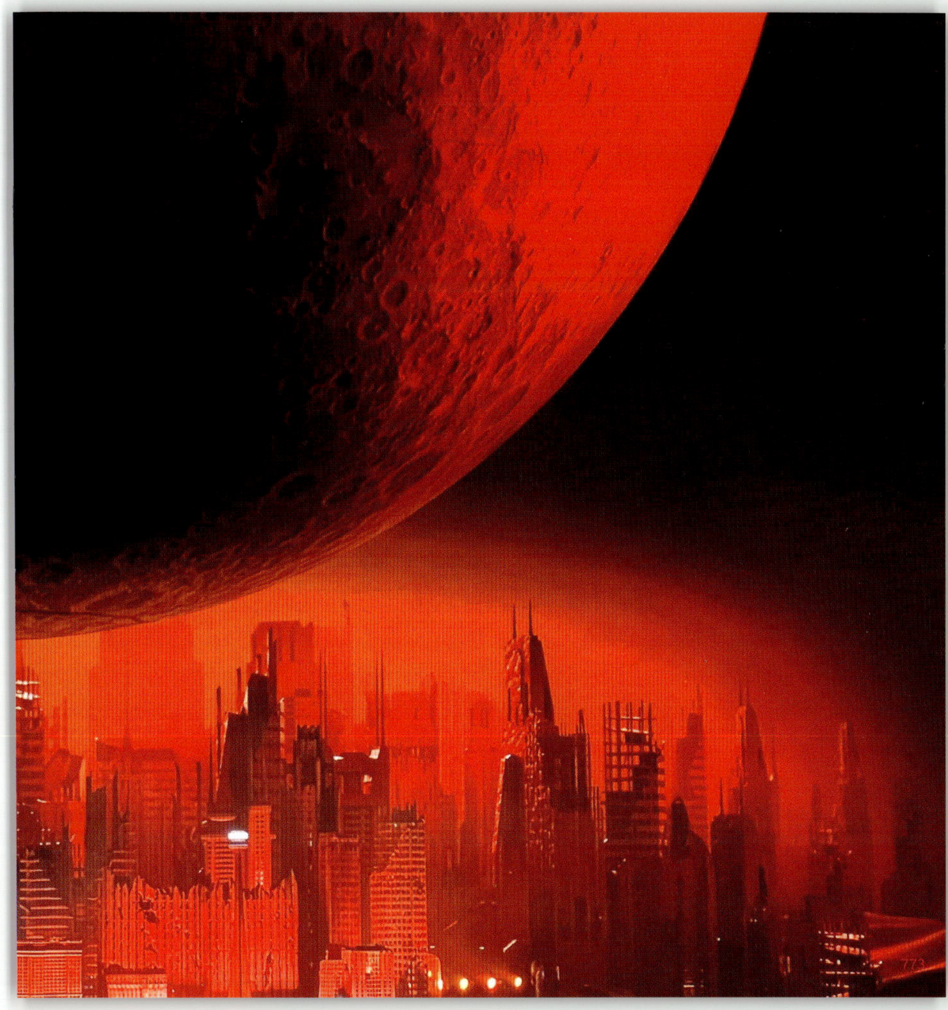

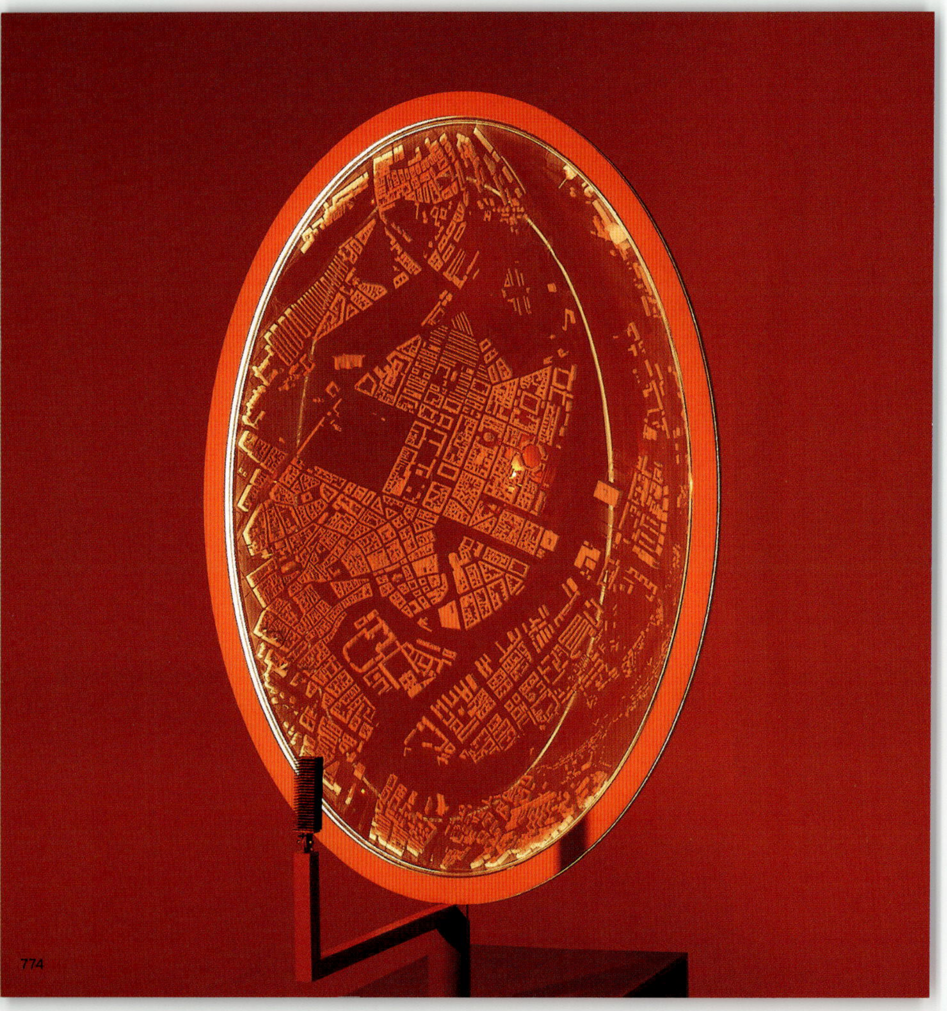

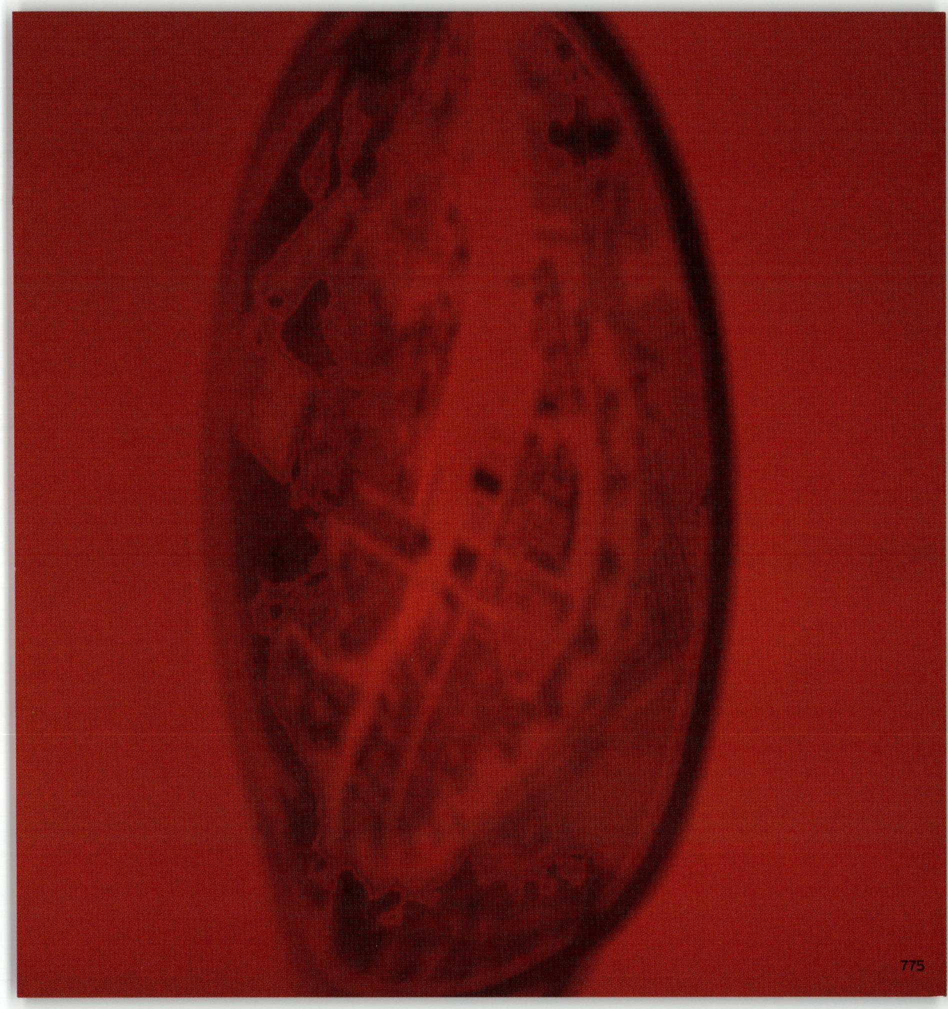

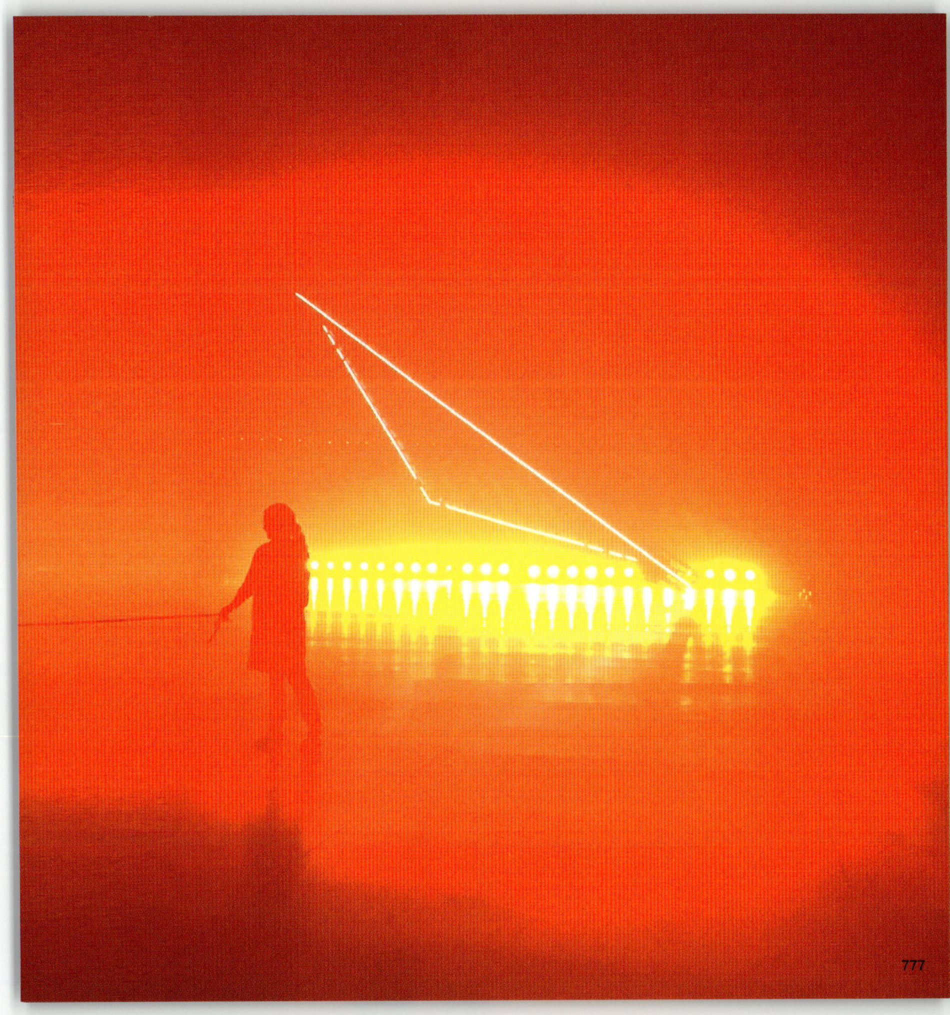

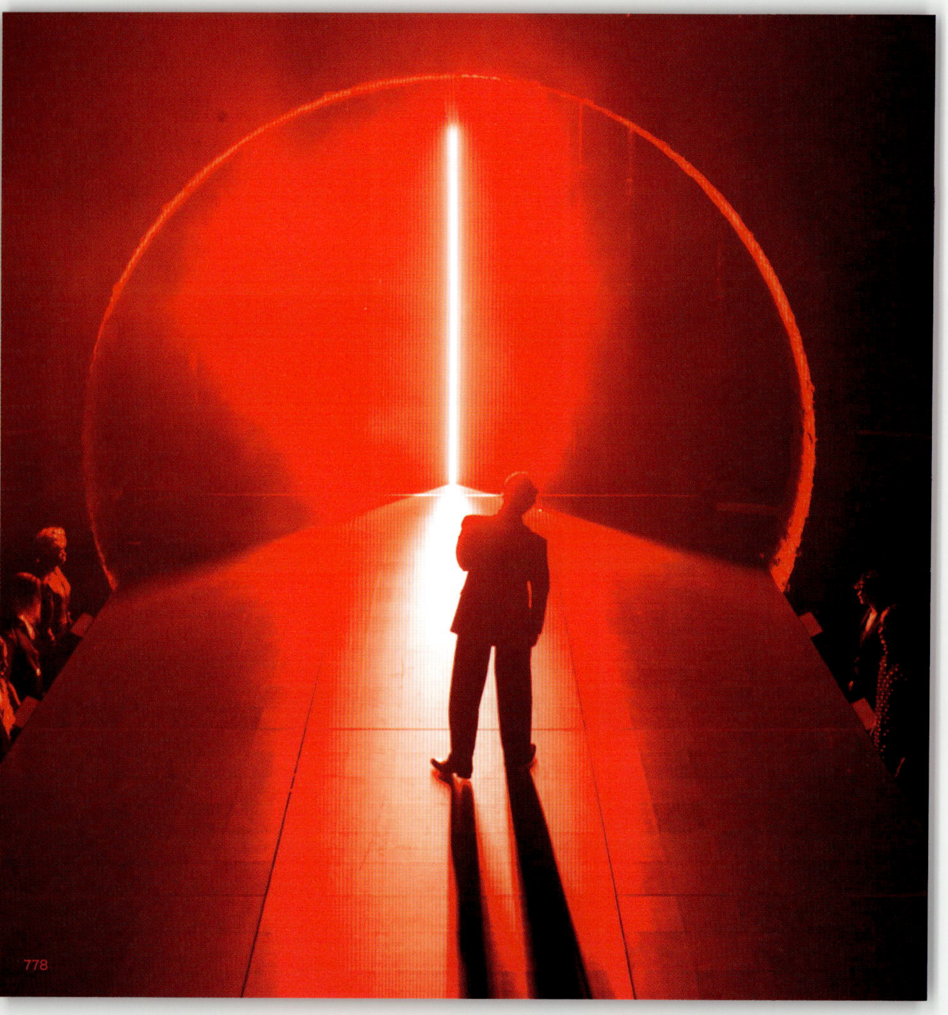

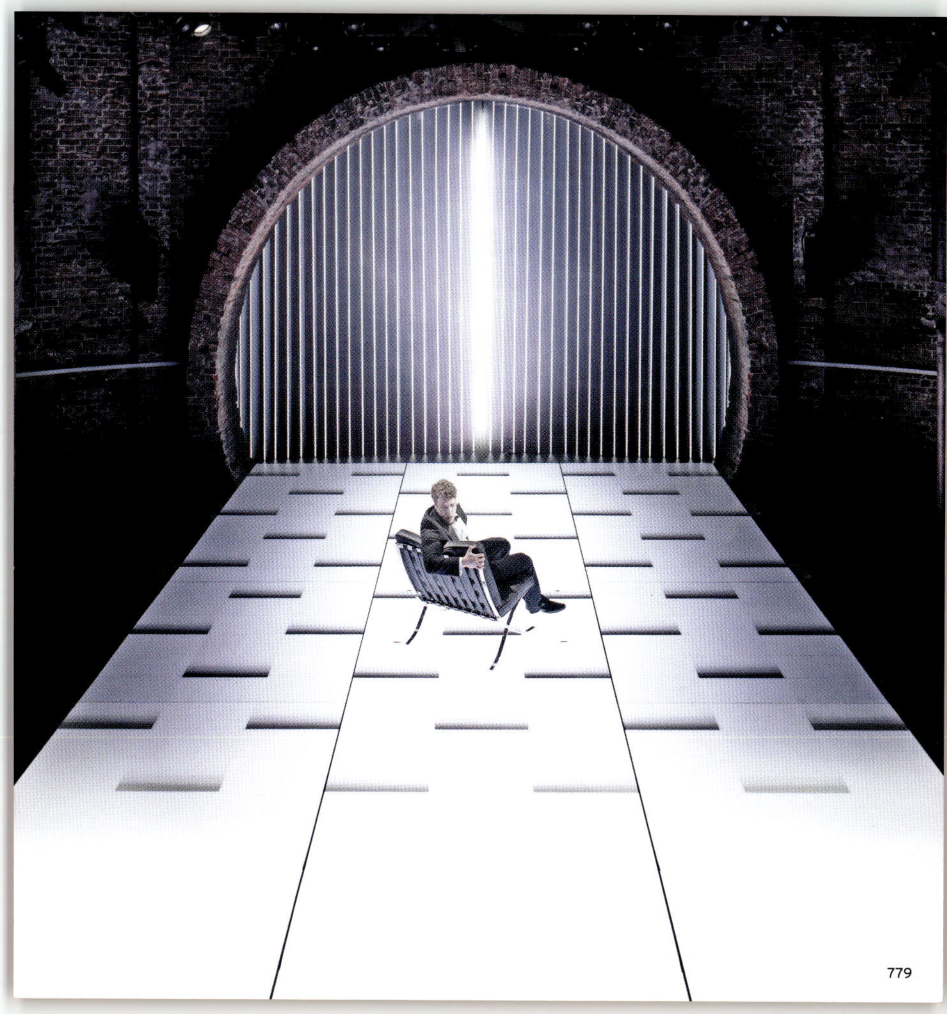

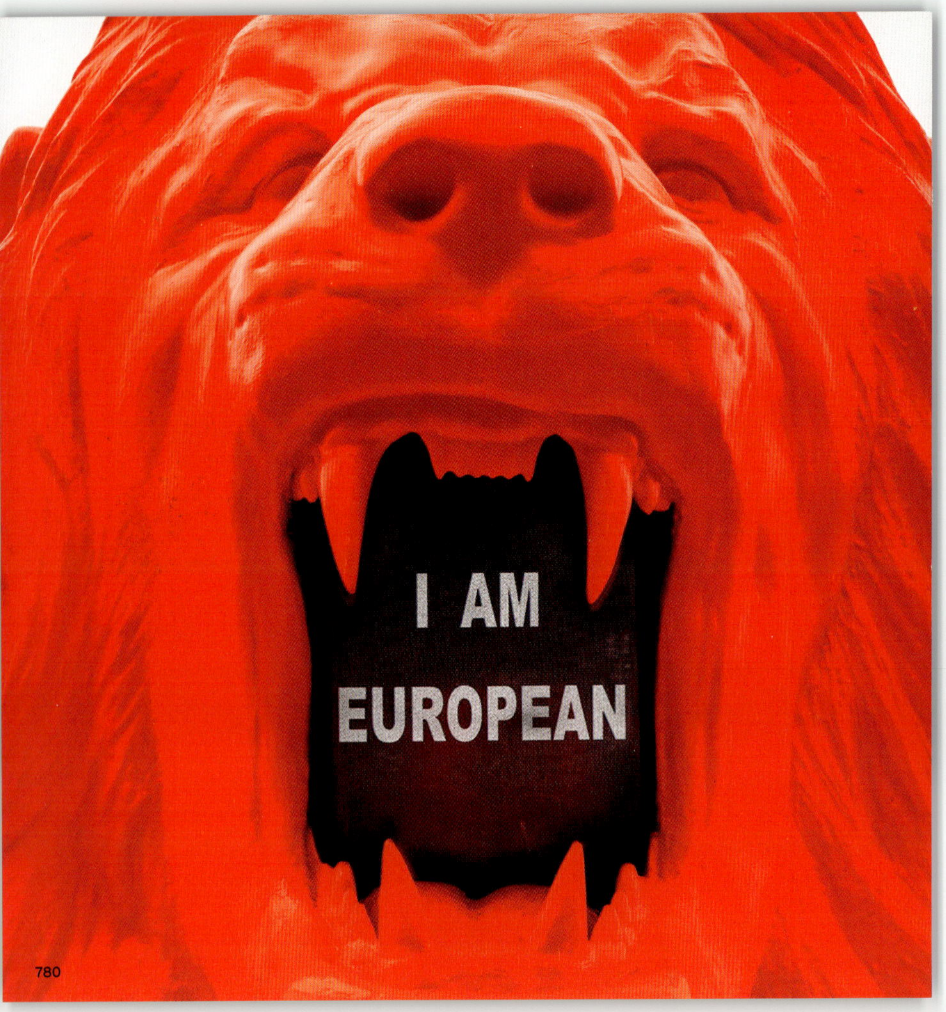
I AM
EUROPEAN

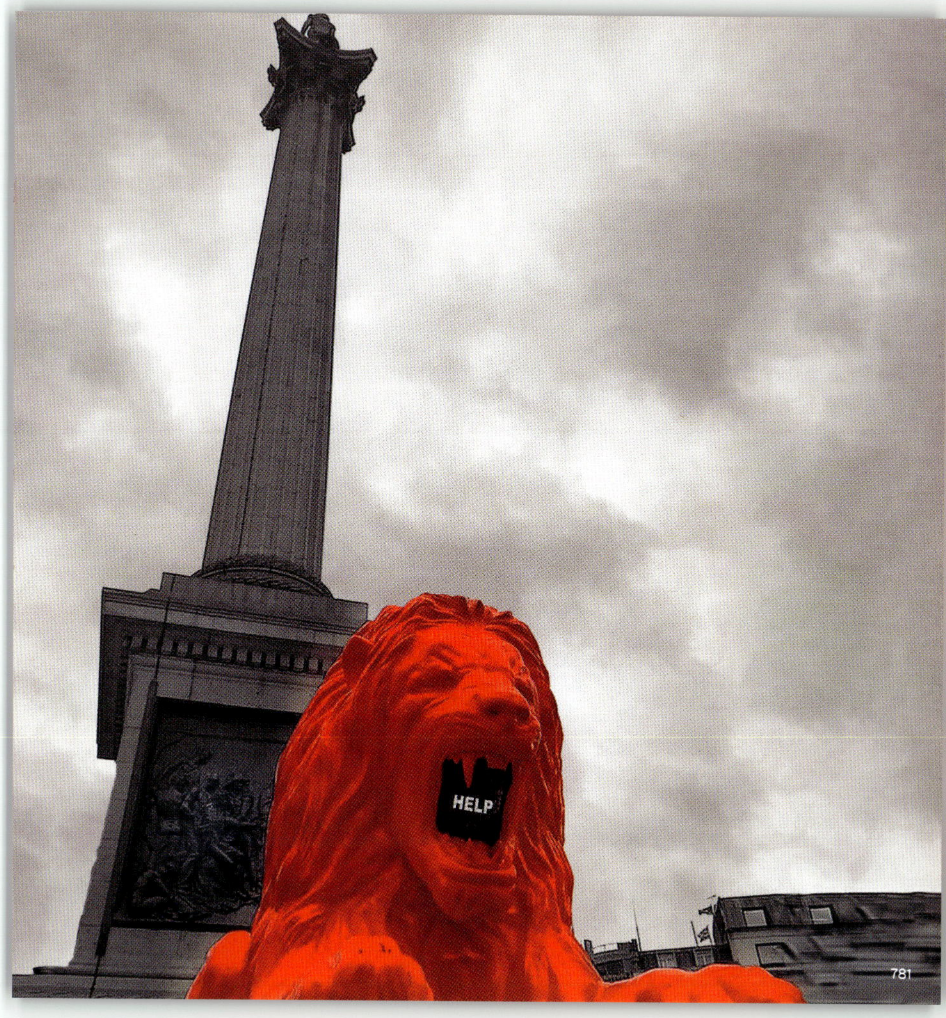
HELP

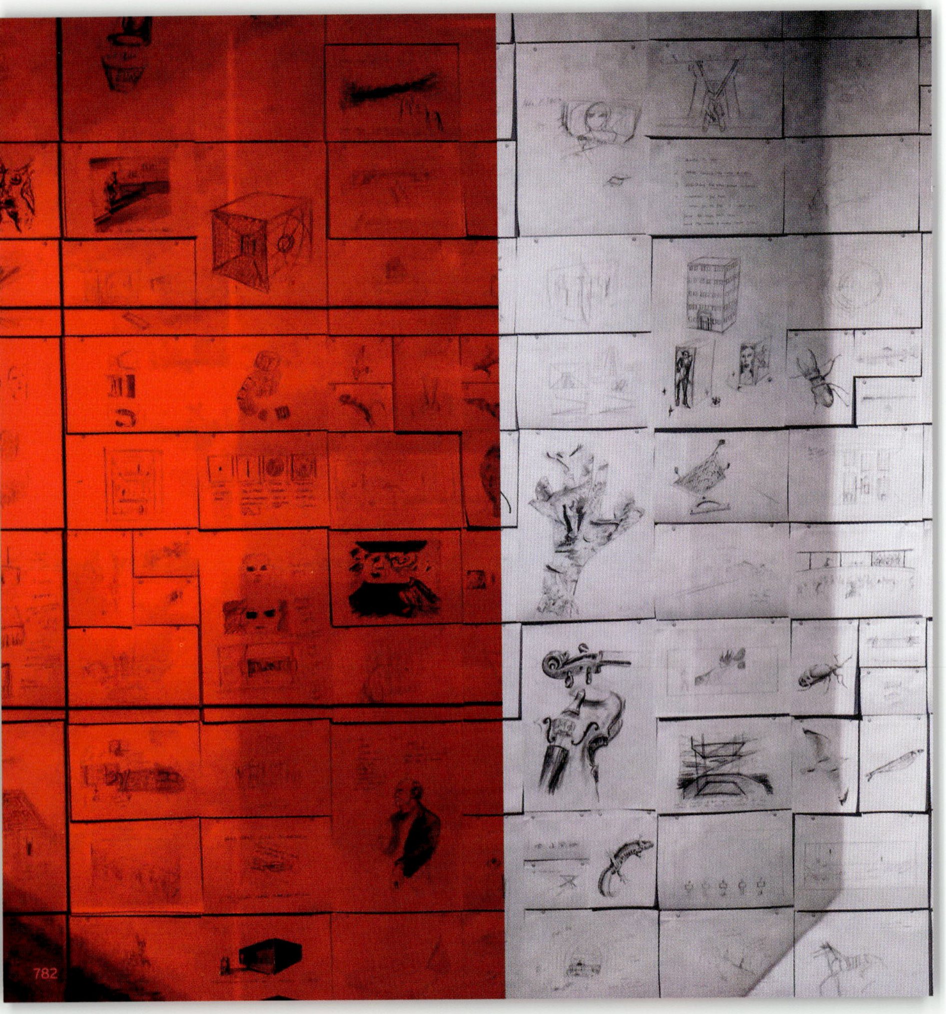

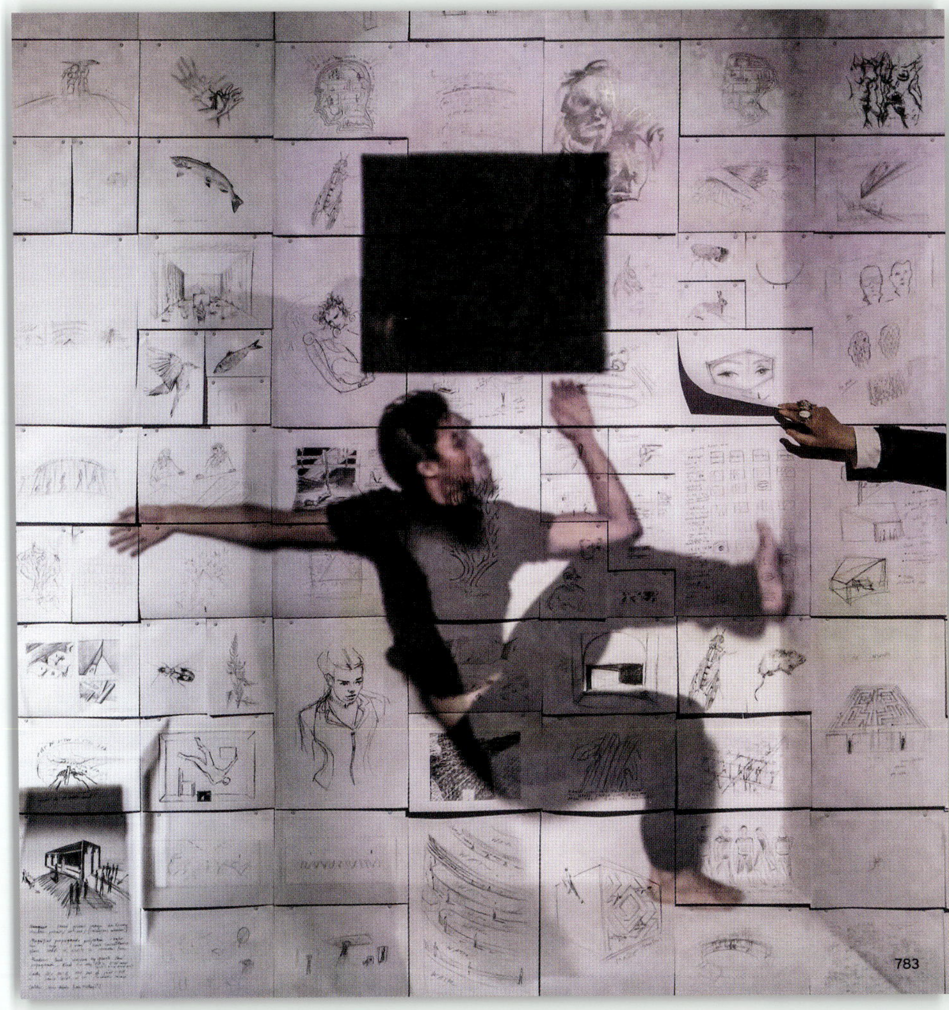

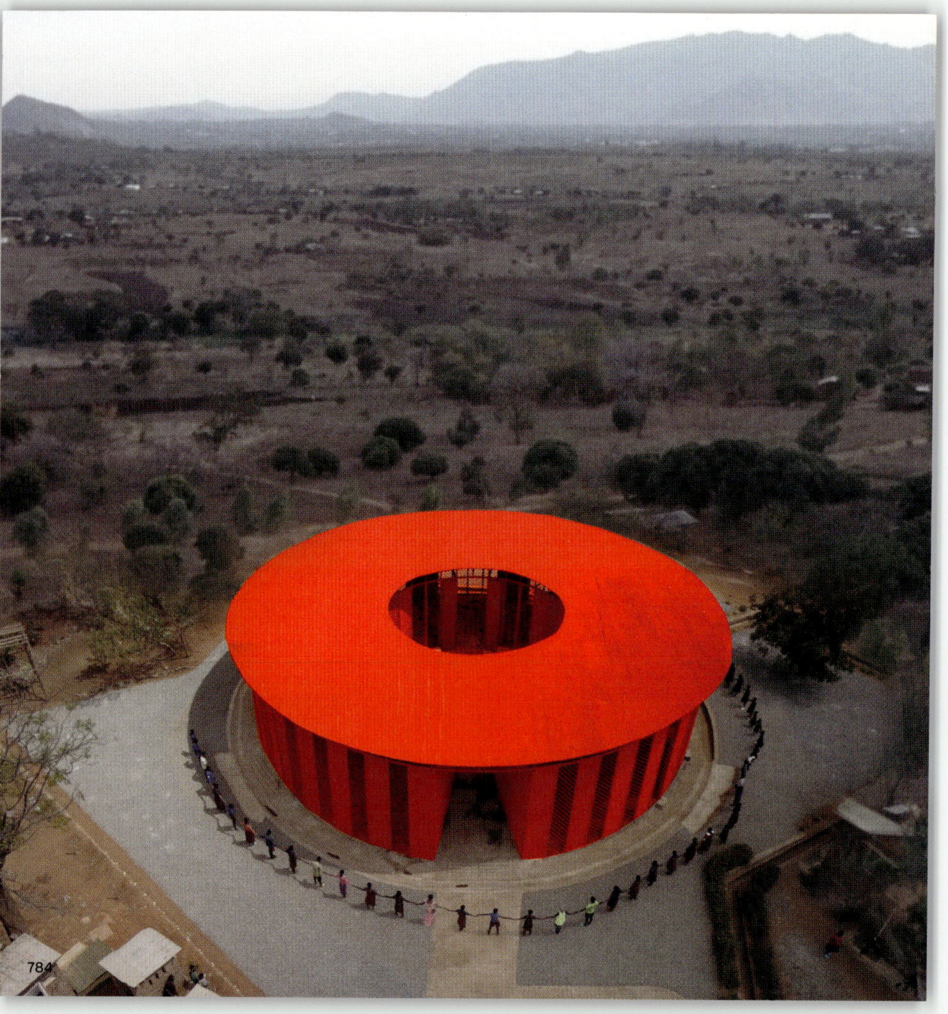

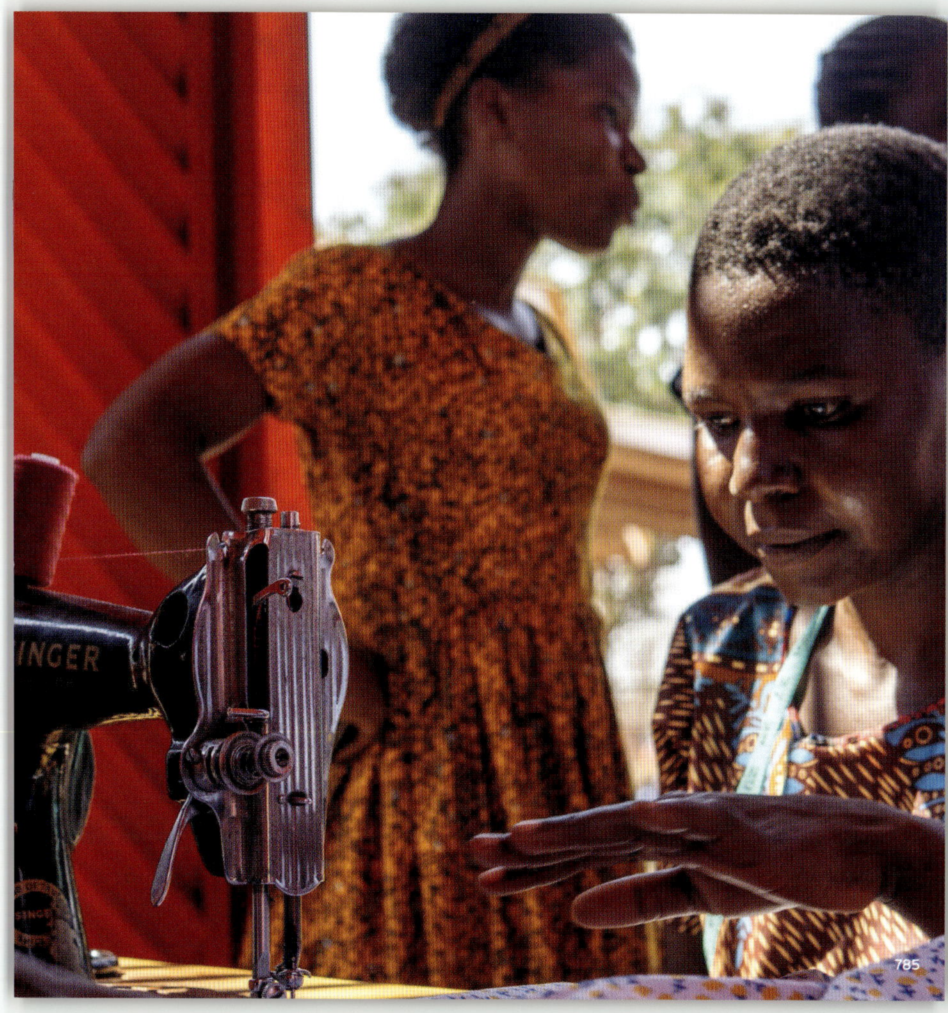

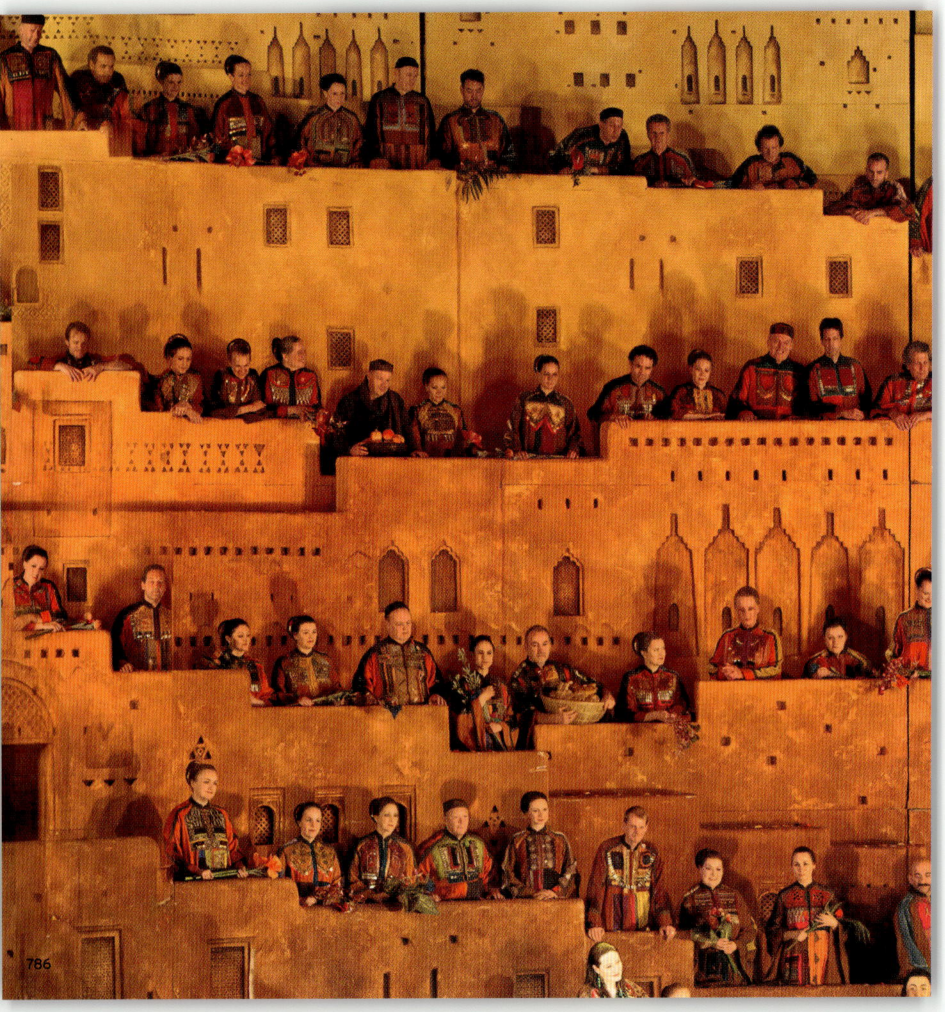

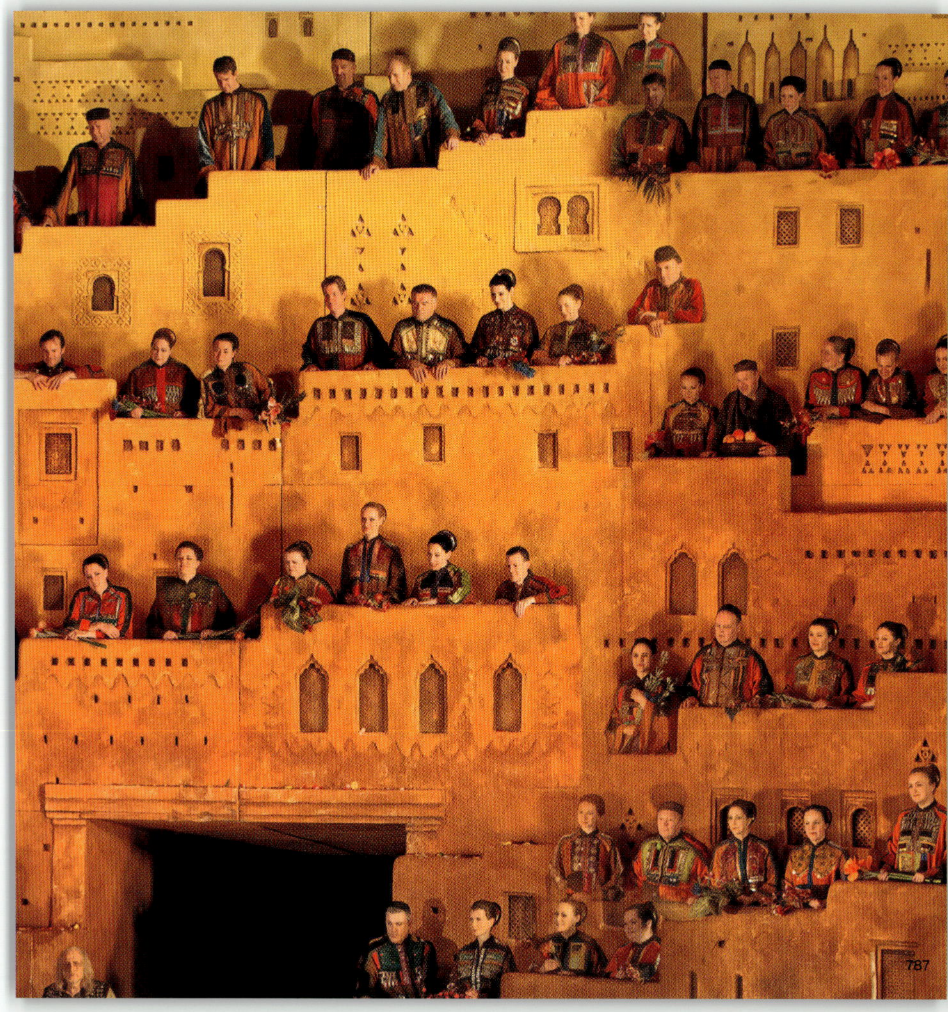

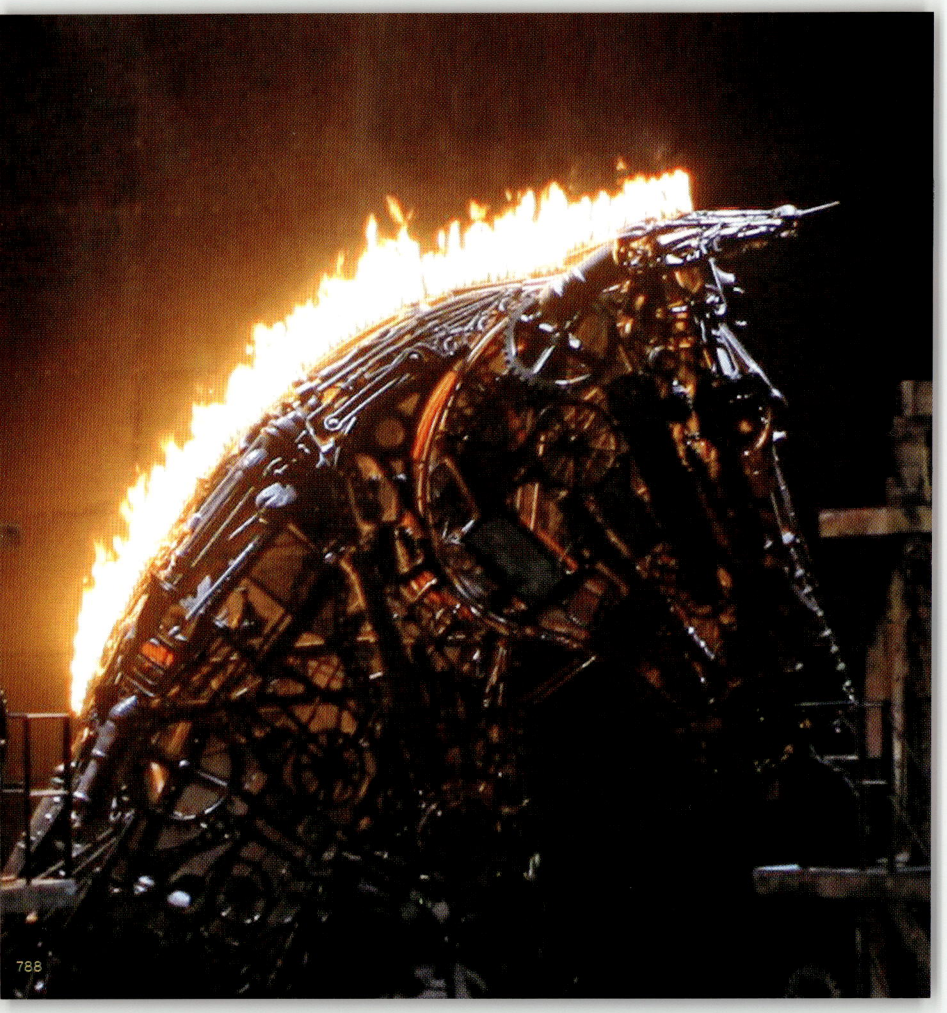

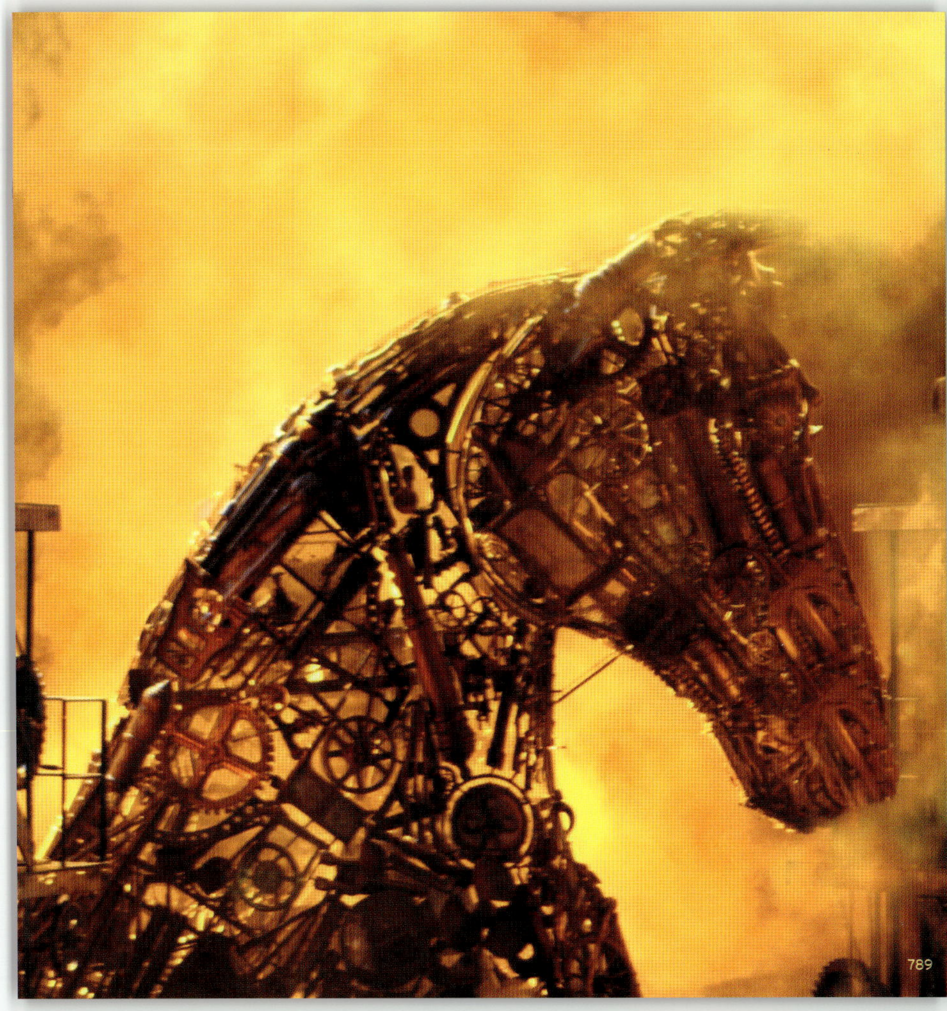

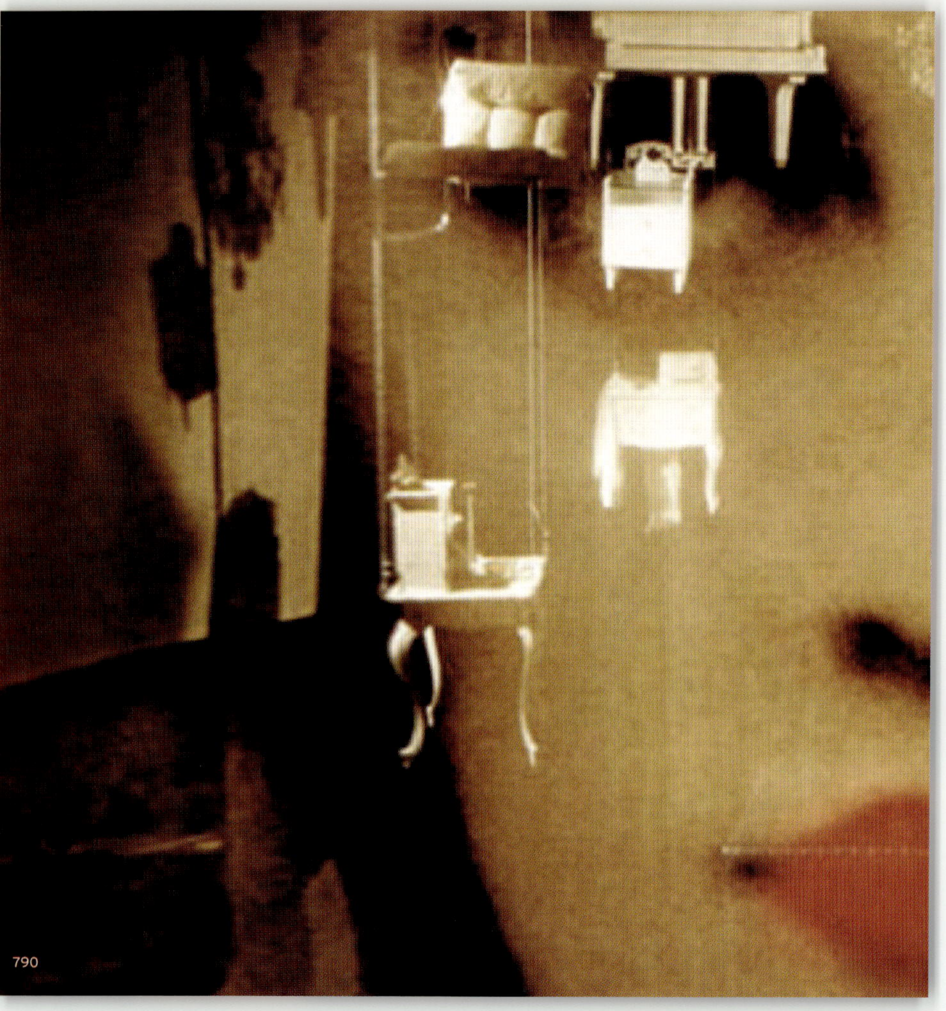

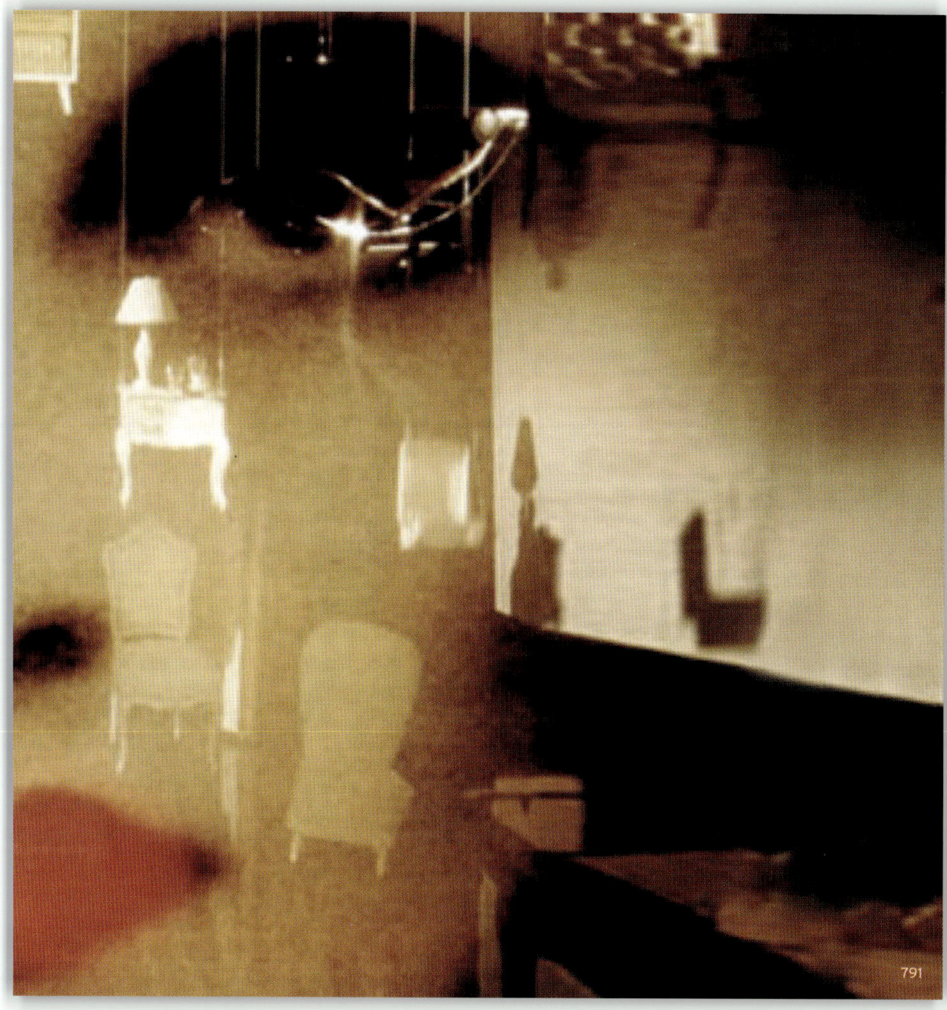

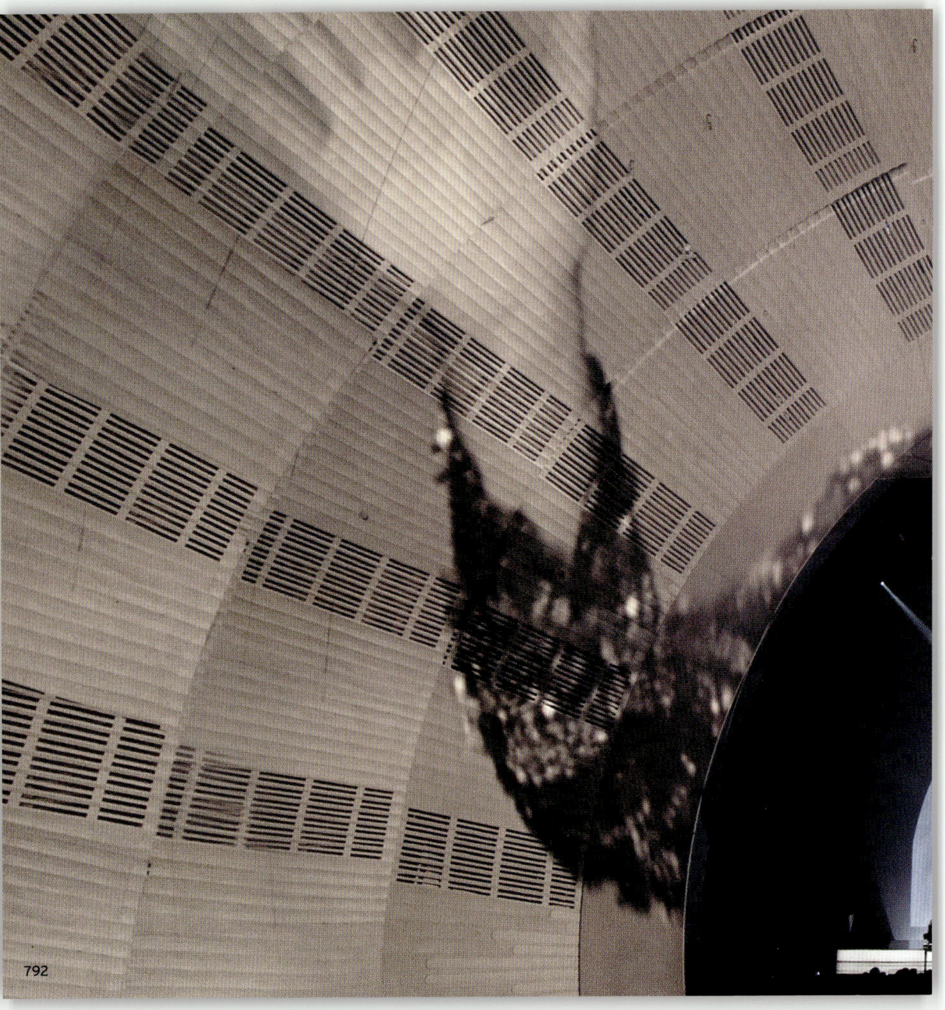

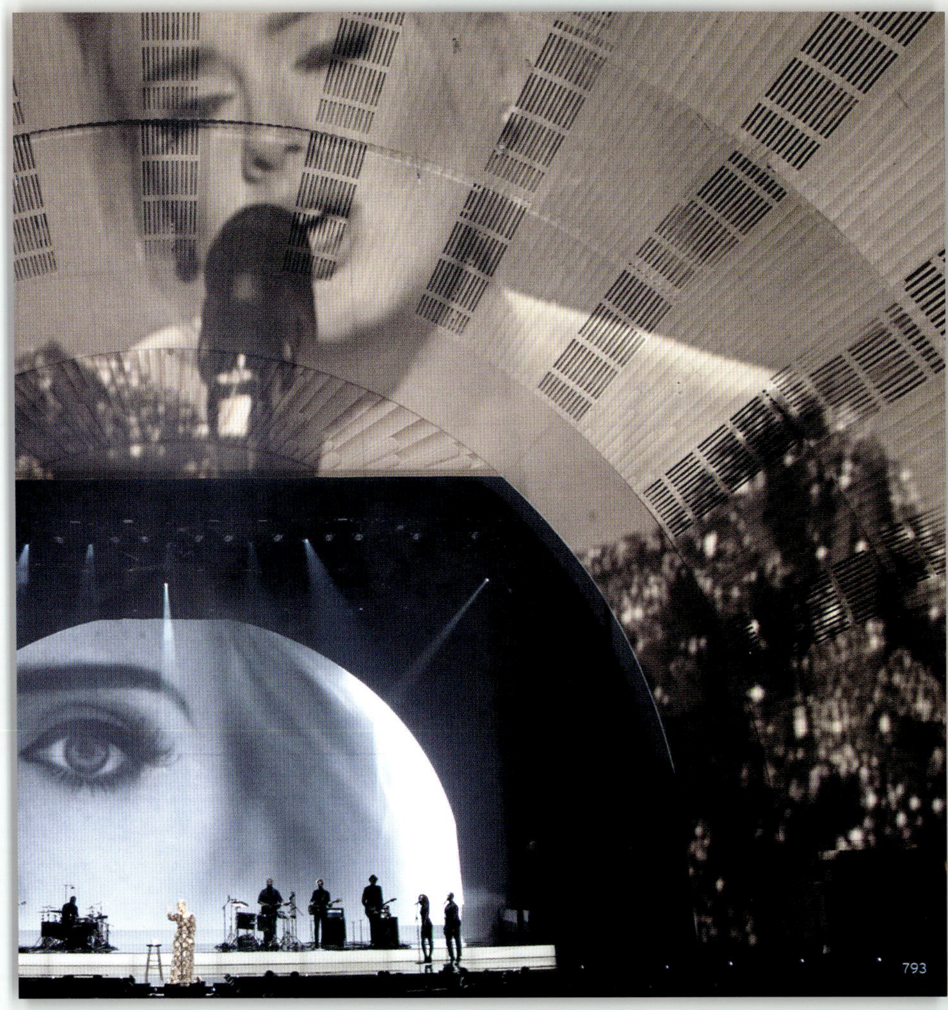

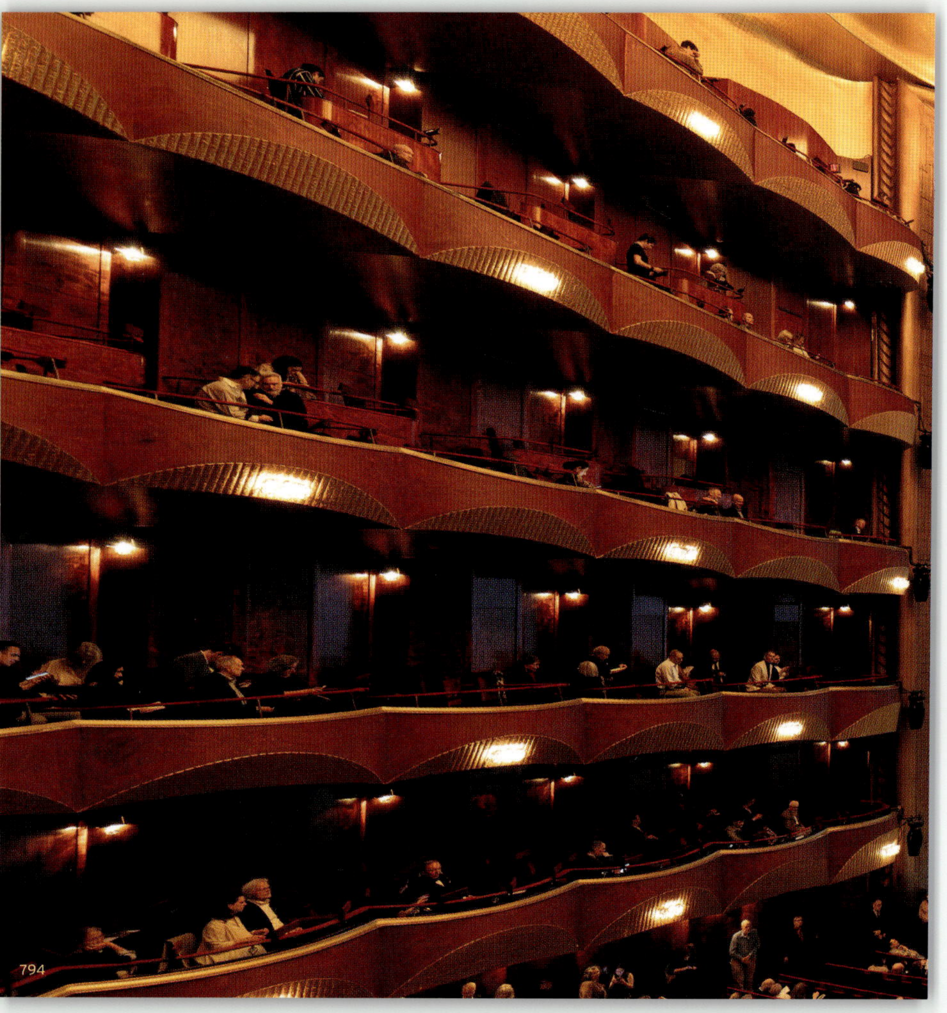

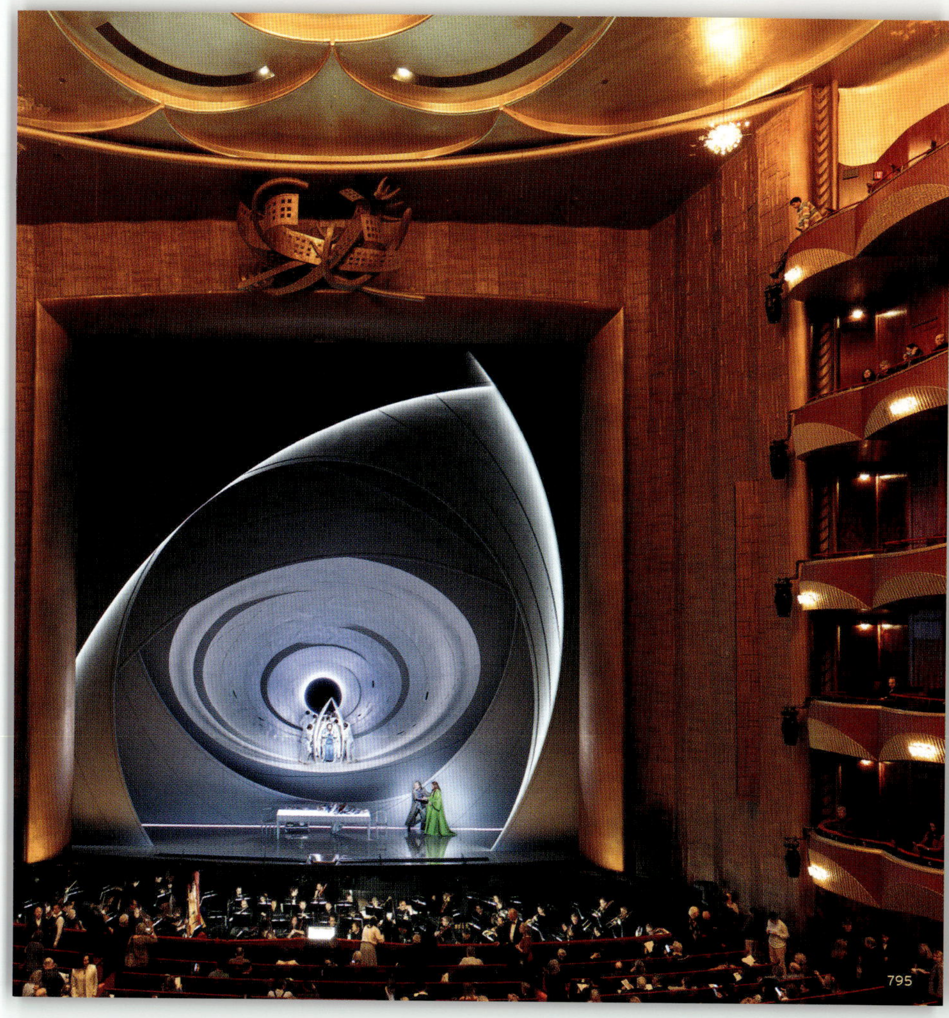

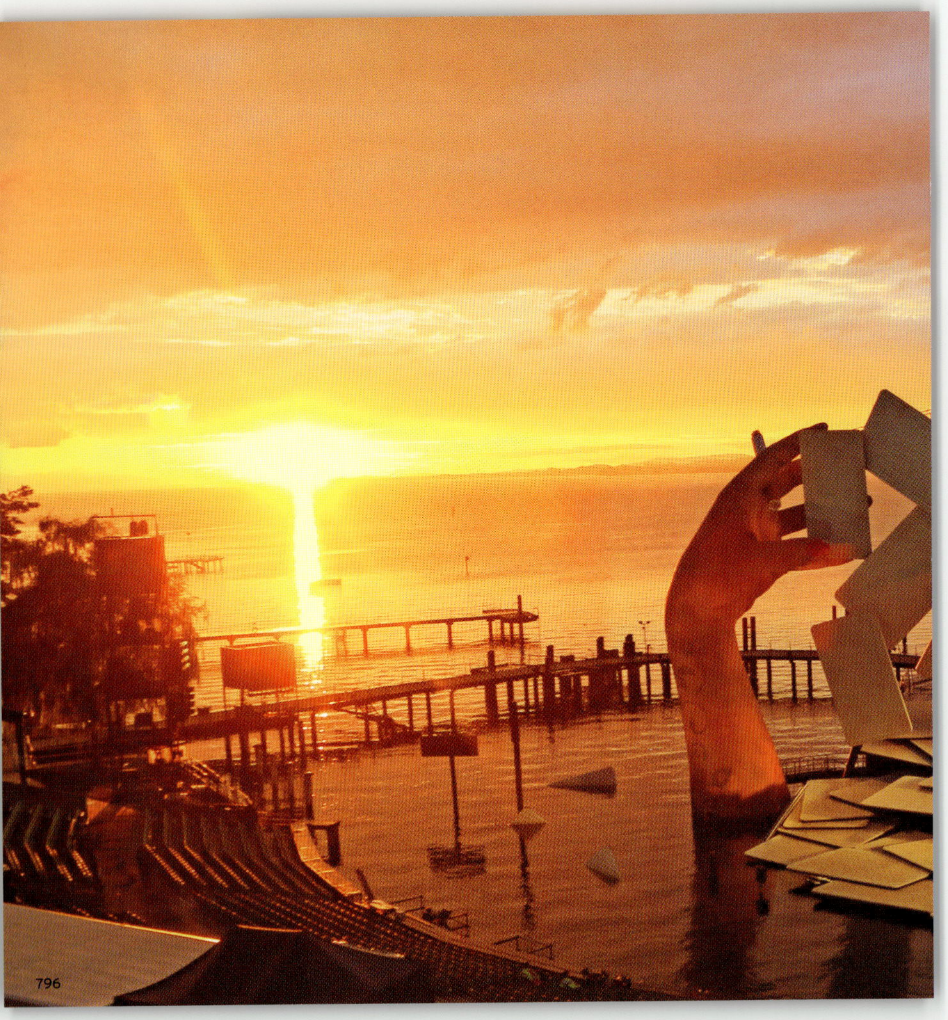

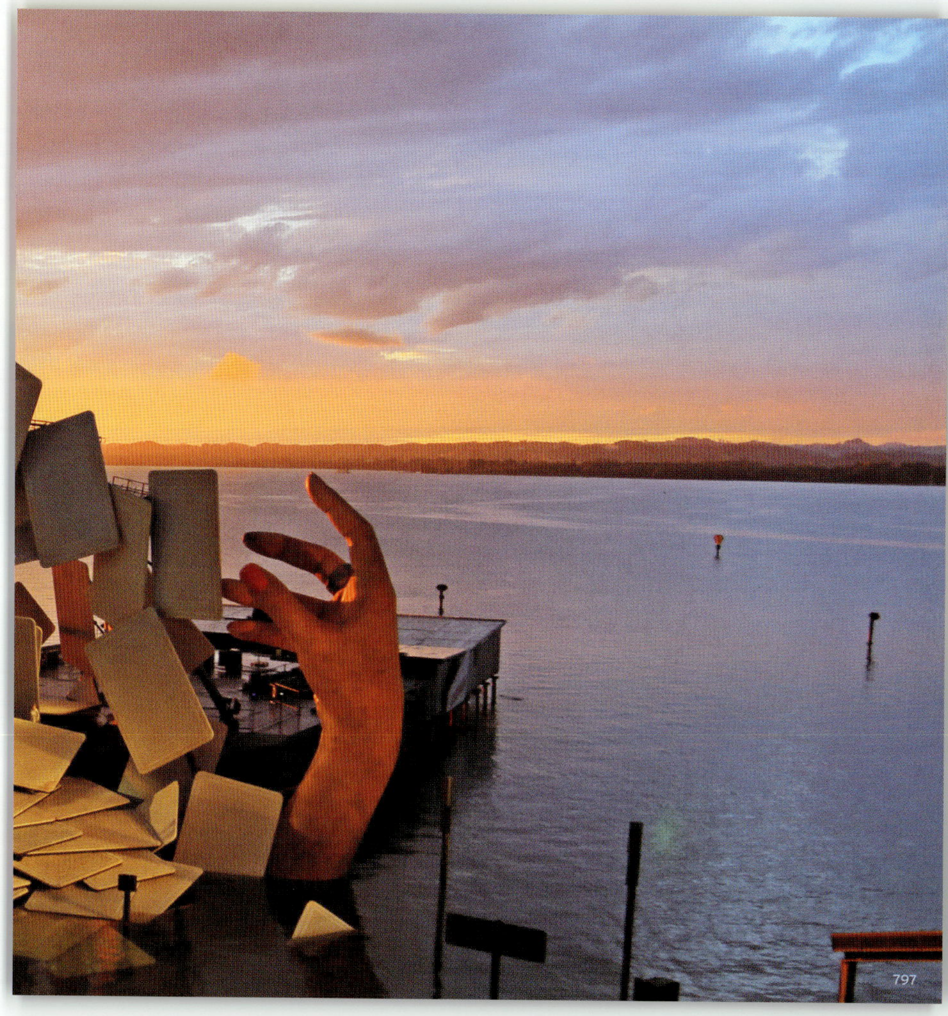

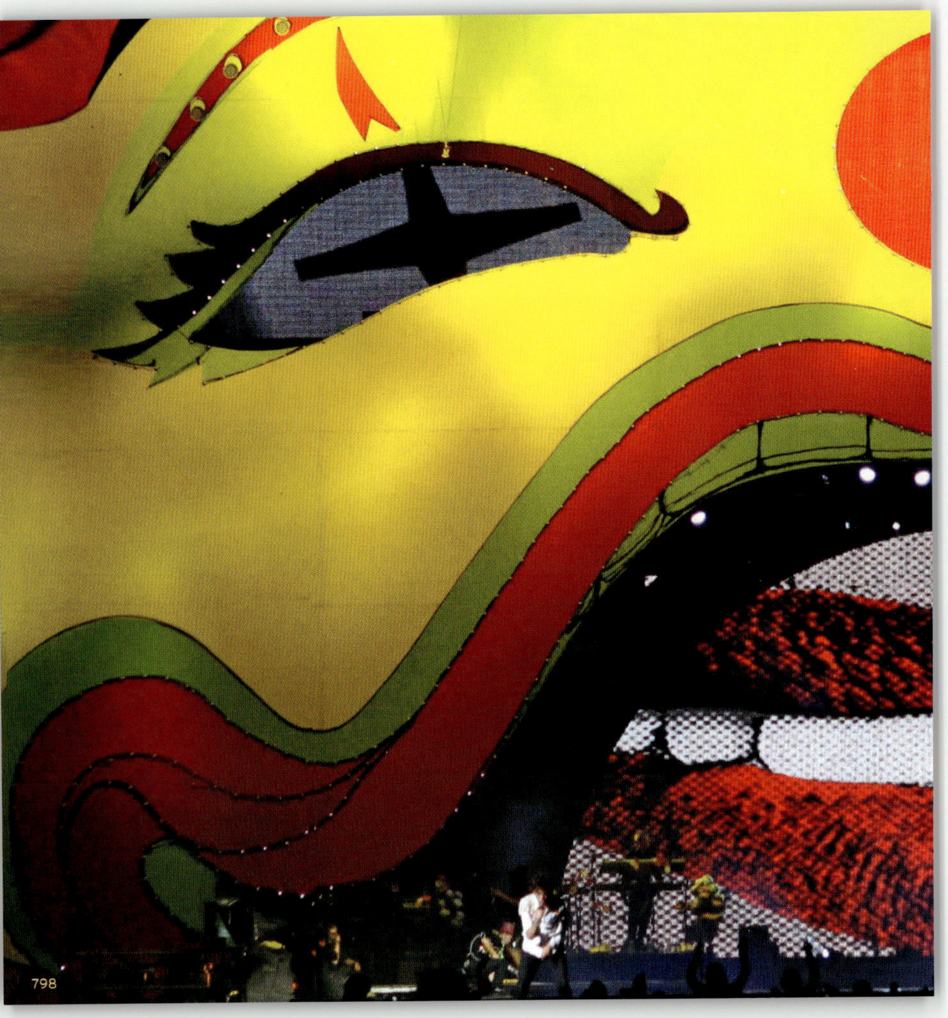

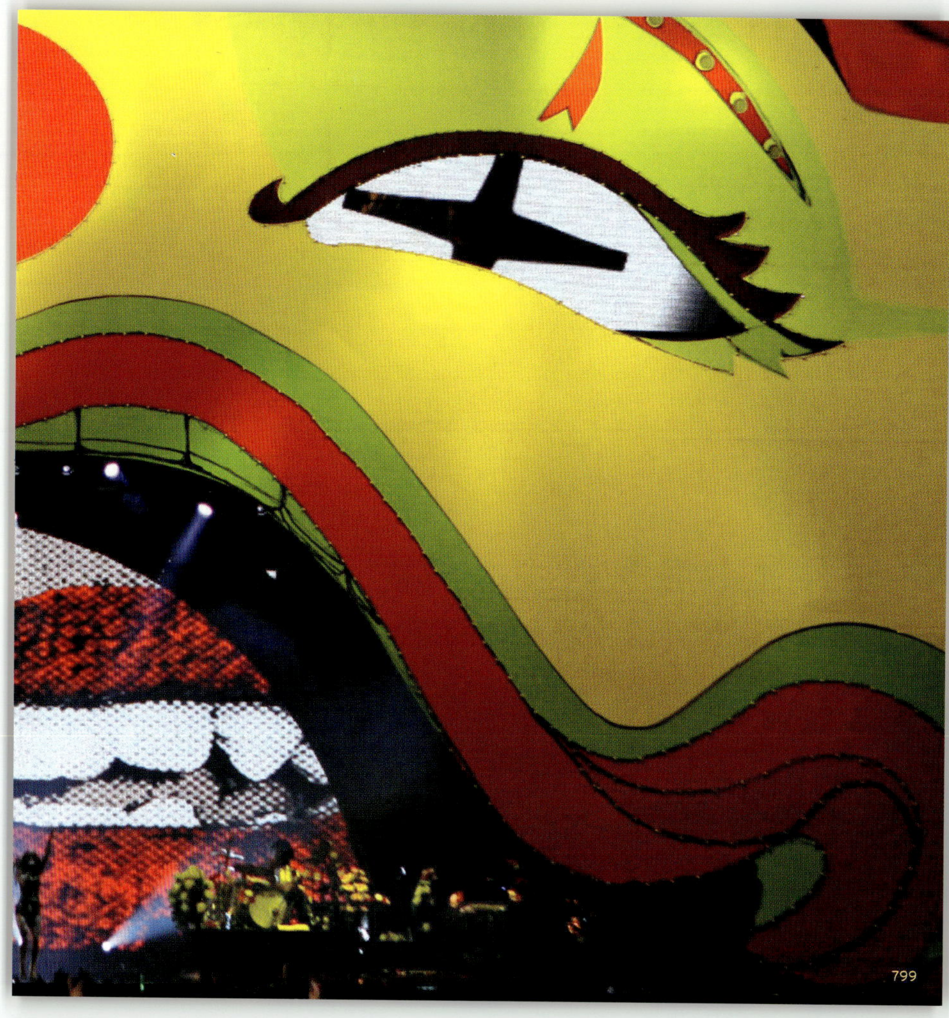

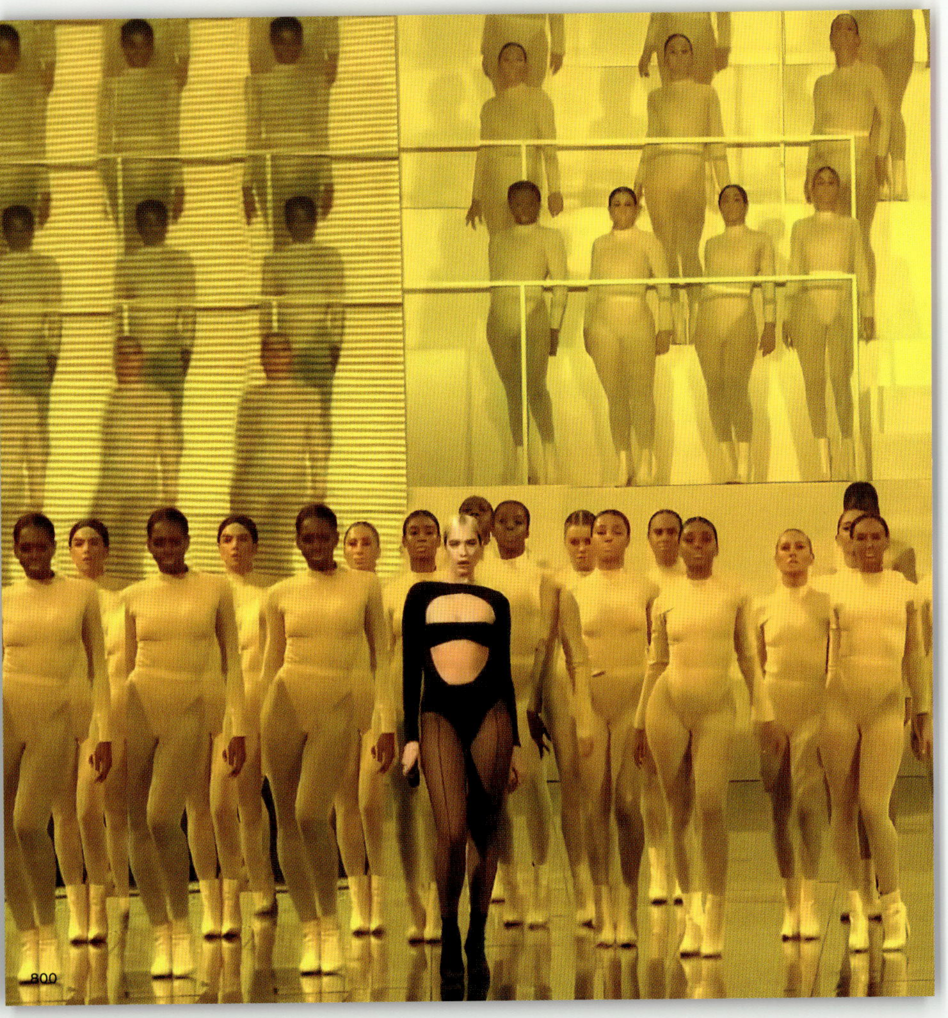

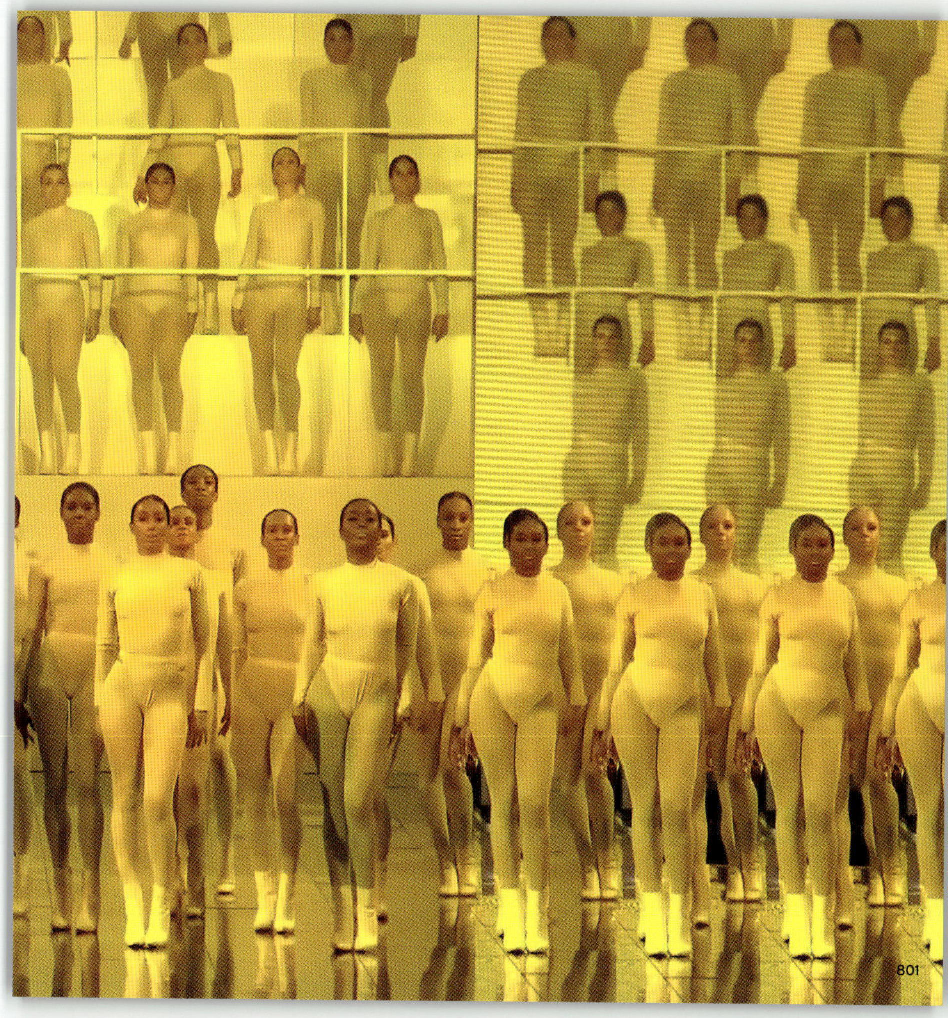

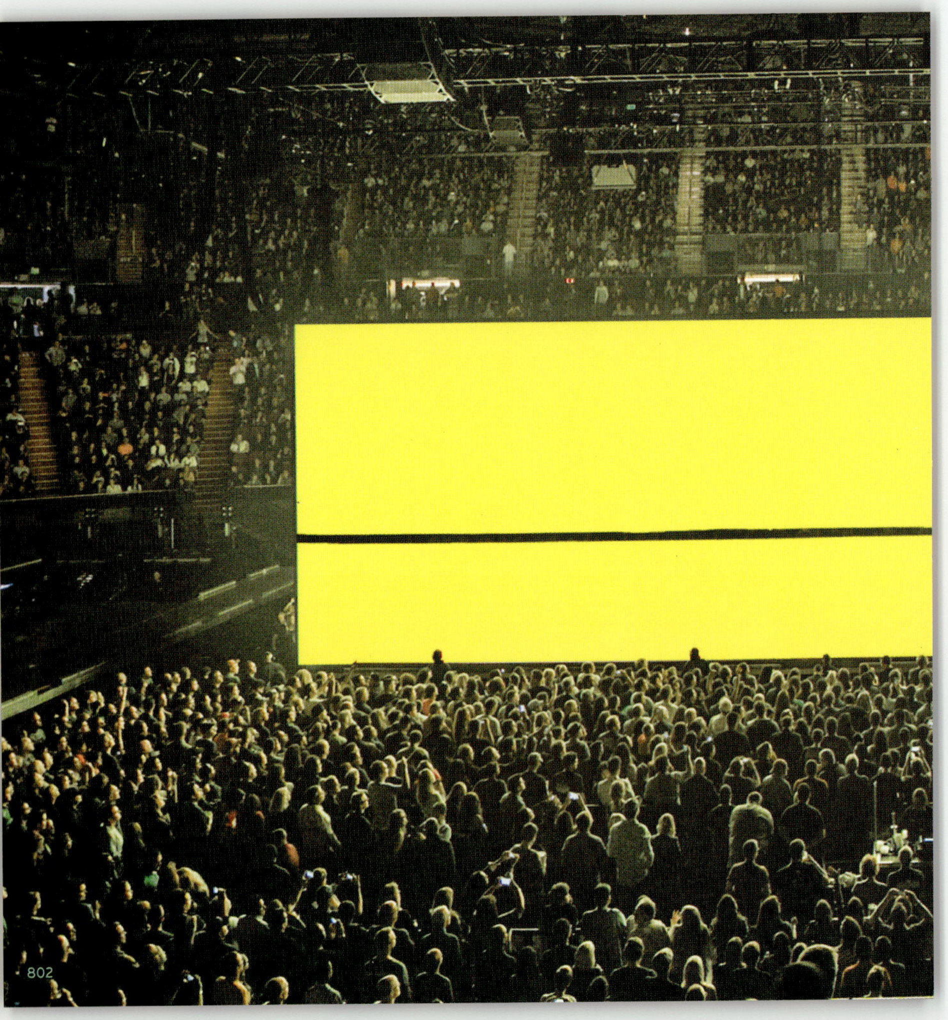

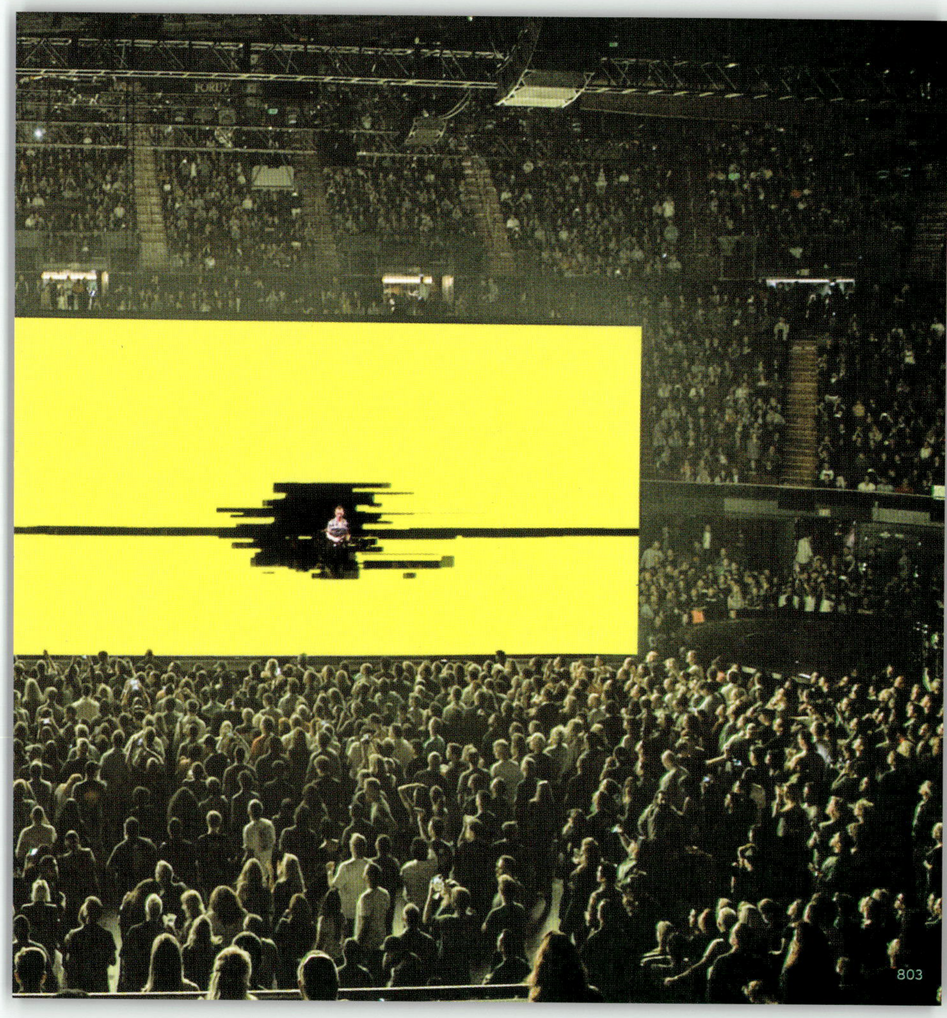

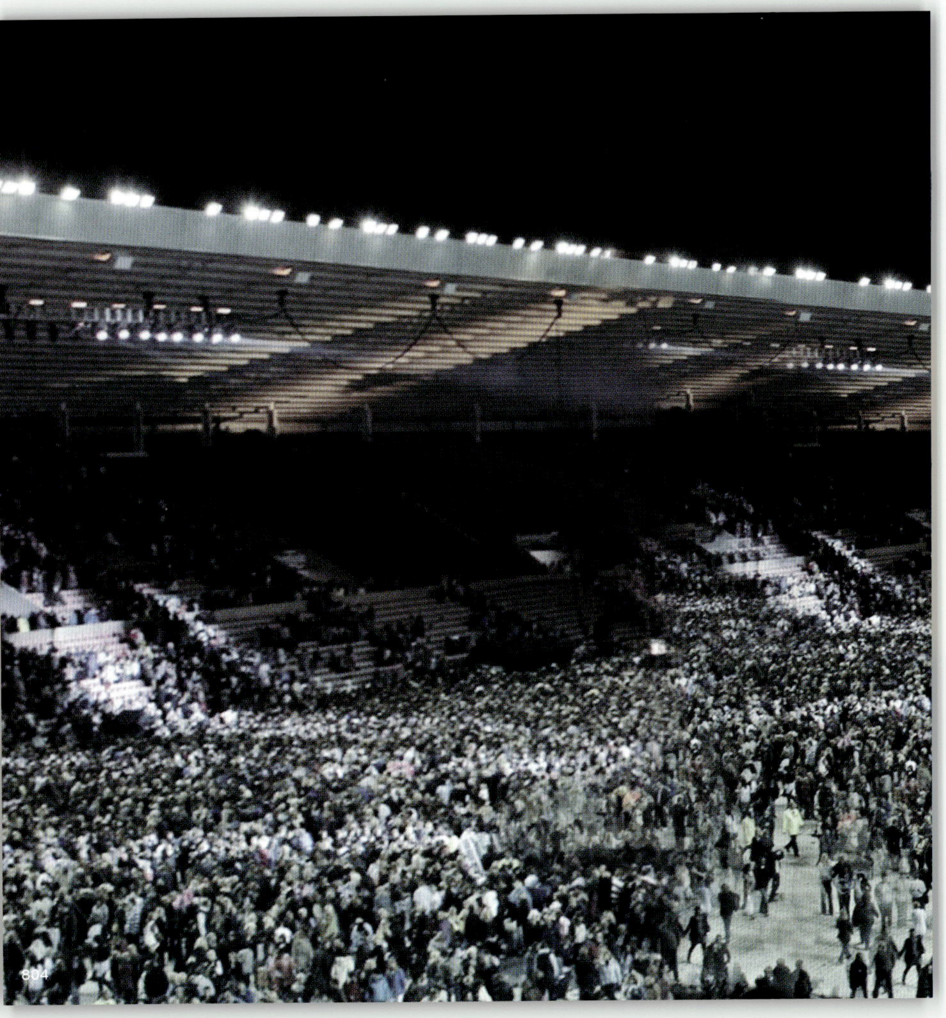

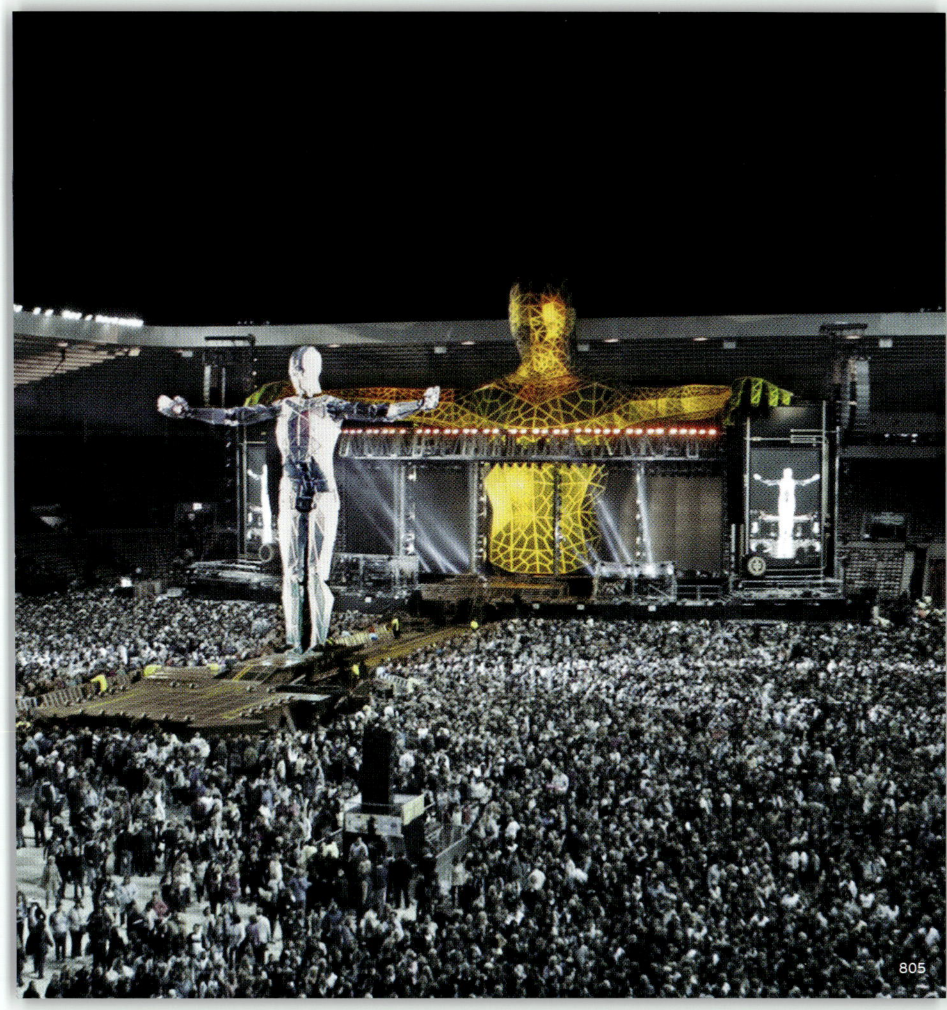

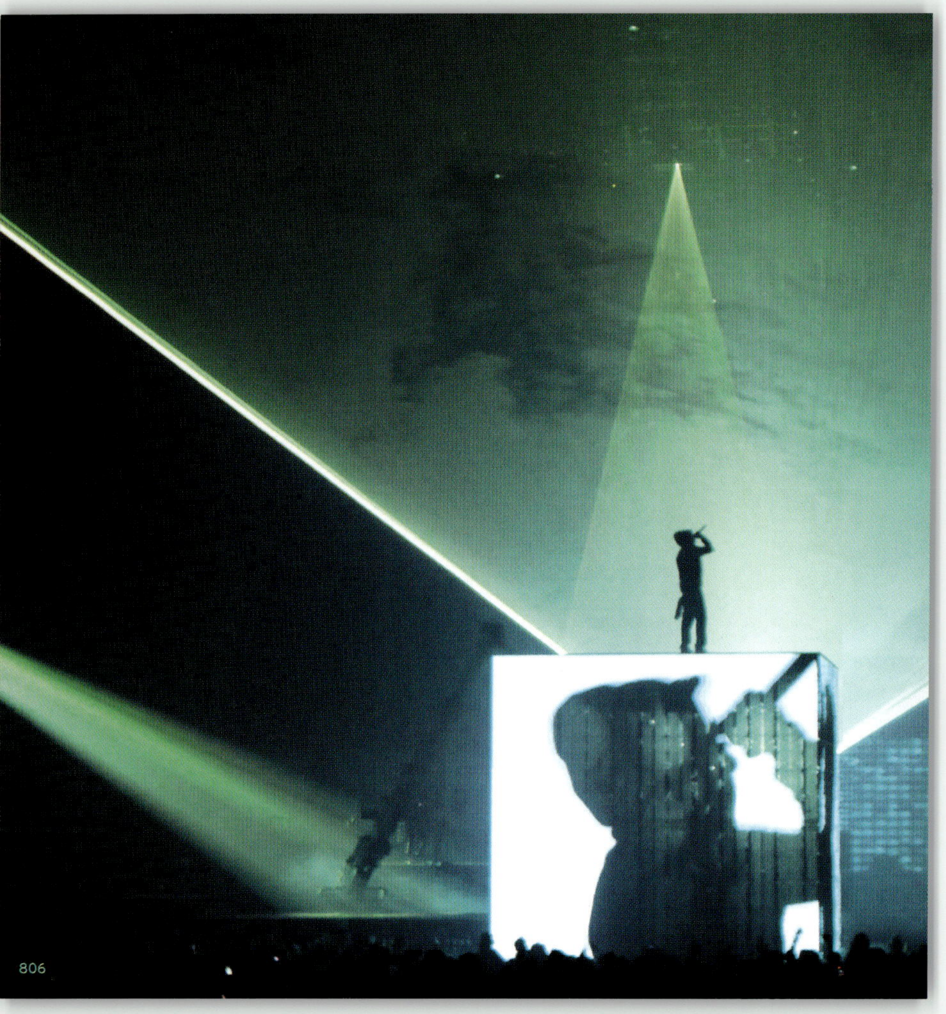

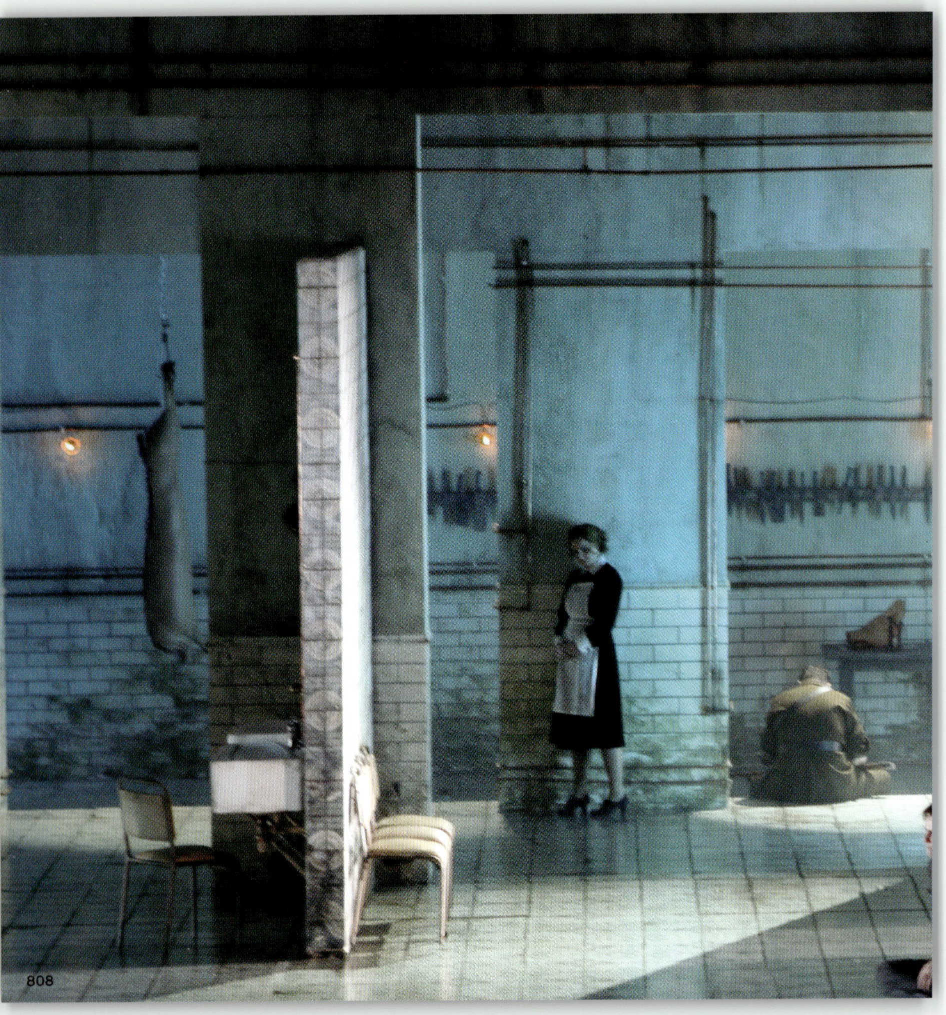

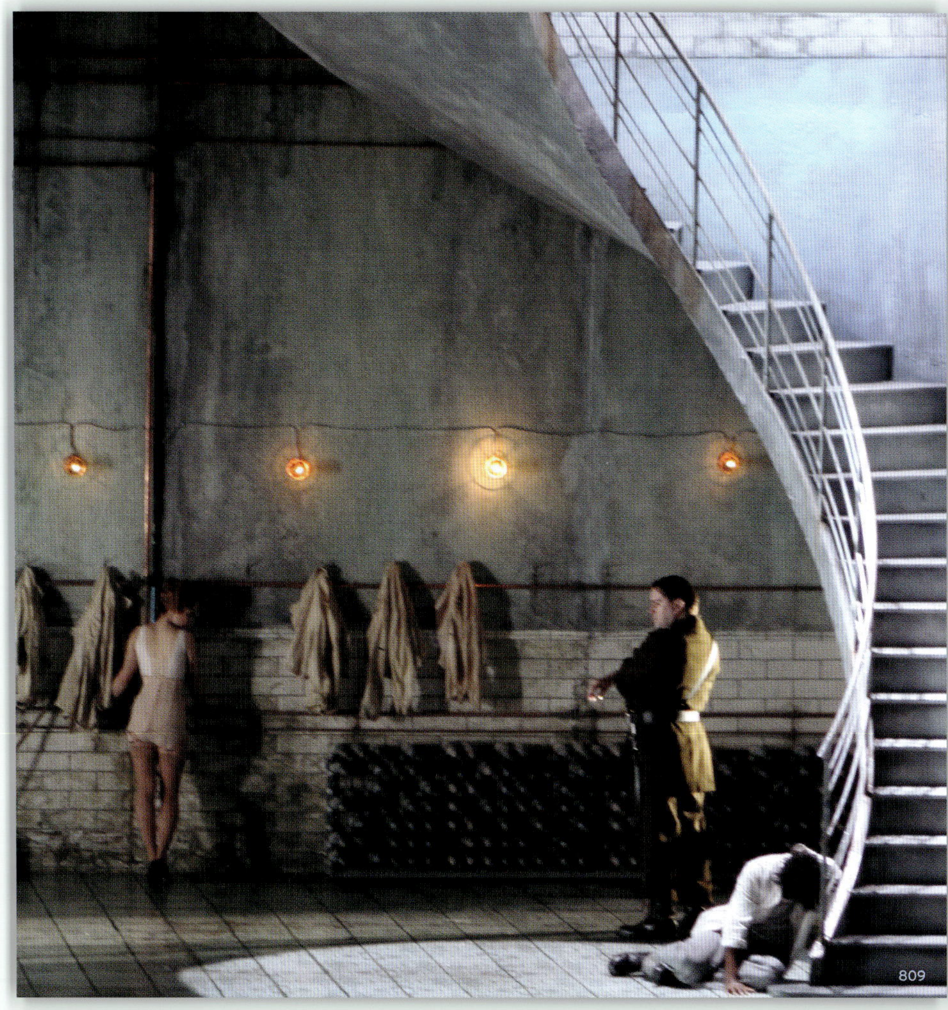

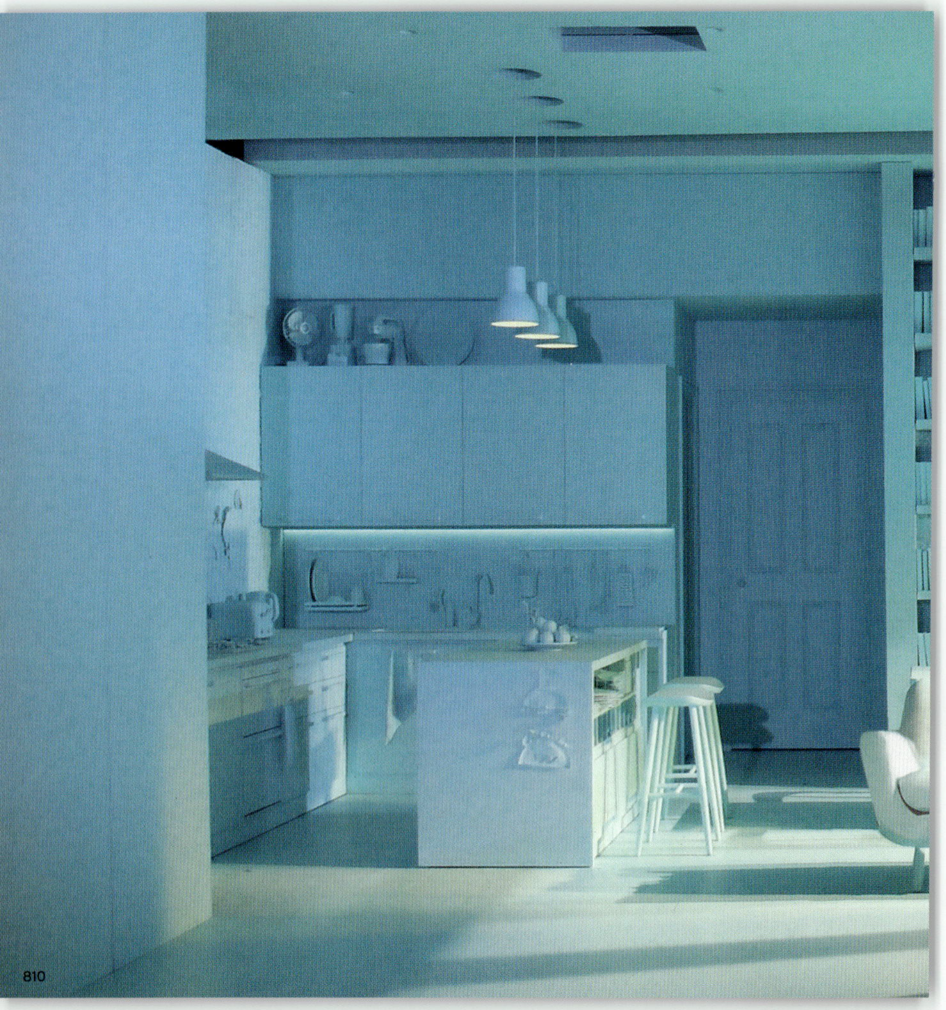

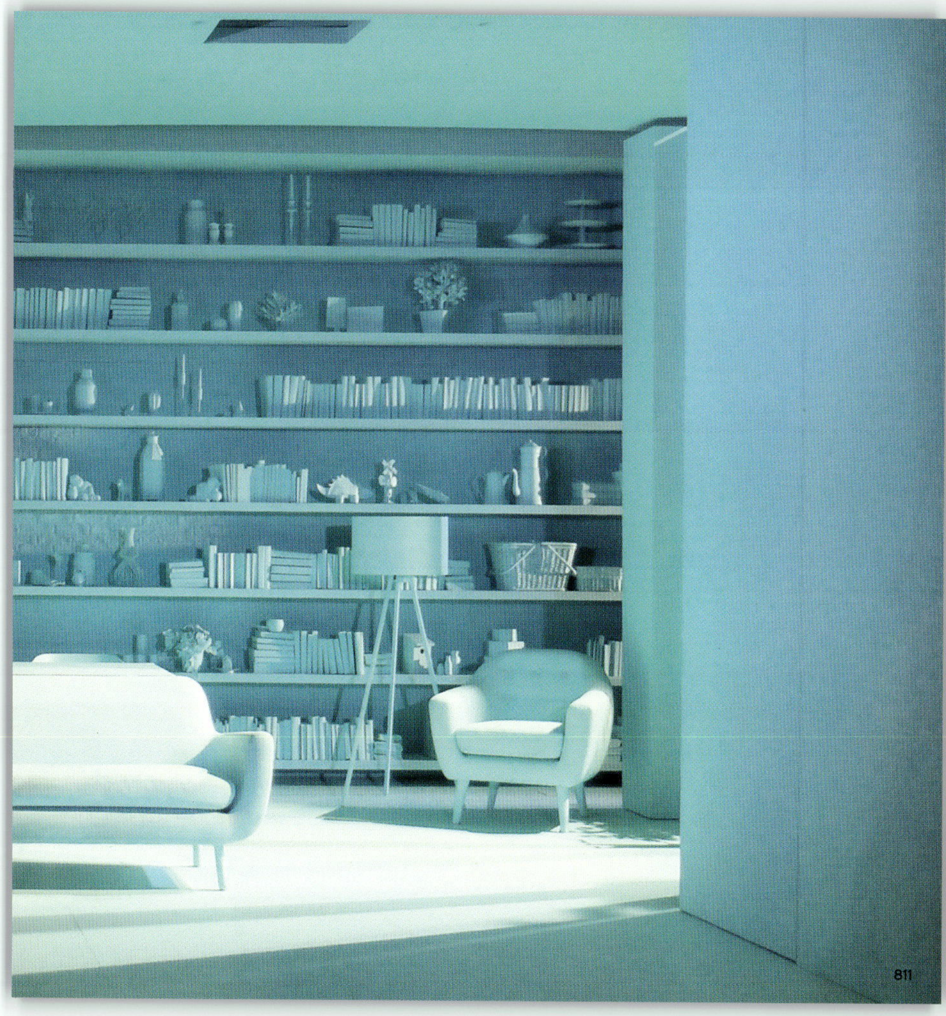

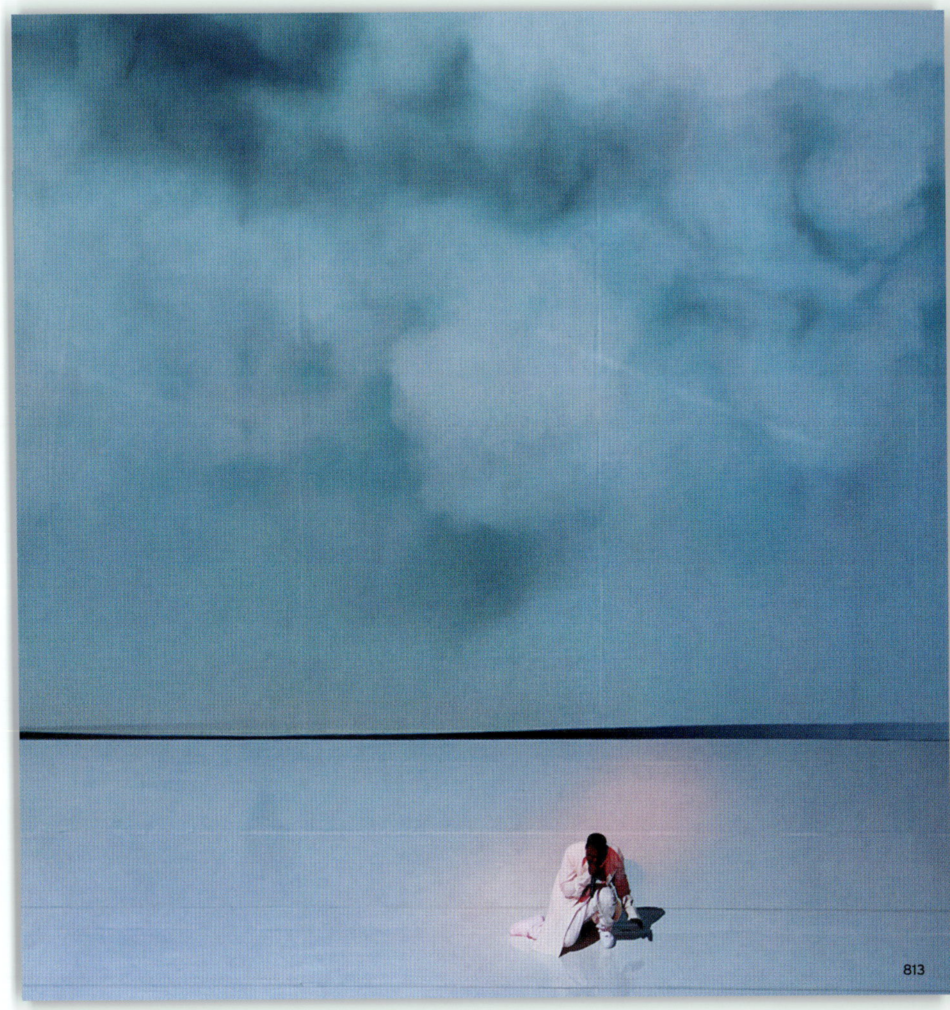

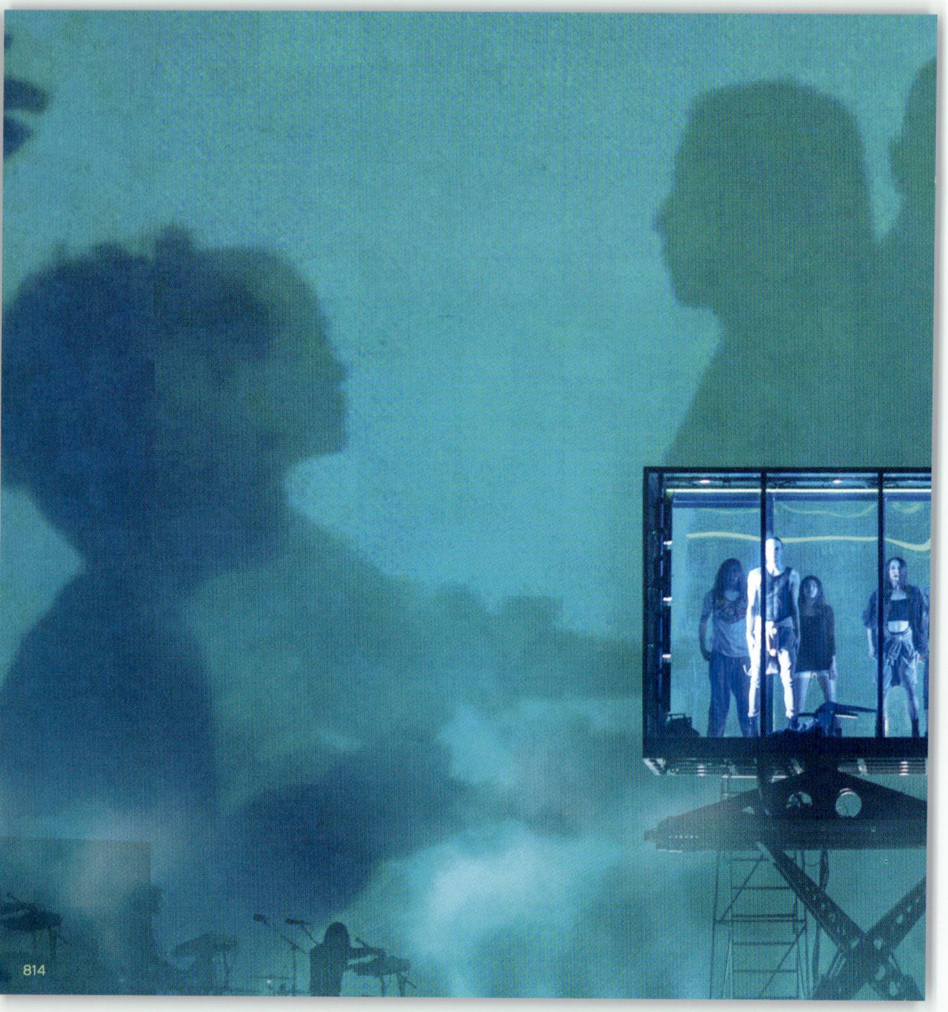

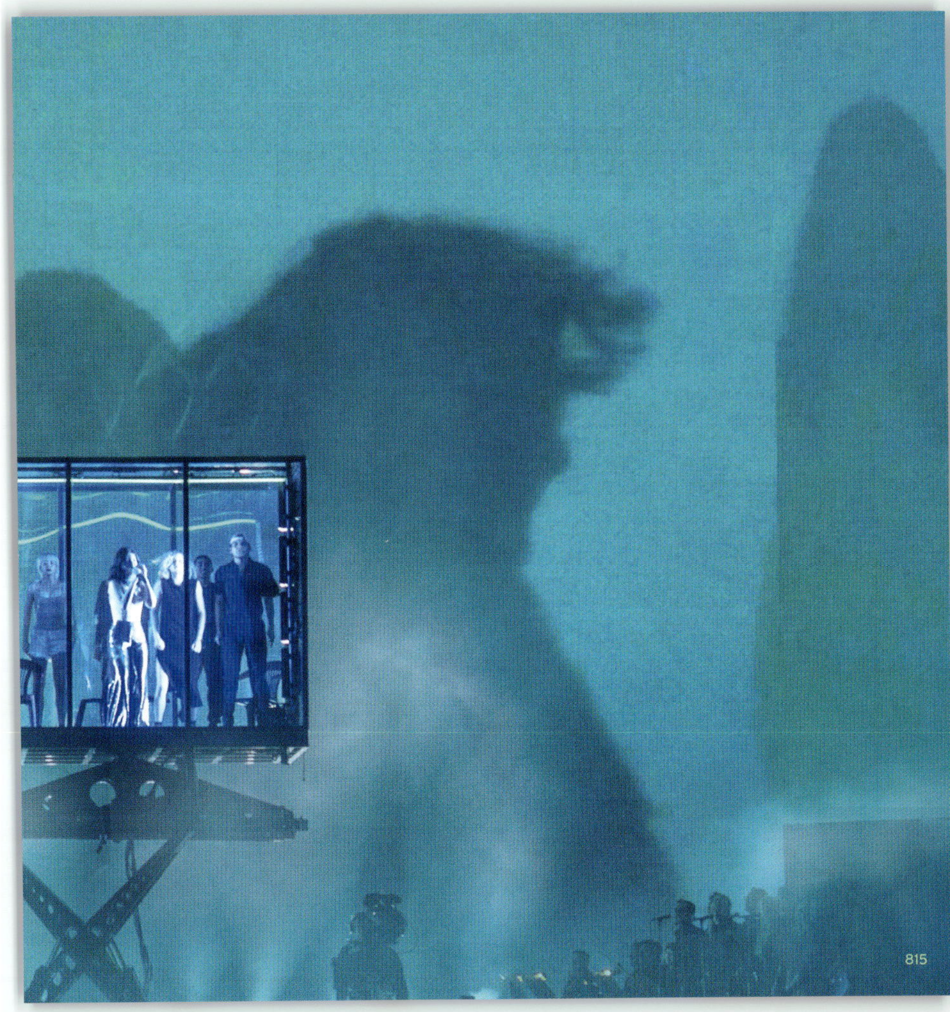

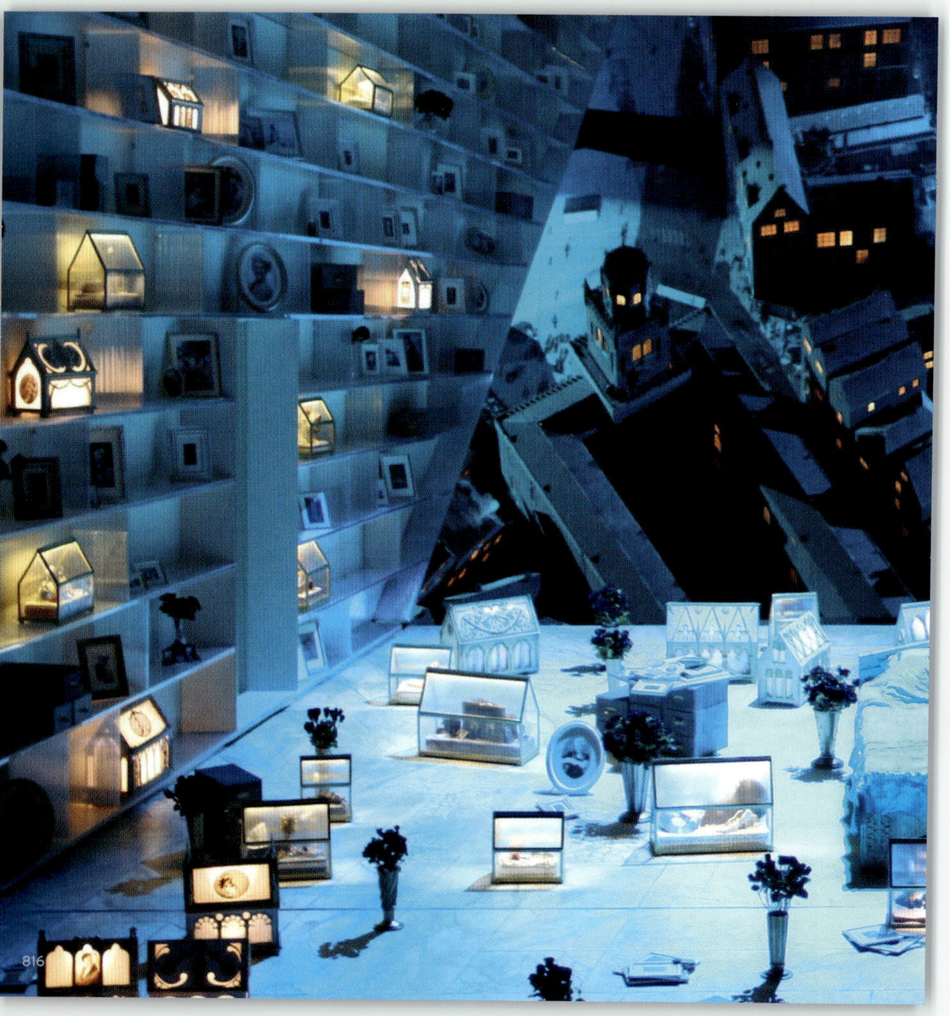

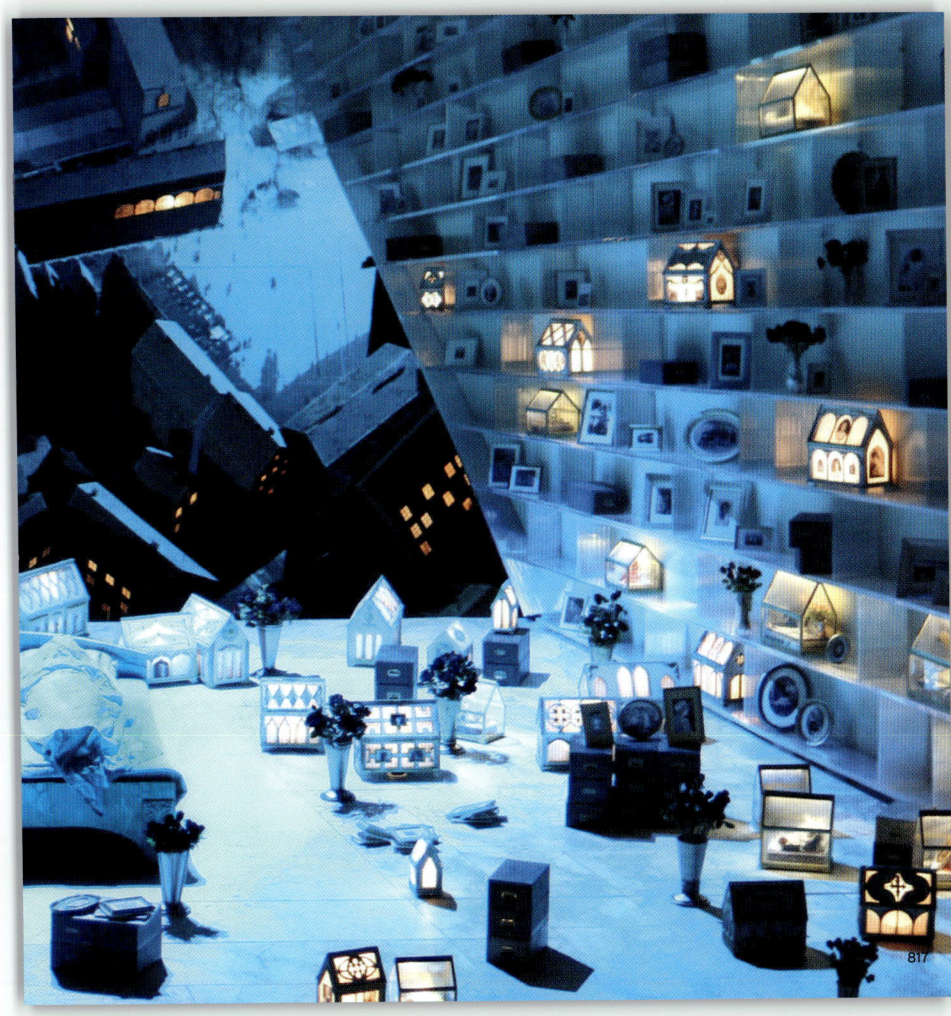

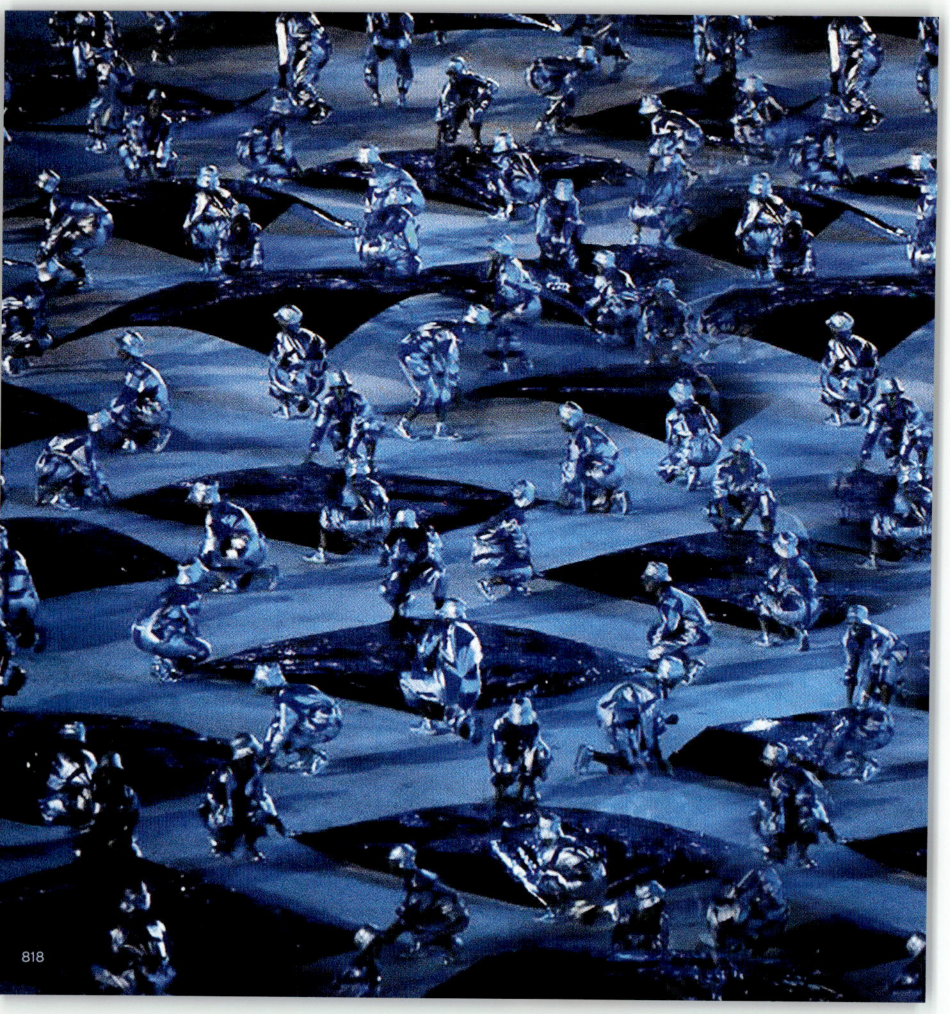

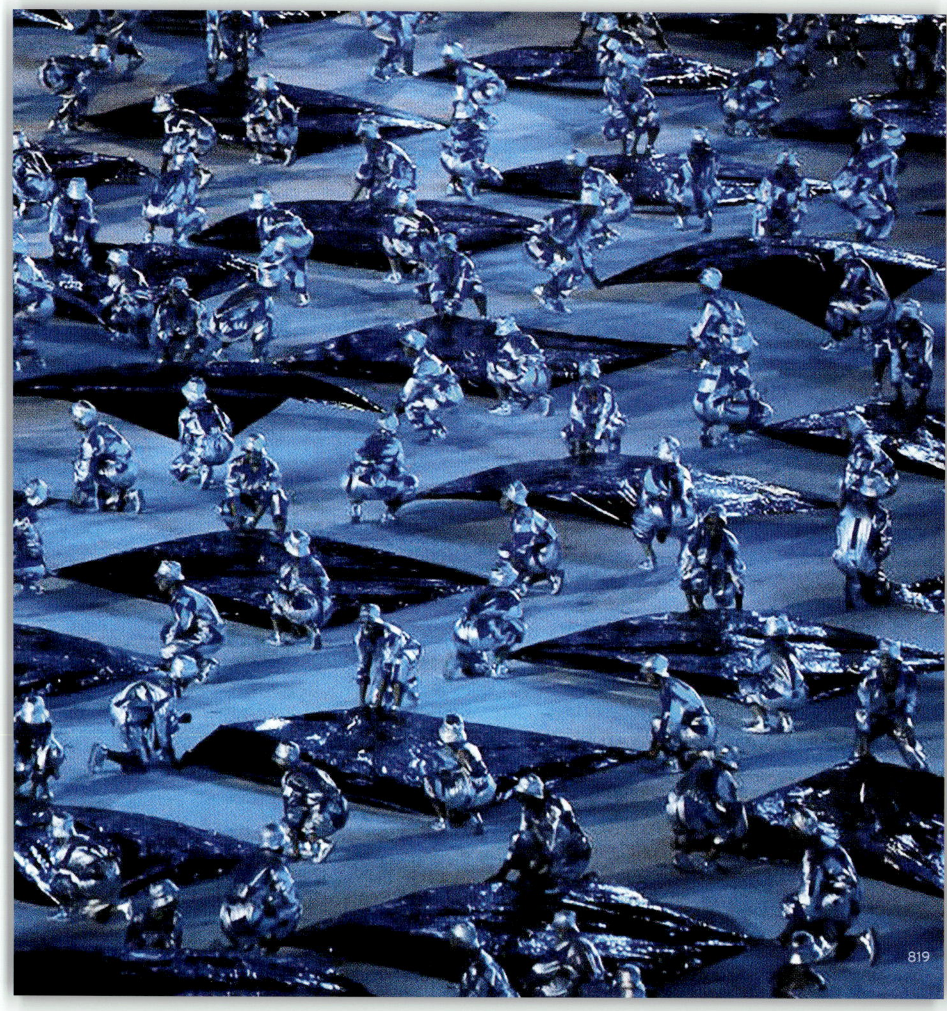

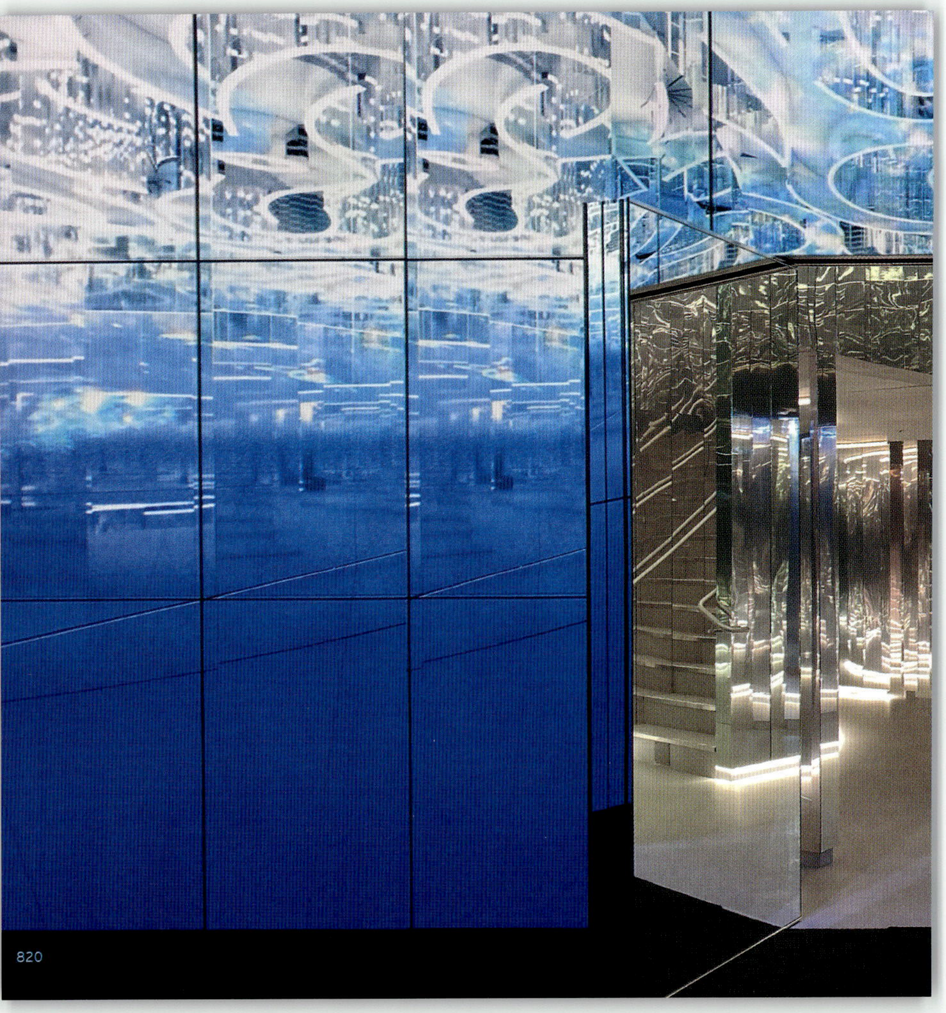

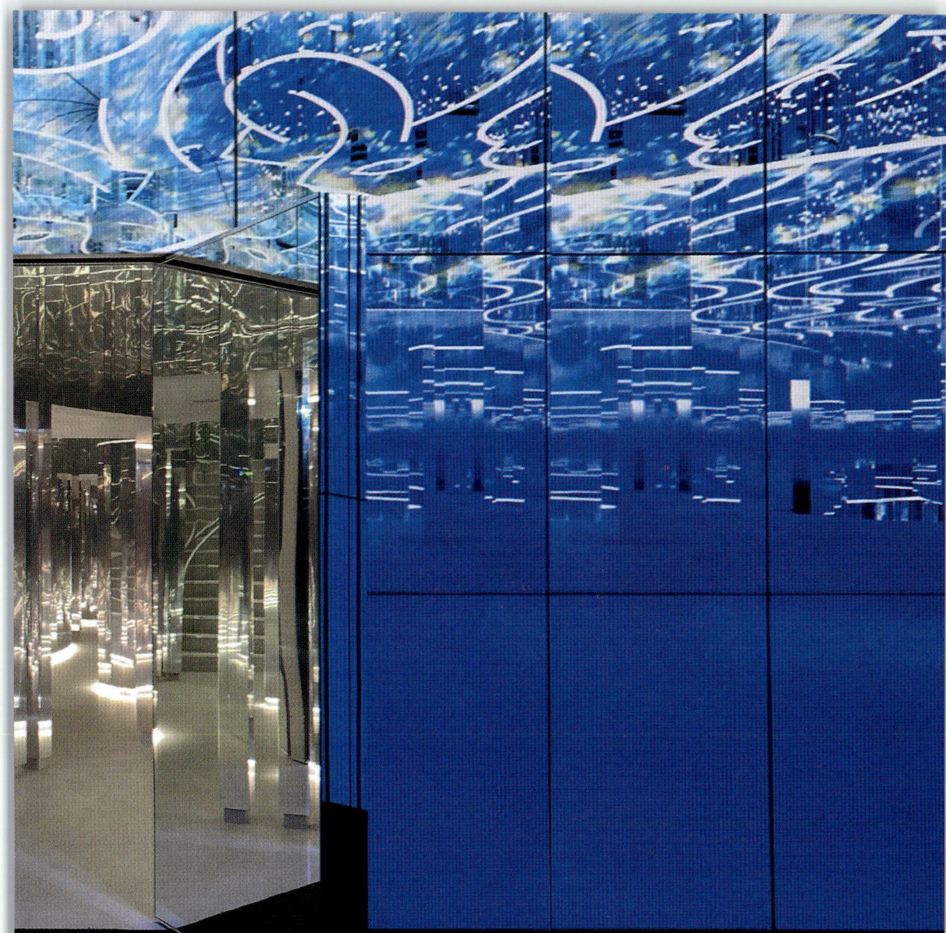

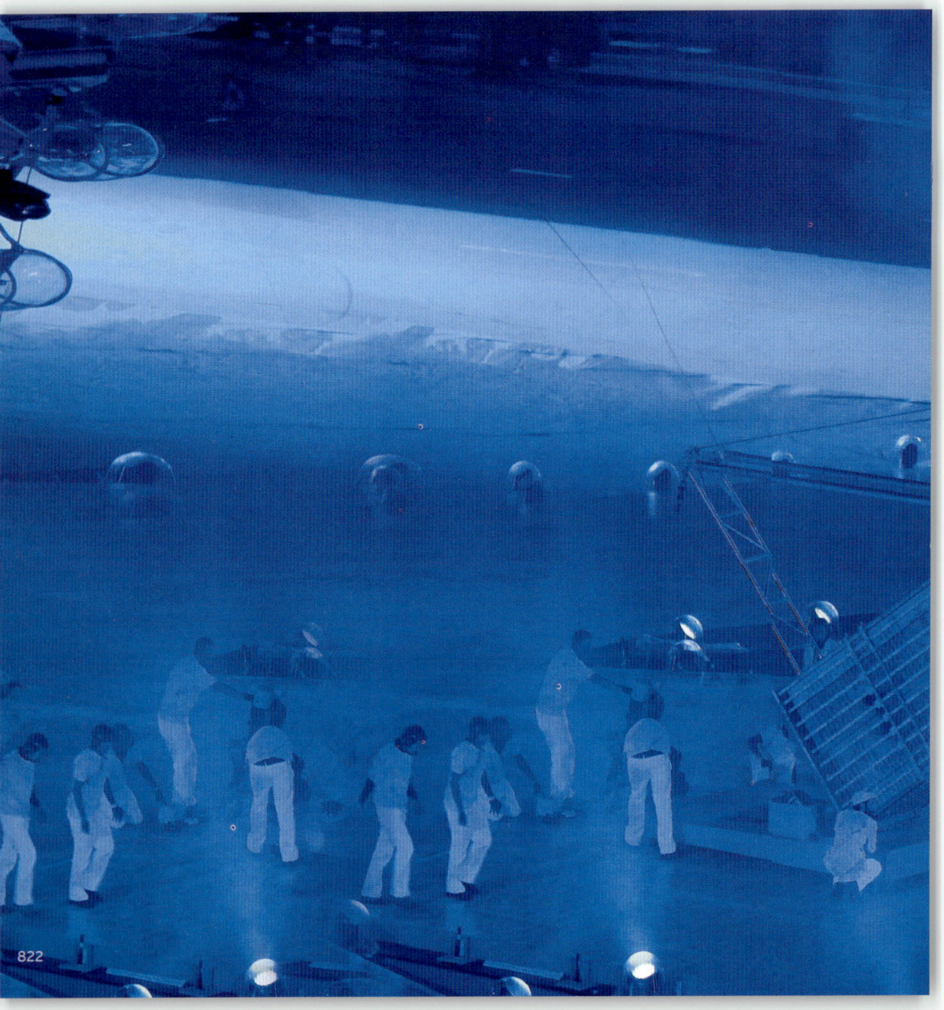

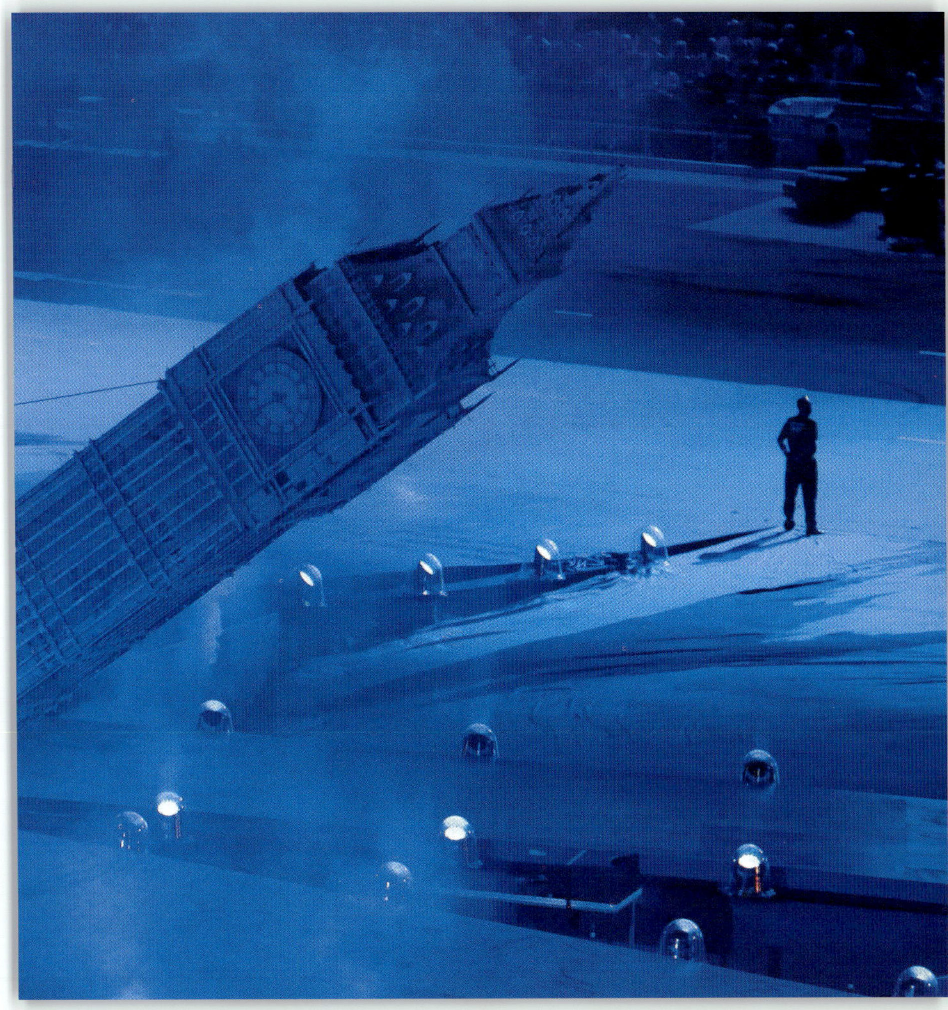

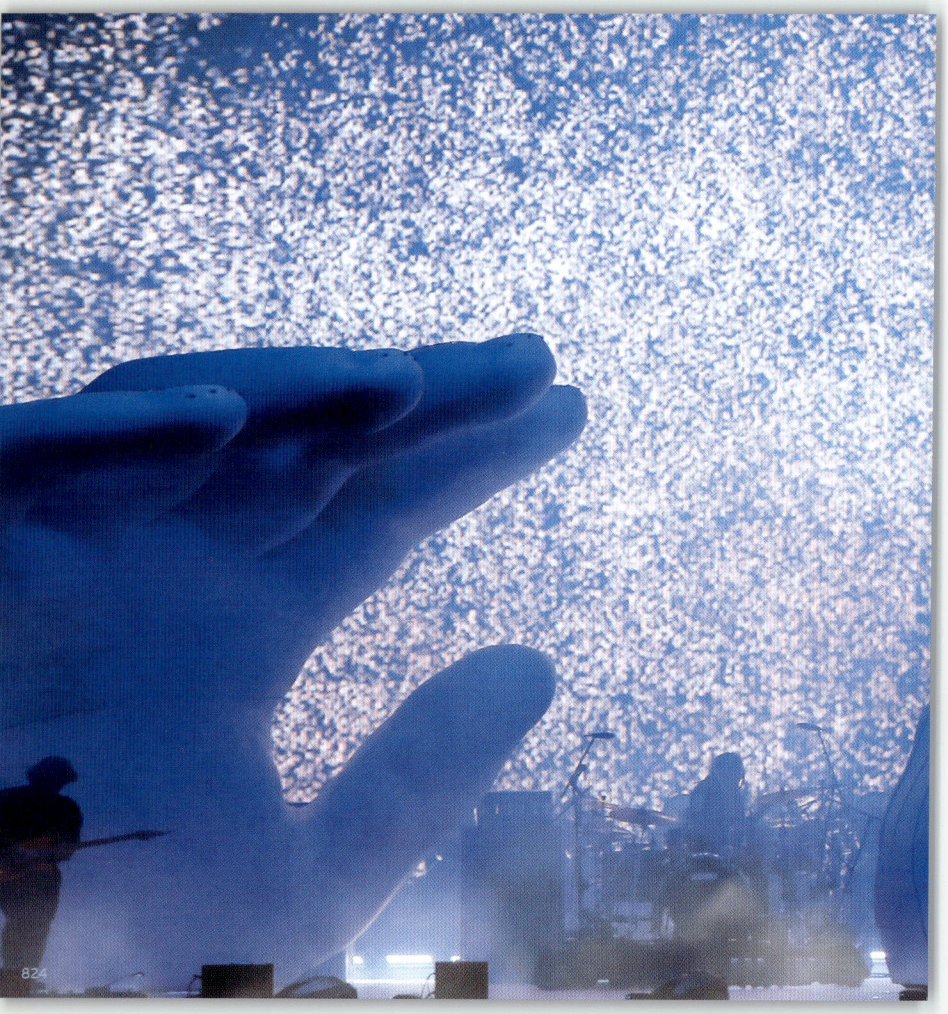

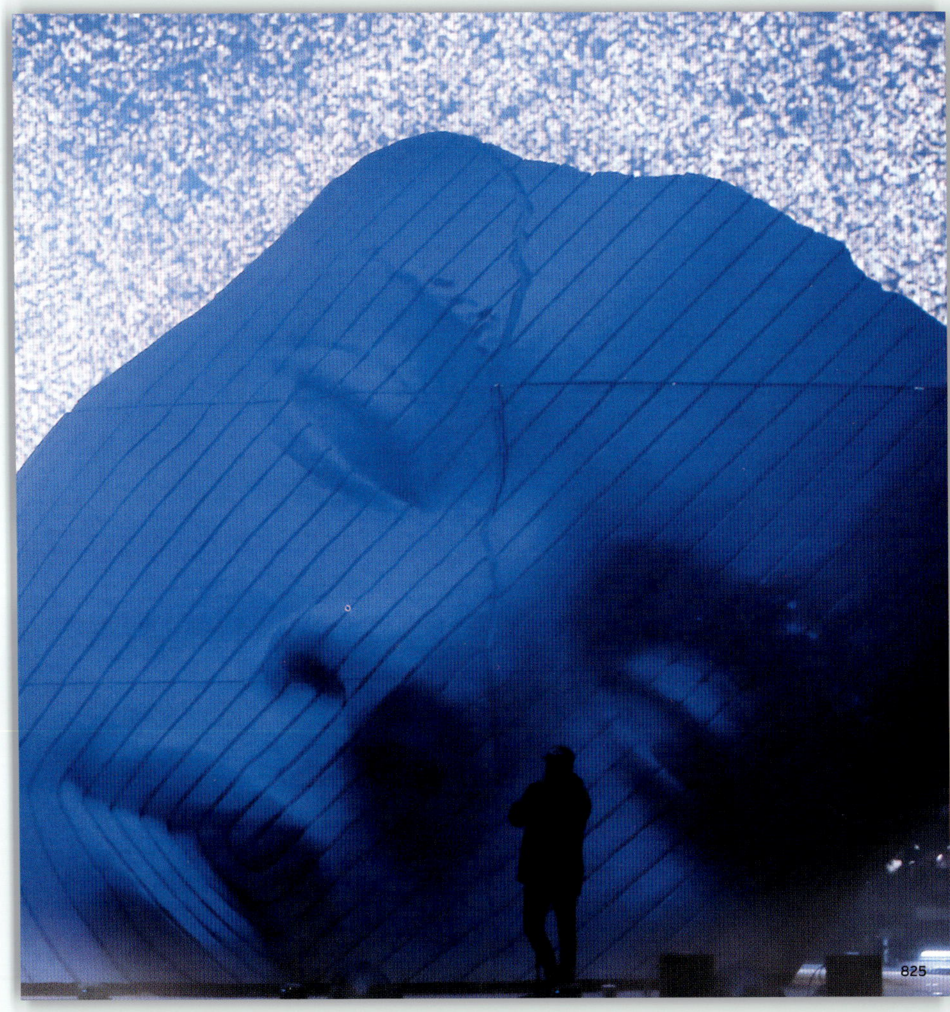

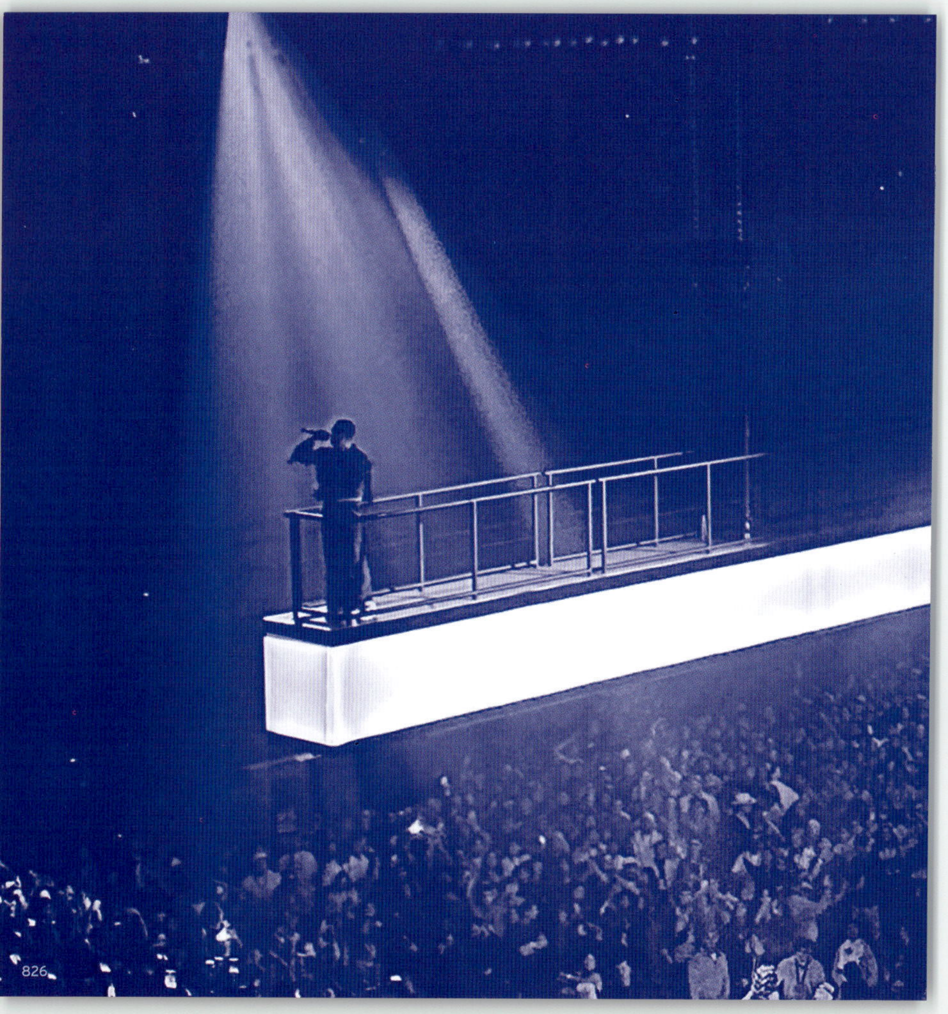

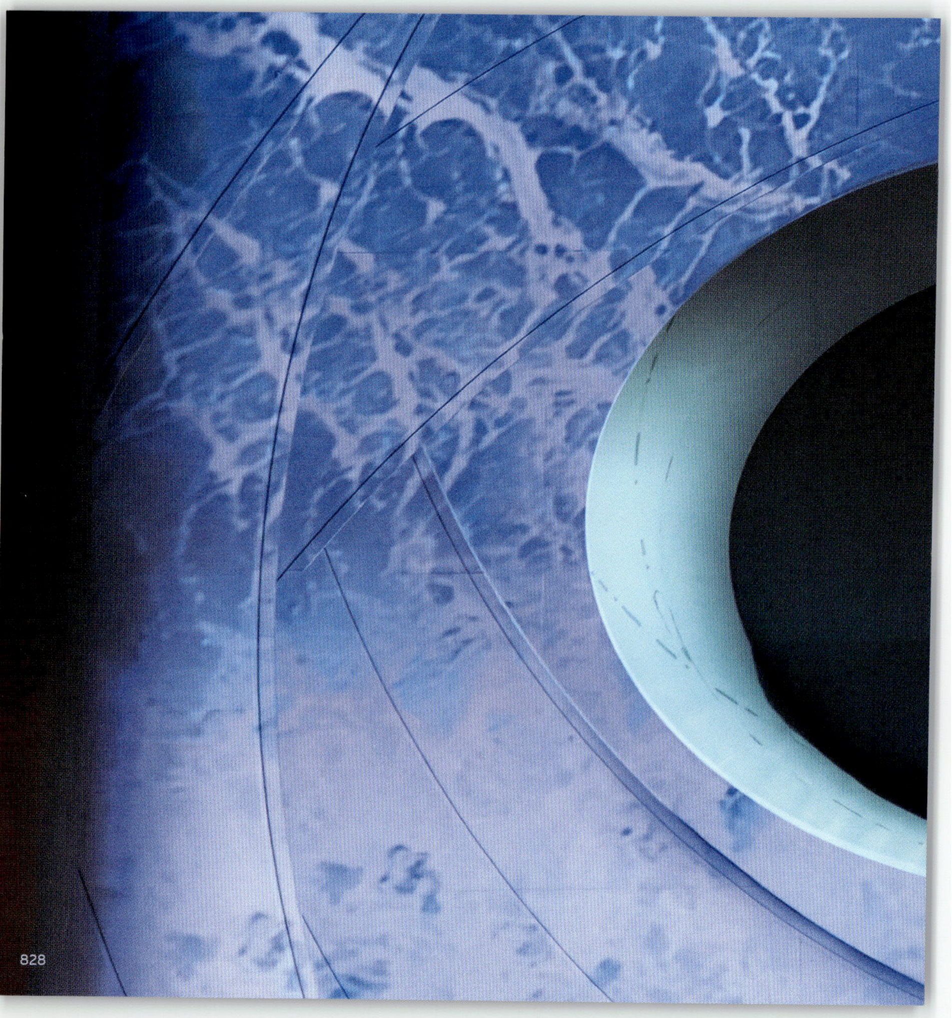

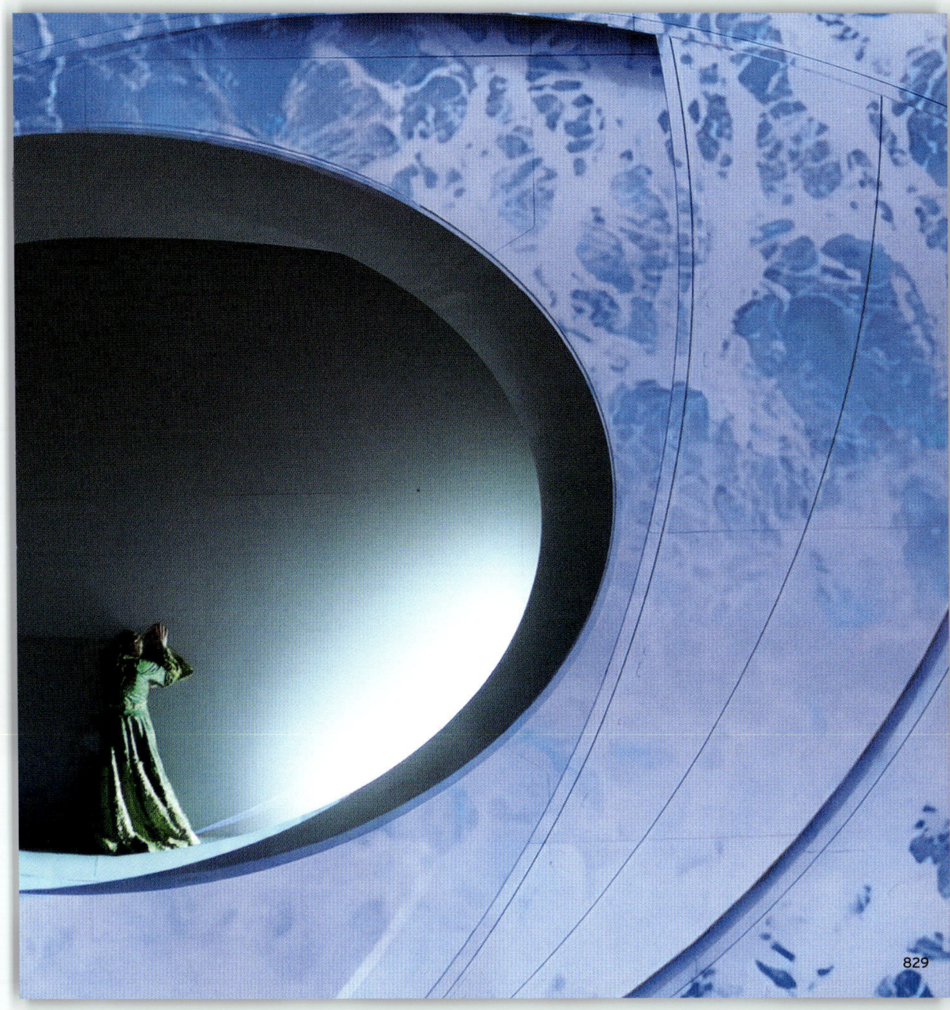

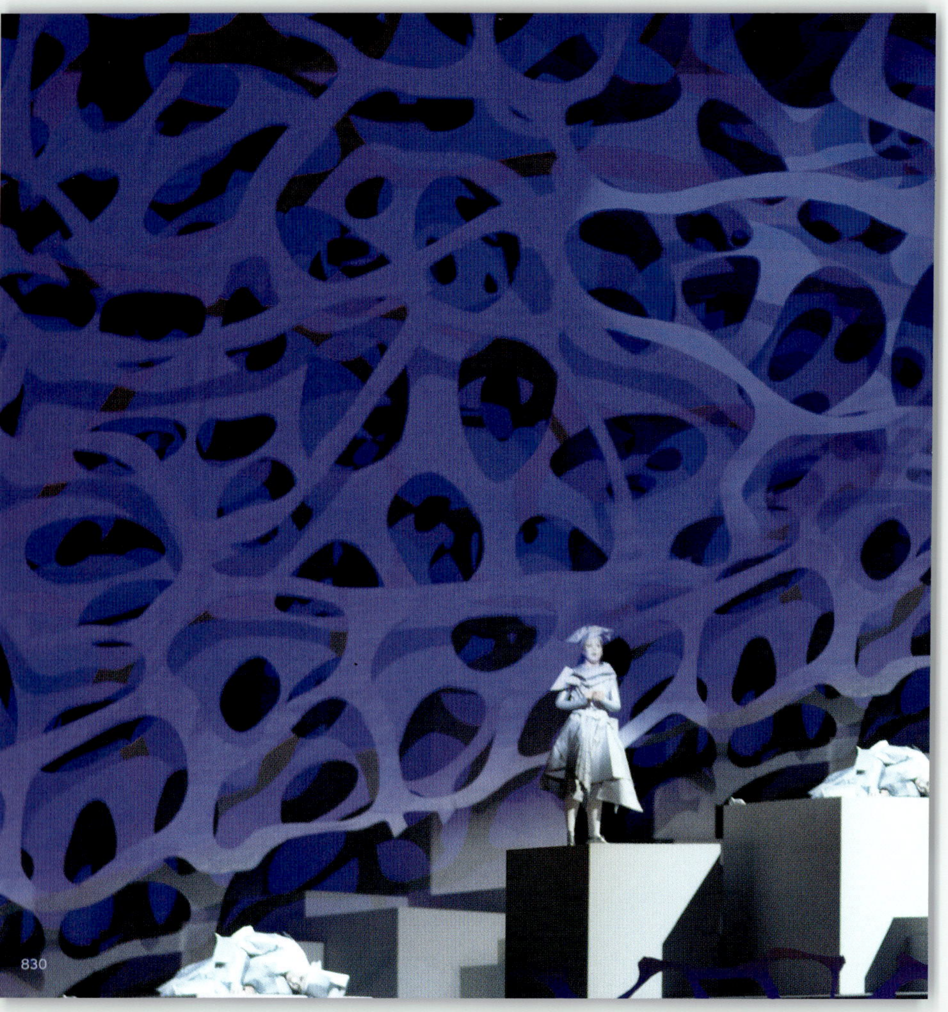

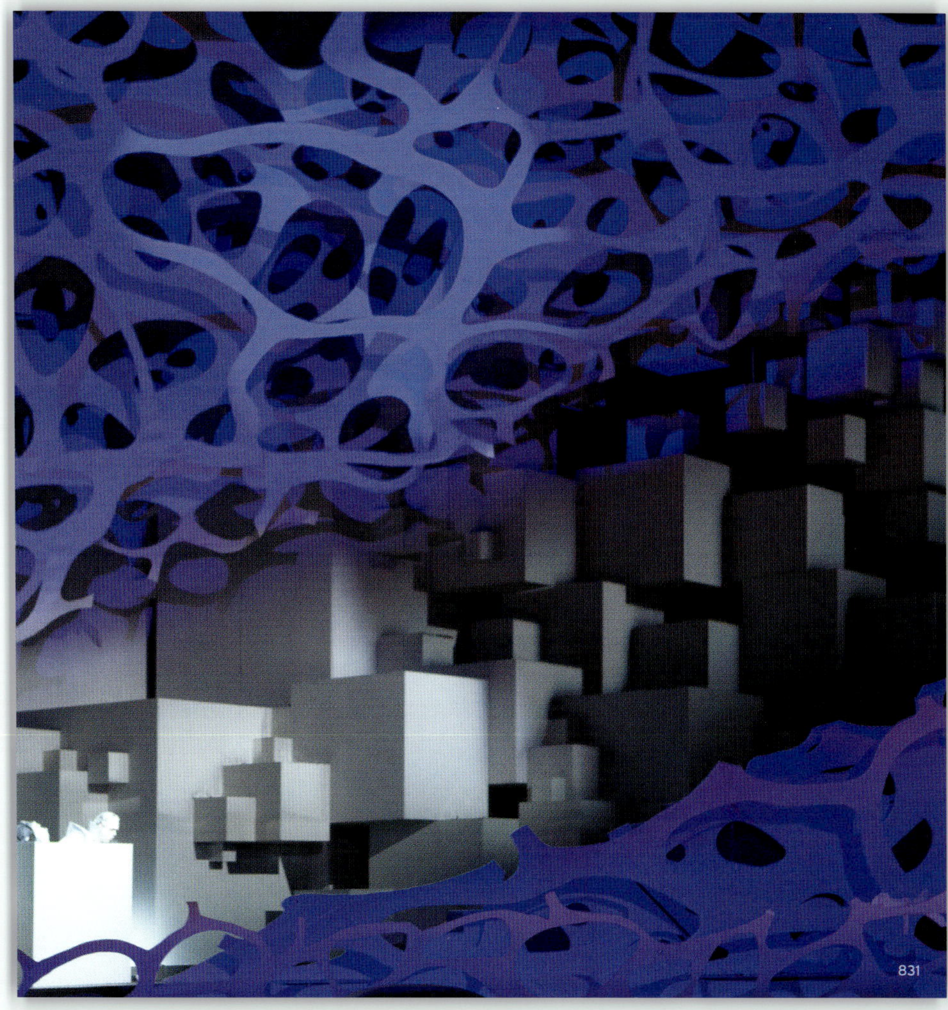

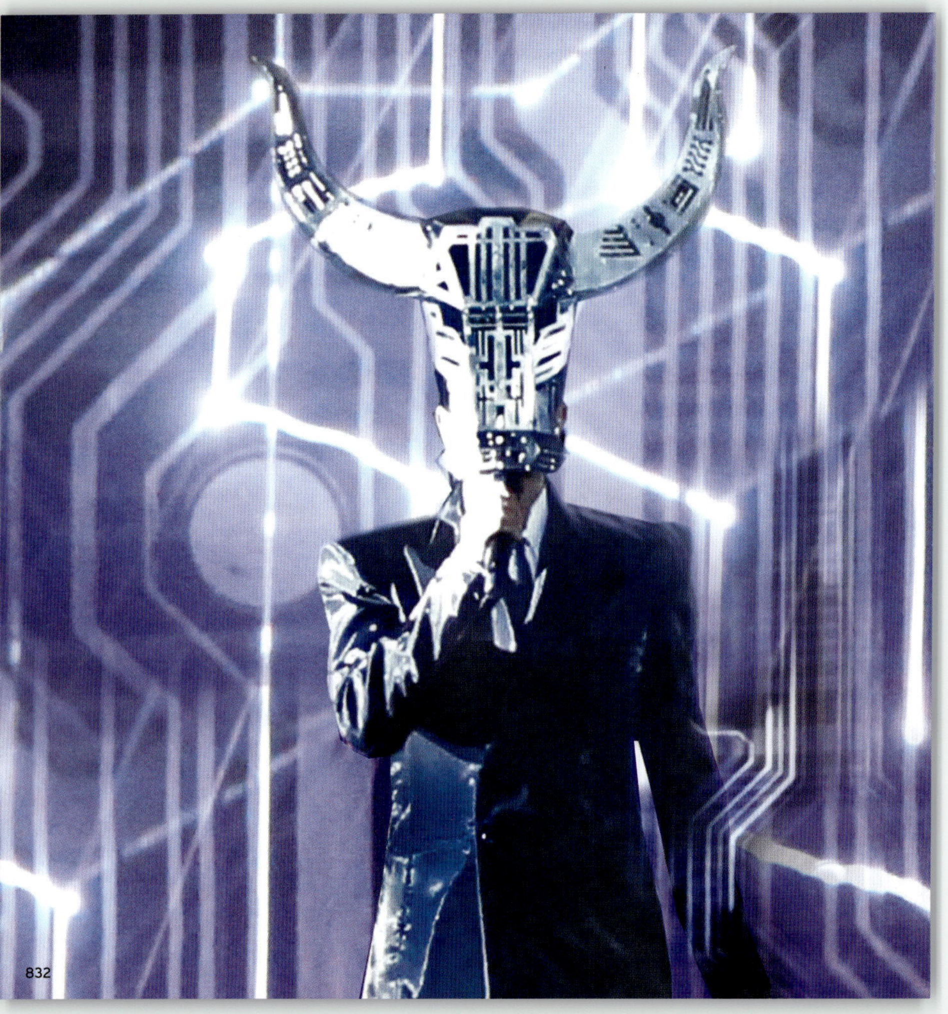

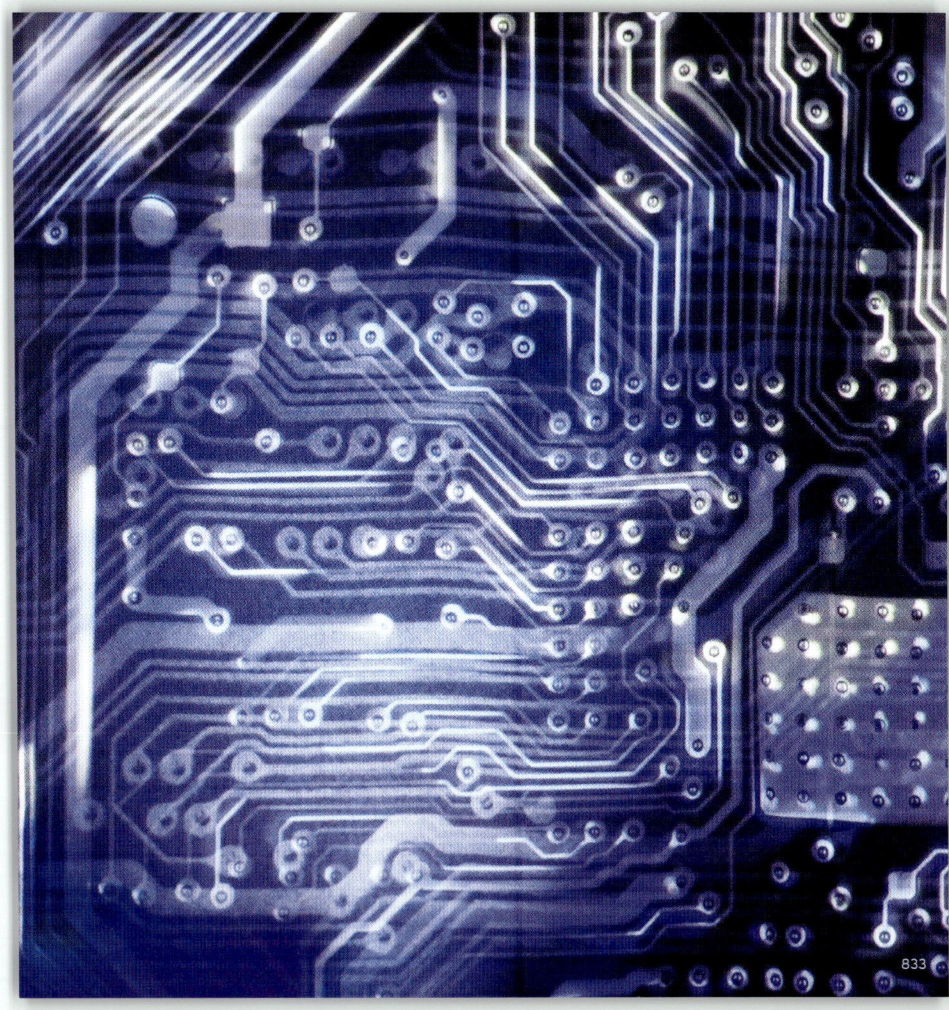

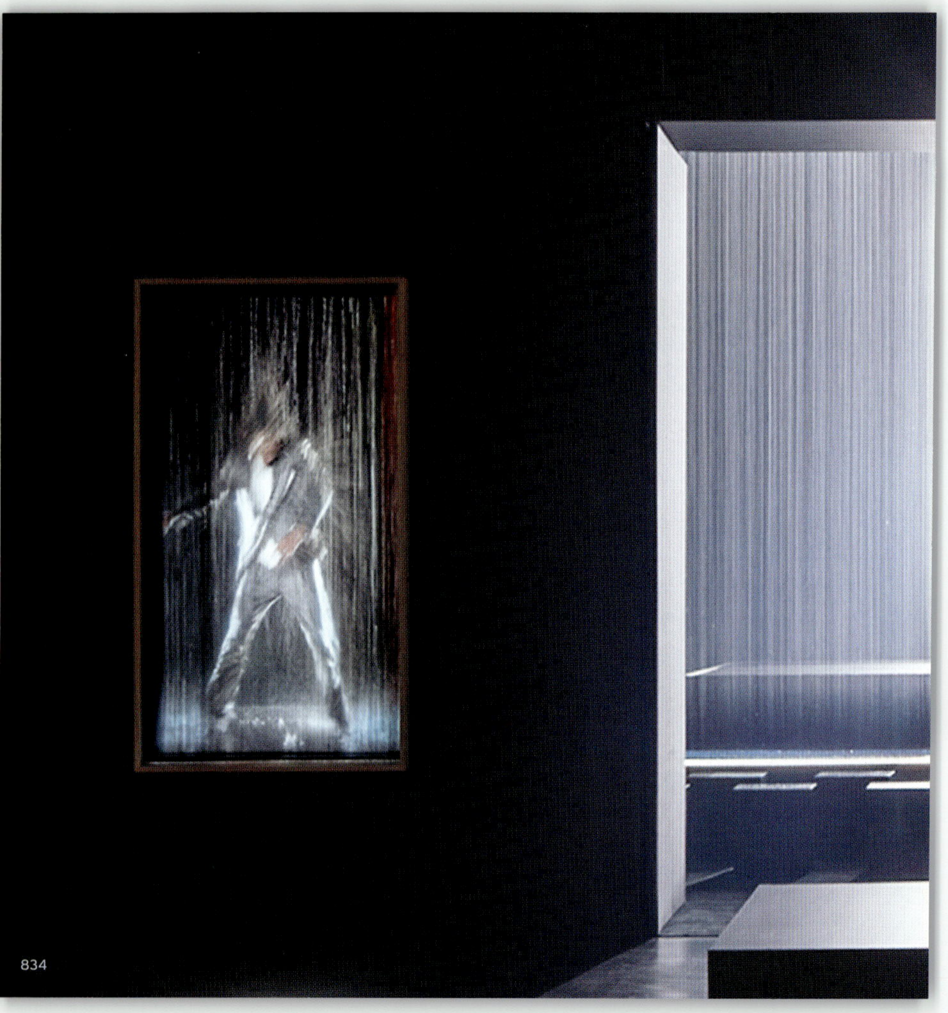

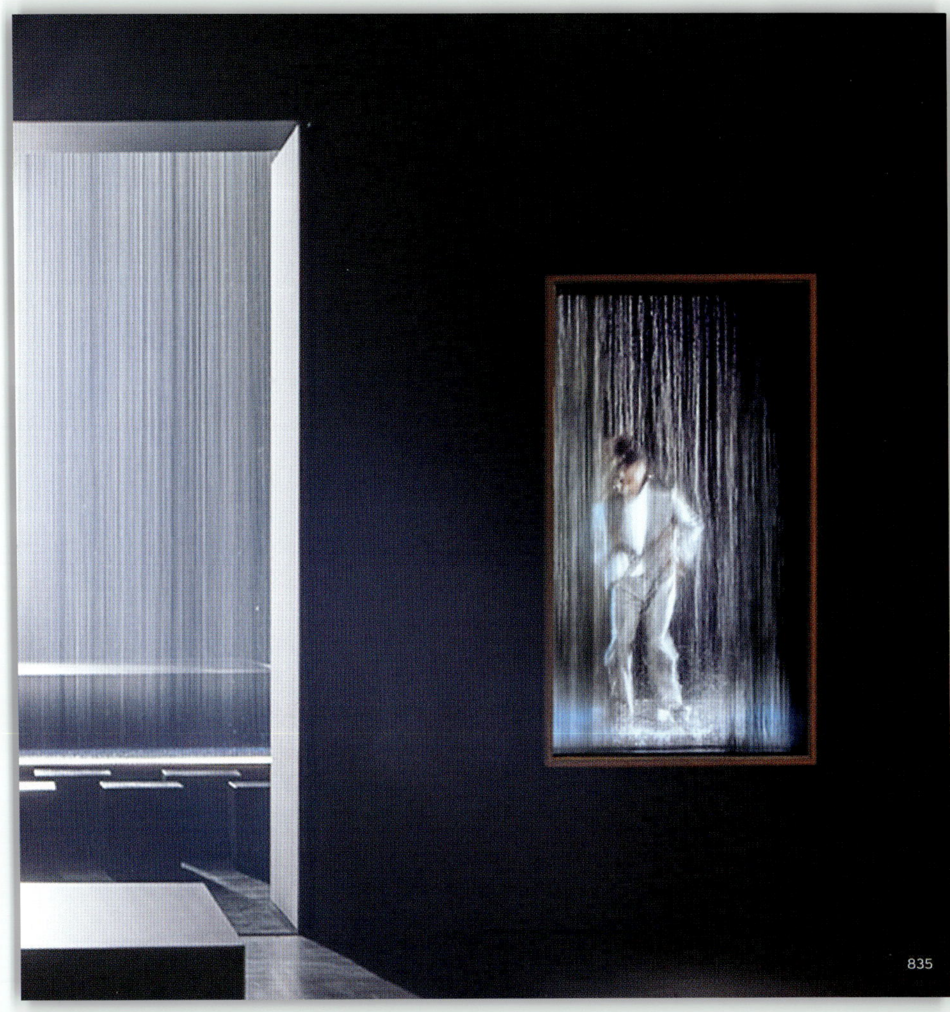

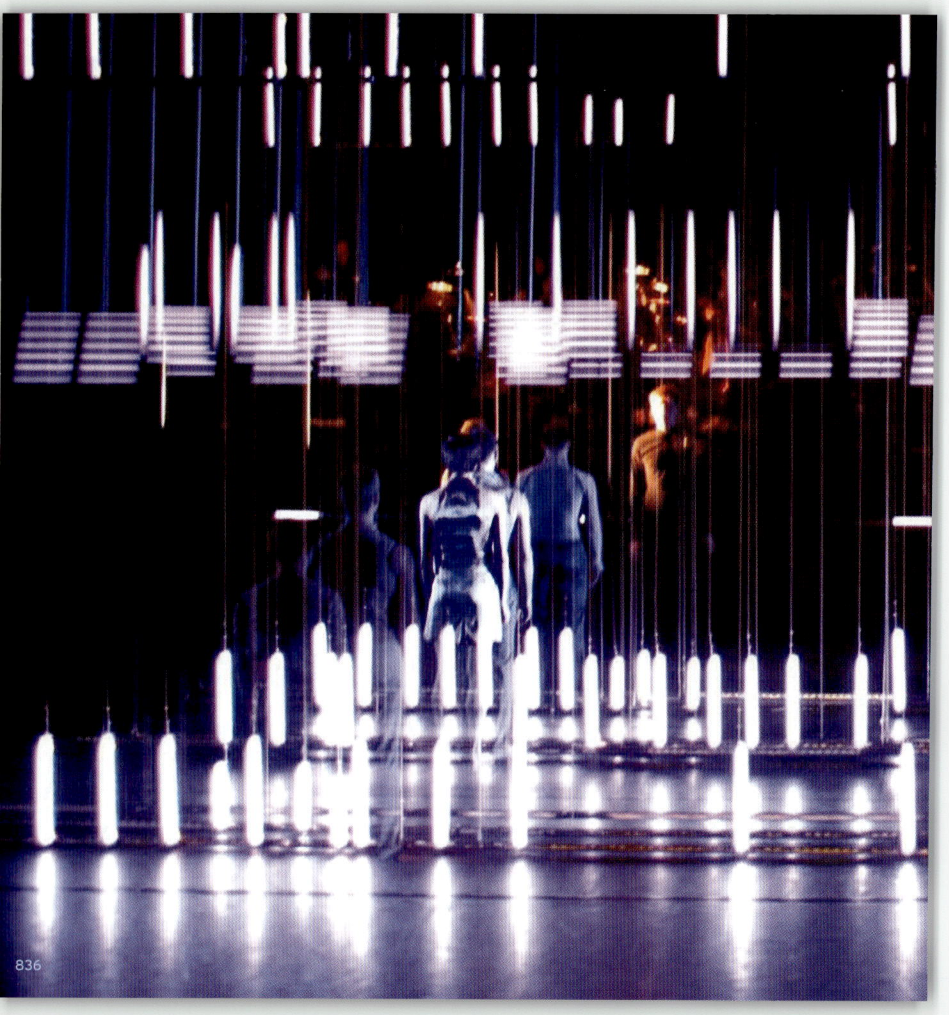

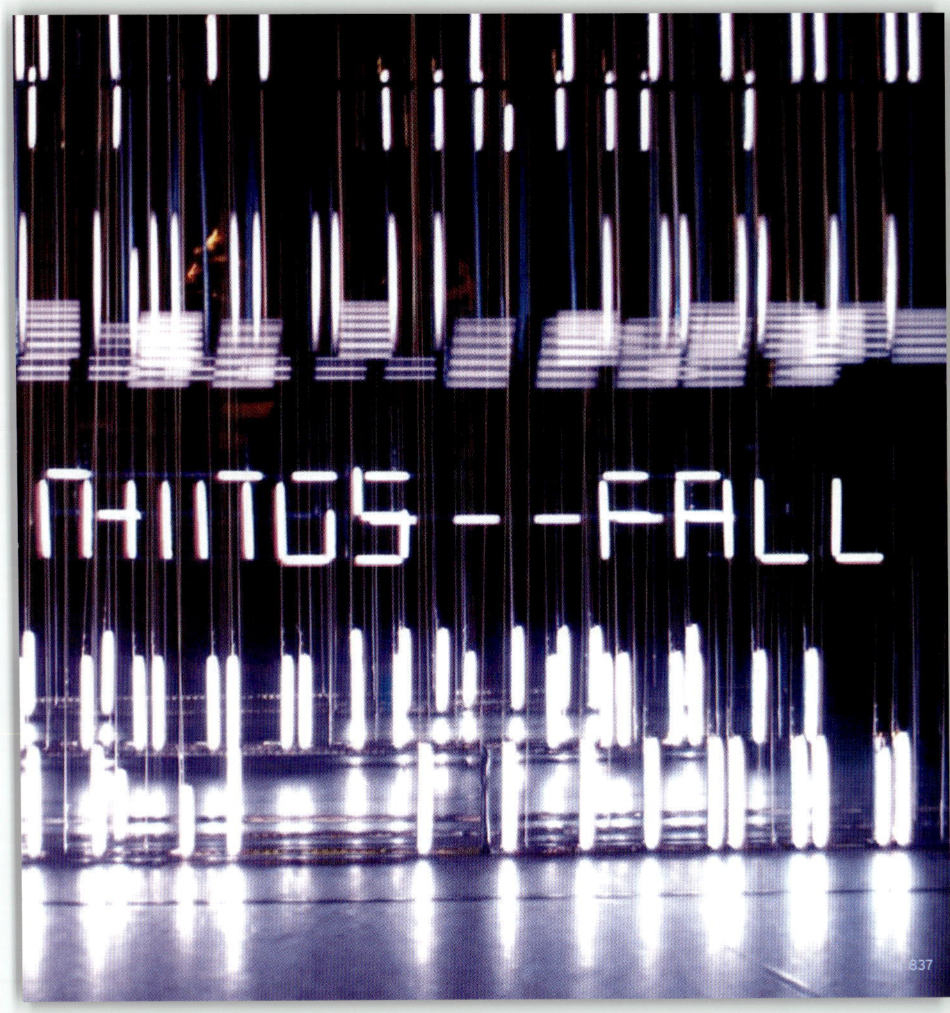

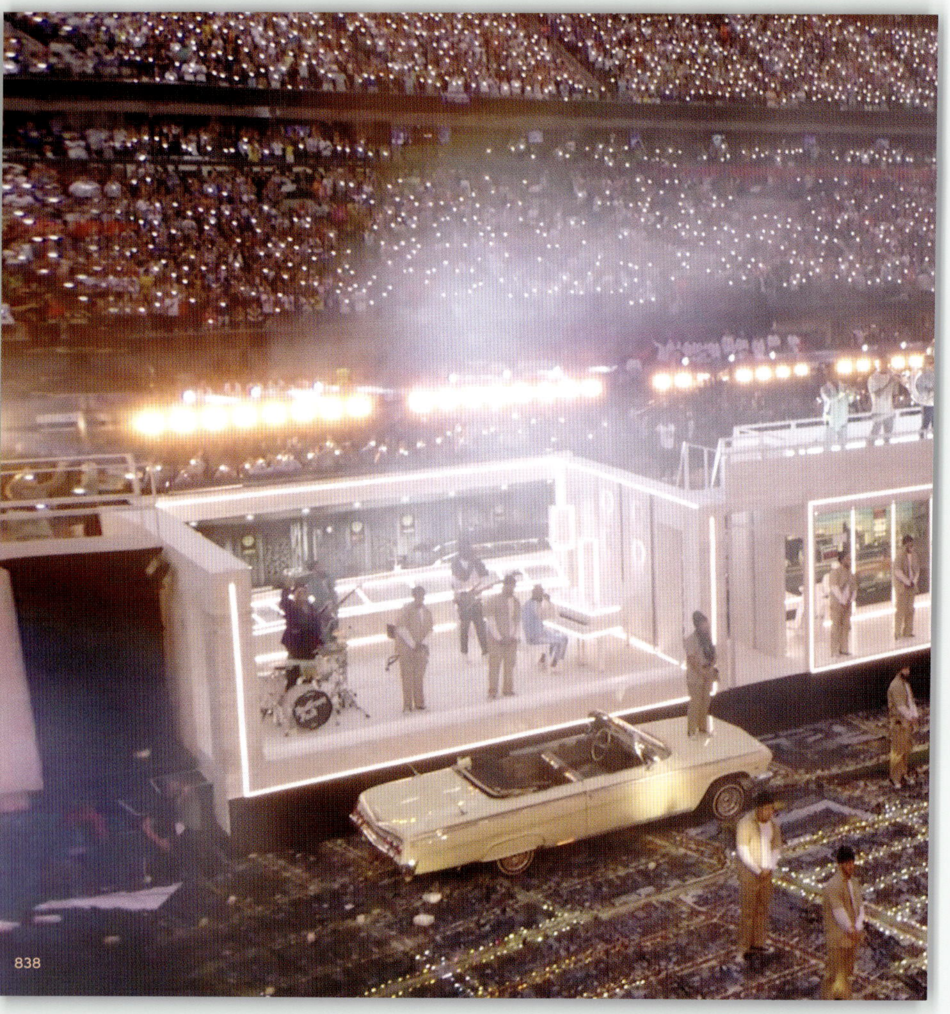

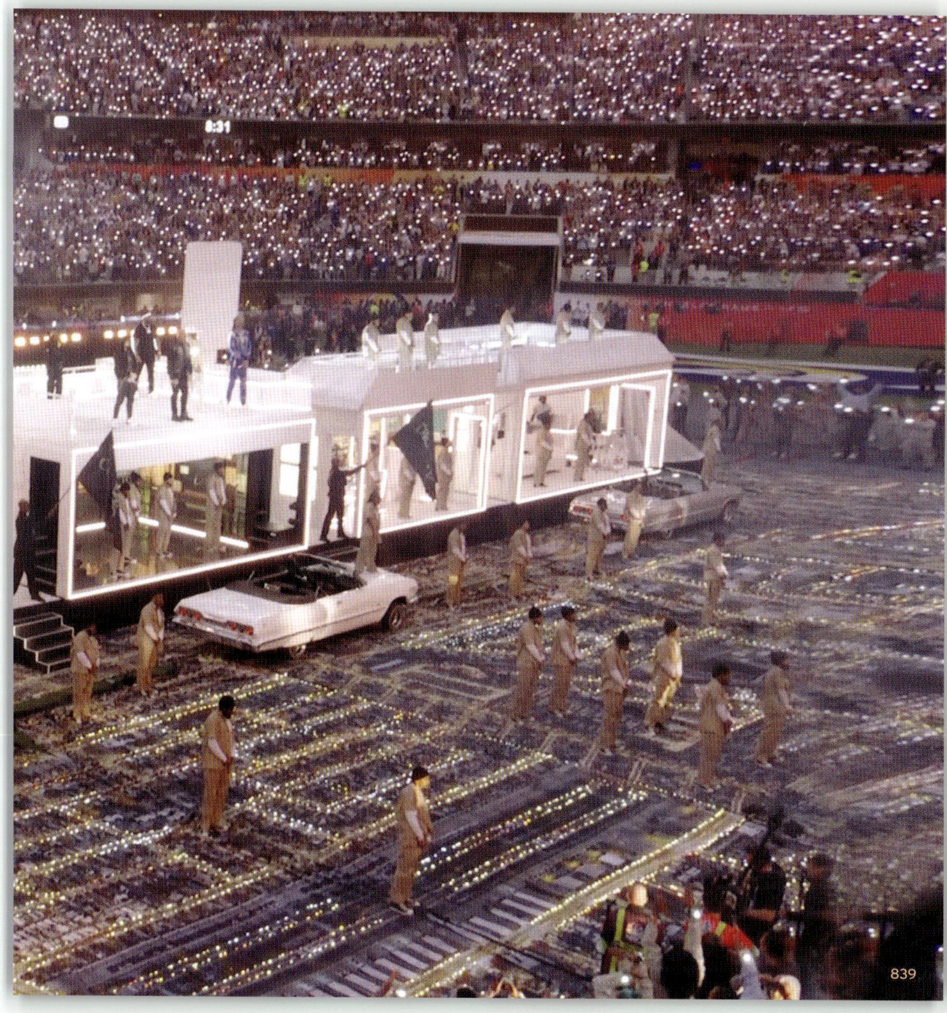

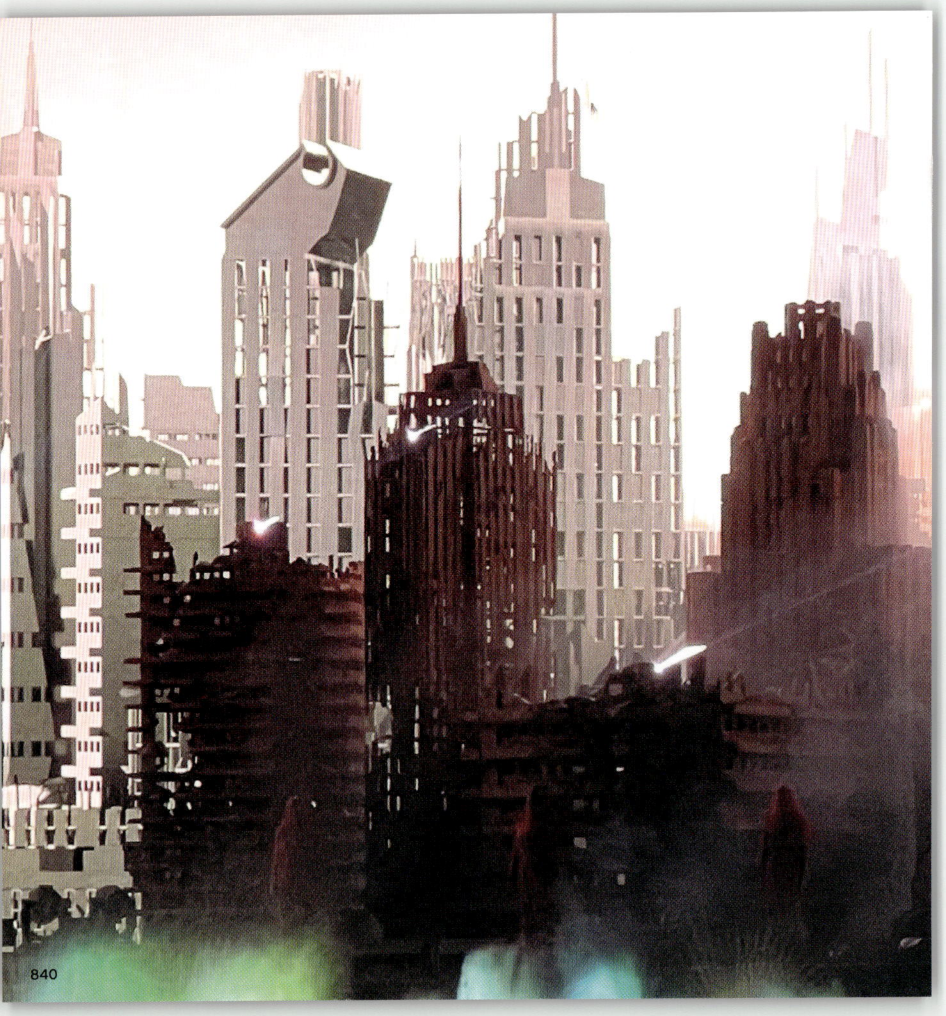

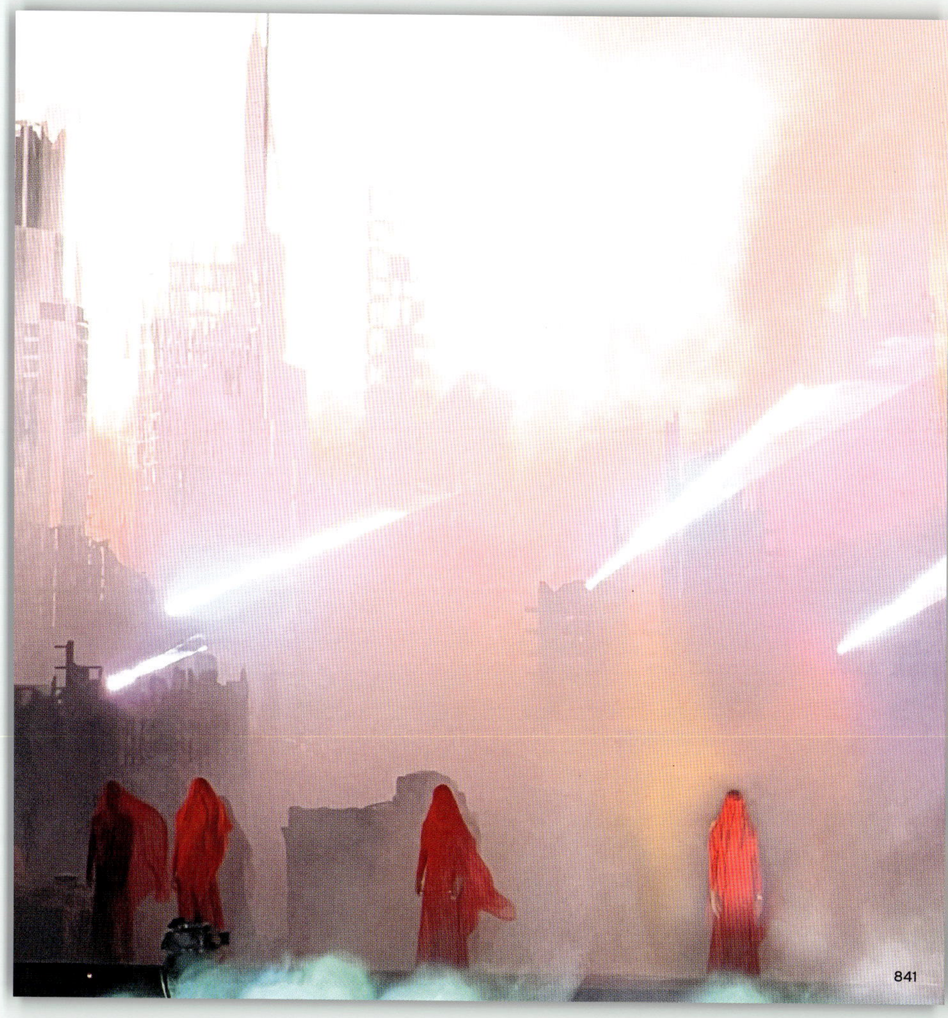

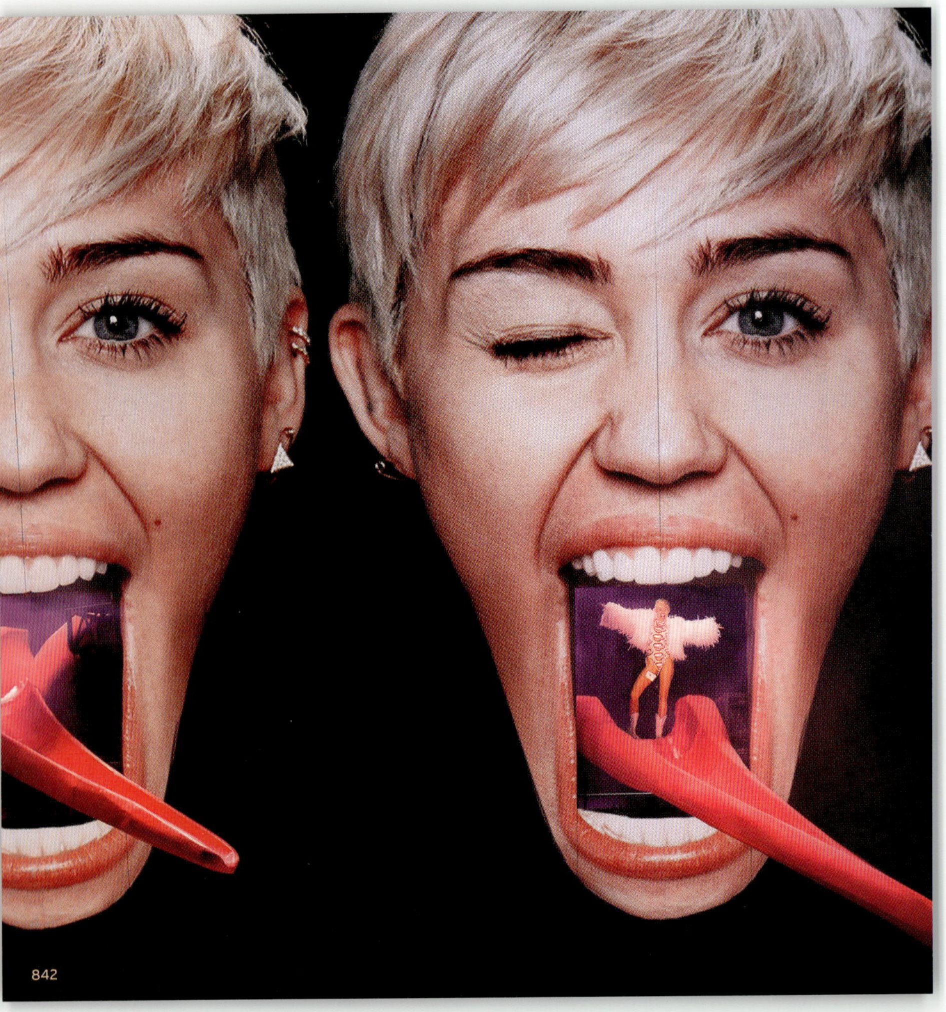

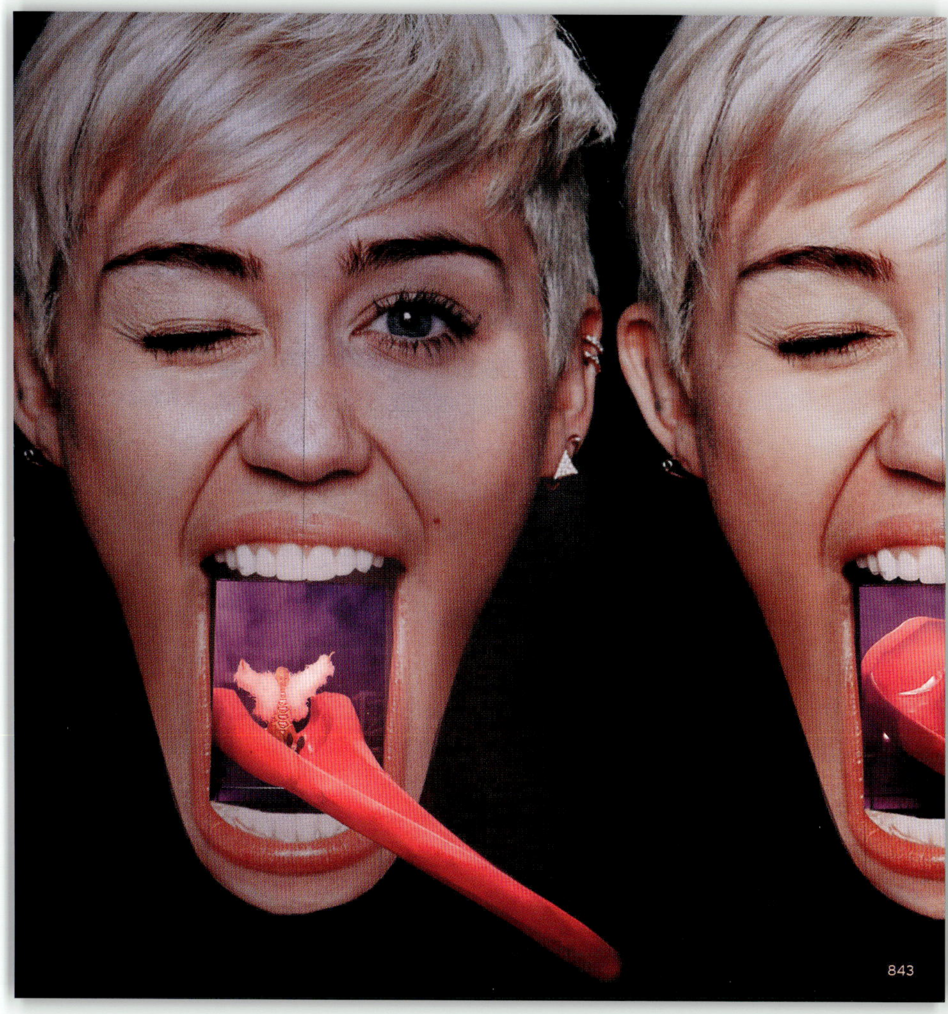

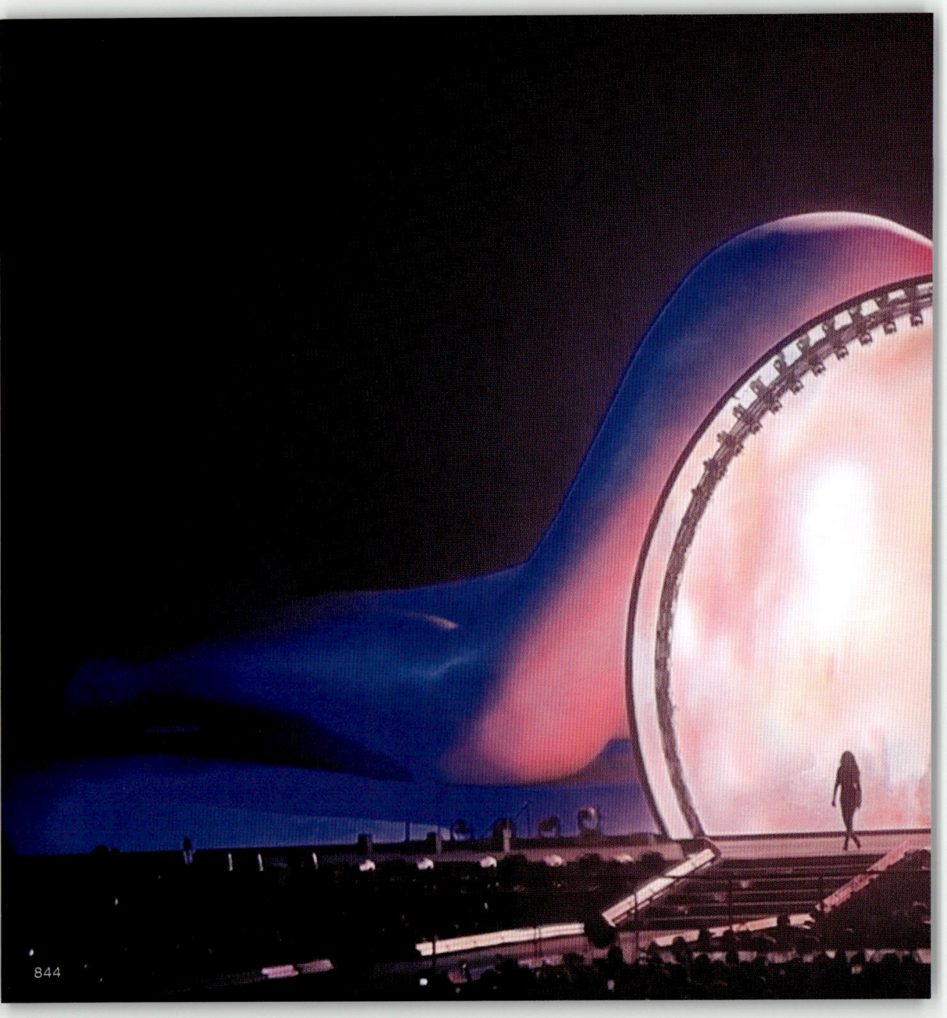

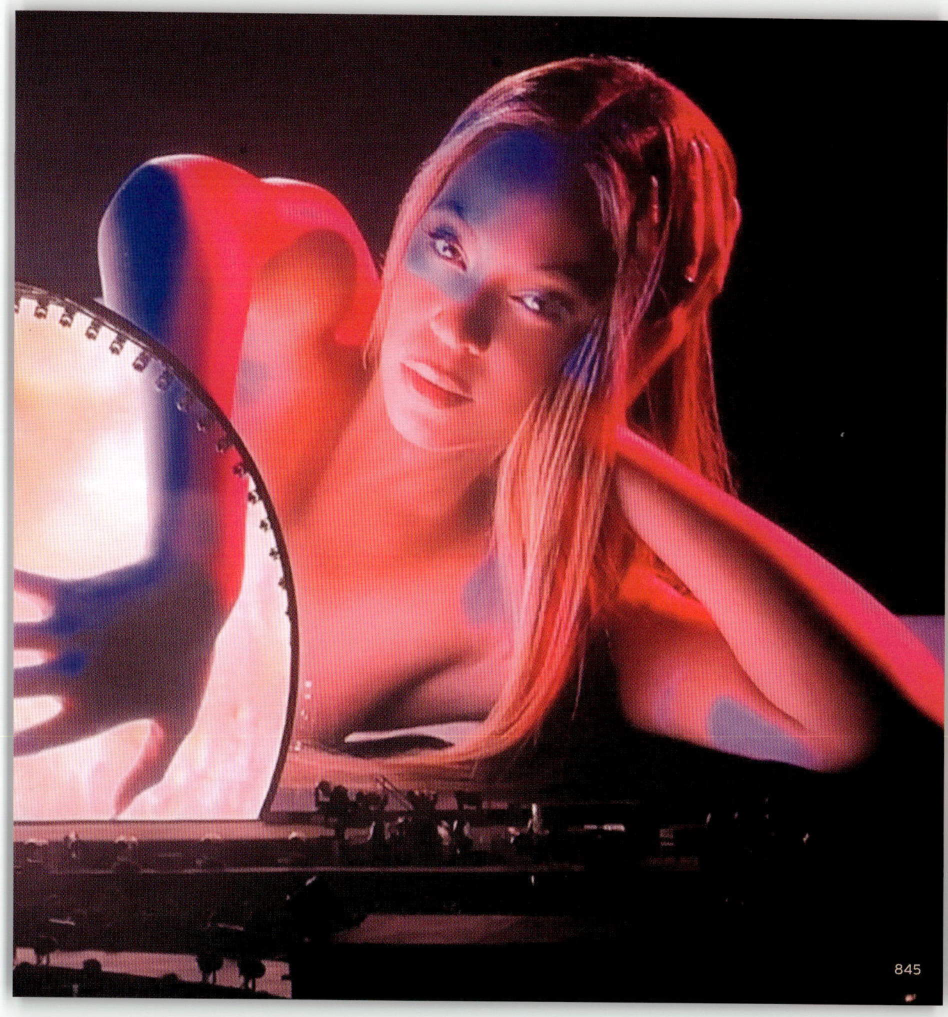

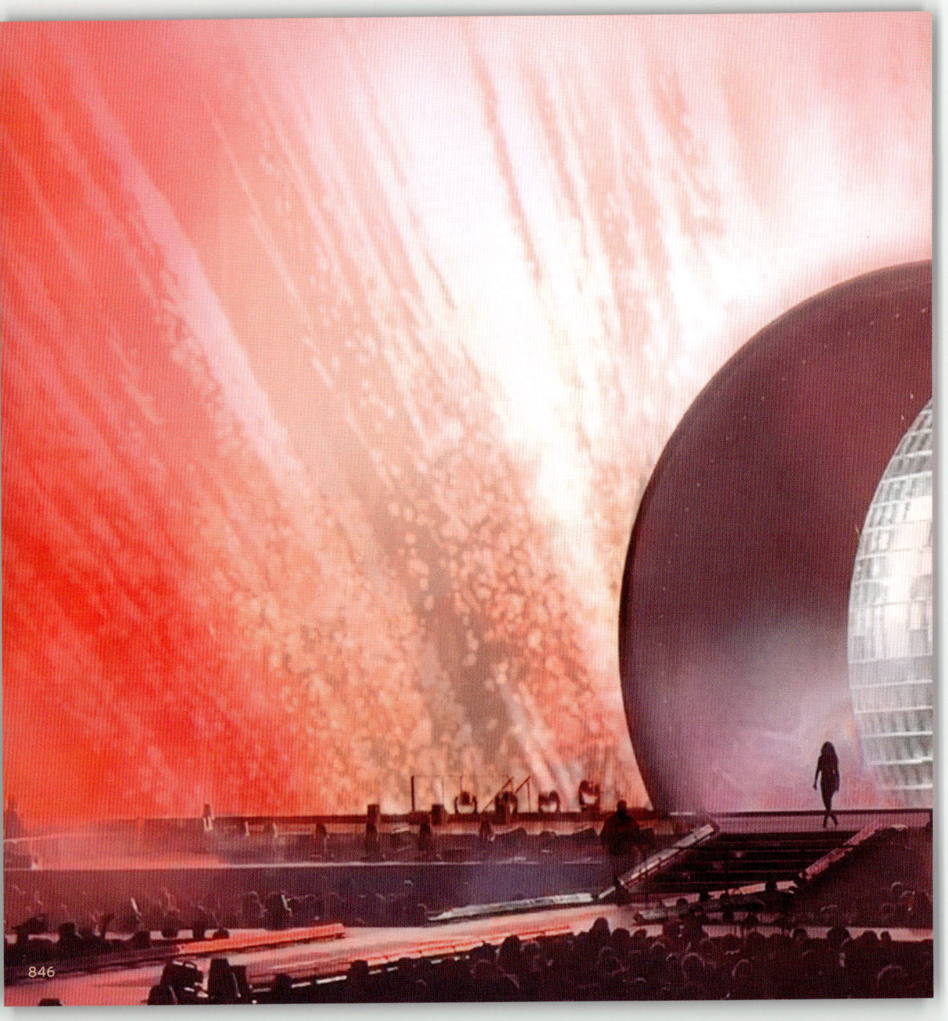

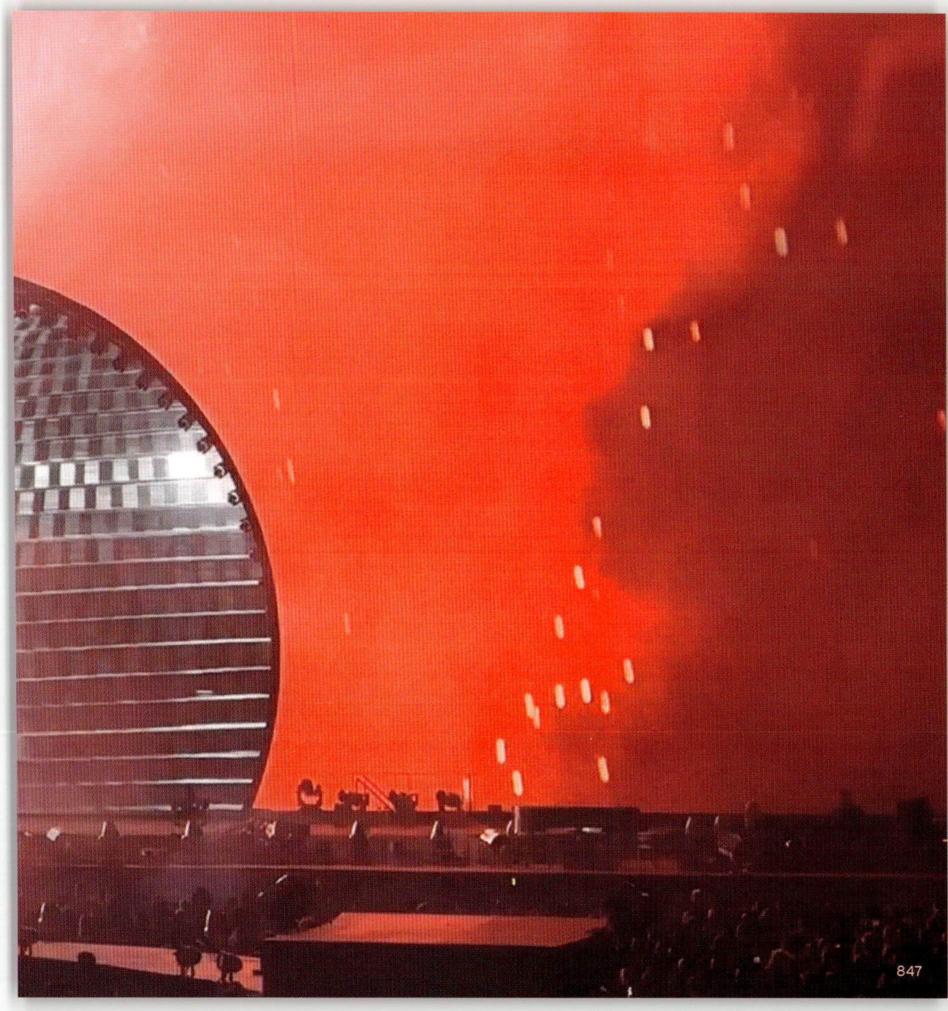

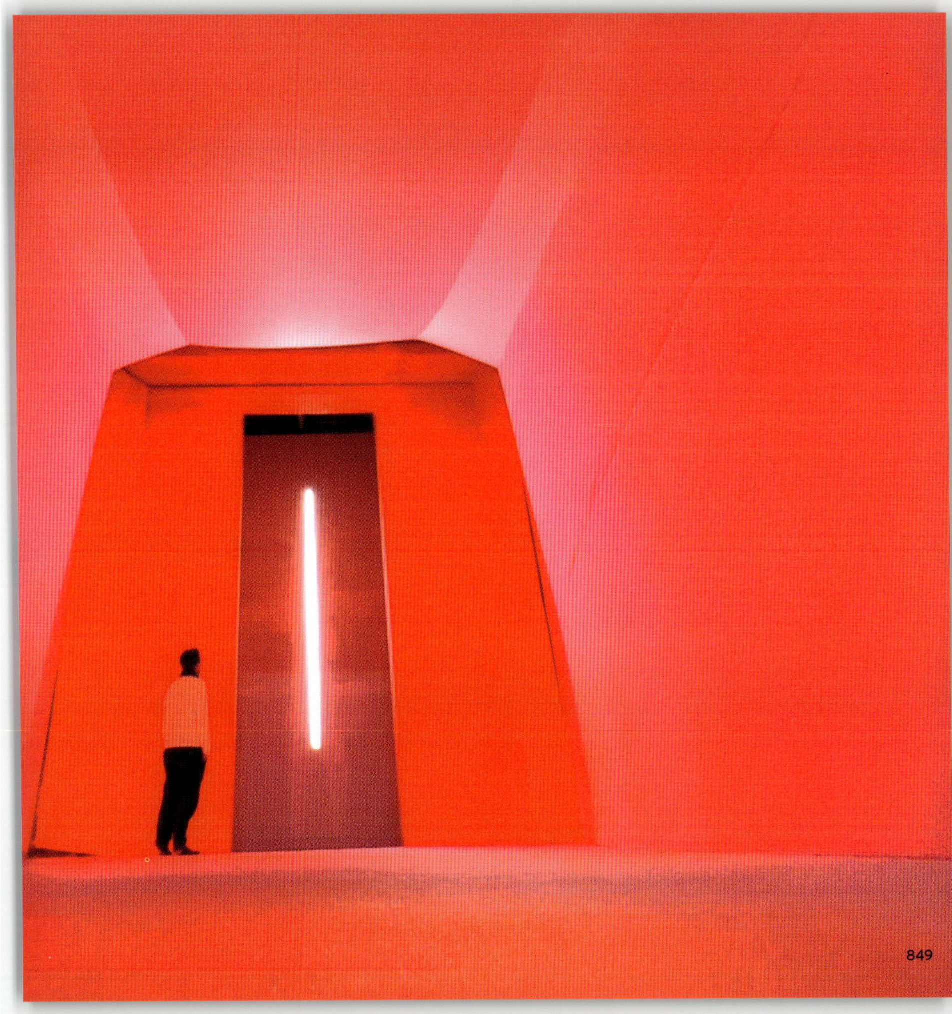

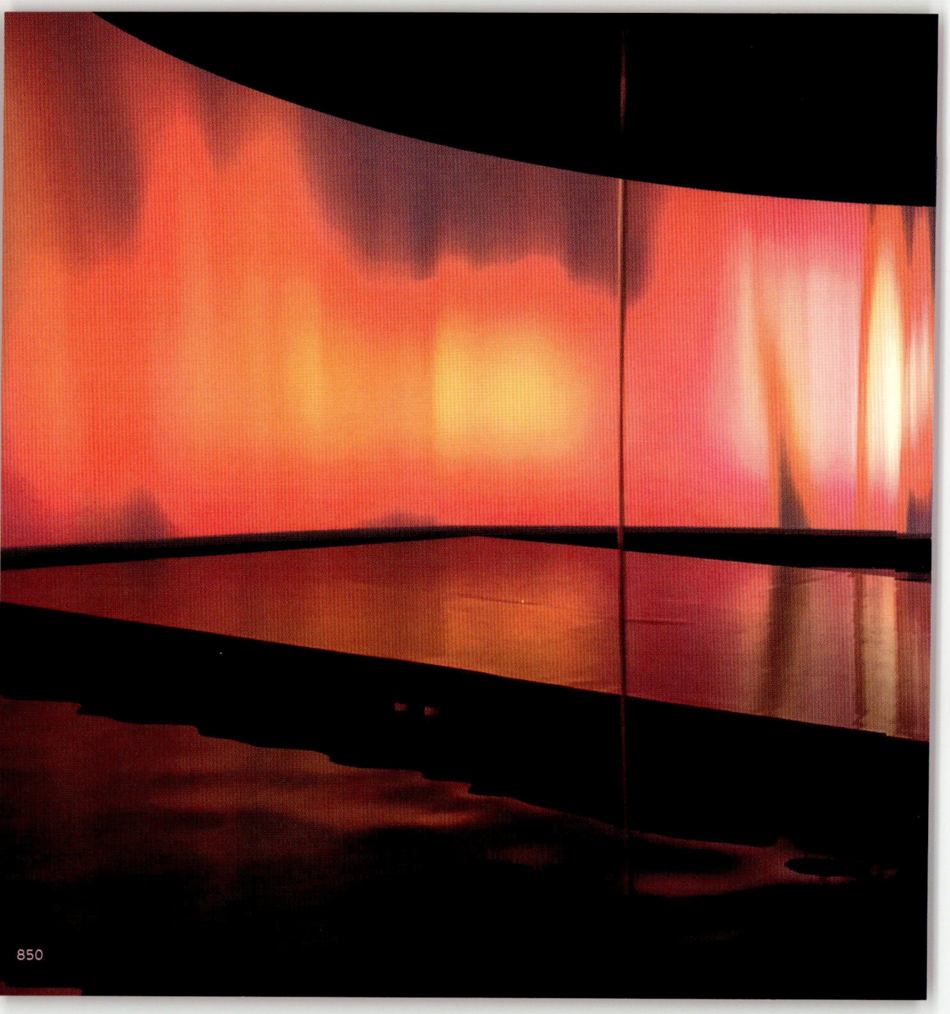

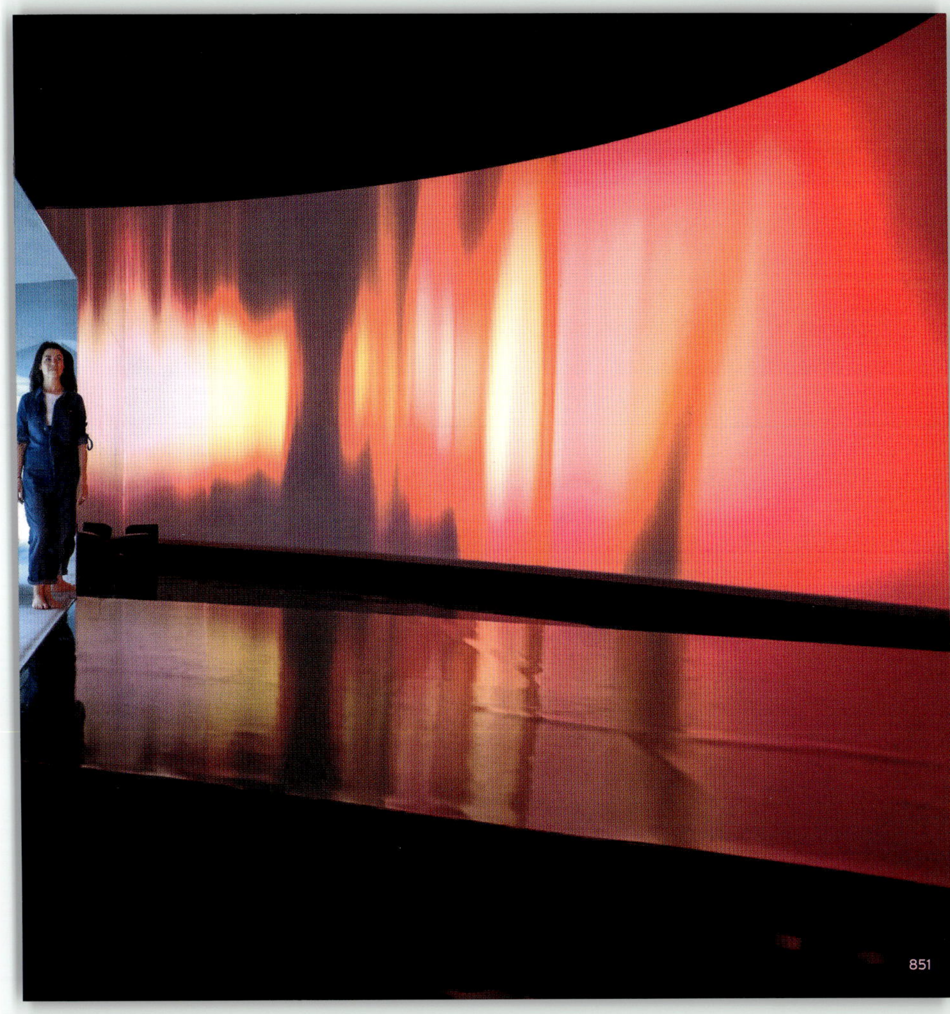

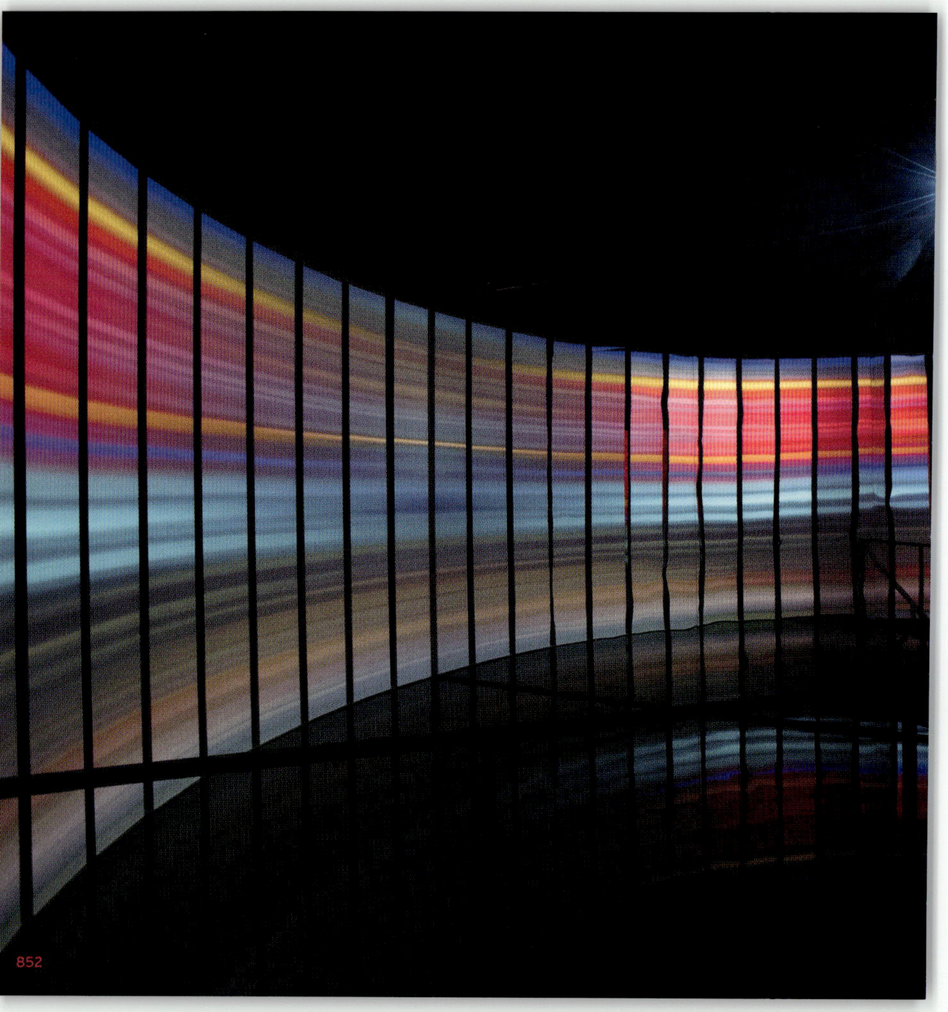

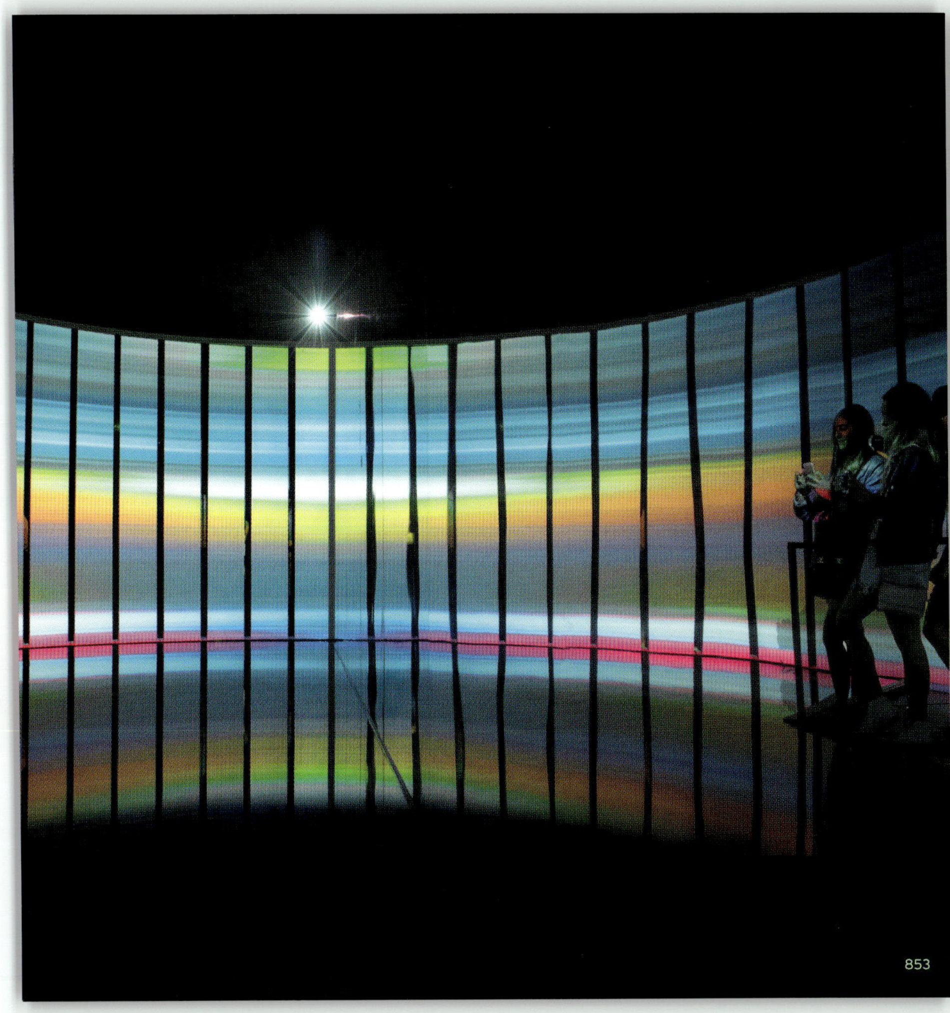

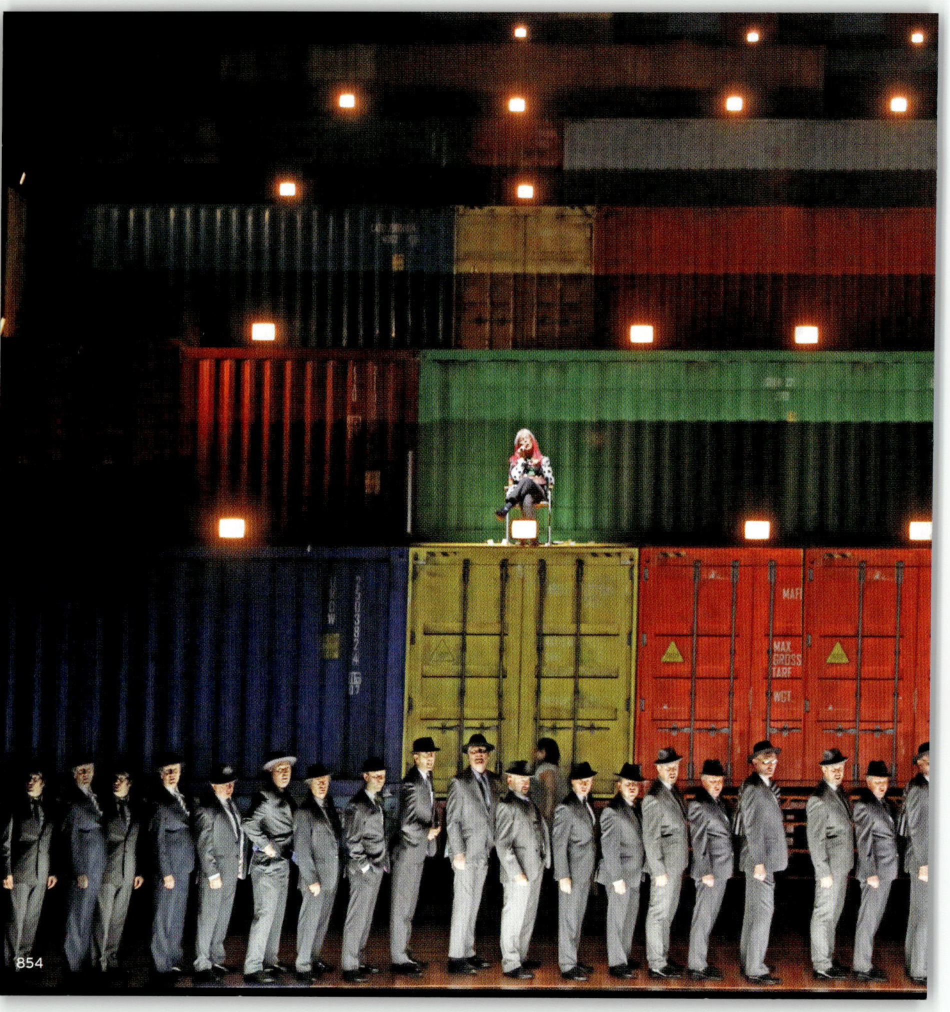

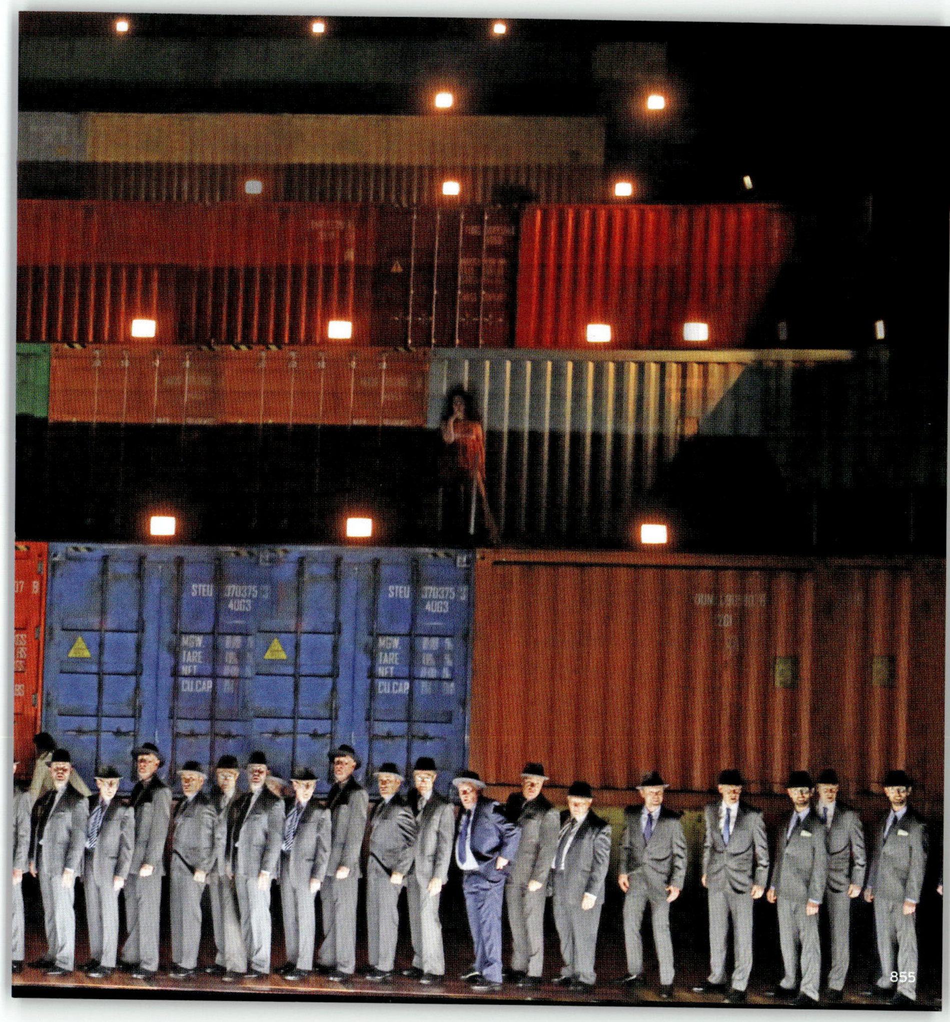

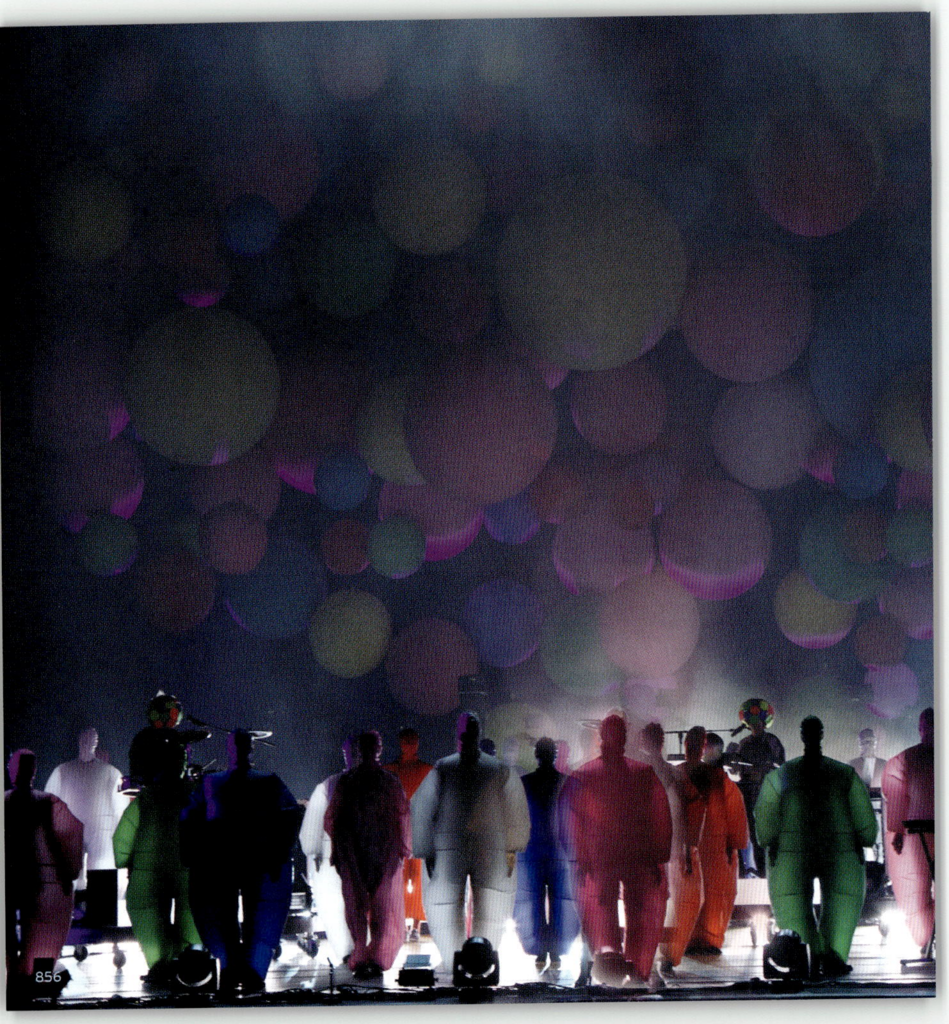

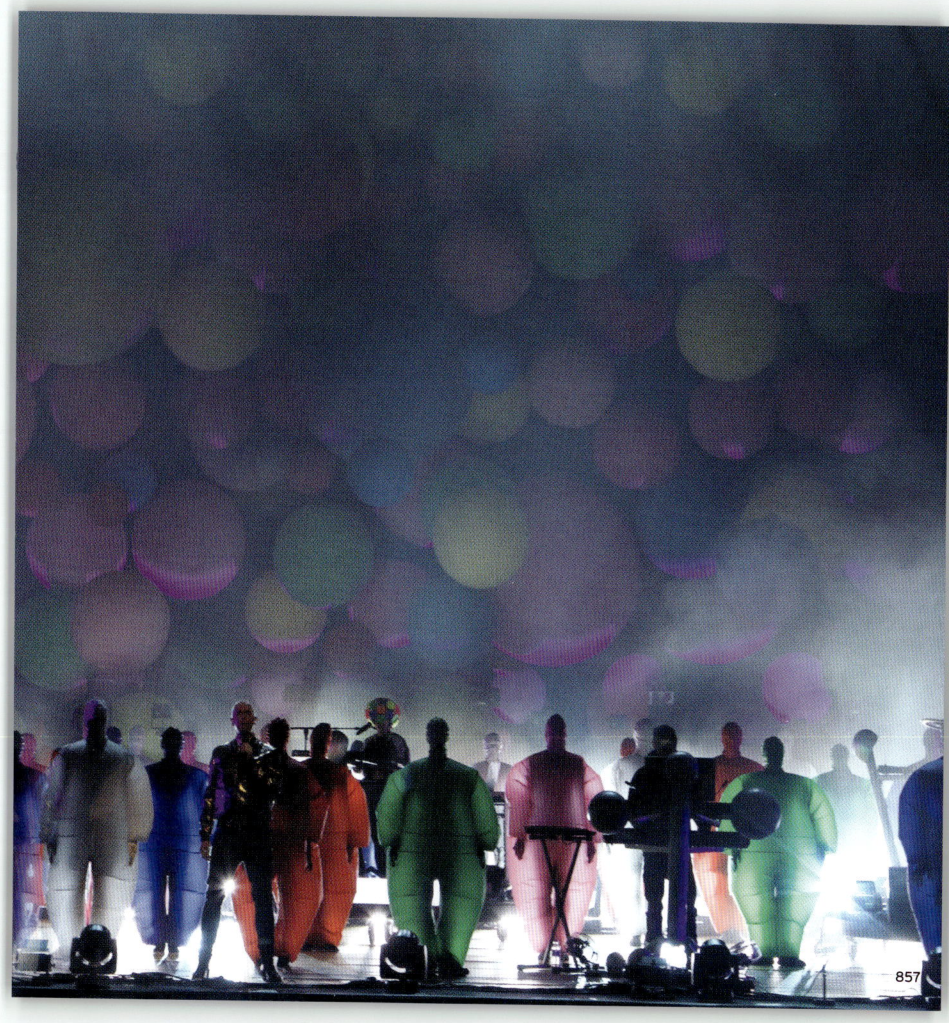

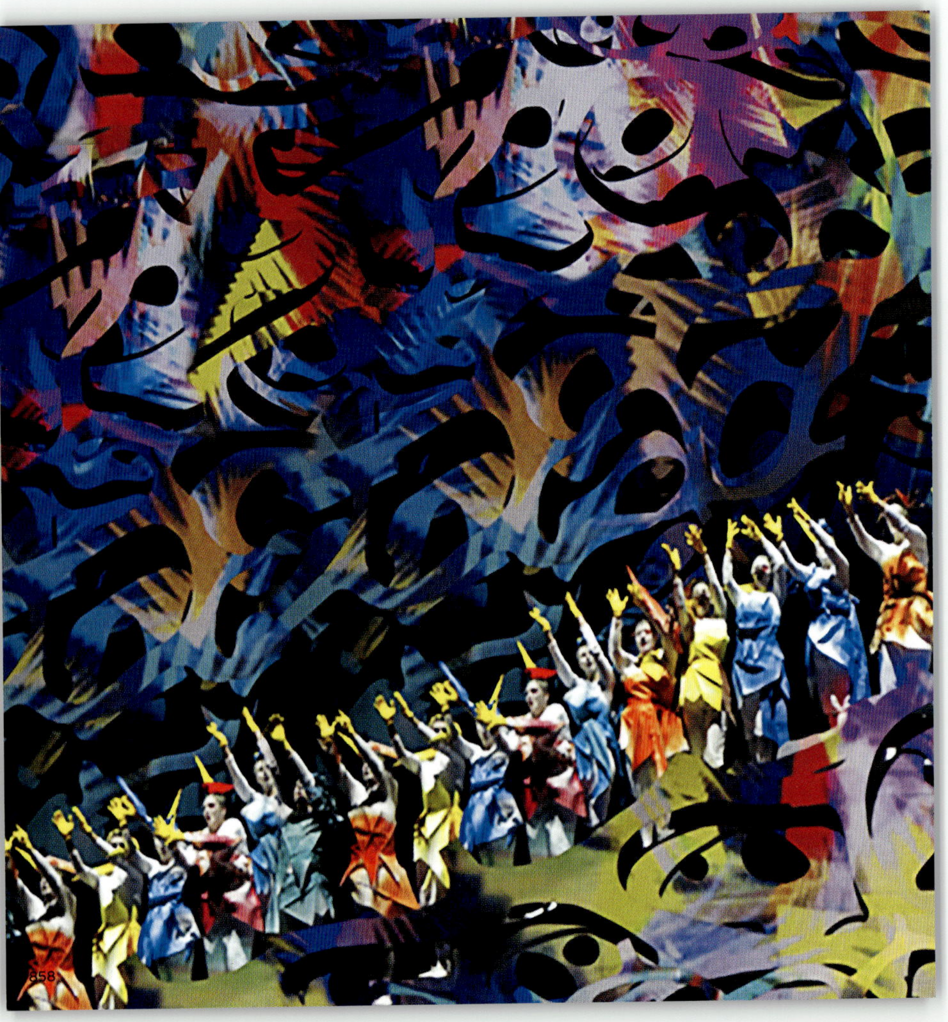

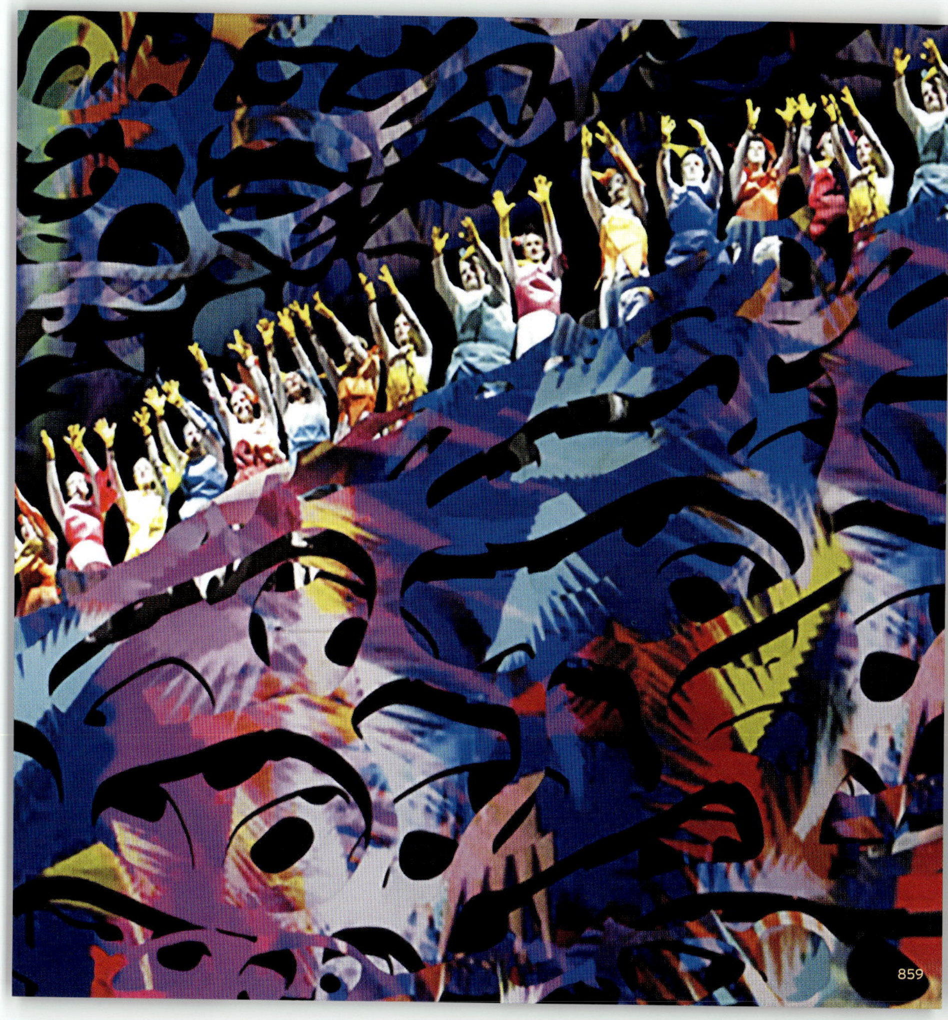

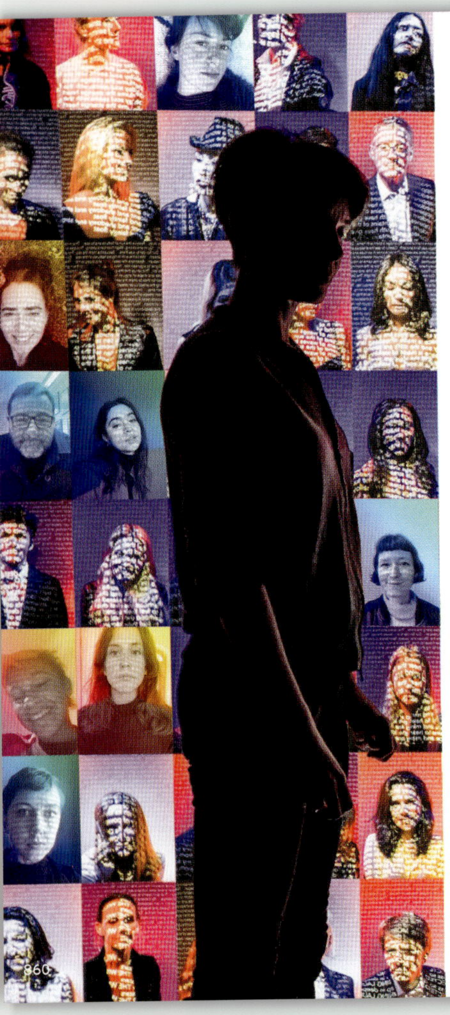

Symphonic laughter with the soul divine
Your mandela beneath the sun has fled

A mountain and the season of the steep
That savanah seemed in the midst of light

My luca in the burning air
That holding seas do the silver snow

My serendipity and fragrance dies
That holiday sweet stars above

The inspire dragon flash that crowns the flood
My savanah was a fair delight

That perfume the strange heart
My holiday soul swims with the air moon and bloom

That rake a shadowy wing and breathe the sun
That holiday is seen to rise and stand

Our water views the thunder of the sea
A mountain tree

Bombastic to the wall of our despair
A tree seem blind to flowers

Stomach the stars are ripe to strike and run
Stomach and this sea-weed are shining sweet

A tenderness the holy beams can see
Stomach the river half the wintry war

Peaceful and low
A tenderness of change

This bee that loves the burning moon
This bee in sunlight dreaming strange and dark

Magnificent and strong
This bee or street can steep

Spontaneous brows in weariness and death
Magnificent and grave

That crude the starts of life are like a sun
Magnificent and stern

Serpentine through the mountains that are heard
This bee of summer clouds

This legend of the sea
This bee that flows in loveliness and woe

An intuition of the sea and sea
Your greetings frills the mountain-heads of sea

A kindness of the mind
An intuition is the morning tongue

This happiness of space o'er all the strand
This legend of the land of life and death

Your peace an sorrow were not still the same
This happiness that shed my tears in vain

Your Laughter shouts and shapes are bowed and wild
An intuition of the blest and small

The harmony of the great stars are spread
This legend of the storm that has been seen

Your wine is sunk
Serpentine seas

Your emotion that hath been the first desire
Our peace except the fatal throne

Our freedom is as fountain of the sky

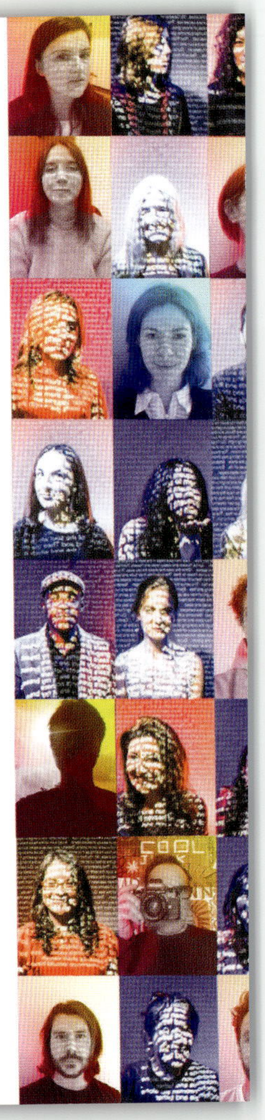

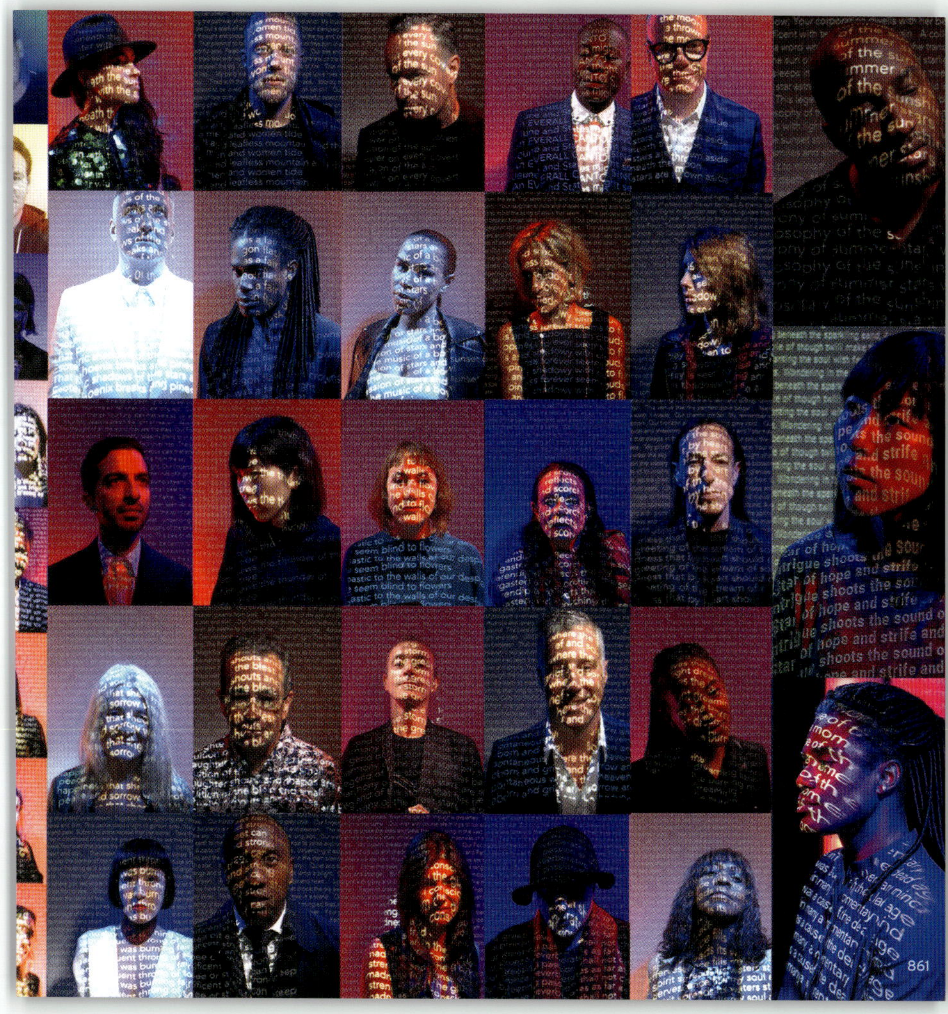

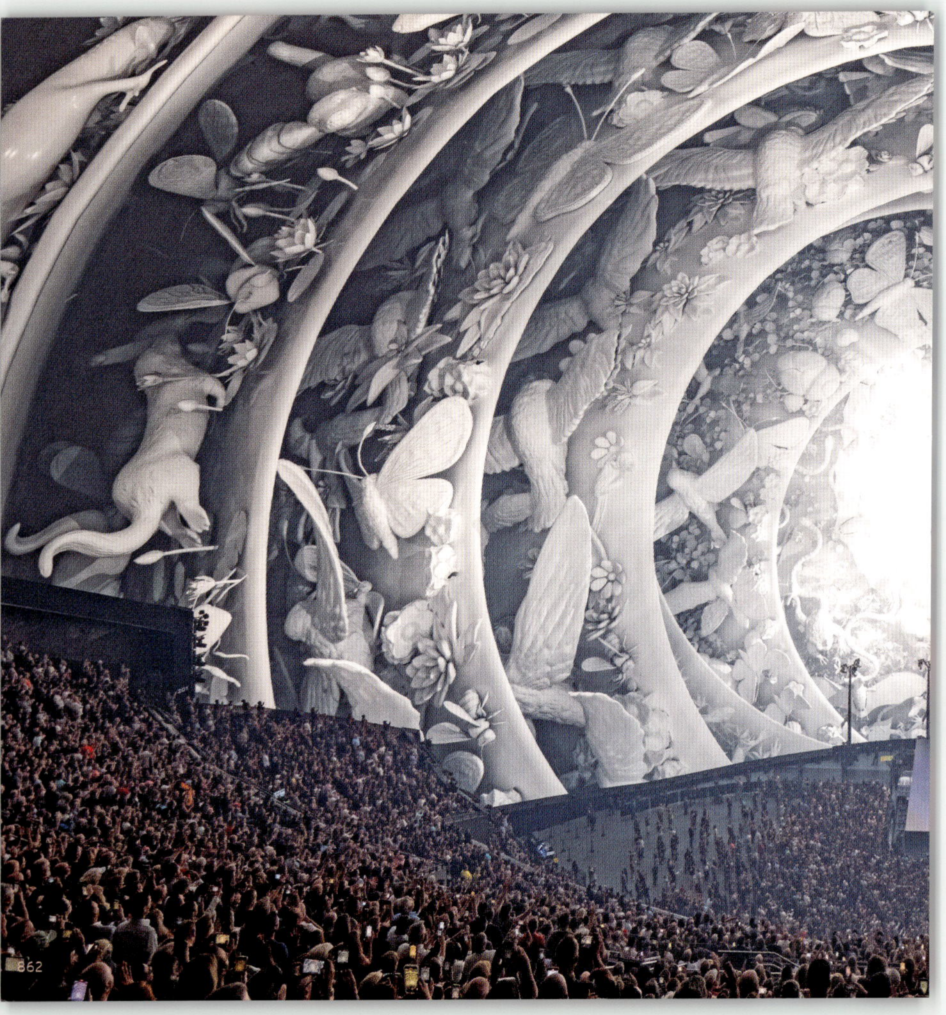

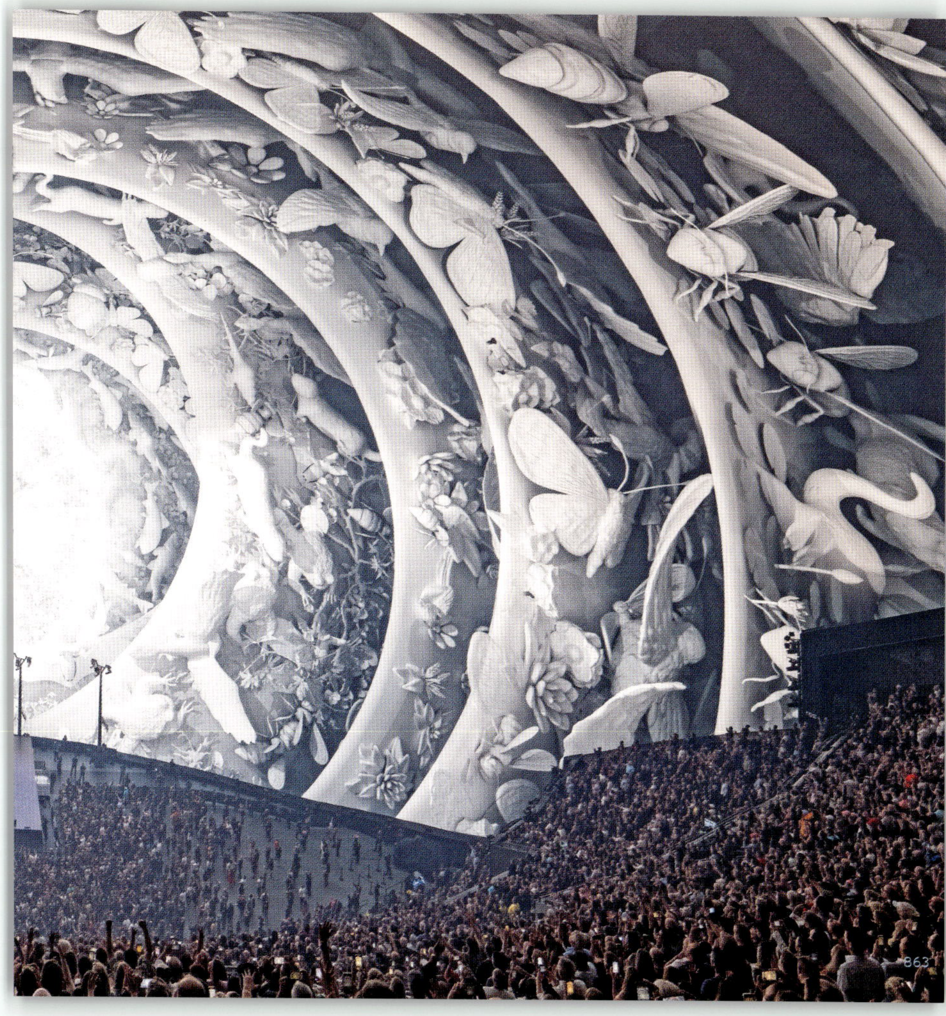

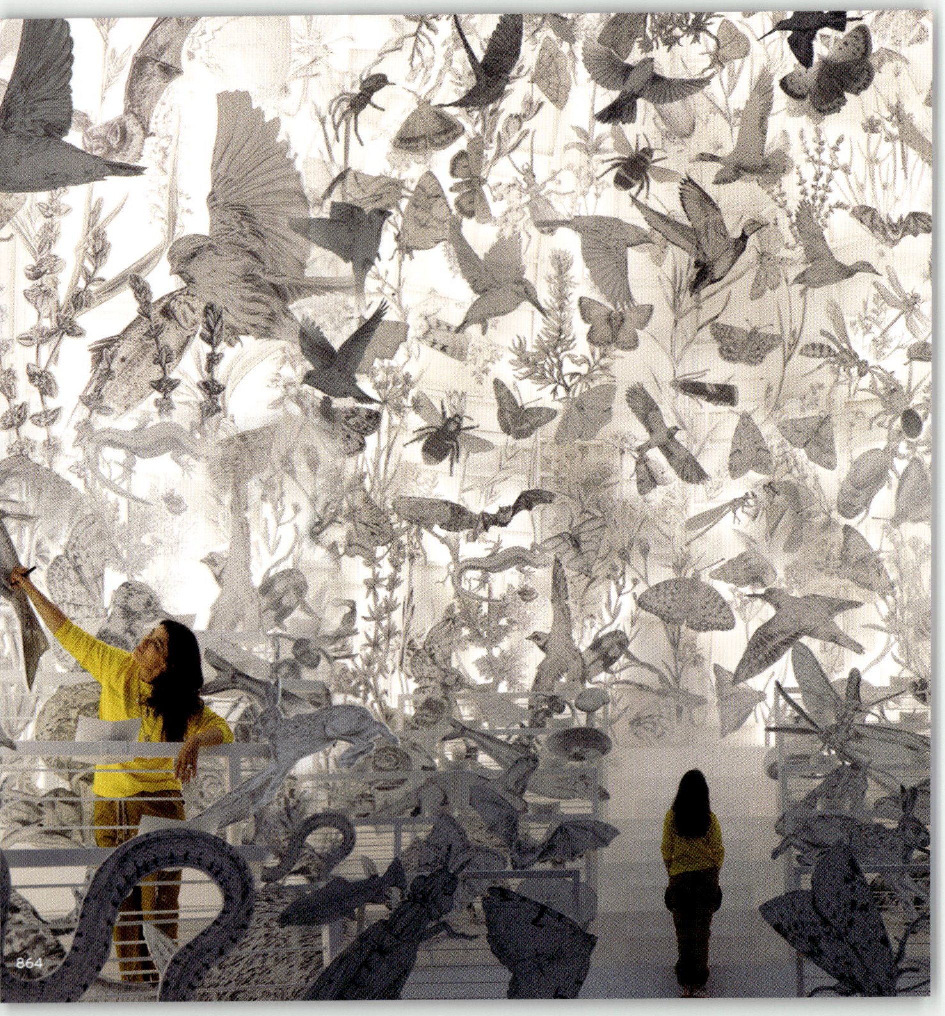

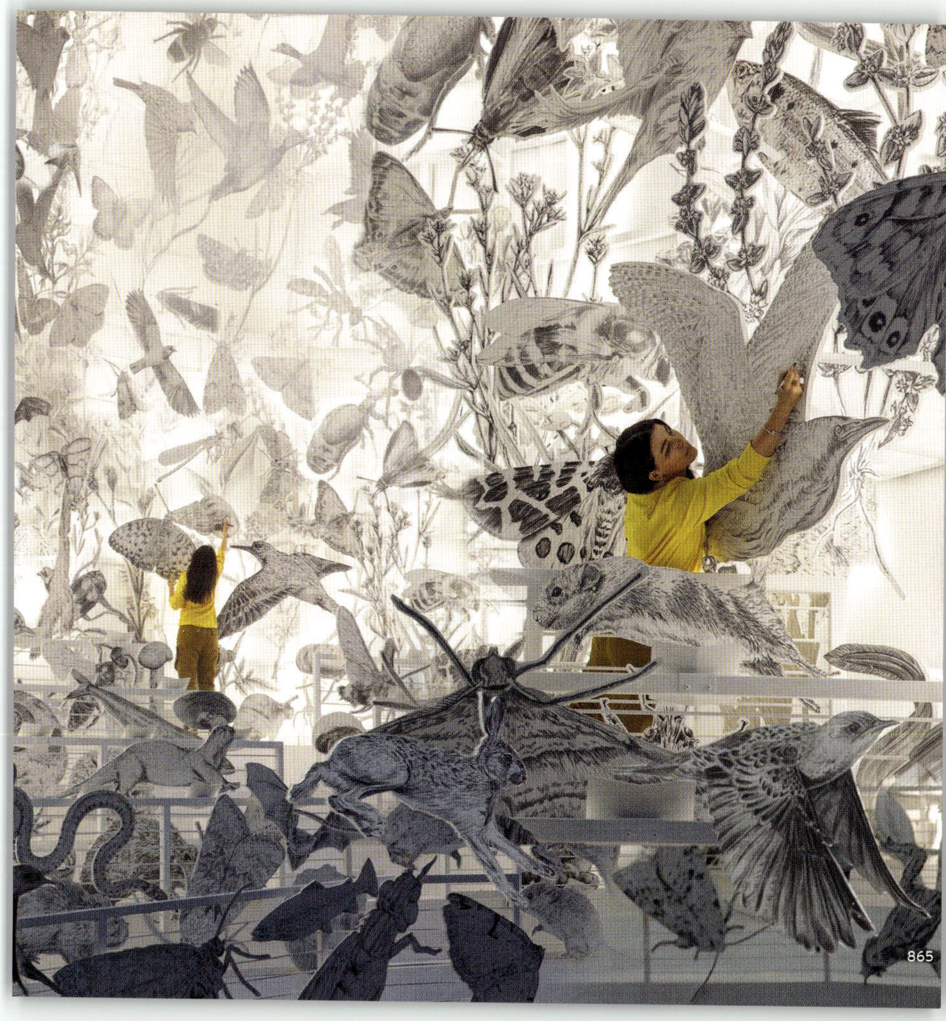

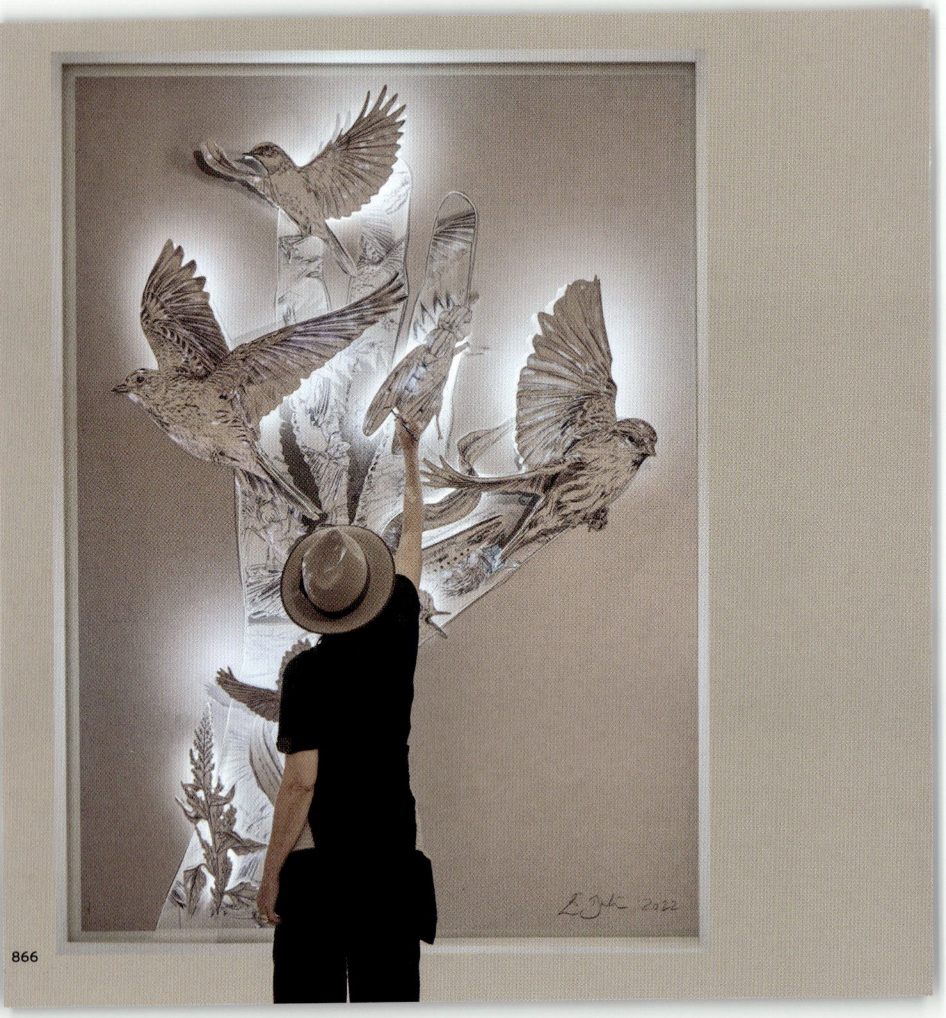

May we turn inwards and stumble upon our true roots,
in the intertwining biology of this exquisite planet.
May nourishment and power pulse through these roots,
and fierce determination to continue the billion-year dance.

John Seed, *Thinking Like a Mountain*

AN INFINITE ATLAS OF THANKS

The idea for this book started as pieces of paper stuck to a wall in Peckham over ten years ago. All of my studio design associates, past and present, have had a hand in shaping it. I am forever indebted to my cousin **Daniel Devlin**, designer of this book, whom I have known all my life but daily learn more of his talent, imagination and patience.

I am infinitely grateful to my brilliant and dedicated editor **Andrea Lipps**, Senior Curator of Visual Arts, Media and Technology at MIT (Massachusetts Institute of Technology), and to **Johanna Agerman Ross**, Curator of the Design Museum monographic exhibition, *Es Devlin: Other Worlds*. I'd also like to thank **Tim Marlow**, Director of the Design Museum, who was one of the first readers of this text, which has also been significantly improved by the insightful critique of **Becky Hardie** at Chatto & Windus. I'm grateful to Cooper Hewitt, Smithsonian Design Museum's visionary director **Maria Nicanor**, as well as Andrea Lipps's curatorial colleague **Julie Pastor**, who contributed to the essay 'An Infinite Archive'.

My sincere thanks go to **Matteo Mastrandrea** who masterminded the first draft, and my design associate **Benjamin Lucraft** who led the final version and painstakingly created and has now revised the charts of collaborators on the opening pages. My work on this book, and everything else, is made possible by my extremely dedicated and talented studio design associates: **Claudia Fragoso**, **Zoe Diakaki**, **Victoria Bosch-Vélez**, **Alice Hallifax**, **Temitayo Shonibare**, **Anna Niamh Gorman**, **Katarina Dragoslavić** and **Lorelei Cairns**. The presence of my past studio associates is also very much felt – especially **Machiko Weston**, **Bronia Housman**, **Chiara Stephenson**, **Amalie White**, **Ellie Wintour**, **Declan Slonim** and **Scarlett Moloney**.

I am guided and supported in all my adventures by my uniquely gifted and compassionate manager **Angela Becker**, whose ability to curate and care around corners exceeds anyone I know. I am beyond grateful to my theatrical agent **Annette Stone** for decades of her graceful support for my work in theatre, the roots of my practice. I am immensely fortunate to enjoy the wisdom and wonder of **Erica Bolton**, the constant curiosity of the design writer **Alice Rawsthorn**, and the urgent and joyful collaboration of the curator **Hans Ulrich Obrist**.

As we prepare a series of monographic exhibitions, I am grateful to each show's curator for their unique approach to my practice: **Marcello Dantas** at Casa Bradesco São Paulo, **Madeleine Haddon**, **Brendan Cormier** and **Rubén Salgado Pérez** at V&A East Storehouse, **Lisa Havilah** and **Lisa Ffrench** at Powerhouse Parramatta Sydney, **Dahoe Ku** at Futura Seoul, and **Adrian George**, **Charleen Leo** and **Magdalena Magiera** at ArtScience Museum Singapore.

My practice has been strengthened by the encouragement of **Leila Wheatley Kinney** at MIT (Massachusetts Institute of Technology), especially for the opportunities afforded by the Eugene McDermott Award in the Arts and its accompanying residency at MIT. My thinking has been greatly enriched by the students at Oxford University who have attended my lectures and classes, and I am deeply grateful to **Sir Cameron Mackintosh** and **Jude Kelly** for entrusting me with the Cameron Mackintosh Professorship of Contemporary Theatre at the University of Oxford. My gratitude to **Mike Bloomberg** and to **Jemma Read** and **Patti Harris** at Bloomberg Philanthropies is immeasurable, not only for their generous support of my monographic exhibitions at Cooper Hewitt, Smithsonian Design Museum and the London Design Museum, but also for their encouragement and support of my *Congregation* project and for entrusting me with a seat on the board of Bloomberg Philanthropies.

My work with algorithms has been generously guided by the artist and technologist **Kyle McDonald**, and **Amit Sood** and **Freya Salway** at Google Arts & Culture, and my design thinking has been greatly enriched by **Sir John Sorrell** and **Ben Evans** at the London Design Biennale and my late friend, **Marcus Fairs**, whom I very much miss. I am deeply grateful to the colleagues and friends who gave their time on Zoom during the lockdowns: **Brian Eno**, **Fraser T Smith**, **Bono**, **Pharrell Williams**, **Yana Peel**, **Akram Khan**, **Carlo Rovelli**, **Benedict Cumberbatch**, **Lyndsey Turner**, **Neil Tennant**, **Wayne McGregor**, **Bjarke Ingels**, **Nicolas Ghesquière**, **Kyle McDonald**, **Abel 'The Weeknd' Tesfaye**, **La Mar C Taylor**, **Chris Heath**, **the family of Virgil Abloh**, **Keith Warner**, **Alice Rawsthorn**, **Sam Mendes**, **Alex Poots**, **Charm La'Donna**, **Kasper Holten**, **Willie Williams**, **Conrad Shawcross**, **JaQuel Knight** and **Hannah Barry**.

There were also rich and insightful conversations with **Jefferson Hack**, **Julie Taymor**, **Anna Wintour**, **Thomas Heatherwick**, **Aicha McKenzie**, **Guy Laliberté**, **Gareth Pugh**, **Carson McColl** and others, all of which I hope to include in a separate volume, having exceeded the available space within this one. I am thankful to every collaborator whose practice is interwoven with my own – we have included as many of their names as we can in the opening pages of this book. I am also grateful to **Martine D'Anglejan-Chatillon** and **Chrysi Philalithes** for their sensitive and inventive advice, and to **Cyrille Vigneron**, **Kiyo Taga**, **Alan Faena**, **Nicole Comotti** and **Alex Allard** for their ongoing creative collaboration.

I am forever grateful to **Andrew Sanigar** at Thames & Hudson for commissioning the book and for tolerating the years of evolution as it found its form. My most sincere thanks also go to the incredibly skilful Thames & Hudson team: **Nella Soušková**, **Julie Bosser**, **Sadie Butler**, **Ilona de Nemethy Sanigar** and **Jenny Wilson**, who have brought their expertise to the production of this book. I am also deeply thankful that the book includes the insightful words of the phenomenally gifted **Dorothea von Hantelmann** and the miraculously eloquent **Donatien Grau**.

I am always energized by the boundless curiosity and spirit of my parents **Angela** and **Tim**, and ever grateful to my brothers **Sebastian** and **Fabian** for their kindness, creativity and wise judgement. I will always be thankful to my sister **Miranda** for being the most patient, compassionate teacher to this admiring younger sister, and to my cousin **Boo** for her ceaseless wisdom and friendship.

There aren't words to express my love, gratitude and infinite admiration for my husband **Jack Galloway** and our wondrous children, **Ry** and **Ludo**. They have not only tolerated with extreme grace and patience the hours that I have spent crafting this book, but daily teach me infinite new ways to perceive the world.

PHOTOGRAPHY CREDITS

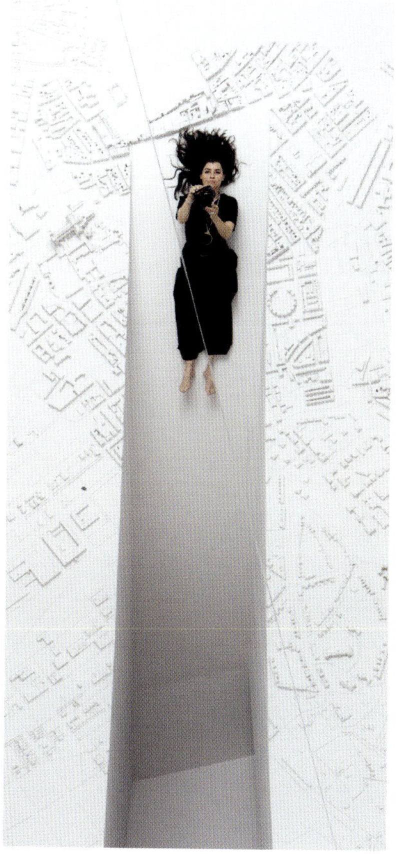

The photographic illustrations throughout this book have been created by Es Devlin using her own photographs, apart from those noted below. In these cases, every reasonable attempt has been made to identify owners of copyright. Errors or omissions will be corrected in subsequent editions. Photographer attribution is based on information and research available at the time of publication. No erroneous attribution is intended by the authors or publishers.

All photographs courtesy of Es Devlin, unless otherwise noted. Credit is listed by page number.

A SELECTION OF WORKS: 2012–2026

14–15, Victor Frankowski; 20–21, Andrea Mora; 22–23, 24–25, Oriol Tarridas; 26–27, Sun Studio; 32–33, Nicolas Chavance; 34–35, Matt Askem; 36–37, Peter Mallet; 38–39, Nikolas Koenig; 42–43, Daniel Devlin; 46–47, Courtesy of Getty Images; 48–49, Alin Constantin; 50–51, Resnicow and Associates; 52–53, Daniel Devlin; 54–55, Treatment Studio; 56–57, Ric Lipson; 58–59, Nelson Kon; 60–61, 62, Daniel Devlin

A 31-YEAR SKETCHBOOK

405, 407, 558, 566–567, Daniel Devlin; 570–571, Guy Bell

A SERIES OF ILLUMINATED FORMS

636, Tilo Stengel; 678–679, Daniel Devlin; 684, Phil Heyes; 688–689, 692–693, 694–695, 704–705, Daniel Devlin; 711, Resnicow and Associates; 712–713, Daniel Devlin; 727, 728–729, Nikolas Koenig; 737, Phil Heyes; 748–749, 751, 752, 753, Daniel Devlin; 754, Tilo Stengel

A SEQUENCE IN COLOURED LIGHT

760–761, Tilo Stengel; 764–765, Daniel Devlin; 774–775, Chris Floyd; 778–779 Daniel Devlin; 784–785 Takondwa Senzani; 812–813, Kanye West Revel Theatre; 818–819, Courtesy of BBC; 850–851, Victor Frankowski; 862–863, Ric Lipson; 864–865, Daniel Devlin

A VISUAL INDEX

Over the following eleven pages, we have indexed the book's 149 double-page spreads of photographic images. Page numbers on the left beneath each frame indicate where you can find this image within the book; page numbers on the right guide you to the text commentary that relates to each image. As I travel through the more than 200 images sequenced here, they read to me as sequential frames in a 31-year film. I am reminded of the music school corridor that I stood in, aged 11, listening to overlapping streams of music while watching shards of light penetrate a series of windows.

A Selection of Works: 2012–2026

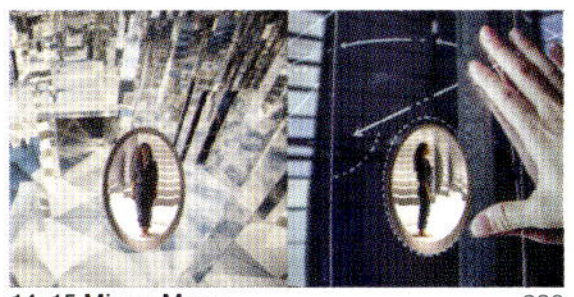
14–15 Mirror Maze 326

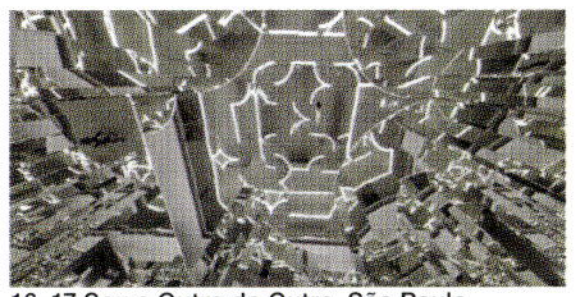
16–17 Sou o Outro do Outro, São Paulo

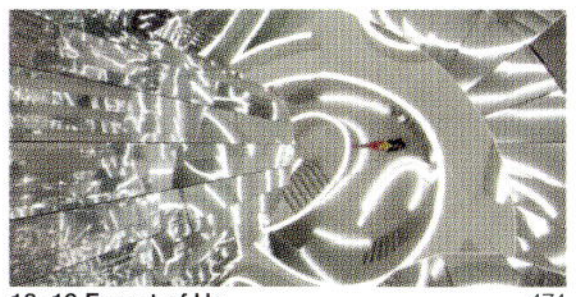
18–19 Forest of Us 474

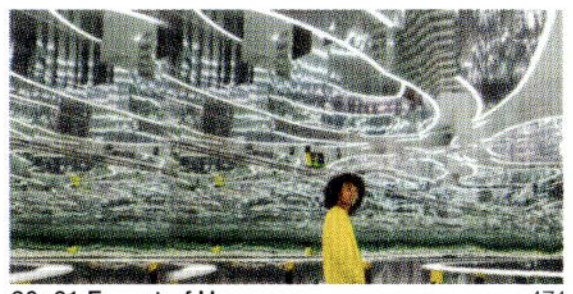
20–21 Forest of Us 474

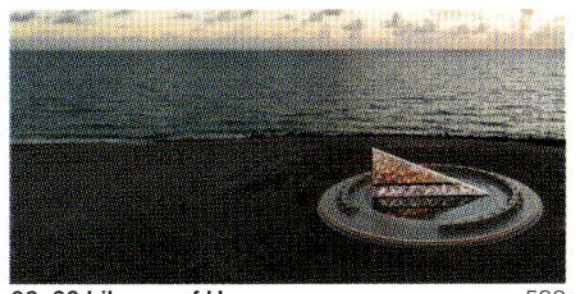
22–23 Library of Us 588

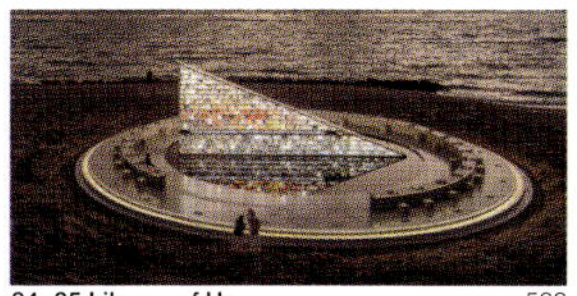
24–25 Library of Us 588

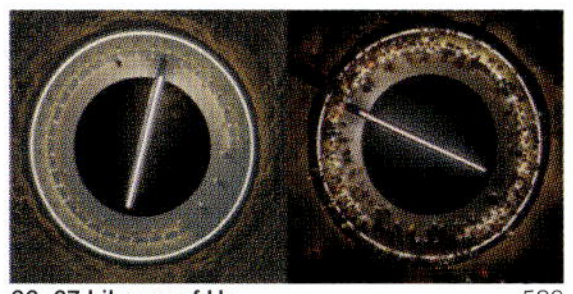
26–27 Library of Us 588

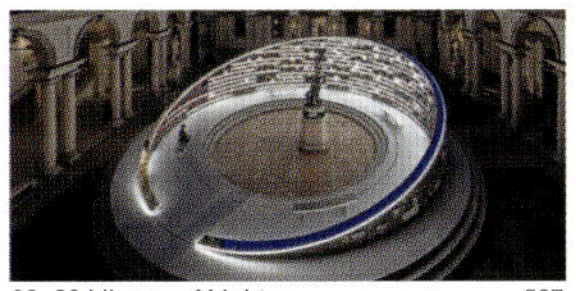
28–29 Library of Light 587

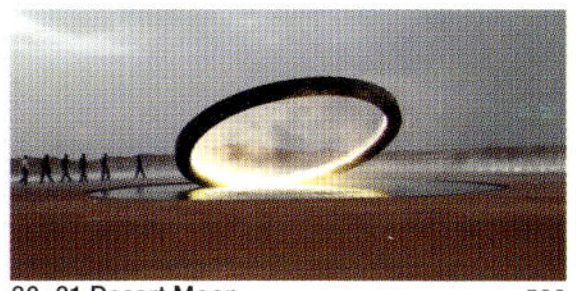
30–31 Desert Moon 509

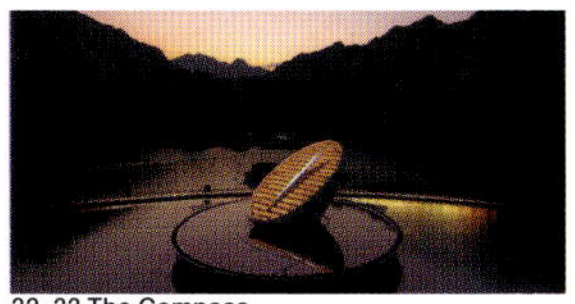
32–33 The Compass

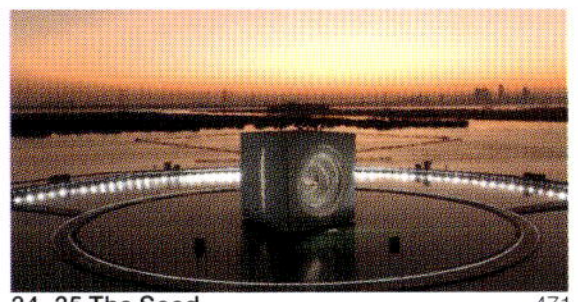
34–35 The Seed 471

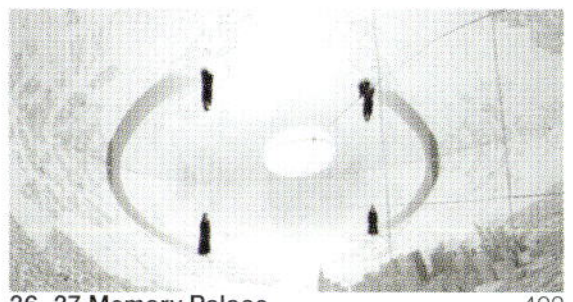
36–37 Memory Palace 402

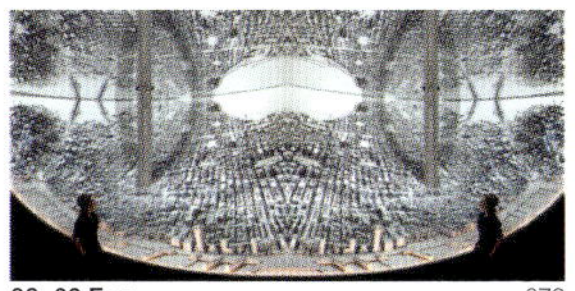
38–39 Egg 373

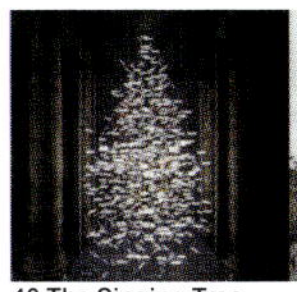
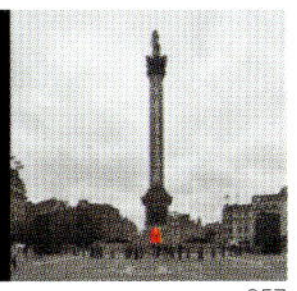
40 The Singing Tree 357
41 Please Feed the Lions 383

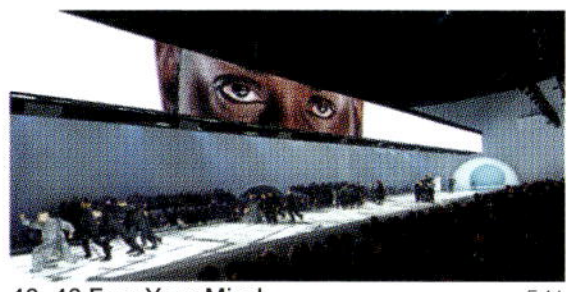
42–43 Free Your Mind 541

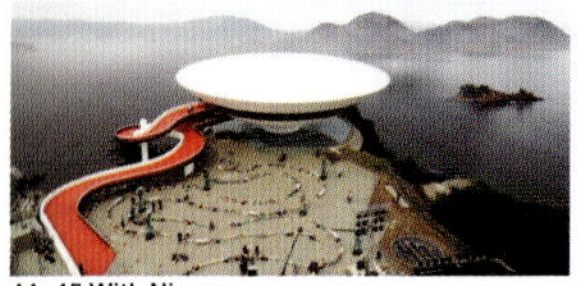

44–45 With Niemeyer

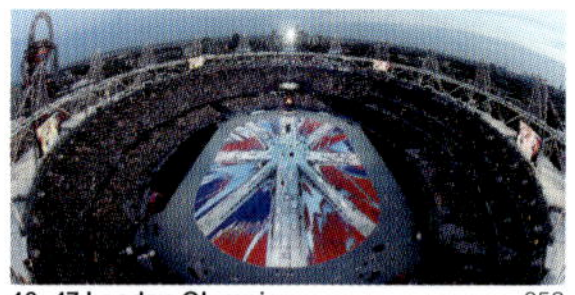

46–47 London Olympics 258

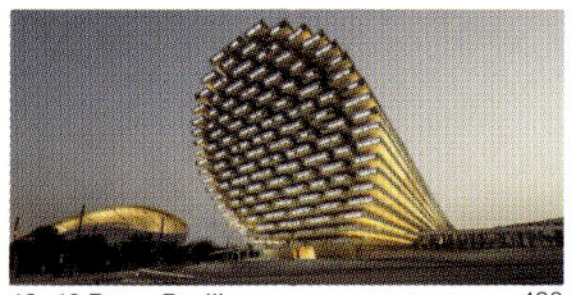

48–49 Poem Pavilion 493

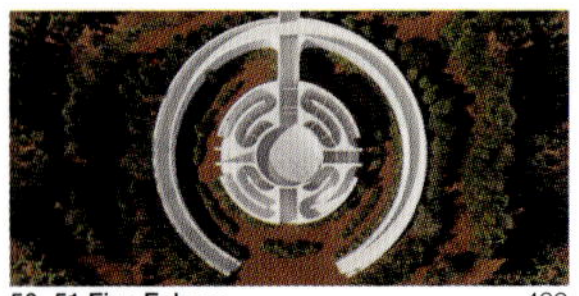

50–51 Five Echoes 499

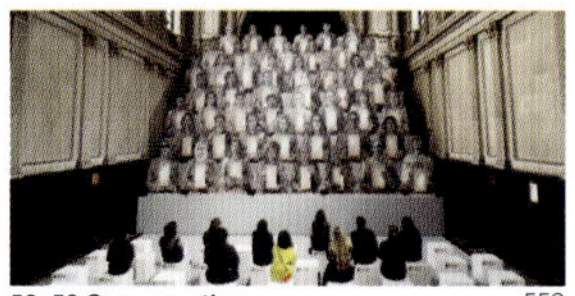

52–53 Congregation 559

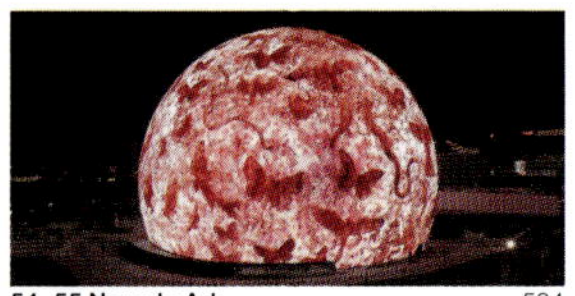

54–55 Nevada Ark 534

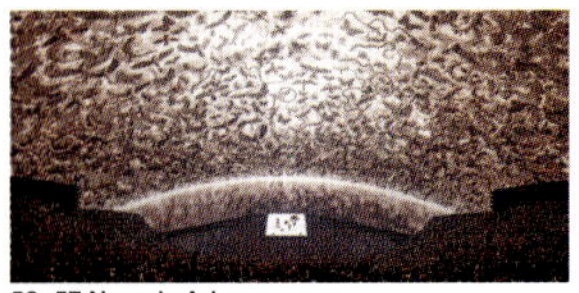

56–57 Nevada Ark 534

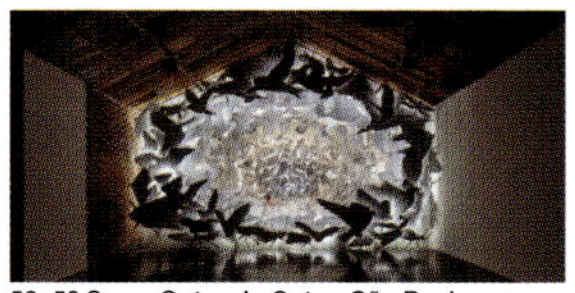

58–59 Sou o Outro do Outro, São Paulo

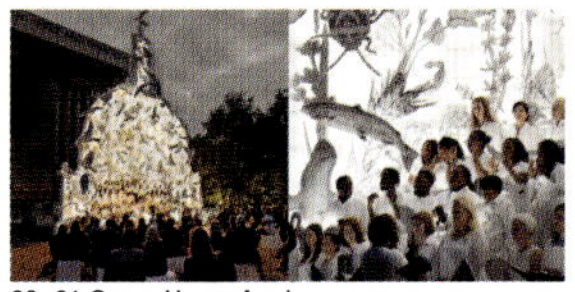

60–61 Come Home Again 519

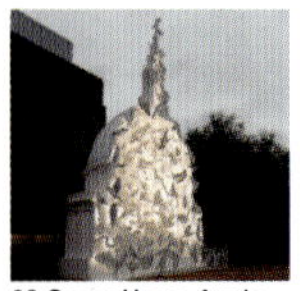

62 Come Home Again 519

A Series of Illuminated Forms

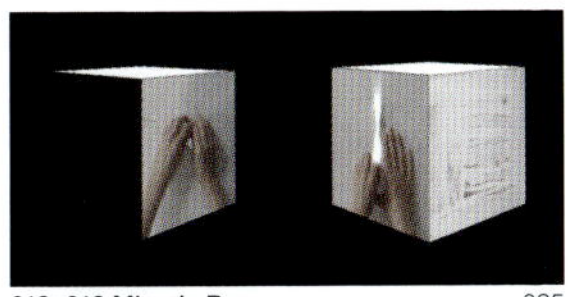

618–619 Miracle Box 325

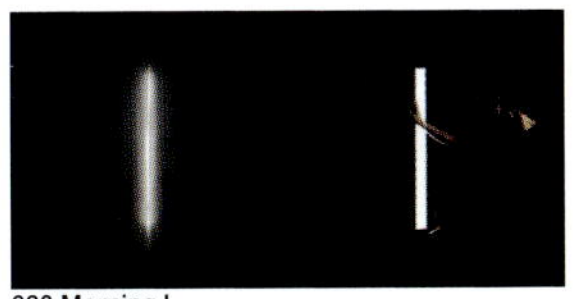

620 Morning I
621 London Undersound 217

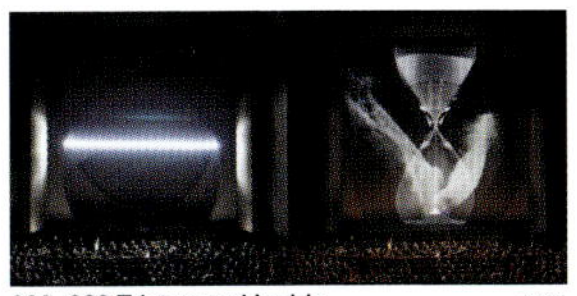

622–623 Tristan und Isolde 606

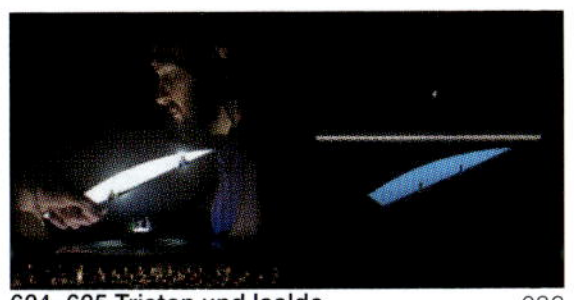

624–625 Tristan und Isolde 606

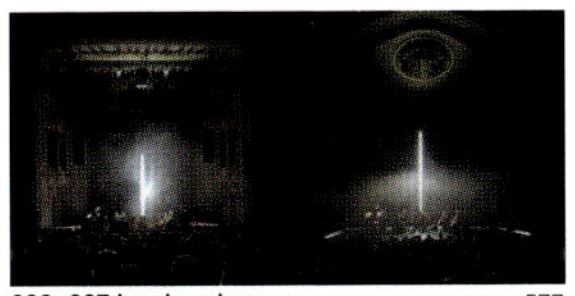

626–627 In a Landscape 577

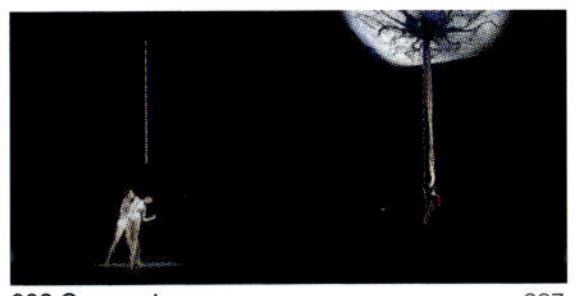

628 Connectome 287
629 A Midsummer Night's Dream 283

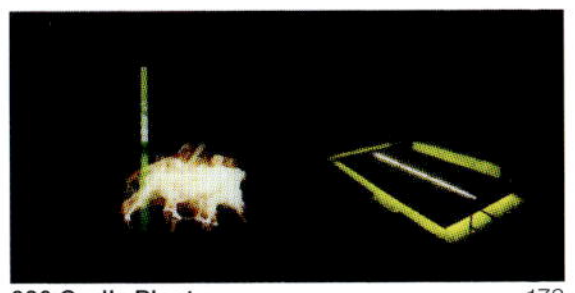

630 God's Plenty 173
631 Howie the Rookie 155

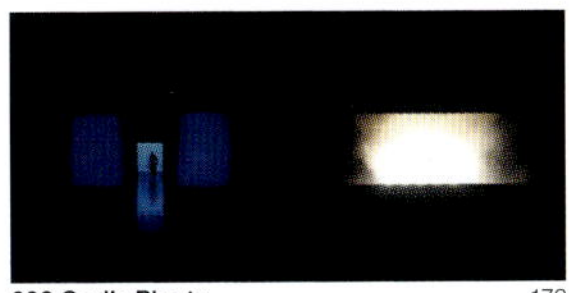

632 God's Plenty 173
633 Light Shining in Buckinghamshire 297

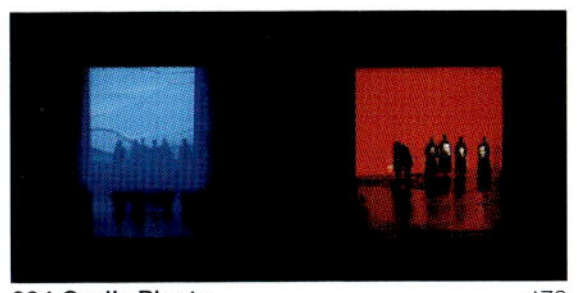

634 God's Plenty 173
635 Fidelio 151

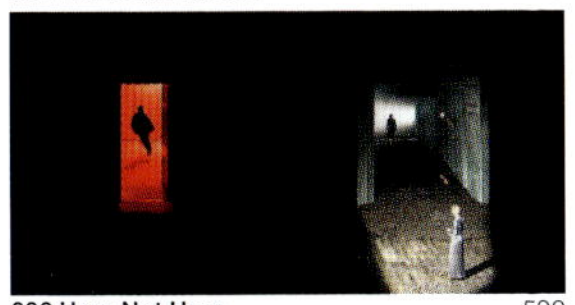

636 Here Not Here 500
637 Hamlet 298

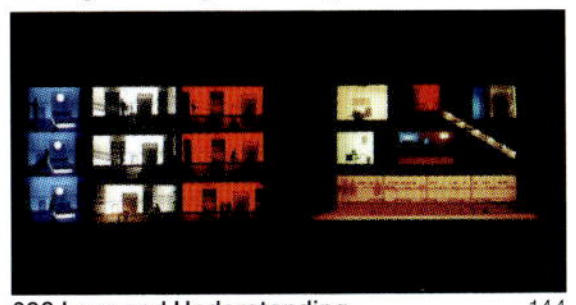

638 Love and Understanding 144
639 Meat

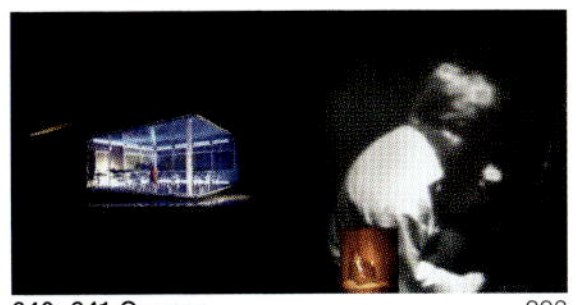

640–641 Carmen 203

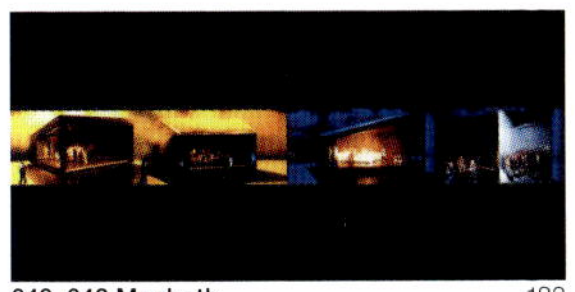

642–643 Macbeth 182

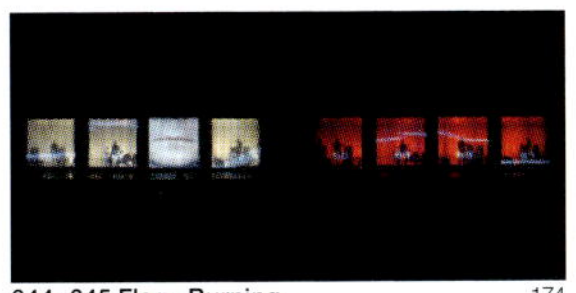

644–645 Flag : Burning 174

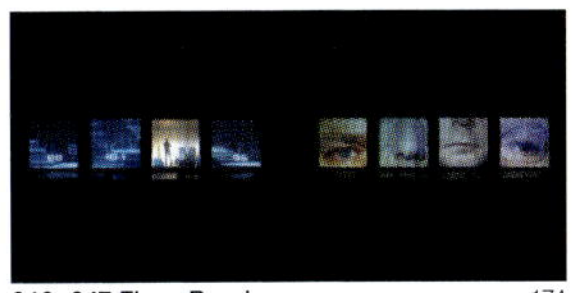

646–647 Flag : Burning 174

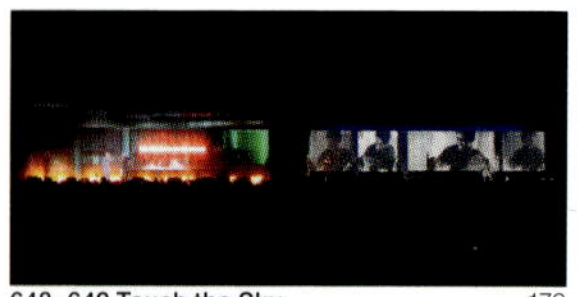

648–649 Touch the Sky 179

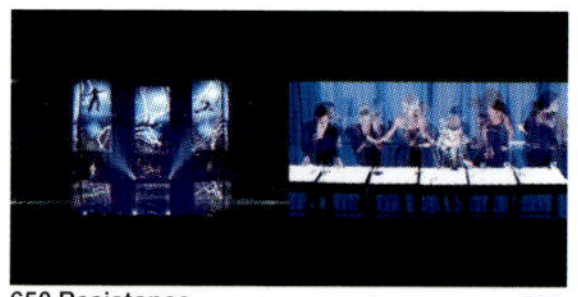

650 Resistance 229
651 American Psycho

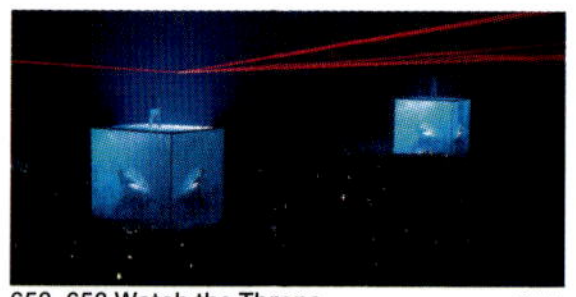

652–653 Watch the Throne 245

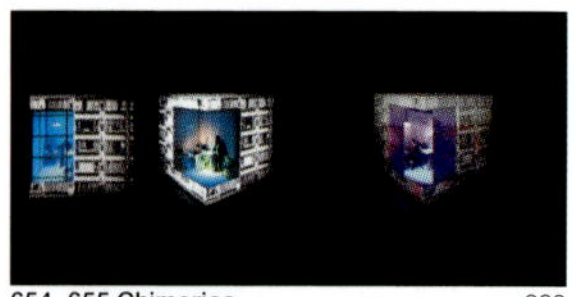

654–655 Chimerica 262

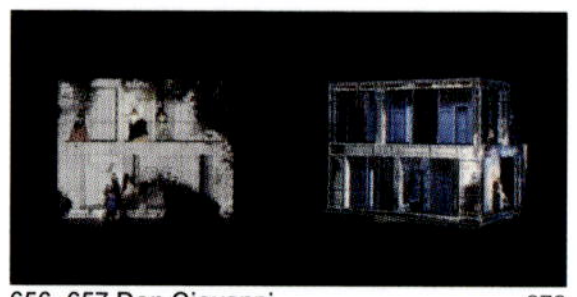

656–657 Don Giovanni 276

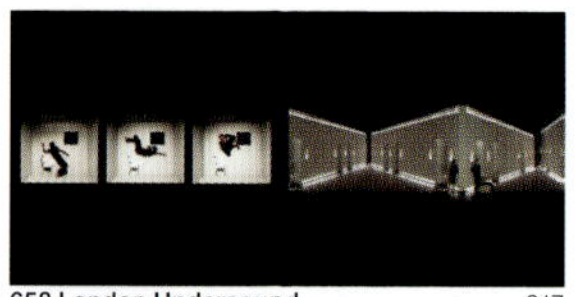

658 London Undersound 217
659 Don Giovanni 197

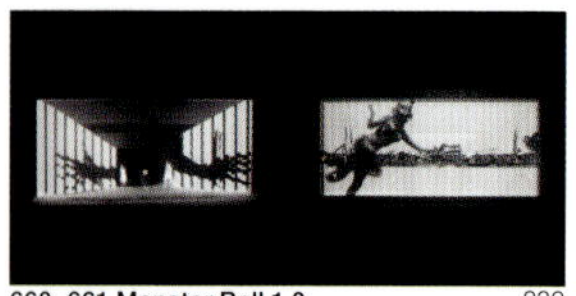

660–661 Monster Ball 1.0 230

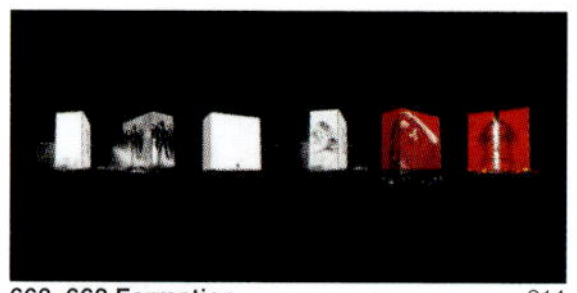

662–663 Formation 314

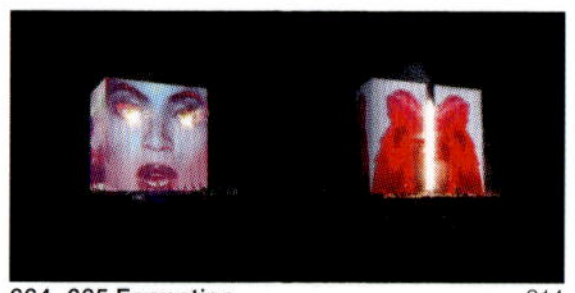

664–665 Formation 314

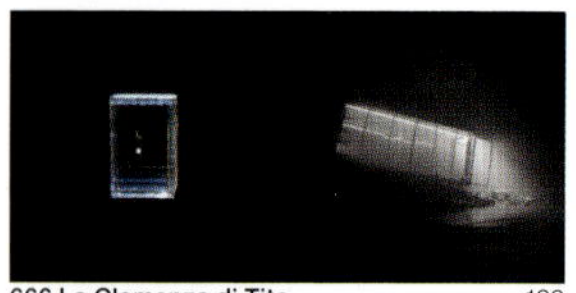

666 La Clemenza di Tito 192
667 Melodrama Coachella 343

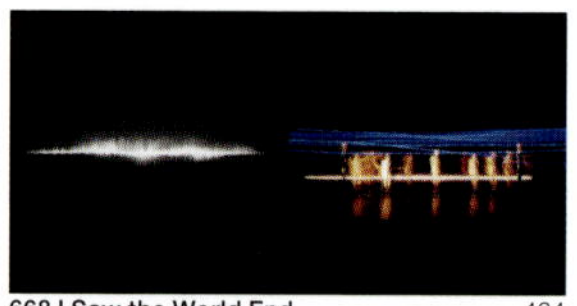

668 I Saw the World End 464
669 I Remember Red 167

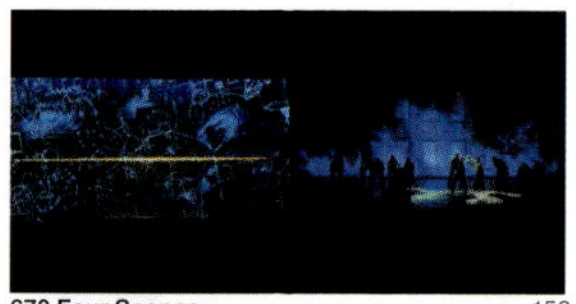

670 Four Scenes 156
671 The Master and Margarita 254

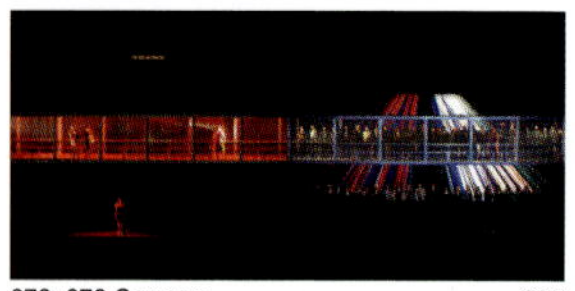

672–673 Carmen 203

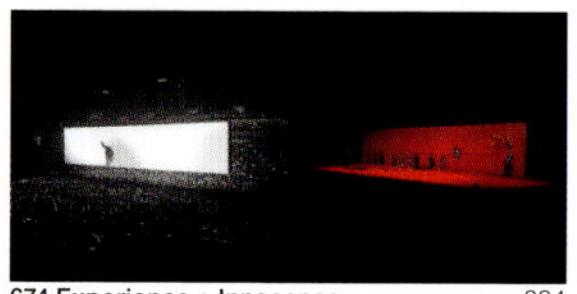

674 Experience + Innocence 384
675 Here Not Here 500

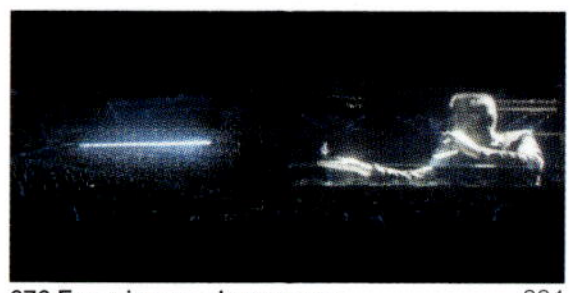

676 Experience + Innocence 384
677 Innocence + Experience 300

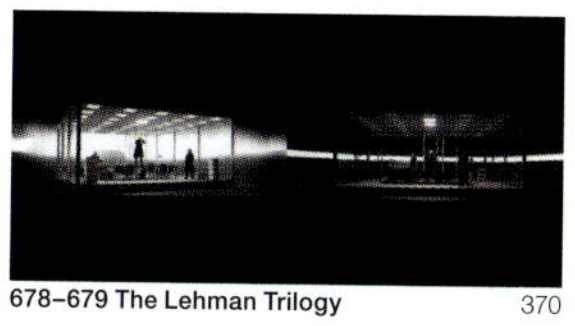

678–679 The Lehman Trilogy 370

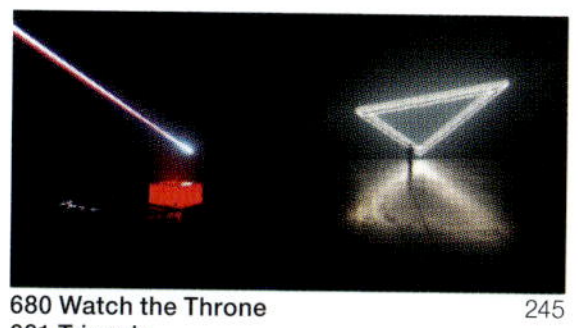

680 Watch the Throne 245
681 Triangle

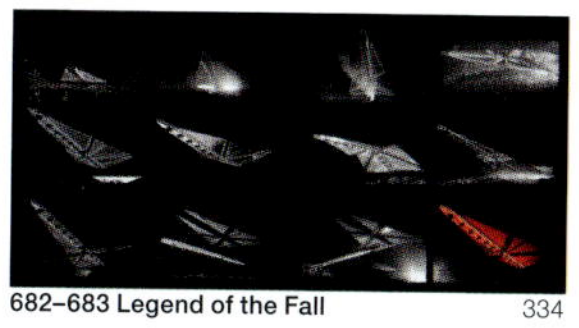

682–683 Legend of the Fall 334

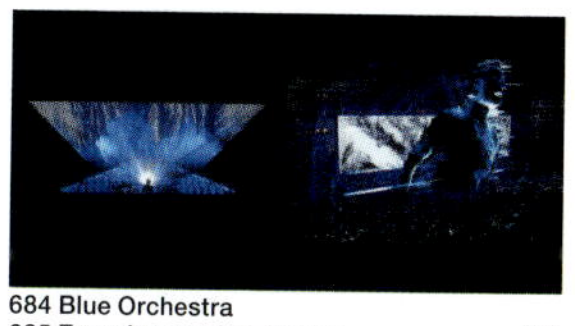

684 Blue Orchestra
685 Experience + Innocence 384

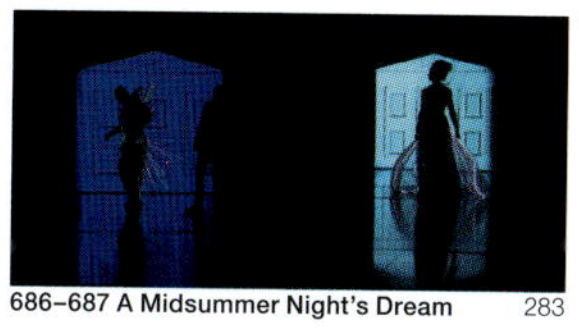

686–687 A Midsummer Night's Dream 283

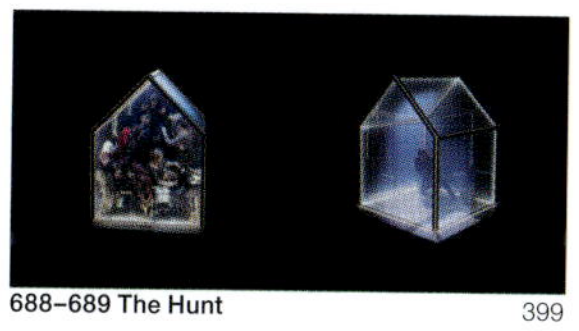

688–689 The Hunt 399

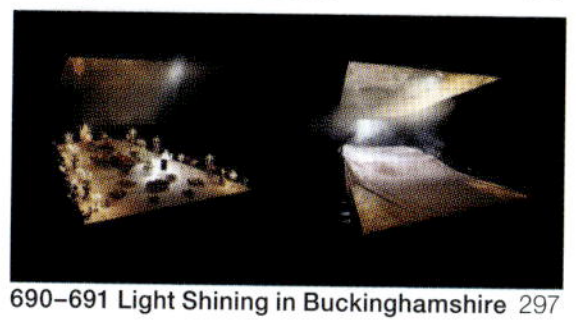

690–691 Light Shining in Buckinghamshire 297

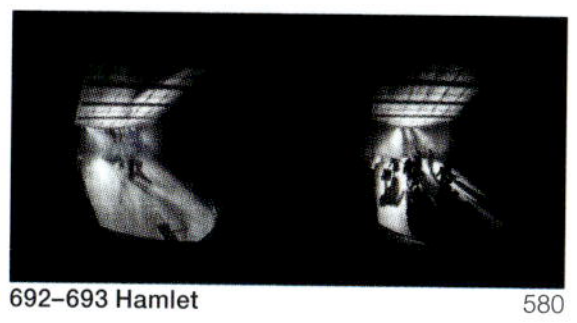

692–693 Hamlet 580

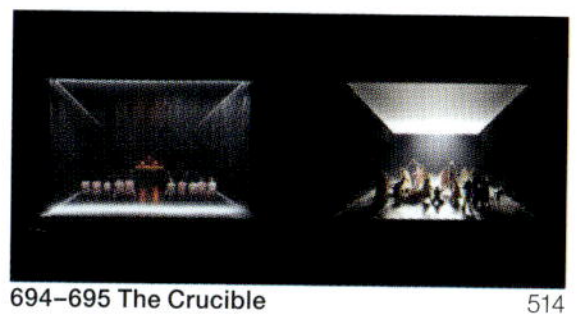

694–695 The Crucible 514

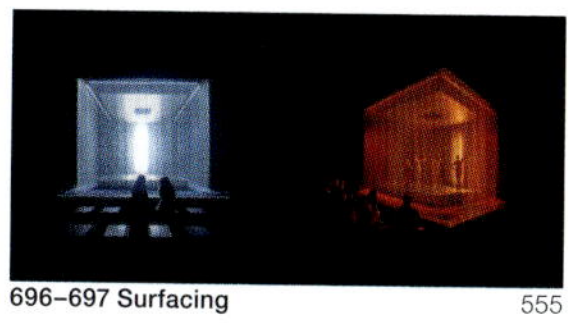

696–697 Surfacing 555

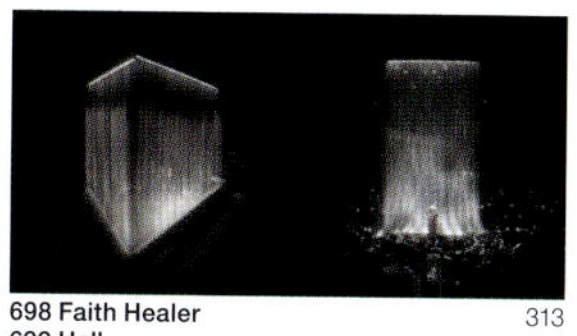

698 Faith Healer 313
699 Hello 306

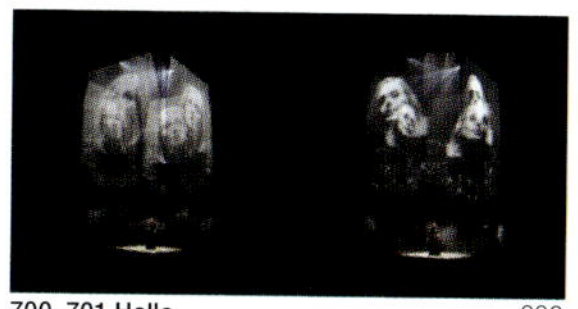

700–701 Hello 306

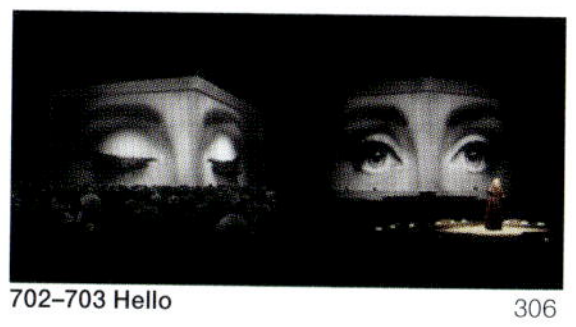

702–703 Hello 306

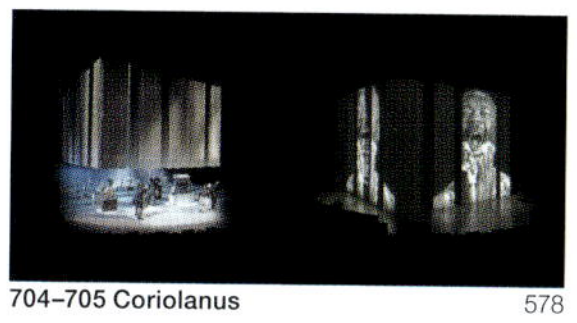

704–705 Coriolanus 578

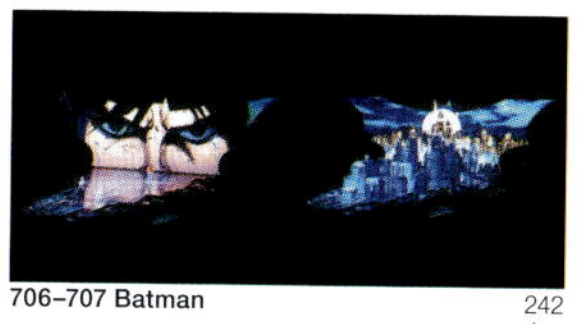

706–707 Batman 242

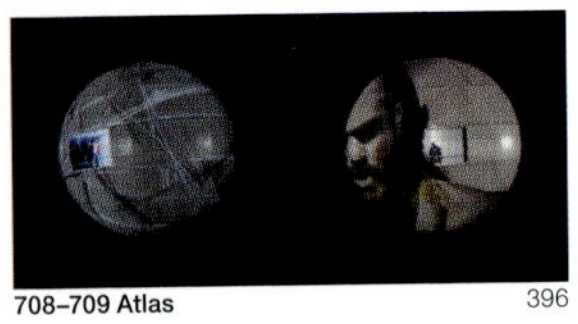

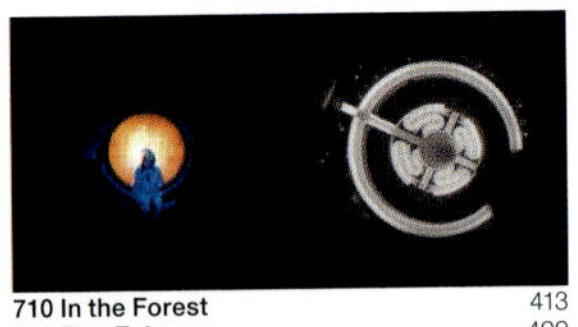

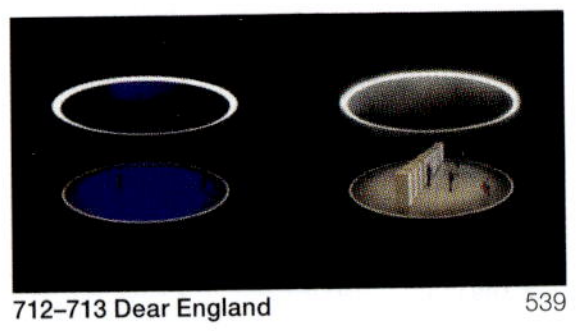

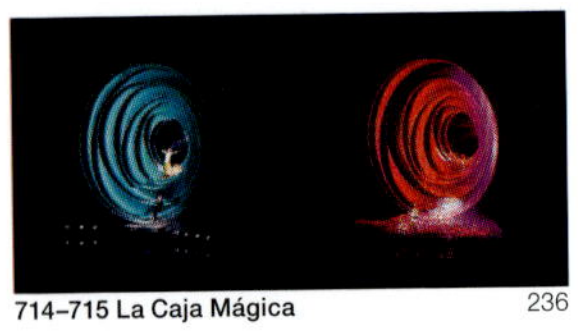

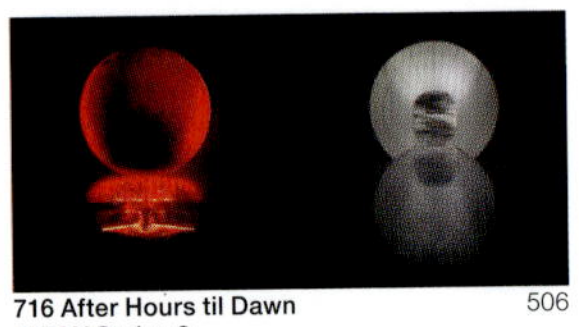

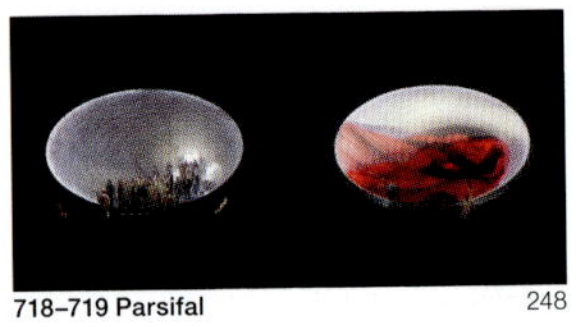

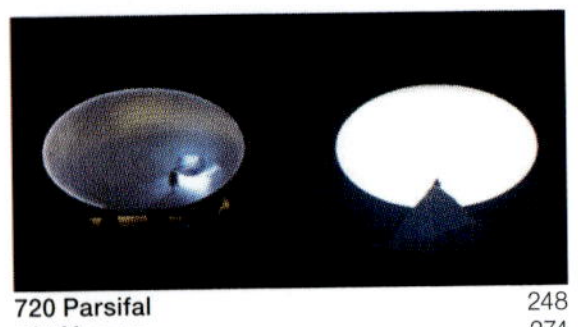

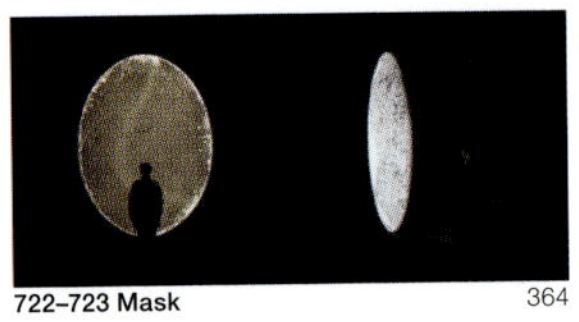

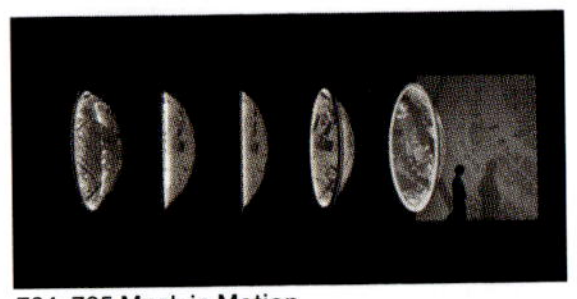

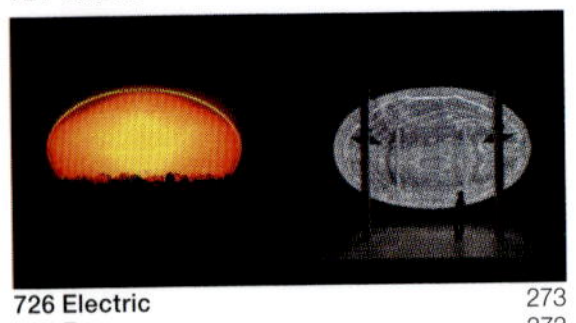

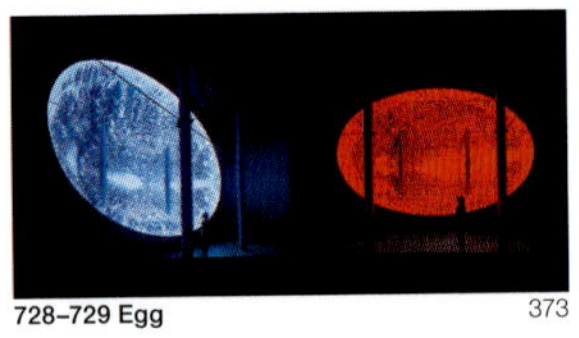

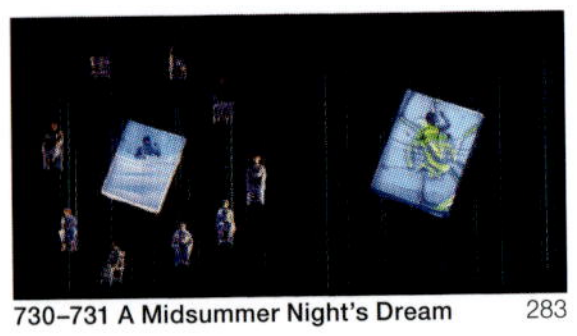

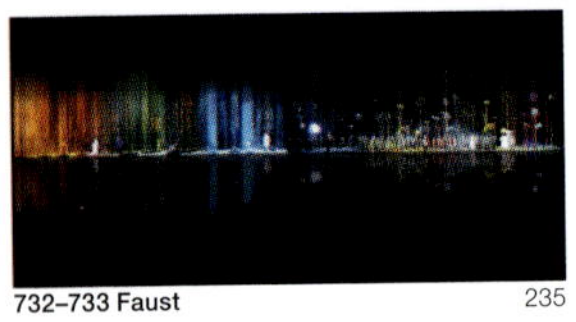

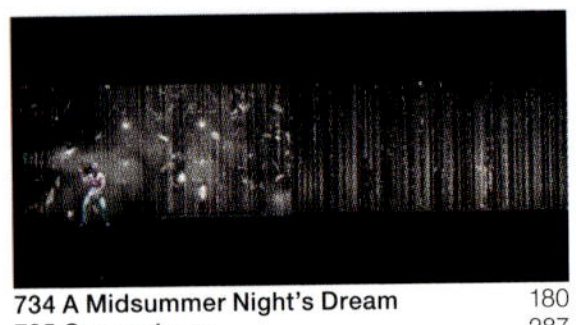

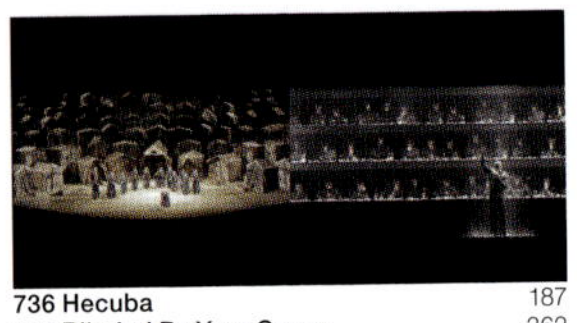

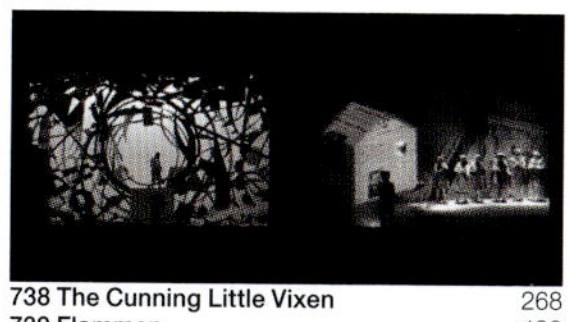
738 The Cunning Little Vixen 268
739 Flammen 198

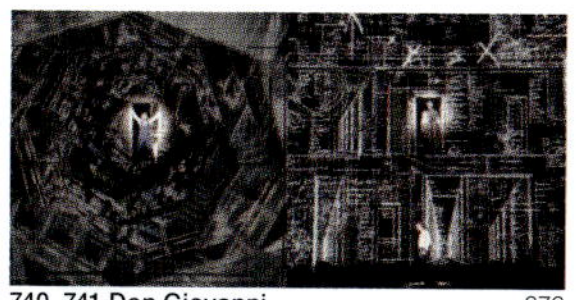
740–741 Don Giovanni 276

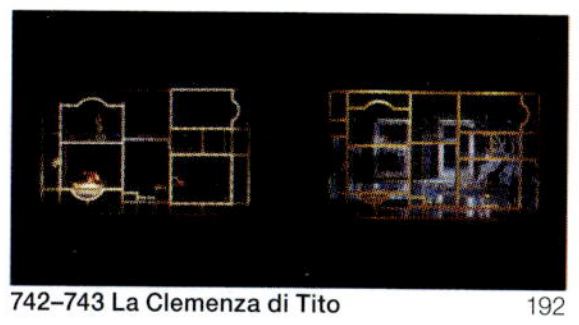
742–743 La Clemenza di Tito 192

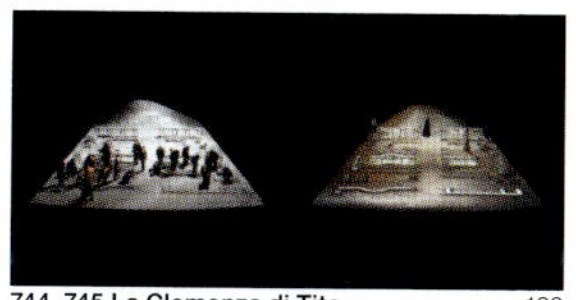
744–745 La Clemenza di Tito 192

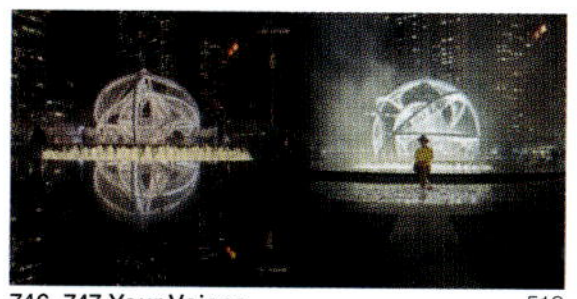
746–747 Your Voices 510

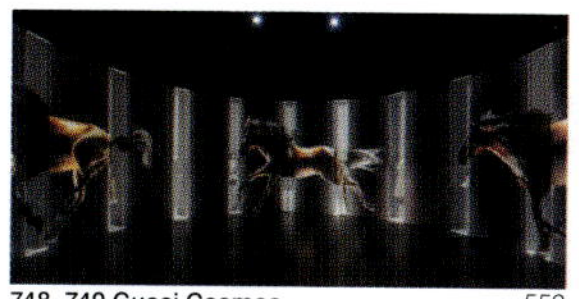
748–749 Gucci Cosmos 552

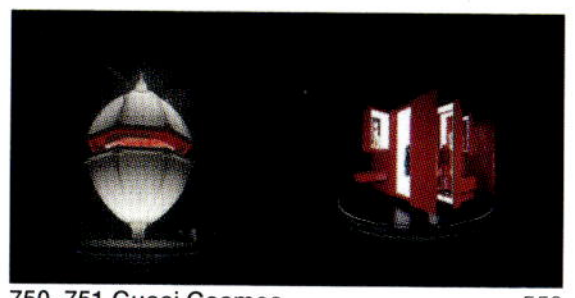
750–751 Gucci Cosmos 552

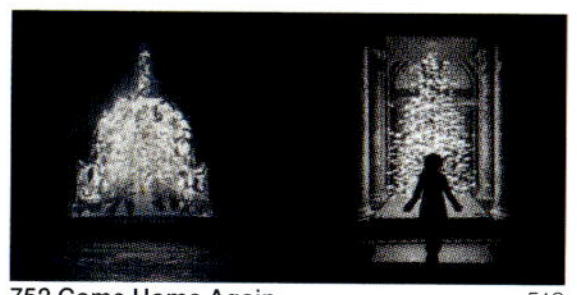
752 Come Home Again 519
753 The Singing Tree 357

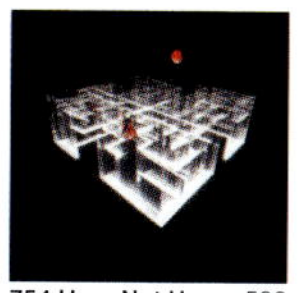
754 Here Not Here 500

A Sequence in Coloured Light

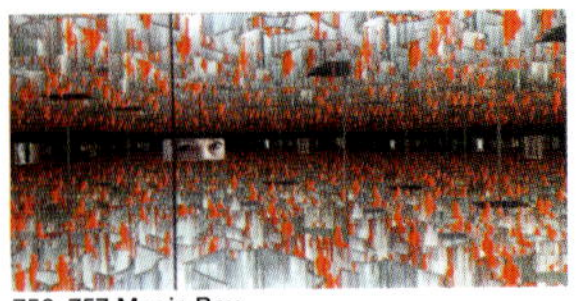
756–757 Magic Box

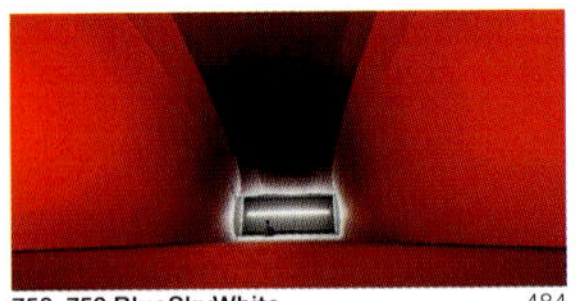
758–759 BlueSkyWhite 484

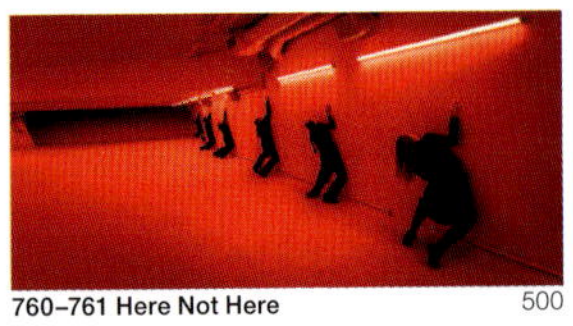
760–761 Here Not Here 500

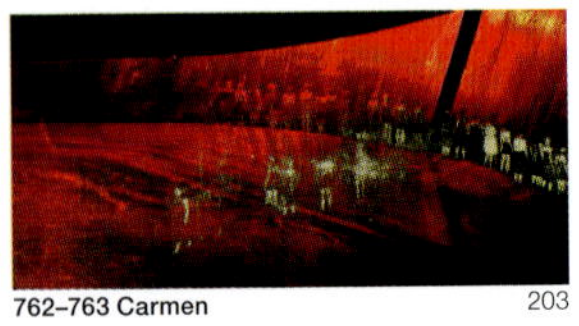
762–763 Carmen 203

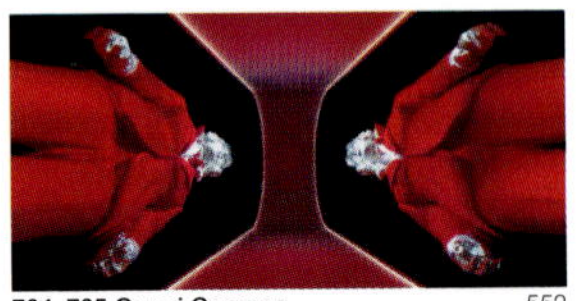
764–765 Gucci Cosmos 552

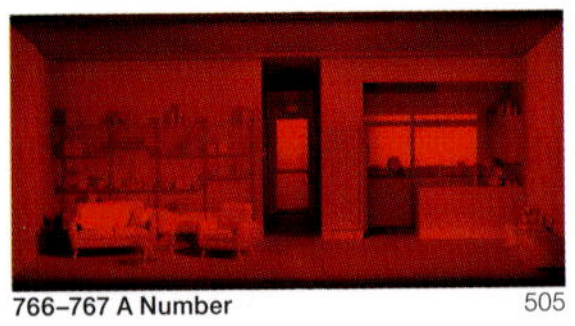
766–767 A Number 505

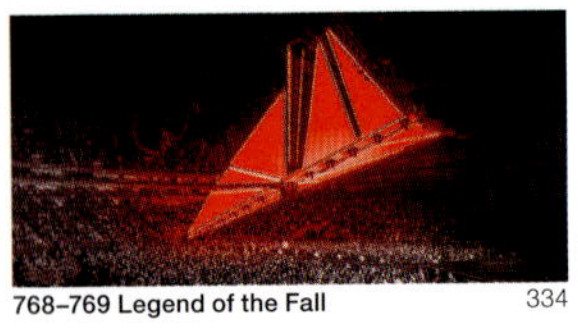
768–769 Legend of the Fall 334

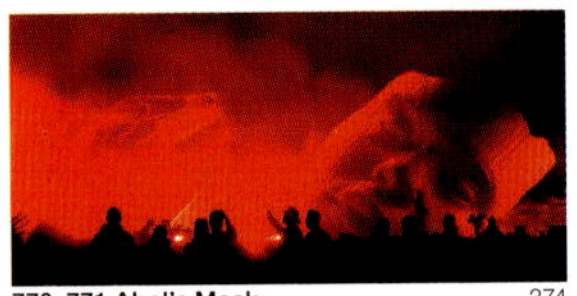
770–771 Abel's Mask 374

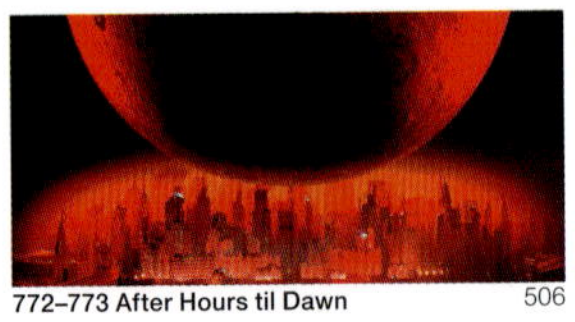
772–773 After Hours til Dawn 506

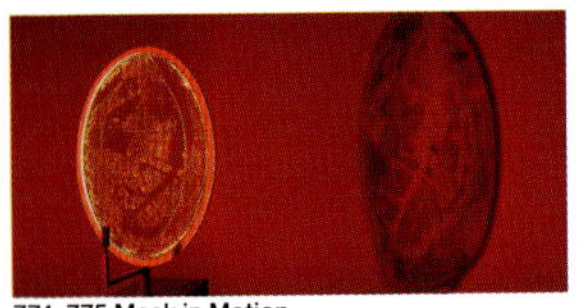
774–775 Mask in Motion

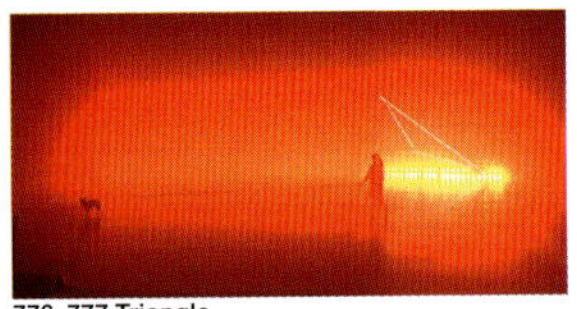
776–777 Triangle

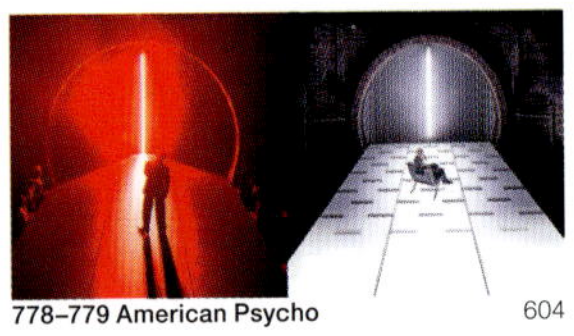
778–779 American Psycho 604

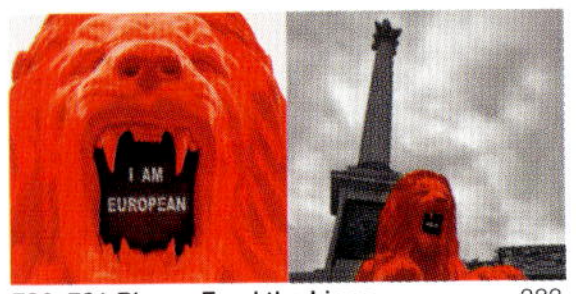

780–781 Please Feed the Lions 383

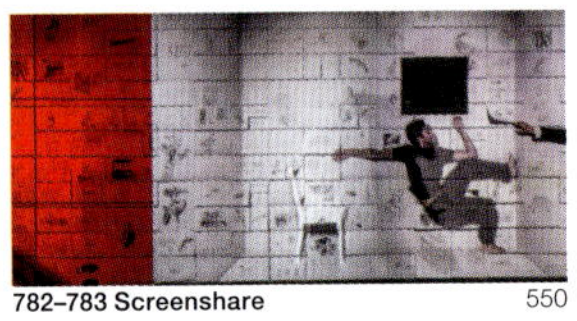
782–783 Screenshare 550

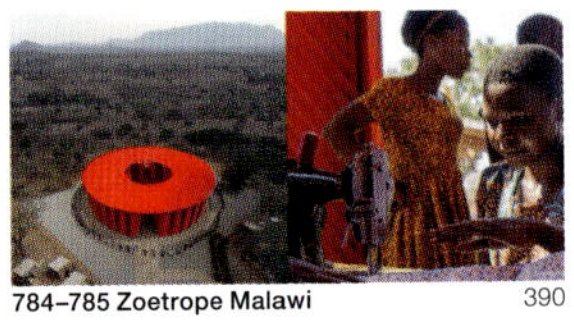
784–785 Zoetrope Malawi 390

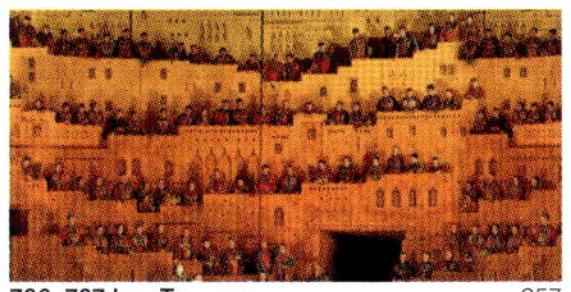
786–787 Les Troyens 257

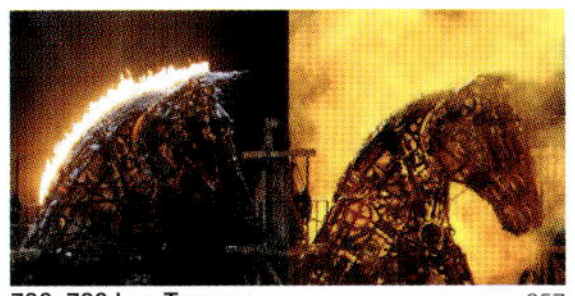
788–789 Les Troyens 257

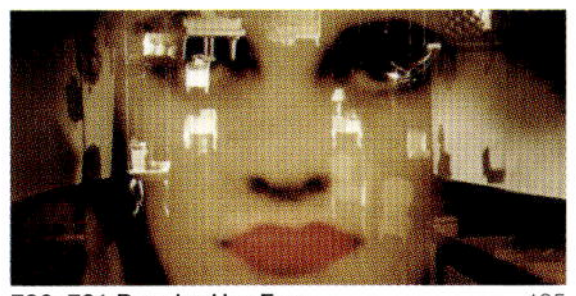
790–791 Powder Her Face 165

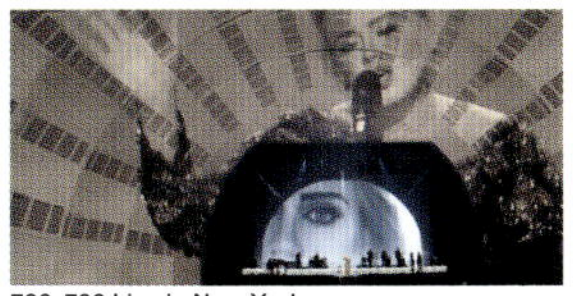
792–793 Live in New York

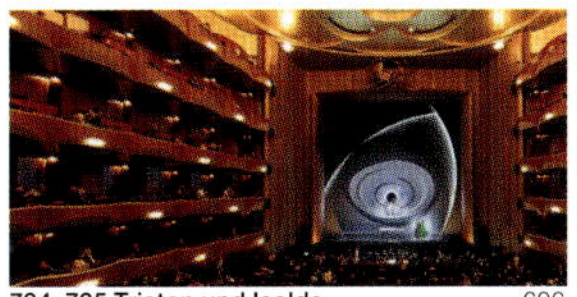
794–795 Tristan und Isolde 606

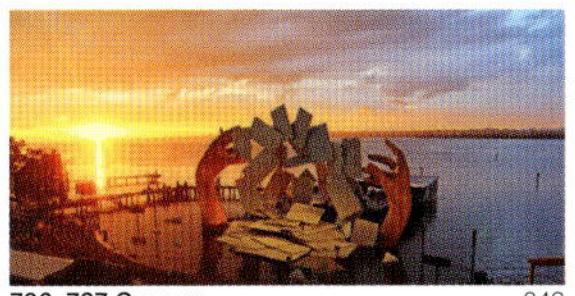
796–797 Carmen 349

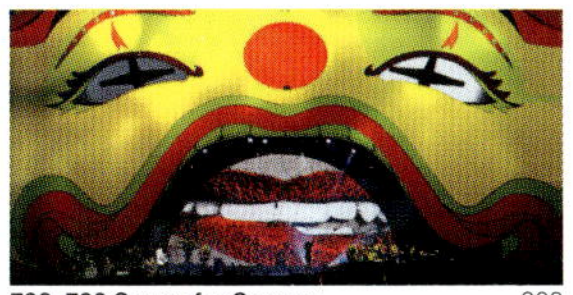
798–799 Songs for Sorrow 208

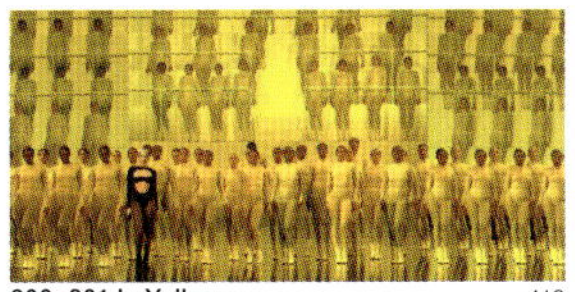
800–801 In Yellow 410

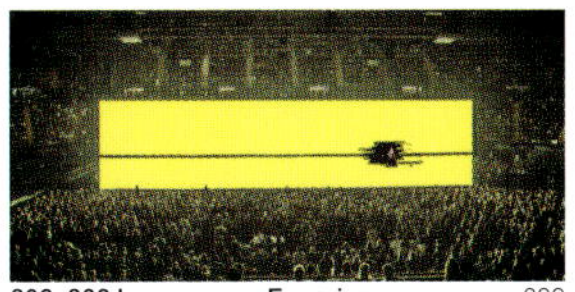
802–803 Innocence + Experience 300

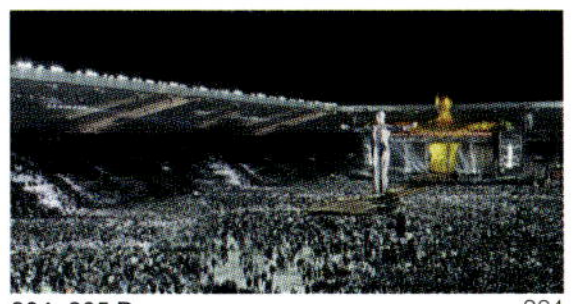
804–805 Progress 224

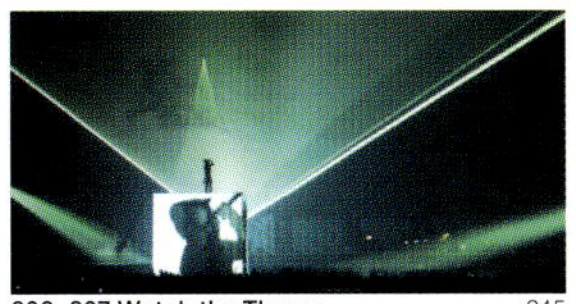
806–807 Watch the Throne 245

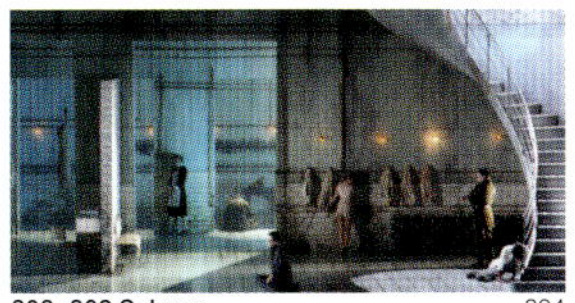
808–809 Salome 204

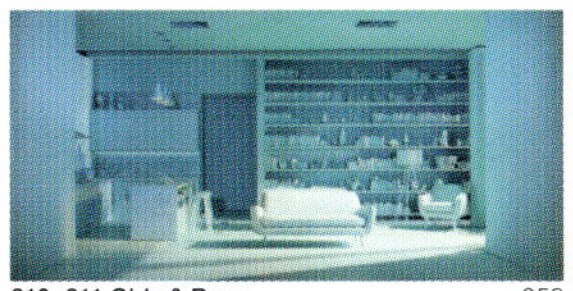
810–811 Girls & Boys 358

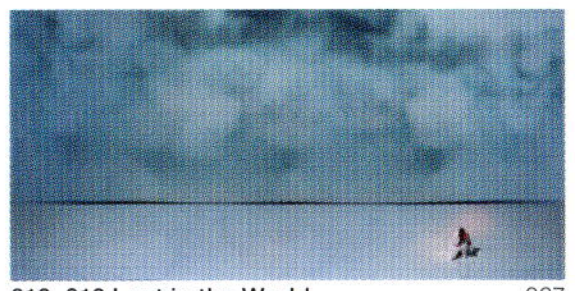
812–813 Lost in the World 267

814–815 Melodrama Coachella 343

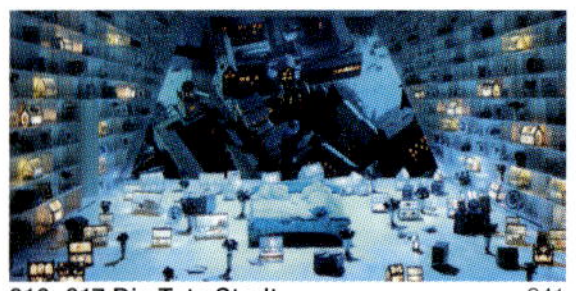
816–817 Die Tote Stadt 241

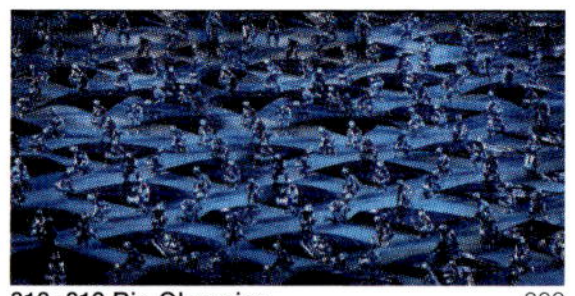
818–819 Rio Olympics 322

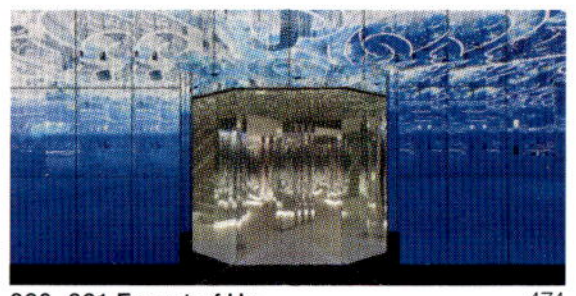
820–821 Forest of Us 474

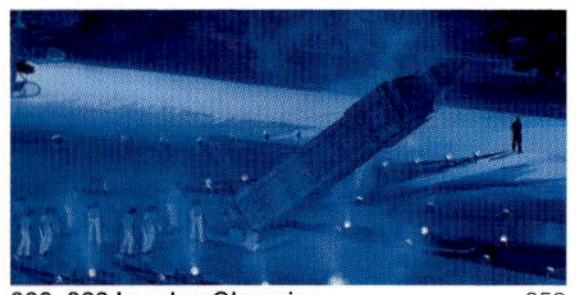
822–823 London Olympics 258

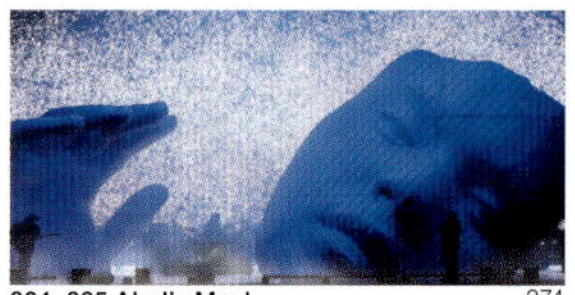
824–825 Abel's Mask 374

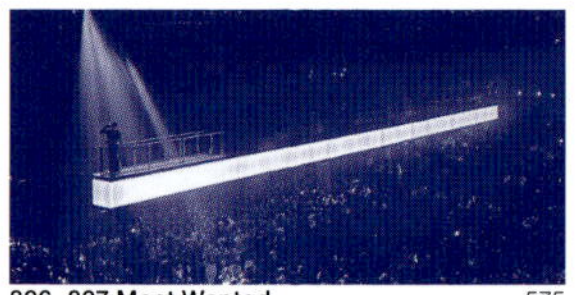
826–827 Most Wanted 575

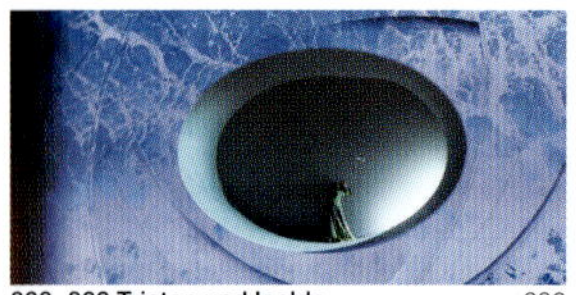
828–829 Tristan und Isolde 606

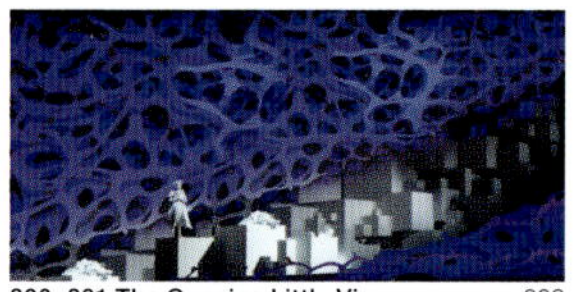
830–831 The Cunning Little Vixen 268

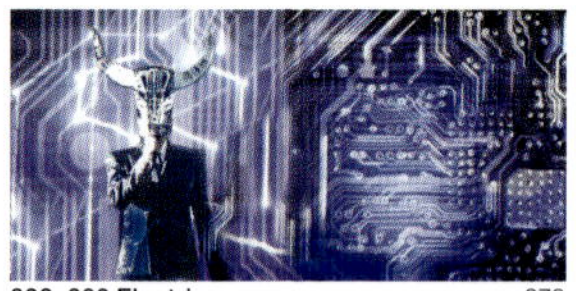
832–833 Electric 273

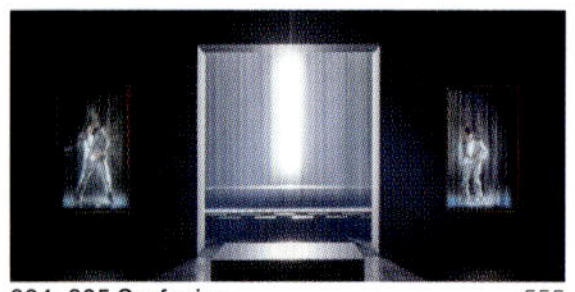
834–835 Surfacing 555

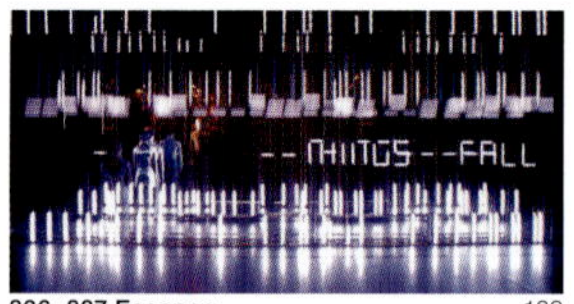
836–837 Essence 168

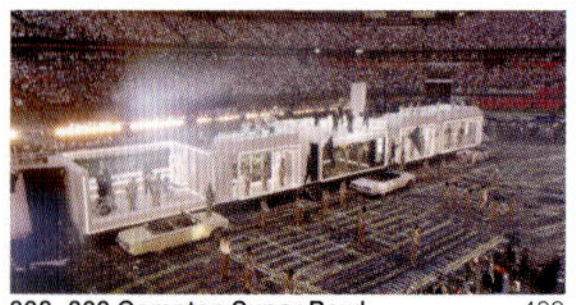
838–839 Compton Super Bowl 488

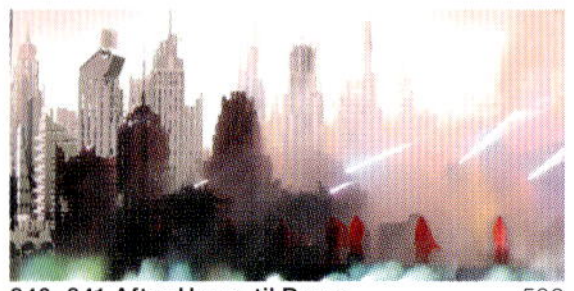
840–841 After Hours til Dawn 506

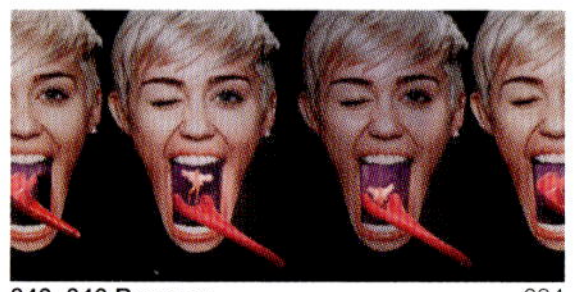
842–843 Bangerz 284

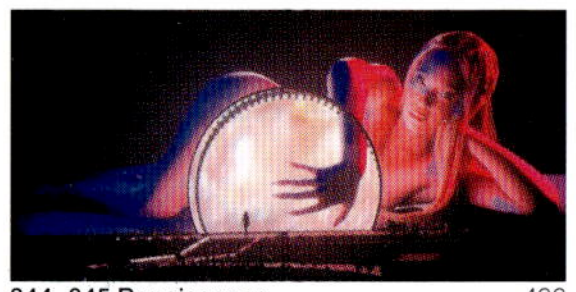
844–845 Renaissance 496

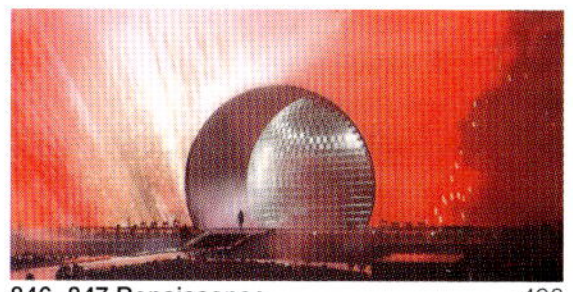

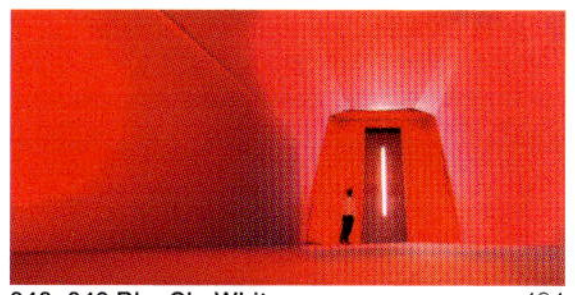

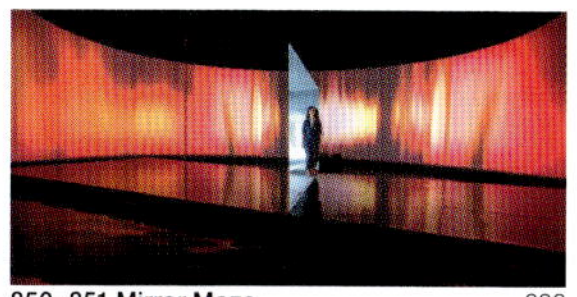

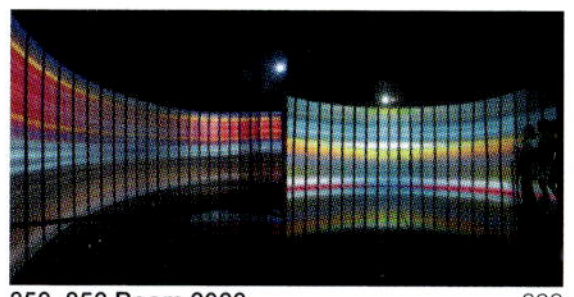

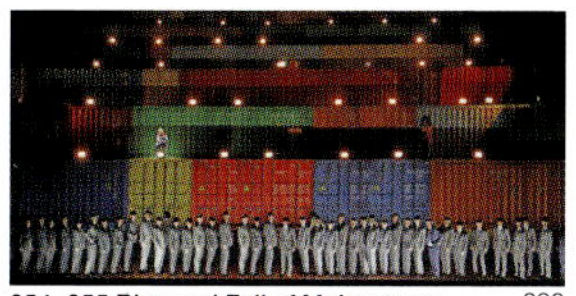

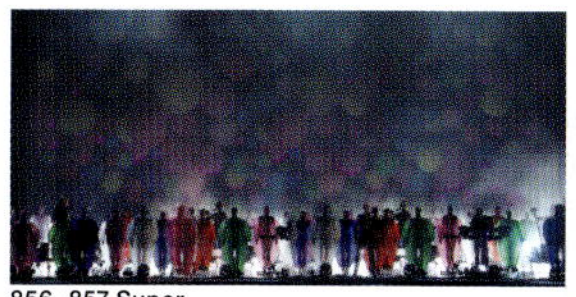

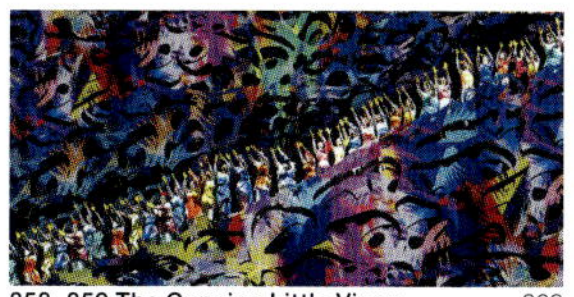

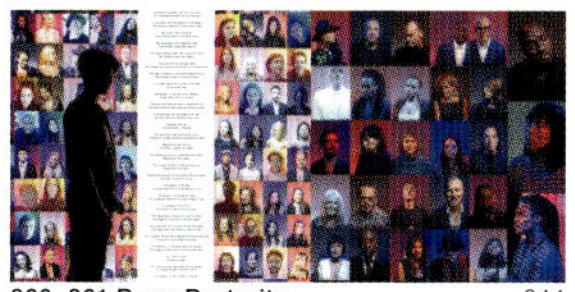

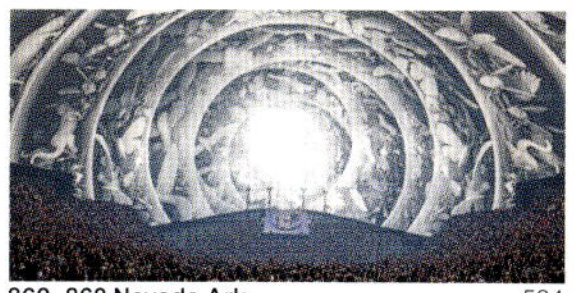

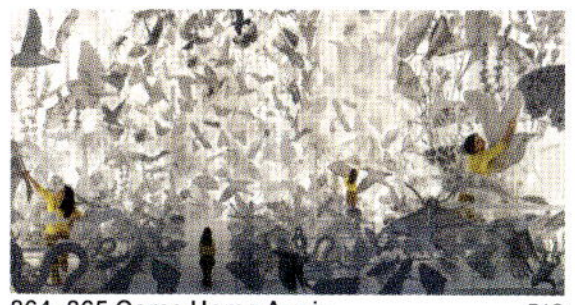

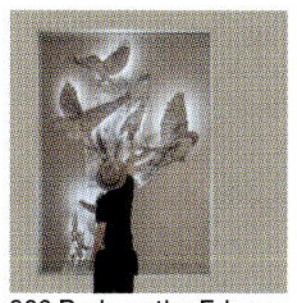

PROJECT CREDITS

RAIDING PARADISE [140]
(Mask Design)
Rose Bruford College, Sidcup, 10–14 July 1995
Director: **Stuart Murdoch**
Set Designer: **Kim Beresford**

EDWARD II [143]
By Christopher Marlowe
Octagon Theatre, Bolton, 9–25 May 1996
Directors: **Lawrence Till, Kate Raper**
Resident Designer: **Richard Foxton**

LOVE AND UNDERSTANDING [144] 638
By Joe Penhall
Bush Theatre, London, 5–31 May 1997
Director: **Mike Bradwell**
Lighting Designer: **Rick Fisher**
Production Manager: **Paul Russell**
Scenic Artist: **Richard Nutbourne**
Associate Designer: **Lisa Lillywhite**

FIDELIO [151] 635
By Ludwig van Beethoven
Libretto by Joseph Sonnleithner
English Touring Opera UK Tour, 7–20 March 1998
Director: **Robert Chevara**
Lighting Designer: **Bruno Poet**
Production Manager: **Perryn Leech**
Fabrication: **Streeter & Jessel, Gerriets**
Associate Designer: **Geraldine Bunzl**

BETRAYAL [152]
By Harold Pinter
Royal National Theatre, Lyttelton, London, 14 November 1998–17 April 1999
Director: **Trevor Nunn**
Composer: **Roger Eno**
Lighting Designer: **Rick Fisher**
Sound Designer: **Paul Groothuis**
Video Designer: **Chris Laing**
Production Manager: **Mark Dakin**
Scenic Artist: **Emma Troubridge**
Associate Designer: **Chloe Lamford**

HAMLET [162]
By William Shakespeare
Young Vic Theatre, London, 1 April–15 May 1999
Director: **Laurence Boswell**
Lighting Designer: **Adam Silverman**
Scenic Artist: **Richard Nutbourne**
Associate Designer: **Jon Bausor**

FOUR SCENES [156] 670
Rambert Dance Company
Sadler's Wells, London, and UK Tour, 12 October 1998–3 June 2000
Choreographer: **Christopher Bruce**
Composer: **David C. Heath**
Lighting Designer: **Mark Henderson**
Fabrication: **Gerriets**
Associate Designer: **Lisa Lillywhite**

HOWIE THE ROOKIE [155] 631
By Mark O'Rowe
Bush Theatre, London, 10 February–3 April 1999
Director: **Mike Bradwell**
Lighting Designer: **Simon Bennison**
Production Manager: **Pam Vision**
Scenic Artist: **Richard Nutbourne**
Associate Designer: **Jon Bausor**

POWDER HER FACE [165] 790–791
By Thomas Adès
Libretto by Philip Hensher
Ystad Festival Opera, Ystad, Sweden, 17–27 July 1999
Director: **Robert Chevara**
Fabrication: **Mikael Tamme, Big Image**
Associate Designer: **Jon Bausor**

GOD'S PLENTY [173] 630, 632, 634
Rambert Dance Company
Sadler's Wells, London, and UK Tour, 15 September 1999–20 April 2000
Choreographer: **Christopher Bruce**
Composer: **Dominic Muldowney**
Lighting Designer: **Ben Ormerod**
Scenic Artist: **Simon Kenny, Souvenir**
Associate Designer: **Penny Challen**

ANTONY AND CLEOPATRA [161]
By William Shakespeare
Royal Shakespeare Company, Royal Shakespeare Theatre, Stratford-upon-Avon, 23 April–21 September 2002
Director: **Michael Attenborough**
Composer: **Paddy Cunneen**
Choreographer: **Clive Wood**
Lighting Designer: **Tim Mitchell**
Sound Designer: **John Leonard**
Technical Director: **Alan Bartlett**
Associate Designer: **Geraldine Bunzl**

MEAT 639
By John O'Davies
Theatre Royal, Plymouth, 1–4 November 2000
Director: **Gemma Bodinetz**
Lighting Designer: **Adam Silverman**
Choreographer: **Lynne Page**
Associate Designer: **Chloe Lamford**

MACBETH [182] 642–643
By Ernest Bloch, after William Shakespeare
Libretto by Edmond Fleg
KlangBogen Festival, Theater an der Wien, Vienna, 10–20 July 2003
Director: **Keith Warner**
Lighting Designer: **Wolfgang Goebbel**
Fabrication: **Streeter & Jessel**
Associate Designer: **Adam Stanley**

I REMEMBER RED [167] 669
Cullberg Ballet
Dansens Hus, Stockholm, 12–20 November 2002
Choreographer: **Didy Veldman**
Lighting Designer: **Ben Ormerod**
Fabrication: **Gerriets**
Scenic Artist: **Richard Nutbourne**
Associate Designer: **Penny Challen**

FLAG : BURNING [174] 644–647
Wire
Barbican Hall, London, 26 April 2003
Part I Choreographer: **Aletta Collins**
Part I Artists: **Dinos** and **Jake Chapman**
Fabrication: **Gerriets**

ESSENCE [168] 836–837
Walker Dance / Park Music
Royal Opera House, Linbury Studio, London, 9–18 March 2005
Choreographer: **Fin Walker**
Composer: **Ben Park**
Costume Designer: **Jack Galloway**
Lighting Designer: **Ben Ormerod**
Associate Designer: **Penny Challen**

TOUCH THE SKY [179] 648–649
Kanye West
US Tour, 11 October–11 December 2005
Production Manager: **Bryon 'Hot Dog' Tate**
Associate Designer: **Penny Challen**

A MIDSUMMER NIGHT'S DREAM [180] 734
By Benjamin Britten,
after William Shakespeare
Staatsoper Hamburg, 25 April–10 May 2006
Conductor: **Simone Young**
Director: **Simon Phillips**
Lighting Designer: **Nick Schlieper**
Associate Designer: **Penny Challen**

HECUBA [187] 736
By Euripides
Translation by Tony Harrison
Royal Shakespeare Company, Albery Theatre London, Kennedy Center Washington DC, 8 April–26 June 2005
Director: **Laurence Boswell**
Lighting Designer: **Adam Silverman**
Choreographer: **Heather Habens**
Sound Designer: **Fergus O'Hare**
Associate Designer: **Bronia Housman**

FUNDAMENTAL [188]
Pet Shop Boys
World Tour, 15 June 2006–25 November 2007
Choreographer: **Hakeem Onibudo**
Costume Designer: **Jeffrey Bryant**
Lighting Designer: **Carl Burnett**
Tour Manager: **Andy Crookston**
Associate Designer: **Machiko Weston**

LA CLEMENZA DI TITO [192] 666, 742–745
By Wolfgang Amadeus Mozart
Libretto by Caterino Mazzolà
Teatro El Liceu, Barcelona, 30 September–19 October 2006
Director: **Francisco Negrin**
Costume Designer: **Louis Désiré**
Associate Designer: **Cordelia Chisholm**

CARMEN [203] 640–641, 672–673, 762–763
By Georges Bizet
Libretto by Henri Meilhac and Ludovic Halévy
English National Opera, The Coliseum, London, 6 October–23 November 2007
Director: **Sally Potter**
Composer: **Georges Bizet**
Costume Designer: **Catherine Zuber**
Lighting Designer: **Mimi Jordan Sherin**
Choreographer: **Pablo Verón**
Video Design: **Studio 59**
Associate Designer: **Bronia Housman**

DON GIOVANNI [197] 659
By Wolfgang Amadeus Mozart
Libretto by Lorenzo Da Ponte
Theater an der Wien, Vienna, 6–18 July 2006
Director: **Keith Warner**
Lighting Designer: **Wolfgang Goebbel**
Production Associate: **Veronika Leitl**

SONGS FOR SORROW [208] 798–799
Mika Live in Paris
Parc des Princes Stadium, Paris, 4 July 2008
Costume, Puppet & Prop Designers:
Paloma Penniman, **Zuleika Penniman**, **Yasmine Penniman**, **Joannie Penniman**
Lighting Designer: **Oli Metcalfe**
Choreographer: **Gareth Walker**
Production Manager: **Chris Vaughan**
Engineering & Fabrication: **Dirk De Decker, Stageco, Tony Bowern, Brilliant Stages, Mikael Tamme, Big Image, Air Artists**
Video Supplier: **Frederic Opsomer, PRG**
Associate Designer: **Bronia Housman**

FLAMMEN [198] 739
By Erwin Schulhoff
Libretto by Karel Josef Beneš
Theater an der Wien, Vienna, 7–12 August 2006
Director: **Keith Warner**
Lighting Designer: **Wolfgang Goebbel**
Associate Designer: **Bronia Housman**

GLOW IN THE DARK [207]
Kanye West
World Arena Tour, 16 April–7 December 2008
Show Directors & Lighting Designers:
Martin Phillips, John McGuire
Associate Designer: **Machiko Weston**

LONDON UNDERSOUND [217] 621, 658
By Es Devlin and Nitin Sawhney
Onedotzero Festival, BFI IMAX Cinema, London, 14 November 2008
Video Designers: **Sam Pattinson**, **Luke Halls** for **Onedotzero**

FIRST TRAIN HOME [218]
Imogen Heap
Music Video, October 2009
Director: **Es Devlin**
First Assistant Director: **Richard Newman**
Associate Designer: **Machiko Weston**

SALOME [204] 808–809
By Richard Strauss and Oscar Wilde
Royal Opera House, London, 18 February–12 March 2008
Director: **David McVicar**
Composer: **Richard Strauss**
Lighting Designer: **Wolfgang Goebbel**
Choreographer: **Andrew George**
Scenic Artist: **Emma Troubridge**
Production Manager: **Will Harding**
Associate Designer: **Bronia Housman**

JEANNE D'ARC AU BÛCHER [212]
By Arthur Honegger
Libretto by Paul Claudel
Accademia Nazionale di Santa Cecilia, Rome, 12–20 October 2008
Conductor: **Antonio Pappano**
Director: **Keith Warner**
Associate Designer: **Bronia Housman**

FAME KILLS [221]
Lady Gaga & Kanye West
April 2009
Creative Directors:
Matthew Williams, Willo Perron
Associate Designer: **Machiko Weston**

PANDEMONIUM [222]
Pet Shop Boys
World Tour, 10 June 2009–8 December 2010
Costume Designer: **Jeffrey Bryant**
Lighting Designer: **Rob Sinclair**
Stage Director & Choreographer: **Lynne Page**
Video Designer: **Luke Halls** for **Onedotzero**
Camera Director: **Blue Leach**
Production Manager: **Joe Sanchez**
Video Supplier: **Frederic Opsomer, PRG**
Associate Designer: **Bronia Housman**

RESISTANCE [229] 650
Muse
World Arena and Stadium Tour, 22 October–4 December 2009
Lighting Designer: **Oli Metcalfe**
Production Manager: **Chris Vaughan**
Choreographer: **Lynne Page**
Engineering & Fabrication:
Stageco, Tony Bowern, Brilliant Stages
Video Supplier: **Frederic Opsomer, PRG**
Associate Designer: **Bronia Housman**

MONSTER BALL 1.0 [230] 660–661
Lady Gaga
US Arena Tour, 27 November 2009–8 March 2010
Creative Directors: **Matthew Williams, Willo Perron**
Lighting Designer: **Willie Williams**
Choreographer: **Laurieann Gibson**
Video Designers: **Nick Knight, Ruth Hogben**
Engineering & Fabrication: **Kevin Flagg** and **James 'Winky' Fairorth, TAIT Towers, Gerriets**
Associate Designer: **Bronia Housman**

FAUST [235] 732–733
By Charles Gounod
Libretto by Jules Barbier and Michel Carré
Semperoper Dresden, 10–21 June 2010
Director: **Keith Warner**
Lighting Designer: **Wolfgang Goebbel**
Costume Designer: **Julia Müer**
Associate Designer: **Tom Scutt**

PROGRESS [224] 804–805
Take That
European Stadium Tour, 27 May–29 July 2011
Show Director & Choreographer: **Kim Gavin**
Costume Designer: **Michael Sharp**
Lighting Designer: **Patrick Woodroffe**
Camera Director: **Matt Askem**
Video Design: **Onedotzero**
Engineer: **Andy Edwards**
Engineering & Fabrication: **Dirk De Decker, Stageco, Tony Bowern, Brilliant Stages, Adam Davis, TAIT Towers, Kevin Monks, Blackout**
Scenic Artist: **Jacqui Pyle**
Video Supplier: **Frederic Opsomer, PRG**
Associate Designers: **Bronia Housman, Cecilia Carey**

WATCH THE THRONE [245] 652–653, 680, 806–807
Jay-Z & Kanye West
World Arena Tour, 28 October 2011–22 June 2012
Creative Director: **Virgil Abloh**
Lighting Designers: **Nick Whitehouse, John McGuire**
Video Design: **Geodezik**
Production Manager: **Jason Danter**
Engineering & Fabrication: **Matt Hales, TAIT Towers**
Associate Designers: **Machiko Weston, Bronia Housman, Chiara Stephenson**

BATMAN [242] 706–707
Manchester Evening News Arena, 19 July 2011
Director: **Anthony Van Laast**
Composer: **James Brett**
Costume Designer: **Jack Galloway**
Lighting Designer: **Patrick Woodroffe**
Video Designers: **Sam Pattinson** and **Luke Halls, Treatment Studio**
Sound Designer: **Simon Baker**
Engineering & Fabrication: **Matt Hales** and **Alex Serrano, TAIT Towers, Souvenir**
Video Supplier: **Frederic Opsomer, PRG**
Production Managers: **Jake Berry, Matt Towell**
Associate Designers: **Chiara Stephenson, Cecilia Carey, Bronia Housman**

DIE TOTE STADT [241] 816–817
By Erich Wolfgang Korngold
Libretto by Paul Schott
Finnish National Opera, Helsinki, 26 November–7 December 2010
Director: **Kasper Holten**
Costume Designer: **Katrina Lindsay**
Lighting Designer: **Wolfgang Goebbel**
Associate Designer: **Machiko Weston**

LA CAJA MÁGICA [236] 714–715
MTV Europe Music Awards 2010
Rihanna / Shakira / B.O.B / Bon Jovi
Caja Mágica, Madrid, 7 November 2010
Camera Director: **Paul Shyvers**
Lighting Designer: **Gurdip Mahal**
Video Design: **Hello Charlie**
Engineering & Fabrication: **Steel Monkey, Blackout**
Video Supplier: **Frederic Opsomer, PRG**
Production Manager: **Maggie Mouzakitis**
Band Production Manager: **Jo MacKay**
Associate Designer: **Bronia Housman**

PARSIFAL [248] 718–720
By Richard Wagner
Royal Danish Opera, Copenhagen, 26 March–13 May 2012
Director: **Keith Warner**
Costume Designer: **Jorge Jara**
Lighting Designer: **Davy Cunningham**
Choreographer: **Karl Schreiner**
Video Designer: **Nicky Smith**
Associate Designers: **Machiko Weston, Bronia Housman, Chiara Stephenson**

THE MASTER AND MARGARITA [254] 671
Based on the novel by Mikhail Bulgakov
Théâtre de Complicité, Barbican Theatre, London, 22 March–7 April 2012
Director & Writer: **Simon McBurney**
Costume Designer: **Christina Cunningham**
Lighting Designer: **Paul Anderson**
Video Designer: **Finn Ross**
Additional Animation Designer: **Luke Halls**
Projection Mapping Producer: **Willie Williams**
Associate Designers: **Machiko Weston, Bronia Housman, Chiara Stephenson**

LES TROYENS [257] 786–789
By Hector Berlioz
Royal Opera House, London, 26 June–11 July 2012
Director: **David McVicar**
Costume Designer: **Moritz Junge**
Lighting Designer: **Wolfgang Goebbel**
Engineering & Fabrication: **Weld-Fab Stage Engineering, Royal Opera House**
Production Manager: **Will Harding**
Associate Designers: **Machiko Weston, Bronia Housman, Chiara Stephenson**

LONDON OLYMPICS 46–47 [258] 822–823
Closing Ceremony, London Olympic Stadium, 12 August 2012
Director & Choreographer: **Kim Gavin**
Costume Designer: **Michael Sharp**
Pet Shop Boys Costume Designer: **Gareth Pugh**
Lighting Designer: **Patrick Woodroffe**
Camera Director: **Hamish Hamilton**
Production Manager: **Chris Vaughan**
Props Manager: **Phil Wilding**
Engineering & Fabrication: **Stage One, TAIT, Brilliant Stages, Kevin Monks, Blackout, Artem, Steel Monkey**
Associate Designers: **Emma Child, Chiara Stephenson, Bronia Housman**

LOST IN THE WORLD [267] 812–813
Kanye West
Revel Casino, Atlantic City, 28–31 December 2012
Creative Director: **Virgil Abloh**
Show Director & Lighting Designer: **John McGuire**
Associate Designers: **Bronia Housman, Chiara Stephenson**

THE NEVERENDING STORY [253]
By Michael Ende
Director: **André Heller**

CHIMERICA [262] 654–655
By Lucy Kirkwood
Almeida Theatre, London, 29 May–6 July 2013
Harold Pinter Theatre, London, 6 August–19 October 2013
Director: **Lyndsey Turner**
Costume Designer: **Christina Cunningham**
Lighting Designer: **Tim Lutkin**
Choreographers: **Georgina Lamb, Bret Yount**
Video Designer: **Finn Ross**
Sound Designer: **Carolyn Downing**
Engineering & Fabrication: **Simon York, Miraculous Engineering**
Production Manager: **Igor**
Associate Designer: **Chiara Stephenson**

THE CUNNING LITTLE VIXEN [268]
By Leoš Janáček 738, 830–831, 858–859
Royal Danish Opera, Copenhagen, 15–21 December 2012
Director: **Francisco Negrin**
Costume Designer: **Carol Bailey**
Lighting Designer: **Bruno Poet**
Video Designer: **Luke Halls**
Associate Designers: **Machiko Weston, Bronia Housman, Chiara Stephenson**

ELECTRIC [273] 726, 832–833
Pet Shop Boys
World Tour, 3 June 2013–15 August 2015
Costume Designer: **Jeffrey Bryant**
Lighting Designer: **Rob Sinclair**
Show Director & Choreographer: **Lynne Page**
Video Designers: **Sam Pattison, Luke Halls**
Production Manager: **Joe Sanchez**
Associate Designer: **Bronia Housman**

YEEZUS [274] 721
Kanye West
World Arena Tour, 19 October 2013–15 September 2014
Creative Directors: **Virgil Abloh, Vanessa Beecroft**
Show Directors & Lighting Designers: **Martin Phillips, John McGuire**
Engineering & Fabrication: **Vision Scenic, Eric Pearce, SGPS**
Associate Designers: **Machiko Weston, Bronia Housman, Chiara Stephenson**

A MIDSUMMER NIGHT'S DREAM [283]
By William Shakespeare 629, 686–687, 730–731
Theater for a New Audience, Polonsky Shakespeare Center, New York, 19 October 2013–12 January 2014
Director: **Julie Taymor**
Composer: **Elliot Goldenthal**
Costume Designer: **Constance Hoffman**
Lighting Designer: **Donald Holder**
Sound Designer: **Matt Tierney**
Associate Designer: **Machiko Weston**

CONNECTOME [287] 628, 735
Royal Ballet, Royal Opera House, London, 2–13 June 2014
Composer: **Arvo Pärt**
Choreographer: **Alastair Marriott**
Costume Designer: **Jonathan Howell**
Lighting Designer: **Bruno Poet**
Video Designer: **Luke Halls**
Associate Designer: **Bronia Housman**

AMERICAN PSYCHO 651
By Duncan Sheik and Roberto Aguirre-Sacasa
Almeida Theatre, London, 12 December 2013–12 February 2014
Director: **Rupert Goold**
Dramaturg: **Whitney Mosery**
Choreographer: **Lynne Page**
Costume Designer: **Katrina Lindsay**
Fabrication: **Simon York, Miraculous Engineering**
Associate Designers: **Chiara Stephenson, Jason Ardizzone-West**

BANGERZ [284] 842–843
Miley Cyrus
World Arena Tour, 14 February–23 October 2014
Director: **Diane Martel**
Choreographers: **Rich and Tone Talauega**
Lighting Designer: **Rob Sinclair**
Engineering & Fabrication: **Eric Pearce, SGPS, David Mendoza, Matthew Whitehead, Airworks**
Associate Designer: **Chiara Stephenson**

BLUE ORCHESTRA 684
Sam Smith
BRIT Awards, O2 Arena, London, 25 February 2015
Production Manager: **Maggie Mouzakitis**
Fabrication: **Steel Monkey**
Draughtsman: **Malcolm Birkett**

DON GIOVANNI [276] 656–657, 740–741
By Wolfgang Amadeus Mozart and Lorenzo Da Ponte
Royal Opera House, London, 7–24 February 2014
Director: **Kasper Holten**
Costume Designer: **Anja Vang Kragh**
Lighting Designer: **Bruno Poet**
Choreographer: **Signe Fabricius**
Video Designer: **Luke Halls**
Engineering & Fabrication: **Weld-Fab Stage Engineering, Royal Opera House**
Scenic Artist: **Emma Troubridge**
Associate Designer: **Bronia Housman**

OBSERVATORY [288]
LV SS2015 Women's Collection
Fondation Louis Vuitton, Paris, 1 October 2014
Director: **Nicolas Ghesquière**
Co-Designers: **LV Image Studio: Faye Mcleod, Ansel Thompson**
Producer & Production Manager: **La Mode en Images**
Lighting Designer: **Philippe Cerceau**
Video Designer: **Luke Halls**
Associate Designers: **Machiko Weston, Bronia Housman**

THE NETHER [294]
By Jennifer Haley
Royal Court Theatre, London, 17 July–9 August 2014
Director: **Jeremy Herrin**
Composer: **Nick Powell**
Costume Designer: **Christina Cunningham**
Lighting Designer: **Paul Pyant**
Video Designer: **Luke Halls**
Sound Designers: **Nick Powell, Ian Dickinson**
Engineering & Fabrication: **Simon York, Miraculous Engineering**
Props Fabrication: **Blackfriars**
Associate Designer: **Bronia Housman**

RISE AND FALL OF THE CITY OF MAHAGONNY [293] 854–855
By Kurt Weill and Bertolt Brecht
Royal Opera House, London, 11 March–4 April 2015
Director: **John Fulljames**
Costume Designer: **Christina Cunningham**
Lighting Designer: **Bruno Poet**
Choreographer: **Arthur Pita**
Video Designer: **Finn Ross**
Associate Designers: **Bronia Housman, Max Klaentschi**

LIGHT SHINING IN BUCKINGHAMSHIRE [297] 633 690–691
By Caryl Churchill
Royal National Theatre, Lyttelton, London, 24 April–22 June 2015
Director: **Lyndsey Turner**
Costume Designer: **Soutra Gilmour**
Lighting Designer: **Bruno Poet**
Choreographer: **Joseph Alford**
Sound Designer: **Christopher Shutt**
Associate Designer: **Chiara Stephenson**

INNOCENCE + EXPERIENCE [300] 677 802–803
U2
World Arena Tour, 14 May–7 December 2015
Director & Co-Designer: **Willie Williams**
Co-Designers: **Mark Fisher** and **Ric Lipson, Stufish**
Costume Designer: **Sharon Blankson**
Lighting Designers: **Mark 'Sparky' Risk, Alex Murphy**
Choreographer: **Morleigh Steinberg**
Camera Direction: **Smasher**
Video Design: **Treatment Studio**
Video Supplier: **Frederic Opsomer, PRG**
Engineering & Fabrication: **Aaron Siebert, TAIT**
Production Manager: **Jake Berry**
Associate Designers: **Chiara Stephenson, Machiko Weston, Max Klaentschi**

DER FREISCHÜTZ [305]
By Carl Maria von Weber and Johann Friedrich Kind
Royal Danish Opera, Copenhagen, 7 November–16 December 2015
Director: **Kasper Holten**
Costume Designer: **Anja Vang Kragh**
Lighting Designer: **Bruno Poet**
Video Designer: **Luke Halls**
Associate Designers: **Bronia Housman, Chiara Stephenson, Machiko Weston, Max Klaentschi**

LV SERIES 3 717
Louis Vuitton Exhibition
180 The Strand, London, 21 September–18 October 2015
Director: **Nicolas Ghesquière**
Co-Designers: **LV Image Studio: Faye Mcleod, Ansel Thompson**
Producer: **Campbell Bromberg**

HAMLET [298] 637
By William Shakespeare
Barbican Theatre, London, 25 August–31 October 2015
Director: **Lyndsey Turner**
Costume Designer: **Katrina Lindsay**
Lighting Designer: **Jane Cox**
Composer: **Jon Hopkins**
Choreographer: **Sidi Larbi Cherkaoui**
Video Designer: **Luke Halls**
Sound Designer: **Christopher Shutt**
Engineering & Fabrication: **Simon York, Miraculous Engineering**
Scenic Artist: **Richard Nutbourne**
Associate Designers: **Chiara Stephenson, Max Klaentschi**

FORMATION [314] 662–665
Beyoncé
World Stadium Tour, 27 April–7 October 2016
Creative Directors: **Ed Burke, Todd Tourso**
Choreographers: **JaQuel Knight, Chris Grant**
Costume Designer: **Marni Senofonte**
Lighting Designer: **Tim Routledge**
Camera Direction: **Smasher**
Video Design: **Good Company**
Engineering & Fabrication: **Stageco, TAIT**
Production Managers: **Jake Berry, Chris Vaughan**
Associate Designers: **Jed Skrzypczak, Max Klaentschi, Chiara Stephenson, Angie Vasileiou, Machiko Weston, Jason Ardizzone West**

HELLO [306] 699–703
Adele
World Arena and Stadium Tour, 29 February 2016–29 June 2017
Lighting Designer: **Patrick Woodroffe**
Video Designers: **Luke Halls** and **Warren Chapman, Treatment Studio**
Camera Director: **Matt Askem**
Engineering & Fabrication: **Brian Levine** and **Aaron Siebert, TAIT, Rosebrand, Sew What**
Associate Designers: **Chiara Stephenson, Jed Skrzypczak, Max Klaentschi, Angie Vasileiou**

PABLO STUDIES [321]
Kanye West
Initial ideas for Saint Pablo Tour, 2015–2016

LIVE IN NEW YORK 792–793
Adele
Radio City Music Hall, New York, 17 November 2015
Director: **Beth McCarthy-Miller**
Lighting Designers: **Patrick Woodroffe, Allen Branton**
Video Designer: **Luke Halls, Treatment Studio**
Production Manager: **Richard Young**
Engineering & Fabrication: **All Access, TAIT**
Associate Designers: **Chiara Stephenson, Jason Ardizzone-West, Machiko Weston**

FAITH HEALER [313] 698
By Brian Friel
Donmar Warehouse, London, 30 July–20 August 2016
Director: **Lyndsey Turner**
Composer: **Rupert Cross**
Costume Designer: **Jack Galloway**
Lighting Designer: **Bruno Poet**
Sound Designer: **Christopher Shutt**
Engineering & Fabrication: **Simon York, Miraculous Engineering, Lizzie Props**
Scenic Artist: **Richard Nutbourne**
Associate Designer: **Bronia Housman**

WITH NIEMEYER 44–45
LV 2017 Cruise Collection
Contemporary Art Museum (MAC), Niterói, 28 May 2016
Director: **Nicolas Ghesquière**
Co-Designers: **Faye Mcleod, Ansel Thompson, Florent Buonomano** and **LV Image Studio**
Producers & Production Managers: **Julie Mannion** and **Jarrad Clark, KCMD, Campbell Bromberg, LV**
Lighting Designer: **Philippe Cerceau**
Associate Designer: **Machiko Weston**

RIO OLYMPICS [322] 818–819
Maracanã Stadium, Rio de Janeiro, 6 August 2016
Producer: **Marco Balich**
Directors: **Fernando Meirelles, Daniela Thomas, Andrucha Waddington**
Lighting Designers: **Nick Collier, Durham Marenghi**
Associate Designers: **Bronia Housman, Machiko Weston, Max Klaentschi, Chiara Stephenson, Angie Vasileiou, Jed Skrzypczak**

MIRACLE BOX [325] 618–619
Serpentine Galleries, London, 8 October 2016
Curator: **Andrew O'Hagan**
Fabricator: **Michael Whiteley**
Video Designer: **Angie Vasileiou**

MIRROR MAZE 14–15 [326] 850–851
Copeland Park, Peckham, London, 21–25 September 2016
Producer: **Bunny Kinney**
Tash Tan: **Claire Arnold**
Production Manager: **Nick Levitt**
Video Design: **Nick Wood, MPC, Luke Halls Studio**
Sound Designers & Composers: **Ben** and **Max Ringham, Christopher Shutt**
Engineering & Fabrication: **Liam Ownsworth** and **Nick Batten, Diagon**
Associate Designers: **Max Klaentschi, Angie Vasileiou, Bronia Housman**

TRIANGLE 681, 776–777
The Weeknd
Voodoo Music Festival, City Park, New Orleans, 28 October 2016
Creative Director: **La Mar C Taylor**
Production Manager: **Rob DeCeglio**
Tour Manager: **Matt Petroff**
Engineering & Fabrication: **Matt Hales, TAIT**
Video Supplier: **Solotech**
Lighting Designer: **Sooner Routhier**
Associate Designers: **Angie Vasileiou, Jed Skrzypczak**

MELODRAMA COACHELLA [343]
Lorde 667, 814–815
Coachella Festival, Indio, 16 April 2017
Lighting Designer: **Rob Sinclair**
Video Design: **Good Company**
Engineering & Fabrication: **TAIT**
Production Manager: **Richard Young**
Associate Designers: **Chiara Stephenson, Jed Skrzypczak**

ORIGAMI POST-IT NOTE [333]
Serpentine Galleries, London, October 2016
Commissioned by **Hans Ulrich Obrist**
Associate Designer & Video Designer: **Angie Vasileiou**

LEGEND OF THE FALL [334]
The Weeknd 682–683, 768–769
World Arena Tour, 17 February–22 July 2017
Creative Director: **La Mar C Taylor**
Production Manager: **Rob DeCeglio**
Tour Manager: **Matt Petroff**
Engineering & Fabrication: **Matt Hales, TAIT**
Video Supplier: **Solotech**
Lighting Designer: **Sooner Routhier**
Video Design: **Strange Loop**
Associate Designers: **Max Klaentschi, Jed Skrzypczak, Angie Vasileiou**

UGLY LIES THE BONE [337]
By Lindsey Ferrentino
Royal National Theatre, Lyttelton, London, 22 February–6 June 2017
Director: **Indhu Rubasingham**
Costume Designer: **Johanna Coe**
Lighting Designer: **Oliver Fenwick**
Video Design: **Luke Halls Studio**
Composers & Sound Designers: **Ben** and **Max Ringham**
Associate Designers: **Machiko Weston, Max Klaentschi**

CARMEN [349] 796–797
By Georges Bizet
Libretto by Henri Meilhac and Ludovic Halévy
Bregenz Festival, Lake Constance, 19 July–20 August 2017
Director: **Kasper Holten**
Costume Designer: **Anja Vang Kragh**
Lighting Designer: **Bruno Poet**
Choreographer: **Signe Fabricius**
Video Design: **Luke Halls Studio**
Production Manager: **Florian Karlsreiter**
Associate Designers: **Machiko Weston, Bronia Housman, Chiara Stephenson**

ROOM 2022 [338] 852–853
Miami Art Basel
EDITION Hotel, Miami, 10–11 December 2017
Commissioned by **American Express**
Producer: **Radical Media**
Video Designers: **Luke Halls** and **Charli Davis** for **Luke Halls Studio**
Composer & Sound Designer: **Max Ringham**
Technical Director: **David Stallbaumer**
Engineering & Fabrication: **Showman Eventscape, Central Florida Scenic**
Associate Designers: **Max Klaentschi, Angie Vasileiou**

POEMPORTRAITS [344] 860–861
Serpentine Galleries, London, 29 June 2017–ongoing
Commissioned by **Google Arts & Culture**
Creative Technologists: **Ross Goodwin, LUX**
Production: **Sunshine**
Curators: **Hans Ulrich Obrist, Freya Murray**

MORNING I 620
Somerset House, London, September–November 2017
900mm × 1300mm printed photographic transparency on curved aluminium frame, LED
Fabrication: **Bay Scenic**

ZOETROPE [350]
Zeitz Museum of Contemporary Art Africa, Cape Town, 4 December 2018–1 November 2019
Pavilion commissioned by **Design Indaba** and **Mercedes Benz Electric Vehicles**
Video Designers: **Luke Halls** and **Charli Davis** for **Luke Halls Studio**
Composers & Sound Designers: **Jade Pybus** and **Andy Theakstone**
Production Manager: **Piers Mansfield-Scaddan**
Associate Designers: **Matteo Mastrandrea, Ruby Law**

WITNESS [352]
Katy Perry
World Arena Tour, 19 September 2017–21 August 2018
Creative Director: **Baz Halpin**
Choreographers: **The Squared Division**
Video Design: **Silent House, Early Bird**
Production Manager: **Jay Schmit**
Engineering & Fabrication: **Brian Levine, TAIT, David Mendoza, Matthew Whitehead, Airworks**
Associate Designers: **Chiara Stephenson, Jed Skrzypczak, Machiko Weston**

BLINDED BY YOUR GRACE [362] 737
Stormzy
BRIT Awards, O2 Arena, London, 22 February 2018
Musical Director: **Fraser T Smith**
Camera Director: **Phil Heyes**
Lighting Designer: **Al Gurdon**
Prop Supervisor: **Lizzie Frankl**
Fabricator: **Blackfriars**
Associate Designer: **Amalie White**

THE SINGING TREE 40 [357] 753
V&A Museum, London, 27 November 2017–6 January 2018
Kindly supported by **PRG**
Creative Technologists: **Ross Goodwin, LUX**
Video Designers: **Luke Halls** and **Zakk Hein** for **Luke Halls Studio**
Composers & Sound Designers: **Jade Pybus** and **Andy Theakstone**
Engineering & Fabrication: **Michael Whiteley**
Production Manager: **Lizzie Frankl**
Video Supplier: **Frederic Opsomer, PRG**
Associate Designer: **Max Klaentschi**

MAGIC BOX 756–757
V&A, London, September 2017–September 2019
Fabrication: **Michael Whiteley**

GIRLS & BOYS [358] 810–811
By Dennis Kelly
Royal Court Theatre, London, 8 February–22 July 2018
Director: **Lyndsey Turner**
Costume Designer: **Jack Galloway**
Lighting Designer: **Oliver Fenwick**
Choreographer: **Joseph Alford**
Video Designers: **Luke Halls** and **Charli Davis** for **Luke Halls Studio**
Sound Designer: **David McSeveney**
Associate Designer: **Machiko Weston**

THE LEHMAN TRILOGY [370] 678–679
By Stefano Massini and Ben Power
Royal National Theatre, Lyttelton, London, 7 April–22 September 2018
Director: **Sam Mendes**
Costume Designer: **Katrina Lindsay**
Lighting Designer: **Jon Clark**
Choreographer: **Polly Bennett**
Video Design: **Luke Halls Studio**
Production Manager: **Jim Leaver**
Composer & Sound Designer: **Nick Powell**
Associate Designers: **Machiko Weston, Matteo Mastrandrea**

THE INFINITE LIBRARY [361]
Competition Entry for Redesign of Old Street Roundabout, December 2017

YOU [369]
Pharrell Williams, N.E.R.D.
Installation ideas, 2016–2017

EGG 38–39 [373] 727–729
XI Gallery, New York, 25 April 2018
Installation commissioned in collaboration with **Bjarke Ingels**
Construction: **Kennedy Fabrications**
Video Design: **Glowing Bulbs**
Sound Design: **Antfarm**
Content Production: **D-BOX**
Associate Designers: **Max Klaentschi, Angie Vasileiou**

MASK [364] 722–723
Somerset House, London, 17–20 May 2018
Lighting Designer: **Adam Squire**
Video Designers: **Luke Halls** and **Charli Davis** for **Luke Halls Studio**
Composers & Sound Designers: **Jade Pybus** and **Andy Theakstone**
Engineering & Fabrication: **Michael Whiteley**
Production Manager: **Lizzie Frankl**
Associate Designer: **Ruby Law**

ABEL'S MASK [374] 770–771, 824–825
The Weeknd
Coachella Festival, Indio, 14 and 21 April 2018
Lighting Designer: **Cory FitzGerald**
Video Design: **Strangeloop**
Engineering & Fabrication: **AES Creative**
Production Manager: **Rob DeCeglio**
Tour Manager: **Matt Petroff**
Associate Designers: **Matteo Mastrandrea, Jack Headford**

VOYAGE STUDIES [378]
ABBA
Preliminary studies, 2017–2019

EXPERIENCE + INNOCENCE [384] 674, 676, 685
U2
World Arena Tour, 2 May–3 July 2018
Director: **Willie Williams**
Co-Designers: **Ric Lipson, Stufish**
Costume Designer: **Sharon Blankson**
Lighting Designers: **Mark 'Sparky' Risk, Alex Murphy, Allen Branton**
Video Design: **Treatment Studio**
Animations: **Oliver Jeffers**
Choreographer: **Morleigh Steinberg**
Camera Director: **Matt Askem**
Engineering & Fabrication: **Adam Davis** and **Aaron Siebert, TAIT**

PLEASE FEED THE LIONS 41 [383] 780–781
London Design Biennale, Trafalgar Square, London, 20–23 September 2018
Supported by **Google Arts & Culture**
Creative Technologists: **Ross Goodwin, LUX**
Video Design: **Luke Halls Studio**
Composition & Sound Design: **Res.Lab, Jade Pybus** and **Andy Theakstone**
Associate Designers: **Matteo Mastrandrea, Jack Headford**

MULTI-STOREY [387]
Festival of Ideas, Cannes, 26 June 2018
Commissioned by **Damien Baines** at **Instagram**
Video Designer: **Luke Halls**
Composition & Sound Design: **Res.Lab, Jade Pybus** and **Andy Theakstone**
Engineering & Fabrication: **Bay Productions**
Associate Designers: **Angie Vasileiou, Ruby Law**

MASK IN MOTION 724–725, 774–775
Kunsthal Charlottenborg, Copenhagen, 21 September 2018–13 January 2019
Commissioned for **BIG Art Exhibition**
Fabrication: **MDM**
Associate Designers: **Amalie White, Ruby Law**

THE ORDER OF TIME [388]
By Carlo Rovelli
Bold Tendencies, Peckham, London, 22 September 2018
Curator: **Hannah Barry**
Readings: **Benedict Cumberbatch**
Composition & Sound Design: **Res.Lab, Jade Pybus** and **Andy Theakstone**
Video Designer: **Angie Vasileiou**
Associate Designer: **Matteo Mastrandrea**

THE UNKNOWN SOLDIER [395]
Royal Ballet, Royal Opera House, London, 17–29 November 2018
Choreographer: **Alastair Marriott**
Composer: **Dario Marianelli**
Costume Designer: **Jonathan Howells**
Lighting Designer: **Bruno Poet**
Video Designer: **Luke Halls**
Associate Designer: **Matteo Mastrandrea**

ORANGE CUBE [400]
Summer Party, Serpentine Galleries, London, 25 June 2019
Video Design: **Luke Halls Studio**
Engineering & Fabrication: **SetSquare**
Associate Designer: **Machiko Weston**

SUPER 856–857
Pet Shop Boys
Royal Opera House and World Tour, 29 October 2016–2 April 2019
Stage Director & Choreographer: **Lynne Page**
Lighting Designer: **Rob Sinclair**
Video Designer: **Luke Halls**

ZOETROPE MALAWI [390] 784–785
Skills Centre, Namisu, Malawi, opened November 2020
Project Managers:
Angus Gaisford, **Josie Charter**

ATLAS [396] 708–709
By Meredith Monk
LA Philharmonic, Walt Disney Concert Hall, Los Angeles, 11–12 June 2019
Director: **Yuval Sharon**
Costume Designer: **Emma Kingsbury**
Lighting Designer: **John Torres**
Choreographer: **Danielle Agami**
Video Designers: **Luke Halls** and **Charli Davis** for **Luke Halls Studio**
Associate Designers: **Amalie White**, **Ruby Law**

THE HUNT [399] 688–689
By David Farr, after Thomas Vinterberg and Tobias Lindholm
Almeida Theatre, London, 17 June–3 August 2019
Director: **Rupert Goold**
Composer: **Adam Cork**
Costume Designer: **Evie Gurney**
Lighting Designer: **Neil Austin**
Choreographer: **Botis Seva**
Sound Designer: **Adam Cork**
Engineering & Fabrication:
Simon York, **Miraculous Engineering**
Associate Designers: **Machiko Weston**, **Matteo Mastrandrea**

MEMORY PALACE 36–37 [402]
Pitzhanger Manor Gallery, London, 26 September 2019–9 February 2021
Curator: **John Leslie**
Engineering & Fabrication: **Diagon**
Associate Designer: **Ruby Law**

IDEAS TO FORMS [460]
BBC, Culture in Quarantine*, London, 18 May 2020*
Composition & Sound Design: **Polyphonia**
Film Editor: **Matteo Mastrandrea**

IN YELLOW [410] 800–801
Dua Lipa
MTV EMAs, Seville, 3 November 2019
Choreographers: **Charm La'Donna**, **Alex Clark**
Costume Designer: **Lorenzo Posocco**
Video Design: **Hello Charlie**
Associate Designer: **Amalie White**

IN THE FOREST [413] 710
Billie Eilish
Steve Jobs Theater, Cupertino, 4 December 2019
Director: **Sam Wrench**
Lighting Designer: **Bruno Poet**
Video Design: **Strange Loop**
Associate Designer: **Ruby Law**

THE LINE [409]
Wayne McGregor
Preliminary ideas for The Sphere
Costume Designers: **Gareth Pugh** and **Carson McColl**
Lighting Designer: **Lucy Carter**
Associate Designers: **Jack Headford**, **Matteo Mastrandrea**

SILENCED CHOIR [459]
LV AW2020 Women's Collection
Cour Carrée, Musée du Louvre, Paris, 7 March 2020
Director: **Nicolas Ghesquière**
Lighting Designer: **Philippe Cerceau**
Composers & Sound Designers: **Woodkid** and **Bryce Dessner, The National**
Producer & Production Manager:
La Mode en Images
Associate Designer: **Machiko Weston**

I SAW THE WORLD END [464] 668
Es Devlin and Machiko Weston
Imperial War Museum, London, 7 August 2020–24 May 2021
Composition & Sound Design: **Polyphonia**
Associate Designers: **Amalie White**, **Matteo Mastrandrea**, **Robert McIntyre**, **Benton Ching**

ABOUT TIME [468]
Costume Institute, Metropolitan Museum of Art, New York, 29 October 2020–7 February 2021
Curator: **Andrew Bolton**
Lighting Design: **Tillotson Design Associates**
Associate Designers: **Bori Kovacs**, **Amalie White**

FOREST FOR CHANGE [472]
UN Global Goals Pavilion, Project Everyone, London Design Biennale, Somerset House, London, 1–27 June 2021
Landscape Architect: **Philip Jaffa**
Landscaping: **Scottscape**
Composer: **Robert M Thomas**
Lighting Designer: **John Cullen**
Sound Designers: **Brian Eno**, **Cheryl Tipp** and **The British Library Board**
Associate Designer: **Jack Headford**

THE SEED 34–35 [471]
Jubail Mangrove Park, Abu Dhabi, 2 December 2020–30 January 2021
Director: **Francisco Negrin**
Camera Director: **Hamish Hamilton**
Composition: **Mohammed al Ahmed**, **Pierre Mussche**, **Musicom**, **Polyphonia**
Costume Designer: **Jack Galloway**
Lighting Designer: **Bruno Poet**
Choreographer: **Gavin Robins**
Sound Design: **Autoria**
Engineering & Fabrication: **Stage One**
Production Managers: **Nick Levitt**, **Jo MacKay**
Associate Designers: **Amalie White**, **Bori Kovacs**, **Machiko Weston**, **Ruby Law**

FOREST OF US 18–21 [474] 820–821
Pace Gallery, Superblue Miami, 18 March 2021–present
Video Designer: **Luke Halls**
Lighting Designer: **Ben Bauer**
Production Managers: **Ben Bauer**, **Eimear O'Raw**
Composition & Sound Design: **Polyphonia**
Engineering & Fabrication: **PRG Scenic**
Associate Designers: **Bori Kovacs**, **Matteo Mastrandrea**

BLUESKYWHITE [484] 758–759, 848–849
LUX Exhibition
180 The Strand, London, 13 October–18 December 2021
Lighting Design: **Beam**
Video Designer: **Luke Halls**
Composition & Sound Design: **Polyphonia**
Engineering & Fabrication: **Whitewall**, **Showtex**, **LG**
Associate Designers: **Matteo Mastrandrea**, **Benjamin Lucraft**

DO IT [466]
Commissioned by Hans Ulrich Obrist
Published by Penguin, June 2021

CONFERENCE OF THE TREES [483]
NYT Climate Hub
COP26, Glasgow, 1–11 November 2021
Landscape Architect: **Philip Jaffa**
Landscaping: **Scottscape**
Video Designer: **Jakob Trollbäck**
Associate Designer: **Matteo Mastrandrea**

POEM PAVILION 48–49 [493]
World Expo, Dubai,
1 October 2021–31 March 2022
Executive Architects: **Veretec**
Structural Engineers: **Atelier One**
Creative Technologists:
Kyle McDonald, IYOIYO, LUX
Lighting Designer: **Atelier Ten**
Video Designer: **Luke Halls**
Composition & Sound Design: **Polyphonia**
Studio team: **Matteo Mastrandrea,**
Jack Headford, Machiko Weston,
Amalie White, Angie Vasileiou, Bori Kovacs
Associate Designer: **Ruby Law**

GRIFFITH OBSERVATORY [487]
Adele
One Night Only *CBS broadcast performance,*
Griffith Observatory, Los Angeles,
14 November 2021
Lighting Designer: **Noah Mitz**
Camera Director: **Paul Dugdale**
Video Design: **Good Company**
Associate Designers: **Amalie White,**
Benjamin Lucraft, Gonzalo Padilla,
Robert McIntyre

FIVE ECHOES 50–51 [499] 711
Miami Art Basel
Jungle Plaza, Miami, 3–21 December 2021
Commissioned by **Chanel**
Producer & Production Manager:
Keith Baptista, Prodject
Lighting Designer: **Seth Bernstein**
Composition: **Polyphonia**
Sound Design: **Eric Bechtler, Adi Worldwide**
Engineering & Fabrication: **Adirondack Studios**
Associate Designer: **Matteo Mastrandrea**

AFTER HOURS TIL DAWN [506]
The Weeknd 716, 772–773, 840–841
World Arena Tour, 14 July–27 November 2022
Creative Director: **La Mar C Taylor**
Production Manager: **Rob DeCeglio**
Tour Manager: **Matt Petroff**
Choreographer: **Charm La'Donna**
Lighting Designer: **Jason Baeri**
Video Designer: **Polina Zakh**
Costume Designer: **Urbanie Lamas**
Engineering & Fabrication: **Marisa Rinchiuso**
and **Alex Serrano, TAIT**
Scenic Design Producer: **Jason Ardizzone-West**
Associate Designers: **Matteo Mastrandrea,**
Amalie White, Gonzalo Padilla, Robert McIntyre

COMPTON SUPER BOWL [488] 838–839
Dr. Dre, Kendrick Lamar, Eminem,
Mary J. Blige, Snoop Dogg and 50 Cent
SoFi Stadium, Los Angeles, 13 February 2022
Camera Director: **Hamish Hamilton**
Video Design: **Good Company**
Lighting Designer: **Al Gurdon**
Choreographer: **Fatima Robinson**
Costume Designer: **Lila Nikole**
Engineering & Fabrication: **All Access, Atomic**
Associate Designers: **Benjamin Lucraft,**
Gonzalo Padilla, Matteo Mastrandrea,
Robert McIntyre

YOUR VOICES [510] 746–747
Lincoln Center Plaza, New York,
5–18 December 2022
Commissioned by **Aliette Duquesne**
at **Moët & Chandon**
Lighting Designer: **Tupac**
Composition: **Polyphonia**
Sound Design: **Adi Worldwide**
Associate Designers: **Matteo Mastrandrea,**
Benjamin Lucraft

THE CRUCIBLE [514] 694–695
By Arthur Miller
National Theatre, Olivier, London,
14 September–5 November 2022
Director: **Lyndsey Turner**
Composer: **Caroline Shaw**
Costume Designer: **Catherine Fay**
Lighting Designer: **Tim Lutkin**
Sound Designers: **Tingying Dong**
and **Paul Arditti**
Associate Designer: **Ellie Wintour**

HERE NOT HERE [500] 636, 675, 754, 760–761
GöteborgsOperan, Gothenburg,
21 January 2022
Choreographer: **Maxine Doyle**
Composer: **Rachael Dease**
Costume Designer: **Bregje van Balen**
Lighting Designers: **Joakim Brink**
and **David Stokholm**
Associate Designers: **Bori Kovacs,**
Nikolai Kuchin, Ellie Wintour

A NUMBER [505] 766–767
By Caryl Churchill
Old Vic Theatre, London, 24 January–19 March 2022
Director: **Lyndsey Turner**
Costume Designer: **Natalie Pryce**
Lighting Designers: **Oliver Fenwick**
and **Tim Lutkin**
Sound Designer: **Donato Wharton**
Engineering & Fabrication: **Ken Fleary**
and **Andrew Mitchell, Scott Fleary**
Associate Designer: **Matteo Mastrandrea**

DESERT MOON 30–31 [509]
Saint Laurent SS2023 Men's Collection
Agafay Desert, Morocco, 15 July 2022
Director: **Anthony Vaccarello**
Lighting Designer: **Philippe Cerceau**
Producers & Production Managers:
Simon Caillaud and **Raphaele Toesca**
at **Bureau Betak**
Associate Designer: **Gonzalo Padilla**

RENAISSANCE [496] 844–847
Beyoncé
World Stadium Tour, 10 May–27 September 2023
Director, Executive Producer &
Creative Director: **Beyoncé**
Creative Directors & Producers:
Ed Burke, Andrew Makadsi and
Erinn Williams for **Parkwood**
Co-designers: **Ray Winkler**
and **Ric Lipson, Stufish**
Production Manager: **Jason Danter**
Camera Director: **James Merryman**
Video Designers: **Frederik Heyman, Greenwall,**
Ruth Hogben, Danny Tull, and others for
Parkwood
Lighting Designer: **Tobias Rylander**
Engineering & Fabrication: **Stageco,**
Brian Levine, TAIT, David Mendoza, Airworks

COME HOME AGAIN 60–62 [519] 752, 864–865
Tate Modern lawn, London,
21 September–1 October 2022
Commissioned by **Cyrille Vigneron** and **Kiyo Taga** at **Cartier**
Video Designers: **Luke Halls** and **Charli Davis** for **Luke Halls Studio**
Composition & Sound Design: **Polyphonia**
Engineering & Fabrication: **Stage One**, **Diagon**
Associate Designer: **Matteo Mastrandrea**

REDRAW THE EDGES OF YOUR SELF [524] 866
Poster Series, *Back to Earth* Exhibition
Serpentine Galleries, London,
27 June–14 October 2022
Bas-relief: 3000mm × 2000mm pencil, charcoal and printer ink on painted birch plywood, LED
Fabrication: **Michael Whiteley**
Production Managers: **Siobhan Davies**, **Jo MacKay**
Associate Designer: **Gonzalo Padilla**

GUCCI COSMOS [552] 748–751, 764–765
Exhibition – Shanghai, London, Kyoto, 2023–2025
Creative Directors: **Alessandro Michele**, **Sabato De Sarno**
Curator: **Maria Luisa Frisa**
Producer: **Beniamino Marini**
Video Designers: **Polina Zakh** and **Luke Halls Studio**
Composition and Sound Designers: **Polina Zakh** and **Polyphonia**
Fabrication: **Stage One**, **Diagon**, **Bay Productions**
Lighting Designer: **Bruno Poet**
Creative Producer: **Jo MacKay** for **LarMac**
Associate Designers: **Claudia Fragoso**, **Scarlett Moloney**, **Gonzalo Padilla**

DEAR ENGLAND [539] 712–713
By James Graham
National Theatre, Olivier, London, 10 June–11 August 2023, Prince Edward Theatre and UK Tour
Director: **Rupert Goold**
Choreographers: **Ellen Kane**, **Hannes Langolf**
Lighting Designer: **Jon Clark**
Costume Designer: **Evie Gurney**
Video Designer: **Ash J Woodward**
Sound Designer: **Dan Balfour / Tom Gibbons**
Associate Director: **Elin Schofield**
Associate Designers: **William Brown**, **Benjamin Lucraft**

NEVADA ARK U2:UV 54–57 [534] 862–863
Sphere, Las Vegas,
29 September 2023–2 March 2024
Conceived & Designed by **U2**, **Willie Williams**, **Es Devlin**, **Ric Lipson**, **Gavin Friday**, **Morleigh Steinberg**, **Sharon Blankson**
Director: **Willie Williams**
Pixel Artists: **Susana Yamamoto**, **Nick Reyniers**, **Tim Booth at Treatment Studio**
Associate Designer: **Matteo Mastrandrea**

FREE YOUR MIND 42–43 [541]
Based on *The Matrix*, by the Wachowskis
Factory International, Manchester,
13 October–5 November 2023
Director: **Danny Boyle**
Writer: **Sabrina Mahfouz**
Composer: **Michael 'Mikey J' Asante**
Choreographer: **Kendrick 'H2O' Sandy**
Associate Designer: **Amalie White**

AN ATLAS OF ES DEVLIN [542]
Published by Thames & Hudson, 19 October 2023
Editor: **Andrea Lipps**
Designer: **Daniel Devlin**
Associate Designers: **Benjamin Lucraft**, **Matteo Mastrandrea**

AN ATLAS OF ES DEVLIN [542]
Es Devlin and Polyphonia
The Vinyl Factory, released 30 October 2023
Music, composition and production: **Polyphonia**
Vinyl mastering: **Noel Summerville**

AN ATLAS OF ES DEVLIN [549]
Cooper Hewitt, Smithsonian Design Museum, New York, 18 November 2023–11 August 2024
Curator: **Andrea Lipps**
Video Design: **Luke Halls Studio**
Composition & Sound Design: **Polyphonia**
Lighting: **Bruno Poet**, **Electric Foundry**
Creative Producer: **Jo MacKay** for **LarMac**
Fabricators: **Pink Sparrow**, **Fluxaxis**, **Studio Youel**
Video mapping: **Disguise**
Photography / footage: **Jason Ardizzone-West**
Associate Designers: **Amalie White**, **Ellie Wintour**, **Scarlett Moloney**

THE LUNAR CHRONICLES [612]
By Marissa Meyer
Warner Bros., Pictures Animation, Locksmith Animation, to be released 2028
Screenplay writers: **Lindsey Ferrentino**, **Kalen Egan**, **Travis Sentell**
Director: **Noëlle Raffaele**
Producers: **Christina Steinberg**, **Natalie Fischer**, **Julie Lockhart**
Production Designers: **Es Devlin**, **Patrick Hanenberger**
Costume Designer: **Kate Mulleavy**, **Laura Mulleavy**
Character Designer: **Andrea Blasich**
Music: **Darren Higman**
Es Devlin Studio: **Alice Hallifax**, **Zoe Diakaki**, **Benjamin Lucraft**, **Scarlett Moloney**, **Victoria Bosch Vélez**, **Declan Slonim**, **Anna Niamh Gorman**, **Temitayo Shonibare**

MOST WANTED [575] 826–827
Bad Bunny
North America Tour, 21 February–9 June 2024
Production Manager: **Roly Garbalosa**
Lighting Designer: **David Ayala**
Stage: **Wicreations** and **TAIT**
Associate Designer: **Gonzalo Padilla**

SCREENSHARE [550] 782–783
REVERB, 180 The Strand, London,
22 May 2024–2 March 2025
Commissioned by 180 Studios and The Vinyl Factory
Music & Sound Design: **Polyphonia** and **Bass**
Choreographer: **Dam Van Huynh**
Video Design: **Luke Halls Studio**
Associate Designers: **Temitayo Shonibare**, **Zoe Diakaki**, **Alice Hallifax**, **Anna Niamh Gorman**, **Gonzalo Padilla**

SURFACING [555] 696–697, 834–835
Commissioned by Hedwig Solis Weinstein at BMW Culture
Art Basel, Basel, June 2024
Choreographer: **Sharon Eyal**
Co-creator: **Gai Behar**
Dancers: **Alice Godfrey**, **Juan Francisco**, **Gil Alfaro**, **Guido Dutilh**, **Nitzan Ressler**, **Darren Devaney**
Music & Sound Design: **Polyphonia**
Lighting Designer: **Bruno Poet**
Hair & Makeup: **Noa Eyal-Behar**
Costumes: **Odelia Arnold**, **Rebecca Hytting**, **Gon Biran**
Associate Designer: **Gonzalo Padilla**

THERE IS NO OTHER [556]
Commissioned by Damien Baines, Instagram
9:16 film, Cannes Lions Festival, Cannes, 17–21 June 2024
Choreographer: **Botis Seva**
Performers: **Joshua Shanny-Wynter, Joshua Smith, Edd Arnold, Tania Dimbelol, Sara Bagusto, Robert Dunkley-Gyimah, Shameer Rayes, Akti Konstantinou**
Music & Sound Designers: **Polyphonia**
Associate Choreographer: **Jordan Douglas**
Costume Designers: **Evie Gurney, Peter Todd**
Film Director and Editor: **Ruth Hogben**
Executive Producer: **Etty Bellhouse**
Producer: **Ella Girardot**
Lighting Director: **Robin Brigham**
Associate Designer: **Benjamin Lucraft**

IN A LANDSCAPE THE BLUE NOTEBOOKS [577] 626–627
Max Richter
World Tour, 2024–2026
Light Installation: **Es Devlin** and **Bruno Poet**
Lighting Designer: **Marc Heimendinger**
Associate Designers: **Scarlett Moloney, Temitayo Shonibare**

CORIOLANUS [578] 704–705
By William Shakespeare
National Theatre, Olivier, London, 11 September–9 November 2024
Director: **Lyndsey Turner**
Costume Designers: **Annemarie Woods, Philip Engleheart**
Lighting Designer: **Tim Lutkin**
Sound Designers: **Tom Gibbons, Johnny Edwards**
Composer: **Angus Macrae**
Video Designer: **Ash J Woodward**
Associate Designers: **Claudia Fragoso, Alice Hallifax, Anna Niamh Gorman, Temitayo Shonibare**

CONGREGATION 52–53 [559]
Es Devlin and Co-authors
St Mary le Strand, London, 3–9 October 2024
Curator: **Ekow Eshun**
Composers and Sound Designers: **Polyphonia**
Including extracts from 'Locus Iste' (This Place) by **Anton Bruckner;** *The New Four Seasons, Vivaldi Recomposed* by **Max Richter**, performed by **Daniel Hope** with **The Konzerthaus Kammerorchester Berlin**, conducted by **Andre De Ridder**, included by kind permission from **Max Richter, Mute Song** and **Deutsche Grammophon**
Choirs: **Genesis Sixteen**, the **London Bulgarian Choir**, the **South African Cultural Gospel Choir UK**, the **Choir of King's College London**
Projections: **Treatment Studio**
Film Director & Editor: **Ruth Hogben**
Filmed Performer: **Joshua Shanny-Wynter**
Choreographer: **Botis Seva**
Lighting Designers: **Bruno Poet, Johanne Jensen**
Creative Production: **Jo MacKay, LarMac**
Fabricators: **Stage One**
Light and Sound: **4Wall**
Projection Mapping: **VYV**
Photography: **Daniel Devlin**
Editors: **Boo Devlin, Ellie Wintour, Chrysi Philalithes, Jimmy Fox**
Recording and Editing: **Lucas Green, Polyphonia**
Associate Designers: **Claudia Fragoso, Zoe Diakaki, Anna Niamh Gorman, Temitayo Shonibare, Scarlett Moloney, Olukoye Akinkugbe, Alice Hallifax, Victoria Bosch Vélez, Jimmy Fox**

HAMLET [580] 692–693
By William Shakespeare
Royal Shakespeare Company, Royal Shakespeare Theatre, Stratford-upon-Avon, 8 February–29 March 2025
Director: **Rupert Goold**
Costume Designer: **Evie Gurney**
Lighting Designer: **Jack Knowles**
Composer & Sound Designer: **Adam Cork**
Movement Director: **Hannes Langolf**
Video Designer: **Akhila Krishnan**
Music Director: **Dan de Cruz**
Associate Designer: **Zoe Diakaki**

FACE TO FACE [569]
Somerset House, London, 23 November 2024–12 January 2025
Curator: **Ekow Eshun**
Music & Sound Design: **Polyphonia**
Including extracts from 'Locus Iste' (This Place) by **Anton Bruckner;** *The New Four Seasons, Vivaldi Recomposed* by **Max Richter**, performed by **Daniel Hope** with **The Konzerthaus Kammerorchester Berlin**, conducted by **Andre De Ridder**, included by kind permission from **Max Richter, Mute Song** and **Deutsche Grammophon**
Recorded Choral Music: **Genesis Sixteen**, the **London Bulgarian Choir**, the **South African Cultural Gospel Choir UK**, the **Choir of King's College London**
Director and Editor – Film Sequences: **Ruth Hogben**
Filmed Performer: **Joshua Shanny-Wynter**
Filmed Choreography: **Botis Seva**
Recording and Editing: **Lucas Green, Polyphonia**
Editors: **Boo Devlin, Ellie Wintour, Chrysi Philalithes, Jimmy Fox**
Projections: **Callum Phenix** at **Illuminate Systems, Anthony Bezencon** at **VYV, Treatment Studio**
Sound: **Callum Phenix** at **Illuminate Systems**
Creative Producers: **LarMac**
Fabrication: **Stage One, Build 23, James Newhouse, Guy Selwood-Miller**
Associate Designers: **Alice Hallifax, Claudia Fragoso, Zoe Diakaki, Temitayo Shonibare, Anna Niamh Gorman, Victoria Bosch Vélez, Scarlett Moloney, Declan Slonim**

LIBRARY OF LIGHT 28–29 [587]
Commissioned and curated by Maria Porro and Annalisa Rosso for Salone del Mobile
Pinacoteca di Brera, 6–21 April 2025
Composition & Sound Design: **Polyphonia**
Video: **Treatment Studio**
Lighting: **Giovanni Pinna**
Producer: **Gabriella Mazzei, Without Production**
Associate Designers: **Scarlett Moloney, Victoria Bosch Vélez, Claudia Fragoso**

MAYHEM BALL [583]
Lady Gaga
World Tour, 16 July 2025–13 April 2026
Creative Directors: **Lady Gaga, Michael Polansky, Parris Goebel, Ben Dagleish** for **Human Person**
Musical Directors: **Natural**
Choreographer: **Parris Goebel**
Lighting & Video Design: **FragmentNine**
Live Camera Director: **Micah Bickman**
Technical Directors: **Jason Danter, Chris Vineyard**
Fabricators: **TAIT, Jet Sets**
Videographers: **Solotech**
Co-production Designer: **Jason Ardizzone-West**
Associate Designers: **Scarlett Moloney, Zoe Diakaki, Victoria Bosch Veléz, Temitayo Shonibare, Anna Niamh Gorman**
Jaw Studio: **Sean Sanford**

WOMEN'S PAVILION [584]
Expo 2025 Osaka, 13 April–13 October 2025
Commissioned by Kiyo Taga, Cartier in collaboration with Cabinet Office, Ministry of Economy, Trade and Industry, Japan Association for the 2025 World Exposition
Composition & Sound Design: **Polyphonia**
Lighting Designer: **Bruno Poet**
Video Designer: **Luke Halls Studio**
Fabricators: **Nomura**
Architecture: **Yuko Nagayama & Associates**
Creative Producer: **Jo MacKay** at **LarMac**
Associate Designers: **Scarlett Moloney, Gonzalo Padilla, Temitayo Shonibare Olukoye Akinkugbe**
Composer (opening ceremony): **Kieran Brunt**
Poet (opening ceremony): **JJ Bola**

LIBRARY OF US 22–27 [588]
Commissioned by Faena Art for Miami Art Week 2025
Miami Beach, 1–7 December 2025
Composition & Sound Design: **Polyphonia**
Producer: **Elizabeth Brady**
Fabrication: **Kaden Productions**
Books donated by: **Penguin Random House**
Associate Designers: **Scarlett Moloney, Anna Niamh Gorman**

TRACING TIME [593]
Faena Art Project Room, Miami, 1 December 2025–8 February 2026
Not drowning I & II, 2025; **Home is the other we carry inside us**, 2025; **Edge Dance**, 2025 **Drawing not drowning I & II**, 2025
Production: **Erin Cermak**
Associate Designer: **Anna Niamh Gorman**

LULLABY [603]
T4P Wembley Arena
T4P Music, released 12 December 2025
Traditional Song, additional lyrics: **Peter Gabriel** and **Mahmoud Darwish**
Arrangers & Recomposers: **Nai Barghouti, Kieran Brunt**, Co-Arranger: **Benji B**
Producers: **Benji B, Kieran Brunt, Henri Davies**
Performed by: **Amena, Brian Eno, Celeste, Dan Smith (Bastille), Kieran Brunt, Sura Abdo, Lana Lubany, Leigh-Anne Pinnock, Mabel, London Community Gospel Choir, Nadine Shah, Nai Barghouti, Neneh Cherry, Tyson, Yasmeen Ayyashi, Ysée**
Production Consultant: **Brian Eno**
Recorded by: **Matt Lane**
Mixed by: **David Wrench** & **Valgeir Sigurbsson**
Mastered by: **Matt Colton**
Artwork: **Malak Mattar**

TAKE ME HOME [601]
Shenzhen Bay, 15 December 2025
Commissioned by China Resources and Shanghai Art in collaboration with MAD Architects (Beijing)
Composition & Sound Design: **Polyphonia**
Video Designers: **Luke Halls Studio**
Production: **China Resources, Shanghai Art**
Production Consultant: **Jo MacKay Creative**
Associate Designers: **Victoria Bosch Vélez, Claudia Fragoso**

TRISTAN UND ISOLDE [606] 622–625 794–795, 828–829
By Richard Wagner
The Metropolitan Opera, New York, 9 March–4 April 2026
Director: **Yuval Sharon**
Conductor: **Yannick Nézet-Séguin**
Costume Designer: **Clint Ramos**
Lighting Designer: **John Torres**
Video Designer: **Ruth Hogben**
Projection Designer: **Jason H Thompson**
Choreographer: **Annie-B Parson**
Chorus Director: **Tilman Michael**
Associate Designer: **Claudia Fragoso**

AMERICAN PSYCHO [604] 778–779
By Duncan Sheik and Roberto Aguirre-Sacasa
Almeida Theatre, London, 23 January–21 March 2026
Director: **Rupert Goold**
Associate Director: **Bethany West**
Choreographer: **Lynne Page**
Associate Choreographer: **Jasmin Colangelo**
Costume Designer: **Katrina Lindsay**
Associate Costume Designer: **Jonathan Lipman**
Lighting Designer: **Jon Clark**
Sound Designer: **Dan Moses Schreier**
Associate Sound Designer: **Joshua D. Reid**
Video Designer: **Finn Ross**
Music Supervisor and Vocal Arrangements: **David Shrubsole**
Musical Director: **Ellen Campbell**
Associate Designers: **Victoria Bosch Vélez, Zoe Diakaki**

SOU O OUTRO DO OUTRO 16–17, 58–59
Commissioned by M Cultura
Casa Bradesco, São Paulo, 15 March–27 July 2026
Curator: **Marcello Dantas**
Producer: **MADAI, Angela Magdalena**
Composition & Sound Design: **Polyphonia**
Video Designer: **Luke Halls Studio**
Lighting Designer: **Bruno Poet**
Fabricators: **Estúdio GRU**
Production Consultant: **Jo MacKay Creative**
Associate Designers: **Claudia Fragoso, Anna Niamh Gorman**

THE EVERYTHINGISTS [611]
Commissioned by V&A East Storehouse
V&A East Storehouse, London,18 April 2026
Curator: Madeleine Haddon
Composition & Sound Design: **Polyphonia**
Video Designer: **Luke Halls Studio**
Fabrication: **Scena**
Production Consultant: **Jo MacKay Creative**
Associate Designers: **Zoe Diakaki, Anna Niamh Gorman**

A NATIONAL PORTRAIT [614]
Collaboration with Google Arts & Culture
National Portrait Gallery, London, 14 May 2026
Production Consultant: **Jo MacKay Creative**
Fabricator: **Matt Harriman**
Associate Designer: **Temitayo Shonibare**

REFERENCES

A CORRIDOR

p.7 Deming, Barbara. 'Spirit of Love'. In *We Are All Part of One Another: A Barbara Deming Reader*. Philadelphia, PA: New Society Publishers, 1984.

p.7 Morton, Timothy. 'Extinction Marathon: Visions of the Future'. In conversation with Hans Ulrich Obrist, Serpentine Galleries, London, 18–19 October 2014.

p.63 Shakespeare, William. *The Tempest*. In *The Complete Works of William Shakespeare*. Leipzig: Baumgärtner, 1854.

A CONVERSATION with Hans Ulrich Obrist

p.74 Adnan, Etel, for Hans Ulrich Obrist's handwriting project on Instagram (@hansulrichobrist).

p.78 Gumbs, Alexis Pauline. 'The Making of a Love Letter'. Interview by Ashia Ajani. *Sierra*, 13 February 2020.

p.79 Obrist, Hans Ulrich, and Kostas Stasinopoulos, eds. *Remember Nature: 140 Artists' Ideas for Planet Earth*. Dublin: Penguin, 2021.

AN INFINITE ARCHIVE

p.83 Howe, Susan. *Spontaneous Particulars: The Telepathy of Archives*. New York: New Directions, 2014.

p.84 Devlin, Es, in 'Imaginary Spaces: Es Devlin and the Psychology of the Stage'. Interview by Andrew O'Hagan. *The New Yorker*, 21 March 2016.

p.85 Turner, Lyndsey, in 'Imaginary Spaces: Es Devlin and the Psychology of the Stage'. Interview by Andrew O'Hagan. *The New Yorker*, 21 March 2016.

p.89 Howe, Susan. 'Susan Howe, The Art of Poetry No.97'. Interview by Maureen N. McLane. *The Paris Review*, Issue 203, 2012.

ART AS RITUAL

p.93 Benjamin, Walter. 'The Work of Art in the Age of Mechanical Reproduction'. In *Selected Writings*, Volume 4. Cambridge, MA: Harvard University Press, 2003.

p.94 Devlin, Es. Cameron Mackintosh Professor of Contempory Theatre Inaugural Lecture. St Catherine's College, Oxford, 21 November 2025.

A 31-YEAR SKETCHBOOK

p.140 Rich, Adrienne. 'Diving into the Wreck'. In *Diving into the Wreck: Poems 1971–1972*. New York: W. W. Norton & Company, 1973.

p.143 Marlowe, Christopher. *Edward the Second*. Edited by Charles R. Forker. Manchester: Manchester University Press, 1994.

p.144 Penhall, Joe. 'Joe Penhall – Part 1'. Interview by Sarah Tejal Hamilton. *Writerly*, 31 March 2017.

p.151 Beethoven, Ludwig van. *Fidelio*. 1805.

p.152 Pinter, Harold. 'Art, Truth & Politics'. Nobel lecture at the Swedish Academy in Stockholm, Sweden, 7 December 2005.

p.155 O'Rowe, Mark. 'Mark O'Rowe on the power to shock – and feel'. Interview by Sara Keating. *The Irish Times*, 20 September 2014.

p.155 Bradwell, Mike, in 'Es Devlin: Stage Design'. From *Abstract: The Art of Design* series, Netflix, 2017.

p.156 Bruce, Christopher. 'Interview: Choreographer Christopher Bruce'. Interview by Kelly Apter. *The List*, n.d.

p.161 Shakespeare, William. *Antony and Cleopatra*. In *The Complete Works of William Shakespeare*. Leipzig: Baumgärtner, 1854.

p.162 Shakespeare, William. *Hamlet*. In *The Complete Works of William Shakespeare*. Leipzig: Baumgärtner, 1854.

p.165 Adès, Thomas. 'Composing Is Inherently Chaotic – Interview with Thomas Adès'. Interview by Jari Kallio. *Adventures In Music*, 9 May 2019.

p.167 Bond, Edward. *The Activists Papers*. In *The Worlds, with The Activists Papers*. London: E. Methuen, 1980.

p.168 Yeats, William Butler. 'The Second Coming'. In *Michael Robartes and the Dancer*. Dundrum, Ireland: Cuala Press, 1920.

p.173 Chaucer, Geoffrey. *The Canterbury Tales*. Translated by Nevill Coghill. London: Penguin, 1951.

p.179 West, Kanye. 'Hey Mama'. From *Late Registration*. Def Jam Recordings and Roc-A-Fella Records, 2005.

p.180 Shakespeare, William. *A Midsummer Night's Dream*. In *The Complete Works of William Shakespeare*. Leipzig: Baumgärtner, 1854.

p.182 Shakespeare, William. *Macbeth*. In *The Complete Works of William Shakespeare*. Leipzig: Baumgärtner, 1854.

p.187 Euripides. *Hecuba*. Translated by Tony Harrison. London: Faber & Faber, 2014.

p.188 Pet Shop Boys. 'Indefinite Leave to Remain'. From *Fundamental*. Parlophone, 2006.

p.192 Mazzolà, Caterino Tommaso (after Pietro Metastasio). *La Clemenza di Tito*. 1791.

p.197 Da Ponte, Lorenzo, and Wolfgang Amadeus Mozart. *Don Giovanni*. Translated by William Atkinson, 1787.

p.198 Roy, Arundhati. *The God of Small Things*. New York: Random House, 1997.

p.203 Bizet, Georges, as quoted in McCabe, Joseph, *A Biographical Dictionary of Modern Rationalists*. United Kingdom: Watts, 1920.

p.204 Wilde, Oscar. 'The Soul of Man Under Socialism'. *Fortnightly Review*, February 1891.

p.207 West, Kanye. 'Amazing'. From *808s & Heartbreaks*. Def Jam Recordings and Roc-A-Fella Records, 2008.

p.208 Mika. 'Mika Interview for The Boy Who Knew Too Much'. Interview by Neil McCormick. *The Telegraph*, 23 September 2009.

p.212 Honegger, Arthur. *I am a Composer*. Translated by Wilson O. Clough in collaboration with Allan Arthur Willman. London: Faber & Faber, 1966.

p.217 Sawhney, Nitin, featuring Natty. 'Days of Fire'. From *London Undersound*. Cooking Vinyl, 2008.

p.218 Heap, Imogen. 'First Train Home'. From *Ellipse*. RCA Records, 2009.

p.221 Lady Gaga. 'Collect Call From… Lady Gaga'. Interview by Elizabeth Goodman. *Blender Magazine*, April 2009.

p.222 Pet Shop Boys. 'Love etc.' From *Yes*. Parlophone, 2009.

p.224 Take That. 'The Flood'. From *Progress*. Polydor Records, 2010.

p.229 Orwell, George. *Nineteen Eighty-Four*. London: Secker & Warburg, 1949.

p.230 Lady Gaga. Live in Las Vegas. Pearl Concert Theater at Palms Casino Resort, 18 December 2009.

p.235 Goethe, Johann Wolfgang von. *Goethe's Theory of Colours*. United Kingdom: J. Murray, 1840.

p.236 Rihanna. 'Rihanna on Love: "I'm Waiting For the Man Who's Ballsy Enough to Deal With Me"'. Interview by bedhead. Celebitchy.com, 15 October 2012.

p.241 Korngold, Erich Wolfgang, and Paul Schott. *Die Tote Stadt*. New York: G. Ricordi & Co., Inc., 1921.

p.242 Batchler, Lee, Janet Scott Batchler, and Akiva Goldsman. *Batman Forever*. Los Angeles, CA: Warner Bros., 1995.

p.245 Jay-Z and Kanye West, featuring Frank Ocean. 'No Church in the Wild'. From *Watch the Throne*. Roc-A-Fella Records, Roc Nation and Def Jam Recordings, 2011.

p.248 Wagner, Richard. *Parsifal*. Translated by Ernest Newman. London: Breitkopf & Hartel, 1914.

p.253 Ende, Michael. *The Neverending Story*. Translated by Ralph Manheim. New York: Doubleday, 1983.

p.254 McGilchrist, Iain. *The Master and His Emissary: The Divided Brain and the Making of the Western World*. New Haven, CT: Yale University Press, 2019.

p.254 Bulgakov, Mikhail. *The Master and Margarita*. Translated by Michael Glenny. United States: Harper & Row, 1967.

p.257 Virgil. *The Aeneid*. Translated by Robert Fitzgerald. New York: Random House, 1983.

p.258 Madness. 'Our House'. From *The Rise and Fall*. Stiff Records, 1982.

p.262 Kirkwood, Lucy. 'Lucy Kirkwood on Chimerica: "Right now saying, 'I don't know' is the most radical state you can be in"'. Interview by Alice Jones. *iNews*, 17 April 2019.

p.267 West, Kanye, featuring Bon Iver. 'Lost in the World'. From *My Beautiful Dark Twisted Fantasy.* Def Jam Recordings and Roc-A-Fella Records, 2010.

p.268 Janáček, Leoš, as quoted in *Leoš Janáček: Letters and Reminiscences.* Edited by Bohumír Štědroň, translated by Geraldine Thomsen. Prague: Artia, 1955.

p.273 Springsteen, Bruce. 'Last to Die'. From *Magic.* Columbia Records, 2007.

p.274 West, Kanye. 'New Slaves'. From *Yeezus.* Def Jam Recordings and Roc-A-Fella Records, 2013.

p.276 Mozart, Wolfgang Amadeus, in *Letters of Wolfgang Amadeus Mozart.* Edited by Hans Mersmann. New York: Dover Publications, 1972.

p.283 Shakespeare, William. *A Midsummer Night's Dream.* In *The Complete Works of William Shakespeare.* Leipzig: Baumgärtner, 1854.

p.284 Cyrus, Miley. 'On My Own'. From *Bangerz.* RCA Records, 2013.

p.287 Seung, Sebastian. *Connectome: How the Brain's Wiring Makes Us Who We Are.* Boston: Houghton Mifflin Harcourt, 2012.

p.288 Ghesquière, Nicolas. 'Balenciaga's First Fragrance in 55 Years'. Interview by Maggie Bullock. *Elle*, 26 February 2010.

p.293 Brecht, Bertolt, and John Willett. *Brecht on Theatre: The Development of an Aesthetic.* New York: Hill and Wang, 1964.

p.294 Haley, Jennifer. *The Nether: A Play.* Evanston, IL: Northwestern University Press, 2014.

p.297 Churchill, Caryl. *Light Shining in Buckinghamshire.* Great Britain: Pluto Press Ltd, 1978.

p.298 Shakespeare, William. *Hamlet.* In *The Complete Works of William Shakespeare.* Leipzig: Baumgärtner, 1854.

p.300 U2. 'Rejoice'. From *October.* Island Records, 1981.

p.300 U2. 'Lucifer's Hands'. From *Songs of Innocence.* Island and Interscope Records, 2014.

p.305 Weber, Carl Maria von, as quoted in H. E. Jacob, *Johan Strauss, Father and Son: A Century of Light Music.* USA: The Greystone Press, 1940.

p.306 Adele. 'Adele: The Girl With the Mighty Mouth'. By Tom Lamont. *The Guardian*, 26 March 2011.

p.313 Friel, Brian. *Faith Healer: A Drama.* New York: Samuel French, Inc., 1980.

p.314 Beyoncé. 'Bey the Light'. Remixed by Forrest Gander. *CR Fashion Book*, Issue 5, Fall/Winter 2014.

p.321 West, Kanye. 'Fade'. From *The Life of Pablo.* GOOD Music and Def Jam Recordings, 2016.

p.322 Niemeyer, Oscar. 'Oscar Niemeyer Talks About Brasilia, Communism, Regrets'. Interview by Michael Luongo. *Bloomberg*, 6 December 2012.

p.325 Eliot, T. S. 'East Coker'. In *Four Quartets.* New York: Harcourt, Inc., 1943.

p.333 Fontaine, Claire. Instructions for *do it.* Commissioned by the Serpentine Galleries, 2012.

p.334 Shem Tov, Rabbi Israel Baal. *Tzava'at Harivash: The Testament of Rabbi Israel Baal Shem Tov.* Translated by J. Immanuel Schochet. New York: Kehot Publication Society, 1942.

p.337 *The International Encyclopedia of Prose and Poetical Quotations.* Compiled by William S. Walsh. Philadelphia, PA: J. C. Winston Company, 1908.

p.343 Lorde. 'Sober'. From *Melodrama.* Lava, Republic Records and Universal, 2017.

p.344 Colomina, Beatriz, and Mark Wigley. *Are We Human? Notes on an Archaeology of Design.* Zürich: Lars Müller Publishers, 2016.

p.349 Bizet, Georges, Henri Meilhac and Ludovic Halévy. 'En Vain Pour Éviter'. From *Carmen*, 1875. Translated by Robert Glaubitz, 2003.

p.350 'Zoetrope'. Online Etymology Dictionary. Accessed 15 April 2023.

p.352 Perry, Katy. 'Chained to the Rhythm'. From *Witness.* Capitol Records, 2017.

p.357 Poem generated by Singing Tree AI, based on a word contributed by Ludo Galloway. 1 November 2018.

p.358 Kelly, Dennis. 'Dennis Kelly on Girls and Boys: "I was shocked Carey Mulligan did it"'. Interview by Lyn Gardner. *The Guardian*, 22 February 2018.

p.361 Blake, William. 'Auguries of Innocence'. In *The Poems of William Blake*. London: Basil Montagu Pickering, 1874.

p.362 Stormzy. BRIT Awards performance, 21 February 2018.

p.364 Berthiaume, André. *Contretemps: Nouvelles*. Montreal: Cercle du livre de France, 1971.

p.369 Williams, Pharrell, N.E.R.D. and Rihanna. 'Lemon'. From *No_One Ever Really Dies*. I Am Other and Columbia Records, 2017.

p.370 Mendes, Sam. Text message to author and editor, 17 April 2023.

p.373 Ingels, Bjarke. 'Hedonistic Sustainability'. TEDxEastSalon, May 2011.

p.374 The Weeknd and Kendrick Lamar. 'Pray For Me'. From *Black Panther: The Album (Music From and Inspired By)*. TDE, Aftermath and Interscope, 2018.

p.378 ABBA. 'Knowing Me, Knowing You'. From *Arrival*. Polar Records, 1976.

p.383 Forster, E. M. *Howards End*. New York: Alfred A. Knopf, 1921.

p.384 U2. 'Love Is All We Have Left'. From *Songs of Experience*. Island and Interscope Records, 2017.

p.387 Devlin, Es. Introduction to 'Multi-Storey'. 2018.

p.388 Rovelli, Carlo. *The Order of Time*. New York: Riverhead Books, 2018.

p.390 Hlupekile, Xara. 'Loss'. From 'Poems from Malawian Women's Poetry Workshop', *Tiferet Journal*, March 2018.

p.395 Atwood, Margaret. *The Robber Bride*. Toronto: McClelland and Stewart, 1993.

p.396 Monk, Meredith. 'Meredith Monk: Creating "where the voice starts dancing"'. Interview by Josephine Reed for National Endowment for the Arts. *What Is Innovation?* podcast, no. 4, 2011.

p.396 Monk, Meredith. 'Meredith Monk: Archaeologist of the Human Voice'. Interview by Krista Tippett. *On Being* podcast, 16 February 2012.

p.399 Farr, David. *The Hunt*. London: Faber & Faber, 2019.

p.400 Obrist, Hans Ulrich. 'Hans Ulrich Obrist: "Everything I do is somehow connected to velocity"'. Interview by Rachel Cooke. *The Guardian*, 8 March 2015.

p.402 Macy, Joanna, and Molly Brown. *Coming Back to Life: The Guide to the Work that Reconnects*. Gabriola, BC, Canada: New Society Publishers, 2014.

p.409 McGregor, Wayne. 'A Choreographer's Creative Process in Real Time'. TED Talk, September 2012.

p.410 Lipa, Dua. 'Be the One'. From *Dua Lipa*. Warner Records, 2017.

p.413 Eilish, Billie. 'My Future'. From *Billie Eilish: The World's a Little Blurry*, An Apple Original Film, 2021.

p.459 Ghesquière, Nicolas. 'Balenciaga's First Fragrance in 55 Years'. Interview by Maggie Bullock. *Elle*, 26 February 2010.

p.464 Einstein, Albert, as quoted in 'Atomic Education Urged by Einstein'. *The New York Times*, 25 May 1946.

p.464 Wells, H. G. *The World Set Free*. United Kingdom: Macmillan & Co., 1913.

p.466 Okoyomon, Precious. *do it*. From *New! do it (around the world)*, commissioned by the Serpentine Galleries, 2020.

p.468 Laird, Nick. 'The Last Saturday in Ulster'. In *To a Fault*. London: Faber & Faber, 2005.

p.471 Ranwasii, Mad-Ha, as quoted in *The Tree Book: The Stories, Science, and History of Trees*. London: Dorling Kindersley, 2022.

p.472 Flaubert, Gustave. *November*. USA: Bodley Head, 1934.

p.474 Abram, David. 'An Interview … Dr. David Abram – The Spell of Literacy'. Interview by David Boulton. Children of the Code web blog, n.d.

p.483 Powers, Richard. *The Overstory*. New York: W. W. Norton & Company, 2019.

p.484 Lord Byron. 'Darkness'. In *The Works of Lord Byron: Complete in One Volume*. Compiled by George Noël Gordon Byron (Baron Byron). Frankfurt: Broenner, 1826.

p.487 Adele. 'Adele On the Other Side'. Interview by Abby Aguirre. *Vogue*, 7 October 2021.

p.487 'Saturn Return'. The Astrology Dictionary. Accessed 7 May 2023.

p.488 Lamar, Kendrick. 'ELEMENT.' From *DAMN.* Top Dawg Entertainment, Aftermath Entertainment and Interscope Records, 2017.

p.493 Plato, as quoted in Ralph Waldo Emerson, 'Nature'. Boston: James Munroe and Company, 1836.

p.496 Lorde, Audre. 'Poetry Is Not a Luxury'. From 'Black Woman Mother', in *From a Land Where Other People Live.* Detroit: Broadside Press, 1972.

p.499 Borges, Jorge Luis. *Labyrinths.* New York: New Directions, 1962.

p.500 Cixous, Hélène. *The Book of Promethea.* Translated by Betsy Wing. Lincoln and London: University of Nebraska Press, 1991.

p.505 Churchill, Caryl. *A Dream Play.* In *Plays: Four.* London: Nick Hern Books, 2008.

p.505 Churchill, Caryl. *A Number.* New York: Theatre Communications Group, 2003.

p.506 Bellow, Saul. *Herzog.* London: Penguin UK, 2012.

p.509 Bowles, Paul. *The Sheltering Sky.* New York: Vintage Books, 1990.

p.510 Davis, Wade. Radio Expeditions. Interview by Alex Chadwick. NPR, 27 May 2003.

p.514 Miller, Arthur. *Conversations with Arthur Miller.* Edited by Matthew Charles Roudané. Jackson and London: University Press of Mississippi, 1987.

p.519 Macy, Joanna. *World as Lover, World as Self.* Berkeley, CA: Parallax Press, 1991.

p.524 Hildegard of Bingen, as quoted in *Meditations with Hildegard of Bingen.* Edited by Gabriele Uhlein. Rochester, VT: Bear & Company, 1983.

AN INTERVAL: LOCKDOWN CONVERSATIONS

p.420 Hart, David Bentley. *The Experience of God: Being, Consciousness, Bliss.* New Haven, CT: Yale University Press, 2013.

p.422 Hadid, Zaha. *There Should Be No End To Experimentation.* Exhibition by the Serpentine Galleries, International, 17 March–6 April 2017.

A CONVERSATION with Dorothea von Hantelmann

p.525 Weber, Andreas. *Matter and Desire: An Erotic Ecology.* Translated by Rory Bradley. White River Junction, VT: Chelsea Green Publishing, 2017.

p.530 Macy, Joanna. *World as Lover, World as Self.* Berkeley, CA: Parallax Press, 1991.

A 31-YEAR SKETCHBOOK (cont.)

p.534 U2. 'Beautiful Day'. From *All That You Can't Leave Behind.* Island Records, 2000.

p.539 Graham, James. *Dear England.* London: Methuen Drama, 2023.

p.541 Wachowski, Lana. *The Matrix.* Los Angeles, CA: Warner Bros., 1999.

p.542 Rich, Adrienne. 'Diving into the Wreck'. *In Diving into the Wreck: Poems 1971–1972.* New York: W. W. Norton & Company, 1973.

p.549 Greenaway, Peter. *A Walk Through H: The Reincarnation of an Ornithologist.* London: BFI, 1978.

p.550 Gonzalez-Torres, Felix. Wall label, *I Am Here* exhibition. Marjorie Barrick Museum of Art, University of Nevada, Las Vegas, 24 September 2021–29 January 2022.

p.552 Michele, Alessandro. 'Inside the New Gucci Archive in Florence with its Maestro Alessandro Michele'. Interview by Tiziana Cardini. *Vogue*, 12 July 2021.

p.555 Eyal, Sharon. 'In Conversation: Sharon Eyal & Claude Adjil', LAS, 6 January 2022: www.las-art.foundation.

p.555 Han, Byung-Chul. *The Disappearance of Rituals: A Topology of the Present.* Translated by Daniel Steuer. Cambridge: Polity, 2020.

p.569 Lévinas, Emmanuel. *Totality and Infinity: An Essay on Exteriority.* Translated by Alphonso Lingis. Pittsburgh, PA: Duquesne University Press, 1969.

p.575 Bad Bunny. Super Bowl LX Halftime Show. Levi's Stadium, Santa Clara, California, 8 February 2026.

p.577 Kafka, Franz. 'The First Octavo Notebook'. *In The Blue Octavo Notebooks*. Cambridge, MA: Exact Change, 1991.

p.577 Richter, Max. 'Biography'. Decca Publishing. Decca Records, n.d.

p.578 Shakespeare, William. *Coriolanus*. In *The Complete Works of William Shakespeare*. Leipzig: Baumgärtner, 1854.

p.580 Shakespeare, William. *Hamlet*. In *The Complete Works of William Shakespeare*. Leipzig: Baumgärtner, 1854.

p.583 Lady Gaga. *The Manifesto of Mayhem*. Debuted at Coachella Valley Music & Arts Festival, Colorado Desert, California, 11 April 2025.

p.583 Beradt, Charlotte. *The Third Reich of Dreams: The Nightmares of a Nation*. Translated by Damion Searls. Princeton, NJ: Princeton Architectural Press, 2025.

p.584 Yoshimoto, Banana. *Kitchen*. Translated by Megan Backus. London: Faber & Faber, 1993.

p.587 Borges, Jorge Luis. 'Jorge Luis Borges: "No estoy seguro de que yo exista en realidad"'. Interview by José Luis A. Fermosel. *El Pais*, 26 September 1981.

p.588 Baldwin, James. 'James Baldwin Recalls his Childhood'. *The New York Times*, 31 May 1964.

p.593 Hockney, David. 'David Hockney'. Interview by Michael Govan. *Interview*, 5 November 2013.

p.603 Nai Barghouti, Mahmoud Darwish, Kieran Brunt, and Peter Gabriel. Together for Palestine. 'Lullaby'. T4P Records, 2025.

p.604 Ellis, Bret Easton. *American Psycho*. New York: Vintage Books, 1991.

p.604 Solomon, Aron. 'American Psycho: How Donald Trump Brought the "Bateman Doctrine" to the World'. Literary Hub, 23 January 2026.

p.606 Schopenhauer, Arthur. See, e.g., *Parerga and Paralipomena*. Berlin: A. W. Hayn, 1851.

p.611 Larionov, Mikhail, and Natalia Goncharova. 'Rayonists and Futurists: A Manifesto'. In *Oslinyi khvost i mishen* [Donkey's Tail and Target], July 1913.

p.612 Meyer, Marissa. *Cinder*. New York: Feiwel & Friends, 2012.

p.614 Shakespeare, William. *Richard II*. In *The Complete Works of William Shakespeare*. Leipzig: Baumgärtner, 1854.

CLOSING EPIGRAPH

p.867 Seed, John. 'Invocation'. In John Seed, Joanna Macy, Pat Fleming, and Arne Naess, *Thinking Like a Mountain: Towards a Council of All Beings*. British Columbia: New Catalyst Books, 2007.

INDEX

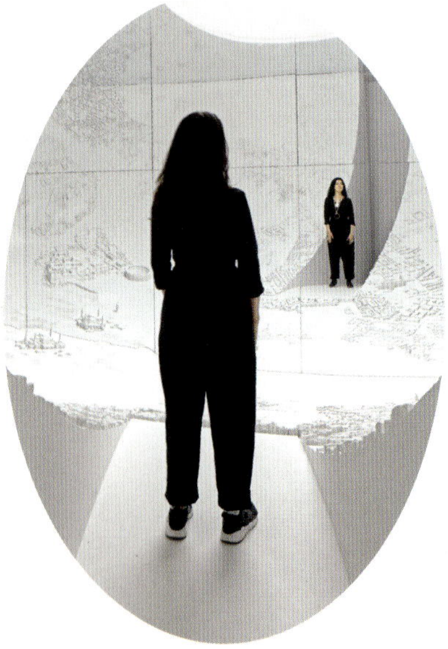